The Bible in American Law and Politics

The Bible in American Law and Politics

A Reference Guide

John R. Vile

ROWMAN & LITTLEFIELD
Lanham • Boulder • New York • London

Published by Rowman & Littlefield
An imprint of The Rowman & Littlefield Publishing Group, Inc.
4501 Forbes Boulevard, Suite 200, Lanham, Maryland 20706
www.rowman.com

6 Tinworth Street, London SE11 5AL, United Kingdom

British Library Cataloguing in Publication Information Available

Library of Congress Cataloging-in-Publication Data Available
ISBN 978-1-5381-4166-3 (cloth)
ISBN 978-1-5381-4167-0 (electronic)

Ecclesiastes 12:12

Contents

Topical List of Entries

Introduction

This volume follows four prior reference books that I have recently authored relative to American symbols. The first was on the U.S. flag, the second on the Declaration of Independence, the third on the Liberty Bell, and the fourth on the national anthem. Whereas these prior books dealt with symbols that were distinctive to America, I recognize that the United States has no monopoly on the Bible or its interpretation. By the same token, I believe that American uses of the Bible can cast significant light on both its history and its self-understanding, particularly during the colonial, founding, and antebellum years.

The Role of the Bible in America

In reviewing Donald S. Lutz's survey of political literature in America from 1760 to 1805, Professor Daniel Dreisbach of American University observes that the Bible was "cited more frequently than any European writer or even any European school of thought such as the Enlightenment or Whig intellectual tradition" (Dreisbach 2014, 146). He further observes that an examination of inventories of individuals who died in the eighteenth century indicates that "the Bible was the most accessible book in late-eighteenth-century America" (147). Professor Mark David Hall of George Fox University notes that "Connecticut required families to own Bibles, and it demanded that towns have schools so that citizens would be able to read them" (2013, 32). Moreover, however much biblical literacy has declined in recent years, Americans remain a religious people, and much current political debate can be related either directly or indirectly to biblical themes. A Museum of the Bible now draws many visitors near the national mall in Washington, DC, while the American Bible Society has recently opened an exhibition on the Bible near Independence Hall in Philadelphia where the nation was born and its constitution formulated.

I realize that a volume on the Bible in American law and politics merely scratches the surface with regard to the role of the Bible in American life and, indeed, in Western civilization. The Torah and other Hebrew writings that Christians call the Old Testament were the foundation of Jewish life and culture. The Bible, expanded to include the New Testament, is the basis of Christianity. Islam also draws many of its stories from the Bible, especially as orally transmitted (Griffith 2013). The Protestant Reformation was based on the doctrine of *sola scriptura,* or the belief that the Bible alone was the only sure guide to Christian life and practice, a conviction that Puritans brought with them to North America. Biblical scenes have been the subject of numerous works of art, the Bible has inspired and been the subject of many musical compositions, and cultural manifestations are as pervasive as Gideon Bibles in motel rooms; the Ark Encounter in Williamstown, Kentucky; the Holy Land Experience theme park in Orlando, Florida; the Bible Museum in Washington, DC (see Bielo "Materializing the Bible"); WWJD (What Would Jesus Do) bracelets and the corresponding HWLV (He Would Love First) on the arms of teenagers; bumper stickers ("God said it, I believe it, that settles it"); cartoons; T-shirts; and the like.

Most people who read the Bible probably do not go there chiefly to settle political or legal issues, and most readers likely revere the Bible less because of persuasive arguments on its behalf or because of its perceived connection to American law and politics than for the comfort and inspiration they find for their daily lives. It has even been reported that as he approached the end of his life, W. C. Fields, who had a reputation for dissolute behavior, began reading the Bible in order to look for loopholes! From a more serious standpoint, many people, especially Protestant evangelicals, are likely to view the key doctrines of their faith as grounded on the Bible.

The Author's Experience with the Bible

In filling out a questionnaire connected to this book, I was asked to list all the contributors. I listed myself both as the "sole" author and the "soul" author because, as much as any of my works, I have put both heart and soul into this book. If readers will permit me to transition from pun to oxymoron, I consider the subjects of the volume to be transcendently practical.

As a child of Protestant Christian parents whose original intention was to be foreign missionaries and whose lives were structured around their faith, I remember singing the words and sounding out the letters of the Bible to a chorus that said,

> The B-I-B-L-E,
> Yes, that's the book for me!
> I stand alone on the Word of God,
> The B-I-B-L-E!

In singing "Jesus Loves Me," I further learned that this great truth was grounded in the knowledge that "the Bible tells me so." Yet another song that we sang, reflecting Psalm 119:105, suggested that "Thy word is a lamp to my feet, a light to my path always" and observed that learning Scripture was important "that I might not sin; that I might sin against Thee."

Almost any time my parents sent a card or signed a guest book, whether for a wedding funeral, open house, or other occasion, they left a reference to a Bible verse, a practice I have followed with what I hope will be considered good humor (it's actually a verse my mother has cited to me a number of times) in this volume. A friend told me about a woman who had forgotten what favorite verse she had taken upon her Lutheran confirmation and called her sister only to be told that it was Proverbs 26:11, which more refined readers may prefer not to read!

In addition to its moral and religious guidance, as I grew older I realized that the Bible was also sometimes regarded as a guide to the future or even as an object of magic. On the last days of the many revival meetings that I attended as a boy, evangelists explained that Russia, China, and the United States were all the subjects of such biblical books as Daniel, Ezekiel, and Revelation and that nations were even then preparing for the final battle of Armageddon. By the time a representative of the Gideons came to church to tell how a soldier in Vietnam was miraculously saved when a bullet intended for his body instead hit the pocket New Testament in his vest, I was old enough to wonder whether another book might have served the same purpose, but I learned that one should reverently and ceremoniously burn an outworn Bible much as one might dispose of a tattered flag.

Although I knew from a young age that the Bible was composed of two central parts, both of which contained many books (although the epistles are better characterized as letters) the names of which we were encouraged to learn in order (a process now made easier by a song), like most people, I chiefly approached the Bible as a single "holy" book, with a coherent theme. I soon learned that even people within the same denomination often differed in their interpretations of various passages and in their explanation of how seemingly contradictory or obscure passages should be interpreted in relation to one another.

Denominations even had particular translations of the Bible that they approved. When I was growing up, ours favored the King James Version, although, for reasons I still do not completely understand, many also liked *The Living Bible*, which did not even pretend to be a translation but a paraphrase. Moreover, the story of Adam and Eve's temptation in the Garden of Eden and of Jesus's temptations in the wilderness revealed that even Satan can quote Bible verses and served as a perpetual warning against misinterpreting Scriptures.

Had I been more closely attuned to the controversies that had been generated by the civil rights movement that developed in the wake of World War II and the Supreme Court decision in *Brown v. Board of Education* in 1954, I might also have wondered why churches in our neighborhood were all white or all black. I heard the story of Moses many times as a child, and the cross was a central motif of our teachings, and yet I do not ever remember either story being applied, as it surely was being applied in black churches and some more theological liberal Protestant churches, to the African American struggle for racial justice, which we often associated with communists and other outside agitators.

As a Protestant Christian who has been teaching Sunday school lessons from the Bible for about forty years and preparing weekly sermons from the Bible for almost twenty, I remain deeply committed to the Bible as a sure guide to faith and practice. As a political scientist, I am also fascinated by the manner in which individuals have interpreted the Bible throughout our history. Moreover, as biblical literacy has declined, I am concerned that Americans may be increasingly unaware of the manner in which biblical themes, as well as specific chapters and verses, and arguments about them, have shaped our own heritage. Perhaps we are now in the position of Europeans about whom Benjamin Franklin wrote in 1781 when he explained, "It was not necessary in New England, where everybody reads the Bible, and is acquainted with Scripture phrases, that you should note the texts from which you took them; but I have observed in England, as well as in France, that verses and expressions taken from the sacred writings and not known to be such, appear very strange and awkward to some readers; and I shall therefore in my edition take the liberty of marking the quoted texts in the margins" (Hall 2019, 30).

I am reminded of scholars who for many years missed many of the biblical references in George Washington's thought because he rarely cited chapter and verse, and they didn't recognize his expressions as biblical. In David Daniell's magnificent study of the Bible in English, after mentioning the "Bible-blindness of so many scholars," he cites a 650-page collection of documents from the Great Awakening from two eminent scholars, who admit that they have removed without notice what they considered to be "a superfluity of Scriptural citations" (2003, 552). In a similar vein, during the administration of George W. Bush, evangelicals throughout the nation often recognized biblical allusions in his speeches long before commentators at the *New York Times* and other mainstream sources did so. It was almost as though he were talking in a language that they did not understand (Berlinerblau 2013, 211). Illustrating yet a different problem, there are any number of books that seek to prove that America is a Christian nation, that its laws are founded on the Ten Commandments, or that most, if not all, American founders were Christians, simply by stringing together quotations from laws, cases, or prominent individuals from American history without regard to context or possible political motivations.

Rhetorical Uses of the Bible

In his classic study of the use of the Bible during the American founding era, Professor Daniel Dreisbach observes that it was used then, as it has been used since, for a variety of purposes. Acknowledging that his own list is overlapping and not intended to be exhaustive, Dreisbach cites five such uses that he thinks have been particularly prominent. They are:

> (1) To enrich a common language and cultural vocabulary through distinctively biblical allusions, phrases, figures of speech, symbols, proverbs, aphorisms, and the like; (2) to enhance the power and weight of rhetoric through its identification with a venerated, authoritative text; (3) to identify and define normative standards and transcendent rules for ordering and judging public life; (4) to illuminate the role of Providence in the affairs of men and nations and, specifically, America's place in providential history; and (5) to gain insights into the character and designs of God, especially as they pertain to His dealings with humankind. (Dreisbach 2017, 72–73)

In a caution that would arguably apply to any period in American history, after illustrating each of these uses, Dreisbach warns against "a misunderstanding of the Scripture's role in the discourse of the founders" (2017, 93). He thus notes, "To interpret biblical language as purely stylistic or rhetorical . . . could lead to the cynical conclusion that the founders employed the Bible only for temporal political advantage and that their invocations of the Bible were merely playing to the prejudices of bible-reading people" (93). Likewise, the opposite error is "to read all invocations of biblical language as direct, literal appeals to transcendent, divine claims," which he believes "ignores the nature of political rhetoric and could lead to an erroneous conclusion that the founders were driven by a theocratic, even messianic, vision of America" (93).

In a study of the early republic, John F. Berens warns that "one element in the political rhetoric of the era was the employment of providential concepts for partisan ends," which he attributes to both major political parties of the day (1978, 10).

Through writing this volume, I have become increasingly cognizant of the need to interpret the Bible, and references to the Bible, with great care. I recognize both that an individual proof text or texts may often be in tension or conflict with larger biblical themes and that larger themes may often require more than a reference to a single text or texts. During the Trump administration, I have also been perplexed at the manner in which individuals whom I had previously believed to be faithful to biblical principles of civility and righteousness in governmental leaders were so seemingly willing to discard or ignore them for a taste of political power or the achievement of immediate policy objectives.

Apart from such observations, and arguably in contrast to the Bible itself, this book has no grand theme other than that of demonstrating the pervasiveness of biblical citation and argumentation throughout American history. If, as I believe, the Bible is true, and certain understandings of its text are more accurate and more in tune with God's will than others, then many of these interpretations have been wrong if for no other reason than that they have been contradictory. No one appears to have understood this better than President Lincoln, who recognized that citizens of the North and the South read the same Bible and prayed to the same God while coming to radically different conclusions about their application to slavery. As I have written this book, I have sought to cultivate what I consider to be Lincoln's own humility in recognizing that it is not always possible to ascertain God's designs but that we remain obligated to pursue them with the best understanding that we can and that such understanding often begins with careful study of the Bible.

In reflecting on the Museum of the Bible, Professor Richard Gamble has observed that although most historians have asked "what impact the Bible has had on American history," if they asked instead "what Americans did to the Bible, they would uncover a story filled with active players who have quoted, interpreted, reinterpreted, and applied the Bible" (Gamble 2019, 242). This book is an attempt to illustrate both how the Bible has influenced America and how Americans have interpreted, and sometimes misinterpreted, the Bible. I think it is important to heed the warning of Paul Hanson that a study of the Bible suggests "that political strategies will continue to avoid static imposition of a timeless blueprint and instead justify political positions on the basis of the criterion of their adequacy in representing God's governance of justice and mercy within specific historical and geographical settings" (2010, 25).

Organization of This Book

I have organized this book, like my other four recent reference books, alphabetically so that readers can quickly find essays on topics of interest. I have included references and suggestions for further reading in each essay as well as cross references to further essays. This book includes a timeline, a topical table of contents, a massive bibliography, and both a general index and an index to specific Bible chapters and verses that I have cited.

Key Topics

As its title suggests, the two most prominent topics of this book seek to relate the Bible to American law and politics. Each of these topics is quite broad, but many essays fall into general categories. There are, of course, court cases that specifically address the Bible, typically in public schools or in other public settings, but I have kept these to a minimum both because most do not directly quote the Bible and because I think they are much better treated in the *Encyclopedia of the First Amendment*, to which I contributed, and which is now accessible online (the First Amendment Encyclopedia). Proponents of numerous causes have associated them with biblical interpretations. Such causes include slavery, temperance, women's rights, civil rights, and such issues as abortion, same-sex marriage, and the like.

I have included essays on numerous speeches and documents in U.S. history (typically listed under either the speaker or a prominent analogy like the City upon a Hill) that either rely upon or cite biblical passages. I have also identified a number of key individuals whose writings and speeches are not only religious but distinctively biblical, but, in this respect, I fear that I have barely scratched the surface and that I have undoubtedly left out many such individuals whose lives and political views have been guided by biblical principles. In some cases, I have separate entries on speeches by the same individual because I think that readers might be more likely to look up a speech, for example, the Gettysburg Address or Lincoln's second inaugural address, by its title than its author.

There are so many denominations within the United States that it would be difficult to cover them all, but I have included some essays on denominations whose interpretations of the Bible have been most influential or whose interpretations have sometimes brought their adherents to court. Unlike the *Encyclopedia of the First Amendment*, to which I continue to contribute, this book does not address church/state issues, with which I remain fascinated, unless they specifically involve biblical interpretations.

In contrast to some earlier volumes, however, this is not a book about the Bible and American culture per se, but it is specifically limited to the Bible in law and politics. Every Sunday, pastors generate thousands of sermons, most of which remain unpublished. As a general rule, I have not specifically referred to sermons unless they specifically related to issues of law and politics and unless they appear to have been more widely disseminated. As I approached the already generous word limit that my publisher provided, I further had to delete a number of entries that I had originally planned, but many of which, thankfully, are at least discussed in passing in existing essays. I am sure that there are many men and women of faith who have cited the Bible as they dealt with political and legal concerns that I have missed, but I continue to hope that this volume might provide at least a guide for those interested in similar scholarly endeavors.

Bible Translation

Although the number of Bible translations has multiplied in recent years, unless the source I am quoting does otherwise, I almost always cite the language of the King James Version. I have done so not because I believe it is necessarily the most accurate (although it had the advantage of having been translated directly from original texts) but because it remains among the most lyrical and has certainly been the most pervasive in U.S. history. I recognize that it is ultimately a translation, which derives its authority from its ability to convey the original meanings of the biblical languages in which it was originally written.

I know that there are religions that are active in the United States that have sacred texts other than, or in addition to, the Christian Bible, probably most notably the Koran, and there are some societies that can better be studied through the influence of that book (although it was itself influenced by the Bible) or religious texts other than the Christian Bible. If there were a volume that describes the influence of this text on American law and politics, I would most assuredly add it to my library, just as I would be delighted to find a volume similar to my own on the influence of the Bible in English law and politics. My research, however, indicates that the Bible has always had, and continues to have, a fairly unique place in American law and politics and although I do refer to a number of alternate texts (Elizabeth Cady Stanton's *The Woman's Bible*, the Jefferson Bible, the Book of Mormon, and others), they are not the primary subject of this volume.

Audience for This Book

I believe that this book will interest students of the Bible, students of American law and politics, historians, lawyers, theologians, and lay persons. As I think back on my own years as both an undergraduate and a graduate student, I wish there had been such a book available while I was seeking topics for term papers and for my own dissertation. I do not recall even thinking about writing my dissertation on some of the biblical topics that I have discovered while writing this book and that, in retrospect, might have proven to be better topics. I will consider this book to be a success if it might scout out the scholarly landscape for future studies relating law and politics to the Bible.

As with my previous books, this should be of particular help to reference librarians and especially appropriate for high school and public libraries, for college and university libraries, and for more specialized collections on law, theology, and history. Like the Bible itself, it is my hope that the volume is understandable enough to be read with profit both by laypersons and by scholars and theologians.

Acknowledgments

I have consulted with numerous scholars on my campus about the subject of this volume and owe particular thanks to Dr. Rebekkah King, Dr. Philip Phillips, Dr. Ryan Korstange, Dr. Cheryl Torsney, and Dr. Fred Rolater. I owe even more to my wife, who has endured more than her fair share of conversations on the subject over the past year. An undergraduate, Hailey Clark, further helped with proofing the manuscript. As always, I remain particularly indebted to the individuals at the Walker Library at the Middle Tennessee State University, and especially to those in the interlibrary loan office.

I am especially grateful to have found a publisher who was willing to take a volume of this length and owe special thanks to acquisitions editor Jon Sisk. I would also like to thank copy editor Krishnaa Lakshmanan.

For Reference and Further Reading

Berens, John F. 1978. *Providence & Patriotism in Early America, 1640–1815*. Charlottesville: University Press of Virginia.

Berlinerblau, Jacques. 2013. "The Bible in the Presidential Elections of 2012, 2008, 2004, and the Collapse of American Secularism." *Interested Reader: Essays on the Hebrew Bible in Honor of David J.A. Clines*. Atlanta, GA: Society for Biblical Literature, pp. 197–218.

Bielo, James. "Materializing the Bible." https://www.materializingthebible.com/.

Daniell, David. 2003. *The Bible in English: Its History and Influence*. New Haven, CT: Yale University Press.

Driesbach, Daniel L. 2014. "The Bible and the Political Culture of the American Founding." *Faith and the Founders of the American Republic*, ed. Daniel L. Dreisbach and Mark David Hall. New York: Oxford University Press, pp. 144–73.

Dreisbach, Daniel L. 2017. *Reading the Bible with the Founding Fathers*. New York: Oxford University Press.

The First Amendment Encyclopedia. Middle Tennessee State University. https://www.mtsu.edu/first-amendment/encyclopedia.

Gamble, Richard M. 2019. *A Fiery Gospel: The Battle Hymn of the Republic and the Road to Righteous War*. Ithaca, NY: Cornell University Press.

Griffith, Sidney H. 2013. *The Bible in Arabic: The Scriptures of the "People of the Book" in the Language of Islam*. Princeton, NJ: Princeton University Press.

Hall, Mark David. 2013. *Roger Sherman and the Creation of the American Republic*. New York: Oxford University Press.

Hall, Mark David. 2019. *Did America Have a Christian Founding? Separating Modern Myth from Historical Truth*. Nashville, TN: Nelson Books.

Hanson, Paul D. 2010. *Political Engagement as a Political Mandate*. Cambridge, UK: James Clarke.

Timeline

ca. 405	St. Jerome publishes a complete translation of the Bible into Latin. His version will be a primary means to accessing the Bible for individuals unfamiliar with Hebrew and Greek for the next thousand years.
1378	John Wycliffe publishes *De veritate Sacrae Scripturae* (*On the Truth of Sacred Scripture*).
1388	Followers of John Wycliffe publish the first complete English edition of the Bible from the Latin Vulgate.
1453	Johannes Gutenberg invents the printing press. The first book that he prints, in Latin, is the Bible. The fall of Constantinople (today's Istanbul) sends scholars of Greek westward.
1492	Christopher Columbus, who was seeking to get to China by sailing west from Europe, leads the first of four voyages to America. Spain expels all Jews.
1517	Martin Luther nails theses on a church door and initiates the Protestant Reformation.
1522	Martin Luther publishes the first New Testament in German.
1525	William Tyndale publishes an English New Testament based on Erasmus's Greek.
1534	King Henry VIII of England breaks with the Catholic Church and creates the Church of England.
1535	Miles Coverdale, a student of Tyndale, produces an English Bible.
1540	First authorized English version of the Bible (variously known as the Great Bible, the Cromwell Bible, or the Cranmer Bible) is published based largely on an earlier translation by William Tyndale.
1560	Exiles from England in Switzerland publish the Geneva Bible in English. It is the first English Bible with verse numbers.
1603	British settlers land in Jamestown, Virginia.
1604	The Hampton Court Conference decides to translate the Bible into English.
1609–1610	The Rheims-Douai Bible becomes the first Roman Catholic Bible published in English.
1611	The King James Version of the Bible is published in England. It is compiled by forty-seven scholars and polished by Miles Smith, widely known for his knowledge of ancient languages.
1618	Beginning of the Thirty Years' War pitting Protestants against Catholics in Europe.
1620	Pilgrims land in North America seeking freedom to practice their religion and enter into the Mayflower Compact. Viewing themselves as the New Israel, they often look upon Native Americans as Canaanites whom they have the right to destroy.

1630	John Winthrop composes his "Model of Christian Charity."
1635	Roger Williams is banished from the Massachusetts Bay Colony.
1637	Puritans burn about five hundred Native Americans to death at Mystic, Connecticut, justifying their actions on the basis of the Old Testament.
1639	Settlers in Connecticut compose the Fundamental Orders of Connecticut.
1640	Publication of *The Bay Psalm Book*.
1644	Roger Williams publishes a pamphlet advocating religious liberty against John Cotton.
1647	Massachusetts adopts the Old Deluder Satan Law requiring that towns of fifty or more households establish schools to teach reading and writing.
1663	John Eliot publishes the first Bible in America, a translation into Wopanaak for local Native Americans, printed in Cambridge, Massachusetts.
1678	First publication of John Bunyan's *Pilgrim's Progress*.
1683	Algernon Sidney is executed for conspiring against King Charles II.
1688	The "Glorious Revolution" replaces a Catholic king with a Protestant one.
1739	Revivalist George Whitefield comes to America and launches the First Great Awakening that continues into the next decade.
1743	Christopher Sauer publishes the first German Bible (Luther's translation) in America.
1754	Beginning of the French and Indian War.
1763	The end of the French and Indian War ends up with the French transfer of Canada to Great Britain.
1765	The British Parliament imposes the stamp tax on its North American colonies.
1768	Boston, Braintree, Charleston, and Lexington, Massachusetts, all declare a day of fasting and prayer to protest the coming of British troops.
1770	British fire on Americans in the so-called Boston Massacre.
1774	Rev. Jacob Duché reads a biblical passage and delivers a prayer before the First Continental Congress.
	Virginia declares June 1 as a day of fasting and prayer.
1775	Patrick Henry gives his famous "Give me liberty or give me death" speech at St. Johns Church in Richmond, Virginia.
	Fighting breaks out at Lexington and Concord between American and British troops.
	The Continental Congress declares July 20 as a day of humiliation and prayer.
	On July 29, the Continental Congress creates the American chaplaincy.
1776	Thomas Paine publishes *Common Sense*, in which he argues from Scripture that God opposed monarchy.

	Lutheran pastor Peter Muhlenberg is said to have taken off his clerical garb at the end of a sermon to his Woodstock, Virginia, congregation to reveal that he has signed up as an officer in the state militia.
	Thomas Jefferson authors and the Second Continental Congress adopts the Declaration of Independence.
1781	General Charles Cornwallis surrenders British troops to George Washington at Yorktown, Virginia.
1782	Robert Aitken publishes the first full-length Bible in the United States, the only such Bible ever to be officially authorized by Congress.
1783	The Treaty of Paris brings an official end to the Revolutionary War.
1786	The Virginia legislature adopts Jefferson's "Bill for Establishing Religious Freedom," which disestablished the state church.
1787	Delegates from twelve states meet in Philadelphia to draw up a new Constitution to replace that under the Articles of Confederation.
1789	George Washington is inaugurated as the first U.S. president.
1790	Matthew Carey of Philadelphia publishes the first edition of the "Douai" (Catholic) Bible, and only the second Bible in English, in America.
1791	Ratification of the first ten amendments, now referred to as the Bill of Rights.
1794	Thomas Paine released the first part of *The Age of Reason*, which attacks the trustworthiness of the Bible.
1801	As many as twenty-five thousand people gather for revival services in Cane Ridge, Kentucky.
1802	On New Year's Day, the Baptist leader John Leland delivers a 1,235-pound mammoth cheese to the White House with the words "Rebellion to tyrants is obedience to God."
1804	Founding of the British and Foreign Bible Society.
1808	Charles Thomson, former secretary of the Continental Congress, publishes the first English translation of the Greek Septuagint.
	U.S. bans slave trade.
1812	Beginning of America's second war with Great Britain.
1814	Francis Scott Key writes "The Star-Spangled Banner."
	Biblica Hebraica becomes the first Hebrew Bible published in the United States.
1816	The American Bible Society is organized.
1820	The Missouri Controversy exposes deepening divisions in the United States over slavery.
1826	In what many citizens interpret as a providential sign, both Thomas Jefferson and John Adams die on the fiftieth anniversary of the signing of the Declaration of Independence.
1827	Presbyterian Ezra Stiles Ely calls upon Protestant Christians to form "a Christian party in politics."
1830	First publication of the Book of Mormon.

1831	James Monroe dies on the anniversary of the signing of the Declaration of Independence.
	William Lloyd Garrison publishes the first issue of his abolitionist news magazine, *The Liberator*.
	Nat Turner leads a slave rebellion in Virginia.
1833	Great Britain bans slavery within all its territories.
	Noah Webster publishes a revised edition of the King James Bible.
	Massachusetts becomes the last state to disestablish its official church.
1834	James Madison composes his "Advice to My Country" with its reference to a serpent in paradise.
1836	The American Temperance Union is formed.
1842	A Dominican friar publicly burns some Bibles in Champlain, New York, that had been distributed by a Protestant Bible society.
1843	Date first predicted by William Miller for the second coming to Earth of Christ.
1844	Anti-Catholic riots break out in Philadelphia, in part stimulated by whether public schools should continue to read from the King James Version of the Bible.
	Joseph Smith runs as an independent for president but is killed by a mob in Illinois.
	Individuals gather to await the second coming of Christ, which was predicted by William Miller; this is sometimes called the Great Disappointment.
1848	The American Missionary Association starts a fund to provide the Bible to southern slaves.
1852	Frederick Douglass uses the Fourth of July to deliver a Scripture-laden sermon condemning slavery.
	The Church of Jesus Christ of Latter-Day Saints (LDS) announces that it accepts plural marriages.
1853	Isaac Lester publishes the first Jewish translation of the Hebrew Scriptures into English.
1859	Biologist Charles Darwin publishes *On the Origin of Species*, which undermines traditional interpretations of the biblical book of Genesis.
1861	Abraham Lincoln becomes the first Republican president of the United States.
	Beginning of the Civil War.
	First Bibles ever published in the South are published by the Southwestern Publishing House in Nashville.
1863	Lincoln delivers the Gettysburg Address.
1865	Lincoln gives his second inaugural address.
1865	End of the Civil War.
	Assassination of President Abraham Lincoln.
	Adoption of the Thirteenth Amendment prohibiting slavery.
1867	The first of numerous meetings of the Bible and Prophecy Conference Movement.

1868 Adoption of the Fourteenth Amendment providing citizenship for all persons born or naturalized in the United States and guaranteeing them certain fundamental rights.

1872 The Ohio Supreme Court upholds a decision by the Cincinnati School Board to remove the Bible from the public school curriculum.

1874 Creation of the Women's Christian Temperance Union.

1875 Mary Baker Eddy publishes *Science and Health.*

1876 Catholic bishop James Gibbons of Richmond, Virginia, publishes *The Faith of Our Fathers: Being a Plain Exposition and Vindication of the Church Founded by Our Lord Jesus Christ.*

The American Publishing Company of Hartford, Connecticut, publishes the first complete translation of the Bible into English by a woman, Julia E. Smith.

1878 William L. Blackstone publishes *Jesus Is Coming,* which raises millennial expectations.

The Niagara Conference adopts a fourteen-point creed that serves as a foundation for twentieth-century Protestant fundamentalism.

1879 Henry George publishes *Progress and Poverty* advocating a single land tax.

1880 Founding of the American branch of the Salvation Army.

1881 First publication of the Revised Version of the Bible in America.

1883 Mary Baker Eddy publishes her *Key to the Scriptures,* which becomes the basis of Christian Science.

1890 Wilford Woodruff, the LDS president, says that God had instructed him that his church should abandon polygamy.

1891 The Blackstone Petition is presented to President Harrison, calling upon him to call a conference in support of resettling the Jewish in Palestine.

1893 The Anti-Saloon League is formed.

1896 Utah, whose entry had been long delayed by concern over prior Mormon beliefs in polygamy, is admitted as the forty-fifth state after its leaders renounce this doctrine.

1898 Numerous pastors view the Spanish-American War as a way of fulfilling America's destiny to spread liberty and Christianity.

1899 The Gideons are founded in Janesville, Wisconsin, for the purpose of distributing copies of the Bible for free.

1901 Publication of the American Standard Version of the Bible, revising King James.

1906 Sermons by William J. Seymour initiate the Azusa Street revivals in southern California.

1909 The publication of the Scofield Reference Bible, the notes to which furthered the ideas of premillennial dispensationalism.

1910–1915 Princeton University professors and others publish a twelve-volume collection known as *The Fundamentals: A Testimony to the Truth* that lays the basis for American fundamentalism.

1917 The United States enters World War I on the side of the Allies.

The Jewish Publication Society publishes a translation of the Hebrew Bible into English.

1919 The Eighteenth Amendment provides for national alcoholic prohibition.

American fundamentalists, convened by William Bell Riley, gather in Philadelphia to form the World's Christian Fundamentals Association.

1920 The Nineteenth Amendment, prohibiting discrimination against women in voting, is adopted.

1923 Professor Edgar J. Goodspeed of the University of Chicago publishes the first so-called American version of the New Testament but is widely criticized for using idioms.

1925 The Scopes Trial highlights the widening gaps between American fundamentalism and liberalism.

1929 The collapse of the stock market signals the beginning of the Great Depression.

1933 Franklin D. Roosevelt gives his first presidential inaugural address.

1941 President Roosevelt proclaims the week of Thanksgiving to be National Bible Week.

1945 The dropping of two atomic bombs on Japanese cities provides a prototype for another way that the world might one day end.

1947 First publication of the Revised Standard Version of the New Testament in the United States.

1948 The modern state of Israel is created and is quickly recognized by President Harry S. Truman. This development stirs increased millennial expectations.

1950 L. Ron Hubbard first publishes his *Dianetics: The Modern Science of Mental Health*.

1952 Publication of the Revised Standard Version of the Bible is endorsed by the National Council of Churches.

1953 The first National Prayer Breakfast is held.

1954 Congress adds the words "Under God" to the pledge to the American flag.

The U.S. Supreme Court rules that racial discrimination violates the equal protection clause of the Fourteenth Amendment to the U.S. Constitution.

1960 John F. Kennedy becomes the first Roman Catholic to be elected as U.S. president.

1962 The U.S. Supreme Court declares that public devotional prayer is unconstitutional in state-supported schools.

1963 President John F. Kennedy is assassinated.

The U.S. Supreme Court outlaws devotional readings of the Bible in public schools.

1966 The American Bible Society publishes Today's English Version of the Bible, the New Testament part of which is entitled *Good News for Modern Man*.

1967	Israel defeats an Arab attack and takes new territory including Jerusalem, sparking hopes among evangelical Christians that they might rebuild the temple and hasten the second coming of Christ.
1970	Hal Lindsey publishes *The Late Great Planet Earth*, stirring renewed millennial expectations.
1973	The U.S. Supreme Court legalizes most abortions in the first and second trimesters of pregnancy.
1974	President Richard M. Nixon resigns from office after impeachment proceedings begin in the aftermath of the Watergate scandal.
1976	The United States celebrates the bicentennial of the Declaration of Independence.
	Jimmy Carter defeats Gerald Ford for the presidency. *Newsweek* magazine declares 1976 to be the "Year of the Evangelical."
1977	Dr. James Dobson creates Focus on the Family.
1979	Rev. Jerry Falwell founds the Moral Majority, designed to support conservative causes.
1983	President Ronald Reagan delivers his "Evil Empire" Speech.
	President Reagan, at congressional request, declares the Year of the Bible.
1985	The Jewish Publication Society publishes a translation of the Hebrew Bible into English called the *Tanakh*.
1986	President Ronald Reagan inscribes a Bible for Oliver North to deliver to Iranians with whom he was negotiating the sale of weapons in exchange for the release of hostages in Lebanon.
1987	The United States celebrates the bicentennial of the U.S. Constitution.
2008	Barack Obama becomes the first African American to be elected as president of the United States.
2012	Republicans nominate Mitt Romney, a member of the Church of Jesus Christ of Latter-Day Saints, for president, but he loses the election to Barack Obama.
2016	Donald J. Trump is elected as president.
	The American Bible Society moves its headquarters from New York to Philadelphia.
2017	The Museum of the Bible opens in Washington, DC.
	President Trump decides to move the U.S. embassy in Israel from Tel Aviv to Jerusalem.
2019	President Trump faces impeachment charges over whether he withheld money from Ukraine until it agreed to investigate the son of a Trump political opponent.
2020	The American Bible Society plans to open its Faith and Discovery Center in Philadelphia, near Independence Hall.

For Reference and Further Reading

Hallihan, C. P. 2010. *The Authorised Version: A Wonderful and Unfinished History*. London: Trinitarian Bible Society.

• A •

Abington v. Schempp (1963)

Just a year after the U.S. Supreme Court struck down the daily recitation of a prayer in public schools in *Engel v. Vitale*, the court extended this prohibition to a daily reading from the Bible by students without comment. This practice had been challenged by the Schempp family in Pennsylvania, who were Unitarians, and by Madalyn Murray and her son in Maryland, who were professed atheists. Although generally using the King James Version of the Bible, both school districts had permitted the use of alternate translations and had exempted students who chose not to participate.

Justice Tom Clark delivered the majority opinion for the U.S. Supreme Court based on the establishment clause of the First Amendment as applied to the states through the due process clause of the Fourteenth Amendment. Although the states had argued that the practice of reading the Bible was designed to perpetuate such secular purposes as "the promotion of moral values, the contradiction to the materialistic trends of our times, the perpetuation of our institutions and the teaching of literature" (1963, 223), Clark observed,

> Surely the place of the Bible as an instrument of religion cannot be gainsaid, and the State's recognition of the pervading religious character of the ceremony is evident from the rule's specific permission of the alternative use of the Catholic Douay version as well as the recent amendment permitting nonattendance at the exercises. None of these factors is consistent with the contention that the Bible is here used either as an instrument for nonreligious moral inspiration or as a reference for the teaching of secular subjects. (1963, 224).

Accepting that the practice of Bible reading might be considered a fairly "minor" encroachment of the First Amendment, Clark feared that a breach "that is today a trickling stream may all too soon become a raging torrent" (1963, 225).

Clark did indicate that the court's decision was not intended to prevent the teaching of the Bible as part of "comparative religion or the history of religion": "It certainly may be said that the Bible is worthy of study for its literary and historic qualities. Nothing we have said here indicates that such study of the Bible or of religion, when presented objectively as part of a secular program of education, may not be effected consistently with the First Amendment" (225).

Justice William Brennan's concurring opinion is frequently quoted. He noted that Bible reading and prayer had long been part of the public school curriculum, but that education had changed substantially as had its religious makeup. He observed that individuals like Horace Mann had once contrasted reading the Bible to what they considered to be more "sectarian" practices (270). However, even though "the religious aims of the educators who adopted and retained such exercises were comprehensive, and in many cases quite devoid of sectarian bias . . . the crucial fact is that they were nonetheless religious" (271). Surveying past controversies at the state level that had involved Bible reading in schools, Brennan cited a variety of decisions that had decided to ban the practice. Although he did not doubt that morning devotional exercises might have some secular benefits, he observed, "To the extent that only religious materials will serve this purpose, it seems to me that the purpose as well as the means is so plainly religious that the exercise is necessarily forbidden by the Establishment Clause" (280). He observed that there were even devout Christians who found public readings of the Bible to be offensive and that attempts to excuse children from such devotional exercises often stigmatized them. Like the majority, however, Brennan did not think the decision foreclosed "teaching *about* the Holy Scriptures or about the differences between religious sects in classes in literature or history" (300).

Justice Potter Stewart, who wrote the only dissenting opinion, believed that it should be possible to maintain Bible readings without having them seem coercive or stigmatizing to those who did not participate.

The majority's decision in this case was consistent with an earlier decision in *McCollum v. Board of Education* (1948), in which the Supreme Court had outlawed use of public school facilities to provide religious instruction. In *Zorach v. Clauson* (1952), the court had permitted so-called released time arrangements in which public school children were dismissed during the school day for such instruction at off-campus sites.

See also Bible Reading in Public Schools

For Reference and Further Reading

Abington School District v. Schempp, 374 U.S. 202 (1963).
The Bible in the Public Schools. 1870. Cincinnati, OH: Robert Clarke Reprint; New York: Da Capo Press, 1967. Introduction by Robert G. McCloskey.
Engel v. Vitale, 370 U.S. 421 (1962).
McCollum v. Board of Education, 333 U.S. 203 (1948).
Zorach v. Clauson, 343 306 (1952).

Abortion

Conflicts over governmental regulations of abortion in the United States have been among the most contentious of any that have roiled American law and politics in the last fifty years. Long the subject of common law decisions and varied state regulations, which had eased in many states, the U.S. Supreme Court entered the area with its path-breaking decision in *Roe v. Wade* in 1973, which allowed most abortions through the first and second trimesters of pregnancy and some during the third. The decision has failed to stop the debate between abortion opponents, who describe themselves as pro-life, and those, describing themselves as pro-choice, who believe the decision is one to be made by a woman and her doctor. A leading scholar of constitutional law refers to this conflict as "the clash of absolutes" (Tribe 1990).

Striking down a Texas law limiting abortion, the court, in an opinion authored by Justice Harry Blackmun, noted that there was wide disagreement over the status of a fetus, but that the reference to persons in the Fourteenth

Amendment to the U.S. Constitution ("all persons born or naturalized in the United States") appeared to refer to postnatal life. In examining abortion laws in U.S. history, Blackmun concluded that most had been enacted to protect the lives of expectant women at a time prior to antiseptics, when the risk of abortion was often greater than the risk of childbearing. Conceiving of the protection of women as the primary goal of such laws, Blackmun thought that modern science now made abortion much safer. In a complex ruling, he thus ruled that a woman should have an unfettered right to abortion during the first trimester (three months) of pregnancy, that the state could enact legislation to ensure that women's health was protected during such procedures during the second trimester, and that only in the third trimester (the point during which a fetus would be viable outside the womb) would the state be able to limit abortion, albeit with exceptions for cases involving the life or health of the mother.

In subsequent decisions, however, most notably *Planned Parenthood of Southeastern Pennsylvania v. Casey* (1992), the court, while affirming the central holding in *Roe,* has enabled states to add waiting periods and other restrictions, the limits of which states have begun to test.

The Roman Catholic Church has long held that human life begins at conception, and Catholics were among abortions' most vocal opponents, with mainline and Protestant churches initially taking a far more positive attitude toward the opinion, which most thought avoided outright abortion on demand. In time, however, evangelicals, many influenced by Francis Schaeffer, began to see the abortion decision as a sign of cultural decline, not only because it seemed to provide a way for individuals to deal with the consequence of childbirth outside of marriage, but also because they thought it was a denial of human dignity.

Historically, Roman Catholics have often pitched arguments on social policies in terms of natural law thinking, which they buttress with modern scientific research, and they largely continue to do so. Pope John Paul II's *The Gospel of Life* (1995), in which he treats the issues of abortion, euthanasia, and the death penalty, also cites many Scriptures. Fundamentalists and evangelicals tend to resort to Scriptures in treating such issues (Dillon 1995).

As it turns out, however, the Bible does not directly mention the practice of abortion (Luo 2005), and opponents have had to argue from analogous situations or more general biblical principles. One analogous situation, which suggests that a fetus is not fully human, is found in Exodus 21:22–23, where a man strikes another man's pregnant wife, causing a miscarriage, and he is obligated to pay a monetary penalty to her husband; the Septuagint translation of this passage further distinguished between an "unformed and a formed fetus" ("Abortion in the Bible" 1980, 221).

Both Catholics and evangelicals often cite the commandment against murder in Exodus 20:13 as well as Deuteronomy 30:19, in which God tells Moses that "I have set before you life and death, blessing and cursing: therefore choose life, that both thou and thy seed may live." They are also fond of Psalm 139:13–14: "thou has covered me in my mother's womb. I will praise thee; for I am fearfully and wonderfully made" and Jeremiah 1:5: "Before I formed thee in the belly I knew thee; and before thou camest forth out of the womb I sanctified thee, and I ordained thee a prophet unto the nations." Similarly, the New Testament describes both John the Baptizer and Jesus in the womb (Jelen 1992, 141). Those who believe that unborn children bear God's image further cited the admonition in Proverbs 31:8 to speak on behalf of those who are needy (Rosati 2019, 16).

One evangelical treatment of the subject, which, like corresponding arguments from Roman Catholics, devotes attention to the position of the early church on the subject, suggests that larger biblical themes might be a more important resource for those opposing abortion than specific proof texts. It specifically lists the doctrines of "Creation," "Incarnation," "Neighbor love," "Enemy love," "Peace," "Justice," "Liberation," "Quality of Life," and "Freedom, conscience and rights" (Gorman 1982, 97–99).

One of the great difficulties in this area, as in others that touch personal morality, is the recognition that even if abortion is identified as a moral wrong, this does not necessarily mean that it is the government's responsibility to legislate against it or that it can necessarily do so effectively. Those who favor leaving the decision to women point out that in the years prior to the legalization of abortion, many women sought back-alley abortions that often posed serious threats to their health. A number of politicians, among them Mario Cuomo, one-time governor of New York who was a professing Catholic, distinguished their own personal morality from state policy.

See also Manhattan Declaration: A Call of Christian Conscience; Schaeffer, Francis; Ten Commandments

For Reference and Further Reading

"Abortion in the Bible." 1980. *Social Sciences*. 55 (Autumn): 221.

Balkin, Jack, ed. 2007. *What Roe v. Wade Should Have Said: The Nation's Top Legal Experts Rewrite America's Most Controversial Decision*. New York: NYU Press.

Dillon, Michele. 1995. "Religion and Culture in Tension: The Abortion Discourses of the U.S. Catholic Bishops and the Southern Baptist Convention." *Religion and American Culture: A Journal of Interpretation* 5 (Summer): 159–80.

Douthat, Ross. 2019. "The Abortion Mysticism of Pete Buttigieg." *New York Times*. September 17.

Gorman, Michael J. 1982. *Abortion and the Early Church: Christian, Jewish and Pagan Attitudes in the Greco-Roman World*. Downers Grove, IL: InterVarsity Press.

Jelen, Ted G. 1992. "The Clergy and Abortion." *Review of Religious Research* 34 (December): 132–51.

John Paul II. 1995. *The Gospel of Life (Evangelium Vitae)*. New York: Random House.

Luo, Michael. 2005. "On Abortion, It's the Bible of Ambiguity." *New York Times*. November 13.

Planned Parenthood of Southeastern Pennsylvania v. Casey, 505 U.S. 833 (1992).

Roe v. Wade, 410 U.S. 113 (1973).

Rosati, Kelly. 2019. "Today's Abortion Conversation: Where Do We Go from Here?" *Evangelicals* 5 (Fall): 14–17.

Tribe, Laurence H. 1990. *Abortion: The Clash of Absolutes*. New York: W.W. Norton.

Adams, Jasper

Although America is often called a Christian nation, it is also said to have a "godless Constitution" (Kramnick and Moore 1996). The First Amendment to the U.S. Constitution clearly prohibits Congress from adopting an "establishment of religion," while also protecting its free exercise. The first clause did not initially prohibit the continuation of the remaining state establishments, and controversy remained over how state establishments fit with the absence of a national one.

To this confusion was added a dispute, chiefly between Joseph Story (1779–1845), a Supreme Court justice, Harvard law professor, and legal commentator who, with some other judges, had contended that Christianity was part of American common law, and Thomas Jefferson, who just as emphatically believed that it was not. At about the same time, controversy developed over whether it was appropriate for Congress to allow processing and delivery of mail on Sundays, which is the traditional Christian Sabbath.

This provided the context for a widely disseminated sermon by Jasper Adams (1793–1841), a South Carolina pastor and president of the College of Charleston, which he delivered before the Convention of the Protestant Episcopal Church of South Carolina on February 13, 1833. It was entitled "The Relation of Christianity to Civil Government in the United States," and, it addition to being printed that same year, it has been reprinted in a book edited by Professor Daniel Dreisbach (1996).

Adams prefaced his sermon with three biblical texts: 1 Peter 3:15, which urged believers to give an account of themselves; Proverbs 14:34: "Righteousness exalteth a nation, but sin is a reproach to any people"; and Revelation 9:15: "The kingdoms of this world are become the kingdoms of our Lord and of his Christ; and he shall reign for ever and ever." Anticipating that Christianity would one day become universal, Adams observed that "there is no possible form of individual or social life, which it is not fitted to meliorate and adorn" (Dreisbach 1996, 39). Noting that the Hebrew nation had combined church and state, Adams viewed Constantine's elevation of Christianity as the official religion of the Roman Empire as the fulfillment of Isaiah 49:23, which had predicted a time when kings and queens would become nursing fathers and mothers. In contrast to many Protestants who saw this as the beginning of what they considered to be the despotism of the Roman Catholic Church, Adams believed that the problem was not governmental recognition of Christianity per se but a recognition of one particular form of Christianity over another.

Adams proceeded to muster evidence to show the connections between governments in America and Christianity in defense of the argument that the Constitution did not intend "to renounce all connexion with the Christian religion," but simply "to disclaim all preference of one sect of Christians over another" (Dreisbach 1996, 43). He further posited that this demonstration "has become important to the religion, the morals, the peace, the intelligence, and in fact, to all the highest interests of this country" (Dreisbach 1996, 43).

Adams began by looking at colonial charters and related documents, which he believed demonstrated that colonists had come to America in pursuit of religious freedom and that their success had largely depended on the spread of churches. He discerned the same pattern in the development of state constitutions and even the U.S. Constitution. As to the former, he observed that many of them specifically recognized Christianity, and that they provided for the observance of Sunday as a day of rest and worship. As to the U.S. Constitution, it not only exempted Sunday from the days that the president had to veto a bill but had, in its attestation clause, specifically referred to "*the year of our Lord,* 1787" (Dreisbach 1996, 63). Adams thought this clause was especially significant: "In the clause printed in Italic letters, the word *Lord* means the Lord Jesus Christ, and the word *our* preceding it, refers back to the commencing words of the Constitution: to wit, 'We the people of the United States' " (Dreisbach 1996, 63). He therefore concluded that, while providing for the free exercise of religion, "THE PEOPLE OF THE UNITED STATES HAVE RETAINED THE CHRISTIAN RELIGION AS THE FOUNDATION OF THEIR CIVIL, LEGAL AND POLITICAL INSTITUTIONS; WHILE THEY HAVE REFUSED TO CONTINUE A LEGAL PREFERENCE TO ANY ONE OF ITS FORMS OVER THE OTHER" (Dreisbach 1996, 46).

Recognizing that the U.S. Constitution was primarily concerned with civil matters and that the First Amendment had recognized the free exercise of religion, Adams argued that it had otherwise left the prior relationship between church and state where it had been under the colonial charters and state constitutions. In a footnote, he likened this connection to that between the principles of the Declaration of Independence, which were largely found *sub silentio* within the Constitution (Dreisbach 1996, 47). Moreover, he pointed to a variety of congressional laws providing for days of prayer and thanksgiving, providing chaplains for the military and the like that showed such continuing church–state associations. Such cooperation was consistent with the admonition in Psalm 127:1 that "except the Lord build the house, they labour in vain that build it" (Dreisbach 1996, 48). In his notes, Adams argued that the recent congressional act requiring postal employees to deliver mail on all days of the week was "unconstitutional, and ought to be rescinded" (Dreisbach 1996, 65). Concluding that "Christianity is the established religion of the nation," Adams noted in a footnote that "the term 'established' is here used . . . in its usual and not in its legal or technical sense" (Dreisbach 1996, 49, n. 27).

Contesting the notion that there should be no connection between the government and Christianity, Adams pointed to its varied social benefits and concluded that "no nation on earth, is more dependent than our own, for its welfare, on the preservation and general belief and influence of Christianity among us" (Dreisbach 1996, 51). Men will either be governed by "physical force" or "by religious and moral principles pervading the community, guiding the conscience, enlightening the reason, softening the prejudices, and calming the passions of the multitude" (Dreisbach 1996, 53). It was thus logical to conclude, "We must be a Christian nation, if we wish to continue a free nation" (Dreisbach 1996, 52). Those who allowed the demise of Christianity through indifference would be culpable of sin and would be responsible for the rise of infidelity, whose political fruits were well known. Christianity had saved newborns from exposure, had secured society by establishing family ties, had provided for a day of rest, had ameliorated the tyranny of masters over the slaves, and had been responsible for the establishment of hospitals and asylums. "By excluding a Supreme Being, a superintending Providence, and a future state of rewards and punishments, as much as possible, from the minds of men, it [infidelity] will destroy all sense of moral responsibility" (Dreisbach 1996, 56).

Adams sent copies of his sermon to a number of contemporary political luminaries whose responses are interesting in their own right. Chief Justice John

Marshall thus noted, "The American population is entirely Christian, & with us, Christianity & Religion are identified" (Dreisbach 1996, 113). Justice Joseph Story was pleased to see that Adams had agreed with his view that Christianity was embedding in the common law. Although James Madison continued to insist that religion did not need any state support in order to flourish, rather than citing Jefferson's noted metaphor of a wall of separation between church and state, he observed that "it may not be easy in every possible case, to trace the line of separation, between the rights of Religion & the Civil authority, with such distinctness, as to avoid collisions & doubts on unessential points" (Dreisbach 1996, 120).

The most extended response to Adams's essay was a review essay entitled the "Immunity of Religion" that was initially published in the *American Quarterly Review* and was probably authored either by Thomas Cooper, a resident of Philadelphia, or Randell Hunt, who had been among Adams's students. Although complimenting Adams on his scholarship and probity, the author argued that Adams "has endeavoured to overturn one of the main pillars of our liberty" by invading and attempting "to destroy freedom of conscience, and on its ruins to erect intolerance and odious discriminations for religion's sake" (Dreisbach 1996, 127). Curiously, however, the essay begins with a defense of "the truth of the Christian Scriptures" (Dreisbach 1996, 127).

The main argument of the essay, however, was the danger of combining church and state, which the author believed would inevitably lead to "discrimination in civil rights" and the allocation of benefits and punishments based on beliefs (Dreisbach 1996, 128). The critic argued that there was no real difference between preferring Christianity to other religions than there was to preferring Protestantism to Catholicism, or to Unitarianism. The role of government was limited: "Civil government is intended for the regulation of social man—for the promotion and security of human happiness here on earth. It is intended for this world—not the next. It should protect us in the enjoyment of our personal rights and property. It should not interfere with our opinions and faith. Its business is with our temporal or present interests, not with our future or eternal welfare" (Dreisbach 1996, 131). The author further argued that because humans cannot help what they believe, they should not be accountable to government for such beliefs. Moreover, "Christianity stands in need of no unequal protection" (Dreisbach 1996, 123).

Reviewing Adams's arguments individually, the author argued that colonial charters had little relevance to the issue of a national religion, although colonists did demonstrate the dangers of religious persecution. Moreover, most states had eliminated their religious establishments. Perhaps seeking to answer Adams's capitalizations with his own, the writer concluded that "THE PEOPLE OF THE SEVERAL STATES—ALTHOUGH A VAST MAJORITY OF THEM WERE CHRISTIANS—RESOLVED, IN FRAMING THEIR CONSTITUTIONS, TO DESTROY ALL CONNEXIONS BETWEEN CHURCH AND STATE" (Dreisbach 1996, 140).

The reference to the year of our Lord in the constitutional attestation clause was "a mere mode of speech" and hardly an attempt to establish Christianity, as is evident by the First Amendment (Dreisbach 1996, 141). The author further disputed Adams's interpretation of the Constitution of South Carolina and noted that many common law doctrines were developed at the time when the Roman Catholic Church, whose doctrines were later pronounced "idolatrous and damnable," was dominant (Dreisbach 1996, 147). The essay concluded with the observation that "Christianity requires no aid from force or persecution. She asks not to be guarded by fines and forfeitures. She stands secure in the armour of truth and reason. She seeks not to establish her principles by political aid and legal enactments. She seeks mildly and peaceably to establish them in the hearts of the people" (Dreisbach 1996, 150).

See also Common Law; Madison, James; Sunday Mail Delivery

For Reference and Further Reading

Dreisbach, Daniel L., ed. 1996. *Religion and Politics in the Early Republic: Jasper Adams and the Church-State Debate.* Lexington: University Press of Kentucky.

Kramnick, Isaac, and R. Laurence Moore. 1996. *The Godless Constitution: The Case Against Religious Correctness.* New York: W.W. Norton.

Adams, John

John Adams (1735–1826) was among the most important of America's Founding Fathers. Born in Massachusetts to a long line of Puritans, Adams might well have gone into the ministry had he not attended Harvard University and decided instead to pursue law. He married Abigail Smith, the daughter of a preacher, and established a practice but, despite his defense of the British soldiers charged with murder in the Boston Massacre, he quickly became one of America's leading advocates of independence from Great Britain.

One of the most active members of both the First and Second Continental Congresses, Adams served on the committee charged with drafting the Declaration of Independence but left the primary task of writing to Thomas Jefferson, with whom he would remain friends throughout much of his life, until they later joined opposing political parties. Adams would go on to serve as an American diplomat in France during the Revolutionary War, as the nation's first vice president under George Washington, as a leader of the Federalist Party (where, however, he was often at odds with Alexander Hamilton), and as the nation's second president, where he successfully avoided a shooting war with France but was defeated for reelection by Democratic-Republicans lead by Thomas Jefferson and James Madison.

Norman Cousins observed that Adams has been variously identified as "a Puritan, Deist, Orthodox Christian, and Humanist" (1958, 75). His Puritanism was perhaps most evident in his moral earnestness, his view that human nature was sinful, and in his desire not to waste time (Fielding 1940, 40). Like both Christians and Deists, Adams believed that God created the world. With Christians, he extolled the Bible and believed in the miracles of Jesus, but with Deists, he did not believe that his death on the cross secured individual salvation. Although Adams believed that God had raised Jesus from the dead, he did not believe that this proved him to be divine (Frazer 2012, 109). Gregg Frazer (2012) believes that he was what he described as a "theistic rationalist," who honored both reason and revelation but considered reason the superior of the two.

Adams believed in the importance of virtue to the success of republican government, and he believed that the teachings of the Bible promoted such virtue. In an entry in his diary dated February 22, 1756, Adams thus wrote,

> Suppose a nation in some distant region should take the Bible for their only law-book, and every member should regulate his conduct by the precepts there exhibited! Every member would be obliged, in conscience to temperance and frugality and industry; to justice and kindness and charity towards his fellow men; and to piety, love and reverence towards Almighty God. In this commonwealth, no man would impair his health by gluttony, drunkenness, or lust; no man would sacrifice his most precious time to cards or any other trifling and mean amusement; no man would steal, or lie, or in any way defraud his neighbor, but would live in peace and good will with all men; no man would blaspheme his Maker or profane his worship; but a rational and manly, a sincere and unaffected piety and devotion would reign in all hearts. What a Utopia; what a Paradise would this region be! (Cousins 1958, 81)

Adams's argument for biblical miracles had a rational basis: "The great and Almighty author of nature, who at first established those rules which regulate the World, can as easily Suspend those Laws whenever his providence sees sufficient reason for such suspension. This can be no objection, then, to the miracles" (Frazer 2012, 109).

Acknowledging in a letter to Samuel Miller dated July 8, 1820, that his immediate ancestors had all been Calvinists and that "I have never known any better people than the Calvinists," he further said that "I must acknowledge that I cannot class myself under that denomination" (Cousins 1958, 111). He believed the doctrine that God elected some to salvation and others to damnation was pernicious because it undercut "the practice of virtue" and rendered "all prayer futile and absurd" (Frazer 2012, 116–17). He extolled the Puritan framers, however, for eliminating the religious hierarchy that had characterized the Roman Catholic and Anglican churches. Citing an anecdote that he attributed to George Whitefield, Adams said that he joined company with all of those, identified in the words of Peter to Cornelius, the Roman centurion, in Acts 10:35: "He who feareth God and worketh righteousness, shall be accepted of him" (Frazer 2012, 120).

With many Deists, Adams admired Jesus as a great moral teacher. He further said that "the Ten Commandments and the Sermon on the Mount contain my religion" (Frazer 2012, 118). Like other Deists, Adams rejected the idea of the Trinity and was a member of a Unitarian church (Frazer 2012, 121). Indeed, Adams was so dismissive of the idea of the Trinity that he said he could not believe it even if Moses had brought the news down from Mount Sinai (Frazer 2012, 121–22)!

One of the great ironies of Adams's beliefs is that many Federalist partisans in the presidential election of 1800 railed against Jefferson because of his alleged heterodoxy, which seems to have been equally shared with Adams. Their correspondence, which they resumed after both had left the presidency, was largely resumed through the efforts of Dr. Benjamin Rush, who often discussed religious matters with them.

The Adams family was one of the most distinguished in U.S. history. John's wife urged him to consider the rights of women. Their son, John Quincy Adams, became the sixth president and a long-term congressman who distinguished himself by his opposition to slavery.

See also Adams, John Quincy; Deism; Jefferson Bible

For Reference and Further Reading

Cousins, Norman, ed. 1958. "In God We Trust": *The Religious Beliefs and Ideas of the American Founding Fathers*. New York: Harper & Brothers.
Fielding, Howard Ioan. 1940. "John Adams: Puritan, Deist, Humanist." *Journal of Religion* 20 (January): 33–46.
Frazer, Gregg L. 2012. *The Religious Beliefs of America's Founders: Reason, Revelation, and Revolution*. Lawrence: University Press of Kansas.
Sutter, Richard L. 1976. "The Divine Dimension: John Adams and Religion in America." *Humboldt Journal of Social Relations* 4 (Fall/Winter): 42–46.

Adams, John Quincy

John Quincy Adams (1767–1848), America's sixth president, only one of two who was himself the son of another president, spent a lifetime in public service. Prior to serving as president, he served as a U.S. senator, was appointed to a number of ambassadorial posts, and served as James Monroe's secretary of state. After serving for a single term as president, he served from 1831 to 1848 in Congress, where he largely distinguished himself for his opposition to slavery. Adams served for a time as the vice president of the American Bible Society (*Presidential Inaugural Bibles* 1969, 20).

Adams made it a practice to begin reading through the Bible once each year. After finishing the task in September one year, he decided that he would begin again, this time in French (Cook 2013, 217). Beginning in September 1811 and continuing for about two years, during which time Adams was an ambassador to Russia, he wrote a series of nine letters to one of his sons who was at school in Massachusetts. These letters were published on the year of his death and gives one of the most complete views of any U.S. president on the Bible.

In the first letter, Adams reported his pleasure in hearing that his son was reading a chapter of the Bible to an aunt: "for so great is my veneration for the Bible, and so strong my belief, that when duly read and meditated on, it is of all books in the world, that which contributes most to make men good, wise, and happy" (Adams 1848, 9). Adams indicated that he read four or five chapters of the Bible every morning and hoped that his son would continue reading it with the goal of improving in both "wisdom and virtue" (11). Observing that he was sometimes distracted from his reading by pain, passion, pleasure, or dissipation (14), he realized that such excuses were inadequate and hoped that his son would learn to govern himself through disciplined reading. Indicating that Scriptures contained world history, the history of Israel, "a system of religion, and of morality" (20), suggested that he would explicate it further in letters to come.

In the second letter, Adams wrote, "My idea of the Bible as a Divine Revelation, is founded upon its practical use to mankind, and not upon metaphysical subtleties" (22). Adams believed its three main doctrines, all of which furthered morality, were "the existence of a God," "the immortality of the Human soul," and "a future state of rewards and punishments" (22–23). He further thought that "it is possible to believe them all without believing that the Bible is a Divine revelation" (23). The very existence of the world pointed beyond itself to a Creator, the nonmaterial nature of consciousness pointed to its spirituality and immortality, and the goodness of God suggested that there must be justice in the life to come (23–24). Adams believed, however, that Scripture presented such ideas with much greater clarity. The opening words of Genesis portray a God far above any conceptions of prior civilization. Noting that there had always been those "who cavil at some of the particular details of this narration" (28), Adams acknowledged both that "much of it is clearly figurative and allegorical" and that it is difficult "to distinguish what part of it is to be understood in a literal and not in a symbolical sense" (29). He thought it clear, however, that the Bible taught that obedience to God and His will was a virtue that humans should pursue.

Drawing from the language of 2 Timothy 3:17, Adams urged his son to read the Bible so as to be "thoroughly furnish[ed] . . . unto all good works" (34). Adams then further distinguished the universal history found in the first eleven chapters of Genesis from the history of Abraham and his family that followed, promises that Adams believed were fulfilled in Christ (38). Believing that it was "immaterial" whether the story of the Garden of Eden in Genesis was "literal or allegorical" (40), Adams believed that its central theme was the necessity of obedience to God. Whereas Adam and Eve were initially told simply what not to do, Abraham faced a greater task in obeying God by leaving his family and even being willing to sacrifice his son.

Adams's fourth letter continued his understanding of the connection between Abraham and his family and its role "as the means in the ways of God's providence, for producing the sacred person of Jesus Christ, through whom the perfect sacrifice of atonement for the original transgression of man should be consummated, and by which 'all the families of the earth should be blessed'" (Adams 1848, 48, repeating a biblical phrase found in both Genesis 12:3 and 22:18). Whereas his father is generally considered to have been a Deist, John Quincy Adams even suggested that there might be intimations of the Trinity in the book of Genesis (49). In addition to obedience, Adams believed that the story of Abraham evidenced God's justice, which was tempered with mercy (50–51). Continuing with the story of Joseph, Adams indicated that biblical stories "have an air of reality about them which no invention could imitate" (52) and pointed to the need for the law of Moses, which would continue to guide the people through Joshua and subsequent judges and through Assyrian and Babylonian captivities.

Adams's fifth letter focused on Moses. Noting that "human legislators can undertake only to prescribe the actions of men: they acknowledge their inability to govern and direct the sentiments of the heart," Adams observed that one of the strengths of the Ten Commandments is that they sought to govern both (62). Recognizing that the law of Moses was directed to a particular people, he believed that "it was destined to be partly suspended and improved into absolute perfection many ages afterward by the appearance of Jesus Christ upon earth"

(64). He attributed the longevity of the Mosaic law to its excellence, observing that "the first four commandments are religious laws, the fifth and tenth are properly and peculiarly moral and domestic rules; the other four are of the criminal department of municipal laws" (69).

In Adams's sixth letter, he tied the Jewish law to the idea "of a covenant or compact between the Supreme Creator and the Jewish people," which he furthered noted was sanctioned "by the blessing and the curse" with which the commandments had been accompanied (75). Adams further attempted to outline the rest of the Old Testament, even mentioning the apocryphal books in the process (83).

Adams's seventh letter pointed to some defects in Mosaic institutions, namely, "the want of a sufficient sanction," their lack of "universality," "the complexity of the objects of legislation," and the overemphasis on religious rites (85–89). Jesus perfected the law by introducing a more universal law with divine sanction that separated his kingdom from that of the world, and nailed ancient rites to the cross (89). Adams preferred to address the contribution of Jesus "not as the scheme of redemption to mankind from the consequences of original sin, but as a system of morality for regulating the conduct of men on earth" (89). He believed this moral system sought to strive for absolute perfection, like that which he believed Jesus had himself achieved (90). In contrast to some religious writers, Adams believed that Christ had proclaimed new standards of morality which "as far exceeds any discovery in the physical laws of nature, as the soul is superior to the body" (94). He believed that Christ had exercised authority such as only a "Redeemer" could do (95).

In his eight letter, Adams proceeded to discuss the Sermon on the Mount as recorded in Matthew 5–7. Again differing from some who believed that Jesus had presented a religion of weakness, Adams observed Jesus's own assertiveness and courage, which was subsequently reflected in the acts of his disciples. He gave particular attention to how "bold, inflexible, tenacious, and intrepid" St. Paul was and to how Peter was known as a rock (107).

In his ninth and final letter in the series, Adams addressed the Bible as literature. In the process, he discussed the five books of Moses (some of which he thought may have originated from Egypt), the poetry and wisdom literature of the Old Testament, the gospels, the book of Acts, the epistles, and the Apocalypse of John (the book of Revelation). Doubting that the style of the Bible could be easily copied "without great affectation," he observed,

> But for pathos of narrative; for the selections of incidents that go directly to the heart; for the picturesque of character and manner; the selection of circumstances that mark the individuality of persons; for copiousness, grandeur, and sublimity of imagery; for unanswerable cogency and closeness of reasoning; and for irresistible force of persuasion: no book in the world deserves to be so unceasingly studied, and so profoundly meditated upon as the Bible. (Adams 1848, 118–19)

Again recommending the reading of the Bible, Adams warned, "Be careful of all not to let your reading make you a pedant, or a bigot; let it never puff you up with pride or a conceited opinion of your own knowledge, nor make you intolerant of the opinions which others draw from the same source, however different from your own" (121). He further hoped that "the merciful Creator, who gave the Scriptures for our instruction, bless your study of them, and make them to you 'fruitful of good works'" (121).

After Adams successfully secured the freedom of the Mendi people aboard *La Amistad*, who had successfully revolted against their captors in a case that reached the U.S. Supreme Court, and were the subject of a movie by Steven Spielberg, they presented him with a Bible that is on display at the Old House at the Adams National Historic Park in Quincy, Massachusetts. It bears the following inscription:

> We are about to go home to Africa. We go to Sierra Leone first, and then we reach Mendi very quick. When we get to Mendi we will tell the people of your great kindness. Good missionary will go with us. We shall take the Bible with us. It has been a precious book in prison, and we love to read it now we are free! Mr. Adams, we want to make you a present of a beautiful Bible! Will you please to accept it, and when you look at it or read it, remember your poor and grateful clients?...
> For the Mendi people. CINQUE, KINNA, KALE.
> Boston, Nov. 6, 1841. (Preble, "The Mendi Bible")

See also Moses; Ten Commandments

For Reference and Further Reading

Adams, John Quincy. 1848. *Letters of John Quincy Adams, to His Son, on the Bible and Its Teachings*. Auburn, NY: Derby, Miller. PDF accessed through Google.

Cook, Jane Hampton. 2013. *American Phoenix: John Quincy and Louisa Adams, the War of 1812, and the Exile That Saved American Independence*. Nashville, TN: Thomas Nelson.

Georgini, Sara. 2019. *Household Gods: The Religious Lives of the Adams Family*. New York: Oxford University Press.

Georgini , Sara. 2013. "John Quincy Adams at Prayer." *Church History* 83 (September): 649–58.

Preble, Peter M. "The Mendi Bible." http://www.frpeterpreble.com/2014/07/mendi-bible.html. Accessed May 23, 2019.

Presidential Inaugural Bibles: Catalogue of an Exhibition, November 17, 1968 *through February 23, 1969*. 1969. Washington, DC: Washington Cathedral.

Adams, Samuel

One of the firebrands of the American Revolution was Samuel Adams (1722–1803) of Massachusetts. The Harvard-educated journalist and agitator was an early advocate of independence. He was prominent in the Sons of Liberty and helped organize the so-called Boston Tea Party in protest against Parliament's tax on tea, and committees of correspondence to communicate with other colonies. The British were actually seeking John Hancock and him when Americans and the British engaged in their first combat at Lexington and Concord.

Adams came from a long line of Puritan forbears but had come to put special value on both political and religious liberty. His sentiments were close to those that would today be identified as evangelical Christianity. As Mitt

Romney would later note in explaining his own faith, however, when the First Continental Congress was meeting in 1774 and there was concern that the delegates were too religiously divided to invite a chaplain to pray, Adams broke the logjam by stating that he was willing for any man of piety who was a patriot (Romney 2007).

On August 1, 1776, Adams delivered a speech from the steps of the Pennsylvania State House (today's Independence Hall), where he supported the Declaration of Independence that the delegates would sign the next day. His speech consisted in both appeals to common sense, to history, and to Scripture. Like many Protestants of his day, Adams associated "popery in religion" with "the popery of politics." By contrast, he observed that America's founding fathers "opened the Bible to all, and maintained the capacity of every man to judge for himself in religion." If "Heaven hath trusted us with the management of things for eternity," how much more should man have control over his own government? He referred to such a development as "the reign of political Protestantism." Using the language of Hebrew prophets, Adams observed, "We have explored the temple of royalty, and found that the idol we have bowed down to, has eyes which see not, ears that hear not our prayers, and a heart like the nether millstone." In language that reflected that of Thomas Paine's *Common Sense*, he further observed, "We have this day restored the Sovereign, to whom alone men ought to be obedient. He reigns in Heaven, and with a propitious eye beholds his subjects assuming that freedom of thought, and dignity of self-direction which He bestowed on them." Paraphrasing both Psalm 113:3 and the Lord's Prayer, he added, "From the rising to the setting sun, may His kingdom come." Shortly thereafter, he utilized another common biblical theme by expressing pity for "those who are yet in darkness."

Pointing to men's "equal right to happiness," Adams questioned why God would bestow greater value on tyrants than on those, identified in Micah 6:8, "who do justice, love mercy, and walk humbly with their God." Professing that he had previously venerated the subjects of Britain "as branches of the same parental trunk, and partakers of the same religion and laws," he believed that all that was left was a lifeless body. He went on to detail how the British had involved Americans in their wars, and how these had become destructive to "political right and public happiness." He further detailed how it had been overcome with the corruption of "venality, luxury, and vice" at a time where America remained "an asylum on earth, for civil and religious liberty." Using another biblical analogy from Isaiah 33:2 and 40:10–11, Adams proclaimed that "it is not our own arm which has saved us," as he warned that we should not turn back to this "political Sodom," lest like Lot's wife (Genesis 19) (turned into a pillar of salt) "we perish and become a monument of infamy and derision to the world!"

Much like Paine, Adams argued that it was impossible to "unite the supremacy of Great Britain and the liberty of America." It was improper for an island to be governing a continent. It was time to escape the "convulsions of elective monarchies" and "hereditary succession."

Returning to the theme of political popery, Adams accused English Protestant reformers of leaving the people "under the domination of human systems and decisions, usurping the infallibility which can be attributed to Revelation alone." Instead of "possessing the pure religion of the gospel," other nations are governed by "infidels who deny the truth, or politicians who make religion a stalking horse for their ambition, or professors, who walk in the trammels of orthodoxy, and are more attentive to traditions and ordinances of men than to the oracles of truth." Support of "unbounding religious freedom . . . will bring with her in her train, industry, wisdom and commerce."

Much as Jefferson had done in the Declaration of Independence, Adams went on to blame the English for a host of atrocities including releasing "the merciless savages to riot in the blood of their brethren—who have dared to establish popery triumphant in our land—who have taught treachery to your slaves, and courted them to assassinate your wives and children." Having argued that America had adequate resources, and hopes of foreign aid, to defeat the British, he also believed that they "can look up to heaven for assistance."

Quoting from another speech that Adams gave in late September 1777 before the Continental Congress, Mark Noll added references to show how pervasively some of Adams's speeches were salted with biblical language:

> Let us awaken then, and evince a different spirit,—a spirit that shall inspire the people . . . to persevere in this glorious struggle, until their rights and liberties shall be established on a rock [see Mt 7:25] . . . We have appealed to Heaven for the justice of our cause, and in Heaven we have placed our trust. Numerous have been the manifestations of God's providence in sustaining us. In the gloomy period of adversity [echoing Eccl 7:14], we have had "our cloud by day and pillar of fire by night" [quoting Ex 13:21-22]. We have been reduced to distress, and the arm of Omnipotence [echoing Psm 44:3; and 136:12] has raised us up. Let us still rely in humble confidence on Him who is mighty to save [quoting Isa 63:1]. Good tidings [See Lk 2:10 and many other passages] will soon arrive. We shall never be abandoned by Heaven while we act worthy of its aid and protection. (Noll 2016, 277)

Adams later supported the adoption of the U.S. Constitution with the hopes that a bill of rights would be added, but sought to create something of a "Christian Sparta" in his home state, which still had an established church. He also sought to ban theater performances in Boston and was fond of issuing days of thanksgiving and fasting (Stoll 2018).

See also Common Sense (Thomas Paine); Declaration of Independence; Revolutionary War

For Reference and Further Reading

Adams, Samuel. August 1, 1776. "'American Independence' Samuel Adams Speech—August 1, 1776." http://www.revolutionary-war-and-beyond.com/american-independence-speech-by-samuel-adams-august-1-1776.html. Accessed April 9, 2019.

Noll, Mark. 2016. *In the Beginning Was the Word: The Bible in American Public Life, 1492–1783.* New York: Oxford University Press.

Romney, Mitt. December 6, 2007. "Transcript: Mitt Romney's Faith Speech." *NPR*. https://www.npr.org/templates/story/story.php?storyID=16969460.

Stoll, Ira. May 3, 2018. "The Revolutionary Gospel According to Samuel Adams." HistoryNet. https://www.historynet.com/revolutionary-gospel-according-samuel-adams.htm.

Africana Movement

Through much of early American history, select Bible verses were used to suggest that African Americans had borne the curse of blackness that they believed had been given to Ham, one of the sons of Noah, for viewing his father's nakedness when he was drunk.

African American defenders, in turn, often compared themselves to the children of Israel, who had suffered servitude in the land of Egypt before Moses led them to the Promised Land of Canaan. In time, an Africana movement developed within the United States that emphasized a very ambiguous verse in Psalm 68:31, an apparent reference to a time when other nations would come to Israel to worship the God, which in the King James Version said, "Princes shall come out of Egypt: Ethiopia shall soon stretch out her hands unto God."

In time, this developed into a Black nationalist ideology, associated with such individuals as Bishop Henry M. Turner (1834–1915) and Marcus Garvey (1887–1940), that two scholars have described as follows:

> It celebrated the sovereignty of God as the one who allowed the enslavement of Africans in order for them to become "civilized" and Christianized by the Europeans who oppressed them. It also hailed the providence of God, who would soon deliver Africans and give them an opportunity to exercise their superior genius in the reordering of the world. At the same time it both provided a theological legitimization for the horrors of slavery and it decried slavery as a crime against a once-and-soon-again-to-be-great people. As presented in the distinctive rendering of the King James Version, this text served as a prophecy of God's impending activity in the very near future; it was an eschatological foretelling of a return to prominence and purpose of a debased and humiliated people. (Powery and Sadler 2016, 17)

See also Curses on Cain, Ham, and the Canaanites; Moses as Political Archetype

For Reference and Further Reading

Powery, Emerson B., and Rodney S. Sadler Jr. 2016. *The Genesis of Liberation: Biblical Interpretations in the Antebellum Narratives of the Enslaved.* Louisville, KY: Westminster John Knox Press.

Ahasuerus as Political Archetype

Prior to the publication of Thomas Paine's *Common Sense* in January 1776, most American colonists appear to have maintained their loyalty to King George III. They largely blamed their troubles either on bad advice that he received from his ministers and counselors or on Parliament, which the colonists thought had no right to tax them.

In doing so, Americans looked for ancient parallels, including those in the Bible. They found one such parallel in the Old Testament book of Esther. It detailed how Esther and her uncle Mordecai had saved the Israelites from Haman, a counselor of King Ahasuerus of the Medes and Persians, who had conspired to destroy the Jews after Mordecai had refused to bow to him.

In the period leading up to America's break with the king in the Declaration of Independence, a number of writers compared George III to Ahasuerus and

Haman to Lord Bute, Lord North, or other counselors or generals (Shalev 2013a, 31). In this interpretation, which overlapped with republican notions of the dangers of corruption, Haman had become corrupt and had misinformed the king of the situation in order to enhance his own power and influence and to pursue a personal vendetta.

See also Common Sense (Thomas Paine)

For Reference and Further Reading

Shalev, Eran. 2013a. *American Zion: The Old Testament as a Political Text from the Revolution to the Civil War*. New Haven, CT: Yale University Press.

Shalev, Eran. 2013b. "Evil Counselors, Corrupt Traitors, and Bad Kings: The Hebrew Bible and Political Critique." *Resistance to Tyrants, Obedience to God: Reason, Religion and Republicanism at the American Founding*, ed. Dustin Gish and Daniel Klinghard. Lanham, MD: Lexington Books, pp. 105–24.

Aitken Bible

During the colonial era, the British, who viewed the colonies as a source of raw materials rather than as a rival manufacturing center, prohibited the printing of Bibles in America. As war broke out between the colonies and Britain, there was a perceived shortage.

In July 1777, Francis Alison, the pastor of Philadelphia's First Presbyterian Church, drew up a petition, signed by two colleagues, urging Congress to authorize an American printing but suggesting that "unless the sale of the whole Edition belong to the Printer, & he be bound under sufficient Penalties, that no copy be sold by him, nor any Retailer under him, at a higher price than that allowed by this honourable house, we fear that ye whole impression would soon be bought up, & sold again at an exorbatant price, which would frustrate your pious endeavours & fill ye Country with Just complaints" (quoted in Pears 1939, 226). Believing that proper types for such printing were unavailable in America, Congress ordered the committee to fulfill this need by importing twenty thousand Bibles from Holland or Scotland, but was prevented by the war from doing so.

Prior to the British capture and occupation of Philadelphia in 1776, a local Scottish Presbyterian binder, printer, and book seller named Robert Aitken (1735–1802), who worked in Philadelphia from 1771 to 1802, and was later succeeded by his daughter Jane (Spawn and Spawn 1963, 424, 428), printed a King James Version copy of the New Testament, which he had already begun to sell. On January 21, 1781, he appealed to Congress to support his publication of both Old and New Testaments. In his memorial to Congress, he observed,

> That in every well regulated Government in Christendom The Sacred Books of the Old and New Testament, commonly called the Holy Bible, are printed and published under the Authority of the Sovereign Powers, in order to prevent the fatal confusion that would arise, and the alarming Injuries the Christian Faith might suffer from the spurious and erroneous Editions of Divine Revelation. That your Memorialist has no doubt but this work is an Object worthy the attention of the Congress of the United States of America, who will not neglect spiritual security, while they are virtuously contending for temporary blessings. (Pears 1939, 229)

Noting that he had already "made considerable progress in a neat Edition of the Holy Scriptures for the use of schools," he indicated that he was "cautious of suffering [allowing] his copy of the Bible to Issue forth without the sanction of Congress" (Pears 1939, 229). He further wanted Congress to advance money for this purpose.

Although Congress neither advanced money to Aitkin for this purpose nor offered to purchase his Bibles, a committee, which included two congressional chaplains, did examine the Bible for accuracy, and on September 10, 1782, Congress adopted its first and only such endorsement of such a publication:

> Whereupon, Resolved, That the United States in Congress assembled highly approve the pious and laudable undertaking of Mr. Aitken, as subservient to the interest of religion, as well as an instance of the progress of arts in this country, and being satisfied from the above report of his care and accuracy in the execution of the work, they recommend this edition of the Bible to the inhabitants of the United States, and hereby authorize him to publish this Recommendation in the manner he shall think proper. (Pears 1939, 234)

In a subsequent advertisement, which appeared in the *Freeman's Journal* of September 25, 1782, Aitken published an advertisement. It stated,

> The serious Christian will be pleased to find, that the scarcity of Bibles, of which he has so long had reason to complain, is now removed; and the patriot will rejoice at the advance in the arts, which has at length produced The First Edition of the Holy Scriptures, in the English language, ever printed in America; each of these will allow the merit due to so capital an undertaking; and the trader will find his interest in affording his patronage and encouragement to this work, as several circumstances, particularly the largeness of the type, and the remarkable good quality of the paper, render this edition superior to any of the same size important from Europe. (Pears 1939, 235)

Aitkin further indicated that the Bibles were available "either bound or in sheets" or as large family Bibles (Pears 1939, 235).

A further communication appeared in the *Freeman's Journal* dated November 20, 1782, noting that apart from a German Bible and an Indian Bible, this was the first such Bible printed in America, and that given that even "the very paper that has received the impression of these sacred books was manufactured in Pennsylvania, the whole book is, therefore, purely American, and has risen, like the fabled Phoenix, from the ashes of that pile in which our enemies supposed they had consumed the liberties of America" (Pears 1939, 237).

Aitken had hoped that Congress might buy a copy for each of those who had served under him, but although he said that "it would have pleased me well, if Congress had been pleased to make such an important present to the brave fellows who have done so much for the security of their country's rights and establishment," he indicated that it was now too late to do so since most of them had been released (Pears 1939, 238).

In 1789, prior to the establishment of copyright laws, Aitken asked Congress to give him the exclusive right to publish Bibles in the United States for the next fourteen years, but it did not do so, and editions by other publishers quickly followed (Pears 1939, 240). James H. Smylie claims that Aitken "never recovered his investment" (1997, 153). Matthew Carey observed that as soon as the Revolutionary War ended and Bibles could be imported, "Bibles were imported on a large scale, somewhat superior in quality and at a far lower price, so that he lost the sale of his, or if he sold, it was at a considerable loss" (quoted in Carter 2007, 453).

It is important to recognize that Aitken's request for government authorization and subsidy came prior to the adoption of the First Amendment, which limits the governmental "establishment" of religion. Although Aitken is believed to have printed as many as ten thousand copies, relatively few remain, and they are highly valued ("Aitken's Bible Endorsed by Congress").

When approached by Christopher Talbot about publishing a Catholic version of the Bible, Talbot reported that "in a holy fit of zeal," Carey had said "that he would rather print the woman of pleasure, than such a pestiferous, idolatrous book" (quoted in Carter 2007, 453–54).

See also King James Version of the Bible; Revolutionary War

For Reference and Further Reading

"Aitken's Bible Endorsed by Congress." Free Republic. www.freerepublic.com/focus/f-news/2722475/posts. Accessed March 25, 2019.

Carter, Michael S. 2007. "'Under the Benign Sun of Toleration': Matthew Carey, the Douai Bible, and Catholic Print Culture, 1789–1791." *Journal of the Early Republic* 27 (Fall): 437–69.

Davis, Deric H. 2000. Religion and the Continental Congress, 1774–1789: *Contributions to Original Intent*. New York: Oxford University Press.

Hogue, William M. 1991. "An Authorized Bible for America." *Anglican and Episcopal History* 60 (September): 361–82.

Pears, Thomas C., Jr. 1939. "The Story of the Aitken Bible." *Journal of the Department of History (the Presbyterian Historical Society) of the Presbyterian Church in the U.S.A.* 18 (June): 225–41.

Smylie, James H. 1997. "America's Political Covenants, the Bible, and Calvinists." *Journal of Presbyterian History* 75 (Fall): 153–64.

Spawn, Willman, and Carol Spawn. 1963. "The Aitken Shop: Identification of an Eighteenth-Century Bindery and Its Tools." *Papers of the Bibliographical Society of America* 57 (Fourth Quarter): 422–37.

Sweet, William W. 1935. "The English Bible in the Making of America." *Christian Education* 19 (October): 9–13.

Alternate Scriptures

Although the focus of this work is on the Bible consisting of the Old and New Testaments, and its role in U.S. law and politics, it is important to recognize that there are alternate scriptural texts that are considered as inspired holy books by other religions and that a number of these have been homegrown.

Jews rely not only on the Scriptures that Christians call the Old Testament but also on interpretations found in the Talmud. Muslims subscribe to the Koran, which they believed God directly dictated to the prophet Muhammad. In contrast to the general Christian willingness to accept translations of Scripture, some Muslims believe that the Koran should not be translated but can only be efficacious in its original Arabic. Hindus consider the Bhagavad Gita to be their Scripture. Both of these Scriptures have been used when members of Congress have taken their oaths to support the U.S. Constitution. In addition, some individuals have avoided holy books altogether, preferring to put their hand on the Constitution or another legal text.

In a study of the National Prayer Breakfast, Jonathan Peterson observes that President Clinton was the first to refer specifically to a text other than the Bible when he referred to a version of the Golden Rule in the Koran and to its teaching "that God created nations and tribes that we might know one another, not that we might despise one another" (2017, 220). Similarly, at the Prayer Breakfast in 2014, President Obama observed that "the Koran instructs: 'Stand out firmly for justice' " (220).

Within the U.S. context, there are some religions, which have had impacts on U.S. politics, that have relied on supplemental texts. They arose within what Lydia Willsky identifies as a "plain Bible" culture, which she associates with "three mutually reinforcing assumptions," namely "that the Bible was *clear* in meaning, *persuasive* in message and *authoritative* in truth claims" (2014, 15). These assumptions were, in turn, often tied to Common Scottish Sense philosophy, which had taught "that truth was knowable through the senses, and that inductive reasoning from observation was the best means for gaining knowledge of truth" (Willsky 2014, 17).

Joseph Smith (1804–1844) questioned this view as he observed the wide variety of interpretations of the same Scripture. Interestingly, by his own account, it was this very Scripture that pointed to a solution. After reading James 1:5, which states, "If any of you lack wisdom, let him ask of God, that giveth to all men liberally, and upbraideth not; and it shall be given him" (cited in Willsky 2014, 19), Smith began to do so. He eventually had a number of revelations that led, by his account, to the translation of golden plates, which he interpreted through two stones called the Urim and Thummin, which were themselves biblical names (Samuel 14:41 and Exodus 28:13–30). In addition to the Book of Mormon, which was first published in 1830, Smith later added the Doctrine and Covenants (1835) and a Book of Abraham (1842), all of which were written in King James English. Somewhat later, the Reorganized Church of Jesus Christ of Latter-Day Saints added his Inspired Version of the Bible, which not only reinterpreted but sometimes added to that Document Scriptures (like revelations to Enoch) that he thought had been lost. In studying this document, Philip Barlow observes that Smith's alterations fell into a number of distinct categories: "long additions that have little or no biblical parallel"; "theological change"; "interpretive additions"; "harmonization"; "grammatical changes, technical clarifications, and modernization of terms" (1990, 55–57). Philip Barlow believes that Smith "was an authentic, nineteenth-century, Bible-believing Christian" but that he was distinctive in that he was not convinced of the Bible's "sufficiency" (1989, 762).

Mary Baker Eddy (1821–1910) added yet another book that has served Christian Scientists when she authored *Science and Health*, which seeks to exegete Scriptures by interpreting them in a more spiritualistic fashion. Eddy, too, appears to have been launched on her quest while reading on a hospital bed the words of Matthew 9:2: "And, behold, they brought to him a man sick of palsy, lying on a bed: and Jesus, seeing their faith said unto the sick of the palsy: Son, be of good cheer: thy sins be forgiven them" (quoted in Willsky 2014, 24). This document often quoted from the Scriptures that it sought to interpret.

Seventh Day Adventists, which grew out of the millennial Millerite movement, and who argue that Christians should honor Saturday, rather than Sunday, as the Sabbath, accept the writings of Ellen G. White (1827–1915) as prophetic. They included commentaries on the Old and New Testaments as well as the life of Christ.

A non-Christian religious book that has enjoyed considerable success since its initial publication in 1950 is L. Ron Hubbard's (1911–1986) *Dianetics: The Modern Science of Mental Health*. This has become the bedrock for Scientology. Another book that was published soon thereafter was Sun-Myung Moon's *The Divine Principle*, which is a central text for the Unification Church (Gutjahr 2001, 353–54). From quite a different perspective, Anton Szazndor LaVey published *The Satanic Bible* in 1969 (Gallagher 2013).

Willsky points out that the writer Henry David Thoreau (1817–1862), usually identified with the New England transcendentalist movement, took the idea of Scriptures to yet another level when in 1859 he authored a personal bible entitled *Wild Fruits* that was not widely known until its publication in 2000. Unlike the Mormon or Christian Science Scriptures, it is not clear that he intended for this to be authoritative for others. Other Bibles that have been reprinted, but not embraced by any particular group of believers, include the Jefferson Bible and the Women's Bible edited by Elizabeth Cady Stanton. Professor Paul C. Gutjahr observes that John Ballou Newbrough (1828–1891) published his *OAHSPE*, which he said he received through channeling in 1882 and that Philemon Stewart, a Shaker, published a text through channeling entitled *A Holy, Sacred and Divine Rolle and Book; from the Lord God of Heaven, to the Inhabitants of Earth* in 1843 (Gutjahr 2001, 345). The Jehovah's Witnesses are known for their *New World Translation* of the Bible, which they first published in 1960 (Gutjahr 2001, 345).

Apart from serving as books on which individuals might take oaths of office, it does not appear that any of these books have been extensively quoted by politicians, apart perhaps from those who might be addressing audiences of Muslims, Mormons, or Christian Scientists. It seems highly doubtful that many individuals outside of these denominations are familiar with these Scriptures or would be likely to recognize them. Given the current religious configuration of the United States, this seems unlikely to change in the near future. Especially in the case of those, like Mitt Romney, who view their own holy books as supplemental to the Bible, it would seem more useful to cite the text that most members of the public would recognize than one that would only appeal to adherents of a single faith.

A recent collection of the favorite Scriptures of one hundred American leaders notes that John Adams enjoyed quoting the introduction of the Shasta, a Hindu Scripture translated from Sanskrit that said,

> God is one, creator of all, universal sphere, without beginning, without end. God governs all the creation by a general providence, resulting from his eternal designs. Search not the essence and the nature of the Eternal, who is one; your

> research will be vain and presumptuous. It is enough, that, day by day and night by night, you adore his power, his wisdom, and his goodness, in his works." (Winder 2019, 2)

The book cites favorite Scriptures from other leaders from the writings of Muhammad and Joseph Smith, the Bhagavad Gita (a Hindu text that had some influence on American Transcendentalism and that has been emphasized by the Hare Krishnas), the Dharma (Gautama Buddha), and others.

See also Church of Jesus Christ of Latter-Day Saints; Congressional Oaths of Office; Jefferson Bible; Muhammad, Elijah; Stanton, Elizabeth Cady

For Reference and Further Reading

Barlow, Philip L. 1989. "Before Mormonism: Joseph Smith's Use of the Bible, 1820–1829." *Journal of the American Academy of Religion* 57 (Winter): 739–71.

Barlow, Philip L. 1990. "Joseph Smith's Revision of the Bible: Fraudulent, Pathologic, or Prophetic?" *Harvard Theological Review* 83 (January): 45–64.

"Forum: American Scriptures." 2011. *Religion and American Culture: A Journal of Interpretation* 21 (Winter): 1–38.

Gallagher, Eugene V. 2013. 2013. "Sources, Sects, and Scripture: The Book of Satan in *The Satanic Bible*." *The Devil's Party: Satanism in Modernity*, ed. Per Faxneld and Jesper A. Peterson. New York: Oxford University Press, pp. 103–22.

Gutjahr, Paul C. 2012. *The "Book of Mormon": A Biography*. Princeton, NJ: Princeton University Press.

Gutjahr. Paul C. 2001. "Sacred Texts in the United States." *Book History* 4: 335–70.

Peterson, Jonathan. R. 2017. "The Religious Content of the Presidents' Remarks at the National Prayer Breakfast, 1953–2016." *Congress & the Presidency* 44(2): 212–34.

Willsky, Lydia. 2014. "The (Un)Plain Bible: New Religious Movements and Alternative Scriptures in Nineteenth-Century America." *Nova Religio: The Journal of Alternative and Emergent Religions* 17 (May): 13–36.

Winder, Mike. 2019. *Favorite Scriptures of 100 American Leaders*. Springville, UT: Plain Sight.

America as New Israel

The fact that Christians divide the Bible into Old and New Testaments is but one indication that this book (or collection of books) focuses on two distinct but related subjects. Most, albeit not all, of the Old Testament describes God's dealings with the nation of Israel, which it presents, as a chosen people. Thus, Deuteronomy 7:6 observes that "thou are an holy people unto the LORD thy God: the LORD thy God hath chosen thee to be a special people unto himself, above all people that are upon the face of the earth." Most of the New Testament deals with the life of Jesus (who, as a Jew, would have been part of this Israel) and the founding of the church, which is often presented as a New Israel, and which is further described as inheriting many of the blessings and obligations of its predecessor. Matthew 16:18 thus notes Jesus's intention to found the church upon a rock "and the gates of hell shall not prevail against it."

As Christianity later split into Catholic and Protestant divisions, which would themselves break into many additional subdivisions including the Church of England, it was common for its members to understand themselves as continuing to perpetuate the struggles and blessings of their spiritual forbears, who did not, at the time, have their own homeland. Richard Hughes notes that William Tyndale (ca. 1494–1534), who translated the Bible into English, was especially interested in the idea of the covenant between God and Israel as described in Deuteronomy 28 and that he was further struck with "the twin themes of chosen people and covenant," which he applied to England (2009, 21).

As Puritans sought to purify this Church, they regarded themselves as having a special mission, which those who came to America hoped might find its full fulfillment there. This mission is often epitomized in John Winthrop's speech entitled "A Model of Christian Charity," in which, citing an analogy from Jesus's Sermon on the Mount, he referred to America as "a city upon a hill" that could serve as a model for others. Puritans, and later American revolutionaries, would compare themselves to Jews who had crossed the Red Sea in order to enter their own promised land, a motif that both Benjamin Franklin and Thomas Jefferson would contemplate as part of the American Seal. In 1784, Timothy Dwight (1752–1817), a congressional minister, authored a massive work on American history entitled *The Conquest of Canaan*. There had, of course, been those who had questioned the connection between America and Israel, perhaps most notably Roger Williams, who had observed, "The State of the land of Israel, the Kings and people thereof in Peace & War, is proved figurative and ceremonial, and no pattern nor precedent for any Kingdom or civil state in the world to follow" (quoted in Hughes 2009, 25).

Still, long after many Americans had shed many of the beliefs that were tied to Puritanism, they continued to think of themselves as a "chosen people," or as God's New Israel, with the earlier religious mission often melded into the mission of advancing knowledge and liberty. John Berens observes that what he calls American "providentialism" was often at odds with European Enlightenment thinking, which largely divorced world events from God's design. Berens tied this providentialism to five themes, which he identified as follows: "(1) the motif of America as God's New Israel; (2) the jeremiad tradition; (3) the deification of America's founding fathers; (4) the blending of national and millennial expectations; and (5) providential history and historiography" (1978, 2).

Writing in "A Dissertation on the Feudal Law," John Adams described the settling of America as "the opening of a grand scene and design in Providence for the illumination of the ignorant and the emancipation of the slavish part of mankind all over the earth" (quoted in Richard 2016, 140). In 1783 Ezra Stiles, the president of Yale, delivered a message entitled "The United States Elevated to Glory and Honor," in which he elaborated on what he perceived to be America's link to Israel. In his Second Inaugural Address in 1805, President Thomas Jefferson observed that he would need the help "of that Being in whose hands we are, who led our forefathers, as Israel of old, from their native land and planted them in a land flowing with all the necessaries and comforts of life" (quoted in Richard 2016, 144). In later years, America would consider their conquest of the American West as a "manifest destiny," and their obligation to foreign colonies like the Philippines to Christianize them. Mormonism would further emerge as a distinct American religion, which was based in part on the belief that Jesus had come to America to reveal Himself to the lost tribes of the house of Israel.

In *White Jacket*, American novelist Herman Melville wrote, "Escaped from the house of bondage, we Americans are the peculiar, chosen people—the Israel of our time; we bear the ark of the liberties of the world" (quoted in Hughes 2009, 24). Harriet Beecher Stowe observed that early Americans "spoke of Zion and Jerusalem, of the God of Israel, the God of Jacob, as much as if my grandfather had been a veritable Jew; and except for the closing phrase, 'for the sake of thy Son, our Saviour,' might all have been uttered in Palestine by a well-trained Jew in the time of [King] David" (quoted in Shalev 2013, 155).

Notably, England and America are not the only nations to embody the notion that they are a chosen people. The Confederate States of America sought to emphasize what it believed to be its special ties to God by specifically referring to God in its constitution. Such a notion was embraced by the Dutch, French, and Germans, known as Afrikaners, who settled in South Africa and long practiced a policy of racial separation and discrimination (Hughes 2009, 28). In a more secular context, fascist nations have considered themselves to be the protectors of a favored race while communist nations have believed themselves to be the unique representatives of the proletariat class.

Perhaps because of the way they identify their own founding with that of ancient Israel, Americans have generally supported the reestablishment of a Jewish state in Israel, with the United States being one of the first nations to recognize that state when it was founded in 1948. Modern American Jews and evangelical Christians, many of whom believe the nation's reestablishment was a fulfillment of biblical prophecies, are often very supportive of that country.

See also Confederate States of America; Great Seal of the United States of America; Model of Christian Charity (Winthrop); Moses as Political Archetype; Political Hebraism; Williams, Roger; Zionism

For Reference and Further Reading

Ahlstrom, Sydney E. 1976. "The Religious Dimension of American Aspiration." *Review of Politics* 38 (July): 332–42.

Berens, John F. 1978. *Providence & Patriotism in Early America, 1640–1815.* Charlottesville: University Press of Virginia.

Goldman, Shalom. 2014. " 'God's New Israel': American Identification with Israel Ancient and Modern." *The Bible in the Public Square: Its Enduring Influence in American Life*, ed. Mark A. Chancey, Carol Meyers, and Eric M. Meyers. Atlanta, GA: Society of Biblical Literature, pp. 81–92.

Guyatt, Nicholas. 2007. *Providence and the Invention of the United States, 1607–1876.* New York: Cambridge University Press.

Hughes, Richard T. 2009. *Christian America and the Kingdom of God.* Champaign: University of Illinois Press.

LaFontaine, Charles V. 1976. "God and Nation in Selected U.S. Presidential Inaugural Addresses, 1789–1945: Part One." *Journal of Church and State* 18 (Winter): 39–60.

LaFontaine, Charles V. 1976. "God and Nation in Selected U.S. Presidential Inaugural Addresses, 1789–1945: Part Two." *Journal of Church and State* 18 (Autumn): 503–21.

Mead, Walter Russell. 2008. "The New Israel and the Old: Why Gentile Americans Back the Jewish State." *Foreign Affairs* 87 (July–August): 28–46.

Richard, Carl J. 2016. *The Founders and the Bible.* Lanham, MD: Rowman & Littlefield.

Shalev, Eran. 2013. *American Zion: The Old Testament as a Political Text from the Revolution to the Civil War.* New Haven, CT: Yale University Press.

American Bible Society

One of the organizations that has done the most to promote the distribution of the Bible throughout the United States and the world is the American Bible Society (ABS). Preceded by a number of state organizations, the Society was founded in New York in 1816 largely by Federalist evangelicals who thought that a wider effort was required. American statesmen who were involved in founding or serving in the Society in its early years included its first president, Elias Boudinot, as well as John Jay (the first chief justice of the U.S. Supreme Court), Charles Cotesworth Pinckney (a delegate to the Constitutional Convention of 1787), John Quincy Adams, DeWitt Clinton (a New York governor), Rufus King (another delegate to the Constitutional Convention), Marquis de Lafayette, and Francis Scott Key, who authored "The Star-Spangled Banner" (Fea 2016, 21).

These men were not only committed to the spread of the gospel but were also firmly convinced that greater biblical literacy would lead to greater citizen virtue at home and to the spread of Western civilization abroad. Although they were willing to work with Roman Catholics, they originally published only King James Versions of the Bible, albeit without notes or comments. The later stipulation was based on the idea that "the Bible's salvific message was self-evident in the words of the inspired text" and was designed to create unity among differing Protestant sects (Fea 2016, 63).

An address published by the Society along with its Constitution observed that "the times are pregnant with great events" and that hopes follow "a period of philosophy, falsely so called, and has gone in the track of those very schemes which, under the imposing names of reason and liberality, were attempting to seduce mankind from all which can bless the life that is, or shed a cheering radiance on the life that is to come" (1816, 13–14). In language that remains familiar in the twenty-first century, members expressed their desire to "fly to the aid of all that is holy, against all that is profane; of the purest interest of the community, the family, and the individual, against the conspiracy of darkness, disaster, and death" (14). The address said that "no spectacle can be so illustrious in itself, so touching to man, or so grateful to God, as a nation pouring forth its devotion, its talent, and its treasures, for that kingdom of the Saviour which is righteousness and peace" (15). This magnitude of the task was exacerbated by the immensity of the growing nation and its population "and the dreadful consequences which will ensue from a people's outgrowing the knowledge of eternal life; and reverting to a species of heathenism, which shall have all the address and profligacy of civilized society, without any religious control" (17). The final paragraph firmly placed the Society within the vision that Puritans had brought to American shores and ended with a quotation from Habakkuk 2:14:

> We shall set forward a system of happiness which will go on with accelerated motion and augmented vigour, after, we shall have finished our career; and confer upon our children, and our children's children, the delight of seeing the wilderness turned into a fruitful field, by *the blessing of God upon that seed which their fathers sowed, and themselves watered. In* fine we shall do our part toward that expansion and intensity of light divine, which shall visit, in its progress, the

> palaces of the great, and the hamlets of the small, until the whole "earth be full of the knowledge of Jehovah, as the waters cover the sea." (1816, 20)

Fea notes that supporters like Peter Jay saw the distribution of Bibles as a way of hastening the second coming of Jesus while individuals like Elias Boudinot believed that the imminence of this coming required special efforts to reach as many lost souls in the interim as possible (2016, 27). Supporters identified biblical themes with American principles of liberty. An 1830 circular entitled "The Bible: A Religious Constitution" thus described Scriptures as a "bill of rights dictated by the Holy Spirit—a charter granted by the Deity himself"; it described the Bible as a Christian "Magna Carta" (quoted in Fea 2016, 66).

In 1852, the Society apparently decided to issue a "standard" version of the King James Version, which included making a few changes to the text (Hogue 1991, 370). This stirred controversy among members of the Episcopal Church, which believed that its mother church in England had guardianship of this translation (370). In time, the ABS withdrew its standard edition and acceded to the standard of "authorized British presses" (quoted in Hogue 1991, 373).

The ABS typically sold its Bibles through state and local auxiliaries, making several major pushes to reach areas of the nation, like the South or the western frontier, which they believed had been underserved. In time, these efforts extended to immigrants, whom the Society thought were in special need of acculturating to American Protestant ideals. The Society also distributed Bibles abroad. Typically, the Society viewed its activities in distributing Bibles to be somewhat distinct from the job of missionaries, who were there specifically to make converts to their denominations.

Through the early part of the twentieth century, the ABS largely worked with mainline Protestant denominations, but beginning in the 1970s and 1980s, as the membership of these denominations declined, the ABS took a turn in a more evangelical direction. Not all evangelicals were pleased when the Society reversed its prior policy and published its own Today's English Version of the Bible, the New Testament of which was distributed under the title of *Good News for Modern Man*, which was based on the idea of "dynamic equivalence" rather than on word-for-word translation. The Society produced a special Eisenhower Memorial Edition of this Bible as well as portions of Scripture to be distributed at Independence Hall during the American Bicentennial celebrations of 1976.

Although the Society had largely judged its prior successes by the number of Scriptures it distributed, it became increasingly concerned about biblical illiteracy and therefore dropped its earlier policy about printing Bibles with commentary or comment and instead expressed its purpose as that of making "the Bible available to every person in a language and format each can understand and afford so that all may experience its life-changing message" (Fea 2016, 302).

In the summer of 2015, the Society moved its national headquarters to Philadelphia, where it plans to open a Faith and Liberty Discovery Center beginning in 2020. It will feature a two-story sculpture that symbolically represents the Bible, the Declaration of Independence, and the U.S. Constitution. Roy Peterson, the CEO of the organization, introduced a statement of faith similar to the Nicene Creed affirming orthodox Christian doctrines, and also calling for all employees to be involved in a local church and to "refrain from sexual contact outside the marriage covenant," which it defined as being exclusively between a man and a woman (cited in Shimron 2018). A number of employees left after this policy was enacted.

See also Boudinot, Elias

For Reference and Further Reading

Constitution of the American Bible Society, Formed by a Convention of Delegates, Held in the City of New York, May, 1816, Together with Their Address to the People of the United States; A Notice of Their Proceedings, and a List of Their Officers. 1816. New York: G.F. Hopkins.

Fea, John. 2016. *The Bible Cause: A History of the American Bible Society*. New York: Oxford University Press.

Glynn, Tom. 2015. *Reading Publics: New York City's Public Libraries, 1754–1711*. New York: Fordham University. [Chapter 4: "The Biblical Library of the American Bible Society: Evangelicalism and the Evangelical Corporation," pp. 101–17.]

Hogue, William M. 1991. "An Authorized Bible for Americans." *Anglican and Episcopal History* 60 (September): 361–82.

Jackson, Kent P. 2014. "The Cooperstown Bible." *New York History* 95 (Spring): 243–70.

McKivigan, John R. 1982. "The Gospel Will Burst the Bonds of the Slave: The Abolitionists Bibles for Slaves Campaign." *Negro History Bulletin* 45 (July–August–September): 62–64, 77.

Mondon, Marielle. 2018. "American Bible Society to Open $60 Million Religious Center on Independence Mall in 2020." *PhillyVoice*. December 7.

Shimron, Yonat. 2018. "Employees Quit American Bible Society over Sex and Marriage Rules." *Religion News Service*. May 29. https://religionnews.com/2018/05/29/american-bible-society-to-require-regular-church-attendance-strict-sexuality-codes/.

Taylor, Justin. 2016. "An Interview with John Fea on His New History of the American Bible Society." March 23. https://www.thegospelcoalition.org/blogs/justin-taylor/an-interview-with-john-fea-on-his-new-history-of-the-american-bible-society/.

American Exceptionalism

One idea that has been prominent through much of American history is the idea that America is an exceptional nation with a special God-ordained mission, variously described as that of spreading liberty, advancing civilization, or otherwise aiding in human progress. This sense of mission is often tied in popular discourse to 2 Chronicles 7:14, in which God, speaking to Solomon, proclaims, "If my people who are called by my name will humble themselves and pray, and seek my face, and turn from their wicked ways, then I will hear from heaven, and I will heal their land." In such an interpretation, the American people become the New Israel or the new church that will inherit God's blessings and share them with the rest of the world.

In its mildest form, this idea touts America as an example for others to follow and urges the people to sacrifice on behalf of the freedom of others. The view can, however, also be used to justify American expansion into the West (manifest destiny) or even the American acquisition of colonies in the wake of the Spanish-American War.

The notion of exceptionalism seems to derive in part from the Puritan idea of a covenantal people, who are the recipient of God's special blessings. One foundation for such a belief is John Winthrop's "City upon a Hill" speech in which, using an example from Jesus's Sermon on the Mount, Winthrop argued that the rest of the world would be watching the new colony to see whether or not it would succeed. Although Winthrop's focus was less on a nation state than on the Puritan church, his words have subsequently been used by Presidents John F. Kennedy and Ronald Reagan to justify a robust American foreign policy that promotes American freedoms and values.

Pointing to Puritan unwillingness to extend religious freedom to those outside the Puritan fold, historian Mark Noll has argued that the notion of American exceptionalism might better be traced to the circular letter that George Washington sent to the states when resigning his military commission in 1783 to return to private life (Noll 2012). Observing that "we shall have equal occasion to felicitate ourselves on the lot which Providence has assigned to us," Washington observed, with greater emphasis on human flourishing than on the glory of God, that, having achieved their independence, Americans "are, from this period, to be considered as the Actors on a most conspicuous Theatre, which seems to be peculiarly designated by Providence for the display of human greatness and felicity" (Washington 2015, 128). He further observed that "Heaven has crowned all its other blessings, by giving a fairer opportunity for political happiness, than any other Nation has ever been favored with" (Washington 2015, 128). Washington thought the time was auspicious both because of reason and revelation:

> The foundation of our Empire was not laid in the gloomy age of Ignorance and Superstition, but at an Epocha when the rights of mankind were better understood and more clearly defined, than at any former period, the researches of the human mind, after social happiness, have been carried to a great extent, the Treasures of knowledge, acquired by the labours of Philosophers, Sages and Legislatures, through a long succession of years, are laid open for our use, and their collected wisdom may be happily applied in the Establishment of our forms of Government; the free cultivation of Letters, the unbounded extension of commerce, the progressive refinement of Manners, the growing liberality of sentiment, and above all, the pure and benign light of Revelation, have had a meliorating influence on mankind and increased the blessings of Society. (Washington 2015, 128).

In seeking to take advantage of God's providential blessings, Washington argued for the importance of "an indissoluble Union," "a sacred regard to Public Justice," "the adoption of a proper Peace Establishment," and "the prevalence of that pacific and friendly Disposition, among the people of the United States, which will induce them to forget their local prejudices and policies, to make those mutual concessions which are requisite to the general prosperity, and in some instances, to sacrifice their individual advantages to the interest of the Community" (Washington 2015, 130).

Even though the U.S. Constitution does not mention God, and the First Amendment prohibits the establishment of religion, many early American history texts argued both that God had intervened to help the United States achieve its independence and that Americans thus occupied a higher moral ground than other nations. John Fea thus notes that in Mercy Otis Warren's *History of the Rise, Progress and Termination of the American Revolution*, which she first published in 1805, she both attributed American independence to a "superintending Providence" and said that the "religious and moral character of Americans yet stands on a higher grade of excellence and purity than that of most other nations" (Fea 2016, 9). Perhaps even more shockingly, Emma Willard's *History of the United States*, which was first published in 1826, describes the thinning of Native Americans through disease as a providential provision for "exchanging, upon these shores, a savage for a civilized people" (Fea 2016, 11). Later in the nineteenth century, the notion of American mission was often fueled by secular ideas of progress, by Hegelian ideas of an immanent world spirit, and even by social Darwinism (Ceaser 2012, 19–20).

During the Civil War, both sides portrayed themselves as the heirs of this legacy, with Northerners touting their opposition to slavery and the Confederate States of America pointing to the reintroduction of God within the preamble of their revised constitution. Many leaders of the social gospel movement portrayed World War I as a war for righteousness (Gamble 2003), while World War II pitted America against totalitarian powers and the Cold War pitted it against godless communism. This opposition was highlighted by the congressional introduction of the words "under God" into the pledge of allegiance to the U.S. flag in 1954. President Reagan, who was quite fond of the "city upon a hill" analogy, further labeled the former Soviet Union as the "evil empire," while George W. Bush later labeled Iraq, Iran, and North Korea as constituting an "axis of evil."

It thus seems clear that the idea of American exceptionalism can be used either to remind Americans that much of their prosperity and success has been a gift of grace and to inspire them to seek similar goals for other nations, or a way of emboldening them to absolutize their own values and to assume that their policies must therefore reflect God's will.

See also America as New Israel; City upon a Hill; Under God; U.S. Constitution; Washington, George

For Reference and Further Reading

Ceaser, James W. 2012. "The Origins and Character of American Exceptionalism." *American Political Thought* 2 (Spring): 3–28.

Fea, John. 2016. *Was America Founded as a Christian Nation?: A Historical Introduction*, rev. ed. Louisville, KY: Westminster John Knox Press.

Gamble, Richard M. 2003. *The War for Righteousness: Progressive Christianity, the Great War, and the Rise of the Messianic Nation*. Wilmington, DE: ISI Books.

Noll, Mark A. 2012. " 'Wee Shall Be as a Citty upon a Hill': John Winthrop's Non-American Exceptionalism." *Review of Faith & International Affairs* 10 (Summer): 5–11.

Shalev, Eran. 2013. *American Zion: The Old Testament as a Political Test from the Revolution to the Civil War*. New Haven, CT: Yale University Press.

Washington, George. 2015 [1793]. "George Washington's Circular Letter to the States." *Founding Documents of America: Documents Decoded*, ed. John R. Vile. Santa Barbara, CA: ABC-CLIO, pp. 127–32.

American Patriot's Bible

In today's market, it is common to find a variety of Bibles aimed at particular audiences. In addition to the wide range of English translations, publishers feature children's Bibles (often in cartoon form), study Bibles by various pastors and commentators (often with maps and other historical information), Bibles for women, and Bibles for other niche markets. Groups like the Gideons, who regularly engage in evangelism by distributing Bibles, often design special covers for students, nurses, members of the military, or members of other groups.

In 1969, the American Bible Society published its translation of the Bible, *Good News for Modern Man: Dwight D. Eisenhower Memorial Edition* with a picture of the president on the back cover and the words, "the Bible is endorsed by the ages. Our civilization is built upon its words. In no other book is there such a collection of inspired wisdom, reality and hope." Over a hundred thousand individuals purchased copies (Fea 2016, 294).

In 1975, the American Bible Society published portions of Scripture entitled "Faith, Justice, and Repentance" and pitched as "a Bible-based 'Call to the Nation'" (Fea 2016, 295). In addition to publishing bicentennial editions of the Bible, it also published "'One Nation Under God,' a meditation on Psalm 33:6–22 ('happy is the nation whose God is the Lord') that connected the Bible to the Pledge of Allegiance; 'Sing a New Song' (Psalms 95 through 100), a reminder of the role of the Bible in the culture of Puritan New England; and 'Plead My cause, O Lord' (Psalm 35), a portion designed to draw attention to the psalm and prayer that Rev. Jacob Duché prayed at the opening of the First Continental Congress in Philadelphia in September 1774" (Fea 2016, 295). In 1976, the Society followed up with a publication of Isaiah 61:1–4, and its description of the Year of Jubilee, entitled "Proclaim Liberty throughout the Land," with a photo of the Liberty Bell on the cover, which was distributed at the Independence National Historical Park during July (296).

In 1983, the National Publishing Company published a commemorative edition of the Bible for the bicentennial of the U.S. Constitution, which was to be celebrated in 1987. It contained the outline of Independence Hall on the cover and an introductory essay on the "Genesis of the Constitution of the United States of America." The Masons, who require a belief in God (albeit not in the divinity of Christ), have a special edition of the King James Version of the Bible that they present to new members and that features pictures of Jesus as well as information on American presidents who were Masons.

In 2009, Thomas Nelson published the *American Patriot's Bible*, which was edited by Richard Lee, a Southern Baptist minister. Using the Revised King James Version, Lee's Bible is described on the Amazon.com website as "THE ONE BIBLE THAT SHOWS HOW A LIGHT FROM ABOVE SHAPED OUR NATION." The description further observes, "Never has a version of the Bible targeted the spiritual needs of those who love our country more than The American Patriot's Bible. This extremely unique Bible shows how the history of the United States connects the people and events of the Bible to our lives in a modern world. The Story of the United States is wonderfully woven into the teachings of the Bible and includes a beautiful full-color family record section, memorable images from our nation's history and hundreds of enlightening articles which complement the New King James Version Bible text."

The front cover features pictures of an American flag, various monuments in the nation's capital, a sketch of the Pilgrims landing in Massachusetts with the Mayflower in the background, and a painting of George Washington praying at Valley Forge against a background of the Declaration of Independence. There is a picture of the Statue of Liberty on the book's spine, and of the monument of Marines planting the American flag on Iwo Jima on the back cover, which also includes a quotation from President Ronald Reagan. A scan through the Amazon preview reveals insets on "The Right to a God-Centered Education," "The Abrahamic Covenant," "The Battle Hymn of the Republic," "The Right to Bear Arms," "The Barbary Pirates," and similar entries.

The unnumbered preparatory materials include "The Seven Principles of the Judeo-Christian Ethic." These themes and their accompanying Scriptures are as follows: "The Dignity of Life" (Exodus 20:13 and Matthew 22:39); "The Traditional Monogamous Family" (Genesis 2:23,24) (a later entry on p. 1116 describes "The Bible and Marriage"); "A National Work Ethic" (2 Thessalonians 3:10); "The Right *to a* God-Centered Education" (Ephesians 6:4); "The Abrahamic Covenant"; "Common Decency" (Matthew 22:39); and "Our Personal Accountability *to* God." Just over halfway through the Bible is a page describing "The Censoring of Religious Activities in Public Schools," which portrays the U.S. Supreme Court decisions with respect to prayer, Bible reading, and the posting of the Ten Commandments as an unwarranted and unprecedented reading of "separation of church and state" into the First Amendment (2009, 731).

Although the Amazon website has many favorable reader reviews, many commentators are wary of associating Holy Scriptures with a single nation. Others were particularly concerned about the juxtaposition of a military image at the beginning of the gospels, which are more typically associated with peace (Kaylor 2009).

There is certainly a sense in which the *American Patriot's Bible* further advances the idea that America is a providential "city upon a hill" with a special mission, but most Christian theologians would see Christianity, rather than America, as the heir of ancient Israel. Moreover, such a Bible could obviously prove troubling either to minority groups within the United States who believe that the government has treated them unjustly or to foreign nations who believe that America has confused its own national interests with the will of God.

The *Patriot's Bible* is far from the only specialty publication. Philip L. Barlow has observed, "Both testaments of *The Green Bible* are printed with soy-based ink on recycled paper within a cotton/linen cover, a green-letter edition highlighting passages that depict God's care for creation" ("Forum" 2011, 9). Moreover, in 2014, David Barton published *The Founders' Bible*, highlighting his view that most of America's founding fathers were Christians.

See also America as New Israel; City upon a Hill; Conservative Bible Project; Founders' Bible; Geneva Bible

For Reference and Further Reading

Boyd, Greg. July 5, 2018. "The Patriot's Bible—Really?" Re Knew. https://reknew.org/2018/07/the-patriots-bible-really/. Accessed April 17, 2019.

Fea, John 2016. *The Bible Cause: A History of the American Bible Society*. New York: Oxford University Press.

"Forum: American Scriptures." 2011. *Religion and American Culture: A Journal of Interpretation* 21 (Winter): 1–38.

Kaylor, Brian. May 22, 2009. "Publisher's 'American Patriot's Bible' Draws Strong Criticism." EthicsDaily.com. https://ethicsdaily.com/publishers-american-patriots-bible-draws-strong-criticism-cms-14259/.

Lee, Richard G., ed. 2009. *The American Patriot's Bible: The Word of God and the Shaping of America*. Nashville, TN: Thomas Nelson.

Antichrist

2 John 1:7 refers to the spirit of the "Antichrist," and numerous Scriptures from the book of Revelation refer to a "man of sin" as someone who will oppose Christ in the last days. The term "Antichrist" has been used both to refer to a particularly evil man who will emerge in the end of times and to a succession of leaders who have opposed Christ.

Written in code at a time when Christians were facing persecution, the biblical book of Revelation identifies Babylon, an ancient pagan city, as sitting on seven hills. This was an obvious reference to Rome; the emperor Nero, who persecuted Christians, would have been an obvious Antichrist. Because the Roman Empire was succeeded by the Roman Catholic Church, the headquarters of which (Vatican City) is also in Rome, it was easy for Protestant reformers from Martin Luther forward to identify the pope as an Antichrist.

Indeed, in a forum to which he contributed, Professor Paul S. Boyer observed that the notes to the Geneva Bible, which was published in English in 1560, explained the passage in Revelation 17:3–4, which describes a woman clothed in purple and scarlet and drinking from a cup of abominations and fornications, by saying, "This woman is the Antichrist, that is, the Pope with ye whole bodie of his filthie creatures" ("Forum" 2011, 18). The Puritans brought this idea with them to the new world, with Jonathan Edwards being among those who believed that the Reformation marked the beginning of the last days in which Catholicism would be overthrown. From such a perspective, which does much to explain conflicts over reading the Bible in public schools in the nineteenth and twentieth centuries, Protestants often regarded Catholics less like fellow Christians than like the antithesis to Christ.

During the American Revolution, some Patriots identified King George III as the Antichrist (Burke 2013). This link may have been furthered by the Quebec Act, in which Britain had acknowledged the Catholic Church in Canada. Internationally, Tsar Alexander was among those who identified Napoleon as a possible Antichrist (Carter 2012).

During World War II, a number of commentators identified Hitler or Mussolini as the Antichrist (Carter 2012; Poole 2009, 145). The subsequent Cold War led others to associate the Antichrist with Russia, whose communist ideology was atheistic. Speculation that U.S. secretary of state Henry Kissinger, who had helped open diplomatic relations with communist China, might be the Antichrist in time gave way to the idea that Soviet premier Mikhail Gorbachev, with a distinct birthmark on his forehead that some likened to the biblical "mark of the beast," might be (Carter 2012).

There is not much distance between the view that the pope and Roman Catholics represent the Antichrist and the view that Muslims, who do not accept the divinity of Christ, are in fact Antichrists (Burke 2013). Such usage may, in fact, date back to the Crusades (Burke 2013). Professor Boyer observed that, in the events leading up to the 1990–1991 and the 2011 invasions of Iraq (the home of ancient Babylon), a number of prophetic writers identified Iraqi leader Saddam Hussein as the Antichrist ("Forum" 2011, 15).

Deeply suspicious of talk of a New World Order, which writers on prophecy have often tied to the United Nations, the Council on Foreign Relations, and the Trilateral Commission, a number of such writers (many of whom may have been drawing from the idea that Obama, whose middle name was Hussein, had been born abroad and/or that he was a Muslim) identified Obama as the Antichrist. Indeed, Boyer reports that a Google search conducted in 2010 produced 8,170,000 hits by matching the keywords "Obama" and "Antichrist" ("Forum" 2011, 14). Apparently, every president from Franklin D. Roosevelt through Obama, other than President Ford, was at one time or another also labeled an Antichrist (Carter 2012).

Clearly, the use of such imagery can be adapted to a variety of contexts and tends to lead to political polarization.

See also Edwards, Jonathan; Obama, Barack; Puritans; Satan

For Reference and Further Reading

Burke, Daniel. February 7, 2013. "How the Antichrist Reflects an Era's Anxieties." The Christian Century. https://www.christiancentury.org/article/2013-02/how-antichrist-reflects-eras-anxieties.

Carter, Joe. 2012. "The 7 Most Popular Contenders for the Title 'Antichrist.'" The Gospel Coalition. November 16. https://www.thegospelcoalition.org/article/the-7-most-popular-contenders-for-the-antichrist/.

"Forum: American Scriptures." 2011. *Religion and American Culture: A Journal of Interpretation* 21 (Winter): 1–38.

Poole, W. Scott. 2009. *Satan in America: The Devil We Know*. Lanham, MD: Rowman & Littlefield.

Pyszczynski, Tom, Carl Henthron, Matt Motyl, and Kristel Gerow. 2010. "Is Obama the Anti-Christ? Racial Priming, Extreme Criticisms of Barack Obama, and Attitudes toward the 2008 US Presidential Candidates." *Journal of Experimental Social Psychology* 46: 863–66.

Apess, William

William Apess (1798–1839), although of mixed blood, identified himself with the Pequot. Indentured as a youth to white families, Apess served for a time in the American militia during the War of 1812. After leading a fairly dissolute life, which he described in his autobiography *The Forest: The Experience of William Apess, a Native of the Forest, Comprising a Notice of the Pequod Tribe of*

Indians, the first known autobiography by such a Native American, which was published in 1829, Apess converted and was ordained as a Methodist minister (Tiro 1996).

Much as abolitionist writers were citing Scriptures to condemn slavery, Apess cited Scripture to rail at discrimination against his own people and other peoples of color. He put particular blame on the Puritans, perhaps in part because he was from Massachusetts but probably also because they had been so reputed for their probity and godliness.

Although some versions have edited out a number of his biblical references, Apess's sermon "An Indian's Looking-Glass for the White Man," which was originally published as an epilogue to *The Experience of Five Christian Indians of the Pequod Tribe* (1833), relied quite heavily on the Bible.

Apess began by identifying God as "the maker and preserver both of the white man and the Indian." From here he described the miserable state of so many Native Americans, which he believed stemmed from the government's failure to extend them equal rights and privileges and from simple prejudice based on their skin color. Ironically, God had chosen to create many more individuals of color than whites, and, in terms of character, it was whites who one could charge "with robbing a nation almost of their whole Continent, and murdering their women and children, and then depriving the remainder of their lawful rights" as well as enslaving African Americans and subjecting them "under the lash with hunger and fatigue under the scorching rays of a burning sun."

The Bible admonishes Christians "to follow Jesus Christ and imitate him and have his Spirit." Apess said that the Bible reveals this in Jesus's summary of the Ten Commandments in Matthew 22:37–40, and in numerous verses dealing with the need for Christian love and charity as in John 13:35; 1 John 4:29; 1 John 3:18; 1 Peter 1:22; 1 John 4:20; and 1 John 3:15. Apess further cited Romans 13:9, which says, "Now if any man have not the spirit of Christ, he is none of his."

Apess proceeded to point out that, as Jews, Jesus and his disciples were not white and asked rhetorically when Jesus had ever taught his disciples "that they ought to despise one because his skin was different from theirs?" In an indirect reference to 1 Samuel 16:7, Apess further pointed out that God looked on the heart rather than on outward appearances, and cited a passage quite familiar to abolitionists, namely that "Where there is neither Greek nor Jew, circumcision nor uncircumcision, Barbarian nor Scthian, bond nor free—but Christ is all and in all" (Colossians 3:11). He further contended that missionary societies were degrading rather than elevating Native Americans.

Apess further pointed to Acts 10:34, which indicated that "God is no respecter of persons." Such Scripture was contrary to state laws that prohibited intermarriage between whites and Native Americans and inconsistent with the fact that whites had themselves often chosen Native American mates.

Accusing whites of degrading and robbing Native Americans, Apess noted that there were some American statesmen who did not mock them, and evoked the compassion of the Good Samaritan (Luke 10:25–37). He ended with, "Do not get tired ye noble-hearted—only think how many poor Indians want their wounds done up daily; the Lord will reward you, and pray you stop not till this tree of distinction shall be leveled to the earth, and the mantle of prejudice torn from every American heart—then shall peace pervade the Union."

Relying more on history than on Scripture, Apess delivered his "Eulogy on King Philip" on January 26, 1836, which in many ways resembles more traditional jeremiads (Bizell 2006). Comparing this Native American king to George Washington, Apess described in vivid detail the manner in which the Puritans had treated Native Americans as less than equals. He reversed the tables of historians who had described Native Americans as savages by detailing how the Puritans had prayed for their deaths and committed many massacres against them. Much like Frederick Douglass in his "What to the Slave in the Fourth of July," Apess described both the day that the Pilgrims landed at Plymouth Rock and Independence Day as "days of mourning and not of joy" (Apess 1836).

See also Douglass, Frederick; Native American Indians; Prophets and Jeremiads; Puritans

For Reference and Further Reading

Apess, William. 1833. "An Indian's Looking-Glass for the White Man." University of Houston Clear Lake. http ://coursesite.uhcl.edu/HSH/Whitec/texts/Amerind/apesslkggls.htm. Note: Because this text leaves out many of Apess's references to the Bible, I have supplemented it with https://www.youtube.com/watch?y=NiY5ef4hWTO.

Apess, William. 1836. "Eulogy on King Philip." Voices of Democracy: The U.S. Oratory Project. https://voicesofdemocracy.umd.edu/apess-eulogy-speech-text/.

Bizell, Patricia. 2006. "(Native) American Jeremiad: The 'Mixedblood' Rhetoric of William Apess." *American Indian Rhetoric of Survivance: Word Medicine, Word Magic*, ed. Ernest Stromberg. Pittsburg, PA: University of Pittsburgh Press, pp. 34–49.

Goodnight, Ethan. 2017. "William Apess, Pequot Pastor: A Native American Revisioning of Christian Nationalism in the Early Republic." *Religions* 8(18): 17pp. https://www.mdpi.com/2077-1444/8/2/18/pdf.

Tiro, Karim M. 1996. "Denominated 'SAVAGE': Methodism, Writing, and Identity in the Works of William Apess, a Pequot." *American Quarterly* 48 (December): 653–79.

Articles, Laws, and Orders, Divine, Politic, and Martial for the Colony in Virginia (1610)

Although it has received far less attention than the laws of New England, the Articles, Laws, and Orders, Divine, Politic, and Marital for the Colony that were issued in Virginia in 1610 have similar scriptural foundations and supports.

Brent Tarter has noted that this set of orders was "the earliest extant English-language body of laws in the western hemisphere," but is careful to add that "it was not a legal code in the modern sense. No legislation created it, and no court enforced it" (Tarter n.d.). Although often associated with Governor Thomas Dale, the orders, which came at a very troubling time in Virginia's early history, appear to have originated with a number of military men. Moreover, in contrast to studies that suggest that colonists carried the common law with them to America, these fairly draconian laws appear more similar to regulations that had been used to govern other colonies, with relatively few free men, than those that are associated with the common law (Konig 1982). It is not always clear whether the regulations applied to citizens in general or only to those who were in the militia, which might, however, have included most adult males.

The most obvious features of the regulations was the manner in which they depend so heavily on the Ten Commandments and how many violations of these commandments are in turn linked to the death penalty. The first of thirty-seven numbered sections begins by observing that humans owe the highest allegiance to "the King of kings, the commaunder of commanders, and Lord of Hostes" (1611). This leads to regulations against speaking "impiously or maliciously, against the holy and blessed Trinitie," or "against the knowne Article of the Christian faith, upon paine of death" (1611). Section 3 specifically provides that those who take God's name in vain or "use unlawful oaths" are subject to having a bodkin thrust through their tongue or, upon multiple offenses, even death.

Subjects are compelled to go to church twice a day and, consistent again with the Ten Commandments, to observe the Sabbath. Section 8 punished murder with death, with other severe penalties for sodomy, fornication, or sacrilege. Section 10 provided penalties for theft, and Section 11 for bearing false witness. There were additional sanctions for trading with Native American Indians or with visiting shipmen, which were, in turn, tied to the sin of covetousness.

Perhaps reflecting the state of near starvation in the colony, the law limited the killing of domestic farm animals that could be bred to increase the colony's stock. There were additional sanitary regulations limiting the distance within which one could wash clothes or utensils or relieve oneself near a street or well.

Section 25, which is one of the more interesting, provided that "every man shall have an especiall and due care, to keepe his house sweete and cleane, as also so much of the streete, as lieth before his door, and especially he shall so provide, and set his bedstead whereon he lieth, that it may stand three foote at least from the ground, as will answere the contrarie at at a martiall Court." A number of penalties involved cutting off the ears of offenders or requiring their work in ship alleys.

See also Capital Punishment; Massachusetts Body of Liberties; Ten Commandments

For Reference and Further Reading

"Articles, Laws, and Orders, Divine, Politic, and Martial for the Colony in Virginia." 1611. Teaching American History. https://teachingamericanhistory.org/library/document/articles-laws-and-orders-divine-politic-and-martial-for-the-colony-in-virginia/.

Konig, David Thomas. 1982. "'Dale's Laws' and the Non-Common Law Origins of Criminal Justice in Virginia." *American Journal of Legal History* 26 (October): 354–75.

Tarter, Brent. n.d. "Laws Divine, Morall and Martiall." Encyclopedia Virginia. https://www.encyclopediavirginia.org/Lawes_Divine_Morall_and_Martiall.

Articles of Confederation

Even before it was officially ratified in 1781, the Articles of Confederation, which was proposed by the Second Continental Congress in 1777, served as the model for the government of the United States that lasted until the implementation of the Constitution that was produced by the Constitutional Convention of 1787 in 1789. The Articles specifically referred to God as "The Great Governor of the World" (Solberg 1958, 51).

Although the document appears to have been chiefly the result of expedience rather than a conscious imitation of biblical government, the Articles and the thirteen states that composed it resembled the government of the twelve tribes of Israel as described in the biblical book of Judges during the period between the death of Joshua (the successor to Moses) and the introduction of kingship in a number of ways (Shalev 2013, 50–83).

Just as primary power rested within individual tribes during the period of judges, so too the Articles of Confederation vested primary sovereignty within the states rather than in its unicameral Congress in which states were equally represented. There was no independent executive power, like later Jewish kings, nor was there an independent judiciary. A majority of nine states was required to adopt most matters of policy under the Articles, and constitutional amendments required unanimous state consent. The national Congress did not have the power exercised by the current body to act directly upon individuals as in taxing them directly or drafting them into military service, nor did it control interstate and foreign commerce.

The Congress that met from the time of American independence until the adoption of the new Constitution did engage in a number of activities related to the Bible. Although it ultimately adopted a different seal, both Benjamin Franklin and Thomas Jefferson, drawing from the Bible, had proposed seals that likened America's revolutionary struggle to that of Moses and the Jewish people in Israel. Congress had begun the practice of inviting chaplains to deliver prayers during the First Continental Congress, at which Jacob Duché had linked the cause of America to that of the Israelites as described in Psalm 35:1.

Consistent with biblical calls for repentance, Congress adopted a number of Fast and Thanksgiving Proclamations and hired chaplains with the hope of encouraging morality among troops. Concerned about the fact that Americans were now cut off from the supply of Bibles that had previously been published in Great Britain, the Congress, which had actually considered issuing a license to a publisher for a single authorized edition (Hogue 1991, 364–65; Gaines 1950/1951), eventually endorsed the publication of a Bible by Robert Aitken of Philadelphia. Congress also sought to encourage literacy by establishing schools in the Northwest Territories.

Ultimately, the people replaced the Articles of Confederation, much as Jews had earlier sought a king, because they found it inadequate to assure justice at home or to preserve the nation's standing abroad. Shay's Rebellion that occurred in the winter of 1786–1787 further suggested that Congress could not adequately protect the states against anarchy (Blau 1987). Largely as a result of their negative experience under King George III, Americans chose to replace their confederal government with a federal one, in which power was divided among three coordinate branches, rather than following the example of the ancient Israelites in establishing a hereditary monarchy.

See also Aitken Bible; First Continental Congress; Forms of Government; Great Seal of the United States; Hebraic Constitutionalism; U.S. Constitution; U.S. Constitutional Convention

For Reference and Further Reading

Blau, Joseph L. 1987. "Government or Anarchy? In the Debates on the Constitution." *Transactions of the Charles S. Peirce Society* 23 (Fall): 507–19.

Dougherty, Keith I. 2001. *Collective Action under the Articles of Confederation.* Cambridge: Cambridge University Press.

Gaines, William H., Jr. 1950/1951. "The Continental Congress Considers the Publication of a Bible, 1777." *Studies in Bibliography* 3: 274–81.

Hogue, William M. 1991. "An Authorized Bible for Americans." *Anglican and Episcopal History* 60 (September): 361–82.

Jensen, Merrill. 1966. *The Articles of Confederation.* Madison: University of Wisconsin Press.

"Religion and the Founding of the American Republic: Religion and the Congress of the Confederation." Library of Congress Exhibitions. https://www.loc.gov/exhibits/religion/rel04.html.

Shalev, Eran. 2013. American Zion: The Old Testament as a Political Text from the Revolution to the Civil War. New Haven, CT: Yale University Press.

Solberg, Winton U., ed. 1958. *The Federal Convention and the Formation of the Union of the American States.* Indianapolis, IN: Bobbs-Merrill.

Vile, John R., and Andrew Foshee. 1988. "Domestic Politics in the Book of Judges: The Story of Gibeah." *Journal of Political Science* 16 (Spring): 33–42.

Ashcroft, John

After serving as attorney general, governor, and U.S. senator from Missouri, John Ashcroft (b. 1942) served as the first U.S. attorney general under President George W. Bush during the terrorist attacks of September 11, 2001. A graduate of Yale University who earned his law degree at the University of Chicago, Ashcroft was a polarizing figure who was often caricatured for his religious beliefs.

Ashcroft is the son and grandson of Assembly of God (a charismatic denomination whose detractors sometimes describe members as "holy rollers") pastors, with his father serving as the president of Evangel University, a liberal arts college sponsored by the Assemblies of God. As a young man, Ashcroft performed southern gospel music and was known for authoring an anthem called "Carry the Cross," which was largely based on Ephesians 6:12. Its words were as follows: "We wrestle not against flesh and blood/ But the darkness of this world./ Put on the whole armor of our God,/ Let his banner of love be unfurled./ I want to carry the cross for the Savior/ I want to carry his cross; that's my goal" (quoted in Goodstein 2001). In giving a speech to students at Bob Jones University in 2001, Ashcroft cited with satisfaction the slogan of some patriots in the American revolution that "We have no king but Jesus" (Larry King Live 2001). On other occasions, however, Ashcroft observe, that "It's against my religion to impose my religion on others" (Goodstein 2001), and despite his own ideological convictions, as attorney general, Ashcroft acted fairly pragmatically (Rosen 2004).

Ashcroft established a reputation for opposing smoking, drinking, dancing, premarital sex, needle exchanges, homosexuality, abortion, and pornography and for holding Bible studies and prayer meetings in his office. Some ridiculed the fact that, consistent with Assembly of God theology, his father chose to anoint him with oil when he accepted public offices. This combined with a statement that "I think all we should legislate is morality" (balanced by "what we can't legislate is spirituality") led to strong but ultimately ineffective opposition to his confirmation as attorney general by those who thought that his policies might be too rigid.

Like President Bush, Ashcroft was deeply affected by the 9/11 terrorist attacks, and he considered his central role to be that of preventing further ones. Again, some opponents were particularly critical of the USA Patriot Act, which they feared might be misused in the future.

Drawing from the Bible, Ashcroft is known for saying that "for every crucifixion, there is a resurrection." After he lost a Senate race to the widow of the candidate whom he had opposed, Ashcroft refused to contest the election and soon found himself appointed as the state auditor of Missouri (Haddock 2002). Visited by presidential aides while he was sick in the hospital, Ashcroft, in conjunction with James Comey and Bob Mueller, refused to oppose reauthorization of practices that he thought might be illegal (Salon Staff 2007).

See also Bush, George W.

For Reference and Further Reading

Ashcroft, John, with Gary Thomas. 1998. *Lessons from a Father to His Son*. Nashville, TN: Thomas Nelson.

Eggen, Dan. 2001. "Ashcroft's Faith Plays Visible Role at Justice." *Washington Post*. May 14.

Goodstein, Laurie. 2001. "Ashcroft's Life and Judgments Are Steeped in Faith." *New York Times*. January 14.

Haddock. Vicki. 2002. "Son of a Preacher Man / How John Ashcroft's Religion Shapes His Public Service." SFGATE. August 4. https://www.sfgate.com/opinion/article/Son-of-a-Preacher-Man-How-John-Ashcroft-s-2787948.php.

Jones, Bob. 2001. "Man of the Law." *World Magazine*. December 22. https://world.wng.org/2001/12/man_of_the_law.

Larry King Live. January 12, 2001. "What Did John Ashcroft Say at Bob Jones University?" CNN.com transcripts. http ://transcripts.cnn.com/TRANSCRIPTS/0101/12/lkl.00.html.

Rosen, Jeffrey. April 2004. "John Ashcroft's Permanent Campaign." *The Atlantic*. https://www.theatlantic.com/magazine/archive/2004/04/john-ashcroft-s-permanent-campaign/302926/.

Salon Staff. 2007. "The Hospital Room Showdown." Salon. May 15. https://www.salon.com/2007/05/15/comey_testimony/.

• B •

Backus, Isaac

Isaac Backus (1724–1806) was the long-time minister of the Middleborough First Baptist Church in Massachusetts and, along with Roger Williams and John Leland, was among the most persistent and effective advocates for separating church and state. From 1777 to 1796, Backus published a three-volume *History of New England, with Particular Reference to the Denomination of Christians called Baptists* (Wood 1977). A much shorter work is one that he wrote in 1773 on the eve of the American Revolution against assessments on behalf of the established Congregational Church. Somewhat like a sermon, the cover page referred to Galatians 5:13, which says, "Brethren, ye have been called unto Liberty; only use not Liberty for an occasion to the Flesh, but by love serve one another."

Backus's 1773 essay is prefaced with an introduction that denies any opposition between true liberty and government. Backus argues, "The true liberty of man is, to know, obey and enjoy his Creator, and to do all the good unto, and enjoy all the happiness with and in his fellow-creatures that he is capable of; in order to which the law of love was written in his heart, which carries in it's nature union and benevolence to being in general, and to each being, in particular, according to it's nature and excellency" (1773, 331). Recounting the story of Adam and Eve in the Garden of Eden, Backus believed that adherence to law actually preceded the fall of man, and that according to 2 Peter 2:18, continuing obedience to law is necessary to secure human flourishing.

Citing 2 Peter 2:13–14, Backus acknowledged the obligation of Christians to follow governmental authority while also pointing out that Colossians 2:20, 22 warns against being "subject to ordinances, after the doctrines and commandments of men" (335). Civil offices should foster responsible behavior toward neighbors whereas "church government respects our behavior toward God as well as man" (336). The Bible thus distinguishes between behavior toward the king and the state and behavior toward the church and toward Christ. As Backus interprets Matthew 23:1–6, Luke 22:25–27, and John 18:36–37, God's kingdom is not of this world, and is therefore not subject to human authority. In words that would probably resonate beyond fellow Baptists, Backus traced the decline of the church and the rise of "hellish tyranny" under the popes, which Protestant reformers had resisted to developments in the aftermath of the decision of Constantine to make Christianity the official religion of Rome (338).

Whereas the colonial legislature claimed the power to compel every town to support public worship by paying taxes for the support of ministers, Backus noted that such support went only to "pedobaptists," that is, to those who, unlike Baptists, supported infant baptism. Disputing the tie that the established church drew between this covenant and Old Testament circumcision, Backus's main point was that each church should be able to appoint its own minister, with greater regard to their spiritual gifts and calling than to their formal theological education (340). Those who serve as pastors are not the "king's minister[s]," but God's (42). Nor does the majority have the right, with regard to such matters of conscience, to dictate to the minority. Backus effectively accused the Puritans of treating dissenters with the same kind of contempt as the Anglican Church had treated the Puritans before they left for America (344).

In a final section of his writing, Backus detailed the way that Baptists have suffered under such rules, with some of them actually being imprisoned for either refusing to pay the tax for preachers of other denominations or refusing to register themselves, or being unable to get recognition of their ministers, in order to get special exemptions. Again speaking in language that might appeal to a wider audience, Backus claimed that it is "high time now to awake, and seek for a more thorough reformation" (356). Churches should be accountable only to Christ, the head of the church, and not to civil authorities.

In his conclusion, Backus appealed again to "equal liberty of conscience" (32). Moreover, he tied the cause of Baptists to the developing colonial case against Great Britain: "as the present contest between Great-Britain and America, is not so much about the greatness of the taxes already laid, as about a submission to their taxing power; so (though what we have already suffered is far from being a trifle, yet) our greatest difficulty at present concerns the submitting to a taxing power in ecclesiastical affairs" (364). The money set aside for pastors should be "sacrifices" (Hebrews 13:15–16) rather than governmental compulsions (366). Noting that the New England fathers are not the only ones to have sought such taxation, he observed that "our veneration for their memory, is so far from reconciling us to [them?], that it fills us with greater detestation of, that mystery of iniquity, which carried them into such acts or imposition and persecution as have left a great blemish upon their character" (367).

See also Baptists; Leland, John; Williams, Roger

For Reference and Further Reading

Backus, Isaac. 1773. *An Appeal to the Public for Religious Liberty, against the Oppressions of the Present Day*. Boston: John Boyle. Reprinted in Sandoz, Ellis, ed. 1991. *Political Sermons of the Founding Era, 1730–1804*. Indianapolis: Liberty Fund, pp. 327–68.

McLoughlin, William G. 1967. *Isaac Backus and the American Pietistic Tradition*. Boston: Little, Brown.

Richards, Peter Judson 2001. "'A Clear and Steady Channel': Isaac Backus and the Limits of Liberty." *Journal of Church and State* 43 (Summer): 447–82.

Wood, Jerome H., Jr. 1977. "For Truth and Reputation: The New England Friends' Dispute with Isaac Backus." *New England Quarterly* 50 (September): 458–83.

Baptists

The nation's largest Protestant denomination with over sixteen million members is the Southern Baptist Convention. It is only one of a number of Baptist groups, almost all of which take a high view of biblical inspiration and of the importance of the Bible as a guide to personal conduct. In contrast to both the Episcopal and Presbyterian traditions, Baptists reject any hierarchy above local churches.

Similarly, Baptists generally eschew creeds, fearing that they might displace emphasis on Scriptures. Like the Restoration movement, often associated with Churches of Christ and Disciples of Christ, Baptists try to replicate the early church, with the so-called Landmarkism movement within the group actually claiming that the early church was Baptistic rather than Catholic in orientation (Hudnut-Beumler 2018, 70).

Essentially an offshoot of Puritanism, Baptists had distinctive views of baptism, which they consider to be an ordinance that does not have saving value but that provides testimony to an inward conversion. Consistent with their view of Scripture, they believe that such baptism should be by full immersion in water (rather than by sprinkling) and that, because it is a symbol of an inward work, it should not be performed (as Puritans did) on infants but only on those who can make a conscious decision to follow Christ.

Although they were otherwise fairly theologically close to the Puritans, Roger Williams, who is often identified as the first Baptist in America, was expelled from the Massachusetts colony and went on to found the state of Rhode Island. Perhaps in part because they were members of such a minority, Baptists were among the first to advocate for separation of church and state, particularly with respect to an established church or using tax money for its support; they believed that such support invariably led to the corruption of the church's mission, which was called, consistent with Galatians 1:4 and 2 Corinthians 6:17, to avoid worldliness. This view was forcefully articulated by John Leland and Isaac Backus and embodied in the establishment clause of the First Amendment. James Madison had been particularly appalled by the incarceration of Baptist pastors in Culpepper, Virginia, for preaching without licenses from what was then the established church of the state.

Baptists and Methodists—a movement founded by John Wesley (1703–1791), which, like Puritanism, was originally designed to refine the Episcopal Church rather than to establish a new denomination—were at the forefront of revivalist campaigns during the Second Great Awakening in the early nineteenth century, which often depended on ministers whose qualifications centered on their perceived sense of calling to the ministry rather than on theological education. Although some Baptists were strict Calvinists who believed in double predestination (neither the elect nor the nonelect could change their eternal destinies), revivalists tended to lean toward the Arminian view that individuals had a choice as to whether to accept or reject salvation by believing in Christ. This has been true of subsequent Baptist evangelists like Billy Graham. Like other major denominations of the day, Baptists broke into Northern and Southern wings on the basis of biblical interpretations opposing or supporting slavery.

Baptists believe it is the duty of every Christian to help spread the gospel, and they have been active in mission movements. They have traditionally advocated strict modes of personal behavior and in earlier years often expelled members who fell short of such standards. Although some have since liberalized these views, Bill Leonard observes that their "sin-list" typically "included alcohol, illicit sex, gambling, card playing, dancing, motion pictures, tobacco, tattoos, rock music, and assorted other public and private evils" (2005, 232). In the nineteenth century, Baptists were strong advocates of temperance and often included a temperance pledge as part of their qualifications of membership. In the twentieth century, they have joined battles against pornography, sponsored a "true love waits" campaign designed to combat premarital sex, and generally have opposed same-sex marriage. Many have also opposed liberal abortion laws. Unlike many other denominations, Baptists put primary emphasis on the power of each individual congregation, and while associations of such churches may from time to time expel or disassociate themselves from a particular congregation, they cannot otherwise exercise power over it. Recent years have witnessed deep divisions within the Southern Baptist Church (Barnhart 1986).

In the 1970s, Baptist minister Jerry Falwell helped create the Moral Majority, which emphasized opposition to moral vices and a number of today's megachurches are led by Baptist pastors. In more recent years, the Westboro Baptist Church in Kansas, a small independent Primitive Baptist congregation that believes that God has chosen his elect and brings judgment on all others, has garnered headlines by demonstrating at funerals of American soldiers and proclaiming that their deaths are a result of God's condemnation of a nation that permits homosexuality and other behavior that its members consider to be immoral. The U.S. Supreme Court ruled that the First Amendment shielded its members from civil liability for such actions in *Snyder v. Phelps* (2011). Its pastor Fred Phelps, who was also a civil rights attorney, died in 2014.

See also Backus, Isaac; Falwell, Jerry; Graham, Billy; Leland, John; Madison, James; Puritans; Williams, Roger

For Reference and Further Reading

Barnhart, Joe Edward. 1986. *The Southern Baptist Holy War*. Austin: Texas Monthly Press.

Barrett-Fox, Rebecca. 2016. *God Hates: Westboro Baptist Church, American Nationalism, and the Religious Right*. Lawrence: University Press of Kansas.

Canipe, Lee. 2011. *A Baptist Democracy: Separating God and Caesar in the Land of the Free*. Macon, GA: Mercer University Press.

Hudnut-Beumler, James. 2018. *Strangers and Friends at the Welcome Table: Contemporary Christianities in the American South*. Chapel Hill: University of North Carolina Press.

Leonard, Bill J. 1987. "Independent Baptists: From Sectarian Minority to 'Moral Majority." *Church History* 56 (December): 504–17.

Leonard, Bill J. 2005. *Baptists in America*. New York: Columbia University Press.

McLoughlin, William G. 1991. *Soul Liberty: The Baptists' Struggle in New England, 1630–1833*. Hanover, NH: Brown University Press.

Rosen, Leo, ed. 1975. *Religions of America*. New York: Simon & Schuster.

Snyder v. Phelps, 562 U.S. 433 (2011).

Battle Hymn of the Republic

The Battle Hymn of the Republic is also among the nation's most biblically inspired songs. It was adopted from "Say, Brothers, Will You Meet / On Canaan's Happy Shore." Described as "a Southern camp-meeting spiritual," it was first published by the Methodist circuit-rider Stith Mead in a hymnbook in 1807 under the title "Grace Reviving in the Soul" (Stauffer 2015, 124). In its original form, it was structured as a call-and response with the question, "O brothers will you meet me, On Canaan's happy shore?" met with the response, "By the grace of God I'll meet you, On Canaan's happy shore." The chorus intoned:

> We'll shout and give him glory, we'll shout and give him
> glory,
> We'll shout and give him glory, for glory is his own. (Stauffer 2015, 124)

This song, in turn, underwent a metamorphosis into "John Brown's Body." One of the catalysts to the Civil War was a raid by John Brown and his sons (who had previously been active in Kansas) on the federal arsenal at what was then Harper's Ferry, Virginia (now West Virginia), in an attempt to spark a slave uprising. After he was captured and hanged, Brown became a martyr for the anti-slavery cause.

The 2nd Battalion, which was also known as the Tigers, was garrisoned in Boston at the start of the war. It included a Scottish immigrant, who was also named John Brown. His comrades, with whom he had formed a choral group, used to tease him about how he could be John Brown when Brown's body was "mouldering in the grave" (Stauffer 2015, 128). After the Tiger regiment merged with the Massachusetts 12th Regiment, it adopted the John Brown Song as its anthem, an arrangement by C. B. March that C. S. Hall, a Boston abolitionist, published in 1861. The verses that praised Brown as "a soldier in the army of the Lord" proclaimed that "His soul's marching on!" (130). Despite a very jaunty beat, the words were fairly coarse.

In November 1861, Julia Ward Howe (1819–1910), a poetess and social activist who was married to Samuel Gridley Howe, who was a member of the U.S. Sanitary Commission, visited troops in Washington, DC. After she joined them in singing "John Brown's Body," her Unitarian minister James Freeman Clarke encouraged her to write more appropriate words for the song. That evening in the Willard Hotel in Washington, DC, she wrote out the lyrics to what is sometimes referred to by its opening line, "Mine Eyes Have Seen the Glory of the Coming of the Lord," but probably more often simply as "The Battle Hymn of the Republic."

There were a number of other contemporary army and battle hymns, including an "Army Hymn" by Oliver Wendell Holmes Sr., and John Greenleaf Whittier's "Ein Feste Burg ist unser Gott," which bore the same time as Luther's "A Mighty Fortress Is Our God" (Gamble 2019, 56–57). Holmes's hymn had included a reference to the pillar of cloud and of fire that had guided Moses in the wilderness (58).

Drawing from the biblical book of Revelation and other scriptural passages (Snyder 1951), as well as from "an extensive popular culture in which biblical imagery was omnipresent" (Fahs 2001, 79), the first verse proclaimed,

> Mine eyes have seen the glory of the coming of the Lord:
> He is trampling out the vintage where the grapes of wrath are stored;
> He has loosed the fateful lightning of His terrible swift sword:
>
> His truth is marching on. (Gamble 2019, ix)

In February 1862, the *Atlantic Monthly* published this and four other verses on its front page.

The song, which is one of the most religious of songs that are sometimes sung in a secular setting, takes its imagery of the winepress of wrath, and "the fateful lightning of His terrible swift sword," from Revelation 14 and 19. This book, which describes the end of times, is particularly appropriate because it reflected the manner in which many individuals interpreted the Civil War in apocalyptic terms, the conclusion of which they hoped would bring about a new age of peace and prosperity (Stauffer 2015, 134). Gamble observes, "Protestant Americans, and Christians in general, would have understood Howe's 'coming of the Lord' to mean the Second Coming of Christ. The more orthodox their theology, the more literal this coming in glory would be to them. Whether postmillennialist, premillennialist, or amillennialist, liberal or conservative, they would have imagined Christ the Lord returning to judge the world in righteousness" (2019, 53).

The second verse evoked the camps of the Union armies with the Old Testament image of an altar, which was a place of sacrifice:

> I have seen him in the watch-fires of a hundred circling camps;
> They have builded him an altar in the evening dews and damps;
> I have read his righteous sentence by the dim and flaring lamps:
>
> His day is marching on. (Gamble 2019, ix)

The third verse continued,

> I have read a fiery gospel writ in burnished rows of steel:
> "As ye deal with my contemners, so with you my grace shall deal;
> Let the hero, born of woman, crush the serpent with his heel,
>
> Since God is marching on." (Gamble 2019, ix)

This verse's reference to the hero crushing the serpent's head is a reference to Genesis 3:15, in which God, after condemning Satan for tempting Eve, said, "And I will put enmity between thee and the woman, and between thy seed and her seed; it shall bruise thy head, and thou shalt bruise his heel." Christians have traditionally interpreted this passage as the "*protoevangelium*, the first announcement of the gospel" portending Jesus as the seed of woman who would conquer Satan, although some of Howe's friends thought that the hero to whom Howe referred was not Jesus but John Brown (Gamble 2019, 59, 62).

The fourth verse continued with images that evoked both the trumpets of battle and the trumpet that would call for a final judgment where God would judge all men:

> He has sounded forth the trumpet that shall never call retreat;
> He is sifting out the hearts of men before His judgment-seat:
> Oh, be swift, my soul, to answer Him! Be jubilant, my feet!
>
> Our God is marching on. (Gamble 2019, ix)

The last verse would have special appeal to most Christians. It proclaimed,

> In the beauty of the lilies Christ was born across the sea,
> With a glory in his bosom that transfigures you and me:
> As he died to make men holy, let us die to make men free,
> While God is marching on. (Gamble 2019, ix)

Stauffer observes that the song was at once "a heroic song, an inspirational song, a revenge song, and a comradeship song" (2015, 136). Although chiefly sung by Northern soldiers, many of whom also continued to sing "John Brown's Body," the song gained wider acceptance in the 1880s as the nation sought reconciliation. As Stauffer explains, "Southerners, too, believed that they had fought for God and freedom" (139). Gamble observes that the hymn has been published in more than "470 hymnbooks, gospel songbooks, Sunday School supplements, and patriotic collections for the use of churches" since the Civil War, and been used by a wide variety of denominations (2019, 67).

The University of Georgia later adopted the song as its battle hymn, as did the Progressive Party—Theodore Roosevelt wanted it to be adopted as the national anthem—and the Industrial Workers of the World (IWW). The song was a favorite of evangelists Billy Sunday and Billy Graham as well as of civil rights leader Dr. Martin Luther King Jr., who quoted the first verse in his speech at the Alabama capital in March 1965 (Stauffer 2015, 140–41). It has special appeal among those who believe they are fighting for a holy cause, and is commemorated by carvings on seven pillars in the Lincoln Bay of the National Cathedral in Washington, DC. The African American singer Mahalia Jackson, who was active in the civil rights movement, did much to popularize the song with her varied renditions (Collins 2003, 58–61).

Arguing that it has become a kind of "unofficial anthem" for America, historian John Stauffer offers several reasons for its popularity. He believes that by distinguishing "us" and "them," it makes a good song for war. He further argues that it exemplifies American civil religion, that it has been "immensely adaptable," that it "exploits the millennialist strain in American culture," that it is "aspirational," and that it "is a musical masterpiece" (2015, 144–45).

Grant Shreve notes that the opening line of "The Battle Hymn of the Republic" is engraved on the base of a statue by Donald Harcourt De Lue at the Normandy American Cemetery and Memorial in Coleville-sur-Mer entitled "The Spirit of American Youth Rising from the Waves." Shreve observes that "De Lue's use of the poem's line transforms into a testament to the promises of internationalism after World War II" (2017).

See also Brown, John; Civil War; King, Martin Luther, Jr.

For Reference and Further Reading

Collins, Ace. 2003. *Songs Sung Red, White, and Blue: The Stories behind America's Best-Loved Patriotic Songs*. New York: HarperCollins.

Fahs, Alice. 2001. *The Imagined Civil War: Popular Literature of the North and South, 1861–1865*. Chapel Hill: University of North Carolina Press.

Gamble, Richard M. 2019. *A Fiery Gospel: The Battle Hymn of the Republic and the Road to Righteous War*. Ithaca, NY: Cornell University Press.

Lyons, John Henry. 1942. *Stories of Our American Patriotic Songs*. New York: Vanguard Press.
McConathy, Osbourne, Russell V. Morgan, James L. Mursell, Marshall Bartholomew, Mabel E. Bray, W. Otto Miessner, and Edward Bailey Birge. 1946. *New Music Horizons*. Fifth Book. New York: Silver Burdett.
Sanders, Mary. 2016. "A Mighty Fortress Is Our Battle Hymn of the Republic: Episcopal Liturgy and American Civil Religion in the National Prayer Service on 14 September 2001." *Anglican and Episcopal History* 85 (March): 63–86.
Shreve, Grant. October 20, 2017. "The Long, Winding History of the 'Battle Hymn of the Republic.'" JSTOR Daily Newsletter. https://daily.jstor.org/the-long-winding-history-of-the-battle-hymn-of-the-republic/.
Snyder, Edward D. 1951. "The Biblical Background of the 'Battle Hymn of the Republic.'" *New England Quarterly* 24 (June): 231–38.
Spofford, Ainsworth R. 1904. "The Lyric Element in American History." *Records of the Columbia Historical Society, Washington, DC* 7: 211–36.
Stauffer, John. 2015. "'The Battle Hymn of the Republic': Origins, Influence, Legacies." *Exploring Lincoln: Great Historians Reappraise Our Greatest President*, ed. Harold Holzer, Craig L. Symonds, and Frank J. Williams. New York: Fordham University Press, pp. 123–45.
Stauffer, John, and Benjamin Soskis. 2013. *The Battle Hymn of the Republic: A Biography of the Song That Marches On*. New York: Oxford University Press.
Vile, John R. 2020. *America's National Anthem: The Star-Spangled Banner in U.S. History, Culture, and Law*. Santa Barbara, CA: ABC-CLIO. [Note: This essay closely follows the one in this book.]

Beecher, Catharine E.

Catharine E. Beecher (1800–1878) was a noted nineteenth-century educator who was the daughter of Pastor Lyman Beecher and the sister of Harriet Beecher Stowe, the author of *Uncle Tom's Cabin*.

Beecher became disturbed by William Lloyd Garrison's call for immediate abolitionism, and by the lectures that Sarah and Angelina Grimke were giving on the subject to popular audiences. She wrote an essay specifically addressed to Angelina as to why she thought it was inappropriate either to join such an anti-slavery society or to advocate on its behalf. In so doing, she differed with the Grimke sisters not only on abolitionism but also on appropriate female roles. Although Beecher did not cite nearly as many Scriptures as Angelina had done in her *Appeal to Christian Women of the South*, she certainly relied heavily on what she believed was the general view of the Bible with respect to such roles.

Much of Beecher's arguments centered on methods. She simply did not think that organizing in one part of the country against perceived sins in another was likely to accomplish much, nor did she think that calls for immediate abolitionism were either practical in and of themselves or likely to engender goodwill among slave slates. She contrasted the tendency of such rhetoric to result in partisan disputes with the way that William Wilberforce (1759–1833) and others had eliminated slavery within the English colonies. Pointing to the "party spirit" that abolitionists fostered, Beecher observed that "such objects as the circulation of the bible, the extension of the Gospel, the promotion of Temperance and other benevolent associations, good men can unite in, without throwing themselves into the heart of party conflict" (1837, 93).

Beecher had serious reservations about women entering such a world. Her arguments are indeed quite close to those that John Winthrop made in his "'Little Speech' on Liberty" in 1645 and consistent with the observations of Catherine Gardner that "Beecher's moral world is a strictly hierarchical world" (2004, 4). Without making specific reference to Scripture, Beecher thus observed that "it is the grand feature of the Divine economy, that there should be different stations of superiority and subordination, and it is impossible to annihilate this beneficent and immutable law" (1837, 97). Just as children are subject to their parents, students to their teachers, and servants to their masters, so too wives should be subordinate to their husbands:

> In this arrangement of the duties of life, Heaven has appointed to one sex the superior, and to the other the subordinate station, and this without any reference to the character or conduct of either. It is therefore as much for the dignity as it is for the interest of females, in all respects to conform to the duties of this relation. And it is as much a duty as it is for the child to fulfil similar relations to parents, or subjects to rulers. (Beecher 1837, 99)

Noting that "it is Christianity that has given to woman her true place in society," Beecher observed that "it is the peculiar trait of Christianity alone that can sustain her therein. 'Peace on earth and good will to men' [Luke 2:14] is the character of all the rights and privileges, the influence, and the power of woman" (99). Whereas men might participate in the hurly-burly of politics, "woman is to win every thing by peace and love; by making herself so much respected, esteemed and loved, that to yield to her opinions and to gratify her wishes, will be the free-will offering of the heart" (100). By contrast, "if petitions from females will operate to exasperate; if they will be deemed obtrusive, indecorous, and unwise, by those to whom they are addressed . . . then it is neither appropriate nor wise, nor right, for a woman to petition for the relief of oppressed females" (102–3). Recognizing that some might cite the biblical Queen Esther as a call to female political participation, Beecher responded, "When a woman is placed in similar circumstances, where death to herself and all her nation is one alternative, and there is nothing worse to fear, but something to hope as the other alternative, then she may safely follow such an example" (103). However, "in this country, petitions to congress, in reference to the official duties of legislators, seem, IN ALL CASES, to fall entirely without the sphere of female duty. Men are the proper persons to make appeals to the rulers whom they appoint" (104).

Beecher believed that women could take on the noble role of educating children while men educate older children and other men and participate in public affairs: "If the female advocate chooses to come upon a stage, and expose her person, dress, and elocution to public criticism, it is right to express disgust at whatever is offensive and indecorous, as it is to criticize the book of an author, or the dancing of an actress, or any thing else that is presented to public observation" (120). Following the spirit of 1 Corinthians 13 (the chapter on the virtue of love, or charity), women should "quietly" hold their own opinions and seek to promote "a spirit of candour, forbearance, charity, and peace" (128).

Acknowledging that the Bible sometimes calls upon individuals to serve the role of "*reprovers*" (145), Beecher said that Scripture "unequivocally point[s] out those qualifications which alone can entitle a man to do it" (146). Men should themselves follow "the example of the Redeemer of mankind" (150), in imitating his gentleness, his pity, and his love (151).

See also City upon a Hill; Esther as Political Archetype; Grimke, Angelina; Grimke, Sarah M. (An Epistle to the Clergy of the Southern States); Grimke, Sarah M. (Letters on the Equality of the Sexes); Slavery

For Reference and Further Reading

Beecher, Catharine E. 1837. *An Essay on Slavery and Abolitionism with Reference to the Duty of American Females*, 2nd ed. Philadelphia: Henry Perkins; Boston: Perkins & Marvin.

Gardner, Catherine Villanueva. 2004. "Heaven-Appointed Educators of Mind: Catharine Beecher and the Moral Power of Women." *Hypatia* 19 (Spring): 1–16.

Beecher, Henry Ward

Preachers have influenced thinking about politics in America from the time of the Pilgrims to the present. Some, like Jonathan Edwards, are original thinkers, while other are better at reflecting changes in contemporary opinions. One of the most influential nineteenth-century preachers was Henry Ward Beecher (1813–1887), a Congregationalist who pastored the Plymouth Church in Brooklyn and routinely spoke to Sunday audiences of two thousand to three thousand people. He was from a family of pastors and brother to Harriet Beecher Stowe, who authored *Uncle Tom's Cabin*.

During the Civil War, Beecher published a series of sermons under the title of *Freedom and War* that showed his evolving thinking on the subject of slavery. Unlike some of his colleagues, Beecher began by taking a relatively moderate view of slavery, believing that it was a moral evil but uncertain how it should be eliminated and unwilling to put all the blame on the South. After Southern forces fired on Fort Sumter and sought to leave the Union, however, he became increasingly convinced that slavery needed to be eliminated, and he increasingly portrayed Northern forces as aligned with good and Southern forces with the devil.

At a time when sermons often lasted two hours, Beecher would often reason from a relatively obscure biblical passage to contemporary issues, typically bringing in arguments from natural law and from a variety of other sources as well (Chesebrough and McBride 1990, 278). The first sermon in his book was entitled "The Nation's Duty to Slavery" and was taken from Jeremiah 6:16–19, which described how Jeremiah had sounded the trumpet of impending doom and the people had refused to listen (1863, 1). His specific subject was John Brown, whom Beecher believed had become transformed from a somewhat unbalanced prophet to a martyr for the cause of liberty.

Beecher's second chapter was based on the description in Luke 4:17–19 of Jesus appearing in a synagogue and proclaiming that he was fulfilling Scripture that called for preaching deliverance and setting the oppressed at liberty. In this sermon, Beecher argued against compromising with the South in order to avoid war. His next sermon, built around the story of Jesus calming a storm on the Lake of Galilee in Mark 4:37–39, was something of a jeremiad in that it pointed to a variety of national sins including not only slavery but also American aggression against Native Americans and Mexicans. Like Lincoln, Beecher recognized that both North and South had been complicit in establishing and perpetuating slavery. His denunciation of certain interpretations of the Bible were harsh: "If men can make the Bible teach me to disown childhood; if men can make the Bible teach me that it is lawful to buy and sell man, that marriage is impracticable between slaves, that laws cannot permit any custom which would hinder the easy sale of such property," then they should be driven from the temple (79). He further observed "that wherever you have had an untrammeled Bible, you have had an untrammeled people; and . . . wherever you have had a Bible shut up, you have had a shut-up people" (80). He ended this sermon by comparing the need to awaken liberty to Jesus's raising of Lazarus from the dead (82).

Writing on the verge of impending war, Beecher drew from Exodus 14:15 urging the nation, which he likened to the children of Israel pressed up against the Red Sea, to move forward and resist Southern interpretations of the Bible as teaching "the religion of servitude" (98). Beecher was especially outraged by Southern deprecations of the flag at Fort Sumter, and "The National Flag," perhaps the most impressive of Beecher's essays, followed and was based on Psalm 9:4, which referred to fighting under a banner of truth. He even compared the sight of the flag to biblical prophecies portraying the Messiah as a light shining in the darkness (124).

A sermon based on Deuteronomy 23:14, which referred to God as being in the midst of the camp, reflected contemporary fears of the moral dangers of army life. The next sermon, based on an encounter between Elisha the prophet and Joash, the King of Israel as recorded in 2 Kings 13:14–19, argued for the continuing vigor of the administration of government.

Although the eighth sermon was entitled "Moses and Duties of Emancipation," it began with a reference to the prophet Samson in Judges 14:8. Here Beecher quoted from a speech by Alexander Stephens, the vice president of the Confederate States, in which Stephens, relying on a biblical analogy generally understood to refer to the Messiah, had argued that the belief in racial inequality was the cornerstone of that government (179). Beecher's ninth sermon dealt with "The Church's Duty to Slavery" and was based on Jesus's teaching from Matthew 20:25–28, in which he contrasted Christ-like servant leadership with the way that Gentile princes ruled over their people (200). Although otherwise praising Abraham Lincoln, Beecher took a firm stance against recolonizing African Americans, unless they chose such a course for themselves.

Quoting from a Presidential Proclamation of May 19, 1862, in which President Lincoln expressed willingness to cooperate with states that were willing to begin a process of voluntary compensated emancipation, Beecher cited Isaiah 42:10–12 and compared this to "The Beginning of Freedom" because it demonstrated that a national leader had finally recognized the need to abolish the institution (223). Recognizing that the passage was filled with poetic imagery, in a sermon on "The Success of American Democracy," Beecher began with a passage from Daniel 11:9–17, which referenced a war between a northern and a southern kingdom (248).

Returning in the next chapter on "Christianity in Government" to Luke 4:18–19 (1863, 270), Beecher described the duty of Christian governments to provide for the weak and poor. Expressing reservations about whether emancipation would bring social equality, and using the N-word so predominately employed in the South at the time, Beecher said that Christ died as much for them as he did for whites (292). This was followed by a sermon taken from a single clause in 2 Peter 2:10 that warned against speaking evil of governmental officials (294).

While Lincoln often mused about whether God was using the Civil War as a form of national punishment, Beecher was much more explicit about this in a sermon drawn from 1 Chronicles 29:10–13, on "National Injustice and Penalty" (311). There he observed that "if it is possible for a nation to sin, it must be when it has been led systematically to violate all the natural rights of a whole race or people; and American slavery, by the very definition of our jurists, is the deprivation of men of every natural right" (318). He argued that slavery violated the right of individuals to their own labor, worked against stable family life, perpetuated ignorance, demeaned human life, ensconced an evil as a good, and brought God's judgment on the nation (320–26). He concluded that "God is pouring out the vial of his wrath; and bearing witness, tremendous witness, by war, against slavery, and against the cruel wickedness of men that perpetuate it" (332).

Beecher drew his sermon "The Ground and Forms of Government" from Job 34:30, warning against the reign of hypocrites (341). Describing republican government as "the noblest and the best," Beecher contrasted it to the aristocratic government of the Confederate States and to the despotisms of other nations (250).

As the war progressed, Beecher sharpened his attack on the Confederacy. Basing a sermon on "Our Good Progress and Prospects" on the story of Jesus casting out a demon from a boy in Mark 9:26–27, Beecher likened that demon to American slavery (368) and lauded Lincoln's Emancipation Proclamation. A sermon on "Liberty under Law," which drew from Galatians 5:18, again also drew from natural law (396) to argue that no one should be subject to bondage to another.

As he reached the last sermon, Beecher evoked a long passage from Revelation 18:1–8 describing Babylon, which he applied to any regime that violated justice and emphasized commerce over human rights (420). The prospect of emancipation had finally revealed the wide gap between "the great cause of God in modern civilization and the cause of the Devil" (433). He ended with the hope that slavery "and those who uphold it" might perish (445).

See also Brown, John; Declaration of Independence; Lincoln, Abraham; Prophets and Jeremiads; Slavery; Stevens, Alexander H. (The Cornerstone Speech); Stowe, Harriet Beecher; U.S. Flag

For Reference and Further Reading

Beecher, Henry Ward. 1863. *Freedom and War. Discourses on Topics Suggested by the Times*. Boston: Ticknor and Fields.

Cheesebrough, David B., and Lawrence W. McBride. 1990. "Sermons as Historical Documents: Henry Ward Beecher and the Civil War." *History Teacher* 23 (May): 275–91.

Benefit of Clergy

Although colonial codes of justice were often quite rigid by comparisons to those of today, judges and juries sometimes worked to avoid their more severe consequences, and there were a number of legal remedies that defendants could employ. One such mechanism was known as the benefit of clergy and was applied to some of the soldiers who had been convicted of manslaughter in the so-called Boston Massacre. After claiming benefit of clergy, they were branded on their hand and released.

The mechanism appears to have originated in England, where ordained clergymen could claim exemption from civil jurisdiction in preference for ecclesiastical jurisdiction. In time, this privilege was extended to individuals, clergymen or not, who were convicted of a broad range of felonies. Originally, after they made the claim, they were asked to read a passage of Scripture (thus initially applying only to those who were literate), and then branded rather than given the stiffer punishment. Typically, one could only evoke the benefit of clergy for one offense.

This workaround appears to have been based on Psalm 105:15, which admonished, "Touch not mine anointed, and do my prophets no harm" (Skousen 2008, 7), but this tie arguably applied far more clearly to the benefit's initial desire to exclude clergymen from ecclesiastical jurisdiction than of its later use in mitigating punishments.

Although originating in England, the practice was continued in the American colonies, with one scholar observing that it remained "a fundamental feature of the criminal law in Maryland and Virginia" up through about the end of the eighteenth century (Sawyer 1990, 67). He further observed that the colonies used the mechanism not simply because it was English but because it proved just as useful in mitigating the harsher elements of the law.

See also Criminal Law

For Reference and Further Reading

Sawyer, Jeffrey K. 1990. "'Benefit of Clergy' in Maryland and Virginia." *American Journal of Legal History* 34 (January): 79–68.

Skousen, Lesley. 2008. "Redefining Benefit of Clergy during the English Reformation: Royal Prerogative, Mercy, and the State." Thesis for MA in history at the University of Wisconsin.

Benezet, Anthony

Anthony Benezet (1713–1784) was a Pennsylvania Quaker who had immigrated to America from France. A friend of Benjamin Rush's, Benezet served as a school teacher and reformer who advocated for the education of women and African Americans and was very active in the early anti-slavery movement. Even though Pennsylvania had been founded as a haven for individuals of all faiths, American Patriots often resented the refusal of Quaker neighbors who failed to take up arms against those that the Patriots considered to be common enemies.

In one of Benezet's most important essays, his "Serious Considerations on Several Important Subjects," which was printed in 1778, he laid out the case for

Christian pacifism and other reforms. Mark Noll has observed that the work "devoted thirteen pages to slavery, in which Scripture was prominent; seven pages against drink, in which an appeal to Scripture was mostly absent; and about twenty-eight pages on warfare, again relentlessly biblical" (2016, 275).

As Noll indicates, Benezet's indictment of war was particularly dominated by Scriptures. Believing that Christians were called to emulate Christ and to obey his commandment to love one another and follow his counsel in the Sermon on the Mount, Benezet contrasted this with the death and destruction that accompany war. Citing James 4, he further associated war with human lust and with the inability to trust God. Christians are called upon to love and pray for their enemies rather than destroying them, whereas war proceeds from man's fallen nature and that which is carnal. Benezet was particularly concerned that deaths caused by war shortened the time that sinners would otherwise have to repent and receive redemption. It is further inconsistent with the prophecy in Isaiah 2:4 that describes God's kingdom, for which Jesus urged Christians to pray, as one where nations have beaten their swords into plowshares and their spears into pruning hooks.

Although Benezet's words against slavery were also scripturally based, at the beginning of this section of his narrative, he quoted statements from the Declaration of Independence and the Virginia Declaration of Rights that indicated that all men are created equal while indicating that failure to live up to such proclamations "is likely to be one of the principal causes of those heavy judgments, which are now so sensibly displayed over the Colonies" (1778, 29). Whereas Scripture (Isaiah 1:17) called upon people "to seek judgment, to relieve the oppressed; to plead for the fatherless, and to judge for the widow" (30), slavery elevated the pursuit of profit over such ideals. Scripture (Jeremiah 34:17) thus condemned the people for not hearkening unto God "in proclaiming liberty every one to his brother, and every man to his neighbor" (32). If people continued to withhold love and compassion, and continue to act the part of "menstealers," they would be judged like the ancient cities of Sodom and Gomorrah.

Benezet's remarks on "spirituous liquors" (40) focused not on alcohol in general but on distilled beverages, which Benezet thought were especially detrimental to health and morals and which spiritually enslave men. In an interesting twist, he also associated the practice with other ills:

> Besides that it would discourage the distillation of rye and other grain; a practice which is not only a great hurt to the poor in raising the price of bread but must also be very offensive to God the great and good father of the family of mankind, that people should in their earthly and corrupt wisdom, pervert their Maker's benevolent intention, in converting the grain he hath given to us as the staff of life, unto a fiery spirit, so destructive of the human frame and attended with the other dreadful consequences already mentioned. (1778, 44)

Benezet was particularly skeptical of claims that distilled alcohol eased earthly labors, but pointed out that even if they did so, "they must nevertheless waste the powers of life, and of course occasion premature old age" (45). Benezet further cited Paul's admonition in 1 Corinthians 8:13 that "if meat make my brother to offend I will eat no flesh while the world stands, lest I make my brother to offend," which he though equally applied to strong drink (47).

See also Declaration of Independence; Quakers; Rush, Benjamin; Slavery

For Reference and Further Reading

Benezet, Anthony. 1778. "Serious Considerations on Several Important Subjects." Philadelphia: Joseph Crukshank. https://quod.lib.umich.edu/cgi/t/text/text-idx?c=evans;cc=evans;rgn=main;view=text;idno=N12457.0001.001. Accessed April 19, 2019.

Bruns, Roger A. 1976. "A Quaker's Antislavery Crusade: Anthony Benezet." *Quaker History* 65 (Autumn): 82–92.

Noll, Mark A. 2016. *In the Beginning Was the Word: The Bible in American Public Life, 1492–1783.* New York: Oxford University Press.

Beveridge, Albert J.

Albert J. Beveridge (1862–1927) was an Indiana Republican who served in the U.S. Senate from 1899 to 1911. A graduate of DePaul University, Beveridge became a leader in the Progressive movement and a strong advocate of American imperial expansion in the aftermath of the Spanish-American War. He also established himself as a historian with a classic work on Chief Justice John Marshall.

In 1907, he published a work entitled *The Bible as Good Reading,* in which he tried to demonstrate that the English version of the Bible was one of the finest works of literature ever written. He put particular emphasis on short stories like the account of David killing Goliath, the story of Esther's patriotism, the stories of Moses, and the life of St. Paul. He praised the wisdom of the laws of Moses and their superiority to all but the most recent systems. He lauded the wisdom of King Solomon as expressed in the book of Proverbs, the Jewish judicial system, and by what he perceived to be the Bible's "tendency toward liberty—even toward democracy" (1907, 69). He was also impressed by the provision for a Year of Jubilee in which slaves were to be set free and "there is to be a new deal all around" (75). Beveridge presented the biblical Joseph not simply as a "dreamer" but also as a "doer" and praised St. Paul's oratory, particularly as demonstrated by his speech on Mars Hill in Athens.

Perhaps as much as any twentieth-century politician, Beveridge took seriously the idea that America was a chosen nation with a unique providential destiny. In the aftermath of the Spanish-American War (1900), he thus argued that "God . . . has marked us as His chosen people, henceforth to lead in the regeneration of the world," and that this destiny involved holding the Philippines. Lambasting those who opposed the war against Filipino independence, Beveridge paraphrased one of Jesus's sayings on the cross in Luke 23:34 to say "that our brothers knew not what they did."

Whereas the vision of American revolutionaries was that of spreading liberty, Beveridge only wanted to do so in a limited sense because he did not believe the Filipino "children," as "Orientals," were capable of self-government. They had "not yet mastered the alphabet of freedom." What America could give the Philippines "involves government, but not necessarily self-government. It means law. First of all, it is a common rule of action, applying equally to all within its limits. Liberty means protection of property and life without price, free speech without intimidation, justice without purchase or delay, government without favor or favorites." Beveridge observed that "the Declaration of Independence does not forbid us to do our part in the regeneration of the world." It "applies only to people capable of self-government." The U.S. flag was on the march and should never retreat.

As he progressed, Beveridge continued to elevate the nation and its implied powers. Noting that "the written Constitution is but the index of the living Constitution," he observed, "The nation alone is immortal. The nation alone is sacred." The nation was, in turn, tied to race: "It is racial. God has not been preparing the English-speaking and Teutonic peoples for a thousand years for nothing but vain and idle self-contemplation and self-admiration. NO! He has made us the master organizers of the world to establish system where chaos reigns."

In a paragraph that ended with a quotation from one of Jesus's parables as recorded in Matthew 25:21, Beveridge observed that God "has marked the American people as His chosen nation to finally lead in the regeneration of the world. This is the divine mission of America, and it holds for us all the profit, all the glory, all the happiness possible to man. We are the trustees of the world's progress, guardians of its righteous peace. The judgment of the Master is upon us. 'Ye have been faithful over a few things; I will make you ruler over many things.'" He subsequently referred to America's duty as "a holy trust" and professed to see "the hand of God" in this destiny.

Perhaps paraphrasing Isaiah 41:1, Beveridge observed, "We will renew our youth at the fountain of new and glorious deeds." Continuing, he observed that "where dwells the fear of God, the American people move forward to the future of their hope and the doing of His work."

Beveridge managed to combine traditional notions of America's destiny with a version of social Darwinism that showed how political progressivism could sometimes morph into expansionistic imperialism with a racial twist. Although not all supported American control over the Philippines, Lyman Abbott (1835–1922) and other progressive pastors of the day also associated American participation in the war as a way to fulfill its mission as God's chosen nation to spread liberty and Christianity (Wetzel 2012). Other Progressive members of the clergy shared similar sentiments. In 1898, Pastor L. B. Hartman observed, "Thus without the least consciousness of presumption or extravagance we recognize our republic as the politico-religious handmaid of Providence in the aggressive civilization of the world" (quoted in McDougall 2019, 123). Similarly, an Episcopal rector named William S. Rainsford observed, "This war has not been cunningly devised by the strategists. America is being used to carry on the work of God in this war, which no politician could create, control, or gainsay" (quoted in McDougall 2019, 123).

See also City upon a Hill; Colonization

For Reference and Further Reading

Beveridge, Albert J. 1900. "U.S. Senator Albert J. Beveridge Speaks on the Philippine Question, U.S. Senate, Washington, D.C., January 9, 1900." https://china.usc.edu/us-senator-albert-j-beveridge-speaks-philippine-question-us-senate-washington-dc-january-9-1900. Accessed April 17, 2019.

Beveridge, Albert J. 1907. *The Bible as Good Reading*. Philadelphia: Henry Altemus.
Inabinet, Brandon. 2007. "Albert J. Beveridge, 'March of the Flag' (16 September 1898)." *Voices of Democracy* 1 (June): 148–64.
McDougall, Walter A. 2019. *The Tragedy of U.S. Foreign Policy: How America's Civil Religion Betrayed the National Interest*. New Haven, CT: Yale University Press.
Wetzel, Benjamin J. 2012. "Onward Christian Soldiers: Lyman Abbott's Justification of the Spanish-American War." *Journal of Church and State* 54 (Summer): 406–25.

Bible Balloon Project

One of the more bizarre initiatives endorsed by the U.S. national government was the Bible Balloon Project hatched by evangelist Billy James Hargis and Rev. Carl McIntyre, both right-wing fundamentalist pastors with broad radio audiences (Jordan 2013, 67). Begun in 1953 and continuing for the next four years, this project sought to float helium balloons from West Germany into Eastern European nations controlled by the Soviet Union with Bible tracts and Scriptures. It followed earlier messages of friendship that had been launched by balloon in August 1951, which, in part, conveyed what the *New York Times* described as "the frequencies and broadcast schedules of Western radio stations" ("Balloon Barrage Grows" 1951).

Although this would not seem to be a particularly effective method of propaganda, a later report noted that eight Russian planes had sought to shoot the balloons down ("Reds Shoot at Balloons" 1951). After reports that the Eisenhower administration had opposed including Bibles, Dr. James B. Conant, the U.S. high commissioner, sent a note indicating that the president considered the project to be "a laudable private undertaking" ("Bible 'Airlift' Lauded" 1953).

In 1951, President Harry S. Truman had created the Psychological Strategy Board (PSB), which included the use of religious appeals in combating "godless" communism (Herzog 2012, 55–56). Eisenhower had continued this approach, which had included operating 165 "information centers" around the world for foreigners. One scholar notes, "Ample quantities of the Bible began arriving, along with subscriptions to religious periodicals like *Christian Century*, *Commonweal*, and *Commentary*. The State Department also sent periodic religious news dispatches to its embassies, complete with analyses of each event's implications for Communists. The Voice of America (VOA) enlisted the aid of religious leaders, who broadcast messages into nations under Communist control" (Herzog 2012, 56–57).

Consistent with this emphasis, Congress added the words "under God" to the pledge to the U.S. flag in 1954.

In addition to the Bible Balloon Project, numerous private religious organizations in the United States and in Western European nations sought to smuggle Bibles into the Soviet Union and Eastern Bloc nations, although their efforts were often exaggerated (Boel 2014; Gouverneur 2007).

Apparently, balloons and smuggling are currently both being used to smuggle books into communist North Korea (McKay 2017).

See also Communism and Anti-Communism; Under God

For Reference and Further Reading

"Balloon Barrage Grows." *New York Times*, August 19, 1951.
"Bible 'Airlift' Lauded." *New York Times*, September 5, 1953.
Boel Bent. 2014. "Bible Smuggling and Human Rights in the Cold War." *Transnational Anti-Communism and the Cold War: Agents, Activities, and Networks*, ed. Luc van Dongen, Stephanie Roulin, and Giles Scott-Smith. New York: Palgrave Macmillan, pp. 263–75.
Gouverneur, Joe. 2007. "Underground Evangelism: Missions during the Cold War." *Transformation* 24 (April): 80–86.
Herzog, Jonathan P. 2012. "From Sermon to Strategy: Religious Influence on the Formation and Implementation of US Foreign Policy in the Early Cold War." *Religion and the Cold War: A Global Perspective*, ed. Philip E. Muehlenbeck. Nashville, TN: Vanderbilt University Press, pp. 44–64.
Jordan, Richard Lawrence. 2013. *The Second Coming of Paisley: Militant Fundamentalism and Ulster Politics*. New York: Syracuse University Press.
McKay, Hollie. 2017. "Operation Bible Smuggling: How Christian Texts Infiltrate North Korea." *World*. October 9.
"Reds Shoot at Balloons." *New York Times*, August 28, 1951.

Bible Burnings

One way to express one's disgust with a writing is to burn it. Burning manuscripts dates far back into antiquity, with some such burnings being intentional and others simply the result of war (Boissoneault 2017). The burnings of the library at Alexander in 48 BC and AD 640 are similar to recent attempts to destroy libraries in Mali and Timbuktu in 2012.

The First Amendment to the Constitution provides for freedom of speech and press, but it does not prevent individuals from burning holy books that they own any more than it would prevent them from burning flags. Early in the twentieth century, however, the New York Society for the Suppression of Vice headed by Anthony Comstock (1844–1915) often burned books that they considered to be pornographic.

The emotional effect of burning a holy book can be particularly intense, and may thus draw disproportionate attention. There was a strong outcry when, in 2008, the U.S. military burned Bibles at the Bagram Air Base in Afghanistan for fear that they would be used to proselytize Muslims in violation of military protocols (Starnes 2012).

The Catholic Church sometimes burned books along with heretics, including individuals like Giordano Bruno and Jan Hus, the former for his Copernican cosmology, and the latter for his attack on such practices as the giving of indulgences (Boissoneault 2017). They sometimes also burned translations other than the Latin Vulgate.

In 2009, the Amazing Grace Baptist Church in Canton, North Carolina, announced that it was going to burn English translations other than the King James Version of the Bible on Halloween. They also planned to burn books by other Christian authors such as Billy Graham, Rick Warren, and others (Chivers 2009).

In 2012, Terry Jones, the pastor of the Dove World Outreach Church in Florida, who had previously stopped early attempts, publicly burned a Koran to protest the Iranian imprisonment of a Christian pastor, Youcef Nadarkhani (Sheridan 2012).

See also Fundamentalists; Pornography

For Reference and Further Reading

Boissoneault, Lorraine. 2017. "A Brief History of Book Burning, from the Printing Press to Internet Archives." *Smithsonian*. August 31. https://www.smithsonianmag.com/history/brief-history-book-burning-printing-press-internet-archives-180964697/.

Chivers, Tom. 2009. "North Carolina Church Plans Halloween Bible Burning." *Telegraph*. October 16. https://www.telegraph.co.uk/news/religion/6346662/North-Carolina-church-plans-Halloween-Bible-burning.html.

Corn-Revere. Robert. 2014. "Bonfires of Insanity: A History of Book Burnings from Nazis to ISIS." Daily Beast. February 28 [updated April 14, 2017]. https://www.thedailybeast.com/bonfires-of-insanity-a-history-of-book-burnings-from-nazis-to-isis.

Sheridan, Michael. 2012. "Florida Pastor Terry Jones Burns Copies of Koran outside Church." *New York Daily News*. April 29. https://www.nydailynews.com/news/national/florida-pastor-terry-jones-burns-copies-koran-church-article-1.1069458.

Starnes, Todd. 2012. "The Day the U.S. Military Burned the Bible in Afghanistan." Fox News. March 2 [updated May 7, 2015]. https://www.foxnews.com/opinion/the-day-the-us-military-burned-the-bible-in-afghanistan. Accessed March 31, 2019.

Bible Signings

In March 2019, President Donald J. Trump signed Bibles at an Alabama church where he visited victims of a recent tornado.

The practice was not new to Trump, although he may have taken it up a notch by signing on the outside cover rather than on the inside. President Franklin D. Roosevelt signed the family Bible of Frank Murphy after he took his oath as U.S. attorney general. President Ronald Reagan signed a Bible that he sent to Iranian officials in 1986. Other presidents who are known to have signed Bibles include Harry S. Truman, Jimmy Carter, and Bill Clinton.

A lot of the controversy has centered on whether observers believe that the Bible signings were done for purely political purposes or as a way of connecting to those who asked for such signatures. Bill Leonard, the dean of the Wake Forest School of Divinity, observed that signing Bibles is a southern tradition, whereas Wayne Flynn, a professor emeritus at Auburn University, described Trump's actions as "right next to a sacrilege" (Roach 2019). In an indication that his judgment may have been more about the signer than the practice itself, however, Flynn said, "If Jimmy Carter had signed a Bible . . . I would have no problems with that" (Roach 2019). Hershael York, from the School of Theology at Southern Baptist Theological Seminary, observed that there was nothing objectively sinful about the practice, although some individuals would be more comfortable with it than others.

Although the practice is not quite the same, both Americans and their British forbearers have long used Bibles, which themselves detail numerous genealogies of the Jewish people, to record family births and deaths (Wulf 2012). Moreover, incoming justices of the U.S. Supreme Court sign the flyleaf of a Bible that John Marshall Harlan I donated to the court in 1906.

See also Harlan Bible; Trump, Donald J.

For Reference and Further Reading

Mcdermott, Jennifer. 2019. "Some Cheer, Some Decry Trump's Signing of Bibles." *The Tennessean*. March 11, 16A.
Roach, David. 2019. "Trump's Bible Signing Called Southern Tradition." Baptist Press. March 11. www.bpnews.net/52551/trumps-bible-signing-called-souther-tradition.
Wulf, Karin. 2012. "Bible, King, and Common Law: Genealogical Literacies and Family History Practices in British America." *Early American Studies* 10 (Fall): 467–502.

Bible Study Groups among Governmental Officials

From the time of the Reformation, Protestants have placed special emphasis on the study of the Bible. This emphasis has been accentuated during the Trump administration with the establishment of what is believed to be the first Bible study among cabinet members in the past hundred years.

Created by Ralph Drollinger (b. 1954), a former basketball player who has helped establish Capitol Ministries, which is now in forty-three U.S. state capitols and twenty foreign legislatures, Drollinger's studies, which take a verse-by-verse approach to Scripture, have been contrasted with what he apparently considers to be the "candy floss Christianity—big, sweet, unsubstantial"—of the National Prayer Breakfast, which is run by The Fellowship (Amos 2018). The establishment of the cabinet study followed the establishment of similar studies in the U.S. House of Representatives and Senate. Vice President Mike Pence sponsors the cabinet group and apparently helped select a core of initial members who have included former attorney general Jeff Sessions, Secretary of State Mike Pompeo, Secretary of Education Betsy DeVos, former health secretary Tom Price, former secretary of homeland security Kirstjen Nielsen, and former energy secretary Rick Perry.

Critics have questioned Drollinger's policy excluding women from directing such Bible studies as well as his criticism of same-sex marriage and of the Roman Catholic Church, which he is quoted as saying "is one of the primary false religions of the world" (Gander 2018). Drollinger has likened Pence to such figures as Joseph, Mordecai, and Daniel, who have exercised godly influences from the number two position in government, and Trump to Samson, the biblical strongman (CBN News 2017). One reporter has linked former attorney general Jeff Sessions's justification of separating immigrant families at the border to one of Drollinger's Bible studies, which emphasized both corporal punishment and the necessity of obedience to law (Seidel 2018). Responding to critics, Drollinger has said that he believes in the separation of church and state but does not believe that "institutional separation" requires "influential separation" (Amos 2018).

See also Corporal Punishment; Immigration; National Prayer Breakfast; Pence, Mike; Perry, Rick; Pompeo, Mike; Trump, Donald J.

For Reference and Further Reading

Amos, Owen. 2018. "Inside the White House Bible Study Group." BBC. April 8. https://www.bbc.com/news/world-us-canada-43534724.

CBN News. 2017. "Bible Studies at the White House: Who's Inside This Spiritual Awakening?" July 31. https://www1.cbn.com/cbnnews/politics/2017/july/bible-studies-at-the-white-house-whos-at-the-heart-of-this-spiritual-awakening.
Gander, Kashmira. 2018. "White House Bible Study Led by Pastor Who Is Anti-Gay, Anti-Women and Anti-Catholic." *Newsweek*. April 11. https://www.newsweek.com/white-house-bible-group-led-pastor-anti-gay-anti-women-anti-catholic-881860.
Seidel, Andrew L. 2018. "The White House Bible Study Group That Influenced Trump's Family Separation Policy." ThinkProgress. June 19. https://thinkprogress.org/white-house-bible-study-group-trump-child-separation-policy-24de236c4824/.

Black, Hugo L.

Hugo Lafayette Black (1886–1971) was one of the longest-serving and most notable Supreme Court justices of the twentieth century; he served from 1937 until shortly before his death in 1971. Born in Clay County, Alabama, Black established himself as a trial attorney, as a congressional investigator, and as a strong supporter of Franklin D. Roosevelt's New Deal programs before Roosevelt appointed him to the court. Black appeared in a national radio address to explain, albeit not to deny, his prior membership in the Ku Klux Klan, and went on both to uphold many New Deal laws and to gain a reputation for being a champion of constitutional provisions, especially those in the Bill of Rights.

Black became known as something of a constitutional fundamentalist in that he believed that the Constitution should be interpreted quite literally and resisted what he believed to be calls to expand even civil rights and liberties beyond the constitutional text. After thus fighting to expand the right to counsel and other rights, Black dissented from the majority decision in *Griswold v. Connecticut* (1965), which recognized a constitutional right to privacy. Similarly, although Black outlined a fairly absolutist position with regard to protections for freedom of speech and press, in his later years, he opposed decisions that would have widened this protection to symbolic speech. Black, however, believed that the Fourteenth Amendment intended to apply, or "incorporate," the provisions of the Bill of Rights to state as well as national governments, even though this amendment does not explicitly say so.

Black was known for his view, which he attributed to Roger Williams and to Thomas Jefferson, that the First Amendment established a "wall of separation between church and state." He outlined this strict position in *Everson v. Board of Education* (1947), even though he did in that case allow a state to provide transportation for students attending parochial schools. Black strongly supported decisions banning public prayer and Bible readings from public schools.

Black led Bible classes at Birmingham's First Baptist Church for fifteen years beginning in the 1910s, and he told his students that "the Bible penetrated the trackless forests with the pioneers and strengthened the sturdy character of our early settlers" (Newman 2017). Although Black had graduated from the University of Alabama School of Law, after he joined the Supreme Court, he bought numerous classics and engaged in an extensive course of reading and study that he believed to be essential for his new job. William Domnarski observed that "among his hundreds of opinions are dozens of references to figures such as Tacitus, Plutarch, Plato, Jefferson, Macaulay, *Pilgrim's Progress*, and the Bible" (2006, 115).

Because he was such a strict separationist, Black sometimes received critical letters. In one case he apparently replied to an Alabama woman who condemned him to hell for his opinion on school prayer by observing that if she would consult the Bible, she would find that individuals were admonished to "pray in your own closet [from Matthew 6:6]" (Newman 2017). After Byron White was appointed to the court after the Supreme Court's decision in 1963 banning devotional Bible reading, White quipped that "I had to borrow this Bible. The only one left in the Supreme Court was Potter Stewart's" (Newman 2017), Stewart having been the only dissenter in that case.

One might argue that Black transferred much of his early faith in the Bible and in Christianity to the Constitution and the court. In 1968, Black gave a series of three lectures at the Columbia University School of Law, which were subsequently published in a book that Black titled *A Constitutional Faith*. After expressing gratitude for the opportunities that his public life had brought and the Constitution that had made it possible, he observed, "That Constitution is my legal bible; its plan of our government is my plan and its destiny my destiny. I cherish every word of it, from the first to the last, and I personally deplore even the slightest deviation from its least important commands" (1968, 66).

See also Abington v. Schempp (1963)

For Reference and Further Reading

Black, Hugo LaFayette. 1968. *A Constitutional Faith*. New York: Alfred A. Knopf.

Domnarski, William. 2006. *The Great Justices, 1941–54: Black, Douglas, Frankfurter, and Jackson in Chambers*. Ann Arbor: University of Michigan Press.

Levinson, Sanford. 1979. "'The Constitution' in American Civil Religion." *Supreme Court Review* 1979: 123–51.

Newman, Roger. 2017. "When It Was Done Right: Justice Hugo Black, Religion and Alabama." *New American Journal*. December 5. https://www.newamericanjournal.net/tag/roger-newman/. Accessed April 22, 2019.

Blasphemy Laws

See Updegraph v. Commonwealth (1824)

Booker, Cory

Cory Booker (b. 1969) is an African American politician. He was educated at Stanford University, the Queens College at Oxford, and at Yale Law School. A former mayor of Newark, New Jersey, he is now a U.S. senator from that state who is vying for the Democratic nomination for U.S. president.

Although he identifies as a Baptist, Booker is quite familiar with Jewish theology, having had a number of friends who were Jewish rabbis. In thus responding to President Trump's comment that Jews who voted for Democrats were disloyal, he responded, "Tzedakah, chesed," and followed with, "Those are ideas about justice and decency and kindness and mercy. We need to get back to those values" (Medina 2019). At Oxford he joined Shmuley Boteach, an American rabbi reaching out to nonpracticing Jews, and became a member of the L'Chaim Society that Boteach founded (Medina 2019). Similarly, at Yale, he cofounded a similar society with a Hasidic rabbi named Shmully Hecht (Rosenberg 2013).

Booker has a stack of religious books on his desk that include "the New Testament, the Tanakh, the Quran and the Bhagavad Gita"; he appears quite comfortable with religious diversity and carries both a Spanish prayer card and an index card with the text of Isaiah 40:31 likening those who wait on God to soaring eagles (Rosenberg 2013). He has been described as "a churchgoing Baptist who teaches Torah like an amateur rabbi. He abstains from alcohol like Muslims and Mormons. He is a vegetarian who meditates and quotes Eastern religious texts" (Rosenberg 2013).

Seemingly much more comfortable with both his own Christian upbringing and religious discourse in general than was Barack Obama, one journalist has described him as a potential "Candidate of the Christian Left" (Kilgore 2018). As a possible heir to the progressive politics of Dr. Martin Luther King Jr., he had advocated bipartisanship, indicating that "my faith tradition is love your enemies. It's not complicated for me, if I aspire to be who I say I am. I am a Christian American. Literally written in the ideals of my faith is to love those who hate you" (Kilgore 2018).

See also Baptists; Judaism; King, Martin Luther, Jr.; Obama, Barack

For Reference and Further Reading

Kilgore, Ed. 2018. "Is Cory Booker the Candidate of the Christian Left?" *Intelligencer*. December 17. http ://nymag.com/intelligencer/2018/12/is-cory-booker-the-candidate-of-the-christian-left.html.

Medina, Jennifer. 2019. "The Yom Kippur Prayer on Cory Booker's Lips." *New York Times*. October 8. https://www.onenewspage.com/n/US/1zkk83f4ch/The-Yom-Kippur-Prayer-on-Cory-Booker.htm.

Rosenberg, Yair. 2013. "New Jersey Senate Candidate Cory Booker Knows His Torah, So What?" *The Tablet*. https://www.tabletmag.com/jewish-news-and-politics/140767/cory-bookers-jewish-story.

Borowicz, Stephanie

On March 25, 2019, Pennsylvania state Republican representative Stephanie Borowicz delivered the opening prayer at a session of the state legislature that also marked the first time that a Muslim representative, Movita Johnson-Harrell, who had brought fifty-five guests with her (most of whom were Muslim), was being sworn into office with her hand on the Koran.

Borowicz's prayer, which lasted about 100 seconds, was noted for citing Jesus at least thirteen times (Dicker 2019). It is also notable for including a number of Christian Scriptures in what some considered to be a weaponized way.

Borowicz began by saying, "I, Jesus, am your ambassador here today, standing here representing you, the King of kings, the Lord of lords." She likely took the term "ambassador" from 2 Corinthians 5:20, which refers to being "ambassadors for Christ" and the designation of God from 1 Timothy 6:15, Revelation 17:14, and Revelation 19:16, which also refer specifically to Jesus. After saying that America's founding fathers had attempted to base the nation on "your principles and your words, and your truths" (quoted in Barillas 2019), she continued, "God forgive us—Jesus—we've lost sight of you, we've forgotten you, God, in our country, and we're asking you to forgive us" (Thebault 2019). She followed by quoting 2 Chronicles 7:14, which says, "If my people, which are called by my name, shall humble themselves, and pray, and seek my face, and turn from their wicked ways; then I will hear from heaven, and will forgive their sin, and will heal their land." Although many Muslims would undoubtedly share in the sentiments expressed in this verse, it seems likely that some members of the audience might have interpreted the admission of a Muslim as the sin at issue.

Borowicz further praised President Trump for recognizing Israel. She ended with a quotation from Philippians 2:10, "I claim all these things in the powerful name of Jesus, the one who, at the name of Jesus, every knee will bow, and every tongue will confess, Jesus, that you are Lord, in Jesus' name" (Thebault 2019).

Although the Supreme Court upheld the practice of prayer in state legislature in the case of *Marsh v. Chambers* (1983), the general expectation is that the individual giving the prayer will do so in a nonpartisan and nonsectarian manner. Although outsiders are instructed to pray in that manner, members are not apparently given the same instructions.

A number of fellow legislators considered the prayer to be Islamophobic, disrespectful, and inappropriate. Rep. Movita Johnson-Harrell observed that "I came to the Capitol to help build bipartisanship and collaborations regardless of race or religion to enhance the quality of life for everyone in the Commonwealth." Democrat representative Frank Dermody reacted to the prayer by saying, "Prayer should never divide us. It should bring us together." Rep. Jordan Harris tweeted, "Prayer should never be weaponized, especially on a celebratory day" (quoted in Barillas 2019). As for Borowicz, she responded, "That's how I pray every day . . . I don't ever apologize for praying" (all three quotations found in Dicker 2019). At least one Christian news site portrayed the criticisms as a way of persecuting Borowicz (Barillas 2019).

See also Trump, Donald J.

For Reference and Further Reading

Barillas, Martin M. 2019. "U.S. Legislator Persecuted for Praying to Jesus before Swearing In of Muslim." LifeSite News. March 27. https://www.lifesitenews.com/news/u.s.-legislator-prays-to-jesus-before-swearing-in-of-muslim-and-is-accused-of-islamophobia. Accessed March 30, 2019.

Dicker, Ron. 2019. "Lawmaker's Prayer Mentions Jesus 13 Times before Muslim Colleague Is Sworn In." HuffPost. March 27. https://www.yahoo.com/huffpost/lawmaker-apos-prayer-mentions-jesus-113436078.html.

Thebault, Reis. 2019. "GOP Legislator Prays for Forgiveness before Pennsylvania's First Muslim Woman Swears In." *Governing*. March 27. https://www.governing.com/topics/politics/GOP-Legislator-Prays-for-Forgiveness-Before-Pennsylvanias-First-Muslim-Woman-Swears-In.html.

Boucher, Jonathan

Numerous historians have noted the effect that preachers had on stirring patriotic sentiments that led to the U.S. Revolutionary War, but it is important to keep in mind that pastors were split on both the legitimacy of the colonial cause and on the proper measures for them to take. Anglican priests often faced particular difficulties because their church was the official Church of England, and they were sworn to uphold the English king. Not nearly as many of their sermons survive as those of Patriot preachers, but those that do are quite instructive.

One of the most forceful Anglican priests who opposed the Patriot side in the American Revolution was Jonathan Boucher (1738–1804), who, after giving a series of sermons urging the cause of passive obedience and nonresistance, left for England at the beginning of the conflict but continued to survey the situation from afar. In 1793, he published a series of thirteen sermons that he had given in the years from 1763 to 1775 with respect to this topic, each with appropriate scriptural citations. They included the following discourses: "On the Peace" (Isaiah 2:4); "On Schisms and Sects" (Judges 17:5–6); "On the American Episcopate" (Isaiah 5:5–7); "On the Character of Absalom" (2 Samuel 18:33); "On the Character of Ahitophel" (2 Samuel 17:23); "The Dispute between the Israelites and Their Two Tribes and an Half, Respecting Their Settlement beyond Jordan" (Joshua 22:22); "On Civil Liberty; Passive Obedience, and Non-Resistance" (Galatians 5:1); and "A Farewell Sermon" (Nehemiah 6:10–11).

There is general consensus that the twelfth sermon, "On Civil Liberty; Passive Obedience, and Non-Resistance," is the most relevant in expressing Boucher's view on the Revolution. Moreover, it has the advantage of responding to a sermon by Jacob Duché, who (while he would later join the British side) had invoked God's help in the First Continental Congress for the Patriot side.

One of the fascinating aspects of Boucher's sermon is that he had lived in Virginia and Maryland and tutored George Washington's stepson. Boucher admired and actually dedicated his discourses to George Washington even though they had been on opposite sides of the revolutionary conflict.

Boucher chose for his text the words of Galatians 5:1, which admonished Christians to "stand fast, therefore, in the liberty wherewith Christ hath made us free." This was a popular Patriot text, which Duché and other Patriot advocates had cited. Boucher believed that in so doing they had taken the text out of context, and he cited both the words of the catechism that promoted the duty of "honouring and obeying the king, and all that are put in authority under him" and St. Paul's injunction in Titus 3:1 "to be subject to principalities and powers, to obey magistrates, and to be ready to every good work" (1793, 498).

Recognizing that some individuals had complained about preaching about politics, Boucher observed that their real quarrel was not with politics per se but with "unpopular politics" (499), whose spokesmen called for obedience to existing governments. He linked those who called for violent resistance to ancient Jewish zealots, and he argued that Paul and other biblical writers had not used the word "liberty" to mean "civil liberty," which Boucher thought was nowhere to be found in Scripture (505), but the liberty of "the spiritual or religious kind" (506). For Jews, liberty was liberty "from the burthensome services of the ceremonial law" while for Christians "it meant a freedom from the servitude of sin" (504).

According to Boucher, the gospel writers "make no manner of alteration in the nature or form of Civil Government; but enforce afresh, upon all Christians, that obedience which is due to the respective Constitutions of every nation in which they may happen to live" (506). He further argued that "obedience to Government is every man's duty, because it is every man's interest: but it is particularly incumbent on Christians" and "is enjoined by the positive commands of God" (507–8). For Boucher such obedience was essential to the rule of law.

Opposing secular writers, especially John Locke (a favorite among revolutionaries), who would base government on conceptions of "the common good" (512), Boucher thought this was too vague and unstable a standard. He was equally dismissive of the idea, which the Declaration of Independence affirmed, that government was formed by a compact or that individuals were equal: "Man differs from man in every thing that can be supposed to lead to supremacy and subjection, *as one star differs from another star in glory*" (514–15). Government based on continuing consent carries "the seeds of it's decay in it's very constitution" (518). Siding with Sir Robert Filmer against Locke, Boucher thought that God had created men in society and that Adam, as "the first father[,] was the first king" over both his wife and children (525).

Boucher further evoked the example of Jesus to argue against anything other than passive nonresistance—disobeying laws that commanded individuals from doing wrong but taking the appropriate penalty. In surveying Scriptures, Boucher therefore observes, "It no where appears, that either our Saviour, or any of his apostles, ever did interfere with the affairs of any government, or the administration of any government, other than by submitting to them" (540). Quoting Jesus's dictum in Matthew 22:21 to "render unto Caesar the things that are Caesar's," Boucher observed "that it is enough for the disciple to be as his master, and the servant as his lord" (342).

No government will ever be perfect, but by nature it is "absolute and irresistible" (345), and it is up to citizens to obey in order to avoid calamities. Government needs to be supreme and, in America, this supremacy is vested in "the King and the Parliament" (554). Moreover, it is unwise to revolt "on account of an insignificant duty on tea" (554), however irritating it might be.

See also Declaration of Independence; First Continental Congress; Revolutionary War

For Reference and Further Reading

Berens, John F. 1978. "'A God of Order and Not of Confusion': The American Loyalists and Divine Providence. 1774–1783." *Historical Magazine of the Protestant Episcopal Church* 47 (June): 211–19.

Boucher, Jonathan. 1793. *A View of the Causes and Consequences of the American Revolution; in Thirteen Discourses, Preached in North America between the Years 1763 and 1775: With an Historical Preface.* London: G.G. and J. Robinson. [Note: Readers may find an excerpted copy of Boucher's sermon on Civil Liberty, Passive Obedience, and Nonresistance at the Constitution Society website at https:///www.constitution.org/bcp/nonresis.htm.]

Frazer, Gregg L. 2018. *God against the Revolution: The Loyalist Clergy's Case against the American Revolution*. Lawrence: University Press of Kansas.
Noll, Mark A. 2016. *In the Beginning Was the Word: The Bible in American Public Life, 1492–1783*. New York: Oxford University Press.

Boudinot, Elias

Elias Boudinot (1740–1821) was an early American statesman who was born in Philadelphia, attended the College of New Jersey (today's Princeton), and studied law under Richard Stockton, who would later become his brother-in-law. He served on a Committee of Correspondence and as a member of the New Jersey provincial assembly and was appointed by General George Washington to serve as a commissary general for British prisoners. He also served in the Continental Congress, where Congress elected him president for the year 1783, and where he introduced a call for a national day of thanksgiving. He was elected to three terms as a member of the U.S. House of Representatives, signed the Treaty of Paris that ended the Revolutionary War, and headed the U.S. Mint.

Boudinot became an ardent Federalist who was strongly opposed to the secular forces unleashed by the French Revolution, which he feared would flourish in America with the election of Thomas Jefferson, whom he considered to be a Deist. More generally, Boudinot feared the decline of public virtue in the United States. In retirement, he helped found and served as the first president of the American Bible Society, through which he thought that the spread of the Bible and of Christianity might bring soon the return of Jesus to earth.

An orthodox Presbyterian, Boudinot had been baptized by George Whitefield (1714–1770) and grew up under the preaching of the revivalist Gilbert Tennent (1703–1764). Boudinot was clearly shocked when Thomas Paine, who had utilized the Bible in *Common Sense*, to argue against the institution of hereditary kingship, published *The Age of Reason*, in which he attacked the authority of the Bible and many other orthodox Christian doctrines.

Boudinot was especially concerned about how such infidelity might affect the morals of America's youth. In a letter to his daughter, Boudinot observed, "I confess that I was much mortified to find the whole force of this vain man's genius and art pointed at the youth of America. . . . This awful consequence created some alarm in my mind lest at any future day, you, my beloved child, might take up this plausible address of infidelity; and for want of an answer at hand to his subtle insinuations might suffer even a doubt of the truth, as it is in Jesus, to penetrate your mind" (DeMar n.d., viii).

Boudinot's refutation is saturated with references to classical historians and contemporary thinkers as well as with scriptural references and scriptural quotations. Indeed, in his dedication, he refers to the Bible as "the Alpha and Omega of knowledge," a term that the Bible (Revelation 1:8; 21:6; and 22:13) uses for Jesus (1801, xxii).

Paine sought to dismiss most biblical accounts on the basis that they were based upon hearsay by individuals who are not alive to be questioned. By contrast,

Boudinot sought to argue that the biblical record, which had been based on hundreds of witnesses, was superior to most other historical accounts upon which scholars commonly rely and had been validated by prophecy. He thus sought to uphold accounts of the virgin birth of Jesus, the divine mission of Christ, the Trinity (which Boudinot believed had been shared by other early religions), the resurrection and ascension of Christ, and the authenticity of the books of both the Old and New Testaments. In arguments that continue to be a part of modern apologetics, Boudinot believed it was contradictory to argue, as Paine had done, that the ethics of Jesus and his disciples were a great advance, while then denying the claims to deity that he believed Jesus had made and suggesting that his disciples had perpetuated a fraud when they argued for Jesus's resurrection and ascension. Referring to a wide variety of statements that the gospels had attributed to Jesus, Boudinot rhetorically asked, "Can that man be a virtuous and amiable man—a preacher and practice of the most benevolent morality, not exceeded by any—and yet in the opinion of this writer, be guilty of imposing on his followers, by assuring them that 'He was before the foundation of the world—that he was the birth born of every creature—that he was sent of God—came down from Heaven—that he was the only begotten Son of God—that God was his father' " (1801, 85). Boudinot observed that "the denial of the principal events and historical occurrences of the life of Jesus Christ, as recorded by the evangelists, necessarily implies a miracle equal to the affirmation of them" (91). Boudinot also challenged Paine, who remained a Deist, to explain evil without the doctrine of original sin (125).

Although *The Age of Reason* sold well in America, it would appear that many more Americans identified with the view expressed by Boudinot and other critics than with Paine, who died in relative obscurity and who continued to be a favorite whipping boy of those who opposed biblical infidelity.

See also American Bible Society; *Common Sense* (Thomas Paine); Jefferson Bible

For Reference and Further Reading

Boudinot, Elias. 1801. *The Age of Revelation: Or, The Age of Reason Shewn to Be an Age of Infidelity*. Philadelphia: Asbury Dickins. Reprinted by Power Springs, GA: American Vision Press.

DeMar, Gary. n.d. "Foreword" to Boudinot, Elias. 1802. *The Age of Revelation: Or, The Age of Reason Shewn to Be an Age of Infidelity*. Philadelphia: Asbury Dickins. Reprinted by Power Springs, GA: American Vision Press, pp. vii–xiv.

Den Hartog, Jonathan. 2014. "Elias Boudinot, Presbyterians, and the Quest for a 'Righteous Republic.' " *Faith and the Founders of the American Republic*, ed. Daniel L. Dreisbach and Mark David Hall. New York: Oxford University Press, pp. 253–76.

Den Hartog, Jonathan J. 2015. *Patriotism & Piety: Federalist Politics and Religious Struggle in the New American Nation*. Charlottesville: University of Virginia Press.

Flick, Stephen. n.d. "Elias Boudinot: Building America on Christ." Christian Heritage Fellowship. https://christianheritagefellowship.com/elias-boudinot-building-america-on-christ/. Accessed May 9, 2019.

Keane, John. 1995. *Tom Paine: A Political Life*. Boston, MA: Little, Brown.

Staloff, Darren. 2014. "Deism and the Founders." *Faith and the Founders of the American Republic*. New York: Oxford University Press, pp. 13–33.

Bradley, Joseph P.

Joseph P. Bradley (1813–1892) was appointed by President Ulysses S. Grant to the Supreme Court in 1870 and served there until his death. Raised in the Dutch Reformed Church, he initially studied for the ministry at Rutgers before pursuing the study of law and developing a national reputation in patent and railroad law. A selection of his writings published after his death contains a long section dealing with his view on religious and moral issues, in which he both articulated his admiration for the Bible and indicated that he believed that God continued to reveal himself through nature and through other extra-biblical writings.

In an opening letter in this section, he indicated that he did not consider the omission of an explicit acknowledgement of God in the Constitution to demonstrate "hostility to religion" but rather "as showing a fixed determination to leave the people entirely free on the subject" (Bradley 1902, 358). For this reason, he did not support the so-called Christian Amendment, which had been supported by his colleague Justice William Strong.

Bradley further explored such esoteric topics as the dimensions and layout of Noah's Ark, the history of English translations of the Bible (despite his liberalism, Bradley was a strong defender of the elegance of the King James Version), and the likely year and date of the crucifixion and resurrection of Jesus. He also explicated the Lord's Prayer and four points that he believed constituted "the whole essence of the Christian religion," namely:

1. God's existence, fatherhood and loving kindliness to all, and hence His attention to our wants and prayers.
2. The equality and brotherhood of all men, and hence the duty of Universal Charity.
3. The prime importance of our spiritual nature, and hence the secondary importance of sensuous and material things.
4. The need of God's forgiveness and help, and hence the hopelessness of an unforgiving spirit. (Bradley 1902, 369)

In writing about the Bible, Strong described it as "a valuable repository." He specifically commended "the devotional fervor of the Psalms, the sententious wisdom of the book of Proverbs, and the profound reflections of Ecclesiastes," as well as the "exalted moral exhortation and instruction" of the prophets, and "the simple and searching lessons of faith, sincerity, purity of heart and universal charity of the New Testament" (370). Bradley thought that it was possible to commend the Bible "without entering into the question of special revelation and miracles, which have so much agitated both the curious inquirers and the superstitious devotees of the Christian world" (370–71). Moreover, such an approach "is consistent with the free and intelligent use of all similar aides to virtue and spiritual elevation to be found in the sayings of the great and good of all nations and times" (371). In another essay entitled "Inerrant or Infallible Bible," Bradley observed, "The Spirit of God moves upon the ocean of human thought, ever evolving light and truth, which concreted in words of immortal power, becomes stereotyped upon the consciousness of the nations, consecrated by antiquity into the forms of sacred learning, and hallowed by all holy and religious associations" (401–2).

Suggesting that those with superior wisdom should tolerate attempts to incorporate biblical teachings into doctrines, in another essay, Bradley observed that "if we do not believe in miracles, we may well believe in the vast importance and benefit of those hoary traditions of Divine influence which have become as effective for good with the great mass of mankind as if they were based on the most certain deductions of reason and experience" (404). In a similar vein, Bradley observed,

> Until the world is ready for the truth, it is not safe to communicate it, except to the select view who can be trusted to embrace and guard it; that select few who are governed by inherent and unbending rectitude. The wise man will continue to respect and observe the laws, usages and modes which prevail, and which society regards as essential to the conservation of order and morality. Mankind in general can only be gradually awakened to truth. The light of science will, in the end, quench the farthing candles of error and superstition. (Bradley 1902, 406)

Believing that Jesus had largely freed his followers from strict observance of the Sabbath, Bradley thought "that civil society has a right to enact wholesome laws on the subject is manifest both from the sayings of Christ and from the incalculable benefits which society derives from the institution" (410).

Arguing that the primary goal of religion was not "to avoid eternal misery and obtain eternal happiness," he said that "its true object is to make men better, or rather, to make them good—a word which includes every virtue" (424). In this same essay, he observed that "a belief in an officious God is absolutely necessary to elevate and purify the masses" (426).

Bradley thought that there should be progress "in religious science" just as in other areas; this, in turn, required rejecting "the theory that revelation of Divine truth was miraculously made to these men at first hand and has never been made except through Hebrew prophets and seers" (428). He specifically argued that "every page of Nature's great Book" refused the "narrow theory of a six day's creation" (428–29). Bradley further said that the only dogma that Jesus taught was "that God is our Father and that we are all brethren" (481).

In an essay dated July 4, 1871, Bradley recorded some "Esoteric Thoughts on Religion and Religionism," which concluded with the thought that "it is for us, through all difficulties and temptations, to pursue an honorable, dignified, truthful and loving life, so that whenever our task is done, we may depart amidst the blessings of mankind and be remembered for our good deeds. *This is my religion*" (435).

See also Christian Amendment; King James Version of the Bible; Sunday Closing Laws

For Reference and Further Reading

Bradley, Joseph P. 1902. *Miscellaneous Writings of the Late Hon. Joseph P. Bradley*, ed. and compiled by Charles Bradley. Newark, NJ: L. J. Hardham.

Hitchcock, James. 2004. *The Supreme Court and Religion in American Life: From "Higher Law" to "Sectarian Scruples."* Vol. II of 2 vols. Princeton, NJ: Princeton University Press.

Brewer, David J.

David J. Brewer (1837–1910) was among the most biblically literate of those who have served as justices of the United States. The son of a Congregationalist minister who had served as a missionary to Turkey and been active in the abolitionist movement, Brewer was educated at Yale University. There he was particularly influenced by Professor (and later president) Theodore Dwight Woolsey, who combined a strong commitment to Christianity with the belief that individuals were free moral beings (Hylton 1998, 420).

In *Church of the Holy Trinity v. United States* (1892), Brewer described the United States as a "Christian nation," but part of what he thought made it Christian was its commitment to religious liberty. In interpreting the Constitution, Brewer emphasized the principles articulated in the first paragraph of the Declaration of Independence.

Brewer was fond of giving speeches, and, in a review of his faith, Linda Przybyszewski observes that Brewer "often quoted from the Christian Bible and popular Protestant hymns" (2000, 231). In a speech defending free enterprise, Brewer cited Micah 4:4 and its reference to individuals being able to sit under their own vine and fig trees (2000, 231). In a speech entitled "The Religion of a Jurist," Brewer quoted Paul (1 Corinthians 15:53) in saying, "For this corruptible must put on incorruption, and this mortal must put on immortality" (2000, 234). In defending toleration, he observed Jesus's statement to Pilate in John 18:36 that "my kingdom is not of this world" (2000, 238). In a speech to the Sons of the Pilgrims of Charleston, South Carolina, Brewer likened the founding of America to Abraham's journey to Canaan (2000, 238). In opposing excessive police powers, he said, "My heart responds to the gentle invitation of the Man of Galilee [Matthew 11:28], 'Come unto me all ye that labor and are heavy laden and I will give your rest" (2000, 239). In that same speech, he said that he believed "in the liberty of the soul, subject to no restraint but the law of love, and in the liberty of the individual, limited only by the equal rights of his neighbor" (2000, 239).

In his book describing the United States as a Christian nation, after observing that "the Bible is the Christian's book," Brewer continued,

> No other book has so wide a circulation, or is so universally found in the households of the land. During their century of existence the English and American Bible Societies have published and circulated two hundred and fifty million copies, and this represents but a fraction of its circulation. And then think of the multitude of volumes published in exposition, explanation and illustration of that book, or some portion of it. (1905, 39)

Later in the book, Brewer opined, quoting from Proverbs 14:34, "It needs no declaration of Scripture to convince that 'righteousness exalteth a nation; but sin is a reproach to any people.' In so far, therefore, as the principles and precepts of

Christianity develop righteousness in the individual, to the same extent will a similar result be found in the life of the nation" (1905, 75). Still later, urging his readers to cultivate Christian homes, he urged them to "crown all these with the inspirations which come from Christianity, place the Bible on your table and enshrine the Master in your heart and you may be sure you are building up a home which will be not merely peace and blessing to you, but also for the strength and glory of the republic" (98).

Przbyszewski points out that Brewer cared little about religious doctrine but believed in a God who would sustain people through trials and right all wrongs. As a postmillennialist, Brewer believed that America could hasten the millennial rule of Christ on earth. This appears to have stimulated his work on behalf of international law. Brewer, however, opposed American foreign imperialism.

See also Declaration of Independence

For Reference and Further Reading

Barka, Mokhtar Ben. 2011. "The Christian Nation Debate and the U.S. Supreme Court." *European Journal of American Studies*. Special Issue: Oslo Conference. https://journals.openedition.org/ejas/8882.

Brewer, David J. 1905. *The United States: A Christian Nation*. Philadelphia: John C. Winston.

Church of the Holy Trinity v. United States, 143 U.S. 457 (1892).

Hylton, J. Gordon. 1998. "David Josiah Brewer and the Christian Constitution." *Marquette Law Review* 82 (Winter): 417–25.

Przbyszewski, Linda. 2000. "The Religion of a Jurist: Justice David J. Brewer and the Christian Nation." *Journal of Supreme Court History* 25 (November): 228–42.

Brown, John

John Brown (1800–1859) was one of America's most radical abolitionists. He led a hardscrabble life that was filled with numerous business failures, law suits, and the loss of several infant children that may have further radicalized him.

In addition to leading the massacre of men and boys at Pottawatomie Creek in Kansas in retaliation for proslavery attacks on Lawrence, Kansas, and conducting a raid into Missouri in which a slave owner was killed and eleven slaves freed, Brown led the raid on the federal arsenal at Harper's Ferry, Virginia (today's West Virginia), in an unsuccessful effort to spark a slave rebellion. In the trial that followed, Brown successfully elevated his profile from that of a terrorist to that of a martyr reading and carefully marking his Bible and identifying himself with prior Christian martyrs, including Jesus.

Whereas many abolitionists espoused a more liberal theology, Brown was a strong Calvinist who believed in the doctrine of original sin and read the sermons of Jonathan Edwards. Although Brown's espousal of violence might seem better to fit the God of the Old Testament than the New, Professor Louis DeCaro argues that Brown's vision "was premised upon a thoroughly biblical spirituality rooted theologically and ethically in the teachings of Jesus and the apostles as much as the Hebrew prophets and Old Testament accounts regarding the slaying of pagan tribes" (2002, 5). DeCaro further noted, "As an evangelical Christian, he not only read the Bible as God's word, he read the Bible as *God's word to John Brown*. He believed that the Scriptures continued to speak to life situations, radiating fresh truth and directives without obscuring its original and primary meaning" (5). In similar fashion, another scholar has observed that "Brown's deterministic Calvinism was tempered by antinomian and perfectionist views held in common with many other abolitionists and religious reforms of his day. Antinomianism, an anti-clerical Protestant heresy with a long life, held that in matters of faith each soul was in direct communication with God outside any church or minister's discipline" (Fellman 2010, 22).

Brown's moralism was evident in a provisional constitution that he drew up for the free state that he anticipated would grow from his raid at Harper's Ferry. It prohibited "profane swearing, filthy conversation, indecent behavior, indecent exposure of the person, or intoxication or quarreling" or "unlawful intercourse of the sexes" (Fogleson and Rubenstein 1969, 47). It also provided for setting aside Sunday for rest and for "moral and religious instruction and improvement, relief of the suffering, instruction of the young and ignorant, and the encouragement of personal cleanliness" (57–58).

In 1859, Brown published "A Declaration of Liberty by the Representatives of the Slave Population of the United States of America" that was patterned on the Declaration of Independence. It referred to "the enormous sin of Slavery," stated, in words close to those that Thomas Jefferson had once voiced, that "I tremble for my Country, when I reflect, that God is just; And that his justice; will not sleep forever," and ended with the dramatic words, "Hung be the Heavens in Scarlet" (Brown 1859).

When asked by a bystander at his trial what principles motivated him, Brown responded, "Upon the golden rule. I pity the poor in bondage that have none to help them; that is why I am here; not to gratify any personal animosity, revenge or vindictive spirit. It is my sympathy with the oppressed and the wronged, that are as good as you and as precious in the sight of God" (Fellman 2010, 39). In making a statement before the court that sentenced him to death, Brown said,

> This Court acknowledges, too, as I suppose, the validity of the law of God. I see a book kissed, which I suppose to be the Bible, or at least the New Testament, which teaches me that all things whatsoever I would that men should do to me, I should do even so to them. I endeavored to act up to that instruction. I say I am yet too young to understand that God is any respecter of persons. I believe that to have interfered as I have done, as I have always freely admitted I have done in behalf of His despised poor, is no wrong, but right. (Fellman 2010, 42)

Brown believed deeply that sin required blood atonement. In disciplining one of his children, he kept an account of his offenses, and, after giving him a number of lashes, then bared his own back for his son to inflict upon him the balance of the judgment (Fellman 2010, 23). An early disciple of Brown summed up his theology with the verse, "Without the shedding of blood there is no remission of sin [Hebrews 9:22]" (Gilpin 2013).

A biographer of Brown notes that the Bible that Brown read in prison was a King James Version, which was printed by the American Bible Society. He gave it to his baker, John F. Blessing, with his best wishes and added that "there is no commentary in the world so good in order to a right understanding of this blessed book as an honest Childlike and teachable Spirit" (DeCaro 2007). Altogether he had dog-eared thirty-five pages, with nine in the Old Testament. In an earlier Bible that he had owned, Brown had marked passages in Genesis, Exodus, Leviticus, Deuteronomy, Job, Proverbs, Ecclesiastes, Isaiah, Jeremiah, and Ezekiel in the Old Testament and Matthew and Revelation in the New Testament (DeCaro 2007).

See also Slavery; Violence

For Reference and Further Reading

Brown, John. 1859. "A Declaration of Liberty by the Representatives of the Slave Population of the United States of America." Digital History. www.digitalhistory.uh.edu/active_learning/explorations/brown/planning3.cfm.

DeCaro, Louis A., Jr. 2002. *"Fire from the Midst of you": A Religious Life of John Brown.* New York: New York University Press.

DeCaro, Louis A., Jr. 2007. "John Brown the Abolitionist—A Biographer's Blog." May 6. http ://abolitionist-john-brown.blogspot.com/.

Fellman, Michael. 2010. *In the Name of God and Country: Reconsidering Terrorism in American History.* New Haven, CT: Yale University Press.

Fogleson, Robmer M., and Richard E. Rubenstein. 1969. *Mass Violence in America: Invasion at Harper's Ferry.* New York: Arno Press.

Gilpin, R. Balkeslee. 2013. "John Brown, Religion and Violent Abolition: 'Choose You This Day Whom You Will Serve.'" HuffPost. January 22. https://www.huffpost.com/entry/john-brown-religion-and-violent-abolition_b_2527903.

Bryan, William Jennings

William Jennings Bryan (1860–1925) was one of America's most important progressive Democrats who was especially known for his oratory. After earning a degree at Illinois College, Bryan received a law degree from Northwestern University. Elected to the U.S. House of Representatives from Nebraska in 1890, he garnered the Democratic nomination for president in 1896 after giving his "Cross of Gold" speech in which he argued for the freer coinage of money rather than following the existing gold standard, which he thought was hurting farmers. His most immortal lines, which drew directly from the gospel stories of the crucifixion of Jesus, were at the end of this speech in which he said, "You shall not press down upon the brow of labor this crown of thorns, you shall not crucify mankind upon a cross of gold" (quoted in Noll 2011, 256); in his keynote address to the Democrat National Convention in 1956, Tennessee governor Frank G. Clement would recycle the analogy in saying, "You will not crucify the American farmer on a Republican cross of gold" (Lawrence 1956). Bryan was renominated in both 1900 and 1908 but lost these elections as well.

Bryan opposed American foreign expansionism in the wake of the Spanish-American War. He later resigned as Woodrow Wilson's secretary of state because Bryan wanted to maintain the policy of neutrality in World War I that Wilson had favored in his first term. In a speech marking the three hundredth anniversary of the King James Version of the Bible in 1911, Bryan had argued forcefully for the idea that the Bible was not the mere work of man but the inspired word of God. Mark Noll has observed that Bryan not only praised the Bible as "the foundation of our statute law," the source of "the rules for spiritual growth" and the world's best "code of morality," but that he stressed that, above all, it presented "the story of him who is the growing figure of all time, whom the world is accepting as Saviour and as the perfect example" (2011, 255).

Bryan was a Cumberland Presbyterian and Congregationalist who believed strongly in the Bible and who thought that it was under attack by the theory of evolution, as advanced by Charles Darwin, Aldous Huxley (Darwin's so-called bull-dog), and others. He was even more concerned about the less scientific doctrine of social Darwinism that attempted to apply insights from biology to human social interactions. In explaining how he could combine what historian Willard Smith describes as "economic liberalism with religious liberalism," Bryan explained, "People often ask me why I can be a progressive in politics and a fundamentalist in religion. The answer is easy. Government is man made and therefore imperfect. . . . If Christ is the final word, how may any one be progressive in religion? I am satisfied with the God we have, with the Bible and with Christ" (Smith 1966, 41–42). Explaining his earnestness for democracy, Bryan said that just as a good sermon stressed the Ten Commandments, the Sermon on the Mount, and Christ's command to love one's neighbor, so too "a good democratic speech is built upon the doctrine of human brotherhood, equal rights, and self government" (Smith 1966, 43).

Although the grilling that Bryan received via attorney Clarence Darrow during the Scopes Trial in Tennessee in 1925 with regard to the state's right to teach the theory of evolution in public schools suggested that he did not know the answer to many biblical conundrums (and that he did not equate the "days" in the Genesis account with actual physical days), the speech that Bryan prepared for trial as a closing argument, which was precluded from giving by Darrow's decision to accept Scopes's guilt, is far more nuanced. It shows that Bryan was deeply concerned about the social implications of the theory and that although he was not advocating the teaching of religion in public schools, he viewed the issue from the populist perspective as to whether citizens had the right to exclude what they considered to be anti-religious materials from public school classrooms.

Early in his speech, Bryan claimed that Christianity was a patron of learning but that Christians believed that "the fear of the Lord is the beginning of wisdom [Proverbs 9:10]" and that "they therefore opposed the teaching of guesses that encourage godlessness among the students" (Bryan 1925). Believing that "divine truth . . . comes by inspiration from God Himself," Bryan thought that it was superior to mere hypotheses that he thought the theory of evolution represented (Bryan 1925). Moreover, the law at issue did not prohibit the teaching of evolution per se, but only the teaching that such evolutionary processes had included mankind.

Bryan believed that, by omitting God, teaching evolution was equivalent to teaching an anti-religion, or what later evangelicals would refer to as "secular humanism." Bryan thus said that "before accepting a new philosophy of life built upon a materialistic foundation, we have reason to remand something more than guesses: 'we may well, suppose' is not a sufficient substitute for 'thus saith the Lord,'" a common biblical saying of the prophets (Bryan 1925).

Bryan broke his criticisms of evolution into several indictments. He argued first that "it disputes the truth of the bible account of man's creation and shakes faith in the Bible as the word of God" (Bryan 1925). Tracing Darwin's own journey from faith to skepticism, Bryan further argued that the theory of evolution, "carried to its logical conclusion, disputes every vital truth of the Bible" (Bryan 1925). In a somewhat circular argument, Bryan argued that miracles are possible and that "the same evidence that establishes the authority of the Bible establishes the truth of the record of miracles performed" (Bryan 1925). Quoting from Luke 17:1–2, which had been one of Abraham Lincoln's favorites, Bryan observed, "It is impossible but that offenses will come; but woe unto him through whom they come. It were better for him that a millstone were hanged about his neck, and be cast into the sea, than that he should offend one of these little ones" (Bryan 1925).

Prior to the Scopes Trial, Clarence Darrow had successfully defended Nathan Leopold and Richard Loeb against the death penalty for the murder of a fellow teenager, Bobby Frank, partly on the basis that their prior education, including reading Frederick Nietzsche, had led to their crime. Tying this view to that of biological determinism (an interesting materialistic echo to Calvinistic predestination), Bryan argued that this was a "damnable philosophy," similar in its materialistic emphasis to Darwinism. In a memorable, but sometimes mocked, line, Bryan said that he did not want students "to lose sight of the Rock of Ages [a reference to Christ] while they study the age of rocks" (Bryan 1925).

As a progressive reformer who shared some views with the social gospel movement, Bryan further argued that "by paralyzing the hope of reform," the theory of evolution "discourages those who labor for the improvement of man's condition" (Bryan 1925). Whereas Christianity promised the hope of redemption, evolution depended on "scientific breeding" and "eugenics"; such a philosophy had no place for such biblical stories as that of the redemption of the prodigal Son (Bryan 1925).

Again, emphasizing that his central concern was less with biology than with social Darwinism, Bryan believed that the teaching of evolution would undermine love by teaching "a struggle of tooth and claw" (Bryan 1925). Drawing from his own pacifist roots, Bryan feared that science was both generating war and making it more deadly.

As he came to his summation, which repeated the words of the song "Faith of Our Fathers," Bryan employed two classical images, one from Elijah's confrontation in the Old Testament with idol worshippers (1 Kings 18:1–45) and the other from Jesus's confrontation with Pilate (John 18:28–40), to say that "it is again a choice between God and Baal; it is also a renewal of the issue in Pilate's court." The question of "What shall I do with Jesus" must be answered. If the jury were to repudiate the law at issue, "there will be rejoicing wherever God is repudiated, the Saviour scoffed at and the Bible ridiculed" (Bryan 1925).

Because Bryan died five days after the trial, he never had a chance to give this speech in person, but it remains a reminder that it was possible for political progressives to be biblical conservatives and a testament to the fact that biological evolution has sometimes been the guise for social theories that could undermine both faith in the Bible and efforts to help the weak and helpless.

See also Fundamentalism; Scopes Trial; Social Gospel

For Reference and Further Reading

Bryan, William Jennings. 1925. "Text of Closing Statement of William Jennings Bryan at the trial of John Scopes, Dayton, Tennessee, 1925." http://www2.csudh.edu/oliver/smt310-handouts/wjb-last/wjb-last.htm.

Lawrence, W. R. 1956. "Democratic Keynote Talk Assails Nixon as 'Hathet Man' of G.O.P.; Lays 'Indifference' to President." *New York Times*. August 14.

Noll, Mark A. 2011. "William Jennings Bryan, Theodore Roosevelt, Woodrow Wilson and the King James Version of the Bible." *Theology* 114(4): 251–59.

Smith, Willard H. 1966. "William Jennings Bryan and the Social Gospel." *Journal of American History* 53 (June): 41–60.

Bush, George W.

George W. Bush (b. 1946) served as the forty-third president of the United States from 2001 to 2009, a time marked both by the terrorist attacks of September 11, 2001, and the second American invasion of Iraq.

A graduate of Yale University, a former governor of Texas, and the son of former president George Herbert Walker Bush, Bush, who was raised in both the Presbyterian and Episcopalian Churches, is, with his wife, a Methodist. He describes how in 1986 he overcame alcoholism after a visit from evangelist Billy Graham. He said that he subsequently felt a call to run for president after hearing his pastor tell how the nation needed modern leaders like Moses and his mother told him, "He was talking to you" (Siker 2006). As governor, Bush supported a prison program that sought to rehabilitate prisoners through Bible reading and prayer (Goodstein 2000), and he declared June 10, 2000, to be "Jesus Day" (Siker 2006).

Supported by many evangelical Christians, during a debate with fellow Republican presidential aspirants during the 2000 presidential campaign, Bush said that Jesus was his favorite political philosopher. Bush read the Bible regularly. He told a reporter that his recommitment to Jesus was "one of the defining moments of my life," and that "from Scripture you can gain a lot of strength and solace and learn life's lessons. That what I believe, and I don't necessarily believe every single word is literally true" (quoted in Goodstein 2000).

Although he kept his family Bible on which he took his oath closed to shield it from rain during his first presidential inauguration, he opened it to Isaiah 40:31 for his second one (Winder 2019, 20). That verse highlighted what had become another American symbol, by proclaiming, "But they that wait upon the Lord shall renew their strength; they shall mount up with wings as eagles; they shall run, and not be weary; and they shall walk, and not faint."

Bush had run on a platform of "compassionate conservatism" and thought that private religious groups could often administer programs better than governmental bureaucracies. In his first inaugural address, Bush made an indirect reference to Jesus's story of the Good Samaritan (Luke 10:25–37) when he said, "I can pledge our nation to a goal: When we see that wounded traveler on the road to Jericho, we will not pass to the other side," and soon after his election he created a faith-based initiative office (Heltzel 2009, 108).

At a memorial service at the National Cathedral for the victims of 9/11, Bush cited Romans 8:38–39 to assure the audience that nothing could separate God's people from their love. As president, Bush connected to earlier notions of American providentialism. In his first inaugural address, he thus observed,

> We have a place, all of us, in a long story. A story we continue, but whose end we will not see. It is the story of a new world that became a friend and liberator of the old, a story of a slave-holding society that became a servant of freedom, the story of a power that went into the world to protect but not possess, to defend but not to conquer. It is the American story. A story of flawed and fallible people, united across the generations by grand and enduring ideals. (Smith 2008, 283)

In a speech that he gave in 2002 on Israel and Palestine, he quoted from Deuteronomy 30:19: "I have set before you life and death; therefore choose life" (Siker 2006).

Bush was known for salting his speeches with references to songs and biblical passages with which evangelical Christians were often familiar, but which it sometimes took the news media some time to discover. In a speech commemorating the second anniversary of the 9/11 attacks, Bush ended with, "This ideal of America is the hope of all mankind . . . That hope still lights our way. And the light shines in the darkness. And the darkness will not overcome it." This paraphrase of John 1:4–5 is from a passage used to describe Jesus and to identify Him with the Creator of the universe, a parallel that one theological studies professor calls "astonishing" because Bush moved "from nationalism to idolatry, envisioning America as the Word made flesh" (Siker 2006). Critics attribute Bush's tendency to moralize with his invasion of Iraq and with other aggressive foreign policy moves.

Others, however, have suggested that Bush's conception of the Bible was fairly bland. Summarizing four articles designed to discuss Bush's Bible, one scholar says that "Bush's Bible (as referenced politically and publicly) hardly exists as an actual corpus. It seems to amount to little more than a few scattered references to the Prophets (in a vague name-dropping sense); a range of quasi-biblicisms that seem to aspire to imitate the paradoxical language of the gospels (such as 'We exercise power without conquest, and we sacrifice for the liberty of strangers'); a few crypto-biblical and crypto-theological references to the 'Author of Liberty'; the democratic-Christian mission against 'tyrants' and the commission by a vaguely theologized 'history'; and the deliberately apocalyptic noun-ing of evil" (Sherwood 2006, 48). This scholar suggested that Bush's Bible was the Liberal Bible, exemplified by the philosophy of John Locke rather than what she describes as the Absolute Monarchist's Bible of seventeenth-century Britain, or the "republican, anti-monarchical, radical Bible" that grew out of reaction to it (Sherwood 2006, 51).

See also Eagle as American Symbol; Graham, Billy; Jesus; Presidential Inaugural Bible Verses

For Reference and Further Reading

Davis. Derek H. 2006. "President George Bush: America's Pastor in Troubled Times?" Society of Biblical Literature. May. https://www.sbl-site.org/publications/article.aspx?ArticleId=153.

Goodstein, Laurie. 2000. "The 2000 Campaign: The Philosophy: Conservative Church Leaders Find a Pillar in Bush." *New York Times*. January 23.

Heltzel, Peter Goodwin. 2009. *Jesus and Justice: Evangelicals, Race, and American Politics*. New Haven, CT: Yale University Press.

Sherwood, Yvonne. 2006 "Bush's Bible as a Liberal Bible (Strange Though That May Seem)." *Postscripts: The Journal of Sacred Texts and Contemporary Worlds* 2(1): 47–58.

Siker, Jeffrey. 2006. "President Bush, Biblical Faith, and the Politics of Religion." Society of Biblical Literature. May. https://www.sbl-site.org/publications/article.aspx?ArticleId=151. Accessed May 27, 2019.

Smith, Rogers M. 2008. "Religious Rhetoric and the Ethics of Public Discourse: The Case of George W. Bush." *Political Theory* 36 (April): 272–300.

Winder, Mike. 2019. *Favorite Scriptures of 100 American Leaders*. Springville, UT: Plain Sight.

Buttigieg, Pete

Pete Buttigieg (b. 1982), the mayor of South Bend, Indiana, who sought the Democratic nomination for president in 2020, is an openly gay married man and an Episcopalian. He grew up in South Bend, which is the home of Notre Dame University, where his parents were professors, and he attended St. Joseph High School (Burke 2019). He is a graduate of Harvard University, where he studied under Sacvan Bercovitch, who specialized in Puritanism, and subsequently attended Pembroke College on a Rhodes Scholarship where he traces his own spiritual awakening.

In part because he comes from the same state as Vice President Mike Pence, who has much more conservative political and religious views, the two have sometimes been at political loggerheads. At one point Buttigieg said that if Pence had a problem with him, "your problem is not with me—your quarrel, sir, is with my creator" (Cole 2019).

Buttigieg has identified two favorite Bible verses. The first is Matthew 25:40, which says, "Whatever you did for one of the least of these . . . you did for me." The second is Matthew 6:5, which says, "And when you pray, do not be like the hypocrites, for they love to pray standing in the synagogues and on the street corners to be seen by others" (Powers 2019).

Asked about the tension between being gay and identifying as a Christian, Buttigieg observed, "It can be challenging to be a person of faith who's also part of the LGBTQ (Lesbian, Gay, Bisexual, Transsexual, Queer) community and yet, to me, the core of faith is regard for one another. And part of God's love is experienced, according to my faith tradition, is in the way that we support one another and, in particular, support the least among us" (quoted in Rocha 2019). Further explaining his view of Scripture, Buttigieg observed,

> When I think about where most of Scripture points me, it is toward defending the poor, and the immigrant, and the stranger, and the prisoner, and the outcast, and those who are left behind by the way society works. And what we have now is this exaltation of wealth and power, almost for its own sake, that in my reading of Scripture couldn't be more contrary to the message of Christianity. So I think it's really important to carry a message (to the public), knitting together a lot of groups that have already been on this path for some time, but giving them more visibility in the public sphere. (Powers 2019)

In the second debate among Democratic contenders for president in 2019, Buttigieg quoted Proverbs 14:31 when he said, "The minimum wage is just too low. And so-called conservative Christian senators right now in the Senate are blocking a bill to raise the minimum wage when Scripture says that, 'Whoever oppresses the poor taunts their maker' " (Parke, 2019).

Although Peter Wehner has expressed concern that Buttigieg's remark that "Christian faith is going to point you in a progressive direction" subordinated Scripture to political ideology, Buttigieg has supported separation of church and state. He has further stated that "I get that one of the things about Scripture is different people see different things in it. But, at the very least we should be able to establish that God does not have a political party" (Rocha 2019). Evangelist Franklin Graham, who tweeted, "As a Christian, I believe the Bible which defines homosexuality as a sin, something to be repentant of, not something to be flaunted, praised or politicized," responded that Buttigieg was right in believing that "God doesn't have a political party. But God does have commandments laws & standards He gives us to live by" (Gomez 2019).

In May 2019, Buttigieg and his husband visited Jimmy Carter's Sunday school class where Carter asked him to read the day's Scripture (Reeves 2019). In an interview on the Today Show on May 7, 2019, Buttigieg suggested that if God were to have a political affiliation, he did not think it would "be the one that sent the current president into the White House" (Mercia 2019).

See also Carter, Jimmy; Pence, Mike; Same-Sex Marriage

For Reference and Further Reading

Burke, Daniel. 2019. "How Pete Buttigieg Found God." CNN Politics. August 17. https://www.cnn.com/2019/08/16/politics/pete-buttigieg-religious-journey/index.html.

Cole, Devan. 2019. "Buttigieg to Pence: 'If You Got a Problem with Who I Am, Your Problem Is Not with Me—Your Quarrel, Sir, Is with My Creator." CNN. April 8. https://www.cnn.com/2019/04/08/politics/pete-buttigieg-mike-pence/index.html.

Douthat, Ross. 2019. "The Abortion Mysticism of Pete Buttigieg." *New York Times*. September 17.

Gomez, Justin. 2019. "Franklin Graham Attacks Pete Buttigieg for Being Gay, Says He Should Repent." ABC News. April 25. https://abcnews.go.com/Politics/franklin-graham-attacks-pete-buttigieg-gay-repent/story?id=62625378&cid=clicksource_4380645_null_twopack_hed.

Mercia, Dan. 2019. "Pete Buttigieg: God Doesn't Belong to a Political Party, but 'I Can't Imagine' God Would Be a Republican." CNN. May 7. https://www.cnn.com/2019/05/07/politics/pete-buttigieg-god-political-party-republican/index.html. Accessed May 7, 2019.

Parke Caleb. 2019. "Pete Buttigieg Uses Bible Verse to Slam 'So-Called Conservative Christian' Republicans during Debate." Fox News. July 29. https://www.foxnews.com/politics/pete-buttigieg-democratic-debate-2020-bible-republicans-christian.

Peters, Jeremy W. 2019. "Pete Buttigieg, Gay and Christian, Challenges Religious Right on Their Own Turf." *New York Times*. April 10. https://www.nytimes.com/2019/04/10/us/politics/pete-buttigieg-sexuality-religion.html. Accessed April 11, 2019.

Powers, Kirsten. 2019. "Mayor Pete Buttigieg's Countercultural Approach to Christianity Is What America Needs Now." *USA Today*. April 4. https://www.usatoday.com/story/opinion/2019/04/03/mayor-pete-buttigieg-christian-right-2020-democratic-primary-trump-column/3342767002/.

Reeves, Jay. 2019. "Buttigieg, Husband Attend Jimmy Carter's Sunday School Class." ABC News. May 5. https://abcnews.go.com/Politics/wireStory/buttigieg-husband-attend-jimmy-carters-sunday-school-class-62836105.

Rocha, Veronica. 2019. "Pete Buttigieg: 'God Doesn't Have a Political Party.'" CNN. April 23. https://www.cnn.com/2019/04/23/politics/buttigieg-god-political-party/index.html.

Wehner, Peter. 2019. "Pete Buttigieg's Very Public Faith Is Challenging Assumptions." *The Atlantic*. April 10. https://www.theatlantic.com/ideas/archive/2019/04/buttigieg-wrong-about-christianity-and-progressivism/586810/.

• C •

Capital Punishment

As with the issue of slavery, individuals who favor and disfavor governmental imposition of the death penalty both have favorite biblical proof tests.

Dan Van Ness, the former president of the Justice Fellowship, identifies and summarizes views of Scripture into three categories. The favorite text of those who believe that Scripture mandates capital punishment is Genesis 9:6, where, after destroying all but eight people in a flood, God provided that "whoever sheds the blood of man, by man shall his blood be shed; for in the image of God has God made man." Moreover, because God gave this instruction prior to the Mosaic law, it "apparently had universal application" (Van Ness n.d.). As American Puritans observed in formulating their own laws, the Mosaic law provided for the offenses of "murder (not accidental killings), striking or cursing a parent, kidnapping, adultery, incest, bestiality, sodomy, rape of a betrothed virgin, witchcraft, incorrigible delinquency, breaking the Sabbath, blasphemy, sacrificing to false gods, oppressing the weak, and other transgression (See Exod. 21, 23, 35; Lev. 20 & 24; Deut. 21–24)" (Van Ness n.d.). While speaking more closely to permission, rather than to mandate, Romans 13:1–7 takes it for granted that government has the right to "bear the sword."

Those believing that the weight of Scripture prohibits capital punishment distinguish the use of the penalty in a theocracy, like Israel, where people were collectively responsible for cleansing the land of slain blood, from others where God is not considered the direct ruler. They may further argue from Hebrews 9:14 that God has already vindicated the value of human life through Jesus's death on the cross, or that the New Testament virtues of forgiveness and the "willingness to suffer evil rather than resist it by force" prevail over Old Testament practices (Van Ness n.d.).

Those who take the middle ground that the Bible permits capital punishment without requiring it can point to biblical limitations on the penalty, for individuals such as Cain, Moses, and David who were not punished for their murders, as well as to the previously cited passage from Romans 13 (Van Ness n.d.). One writer thus notes that modern readers must "distinguish between descriptive Bible content (that simply describes, in a historical sense, the state of things in Bible times, without necessarily requiring it of believers today) and prescriptive Bible content (that imparts an authoritative command or guidelines for Christians of all eras)" (Rau 2011).

Perhaps as important as whether the Bible mandates or permits capital punishment are the ways that Scripture limited such punishments through principles such as proportionality (Exodus 21:23–25), certainty of guilt (the two-witness rule delineated in Deuteronomy 17:6 and Numbers 35:30), intent (as evidenced by the creation of cities of refuge), due process requirements, and expressions—like that in Ezekiel 33:11—of God's reluctance to punish (Van Ness n.d.).

Historically, some of the leading exponents of opposition to capital punishment have been motivated by Christian principles. Dr. Benjamin Rush was among early Americans who sought to replace the death penalty, and especially public executions, with incarceration. He cited Matthew 16:26: "The Son of Man came not to *destroy* men's lives, but to *save* them" (Vile 2019, 192). There was an anti-gallows movement that lasted from the writing of the Constitution to the Civil War, peaking in the 1840s, in which individuals citing such diverse sources as the Bible, the writings of the Italian criminologist Cesare Beccaria (1738–1794), romanticism, Quaker thought, and utilitarian philosophers offered a variety of arguments opposing capital punishment. Although a few states actually eliminated the death penalty, it was more common for states to circumscribe the offenses for which it could be imposed and to limit its public displays (Davis 1957).

Debates over capital punishment were renewed in the twentieth century, in which courts restricted the punishment to cases of capital murder and insisted on greater procedural protections. In *Furman v. Georgia* (1972), the U.S. Supreme Court ruled that the death penalty, as it was then being imposed, violated the prohibition against cruel and unusual punishment in the Eighth Amendment, which is applied to the states through the Fourteenth. A majority of states, however, responded by passing laws dividing capital trials into separate guilt and innocence and punishment stages, mandating consideration of aggravating and mitigating circumstances, and providing automatic appeals. The court upheld such laws in *Gregg v. Georgia* (1976). Continuing points of dispute involve whether retribution is an appropriate approach to punishment, whether the penalty serves as a deterrent to other crimes, and whether the penalty can be administered in a nonracially discriminatory manner. One difficulty with the death penalty is that, once administered, it is irrevocable. Moreover, Christians believe that Jesus, an innocent man, was one of its victims (Osler 2009).

It has been argued that the standard for criminal punishments, "beyond a reasonable doubt," was developed in part for Christian jurors who feared that if they inadvertently condemned an innocent person to death, they were committing a mortal crime (Whitman 2008).

Although lawyers have long cited biblical passages in attempting to persuade jurors either to inflict or to spare defendants, in *People v. Harlan* (2005), Colorado invalidated a death sentence when a juror brought a Bible into the jury room during deliberations, although appellate courts sometimes rule that judicial references to the Bible during sentencing have been harmless errors. A central concern has been that jurors are limited by rules of evidence to the evidence that is presented to them and the fear that jurors will be unduly swayed by references to holy writ (Hudson 2005). This would typically nor prevent a juror from verbally citing Scripture in support or opposition to inflicting the death penalty (Wojdacz n.d.; Sporn 2009).

Judge Tammy Kemp stirred criticism that she was engaged in proselytizing and crossing the line between church and state in October 2019 when she gave a Bible to police officer Amber Guyger, who had been convicted of killing a neighbor, Botham Jean, after walking into the wrong apartment that she thought was her own (Holcombe 2019).

See also Criminal Law; Puritans; Quakers; Rush, Benjamin

For Reference and Further Reading

Davis, David Brion. 1957. "The Movement to Abolish Capital Punishment in America, 1787–1861." *American Historical Review* 63 (October): 23–46.

Furman v. Georgia, 408 U.S. 238 (1972).

Gregg v. Georgia, 428 .S. 153 (1976).

Hudson, David L., Jr. 2005. "The Bible Tells Them So." *ABA Journal*. July 28. www.abajournal.com/magazine/article/the_bible_tells_them_so.

Holcombe, Madeline. 2019. "Judge Who Gave Convicted Murderer Amber Guyger a Bible Is Accused of Bridging the Church-State Divide." CNN. October 4. https://www.cnn.com/2019/10/04/us/guyger-judge-freedom-religion/index.html.

Osler, Mark. 2009. *Jesus on Death Row: The Trial of Jesus and American Capital Punishment*. Nashville, TN: Abington Press.

People v. Harlan, 209 P.3d616 (2005).

Rau, Andy. 2011. "What Does the Bible Say about Capital Punishment?" Bible Gateway Blog. September 27. https://www.biblegateway.com/blog/2011/09/what-does-the-bible-say-about-capital-punishment/.

Sporn, Jeremy B. 2009. "Legal Injection? The Constitutionality of the Bible in Capital Sentencing Deliberations." *Tulane Law Review* 83: 813–51.

Van Ness, Dan. n.d. "A Biblical Perspective on the Death Penalty." Prison Fellowship. https://www.prisonfellowship.org/resources/advocacy/sentencing/the-death-penalty/.

Vile, John R. 2019. *A Constellation of Great Men: Exploring the Character Sketches of Dr. Benjamin Rush of Pennsylvania of the Signers of the Declaration of Independence*. Clark, NJ: Talbot.

Whitman, James Q. 2008. *The Origins of Reasonable Doubt: Theological Roots of the Criminal Trial*. New Haven, CT: Yale University Press.

Wojdacz, Mariah. n.d. "Should Bibles Be Present in a Jury Deliberation Room?" LegalZoom. https://www.legalzoom.com/articles/should-bibles-be-present-in-a-jury-deliberation-room.

Carey, Matthew

Matthew Carey (1760–1839) was an Irish-born publisher who, after being persecuted for his anti-British sentiments, fled first to France, where he struck up a friendship with Benjamin Franklin, and then to Philadelphia, where the Marquis de Lafayette gave him money to set up his business. He began publishing the *Pennsylvania Herald* in 1785 and subsequently published the *Columbian Magazine* and the *American Museum* as well as a variety of books. He is best known for publishing the Douai (Roman Catholic version translated from St. Jerome's Latin Vulgate) Bible in 1790, which was largely sold by subscription. This volume had first been translated by Gregory Martin at the University of Douai at Rheims in 1582 (New Testament) and 1609 (the entire Bible), but Carey patterned his Bible after the second edition that Richard Challoner had published in England in 1764.

Although he appears to have published no more than five hundred volumes (Daniell 2003, 625), the interest that his Bible generated suggests that Protestants mistook the Roman Catholic mistrust of the King James Version of the Bible with a more general distrust of Holy Writ itself (Carter 2007, 448).

Prior to the American Revolution, Britain held a monopoly on the printing of English Bibles for America, and Carey's was only the second such Bible printed in America—the first having been the so-called Aitken Bible. To encourage sales, Carey appealed to Catholics by suggesting that such purchases would "evince their determination to shew their reverence for the Holy Scriptures—and to prove the futility of the charge, that they are forbidden the use of the sacred volume" (quoted in Carter 2007, 459). While advertising that the Douai Bible was superior to the King James Version, in an address "To the Protestants of the United States," he also suggested that "liberal-minded protestants who glory in the influence of the benign sun of toleration will probably be happy in an opportunity of uniting their names of the Roman catholics who have supported this work, and thus evincing, that they are superior to that wretched—that contemptible prejudice, which confines its benevolence within the narrow pale of one religious denomination, as is the case of bigots of every persuasion" (quoted in Carter 2007, 459–60).

Although he retained his own Roman Catholic faith, Carey went on to print numerous editions of the King James Bible, often containing detailed commentary and semi-salacious prints (Daniell 2003, 629). Among his salesmen was Parson Mason Weems (1759–1825), who later wrote a biography of George Washington that included the legend of refusing to lie about chopping down a cherry tree in his youth.

Carey served as the secretary of the society for establishing Sunday Schools and was an advocate of religious pluralism (Carter 2007, 465). He thought that knowledge of religion was a way of promoting citizen virtue.

See also Aitken Bible; Roman Catholics

For Reference and Further Reading

Carter, Michael S. 2007. "'Under the Benign Sun of Toleration': Matthew Carey, the Douai Bible, and Catholic Print Culture, 1789–1791." *Journal of the Early Republic* 27 (Fall): 437–69.

Daniell, David. 2003. *The Bible in English: Its History and Influence.* New Haven, CT: Yale University Press.

Falls, Thomas B. 1942. "The Carey Bible." *Records of the American Catholic Historical Society of Philadelphia* 53 (June): 111–15.

Carson, Ben

Dr. Ben Carson (b. 1951) is a former pediatric neurosurgeon at Johns Hopkins University who serves as the Secretary of Housing and Urban Development under President Trump. Carson, who is African American and a Seventh-Day Adventist, grew up in a rough neighborhood in Detroit, Michigan, but succeeded, largely with his single mother's inspiration, in achieving academically and graduating from Yale University and the University of Michigan Medical School.

Carson vied unsuccessfully for the 2016 Republican presidential nomination. Known as a conservative who attends a weekly Bible study and proudly displays his faith, he spoke both at the 1997 and the 2013 National Prayer Breakfasts. Carson's middle name is Solomon, and he appears to quote more frequently from the book of Proverbs, which is attributed to Solomon, than from any other book. In his second speech at the National Prayer Breakfast, three of his four texts were from Proverbs (11:9; 11:12; and 11:25), and the last was 2 Chronicles 7:14: "Then if my people who are called by my name will humble themselves and pray and seek my face and turn from their wicked ways, I will hear from heaven and will forgive their sins and heal their land" (cited in Carson 2014, ix). Carson's favorite verse, from Proverbs 22:4, says that "by humility and the fear of the Lord are riches, and honour, and life" (Winder 2019, 25).

In a book that he wrote prior to his 2016 campaign, Carson highlighted each chapter with a passage from Proverbs. Although he continually lauded the value of education in combatting ignorance, in his book, Carson presented his own political stances simply as common sense, which he often contrasted to what he referred to as the views of "the secular progressive movement," which he portrayed as attempting to expunge all biblical references and teachings from the public square (Carson 2014, 41). He opposed Obamacare as giving important health-care decisions to the government rather than to private individuals, advocated a simple flat tax based on the principle of biblical tithing, opposed welfare for able-bodied individuals who could provide for themselves, and generally argued for moderation and civil discourse. Carson believes that individuals should care for themselves and their families rather than over-relying on the government to do so.

Carson generally takes a fairly literal view of the Bible and bemoans what he believes is the nation's departure from this belief. He noted, "For years, most Americans have turned to a belief in God and the Bible for answers. From the Creation story to the Ten Commandments to the Gospels to the Epistles, the Bible provided an explanation for the meaning of life and instructed us in moral principles. We held to a Judeo-Christian standard while respecting the beliefs of those who didn't share them" (Carson 2014, 192). By contrast, he observed that "today, fewer people believe in the Bible, or even in absolute truth, and our rejection of an objective moral standard has thrown our society into disarray. If in fact we do really believe in God and His Word, many of the moral 'gray' issues of today become black and white" (Carson 2014, 193). Citing the prohibition in Exodus against murder and the admonition in Matthew 22:39 to "love your neighbor as yourself," Carson indicated that "abortion is rarely a moral option" (Carson 2014, 193). Similarly, he opposed homosexual conduct, expressed his belief in creationism without taking a position on the age of the earth, and argued that "many of our laws are based on the Ten Commandments" (Carson 2014, 200).

Carson is often known for making provocative off-the-cuff remarks, sometimes involving matters of religion and morality (Gass 2015). Critics like Bible scholar Pete Enns, while lauding Carson as a good man, charge that he often simplifies or misapplies biblical truths, as when Carson tweeted, "It is important to remember that amateurs built the Ark and it was the professionals that built the Titanic." Enns also questions whether one can apply the principle of the biblical tithe to contemporary society.

See also Abortion; Creationism and Evolution; Ten Commandments

For Reference and Further Reading

Carson, Ben, with Candy Carson. 2014. *One Nation: What We Can All Do to Save America's Future.* New York: Sentinel.

Devi, Gayatri. 2014. "Candidates Use the Bible to Justify Their Views. We Must Respond with Reason." *The Guardian*. November 5. https://www.theguardian.com/commentisfree/2015/nov/05/candidates-bible-views-noahs-ark-donald-trump-ben-carson. Accessed May 29, 2019.
Enns, Pete. "Ben Carson and the Bible: Maybe He Should Get a Second Opinion." https://peteenns.com/ben-carson-and-the-bible-maybe-he-should-get-a-second-opinion/.
Gass, Nick. 2015. "Ben Carson's 15 Most Controversial Quotes." Politico. October 9. https://www.politico.com/story/2015/10/ben-carson-controversial-quotes-214614. Accessed May 29, 2019.
Winder, Mike. 2019. *Favorite Scriptures of 100 American Leaders*. Springville, UT: Plain Sight.

Carter, Jimmy

Jimmy Carter (b. 1924), who served a term as president of the United States from 1977 to 1981, was a long-time Southern Baptist. He came into office as a professed evangelical Christian but found that after a single presidential term, he was outflanked by Ronald Reagan, whose rhetoric and policies (especially on issues like abortion, prayer in schools, and opposition to the Equal Rights Amendment) had greater appeal to the evangelical right and to such organizations as the National Christian Action Coalition, the Moral Majority, the Religious Roundtable, and Christian Voice (Smith 2006, 318; also see Freedman 2005).

Raised in a small town in Georgia, Carter had a conversion experience at a revival meeting as an eleven-year-old and was baptized. He was accepted into the Naval Academy where he taught Sunday school, a practice that he has continued through most of his life (Holmes 2012, 148–49). After serving in the Georgia state legislature, Carter was devastated when he was defeated by segregationist Lester Maddox in a race for governor, but he engaged in mission work and resumed Bible reading after being challenged by his sister who was an evangelist, and by a sermon that asked "If You Were Arrested for Being a Christian, Would There Be Any Evidence to Convict You?" (Holmes 2012, 152).

As an evangelical Christian, Carter considered politics to be a vocation, or form of ministry, and believed faith to be "not just a noun but also a verb" (Berggren 2005, 44–45). He further identified his role as president as that of being "First Servant" (Berggren 2005, 46). Perhaps because, as a Baptist, Carter put strong emphasis on the separation of church and state, he did not use religious rhetoric as frequently as such successors as Ronald Reagan and George W. Bush. He did, however, invite Martin Luther King Sr. to preach at a People's Prayer Service that he held on the steps of the Lincoln Memorial (Holmes 2012, 154–55). In his presidential inaugural address, he opened the Bible on which he took his oath to Micah 6:8: "He hath shewed thee, O man, what is good; and what doth the Lord require of thee, but to do justly, and to love mercy, and to walk humbly with thy God" and cited this passage in his address. Carter faithfully attended church throughout his presidency.

Identified by Berggren as one who preferred the role of a prophet to that of a priest or pastor, Carter is particularly known for advocating energy independence at a time when the nation was more preoccupied with high inflation, unemployment, and interest rates, and for identifying a "crisis of confidence" in the American people, which he thought came in part from forsaking traditional values. Although he stressed humility, he sometimes came across as someone who was holier than thou, especially in his relations with Congress, whose members he thought were too focused on the personal interests of their states and districts.

Carter often rested on universalistic themes of equality and liberty, which he found in the Declaration of Independence and other founding documents, but he believed these were firmly grounded in Scripture. In a speech to the World Jewish Congress, in 1977, Carter thus said,

> In large measure, the beginnings of the modern concept of human rights go back to the laws and the prophets of the Judeo-Christian traditions. I've been steeped in the Bible since early childhood, and I believe that anyone who reads the ancient words of the Old Testament with both sensitivity and care will find there the idea of government as something based on a voluntary covenant rather than force—the idea of equality before the law and the supremacy of law over the whims of any ruler; the idea of the dignity of the individual human being and also of the individual conscience; the idea of service to the poor and to the oppressed; the ideas of self-government and tolerance and of nations living together in peace, despite differences of belief. (Flowers 1983, 128)

Although he enjoyed reading Reinhold Niebuhr, who was known for his political realism, Carter believed that the Sermon on the Mount and the Golden Rule provided guidance on matters of foreign policy, which his critics believed to be naïve. Carter put the advancement of human rights at the top of his foreign policy agenda but combined this emphasis with the biblical maxim from Matthew 7:1, "Judge not, that ye be not judged" (Berggren 2005, 56). Carter negotiated a treaty returning control of the Panama Canal to the nation of Panama, largely because he thought it was the right thing to do, and extended amnesty to nonviolent individuals who had fled the country rather than be drafted to serve in the war in Vietnam. Iranian revolutionaries held fifty-two Americans hostage during the last two years of Carter's administration, and a mission that he sent to free them resulted in American casualties.

Carter spent almost two weeks negotiating directly with the leaders of Israel and Egypt in order to secure peace in the Middle East. In his book *The Blood of Abraham*, Carter, explained, "For me there is no way to approach or enter Israel without thinking first about the Bible and the history of the land and its people. The names and images have long been an integral part of my life as a Christian"; he further observed that "the power of faith is a unifying bond between Christian and Jew and between the heroes of ancient Israel and those of New Testament times" (quoted in Berggren 2005, 57). Citing the story of Cain killing his brother Abel in Genesis 4, Carter observed, "The blood of Abraham, God's father of the chosen, still flows in the veins of Arab, Jew, and Christian, and too much of it has been spilled in grasping for the inheritance of the revered patriarch in the Middle East. The spilled blood in the Holy Land still cries out to God—an anguished cry for peace" (quoted in Berggren 2005, 59). During his negotiations with the leaders of Egypt and Israel, Carter quoted the words of Jesus from the Sermon on the Mount as recorded in Matthew 5:9: "Blessed are the peacemakers, for they shall be called the children of God" (Holmes 2012, 160).

Carter is often cited as one of America's best ex-presidents, engaging with Habitat for Humanity and launching projects through the Carter Center to monitor elections and improve international well-being, perhaps most notably in its attempt to eliminate the parasitic Guinea worm. He received a Nobel Peace Prize in 2002, primarily for his work as president in promoting Middle East peace. In his acceptance speech, Carter observed,

> I worship Jesus Christ, whom we Christians consider to be the Prince of Peace. As a Jew, he taught us to cross religious boundaries, in service and in love. He repeatedly reached out and embraced Roman conquerors, other Gentiles, and even the more despised Samaritans.
>
> Despite theological differences, all great religions share common commitments that define our ideal secular relationships. I am convinced that Christians, Muslims, Buddhists, Hindus, Jews, and others can embrace each other in a common effort to alleviate human suffering and to espouse peace. (quoted in Holmes 2012, 172)

Before, during, and after he became president, Carter led Sunday school classes. Meir Soloveichik (2018) believed that some of Carter's lessons, especially during his presidency, suggested that he thought that his knowledge of the Bible was more important than political skill or diplomacy and that some of his interpretations, especially of the death of Jesus, were culturally insensitive.

Carter continued teaching Sunday school at the Maranatha Baptist Church in Plains, Georgia, where he also served as a handyman. He has drawn his lessons from both the Old and New Testaments. His classes have become a major tourist attraction in his hometown. The church where he has taught has since left the Southern Baptist Convention for the Cooperative Baptist Fellowship. Allowing for the ordination of women and the separation of church and state, this group distances itself from the view that the Bible is "inerrant" or without error, albeit on what it believes to be biblical grounds: "The Bible neither claims nor reveals inerrancy as a Christian teaching. Bible claims must be based on the Bible, not on human interpretations of the Bible" (quoted in Holmes 2012, 169).

Among the latest individuals to attend this class was Democratic presidential candidate Pete Buttigieg and his husband, Chasten, whom Carter called upon to read Scripture (Reeves 2019).

See also Buttigieg, Pete; Evangelicals; Niebuhr, Reinhold; Zionism

For Reference and Further Reading

Banks, John. 2019. "Visiting Jimmy Carter's Sunday School Class Has Become an American Pilgrimage." *Dallas News*. February 17. https://www.dallasnews.com/opinion/commentary/2019/02/17/visiting-jimmy-carters-sunday-school-class-become-american-pilgrimage. Accessed May 6, 2019.

Berggren, D. Jason. 2005. "'I Had a Different Way of Governing': The Living Faith of President Carter." *Journal of Church and State* 47 (Winter): 43–61.

Carter, Jimmy. 1996. *Living Faith*. New York: Random House.

Flippin, J. Brooks. 2011. *Jimmy Carter, the Politics of Family, and the Rise of the Religious Right*. Athens: University of Georgia Press.

Flowers, Ronald B. 1983. "President Jimmy Carter, Evangelicalism, Church-State Relations, and Civil Religion." *Journal of Church and State* 25 (Winter): 113–32.

Freedman, Robert. 2005. "The Religious Right and the Carter Administration." *The Historical Journal* 48 (March): 231–60.
Holmes, David L. 2012. *The Faiths of the Postwar Presidents*. Athens: University of Georgia Press.
Reeves, Jay. 2019. "Buttigieg, Husband Attend Jimmy Carter's Sunday School Class." ABC News. May 5. https://abcnews.go.com/Politics/wireStory/buttigieg-husband-attend-jimmy-carters-sunday-school-class-62836105.
Smith, Gary Scott. 2006. *Faith and the Presidency*. New York: Oxford University Press.
Soloveichik, Meir Y. 2018. "Jimmy Carter: The Sunday-School Years." JewishPress.com. October 28. https://www.jewishpress.com/indepth/opinion/jimmy-carter-the-sunday-school-years/2018/10/28/.

Cartoons

One indication of the continuing influence of the Bible on American understandings may be found in the number of cartoons that reference biblical themes or figures.

Many recent cartoons, which can be accessed at PoliticalCartoons.com, center on President Trump. A cartoon by Dave Granlund published on January 11, 2017, shows Trump about to take an oath on his book *The Art of the Deal*. A second by J. D. Crowe dated March 9, 2019, shows him labeling commandments against adultery, theft, and false witness as "Fake News." Another by John Darkow published on March 11, 2019, shows Trump signing a Bible while one woman comments that he is using the same pen that he used to sign hush money payments to porn stars. Pat Bagley has another cartoon in which Rudolph Giuliani warns, "It's a trap," as Trump is asked to swear (presumably as part of the Mueller investigation) on the Bible.

There were a number of cartoons that pictured Barack Obama standing by Abraham Lincoln as Obama took the oath on Lincoln's Bible. Another by Yaakov Kirschen, which seems equally applicable to Trump, and perhaps to presidents in general, has Obama telling the chief justice as he takes his oath that the Bible is specifically about him.

Some highlight the practice of using proof texting to justify immigration or other policies. A number cite former attorney general Jeff Sessions's attempt to use the Bible to justify separating families at the border, with some focusing specifically on Jesus's being taken by government officials from his manger.

A cartoon by Pat Bagley from June 4, 2015, indicates that Bible marriage often involved plural marriages or concubines. Another, also by Bagley, observes that Jesus spoke as often about the sin of homosexuality as he did about homosexuality, namely, not at all.

Some cartoons reference foreign policy. A cartoon by Dario Castillejos labeled "Israel Proportional Response" shows an Israeli Goliath swinging a huge slingshot to overwhelm a small Palestinian.

A number of cartoons observe what industrialization and pollution have done to the environment.

A study of sixty-five thousand syndicated cartoons that appeared in the *Los Angeles Times* from mid-1979 through mid-1987 found that 7.1 percent of religious cartoons made "humorous use of Biblical stories, characters and sayings" (Lindsey and Heeren 1992, 75). The authors of the study noted, "The most common and repeatedly used Biblical narratives that become objects for cartoonists' pens are the accounts of Adam and Eve in the Garden of Eden, Noah and the flood, and Moses in his role as recipient of the Ten Commandments. In addition to these contexts a variety of other less frequently used stories include Jonah, David and Goliath, the Last Supper and the Sermon on the Mount" (75). The authors observed that "the Bible provides a background of knowledge, a resource, against which cartoonists can communicate their humor to readers" (75). They further observed that "placing moderns in Biblical situations facilitates commentary on current events, as well as on our distinctly modern consciousness" (75).

In 2014, Robert M. Price published *The Politically Correct Bible*, with a cover picturing Jesus as an African American with women, a Native American Indian Chief, a Muslim woman, and others celebrating the Last Supper.

See also Obama, Barack; Sessions, Jeff; Ten Commandments; Trump, Donald

For Reference and Further Reading

Lindsey, Donald B., and John Heeren. 1992. "Where the Sacred Meets the Profane: Religion in the Comic Pages." *Review of Religious Research* 34 (September): 63–77.
PoliticalCartoons.com. https://politicalcartoons.com/?s=bible. Accessed May 24, 2019.
Price, Robert M. 2014. *The Politically Correct Bible*. eBookIt.com.

Chavez, Cesar

Cesar Chavez (1927–1993) is the best-known Hispanic American activist and was posthumously awarded the Presidential Medal of Freedom. Born in Yuma, Arizona, to a middle-class family that fell on hard times, Chavez spent most of his teen years as a migrant laborer where he was deeply affected by "Abulita Theology," that is, teachings of the Catholic Church that his grandmother, Mama Tella, who had been raised in a convent where she learned theology, had passed down to him (Romero 2017, 27). After serving in the military, Chavez returned to California, where he became a community organizer and was instructed in Catholic social thought by a white Catholic clergyman, Father Donald McDonnell.

In 1962, Chavez began organizing farm workers, in time leading a successful five-year strike against grape growers and helping to organize the United Farm Workers Organizing Committee. Chavez's faith played a major role. Chavez drew from Roman Catholic social teachings, including nonviolence and God's concern for the poor and lowly; incorporated elements of Catholic ritual into his protests; and drew from Scriptures for inspiration.

Chavez patterned some of his protests around the "peregrinacion," or penitential march, which was led by a Catholic priest, begun with prayer, accompanied by a banner of the Virgin of Guadalupe, and concluded with the celebration of a Catholic mass. He fasted after the movement turned violent in order to bring his followers back to their commitment to nonviolence.

Chavez's grandmother had taught him to follow Jesus's admonition in the Sermon on the Mount to turn the other cheek and to find alternate methods of resolving disputes (Romero 2017, 34). Speaking to the *National Catholic Reporter*, Chavez described the influence of the Beatitudes about which Jesus spoke in this sermon as follows:

> The Beatitudes make natural good sense to the poor. We, of course, do not analyze the words and the meanings in the way scholars do. Jesus' words fit his life and therefore the meaning of his words appear to be obvious to us. He spent his life with the poor, the sick, the outcasts, the powerless people. He attacked the wealthy and the powerful. He is with us. We feel he is our friend, our advocate, our leader. (Piar 1996, 117)

Like Martin Luther King Jr., Chavez stressed the importance of nonviolence. Describing important influences on his approach to nonviolence, Chavez said, "Moses is about the best example, and the first one. Christ is also a beautiful example, as is the way Christians overcame tyranny. They needed over three hundred years, but they did it" (quoted in Romero, 2017, 34).

Chavez justified his belief that God was especially interested in farm workers by citing James 5:4–6: "Listen! The wages of the laborers who mowed your fields, which you kept back by fraud, cry out, and the cries of the harvesters have reached the ears of the Lord of hosts. You have lived in luxury and in pleasure; you have fattened your hearts in a day of slaughter. You have condemned and murdered the righteous one, who does not resist you" (35).

Beginning with the defeat of a California referendum Proposition 14, which would have strengthened the role of union organizers among farm workers, the United Farm Workers declined, and Chavez tried to build a religious order around himself and Synanon, which was associated with New Age religion (37). Chavez's associates also accused him of becoming autocratic and unwilling to listen to others. His most successful efforts at labor organizing, however, had a distinctly Christian, and biblical, cast.

See also Civil Disobedience; Moses as Political Archetype; Roman Catholics

For Reference and Further Reading

Piar, Carlos R. 1996. "Cesar Chavez and La Causa: Toward a Hispanic Christian Social Ethic." *Annual of the Society of Christian Ethics*. 16: 103–20.

Romero, Robert Chao. 2017. "The Spiritual Praxis of Cesar Chavez." *Perspectivas* 14 (Spring): 24–39.

Cherokee Removal

One of the causes that motivated a number of nineteenth-century American Protestants was that of the forced removal of Native American Cherokee Indians from Georgia to modern-day Oklahoma. American missionaries to the Cherokees did their best to protest against this removal that resulted in many deaths and that remains one of the most tragic chapters in American history, but President Andrew Jackson cooperated with authorities in Georgia to effect this action, which the U.S. Supreme Court was helpless to prevent.

One of the most vocal opponents of this action was Jeremiah Evarts (1791–1831), a Vermont-born lawyer and missionary who served as an officer for the

American Board of Commissioners for Foreign Missions. He wrote a series of essays under the name of William Penn explaining its injustices. Although a great number of the essays were devoted to explicating Cherokee rights under treaties and international law, he made a number of arguments from Scripture.

Indeed, in the first of his essays, he likened the attempt to remove the Cherokees to the story of Ahab's seizure of Naboth's vineyard (aided by his wife Jezebel) as described in 1 Kings 21:1–16 (Evarts 1829, 5). Evarts further tied injustice to God's judgment. After noting that America would suffer in the eyes of other nations if it acted unjustly, he further observed,

> There is a higher consideration still. The Great Arbiter of Nations never fails to take cognizance of national delinquencies. No sophistry can elude his scrutiny; no array of plausible arguments, or of smooth but hollow professions, can bias his judgment; and he has at his disposal most abundant means of executing his decisions. In many forms, and with awful solemnity, he has declared his abhorrence of oppression in every shape; and especially of injustice perpetrated against the weak by the strong, *when strength is in fact made the only rule of action.* (Evarts 1829, 5–6)

He further cited the words of Micah 6:8 in reference to the obligation "to *do justly, love mercy, and walk humbly with their God*" (Evarts 1829, 6).

Evarts's second essay combined biblical and natural rights principles. He thus observed, "The Cherokees are human beings, endowed by their Creator with the same natural rights as other men" (Evarts 1829, 7). He noted that they had adopted an agricultural lifestyle and established schools, and that many had become Christians.

Meticulously defending the rights of the Cherokees under treaties and both national and international law, Evarts once again called upon God:

> If this case should unhappily be decided against the Cherokees, (which may Heaven avert!) it will be necessary that foreign nations should be well aware, that the People of the United States are ready to take the ground of fulfilling their contracts so long only, as they can be overawed by physical force; that we as a nation, are ready to avow, that we can be restrained from injustice *by fear alone*; not the fear of God, which is a most ennobling and purifying principle; not the fear of sacrificing national character, in the estimation of good and wise men in every country, and through all future time; not the fear of present shame and public scorn; but simply, and only, the fear of bayonets and cannon. (Evarts 1829, 46)

Further summarizing the view of the Cherokees in his fifteenth essay, Evarts observed,

> We do not profess to be learned in the law of nations; but we read the Bible, and have learned there some plain principles of right and wrong. The Governor of the world gave us this country. We are in peaceable possession. We have never acknowledged any earthly lord, or sovereign. If our Creator has taken away our land and given it to you, we should like to see some proof of it, beside your own assertion. We have read in the book, which we understand you to acknowledge as the word of God, that "to oppress a stranger wrongfully" [Ezekiel 22:29] is a mark of great national wickedness. (Evarts 1829, 55)

In what should have appealed to a largely Protestant audience, in his sixteenth essay, Evarts observed that Queen Elizabeth was imitating the pope when she tried to claim North America, just as the pope had sought to divide South America between Spain and Portugal (58). In a later essay, Evarts linked the whites' desire for Cherokee lands to the biblical sin of covetousness, which is delineated in the Ten Commandments (88).

In his twenty-third essay, Evarts argued that Christianity is both "the basis of the present law of nations" and "a part of the common law." He, in turn, linked both to the Golden Rule of treating others as one desired to be treated (95).

Almost as if imitating his namesake, the prophet Jeremiah, Evarts observed that "the memory of these transactions will not be forgotten. A bitter roll will be unfolded, on which *Mourning, Lamentation, and Woe to the People of the United States* will be seen written in characters, which no eye can refuse to see" (100). He then quoted from Deuteronomy 27:17–19: "*Cursed be he, that removeth his neighbor's landmark: and all the people shall say, Amen. Cursed be he, that maketh the blind to wander out of the way: and all the people shall say, Amen. Cursed be he that perverteth the judgment of the stranger, fatherless, and widow: and all the people shall say, Amen*" (Evarts 1829, 100–1).

After again suggesting that God would judge the nation if it went forward with this plan, Evarts proceeded to elaborate with an apparent reference to Deuteronomy 19:14, which warned against removing boundary stones:

> It is now proposed *to remove the landmarks*, in every sense;—to disregard territorial boundaries, definitely fixed, and for many years respected;—to disregard a most obvious principle of natural justice, in accordance with which the possessor of property is to hold it, till some one claims it, who has a better right;—to forget the doctrine of the law of nations, that engagements with dependent allies are as rigidly to be observed, as stipulations between communities of equal power and sovereignty;—to shut our ears to the voice of our own sages of the law, who say that Indians have a right *to retain possession of their land and to use it according to their discretion*, antecedently to any positive compacts; and, finally, to dishonor Washington, the Father of his country,—to stultify the Senate of the United States during a period of thirty-seven years,—to burn 150 documents, as yet preserved in the archives of State, under the denomination of treaties with Indians, and to tear out sheets from every volume of our national statute-book and scatter them to the winds. (Evarts 1829, 101)

Evarts ended by quoting Thomas Hooker to indicate that the seat of law is found in "the bosom of God" and that it is "the mother of their peace and joy" (101).

See also Common Law; Jezebel as Political Archetype; Judgment; Native American Indians

For Reference and Further Reading

Andrew, John A. 1992. *From Revivals to Removal: Jeremiah Evarts, the Cherokee Nation, and the Search for the Soul of America*. Athens: University of Georgia Press.

[Evarts, Jeremiah]. 1829. *Essays on the Present Crisis in the Condition of the American Indians: First Published in the National Intelligencer, under the Signature of William Penn*. Boston: Perkins & Marvin.

West, John G., Jr. 1996. *The Politics of Revelation and Reason: Religion and Civic Life in the New Nation*. Lawrence: University Press of Kansas.

Chosen People

See America as New Israel

Christian Amendment

The Ten Commandments resemble a treaty between God and his people, and their introduction, as recorded in Exodus 20, begins with God saying, "I am the LORD thy God." Although some defenders of the idea that America was a Christian nation found meaning in the fact that the attestation clause of the U.S. Constitution referred to "the year of our LORD," some religious groups thought the nation could never secure God's blessings without more explicitly mentioning Him. The Reformed Presbyterian Church, with roots in the Scottish Covenant tradition, launched an initiative to see that the U.S. Constitution specifically acknowledged God. John Alexander, a layman, proposed to a convention of the National Association to Secure the Religious Amendment of the Constitution (later called the National Reform Association) meeting in Zenia, Ohio, in February 1863 that such an amendment acknowledge "the rulership of Jesus Christ and the supremacy of the divine" (Borden 1979, 159).

Particularly prominent during the 1870s, this movement presented a petition of more than thirty-five thousand signatures to Congress but met with increasing concerns that the proposed amendment, especially as worded to recognize Jesus Christ, might violate the separation of church and state. Such proposals continued, however, with support from the National Association of Evangelicals and other groups. In 2000, the platform of a group calling itself the Constitution Party observed as follows:

> The U.S. Constitution established a Republic under God, rather than democracy; our Republic is a nation governed by a Constitution that is rooted in Biblical law, administered by representatives who are Constitutionally elected by the citizens; [and] in a Republic governed by Constitutional law rooted in Biblical law, all Life, Liberty and Property are protected because law rules. (Vile 2015, I: 72)

See also Findley/Wylie Debate over "The Two Sons of Oil"; Ten Commandments; U.S. Constitution

For Reference and Further Reading

Borden, Morton. 1979. "The Christian Amendment." *Civil War History* 25 (June): 156–67.

Jacoby, Stewart O. 1984. "The Religious Amendment Movement: God, People and Nation in the Gilded Age." 2 vols. PhD diss., University of Michigan.

Kabala, James S. 2013. *Church-State Relations in the Early American Republic, 1787–1846*. Brookfield, VT: Pickering and Chatto.

Vile, John R. 2015. *Encyclopedia of Constitutional Amendments, Proposed Amendments, and Amending Issues, 1789–2015*. 2 vols., 4th ed. Santa Barbara, CA: ABC-CLIO.

Christian Reconstructionism

Throughout Christian history, theologians and political leaders have sought to ascertain the degree to which biblical laws and admonitions should be enacted into laws and the degree to which they should apply to non-Christians. American Puritans probably came as close as any group to using biblical laws as the basis of colonial laws. They further limited voting rights to those who were church members.

Rousas John Rushdoony (1917–2001) has laid the philosophical foundation for reinstituting such a polity within the United States in what is generally recalled Christian Reconstructionism, or Theonomy. The son of an Armenian immigrant, Rushdoony was educated at the Westminster Theological Seminary (a breakaway from Princeton Theological Seminary) and served as founder and president of the Chalcedon Foundation, which was named after an early creed that reiterated that Jesus was both fully God and fully man. Influenced by the idea of presuppositionalism, which he learned from Professor Cornelius Van Til (1895–1987) at Westminster Seminary, Rushdoony argued that believers, who followed the Bible, had little in common with those who did not. It became the responsibility of the former to exercise dominion over all creation in accord with the mandate that God gave to Adam in Genesis 1:28 and reaffirmed in the covenant with Noah in Genesis 9:1–3, and in Psalm 8:6–8. Rushdoony was a prolific writer whose most important work, *The Institutes of Biblical Law*, first published in 1973 and patterned on John Calvin's classic *Institutes of the Christian Religion* (1536), describes in detail how each of the commandments would be applied.

Many Reconstructionists believe that America is a Christian nation and that states and localities are responsible for enforcing the Ten Commandments, including capital punishment (stoning) not only for offenses like murder but also for blasphemy and disrespect for parents. Molly Worthen has summarized the tenets of Christian Reconstructionism as follows:

> A Calvinistic notion of regeneration, or salvation by God-given grace; a postmillennial eschatology predicting that Jesus Christ's second coming will occur after a thousand-year reign of the saints, thus requiring Christians to act now to bring about that reign; presuppositional apologetics; an anti-statist worldview requiring "decentralized social order where civil government is only one legitimate government among many"; and finally, "continuing validity and applicability of the whole law of God" (Worthen 2008, 401)

Worthen further observes that the rule of God's law would include not only the Ten Commandments but also some six hundred other rules that accompanied them (401).

Frederick Clarkson observes that there are both "hard and soft Dominionists," but that they are bound together by three views:

1. Dominionists celebrate Christian nationalism, in that they believe that the United States was, and should once again be, a Christian nation. In this way, they deny the Enlightenment roots of American democracy.
2. Dominionists promote religious supremacy, insofar as they generally do not respect the equality of other religions, or even other versions of Christianity.
3. Dominionists endorse theocratic visions, insofar as they believed that the Ten Commandments, or "biblical law," should be the foundation of

> American law, and that the U.S. Constitution should be seen as a vehicle for implementing biblical principles. (Clarkson 2011)

Rushdoony was a particular foe of public education, which he associated with secular humanism, and he helped lay the groundwork for the Protestant Christian homeschool movement. Believing that the purpose of government was to establish justice rather than to embody love, he further argued that law should focus on punishment rather than on rehabilitation. Rushdoony, who opposed racial desegregation, believed that the purpose of law was not to equalize individuals but to form a "separate" people in a covenantal relationship with God (Worthen 2008, 419). As in Puritan thought, Rushdoony had little respect for diversity, viewing law itself as what he described as "*a state of war*; it is the organization of the powers of civil government to bring the enemies of the law-order to justice" (Worthen 2008, 421).

Rushdoony's thought has been proponed by a number of followers, including his son-in-law Gary North, an economist with whom he was estranged. Reconstructionism has had the greatest influence on the Christian right, influencing such individuals as Herb Titus, who helped found the law school at Pat Robertson's Regent University; Gary DeMar, who heads American Vision; Roy Moore, the Alabama judge best known for installing a large monument to the Ten Commandments in the Alabama Supreme Court; Randall Terry, who headed Operation Rescue in opposing abortion; Texas senator Ted Cruz; former Kansas senator Sam Brownback; former televangelist D. James Kennedy; and others (Sugg 2005; Clarkson 2011).

Bill Strittmatter, the pastor of the Church of Jesus Christ in Lakemore, Ohio, published a pamphlet, probably in the early 1970s, entitled "A Christian Constitution and Civil Law for the Kingdom of Heaven on Earth," in which he attempted to base a proposed national constitution on the Ten Commandments. It was based on the idea that the United States was a Christian nation (Vile 2014, 122).

See also Capital Punishment; Covenants, Compacts, Contracts, and Constitutions; Moore, Roy; Puritanism; Ten Commandments

For Reference and Further Reading

Clarkson, Frederick. 2011. "The Rise of Dominionism—Remaking America as a Christian Nation." *Public Eye Magazine*. April 12. www.spaulforrest.com/2011/04/rise-of-dominionism-remaking-america-as.html.

Sugg, John. December 2005. "A Nation under God." Mother Jones. https://www.motherjones.com/politics/2005/12/nation-under-god/.

Vile, John R. 2014. *Re-Framers: 170 Eccentric, Visionary, and Patriotic Proposals to Rewrite the U.S. Constitution*. Santa Barbara, CA: ABC-CLIO.

Worthen, Molly. 2008. "The Chalcedon Problem: Rousas John Rushdoony and the Origins of Christian Reconstructionism." *Church History* 77 (June): 399–437.

Church of Jesus Christ of Latter-Day Saints

The Church of Jesus Christ of Latter-Day Saints, colloquially known as the Mormons or the LDS, is an indigenous American religion that grew out of visions of Joseph Smith of Palmyra, New York. By his testimony, an angel named Moroni appeared to him and revealed the presence of golden plates that, with the help of the Urim and Thummin, parts of the priestly vestments mentioned in the Old Testament, he was able to translate as the Book of Mormon, which was first published in 1830.

This book, which has since been recognized as an additional Scripture by the LDS, described how a Hebrew prophet named Lehi, with the help of his sons Laman and Nephi, fled before King Nebuchadnezzar attacked Jerusalem in 586 BC and sailed to America. Nephi's sons remained godly whereas the sons of Laman were unrighteous and were cursed by God with darker skin (Wood 2000, 170–71). After Jesus was crucified, he came to America to preach to both peoples and initiated a period of peace that lasted until the Lamanites finally wiped out the Nephites in the fifth century AD, leaving Moroni to write their history, which Smith later recovered.

Like other Restorationist movements of his day, Smith sought to restore religious practice to that of the Old Testament and the early church. The church puts great emphasis on its temples, where couples can be married for eternity. To this day, the church has a hierarchical arrangement that allows, like the Book of Mormon, for continuing revelation. According to Timothy Wood, Smith had a looser conception of monotheism that essentially regarded the differences between God and man more as what Wood describes as "differences in degree, not of essence" (Wood 2000, 173). In time, believers could progress into godhead; unions that were blessed in the temple would be united forever in heaven. LDS members are to refrain from tea, coffee, tobacco, and alcohol.

The LDS Church regards the translations and writings of Joseph Smith as revelations that supplement the Bible, which they also revere, but the translation of which they believe has been corrupted over time. In addition to translating the Book of Mormon, Smith also wrote the *Doctrine and Covenants*, *The Pearl of Great Price*, and his own emendations of the King James Bible (Joseph Smith Translation, or JST). One scholar observes that this retranslation "was not a traditional rendering of the text. The project bore a certain resemblance to targumic translation, a tradition of expansive interpretation that often meant the pursuit not just of what the Bible had originally said, but of what the Bible should have said" (Holland 2017, 617). He further observed that "Smith's translation of the Bible not only altered certain phrases and reworked particular passages; it created entire new chapters. Engagement with the text became the setting for both exegesis and ongoing revelation. Most of the textual changes that emerged from his translation drew more heavily from Smith's sense of inspiration than his philology" (617). Two scholars who have studied the subject observe, "While expressing a strong and basic general belief in the Bible, early Mormon leaders limited the authority of the Bible by (1) promulgating an extra-Biblical canon, (2) placing primacy on living prophets over received Scriptures, (3) representing Scripture as but one source of truth among others, (4) stressing the corruptions in the received text of the Bible, and (5) dismissing portions of it as uninspired" (Mauss and Barlow 1991, 406). As the LDS Church has become more conservative in recent years, it has joined fundamentalist Protestant churches in recognizing the King James Version of the Bible as the most accurate (Mauss and Barlow 1991).

The LDS Church encountered significant resistance in its early years, both from those who believed that the existing Bible was complete and from those who were concerned that the tight-knit communities, often composed of a high number of immigrants, formed in a tight hierarchy threatened traditional republican ideals of government. In 1838, Missouri governor Lilburn Boggs ordered the Church to leave the state or be met with force. Church members then moved to Nauvoo, Illinois, where they built another temple. It was there that Joseph Smith launched a bid for the presidency before being assassinated by a local mob.

In time, the LDS Church moved to Salt Lake City, Utah, where it established its national headquarters and build its most impressive temple. It was there that Brigham Young, who had succeeded Smith as the head of the Church, announced that the LDS had embraced polygamy, a practice that, although not uncommon in the lives of some Old Testament patriarchs, many Americans associated with slavery and with uncivilized nations. Although the United States had to this point left matters of family law to the states, it adopted the Morrill Act and others that sought to limit such practice in Utah and other areas that remained territories and arrested many members for violating the law. In *Reynolds v. United States* (1879), the U.S. Supreme Court upheld the law against charges that it violated the establishment clause of the First Amendment by arguing that while leaving individual beliefs intact, the amendment did not prohibit the regulation of conduct. Perhaps because of this and similar decisions, the nation did not adopt a constitutional amendment prohibiting the practice.

In 1890, the Church announced an official end to polygamy, and in 1891, it dissolved its People's Party. In 1896, Utah was admitted into the Union as the forty-fifth state. Even in 1902, however, the U.S. Senate questioned whether Reed Smoot, who was one of the LDS apostles, should be permitted to sit in this body. Although the Senate ultimately ruled in his favor, Mormon candidates for nationwide office have faced concerns, similar to those once expressed about Roman Catholics, about their independence from the Church.

In recent years, the LDS Church has become increasingly identified with the Republican Party and with conservative ideology. Its members have taken strong stands against same-sex marriage and abortion. In 2008, Mitt Romney, a member, won the Republican nomination for president.

See also Alternate Scriptures; Polygamy; Roman Catholics; Romney, Mitt; Smith, Joseph

For Reference and Further Reading

Campbell, David E., and J. Quin Monson. "Dry Kindling: A Political Profile of American Mormons." *From Pews to Polling Places: Faith and Politics in the American Religious Mosaic*, ed. J. Matthew Wilson. Washington, DC: Georgetown University Press, pp. 105–29.

Cannon, Mark W. 1961. "The Crusades against the Masons, Catholics, and Mormons: Separate Waves of a Common Current." *Brigham Young University Studies* 3 (Winter): 23–49.

Dias, Elizabeth. 2019. "'Mormon' No More: Faithful Reflect on Church's Move to Scrap a Moniker." *New York Times*. June 29.

Gordon, Sarah Barringer. 2002. *The Mormon Question: Polygamy and Constitutional Conflict in Nineteenth-century America*. Chapel Hill: University of North Carolina Press.
Holland, David. 2017. "The Bible and Mormonism." *The Oxford Handbook of the Bible in America*, ed. Paul C. Gutjahr. New York: Oxford University Press, pp. 611–26.
Mauss, Armand L., and Philip L. Barlow. 1991. "Church, Sect, and Scripture: The Protestant Bible and Mormon Sectarian Retrenchment." *Sociological Analysis* 52 (Winter): 397–414.
Reynolds v. United States, 98 U.S. 145 (1879).
Talbot, Christine. 2013. *A Foreign Kingdom: Mormons and Polygamy in American Political Culture, 1852–1890*. Champaign: University of Illinois Press.
Turner, John G. 2012. *Brigham Young: Pioneer Prophet*. Cambridge, MA: Harvard University Press.
Wood, Timothy L. 2000. "The Prophet and the Presidency: Mormonism and Politics in Joseph Smith's 1844 Presidential Campaign." *Journal of the Illinois State Historical Society* 93 (Summer): 167–93.

Cincinnati Bible War of 1869

Although the U.S. Supreme Court did not outlaw devotional Bible reading in public schools until its decision in *Abington v. Schempp* in 1963, the issue had flared in a number of cities during the nineteenth century including Philadelphia, New York, and Cincinnati. The latter controversy generated an opinion by the Ohio Supreme Court upholding a decision by the Cincinnati Board of Education to discontinue the use of the King James Bible and other devotional exercises in the public schools.

In the years leading up to this decision, public schools had opened the school day with readings from the King James Bible (KJV). They considered such teaching important to socializing immigrant children, especially those from Roman Catholic countries. Although it exempted students whose parents objected to the KJV, they did not permit them to bring the Catholic Douay Bible because it contained commentary that school officials believed was sectarian in nature. Most Protestants considered the KJV to be nonsectarian because it was acceptable to most Protestant denominations. Catholics generally opposed it because they did not think it was a good translation, because it left out some books that Catholics accepted, and because they thought it should be accompanied by Catholic commentary.

Cincinnati Catholics led by Archbishop John B. Purcell (1800–1883) had developed their own school system but at one point offered to merge the two systems if the Bible were removed from both. Although this plan fell through, in part because Catholics did not think that education should be divorced from religious training, the school board adopted two resolutions:

> *Resolved*, That religious instruction and the reading of religious books, including the Holy Bible, are prohibited in the common schools of Cincinnati, it being the true object and intent of this rule to allow the children of the parents of all sects and opinions, in matters of faith and worship, to enjoy alike the benefits of the common-school fund.

> *Resolved*, That so much of the regulations on the course of study and the text-books in the intermediate and district schools as reads as follows, "The opening exercises in every department shall commence by reading a portion of the Bible by or under the direction of the teacher, and appropriate singing by the pupils," be repealed. (*Board of Education of Cincinnati v. Minor* 1872, 211)

This stirred considerable anger, especially among members of the Protestant clergy, who viewed America as a Christian nation and continued to view any Catholic efforts to defend their own view points as being directed by the pope. Opponents to the resolutions were able to win a two-to-one victory in the Hamilton County Superior Court.

When the case reached the Ohio Supreme Court, future U.S. Supreme Court justice Thomas Stanley Matthews, a Presbyterian elder, was among those who argued for reversing its decision, which is what that court did. Although much of the argument centered on whether curricular decisions were best vested in the school board or in the court, the decision hinged in large part on a provision of the Ohio Constitution, similar to that in the Northwest Ordinance of 1787, that, after providing that "all men have a natural and indefeasible right to worship Almighty God according to the dictates of their own conscience," went on to provide that "religion, morality, and knowledge, however, being essential to good government, it shall be the duty of the general assembly to pass suitable laws to protect every religious denomination in the peaceable enjoyment of its own mode of public worship, and to encourage schools and the means of instruction" (*Board v. Minor* 1872, 241). Supporters of religious exercises believed this provision was a positive injunction requiring the teaching of the Bible.

Justice John Welch, who wrote the decision on behalf of the Ohio Supreme Court, disagreed. Recognizing the state's mandate to promote "religion, morality, and knowledge," he pointed out, "There is no direction given as to what system of general knowledge, or of religion or morals, shall be taught; nor as to what particular branches of such system or systems shall be introduced into the 'schools'; nor is any direction given as to what other 'means of instruction' shall be employed" (*Board v. Minor* 1872, 244). Whether consciously or unconsciously echoing Pilate's rhetorical question to Jesus as recorded in John 18:38, Welch continued, "To enjoy 'instructions' in 'knowledge,' the knowledge of *truth* in all its branches—religious, moral, or otherwise—is one thing; and to declare *what is* truth—truth in any one, or in all departments of human knowledge—and to enjoin the teaching of *that*, as truth, is quite another thing" (*Board v. Minor* 1872, 244).

Welch was quite cognizant that it was difficult to separate religious prejudices and convictions from public policies. He observed, however, that it was possible to distinguish the constitution's regard for the value of religion in general from that of the Christian religion in particular. Pointing to both state and national constitutions, he observed that "neither the word 'Christianity,' 'Christian,' nor 'Bible,' is to be found in either. When they speak of 'religion,' they must mean the religion of man, and not the religion of any class of men. When they speak of 'all men' having certain rights, they cannot mean merely 'all Christian men.'

Some of the very men who helped to frame these constitutions were themselves not Christian men" (*Board v. Minor* 1872, 246).

Countering the argument that the constitution must mean Christianity because it is part of the common law, Welch observed, "If Christianity is a *law* of the state, like every other law, it much have a *sanction*" (247). Because the nation consists of a largely Christian people, however, it is especially offensive to try to enforce Christianity on others. Paraphrasing Jesus's words as recorded in Matthew 26:52, Welch observed, "True Christianity asks no aid from the sword of civil authority. It began without the sword, and wherever it has taken the sword it has perished by the sword" (247). Almost as though he were summarizing a long-standing Protestant critique of Catholicism, Welch observed that "legal Christianity is a solecism, a contradiction of terms" (248). In his view, "Religion is the parent, and not the offspring, of good government"; likely paraphrasing Jesus's words in Matthew 6:33, Welch added, "Its Kingdom is to be *first* sought, and good government is one of those things which will be added thereto" (249). If the public schools were to teach Christianity as the true religion, all teachers would have to be Christians, and the very act of teaching their own religion would be to violate the Golden Rule of treating others with respect.

Countering arguments that omitting the teaching of the Bible would give control of the schools to "infidel sects," Welch observed, "The only fair and impartial method, where serious objection is made, is to let each sect give its own instructions, elsewhere than in the state schools, where of necessity all are to meet; and to put disputed doctrines of religion among other subjects of instruction, for there are many others, which can more conveniently, satisfactorily, and safely be taught elsewhere" (253). He further cited James Madison as one of the founders who supported this position.

Controversy continued even after this decision when the city attempted to tax the property of parochial schools, only to be overturned by a court decision in *Purcell v. Gerke* (1874).

See also Abington v. Schempp; King James Bible; Philadelphia Bible Wars

For Reference and Further Reading

Board of Education of Cincinnati v. Minor, 23 Ohio St. 211 (1872).

DePalma, Margaret. 2003. "Religion in the Classroom: The Great Bible Wars in Nineteenth Century Cincinnati." *Ohio Valley History* 3 (Fall): 17–36.

Mach, Andrew. 2015. "'The Name of Freeman Is Better than Jesuit': Anti-Catholicism, Republican Ideology, and Cincinnati Political Culture, 1853–1854." *Ohio Valley History* 15 (Winter): 3–21.

Moore, R. Laurence. 2000. "Bible Reading and Nonsectarian Schooling: The Failure of Religious Instruction in Nineteenth-Century Public Education." *Journal of American History* 86 (March): 1581–99.

Newsome, Michael Dehaven. 2002. "Common School Religion: Judicial Narratives in a Protestant Empire." *Southern California Interdisciplinary Law Journal* 11: 219–337.

Purcell v. Gerke, 25 Ohio St. 229 (1874).

Throckmorton, Warren. 2011. "The Cincinnati Bible Wars: When the KJV Was Removed from Public Schools." The Christian Post. May 4. https://www.christianpost.com/news/the-cincinnati-bible-wars-when-the-kjv-was-removed-from-public-schools.html.

Citizenship

One of the arguable defects of the original U.S. Constitution is that although it indicated a difference between a "natural-born" citizen and those who were naturalized, it did not provide a definition of which groups qualified for either (Vile 2016). Nor did it indicate whether it was possible for an individual to be a citizen or a resident of a state without thereby also being a citizen or resident of the United States. In the Dred Scott decision of 1857, the U.S. Supreme Court ultimately decided that blacks were not and could not be citizens of the United States (and thus part of "We the People"). After the Civil War, the adoption of the Fourteenth Amendment (1868) subsequently overturned this decision and declared that all persons born or naturalized within the United States were citizens thereof.

Although English law had suggested that subjects born within the realm were forever subjects thereof, America necessarily adopted a more flexible approach, which permitted individuals who immigrated to the United States to become citizens and those who chose to leave to become citizens elsewhere. Michael Walzer has observed that biblical covenants were sometimes associated with descendants of a particular person, such as Abraham, and at other times extended to a "mixed multitude" (Walzer 2012, 2), such as those who accompanied Moses out of Israel. This led to two different models of citizenship: "There is a permanent, built-in tension between the birth model and the adherence model. The first favors a politics of nativism and exclusion (as in the books of Ezra and Nehemiah), the second a politics of openness and welcome, proselytism and expansion (and even forced conversion), as in the stories of Ruth" (Walzer 2012, 3) and, he might have added, Rahab.

In examining the controversies over citizenship that led up to the Civil War, Carrie Hyde believes that Philippians 3:20 may have played a part in American understandings. Although the King James Version read that "our conversation is in heaven; from whence also we look for the Saviour, the Lord Jesus Christ," in the early part of the nineteenth century, the word "conversation"—which had ceased to mean who a person was rather than what they said, which came from the Greek word *politeuma*, the origins of the word "politics"—was increasingly translated as, and understood to mean, "citizenship." It was thus so translated in the Bible published in 1808 by Charles Thomson, the former secretary of the Continental Congress (Hyde 2018, 55, 58).

This new understanding had two consequences that Hyde traces through such works of literature as David Walker's *Appeal to the Coloured Citizens of the World* (1829) and Harriet Beecher Stowe's *Uncle Tom's Cabin* (1852) and *Dred* (1856). One was to suggest worldly disengagement emphasizing the world to come, and perhaps even justifying earthly injustices like those perpetrated by the institution of slavery as a way to prepare one for a better life to come. The other, however, was to pose a more perfect heavenly citizenship against a deficient idea of citizenship such as that perpetuated under slavery. In Hyde's words, "the value of theological models of citizenship . . . is that they provided a clear alternative to the convention-bound structure of positive law" (2018, 61). For those who recognized that the kingdom of heaven would consist of members of all races, it seemed only logical that they should also be included as citizens in an ideal republic. Moreover, to the extent that the American polity extended protections to all, it could further be identified with the heavenly city or New Jerusalem to come.

See also Slavery; Stowe, Harriet Beecher; Thomson, Charles; Walker, David

For Reference and Further Reading

Hyde, Carrie. 2018. *Civic Longing: The Speculative Origins of U.S. Citizenship.* Cambridge, MA: Harvard University Press.

Vile, John R., ed. 2016. *American Immigration and Citizenship: A Documentary History.* Lanham, MD: Rowman & Littlefield.

Walzer, Michael. 2012. *In God's Shadow: Politics in the Hebrew Bible.* New Haven, CT: Yale University Press.

City upon a Hill

Few, if any, metaphors have better encapsulated the thought of American Pilgrims than an image from John Winthrop's Scripture-laden essay (usually described as a sermon) from 1630, delivered aboard the ship *Arbella* or possibly simply circulated in written form (Rodgers 2018, 27–28), entitled "A Model of Christian Charity."

Winthrop's speech reflected the fact that Puritans considered themselves, like ancient Israelites, to be in a special agreement, or covenant, with God: "Thus stands the cause between God and us. We are entered into covenant with Him for this work, we have taken out a commission, the Lord hath given us leave to draw our own articles we have professed to enterprise these actions upon these and these ends, we have hereupon besought Him of favor and blessing" (Vile 2015, 20). Like covenants within the Old Testament, such a covenant required the Pilgrims to keep their side of the agreement lest "the Lord will surely break out in wrath against us, be revenged of such a perjured people, and make us known the price of the breach of such a covenant" (Vile 2015, 20).

Although he did not cite chapter and verse, Winthrop quoted from Micah 6:8 about the responsibility of the people "to do justly, to love mercy, to walk humbly with our God" (Vile 2015, 20). As he ended his speech, Winthrop exhorted his fellow passengers with a phrase that he borrowed from Jesus's Sermon on the Mount in Matthew 5:14. After he said that his followers should be "the light of the world," Winthrop observed that

> we must consider that we shall be as a city upon a hill, the eyes of the people are upon us. So that if we shall deal falsely with our God in this work we have undertaken and so cause Him to withdraw His present help from us, we shall be made a story and a byword throughout the world, we shall open the mouths of enemies to speak evil of the ways of God, and all professors for God's sake, we shall shame the faces of many of God's worthy servants and cause their prayers to be turned into curses upon us till we be consumed out of the good land whither we are going. (Vile 2015, 21)

Winthrop drew from Moses's words to Israel in Deuteronomy 30:15–16 when he observed, "Beloved there is now set before us life and good, death and evil, in that we are commanded this day to love the Lord our God, and to love one another, to walk in His ways and to keep His commandments and His ordinance, and His laws, and the article of our covenant with Him that we may live and be multiplied, and that the Lord our God may bless us in this land whither we go to possess it" (Vile 2015, 21). Winthrop thus further identified New England as a type of New Israel with the trip from the Netherlands to the United States being likened to that of Moses and his people crossing the Red Sea.

Although this speech is sometimes interpreted as the beginning of American exceptionalism that portrays the nation as uniquely ordained and blessed by God, Winthrop clearly suggested that if the colony were to remain in God's graces, it would need to be faithful to Him. Being an exceptional settlement could easily bring about curses as well as blessings if the Pilgrims do not keep up their side of the covenant.

As a native of Massachusetts, John F. Kennedy was particularly fond of the city-on-the-hill analogy and used it in a speech that he gave to his constituents before leaving for Washington, DC. Citing Winthrop's reference to this city, Kennedy observed, "Today the eyes of all the people are truly upon us—and our governments, in every branch, at every level, national, state, and local, must be as a city upon a hill—constructed and inhabited of men aware of their great trust and their great responsibilities." Like the Pilgrim settlers, Kennedy said it was important for modern leaders to be men of courage, judgment, integrity, and dedication (Kennedy 1961).

President Ronald Reagan was especially enamored with the central metaphor in Winthrop's speech, which Reagan typically stated as "a shining city upon a hill." As he employed the phrase, however, the image became transformed from what Daniel Rodgers describes as a "fragile possibility to an enduring fact" (2018, 244–45).

This was probably most evident in a speech that Reagan gave to celebrate the centennial of the Statue of Liberty on July 23, 1986. Calling the ship from which Winthrop delivered the speech as the *Arabella* rather than the *Arbella*, and at one point incorrectly identifying the Puritans as Quakers, Reagan explained, "A little group of Puritans huddled on the deck. And then John Winthrop, who would later become the first governor of Massachusetts, reminded his fellow Puritans there on that tiny deck that they must keep faith with their God, that the eyes of all the world were upon them, and that they must not forsake the mission that God had sent them on, and they must be a light unto the nations of all the world—a shining city upon a hill" (speech in Balmer 2008, 213). Further elaborating his belief in American exceptionalism, Reagan intoned, "Call it mysticism if you will, I have always believed there was some divine providence that placed this great land here between the two great oceans, to be found by a special kind of people from every corner of the world, who had a special love for freedom and a special courage that enabled them to leave their own land, leave their friends and their countrymen, and come to this new and strange land to build a New World of peace and freedom and hope" (Balmer 2008, 213)

In associating the city-on-the-hill analogy with American exceptionalism, Professor Patrick Deneen has delineated four types of vision. He describes the vision of John Winthrop, like Nathaniel Nile's sermon, as "Two Discourses on

Liberty," and some Anti-Federalist writings as examples of what he calls communal perfectionism. He believes that George Washington's Farewell Address and John Quincy Adams's speech on July 4, 1821, were what he describes as liberal isolationism, which focused chiefly on America's role as an example to other nations. Deneen believes, however, that there was a fine line between liberal isolationism and liberal expansionism, both at home (as in manifest destiny) and abroad, as in the American acquisition of colonies after the Spanish-American War and in Ronald Reagan's own vision of the shining city on a hill. Finally, Deneen identifies a category that he calls global communalism, which looks forward to expanded internationalism. Deneen posits that all four forms of American exceptionalism depart from the Augustinian distinction between the city of God, which consists of members of the church, and the city of man, or earthy kingdoms, none of which Augustine thought could claim a heavenly mission (Deneen 2012, 49).

See also American Exceptionalism; Covenants, Compacts, Contracts, and Constitutions; Kennedy, John F.; Model of Christian Charity; Moses; Pilgrims; Reagan, Ronald (Evil Empire Speech)

For Reference and Further Reading

Balmer, Randall. 2008. *God in the White House: A History; How Faith Shaped the Presidency from John F. Kennedy to George W. Bush*. New York: HarperOne.

Deneen, Patrick K. 2012. "Cities of Man on a Hill." *American Political Thought* 2 (Spring): 29–52.

Dunn, Richard S. 1987. "An Odd Couple: John Winthrop and William Penn." *Proceedings of the Massachusetts Society*, Third Series 99: 1–24.

Holland, Matthew S. 2007. *Bonds of Affection: Civic Charity and the Making of America—Winthrop, Jefferson, and Lincoln*. Washington, DC: Georgetown University Press.

Johnson, Paul. 1995. "God and the Americans: The City upon a Hill." *Commentary* 99 (January): 25–32.

Kennedy, John F. 1961. "The City upon a Hill Speech." John F. Kennedy Presidential Library and Museum. January 9. https://www.jfklibrary.org/learn/about-jfk/historic-speeches/the-city-upon-a-hill-speech.

Morgan, Edmund S. 1958. *The Puritan Dilemma: The Story of John Winthrop*. Boston: Little, Brown.

Noll, Mark A. 2012. "'We Shall Be as a City upon a Hill': John Winthrop's Non-American Exceptionalism." *Review of Faith & International Affairs* 10 (May 24): 5–11.

Rodgers, Daniel T. 2018. *As a City on a Hill: The Story of America's Most Famous Lay Sermon*. Princeton, NJ: Princeton University Press.

Schweitzer, Ivy. 2005. "John Winthrop's 'Model' of American Affiliation." *Early American Literature* 40(3): 441–69.

Vile, John R., ed. 2015. *Founding Documents of America: Documents Decoded*. Santa Barbara, CA: ABC-CLIO.

Civil Disobedience

Christian leaders throughout history have generally advocated obedience to laws, especially those that were legally enacted for the common good. In the Sermon on the Mount, Jesus is quoted as saying, "Resist not evil" (Matthew 5:39). In Matthew 22:21, Jesus urged followers to "render to Caesar the things that are

Caesar's; and to God the things that are God's," and, in the opening verses of Romans 13, Paul urged Christians to submit to governing authorities.

There are occasions in both the Old and New Testaments, however, that also praise those who have stood up to injustice and disobeyed unjust laws. Exodus praised midwives who refused to carry out orders to slay newborn Hebrew boys. The book of Daniel recorded that his three friends were willing to be cast into a fiery furnace rather than bow down to an idol. King Saul's own bodyguards refused to carry out his order to kill priests who had fed David, while Hebrew kings were instructed to write out passages from the law to which they were bound to adhere (Waskow n.d.).

In the New Testament, after religious leaders cautioned early Christians against preaching the gospel, Peter responded in Acts 5:29, "We must obey God rather than men" (Blankley 2012). Historically, Christians have suffered martyrdom rather than surrendered their faith.

Many individuals fled to the United States for refuge after being persecuted for their beliefs. Quakers had been harassed for their refusal to duff their hats to rulers, while Puritans hoped to found a purer church than they had left in England.

Henry David Thoreau's essay "Resistance to Civil Government," better known today as "Civil Disobedience," which was published in 1849, is one of the more articulate defenses of civil disobedience. In Thoreau's case, he had refused to pay a poll tax during the Mexican-American War, which he considered to be an attempt at expanding American slave power (Perry 2013, 94–125). Although his perspective was largely that of libertarian individualism, numerous Christians expressed their unwillingness in the years leading up to the U.S. Civil War to help enforce fugitive slave laws. One pastor, J. C. W. Pennington, likened such participation to Judas's decision to betray Jesus for thirty pieces of silver (Perry 2013, 111). In so doing, opponents of the laws that required the return of escaped slaves appealed to a higher moral law, much as they believed American revolutionaries had done in an earlier generation.

In the years leading up to the adoption of the Nineteenth Amendment in 1920, American suffragists practiced civil disobedience in order to highlight the cause of women's voting.

During the civil rights movement in the 1950s and 1960s, Dr. Martin Luther King Jr. combined the idea of nonviolent resistance and civil disobedience. He eloquently defended his views in his "Letter from a Birmingham Jail," which he wrote in response to a number of pastors and religious leaders who had accused him of being an outsider who was stirring up violence, after he was imprisoned for failing to get a permit to demonstrate.

Justifying his action in part on the basis of his presidency of the Southern Christian Leadership Conference, King cited a number of biblical precedents: "Just as the eighth-century prophets left their little villages and carried their 'thus saith the Lord' far beyond the boundaries of their hometowns; and just as the Apostle Paul left his little village of Tarsus and carried the gospel of Jesus Christ to practically every hamlet and city of the Greco-Roman world, I too am compelled to carry the gospel of freedom beyond my particular hometown" (King 1963).

Responding to those who urged him to "wait," he cited the aphorism that "justice too long delayed is justice denied." He further sought to tie civil disobedience to the principles embodied both in the Declaration of Independence and in Scripture. With St. Augustine, King observed that "an unjust law is no law at all." Drawing on St. Thomas Aquinas, King said that human laws that were not rooted "in eternal and natural law" called for disobedience (King 1963). Drawing from the biblical book of Daniel, he further cited "the refusal of Shadrach, Meshack, and Abednego to obey the laws of Nebuchadnezzar because a higher moral law was involved," as well as "early Christians, who were willing to face hungry lions and the excruciating pain of chopping blocks before submitting to certain unjust laws of the Roman Empire" (King 1963).

King believed that laws mandating segregation were wrong and represented the unjust will of the majority forcing themselves on a racial minority. Rejecting the accusation that he was an extremist, King contrasted his own nonviolent approach, which he grounded on the New Testament and on the philosophy of Mahatma Gandhi, with the militant national of Elijah Muhammad and his movement:

> Was not Jesus an extremist in love?—"Love your enemies, bless them that curse you, pray for them that despitefully use you." Was not Amos an extremist for justice?—"Let justice roll down like waters and righteousness like a mighty stream" [Amos 5:24]. Was not Paul an extremist for the gospel of Jesus Christ?—"I bear in my body the marks of the Lord Jesus" [Galatians 6:17]. Was not Martin Luther an extremist?—"Here I stand; I can do not other so help me God." Was not John Bunyan an extremist?—"I will stay in jail to the end of my days before I make a mockery of my conscience." Was not Abraham Lincoln an extremist?—"This nation cannot survive half-slave and half free." Was not Thomas Jefferson an extremist?—"We hold these truths to be self-evidence, that all men are created equal." (King 1963)

In the 1960s, a number of individuals who opposed being drafted into the armed forces did so on the basis that because the war was unjust, it would be immoral for them to serve. Many received inspiration from William Sloane Coffin Jr. (1924–2006), who was the chaplain at Yale University and who was himself brought to trial for encouraging draft resistance (Goldstein 2004, 183–224). Coffin especially liked to quote Amos 5:24, indicating that it was the "preacher's job to call for justice to roll down like mighty waters. The politician's job was to work out the irrigation system" (Goldstein 2004, 222).

See also King, Martin Luther, Jr.; Natural Law; Puritans; Quakers

For Reference and Further Reading

Allen, Barbara. 2000. "Martin Luther King's Civil Disobedience and the American Covenant tradition." *Publius* 30 (Autumn): 71–113.

Areshinze, Giorgi. 2016. *Democratic Religion from Locke to Obama: Faith and the Civil Life of Democracy*. Lawrence: University Press of Kansas.

Blankley, Bethany. 2012. "The Biblical Civil Disobedience Mandate." HuffPost. February 6 [updated April 7, 2012]. https://www.huffpost.com/entry/biblical-civil-disobedience-mandate_b_1249785.

Goldstein, Warren. 2004. *William Sloane Coffin Jr.: A Holy Impatience*. New Haven, CT: Yale University Press.
King, Martin Luther, Jr. August 1963. "Letter from Birmingham Jail." https://web.cn.edu/kwheeler/documents/Letter_Birmingham_Jail.pdf.
Perry, Lewis. 2013. *Civil Disobedience: An American Tradition*. New Haven, CT: Yale University Press.
Waskow, Arthur O. n.d. "Civil Disobedience in the Bible." https://www.myjewishlearning.com/article/civil-disobedience-in-the-bible/.

Clark, Champ

Champ Clark (1850–1921) was a member of the House of Representatives from Missouri who served from 1897 to 1921 and was Speaker of the House from 1911 to 1919. Born in Kentucky, Clark earned his undergraduate degree from Bethany College, which had been founded by Alexander Campbell, who founded the Disciples of Christ, which Clark joined. Clark studied law at the University of Cincinnati. He unsuccessfully sought the Democratic nomination for president in 1912 but lost to Woodrow Wilson and later opposed Wilson's call for U.S. entry into World War I.

Clark was widely known for his oratory, and for many years held the record for the longest speech ever given before Congress. Umphrey Lee observed that Clark "was proud of the statement that he quoted the Bible oftener and more accurately than any other man in Congress" (1935, 19). Similarly, Clark's biographer observes that "Champ Clark is the most competent and thorough Bible student in public life to-day. His speeches, orations, and lectures are replete with accurate and apropos bible quotations" (Webb 1912, 22).

Champ told his biographer that his father wanted him to read the Bible, but that when Champ refused, he bought him a "vest-pocket volume" with the Articles of Confederation, the Declaration of Independence, and Washington's Farewell Address, and said, "My son, as you will not read your Bible, here is the next best book; study it" (Webb 1912, 23). Later refusing to give in to his son's desire to read novels, but indulging his interest in histories and biographies, his father provided him with a copy of William Wirt's *Life of Patrick Henry*. Enamored with Henry's speech at St. John's Church, Clark was especially mesmerized by the words, "The race is not always to the swift, nor the battle to the strong [Ecclesiastes 9:11]." Telling his father how enamored he was with these words, Clark said that his father responded, "My son, King Solomon, and not Patrick Henry, wrote that sentence that you admire so much. Read your Bible as eagerly as you do your histories and biographies, and you will find hundreds of others fully as magnificent" (Webb 1912, 24). Clark reported that "I took him at his word, and have been reading the Bible ever since, which constantly increasing profit and delight. To say nothing of its religious value, it is the best book in the world to quote from. Whatever knowledge I have of it dates from the day that my father placed William Wirt's 'Life of Patrick Henry' in my hands" (Webb 1912, 24–25).

See also Henry, Patrick; Wilson, Woodrow

For Reference and Further Reading
Lee, Umphrey. 1935. "The English Bible and American Public Men." *Christian Education* 19 (October): 18–21.
Webb, W. L. 1912. *Champ Clark*. New York: Neale Publishing Company.

Climate Change

There is a rising scientific consensus that the earth is warming as a result of the increased burning of fossil fuels, which is increasing the level of carbon dioxide in the atmosphere. There is further widespread scientific agreement that this gas traps radiation in the atmosphere, creating global warming; that such warming is having serious negative environmental consequences; and that steps need to be taken to combat them. Scientists believe that global warming is exaggerating existing weather patterns, resulting in greater flooding, especially in low-lying areas, more intense fires and storms, and the like. The dangers of global warming are often presented in apocalyptic language that resembles the biblical terminology that evangelists once used to describe the end of the world (Lilly 2016).

A fair number of people, typically political conservatives who are generally wary of increased governmental initiatives, however, have rejected such claims outright. Others have argued that they are exaggerated, have suggested that they might be the result of unknown phenomena that are not so directly connected to human actions, or have argued either that combatting global warming might have adverse economic consequences or that funds spent to reduce global warming could better be spent in other ways (Alumkal 2017).

Support for this position might be fueled in part by conservative interpreters of the Bible who believe that Genesis teaches a literal six-day creation and who therefore suspect that scientists might have a hidden agenda in advancing theories of global warming just as they believe they did in advancing the theory that humans evolved from other forms of animal life. Critics are particularly suspicious of individuals who in their judgment seek to deify the earth or nature in an attempt to elevate attention to the environment. Some may, indeed, believe that Christ's second coming might be so imminent as to think that it is pointless to worry about such long-run dangers (Delgado 2017, 17). Others believe that advocates of global warming are showing a lack of faith in the resilience of God's creation as evidenced in Psalm 19:1–6 and its own self-correcting mechanisms. Moreover, some have argued that God's promise to Noah in Genesis 9:11–12, 15–16 that he will never again cover the earth with water would preclude the kind of flood levels that some scientists have predicted (argument cited in Alumkal 2017, 165).

The Bible contains many accounts of natural disasters. While some, like the flood from which Noah and his family escaped on an ark, or the destruction of Sodom and Gomorrah, were attributed to God's wrath against man's sins, they were initiated by God rather than through direct human causes. One scholar has thus noted that "the biblical apocalypse posits humanity at the center of the universe and upholds the notion of a Creator who intervenes in history on behalf of humans. This God bends nature to his service, causing both hellscape and

New Jerusalem to emerge in the story of humankind. In contrast, Enlightenment science's appeal to apocalyptic language has no subject and no body. It tells no history, elicits no desire, and offers no catharsis. Its crisis is measured in meters, not monsters" (Lilly 2016, 368–69).

Much of the biblical arguments relative to global warming have centered on two passages, both of which come from the creation accounts (McCammack 2007, 648). Genesis 1:28 gives humans dominion over the environment: "Be fruitful and increase in number; fill the earth and subdue it. Rule over the fish of the sea and the birds of the air and over every living creature that moves on the ground." Genesis 2:15, however, indicates that human beings serve as stewards of creation: "The LORD God took the man and put him in the Garden of Eden to work it and take care of it."

One perceived threat of global warming is that its negative consequences will fall both on the most vulnerable nations of the world and on the most vulnerable individuals within such nations. This seems to be a major theme in a report by the Evangelical Climate Initiative entitled "Climate Change: An Evangelical Call to Action," which ties concern for climate change both with biblically based concerns for the poor and with the Christian call to love one's neighbors. Texas Tech professor Katharine Hayhoe (2019) cites 2 Timothy 1:7 in an attempt to persuade theological evangelicals thinking about climate change that Christians should have a spirit of love and power rather than one of fear.

See also Judgment; Natural Disasters

For Reference and Further Reading

Alumkal, Anthony. 2017. *Paranoid Science: The Christian Right's War on Reality*. New York: New York University Press.

Delgado, Sharon. 2017. *Love in a Time of Climate Change*. Minneapolis, MN: Augsburg Fortress.

Evangelical Climate Initiative. n.d. "Climate Change: An Evangelical Call to Action." https://www.npr.org/documents/2006/feb/evangelical/calltoaction.pdf.

Hayhoe, Katharine. 2019. "Caring about Climate Change Is the Christian Thing to Do." *New York Times*. October 31.

Lilly, Ingrid Esther. 2016. "The Planet's Apocalypse: The Rhetoric of Climate Change." *Apocalypses in Context: Apocalyptic Currents through History*, ed. Kelly J. Murphy and Justin Jeffcoat Schedtler. Minneapolis, MN: Augsburg Fortress, pp. 359–79.

McCammack, Brian. 2007. "Hot Damned America: Evangelicalism and the Climate Change Policy Debate." *American Quarterly* 49 (September): 545–668.

Clinton, Bill (New Covenant)

On July 17, 1992, William Jefferson (Bill) Clinton (b. 1946), a former governor of Arkansas, accepted the nomination of the Democratic Party to run for president. He had emerged from a large field of Democrats and went on to win against President George H. W. Bush, who, while having successfully repelled the Iraqi attack on Kuwait, was not perceived as having done as good a job with the domestic economy.

Both Clinton and his vice president, Al Gore Jr., were raised as Southern Baptists. According to 1 Corinthians 13:13, the three great Christian virtues are faith, hope, and charity (love). Just as Barack Obama would later write a book called *The Audacity of Hope*, so too Clinton capitalized on this virtue by referencing the name of the town of Hope where he grew up. As a candidate with a better common touch than his Republican rival, Clinton was able to identify with small-town America, observing in his acceptance speech that he learned "more about equality in the eyes of the Lord than all my professors at Georgetown; more about the intrinsic worth of every individual than all the philosophers at Oxford [Clinton had been a Rhodes Scholar], more about the need for equal justice under the law than all the jurists at Yale Law School." Clinton observed, "For too long, those who play by the rules and keep the faith have gotten the shaft. And those who cut corners and cut deals have been rewarded."

Pointing to his own successes with the economy in Arkansas, Clinton called for "a new approach to government." Whereas previous presidents had talked about a New Deal (Franklin D. Roosevelt), a New Frontier (John F. Kennedy), or a Great Society (Lyndon B. Johnson), Clinton called his own approach "a New Covenant, a solemn agreement between the people and their government, based not simply on what each of us can take, but what all of us must give to the nation." Although the covenant Clinton described was thus between the people and their government rather than between the people and God, it nonetheless reached back not only to social contract philosophers like John Locke but also to America's Pilgrim fathers, who patterned their own government on the laws of Israel that they traced back to the covenant they had made with God at Sinai. Christians divide their Scriptures into the Old and New Testaments, which are also often referred to as the Old and New Covenants.

President Bush was known for having difficulty with what he sometimes called "the vision thing." Clinton gamely capitalized on this by quoting "Scripture," without mentioning the chapter and verse of the biblical maxim in Proverbs 29:18, that "where there is no vision, the people perish." He cited this phrase three times within as many paragraphs.

Most of the rest of Clinton's speech focused on outlining this New Covenant, which was based on balancing rights with responsibilities in fields as diverse as college opportunity, health care, taxation, welfare, defense, and the like. Rather than dividing the nation into "us" versus "them," Clinton further associated his new covenant with the words of the Pledge of Allegiance to "one nation, under God, indivisible, with liberty, and justice for all." Somewhat paraphrasing 1 Corinthians 2:9, Clinton observed, "As the Scripture says, our eyes have not yet seen, nor our ears heard nor our minds imagined what we can build." Envisioning such a better future, Clinton said that "every one of us has a personal, moral responsibility to make it so." He ended his speech with another mention of the "New Covenant," and, just before "God bless you, and God bless America," with "I still believe in a place called Hope."

Although Clinton's two terms were a time of relative prosperity, he became entangled in a sexual scandal with a White House intern that led to his eventual impeachment, albeit not his removal from office. He used one of his appearances at a National Prayer Breakfast to express contrition and seek forgiveness for this behavior (Ofulue 2002).

After extensive analysis of Clinton's policies and rhetoric, Robert Durant has concluded that his New Covenant lent a philosophical consistency to Clinton's vision that observers often missed. He believes this occurred largely because, while Clinton used such individual terms as opportunity, responsibility, and community, he often failed to link them together in his rhetoric or to tie them specifically to his vision of the New Covenant (Durant 2006).

Analyzing Clinton's rhetoric as president, Robert Linder concluded that he appeared as president to be the pastor not only of the nation but also of the world. Linder noted that in his first inaugural address, Clinton referred to the Scripture, found in Galatians 6:9, "let us not be weary in well-doing, for in due season, we shall reap if we faint not" (1996, 743). In a speech at the Israeli Embassy in Washington, DC, on March 5, 1996, for victims of a terrorist bombing in Israel, Clinton argued that "the fundamental differences are no longer between Jews and Arabs, or Protestants and Catholics, or Muslims and Serbs and Croats" but "between those who embrace peace and those who would destroy it; those who look to a future of hope and those who are trapped in a past of hatred; those who open their arms and those who insist on clenching their fists" (Linder 1996, 747).

See also Clinton, Bill (Speech of Contrition at National Prayer Breakfast); Contract, Covenant, and Constitution

For Reference and Further Reading

Clinton, Bill. 1992. "In Their Own Words: Transcript of Speech by Clinton Accepting Democratic Nomination." *New York Times*. July 17. https://www.nytimes.com/1992/07/17/their-own-words-transcript-speech-clinton-accepting-democratic-nomination.html. Accessed March 31, 2019.

Durant, Robert F. 2006. "A 'New Covenant' Kept: Core Values, Presidential Communications, and the Paradox of the Clinton Presidency." *Presidential Studies Quarterly* 36 (September): 345–72.

Linder, Robert D. 1996. "Universal Pastor: President Bill Clinton's Civil Religion." *Journal of Church and State* 38 (Autumn): 733–49.

Ofulue, Nneka Ifeoma. 2002. "President Clinton and the White House Prayer Breakfast." *Journal of Communication and Religion* 25(1): 49–63.

Clinton, Bill (Speech of Contrition at National Prayer Breakfast)

When he accepted the nomination of the Democratic Party for the presidency in 1992, William Jefferson (Bill) Clinton indicated that he intended to establish a "new covenant" between the American people and their government that would be based on both rights and responsibilities. In time, however, Clinton became caught up in a sexual scandal with a White House intern named Monica Lewinsky, which he had vigorously denied but which was revealed in excruciating detail by Special Prosecutor Kenneth Starr, whose initial charge had been to investigate a land deal in which Clinton had participated.

The same day that Congress released this report, Clinton used the annual prayer breakfast at the White House to give a twelve-minute speech in which he admitted to the affair, expressed contrition for his actions, and pledged to continue his work as president in what was probably the most Scripture-saturated speech of his two-term presidency.

Saying that he had been up late at night "thinking about and praying about what I should say today," Clinton indicated that he had been on "quite a journey" to get "to the rock bottom truth of where I am and where we all are." Acknowledging that he had not previously been "contrite enough," he followed with "I don't think there is a fancy way to say that I have sinned." Clinton seemed to be following David's confession of sin with Bathsheba (and his subsequent complicity in the death of her husband, Uriah) in Psalm 51, where, in verse 1, he had called upon God to "blot out my transgressions," and, in verse 2, to "cleanse me from my sin." Clinton continued: "It is important to me that everybody who has been hurt know that the sorrow I feel is genuine: first and most important, my family; also my friends, my staff, my Cabinet, Monica Lewinsky and her family, and the American people. I have asked all for their forgiveness."

Although Clinton did not mention God as among those against whom he had sinned (by contrast, in addressing God in Psalm 51:4, King David had said "against thee, and thee only have I sinned"), Clinton indicated that he needed "God's help to be the person that I want to be." In addition to his sorrow, he indicated that, if he were to be forgiven, he needed, "genuine repentance—a determination to change and to repair breaches of my own making," and "what my bible calls a 'broken spirit,'" a theme evident in many biblical passages including Psalm 51:57, which refers to "a broken spirit; a broken and a contrite heart." Somewhat later, however, after indicating that while admitting wrong, he was still instructing his lawyers to "mount a vigorous defense," Clinton expressed the hope "that with a broken spirit and a still strong heart I can be used for greater good."

As the speech continued, Clinton indicated that he was seeking pastoral support and prayers and hoped that the nation's children could learn "that integrity is important and selfishness is wrong." He further quoted from the liturgy of Yom Kippur, the Jewish Day of Atonement. In concluding his speech, Clinton referenced without citing chapter and verse Psalm 139:23–24 in saying, "I ask you to share my prayer that God will search me and know my heart, try me and know my anxious thought, see if there is any hurtfulness in me, and lead me toward the life everlasting." He also reflected the words of Psalm 51:10 in asking for "a clean heart," and 2 Corinthians 5:7 in saying, "let me walk by faith and not sight."

Reflecting Jesus's summary of the Ten Commandments, the words of St. Francis, and Psalm 19:14 and Psalm 139:1, 23–24, Clinton ended the text of his formal speech by saying, "I ask once again to be able to love my neighbor—all my neighbors—as my self, to be an instrument of God's peace; to let the words of my mouth and the meditations of my heart and, in the end, the work of my hands, be pleasing. This is what I wanted to say to you today. Thank you. God bless you."

Reactions to the speech varied. Susanne Scholze, from Wooster University, thus cited Clinton's use of Scripture as an example of "hermeneutic abuse," noting that "to use the Bible for such political ends is an abuse of the Bible" (quoted by Herlinger 1998). Members of the National Association of Evangelicals and of the Southern Baptist Convention had refused to attend. By contrast,

Rev. Joan Brown Campbell, the general secretary of the National Council of Churches, said that "I think he was repentant this morning. And for me, that's more important than being sorry" (quoted by Bennet 1998).

At least two articles have explored the parallels between Clinton and the biblical king David (see Vile [1998] and Ofulue 2002). In 1995, Mother Teresa has used her speech before the National Prayer Breakfast to speak out against abortion, during which President Clinton was reported to have "quietly listened" (Winston 2017).

See also Clinton, Bill (New Covenant)

For Reference and Further Reading

Bennet, James. 1998. "Testing of a President: The President; Tearful Clinton Tells Group of Clerics, 'I Have Sinned.'" *New York Times*. September 12. https://www.nytimes.com/1998/09/12/us/testing-president-president-tearful-clinton-tells-group-clerics-have-sinned.html.

Clinton, Bill. 1998. "I Have Sinned." The History Place Great Speeches Collection. September 11. http ://www.historyplace.com/speeches/clinton-sin.htm.

Herlinger, Chris. 1998. "Clinton Tells Religious Leaders: 'I Have Sinned.'" The Layman. September 18. https://layman.org/news61c4/.

Ofulue, Nneka Ifeoma. 2002. "President Clinton and the White House Prayer Breakfast." *Journal of Communication and Religion* 25:1: 49–63.

Vile, John R. [1998]. "David and Ahab, Clinton and Nixon: Contemporary Lessons from Two Biblical Stories." www.leaderu.com/socialsciences/david-ahab.html.

Winston, Diane. 2017. "The History of the National Prayer Breakfast." *Smithsonian Magazine*. February 2. https://www.smithsonianmag.com/history/national-prayer-breakfast-what-does-its-history-reveal-180962017/.

Colonization

Americans like to glorify those, particularly the Pilgrims, who settled in the new land, which many regarded variously as a wilderness or as a new Eden or Canaan. Given the near decimation of the Native American Indian population, it is increasingly difficult fully to credit the biblical rationales that settlers gave for coming to America, but contemporary understandings can equally go awry if they fail to consider biblical motives for such efforts.

In his study of the English Bible in America, David Daniell observed that "the conversion of the pagan inhabitants to Christianity" was "high on the list" of reasons that early explorers gave for coming to America (2003, 392). He cited Dionyse Settle's book of 1577 entitled *A True Reporte of the Laste Voyage made into the West and Northwest Regions, &c. 1577: Worthily atchieued by Capteine Frosbisher* as observing "that by our Christian studie and endeuour, those barbarous, people, people trained up in Paganisme, and infidelitie might be reduced to the knowledge of true religion, and the hope of salvation in Christ our Redeemer" (392). Moreover, a subsequent book, *A report of the voyage and successe thereof, attempted in the yeere of our Lord 1583 by sir Humprey knight, intended to discover and to plant Christian inhabitants in place convenient . . . written by M. Edward Haies, Gentleman*, specifically cited the need to sow the seeds of the gospel among the pagans and cited the call (Matthew 24:14) to preach the gospel through the entire earth, as well as numerous references to the biblical books of Joshua and Judges (419).

That same year, Richard Hakluyt's *Discourse of Western Planting* cited the call for the preaching of the gospel in Romans 10 and the call to seek the kingdom of God in Matthew 6:33 as reasons for colonization (Daniell 2003, 417). The Massachusetts Bay Company's Seal portrayed a Native American uttering the plea of the Macedonian to Paul in Acts 16:9 to "come over and help us" (417).

Although such motives are often attributed chiefly to New England settlers, Daniell observes that they also served as justification for Jamestown and other settlements to the South. Captain John Smith observed that although "religion" was "their colour," the primary aim of those who colonized was "nothing but present profit" (400), but even Smith interpreted the survival of the settlement, much as New Englanders would interpret they own survival, as providential. Moreover, some took solace in Jeremiah 5:14–18, which suggested that the Bible had predicted both "hardships and disasters" for such pilgrims (403). Daniell further notes that the settlers in both the North and the South likely carried Bibles with them, that biblical images of Eden and of a new heaven and a new earth inspired them, and that they looked upon the New World as an opportunity "to remake Christ's church," which many believed had been corrupted both by the papacy and the Church of England (405).

In 1622, the English poet John Donne, who was dean of St. Paul's Cathedral, assured stockholders of the Virginia Company: "You shall have made this Island, which is but as the Suburbs of the old world, a Bridge, a Gallery to the new; to join all to that world that shall never grow old, the Kingdom of Heaven. You shall add persons to this Kingdom, and to the Kingdom of heaven, and add names to the Books of our Chronicles, and to the Book of Life" (Daniell 2003, 417). One of Christopher Columbus's motives for seeking gold in South America was to finance an expedition to free Jerusalem from the Turks and hasten the second coming of Christ. Noting that Spanish and Portuguese explorations were also accompanied by priests, Daniell observed a contrast between what he thought were primarily the "Church-based" efforts of Roman Catholic explorers from the "Bible-based" motives of the English (419).

Daniell is quick to acknowledge that motives were quite mixed, and not always transparent, but cites Professor Perry Miller's assessment that "in their own conception of themselves," planters and their promoters were "first and foremost Christians, and above all militant Protestants" (420). As later critics such as William Apess would point out, this latter aspect could become particularly disturbing when settlers cited passages from the biblical conquest of Canaan to justify almost unspeakable atrocities during Indian wars. These were often linked to ideas that Native American Indians were both pagan and sexually immoral (Stevens 1993).

Daniell observes that in his history *Of Plymouth Plantation*, William Bradford quoted extensively from, without citing, Psalm 107, which, in applying its description of God's deliverance of the Israelites from Egypt, became known as "the settlers' psalm" (Daniell 2003, 432).

Throughout the nineteenth century, Americans continued to use the concept of manifest destiny to justify their expanse across the continent and their dispossession of Native Americans from their path. At the end of the Spanish-American War, which was supported by many advocates of the social gospel, President William McKinley further used the desire to convert Philippine natives as a justification for American occupation of those islands.

See also America as New Israel; City upon a Hill; Apess, William; Columbus, Christopher; McKinley, William; Manifest Destiny; Native American Indians; Puritans; Social Gospel

For Reference and Further Reading

Daniell, David. 2003. *The Bible in English: Its History and Influence.* New Haven, CT: Yale University Press.

Stevens, Paul. 1993. "'Leviticus Thinking' and the Rhetoric of Early Modern Colonialism." *Criticism* 35 (Summer): 441–61.

Colson, Chuck

Chares (Chuck) Colson (1931–2012) transitioned from serving as White House counsel and being one of President Richard Nixon's "hatchet men" (the first to be imprisoned) to being a prominent evangelical leader and head of the Prison Fellowship, which had sought to provide spiritual help to individuals who are incarcerated.

Born in Massachusetts and educated at Brown University and George Washington University, where he received his law degree, he served in the Marine Corps, served in a number of governmental positions, and founded a law firm before joining the Nixon administration.

Perhaps best known in the White House for compiling the president's so-called enemies list, Colson pled guilty for having arranged the raid of the psychiatrist office of Daniel Ellsberg, who had leaked the Pentagon Papers, and served a prison term.

Raised as an Episcopalian and married to a Roman Catholic, God was not a major part of his life until he read C. S. Lewis's *Mere Christianity* and became convinced that, if the testimony of the Bible were true, then Jesus was either the Son of God or a lunatic. Relying upon John 10:30 and convinced that Jesus was the former, Colson recorded that he had a conversion experience, which he recounted in his best-selling book (Colson 1976, 125–30). One lesson that Colson said he had learned from the Watergate experience was that "a lie cannot live for long" (Hyer 1983).

In addition to providing him with increased skepticism about human nature and the dangers of human power and pride, Colson's conversion appeared to have reinforced many of his conservative views opposing abortion on demand and same-sex marriage, and his fear that the culture was in moral decline. He took, however, a more liberal stance on matters of criminal justice. As Tanya Erzen has observed, "He opposes mandatory minimum sentencing laws that send people to prison for first-time drug offenses and is an advocate of better work-release and after-care programs for prisoners. Colson promotes rehabilitation, restorative justice, and the improvement of living conditions in prisons as long as the rehabilitation entails a conversion to evangelical Christianity" (2007, 1003).

Colson has founded Prison Fellowship Ministries and the InnerChange Freedom Initiative, which are designed to provide rehabilitation for prisoners based on conversion experiences and Bible studies (Sullivan 2009, 66).

Colson authored and coauthored numerous books about developing a Christian worldview that could be applied to the whole of life, often citing numerous philosophers to buttress his defenses of Christianity (Colson and Pearcey 1999; Colson and Vaughn 1992). In an essay in which Colson began by saying that "I believe in biblical inerrancy, the sufficiency of scripture, and the doctrine the Reformers called *Sola Scriptura*," he proceeded to say that "while we have to be immersed in scripture and understand it fully, we also have to know when and how to use it in public discourse" (Colson 2011). Pointing out that C. K. Chesterton when asked what book he would most like to have if he were shipwrecked on a desert island responded with Thomas's *Guide to Practical Shipbuilding* rather than, as expected, the Bible, Colson argued that starting a conversation with "the Bible says" may cause people to stop listening. He observed that in giving his speech at Mars Hills in Athens, which is recorded in Acts 17:16–34, the apostle Paul quoted Greek poets and used what "the Reformers called common grace, or what historically has been called natural law" rather than simply quoting from Scriptures (Colson 2011).

Colson was one of the authors of the Manhattan Declaration of 2009 in which evangelicals, Roman Catholics, and Orthodox Christians joined in support of "the sanctity of human life, traditional marriage and religious freedom" (Brant n.d.). He was the recipient of the Templeton Prize for Progress in Religion in 1993.

See also Evangelicals; Manhattan Declaration: A Call of Christian Conscience; Natural Law

For Reference and Further Reading

Brant, Ginny Dent. n.d. "Lessons from Chuck Colson: A Heaven-Bent Transformer of This World." CBN.com. https://www1.cbn.com/spirituallife/lessons-from-chuck-colson.

Chua-Eoan, Howard. 2012. "The Watergate Dirty Trickster Who Found God: Charles Colson (1931–2012)." *Time*. April 21.

Colson, Charles W. 1976. *Born Again*. Old Tappan, NJ: Chosen Books (Distributed by Fleming H. Revell).

Colson, Chuck. 2011. "Making the Case: Don't Quote the Bible?" Christian Headlines. April 27. https://www.christianheadlines.com/columnists/breakpoint/making-the-case-don-t-quote-the-bible.html.

Colson, Charles, with Ellen Santilli Vaughn. 1992. *The Body*. Dallas, TX: Word Publishing.

Colson, Charles, and Nancy Pearcey. 1999. *How Now Shall We Live?* Wheaton, IL: Tyndale House.

Erzen, Tanya. 2007. "Testimonial Politics: The Christian Right's Faith-Based Approach to Marriage and Imprisonment." *American Quarterly* 59 (September): 991–1015.

Hyer, Majorie. 1983. "Colson Preaches That Watergate Proves the Bible." *Washington Post*. September 28.

Sullivan, Winnifred Fallers. 2009. *Prison Religion: Faith-Based Reform and the Constitution*. Princeton, NJ: Princeton University Press.

Columbus, Christopher

Christopher Columbus (1451–1506) is credited with the European "discovery" of America, in the first of four trips that he made on behalf of King Ferdinand and Queen Isabella of Spain in 1492. Long lauded, especially by Americans of Italian descent, for this discovery, in more recent years, his legacy has been tarnished by the legacy of imperialism, racism, and genocide that his exploration and colonization left in its path.

The Italian-born explorer had actually been seeking to open up trade with China, which he thought that he could reach from Europe by sailing West. Although he does not appear to have been the only individual of his day who believed that the earth was round, he does appear to have thought that the Atlantic Ocean was much smaller and that it could become a highway to the Orient.

Although the remarkable legacy of Columbus has been shadowed by subsequent treatments of the natives in the Caribbean and in Latin America, his primary goal (even when seeking gold) appears to have been motivated by his desire to secure funding for another crusade to capture the Holy Land from the Muslims, convert its inhabitants, and rebuild the temple. All of this was to be done in preparation for the second coming of Christ, which he anticipated would occur in about 150 years.

Both his diary and a book, *Libro de las profecias* (Book of Prophecies), which was not translated into English until 1991, testify to his knowledge of Scripture, especially the book of Revelation (Delaney 2006, 262). His journey to America followed shortly after the expulsion of Jews and Muslims from Spain, and Columbus was highly influenced by the view of Joachim of Fiori (1135–1202) that the world was soon coming to a close. The first sentence of Columbus's book describes its purpose: "Here begins the book, or handbook, of sources, statements, opinions and prophecies on the subject of the recovery of God's Holy City and Mount Zion, and on the discovery and evangelization of the islands of the Indies and of all other peoples and nations" (Delaney 2006, 268). The book further indicates his familiarly both with the fourfold method of biblical interpretation (historical, allegorical, tropological, and anagogical) and "prefigurement," which explains how Old Testament prophecies are fulfilled in the New (Delaney 2006, 268).

Columbus cited a number of prophecies from Isaiah (e.g., Isaiah 51:5b) that focused on the role of islands and often interpreted his discovery of the Americas as the "new heaven and earth" as portrayed in the book of Revelation (Delaney 2006, 269, 271–72). After citing his own knowledge of contemporary science, Columbus said that his primary inspiration and guide had been "the Holy Spirit who encouraged me with a radiance of marvelous illumination from the sacred Holy Scriptures" (Delaney 2006, quoting Columbus's *Libro*, 272).

It is important to understand that Columbus's journey preceded the Protestant Reformation and the resulting split in Christendom. Like Columbus, those (especially the Puritans) who later settled North America brought their own sense of mission and apocalyptic expectations with them (Delaney 2006, 287). They too believed that they came to the New World with a mission and that this mission justified their possession of the land from Native Americans, especially those who refused to convert to Christianity.

See also America as New Israel; Colonization; Puritans

For Reference and Further Reading

Delaney, Carol. 2006. "Columbus's Ultimate Goal: Jerusalem." *Comparative Studies in Society and History* 48 (April): 260–92.
Phillips, William D., Jr. 1992. "Africa and the Atlantic Islands Meet the Garden of Eden: Christopher Columbus's View of America." *Journal of World History* 3 (Fall): 149–64.
Sha'ban, Fuad. 2005. *For Zion's Sake: The Judeo-Christian Tradition in American Culture.* London: Pluto Press.

Common Sense (Thomas Paine)

Even after fighting erupted between American and British troops in April 1775 at Lexington and Concord, many Americans remained loyal to King George III, believing that their quarrel was with the British Parliament and its claims to exercise sovereignty over the colonies, which were not represented in that body. Statesmen like John Adams viewed the British monarchy as part of the "balanced government" consisting of the monarchy, the House of Lords, and the House of Commons, each of which represented different class interests. On August 23, however, the king proclaimed the colonies to be in rebellion, and he followed up with speeches to Parliament supporting its position on October 27, 1775, and again on October 31, 1776 (Vile 2019, 107–10).

Between these two speeches, Thomas Paine (1737–1809), a recent immigrant from Britain, wrote a popular book entitled *Common Sense,* which was designed to question such balanced government in general and monarchy in particular. Although he would later become known as a skeptic for *The Age of Reason,* in *Common Sense,* Paine engaged in fairly extensive biblical exegesis to argue for what Nathan Perl-Rosenthal calls "Hebraic Republicanism" (2009), or the idea that the Old Testament preferred republican government over government by a king.

In *Common Sense,* Paine observed, "In the early ages of the world, according to the scripture chronology, there were no kings, the consequence of which was there were no wars; it is the pride of kings which throws mankind into confusion" (1953, 10). He further observed that "government was first introduced into the world by the heathens, from whom the children of Israel copied the custom. It was the most prosperous invention the devil ever set on foot for the promotion of idolatry" (10). Paine observed that both Gideon and Samuel had opposed the creation of kingship and that "monarchy is ranked in scripture as one of the sins of the Jews, for which a curse in reserve is denounced against them" (11). Citing Gideon's refusal to rule as a king, which is recorded in Judges 8:23, Paine quoted his response to the plea to "Rule thou over us, thou and thy son, and thy son's son," with "I will not rule over you, neither shall my son rule over you. *The Lord shall rule over you*" (11). Similarly, he quoted from 1 Samuel 8, where God tells Samuel that "they have not rejected thee, but they have rejected me, *that I should not reign over them*" and where Samuel warns the people that a king will take their sons and daughters for his work and tax them heavily (12). Paine proceeded to make further arguments about hereditary succession and argued that America was ready for a continental union and had sufficient strength to succeed in a conflict with Great Britain.

Opposing the idea that Britain should be treated as a kind "mother" country, Paine played on Protestant prejudices by associating this term "with a low papistical design of gaining an unfair bias on the credulous weakness of our minds" (21). In another analogy drawn from the biblical book of Exodus, he further compared George III to "the hardened, sullen-tempered Pharaoh of England" (27).

In one of the most dramatic passages of his work, Paine imagined a nation ruled by law rather than by a king: "Yet that we may not appear to be defective even in earthly honors, let a day be solemnly set apart for proclaiming the charter; let it be brought forth placed on the divine law, the word of God; let a crown be placed thereon, by which the world may know that, so far as we approve of monarchy, that in America *the law is king*" (32). This is a scene reminiscent of Moses's destruction of the golden calf in Exodus 32:20 (he had ground it up, sprinkled it in water, and made the people drink it); Paine suggested that "lest any ill use should afterward arise, let the crown at the conclusion of the ceremony be demolished and scattered among the people, whose right it is" (32). Paine further suggested that "nothing can settle our affairs so expeditiously as an open and determined declaration for independence" (43).

Perl-Rosenthal said that Paine's arguments were similar to, and may have been at least partly drawn from, the writings of John Milton (1608–1674), Algernon Sidney (1622–1683), and others but that his Hebraic republicanism was a departure from many other civic republican writers who had accepted monarchy, at least as part of a balanced government. In his *Two Treaties of Government*, John Locke (1632–1704) had, of course, argued against the doctrine of the divine right of kings that Sir Robert Filmer (1588–1653) had advanced in his *Patriarcha*. Perl-Rosenthal further documents how Paine's work prompted a number of published attacks and responses, which further served to focus on biblical arguments both for and against kingship (2009, 537).

In writing the Declaration of Independence, Thomas Jefferson directed his attacks on the British king rather than on Parliament, the authority of which the colonists had already previously rejected.

Later in life, Thomas Paine wrote *The Age of Reason*, which, while affirming basic tenets of Deism, attacked orthodox religion and its biblical foundations. Many Americans, especially those who remembered Paine's arguments from Scripture in *Common Sense*, were shocked by what they considered to be his infidelity. Elias Boudinot was among those who authored attacks on Paine's reasoning.

See also Boudinot, Elias; Declaration of Independence; Gideon; Pharaoh; Political Hebraism

For Reference and Further Reading

Jordan, Winthrop D. 1973. "Familial Politics: Thomas Paine and the Killing of the King, 1776." *Journal of American History* 60 (September): 294–308.

Paine, Thomas. [1776] 1953. *Common Sense and Other Writings*, ed. Nelson F. Adkins. New York: Liberal Arts Press.

Perl-Rosenthal, Nathan R. 2009. "The 'Divine Right of Republics': Hebraic Republicanism and the Debate over Kingless Government in Revolutionary America." *William and Mary Quarterly*, 3rd Series 66 (July): 535–64.
Vile, John R. 2019. *The Declaration of Independence: America's First Founding Document in U.S. History and Culture*. Santa Barbara, CA: ABC-CLIO.

Commonwealth v. Cooke (MA, 1859)

Ever since its decision in *Abington v. Schempp* (1963), the U.S. Supreme Court has invalidated devotional Bible reading in public schools, but it was not always so. In 1859, the Police Court of Boston, Massachusetts, thus upheld the right of a teacher, McLaurin F. Cooke, to inflict corporal punishment on an eleven-year-old boy named Thomas J. Wall after Wall refused to repeat the Ten Commandments. Both his parish priest and his father, who did not accept the King James Version of the Bible from which the commandments were taken, had encouraged Wall to resist. Over the course of half an hour, Cooke had intermittently hit Wall's hand with a rattan stick, approximately three feet in length and three-eighths of an inch think, until he finally compiled. Although his hands had swelled, a doctor believed the injury would not last beyond a day's time.

Written at a time prior to the application of the Bill of Rights to state actions, the judge focused instead on the state laws and on its constitution. He noted that schools were established under authority of state laws, which prohibited the appropriation of state money "to any religious sect, for the maintenance, exclusively, of its own schools" (1859, 420). He further observed that state laws enjoined schools "to exert their best endeavors to impress on the minds of children and youth, committed to their care and instruction, the principles of piety, justice, and a sacred regard to truth, love to their country, humanity and universal benevolence, sobriety, industry, and frugality, chastity, moderation, and temperance, and those other virtues which are the ornaments of human society, and the basis upon which a republican constitution is founded" (420–21). A state law also provided that "the School Committee of each town and city in the Commonwealth, shall require *the daily reading of some portion of the Bible in the common English version*, and shall direct what other books shall be used in the public schools" (421).

The Boston school committee had specifically required that "the morning exercises of all the schools shall commence with reading a portion of the Scripture in each room by the teachers, and the Board recommend that the reading be followed with the Lord's Prayer repeated by the teacher alone, or chanted by the teacher and the children in concert, and that afternoon session close with appropriate singing, and *also that the pupils learn the Ten Commandments, and repeat them once a week*" (421). These laws needed to be measured against the provision in the state constitution that provided:

> That it is the right as well as the duty of all men in society publicly and at stated seasons to worship the Supreme Being, the great Creator and Preserver of the universe. And no subject shall be hurt, molested, or restrained in his person, liberty, or estate, for worshipping God in the manner and seasons most agreeably to the dictates of his own conscience, or for his religious professions or sentiments,

provided he doth not disturb the public peace, or obstruct others in their religious worship. (1859, 421)

Noting that "our schools are the granite foundation on which our republican form of government rests" (1859, 421), the court observed that, if children were to insist only upon reading a particular version of the Bible, this would be to take the decision over the choice of books "from the State government" and place it "in the hands of a few children" (422). If Roman Catholic children could make such a claim, so could Universalists, those who favor sprinkling instead of baptism by immersion, and even those who might think that the Bible points to three gods rather than one. Classifying such deference as "narrow and sectarian," the judge concluded that the state constitution was designed "for the protection of all religions" (422) and "intended to prevent persecution by punishing religious opinions" (423).

Apparently regarding the King James Version of the Bible as nonsectarian (the very point that the student was contesting), the court observed, "The Bible has long been in our common schools. It was placed there by our fathers, not for the purpose of teaching sectarian religion, but a knowledge of God and of his will, whose practice is religion" (423). Pointing out that the law did not require students "to believe it," or "to receive it as the only true version of the laws of God," the court further observed, "The teacher enters into no argument to prove its correctness, and gives no instructions in theology from it. To read the Bible in school for these and like purposes, or to require it to be read without sectarian explanations, is no interference with religious liberty" (423). Moreover, to accept a plea of conscience against reading a particular translation of the Bible would be to open the schools to Jewish requests to read the Bible from scrolls or the original Hebrew. It would be the equivalent to having courts allow oaths "by swearing the Protestant by the uplifted hand, the Roman Catholic upon the Evangelists, the Jew upon the Pentateuch, while facing the East, with his head covered, and refusing to admit the Infidel as a witness at all!" (423).

Answering the argument that the boy was following his father's instructions, the court cited the biblical proverb that a house divided against itself cannot stand (Mark 3:25), to say that the teacher must govern the school just as a father governs the family (424). Were the school to allow students like Wall to use the Douay (Roman Catholic) version of the Bible, it would in fact be to violate the constitutional provision prohibiting tax money to be used for sectarian schools. Over time, an accumulation of such exemptions, like tiny threads woven into large cables to uphold a suspension bridge, would bind church and state together forever (425).

As to punishment, it is limited both at home and at school, but in this case Wall could have ended the punishment sooner by complying, and the punishment did not exceed the bounds "of sound discretion" (426).

The most fascinating aspect of the case is the way that the judge accepted the King James Version of the Bible as nonsectarian because it was used by multiple Protestant denominations, even though it was not accepted by the Catholic Church. It also seems odd that the court did not consider the possibility that Wall might simply have been permitted to remain silent or absent himself during the recitation of the Ten Commandments, which, while presenting its own problems, appears to have been the practice of some schools prior to the decision in *Abington v. Schempp*.

See also Abington v. Schempp (1963); King James Version of the Bible; Roman Catholics; Ten Commandments

For Reference and Further Reading

Cushman, Robert Fairchild. 1955. "Holy Bible and the Public Schools." *Cornell Law Review* 40 (Spring): 475–99.

"In the Police Court of Boston, Massachusetts. April, 1859. Commonwealth, on Complaint of Wall vs. M'laurin F. Cooke." *American Law Register* 7 (May): 417–26. Cited as *Commonwealth v. Cooke*, 7 Am. L. Reg. 417 (Police Court of Boston, MA, 1859).

Communism and Anti-Communism

One of America's most widespread fears throughout the twentieth century was the fear of communism. Largely the brainchild of Karl Marx (1818–1893) and Frederick Engels (1820–1895), who authored *The Communist Manifesto* in 1848, communism advocates public, rather than private, ownership of the major means of production as in capitalist, or free enterprise, systems. Believing that economic matters were paramount, they believed that religion was simply a tool used by the ruling class to stifle dissent.

As an ideology, communism urged members of the working class (the proletariat) to revolt against those who owned property and create a dictatorship of the proletariat that would last until, in a kind of secular utopia, the state withered away. In practice, nations that have attempted to implement communism have concentrated power in a single leader or leaders often at a great cost to human life, liberty, and private property, most notably in the former Soviet Union and its one-time East European puppets, in the People's Republic of China, in North Korea, and in other nations.

Communists seized power in Russia in 1917, causing a concomitant "Red Scare" in the United States during which civil liberties were repressed. On June 25, 1950, North Korea invaded South Korea, and the United States entered conflict under the auspices of the United Nations in a bloody war that eventually included China. That same decade, Senator Joseph McCarthy of Wisconsin led a series of congressional hearings in which he falsely accused many Americans of being communists. Richard Nixon won a Senate election on a strong anti-communist platform and led Senate investigations to uncover communists in government. One reason that Congress added the words "under God" to the pledge to the U.S. flag in 1954 was to highlight the differences between the United States and atheistic communist nations. The United States committed itself to contain communism, which led in part to its long participation in the war in Vietnam. With the fall of the so-called Iron Curtain separating the communist and non-communist European nations in 1989, fears of communism have somewhat abated, and yet North Korea and China still maintain elements of communist ideology that threaten U.S. values.

Although the Bible takes a clear stance against tyranny, or statism, there are passages that are sometimes cited to support communism. Exodus 16:16–18 instructed the Israelites to take no more than was needed when they gathered daily manna. Once the Jews settled in Canaan, land was supposed to remain within tribes and families. Notably, this appears to have been a primary reason that Naboth had refused to sell his vineyard to King Ahab, whose wife had, in turn, arranged for Naboth's death. Jesus often warned about those who stored up earthly treasures (as in Matthew 6:19–20 and Luke 6:24–25), and one of his most vivid stories, that of Lazarus and the rich man (Luke 16:19–31), describes a rich man suffering in the afterlife while a beggar at his gates lives in comfort. Acts 2:44–45 and Acts 4:33–37 describe how early Christians held property in common in order to take care of one another. Peter subsequently pronounced judgment on Ananias and Sapphira in a story recounted in Acts 5:1–11, but this appears based on their false claim to have sold all that they had for the common good rather than on any church-mandated obligation that they do so.

Although many fundamentalists largely withdrew from politics after the Scopes Trial in 1925, one exception was their unrelenting opposition to communism, which they associated with atheism and statism. One leader in this movement was Rev. Carl McIntire (1906–2002), who founded numerous organizations and had a program on more than six hundred radio stations. Although refusing to compromise his hard-shell fundamentalist convictions, McIntire was willing to ally with Catholics and others on this issue (Ruotsila 2012, 388). From the Protestant mainline church, Secretary of State John Foster Dulles (1888–1959) developed a strong anti-communist stance based largely on his belief that communism denied that human beings had been created in God's image and deserved basic human rights.

Communism has not been popular in the United States, and throughout U.S. history, politicians have sought to label their opponents as communists, socialists, or fellow travelers. Southern supporters of segregation often denounced Dr. Martin Luther King Jr., and other civil rights leaders, in such terms. Ironically, King gave a sermon on the subject in Atlanta, Georgia, on August 9, 1953, in which he began with the statement that "communism and Christianity are at the bottom incompatible. One cannot be a true Christian and a true Communist simultaneously" (King 1953). More specifically, King argued that because it left out God and Christ, communism was "avowedly secularistic and materialistic." He further observed that the methods of communism "are diametrically opposed to Christianity." Third, he pointed out that communists subordinated individuals to the state. He did, however, cite the observation of William Temple, a former Archbishop of Canterbury, who had identified communism as something of a "Christian heresy." King thus noted that communists had a concern for social justice and emphasized the need for action. He observed that "we are challenged to dedicate and devote our lives to the cause of Christ as the Communist[s] do to Communism" (King 1953).

See also Fundamentalism; King, Martin Luther, Jr.; Property

For Reference and Further Reading

Cline, Austin. 2019. "What Does the Bible Say about Communism and Socialism?" Learn Religions. March 22. https://www.learnreligions.com/biblical-communism-250944.

Hart, David Bentley. 2017. "Are Christians Supposed to Be Communists?" *New York Times*. November 4.

King, Martin Luther, Jr. 1953. "Communism's Challenge to Christianity." Stanford University: The Martin Luther King, Jr. Research and Education Institute. August 9. https://kinginstitute.stanford.edu/king-papers/documents/communisms-challenge-christianity.
Mulder, John M. 1971. "The Moral World of John Foster Duller: A Presbyterian Layman and International Affairs." *Journal of Presbyterian History* 49 (Summer): 157–82.
Ruotsila, Markku. 2012. "Carl McIntire and the Fundamentalist Origins of the Christian Right." *Church History* 81 (June): 378–407.
Wilcox, Clyde. 1987. "Popular Backing for the Old Christian Right: Explaining Support for the Christian Anti-Communism Crusade." *Journal of Social History* 21 (Autumn): 117–32.

Confederate States of America

Although Abraham Lincoln observed in his second inaugural address that Northerners and Southerners read the same Bible, their interpretations varied significantly on the issue of slavery. Northerners often emphasized the story of Moses and other liberation narratives in Scripture, while Southern slave apologists pointed to verses encouraging slaves to obey their masters. These differences were reflected into the division of major denominations into Northern and Southern wings.

The religious dimension of the Southern case was evident in the preamble to the Constitution of the Confederate States which, while otherwise almost identical to its forbear, explicitly invoked "the favor and guidance of Almighty God" (Vile 2018, 23). The Confederate States further adopted the motto *Deo Vindice* ("God will avenge") and conceived of themselves, much as had the New England Puritans whom Southerners largely despised, as God's chosen people (Stout n.d.). Drawing from biblical passages in Psalm 118:22 and Matthew 21:42, Alexander H. Stephens, the vice president of the Confederacy, stated that the Confederate States repudiated the philosophy of the Declaration of Independence that "all men are created equal," and were instead built upon the "corner-stone" of human inequality (Stephens 1861).

Because most American Bibles had been printed in the North prior to the war, the Southern states faced a shortage both of Bibles and of prayer books (Brydon 1948). The Southwestern Publishing House in Nashville, Tennessee, which was owned by J. R. Graves, W. F. Marks and Company, published the first Bibles to be published in the Confederacy in 1861, but publication ceased when Union troops occupied the city in February 1862.

Perhaps seeking to alleviate this problem, the Confederate Congress enacted a law on October 13, 1862, which provided that "all money and other property bequeathed by any person within the Confederate States, or any State thereof, to the American Bible Society, and which may be liable to sequestration under the laws of the Confederate States, shall be paid and delivered to the Bible Society of the Confederate States of America, as if the same had been bequeathed to said Bible Society of the Confederate States, for the purposes of such bequest" (*Journal of the Congress of the Confederate States of America* 1862, 2:378). President Jefferson Davis vetoed this bill on October 26, 1862. He argued that the Congress had no power to bestow such money as a gift, or to divert it from its beneficiaries, and that it had no way of knowing what the purposes of the American Bible Society might have been (Davis 1862).

Most Southern efforts to import Bibles from England were frustrated by the Northern blockade of Southern ports. As the war increasingly turned against the South, chaplains reported increased revivals among the troops, many of whom developed what has been called "the religion of the 'Lost Cause,'" in which they tried to interpret their suffering and defeat as the pursuit of a higher cause. Southern writers especially glorified General Stonewall Jackson and his Christian faith and used the date of his death by friendly fire (May 10) as the Confederate Memorial Day (Stout n.d.).

The Union victory was interpreted by many former slaves as a recapitulation of the biblical story of Exodus and lifted Southern rules that had made it a crime to teach them how to read and write. Prior to this, even African American preachers were often far more familiar with oral renditions of Scripture than with the written word.

See also American Bible Society; Declaration of Independence; Jackson, Thomas (Stonewall); Lincoln, Abraham (Second Inaugural Address); Slavery; Stephens, Alexander H. (Cornerstone Speech)

For Reference and Further Reading

Brydon, G. MacLaren. 1948. "The 'Confederate Prayer Book,'" *Historical Magazine of the Protestant Episcopal Church* 17 (December): 339–44.

Davis, Jefferson. 1862. "A Veto Message from Jeff. Davis." New York Times Archives. October 26.

Journal of the Congress of the Confederate States of America, 1861–1865 (vol. 2). Reprint by Ithaca, NY: Cornell University Press, 2009.

Rable, George C. 2010. *God's Almost Chosen Peoples: A Religious History of the American Civil War*. Chapel Hill: University of North Carolina Press.

Stephens, Alexander H. 1861. "Cornerstone Speech." American Rhetoric Online Speech Bank. March 21. https://americanrhetoric.com/speeches/alexanderstephenscornerstone.htm.

Stout, Harry S. n.d. "Religion in the Civil War: The Southern Perspective." TeacherServe. https://nationalhumanitiescenter.org/tserve/nineteen/nkeyinfo/cwsouth.htm. Accessed May 24, 2019.

Vile, John R., ed. 2018. *The Civil War and Reconstruction Eras: Documents Decoded*. Santa Barbara, CA: ABC-CLIO.

Congressional Oaths of Office

Although it is common for members of Congress, and other public offices, to take their oaths on the Bible, this is not required by the U.S. Constitution, which specifically prohibits religious tests for office, and individual members sometimes choose other documents.

This was particularly evident in the 116th congressional class that was inaugurated in 2019. Amanda Jackson reports, "More than a dozen documents and books—including the US Constitution, Eastern Orthodox Bible and Quran—were used to swear in officials of various ethnic and religious backgrounds" (2019).

Two Muslim members of the U.S. House of Representatives, Ilham Omar of Minnesota and Rashida Tlaib of Michigan, both swore on the Koran. The former used a Koran that belonged to her grandfather, and the latter used a translation from 1734 that Thomas Jefferson had owned.

Senator Martha McSally of Arizona, a former combat pilot in the Air Force, swore on a Bible recovered from a sailor who was aboard the USS *Arizona* when it was attacked at Pearl Harbor. Senator Kyrsten Sinema of Arizona swore upon copies of the U.S. and Arizona Constitutions, and Senator Mitt Romney of Utah swore on a Bible that his father, a former Michigan governor, had used; he also followed his precedent of adding a special inscription (Schallhorn 2019).

Recent years have witnessed kerfuffles over whether the oath should be administered with or without the words "So help me God" (Edmondson 2019).

See also Bible Signings; Presidential Inaugural Bible Verses

For Reference and Further Reading

Edmondson, Catie. 2019. "'So Help Me God' No More: Democrats Give House Traditions a Makeover." *New York Times.* May 11.

Jackson, Amanda. 2019. "Muslim and Jewish Holy Books among Many Used to Swear-in Congress." CNN. January 3. https://www.cnn.com/2019/01/03/us/congress-swear-in-religious-books-trnd/index.html.

Schallhorn, Kaitlyn. 2019. "New Lawmakers Used Historical Texts, Family Heirlooms during Swearing-In Ceremonies." Fox News. January 4. https://www.foxnews.com/politics/new-lawmakers-used-historical-texts-family-heirlooms-during-swearing-in-ceremonies.

Congressional Resolution on the Ten Commandments (1997)

The Ten Commandments as recorded in Exodus 20 are among the most recognizable sets of ancient laws and are widely accepted as a solid basis for ethical behavior. According to biblical accounts, Moses received the commandments from God at Mount Sinai, and they subsequently became the basis whereby the Hebrew people established a covenant between themselves and God. Although the first part of the Commandments deals chiefly with human obligations to God, the second part deals primarily with relations among individuals. The Puritans who settled in America were especially interested in the Ten Commandments and attempted to model many of their laws on these commandments and their subsequent adumbrations.

Because the Commandments detail relationships to God that are beyond the scope of the government created under the U.S. Constitution (the First Amendment of which prohibits the "establishment" of religion), questions have arisen concerning their placement in governmental buildings. Some judicial decisions have permitted displays of the Commandments when surrounded by other documents, whereas others have generally ruled that standing alone, they give undue preference to Judeo-Christian understandings.

Judge Roy S. Moore of Alabama has been involved in a number of controversies over displays of the Ten Commandments, including a dispute in which an Alabama circuit judge ordered him to remove a copy from his courtroom. As the Alabama Supreme Court (on which he would later serve) issued a stay of this order, the U.S. Congress adopted a resolution supporting his display. Perhaps seeking to support the argument that such displays had a clear secular legislative purpose (one of the three prongs of the Lemon Test that the U.S. Supreme Court often employs to resolve such matters), Congress was intent on supporting arguments that the Ten Commandments were a major source of U.S. law.

In its resolution, Congress accordingly stated both that "the Ten Commandments have had a significant impact on the development of the fundamental principles of Western Civilization" and that they "set forth a code of moral conduct, observance of which is universally acknowledged to promote respect for our system of laws and the good of society." Having highlighted such influences, Congress further resolved that:

1. The Ten Commandments are a declaration of fundamental principles that are the cornerstones of a fair and just society; and
2. The public display, including display in government offices and courthouses, of the Ten Commandments should be permitted.

See also Covenants, Compacts, Contracts, and Constitutions; Moore, Roy; Ten Commandments

For Reference and Further Reading

Green, Steven K. 1999–2000. "The Fount of Everything Just and Right? The Ten Commandments as a Source of American Law." *Journal of Law and Religion* 14(2): 525–58.

H.Con.Res.31—Expressing the sense of Congress regarding the display of the Ten Commandments by Judge Roy S. Moore, a judge on the circuit court of the State of Alabama. 105th Congress (1997–1998). March 5, 1997.

Conservative Bible Project

The Conservative Bible Project was launched in 2009 and continues to this day. The project is the brainchild of Andy Schlafly, the founder of Conservapedia, which he established as an alternative to Wikipedia, the online source that he considered to be too liberal. He is the son of one-time conservative activist Phyllis Schlafly (1924–2016), who was perhaps best known for her opposition to the Equal Rights Amendment.

The project seeks to enlist readers, working from the King James Version of the Bible, to rework the biblical text so as to mitigate against "Liberal Bias" ("Conservative Bible Project"). Other stated goals include those designed to remedy flaws in other translations, which are accused of eliminating gender pronouns, dumbing down the language, undermining the doctrine of hell, and the like. The website thus identifies the need to replace such words as "comrade" with "volunteer"; updating words like "peace," the meaning of which has changed; expressing the truths of "Free Market Parables"; and preferring "Conciseness over Liberal Wordiness" ("Conservative Bible Project"). Schlafly is also concerned about combatting addiction by using the term "gamble" instead of "casting lots"; describing the behavior of the "dishonest" manager described in Luke 16:8 as being "shrewd"; and eliminating "inauthentic passages" such as Jesus's encounter with the adulteress woman or his plea from the cross in

Luke 23:34 for forgiveness for those who knew not what they were doing, which are not found in some of the earliest manuscripts. Although the project is not yet complete, it includes plans to include the apocryphal/Eueterocanonical books, which were traditionally accepted by Roman Catholics and Orthodox believers, and which even some Protestant reformers considered as being "good to read" ("Conservative Bible Project").

Columnist Thomas Fabisiak observes that Schlafly's project bears some resemblance to Thomas Jefferson's attempt to remove miracles from the Bible. He also observed that the project has considered some odd proposals such as translating the word "Pharisee" as "elite" or "self-proclaiming elite" and as anachronistic to the extent that it attempts to read "free market" ideas, which were unknown in Jesus's day, into his parables. Fabisiak (2009) further notes that the passages that Schlafly regards as inauthentic were added long before modern-day liberalism emerged.

An article by the Associated Press (2009) quotes Timothy Paul Jones, a theologically conservative theological professor at the Southern Baptist Theological Seminary in Louisville, Kentucky, as saying, "This is not making scripture understandable to people today, it's reworking scripture to support a particular political or social agenda." It reports that Schlafly responded that "the phrase 'theological conservative' does not mean that someone is political conservative."

In the 1980s and 1990s a group of theologically liberal scholars created the Jesus Seminar in an attempt to come to a consensus about which of the sayings of Jesus were authentic and which were not. A columnist at Beliefnet facetiously described the Conservative Bible Project as "what you'd get if you crossed the Jesus Seminar with the College Republican chapter at a rural institution of bible learnin'" (Weiner 2010).

Writing for Faith Perspectives, Sharon Autenrieth (2009) said that she wanted to treat the project as a joke, but concluded that it was a form of eisegesis or "reading your own opinions and attitudes into scripture" or even making a god of "conservative ideology".

Schlafly's attempt to align the Bible with a contemporary ideology was not, of course, unique. Quoting from an article in the *Gospel Advocate* of August 1822, William Hogue observes that relatively early in U.S. history, a "republican" Bible had been proposed. It would have provided to translate the words "kings, potentates, lords, thrones, etc." with "presidents, senators, statesmen, [and] chairs of state" (Hogue 1991, 380). More recently, the *American Patriot's Bible* contains stories and illustrations about the role of the Bible in American history.

See also American Patriot's Bible; Jefferson Bible

For Reference and Further Reading

Associated Press. 2009. "Conservative Bible Project Aims to Rewrite Scripture to Counter Perceived Liberal Bias." December 4. https://www.nydailynews.com/life-style/conservative-bible-project-aims-rewrite-scripture-counter-perceived-liberal-bias-article-1.431955.

Autenrieth, Sharon. 2009. "Andy Schlafly, Stephen Colbert and the Conservative Bible Project: Is This Self-Parody?" December 10. https://www.stltoday.com/lifestyles/faith-and-values/civil-religion/andy-schlafly-stephen-colbert-and-the-conservative-bible-project-is/article_fa7b86b1-bf3d-5fc4-9ac9-34d65787a9f4.html.

"Conservative Bible Project." Conservapedia. https://www.conservapedia.com/Conservative_Bible_Project. Accessed July 15, 2019.

Fabisiak, Thomas. 2009. "The Conservative Bible Project: Looking for Conservative Diamonds in a Liberal Dung-Hill." Religion Dispatches. October 21. http :// religiondispatches.org/the-conservative-bible-project-looking-for-conservative-diamonds-in-a-liberal-dung-hill/.

Hogue, William M. 1991. "An Authorized Bible for America." *Anglican and Episcopal History* 60 (September): 361–82.

Weiner, Rachel. 2010. "Conservative Bible Project Cuts Out Liberal Passages." HuffPost. March 18 [updated January 4, 2012]. https://www.huffpost.com/entry/conservative-bible-projec_n_310037.

Constitutional Interpretation

If it is a truism that America is a republic that rests on the authority of a written constitution, it has proven equally true that written documents like the Constitution often require interpretation as well as application to issues that its framers could not have envisioned. The U.S. Constitution, sometimes in conjunction with other founding documents, is sometimes referred to as American Scripture, and individuals often refer to their "faith" in the constitutional system much like they would refer to their religious beliefs. It is common for scholars to refer to U.S. presidents or Supreme Court justices as secular priests. Both the Bible (with its Old and New Testaments) and the U.S. Constitution (with twenty-seven amendments and thousands of judicial interpretations) were written over time. Interpretative principles—for example, original intent, emphasis on the meaning of words, comparing texts, and even the idea that both might grow over time—and applications of the two documents are often similar.

Professor Henry Chambers thus observes,

> Similarities between the Bible and the Constitution abound. The Bible is a constitution for Christians. Its theology tells Christians who they are, indicates how Christians should live, and states what Christians should aspire to be. Similarly, the Constitution is the constitution for Americans. It constitutes the United States as a nation and reflects American aspirations. Indeed, some would argue that the Constitution reflects our civil religion. (Chambers 2009, 94)

From a somewhat different perspective, Professor Thomas Grey noted,

> The maxim *vox populi, vox Dei* [the voice of the people is the voice of God] hints at the force of the analogy between Bible and Constitution. Just as Christians and Jews take the word of God as sovereign and the Bible as the word of God, so Americans take the will of the people as sovereign, at least in secular matters, and the Constitution as the most authoritative expression of that popular will. Beyond that, Americans have never regarded the United States Constitution simply as a hierarchically superior statute, which is, by and large, how they view their state constitutions. Rather, it has been, virtually from the moment of its ratification, a sacred symbol, the most potent emblem (along with the flag) of the nation itself. (Grey 1984, 3)

A number of scholars have attempted to compare principles of biblical and constitutional interpretation, which are both known as hermeneutics (see especially Pelikan 2004). One of the best known of these is Sanford Levinson's approach to the subject of constitutional interpretation from the perspective that Roman Catholics and Protestants typically take toward the Bible. In Levinson's schema, Protestants typically emphasize the primary authority of the Bible, which they believe is capable of interpretation by lay persons. By contrast, Roman Catholics emphasize the need for the church to interpret the Bible, often relying on traditions as well as on the language of the Bible itself. Catholics also stress the need for the pope to serve as the ultimate interpreter of this text.

A judge, scholar, justice, or private individual who puts primary emphasis on the text of the Constitution to the exclusion of most other evidence would thus be similar to Protestants who profess to go simply by the words of the Constitution; Justice Hugo Black is a quintessential example of such an approach. Individuals who are willing to cite other documents and rely more strongly on judicial precedents, for example, those who might supplement the Constitution with natural law teachings, would be taking a more Catholic approach. Similarly, individuals who would vest final interpretative power in the U.S. Supreme Court, which probably includes most individuals who have sat on the U.S. Supreme Court, would be taking a position similar to that of Catholics who believe that the pope is the final authority, whereas individuals (e.g., Presidents Andrew Jackson and Abraham Lincoln) who would emphasize the duty of each department of government to interpret the Constitution, if not even private individuals, would be taking a more Protestant view. Individuals may employ a Catholic approach on one side and a Protestant view on the other. They might thus take a Protestant view of the authority of the Constitution and a Catholic view of the role of the Supreme Court in interpreting it, or a more Catholic view of the nature of the Constitution and a more Protestant view of who should interpret it (Levinson 1979).

Issues of both biblical and constitutional interpretation are often difficult in part because both contain general principles. In his famous concurring opinion in the case of *Youngstown Sheet & Tube Co. v. Sawyer*, Justice Robert Jackson observed, "A judge, like an executive adviser, may be surprised at the poverty of really useful and unambiguous authority applicable to concrete problems of executive power as they actually present themselves. Just what our forefathers did envision, or would have envisioned had they foreseen modern conditions, must be divined from materials almost as enigmatic as the dreams Joseph was called upon to interpret for Pharaoh" (1952, 635).

Constitutional interpretation often involves looking not only at powers and limits that the Constitution specifically lists but also those that might be implied. Moreover, arguments for adhering to the original intent of the framers are often balanced by the need for the Constitution to be interpreted organically. Political scientist John Compton has argued that evangelical calls for the elimination of slavery, for temperance, and opposing lotteries led to ideas that the Constitution's protections for private property were not as rigid as had hitherto been argued and resulted in part in the shift to the idea that the Constitution should be interpreted more flexibly as a living document (Compton 2014).

See also Covenants, Compacts, Contracts, and Constitutions; Black, Hugo; U.S. Constitution

For Reference and Further Reading

Chambers, Henry L., Jr. 2009. "Biblical Interpretation, Constitutional Interpretation and Ignoring Text." *Maryland Law Review* 69: 92–114.

Compton, John W. 2014. *The Evangelical Origins of the Living Constitution*. Cambridge, MA: Harvard University Press.

Garet, Ronald R. 2009. "With Radiant Countenance: Creation, Redemption, and Revelation." *Michigan State Law Review* 2002: 289–306.

Grey, Thomas C. 1984. "The Constitution as Scripture." *Stanford Law Review* 37: 1–25.

Kalscheur, Gregory A. 2005/2006. "Christian Scripture and American Scripture: An Instructive Analogy?" *Journal of Law and Religion* 21(1): 101–42.

Konvitz, Milton R. 1998. *Torah and Constitution: Essays in American Jewish Thought*. Syracuse, NY: Syracuse University Press.

Levinson, Sanford. 1979. "'The Constitution' in American Civil Religion." *Supreme Court Review* 1979: 123–51.

Pelikan, Jaroslav. 2004. *Interpreting the Bible and the Constitution*. New Haven, CT: Yale University Press.

Youngstown Sheet & Tube Co. v. Sawyer, 343 U.S. 579 (1952).

Corporal Punishment

Although the U.S. Supreme Court has ruled that flogging and otherwise administering corporal punishment to adults violates the Eighth Amendment's prohibition against cruel and unusual punishments, it still permits corporal punishments in schools with appropriate legal safeguards as well as parental use of such punishment as long as it is reasonable and does not qualify as abuse (Englander 1978, 530). Immigrants sometimes find that punishments accepted in their own culture are often prohibited in America, where punishments that leave bruises may be one sign of potential abuse (Rentein 2010). In Sweden the government has outlawed all such punishment, even by parents.

Such corporal punishments appear to be more common in fundamentalist and evangelical households in the United States than within the general population, although it is much more difficult to ascertain whether there is greater child abuse in such groups (Ellison 1996).

In 2016, an Indiana mother was charged with felony abuse of her seven-year-old son after hitting him with a coat hanger, which resulted in thirty-six bruises (Kauffman 2016). The case gained particularly notoriety when the mother sought protection under Indiana's Religious Freedom Restoration Act. Following the lead of conservative Christians, her lawyer cited the passage in Proverbs 23:13–14 that said that striking a child with a rod might save the child's soul. Such punishments may also be based on the idea that "human nature is fundamentally sinful and corrupt" and that "persons who violate God's rules must be punished" (Ellison 1996, 3).

Psychologist James Dobson is among evangelical leaders who not only cites the passage in Proverbs to justify corporal punishment but also relies on the idea that children have a fallen nature that needs to be disciplined, but he is certainly not alone. Pat Robertson thus observed that while "sexual and physical abuse of children is unlawful, immoral, and deplorable," "loving discipline . . . is absolutely necessary" (Robertson 1984).

Ross Campbell, a Baptist clinical psychiatrist, claims that the rod to which Proverbs referred was not a stick with which to hit a child but the rod that a shepherd uses to guide his sheep (Stephens and Gilberson 2011, 132).

See also Dobson, James; Robertson, Pat

For Reference and Further Reading

Ellison, Christopher G. 1996. "Conservative Protestantism and the Corporal Punishment of Children: Clarifying the Issues." *Journal for the Scientific Study of Religion* 35 (March): 1–16.

Englander, Meryl E. 1978. "The Court's Corporal Punishment Mandate to Parents, Local Authorities, and the Profession." *Phi Delta Kappan* 59 (April): 529–32.

Kauffman, Gretel. 2016. "Is the Bible a Defense for Corporal Punishment of Children?" Christian Science Monitor. September 1. https://www.csmonitor.com/USA/Justice/2016/0901/Is-the-Bible-a-defense-for-corporal-punishment-of-children.

Rentein, Alison Dundes. 2010. "Corporal Punishment and the Cultural Defense." *Law and Contemporary Problems* 73 (Spring): 253–79.

Robertson, Pat. 1984. "Is Physical Punishment of Children Allowed in the Bible?" CBN. https://www1.cbn.com/questions/physical-punishment-allowed-bible.

Stephens, Randall J., and Karl W. Giberson. 2011. *The Anointed: Evangelical Truth in a Secular Age*. Cambridge, MA: Harvard University Press.

Course in Miracles, A (Schucman)

A Course in Miracles is a three-volume text, written in the style of the language of the New Testament and first published by the Foundation for Inner Peace in 1976. It consists of revelations that Dr. Helen Schucman (1909–1981), who earned her PhD at New York University and worked at the Columbia University Medical School and its affiliated Neurological Institute, believed Jesus had channeled to her. In compiling this study course, she had the help of Dr. William Thetford (1923–1988), who was also associated with Columbia and with the Columbia-Presbyterian Hospital, Dr. Kenneth Wapnick (1942–2013), and Judith (Rothstein) Skutch (Whitson) (b. 1931).

Similar to the writings of Mary Baker Eddy's *Science and Health*, and often associated with the New Age philosophy, the book stresses that "nothing unreal exists. Nothing real can be threatened. Herein lies the peace of God" (quoted from its opening words by Kestenbaum 2019). Although Schucman was herself somewhat reluctant to have the work published and did not consider herself to be a spiritual prophet, the work has increased in popularity.

Many people become at least indirectly acquainted with the book during the first televised debate among Democrat candidates for president in 2019 when Marianne Williamson, a spiritual advisor to Oprah Winfrey who is one of the movement's most prolific proponents, and the author of *A Politics of Love*, called out Trump and said that her "love" would prevail over his hate. She is an advocate for a new Department of Peace.

See also Alternate Scripture

For Reference and Further Reading

Kestenbaum, Sam. 2019. "The Curious Mystical Text behind Marianne Williamson's Presidential Bid." *New York Times*. July 5.

Taves, Ann. 2016. *Revelatory Events: Three Case Studies of the Emergency of New Spiritual Paths*. Princeton, NJ: Princeton University Press.

Covenants, Compacts, Contracts, and Constitutions

Both Jews and Christians, particularly those in the Calvinist Reformed tradition, put great emphasis on covenants. The Bible mentions covenants between God and Adam (Genesis 1:28–30), God and Noah (Genesis 9:8–17), God and Abraham (Genesis12–17), the people of Israel under Moses (Exodus 19 and 24) and Joshua (Joshua 23 and 24), and God and David (1 Samuel 7). Biblical passages further describe the renewing of the covenant between God and Israel under King Josiah (2 Kings 23:2–3) and under Ezra (Nehemiah 8–9).

The Christian Bible is further divided between the Old Testament (or covenant) and the New, with Christians often interpreted as having a covenantal relationship with God similar to that which God had with Israel. Individuals such as David and Jonathan often entered into covenants with one another. Marriage can further be classified as such a covenant, whereas matters involving property rights are more likely to be classified as contracts, to which an entire area of law is devoted.

God's giving, and the Jewish reception, of the Ten Commandments through Moses is a classic example of a covenant. Modern scholars have demonstrated that this covenant shared the form of so-called suzerainty treaties, between one dominant ruler (the suzerain) and a vassal state (Coogan 2014, 14; however, note Walzer's reservations in 2012, 7). These are usually based on a template that includes the following elements:

- Identification of the two parties to the agreement; in suzerainty treaties emphasis is on the more powerful ruler.
- A historical summary of the relationship between the two parties; in suzerainty treaties emphasis is on what the more powerful ruler has done for his vassal.
- A list of the obligations that the treaty imposes on both parties, especially on the vassal; these require loyalty to the suzerain and prohibit actions against other vassals of the suzerain.
- The invocation of the gods of both parties as witnesses; in the ancient world, the sacred and the secular were intertwined.
- Curses that the gods will bring down if the terms of the treaty are not kept, and blessings that the gods will bestow if they are. (Coogan 2014, 14–15)

The making, or "cutting," of biblical covenants were often accompanied by animal sacrifice.

Puritans came to America believing that they had a special relationship to God, which was epitomized in John Winthrop's speech of 1630 entitled "The Model of Christian Charity," in which he expressed the hope that the Massachusetts Bay Colony would be a "city upon a hill" spreading God's light to others. A similar view had been expressed in the Mayflower Compact (also known as the Plymouth combination) of 1620 and in the Fundamental Orders of Connecticut of 1639. In a tract on "The Necessity of Reformation," which Increase Mather authored for the Boston Synod in 1679, he suggested that one solution to what he viewed as increasing ungodly behavior was for the people of Massachusetts to renew their covenant (Mather 1679, 12–13).

In time, the notion of covenant became secularized into the idea of contract, as expressed in the writings of such English social contract writers as Thomas Hobbes (1588–1679) and John Locke (1632–1704). American colonists further considered the charters that the British king had issued to them as a form of covenant outlining the respective rights and responsibilities of the parties. Even at a time when the British did not have a single written constitution, American colonists clung to their charters as though they were constitutions with the force of law.

In time, many of the elements and expectations that surrounded covenants and contracts were applied first to state constitutions, which states began to draft on the eve of independence from Britain, and then in the Articles of Confederation and the U.S. Constitution. Professor Donald Lutz lists scores of such constitution-like documents in both Britain and America (1980, 129–33).

Whereas the charters that the king issued were between him and the settlers, later constitutions were among the people themselves. Notably, the preamble of the U.S. Constitution begins with the words, "We the people."

In stressing the importance of precedents when deciding in *Planned Parenthood v. Casey* to affirm earlier decisions allowing women to procure abortions during the first two trimesters of pregnancy, U.S. Supreme Court justices Sandra Day O'Connor, Anthony Kennedy, and David Souter chose to refer back to the idea of a covenant. They thus wrote, "Our Constitution is a covenant running from the first generation of Americans to us and then to future generations. It is a coherent succession. Each generation must learn anew that the Constitution's written terms embody ideas and aspirations that must survive more ages than one. We accept our responsibility not to retreat from interpreting the full meaning of the covenant in light of all our precedents. We invoke it once again to define the freedom guaranteed by the Constitution's own promise, the promise of liberty" (1992, 901).

See also City upon a Hill; Fundamental Orders of Connecticut; Mayflower Compact; Puritans; Ten Commandments; U.S. Constitution

For Reference and Further Reading

Allen, Barbara. 2000. "Martin Luther King's Civil Disobedience and the American Covenant Tradition." *Publius* 30 (Autumn): 71–113.

Coogan, Michael. 2014. *The Ten Commandments: A Short History of an Ancient Text*. New Haven, CT: Yale University Press.

Elazar, Daniel J. 1980. "The Political Theory of Covenant: Biblical Origins and Modern Developments." *Publius* 10 (Fall): 3–30.
Elazar, Daniel J. 1992. "Deuteronomy as Israel's Ancient Constitution: Some Preliminary Reflections." *Jewish Political Studies Review* 4 (Spring): 3–39.
Elazar, Daniel, 1995–1998. *The Covenant Tradition in Politics*. 3 vols. New Brunswick, NJ: Transaction Publishers.
Hall, David W. 2003. *The Genevean Reformation and the American Founding*. Lanham, MD: Lexington Books.
Kammen, Michael. 1980. "From Covenant to Constitution in American Political Thought." *Publius* 10 (Fall): 101–35.
Lutz, Donald S. 1980. "From Covenant to Constitution in American Political Thought." *Publius* 10 (Autumn): 101–33.
Mather, Increase [Boston Synod]. 1679. "The Necessity of Reformation." September 10. Boston: John Foster. Evans Early American Imprint Collection. https://quod.lib.umich.edu/cgi/t/text/text-idx?c=evans;cc=evans;view=toc;idno=N00203.0001.001.
Moots, Glenn A. 2010. *Politics Reformed: The Anglo-American Legacy of Covenant Theology*. Columbia: University of Missouri Press.
Planned Parenthood v. Casey, 505 U.S. 833 (1992).
Reimer, Neal. 1980. "Covenant and the Federal Constitution." *Publius* 10 (Fall): 135–48.
Rothman, Rozann. 1980. "The Impact of Covenant and Contract Theories on Conceptions of the U.S. Constitution." *Publius* 10 (Fall): 149–64.
Smylie, James H. 1997. "America's Political Covenants, the Bible, and Calvinists." *Journal of Presbyterian History* 75 (Fall): 153–64.
Walzer, Michael. 2012. *In God's Shadow: Politics in the Hebrew Bible*. New Haven, CT: Yale University Press.
Williams, Rhys H. 1999. "Visions of the Good Society and the Religious Roots of American Political Culture." *Sociology of Religion* 60 (Spring): 1–34.

Creationism and Evolution

One hot-button issue that confronts state and local governments is the teaching of Darwinian evolution in schools. Long accepted in scientific circles as a comprehensive explanation of the origins and variation of life, the theory posits that all life evolved over millions of years through a process of gradual genetic changes, often connected to the process of natural selection, that led from less complex to more complex life forms.

This explanation conflicts with literal interpretations of the accounts of creation in the opening chapters of the biblical book of Genesis, which describe God as creating life, including the first humans Adam and Eve during a six-day period. Literalists fear that casting any doubt upon this timeline might undermine morality by calling humankind's special creation in the image of God into question and raise doubts about other biblical teachings including those related to personal salvation. A group called Answers in Genesis has opened a "Creation Museum" in Kentucky with a replica of Noah's Ark, which is aligned with this view.

There are variations, however, among even fundamentalist interpreters. These vary from the young-earth creationists (YECs), who are most typically associated with the belief that the earth was created approximately six thousand years ago and who believe that dinosaurs existed on the earth as the same time as humans (Scott 2016, 289). This belief was especially associated with Henry M. Morris, who coauthored with John C. Whitcomb an influential book

(*The Genesis Flood*, which was first published in 1962), founded the Institution for Creation Research (ICR), and believed that most geological phenomena associated with a longer time period could be accounted for by the great flood that the Bible described Noah as surviving.

There are, however, at least two versions of old-earth creationism. Gap creationists posit that there may have been a large time period between the opening verse in Genesis that described God as creating the earth and subsequent verses that may describe a re-creation. Other old-earth creationists, drawing from Psalm 90:4, which says that a day is like a thousand years in the sight of God, suggest that the "days" in Genesis may have been of long duration (Scott 2016, 291).

Still others, most represented by main-line Christian denominations, accept theistic evolution, or the idea that God has used evolution and other naturalistic means to bring life on earth to its current state. Because all of these theories are based more on interpretations of Scripture than on scientific experiment, proponents have had little success in introducing them into public classrooms. Terminology has somewhat changed from that of creationism, to creation science, to Intelligent Design (ID) (Wiley 2009, 105). Advocates of the latter have argued that the intricacy of the universe points to a designer, which most ID advocates associate with the Christian God. Advocates have included Philip Johnson, a law professor at Berkeley who authored *Darwin on Trial*, and Michael J. Behe, a biochemist who authored *Darwin's Black Box: The Biochemical Challenge to Evolution*.

The Scopes Trial of 1925 sought to challenge a Tennessee law that prohibited teaching the view that man had ascended from lower life forms, but it ended up being thrown out on appeal on a technicality. Subsequent laws that have sought to prohibit the teaching of evolution, require that it be presented as a mere theory, or that it be balanced by teachings of creation science or intelligent design have failed on First Amendment grounds (Moore, Jensen and Hatch 2003). Thus, in *Epperson v. Arkansas* (1968), the U.S. Supreme Court struck down an Arkansas law that made it a crime to teach evolution in public schools, and in *Edwards v. Aguillard* (1987) it invalidated a Louisiana law requiring the teaching of "creation science" whenever evolution was taught.

See also Edwards v. Aguillard; *Epperson v. Arkansas*; Scopes Trial

For Reference and Further Reading

Edwards. V. Aguillard, 482 U.S. 578 (1987).

Epperson v. Arkansas, 393 U.S. 97 (1968).

Falk, Daniel K. 2016. "Teaching Evolution versus Creationism." *The Bible in Political Debate: What Does It Really Say?*, ed. Frances Flannery and Rodney A. Werline. New York: Bloomsbury T&T Clark, pp. 113–24.

Moore, Randy, Murray Jensen and Jay Hatch. 2003. "Twenty Questions: What Have the Courts Said about the Teaching of Evolution and Creationism in Public Schools?" *BioScience* 53 (August): 766–71.

Scott, Eugenie C. 2016. "Creationism and Intelligent Design." *How Evolution Shapes Our Lives: Essays on Biology and Society*, ed. Jonathan B. Losos and Richard Lenski. Princeton, NJ: Princeton University Press, pp, 284–99.

Wiley, Tatha. 2009. *Creationism and the Conflict over Evolution*. Cambridge, UK: James Clarke.

Criminal Law

The field of criminal law is vast and the history of the Bible is long. Moreover, both overlap in so many particulars with other bodies of law and other holy writings that it is often difficult to ascertain direct influences with complete certainty. There are certainly some areas, however, where the influences are fairly obvious.

Whereas civil law is initiated by private individuals, criminal law is initiated by governments in hopes of securing justice for citizens, and especially for those who have been victims of violence. The system is predicated on human worth and standards of justice. Thus Genesis 9:6 observes, "Whosoever sheds man's blood, his blood will be shed by man, for God made man in His image." By the same token, the biblical practice of establishing six cities of refuge for individuals who had inadvertently killed someone, which is outlined in Joshua 20, is a model for the modern distinction between murder and involuntary manslaughter.

In ancient societies, including some parts of the Old Testament, justice was largely a private affair, with members of a family or tribe seeking retribution or vengeance for crimes committed against them. Although Old Testament laws providing an "eye for an eye" and a "tooth for a tooth" are often portrayed as overly bloodthirsty, they actually had the effect of limiting such retribution by imposing a measure of proportionality. The Eight Amendment of the U.S. Constitution preventing "excessive fines or cruel and unusual punishments" would fulfill a similar goal. This being said, the Old Testament provided the death penalty for numerous offences, for which it would not today be considered appropriate. Indeed, one of the aspects of the Massachusetts Body of Liberties and early laws in the colonies that were patterned on Old Testament laws was their resort to the death penalty.

One of the Ten Commandments attempted to enhance the criminal justice system by forbidding individuals from engaging in false witness. Even today, witnesses in criminal trials who perjure themselves are subject to punishment. This possibility is affirmed by the oath that witnesses take, typically upon the Bible or other holy book, indicating their responsibility to tell the truth, the whole truth, and nothing but the truth. The book of Susanna, which is sometimes added to the book of Daniel, and which Protestants consider to be apocryphal, is based on Daniel's ability to discern a falsehood and thus save an innocent woman from execution. The Sixth Amendment right to confront witnesses would be an instantiation of this concern for discerning truth.

The Constitution delineates few crimes, but in delineating the crime of treason, it follows the biblical guideline, outlined in Deuteronomy 19:15, of requiring the testimony of two witnesses, thus seeking to make sure that individuals who are falsely accused are not convicted.

Although the norm is not directly embodied in the Constitution, criminal courts in the United States and in Great Britain require that convictions be based on evidence "beyond a reasonable doubt." Although this provision is usually interpreted as a means of assuring that innocent individuals are not convicted, it may serve an additional purpose. Professor James Q. Whitman explains that

Matthew 7:1 had instructed, "Judge not lest ye be judged!" (2008, 3). In Christian thought, falsely convicting an individual was considered to be a mortal sin, and jurors who were fearful for their souls would often exonerate defendants on the basis of very slender doubts. The idea of "reasonable doubt" was used to ensure that jurors did not simply acquit rather than accept their reasonability to do their civic duty. Whitman notes that one of the earliest uses of the concept was during John Adams's defense of the British troops involved in the so-called Boston Massacre (2008, 193).

Professor Mark Osler (2013) has argued that the practice of granting the president the power of clemency, or pardon, to law breakers is an expression of a biblical principle. Jeffrie Murphy has further discussed the role of Christian love and forgiveness in the infliction of criminal punishments (2017, 157–63).

There have been some attempts in American history to criminalize behavior based on biblical injunctions (or their interpretations) that have backfired. The most obvious was probably national alcoholic prohibition, which led to widespread evasion, disrespect for law, and overly intrusive means of enforcement. When laws prohibiting legal abortion were in force, they were often evaded through illegal procedures (Skeel and Stuntz 2006, 829).

See also Adams, John; Benefit of Clergy; Capital Punishment; Massachusetts Body of Liberties; Temperance Movement; Ten Commandments; U.S. Constitution

For Reference and Further Reading

Gaffney, Edward McGlynn, Jr. 1986. "Biblical Law and the First Year Curriculum of American Legal Education." *Journal of Law and Religion* 4(1): 63–95.

Methvin, Thomas J. 2006. "Trial Lawyers and the Biblical Basis for What We Do." *Alabama Association of Justice Journal* 16: 21–27.

Murphy, Jeffrie G. 2017. "Christian Love and Criminal Punishment." *Agape, Justice, and Law: How Might Christian Love Shape Law?*, ed. Robert F. Cochran Jr. and Zachary R. Calo. New York: Cambridge University Press, pp. 151–65.

Osler, Mark. 2013. "A Biblical Value in the Constitution: Mercy, Clemency, Faith and History." *University of St. Thomas Law Journal* 9: 769–82.

Skeel, David A., Jr., and William J. Stuntz. 2006. "Christianity and the (Modest) Rule of Law." *University of Pennsylvania Journal of Constitutional Law* 8: 809–39.

Whitman, James Q. 2008. *The Origins of Reasonable Doubt: Theological Roots of the Criminal Trial.* New Haven, CT: Yale University Press.

Crocker, Hannah Mather

Hannah Mather Crocker (1752–1829) of Massachusetts was the granddaughter of the Puritan minister Cotton Mather, and an early advocate for women's rights who published a book on the subject in 1818. Involved in smuggling messages to revolutionary forces in the American Revolution, Hannah married Joseph Crocker in 1779, and they had ten children during their eighteen-year marriage, which ended with his death. Crocker helped found the St. Anne's Lodge as an alternative to the Masons, who did not accept female members. Often ignored because she did not call, like later women's suffragists, for women to vote or to hold public office, she showed an ability to argue for women's equality from the Bible without unduly threatening existing gender norms.

Crocker prefaced her *Observations on the Real Rights of Women, with Their Appropriate Duties, Agreeable to Scripture, Reason and Common Sense* with the passages from Genesis 2:18 and Genesis 2:23: "And God saw it was not good for man to be alone; and he made him an help meet for him.—and Adam said she is bone of my bones, and flesh of my flesh, therefore she shall be called woman" (Crocker 1818, 71).

In her introduction, Crocker indicated her intention to demonstrate "that though there are appropriate duties peculiar to each sex, yet the wise Author of nature has endowed the female mind with equal powers and faculties, and given them the same right of judging and acting for themselves, as he gave to the male sex" (75). Moreover, agreeing that the Genesis account showed that Eve was the first transgressor and was thus during "the Jewish dispensation" under "the yoke of bondage," she believed this had been ended with "the birth of our blessed Savior, which, according to the promise given, was the seed of the woman, that should bruise the serpent's head [a reference to Genesis 3:15]" (75).

Further citing Genesis 2:18–24 in her first chapter, Crocker observed that woman was made from man's flesh, "to make woman of a more refined and delicate nature, by thus causing the original clay to pass, as it were, twice through his refining hand" (77). Suggesting that Adam may not have clearly passed on God's instruction to Eve and that the situation might have been different had he been present when Satan tempted her, Crocker nevertheless suggested that whatever penalty God may have inflicted was mitigated when Mary gave birth to the Savior. In a passage similar to arguments that Sojourner Truth would later make in her "Aren't I a Woman" speech, Crocker observed, "Herein she is exalted, and fully restored to her original dignity, by being the mother of our blessed Lord and Savior Jesus Christ, according to his human nature. This, surely, must place her equal with man, under the Christian system" (82).

Bowing to contemporary expectations, Crocker did not think that women should seek to challenge men in "the manly art of slaughtering fellow-men" (85), but she did think that "women have an equal right, with the other sex, to form societies for promoting religious, charitable and benevolent purposes" (86–87). Although women should not expect to be lawyers or to excel at gaming tables, "no servile dependence on men can be recommended under the Christian system, for that abolished the law of slavery, and left only a claim on their friendship; as the author of their nature originally intended, they should be the protectors of female innocence, and not the fatal destroyers of their peace and happiness" (87).

Relying upon Galatians 3:28, Crocker wrote that "Christianity has exalted women to true and undisputed dignity in Christ Jesus. As there is neither rich nor poor, bond nor free, there is neither male nor female, in the view of that immortality which is brought to light by the gospel" (90–91). The Bible showed this by focusing on women's faithfulness to Jesus and by recounting how they were first to receive the news of Jesus's resurrection (91–92). The Old Testament further recounted the exploits of the prophet Deborah (perhaps somewhat undermining what Crocker had said earlier about women and battle), of Ruth and Naomi, and in the lives of later Christian wives and mothers, including some European monarchs. In America, Mercy Warren, Abigail Adams, Martha Washington, and Rachel Jackson had provided further examples of Christian women who showed their patriotism. Crocker thus observed, "Agreeably to scripture, the corner stone for permanent happiness must be laid in vital piety, or heart religion, reduced to practice" (114), in which capacities she thought women were equal to men. In quoting Joshua 24:15, Crocker included both partners in the determination to "serve the Lord" (116). As the primary teachers of children, it was particularly important for women to receive appropriate educations. Although Genesis had referred to woman as a "help meet [appropriate]" for man, she should be "not only a help meet, but a woman capable of reasoning and giving advice for mutual happiness" (120). Such "reciprocal exchange of kind attentions" will "constitute the permanent love of our neighbor as ourselves, agreeably to the golden rule of equity [Matthew 7:12]" (121).

Historically, women joined the struggle for independence and prayed "for the peace of our American Israel" (125). True Christians join Christ (his prayer at Gethsemane as recorded in Luke 22:2) in saying "not my will, but thine be done," and "Scripture, reason and common sense dictate the divine right is in women, to promote those fine sympathetic affections that will have a tendency to assist, harmonize and sweeten a religious course of life" (128). "As there is no spiritual distinction of sexes, the twin soul shall there [in heaven] join the general choir of all those who are equally redeemed by the precious blood of Jesus Christ, the Lamb of God" (130).

In an appendix, Crocker extolled great men and women of the Bible, with special emphasis on Isaiah's prophecy of the suffering servant in Isaiah 53. She further embraced King Limuel's description of the good wife and mother in Proverbs 31, including his conclusion, in verse 30, that "favour is deceitful, and beauty is vain, but a woman that feareth the Lord she shall be praised" (136).

See also Sojourner Truth

For Reference and Further Reading

Botting, Eileen Hunt, and Sarah L. Houser. 2006. "'Drawing the Line of Equality': Hannah Mather Crocker on Women's Rights." *American Political Science Review* 100 (May): 265–78.

Crocker, H. Mather. 1818. *Observations on the Real Rights of Women, with Their Appropriate Duties, Agreeable to Scripture, Reason, and Common Sense*. Boston: printed for the author. From *Observations on the Real Rights of Women and Other Writings*, 2011, ed. Constance J. Post. Lincoln: University of Nebraska Press, pp. 71–144.

Curse of Meroz

Sometime a single biblical verse becomes the scaffolding upon which an entire issue can be framed. One such example is the so-called Curse of Meroz. It is taken from the prophet Deborah's song as recorded in Judges 5:23, in which she pronounces a curse on a town that did not participate in the battle that she and Barak won against Sisera, who was fighting on behalf of Jabin, the King of Canaan. The verse says, "'Curse ye Meroz,' said the angel of the LORD, 'curse ye bitterly the inhabitants thereof; because they came not to the help of the LORD, to the help of the LORD against the mighty.'"

During the Puritan Revolution, English Calvinists had invoked the curse against those who had refused to join their cause as had later leaders of the First

Great Awakening in America and participants in the French and Indian War (Shalev 2013, 35–36). During the American Revolution, Patriots invoked the Curse of Meroz to cast aspersions on Tory supporters of Great Britain who either joined the British cause or refused to support their fellow countrymen.

Professor Eran Shalev has noted that this analogy was, in turn, entwined with classical republicanism, which associated civic corruption with the decline of republic governments. Through such a lens, Patriots accused their Tory counterparts, like the residents of Meroz, of cowardice and lack of sympathy for fellow citizens. Even after the Revolution ended, some preachers continued to cite the Curse of Meroz to suggest that Tories should not be welcomed in the new republic (Byrd 2013, 88–91). Democratic-Republican supporters of the War of 1812 also applied the curse to those, whom they labeled as "Tories," who had refused to participate in the war (Berens 1978, 155).

See also French and Indian War; Revolutionary War

For Reference and Further Reading

Berens, John F. 1978. *Providence & Patriotism in Early America, 1640–1815*. Charlottesville: University Press of Virginia.

Byrd, James P. 2013. *Sacred Scripture, Sacred War: The Bible and the American Revolution*. New York: Oxford University Press.

Shalev, Eran. 2013. *American Zion: The Old Testament as a Political Text from the Revolution to the Civil War*. New Haven, CT: Yale University Press.

Curses on Cain, Ham, and the Canaanites

There are times when misinterpretations of the Bible can be as significant as scholarly exegesis, especially when the text is being used to buttress an argument.

There are two such texts that were widely utilized in the slavery debate. One derived from Genesis 4, which, ironically, is also the source for the widely utilized statement, "Am I my brother's keeper?" (4:9). The passage describes how Cain slew his brother Abel and was condemned by God to be a wanderer on the earth. Verse 15 also recorded that God appointed a sign for Cain to prevent others from killing him for his offense. In time, Cain's downcast state became translated as a dark state, which became associated with a dark skin color (Goldenberg 2003, 180). Those advocating slavery could thus argue that in enslaving Africans of color, they were simply furthering God's curse. In addition to the problem of translation, however, this passage presented another problem, namely that according to accounts of the flood, all humanity other than the family of Noah were exterminated from the earth.

Here, yet a second misinterpretation took hold. After the story of the flood, the Bible recounts in Genesis 9 that Noah became drunk and that his son Ham, said in Genesis 9:18 to be the father of Canaan (the land that was to be given to Israel), looked upon his nakedness and was subsequently cursed by Noah. He announced, in verse 25, that "a servant of servants shall he be unto his brethren." Notably, this curse said nothing about skin color, but interpretations connecting blackness with slavery apparently originated in Islamic sources (Goldenberg 2003, 17) and were then taken up by Europeans as a rationalization for enslaving

Africans and later repeated by advocates of slavery in America. James A. Sloan, an American Presbyterian minister, thus observed in 1857,

> Ham deserved death for his unfilial and impious conduct. But the Great Lawgiven saw fit, in his good pleasure, not to destroy Ham with immediate death, but to set a mark of degradation on him. . . . All Ham's posterity are either *black* or dark colored, and thus bear upon their countenance the mark of inferiority which God put upon the progenitor. . . . *Black, retrained, despised, bowed down* are the words used to express the condition and place of Ham's children. Bearing the mark of degradation on their skin. (quoted in Goldenberg 2003, 176).

The argument became circular. Black skin was a curse, slavery was a curse, therefore, those who were black deserved to be enslaved. Theodore Dwight Weld was among those who had observed that God's command had not been to enslave, but to kill, the Canaanites (1839, 79).

See also Africana Movement; Slavery; Smith, Joseph; Walker, David; Weld, Theodore Dwight

For Reference and Further Reading.

Haynes, Stephen R. 2002. *Noah's Curse: The Biblical Justification of American Slavery.* New York: Oxford University Press.

Goldenberg, David M. 2003. *The Curse of Ham: Race and Slavery in Early Judaism, Christianity, and Islam.* Princeton, NJ: Princeton University Press.

Weld, Theodore Dwight. 1838. *The Bible against Slavery: An Inquiry into the Patriarchal and Mosaic Systems on the Subject of Human Rights.* 3rd ed. New York: American Anti-Slavery Society.

Cyrus as Political Archetype

In Isaiah 45:1, the prophet describes Cyrus (ca. 599–600 BC–530 BC), the pagan head of the Persian Empire, as "his anointed" because God used him to restore the Jews in exile in Babylon to Jerusalem where they rebuild their temple. There have been at least three uses of this image in U.S. history.

Thus, in justifying the so-called Blackstone Petition, which was presented to President Harrison in 1891 and again to Woodrow Wilson in 1916 urging the reestablishment of a Jewish state, William E. Blackstone argued that the United States should play the role of Cyrus in restoring the Jews to Israel. Blackstone believed that God had chosen the United States for its moral superiority and that God would judge it if it did not carry out this role (Ariel 2014, 43).

When, against the advice of his own secretary of state and many of his top advisors, Harry S. Truman made the United States the first nation to recognize Israel, he too was likened to Cyrus. Thus, when Israel's chief rabbi visited Truman in 1949, he proclaimed to Truman that "God put you in your mother's womb so you would be the instrument to bring about the rebirth of Israel after two thousand years," after which the rabbi read the words from Ezra 1:2, which said, "The Lord God of heaven hath given me all the kindness of the earth; and He hath charged me to build Him an house at Jerusalem, which is in Judah" (quoted in Benson 1994, 21). In 1953, during a visit to the Jewish Theological

Seminary in New York City, Truman further acknowledged that "I am Cyrus, I am Cyrus!" (Benson 1994, 22).

In more recent years, this analogy has become a common trope, especially among evangelical Christians, many of whom support the Trump presidency despite his perceived character flaws (love of money, sexual indiscretions, abusive rhetoric) because they believe God has chosen him for the job.

This analogy has been used more widely in the wake of Trump's decision to recognize Jerusalem as the capital of Israel. Indeed, on March 5, 2018, Israeli prime minister Benjamin Netanyahu sought to further this comparison in flattering Trump during a trip to Washington, DC:

> I want to tell you that the Jewish people have a long memory. So we remember the proclamation of the great King Cyrus the Great—Persian King. Twenty-five hundred years ago, he proclaimed that the Jewish exiles in Babylon can come back and rebuild our temple in Jerusalem. We remember, 100 years ago, Lord Balfour, who issued the Balfour Proclamation that recognized the rights of the Jewish people in our ancestral homeland.
>
> We remember seventy years ago, President Harry S. Truman was the first leader to recognize the Jewish state. And we remember how a few weeks ago, President Donald J. Trump recognized Jerusalem as Israel's capital. Mr. President, this will be remembered by our people throughout the ages. And as you just said, others talked about it. You did it. (Kilgore 2018)

Tara Burton (2018) observed that the Mikdash Education Center in Israel minted what it described as a commemorative "Temple Coin" depicting busts of Trump in the foreground against that of Cyrus behind him with the words "Cyrus–Balfour–Trump Declaration 1917–2017."

The idea that Trump might be a modern-day Cyrus has been conveyed in a film played before the 2018 midterm elections entitled "The Trump Prophecy." It featured a former firefighter named Mark Taylor who claims that in 2011 God revealed to him that Trump would be elected president (Stewart 2018). The film was produced and supported with the help of students and professors at Liberty University where Jerry Falwell Jr. is president. John Fea, who teaches evangelical history at Messiah College, observes that the Cyrus analogy is "the theopolitical version of money laundering, taking Scripture to . . . clean [up] your candidate" (quoted in Burton 2018).

Ralph Drollinger, who leads Bible studies in the White House, is apparently enamored with the analogy not only to Cyrus but also to that of a "king" (Steward 2018). More generally, it is often associated with a wider "Christian nationalist movement" that Katherine Stewart (2018) describes as "authoritarian, paranoid and patriarchal at its core."

From a somewhat different perspective, a Roman Catholic scholar who is particularly pleased with President Trump's policy of seeking to limit abortion has cited Numbers 11:21–34, in which a prophet's donkey conveys God's word. The scholar observed that "God spoke through the donkey to Balaam, just as God may select and employ any vehicle He so chooses, even the morally imperfect, to make His wishes known or to achieve His designs" (Cathey 2019).

In 1990, Vernon Howell took the name David Koresh, from God's favorite king and from the Hebrew word for Cyrus. Three years later, he and most of his followers, known as Branch Davidians, were killed during a government raid of their compound in Waco, Texas (Corrigan and Neal 2010, 217).

See also Koresh, David; Truman, Harry S.; Trump, Donald; Zionism

For Reference and Further Reading

Ariel, Yaakov. 2014. "Biblical Imagery, the End Times, and Political Action: The Roots of Christian Support for Zionism and Israel." *The Bible in the Public Square: Its Enduring Influence in American Life*, ed. Mark A. Chancey, Carol Meyers, and Eric M. Meyers. Atlanta, GA: Society of Biblical Literature, pp. 37–62.

Benson, Michael T. 1994. "Harry S. Truman as a Modern Cyrus." *Brigham Young University Studies* 34(1): 6–27.

Burton, Tara Isabella. 2018. "The Biblical Story the Christian Right Uses to Defend Trump." Vox. March 5. https://www.vox.com/identities/2018/3/5/16796892/trump-cyrus-christian-right-bible-cbn-evangelical-propaganda.

Cathey, Boyd D. 2019. "Abortion, Balaam's Donkey, and President Donald Trump." *The Remnant*. January 22. https://remnantnewspaper.com/web/index.php/fetzen-fliegen/item/4306-abortion-balaam-s-donkey-and-president-donald-trump.

Corrigan, John, and Lynn S. Neal. 2010. *Religious Intolerance in America: A Documentary History*. Chapel Hill: University of North Carolina Press.

Kilgore, Ed. 2018. "Bibi and the Christian Right Agree: Trump Is the New Cyrus the Great." *Intelligencer*. March 5. http ://nymag.com/intelligencer/2018/03/bibi-and-the-christian-right-trump-the-new-cyrus-the-great.html. Accessed March 27, 2019.

Stewart, Katherine. 2018. "Why Trump Reigns as King Cyrus." *New York Times*. December 31. https://www.nytimes.com/2018/12/31/opinion/trump-evangelicals-cyrus-king.html.

• D •

Danforth, John

John Danforth (b. 1936) is a former attorney general of Missouri who served three terms in the U.S. Senate and briefly as U.S. ambassador to the United Nations. After graduating from Princeton University, he earned both a JD and a Masters of Divinity degree from Yale University. In addition to being a public servant, he is also as an ordained Episcopal priest.

Danforth is a Republican who was particularly known for helping Clarence Thomas (a former member of his staff) achieve confirmation to the U.S. Supreme Court. As one whose faith influenced his own political views, Danforth has become increasingly concerned that individuals, especially on the Christian right, are conflating their own political views with those of the Bible.

Danforth frequently cites the second commandment against idolatry in cautioning against making anything other than God the ultimate value in one's life. In a sermon that he delivered at the Harvard Memorial Church entitled "Parables, Priorities, and Politics," Danforth drew on the parable of the pearl of great price, which is found in Matthew 13:45–46, to argue against recognizing anything but God, and the knowledge of God, as this pearl. He thus cautioned that "some popular idols are money and possessions and status. In recent times, we have added politics to the pantheon" (Danforth 2017). In this sermon he recounted how, when he feared losing his seat in the U.S. Senate, his daughter brought him back to reality by saying, "Well Dad, it's not the World Series" (Danforth 2017). In an interview with National Public Radio, Danforth further described the biblical problem of idolatry as "confusing who you are and what you think with who God is and what God thinks" ("John Danforth on Faith" 2009).

In his sermon at Harvard, Danforth identified four issues that he thought were distorting current American politics. They were "the cost of campaigns," "the duration of campaigns," "the media's exaggeration of politics," and "absolutism," which he associated with demands of "dogmatic purity" from both the left and the right as in what he described as "the Armageddon-like quality of the health care debate" (Danforth 2017).

See also Ten Commandments

For Reference and Further Reading

Danforth, John. 2006. *Faith and Politics: How the "Moral Values" Debate Divides America and How to Move Forward Together*. New York: Viking.

Danforth. John. 2015. *The Relevance of Religion: How Faithful People Can Change Politics*. New York: Random House.

Danforth, John. 2017. "Sermon Delivered by Danforth at Harvard Memorial Church: 'Parables, Priorities, and Politics.'" September 27. Posted by Debra Kennard. https://rap.wustl.edu/sermon-delivered-by-danforth-at-harvard-memorial-church-parables-priorities-and-politics/.

"John Danforth on Faith, Evangelicals and Politics." 2009. NPR Newscast. May 8. https://www.npr.org/templates/story/story.php?storyId=103929890.

Danforth, Samuel

See Errand in the Wilderness

David as Political Archetype

Of all Israel's kings, the one who stands out the most is King David, the shepherd king, who first distinguished himself as a teen who smote the giant Goliath with a slingshot, and who subsequently went on to other military victories after succeeding King Saul. Samuel Davies used David as an example of godly public service in a valedictory address to students at Princeton in 1760. King David is also known for committing adultery with Bathsheba and subsequently putting her husband in harm's way in the battle in which he died, leading to God's judgment on David's house that included a rebellion by his son Absalom.

James P. Byrd has documented how during the Revolutionary War, as in previous wars in the colonies, pastors used David for three main purposes connected to the war. First, many drew from David's confrontation with Goliath in 1 Samuel 17 to encourage soldiers not only to be courageous but also to rely upon God (Byrd 2013, 95–103). At times, they further compared the paganism of Goliath to the perfidy of English generals (99).

Second, many pastors drew from the Psalms, many of which David had written, to inspire troops to wartime violence against the enemy at a time when many were more willing to sacrifice themselves than to kill others. David became a prototype of the spiritual warrior. Pastors thus often cited Psalm 114:1: "Blessed be the LORD my strength which teacheth my hands to war, and my fingers to fight." On occasion, pastors even cited Psalm 137:5: "Happy shall he be, that taketh and dasheth thy little ones against the Stones" (Byrd 2013, 106).

A third use focused on David as king. At the beginning of the controversy between the colonies and Parliament, when many patriots were still urging allegiance to King George III, some pastors used David as an example of a man who respected Saul, even when Saul was seeking his life. A famous embroidery from the time depicted "The Hanging of Absalom," who was variously portrayed as a disloyal son and as an archetype of the oppressed colonies (Byrd 2013, 111–12)—thus in the embroidery the individual thrusting a spear through Absalom is dressed as a British redcoat (Hutson 1998, 36). In time, David's oppressive grandson Rehoboam (the third in the line of Davidic kings) became a symbol for George III (Hutson 1998, 112–13).

See also Davies, Samuel; Revolutionary War

For Reference and Further Reading

Byrd, James P. 2013. *Sacred Scripture, Sacred War: The Bible and the American Revolution.* New York: Oxford University Press.

Carmy, Shalom. 2010. "Personal Ethics, Public Virtue, and Political Legitimacy in Biblical Kings and American Presidents." *Presidential Studies Quarterly* 40 (March): 76–89.

Hutson, James H. 1998. *Religion and the Founding of the American Republic*. Washington, DC: Library of Congress.
Vile, John R. [1998]. "David and Ahab, Clinton and Nixon: Contemporary Lessons From Two Biblical Stories." www.leaderu.com/socialsciences/david-ahab.html.

Davies, Samuel

Samuel Davies (1723–1761) was a Presbyterian minister who preached at the church that Patrick Henry attended when he was a youth and who subsequently became president of the College of New Jersey (today's Princeton).

On September 21, 1760, he delivered a valedictory address to the senior class at Princeton entitled "Religion and the Public Spirit," which was published two years later. It centered on Acts 13:36, in which Paul observed, "For David, after he had served his own generation by the will of God, fell on sleep, and was laid unto his fathers, and saw corruption." At a time when American colonists still recognized the British king, Davies used David as an example of public service that his graduates should imitate. Davies thus lauded King David as an example of "PUBLICK SPIRIT and RELIGION," the first of which David performed "*in serving his Generation*," and the latter of which consisted in doing so "*according to the Will of God*" (Davies 1760, 4). He observed that "so inseparable are these united, that the one cannot exist, in the entire Absence of the other. Public Spirit and Benevolence without Religion, is but a warm affection for the Subjects to the Neglect of their Sovereign; or a Partiality for the Children, in Contempt of their Father, who is infinitely more worthy of Love. And Religion without Publick Spirit and Benevolence, is but a sullen, selfish, sour and malignant Humour for Devotion, unworthy that sacred Name" (4–5). Davies observed that the two are as intertwined with biblical admonitions to love both God and man. Davies emphasized how important it was to "IMBIBE AND CHERRISH A PUBLICK SPIRIT" (7). Much as his Puritan forbears would have done, he admonished graduates to "live not for your selves, but the Publick. Be the Servants of the Church; the Servants of your Country; the Servants of all. Extend the Arms of your Benevolence to embrace your Friends, your Neighbours, your Country, your Nation, the whole Race of Mankind, even your Enemies" (7).

At a time when many emphasized the sovereignty of monarchs, Davies connected kingly leadership with servanthood. Such a spirit of servanthood could be manifested whether graduates chose to become pastors, lawyers, or doctors. Graduating seniors would now take the place of service that had been occupied by the many individuals who had gone before them. They should need the admonition of Ecclesiastes 9:10 that "whatever your Hand findeth to do, do it with your Might, for there is no Work, nor Device, nor Knowledge, nor Wisdom in the Grave, whither you are going" (9). Graduates should act like good and faithful servants whom the master would find at work when he returned. Davies extolled the importance of a new birth saying that "THE NEW BIRTH IS THE BEGINNING OF ALL GENUINE RELIGION AND VIRTUE" (13).

It was important for graduates to recognize the brevity of life and to avoid "sensual Gratification" that has been "the Ruin of many a good Creature," just as it was important to guard against "a Life of Idleness and Trifling" (17).

Especially under the presidency of John Witherspoon, Princeton would be a virtual incubator of statesmen for the American Revolution. Professor Donald D'Elia has called Davies's speech "a handbook of Christian Revolution" (1974, 15). Dr. Benjamin Rush was among the graduates who heard Davies's valedictory address.

See also David as Political Archetype; Henry, Patrick; Puritans; Rush, Benjamin

For Reference and Further Reading

Bost, George H. 1948. "Samuel Davies as President of Princeton." *Journal of the Presbyterian Historical Society* 26 (September): 165–81.

D'Elia, Donald J. 1974. "Benjamin Rush: Philosopher of the American Revolution." *Transactions of the American Philosophical Society* 64: 1–113.

Davies, Samuel. 1760. "Religion and the Public Spirit. A Valedictory Address to the Senior Class, Delivered in Nassau-Hall, September 21, 1760. The Sunday before the Commencement." Portsmouth, NH: Daniel Fowle. Accessed at https://quod.lib.umich.edu/e/evans/N07144.0001.001?rgn=main;view=fulltext.

Days of Humiliation, Fasting, and Thanksgiving

The Bible (and especially the book of Psalms) is filled with references to thanksgiving, and fasts were a way that individuals, especially in Old Testament times, often expressed contrition for sins in hopes of averting the wrath of God. The biblical Feast of Tabernacles, known as the Hebrew Sukkot, during which families built booths of palm branches, was designed both to thank God for bountiful harvests and to recall the years that the children of Israel had wandered in the wilderness after they left Egypt on their way to the promised land of Canaan.

After the Reformation, many Protestant denominations replaced most religious holidays with periodic days of fasting and prayer (Jacobs 2015, 286). These were, in turn, often called in response to natural disasters, outbreaks of disease, or military conflicts that they sometimes interpreted as signs of God's wrath, which the people might abate through repentance. In the New Netherland (today's New York) such proclamations often included biblical quotations and metaphors (287). They were to become most common in the New England states, where early colonists declared their own days of humiliation, fasting, and thanksgiving (Seiglie 2010). Although often cited as the prelude to modern Thanksgiving proclamations, they were far more somber affairs; in January 1697, for example, Judge Samuel Sewall used the day to repent of his role in the Salem witch trials (LaPlante 2007).

As the Revolutionary War approached, these precedents were revived in order to stir popular support. Thus, in 1768, the towns of Boston, Braintree, Charleston, and Lexington, Massachusetts, observed a day of fasting and prayer in anticipation of the arrival of British troops, and southern states followed suit in subsequent months, with Thomas Jefferson, Patrick Henry, and Richard Henry Lee being among those advocating the event in Virginia (Davis 2000, 84).

Not long after fighting had begun at Lexington and Concord, the Second Continental Congress issued a call on June 12, 1775, for a fast day for July 20. It was, quite appropriately, authored by John Witherspoon, the president of the College of New Jersey (today's Princeton), the only clergyman who would sign the Declaration of Independence. Although the call for a fast day never directly quoted Scripture, the declaration was clearly grounded in biblical themes. Beginning with a reference to "the great Governor of the world" who "conducts the course of wisdom" and "influences the minds of men," the proclamation went on to "acknowledge his superintending providence, especially in times of impending danger and publick calamity" (Davis 2000, 85). It reverenced "his immutable Justice" and implored "his merciful interposition for our deliverance," which it hoped to secure by "publick humiliation, fasting and prayer" during which the people would "humbly" beseech God "to forgive our iniquities, to remove our present calamities, to avert those desolating judgments with which we are threatened, and to bless our rightful Sovereign, King George the Third" with wisdom (85). The proclamation further expressed the desire "that virtue and true religion may revive and flourish throughout our land; and that America may soon behold a gracious inter position of her invaded rights, a reconciliation with the Parent state . . . and that her civil and religious privileges may be secured to the latest posterity" (85). It recommended "to Christians of all denominations, to assemble for publick worship, and to abstain from servile labour and recreation on said day" (85). On the designated day, Congress attended Jacob Duché's Episcopalian church in the morning and Dr. Francis Alison's First Presbyterian Church that afternoon (86).

In 1777, Congress issued its first thanksgiving proclamation for December 18, substituting praise, thanksgiving, and prayer for fasting. Sometimes attributed to Richard Henry Lee but probably authored in conjunction with Witherspoon (Mailer 2017, 299), the proclamation began with recognition of "the indispensable duty of all men to adore the superintending providence of almighty God," and with hopes that he would "smile upon us in the prosecution of a just and necessary war" (Davis 2000, 86). This proclamation was even more distinctly Christian than the first, indicating that the people may join in "the penitent confession of their manifold sins" and make "their humble and earnest supplication that it may please God through merits of Jesus Christ, mercifully to forgive and blot them out of remembrance" (86). In a similar vein, the proclamation asked for prosperity "to prosper the means of religion, for the promotion and enlargement of that Kingdom, which consisteth 'in righteousness, peace and joy in the Holy Ghost' [a direct quotation from Romans 14:17]" (87).

One fascinating aspect about congressional declarations is that they apparently prompted George III to declare similar days of fasting and prayer in Great Britain beginning in 1776 and continuing each year, other than 1777, until 1781 (Ippel 1980, 45, 54). Even though the king had issued similar proclamations during previous times of distress, his own proclamations appeared to have stirred a fair amount of criticism within Great Britain. Some believed the king was exercising an inappropriate spiritual power, while others objected to invoking God's help in a bloody war, which not all Britons were convinced was morally justified. Interestingly, pastors in Britain on both sides of the controversy used some of the same texts as those in America who also debated the justice of the war. In 1778, Rev. Benjamin Hutchinson, a vicar from the county of Huntington, objected to being asked to pray for killing others (Ippel 1980, 57). In a sermon published as *The Bible and the Sword,*

Rev. John Fletcher thus justified the day by likening it to the reference in Judges 20 of using the sword against fellow Benjamites, compared the prayer to Aaron and Hur lifting the hands of Moses during the battle against the Amalekites as recorded in Exodus 17, and referenced Paul's teaching in Romans 13 that "the ruler is the minister of God to thee for good, bearing not the sword in vain." (Ippel 1980, 57–58).

A Thanksgiving Day Proclamation by Congress on October 16, 1781, written by John Witherspoon, ended with a paraphrase of Habakkuk 2:14 in hoping that peace would "cause the knowledge of God to cover the earth, as the water covers the seas" (Morrison 1999, 572). The Thanksgiving Day Proclamation of October 11, 1782, further referred to "the practice of true and undefiled religion," a likely reference to James 1:27 (573).

The resolutions of the Continental Congress preceded the adoption of the First Amendment, which prohibited the "establishment" of religion, but both Washington and Adams later issued similar proclamations—with that of John Adams (following the New England models with which he was most familiar) continuing to emphasize repentance, and often being interpreted through partisan lenses as attacking the dissension coming from Democratic-Republican opponents (Dickson 1987). Thomas Jefferson, who held stricter views of separation of church and state, decided not to issue such declarations, and Madison did so somewhat reluctantly, in part justifying his decision as responding to the will of Congress (Fleet 1946, 562).

In time, Abraham Lincoln reestablished the precedent for Fast Day and Thanksgiving Proclamations, many of which (likely with slavery in mind) included calls for repentance over national sins. His proclamation of a National Fast Day on March 30, 1863, specifically acknowledged "the sublime truth, announced in the Holy Scriptures [Psalm 33:12] and proven by all history, that those nations only are blessed whose God is the Lord" (Wilkerson 1991). A contemporary Proclamation for a day of public thanksgiving and praise that was issued by Governor John Andrew of Massachusetts cited at least four different passages from the Psalms (Morris [1864] 2007, 717–20). Subsequent presidents have focused on thanksgiving rather than on fasting and repentance, and the holiday is much more likely to consist of feasting and watching parades and sports events (LaPlante 2007). Courts have accepted these proclamations as an innocuous form of ceremonial Deism.

Sometimes state governors issue proclamations, as did Governor Bill Lee of Tennessee when in October 2019 he invited state citizens to join on October 10 "to fast and to pray for God's favor and blessing on the people of Tennessee" (Meyer 2019, 1). It received mixed reviews in part because of its timing, which fell a day after Yom Kippur, the Jewish Day of Atonement.

See also Adams, John; Election Day Sermons; First Continental Congress; Lincoln, Abraham; Puritans; Revolutionary War; Sewall, Samuel; Witherspoon, John

For Reference and Further Reading

Albala, Ken. 2015. "The Other Side of Thanksgiving: Fasting." *San Francisco Chronicle*. November 20. https://www.sfchronicle.com/opinion/article/The-other-side-of-Thanksgiving-fasting-6644328.php.

Davis, Derek H. 2000. *Religion and the Continental Congress 1774–1789: Contributions to Original Intent*. New York: Oxford University Press.
Dickson, Charles Ellis. 1987. "Jeremiads in the New American Republic: The Case of National Fasts in the John Adams Administration." *New England Quarterly* 60 (June): 187–207.
Fleet, Elizabeth. 1946. "Madison's 'Detached Memoranda.'" *William and Mary Quarterly* 3 (October): 534–68.
Ippel, Henry P. 1980. "Blow the Trumpet, Sanctify the Fast." *Huntington Library Quarterly* 44 (Winter): 43–60.
Jacobs, Jaap. 2015. "'Hot Pestilential and Unheard-Of Fevers, Illnesses and Torments': Days of Fasting and Prayer in New Netherland." *New York History* 96 (Summer/Fall): 284–300.
LaPlante, Eve. 2007. "The Opposite of Thanksgiving." *Boston Globe*. November 18. archive.boston.com/bostonglobe/ideas/articles/2007/11/18/the_opposite_of_thanksgiving.
Mailer, Gideon. 2017. *John Witherspoon's American Revolution: Enlightenment and Religion from the Creation of Britain to the Founding of the United States*. Chapel Hill: University of North Carolina Press; Omohundro Institute of Early American History and Culture.
Meyer, Holly. 2019. "Lee's Prayer, Fasting Day Draws Mixed Responses." *The Tennessean*. October 8, p. 1 and p. 11A.
Morris, Benjamin F. [1864] 2007. *The Christian Life and Character of the Civil Institutions of the United States*. Powder Springs, GA: American Vision.
Morrison, Jeffry Hays. 1999. "John Witherspoon and 'The Public Interest of Religion.'" *Journal of Church and State* 41 (Summer): 551–73.
Seiglie, Mario. 2010. "Is Thanksgiving Rooted in Biblical Festival?" UCG.org. November 12. https://www.ucg.org/the-good-news/is-thanksgiving-rooted-in-a-biblical-festival.
"Thanksgiving Day Proclamations 1789–Present." What So Proudly We Hail. https://www.whatsoproudlywehail.org/curriculum/the-american-calendar/thanksgiving-day-proclamations-1789-present.
Wilkerson, David. 1991. "Proclamations of Days of Thanksgiving, Fasting, and Prayer." February 1. https://worldchallenge.org/newsletter/1991/proclamations-for-days-of-thanksgiving-fasting-and-prayer.

Declaration of Independence

In declaring 1983 to be the "Year of the Bible," President Ronald Reagan observed that "biblical teachings inspired the concepts of civil government that are contained in our Declaration of Independence and the Constitution of the United States" (Fea 2014, 65).

The Second Continental Congress adopted a resolution for independence from Britain on July 2, 1776, and then ratified the Declaration of Independence as an explanation of this decision on July 4. Although Congress appointed a committee to draft the document, Thomas Jefferson was largely responsible for writing the first draft. Congress made many changes, including deleting a section charging King George III with responsibility for perpetuating slavery within the colonies. The most notable section of the Declaration is the opening paragraph that claims that "all men are created equal, that they are endowed by their Creator with certain unalienable rights, [and] that among these are Life, Liberty and the pursuit of Happiness." The document further argued that the people have the right to overthrow and replace a government that does not accomplish these rights and included a long list of grievances that the thirteen colonies had against Great Britain, including war atrocities that had occurred since fighting had commenced (Vile 2019).

Many of the arguments, both for and against independence, prior to the writing and adoption of the Declaration had certainly been based on biblical arguments, and Professor Derek Davis has observed "that a majority of the American people would never have endorsed a colonial separation from the mother country unless they believed it had God's sanction" (2000, 95). John Alvis has further noted, "The Congress and conventions in the colonies made clear from the outset their expectation of a document friendly to scriptural religion from whoever should compose a statement of the colonies' separation from the parent country" (1998, 369).

Altogether, the Declaration contains four references to God. The first reference, the only one initially penned by Thomas Jefferson, referred to "nature and nature's God." Benjamin Franklin is apparently responsible for altering Jefferson's statement "that from that equal creation . . . they derive rights inherent and inalienable" to the second reference in the phrase, "they are endowed by their Creator with rights some of which are certain inherent and unalienable," which Congress further changed to "they are endowed by their Creator with certain unalienable rights" (1994, 472). This is certainly consistent with the biblical view of creation as outlined in the book of Genesis but compatible with the views of "deists, Unitarians, and freethinkers as well" (Fea 2016, 132).

The last paragraph of the Declaration, as amended by Congress, includes an appeal "to the Supreme Judge of the world," which is also consistent with the God of the Bible but would also have appealed to those who might not be orthodox Christians but who still believed "that human beings would be judged in the next life for their moral conduct in this one" (Fea 2016, 132). Another reference to the Founders' "firm reliance on the protection of Divine Providence" appealed both to a "theistic" and "deistic" worldview (Davis 1994, 479) of individuals who thought that God was looking out for the revolutionary clause.

R. L. Bruckberger believes the document represented a prudent compromise between the Puritan tradition, as embodied in such documents as the Mayflower Compact, and Jeffersonian Deism, which was evident in his later abridgements of the Bible. Bruckberger observed that "had the Declaration been written in the strictly Puritan tradition it would probably not have managed to avoid an aftertaste of theocracy and religious fanaticism. Had it been written from the standpoint of the lax philosophy of that day, it would have been a-religious, if not actually offensive to Christians" (1949, 93). Bruckberger points out that the Declaration clearly rejected the idea of "divine right," or the notion that God had specifically ordained George III and commanded allegiance to him. In January 1776, Thomas Paine's *Common Sense* had used biblical arguments to discount this doctrine.

Like earlier covenants and contrasts, the Founders signed the document as witnesses to their action.

See also Common Sense (Thomas Paine); Covenants, Compacts, Contracts, and Constitutions; Jefferson Bible; Revolutionary War; U.S. Constitution; Year of the Bible

For Reference and Further Reading

Alvis, John. 1998. "Milton and the Declaration of Independence." *Interpretation* 24 (Spring): 367–405.

Bruckberger, R. L. 1949. *Image of America*. New York: Viking Press.

Davis, Derek H. 1994. "Religious Dimensions of the Declaration of Independence: Fact and Fiction." *Journal of Church and State* 36 (Summer): 469–82.

Davis, Derek H. 2000. *Religion and the Continental Congress, 1774–1789: Contributions to Original Intent*. New York: Oxford University Press.

Fea, John. 2014. "Does America Have a Biblical Heritage?" *The Bible in the Public Square: Its Enduring Influence in American Life*, ed. Mark A. Chancey, Carol Meyers, and Eric M. Meyers. Atlanta, GA: Society of Biblical Literature, pp. 65–79.

Fea, John. 2016. *Was America Founded as a Christian Nation?: An Historical Introduction*, rev. ed. Louisville, KY: Westminster John Knox Press.

Vile, John R. 2019. *The Declaration of Independence: America's First Founding Document in U.S. History and Culture*. Santa Barbara, CA: ABC-CLIO.

Deists

Although categorical labels frequently lead to overgeneralizations, it is common for individuals to assert that the American founders were Christians; it is also common to see assertions that they were largely Deists. In part because of the imprecision of either term, some individuals may have claimed allegiance to both camps. Historian Joseph Waligore thus refers to Benjamin Franklin as a "Christian Deist" (Waligore 2016). Moreover, American founding fathers differed significantly in their beliefs. John Dickinson of Delaware was influenced by his Quaker beliefs; Roger Sherman shared the faith of his Puritan forbears; John Jay would play a major role in the American Bible Society; James Madison studied under John Witherspoon at the College of New Jersey but often kept his faith fairly private; Benjamin Rush believed in the atonement of Christ and most traditional Christian doctrines but appeared to have become a universalist; Alexander Hamilton appeared to have moved from skepticism to faith; and George Washington often used biblical analogies, while rarely referring directly to Jesus in public documents. Thomas Paine, Benjamin Franklin, John Adams, and Thomas Jefferson are generally classified as Deists, although some expressed elements that suggested that they believed God had intervened on America's behalf.

Certainly, by the time of the American Revolution, and in the years that followed, there were numerous Christians who had departed from the strict predestinationist doctrines of John Calvin. Even American revivalists were stressing not only God's grace but also the need for individuals to respond in faith to His calling. Many Christians were also open to the discoveries of natural science, especially as mediated through the lens of Scottish Common Sense philosophy and even the emphasis by the English philosopher Francis Bacon (1561–1626) on empirical proof. Moreover, some advanced the argument that biblical miracles and the fulfillment of prophecies were further evidences of the truth of Christianity.

Although at least one scholar strongly disagrees (Hefelbower 1920, 217), Deism is often associated with the idea of a watchmaker God, who created the universe to operate according to natural law and then largely withdrew, leaving humankind to their own devices. Thomas Jefferson was among those who believed that the harmony of nature was evidence of a divine Creator, although this doctrine would be somewhat shaken in the nineteenth century by Darwin's theory of evolution. Jefferson believed that Francis Bacon, Isaac Newton, and John Locke had helped convert what had sometimes been known as the Age of Faith into an Age of Reason (Lambert 2003, 161).

Consistent with Jefferson's own trinity of mentors, the central tenets of Deism focused on emphasizing reason and nature as keys to the understanding of God. While Christians had long argued that Christianity was reasonable, Deists were more likely to subject Christian beliefs to crucial scrutiny and even to deny the possibility of special revelation, that is, revelation to a particular people like the Jews. Just as Protestants had used Scriptures to question the accumulated dogmas of the Roman Catholic Church, so too Deists subjected Protestant doctrines to similar scrutiny from the perspectives of reason and nature.

This led many to deny most, if not all, miracles in the Bible, often seeking to provide naturalistic explanations for them. Thomas Jefferson notoriously took scissors to the Bible to exclude the virgin birth, the resurrection of Christ, and similar events that appeared to contradict natural laws. Although Jefferson was among those generally classified as Deists who professed great admiration for Jesus's moral teachings, he also believed that St. Paul and others had distorted them. Thomas Paine was among not only those who believed that the Bible contained errors but also those who believed that it was a tale of violence and debauchery. In his *Age of Reason*, Paine thus charged, "Whenever we read the obscene stories, the voluptuous debaucheries, the cruel and torturous executions, the unrelenting vindictiveness, with which more than half the Bible is filled, it would be more consistent that we called it the word of a demon than the word of god. It is a history of wickedness that has served to corrupt and brutalize mankind" (Jauhiainen 2001, 122). Paine also contested the idea that a just God would allow a perfect son to die (122).

Especially at the national level (some states would retain established religions through the early eighteenth century), both orthodox Christians and Deists generally agreed that because religious beliefs involved individual relationships to God, they were the province of individual choice. Thus Christians and Deists could often agree on the importance of religious freedom. Deists, who were particularly concerned about the social utility of religion, also shared with Christians a concern about citizen virtue and a belief in the immortality of the soul and future rewards and punishment (Morais 1932, 435; Dunn 1984, 10–19).

Largely because there had never been a strong establishment in America, American Deism generally lacked the strong anticlericalism that often characterized Deism in France. When the ideas of the French Revolution began to permeate American politics, however, it was common to lump American Deism with its French counterpart and with atheism and for partisans of the Federalist party like Timothy Dwight and Elias Boudinot to suggest that American adherents (generally identified as Jeffersonian Republicans) were going to confiscate Bibles and approve dissolute living (Den Hartog 2015; Schlereth 2013).

See also Boudinot, Elias; *Common Sense* (Thomas Paine); Ethan Allen Bible; Dwight, Timothy; Franklin, Benjamin; Jefferson Bible; Washington, George

For Reference and Further Reading

Boudinot, Elias. 1801. *The Age of Revelation. Or The Age of Reason Shewn to be an Age of Infidelity*. Philadelphia: Asbury Dickins. Reprinted by Power Springs, GA: American Vision Press.

Den Hartog, Jonathan J. 2015. *Patriotism and Piety: Federalist Politics and Religious Struggle in the New American Nation*. Charlottesville: University of Virginia Press.

Dunn, Charles W., ed. 1984. *American Political Theology: Historical Perspective and Theoretical Analysis*. New York: Praeger.

Hefelbower, S. G. 1920. "Deism Historically Defined." *American Journal of Theology* 24 (April): 217–23.

Jauhiainen, Peter D. 2001. "'Reasoning Out of the Scriptures': Samuel Hopkins, the Theological Enterprise, and the Deist Threat." *Journal of Presbyterian History* 79 (Summer): 119–33.

Lambert, Frank. 2003. *The Founding Fathers and the Place of Religion in America*. Princeton, NJ: Princeton University Press.

Morais, Herbert M. 1932. "Deism in Revolutionary America (1763–89)." *International Journal of Ethics* 42 (July): 434–53.

Schlereth, Eric R. 2013. *An Age of Infidels: The Politics of Religious Controversy in the Early United States*. Philadelphia: University of Pennsylvania Press.

Staloff, Darren. 2014. "Deism and the Founders." *Faith and the Founders of the American Republic*, ed. Mark David Hall and Daniel L. Dreisbach. New York: Oxford University Press, pp. 13–33.

Viney, Donald Wayne. 2010. "American Deism, Christianity, and the Age of Reason." *American Journal of Theology and Philosophy* 31 (May): 83–107.

Waligore, Joseph. 2016. "The Christian Deist Writings of Benjamin Franklin." *Pennsylvania Magazine of History and Biography* 140 (January): 7–29.

Dobson, James

Although he was never ordained, Dr. James Dobson (b. 1936), a child psychologist, has been among America's most influential evangelicals. Born to a third-generation Church of the Nazarene minister, with connection to Wesleyanism and the Holiness movement, Dobson earned his undergraduate degree at Point Loma Nazarene University and a PhD in psychology from the University of Southern California and subsequently served on the faculty in its medical school for almost fifteen years.

In 1970, Dobson authored *Dare to Discipline*, which, with a number of his other books, became a best seller. Contrasting himself with Dr. Benjamin Spock and other child psychologists, Dobson argued for strict discipline including corporal punishment. In 1977, Dobson created Focus on the Family, which broadcast throughout the country and eventually amassed a mailing list of six million persons and operated on an annual budget of $150 million (Heltzel 2009, 92). Its political arms were the Family Research Council (FRC) and the Family Research Council Action.

Dobson became a strong defender of the nuclear family, with its firm roots in the Victorian era. It focused on traditional male and female roles, with the husband providing the leadership and the wife taking primary care of the children.

Dobson was particularly concerned with the feminist movement, which he thought was emasculating males, and which he associated with the rise of other social ills, and he opposed adoption of the Equal Rights Amendment. In addition to giving practical advice about child rearing and other family matters, Dobson, influenced in part by Francis Schaeffer, became increasingly concerned about abortion and about the rising acceptance of homosexuality. Dobson was particularly opposed to the recognition of same-sex marriage and concerned about the increasing role of the national government in American life. Dobson included Albert Mohler, the president of the Southern Baptist Theological Seminary, and Richard Land, the president of the Southern Baptist Convention's Ethics and Religious Liberty Commission, on his board (Heltzel 2009, 96).

Dobson appointed Gary Bauer to head the Family Research Council, which sought to influence public policy on behalf of family issues. Presidents, in turn, sought Dobson's advice and appointed him to a number of national commissions.

While speaking with authority as a psychologist, Dobson believed that his primary authority came from the Bible. In pointing to the importance of the family, he often cited Exodus 20:12, which tied honoring parents to a nation's longevity; in arguing for the authority of the father, he pointed to 1 Timothy 3:4–5; and in arguing for corporal discipline, he cited Proverbs 22:15, all of which he put in the context of Ephesians 5–6 (Stephens and Gilberson 2011, 115–16). Dobson often blended Old Testament passages that emphasized both compassion and judgment. Dobson further used Psalm 51:5, "In sin did my mother conceive me," and Romans 3:23, "For all have sinned, and fallen short of the glory of God," to argue that strong discipline was necessary because children were naturally inclined to rebel (Stephens and Gilberson 2011, 125). He found biblical support for his arguments against homosexual behavior in Leviticus 18:22 and 1 Corinthians 6:9–10 (127).

Dobson's advice often ran counter to that of mainstream psychologists, and even some fellow evangelicals questioned some of his interpretations. Ross Campbell, a Baptist clinical psychiatrist, thus argues that Dobson's evocation of the biblical rod was not intended to be a stick to inflict corporal punishment but to be the rod that shepherds use to guide their sheep (Stephens and Gilberson 2011, 132).

Although he no longer hosts Focus on the Family and he and his supporters appear to have lost the fight against same-sex marriage, Dobson's influence remains strong within the evangelical community. Many students participate in Bring Your Bible to School Day (BYBSD), which Focus on the Family established in 2015 as a way of enhancing Christian witness in public schools (Concannon 2019).

See also Corporal Punishment; Same-Sex Marriage; Schaeffer, Francis

For Reference and Further Reading

Concannon, Cavan. 2019. "Every Day Is Already 'Bring Your Bible to School Day." *Religion & Politics*. October 1. https://religionandpolitics.org/2019/10/01/every-day-is-already-bring-your-bible-to-school-day/.

Heltzel, Peter Goodwin. 2009. *Jesus and Justice: Evangelicals, Race, and American Politics*. New Haven, CT: Yale University Press.

Stephens, Randall J., and Karl W. Giberson. 2011. *The Anointed: Evangelical Truth in a Secular Age*. Cambridge, MA: Harvard University Press.

Douglass, Frederick

The Declaration of Independence is often considered to be the nation's birth certificate. Its adoption on July 4, 1776, is celebrated every Independence Day. In the nineteenth century, it was especially common to accompany this holiday with speeches extolling America's founders and likening America to a New Israel.

One of the most profound of such speeches is the one that Frederick Douglass delivered on July 5, 1852. Douglass was a former slave who had authored his *Narrative of the Life of Frederick Douglass, an American Slave*, which contained numerous biblical allusions, in 1845 (Zeitz 1981). As a former slave and contemporary abolitionist, his attitude diverged from the unmitigated praise for America that was typical for such speeches. As he noted in one of his opening paragraphs, "the distance between this platform and the slave plantation, from which I escaped, is considerable."

As an abolitionist, Douglass was intimately familiar with biblical arguments for and against slavery. His speech utilizes a number of biblical references. One of these is a comparison of the Declaration of Independence and American independence to "what the Passover was to the emancipated people of God. It carries your minds back to the day, and to the act of your great deliverance; and to the signs, and to the wonders, associated with that act, and that day." Lauding this fight against external tyranny, Douglass observed that "blindness" characterizes "tyrants, since Pharaoh and his hosts were drowned in the Red Sea."

Douglass praised the bravery and foresight of "the fathers of this republic" who put the interest of the nation above their own private interests. Perhaps with the biblical passage on the Liberty Bell in mind, Douglass further tied Independence Day to the biblical Year of Jubilee, in which debts were to be forgiven and slaves freed.

Having looked to the past, Douglass turned to the present. Paraphrasing 2 Corinthians 6:2 ("behold, now is the accepted time; behold, now is the day of salvation"), Douglass said, "The accepted time with God and his cause is the ever-living now." As heirs to the Revolution, the present generation had its own obligations. Echoing criticisms that Jesus had lodged against the religious leaders of his day, Douglass observed,

> It was fashionable, hundreds of years ago, for the children of Jacob to boast, we have "Abraham to our father," when they had long lost Abraham's faith and spirit. That people contented themselves under the shadow of Abraham's great name, while they repudiated the deeds which made his name great. Need I remind you that a similar thing is being done all over this country to-day? Need I tell you that the Jews are not the only people who built the tombs of the prophets, and garnished the sepulchers of the righteous? Washington could not die till he had broken the chains of his slaves. Yet his monument is built up by the price of human blood, and the traders in the bodies and souls of men shout—"We have Washington to *our father*."—Alas! That it should be so; yet so it is.

Whereas Jesus had proclaimed in Matthew 11:30 that "my yoke is easy and my burden is light," Douglass observed that were he able to bring his gratitude to the "national altar," his own task would "be light, and my burden easy and delightful." However, "This Fourth [of] July is *yours*, not *mine*." It was as if those who had invited him to speak were mocking him.

At this point Douglas quoted almost verbatim the first five verses of Psalm 137, which are generally understood to express the angst of the children of Israel during their captivity in Babylon:

> By the rivers of Babylon, there we sat down. Yea! We wept when we remembered Zion. We hanged our harps upon the willows in the midst thereof. For there, they that carried us away captive, required of us a song; and they who wasted us required of us mirth, saying, Sing us one of the songs of Zion. How can we sing the Lord's song in a strange land? If I forget thee, O Jerusalem, let my right hand forget her cunning. If I do not remember thee, let my tongue cleave to the roof of my mouth.

There is no way of knowing how many of Douglass's listeners might have known that the psalm ends in verse 9 with a blessing upon those who seize the children of the Babylonians and dash their heads against a rock, but Douglass mercifully (and prudently) omitted this from his quoted passage.

In identifying America, rather than an enemy land, as Babylon (Stowe 2014, 145), Douglass described in great detail the horrors of American slavery, the evils of which he said had been justified "in the name of the constitution and the Bible." He further said that slavery is incompatible with the manhood of the slave, which he contrasted, in biblical language, from the creation stories to "the fowls of the air . . . the cattle on your hills . . . the fish of the sea, and the reptiles that crawl." In an argument that Lincoln would later utilize, Douglass pointed out that "there is not a man beneath the canopy of heaven, that does not know that slavery is wrong *for him*." Drawing from the story of the prophet Elijah's encounter with God in 1 Kings 19:11–13, Douglass said that "we need the storm, the whirlwind, and the earthquake. The feeling of the nation must be quickened; the conscience of the nation must be roused" to "the gross injustice and cruelty" of the nation's actions, which are particularly evident in the nation's "*internal slave trade*." Douglass did not mention that God ultimately spoke to Elijah not through dramatic acts of nature but through a "still small voice" of His Spirit.

Douglass again resorted to the language of Jesus (this time from Matthew 23:23), in noting that "Did this law concern the 'mint, anise, and cumin [a reference to tithing]'—abridge the right to sing psalms, to partake of the sacrament, or to engage in any of the ceremonies of religion, it would be smitten by the thunder of a thousand pulpits." Content with the injustices of the fugitive slave law, the church has shown that it "regards religion simply as a form of worship, an empty ceremony, and *not* a vital principle, requiring active benevolence, justice, love and good will towards man." In a criticism of mere formalities that Jesus had repeatedly echoed from the Hebrew prophets, Douglass said that such religion "esteems sacrifice above mercy; psalm-singing above right doing; solemn meetings above practical righteousness." Further echoing Jesus's words about the

Last Judgment in Matthew 25:35–40, Douglass observed, "A worship that can be conducted by persons who refuse to give shelter to the houseless, to give bread to the hungry, clothing to the naked, and who enjoin obedience to a law forbidding these acts of mercy, is a curse, not a blessing to mankind." Returning to his earlier analogy, Douglass noted that "the Bible addresses all such persons as 'scribes, Pharisees, hypocrites, who pay title of *mint, anise*, and *cumin*, and have omitted the weightier matters of the law, judgment, mercy and faith.' "

Douglass proceeded to describe such behavior as blasphemous. Citing a metaphor from the epistles, Douglass said that ministers who support slavery lack "bowels of compassion." Referencing, without citing the chapter and verse (James 1:27), "that *'pure and undefiled religion'* which is from above," Douglass transitioned to the words of Isaiah 1:13–17, again without the specific reference to chapter and verse:

> Bring no more vain ablations; incense is an abomination unto me: the new moons and Sabbaths, the calling of assemblies, I cannot away with; it is iniquity even the solemn meeting. Your new moons and your appointed feasts my soul hateth. They are a trouble to me; I am weary to bear them; and when ye spread forth your hands I will hide mine eyes from you. Yea! When ye make many prayers, I will not hear. YOUR HANDS ARE FULL OF BLOOD; cease to do evil, learn to do well; seek judgment; relieve the oppressed; judge for the fatherless; plead for the widow.

Noting that it was possible to commit sins of omission as well as those of commission, Douglass effectively contrasted the actions of church leaders who taught *"that we ought to obey man's law before the law of God"* to the words of Peter and the apostles in Acts 5:20 when they were called before Jewish religious authorities.

Contrasting the inaction of American churches with respect to slavery and the slave trade with those in Britain, Douglass further contrasted their attitude towards the words of Paul in Athens, in which (Acts 17:26) he proclaimed " 'that, of one blood, God made all nations of men to dwell on the face of the earth,' and hath commanded all men, everywhere to love one another" with American racism. He also compared this racism with the affirmations in the Declaration of Independence that "all men are created equal" and are equally entitled to fundamental rights. In what appears to be an indirect reference to the story of the Garden of Eden in the biblical book of Genesis, Douglass warned that slavery is "a horrible reptile . . . coiled up in your nation's bosom."

In contrast to those abolitionists who thought that the U.S. Constitution gave sanction to slavery, Douglass believed that the framers did not intend to do so. Moreover, rather than give way to despair, he believed that "there are forces in operation, which must inevitably work the downfall of slavery. 'The arm of the Lord is not shortened' [a reference to Isaiah 59:1], and the doom of slavery is certain." God's fiat " 'Let there be light' [Genesis 1:3] has not yet spent its force. No abuse, no outrage whether in taste, sport or avarice, can now hide itself from the all-pervading light."

Douglass ended by quoting a poem from the abolitionist William Lloyd Garrison, which referred to a worldwide "year of jubilee / When from their galling chains set free, Th' oppress'd shall vilely bend the knee."

In 1849, Douglass participated in a debate with Henry Highland Garnet, an African American Presbyterian minister who advocated slave rebellion and was supporting a campaign to raise money to provide Bibles for Southern slaves. Knowing that masters were sending preachers among their slaves to teach that the Bible commanded them to obey their masters, Douglass, who had himself led Sunday school classes when he was a slave, opposed this measure and barely carried the day by a single vote. Douglass's biographer, Frederic Holland, observed that Douglass had actually been inspired to read through Scripture:

> I remember the first time I ever heard the Bible read, and from that time I trace my first desire to learn to read. I was over seven years old; my master had gone out one Sunday night, the children had gone to bed. I had crawled under the center table and had fallen asleep, when my mistress commenced to read the Bible aloud, so loud that she waked me. She waked me to sleep no more. I have found since that the chapter she then read was the first of Job. I remember my sympathy for the good old man, and my anxiety to learn more about him led me to ask my mistress to teach me to read. (Powery and Sadler 2016, 11)

Whereas a number of radical abolitionists had excoriated both the Bible and the U.S. Constitution for upholding slavery, Douglass resisted. He thus , that "It is no evidence that the Bible is a bad book, because those who profess to believe the Bible are bad. The slaveholders of the South, and many of their wicked allies at the North, claim the Bible for slavery; shall we, therefore, fling the Bible away as a pro-slavery book? It would be as reasonable to do so as it would be to fling away the Constitution" (quoted in Harrill 2000, 160). Tying biblical interpretation to constitutional interpretation, Douglass further mused,

> The constitution is pro-slavery, because men have interpreted it to be pro-slavery, and practice upon it as if it were pro-slavery. The very same thing, sir, might be said of the Bible itself; for in the United States men have interpreted the Bible against liberty. They have declared that Paul's epistle to *Philemon* is a full proof for the enactment of that hell-black Fugitive Slave Bill which has desolated my people for the last ten years in that country. They have declared that the Bible sanctions slavery. What do we do in such a case? What do you do when you are told by the slaveholders of America that the Bible sanctions slavery? Do you go and throw your Bible into the fire? Do you sing out, "No Union with the Bible!"? Do you declare that a thing is bad because it has been misused, abused, and made a bad use of? Do you throw it away on that account? No! You press it to your bosom all the more closely; you read it all the more diligently; and prove from its pages that it is on the side of liberty—and not on the side of slavery. (Harrill 2000, 160–61)

See also Constitutional Interpretation; Garnet, Henry Highland; Slavery

For Reference and Further Reading

Callahan, Allen Dwight. 2006. *The Talking Book: African Americans and the Bible*. New Haven, CT: Yale University Press.

Deacon, Andrea. 2003. "Navigating 'The Storm, the Whirlwind, and the Earthquake': Reassessing Frederick Douglass, the Orator." *Rocky Mountain Review of Language and Literature* 47(1): 65–81.

Douglass, Frederick. July 5, 1852. "What to the Slave in the Fourth of July?" TeachingAmericanHistory.org. http://teachingamericanhistory.org/library/document/what-to-the-slave-is-the-fourth-of-july/. Accessed March 25, 2019.

Harrill, J. Albert. 2000. "The Use of the New Testament in the American Slave Controversy: A Case History in the Hermeneutical Tension between Biblical Criticism and Christian Moral Debate." *Religion and American Culture: A Journal of Interpretation* 10 (Summer): 149–86.

Powery, Emerson B., and Rodney S. Sadler Jr. 2016. *The Genesis of Liberation: Biblical Interpretation in the Antebellum Narratives of the Enslaved*. Louisville, KY: Westminster John Knox Press.

Scheil, Andrew. 2016. *Babylon under Western Eyes: A Study of Allusion and Myth*. Toronto: University of Toronto Press.

Shulman, George. 2008. *American Prophecy: Race and Redemption in American Political Culture*. Minneapolis: University of Minnesota Press.

Stowe, David W. 2014. "History, Memory, and Forgetting in Psalm 137." *The Bible in the Public Square: Its Enduring Influence in American Life*, ed. Mark Chancey, Carol Meyers, and Eric M. Meyers. Atlanta, GA: Society of Biblical Literature, pp. 137–57.

Zeitz, Lisa Margaret. 1981. "Biblical Allusion and Imagery in Frederick Douglass' 'Narrative.'" *CLA Journal* 25 (September): 56–64.

Dow, Lorenzo

Methodist evangelist Lorenzo Dow (1877–1834) provides an example of what Nathan Hatch has described as "both a holy man, who cultivated the image of John the Baptist, and a radical Jeffersonian, who could begin a sermon by quoting Thomas Paine" (1989, 36). Traveling thousands of miles a year and giving numerous sermons, Dow condensed many of his sentiments into his "Analects upon Natural, Social, and Moral Philosophy," which, when published in his collected works, was already in its seventh edition.

Although the opening pages of this essay contained some references to Scripture, they relied far more heavily on the principles of natural rights as articulated in the Declaration of Independence as Dow distinguished between personal rights, social rights, and moral rights. Dow was a strong advocate of religious liberty, which he thought was a much stronger concept than mere religious "toleration": "Intolerance assumes to itself the *right* of withholding *liberty of conscience*. '*Toleration*' assumes the *right* of *granting* it. Both are *despotisms* in their nature. Man worships not himself but his *Maker*; and the liberty of conscience which he claims, is not for the service of himself but of his God" (Dow 1851, 425). Citing numerous Scriptures that showed man's obligations to God, Dow identified religious establishments, including Protestant ones, with the "*Whore of Babylon*" and "*Mother of Harlots*" identified in the biblical book of Revelation (427).

The book of Genesis indicates that God created man in His own image. Moreover, "all men are born *equal*, and with equal natural rights" (429). In arguments that were similar to those that Thomas Paine had articulated in *Common Sense,* Dow argued that the idea of patriarchy is more a matter of custom than a basis for monarchical government, which the Israelites created only in an attempt to imitate the pagan nations around them (430–31). The idea that one generation could be bound, through the doctrine of hereditary succession, to a choice that had been made many generations before them was ludicrous and "inconsistent, both with Scripture and Common Sense" (432). The Emperor Constantine's attempt to make Christianity into the state religion of Rome led to the eventual elevation of the pope and the doctrine of papal infallibility.

In language similar to that which Puritans had employed, Dow considered it providential that God had allowed the discovery of "an uncultivated wilderness" in which "a new world appears" as a "theatre, designed by the governor of the Universe, for the display of some *important* and *grand design,* worthy of *Himself*" (436–37). Although early Puritans persecuted fellow Christians, individuals like William Penn and Lord Baltimore allowed for the free exercise of religion that allowed the "'Moral Law' of Love" to prevail (446). The American Revolution, in its turn, brought about the establishment of republican government in which officials are elected to serve the people and to return to them after their terms expired.

Dow diverged a bit from his main theme in outlining his thoughts on punishments, which he thought could best be carried out through a penitentiary system that adjusted punishments to crimes and which furthered the moral reform of prisoners. Returning to wider political themes, Dow observed, "As it is nowhere said, that Nations in their political capacity, shall be judged in futurity—political evils must be punished here," a principle that he illustrated with reference to both biblical and secular history (451–52).

Christ's Great Commission is to spread the gospel to all nations, and yet even in American homes with Bibles, "many are unacquainted with experimental religion; and even ignorant of the very first principles of the doctrines of Christ" (454). The character of Jehovah, as manifested in Christ, is consistent with "Justice," "Righteousness," "Goodness," "Wisdom," and "Mercy," and Scripture reveals that God rewards and punishes nations with regard to their adherence or departure from such virtues (456–57). "Christ is the MERITORIOUS *cause* of our *redemption*" but "FAITH is the *instrumental cause* of our SALVATION" (459). "Thus the true light of moral *virtue* came by *Revelation,* and is enjoyed by *divine inspiration,* operating on the heart, which all men are under the *restraining* influence of, in a greater or less degree, until the day of their visitation be past" (462).

Reiterating the need for religious freedom and lauding the end of the slave trade, Dow was quite optimistic about America's future: "The spirit of *inquiry,* the spirit of *missionary* is prevailing, together with the translation of the *scriptures* into so many new *languages. Bible societies* are forming to disperse the holy scriptures. Priestcraft is falling, and the power and influence of the established, corrupt, and wicked clergy, is broken and tumbling down. Crown heads are going out of date" (464). Dow believed the "seventh trumpet" outlined in the biblical book of Revelation might already be sounding (465), and ended with literally pages of Scriptures from throughout the Bible, most with millennial themes, ending with Jesus's commission to spread the gospel throughout the world (478).

See also Common Sense (Thomas Paine); Declaration of Independence; Judgment

For Reference and Further Reading

Dow, Lorenzo. 1851. "Analects upon Natural, Social, and Moral Philosophy." 7th ed., enlarged, *History of Cosmopolite: Or, The Writings of Rev. Lorenzo Dow: Containing His Experience and Travels, in Europe and America, Up to Near His Fiftieth Year*. N.p.: J.B. Smith, pp. 417–78.
Hatch, Nathan O. 1989. *The Democratization of American Christianity*. New Haven, CT: Yale University Press.

Dulles, John Foster

John Foster Dulles (1888–1959) was a lawyer who served as secretary of state under President Dwight D. Eisenhower from 1953 until 1959. Born to a father who was a Presbyterian minister and later a seminary professor, Dulles also had a legacy from his grandfather and an uncle, both of whom had served as secretaries of state. Dulles served under the latter, Robert Lansing, at the Versailles Peace Conference at the end of World War I.

Dulles earned his undergraduate degree at Princeton and his law degree at George Washington University and rose to head the New York City law firm of Sullivan and Cromwell, where he specialized in international law. He became an advisor to Republican presidential candidate Thomas Dewey and to U.S. senator Arthur H. Vandenberg, who was influential in establishing the United Nations.

Although Dulles criticized the use of the atomic bomb in Japan, as Eisenhower's secretary of state, he opposed the prior policy of containment and advanced the policy of threatening massive nuclear retaliation to deter communist aggression. Dulles, who was a fiscal conservative, also believed this was much cheaper than building up sufficient military forces for all contingencies.

Prior to becoming secretary of state, Dulles had participated in a number of Christian ecumenical efforts including heading a Commission on a Just and Durable Peace, which had been sponsored by the Federal Council of Churches (FCC), where he had advocated a new international body that would be stronger than the existing League of Nations (Wilsey 2015, 129). Dulles had also attended the conference on "Church, Community and State," which had been held at Oxford in 1937, and where he had advanced the idea that churches could advance peaceful change because they had a higher loyalty than did individual nation-states. Dulles had defended Harry Emerson Fosdick against charges that he was too modernist and cited Fosdick's argument that Jesus was "everlastingly right" in revealing the truth and its positive impact on politics (Dulles 1960, 53).

Much as John Winthrop had done when he envisioned his colony as a city upon a hill, Dulles thus applied Jesus's words in Matthew 5:16 to "let your light so shine before men, that they may see your good works" (Dulles 1960, 55). Similarly, in a paraphrase of Matthew 6:33, to which he often referred, Dulles observed, "It was said by Christ that material things would be added unto those who seek first the Kingdom of God and his righteousness" (60).

A collection of Dulles's writing indicates that he was guided by five major principles, each of which was arguably biblically based: the reality of the moral law; a belief that human beings were children of God, who were made in His image; the importance of the teachings of Jesus; the obligation to act; and the necessity of faith (Van Dusen in Dulles 1960, xviii–xx).

In a speech at Indiana University on "Patriotism and the American Tradition," which he gave on June 12, 1955, Dulles indicated that his favorite Bible verse was Hebrews 12:1, which said, "Seeing that we are compassed about by so great a cloud of witnesses, let us run with endurance the race that is set before us" (Dulles 1960, 39). Toward the end of this speech, he further cited the admonition of Romans 15:1 that "we are all members of one another and that those who are strong ought to bear the infirmities of the weak" (42).

Dulles believed that one of America's greatest weapons was its spiritual heritage, based on the Bible and on principles articulated in the Declaration of Independence and *The Federalist Papers*. He was thus a strong advocate of American exceptionalism and the necessity of basing politics on the moral law. In speaking of "Our Spiritual Heritage" in 1947, Dulles observed, "The moral law is sublimely reflected by the Ten Commandments and by the injunctions [Matthew 22:37, 39]: 'Thou shalt love the God with all they heart, and with all thy soul, and with all thy mind' and 'Thou shalt love thy neighbor as thyself' " (67). Although he further noted that Christians opposed imposing their faith through "violence, coercion and deceit" (68), his rhetoric framed the Cold War as a Manichean contest between Christianity and atheism, which critics thought led to excessive moralism and rigidity.

See also American Exceptionalism; City upon a Hill; Communism and Anti-Communism

For Reference and Further Reading

Dulles, John Foster. 1960. *The Spiritual Legacy of John Foster Dulles: Selections from His Articles and Addresses*, ed. with introduction by Henry P. Van Dusen. Philadelphia: Westminster Press. Van Dusen's introductory essay is from pp. xi–xxii.

Mulder, John M. 1971. "The Moral World of John Foster Dulles: A Presbyterian Layman and International Affairs." *Journal of Presbyterian History* 49 (Summer): 157–82.

O'Gorman, Ned. 2012. *Spirits of the Cold War: Contesting Worldviews in the Classical Age of American Security Strategy*. East Lansing: Michigan State University Press.

Wilsey, John D. 2015. *American Exceptionalism and Civil Religion: Reassessing the History of an Idea*. Downers Grove, IL: IVP Academic.

Dwight, Timothy

An influential Congregational minister who was born in Northampton, Massachusetts, Timothy Dwight (1752–1817) served as a chaplain of the Connecticut Brigade during the Revolutionary War and subsequently wrote an epic narrative of eleven books entitled *The Conquest of Canaan* (1785) seeking to describe American history, before succeeding Ezra Stiles as president of Yale in 1795.

A strong defender of the Connecticut establishment, which included a state church, Dwight became increasingly concerned about what he perceived to be the rise of unbelief, which he, and pastor Jedidiah Morse, associated with the French philosophes and the Revolution that followed. Dwight frequently mixed politics and religion in both his sermons and his speeches to students. On July 4, 1798, he delivered one of his most famous published sermons entitled *The Duty of Americans at the Present Crisis*. At the time, the United States was being led by Federalist John Adams, who was in an undeclared war at sea with the French while supporting the Alien and Sedition Acts that were designed to mute public criticism of the government and decrease immigrant support for the Democratic-Republican Party, which came into power in 1801 with the election of Thomas Jefferson, whom many Federalists believed to be a Deist or infidel.

Dwight's sermon is a notable example of how the clergy, especially in New England, often interpreted American history in light of that of Israel, often while relying on biblical prophecies. In Dwight's case, he chose as a text Revelation 16:12–16, which described the pouring out of the sixth vial of judgment upon the ungodly and the evil spirits (described as frogs), which they unleashed. Dwight focused specifically on the words of verse 15, which proclaimed of Christ, "Behold I come as a thief: Blessed is he that watcheth, and keepeth his garments, lest he walk naked, and they see his shame." Interestingly, Dwight told his audience that instead of canvassing prior interpretations of this passage, "I shall . . . state to you that, which appears to me to be its true meaning."

Believing that the passage spoke of the destruction of ancient Babylon by diverting a river, he believed that Babylon was a figurative symbol for future events, and that it was important to follow the biblical injunction in 1 John 4:1 to "Test the spirits." Dwight believed that each of the periods described in Revelation corresponded roughly to 180-year periods that began at about AD 800; (he thought the sixth vial had in turn begun at about 1687 (which would have been near the beginning of the reign of William and Mary). He believed this time had witnessed the weakening of the Jesuits (Protestants often associated the papacy with Babylon) and the weakening of other "Antichristian secular powers." It had, however, also witnessed the rise of "irreligion and atheism," associated with Voltaire, the philosophes, Masonic societies, and the Order of Illuminati in Bavaria. He associated these developments with mockery of God, denigration of government, the undermining of private property, unchastity, and a host of other evils. Individuals needed to clothe themselves with righteousness to combat the nakedness of such sins.

Dwight advanced five steps that Christians need to take. First, they need to engage in "private, personal obedience and reformation of life; personal piety, righteousness, and temperance." Indeed, he argued "that personal obedience and reformation is the foundation, and the sum, of all national worth and prosperity." Second, he thought that it was important to maintain observance of the Sabbath. Observing that "Religion and Liberty are the two great objects of defensive war," Dwight said that "if our religion were gone, our state of society would perish with it; and nothing would be left, which would be worth defending." Third, he believed that it was important for Christians to separate from infidels, especially those who burned Bibles and otherwise mocked religion. Fourth, he thought it was important to promote national unity. In a biblical analogy from Matthew 12:25 that Abraham Lincoln would later use, Dwight observed that "a house, a kingdom, divided against itself cannot stand." Finally, he thought that it was important to display "unshaken firmness in our opposition." Citing a biblical phrase from Galatians 5:1 that had been popular during the American Revolution, he argued, "We fight for that, for which we can pray. We fight for the lives, the honor, the safety, of our wives and children, for the religion of our fathers, and for the liberty, 'with which Christ hath made us free.'"

Dwight contrasted the "hardy face of freemen, uncorrupted by luxury, unbroken by despotism; enlightened to understand their privileges, glowing with independence, and determined to be free, or die: men who love, and who will defend their families, their country, and their religion." They need not "trust in chariots and in horses" but in "the Lord our God." Lauding Washington, Dwight believed that "you will find scarcely less glorious and wonderful proofs of divine protection and deliverance, uniformly administered through every period of our existence as a people, than shone to the people of Israel in Egypt, in the wilderness and in Canaan." He further anticipated "the conversion of the heathen," the end to slavery, and the decline of Islam and quoted from Nahum 1:2–6 in believing that God's vengeance would wipe out all ungodliness.

Not surprisingly, John Leland and others at odds with the Connecticut establishment defended the Democratic-Republican position, which was more charitable to France (Den Hartog 2015, 61). Pointing to the conspiratorial nature of so much of the thinking of Dwight and Morse, Jonathan Den Hartog (2015) believes that Dwight, Morse, and other Federalist preachers "overplayed their hand" and that their "moderation" failed them much as it failed Adams when he supported the Alien and Sedition Acts.

Dwight continued to be at loggerheads with the Democratic-Republican Party and responded to the call for a national day of prayer and fasting with a series of four sermons in which he accused his countrymen of straying from the faith of their fathers, which he attributed not only to the infidelity of Voltaire and other French intellectuals but also to the rise of party spirit (Imholt 2013, 79–80). He attributed the latter in part to the fact that "we formed our Constitution without acknowledgment of GOD" (quoted in Imholt 2013, 80). Dwight was especially distressed that the war would again involve the United States on the side of France. As distressed as he was by the war, Dwight continued to maintain his postmillennialist view that the universal proclamation of the gospel would ultimately lead to the establishment of Christ's kingdom on earth (Imholt 2013, 83).

See also Adams, John; America as New Israel; Jefferson Bible; Leland, John

For Reference and Further Reading

Berk, Stephen E. 1974. *Calvinism versus Democracy: Timothy Dwight and the Origins of American Evangelical Orthodoxy*. Hamden, CT: Archon Books.

Den Hartog, Jonathan J. 2015. *Patriotism & Piety: Federalist Politics and Religious Struggle in the New American Nation*. Charlottesville: University of Virginia Press.

Dwight, Timothy. July 4, 1798. "The Duty of Americans, at the Present Crisis." https://www.consource.org/document/the-duty-of-americans-at-the-present-crisis-by-timothy-dwight-1798-7-4/. Accessed April 10, 2019.

Imholt, Robert J. 2013. "The Fast Day Sermons of Timothy Dwight." *Connecticut History Review* 52 (Spring): 75–85.

• E •

Eagle as American Symbol

Especially prior to the rise and popularity and the standardization of the U.S. flag, one of America's most ubiquitous symbols has been the American Eagle. The Great Seal of the United States thus depicts an eagle with outstretched wings below a heaven of thirteen stars with a red, white, and blue shield on its chest and clutching an olive branch in one talon and arrows in the other.

Historian David Hackett Fischer has observed that, before settling on the eagle, America had considered the adoption of numerous other animal symbols. These had included the buffalo, the white-tailed deer, and the beaver. He noted that southerners often "preferred to think of themselves as coiled rattlesnakes, angry hornets, infuriated alligators, and snarling wildcats" (2005, 148). Benjamin Franklin suggested the turkey.

The eagle was eventually adopted for a number of reasons. It was a strong bird and could fly high, thus representing both strength and aspiration. Southerners viewed the eagle as "a symbol of honor," while Native Americans saw it as a sign of "courage and strength" (150).

There was, however, also a biblical connection. Fischer observes that the eagle was the figurehead on the *Arbella*, which brought John Winthrop to America and a symbol of "John the Evangelist, and of evangelical Christianity in general" (150). The Bible contained numerous references to similar birds of prey, and a popular verse in America was Isaiah 50:31, which proclaimed that "they that wait upon the LORD shall renew their strength; they shall mount up with wings as eagles; they shall run, and not be weary; and they shall walk, and not faint." Revelation 12:14 further described a woman in great distress (a symbol sometimes appropriated by the Puritans) who was "given two wings of a great eagle, that she might fly into the wilderness, into her place, where she is nourished for a time, and times, and half a time, from the face of the serpent." Samuel Sherwood used this verse in the sermon "The Church's Flight into the Wilderness," which he published in January 1776.

Fischer has observed that depictions of the eagle have varied in U.S. history, with wars typically resulting in more bellicose portrayals than peacetime (2005, 151). When the Apollo 11 mission went to the moon, the crew modified an eagle on the patch designed to symbolize the mission by placing an olive branch in its mouth (Wilson 1984, 222); this symbol of peace originates from the branch that a dove brought to Noah's Ark after the flood as recorded in Genesis 8:11.

See also Puritans; Sherwood, Samuel

For Reference and Further Reading

Fischer, David Hackett. 2005. *Liberty and Freedom*. New York: Oxford University Press.

Wilson, Charles Reagan. 1984. "American Heavens: Apollo and the Civil Religion." *Journal of Church and State* 26 (Spring): 209–26.

Edwards, Jonathan

Jonathan Edwards (1703–1758) was one of America's foremost Congregationalist ministers and theologians. A Connecticut-born graduate of Yale University who spent many years as a pastor in Northampton, Massachusetts, where he also ministered to Native American Indians, he was chosen to head the University of New Jersey (today's Princeton). Edwards is perhaps best known for his sermon "Sinners in the Hands of an Angry God," which is associated with America's First Great Awakening and which depicted unregenerate human beings suspended like spiders over hell fire simply awaiting God's wrath against their sins. This revival, which was accompanied with vivid physical manifestations, is often credited with awakening and empowering common people not only to their own spiritual condition but also to the necessity to promote public righteousness.

An orthodox Calvinist who was familiar with the major theological, scientific, and philosophical writings of his day, Edwards had a high view of Scripture, even when, as in the case of miracles, it appeared in conflict with human reason. At the time of his death, he was working on a *History of the Work of Redemption* and on *The Harmony of the Old and New Testaments* (Marsden 2003, 473).

In 1729, Edwards delivered a fast day sermon entitled "Sin and Wickedness Bring Calamity and Misery," which indicated that personal and public well-being were connected. He used as his text Proverbs 14:34: "Righteousness exalteth a nation: but sin is a reproach to any people." Pointing to the need for citizens and leaders who pursued common interests and rendered impartial judgments, Edwards noted,

> 'Tis God's manner to bring calamities and misery upon a people in judgment for the prevalence of [wickedness amongst them]. 'Tis as God has threatened in his holy Word: God rewards a public righteousness with public rewards and punishes public iniquity with [public judgments], which can be done only in this world. In another world, mankind will be rewarded and punished only as particular persons, for the bonds by which they are united in societies will then be dissolved. Though the guilt of all the sin that is in a nation lies upon particular persons, so that it will all be punished in another world, yet a people are punished as a people only in this world, though it may be with spiritual judgments. The prosperity or adversity of a people in this world is much more universally according to the prevalence [of wickedness amongst them] than [the wickedness] of a particular person. (Edwards 2015, 40)

As a Puritan, Edwards believed strongly in covenantal relationships to God. He also had a strong belief in America's providential destiny. This theme is evident in Edwards's extended defense of the Great Awakening, which had stirred displeasure among "Old Light" Puritans, who were concerned about the emotional outbursts with which it was often associated. Headed with the text of Isaiah 40:3, "Prepare ye the way of the Lord, make straight in the desert a high way for our God," Edwards cited numerous Scriptures that depicted the Awakening as a work of God's Holy Spirit. Moreover, he argued that the revival should not be judged simply by whether individuals liked or disliked the emotional responses that it engendered in converts but according to Scriptures. He thus charged that "many are guilty of not taking the Holy Scriptures as a sufficient and whole rule, whereby to judge of this work" ([1742], 7). In seeking to justify the revival, Edwards put particular emphasis on its positive effect upon young people who had largely forsaken "their frolicking, vain company keeping, night walking, their mirth and jollity, their impure language and lewd songs" and, along with adults, altering their "drinking, tavern-haunting, profane speaking, and extravagance in apparel" (20). Because of the revival, "through the greater part of New England, the Holy Bible is in much greater esteem and use than before" (20) and "poor Indians" and "poor Negroes" had been enlightened (21).

Edwards believed that the Reformation had marked the beginning of the defeat of the Antichrist, whom he associated with the Roman Catholic Church (Marsden 2003, 90), and although he would later express concern over the backsliding from such behaviors, Edwards hoped that the revival might be the beginning of God's work in America. Drawing from Isaiah 60:9, "Surely the isles shall wait for me and the ships of Tarshish first, to bring my sons from afar," which had also inspired Christopher Columbus, Edwards believe that these isles might well be America. Noting that God had created "two great habitable continents, far separated one from the other," he believe that God may well be preparing the new world for the dawn of "the *new heavens and new earth*" ([1742], 33). Just as the biblical Rachel had birthed Joseph and Benjamin after Leah had brought forth Judah and his brothers, so too the new continent might now have its role: "The other continent has slain Christ, and has from age to age shed the blood of the saints and martyrs of Jesus, and has often been as it were deluged with the church's blood. God has therefore probably reserved the honors of building the glorious temple to the daughter that has not shed so much blood, when those times of the peace, prosperity, and glory of the church, typified by the reign of Solomon, shall commence" (34).

Seeing this as establishing a proper balance between the two continents, Edwards observed, "When God is about to turn the earth into a paradise, he does not begin his work where there is some good growth already, but in the wilderness, where nothing grows, and nothing is to be seen but dry sand and barren rocks; that the light may shine out of darkness, the world be replenished from emptiness, and the earth watered by springs from a droughty desert; agreeable to many prophecies of Scripture, as Isa 32:15" (34), others of which he proceeded to delineate. It is easy to see how later Americans might convert some of these millennial expectations from the church to the nation, which they saw as combatting the evil presence of monarchy and tyranny in the Old World.

See also Antichrist; Columbus, Christopher; Covenants, Compacts, Contracts, and Constitutions; Judgment; Prophets and Jeremiads; Puritans

For Reference and Further Reading

Bercovitch, Sacvan. 1968. "The Typology of America's Mission." *American Quarterly* 30 (Summer): 135–55.

Edwards, Jonathan. [1742]. *Some Thoughts Concerning the Present Revival of Religion in New England and the Way in Which It Ought to Be Acknowledged and Promoted, Humbly Offered to the Public in a Treatise on That Subject.* http://www.revival-library.org/index.php/catalogues-menu/1725/some-thoughts-concerning-the-present-revival-of-religion-in-new-england.

Edwards, Jonathan. 2015. "Sermon: 'Sin and Wickedness Bring Calamity and Misery' (1729)." *The Other Jonathan Edwards: Selected Writings on Society, Love, and Justice,*

ed. Gerald McDermott and Ronald Story. Amherst: University of Massachusetts Press, pp. 35–41.
Frykholm, Amy. 2016. *Christian Understandings of the Future: The Historical Trajectory*. Minneapolis, MN: Augsburg Fortress.
Marsden, George M. 2003. *Jonathan Edwards: A Life*. New Haven, CT: Yale University Press.
McDermott, Gerald R. 1991. "Jonathan Edwards, the City on a Hill, and the Redeemer Nation: A Reappraisal." *American Presbyterian* 69 (Spring): 33–47.

Edwards v. Aguillard (1987)

In *Edwards v. Aguillard*, the U.S. Supreme Court upheld decisions by a U.S. district court and a U.S. court of appeals striking down Louisiana's "Balanced Treatment for Creation-Science and Evolution-Science in Public School Instruction" Act as a violation of the establishment clause of the First Amendment as applied to the states through the due process clause of the Fourteenth Amendment. The law did not require public schools to teach evolution, but it did mandate that if a school taught evolution, it also had to teach creation science. All three major monotheistic religions (Judaism, Christianity, and Islam) have taught that God is the creator and sustainer of the universe, although many proponents of these faiths believe that, in the case of life, God may have worked through evolutionary processes. Advocates of creation science typically interpret the opening chapters of the biblical book of Genesis literally, with some believing that God created everything within six days, thus making the earth much younger that most scientists traditionally believe.

In a decision authored by Justice William Brennan, the Court's 7-to-2 majority applied the so-called Lemon Test, which requires that laws challenged as violating the establishment clause must have a clear secular legislative purpose, the primary purpose of which neither advances nor inhibits religion, and which avoids excessive entanglement between church and state. Brennan thought it was obvious that the primary purpose of the law was not its professed purpose of promoting academic freedom but of introducing a particular interpretation of Genesis into the public schools under the guise of teaching science. In this respect, the law shared the infirmities of the Kentucky law invalidated in *Stone v. Graham* (1980), which had required the posting of the Ten Commandments in public schools, and the law invalidated in *Epperson v. Arkansas* (1968), which had prohibited the teaching of evolution in such schools. As the majority viewed the situation, "the Louisiana Creationism Act advances a religious doctrine by requiring either the banishment of the theory of evolution from public school classrooms or the presentation of a religious viewpoint that rejects evolution in its entirety" (*Edwards v. Aguillard*, 1987, 597).

A concurring opinion written by Justice Lewis Powell, and joined by Sandra Day O'Connor, further traced the religious motivations of the law by tying the doctrine of scientific creationism to the Institute for Creation Research in California and the Creation Research Society in Ann Arbor, Michigan. The latter required members to subscribe to a statement of belief indicating that "the Bible is the written word of God, and because it is inspired throughout, all of its assertions are historically and scientifically true," and "that the account of origins in Genesis is a factual presentation of simple historical truth" (quoted at

602). Drawing from the opinion in *Abington School District v. Schempp* (1963), however, Powell indicated that the Court was not saying that the Bible could not be taught in public schools as part of "an appropriate study of history, civilization, ethics, comparative religion, or the like" (*Edwards v. Aguillard* 1987, 608). Justice Byron White also wrote a brief concurring opinion.

Justice Antonin Scalia wrote a dissenting opinion, joined by Chief Justice William Rehnquist, in which Scalia questioned the court's interpretations of the Louisiana legislature's motive in adopting the law. He pointed to scientific testimony that the legislature had elicited in the process of adopting the law, stressing that the establishment clause did not prohibit legislators from acting upon their religious convictions.

See also Abington v. Schempp (1963); Creationism and Evolution; *Epperson v. Arkansas* (1968); *Stone v. Graham* (1980)

For Reference and Further Reading

Abington v. Schempp, 374 U.S. 203 (1963).
Edwards v. Aguillard, 482 U.S. 478 (1987).
Epperson v. Arkansas, 393 U.S. 97 (1968).
Hahn, George E. 1982. "Creation-Science and Education." *The Phi Delta Kappan* 63 (April): 553–55.
McNair, Matthew. 2016. "Rhetorical Continuity: Evolution, Creation Science, and Intelligent Design." *First Amendment Studies in Arkansas*, ed. Stephen A. Smith. Little Rock: University of Arkansas Press, pp. 223–54.
Stone v. Graham, 449 U.S. 39 (1980).

Election Day Sermons

Modern elections and inaugurations come with certain expectations. The latter almost always include prayers by members of the clergy, and with presidential inaugural addresses often salted with references to American ideals. So, too, early American elections, especially in New England, were often highlighted by election sermons.

Unlike today's sermons, most of these lasted about an hour and a half and were often subsequently printed as pamphlets. They generally proceeded from a specific scriptural passage, which they explicated, explaining both the doctrine it advanced and the application to the Christian life. Professor A. W. Plumstead observes that such sermons "were given in Connecticut from 1674 to 1830, in New Hampshire from 1784 to 1831, and in Vermont from 1777 to 1824" and in Massachusetts from 1634 to 1884 (1968, 6).

Plumstead's study of such sermons suggests that "the election sermon tradition started as a defense of theocracy; by the time of the Revolution it was a ready-made vehicle for defining civil liberty and calling for resistance to George III" (7). He further identified a number of prominent motifs in such sermons. Much like the Mayflower Compact, they focused on the idea that the people of New England were a chosen people who had made an errand into the North American wilderness (18–19). Many further emphasized what Plumstead described as "the divine source of government and God's sanction of the study of political science" (19), whose themes were often tied to human depravity (Hall

1996, 14). Many also sought to provide justification for cooperation between church and state (Plumstead 1968, 20). Others also emphasized "the Character of the Good Ruler," with such descriptions taken from Scriptures (22). The need for public virtue was also a frequent theme (Hall 1996, 14).

Many such sermons took the form of jeremiads in which pastors warned that successors to New England's founding fathers were not as godly as their predecessors and needed to repent of their sins in order to secure God's favor in order to remain a city on a hill that could serve others as an example of godly government. At times, pastors would suggest policy reforms, such as further restricting travel on the Sabbath, seeking to rein in excessive time spent at pubs, or even providing restitution for those who had been falsely accused of witchcraft (Plumstead 1968, 34).

See also City upon a Hill; Covenants, Compacts, Contracts, and Constitutions; Mayflower Compact; Prophets and Jeremiads; Puritans; Revolutionary War

For Reference and Further Reading

Hall, David W. 1996. "Introduction: Revolutionary Pulpits." *Election Day Sermons*, ed. David W. Hall. Oak Ridge, TN: Kuyper Institute, pp. 9–26.

Plumstead, A.W. 1968. "An Introductory Essay." *The Wall and the Garden: Selected Massachusetts Election Sermons 1670–1775*, ed. A. W. Plumstead. Minneapolis: University of Minnesota Press, pp. 3–37.

Electioneering

American politicians have been quoting the Bible throughout much of American history, but recent studies indicate that candidates for public office, especially Republicans, may be doing so with greater frequency and in a more targeted fashion.

Professor Jacques Berlinerblau of Georgetown University thus cited numerous examples. They included the following: Democratic aspirant John Edwards citing Matthew 25:45, in which Jesus says that those who ignored "the least of these" also ignored him—a passage also cited by President Barack Obama and used as the name of a Democratic consulting company, the Matthew 25 Network; Rick Santorum sending out a Hanukkah card with Jesus's words in John 8:12: "I am the light of the world"; Herman Cain comparing his call to that of Moses; and Rick Perry claiming that he received a call similar to that reported by Isaiah in Isaiah 6:8; and others (Berlinerblau 2013, 199–202). Berlinerblau further notes that such "Scripture bombing" (202) seems not only more frequent but also more prolonged, possibly signaling that secularism has weakened as a force in U.S. politics. Political scientists John C. Green and James L. Guth further suggest that the 1988 election might have signaled a change in which "the United States is moving away from the ethnocultural foundations of political alignments, based on conflict between religious traditions, toward a more European pattern, in which conservative parties draw heavily from religious groups and leaders, while parties of the left are supported by more secular forces" (1991, 207).

Berlinerblau observes, however, that such scriptural citations must be interpreted cautiously and that whether candidates are "Democrat or Republican, liberal or conservative, Jew or Gentile, we must *never* make the mistake of assuming that their invocation is *not* motivated by political expediency" (2013, 202). He thus argues that just because politicians quote Scripture does not mean that such Scripture drives their political agendas. Indeed, he concludes that "in the main, Bible-thumpin' politicians are all rhetoric, no policy" (205).

Further noting that evangelical Christians generally give greater attention to biblical texts than do Jews (who are more influenced by the Talmudic tradition) and Roman Catholics (who are more influenced by the teachings of the apostolic fathers and the Church), he questions whether Protestants recognize the layers of hermeneutical interpretation that their own readings often impose upon the texts (206–97). He further notes that whereas many politicians traditionally used what he calls "the cite and run" method of scriptural citation rather than any deep exegesis thereof (210), this may be giving way to longer, more extended citations, often with the expectation that the Scriptures are self-interpreting and clearly support the policies the candidate is advocating.

Finally, Berlinerblau cautions that candidates more frequently cite scriptures to whip up their base than to recruit new voters. Moreover, sometimes interpretations of Scripture—as in a Missouri race for the U.S. Senate where a candidate attempted to distinguish "legitimate rape," which he believed rarely led to conception, from false claims of rape that he thought were used to provide an explanation of conception—were quite questionable (214). Using his own biblical analogy, Berlinerblau observed that such rhetoric could be not only "a double-edged sword" but also a "double-edged nuke!" (214).

Berlinerblau believes that Jimmy Carter was among the first to use Scripture in its modern form and that it was furthered by Jerry Falwell's Moral Majority and by the rise of the religious right.

See also Carter, Jimmy; Evangelicals; Falwell, Jerry

For Reference and Further Reading

Berlinerblau, Jacques. 2008. *Thumpin' It: The Use and Abuse of the Bible in Today's Presidential Politics.* Louisville: Westminster John Knox Press.

Berlinerblau, Jacques. 2013. "The Bible in the Presidential Elections of 2012, 2008, and 2004, and the Collapse of American Secularism." *Essays on the Hebrew Bible in Honor of David J.A. Clines*, ed. James K. Aitken, Jeremy M. S. Clines, and Christl M. Maier. Atlanta, GA: Society of Biblical Literature, pp. 197–218.

Brooks, Clem, and Jeff Manza. 2004. "A Great Divide? Religion and Political Change in U.S. National Elections, 1972–2000." *Sociological Quarterly* 45 (Summer): 421–50.

Green, John C., and James L. Guth. 1991. "The Bible and the Ballot Box: The Shape of Things to Come." *The Bible and the Ballot Box: Religion and Politics in the 1988 Election*, ed. by James L. Guth and John C. Green. Boulder: Westview Press, pp. 207–25.

Ely, Ezra Stiles

Ezra Stiles Ely (1786–1861) was a Connecticut-born Presbyterian minister and graduate of Yale University. As the minister of the Seventh Presbyterian Church in Philadelphia, Ely delivered a controversial speech celebrating American independence in 1827 entitled *The Duty of Christian Freemen to Elect Christian Rulers.*

As the title suggests, Ely devoted his sermon, which was later printed and became the subject of considerable controversy, to suggesting that Protestant

Christians should band together politically to elect fellow Christian leaders. Ely's primary biblical text was Psalm 2:10–12: "Be wise now therefore, O ye kings: be instructed, ye judges of the earth. Serve the Lord with fear, and rejoice with trembling. Kiss the Son, lest he be angry, and ye perish from the way; when his wrath is kindled but a little. Blessed are they that put their trust in him." Ely, however, also liberally quoted from other verses in the Psalms and other Scriptures. In particular, he urged that the dictum in Proverbs 3:6, "In all thy ways acknowledge him, and he shall direct thy paths," applied to nations and their leaders as well as to private individuals. Ely also specifically evoked John Winthrop's biblical image of "a city on a hill, which cannot be hid" (Ely 1828, 5).

Denying that he favored a "religious test" for office, such as the U.S. Constitution prohibited, Ely nonetheless set a high standard for those who help public office:

> Our rulers, like any other members of the community, who are under law to God as rational beings, and under law to Christ, since they have the light of divine revelation, ought to search the scriptures, assent to the truth, profess faith in Christ, keep the Sabbath holy to God, pray in private and in the domestic circle, attend on the public ministry of the word, be baptized, and celebrate the Lord's supper. None of our rules have the consent of their Maker, that they should be Pagans, Socinians [deniers of the divinity of Jesus and thus the Trinity], Mussulmen [Muslims], Deists, the opponents of Christianity; and a religious people should never think of giving them permission, as public officers, to be and do, what they might not lawfully be and do, as private individuals. (Ely 1828, 5–6)

It followed that Christians had the duty to elect fellow Christians as rulers.

Some believed that Christians had no business participating in politics, but Ely thought that it was their duty to vote. Indeed, although it is not clear that he was calling for an actual political party, Ely proposed "*a Christian party in politics*, which I am exceedingly desirous all good men in our country should join: not by *subscribing a constitution* and the formation of a new society, to be added to the scores which now exist; but by adopting, avowing, and determining to act upon, truly religious principles in all civil matters" (8). Ely explained that Christians should "never wittingly support for any public office, any person whom they know or believe to sustain, at the time of his proposed election, a bad moral character" (8–9). In addition to disqualifying "confirmed sots [alcoholics]" and convicted criminals, "they ought to render the election of all profane swearers, notorious Sabbath breakers, seducers, slanders, prodigals and riotous persons, as well as *the advocates of dueling*, impracticable" (10). Ely further thought that Christians should indicate that "they will never vote for any one to fill any office in the nation or state, who does not profess to receive the Bible as the rule of his faith" (11).

Noting that three or four of the leading Protestant denominations—he specifically listed "the Presbyterians, the Baptists, the Methodists and Congregationalists" (11)—should band together in common cause, he observed that "the Presbyterians alone could bring half a million of electors into the field, in opposition to any known advocates of Deism, Socinianism, or any species of avowed hostility to the truth of Christianity" (11). He also suggested that

Episcopalians might participate. Even if this occasionally resulted in politicians acting hypocritically, Ely thought that this would be preferable to flaunting their unbelief and/or bad behaviors (13).

Perhaps anticipating criticisms that he was arguing for a breach of the wall of separation between church and state, and perhaps paraphrasing a statement of Thomas Jefferson on religious toleration, Ely observed, "It would pick no infidel's pocket, and break no Jew's neck, if our President should be so singular as to let it be known, that he is a Christian by his Messages, and an advocate for the Deity of Christ by his personal preference of a Christian temple to a Socinian conventicle" (14). In a theme that continues to be prominent in modern discourse, Ely observed that "we are a Christian nation: we have a right to demand that all our rulers in their conduct shall conform to Christian morality; and if they do not, it is the duty and privilege of Christian freemen to make a new and a better election" (14).

Professor Daniel L. Dreisbach believes that Ely's speech, although strongly attacked by those who thought it was advocating a breach in the wall of separation between church and state, may have been in response to contemporary controversies over whether Christianity was embodied in the common law (1996, 11). In what appears to be a tongue-in-check language, Ely himself dedicated his sermon "to those members of the Senate of the State of Pennsylvania, who in February, 1828, signalized themselves, by refusing to grant an act of incorporation to 'The American Sunday School Union'" (1828, unnumbered page after title page), suggesting perhaps that he thought that the legislature had taken scruples against joining church and state too far.

Because Ely had previously written to the newspaper indicting his support for Andrew Jackson (Ely believed that John Quincy Adams was a Unitarian), some individuals also interpreted Ely's speech as an attempt to lend further support to Jackson's candidacy. Ironically, Ely, who appeared to have been almost constantly involved in disputes, was among those who expressed reservations about the morality of Peggy Eaton, the wife of Jackson's secretary of war, which led to her defense by Jackson and the resignations of most members of his cabinet (Dahl 1974).

Dreisbach observes that the impact of Ely's speech was the opposite of what he intended: "The national furor sparked by Ely's suggestion did not subside for decades, and it nourished the suspicion of many that Presbyterian clerics were 'attempting to control the state to further their own schemes' and to exclude non-Christians from full participation in the political process" (1996, 10).

Ely's proposal for a Christian party had a precedent, although he may have been unaware of it. In 1802, Alexander Hamilton, who had suffered some humiliating political defeats, had proposed a "Christian Constitutional Society," which Professors Douglass Adair and Marvin Harvey describe as "a network of interstate political clubs dedicated to the support of Christianity and the United States Constitution against [what he considered to be] the devilish Jeffersonians" (1955, 326). A number of postwar Western European nations had political parties, such as the Christian Democratic Party in Western Germany, which had the title "Christian" in their designations.

See also City upon a Hill

For Reference and Further Reading

Adair, Douglass, and Marvin Harvey. 1955. "Was Alexander Hamilton a Christian Statesman?" *William and Mary Quarterly* 12 (April): 308–29.

Dahl, Curtis. 1974. "The Clergyman, the Hussy, and Old Hickory: Ezra Stiles Ely and the Peggy Eaton Affair." *Journal of Presbyterian History* 52 (Summer): 127–55.

Dreisbach, Daniel L. 1996. "Introduction: A Debate on Religion and Politics in the Early Republic." *Religion and Politics in the Early Republic: Jasper Adams and the Church-State Debate*, ed. Daniel L. Dreisbach. Lexington: University Press of Kentucky, pp. 1–35.

Ely, Ezra Stiles. 1828. *The Duty of Christian Freemen to Elect Christian Rules: A Discourse Delivered on the Fourth of July, 1827*. Philadelphia: William F. Geddes.

Epperson v. Arkansas (1968)

In *Epperson v. Arkansas*, the U.S. Supreme Court ruled that an Arkansas anti-evolution statute of 1928, similar to the so-called Tennessee monkey law that had been at issue in the Scopes Trial, violated the establishment clause of the First Amendment as applied to the states through the due process clause of the Fourteenth Amendment.

Justice Abe Fortas wrote the opinion for the court. He pointed out the law, which made it unlawful for teachers in state schools "to teach the theory or doctrine that mankind ascended or descended from a lower order of animals" or "to adopt or use in any such institution a textbook that teaches" this theory (1968, 98–99). In the case at hand, a biology teacher, Susan Epperson, indicated that she was uncertain whether teaching from a newly adopted book explaining evolution would subject her to punishment or not; parents of a child also filed suit to have the subject taught.

A local chancery court invalidated the law, but the Arkansas Supreme Court overturned the decision and provided only minimal guidance as to how the law, which had not previously been used, would be interpreted so as to prevent the teaching of the theory of evolution or merely whether it would prohibit teaching that the theory were true.

Deciding not to invalidate the law on the basis of its vagueness, Fortas chose instead to invalidate it for violating the principle of neutrality among religions and between religion and irreligion that he associated with the establishment clause. In this case, he decided that the only reason that Arkansas had adopted the law was because evolution "is deemed to conflict with a particular religious doctrine; that is, with a particular interpretation of the Book of Genesis by a particular religious group" (1968, 103). Fortas drew from the decision in *Meyer v. Nebraska* (1923), in which the court had invalidated, albeit on due process grounds, a state law prohibiting the teaching of foreign languages in any school, as well as from *McCollum v. Board of Education* (1948), in which it had prohibited devotional Bible readings in public schools. He thus observed, "While study of religions and of the Bible from a literary and historic viewpoint, presented objectively as part of a secular program of education, need not collide with the First Amendment's prohibition, the State may not adopt programs or practices in its public schools or colleges which 'aid or oppose' any religion" (1968, 107). Fortas saw little difference between this law and the Tennessee monkey law and believed that because "there is no doubt that the motivation for the law was the same: to suppress the teaching of a theory which, it was thought, 'denied' the divine creation of man," the law "cannot be defended as an act of religious neutrality" (109).

In a concurring opinion, Justice Hugo Black indicated that he was unsure whether the case presented a justiciable issue but supported voiding the law for vagueness. Adding a wrinkle to the discussion, he indicated that to the extent that the theory of evolution might be viewed as anti-religious, teaching it might, in fact, ally the state with irreligion against religion (113). In this respect, he concluded, "Unless this Court is prepared simply to write off as pure nonsense the views of those who consider evolution an anti-religious doctrine, then this issue presents problems under the Establishment Clause far more troublesome than are discussed in this Court's opinion" (113). School authorities certainly had power to decide generally which subjects they would teach and which they would not.

Justice John Marshall Harlan and Justice Potter Stewart also wrote short concurring opinions, with the latter indicating that it was one thing for a public school to determine its curriculum and quite another "to make it a criminal offense for a public school teacher so much as to mention the very existence of an entire system of respected human thought" (116).

In *Edwards v. Aguillard* (1987), the Supreme Court subsequently invalidated a Louisiana law that required public schools that taught evolution to accompany it with the teaching of creation science.

See also Abington v. Schempp (1963); Creationism and Evolution; *Edwards v. Aguillard* (1987); Scopes Trial

For Reference and Further Reading

Epperson v. Arkansas, 393 U.S. 97 (1968).
McCollum v. Board of Education, 333 U.S. 203 (1948).
Meyer v. Nebraska, 262 U.S. 390 (1923).
Moore, Randy. 1999. "Creationism in the United States: IV. The Aftermath of Epperson v. Arkansas." *American Biology Teacher* 61 (January): 10–16.

Errand into the Wilderness

One of the more striking figures of speech from early American history is the Puritan image of an errand into the wilderness, which is prominent and may have originated in a published election sermon delivered by Samuel Danforth (1626–1674) in Roxbury, Massachusetts. It is a classic example of the jeremiad, in which a speaker excoriates the people for their sins in the hope that they will repent.

The title page of the sermon referred to the passage in Jeremiah 2:2–5, in which God called to mind a time when Jerusalem (a symbol for Israel as a whole), having emerged from the years in the wilderness under Moses, had now "gone far from me, and have walked after vanity, and are become vain." It was also prefaced with the passage from Matthew 11:7–9, in which Jesus asked what people had expected to see when they went into the wilderness to see John the Baptist. As might be expected from such a product, the speech was suffused with biblical quotations and citations, many taken from the Hebrew prophets.

Drawing from the passage in Matthew 11, Danforth noted that those interested in John had not gone to see "a reed shaken with the wind" or an individual wearing the fine garments of a royal court but a prophet heralding Jesus the Messiah (Danforth 1670, 2–4). Although the ancient people of Israel and those who had sought out John had gone on "their Errand into the Wilderness" to engage in true worship, they had instead ended up worshipping idols and forgetting their "first love [a reference to Revelation 2:4]" (6). Moreover, they had often turned on the prophets and ministers who were "the *faithful Dispensers* of the Gospel" (8).

Much as in John Winthrop's "Model of Christian Charity," Danforth reiterated the noble purposes of those who had first settled Massachusetts, Plymouth, Connecticut, and New Haven. These included the goal of obtaining *"your Liberty to walk in the Faith of the Gospel with all good Conscience according to the Order of the Gospel, and your enjoyment of the pure Worship of God according to his Institution, without humane Mixtures and Impositions"* (11).

One of the more remarkable aspects of this sermon, however, is that one of the sins that Danforth identified is what might be called the sin of tolerance! In apparent references to Anne Hutchinson and others whom the colonies had expelled or executed, Danforth thus observed, "What fervent zeal was there then against Sectaries and Hereticks, and all manner of Heterodoxies. *You could not bear them that were evil,* but tried them that pretended to New Light and Revelations, and found them *liars*" (13).

Tolerance of heretics had been further compounded by iniquities: "Pride, Contention, Worldliness, Covetousness, Luxury, Drunkenness and Uncleanness break in like a flood upon us, and good men grow cold in their love to God and to one another" (14). People who were once known for having "bowels of mercy [Colossians 3:12]" were now constipated (16), having lost sight of their founding: "What is it that *distinguisheth New-England* from other Colonies and Plantations in *America*? Not our transportation over the *Atlantick* Ocean, but the *Ministry* of Gods faithful Prophets, and the fruition of his holy *Ordinances*" (19–20).

The colonists' loss of their first love had resulted in numerous natural disasters that reflected God's wrath upon their sins. Although the situation was dire, there was still time for the colonists to repent.

Rev. Increase Mather (1639–1723) later authored a similar jeremiad on behalf of the Boston Synod in which he not only repeated the terminology of the errand in the wilderness but also reflected upon Jesus's question to those who had sought out John the Baptist (Mather 1679).

One obvious problem with the image of America as a wilderness is that it tended to downplay the fact that, although many had been decimated by European diseases, the continent remained populated with Native American populations. Puritans often analogized such Native Americans to Canaanites or heathen whose elimination was necessary for progress.

See also Hutchinson, Anne; Model of Christian Charity (Winthrop); Native American Indians; Natural Disasters; Prophets and Jeremiads; Puritans

For Reference and Further Reading

Danforth, Samuel. 1670. "A Brief Recognition of New England's Errand into the Wilderness." Cambridge, MA: S.G. and M.F. From Samuel Danforth and Paul Royster (transcriber and editor), "A Brief Recognition of New-Englands Errand into the Wilderness: An Online Electronic Text Edition (1670)." Faculty Publications, UNL Libraries. 35. https://digitalcommons.unl.edu/libraryscience/35.

Mather, Increase [Boston Synod]. 1679. "The Necessity of Reformation." September 10. Boston: John Foster. Evans Early American Imprint Collection. https://quod.lib.umich.edu/cgi/t/text/text-idx?c=evans;cc=evans;view=toc;idno=N00203.0001.001.

Miller, Perry. 1953. "Errand into the Wilderness." *William and Mary Quarterly* 10 (January): 3–32.

Esther as Political Archetype

The biblical book of Esther portrays how Esther, a Jewish orphan who was raised by her uncle Mordecai, becomes the bride of King Ahasuerus (Xerxes) and saves her people from destruction after Xerxes's advisor, Haman, is offended by Mordecai and attempts to wipe out the Jewish people. The story, which bears some parallels to the story of Joseph in Genesis and the story of the Passover in the book of Exodus, is also used to explain the annual Jewish celebration of Purim.

Professor Benjamin R. Hertzberg has pointed out that, while both books describe the Jews in exile, the approach to politics in Esther differs from that in Daniel where Daniel and his exiled friends do not conceal their Jewish identity. Using the terminology of sociologist Max Weber (1864–1920), Hertzberg argues that Esther illustrates "a politics of *responsibility* that enjoins strategic assimilation and concealment to preserve the Jews as a nation," whereas Daniel illustrates a "politics of *conviction*" wherein "the Jews ought to scrupulously and publicly adhere to their law, no matter the consequences" (Hertzberg 2015, 400).

A recent book written by journalist Robert Case entitled *Esther and Trump* illustrates how some evangelical Christians might apply the lessons of Esther to contemporary politics. Using the book to show how "political involvement matters," Case suggested that Christians need to be more like rattlesnakes than like ostriches (Case 2018, 29). This might involve hiding one's Christian identity and deemphasizing outward religious observance in order to rise within the political establishment.

Case appears to attempt to put his own advice into practice. Although he titles the book *Esther and Trump*, he never once mentions Trump's name directly in the text. Early in the book, however, he says that life in Persia under Xerxes, whom he clearly identifies as a tyrant, "is similar to life of faith in a post-Christian American culture ruled by an immoral unbeliever, who is the current secular patron of the sacred Church" (34). He alternates between calling Mordecai the Jew and Haman, his opponent, as Persia's vice president, making it difficult to tell which role he thinks Mike Pence is currently playing.

Jews were clearly a minority within the Persian empire, and Case suggests that such societies often extended protection only "to the extent one agreed with the leaders of the empire" (183). Even though the book of Esther is "neither prophetic nor apocalyptic" (Durbin 2014, 96), Christian American supporters of Israel often liken Haman's hatred to the Jews to that of President Mahmoud Ahmadinejad and other leaders of Iran who had called for the destruction of Israel and which they view as an existential threat to that nation's continuing existence (Durbin 2014, 97). Secretary of State Mike Pompeo has been among those who has suggested that Trump may be a modern Esther called to save the Jews from those who would destroy them.

See also Cyrus as Political Archetype; Pence, Mike; Pompeo, Mike; Trump, Donald

For Reference and Further Reading

Case, Robert. 2018. *Esther and Trump*. Tacoma, WA: Saluda Press.

Durbin, Sean. 2014. "Walking in the Mantle of Esther: 'Political' Action as 'Religious' Practice." *Comprehending Christian Zionism: Perspectives in Comparison*, ed. Goran Gunner and Robert O. Smith. Minneapolis, MN: Augsburg Fortress, pp. 85–124.

Hazony, Yoram. 2007. *The Dawn: Political Teachings of the Book of Esther* (3rd printing). Jerusalem: Shalem Press.

Hertzberg, Benjamin R. 2015. "Daniel, Esther, and the Minority Politics of the Hebrew Bible." *Polity* 47 (July): 397–416.

Ethan Allen Bible

Like contemporary Americans, the Founders often differed profoundly about religious issues. Although it is sometimes difficult to identify the views of individual founders, some were quite vocal. One such individual was Ethan Allen (1738–1789), the Vermont hero of the American Revolution who helped capture Fort Ticonderoga.

In 1784, Allen published a book entitled *Oracles of Reason* under his name, which is often described as Ethan Allen's Bible. This work largely appears to have been the work of Dr. Thomas Young (1732–1777), a leader of the Boston Tea Party, with whom Allen had collaborated as a writer, and whose widow had given him the manuscript upon Young's death. One scholar believes that Allen probably wrote less than one-fifth of the manuscript (Anderson 1937, 694), even though he neither credited Young nor appears to have given any money to his widow. The book, which was divided into thirteen chapters, made a concerted effort to undermine the authority of the Bible, often using biblical texts and examples in the process.

The first chapter of this work stated the purpose of the book to reform mankind "from Superstition and Error," which it argued could only happen through reason. Such reason revealed that there is a noncorporeal God who is perfect and good and whose rationality is reflected in his creation and its laws.

The second chapter devoted to "The Eternity of Creation" sought to debunk Moses's account in the opening chapters of Genesis of the creation of man, while the third chapter was devoted to consideration of "the doctrine of the infinity of evil and of sin." It sought to establish the irrationality of the doctrine of "endless punishment" or the idea that punishments were visited upon man for sins rather than simply because mankind is part of a natural order and thus subject to decay.

Calvinists and others often pointed to the deficiency of human reason in learning about God without the benefit of revelation, but the Allen Bible argued that such reason "is not and cannot be depraved, but that it bears a likeness to divine reason, is of the same kind, and in its own nature as uniform as truth, which is the test of it." The laws of nature and morality are open to human reason through natural law. In contrast to those who lauded the Ten Commandments, Allen and Young suggested, "The moral precepts contained in Moses' Decalogue to the people of Israel, was previously known to every nation under heaven, and in all probability by them as much practiced as by the tribes of Israel." Moreover, its one innovation, the Sabbath, "was an arbitrary imposition of Moses, (as many other of his edicts were) and not included in the law of nature."

Proceeding in Chapter 5 to "supernatural and mysterious revelation in general," the work argued that the only revelation that was necessary for mankind was revealed within nature. It disputed the idea of infallible revelation, noting that even some biblical writers like Paul sometimes seemed uncertain whether they were sharing their own wisdom or that of God.

Chapter 6 proceeded to dispute the idea that miracles might occur in violation of God's laws of nature, without therefore derogating from His perfection: "God, the great architect of nature, has so constructed its machinery, that it never needs to be altered or rectified." The events that appear to be miraculous are simply wonders of nature that people have failed to understand. Jesus himself suggested that his disciples should be able to perform miracles and drink poison, and the authors thus said they were unwilling to believe any of them unless and until they drank poison without ill effect. They further suggested that prayer "is no part of a rational religion, nor did reason ever dictate it," since "to make known our wants to God by prayer, or to communicate any intelligence concerning ourselves or the universe to him, is impossible, since his omniscient mind has a perfect knowledge of all things, and therefore is beholden to none of our correspondence to inform himself of our circumstances, or of what would be wisest and best to do for us."

Many defenders of Christianity relied upon the fulfillment of biblical prophecies, but the authors believed that such prophecies "are most generally so loose, vague and indeterminate in their meaning, or in the grammar of their present translation, that the prophets will as well answer to events in one period of time, as in another, and are equally applicable to a variety of events, which have and are still taking place in the world, and are liable to so many different interpretations, that they are incapable of being understood or explained, except upon arbitrary principles, and therefore cannot be admitted as proof of revelation; as for instance, 'it shall come to pass in the last days, saith God.'" This chapter cast doubt on the fulfillment of prophecy in the book of Revelation, or on the Day of Pentecost as recorded in the biblical book of Acts, and suggested that Jeremiah's anticipation of the Babylonian capture of Israel did not require supernatural revelation. It cast further doubt on whether God would, as Genesis 22 recorded, have commanded Abraham to sacrifice his son Isaac and wondered how Moses could, as in the last chapter of Deuteronomy, have written about his own death and burial. The chapter further pointed to occasions where one biblical writer contradicts another as when Ezekiel (18:2) countermanded the Mosaic dictum that "the fathers have eaten sour grapes and the children's teeth are set on edge." The chapter further questioned the reliability of dreams and visions recorded in Scripture and pointed to early disputes within the church to contradict the idea that the Holy Spirit was at work among its members.

The eighth chapter quoted a wide variety of Scriptures, most from Paul, about the nature of faith and its saving value. By contrast, it argued that "for us to believe such doctrines, or systems of religion, as appears to be credibly recommended to our reason, can no more partake of the nature of goodness or morality, than our natural eyes may be supposed to partake of it in their perception of colors." Again, they relied upon the differences among religious sects as proof that religious traditions were flawed.

Chapter 9 proceeded to dispute the doctrine of the Trinity. It cited Jesus's statement in Matthew 24:36 that no one knew the hour of God's return to suggest that "he was a mere creature" and not the coequal with God.

Chapter 10 raised questions about Moses's account of Adam and Eve in the Garden of Eden. The chapter further questioned whether all human beings were, as Acts 17:26 had written, of "one blood." In highly racist statements, the chapter went on to observe that "the acquaintance, which we have had with the negro nation in particular, fully evinces the absurdity of supposing them to be of the same blood and kindred with ourselves."

Chapter 11 aimed directly at the view that Jesus's sacrifice on the cross could atone for sins of others. It argued that laws of morality demanded that everyone suffer or reap the consequences of their own actions.

Chapter 12 questioned whether, even had Scriptures been originally without error, they could have been transmitted over centuries to men "through all the vicissitudes and alternations of human learning, prejudices, superstitions, enthusiasms and diversities of interest and manners, to our time, so as to present us with a perfect edition from its premised infallible original manuscript copies." Moreover, it declared, "Every commentary and annotation on the Bible, implicitly declares its fallibility; for if the Scriptures remained genuine and entire, they would not stand in need of commentaries and expositions, but would shine in their infallible lustre and purity without them." The chapter similarly derided claims of papal infallibility.

The title of the final chapter indicated that "Morality [is] derived from natural fitness, and not from tradition." It further denied that anyone could know about the afterlife, but suggested that "virtue and vice are the only things in this world, which, with our souls, are capable of surviving death; the former is the rational and only procuring cause of all intellectual happiness, and the latter of conscious guilt and misery; and therefore, our indispensable duty and ultimate interest is, to love, cultivate and improve the one, as the means of our greatest good, and to hate and abstain from the other, as productive of our greatest evil." It concluded that "reason therefore must be the standard by which we determine the respective claims of revelation."

This publication clearly indicated that there was what Matthew Stewart (2014) has identified as a "heretical" strand among leaders of the American republic that is often identified as Deism. Although evangelical Christians and

Deists sometimes worked together on similar political objectives, they often did so from radically different perspectives on the Bible.

See also Deism; Ten Commandments

For Reference and Further Reading

Allen, Ethan [and Thomas Young]. 1784. *Reason: The Only Oracle of Man: A Compendious System of Natural Religion*. Boston: J.P. Mendum, Cornhill, 1854. Accessed at libertyonline.hypermall.com/allen-reason.html on May 10, 2019.

Anderson, George Pomeroy. 1937. "Who Wrote 'Ethan Allen's Bible.'" *New England Quarterly* 10 (December); 685–96.

Stewart, Matthew 2014. *Nature's God: The Heretical Origins of the American Republic*. New York: W. W. Norton.

Walters, Kerry S. 1992. *The American Deists: Voices of Reason and Dissent in the Early Republic*. Lawrence: University Press of Kansas.

Ethiopia as Political Archetype

Sometimes a single biblical verse can take on its own life in politics and popular culture, particularly when combined with other scattered biblical references. Such seems to be the case with Psalm 68:31, which said, "Princes shall come out of Egypt; Ethiopia shall soon stretch out her hands unto God."

The psalm as a whole is generally regarded as a processional hymn that marks either the actual occasion of moving the ark of the covenant from the private home of Obed-Edom to a new Tabernacle that King David had prepared on Mt. Zion, or possibly in an annual celebration of this event (Guthrie 1970, 491). Verse 31 celebrates the day when the enemies of Israel, who had been exacting tribune, will be defeated and the glory of God will spread to other nations, whose leaders will come to Mt. Zion to worship.

As interpreted by many African Americans in U.S. history, instead of being interpreted as pointing "back to Zion," it was interpreted as an oracle that "pointed forward to Ethiopia" (Scott 2004, 138). To this end, Ethiopia became shorthand not for a specific nation in Africa but for Africa as a whole, while "Ethiopia took its place in African-American racial consciousness at the center of a biblical cartography of hope" (139).

In addition to Psalm 68:31, there are numerous other biblical references to Ethiopia, or "Cush" (one of the grandsons of Noah), as the name is sometimes translated. These include the reference in 2 Kings 19:9 to an attack by King Tirkakah of Ethiopia on Assyria, a reference in Isaiah 45:3 to its wealth, a reference in Jeremiah 46:7 to its mighty warriors, and the story recounted in Acts 8 of Philip explaining the Scriptures to an Ethiopian eunuch and baptizing him.

One interpretation of Psalm 68:31, especially identified with white abolitionists, interpreted the passage as an African American plea to whites for deliverance, while another stressed the need for African Americans to deliver themselves (Shilliam 2012). Anthony Benezet, an influential American Quaker, was among the earliest abolitionists to cite this passage, but it was subsequently used by David Walker and Maria Stewart before later being utilized by Marcus Garvey's Universal Negro Improvement Association in the early twentieth century. Some revivalists in the Second Great Awakening early in the nineteenth century saw African American conversions to Christianity as a sign that this Scripture was being fulfilled (Callahan 2006, 140).

In 1896, just as the U.S. Supreme Court was enthroning racial segregation, many African Americans took pride in the Ethiopian defeats of invading Italians, just as African Americans were subsequently outraged by Mussolini's subsequent invasion in 1935 (Callahan 2006, 162, 174–75). Hopes were, however, renewed for the fulfillment of what many considered to be a prophecy during the Cold War as numerous African states declared their independence.

See also Benezet, Anthony; Stewart, Maria; Walker, David

For Reference and Further Reading

Callahan, Allen Dwight. 2006. *The Talking Book: African Americans and the Bible*. New Haven, CT: Yale University Press.

Guthrie, D., and J. A. Motyer, eds. 1970. *The New Bible Commentary*, 3rd ed. Grand Rapids, MI: William B. Eerdmans.

Scott, William. 2004. "The Ethiopian Ethos in African American Thought." *International Journal of Ethiopian Studies* 1 (Winter/Spring): 40–57.

Shilliam, Robbie. 2012. "A Global Story of Psalms 68:31." November 7. https://robbieshilliam.wordpress.com/2012/11/07/a-global-story-of-psalms-6831/.

Walker, Albert B. Cleage, Jr. 2008. "Princes Shall Come Out of Egypt: A Theological Comparison of Marcus Garvey and Reverend Albert B. Cleague Jr." *Journal of Black Studies* 39 (November): 194–251.

Evangelicals

Sometimes individuals from different denominations share more beliefs and behaviors than individuals from within the same denomination. This certainly appears to be true of evangelical Christians.

Professor John Stackhouse, who quotes Anglican John Stott as simply describing evangelicals as "Bible people," associates them with five major beliefs (Stackhouse 2017, 559). The first, expressed in their name, is their emphasis on the evangel, or gospel, as proclaimed through Jesus Christ. Consistent with orthodox creeds, they believe that Jesus was God incarnate who gave his perfect life as a sacrifice, or atonement, for sin on the cross, rose again, and will one day come back to earth for his followers. In a second distinctive, like their Reformation forbears, evangelicals believe the Bible is the written word of God, which is the surest guide to faith and conduct, and which many interpret fairly literally. Evangelicals have been active in Bible translation, with many preferring the King James Version, the New American Standard Version (1960), or the New International Version (1973). Evangelical churches often have Sunday schools or Bible study groups, and their services typically center on a sermon drawn directly from Scriptures. Like fundamentalist predecessors, who once led the battle against the teaching of evolution in public schools, evangelicals often contrast their own views of Scripture to Protestant liberalism, which they believe takes undue liberties with the text and denies its more supernatural elements. Evangelicals from a variety of denominations often gather together for Bible study as part of the Bible Study Fellowship (BSF), which has offices throughout the world, and, at the college level, groups like Campus Crusade for Christ, Intervarsity Christian Fellowship, and other interdenominational fellowships.

Third, evangelicals, who often cite John 3:7 and John 3:16, believe in the necessity of being converted, or "born again," in order to inherit eternal salvation. Many think that belief in Christ is, in fact, the only means of achieving salvation. Although advocating church attendance, tithing, and good works, evangelicals discount reliance upon such behaviors, or upon sacraments, as means to salvation. Billy Graham is an example of an evangelical preacher whose sermons often concentrate on the necessity of a new spiritual birth.

Fourth, consistent with this emphasis, evangelicals believe in the importance of Jesus's Great Commission (Matthew 18:19, Mark 16:15) in spreading the gospel throughout the world. Evangelicals support numerous foreign missionaries. Evangelicals are much more likely to proselytize than others, even sometimes specifically targeting Jews. In recent years, evangelicals have often been supportive of Zionism, believing that the restoration of Jews to Israel is the fulfillment of biblical prophecy.

Fifth, although they are members of such diverse denominations as Baptists, Methodists, Pentecostals, Presbyterians, Episcopalians, and other faiths, they are often willing to cooperate together through such organizations as the American Bible Society, the Gideons, and World Vision either on distributing Bibles or on disaster relief efforts, often seeing the latter as a means of evangelism (Stackhouse 2017, 558–59). Many African Americans are evangelicals, although their voting patterns, which have been heavily in favor of the Democratic Party, are often fairly distinct from those of white evangelicals. There are additional divides between Protestants who identify themselves as charismatics (speaking in tongues, faith healing, and prophecy) and those who do not.

Many evangelicals trace their roots not only through the Protestant Reformation but also through Puritan forbears, and the revival movements known as the First and Second Great Awakenings. The first of these movements is often credited with laying the groundwork for the American Revolution, while the second was an impetus for numerous political reforms including antislavery (though many southern evangelicals remain convinced that the Bible sanctioned this institution), temperance, women's rights, opposition to gambling and lotteries, and the like. Many evangelicals share a theological outlook that is similar, albeit typically more willing to engage with contemporary culture, to that of earlier fundamentalists.

Newsweek magazine declared 1976 to be the year of the evangelical after Jimmy Carter successfully won the presidency after clearly identifying himself as an evangelical Christian. Although his faith clearly influenced his policies, including his efforts to achieve peace in the Middle East, many evangelicals were drawn in the next election to Ronald Reagan. Although he was less openly devout, he more strongly opposed abortion, and he supported prayer and/or Bible reading in public schools, home schooling, and other issues that appealed to many evangelicals, many of whom supported the Moral Majority, which was the brainchild of Rev. Jerry Falwell. Ben Sasse, Mike Huckabee, Pat Robertson, and Ted Cruz are among modern politicians who have self-identified as evangelicals. In recent years, evangelicals have increasingly cooperated with Roman Catholics and with others who share many of their conservative political stances.

With their emphasis on the need for personal conversion and regeneration, evangelicals have often emphasized the importance of character in politics. Many were especially censorious of President Clinton for his lapses in behavior and supported his impeachment. Widespread support among evangelicals for President Donald J. Trump, whose flamboyant lifestyle, brash language, proclivity to prevaricate, appeals to racial divisions, and relative biblical illiteracy are far from evangelical ideals, would appear to indicate that they are far more attracted by his willingness to appoint strong conservatives to the courts, recognize Jerusalem as the capital of Israel, and his appeal to those who are often looked upon as political outsiders than on character per se. Some have tried to minimize this disconnect by likening Trump to King Cyrus, a pagan biblical ruler whom God used for his own purposes. Others find some solace in the fact that Mike Pence is an evangelical who supports what they consider to be traditional family values.

See also American Bible Society; Carter, Jimmy; Cyrus as Political Archetype; Falwell, Jerry; Graham, Billy; Puritans; Robertson, Pat; Trump, Donald J.; Zionism

For Reference and Further Reading

Fitzgerald, Frances. 2017. *The Evangelicals: The Struggle to Shape America*. New York: Simon & Schuster.

Gushee, David P. 2008. *The Future of Faith in American Politics: The Public Witness of the Evangelical Center*. Waco, TX: Baylor University Press.

Howe, Ben. 2019. *The Immoral Majority: Why Evangelicals Choose Political Power over Christian Values*. New York: Broadside Books.

Jen, Joanna Tice. 2019. "'Be Joyful Always!': Twenty-First-Century Evangelical Conceptions of Happiness and Trumpist Politics." *Regimes of Happiness: Comparative and Historical Studies*, ed. Yuri Contreras-Vejar, Joanna Tice Jen, and Bryan S. Turner. New York: Anthem Press, pp. 93–110.

Juzwik, Mary M. 2014. "American Evangelical Biblicism as Literate Practice: A Critical Review." *Reading Research Quarterly* 49 (July/August/September): 335–49.

Kidd, Thomas S. 2019. *Who Is an Evangelical? The History of a Movement in Crisis*. New Haven, CT: Yale University Press.

Linder, Robert D., and Richard V. Pierard. 1978. *Twilight of the Saints: Biblical Christianity and Civil Religion in America*. Downers Grove, IL: InterVarsity Press.

Sider, Ronald J. 2008. *The Scandal of Evangelical Politics: Why Are Christians Missing the Chance to Really Change the World?* Grand Rapids, MI: Baker Books.

Stackhouse, John G., Jr. 2017. "The Bible and Evangelicalism." *The Oxford Handbook of the Bible in America*, ed. Paul C. Gutjahr. New York: Oxford University Press, pp. 558–74.

Wehner, Peter. 2019. "The Deepening Crisis in Evangelical Christianity." *The Atlantic*. July 5. https://www.theatlantic.com/ideas/archive/2019/07/evangelical-christians-face-deepening-crisisi/593353/.

Evolution

See Creationism and Evolution

Execution Day Sermons

Sermons provide quintessential occasions for scriptural citations. One genre of sermon that appears to have been fairly unique to New England and that lasted for roughly 150 years from the 1670s to the 1820s was the so-called execution sermon. It was common for ministers to deliver such sermons both on the Sundays before and on the day of executions, often to large audiences, including those who were condemned to die as well as those who had come to witness the event. Many were subsequently published, often in multiple editions.

Like the jeremiad form in which they were often presented, these sermons enabled pastors to outline the seriousness of the offenses, warn others of the dangers to which sins exposed them, provide a means for the community to renounce the sin, and even offer the condemned a chance to save their souls by repenting of their sins and calling upon God's mercy (Bosco 1978). In the process, ministers might also hope to convert those in the audience who had not yet embraced the Christian faith.

Although pastors were almost always allied with the state in seeking to justify the necessity of strict punishments, over time their arguments somewhat changed. Daniel Cohen notes that in early sermons, pastors cited Scriptures, especially for crimes like "adultery, sodomy, and blasphemy—severely condemned by Scripture, but not then capital under British law" (Cohen 1988, 149). Indeed, the Massachusetts Body of Liberties had specifically cited Scriptures in justifying capital punishment for such crimes. Pastors might also point to special circumstances, like the sermon that Samuel Danforth delivered in 1674 entitled *The Cry of Sodom Enquired Into*, which involved the condemnation of an individual who had committed bestiality with a mare in broad daylight (150). In delivering this sermon, Danforth observed that "the Land cannot be cleansed, until it hath spued out this Unclean Beast" (150).

Over time pastors began devoting greater attention to the manner in which they believed that capital punishment would serve as a deterrent to other potential malefactors and to the importance of societies protecting themselves. This became ever more important as the colonies moved toward the British model, which deemphasized moral failings as detailed in Scriptures and began increasing penalties for property-related crimes like robbery and burglary. In many cases pastors appeared to have arrayed themselves on the side of authorities imposing such penalties in the face of public opinion that capital punishment was too severe for such crimes (Cohen 1988, 155). In cases involving murder, pastors often cited Genesis 9:6: "Whoso sheddeth man's blood, by man shall his blood be shed: for in the image of God made he man."

In another interesting twist, in time, pastors used the establishment of regularized courts following constitutionally prescribed procedures to argue that punishments were appropriate because they had been duly authorized by due process and by a jury of the malefactor's peers (Cohen 1988, 157). Moreover, the popular appetite for stories of such executions appeared to be whetted in time by the publication of such trial proceedings rather than by execution sermons (158).

As public opinion began to turn against capital punishment in the 1830s and 1840s, however, members of the clergy remained on the forefront of those who cited biblical texts to argue for the continuation of this penalty (159).

One of the more fascinating execution sermons was a sermon by Native American Samson Occom (1723–1792) at New Haven's First Congregational Church on September 2, 1773, upon the execution of a fellow Native American, Moses Paul, for murder. Occom organized his sermon around Romans 6:23: "For the wages of sin is death, but the gift of God is eternal life through Jesus Christ our Lord" (Weyler 2013, 137). Attempting to identify Native Americans as fellow descendants of Adam and Eve, Occom condemned not only Indians, like Moses Paul, who had fallen prey to alcohol but also those among his largely white audience who were complicit in selling it to them (Weyler 2013, 142–43).

See also Capital Punishment; Massachusetts Body of Liberties; Native American Indians; Prophets and Jeremiads; Puritans

For Reference and Further Reading

Bosco, Ronald A. 1978. "Lectures at the Pillory: The Early American Execution Sermon." *American Quarterly* 30 (Summer): 156–76.

Cohen, Daniel A. 1988. "In Defense of the Gallows: Justifications of Capital Punishment in New England Execution Sermons, 1674–1825." *American Quarterly* 40 (June): 147–64.

Weyler, Karen A. 2013. *Empowering Words: Outsiders and Authorship in Early America*. Athens: University of Georgia Press.

• F •

Falwell, Jerry

Jerry Falwell (1933–2007) was an independent Baptist minister who founded the Thomas Road Baptist Church in Lynchburg, Virginia, and Liberty University, of which he was president. He also cofounded the Moral Majority in 1979, which was one of the most visible Christian organizations identified with the election of Ronald Reagan in 1980 and the new right.

A graduate of the Baptist Bible College in Springfield, Missouri, Falwell founded the Thomas Road Baptist Church in 1956 and subsequently grew it into a megachurch. He also established "The Old Time Gospel Hour" broadcast from his church to hundreds of television and radio stations, which hewed to the essentials of biblical fundamentalism, with special emphasis on patriotism and the importance of traditionally conceived family life.

Like many other fundamentalists of his day, Falwell believed that the Bible was inerrant, that American society was eroding as the nation strayed from what he believed to have been its biblical foundations, and that revival was necessary to save it. Professor Frances FitzGerald notes that "his lists of national sins included sex education, 'secular humanist' textbooks, the ERA, feminism, abortion, and homosexuality—as well as pornography, drugs, and TV soap operas" (2017, 306).

Like many other white southern fundamentalist preachers of his day, Falwell had opposed racial integration. Despite later denials, Falwell does not initially appear to have been particularly concerned about the U.S. Supreme Court decision liberalizing abortion in *Roe v. Wade* in 1973 (Dowland 2009, 610).

Falwell's greatest innovation may have been his willingness to ally in the Moral Majority, which continued until 1989, with conservative Roman Catholics, Jews, and others whose theology differed from his but who shared his conservative social agenda on such issues as opposition to the Equal Rights Amendment (ERA), the legalization of abortion, and gay marriage. This sometimes brought on the ire of fellow fundamentalists like Bob Jones Jr. (head of the conservative Bob Jones University), who considered this to be unwarranted compromise with liberalism. An early promotional brochure for the Moral Majority described it as "pro-life, pro-family, pro-moral, and pro-America" (Dowland 2009, 614). In recounting a conversation with President Jimmy Carter, Falwell claimed that Carter admitted that he had homosexuals on his staff so he could represent everyone, but Carter produced evidence that he had not said this (625). Although Falwell closely identified with President Reagan, Reagan chose to put far greater emphasis on tax cuts than in efforts to overturn Supreme Court decisions on abortion or prayer in schools, and there were times when the Moral Majority seemed to need Reagan more than he needed its support (Banwart 2013, 152).

Like today's pastor John Hagee, Falwell was a strong supporter of Israel. He believed that its reestablishment as a nation was a fulfillment of biblical prophecy, and he established a strong friendship with Israeli prime minister Menachem Begin, who made the decision to bomb Iraqi nuclear facilities in 1981. Drawing from the promise to Abraham in Genesis 12:3 that God would bless those who blessed him, Falwell said that "you touch the apple of God's eyes when you touch Israel," and he attributed America's greatness to the fact that it had been a haven for Jews (Kincheloe and Staley 1982, 37).

The butt of a very tasteless mock advertisement in Larry Flint's *Hustler* magazine, Falwell unsuccessfully sued and lost in an 8-0 decision by the U.S. Supreme Court. It ruled in *Hustler Magazine v. Falwell* (1988) that because Falwell was a public figure, and no one would be likely to take the advertisement seriously, it was a form of protected speech. On another occasion, Falwell was ridiculed when, in a speech on February 15, 1999, he condemned a Tinky Winky Teletubby doll in a speech for promoting a homosexual lifestyle (Wilcox 2003, 25).

Although Falwell tacked closer to evangelicals than toward fundamentalists, a scholar has observed that "critics included not only leftist evangelicals like Jim Wallis and Ronald Sider, but also moderate academics like Mark Noll, George Marsden, and National Hatch," who warned against "identifying the 'family values' agenda with the gospel" (Dowland 2009, 628).

After his death from a heart attack, his son, Jerry Falwell Jr., who has a law degree, took the reins of Liberty University, where he often invites politicians to speak. He endorsed and has remained one of the most outspoken supporters of President Donald J. Trump, despite Trump's questionable lifestyle and his seeming ignorance of fundamentalist theology. A recent investigation has raised serious questions about Falwell's management of the university, which has continued to grow under his leadership (Ambrosino 2019; French 2019).

See also Abortion; Baptists; Fundamentalists; Hagee, John; Reagan, Ronald

For Reference and Further Reading

Ambrosino, Brandon. 2019. "Someone's Gotta Tell the Freakin' Truth': Jerry Falwell's Aides Break Their Silence." *Politico*. September 9. https://www.politico.com/magazine/story/2019/09/09/jerry-falwell-liberty-university-loans-227914.

Banwart, Doug. 2013. "Jerry Falwell, the Rise of the Moral Majority, and the 1980 Election." *Western Illinois Historical Review* 5 (Spring): 133–57.

Dowland, Seth. 2009. "'Family Values' and the Formation of a Christian Right Agenda." *Church History* 78 (September): 606–31.

FitzGerald, Frances. 2017. *The Evangelicals: The Struggle to Shape America*. New York: Simon & Schuster.

French, David. 2019. "Jerry Falwell Jr. Shows How the Advance of Christendom Can Harm Christianity." *National Review*. September 11. https://www.nationalreview.com/2019/09/jerry-falwell-jr-shows-how-the-advance-of-christendom-can-harm-christianity/.

Hustler Magazine v. Falwell, 485 U.S. 46 (1988).

Kincheloe, Joe L., and George Staley. 1982. "The Menachem Begin-Jerry Falwell Connection: A Revolution in Fundamentalism." *Journal of Thought* 17 (Summer): 35–39.

Leonard, Bill J. 1987. "Independent Baptists: From Sectarian Minority to 'Moral Majority.'" *Church History* 56 (December): 504–17.
Wilcox, Clyde. 2003. "Laying Up Treasures in Washington and in Heaven: The Christian Right and Evangelical Politics in the Twentieth Century and Beyond." *OAH Magazine of History* 17 (January): 23–29.
Winters, Michael Sean. 2012. *God's Right Hand: How Jerry Falwell Made God a Republican and Baptized the American Right*. New York: HarperCollins.

Findley/Wylie Debate over "The Two Sons of Oil"

One of the more obscure Scriptures to enter American political debate was taken from Zechariah 4:14. It refers to two olive trees—often used as a biblical symbol for Israel and sometimes identified with Joshua and Zerubbabel, the first a Jewish priest and the second a descendant of Israel's kings, whom Cyrus appointed over the Jews who returned to Jerusalem.

In an essay that he published in 1803 entitled "The Two Sons of Oil," Samuel Brown Wylie (1773–1852), an Irish-Presbyterian minister of the Reformed Presbyterian Church of the United States, argued that the U.S. government was illegitimate because it failed to recognize God or the sovereignty of Jesus Christ. Moreover, by failing to enforce the Ten Commandments or establish a religion, by allowing atheists to hold office, and by providing for freedom of conscience, the government allowed sin to run rampant (Wedgeworth 2011–2012, 147–48). This argument tapped into centuries of discussion, heighted by the Reformation, about the duty of civil magistrates to enforce the Law of Moses (Avis 1975). Almost in anticipation of the arguments of later abolitionists, Wylie also objected to the Constitution because he believed it sanctioned slavery, and, like other Reformed Presbyterians, he thus urged his readers not to vote, hold office, or participate in the militia.

This essay prompted an extended rebuttal by another former Reformed Presbyterian named William Findley (1741–1821). He had served in the Pennsylvania legislature, opposed ratification of the U.S. Constitution without the addition of the Bill of Rights, and served several terms in the U.S. Congress.

Whereas Wylie had argued that magistrates were obligated to enforce the Ten Commandments, Findley countered that these laws were tied to a specific covenant between God and Israel and were thus not the job of civil magistrates: "Now the intention of the Sinai covenant does not appear to have extended beyond the Israelites themselves; it was addressed solely to them, and calculated to operate within bounds expressly prescribed, and could not be put in operation elsewhere" (Findley 2007, 9). When the Bible referred to Jesus as a king, it referred not to civil rule but to his role within the church. Governments should seek to secure natural rights rather than the law of God, and, in accord with Romans 13 and other verses, citizens should obey governmental officials (30). Findley believed that in seeking to enforce the laws of God through civil power, Wylie was effectively imitating Muslims and Roman Catholics who fruitlessly sought to judge human consciences, which were only knowable by God.

Although Wylie later repudiated his views, Reformed Presbyterians continued throughout the nineteenth century to advocate for an amendment specifically mentioning God in the U.S. Constitution. In more recent times, Christian

Reconstructionists have taken up the cudgels for vesting governments with the power to enforce biblical laws.

See also Christian Amendment; Christian Reconstructionism; Jesus; Moses; Ten Commandments

For Reference and Further Reading

Avis, P. D. L. 1975. "Moses and the Magistrate: A Study in the Rise of Protestant Legalism." *Journal of Ecclesiastical History* 26 (April): 149–72.

Emery, Robert. 2009–2010. "Church and State in the Early Republic: The Covenanters' Radical Critique." *Journal of Law and Religion* 25(2): 487–501.

Findley, William. 2007. *Observations on "The Two Sons of Oil" Containing a Vindication of the American Constitutions, and Defending the Blessings of Religious Liberty and Toleration, against the Illiberal Strictures of the Rev. Samuel B. Wylie*, ed. with an introduction by John Caldwell. Indianapolis: Liberty Fund.

Wedgeworth, Steven. 2011–2012. "'The Two Sons of Oil' and the Limits of American Religious Dissent." *Journal of Law and Religion* 27(1): 141–61.

First Continental Congress

One of the scenes from U.S. history that has been immortalized in stained glass in a window at Philadelphia's Christ Church depicts Rev. Jacob Duché reading Psalm 35 in Carpenter's Hall at the First Continental Congress, which had been called to discuss colonial grievances against the British.

Twelve states (all but Georgia) had sent a total of fifty-six delegates to this Congress, which met in Philadelphia to protest the Coercive (or Intolerable) Acts, which the British had adopted in the wake of the so-called Boston Tea Party, and to author a "Declaration and Resolves" articulating colonial rights. When the Convention began on September 6, 1774, a delegate suggested that the assembly should open with prayer. Although delegates were initially too divided along denominational lines to settle on a clergyman, Samuel Adams suggested inviting Jacob Duché of the neighboring Christ Church. He arrived the next morning in clerical garb and a wig and read Psalm 35 from the Book of Common Prayer's suggested reading for the day. That psalm beings with the verse, "Please my cause, O LORD, with them that strive with me; fight against them that fight against me." John Adams noted in a letter to his wife Abigail that "it seemed as if Heaven had ordained that Psalm to be read on that Morning" (Feiler 2009, 56). Adams had similar praise for Duché's prayer, which departed from the prescribed of the day. Drawing from the spirit of the psalm, Duché called upon God to look down "on these our American States, who have fled to Thee from the rod of the oppressor and thrown themselves on Thy gracious protection, desiring to be henceforth dependent only on Thee. To Thee have they appealed for the righteousness of their cause; to Thee do they now look up for that countenance and support, which Thou alone canst give." He further asked God to take them "under Thy nurturing care; give them wisdom in Council and valor in the field; defeat the malicious designs of our cruel adversaries; convince them of the unrighteousness of their Cause and if they persist in their sanguinary purposes, of our unerring justice, sounding in their hearts, constrain them to drop the weapons of war from their unnerved hands in the day of battle!" ("First Prayer").

Two years later, after Congress adopted the Declaration of Independence on July 4, 1776, Duché met with vestrymen from his church who agreed that he should strike out references to the king from the church's Book of Common Prayer. He subsequently struck out about half a dozen such references and replaced them with references to the U.S. Congress and the welfare of the American people (Feiler 2009, 57).

As colonial fortunes fell, Duché wrote a letter to George Washington urging him to cease hostilities. When Washington released the letter to Congress, Duché sought exile in England, and although he later returned to Philadelphia, he never regained his former standing.

See also Revolutionary War

For Reference and Further Reading

Feiler, Bruce. 2009. *America's Prophet: Moses and the American Story*. New York: William Morrow.

"First Prayer of the Continental Congress, 1774." The Office of the Chaplain, United States House of Representatives. https://chaplain.house.gov/archive/continental.html.

Forms of Government

The thirteen states that formed the original United States began as colonies of Great Britain. Even when they were founded, the power of its monarch was already losing ground to the Parliament, which would in time assert its ultimate political sovereignty, especially over matters of taxation. Governments varied within individual colonies, with Massachusetts and Connecticut being particularly associated with the Puritanism and the legislation of morality. By contrast, Rhode Island (founded by erstwhile Baptist Roger Williams), Pennsylvania (founded by Quaker William Penn), and, for a time, Maryland (founded by Lord Baltimore, who was seeking a haven for Roman Catholics) were associated with religious toleration.

At the outbreak of the American Revolution, these states created the Articles of Confederation in which primary power rested with the states. This government was quite similar to that during the period of the judges after the Jews were delivered out of Egypt and before they created their own monarchy. In 1787, delegates met in Philadelphia to draw up another constitution that created the current democratic-republican (representative) federal government, in which power is more equally shared between the national government and the states, but in which on key issues the federal constitution is considered to be supreme. The government of the Confederate States of America, from 1861 to 1865, was something of a combination of federal and confederal forms, thought to be sanctioned in part by the specific mention of God in its preamble.

Although the Bible, particularly the Old Testament, describes a variety of empires, it does not warrant a single time of regime, and it is doubtful that American statesmen who wanted to live by the Bible could have pointed to particular chapters and verses requiring a particular type. The Bible does, however, make it clear, especially in its prophetic tradition, that any earthly ruler was subject to God, and individuals were ultimately responsible for obeying God rather than men in cases of conflict (Wildavsky 1984).

Paul Hanson has identified six regime types in the Old Testament. He calls the confederal rule of the judges "theocratic" because the individual tribes were understood as being directly accountable to God (2010, 12–14). There was at least some attempt to prescribe the rule of Moses during this period, a law that Massachusetts later tried to incorporate within its own Body of Liberties.

In describing biblical monarchy, Hanson observes, as Thomas Paine would later do, that the prophet Samuel had warned in 1 Samuel 8:17 that kings would bring conscription of men for battle, increased taxes, and even slavery. Hanson observes that only a handful of kings, most notably "Aza, Hezekiah, and Josiah" (16), met biblical standards while the kings lauded as the greatest, notably David and Solomon, had great flaws. Hanson associates monarchy with prophets, who called kings to task and emphasized "worship and mercy and justice" (17).

Hanson also refers to what he calls "the sapiential model" (21), which draws from Hebrew wisdom literature and is similar to what Aristotle described when referring to politics as a form of practical reason. Hanson also offers the "accommodationalist model," which he associates with times of Jewish exile, such as that found in the book of Esther, and the "apocalyptic model" (23, 24), which he says gave hope for the future during times of persecution like that suffered by the early church.

As churches attempted to come up with their own forms of government, they developed three types. The congregational model, which is based on the doctrine of the priesthood of all believers (1 Peter 2:9) and which was particularly popular in New England and is shared by Baptists, Quakers, and other groups, vests primary power within local congregations. It was arguably a model for democratic forms of government elsewhere whose members may, however, unite in various larger associations. The Presbyterian model, which is a type of indirect, or republican, democracy, vests the chief power in church elders, interchurch groups of whom might also meet to settle issues of doctrine. There may be precedent for this in the Council of Jerusalem as described in Acts 15. This model is most closely associated with the denomination that bears its name. The episcopal system, which is most closely associated with the Roman Catholic and Episcopal Churches, strives for greater unity with a system of bishops or archbishops, which in the Catholic Church are headed by the pope in Rome. Such systems rely heavily on the authority vested in the apostles in the New Testament (Morris n.d.).

The Declaration of Independence gave clues as an appropriate secular government by listing the kinds of abuses against which the colonies were rebelling, but focused chiefly on the fact that governments should protect individual liberties and could be changed by the people. The biblical theme that his people were bound to God through covenant, like that which the people of Israel agreed to at Mount Sinai, influenced later ideas that both the powers of government and the rights and liberties of the people should be incorporated into a constitution. The influence of the Bible on specific institutions stemmed not from a particular mandate for one regime over another but from the idea that human nature is so fundamentally flawed that any power must be balanced against others.

In defending dividing the national government into three different branches, James Madison, who had studied under John Witherspoon at the College of New

Jersey, rhetorically asked, "But what is government itself, but the greatest of all reflections on human nature" and noted that "if men were angels, no government would be necessary," but that it was important for government not only "to control the governed" but also "to control itself." He further noted, "A dependence on the people is, no doubt, the primary control on the government; but experience has taught mankind the necessity of auxiliary precautions" (Hamilton, Madison, and Jay [1788] 1961, 322).

The postbellum amendments that the nation adopted from 1865 to 1870 were designed to incorporate ideas of equal protection and due process from the Declaration of Independence, which arguably had their roots both in biblical teachings and in social contract theory, within the Constitution itself. The American judicial system is arranged in a tiered system in a manner similar to that which Moses instituted after receiving advice from his father-in-law Jethro in Exodus 18.

Most alternative forms of government that have been proposed for the United States have been secular models, with many suggesting a parliamentary system like that in Britain rather than our own presidential system of separated powers (Vile 2014).

See also Covenants, Compacts, Contracts, and Constitutions; Declaration of Independence; Human Nature; Madison, James; Massachusetts Body of Liberties; Paine, Thomas; Penn, William; Puritans; U.S. Constitution; Williams, Roger

For Reference and Further Reading

Hamilton, Alexander, James Madison, and John Jay. [1788] 1961. *The Federalist Papers.* New York: New American Library.

Hanson, Paul D. 2010. *Political Engagement as Biblical Mandate.* Cambridge: James Clarke.

Morris, L. n.d. "Church Government." Elwell Evangelical Dictionary. http ://mb-soft.com/believe/text/cgovern.htm.

Vile, John R. 2014. *Re-Framers: 170 Eccentric, Visionary, and Patriotic Proposals to Rewrite the U.S. Constitution.* Santa Barbara, CA: ABC-CLIO.

Wildavsky, Aaron. 1984. *The Nursing Father: Moses as a Political Leader.* Tuscaloosa: University of Alabama Press.

Founders' Bible

Professor Mary Juzwik has observed that "many contemporary Bibles include extra-Biblical material targeted at specific audiences" (2014, 341). *The Founders' Bible* is among the specialty Bibles that attempt to link Scriptures to American law and politics. In addition to numerous illustrations, it contains approximately two hundred articles on related topics and another sixty-five articles on biographies of American founders.

Most of the articles are the work of David Barton, a self-styled historian and founder of Wallbuilders, who is said to have a vault of some two hundred thousand original historical manuscripts and who is widely known for arguing that America is a Christian nation that was largely founded by orthodox Christians. Although he speaks extensively in evangelical circles and is widely admired and quoted, professional historians and fellow evangelical scholars have warned that his scholarship, particularly with regard to Thomas Jefferson, is significantly flawed, so much so that Thomas Nelson withdrew one of the books that he published on the subject (Coulter and Throckmorton 2013; Burton 2018).

The eye-catching cover of *The Founders' Bible* portrays three men in colonial garb in a lantern-lit room with a copy of the Constitution, the Declaration of Independence, and the Bible on the desk before them and a fourth looking out the window at a nearby church. Perhaps as a reminder of the Second Amendment, there is a gun on the wall. The subtitle of the book is *The Origin of the Dream of Freedom*. Likely as a way of further indicating its ties to the nation, the version of the Bible used is the New American Standard Bible, which was sponsored by the Lockman Foundation. The book is colorfully illustrated with sketches by C. Michael Dudash.

Barton has a way of tying together diverse quotations from a variety of individuals (often without providing context) to make his point. His very first essay, "America: A Bible Nation," ties the success of America to the success of the Bible as a publication (ix) and quotes a number of presidential commendations of the value of Scriptures. A later essay describes the history of the English Bible (A-1–A-16 after p. 360). Although the book's title suggests that it is about the American founders, many of the essays are essentially Barton's commentary on contemporary issues. Thus, one of the earliest essays on "Creationism" suggests that American founders accepted creationism over evolution, without recognizing that the term "creationism" is of relatively recent derivation and is often associated with the view, not directly stated in the Bible, that the Earth is relatively young (3–6). An essay on Jamestown says that the marriage of John Rolfe and Pocahontas suggests that their marriage provides "*a model of racial equality and harmony*" (39), while a later essay argues that God used the transportation of slaves to the United States, like the selling of Joseph into slavery in Egypt, for good (75–78).

A story embedded in the account of Exodus associates the Puritan Pilgrims with an "escape from tyranny" (95). Not surprisingly, Barton ties the giving of the Ten Commandments in Exodus 20 with "the Moral Law for Nations" (161). Unsurprisingly, Leviticus 25 provides an occasion for an essay on the Liberty Bell (213–14), while the book of Deuteronomy is punctuated by an essay on "The Source of American Exceptionalism" (281), another tying God's destruction of the world in the Great Flood with capital punishment (321–26), and yet another citing the practice of gleaning as a way to help the poor (337–40). An essay tied to 1 Chronicles 5:22 provides assurance that God sometimes ordains war (611–16). Another essay, tied to Psalm 139, interprets a number of historical writings that deal specifically with abortion after "quickening" as outright bans on the procedure (905–8).

In addition to the previously mentioned essay on the history of the English Bible, there are other long, colorfully illustrated essays on George Washington (after p. 849); the Declaration of Independence (after p. 1032), which a later essay (1964–67) traces not to the Enlightenment but to a book on church government; the phrase "In God We Trust" (after p. 1320); and "Separation of Church and State" (after p. 1656), which questions modern judicial interpretations of the First Amendment.

Matthew 5:16 provides an occasion for an essay on "The Shining City Set on a Hill" (1433–36), Matthew 19 on the harms of divorce (1471–77), and Matthew 20 on the value of "Free-Market Enterprise" (1485–87). Essays accompanying Romans 1:26–27 and 1 Corinthians 6 highlight the sinfulness of homosexuality (1737–43 and 1803–12).

The final essay is an extended essay entitled "America: A Christian Nation" (2091–106) and suggests that anyone who believes otherwise is simply unwilling to acknowledge the truth. It adds that "the best antidote to the current secular progressive revisionist claim that America is not a Christian nation is for citizens (1) to study and know for themselves America's history as a Christian nation, and (2) share that truth with others" (2104).

There will, of course, be many who would, in the least, want to qualify such a characterization with suitable reservations, but the apparent audience for this Bible will likely consist of those who already accept that message and who have no qualms about associating a book designed for individuals throughout the entire world with one exceptional nation.

See also American Patriots' Bible; Founding Fathers

For Reference and Further Reading

Burton, Tara Isabella. 2018. "Understanding the Fake Historian behind America's Religious Right." Vox. January 25. https://www.vox.com/identities/2018/1/25/16919362/understanding-the-fake-historian-behind-americas-religious-right.

Coulter, Michael, and Warren Throckmorton. 2013. "David Barton Is Wrong." World. Faith & Religion. January 22. https://world.wng.org/2013/01/david_barton_is_wrong.

The Founders' Bible: The Origin of the Dream of Freedom. 2012. Signature historian David Barton. Newbury Park, CA: Shiloh Road.

Juzwik, Mary M. 2014. "American Evangelical Biblicism as Literate Practice: A Critical Review." *Reading Research Quarterly* 49 (July/August/September): 335–49.

Taylor, Justin. 2017. "Christian History: How David Barton Is Doing It Wrong." The Gospel Coalition. May 12. https://www.thegospelcoalition.org/blogs/evangelical-history/christian-history-why-david-barton-is-doing-it-wrong/.

Four Horsemen of the Apocalypse

The biblical book of Revelation, which closes the traditional Christian canon, is noted for its vivid imagery. Chapter 6:1–8 describes four horsemen—one white, one red, one black, and one pale—that respectively represent war, famine, pestilence, and death. These symbols have often been used in American history to describe real or anticipated devastation of creation, often connected to God's judgment.

When the U.S. Supreme Court opposed President Franklin Delano Roosevelt's progressive New Deal policies, the press referred to its four most conservative members who were leading this opposition as the Fourth Horsemen. They were Pierce Butler, James Clark McReynolds, George Sutherland, and Willis Van Devanter.

When on June 1, 1950, U.S. senator Margaret Chase Smith of Maine registered her concern on the Senate floor about the manner in which fellow senator Joseph McCarthy and others were falsely labeling opponents as communists or communist sympathizers, she referred to "the Four Horsemen of Calumny—Fear, Ignorance, Bigotry, and Smear" (Smith 1950, 522).

Recent commentators continue this theme. As the 2016 presidential election approached, a writer identified Donald Trump and three allies—former New Jersey governor Chris Christie, former Speaker of the House Newt Gingrich, and former New York City mayor Rudy Giuliani—as "the four horsemen of the GOP's apocalypse" (Cross 2016). By contrast, a writer for the *American Spectator* described four progressive U.S. Democrat representatives who are known for their social media savvy—namely, Alexandria Ocasio-Cortes, Rashida Tlaib, Ayanna Pressley, and Ilham Omar—as "The Four Horsemen of the Democrat Apocalypse" and praised House Speaker Nancy Pelosi for opposing them (Flynn 2019).

Showing that such criticism can be bipartisan in nature, another writer who was anticipating the 2016 election identified Democrat Hillary Clinton with "the white horse of conquest," Republican Donald Trump on the red horse to take away peace, Democrat Bernie Sanders with the black horse of theft, and Chris Christie on the pale horse of death (Jensen 2016).

Many who have voiced concern over climate change have further connected the projected ills these changes are bringing with the Four Horsemen.

See also Climate Change; Judgment

For Reference and Further Reading

Cross, Richard J., III. 2016. "The Four Horsemen of the GOP's Apocalypse." *Baltimore Sun*. November 5. https://www.baltimoresun.com/opinion/op-ed/bs-ed-four-horsemen-20161105-story.html.

Flynn, Daniel J. 2019. "The Four Horsewomen of the Democrat Apocalypse: Pestilence, Family, War, and Death Take a Blow from Nancy Pelosi." *American Spectator*. July 12. https://spectator.org/the-four-horsewomen-of-the-democrat-apocalypse/.

Jensen, Samuel Wean. 2016. "The Four Horsemen of the American Political Apocalypse." The Moral Middle. February 19. https://web.archive.org/web/20160324042730/http :// themoralmiddle.com/the-four-horsemen-of-the-american-political-apocalypse/.

Smith, Margaret Chase. 1950. "Declaration of Conscience." June 1. https://www.senate.gov/artandhistory/history/resources/pdf/SmithDeclaration.pdf.

Franklin, Benjamin

One of the most influential and celebrated American founders was Benjamin Franklin (1706–1790). He rose to riches to become a leading colonial publisher of newspapers, almanacs, and books—including the writings of the evangelist George Whitefield (1714–1770), with whom he was friends (Hoffer 2011). He was also a noted scientist and then retired to devote most of his life to public service, including service as postmaster general. He also founded institutions as diverse as a fire department, a lending library, and a university. He served for many years as a colonial representative to London before being humiliated in Parliament and returning to Philadelphia and supporting the American Revolution. He contributed to the writing of the Declaration of Independence, which he signed and which put him at permanent odds with a Tory son who was serving as governor of New Jersey. During much of the Revolutionary War, Franklin served as an

American ambassador to France, where he made a highly favorable impression on the French imagination and helped secure French help in the war. The oldest member of the Constitutional Convention of 1787, Franklin is quoted more frequently than any other delegate as citing Scripture.

His own religious views have long been the subject of dispute. Although he is often classified as a Deist (one who believed that after creation, God largely stepped aside to let people govern their own affairs), Joseph Waligore has made a convincing case that he came closest to what might be called a "Christian Deist," which he defines as one who privileged natural religion (the use of reason) over revealed religion, who had a special place for Jesus, whose original teachings such Deists believed had been corrupted by priests and other religious leaders, but who believed that God sometimes intervenes in world affairs on behalf of liberty and virtue (2016, 9). Waligore thinks that Franklin's beliefs were most evident in his defense of Rev. Samuel Hemphill, who was eventually expelled from the Presbyterian Church, and that Franklin was likely influenced in his belief by James Pitt of England.

Whatever Franklin may ultimately have believed, he had such a good familiarity with Scripture that at times he was able to perpetrate what Prudence Steiner refers to as "biblical hoaxes." She notes that, in a discussion of John Locke's treatise on religious toleration, Franklin sought to win an argument by referring someone to the 51st chapter of Genesis, a chapter that he himself had written and printed and bound into his copy of the Bible! This pseudo-biblical passage described how God rebuked Abraham for turning away an idolater by pointing out that God had been able to put up with him for 198 years, and as a sinner, Abraham should have been able to host him for at least one night (Steiner 1987, 184).

On another occasion, again translating a Parable on Brotherly Love, which he appears to have taken from the Talmud, into the language of the King James Bible, Franklin attributed conflict among believers not to differences of doctrine but to lack of charity (Steiner 1987, 185).

On yet another occasion, Franklin reworked the opening words of the book of Job so that they applied to the English Court and drew the lesson that one should never trust those in governing positions (Steiner 1987, 189). He also revised and reworked the Lord's Prayer and revised the catechism so that it asked only two questions, namely "What is your duty to God?" and "What is your duty to your neighbor?" (191). Steiner further likens Franklin's famed *Poor Richard's Almanack* to "a new book of Proverbs" (196), while Nancy Galzener observes that Franklin searched "for a religious lowest common denominator, weighted toward the needs of civil society" (2008, 223).

Ministers are fond of quoting a story, which I have been unable to verify from original sources, that Franklin once changed the names in the story recounted in the biblical book of Ruth and read it before an Infidel Society, whose members praised it as one of the best short stories they had heard, only to have Franklin inform them that it came from the book that they had ridiculed. Such a story would not, of course, establish that Franklin accepted the Bible as the inspired word of God but that he recognized that it was a treasure trove of pious civic behavior and of wisdom.

See also Constitutional Convention of 1787; Declaration of Independence; Deism

For Reference and Further Reading

Glazener, Nancy. 2008. "Benjamin Franklin and the Limits of Secular Civil Society." *American Literature* 80 (June): 203–31.
Hoffer, Peter Charles. 2011. *When Benjamin Franklin Met the Reverend Whitefield.* Baltimore, MD: Johns Hopkins University Press.
Shalev, Eran. 2010. "'Written in the Style of Antiquity': Pseudo-Biblicism and the Early American Republic, 1770–1830." *Church History* 79 (December): 800–26.
Steiner, Prudence L. 1987. "Benjamin Franklin's Biblical Hoaxes." *Proceedings of the American Philosophical Society* 131 (June): 183–96.
Waligore, Joseph. 2016. "The Christian Deist Writings of Benjamin Franklin." *Pennsylvania Magazine of History and Biography* 140 (January): 7–29.

Frelinghuysen, Theodore

Theodore Frelinghuysen (1787–1862) was an accomplished statesman and educator who was raised in the Dutch Reformed Church and spent much of his life as a Presbyterian before returning to the church of his youth. A graduate of Princeton University, Frelinghuysen became an attorney, served as an officer during the War of 1812, was selected as attorney general and U.S. senator from New Jersey, and was chancellor of New York University and later president of Rutgers College.

Frelinghuysen had a deep Christian faith rooted in the Bible, and he headed numerous interdenominational groups that sought a variety of political and social reforms. A strong advocate of missions, he served as president of the American Board of Commissioners for Foreign Missions (ABCFM). He was also a prominent member of the American Bible Society (ABS). In this capacity, he lauded "that sacred Book, which reveals the best and only lasting hope for ourselves, our country, and the world" (Eells 1991, 261). He also served as president of the American Tract Society and as vice president of the American Sunday School Union (ASSU), which at the time was deeply devoted to teaching individuals of all classes.

Frelinghuysen was a strong advocate of public education and the temperance movement and favored total abstinence. He served as a member of the executive committee of the American Congressional Temperance Society. He was one of the most vocal opponents of President Andrew Jackson's policy of removing the Cherokee Indians and gave a six-hour speech outlining his opposition (Eells 1991, 265).

Frelinghuysen also considered slavery to be a moral evil, but, in contrast to those who advocated immediate abolitionism, he devoted his efforts to recolonizing freed slaves to Africa and was a strong supporter of the American Colonization Society (ACS). His position stemmed in part from his deep respect for southern culture and for what he believed would be the dire impact of immediate emancipation.

Although Frelinghuysen favored religious freedom, he thought that Thomas Jefferson, Andrew Jackson, and others had pushed the separation of church and state too far in opposing national days of thanksgiving in prayer, the beginning of legislative sessions with prayer, and encouraging commerce on the Sabbath by providing for Sunday mail. He expressed these ideas in a book that he coauthored with Henry Whiting Warner in 1838. In arguments that often resemble those that Ezra Stiles Ely had voiced in *The Duty of Christian Freemen to Elect Christian Rulers*, Frelinghuysen expressed shock that the nation should "be administered with as little avowed deference as possible for those of the supreme being" (1838, 2) or that the Constitution might be interpreted in a manner "unfriendly to religion" (24).

Frelinghuysen believed that most American colonies had been founded by individuals seeking religious freedom and that the belief in the importance of religion and the Bible was embodied in state constitutions. Frelinghuysen further believed that it was possible to distinguish "between legislating *directly for religion*, as an end of jurisdiction, and *keeping it respectfully in view*, while legislating for other ends, the legitimacy of which was unquestioned" (Frelinghuysen and Warner 1838, 111). He proceeded to cite numerous examples of congressional declarations of repentance and thanksgiving, of regulations encouraging members of the military to honor the Sabbath, and the like.

Much like those who had argued that the common law embodied Christian principles, Frelinghuysen pointed to the use of oaths taken upon Bibles in court (131). Associating Christianity with republican virtue, Frelinghuysen thought that governments should do their best to further it. As he viewed the situation, the issue is, "shall the government be administered *as it is, or as it is not?* As a *christian* or a *pagan* government?" (141). Positing that the Bible is true, Frelinghuysen believed that "it is the duty of all men indiscriminately, to cherish the interests of religion in the world" (142). Associating republicanism with Christianity, Frelinghuysen argued that nations, like individuals, were subject to God's judgment, and it was thus appropriate for government to promote Christian principles (145). He observed that "Christianity, besides being itself a revelation, and having in it a revealing principle that tends to enlighten everything else, has a *principle of charity also*, which the press could never supply" (148). He believed this spirit was a major impetus to public education.

Believing that the universal adoption of Christianity would bring great benefits, Frelinghuysen thought that government should seek to allow its truths to expand. He believed that such truth was the enemy of fanaticism and that the spread of biblical knowledge in America was even leavening Roman Catholicism, many of whose members he admired (169–70). He argued that Christianity was "favourable to liberty" (171) and that its influence was a key factor in eliminating the slave trade and polygamy and in undermining the continuation of slavery.

Frelinghuysen attempted to avoid the errors of both theocracy and indifference: "The European statesman hugs the church, and calls it an establishment of *religion*. This is bad enough. American politicians turn religion out of doors, and call it keeping clear of the *church*. This is worse" (186). Frelinghuysen advocated deference to Christianity, the majority religion, but neutrality among Christian sects. Writing about existing laws, particularly at the state level, he thus observed, "So far as they have any the least concern for religion, it is for Christianity only; they know no other faiths. Among the various sects professing this faith, they hold, or aim to hold, an even balance, treating all with like favor, out of a common respect for all, as children of one family. But here they stop. Other religions are protected; this alone is fostered" (193). He specifically applied this doctrine to the issue of Sunday mails.

While recognizing that the Constitution forbade religious test, in his concluding chapter Frelinghuysen said that "I do not say, that persons of know piety should alone be admitted to the people's confidence; but I hope it may be said without offence, that other things being equal, such should be preferred; and this, not for their sake but the country's; not because office is a boon to be given to the worthiest, but a trust, upon the due execution of which the country has every thing at stake" (207).

See also American Bible Society; Cherokee Removal; Jefferson Bible; Slavery; Sunday Mail; Temperance Movement

For Reference and Further Reading

Eells, Robert J. 1987. *Forgotten Saint: The Life of Theodore Frelinghuysen, A Case Study in Christian Leadership*. Lanham, MD: University Press of America.

Eells, Robert J. 1991. "Theodore Frelinghuysen, Voluntaryism and the Pursuit of the Public Good." *American Presbyterians* 69 (Winter): 257–70.

Frelinghuysen, Theodore, and Henry Whiting Warner. 1838. *An Inquiry into the Moral and Religious Character of the American Government*. New York: Wiley and Putnam.

French and Indian War

From 1754 to 1763, militiamen from the thirteen English colonies joined English troops in battling against French Canadians and their Native American allies to the North.

During this war, George Washington made his first foray into military conflict, and at the war's end, Britain took control over Canada, arguably relieving one of the threats to the British colonies that had kept them so closely allied to the mother country. Historian Nathan Hatch (1974) has demonstrated that this war, which was part of a much larger conflict between the English and the French, featured many of the same biblical themes, most notably what he calls "civil millennialism" that would reappear, in a somewhat different form, during the American Revolution.

Prior to the war, Jonathan Edwards and other American theologians were convinced that the First Great Awakening, which was concentrated in the 1730s and 1740s, signaled the beginning of the millennial reign of Christ on earth, which Edwards and others thought would probably begin in America (Hatch 1974, 412). Protestant theologians of the day often associated the coming of the millennium with the defeat of the Antichrist, whom they identified with the Great Whore of Babylon in the book of Revelation, which they in turn identified with the Roman Catholic Church, and the governments, like Spain and France, which supported it.

In 1745, almost ten years prior to the French and Indian War, New England was enraptured by news that New Englanders had captured the French fortress of Louisbourg, which they again associated with the defeat of Catholicism (Hatch 1974, 417). During the French and Indian War, pastors not only in New England, but also in the South, further associated victories against the French with the defeat of the Antichrist and with the spread of both civil and religious liberty. In a sermon that railed against both Catholics and Native American Indians and that would echo themes later emphasized during the Revolutionary War, Samuel Davies (1723–1761), a pastor in Hanover County, Virginia (the home of Patrick Henry), preached a sermon entitled "Religion and Patriotism the Constituents of a Good Soldier," in which he inspired individuals to join the fight with the words of 2 Samuel 10:12: "Be of good Courage, and let us play the men, for our People, and for the Cities of our God" (Byrd 2013, 25). Davies would later cite Jeremiah's exhortation in 48:10 that "cursed be he that keepeth back his Sword from Blood" to urge the troops to even greater efforts (26).

Hatch observes that "clergymen appear to have lost a clear distinction between the kingdom of God and the goals of their own political community. Military victories of Protestants over Catholics, which for earlier New Englanders had been means to the end of worldwide revival, now pointed toward a different end. The idea of a millennium of liberty both civil and religious had captured the clergy's imagination" (1974, 422). They, in turn, began increasingly reading the goal of civil liberty back into their own Puritan founders, who while seeking liberty to pursue their own faith had often been unwilling to extend it to others.

Closely tied to the British during the war against France, the colonists lauded the British Constitution, which they believed displayed God's providence in a manner similar to that which had been displayed within America. Hatch observes that Americans "had scarcely savored victory, however, when the grasping hand of tyranny reappeared in a new and dangerous form," namely the Stamp Act, fears that the English were going to create a system of bishops within the United States, and, in time, the Quebec Act, through which the English recognized the Catholic Church in Canada. During the Revolution, Americans projected many of the fears that they had previously associated with France, to whom they were now allied, onto Britain, associating the war with the protection of both civil and religious liberties.

See also Puritans; Revolutionary War; Roman Catholics

For Reference and Further Reading

Berens, John F. 1978. *Providence & Patriotism in Early America, 1640–1815*. Charlottesville: University Press of Virginia.

Byrd, James P. 2013. *Sacred Scripture, Sacred War: The Bible and the American Revolution*. New York: Oxford University Press.

Hatch, Nathan O. 1974. "The Origins of Civil Millennialism in America: New England Clergymen, War with France, and the Revolution." *William and Mary Quarterly* 31 (July): 407–30.

Fuller (Richard) and Wayland (Francis) Correspondence on Slavery

In his second inaugural address, President Lincoln observed that Northerners and Southerners read the same Bible but aligned themselves on different sides with respect to slavery. Abolitionists often called for immediate emancipation, arguing that all slavery was wrong, while slave apologists, who had once largely classified slavery as a necessary evil, increasingly argued that it was a positive good for both masters and slaves that the Bible approved.

As positions hardened on both sides, dialogue became increasingly difficult, and most Protestant denominations split into northern and southern wings. In a book first published in 1845 and republished on the very eve of the Civil War, however, two Baptist pastors and theologians sought to outline their respective positions in a series of letters that they published, and they did so with grace and dignity.

The correspondence opened with a letter from Dr. Richard Fuller (1804–1876), a former lawyer and pastor of the Baptist church in Beaufort, South Carolina, who helped found the Southern Baptist Convention. He argued against the abolitionist idea that slavery was always sinful. This was followed by a series of eight letters from Dr. Francis Wayland (1796–1865), the president of Brown University and pastor of the First Baptist Church of Providence, Rhode Island, who argued against slavery as in his *Elements of Moral Science* in 1835. These letters were, in turn, followed by a series of six letters from Dr. Fuller further defending slavery and a closing letter from Dr. Wayland reiterating his earlier arguments.

In his opening letter, Dr. Fuller took primary aim at abolitionists and observed that "I find my Bible condemning the abuses of slavery, but permitting the system itself, in cases where its abrogation would be a greater calamity than its existence" (Fuller and Wayland 1860, 4). Accepting the idea that slavery was "an obligation to labor for the benefit of the master, without the contract or consent of the slave" (7), Fuller did not think bondage was in and of itself sinful, although he agreed that it was sinful to treat slaves as mere chattel, without any rights (9). Abuses were "mere accidents of slavery" (10) rather than an essential component thereof.

In his first letter, Wayland clearly separated himself from radical abolitionism, but he noted that at the time the nation adopted the U.S. Constitution, there was a general understanding both that slavery was wrong and that states should eliminate it "as soon as practicable" (15). Given Fuller's definition of slavery, Wayland did not conceive of how such a relationship could be maintained except by force. Although believing that slavery was always a moral evil, Wayland conceded that it might be possible for individuals to hold others in slavery without the guilt of realizing that they were doing wrong (24–25).

In his second letter Wayland argued that slavery violated the biblical commandment to love one's neighbor as himself (31) as well as being contrary to the truths articulated in the Declaration of Independence (33). He cited Acts 17:26 to prove that God had made all people of one blood (26), and John 3:16 to show that God had sent Christ to die on behalf of all (27). It was impossible to follow the biblical admonition to love others while forbidding them to read and thus consigning them "to intellectual and moral imbecility" (29). Slavery was incompatible with the Golden Rule (30), and "the Scriptures frequently allude to the fact, that wrong done by law, that is, by society, is amenable to the same retribution as wrong done by the individual," a principle he tied to Psalm 94:20–23 and Isaiah 10:1–4 (31–32).

In his fourth letter, Wayland returned to his understanding of the Bible, noting that "believing as we both do that the Bible is a perfect rule of duty, if we can ascertain what it teaches, we may reasonably hope that our opinions may yet coincide" (49). Wayland agreed with Fuller that the Bible had sanctioned slavery in the Old Testament, that the Hebrews had held slaves, and that the Mosaic law had permitted slavery. He cautioned, however, that modern Christians could not appropriate divine commandments that were specifically given to the Jews with regard to the Canaanites (50), and he believed that revelation was progressive, which he illustrated by the fact that the Old Testament had also sanctioned divorce and polygamy, neither of which the New Testament approved (56). In the next letter, he suggested that the Bible may have permitted some institutions simply because they could not be eliminated expeditiously, while suggesting that the general principles of Scripture nonetheless pointed toward principles like those embodied in the Declaration of Independence (74).

Wayland's sixth letter carried this argument into the New Testament, again admitting that Jesus had alluded to slavery and that many Scriptures, which he cited at length, had outlined slave duties, while still emphasizing that the Bible was not a book of law but that it set forth universal rules that would be appropriate for subsequent generations (85). Admitting that "the New Testament contains no *precept* prohibitory of slavery," he did not think this settled the matter (89). In his seventh letter, Wayland further observed that the Pharisees had followed the "letter" while often violating the "spirit" of the law (97). As he further explained, "I believe that slavery is forbidden in the Scriptures just as almost every other sin is forbidden; that is, by the inculcation of moral principles which are utterly at variance with it" (106). In his eighth, and final, letter in the series, Wayland further associated slavery with the sexual abuse of African American women by their masters, with depriving slaves of the ability to read and write, and with intrusions upon their worship (113–14). He did acknowledge that exactly how and when slaves should be emancipated was a matter requiring "great practical wisdom" (121).

In responding, Dr. Fuller arguably distanced himself from many Southern contemporaries by presenting himself not as "the eulogist and abettor of slavery" but as an apologist for "an institution transmitted to us by former generations, the existence of which I lament" (128). Associating the origins of slavery with English kings and with northern merchants, he hoped that God was fulfilling Romans 8:28 by assuring that slavery would inure even to the slave's benefit (132). He observed that the Bible had condemned the Gibeonites to perpetual slavery, and that "hot countries cannot be cultivated without negroes" (133). The Anglo-Saxons had the ability to elevate the Negro race, which was far better than giving them "a liberty for which they are wholly unprepared, and which would be only a license for indolence and crime" and converting them "from a contented and cheerful peasantry, into a horde of outlaws . . . with whom the white population could never amalgamate" (136).

Consistent with this analysis, Fuller's second letter compared the relationship between master and slave to that of parents and children (141). In his third letter, Fuller further observed that, despite its references to equality, the Declaration of Independence had neither guaranteed the right to vote to women nor to males under twenty-one years of age (148). Individuals were born into certain stations, including slavery, and the fact that the system of slavery gave masters despotic power did not mean that it was sinful (153). Moreover, the incendiary nature of abolitionist publications was one of the reasons that the South had restricted slave literacy (160).

Fuller's fourth letter focused more specifically on biblical arguments. He saw no incompatibility between the Golden Rule and slavery because he did not believe the Bible outlawed the institution. Moreover, even if the Bible did not justify slavery, that might still make the institution only a matter of indifference (166). Quoting the words of 2 Timothy 2:16–17 about all Scripture being inspired by God (171), Fuller expressed concern about reading one's own philosophy into the text. To interpret the Bible as expansively as Dr. Wayland was to undermine its actual words and to open it up to human caprice. Abraham owned slaves, the Mosaic law (Fuller quoted from numerous biblical passages) permitted slavery, and, in contrast to polygamy and divorce, the New Testament contained no subsequent condemnations of the institution (183).

Fuller's fifth letter, which focused chiefly on the New Testament, warned against interpreting the Bible to support one's preconceived notions. Fuller cited even more passages than had Wayland, in which Scriptures had enjoined slaves to be obedient to their masters, putting particular emphasis on the book of Philemon, in which Paul had returned a slave, Onesimus, to his master (195). The apostles baptized slaves without requiring their masters to free them. If the Bible had intended to eliminate slavery, it would have done so not by articulating general principles but by specific commands and prohibitions (209). Again, Fuller feared elastic interpretations: "'The Times are changed.' What then? Who but sees the inference? It is that the gospel must have an expansion or elasticity, so as to adjust itself to the times. But what if the gospel can by no torture be framed and bent to what anybody and everybody chooses to call 'the times?' Why, then, the gospel is effete, and obsolete, and must be discarded, as it has been by many of the abolitionists" (210–11).

As to his own conduct, Fuller observed that he treated his own slaves with utmost kindness:

> They are placed under a contract, which no instrument of writing could make more sacred. By this contract they, on their part, perform not one half the work done by free laborers; and I, on my part, am bound to employ a missionary to teach and catechize them and their children; to provide them a home, and clothes, and provisions, and fuel, and land to plant for themselves; to pay all medical bills; to guaranty to them all the profits of their skill and labor, in their own time; to protect them as a guardian; and to administer to the wants of the children, and of those that are sick, and infirm, and aged. (1860, 222)

Wayland's final letter reiterated his view that slavery could be a moral evil without slaveholders understanding it to be such, while seeking to respond to Fuller's main arguments for slavery.

Ultimately, the issue of slavery was settled by force of arms and by constitutional amendments rather than through reasoned arguments, but the exchange between Fuller and Wayland remains a model of civility (Finn 2013). In

1859, John Leadley Dagg (1794–1884), the former president of Mercer College, published *The Elements of Moral Science*, in which he repeated many of Fuller's scriptural arguments in justifying slavery (Gardner 1960, 352). There were undoubtedly many other debates between pastors relative to slavery. These included debates between Rev. Jonathan Blanchard, of the Sixth Presbyterian Church of Cincinnati, and what Mark Noll describes as "the moderate emancipationist" (2006, 41) Nathaniel Rice of Cincinnati's Central Presbyterian Church, which were held in four days in October 1845 (Blanchard and Rice 1846).

See also Baptists; Slavery

For Reference and Further Reading

Blanchard, J., and N. Rice. 1846. *A Debate on Slavery Held on the First, Second, Third and Sixth Days of October, 1845, in the City of Cincinnati, between Rev. J. Blanchard, and N.L. Rice*. Cincinnati: Wm. H. Moore; New York: Mark H. Newman.

Finn, Nathan A. 2013. "Francis Wayland and Richard Fuller: Debating Slavery with Christian Civility." Andrew Fuller Center for Baptist Studies. May 10. http://andrewfullercenter.org/articles/blog/2013/05/francis-wayland-and-richard-fuller-debating-slavery-with-christian-civility.

Fuller, Richard, and Francis Wayland. 1860. *Domestic Slavery Considered as a Scriptural Institution: In a Correspondence between the Rev. Richard Fuller of Beaufort, S.C., and the Rev. Francis Wayland, of Providence, R.I.*, rev. and corrected by the authors. New York: Sheldon.

Gardner, Robert. 1960. "A Tenth-Hour Apology for Slavery." *Journal of Southern History* 26 (August): 352–67.

Giles, Kevin. 1994. "The Biblical Argument for Slavery: Can the Bible Mislead? A Case Study in Hermeneutics." *Evangelical Quar*terly 661: 3–17.

Harrill, J. Albert. 2000. "The Use of the New Testament in the American Slave Controversy: A Case History in the Hermeneutical Tension between Biblical Criticism and Christian Moral Debate." *Religion and American Culture: A Journal of Interpretation* 10 (Summer): 149–86.

Noll, Mark A. 2006. *The Civil War as a Theological Crisis*. Chapel Hill: University of North Carolina Press.

Roberts, Kristofer. 2016. "Scripture in the Public Forum: The Fuller-Wayland Letters and the Debate over Domestic Slavery." *Journal of Scriptural Reasoning*. March 9, http :// jsr.shanti.virginia.edu/page/2/?s=Isaiah.

Fundamental Orders of Connecticut

Early American Pilgrims who settled in America brought with them the idea, which they largely borrowed from the Old Testament, that they were a covenantal people. This belief is evident both in the Mayflower Compact of 1620 and in the Fundamental Orders of Connecticut in 1639.

The preamble to the latter document was as follows:

> For as much as it hath pleased Almighty God by the wise disposition of his divine providence so to order and dispose of things that we the Inhabitants and Residents of Windsor, Hartford and Wethersfield are now cohabiting and dwelling in . . . and well knowing where a people are gathered together the word of God requires that to maintain the peace and union of such a people there should be an orderly and decent Government established according to God, to order and dispose of

> the affairs of the people at all seasons as occasion shall require; do therefore associate and conjoin ourselves to be as one Public State or Commonwealth; and do for ourselves and our successors and such as shall be adjoined to us at any time hereafter, enter into Combination and Confederation together, to maintain and preserve the liberty and purity of the Gospel of our Lord Jesus which we now profess, and also, the discipline of the Churches, which according to the truth of the said Gospel is now practiced amongst us; and also in our civil affairs to be guided and governed according to such Laws, Rules, Orders and Degrees as shall be made, ordered, and decreed as followeth. (Vile 2015, 23–24)

David Weir observes that although this preface credits Scripture with ordaining government and was "explicitly Christian," it "gave broad latitude to the general court to discern how Christ and the scriptures were to be worked out in public affairs" (2005, 87). The document proceeded to outline a form of government that distinguished legislative from executive powers. The philosophy of government in the Fundamental Orders was probably best explained in a sermon delivered by Thomas Hooker in 1638.

See also Covenants, Compacts, Contracts, and Constitutions; Hooker, Thomas; Mayflower Compact; Puritans

For Reference and Further Reading

Kendall, Willmoore, and George W. Carey. 1970. *The Basic Symbols of the American Political Tradition*. Baton Rouge: Louisiana State University Press.
Vile, John R., ed. 2015. *Founding Documents of America: Documents Decoded*. Santa Barbara, CA: ABC-CLIO.
Weir, David A. 2005. *Early New England: A Covenanted Society*. Grand Rapids, MI: William B. Eerdmans.

Fundamentalists

Towards the end of the nineteenth and the early twentieth centuries, members of Protestant denominations who were seeking to uphold what they believed to be orthodox interpretations of the Bible often joined together at conferences to articulate their opposition to higher criticism methods of interpreting the Bible, which modernists were embracing and which fundamentalists believed unduly undermined biblical authority.

Although many came from denominations that eschewed formal creeds, lest they replace Scriptures, fundamentalists meeting at the Niagara Bible Conference in 1878 crafted a series of fourteen propositions to which many of them would have agreed. Prefaced by the belief that "so many in the latter times have departed from the faith, giving heed to seducing spirits, and doctrines of devils," the very first proposition focused chiefly on Scripture, citations to which it supplied:

> We believe "that all scriptures is given by inspiration of God," by which we understand the whole of the book called the Bible: nor do we take the statement in the sense in which it is sometimes foolishly said that the works of human genius are inspired, but in the sense that the Holy Ghost gave the very words of the sacred writings to holy men of old; and that His Divine inspiration is not in different degrees, but extends equally and fully to all parts of these writings,

> historical, poetical, doctrinal and prophetical, and to the smallest word, and inflection of a word, provided such word is found in the original manuscripts: 2 Tim. 3:16, 17; 2 Pet. 1:21; 1 Cor. 2:13; Mark 12:16,36; 12:11; Acts 1:16; 2:4. (text found in Unger 1981, 320)

Further statements affirmed the following: the Trinity; God's creation in God's image and his fall into sin; the doctrine of original sin; the need to be born again; the redemptive work of Christ on the cross; salvation by faith alone; the assurance of salvation for believers; the importance of Scriptures in pointing to Jesus; the work of the Holy Spirit; the need for godly living; the resurrection of the body; and the belief in a final judgment (Unger 1981, 320–23).

One of the major challenges to fundamentalism was the theory advanced by Charles Darwin (1809–1882) that all life, including human beings, had originated from a single source. This certainly contradicted any literalistic reading of the creation stories found in the biblical book of Genesis. The more modernists suggested the possibility of theistic evolution and called into question the story of biblical miracles, the more fundamentalists entrenched.

Despite their attempts to ground themselves in classical orthodoxy, Ernest Sandeen has suggested that the fundamentalist worldview was actually strongly shaped by two more recent influences. One was an alliance with theological dispensationalism, which emerged from the thinking of John Nelson Darby (1800–1882) and was conveyed to popular audiences by the *Scofield Reference Bible*, which was first published in 1909. This understanding divided human history into seven dispensations, in each of which God had dealt somewhat differently with man (Sandeen 1967, 68). In part because this view portrayed mankind as being in the next to the last stage, just before God's millennial reign on earth, this view increased expectations of Christ's second return to earth, which many believed would be preceded by the reestablishment of Israel. Thus, quite a number of dispensationalists were also Zionists (68).

Sandeen believes that fundamentalists were also highly influenced by Princeton Theology, which had applied a very rationalistic Newtonian method to theology. Professors such as Charles Hodge (1797–1876), A. A. Hodge (1823–1886), B. B. Warfield (1851–1921), John Gresham Machen (1881–1937), and others had developed what Sandeen describes as "a shock-proof doctrine of Biblical authority" based on the beliefs that "the Bible was 1) verbally inspired, 2) inerrant in its every reference, statistic, and quotation, 3) when first written down on the original autographs" (1967, 74).

From 1910 to 1915, fundamentalists produced a series of pamphlets entitled *The Fundamentals: A Testimony to the Truth*, in which they outlined their central tenets in ninety articles written by sixty-four authors. These have often been taken as the definitive exposition of fundamentalist views.

In addition to battling such social evils as alcohol, gambling, obscenity, and prostitution, fundamentalists were very concerned about teaching morality in public schools. They spearheaded efforts to restrict the teaching of evolution in public schools, in part because this doctrine was associated with Social Darwinism (which applied the doctrine of "the survival of the fittest" to human life) and eugenics. After Clarence Darrow's withering cross-examination of William Jennings Bryan at the Scopes Trial in 1925, fundamentalists were increasingly associated with southern agrarianism, but Sandeen notes that "if one turns to Fundamentalist periodicals and conference platforms, he does not find them dominated by ill-taught stump preachers or demagogues. In the nineteenth century, especially, the proto-Fundamentalists were frequently men in high esteem in their own denominations and communities" (1967, 83).

As fundamentalists largely withdrew from the public arena to build their own Bible schools and other institutions, many remained deeply concerned with moral issues, and with what they perceived to be the rising threat of communism and anarchism (Wilcox 1987). Carl McIntyre (1906–2002) was among the most extreme fundamentalist anti-communists, who was broadcast on more than six hundred television stations and, while remaining doctrinally aloof even from other fundamentalists, sometimes allied with others in his anti-communist crusades (Ruotsila 2012, 2016).

Although Jerry Falwell is often identified as a fundamentalist, over time, his approach came closer to those of evangelicals like Billy Graham who tended to take a somewhat less dogmatic approach to Scripture (especially with respect to biblical prophecy) and a less antagonistic view toward those with rival points of view. Mathews has argued that fundamentalism fueled opposition to the Equal Rights Amendment (1993), and it has likewise led to continuing opposition to same-sex marriage.

See also Communism and Anti-Communism; Creationism and Evolution; Evangelicals; Falwell, Jerry; Graham, Billy; Same-Sex Marriage; Scopes Trial

For Reference and Further Reading

Claxton, Nicholas James. March 2019. "The Niagara Creed: Its History, Theology, and Relevance." Submitted for PhD at Bob Jones University.

Mathews, Donald G. 1993. "'Spiritual Warfare': Cultural Fundamentalism and the Equal Rights Amendment." *Religion and American Culture: A Journal of Interpretation* 3 (Summer): 129–54.

Ruotsila, Markku. 2012. "Carl McIntire and the Fundamentalist Origins of the Christian Right." *Church History* 81 (June): 378–407.

Ruotsila, Markku. 2016. *Fighting Fundamentalist: Carl McIntire and the Politicization of American Fundamentalism*. New York: Oxford University Press.

Russell, C. Allyn. 1976. *Voices of American Fundamentalism: Seven Biographical Studies*. Philadelphia: Westminster Press.

Sandeen, Ernest R. 1967. "Toward a Historical Interpretation of the Origins of Fundamentalism." *Church History* 36 (March): 66–83.

Sutton, Matthew Avery. 2019. "The Day Christian Fundamentalism Was Born." *New York Times*. May 25.

Unger, Walter. 1981. "'Earnestly Contending for the Faith': The Role of the Niagara Bible Conference in the Emergence of American Fundamentalism, 1875–1900." Thesis for doctor of philosophy degree at Simon Fraser University.

Wilcox, Clyde. 1987. "Popular Backing for the Old Christian Right: Explaining Support for the Christian Anti-Communist Crusade." *Journal of Social History* 21 (Autumn): 117–32.

Furman, Richard

Richard Furman (1755–1825) was a gifted orator from Charleston, South Carolina, who was elected as the first president of the Baptist Triennial Conference. He sought respectability for this denomination, which included helping to found the Columbian University in the District of Columbia, which is today's George Washington University (Hatch 1989, 94–95). He also helped found the University of South Carolina.

Furman was a supporter of the Federalist Party who owned slaves and who, in his capacity as head of the South Carolina Baptist Convention, published an exposition, in which he laid out a biblical defense of slavery. The immediate occasion for his exposition was a request for a Day of Public Humiliation and Thanksgiving that followed the detection of the Demark Vesey rebellion that was believed to have posed a direct threat to the lives of many slave owners. It also followed damage from a hurricane.

After addressing the propriety of the Day of Public Humiliation and Thanksgiving, which he supported, Furman noted that abolitionist rhetoric had already penetrated the South:

> Certain writers on politics, morals and religion, and some of them highly respectable, have advanced positions, and inculcated sentiments, very unfriendly to the principle and practice of holding slaves; and by some these sentiments have been advanced among us, tending in their nature, directly to disturb the domestic peace of the State, to produce insubordination and rebellion among the slaves, and to infringe the rights of our citizens; and indirectly, to deprive the slaves of religious privileges, by awakening in the minds of the masters a fear, that acquaintance with the Scriptures, and the enjoyment of these privileges would naturally produce the aforementioned effects; because the sentiments in opposition to the holding of slaves have been attributed, by their advocates, to the Holy Scriptures, and to the genius of Christianity. (Furman 1822, para. 7)

He observed, however, that slavery was prevalent in the Greek and Roman empires and that in writing to the churches, Paul had not demanded their emancipation, and that, had he considered it to be "a moral evil," he would most surely have done so (Furman 1822, para. 9).

Furman further used this to argue against the idea that the biblical Golden Rule invalidated the institution: "But surely this rule is never to be urged against that order of things, which the Divine government has established; nor do our desires become a standard to us, under this rule, unless they have a due regard to justice, propriety and the general good" (para. 11). Elaborating, he said that "if the holding of slaves is lawful, or according to the Scriptures; then this Scriptural rule can be considered as requiring no more of the master, in respect to justice (whatever it may do in point of generosity) than what he, if a slave, could, consistently, wish to be done to himself, while the relationship between master and servant should be still continued" (para. 13). Portraying slaves as part of the owner's family, Furman explained how masters took care of "the children, the aged, the sick, the disabled, and the unruly, as well as those, who are capable of service and orderly, are the objects of his care" (para. 15). By purchasing such individuals, "yet might motives of humanity and even piety have been originally brought into operation in the purchase of slaves, when sold in the circumstances we have described" (para. 18).

Believing that slaves had originally been enslaved rather than being killed in war, Furman further argued that, by accepting such rules of war, the slave "might be said to be made so by his own consent, and by the indulgence of barbarous principles" (para. 16). Just because some slave owners might act as tyrants was no reason to condemn the entire institution of slavery. For many slaves, their transit to America was "the means of their mental and religious improvement, and so of obtaining salvation, as many of themselves have joyfully and thankfully confessed" (para. 18). Those who by excessive zeal preach abolitionism are more likely to bring about "anarchy and blood" rather than "better the state of that people" (para. 28).

Furman believed that Christian benevolence required "consulting the truest and best interests of its objects," and that "while men remain in the chains of ignorance and error, and under the dominion of tyrant lusts and passions, they cannot be free" (para. 20). Even if some individuals might think it would be generous to free the slaves, they cannot compel such generosity on the part of others. Recognizing that there might be a time when it would be possible to provide for such freedom, Furman believed that "they are now in a state of probation; and that God as a Righteous, All-wise Sovereign, not only disposes of them as he pleases and bestows upon them many unmerited blessings and comforts, but subjects them also to privations, afflictions and trials, with the merciful intention of making all their afflictions, as well as their blessings, work Finally for their good" (para. 21).

Baptists and Methodists had both become known for attempting to evangelize slaves, and Furman indicated that he was concerned about "the religious interests of the Negroes," explaining that "though they are slaves, they are also men; and are with ourselves accountable creatures; having immortal souls, and being destined to future eternal award. Their religious interests claim a regard from their masters of the most serious nature; and it is indispensable" (para. 22). Probably with some knowledge of Vesey's own religious justifications, Furman indicated that such interpretations tend "to make servants insubordinate to proper authority," whereas "the influence of a right acquaintance with that Holy Book tends directly and powerfully, by promoting the fear and love of God, together with just and peaceful sentiments toward men, to produce one of the best securities to the public, for the internal and domestic peace of the state" (para. 23). He further noted that the church with which the Vesey insurrectionists had been associated was "an irregular body, which called itself the African Church, and had intimate connection and intercourse with a similar body of men in a Northern City, among whom the supposed right to emancipation is strenuously advocated" (para. 24).

In summary, Furman reiterated "that the holding of slaves is justifiable by the doctrine and example contained in Holy writ; and is, therefore consistent with Christian uprightness, both in sentiment and conduct" (para. 25). He further observed "that slavery, when tempered with humanity and justice, is a state of tolerable happiness; equal, if not superior, to that which many poor enjoy in countries reputed free" (para. 25). Moreover, it is "the positive duty of servants to reverence their master, to be obedient, industrious, faithful to him, and careful of his interests; and without being so, they can neither be the faithful servants of God, nor be held as regular members of the Christian Church" (para. 25). Masters should provide "religious instruction" to slaves, "due care being at the same time taken, that they received their instructions from right sources, and from their connexions, where they will not be in danger of having their minds corrupted by sentiments unfriendly to the domestic and civil peace of the community" (para. 25). Government had an interest in preventing and punishing insurrections, in minimizing oppression by "reasonable, cruel masters," and in affording slaves such religious freedoms "as may comport with the peace and safety of the state" (para. 25).

See also Baptists; Days of Humiliation, Fasting, and Thanksgiving; Slavery; Vesey, Denmark

For Reference and Further Reading

Daly, John Patrick. 2002. *When Slavery Was Called Freedom: Evangelicalism, Proslavery, and the Causes of the Civil War*. Lexington: University Press of Kentucky.

Furman, Richard. [December 24, 1822] 1985. "Exposition of the Views of the Baptists Relative to the Coloured Population of the United States in Communication to the Governor of South Carolina." Reprinted in Roberts, James A. 1985. *Richard Furman: Life and Legacy*. Macon, GA: Mercer University Press, pp. 274–86. Accessed at https://glc.yale.edu/exposition-views-baptists-relative-coloured-population.

Greenberg, Kenneth S. 1976. "Revolutionary Ideology and the Proslavery Argument: The Abolition of Slavery in Antebellum South Carolina." *Journal of Southern History* 42 (August): 365–84.

Hatch, Nathan O. 1989. *The Democratization of American Christianity*. New Haven, CT: Yale University Press.

Morrison, Larry R. 1980. "The Religious Defense of American Slavery before 1830." *Journal of Religious Thought* 37: 16–29. https://www.kingscollege.net/gbrodie/The%20religious%20justification%20of%20slavery%20before%201830.pdf.

• G •

Garfield, James

James A. Garfield (1831–1861), who served as the twentieth president of the United States for only about six months before dying at the hands of an assassin, regularly engaged in preaching prior to his presidency and had an important role in the early development of the Disciples of Christ.

The Disciples (originally also joined with the Christian Church) were part of the Restoration movement initiated by Barton W. Stone (1772–1844) of Lexington, Kentucky, and Alexander Campbell (1788–1866) of Bethany, Virginia (today's West Virginia), which sought to restore primitive Christianity and Christian unity based purely on the Bible. Although they founded their own churches, members did not consider themselves to be a denomination and chided other groups for being so. Members of such denominations, in turn, often believed that the Disciples were overly legalistic, especially on personal matters like drinking, theater performances, levity, and the like.

Garfield was baptized at the age of eighteen, attended Geauga Seminary, Hiram College, and Williams and regularly preached before accepting a position as a professor, and later as president of Hiram College. As a young man, Garfield expressed disgust at the teachings of a traveling atheist named Joseph Treat:

> His principles would arraign the Holy Book of God at the bar and he puts his feeble reason upon the throne to judge it by. Let him raise his insect arm against infinity, and the Almighty, but truth is mighty, eternal, and the Bible firm as the Throne of God shall stand when kingdoms crumble and the planets crash. Its holy truths through ceaseless ages still, shall send a blaze of heavenly light and drive the darkness from the nauseous tomb, and point us to the morning star of God which shall arise from out the tomb and blaze his glories while eternity endures, or God exists in heaven. (Rushford 1977, 33)

Although he seemed initially destined for a career as a pastor, Garfield appeared frustrated by divisions within the religious movement to which he adhered, and became drawn to politics. He was elected to the Ohio legislature before joining the Union Army, where he distinguished himself at a number of battles including the Battle of Chickamauga. He subsequently served in Congress before gaining the Republican nomination in 1880 and narrowly winning the race against General Winfield Scott Hancock. He had strong support among members of Disciples, some of whom, however, opposed political participation of any kind and some of whom thought that he had abandoned his true calling by going into politics. Garfield faithfully attended church during his brief presidency and lingered on several weeks before dying from wounds he received from a disappointed office seeker.

In 1860, Garfield formulated a statement of faith at the dedication of a new Disciples of Christ building. Notably, two of eleven statements focused specifically on the Bible:

1. We call ourselves Christians, or Disciples of Christ.
2. We believe in God the Father.
3. We believe that Jesus is the Christ, the Son of the living God, and our Savior. We regard the divinity of Christ as the fundamental truth of the Christian system.
4. We believe in the Holy Spirit, both as to his agency in conversion and as indwelling in the heart of the Christian.
5. We accept both the Old and the New Testament Scriptures as the inspired Word of God.
6. We believe in the future punishment of the wicked and the future reward of the righteous.
7. We believe that the Deity is a prayer hearing and a prayer answering God.
8. We observe the institution of the Lord's Supper on the Lord's Day. To this table we neither invite nor debar; we say it is the Lord's Supper for all the Lord's children.
9. We plead for the union of God's people on the Bible and the Bible alone.
10. The Christ is our only creed.
11. We maintain that all the ordinances should be observed as they were in the days of the Apostles. (Rushford 1977, 142–43)

After his election, Garfield resisted entreaties by fellow church members for positions within his administration, and he emphasized the importance of civil liberties. A recent book suggests that Garfield would have been much more likely to have pushed for racial justice for African Americans than did his successor Chester A. Arthur (Cohen 2019). When taking his oath, Garfield's Bible was open to Psalm 21:1, which says, "The king's heart is in the hand of the Lord, as the rivers of water he turneth it whithersoever he will." Two of the themes of Garfield's inaugural address were a plea for equal suffrage and "universal education." Saying that it is the "sacred duty of those now living to educate their successors and fit them, by intelligence and virtue, for the inheritance which awaits them," Garfield cited the biblical prophecy (Isaiah 11:6) in "the divine oracle which declares that 'a little child shall lead them,' for our own little children will soon control the destinies of the Republic" (Garfield 1881).

See also Presidential Inaugural Bible Verses

For Reference and Further Reading

Cohen, Jared. 2019. *Accidental Presidents: Eight Men Who Changed America.* New York: Simon & Schuster.

Garfield, James A. March 4, 1881. "Inaugural Address." https://www.bartleby.com/124/pres36.html. Accessed April 29, 2019.

Rushford, Jerry Bryant. August 1977. "Political Disciple: The Relationship between James A. Garfield and the Disciples of Christ." Diss. for PhD at the University of California, Santa Barbara. Accessed through Pepperdine University Digital Commons.

Garnet, Henry Highland (Address to Congress, 1865)

Henry Highland Garnet (1814–1882) was an African American abolitionist who had been born into slavery in Kent County, Maryland, from which he and his family had escaped to New York City. After being educated in free schools, he became a Presbyterian minister. He is best known for giving two speeches. He delivered the first of these, the subject of another essay in this book, in Buffalo, New York, where he urged slaves to rebel. A second, the subject of this essay, was a speech to the U.S. Congress, where he lauded the adoption of the Thirteenth Amendment ending involuntary servitude. This speech is particularly significant because it is the first ever delivered to Congress by an African American. At the time, Garnet was serving as pastor of the Fifteenth Street Presbyterian Church.

Although Garnet's speech was infused with scriptural allusions, he took his primary text from Matthew 23:4, where, in referring to the scribes and Pharisees, Jesus said, "For they bind heavy burdens, and grievous to be borne, and lay them on men's shoulders, but they themselves will not move them with one of their fingers." Garnet thus sought to contract religious "theory" with religious "practice" (1865, 69). Garnet argued that America has its own scribes and Pharisees, namely those who "are intelligent and well-informed," know "the law of nations," including "constitutional law," "common law," the Magna Carta, as well as the Ten Commandments and the Beatitudes, and who may even have descended from the Pilgrims (71) and yet had enslaved "their fellow-men, equal before the Almighty, and made by him of the same blood [a reference to Acts 17:26], and glowing with immortality" (72).

Noting that he had been born into slavery, Garnet observed how slavery had turned what should have been a "paradise" in Maryland into a "despotism" (73). Garnet pointed to the horror of the attempt to "chattelize man; to hold property in human beings" who were "made in the image of God, and for whom Christ died" (73–74). Garnet observed that this institution treated men like beasts, that it began in kidnapping, and that it was tied to numerous other sins including the "disregard of parental authority," the destruction of "the marriage altar" and the cultivation of "prejudice" (77). He further argued, "He seals up the Bible and mutilates its sacred truths, and flies in the face of the Almighty, and impiously asks, *'Who art thou that I should obey thee?'* " (78).

Garnet believed that slavery was a violation of the Golden Rule as well as the judgment of numerous philosophers and statesmen, including King Cyrus, who had said that "to fight in order not to be a slave is noble" (79). Citing numerous American patriots who had made similar statements, Garnet included a reference to the law of Moses in Exodus 21:16 that "whoso stealeth a man, and selleth him, or if he be found in his hand, he shall surely be put to death" (82). In an apparent secularized reference to Psalm 137, Garnet further observed, "When the Muses can no longer decorate her altars with their garlands, then they hang their harps upon the willows and weep" (83). Garnet joyfully described the Thirteenth Amendment as signaling the death of a monster (85).

As he sought to answer the question, "when and where will the demands of the reformers of this and coming ages end?" Garnet looked forward to the time "when all unjust and heavy burdens shall be removed from every man in the land. When all invidious and proscriptive distinctions shall be blotted out from our laws, whether they be constitutional, statute, or municipal laws. When emancipation shall be followed by enfranchisement, and all men holding allegiance to the government shall enjoy every right of American citizenship. When our brave and gallant soldiers shall have justice done unto them" (85–86). Stating that "we ask no special favors, but we plead for justice" (86), Garnet noted that the nation was still paying for its "atonement" (87). Having "begun its exodus from worse than Egyptian bondage," the nation needed to "go forward" and prove "the superiority of our Democratic, Republican Government" (89). In conclusion, he observed that by doing justice to all, "thus shall we give to the world the form of a model Republic, founded on the principles of justice and humanity, and Christianity, in which the burdens of war and the blessings of peace are equally borne and enjoyed by all" (91).

President James Garfield later appointed Garnet as U.S. minister and counsel general to Liberia, but Garnet died shortly after his arrival.

See also Garfield, James; Garnet, Henry Highland ("An Address to the Slaves of the United States," 1843); Slavery

For Reference and Further Reading

Garnet, Henry Highland. 1865. *A Memorial Discourse; by Rev. Henry Highland Garnet, Delivered in the Hall of the House of Representatives, Washington City, D.C. on Sabbath, February 12, 1865, with an Introduction by James McCune Smith, M.D.* Philadelphia: Joseph M. Wilson.

Schor, Joel. 1979. "The Rivalry between Frederick Douglass and Henry Highland Garnet." *Journal of Negro History* 64 (Winter): 30–38.

Garnet, Henry Highland ("An Address to the Slaves of the United States," 1843)

Although largely eclipsed by Frederick Douglass, with whom he was often in conflict, Henry Highland Garnet (ca. 1815–1882) was a noted Presbyterian minister and orator who, in one of his best known speeches, a speech to the National Negro Convention held in Buffalo, New York, in 1843, encouraged American slaves to take up arms to secure their freedom.

Noting that the two groups shared a "common humanity," he observed the "deep gulf" that existed between African Americans who were free and those who were slaves (perhaps a reference to the "great gulf" that Jesus said existed between Lazarus and the rich man in John 5:26). The continuing existence of slavery was the result of "men calling themselves Christians," who possessed "the worst features of corrupt and sordid hearts" motivated by "avarice and lust." Their hearts seemed immune as "the bleeding captive plead his innocence, and pointed to Christianity who stood weeping at the cross."

Observing that "nearly three millions of your fellow citizens are prohibited by law and public opinion, (which in this country is stronger than law,) from reading the Book of Life," Garnet described how American revolutionaries had proclaimed "Liberty or Death," while refusing to extend it to African Americans.

Whereas slave owners quoted Scriptures to urge slaves to obey their masters, Garnet proclaimed that "TO SUCH DEGREDATION IT IS SINFUL IN THE EXTREME FOR YOU TO MAKE VOLUNTARY SUBMISSION." He tied this to God's commandments:

> He requires you to love him supremely, and your neighbor as yourself—to keep the Sabbath day holy—to search the Scriptures—and bring up your children with respect for his laws, and to worship no other God but him. But slavery sets all these at naught, and hurls defiance in the face of Jehovah. The forlorn condition in which you are placed, does not destroy your moral obligation to God. You are not certain of heaven, because you suffer yourselves to remain in a state of slavery, where you cannot obey the commandments of the Sovereign of the universe.

Somewhat tempering his call for rebellion, Garnet argued that as "native born American citizens" (quite similar to the description that the Fourteenth Amendment would later adopt), slaves "are justly entitled to all the rights that are granted to the freest," and they should go to their masters, claim these rights, and offer to continue their work "if they will render to you an equivalent for your service." However, he thought that "you had better all die immediately, than live [as] slaves and entail your wretchedness upon your posterity." In a paraphrase of Hebrews 9:22, which resembled the thinking of John Brown, Garnet observed that "however much you and all of us may desire it, there is not much hope of redemption without the shedding of blood." He further observed that "it is impossible like the children of Israel, to make a grand exodus from the land of bondage. The Pharaohs are on both sides of the blood red waters!"

Garnet proceeded to praise Denmark Vesey, Nat Turner, and others who had led slave revolts. He further noted,

> It is in your power so to torment the God cursed slaveholders that they will be glad to let you go free. If the scale was turned, and black men were the masters and white men the slaves, every destructive agent and element would be employed to lay the oppressor low. Danger and death would hang over their heads day and night. Yes, the tyrants would meet with plagues more terrible than those of Pharaoh. But you are a patient people. You act as though you were made for the special use of these devils. You act as though your daughters were born to pamper the lusts of your masters and overseers. And worse than all, you tamely submit while your lords tear your wives from your embraces and defile them before your eyes.

Garnet concluded his speech by urging the slaves to "trust in the living God. Labor for the peace of the human race, and remember that you are FOUR MILLIONS."

Garnet, described as believing that furnishing the Bible to slaves "was tantamount to making a gift of the book of Southern Christianity that bore the seeds of the regime's undoing" (Callahan 2006, 24), favored such an effort, which Frederick Douglass opposed for fear that slave owners would simply emphasize passages that they believed supported slave obedience.

See also Brown, John; Douglass, Frederick; Moses as Political Archetype; Turner, Nat; Vesey, Denmark

For Reference and Further Reading

Callahan, Allen Dwight. 2006. *The Talking Book: African Americans and the Bible*. New Haven, CT: Yale University Press.

Garnet, Henry Highland. 1843. "An Address to the Slaves of the United States." https://www.blackpast.org/african-american-history/speeches-african-american-history/1843-henry-highland-garnet-address-slaves-united-states/. Accessed April 20, 2019.

Schor, Joel. 1979. "The Rivalry between Frederick Douglass and Henry Highland Garnet." *Journal of Negro History* 64 (Winter): 30–38.

Garrison, William Lloyd

William Lloyd Garrison (1805–1879), who found *The Liberator* in 1831, was one of the most important abolitionists in the years leading up to the Civil War. At a time when other opponents of slavery were considering recolonizing African Americans in Africa or otherwise putting slavery on a path toward gradual extinction, the Massachusetts-born Garrison considered slavery to be such a great evil that it should be eliminated immediately. In this respect, his rhetoric was similar to that of Hebrew prophets (Stafford n.d.).

When Garrison first started his anti-slavery magazine, he appears to have had fairly conventional views of Christianity, but as he found most orthodox clergymen unwilling to embrace his advocacy for immediate emancipation as impractical and likely to end in rebellion or war, he was increasingly drawn toward Unitarianism and Spiritualism. Although he thought it was justified, Garrison did not advocated slave revolts (he did later embrace the justice of the Civil War), and many who adhered to his cause were Quakers. Professor William L. van Deburg notes, "After 1840, the Boston editor continued the criticism of religious 'forms and ceremonies,' 'temple worship,' and Sabbatarianism [which he had previously supported] while broadening his attack to include revivalism, the divine inspiration of the Bible, the ordinance of baptism, and the atoning powers of Christ" (1975, 235). Relying heavenly on the natural rights philosophy in the Declaration of Independence, in contrast to individuals like Frederick Douglass and Abraham Lincoln who attempted to work from within the Constitution to find justifications for ending slavery, Garrison considered it to be "an agreement with hell, a covenant with death."

However he may have departed from orthodox Christian beliefs and did not typically cite biblical chapters and verses, many of Garrison's speeches were soaked in biblical language. Thus in the opening paragraph of his "Extracts from a Fourth of July Oration," Garrison called for immediate emancipation by combining appeals to the truths announced in the Declaration of Independence with those of the Bible: "In the name of the God, who has made us of one blood [Acts 17:26], and in whose image we are created [Genesis 1:27], who came to bind up the broken-hearted, to proclaim liberty to the captives and the opening of the prison to them that are bound [Isaiah 61:1 and Luke 4:18]; I demand the immediate emancipation of those who are pining in slavery on the American soil" ([1852] 1968, 188). A bit later in his speech, he cited the words from Leviticus

25:10 to proclaim liberty "throughout all the land, unto all the inhabitants thereof'" (190) that are inscribed on the Liberty Bell, which had become a prime abolitionist symbol.

As his thought developed, Garrison authored an essay on the "Divine Authority of the Bible." Although his views were quite theologically liberal for his day, they remained respectful and were firmly grounded on what Garrison understood to be "the right of private judgment," which the founders of the Protestant Reformation had recognized and which "leaves the human mind (as it should be left) free to judge of the origin, authenticity, inspiration, authority, [and] value of the Bible, according to its own perception of right, its own conviction of duty" (Garrison [1852] 1968, 221). Pointing to the wide variety of biblical interpretations and attempts to seek "proof-texts in support of their own peculiar faith" within its pages, Garrison said that he would rather "repudiate Protestantism" and "turn Catholic" than to "give up my own independent Judgment, and to pin my faith upon any man's sleeve" (221–22).

Rather than rejecting a book with "an immense amount of truth in it" (222), Garrison sought (not unlike Thomas Jefferson had done at an earlier day) to separate enduring biblical truths from what he considered to be more time-bound teachings, the acceptance of which was based on failure to recognize that scripture "is not one production, but many productions—as it is neither exclusively Jewish nor wholly Christian, but a mixture of both" (223). Garrison believed that too many individuals interpreted the Bible "by imitation, by tradition, by education, by custom" (224). He thought that a true search of Scripture required rejecting both the view of "plenary [complete] inspiration," and the dogma that "the Bible is the only rule of faith and practice; so that whatever it teaches or allows must be right, and whatever forbids must be wrong, independent of all other considerations" (225–26).

Again harkening back to the Reformation, Garrison opposed authoritative "priestly" interpretations of Scripture. Citing the maxim that "the Bible is like a fiddle; you can play any tune on it you please," Garrison further argued that "the Bible does not change, but the interpretations of the Bible are constantly fluctuating" (228).

Garrison thus noted,

> I have lost my traditional and educational notions of the holiness of the Bible, but I have gained greatly, I think, in my estimation of it. As a divine book, I never could understand it; as a human composition, I can fathom it to the bottom. Whoever receives it as his master, will necessarily be in bondage to it; but he who makes it his servant, under the guidance of truth, will find it truly serviceable. (Garrison [1852] 1968, 228)

He ended his oration by further observing,

> I am fully aware how grievously the priesthood have perverted the Bible, and wielded it both as an instrument of spiritual despotism and in opposition to the sacred cause of humanity; still, to no other volume do I turn with so much interest, no other do I consult to refer to so frequently, to no other am I so indebted for light and strength, no other is so identified with the growth of human

> freedom and progress, no other have I appealed to so effectively in aid of the various reformatory movements which I have espoused; and it embodies an amount of excellence so great as to make it, in my estimation, THE BOOK OF BOOKS. (Garrison [1852] 1968, 225)

Although Garrison thus appears to have subjected Scripture to human understandings and morality, he was able to continue to draw from it as a source of wisdom and inspiration.

See also Douglass, Frederick; Jefferson Bible; Liberty Bell; Lincoln, Abraham; Quakers; Slavery

For Reference and Further Reading

Garrison, William Lloyd. [1852] 1968. *Selections from the Writings and Speeches of William Lloyd Garrison*. New York: Negro Universities Press. Reprint of R.F. Wallcut, 1852.

McInerney, Daniel J. 1991. "'A Faith for Freedom': The Political Gospel of Abolition." *Journal of the Early Republic* 11 (Autumn): 371–93.

Stafford, Tim. n.d. "The Abolitionists." *Christian History*. https://christianhistoryinstitute.org/magazine/article/abolitionists.

van Deburg, William L. 1975. "William Lloyd Garrison and the 'Pro-Slavery Priesthood': The Changing Beliefs of an Evangelical Reformer, 1830–1840." *Journal of the Academy of Religion* 43 (June): 224–37.

Geneva Bible

Through much of American history, the primary Bible that most Americans (particularly Protestants) consulted was the Authorized, or King James, Version, which was first published in 1611 during the reign and with the approval of King James I of Britain (James VI of Scotland). It remains a favorite even today, especially among traditional Anglicans and independent Protestant fundamentalists.

Prior to this, the most predominant English translation was the Geneva Bible, which was first published in 1560 and which followed earlier publications by John Wycliffe (1330–1384) in 1388 and by Myles Coverdale (1488–1569) in 1535. The Geneva Bible has special relevance to America because it was the favorite of many early American Pilgrims, especially those who settled in Plymouth, Massachusetts, and was used by John Winthrop in composing his "Model of Christian Charity."

As the name suggests, the Geneva Bible originated in the Swiss city of Geneva, in which the reformer John Calvin (1509–1564) was the central figure. Although drawing from the language of earlier English Bibles, it was translated directly from Greek and Hebrew texts.

Among the most innovative features of the Geneva Bible was that it was the first English Bible to be divided into chapters and verses, it included annotations to the text, and it included numerous cross-references to other Bible verses (Van Engen 2013, 550). It was the primary Bible of the Elizabethan era and helped shape the language used by William Shakespeare. King James was suspicious of the Bible because he believed that it undermined his arguments for the divine right of kings and because he feared that the Bible's emphasis on the sovereignty of God might provide a basis for civil disobedience (the title page pictured Pharaoh pursuing the children of Israel to the Red Sea); he also disliked its use of the word "tyrant" to describe a number of biblical rulers (Van Engen 2013, 551). He was particularly disturbed by the fact that Scottish Presbyterians had used the Geneva Bible to depose and eventually execute Queen Mary (Betteridge 1983, 48). In the 1620s, Britain had actually adopted a ban on printing the Geneva Bible in England (Van Engen 2013, 553). By contrast, the Geneva Bible was the first to be printed in Scotland, which was predominately Presbyterian rather than Anglican, and the Scottish Parliament actually required every substantial householder to buy a copy (Betteridge 1983, 44).

Betteridge notes that the Geneva Bible appeared in three primary forms. Black-letter quartos used gothic type and included concordances with what Betteridge calls "a more obtrusive Puritan bias" (1983, 45). A second form included a revised 1576 New Testament translation by Laurence Tomson and expanded commentary. The third, known as the Geneva-Tomson-Junius version, included what Betteridge described as "a massive and violently antipapal diatribe by Franciscus Junius [1545–1602]," who taught in Leiden (1983, 45). Betteridge observes that the Geneva Bible was "the Elizabethan best seller, the set book of the Scottish reformation, the guide book for the English navigators, [and] the companion of those pilgrims who went to 'the howling wilderness'" (62).

When the King James Version of the Bible was published in 1611, it did not include notes, although many such Bibles are now available.

See also King James Version of the Bible; Model of Christian Charity

For Reference and Further Reading

Betteridge, Maurice S. 1983. "The Bitter Notes: The Geneva Bible and Its Annotations." *Sixteenth Century Journal* 14 (Spring): 41–62.

Daniell, David. 2003. *The Bible in English: Its History and Influence*. New Haven, CT: Yale University Press.

Hallidan, C. P. 2010. *The Authorized Version: A Wonderful and Unfinished History*. London: Trinitarian Bible Society.

Van Engen, Abram C. 2013. "Origins and Last Farewells: Bible Wars, Textual Form, and the Making of American History." *New England Quarterly* 86 (December): 543–92.

George, Henry

Henry George (1839–1897) was one of the most influential journalists and economists in America in the nineteenth century. He is primarily known for his book *Progress and Poverty*, which he published in 1879, and in which, out of concern for the rising gap between the rich and the poor, he advocated a tax on land. He also favored governmental regulation and control of monopolies.

In the year prior to his publication of *Progress and Poverty*, George gave a speech to the Young Men's Hebrew Association of San Francisco lauding Moses and the role he played in leading his people out of Israel:

> To lead into freedom a people long crushed by tyranny; to discipline and order such a mighty host; to harden them into fighting men, before whom warlike

> tribes quailed and walled cities went down; to repress discontent and jealousy and mutiny; to combat reactions and reversions; to turn the quick, fierce of enthusiasm to the service of a stead purpose, required some towering character—a character blending in highest expression the qualities of politician, patriot, philosopher, and statesman. (George [1878] 1956, 4)

George believed that Moses's emphasis on "the rights of man" stood in sharp contrast to the oppression of the Egyptians ([1878] 1956, 6). In addition to being "intellectually great," Moses was "morally great—a statesman aglow with the unselfish patriotism that refuses to grasp a scepter or found a dynasty" (7). George credited Moses with founding "a commonwealth based upon the individual" (8).

George was particularly impressed by the way that the laws of Moses protected individuals of all classes as well as animals by providing a Sabbath day for rest each week. He was also very impressed by Moses's provision for a Year of Jubilee every fiftieth year in which debts would be forgiven and slaves would be freed. He further credited Moses with de-emphasizing life after death (immortality having been a major theme of Egyptian thought) for emphasis on social action in the present.

As one who believed that rents gave some an unfair advantage over others, George lauded Moses for treating the land as "the gift of the Creator to His common creatures, which no one had the right to monopolize" (15). He further praised Moses for rejecting the "blasphemous doctrine preached oft-times even from Christian pulpits—that the want and suffering of the masses of mankind flow from a mysterious dispensation of providence, which we may lament, but can neither quarrel with nor alter" (17). George contrasted Moses's unmarked grave with the pyramids that marked the tombs of the pharaohs, "lest the idolatrous feeling, always ready to break forth, should in death accord him the superstitious reverence he had refused in life" (20).

Durocher observes that George believed strongly in the rights of man as articulated in the Declaration of Independence, the preamble to the U.S. Constitution, and the Declaration of the Rights of Man and of Citizens (1961, 500). Durocher notes that in his *Social Problems*, George further extolled the biblical notion that we are our brother's keeper and the biblical view that we should love our neighbors as ourselves (500, 507).

See also Moses as Political Archetype

For Reference and Further Reading

Durocher, Aurele. 1961. "The Social Ideas of Henry George." *American Journal of Economics and Sociology* 20 (October): 497–512.

George, Henry. "Moses." [1878] 1956. Paramount Pictures. Reprinted from New York: Robert Schalkenbach Foundation.

Shapiro, Aharon H. 1988. "Moses. Henry George's Inspiration." *American Journal of Economics and Sociology* 47 (October): 493–501.

Gideon as Political Archetype

Although it is common to associate the Bible with chapters and verses, sometimes biblical archetypes are more important than specific passages. For many years from the death of Joshua until the kingship of King Saul and his successors, ancient Israel was ruled by judges who filled both military and judicial roles. This period, in which each of twelve tribes largely took care of their own internal affairs, bears a strong resemblance to the government under the Articles of Confederation in the United States (1781–1789) where primary power rested with the states (Vile and Foshee 1988).

One of the greatest of the biblical judges was Gideon, who was also known as Jerubbaal. He helped the Israelites defeat the Midianites and the Amalekites. In addition to his military victories, Gideon (whose name is currently used for a group that distributes Scriptures) was primarily known for his modesty in accepting God's call to lead the armies of Israel, and for his refusal to be king after securing military victories over God's enemies. In a famous passage in Judges 8:23, Gideon is quoted as saying, "I will not rule over you, neither shall my son rule over you: the LORD shall rule over you."

Gideon became a prototype for George Washington, who, like Gideon, expressed reservations about his own ability to lead American forces at the beginning of the Revolutionary War and who turned over his authority to Congress after the American Revolution and returned to private life at his plantation at Mount Vernon. John Murray noted this parallel in a long pamphlet that he published in 1784 entitled *Jerubbaal* (see Shalev 2013, 45). Thomas Paine quoted the same biblical passage in arguing against hereditary monarchy in *Common Sense*, which he published in January 1776. Washington further cemented his own reputation as Gideon when he decided in 1796 not to run for a third consecutive presidential term.

Another common figure to whom Washington was often compared was the Roman Lucius Quinctius Cincinnatus (519–438 BC), who was called from his farm to assume command of Roman forces and returned to his farm after securing this victory (Wills 1984). Professor Eran Shalev (2013) has argued that this points to the convergence of civic republican thinking, which tended to stress citizen virtue and the dangers of corruption, with Christian symbols, which might often have been more familiar to common people than analogies drawn from Greek and Roman history.

See also Common Sense (Thomas Paine); Washington, George

For Reference and Further Reading

Shalev, Eran. 2013. *American Zion: The Old Testament as a Political Text from the Revolution to the Civil War*. New Haven, CT: Yale University Press.

Vile, John R., and Andrew Foshee. 1988. "Domestic Politics in the Book of Judges: The Story of Gibeah." *Journal of Political Science* 16 (Spring): 33–42.

Wills, Garry. 1984. *Cincinnatus: George Washington and the Enlightenment*. New York: Doubleday.

Graham, Billy

William Franklin (Billy) Graham (1918–2018) was among the best-known and respected religious figures of the twentieth century. Born in Charlotte, North Carolina, he briefly attended Bob Jones University and the Florida Bible Institute before getting an undergraduate degree at Wheaton College. There he met his wife, Ruth Bell, the daughter of Presbyterian missionaries to China, where she was born. The college houses a museum in his honor.

Graham identified himself as a Southern Baptist. Although he spent a brief time as president of Northwestern College in Minneapolis, Minnesota, his primary activities were in the field of evangelism. Much like evangelist Dwight L. Moody in the nineteenth century and Billy Sunday in the early twentieth century, Graham conducted a series of crusades in which he often filled stadiums with tens of thousands of people to whom he would present a straightforward biblical message of repentance and salvation, which were followed by altar calls. With the Bible often in hand, Graham was often associated with the phrase "The Bible says" and was rarely given to theological nuance. To the consternation of some of his more conservative supporters, Graham invited all the denominations to join his efforts and sought to direct those without church homes who responded to his altar calls to one of them. He also had respect for Pope John Paul II and other Roman Catholics who had stood up to communism. Graham was a major figure in the establishment of the evangelical magazine *Christianity Today*.

Graham was quite photogenic and came over as very sincere in television. He had something of a breakout moment in the fall of 1949 when, during a month-long campaign in Los Angeles, the publisher William Randolph Hearst ordered his editors to "puff Graham." Hearst did so largely because he perceived Graham's message as a way of rallying the nation against atheistic communism at a time when the United States was involved in an on-going Cold War with this ideology (Miller 2009, 14–15).

Fairly early in his evangelistic campaign, Graham desegregated his crusades. Even before he had eliminated segregated seating, he pronounced that "the audience may be segregated, but there is no segregation at the altar" (Miller 2009, 13). Although Graham would later express concerns over civil disobedience, he invited Martin Luther King Jr. to speak at his New York Crusade in 1957.

Graham kept close guard on his personal life and was never associated with the kinds of sexual and financial scandals that sometimes surrounded other televangelists. Graham was perhaps best known for cultivating relationship from Presidents Harry S. Truman through Barack Obama. He learned an early lesson when he re-created a prayer that he had with President Truman, who thought he was showboating. Graham managed to do better with most subsequent presidents, most of whom appeared to value his personal ministry and some of whom undoubtedly also tried to use him for their political advantage. Graham was especially close to President Lyndon B. Johnson and to the Bushes, and George W. Bush claimed to have had a transformative conversation with him. Graham expressed remorse after being quoted parroting anti-Jewish remarks to President Nixon and was notable among evangelical Christians for not targeting Jews for conversion. Graham, who was arguably politically naïve, was shocked and felt further compromised when the Watergate tapes revealed Nixon's foul language.

Professor Richard V. Pierard observed that Graham "leaned to the conservative side of most issues but avoided extremist positions and modified his views as he became better informed or the mood of the country changed" (1980, 112). Asked in 1952 what he would do were he running for the presidency, he responded, "I would launch out and call people back to God, back to Christ, and back to the Bible" (115).

Because Graham rarely called politicians on the carpet, even when they were leading dictatorships, he succeeded in being able to lead crusades in Eastern European nations. Pierard explains that he conceived of himself as a "New Testament evangelist not an Old Testament prophet" (126).

Graham authored a number of books in which he often tied current world crises to biblical prophecies. His son Franklin (b. 1952) is also an evangelist who was one of the early supporters of the presidency of Donald J. Trump.

See also Baptists; Bush, George W.; Communism and Anti-Communism; Evangelicals

For Reference and Further Reading

"Billy Graham." 2018. Special Issue. *Christianity Today*. https://www.christianitytoday.com/ct/2018/billy-graham.

Gibbs, Nancy, and Michael Duffy. 2008. *The Preacher and the Presidents: Billy Graham in the White House*. New York: Center Street.

Martin, William. 2018. *A Prophet with Honor*, updated ed. Grand Rapids, MI: Zondervan.

Miller, Steven R. 2009. *Billy Graham and the Rise of the Republican South*. Philadelphia: University of Pennsylvania Press.

Pierard, Ricard V. 1980. "Billy Graham and the U.S. Presidency." *Journal of Church and State* 22 (Winter): 107–27.

Great Seal of the United States

The Great Seal of the United States is often displayed with the U.S. flag as a symbol of the nation. The seal, which Congress adopted on June 20, 1782, has two sides. One features an American Eagle with a shield of thirteen white and red vertical stripes on its chest. It holds an olive branch in its right talon and a bundle of thirteen arrows in its left. Its beak holds a scroll inscribed with one of the nation's mottos, "E pluribus unum" (From many one). Above the blue crest over the eagle's head is a depiction of a golden glory breaking through a cloud and surrounded by a constellation of thirteen stars.

On the reverse side is a pyramid with an eye of providence in a triangle and the words "Annuit Coeptis," meaning, as Matthew Franck has explained with the use of brackets, that "[He—or Providence—the subject is understood and not stated] has favored our undertakings" (2016, 265). The base of the pyramid contains the Roman numerals for the year 1776 and below are the words "novus ordo seclorum," meaning "new order of the ages."

The first congressional committee that considered fashioning the great seal was composed of Thomas Jefferson, John Adams, and Benjamin Franklin. At least two of the delegates attempted to symbolize America through a resort to Hebraic symbolism. The venerable Franklin thus proposed a picture of "Moses standing on the Shore, and extending his Hand over the Sea, thereby causing the same to overwhelm Pharaoh who is sitting in an open Chariot, a Crown on his Head and a Sword in his Hand. Rays from a Pillar of Fire in the Clouds reaching to Moses, to express that he acts by Command of the Deity" (Sha'ban 2005, 58). In a similar vein, Jefferson had suggested an allegorical scene depicting "children of Israel in the wilderness, led by a cloud by day and a pillar of fire by night" (58). The final proposal was for a seal that pictured

> Pharaoh sitting in an open Chariot, a Crown on his head and a Sword in his hand passing through the divided Waters of the Red Sea in Pursuit of the Israelites: Rays from a Pillar of Fire in the Cloud, expressive of the divine Presence and Command, beaming on Moses who stands on the shore and extending his hand over the Sea causes it to overwhelm Pharaoh. Motto: Rebellion to Tyrants is Obedience to God. (Sha'ban 2005, 59)

Although this motto was not adopted, it demonstrates how even individuals who are more likely to be classified as Deists rather than an orthodox Christians were aware of biblical imagery, in this case chiefly from the 14th chapter of Exodus, and willing to employ it on behalf of national unity.

See also Deists; Franklin, Benjamin; Jefferson Bible; Moses as Political Archetype

For Reference and Further Reading

Feiler, Bruce. 2009. *America's Prophet: Moses and American Society*. New York: William Morrow.

Franck, Matthew J. 2016. "Christianity and Freedom in the American Founding." *Christianity and Freedom: Vol. I, Historical Perspectives*, ed. Timothy Samuel Shah and Allen D. Hertzke. New York: Cambridge University Press, pp. 264–89.

Hutson, James H. 1998. *Religion and the Founding of the American Republic*. Washington, DC: Library of Congress.

Madan, Rafael Alberto. 2008. "The Sign and Seal of Justice." *Ave Maria Law Review* 7: 123–204.

Sha'ban, Fuad. 2005. *For Zion's Sake: The Judeo-Christian Tradition in American Culture*. Ann Arbor, MI: Pluto Press.

Green Bible

The number of specialty Bibles that appeal to niche markets appear to be expanding, so it is perhaps not surprising that one such Bible, first published in 2008, is entitled *The Green Bible* and is designed to highlight environmental issues. The cover features a picture of a green tree, and, in contrast to so-called Red-Letter Bibles that highlight the words of Jesus in red, this Bible highlights biblical passages that deal with the earth and its environment in green. The version is the New Revised Standard Version. The title page includes both the picture of the tree from the cover and Genesis 1:31: "God saw everything that he had made, and indeed, it was very good."

In contrast to Bibles that intersperse stories and pictures throughout the biblical text, this Bible opens with the "Canticle of the Creatures" by St. Francis of Assisi and "The Clearing Rests in Song and Shade" by Wendell Berry, which are followed by a foreword by Archbishop Desmond Tutu of South Africa, ten essays by a variety of individuals, and a series of quotations entitled "Teachings on Creation through the Ages."

In the introduction entitled "The Power of a Green God," Dr. J. Matthew Sleeth explains how he gave up his medical practice and its accompanying lifestyle in order to seek to save the environment. He focuses on the importance of trees in biblical stories beginning with the story of the Garden of Eden in Genesis (2008, I-17–I-24). In "Reading the Bible through a Green Lens," Professor Calvin B. DeWitt describes the Bible as "a powerful ecological handbook on how to live rightly on earth" (I-25). He further identifies a number of "Stumbling Blocks to Creation's Care," discusses "Now What Must We Do about Creation?" and then presents "Biblical Principles for Creation Care" (I-24–I-34).

The next reading is a message that Pope John Paul II gave on the Celebration of the World Day of Peace on January 1, 1990, and is entitled "Peace with God the Creator, Peace with All of Creation" (I-35–I-42). The pope cited numerous scriptural passages, not only from Genesis but also from other portions of Scripture. Former pastor Brian McLaren follows with an essay, "Why I Am Green" (I-43–I-50). At one point he distinguishes what he believes to be the biblical view that "Nature is our sister" from what he describes as "the essence of all pantheism, evolutionism, and modern cosmic religion . . . that Nature is our mother" (I-45). Acknowledging that a strain of "liberal Christianity was once tempted to become the civil religion of socialism," McLaren suggested it was still possible to "imagine an economy based on stewardship rather than exclusive ownership" (I-47).

Professor Ellen Bernstein presents "Creation Theology: A Jewish Perspective" in the next essay (I-51–I-57). She makes a point of distinguishing what she calls "creation theology" from "creationism" (I-51). She further presents "The Ten Commandments of Creation Theology" (I-52).

Professor Ellen F. Davis's essay on "Knowing Our Place on Earth" focuses on passages from the Old Testament (I-58–I-64). She describes how the Bible attempts to combine discussions of both the physical and the spiritual worlds. In a particularly curious passage, she observes with reference to Eden that "the first human sin, as the Bible represents it, is an eating violation" (I-61).

James Jones, the bishop of Liverpool, follows with an essay entitled "Jesus: Savior of the Earth" (I-65–I-71). He notes the number of occasions that the Bible combines the description of Jesus as "the Son of Man" with mentions of the "Earth" (I-66). Another bishop, Dr. N. T. Wright, follows with a provocative essay entitled "Jesus Is Coming—Plant a Tree!" (I-72–I-85). In what may be the deepest theological essay, Wright argues that the coming of Christ will represent a restoration of earth and the combining of God's heavenly spiritual kingdom with that on earth, in the process parting with many contemporary Christian explanations of eschatology.

Professor Barbara Brown Taylor authors an essay on "The Dominion of Love" (I-86–I-90), in which she emphasizes the need for biblical stewardship of the earth while Gordon Aeschliman, the founding editor of *The Green Cross*, explains how "Loving the Earth Is Loving the Poor" (I-91–I-97). He sought to tie biblical concern for the poor with the Old Testament injunction to allow lands to lie fallow every seventh year.

The end of *The Green Bible* includes "The Green Bible Trail Guide" (1221–35) and a resource guide entitled "Where Do You Go from Here?" (1236–51), which includes a list of faith-based environmental organizations. The Trail Guide associates the themes of "And It Was Good," "Finding God," "Connected to Creation," "Creation Care as Justice," "The Full Impact of Sin," and "The New Earth" to relevant scriptural passages, and "The Green Subject Index" further provides references to relevant biblical passages (1252–70).

See also Climate Change

For Reference and Further Reading

The Green Bible (NRSV). 2008. New York: HarperOne.

Greenleaf, Simon

Legal educators, especially at prestigious law schools, often exercise significant influence on their students. One such educator was Simon Greenleaf (1783–1853), who was one of the founders of Harvard Law School. Born and educated in Massachusetts, he worked in the law office of Ezekiel Whitman in Maine before applying to the bar and eventually becoming a reporter for Maine's Supreme Court before becoming a professor at Harvard in 1833. There he worked closely with Justice Joseph Story in bringing the school into national prominence.

Greenleaf had successfully argued the case of *Charles River Bridge v. Warren Bridge* (1837), involving contract rights, against Daniel Webster, but was probably best known for authoring the first U.S. treatise on the law of evidence, which was the central reference on the subject until John Henry Wigmore's book on the subject supplanted it in 1904. Greenleaf was a pious Episcopalian who remains lauded among contemporary American evangelicals for a work entitled *An Examination of the Testimony of the Four Evangelists by the Rules of Evidence Administered in Courts of Justice*, first published in 1846, which served as a kind of Christian apologetics in defense of the New Testament gospels.

At a time when some skeptics were essentially arguing that anything found in the Bible was a form of hearsay, Greenleaf worked to show that the authors were reliable, that their testimonies reinforced one another, and that they would stand up in courts of law. Like many contemporary evangelicals, he relied strongly on Scottish Common Sense philosophy as well as on the complementary nature of reason and revelation. Howard Schweber has tied Greenleaf to what he referred to as "Protestant Baconianism," which he in turn associated with four major characteristics: "a commitment to natural theology, the doctrine that the study of nature proved religious truths; a commitment to a limited form of inductivism that defined science as fundamentally an exercise in taxonomy; a belief in a grand synthesis that bound all forms of knowledge together in a system of analogies; and a claim that science was a public undertaking that would produce moral and political uplift" (1999, 423).

At one point in his defense of the gospel writers, Greenleaf observed, "By competent evidence is meant such as the nature of the thing to be proved requires; and by satisfactory evidence is meant that amount of proof, which ordinarily satisfies an unprejudiced mind, beyond any reasonable doubt" ([1846] n.d. 28). Perhaps seeking to distinguish the witness of the gospel writers from that of the Book of Mormon, Greenleaf observed that "there is no pretense that they were engraven on plates of gold and discovered in a cave, nor that they were brought from heaven by angels; but they are received as the plain narratives and writings of the men whose names they respectively bear, made public at the time they were written" (10). At another point he observed that "in trials of fact, by oral testimony, the proper inquiry is not whether it is possible that the testimony may be false, but whether there is sufficient probability that it is true" (27).

Greenleaf joined Justice Story and others in believing that the common law was consistent with the principles of Christianity. One of his students, David Cross, thus recorded that Greenleaf said in a lecture, "The Common Law is Christian; It has been baptized" (Blinka 2019, 171).

See also Criminal Law; Torts

For Reference and Further Reading

Blinka, Daniel D. 2007. "The Roots of the Modern Trial: Greenleaf's Testimony to the Harmony of Christianity, Science, and Law in Antebellum America." *Journal of the Early Republic* 27 (Summer): 293–34.

Blinka, Daniel David. 2019. "Harvard's Evangelist of Evidence: Simon Greenleaf's Christian Common Sense." *Great Christian Jurists in American History*, ed. Daniel L. Dreisbach and Mark David Hall. New York: Cambridge University Press, pp. 161–78.

Charles River Bridge v. Warren Bridge 11 Pet. (36 U.S.) 420 (1837).

Greenleaf, Simon. [1846] n.d. *The Testimony of the Evangelists Examined by the Rules of Evidence Administered in Courts of Justice.* Suzeteo Enterprise. [Note: this version is a significantly shortened version of the original.]

Schweber, Howar. 1999. "The 'Science' of Legal Science: The Model of the Natural Sciences in Nineteenth-Century American Legal Education." *Law and History Review* 17 (Autumn): 421–66.

Grimke, Angelina

Angelina Grimke (1805–1879) was a Southern-born woman who moved to Philadelphia and later to Boston where she became a prominent abolitionist and suffragist. She and her older sister, Sarah, were popular public speakers, as was Theodore Dwight Weld, Angelina's husband (Hempton 2008, 70–91). As a reformer, Angelina deftly combined appeals from natural rights with scriptural passages.

In 1836, she authored her *Appeal to Christian Women of the South.* She prefaced it with a passage from Esther 4:13–16, in which Mordecai tells his niece Queen Esther that she will not escape the slaughter of her fellow Jews that Haman has arranged and that she may have become queen of Persia "for such a time as this" (Grimke 1836, 1). Grimke's thirty-six-page letter contains numerous scriptural references designed to show the evils of slavery.

The first portion of her letter referred to her audience as "Sisters in Christ" (1836, 1), with whom she hoped to share her moral light. In so doing, she quoted the language of human equality from the Declaration of Independence while indicating, in very Protestant fashion, that "the Bible is my ultimate appeal in all matters of faith and practice, and it is to this test I am anxious to bring the subject at issue between us" (3). In so doing she began by noting that while Genesis and Psalm 8 indicated that God had given Adam dominion over beasts, neither had vested him with dominion over his fellow man.

Moreover, whatever one might make of the curse upon Canaan (often identified with Ham, the son of Noah), it was a prophecy rather than an invitation to mistreat others. As Lincoln would later do in his second inaugural address, she quoted, without citing, Matthew 18:7: "it must needs be that offences come, but woe unto that man through whom they come" (3). In Grimke's judgment, those who hold slaves can be no more exonerated than those who sought the death of Jesus (4).

Moving on to the biblical patriarchs, Grimke argued that slavery as practiced in the South differed significantly from that as practiced by Abraham and his contemporaries. She thus noted that slave boys were circumcised, just like their masters' sons (thus including them within the covenant), whereas many masters did not extend baptism, which she regarded as the New Testament equivalent, to their slaves. Carefully describing six ways that Hebrews could become slaves—as described in Leviticus 25:38, 47–55; Exodus 21:2–6; and 2 Kings 4:1—she observed that none corresponded to the system of kidnapping that led to African American servitude. Such servitude was more akin to Joseph's brothers selling him into slavery (6). African American slavery actually violated the passage in Exodus 21:16, which proclaimed that "he that stealeth a man, and selleth him, or if he be found in his hand, he shall surely be put to death" (6). Even those that Hebrews held in bondage from other countries were taken in war or bought from heathen and, Grimke believed, held for a limited number of years.

Grimke further cited a host of biblical passages, most from Exodus 20 and 21, which provided legal protections for Hebrew servants. She devoted special attention to Exodus 21:21, in which if a servant survived for a day or more after being struck, the master "shall not be punished for he is his money" (8). Rejecting an interpretation that this proved that slaves were mere things rather than people, she rhetorically asked, "if so, why were so many laws made *to secure their rights as men*, and to ensure their rising into equality and freedom?" (8). With a view to fugitive slave laws, she further pointed to an admonition in Deuteronomy 23:15–16 that prohibited the return of slaves who had left their masters, and cited the celebration of the Year of Jubilee in Leviticus 25:10 (the latter part of which is inscribed on the Liberty Bell) that "ye shall hallow the fiftieth year, and proclaim *Liberty* throughout *all* the land, unto *all* the inhabitants thereof" (9).

Seeking to show how American slavery reduced slaves to objects, Grimke observed numerous ways in which it differed from that in the Bible. She thus argued that it is "hereditary and perpetual"; that slave labor "is compulsory and uncompensated"; that the slave is considered to be "personal chattel" that is "sold or pledged, or leased at the will of his master"; that slaves "can make no contracts and have no legal rights to any property"; that even freed slaves were not permitted to be witnesses against whites in court; that a slave "may be punished at his master's discretion—without trial—without any means of legal redress"; that slaves may not legally resist mistreatment; that slaves "cannot redeem themselves"; that the slave "is entirely unprotected in his domestic relations"; that the laws make manumission difficult; that "the operation of the laws tends to deprive slaves of religious instruction and consolation"; that laws seek to keep slaves "in a state of lowest ignorance"; that they are treated very differently than whites; and that "laws operate most oppressively upon free people of color" (11–12).

Grimke proceeded to refute arguments that Jesus had endorsed slavery. She noted that he lived among Jews who were not, at the time, practicing slavery and thus had no reason to comment on it. She further cited his Golden Rule and asked her readers if they were willing to experience the bondage that they had imposed on others. Animals were rightfully under the dominion of men (and thus had no cause to rebel), but slaves were not. As to arguments that St. Paul had sent Onesimus back to Philemon in the biblical book by the later name, she denied that Paul had exerted any coercion and cited his admonition in Colossians 4:1 to "give unto your servants that which is *just and equal*, knowing that ye also have a master in heaven" (15). She further pointed to the contradiction of despising slave traders while honoring slaveholders.

Having thoroughly indicted slavery and undermined its biblical foundations, Grimke outlined a plan of action. Women should read about slavery, pray about it, speak about it, and act on it (16–17). Noting that much anti-slave literature was banned in the South, Grimke urged women to "search the Scripture [John 5:39]" (17). Women could pray that God would "open the door of freedom" to slaves "without violence or bloodshed" and pray for Northern abolitionists (17). Women should especially speak out against laws that deprived slaves of Scripture much as Roman Catholics were reputed to seek to keep them out of the hands of everyone (17). She further encouraged women to free their own slaves and encourage their husbands and fathers to do the same, even if this brought persecution. She cited numerous individuals, including biblical women like Miriam, Deborah, Huldah the prophetess, Queen Esther, and others who had spoken out and sometimes suffered persecution, or the threat of persecution, for their faithful witness. She further noted the powerful role that women had played in the New Testament.

Grimke pointed to the "dark cloud of vengeance which hangs over our boasting Republic" (24) and decried the attempts by American settlers to reestablish slavery in the Catholic Mexican Republic.

Citing the words (from Daniel 12:4) that "many shall run to and fro, and knowledge shall be increased," which many interpreted as a sign that the end times were approaching, Grimke suggested that because slavery is such "an insurmountable barrier to the increase of knowledge in every community where it exits; slavery, then, must be abolished before this prediction can be fulfilled" (27). Rhetorically asking, "Will the wheels of the millennial car be rolled onward by miraculous power?" she suggested that this was a task for human beings to accomplish (27).

Grimke further likened the freeing of the slaves from ignorance and slavery to Jesus raising his friend Lazarus from the dead. Again, she used a rhetorical question: "Is not Jesus still the resurrection and the life? Did He come to proclaim liberty to the captive, and the opening of prison doors to them that are bound, in vain?" (28).

Appealing again as a Southerner who had joined the Female Anti-Slavery Society of Philadelphia and who had mixed with abolitionists and read their publications, Grimke denied that they were trying to stir up violence among the slaves. She identified slavery as "a national sin" (30) that required immediate action and noted that others who had battled slavery had, like Jesus, been subject to unjust accusations and treatment. Abolitionists were not abusing Southerners but simply playing the role of prophets in seeking to rid the nation of evil.

She signed as "Your sympathizing Friend" (36).

See also Curses on Cain, Ham, and the Canaanites; Declaration of Independence; Jesus; Esther as Political Archetype; Liberty Bell; Slavery

For Reference and Further Reading

Grimke, Angelina Emily. 1836. *Appeal to Christian Women of the South.* New York: American Anti-Slavery Society. Website of National Women's History Museum.

Hempton, David. 2008. *Evangelical Disenchantment: Nine Portraits of Faith and Doubt.* New Haven, CT: Yale University Press.

Sklar, Kathryn Kish. 2007. " 'The Throne of My Heart': Religion, Oratory, and Transatlantic Community in Angelina Grimke's Launching of Women's Rights, 1828–1838." *Women's Rights and Transatlantic Antislavery in the Era of Emancipation*, ed. Kathryn Kish Sklar and James Brewer Stewart. New Haven, CT: Yale University Press, pp. 211–41.

Grimke, Sarah M. (An Epistle to the Clergy of the Southern States)

In 1836, the Southern-born Sarah Moore Grimke (1792–1873), who was, at the time, an abolitionist living in New York, drafted an "epistle," or letter, to clergymen in the South decrying the institution of slavery and urging them to join cause with Northern abolitionists against it. Just as the term "epistle" is used to describe the letters that apostles wrote to the early church, Grimke's arguments show a wide knowledge of Scripture, which were, indeed, her primary source in denouncing slavery.

Like a preacher, Grimke began with a text. She chose Luke 19:41–42, which portrayed Jesus as crying over the sins, and eventual destruction, of Jerusalem. As Jesus had done, she further accused Southerners of seeking to stifle, and even to kill, the prophets among them. Instead, the pastors needed to serve as "watchmen on the walls of Zion [Isaiah 62:6]" as they sought "the right understanding of the sacred volume . . . of the Word of God."

As she recounted the creation of the world in Genesis, Grimke observed that God had created human beings in His image, thus separating him both from other created living beings and from mere things. This uniqueness was so special that God had instructed Noah, in a passage often used to justify capital punishment, to require the lives of both men and beast who killed human beings (Genesis 9:5). She further noted that in Psalm 8, King David has described man as just "a little lower than the angels" and that Jesus had Himself appeared in human flesh. To enslave a fellow human being is to enslave one of the same blood whose very body is "the temple of the Holy Ghost" (1 Corinthians 6:19). She buttressed her argument here, and elsewhere, by quoting from southerners who had questioned the morality and legality of slavery from the floors of southern state legislatures and argued that the institution was contrary to the Golden Rule that Jesus had advocated.

Grimke devoted a good part of her argument to showing that Jewish servitude, which some had used as a justification of slavery in the South, was considerably different, even attempting to parse the words that the Old Testament had used for servants. Addressing arguments from the supposed curse on Canaan, or Ham (one of the sons of Noah whom some believed had been cursed with blackness), Grimke said that the only reason that the Jews were able to slaughter the Canaanites was that God had given them a special commission to do so. She further argued that even if the Bible had prophesied that certain groups of people had been cursed, this did not exonerate those who mistreated them any more than it exonerated the Egyptians who had enslaved the Israelites or the Jews who had participated in the killing of Jesus.

According to Grimke, "the times of our ignorance on the subject of slavery which God may have winked at, have passed away. We are no longer standing unconsciously and carelessly on the brink of a burning volcano." The time had come for repentance from sins for which Jesus had died on the cross.

> What an appalling spectacle do we now present! With one hand we clasp the cross of Christ, and with the other grasp the neck of the down-trodden slave! With one eye we are gazing imploringly on the bleeding sacrifice of Calvary, as if we expected redemption through the blood which was shed there, and with the other we cast the glance of indignation and contempt at the representative of Him who there, made his soul an offering for sin! My Christian brethren, if there is any truth in the Bible, and in the God of the Bible, our hearts hear us witness that he can no more acknowledge us as his disciples, if we willfully persist in this sin, than he did the Pharisees formerly, who were strict and punctilious in the observance of the ceremonial law, and yet devoured widows' houses.

Grimke reiterated the need for repentance, citing the biblical book of Ezra on the importance of prayer and fasting, in order to save the entire land "from blood guiltiness." She further chided the clergy for reports that they were attempting to train their own clergymen so that they would support slavery rather than "the gospel of Jesus Christ, which proclaims LIBERTY TO THE CAPTIVE," a likely reference to the words on the Liberty Bell from Leviticus 25:10. She said that in order to preach slavery the words of the book of the biblical book of James crying out against false dealings (James 5:4) would only be the first casualty: "Multitudes of other texts must be virtually expunged from the Bible of the slave holding minister; every denunciation against oppression strikes at the root of slavery. God is in a peculiar manner the God of the poor and the needy, the despised and the oppressed."

Grimke quoted southern spokesmen to show that slaves were being deprived not only of the ability to read and write but also of knowledge of the gospel. As they sat around their own hearths enjoying their families, pastors should realize that their fellow slaves had similar sentiments towards their own family members. However, "they have no Bibles to read by their own fire-sides—they have no family altars; and when in affliction, sickness, or death, they have no minister to address to them the consolations of the gospel, nor to bury, them with solemn and appropriate services." Citing Southern laws against teaching slaves to read or write, she commented, "Oh, my brethren! When you are telling to an admiring audience that through your instrumentality nearly two millions of Bibles and Testaments have been disseminated throughout the world, does not the voice of the slave vibrate on your ear?"

Grimke remained determined to persist even in the wake of attempts to destroy anti-slave writings. Indeed, she likened attempts to suppress the speech of abolitionists to earlier historical attempts to stamp out distribution of the Bible. Citing the story of Procurator Felix's decision to wait for a more "convenient" day (Acts 24:25) before deciding how to sentence St. Paul, Grimke observed "that prospective repentance and future amendment are destruction to the soul," and recounted the story of a slave owner who beat a slave to death after the slave refused to renounce his faith in God.

Classifying the system of slavery as "necessarily cruel," Grimke compared it to the Catholic inquisition. She further denied that slavery was justified because it "has been entailed upon us by our ancestors." Citing the proverb in Ezekiel 18:2 that "the fathers have eaten sour grapes, and the children's teeth are set on edge," Grimke argued that rather than blaming forefathers for their current situation, those who owned slaves should acknowledge their own sins. Whereas her sister Angelina had in her appeal to Christian Women of the South largely condemned Thomas Jefferson's racist sentiment in his *Notes on the State of Virginia*, Sarah Grimke chose to observe Jefferson's observation in that same work "of the [negative] influence of slavery, on the temper and morals of the master."

Sarah Grimke made a special appeal to fellow Methodists, noting that John Wesley and Adam Clarke had both opposed slavery. She described the institution as "the sin, which the Church is fostering! In her bosom," which she likened both to "leprosy" and to a "monster."

See also Abolitionists; Grimke, Angelina; Slavery

For Reference and Further Reading

Carlacio, Jami. 2002. "'Ye Knew Your Duty, but Ye Did It Not': The Epistolary Rhetoric of Sarah Grimke." *Rhetorical Review* 21(3): 247–63.

Grimke, Sarah M. 1836. "An Epistle to the Clergy of the Southern States." https://en.wikisource.org/wiki/An_Epistle_to_the_Clergy_of_the_Southern_States.

Grimke, Sarah M. (Letters on the Equality of the Sexes)

Sarah Moore Grimke (1792–1837), like her sister Angelina, was a Southern-born abolitionist who was also deeply concerned about women's rights. Prompted in part by Catharine Beecher's defense of traditional female roles and by a Pastoral Letter of the General Association of Congregational Ministers of Massachusetts, Grimke published a series of letters addressed to Mary S. Parker, the president of the Boston Female Anti-Slavery Society, which were collected and published in book form. Altogether, the book consisted of fifteen letters that tied her advocacy of abolitionism to that of women's rights.

Her early letters make the most references to the Bible. In thus addressing "The Original Equality of Woman" in her first letter, Grimke indicated that she knew that she was facing "the perverted interpretation of Holy Writ, which has so universally obtained" (1938, 3) but that she would "depend solely on the bible to designate the sphere of woman, because I believe almost every thing that has been written on this subject, has been the result of a misconception of the simple truths revealed in the Scriptures, in consequences of the false translation of many passages of Holy Writ" (4). Focusing on what she believed was the error of the King James Version of the Bible, she distinguished the errors of the translators from the truth of the original. Moreover, in very Protestant fashion, she said that "I also claim to judge for myself what is the meaning of the inspired writers, because I believe it to be the solemn duty of every individual to search the Scriptures for themselves, with the aid of the Holy Spirit, and not be governed by the views of any man, or set of men" (4).

Beginning with the story of creation in Genesis 1:26–27, Grimke argued that God had created mankind, both male and female, in His image and had given dominion "to both [of them] over every other creature, but not over each other" (4). Grimke further argued that when God created woman, she was "a companion, *in all respects* his equal; one who was like himself *a free agent*, gifted with intellect and endowed with immortality; not a partaker merely of his animal gratifications, but able to enter into all his feelings as a moral and responsible being" (5).

Proceeding to discuss the fall of mankind in Genesis 3, Grimke observed that both Adam and Eve had sinned, and that as a consequence, "they both fell from innocence, and consequently from happiness, *but not from equality*" (7). Recognizing that Genesis 3:16 had indicated that "thou wilt be subject unto thy husband, he will rule over thee," she contended that this was not a "command" but a "prediction" that should not have been translated as a "*shall*" but as a "*will*" (7). As she summarized, "God created us equal;—he created us free agents;—he is our Lawgiver, our King and our Judge, and to him alone is woman bound to be in subjection, and to him alone is she accountable for the use of those talents with which her Heavenly Father has entrusted her. One is her Master even Christ" (8).

Grimke continued this theme in her second letter, "Woman Subject Only to God." Reiterating her analysis of creation, Grimke found similar equality during the time of Noah. "The lust of dominion was probably the first effect of the fall, and as there was no other intelligent being over whom to exercise it, woman was the first victim of this unhallowed passion" (11). Noting that John Quincy Adams had classed women with slaves, she said that, even in "republican America, woman has more or less been made a *means* to promote the welfare of man, without due regard to her own happiness and the glory of God as the end of her creation" (12). As a result of the fall, "the cupidity of man soon led him to regard woman [as they would later regard slaves] as property" (13).

In her third letter, Grimke addressed a Pastoral Letter of the General Association of Congregational Ministers of Massachusetts, whose sentiments she again attributed to improper biblical translations. She believed that Jesus had outlined equal duties for men and women in his Sermon on the Mount. Rejecting the Pastoral Letter's admonition to women to exercise their influence privately and unobtrusively, she observed, "This has ever been the flattering language of man since he laid aside the whip as a means to keep woman in subjection. He spares her body; but the war he has waged against her mind, her heart, and her soul, has been no less destructive to her as a moral being. How monstrous, how anti-christian, is the doctrine that woman is to be dependent on man! Where, in all the sacred Scriptures is this taught?" (17). In a theme to which she will return in later essays, Grimke observed that "he has adorned the creature whom God gave him as a companion, with baubles and gewgaws, turned her attention to personal attractions, offered incense to her vanity, and made her the instrument of his selfish gratification, a plaything to please his eye and amuse his hours of leisure" (17). God expects both men and women to exhibit such fruits of the Spirit as "love, meekness, gentleness, &c. [a reference to Galatians 5:22–23]" (18). Assuming that women can only be instructed by male pastors is to assume "that all pastors are better qualified to give instruction than woman," which she utterly denied (19).

In her fourth letter, Grimke argues that social intercourse between men and women is distorted when males only view women based on their sex. She cited Paul's injunction (Galatians 3:28) that "there is neither Jew nor Greek, there is neither bond nor free, there is neither *male* nor *female*; for ye are all one in Christ Jesus" (24). Nor should woman allow "false delicacy" to lead her "to shun her fallen sister and brother, and shrink from *naming those sins* which she knows exist but which she is too fastidious to labor by deed and by word to exterminate" (25).

After surveying the condition of women throughout the world, Grimke observed in her sixth letter that "there is no natural inferiority in woman. Not that I approve of woman's holding the reins of government over man. I maintain that they are equal, and that God never invested fallen man with unlimited power over his fellow man; and I rejoice that circumstances have prevented woman from being more deeply involved in the guilt which appears to be inseparable from political affairs" (33). More to her point, she observed "that intellect is not sexed" (33).

Discussing the plight of women in the United States, Grimke observed that she once gave herself to fashion and to the idea that the primary goal for a woman was to secure a husband, but that she believed that women should have equal opportunities for an education and that they should receive commensurate pay with men.

Returning to the subject of female dress in her ninth letter, Grimke observed that while women's dress is often compared to that of the adornment of birds and flowers, women were neither (71). Women, like men, are commanded (Romans 12:2) "not to be conformed to this world, but to be transformed by the renewing of her mind, that she may know what is the good and acceptable and perfect will of God" (72).

In her twelfth letter, Grimke elaborated on women's legal disabilities under existing doctrines of coverture and restrictions on women's legal rights and her obligation to accept the chastisements of their husbands. In the letter that followed, she further described marriage as "a *divine ordination*, not a civil contract" (84). Women should have the same right to sign anti-slavery petitions and participate in the anti-slavery cause as men. The biblical commands to honor parents applied equally to mothers and fathers (89). Moreover, consistent with the Ten Commandments, "man shall have no other gods before ME, and woman shall have no other gods before MAN" (90). She recognized that passages in Paul's epistles suggesting that women were to be subject to their husbands were shaped by the fact that "his mind was under the influence of Jewish prejudices respecting women, just as Peter's and the apostles were about the uncleannesss of the Gentiles" (91). Comparing biblical admonitions about the behavior of both men and women, she observed with special reference to Ephesians that the whole work "breathes a spirit of love" (95).

In her penultimate letter, she observed that even religious bodies that allow women to preach have not fully embraced them in such a role. Noting that women like Miriam, Deborah, and Huldah had prophesied in the Old Testament, she observed that both men and women received the Holy Spirit at Pentecost, and that the early church contained prophetesses, deaconesses, and even ministers, as commentators like John Locke and Adam Clarke had recognized (107–9). Grimke argued that 1 Timothy 2:8, which had been used to support the idea that only men could preach, had been misinterpreted because of a punctuation error (112).

In her final letter, Grimke returned to the idea that Adam and Eve were equally guilty of committing the first sin, and that women have been shackled by a *"corrupt public opinion, and a perverted interpretation of the holy Scriptures"* (116). Both men and women have equal rights and equal responsibilities. Instead of taking up collections for the education of male clergymen, members of all-female sewing societies should be insisting on equal education for women. Nor was it necessary for them to invite men to give the opening prayer. Women were equally needed to engage in the cause of abolitionism and the coming of the "kingdom of heaven" (124).

See also Grimke, Angelina; Grimke, Sarah M. (An Epistle to the Clergy of the Southern States)

For Reference and Further Reading

Carlacio, Jami. 2002. "Ye Knew Your Duty, but Ye Did It Not': The Epistolary Rhetoric of Sarah Grimke." *Rhetorical Review* 21(3): 247–63.

Grimke, Sarah Moore. 1838. *Letters on the Equality of the Sexes and the Condition of Woman. Address to Mary S. Parker, President of the Boston Female Anti-Slavery Society*. Boston: Isaac Knapp.

• H •

Hagee, John

John Hagee (b. 1940) is the minister of the Cornerstone Church in San Antonio, Texas, a congregation that grew from his television ministry. Hagee, who is a member of the Assembly of God, is among the most prominent charismatic ministers in the United States and is especially known for his belief, based on Genesis 12:3, that nations that bless Israel will be blessed and that those that do not will be cursed. He has authored at least ten books, most of which focus on prophecy, and one of which (*God's Candidate for America*) specifically endorsed George W. Bush for president.

Hagee founded Christians United for Israel in 2006, has advocated obliterating Iran with nuclear weapons, and has supported President Trump's relocation of the American Embassy in Israel from Tel Aviv to Jerusalem. Hagee has raised a lot of money for Jewish causes, and he has succeeded in drawing prominent American politicians to his church and for making friends with other prominent Israeli politicians.

In contrast to most evangelical Christians, with whom he is often allied on political matters, and to many earlier Christian Zionists, Hagee appears to believe that Jews can achieve salvation apart from personally accepting Jesus as Savior. In a provocative statement that he might have intended to stir interest in one of his books, Hagee denied that Jesus was the Messiah, at least in the sense of being a political deliverer. Given such a view, the Jews had the right to reject him as such (Slick n.d.). Victoria Clark, who thinks that Agee's approach to world politics is akin to "talking Texan" (the title of one of her book chapters), observes that Hagee has disassociated himself from Jews who had coveted to Christianity "because 'the Israelis see those people as traitors'" and that "bringing Jews to Jesus as their messiah would 'muddy the waters in what we're trying to accomplish'" (2007, 276).

Sarah Posner argues that Hagee is associated both with the prosperity gospel, which teaches that God desires to bless Christians with material wealth, and with what she describes as "revelation knowledge," whereby a believer "derives knowledge directly from God, rather than from the senses" (2008). Irvin Chetty further associates Hagee with the New Apostolic Reformation (NAR), which emphasizes "the primacy of the apostle . . . who also functions in the role of a teacher by 'accurately' decoding God's divine blueprint for this season" (2014, 297).

See also Bush, George W.; Prosperity Gospel; Trump, Donald J.; Zionism

For Reference and Further Reading

Bova, Gus. 2018. "Under Trump, Islamophobic Pastor John Hagee's Star Rises Again." *Texas Observer*. August 9. https://www.texasobserver.org/trump-pastor-john-hagee-texas-jerusalem/.

Chetty, Irvin G. 2014. "The New Apostolic Reformation and Christian Zionism." *Journal for the Study of Religion* 27(2): 297–312.
Clark, Victoria. 2007. *Allies for Armageddon*. New Haven, CT: Yale University Press.
Posner, Sarah. 2008. "John Hagee's Controversial Gospel." The American Prospect. March 12. https://prospect.org/article/john-hagees-controversial-gospel.
Slick, Matt. n.d. "John Hagee Denies Jesus Claimed to Be the Messiah." Christian Apologetics & Research Ministry. https://carm.org/john-hagee-denies-jesus-claimed-to-be-the-messiah.

Harlan Bible

Justice John Marshall Harlan (1833–1911) was considered to be a maverick during his tenure on the U.S. Supreme Court from 1877 to 1911, where he was the only justice to dissent from the court's ruling upholding racial segregation in *Plessy v. Ferguson* (1896). He was also known for his deep religious faith. Indeed, fellow justice David Josiah Brewer reputedly "suggested that Harlan had one hand on the Bible, and the other hand on the Constitution when he went to bed each night" (Gordon 2001, 318). Gordon notes that Harlan had grown up in a Presbyterian church in Frankfort, Kentucky, that stressed "the memorization and recitation of Bible verses," that he was a long-time Sunday school teacher, and that he attended Centre College, which was supported by the Presbyterian Church (pp. 323–24). Gordon suggests that if Harlan could speak today, "he would almost certainly tell us that his Presbyterianism was the most important lens through which he viewed the people and events of his life. He would assert that the Bible was a divinely revealed, inerrant, moral guide for human conduct and that he had tried to follow its commands. With his characteristic humor, he might add that his Presbyterian belief in the 'right of private judgment' preordained his remarkable independence of mind on the crucial constitutional questions of his day" (p. 321). Indeed, in responding to an interview, Harlan once said that "I fully believe in both the Bible and the Constitution. . . . I believe that the Bible is the inspired Word of God. Nothing which it commands can be safely or properly disregarded—nothing that it condemns can be justified. No civilization is worth preserving which is not based on the doctrines or teachings of the Bible" (quoted in Gordon 2001, 241–341). Although firm in his beliefs, Harlan also believed strongly in the "sacred right of private judgment," which was a tenet of his church (p. 344).

Harlan saw a clear line between right and wrong, and his approaches to interpreting the Bible and the U.S. Constitution appear to have been closely related and have been linked to his willingness to apply the Reconstruction Amendments strictly. Gordon thus observes, "The fact that Harlan often read the Constitution or statutes literally does not mean that he was necessarily trapped within their letter. He found layers in the Bible, and he accepted that understanding the Founders required that the words of the Constitution be reconciled with the purposes for which the Constitution was created. Although Harlan was prepared for a sophisticated analysis of a text, he was unwilling to abandon its words" (2001, 364). Gordon also persuasively argues that Harlan's support of a strong national government with extensive powers over interstate commerce and in robust state police powers was consistent with the special place that Orthodox Calvinism assigned to the importance of law in guiding human behavior (pp. 366–84).

In 1906, Harlan donated his Oxford Sunday School Teachers Edition of the King James Version of the Bible to the Supreme Court. Each subsequent justice has signed on the Bible's flyleaf, which is now called the "Harlan Bible." A number of the justices have testified to the meaningfulness of this tradition.

A group known as the American Judicial Alliance has subsequently launched a project to donate a Bible to every court in the United States. It has chosen the Thompson Chain Reference Study Bible with a number of blank flyleaf pages for future judges to sign. A statement by Congressman Ted Poe on the Alliance's website says that "American Judicial Alliance's presentation should be required for all Supreme Court nominees and sitting Federal Judges," but such a requirement would appear to conflict with the establishment and free exercises clauses of the First Amendment to the U.S. Constitution.

See also Bible Signings; Constitutional Interpretation; U.S. Constitution

For Reference and Further Reading

"Bible Project." American Judicial Alliance. https://ajatoday.com/bible-project. Accessed April 11, 2019.

Gordon, James W. 2001. "Religion and the First Justice Harlan: A Case Study in Late Nineteenth Century Presbyterian Constitutionalism." *Marquette Law Review* 85 (Winter): 317–422.

Harrison, Benjamin

Benjamin Harrison (1833–1901) served as the twenty-third president of the United States from 1889 to 1893 and was well known for his Presbyterian piety.

The grandson of President William Henry Harrison, who had served only about a month in the White House before dying, Benjamin was born and educated in Ohio (Miami University of Ohio). He studied law under Bellamy Storer of Cincinnati, before moving to Indiana. There he established a successful legal practice and served as a city attorney and in a number of other positions. He enlisted as a colonel in the Union Army and served in the U.S. Senate before being elected as president.

In a college essay written at a time when he may still have been deciding on whether to pursue a career in the ministry or in the law, he observed that it was important to "remember that Civil Society is no less an institution of God than the Church, that society can in no sense exist without government, and that man in the instrumentality appointed to administer this government" (Calhoun 1993, 655). In that same work, he observed that "the religion of Christ claims but one throne, the throne of the heart. The church, as a church, can take no part in the affairs of the state, but individual members of the church as embodying the only true morality and as members of civil society owe to that society of which they form an integral part certain duties for the neglect of which God will not hold them guiltless" (Calhoun 1993, 655). Harrison traced the origins of republican government to Scripture, noting that "not Plato nor [George] Buchanan, nor Locke, but the Word, read with reverence daily in the household, and expounded in the sanctuary, was the chief instructor of the body of colonists in the theories of popular rights" (Calhoun 1993, 657).

Harrison had joined the Republican Party largely as a matter of principle, and in 1876 he said that the party could look back with St. Paul (2 Timothy 4:7) in saying, "I have fought the good fight, I have kept the faith" (Calhoun 1993, 656). As a lawyer and private citizen, Harrison was known for his devotion to his family, for leading daily prayers, for honoring Sunday as a day of rest, and for serving as a Presbyterian elder.

Although he was known for his personal probity, his election was surrounded by charges of corruption. After the election returns came in, Harrison exclaimed, "Providence has given us the victory!" The Republican National Committee chairman, who was more familiar with the behind-the-scenes machinations, later said, "Providence hadn't a damn thing to do with it" (Ringenberg 1986, 186–87). Harrison filled his cabinet with church men, including his postmaster general John Wanamaker (1838–1922), who, like Harrison, was an active member of the Sunday school movement.

When leaving for his inauguration, Harrison observed that "there is a great sense of loneliness in the discharge of high public duties. The moment of decision is one of isolation. But there is One whose help comes even into the quiet chamber of judgment, and to whose wise and unfailing guidance will I look for direction and safety" (Ringenberg 1986, 182). Often identified as a proponent of a civil religion used to unite the people, in a speech marking the centenary of Washington's administration, he expressed the desire "to elevate the morals of our people; to hold up the law as that sacred thing which, like the ark of God of old, may not be touched by irreverent hands, . . . to unite our people in all that makes home comfortable, as well as to give our energies in the direction of material advancement, this service may we render" (Calhoun 1993, 651). As president, in addition to supporting Republican policies typical for his era, Harrison opposed polygamy by upholding legislation and delaying the entry of Utah into the Union, sought to end federal aid to Catholic churches who were aiding in Indian education (probably as a result of his view of strict separation of church and state), and opposed gambling.

After failing to be reelected, Harrison returned to the practice of law and was frequently called upon to speak to a variety of organizations, including religious ones. In 1900, President William McKinley appointed him to the International Court. From April 19 to May 1, 1900, Harrison was the honorary chairman and a delegate from the Presbyterian Church to the Ecumenical Missionary Conference held in Carnegie Hall. In speaking to the conference, he identified "Christ in the heart and His Gospel of love and ministry in all the activities of life" as "the only cure" for world problems (Ringenberg 1986, 187).

Harrison was a proponent of international missionary activities but cautious about American imperialism. He said that because all men were equal in the sight of God: "The highest conception that has ever entered the mind of man is that of God as the Father of all men—the one blood—the universal brotherhood" (Ringenberg 1986, 187).

After he left the presidency, Harrison was given increasingly to delivering jeremiads, which found good reception in the social gospel movement. At one point, he observed that the "only cure" was "Christ in the heart and His gospel of love and ministry in all the activities of life." He further observed, "If you could blot out of your statute books, out of your constitutions, out of your codes of morals, out of your social and family institutions all that is derived from the sacred book, what would there be left to bind society together?" (Calhoun 1993, 663). Professor Charles Calhoun believes that William McKinley and Theodore Roosevelt both followed his belief in the importance of spreading Christianity throughout the world (Calhoun 1993, 664).

See also McKinley, William; Polygamy; Providence; Roosevelt, Theodore; Social Gospel

For Reference and Further Reading

Calhoun, Charles W. 1993. "Civil Religion and the Gilded Age Presidency: The Case of Benjamin Harrison." *Presidential Studies Quarterly* 23 (Fall): 651–67.

Ringenberg, William C. 1986. "Benjamin Harrison: The Religious Thought and Practice of a Presbyterian President." American Presbyterians 64 (Fall): 175–89.

Hatfield, Mark

Although evangelical Christians are often associated with right-wing politics, Mark Hatfield (1922–2011), the two-term Republican governor and five-term U.S. senator from Oregon, proved to be an exception. Educated at Willamette and Stanford Universities, he taught at Willamette before serving in the Oregon state legislature and in subsequent posts, and he resumed his association with a number of institutions of higher learning after leaving the Senate. Both Richard Nixon and George McGovern had considered placing him as vice president on their presidential tickets.

Hatfield, whose colleagues sometimes referred to him as "Saint Mark," established a strong pro-life position. It included opposition not only to abortion but also to capital punishment and to the war in Vietnam. Still, he recognized that people of faith disagreed on issues and opposed one-issue politics (Currie 2011).

In 1973, Hatfield confounded expectations when, at the National Prayer Breakfast, he delivered a speech that departed significantly from the standard fare. Warning of the dangers of "misplaced allegiance, if not outright idolatry," he said that it was critical "to distinguish between the god of an American civil religion and the God who reveals Himself in the Holy Scriptures and in Jesus Christ" (Swartz 2019). Drawing from a manuscript provided by Jim Wallis, a left-wing evangelical who founded the *Sojourners* magazine, Hatfield proceeded to say that "if we pray to the Biblical God of justice and righteousness, we fall under God's judgment for calling upon His name, but failing to obey His commands" (Swartz 2019), and he cited Luke 6:46 on the importance of obeying God.

Further drawing from Isaiah 58:6–7, Hatfield associated acceptable worship with acts of justice and with repentance. He tied them, in turn, to the promise in 2 Chronicles 7:24 that "if my people . . . shall humble themselves, and pray, and seek my face, and turn from their wicked ways, . . . then I will forgive their sins, and will heal their land." This required that the "confessing church" heed the call of Romans 12:2 to transform the world, rather than being conformed to it.

Billy Graham was among those in the audience who later called Nixon to distance himself from Hatfield's message in order to stay in President Nixon's good graces. At least in the eyes of one critic, the National Prayer Breakfast has remained, with relatively few exceptions, "one of polite acquiescence to the Washington establishment, sycophantic cheerleading of one's own party, and partisan critiques of the other party" (Swartz 2019).

See also Abortion; Graham, Billy

For Reference and Further Reading

Currie, Chuck. 2011. "The Christian Faith of Senator Mark Hatfield." HuffPost. August 8. https://www.huffpost.com/entry/christian-faith-mark-hatfield_b_921230.

Eells, Robert, and Bartell Nyberg. 1979. *Lonely Walk: The Life of Senator Mark Hatfield.* Chappaqua, NY: Christian Herald Books.

Greanberg-Michaelson, Wes. 2011. "A Tribute to Mark O. Hatfield." *Sojourners.* August 8. https://sojo.net/articles/tribute-mark-o-hatfield.

Swartz, David. 2019. "The National Prayer Breakfast and Evangelical Prophetic Witness." Patheos. January 30. https://www.patheos.com/blogs/anxiousbench/2019/01/the-national-prayer-breakfast-and-evangelical-prophetic-witness/.

Heaven and Hell

The majority of Americans have long maintained a belief in the afterlife, including a heaven that rewards the godly and faithful and a hell for unrepentant sinners. John 14, as well as a variety of passages in the book of Revelation, is often cited as support for heaven, whereas such passages as Matthew 22:13, Matthew 25:41, the story of Lazarus and the Rich man in Luke 16, and Revelation 21:27 suggest punishment, which many Christians believe to be eternal.

One of America's most famous sermons, Jonathan Edwards's "Sinners in the Hands of an Angry God," sought the conversion of sinners by portraying them as spiders hanging over an open pit and connected only by a slender thread that God could cut at any time. The idea of saving people from eternal torment in hell (as well as promises of heaven) gave a major boost to missionary efforts, like those of the American Bible Society, both within the United States and abroad. Moreover, the idea that the redeemed were citizens of a heavenly city in addition to the nation in which they resided both gave them the possibility of disobeying earthly powers when its demands were thought to be against God, as well as provided a heavenly alternative to current laws (Hyde 2018).

Many American founders, even those who might otherwise have been classified as Deists rather than orthodox Christians, thought that belief in future rewards and punishments was important, in part because of the way it encouraged civic virtue. John Quincy Adams thus identified his belief in "a future state of rewards and punishments" as one of three doctrines—the others were "the existence of a God" and "the immortality of the human soul"—that were central to the Bible and that he thought promoted morality (Adams 1848, 22–23).

At the Constitutional Convention of 1787, George Mason of Virginia, who was on fairly shaky moral ground since he himself owned many slaves, delivered an extensive critique of the institution of slavery. He thus observed, "Slavery discourages arts & manufacturers. The poor despise labor when performed by slaves. They prevent the immigration of Whites, who really enrich & strengthen a Country. They produce the most pernicious effect on manners. Every master of slaves is born a petty tyrant" (Farrand 1966, II: 370). Immediately thereafter, Mason observed that "they bring the judgment of heaven on a Country. As nations can not be rewarded or punished in the next world they must be in this. By an inevitable chain of causes & effects providence punishes national sins, by national calamities" (II: 370). The idea that God would punish nations, especially those in covenant with Him who departed from moral behavior, with foreign invasion and/or natural disasters has a long lineage (Jackson 2007, 44). Methodist evangelist Lorenzo Dow was among those who observed that "as it is nowhere said, that Nations in their political capacity, shall be judged in futurity—political evils must be punished here" (Dow 1851, 451–52).

Kathryn Gin Lum has conducted a comprehensive study of the effect of the belief in hell in America. She believes that many religious and social movements in the early republic were motivated by hopes of saving others from hell fire. During debates over slavery, abolitionists claimed both that keeping slaves in ignorance resulted in their own damnation and that those who participated in the evils of slavery would face hell fire. More generally, she believes that the hope of heaven and the threat of hell were used to promote civic virtue. She notes, "If evangelicals had dropped hell from their worldviews, revivals would not have had life-or-death intensity, missions movements would likely not have taken off, and social reform crusades may not have seemed as immediately pressing" (Lum 2014, 233). Even today, some fundamentalist churches use "hell houses" during the week of Halloween to portray the horrors that they believe await those who become involved in premarital sex, alcohol, smoking, and other dangerous behaviors.

One specific application of a belief in heaven and hell is the system of oaths used both for individuals who assume public office and for those who testify in Court (Dreisbach 2019, 89). Indeed, some political theorists in both England and the United States questioned whether the oath of an individual who did not believe in God, and/or in a future state of rewards and punishments, could be trusted.

See also Adams, John Quincy; American Bible Society; Citizenship; Deism; Edwards, Jonathan

For Reference and Further Reading

Adams, John Quincy. 1848. *Letters of John Quincy Adams, to His Son, on the Bible and Its Teachings*. Auburn, NY: Derby, Miller. PDF accessed through Google.

Dow, Lorenzo. 1851. "Analects upon Natural, Social, and Moral Philosophy." 7th ed., enlarged, *History of Cosmopolite: Or, the Writings of Rev. Lorenzo Dow: Containing His Experience and Travels, in Europe and America, Up to Near His Fiftieth Year*. N.p.: J.B. Smith, pp. 417–78.

Dreisbach, Daniel L. 2019. "Introduction: Christianity and American Law." *Great Christian Jurists in American History*, ed. Daniel L. Dreisbach and Mark David Hall. New York: Cambridge University Press, pp. 1–15.

Farrand, Max, ed. 1966. *The Records of the Federal Convention of 1787*. 4 vols. New Haven, CT: Yale University Press.

Hyde, Carrie. 2018. *Civic Longing: The Speculative Origins of U.S. Citizenship*. Cambridge, MA: Harvard University Press.

Jackson, Brian. 2007. "Jonathan Edwards Goes to Hell (House): Fear Appeals in American Evangelism." *Rhetoric Review* 26(1): 42–59.
Lum, Kathryn Gin. 2014. *Damned Nation: Hell in America from Revolution to Reconstruction*. New York: Oxford University Press.

Henry, Patrick

One of the speeches that is believed to have done the most to spur Virginians to prepare for possible conflict with England was the speech that Patrick Henry gave before the Second Virginia Convention that met on March 20, 1775, at St. John's Church in Richmond.

The speech was so mesmerizing that Colonel Edward Carrington, who had listened to the speech from outside the window, asked that he be buried on that spot when he died (a request that was granted). The speech was not transcribed at the time but was later recreated by William Wirt in an early biography of Henry, in part from recollections of Thomas Jefferson and others who were present for the speech.

At least as Wirt reconstructed the speech, it contained a number of scriptural allusions, which would likely be expected from a lawyer who was known to have been so persuasive before juries. Edmund Randolph had observed that Henry's "figures of speech, when borrowed, were often borrowed from the Scriptures," and compared Henry's work at the Virginia Convention to St. Paul's speech at Athens as recorded in Acts 17 (Cohen 1981, 712).

In words that today seem somewhat ironic coming from a slave owner, Henry posed the issues between the United States and Britain "as nothing less than a question of freedom or slavery." To be silent at such a time was to commit treason against "the Majesty of Heaven," an expression that Henry had gleaned from 1 Chronicles 29:11.

While fellow delegates were holding out the possibility of reconciliation, Henry thought they were guilty of political blindness, like the spiritual blindness described in Jeremiah 5:21 and Ezekiel 12:2, among "those who, having eyes, see not, and, having ears, hear not, the things which so nearly concern their temporal salvation." Professing to be led by "the lamp of experience" (Psalm 119:105 refers to God's words as "a lamp to my feet"), Henry suggested that the only way of judging future British conduct was by past actions, which included building up troops in America and refusing colonial petitions. Whereas those advocating the cause of England were likely to think of Americans as treasonous, Henry reversed the tables by warning, in obvious reference of Judas's betray of Jesus in Matthew 26:48, that they should "suffer not yourselves to be betrayed with a kiss." In terminology that is frequently repeated in the Bible, Henry also warned about "a snare to your feet." Citing a further reference that is found in many Old Testament passages (often with the word "LORD" rather than "God"), Henry concluded, "An appeal to arms and to the God of Hosts is all that is left us!"

The Bible contains many stories of individuals who overcame their adversaries with the help of God. Henry noted that "three millions of people, armed in the holy cause of liberty, and in such a country as that which we possess, are invincible by any force which our enemy can send against us." Taking comfort in what he believed to be the justice of the colonial cause, Henry further noted that "there is a just God who presides over the destinies of the nations; and who will raise up friends to fight our battles for us." He continued with the admonition, a paraphrase of Ecclesiastes 9:11–12, that "the battle, sir, is not to the strong alone; it is to the vigilant, the active, the brave."

In one of the most famous lines of the speech, Henry quoted from the words of the prophet Jeremiah warning against false prophets. Henry noted that "gentlemen may cry Peace, Peace but there is no Peace" and correctly predicted, less than a month from the battles of Lexington and Concord, that "the next gale that sweeps from the north will bring to our ears the clash of resounding arms!" Drawing from Jesus's parable of the owner of the vineyard seeking workers in Matthew 20:6, Henry asked, "Why stand we here idle?" and ended with perhaps the most famous words of his life: "Is life so dear, or peace so sweet, as to be purchased at the price of chains and slavery? Forbid it, Almighty God! I know not what course others may take; but as for me, give me liberty or give me death!"

It seems likely that the latter verse was intended to evoke Joshua 24:14. There Moses's successor, Joshua, asked the people to choose between the pagan gods of their ancestors and the true God and affirmed that "as for me and my house, we will serve the LORD." Like the ancient Israelites, Virginians needed to make a break with the past if they were to have a viable future.

Attuned to various modes of arguments that were employed in the years leading up to the American Revolution, Charles Cohen observes that "the broader significance of the 'Liberty or Death' speech lies in the way it instances the importance of religious as well as political current in the colonists' Revolutionary thought. The bible could teach Virginians a provocative lesson; Jeremiah could unmask a devious conspiracy as effectively as 'Cato' in the *Independent Whig*" (1981, 717).

Distinguishing among various uses of Scripture in rhetoric, Daniel Dreisbach (2017) further observes that Henry "appropriated biblical language, not to draw attention to some specific biblical theme or principle, but to enhance the dramatic appeal and gravity of the rhetoric."

See also Revolutionary War; Slavery

For Reference and Further Reading

"Biblical Reference in Patrick Henry's Speech." Bible and Civil Government. http://bibleandcivilgovernment.com/christian_heritage/patrick_henry_give_me_liberty.php. Accessed March 28, 2019.

Cohen, Charles L. 1981. "The 'Liberty or Death' Speech: A Note on Religion and Revolutionary Rhetoric." *William and Mary Quarterly* 38 (October): 702–17.

Dreisbach, Daniel L. 2017. "The Promises and Perils of Using the Bible in Political Discourse." February. www.bibleinterp.com/articles/2017/02/dre418022.shtml.

Henry, Patrick. 1775. "Give Me Liberty or Give Me Death!" Colonial Williamsburg. https://www.history.org/almanack/life/politics/giveme.cfm.

Heschel, Abraham Joshua

Rabbi Abraham Joshua Heschel (1907–1972) was a Polish-born American rabbi and theologian who taught at the Jewish Theological Seminary of America, authored a number of influential books, and was active in both the civil rights movement (he was by the side of Martin Luther King Jr. on the march from Selma to Montgomery, Alabama) and the movement against American participation in the war in Vietnam.

The Hebrew Scriptures were at the core of Heschel's thought. In his classic *God in Search of Man* (1955), Herschel stressed how the world could never be the same after God's revelation of his laws to Moses on Mount Sinai. In contrast to some of his peers, Heschel also gave prominent attention to the Hebrew prophets.

In accepting the idea of biblical revelation, Heschel argued that it was necessary both to renounce the idea, which he associated with the Deists, of "man's self-sufficiency" and the idea, which he associated with modern natural science, that man was so insignificantly small "in relation to the universe" (1955, 169–70). In contrast to Protestant fundamentalists, Heschel did not believe that revelation should be taken "literally" (178), but he believed that it contained layers of deep meaning that could speak to subsequent generations in new ways.

Heschel sought to apply his knowledge and interpretation of Hebrew Scriptures to the issue of civil rights in a speech that he delivered on January 14, 1963. He began by observing that "the first conference on religion and race" was between Pharaoh and Moses, and that "it was easier for the children of Israel to cross the Red Sea than for a Negro to cross certain university campuses" (Herschel 1963, para. 1). Heschel contrasted the view that all humans descended from Adam and Eve to classifications based on race, and he described racism as being "worse than idolatry. *Racism is Satanism*, unmitigated evil" (para. 6). He further explained that an idol is "any *god who is mine but not yours*, any god concerned with me but not with you, is an idol" (para. 11). He suggested that "what we need is an NAAAP, a National Association for the Advancement of All People" (para. 18).

Drawing from the biblical command to love one's neighbor, Heschel observed, "The Word proclaims: Love thy neighbor! *So we make it impossible for him to be a neighbor*. Let a Negro move into our neighborhood and madness overtakes the residents" (para. 27). He thus deplored racially segregated housing, which he believed deprived African Americans of equal opportunity.

Heschel observed that "in a sense, the calling of the prophet may be described as that of an advocate or champion, speaking for those who are too weak to plead their own cause. Indeed, the major activity of the prophets was *interference*, remonstrating about wrongs inflicted on other people, meddling in affairs which were seemingly neither their concern nor their responsibility" (para. 41). He further cited Isaiah 1:17, admonishing readers to "seek justice, relieve the oppressed, judge the fatherless, plead for the widow." He thus joined Dr. Martin Luther King Jr. in believing that God was concerned with what pastors who had argued against his cause described as "the transitory social problems" (para. 46).

Heschel grounded the claim to civil rights on the claim to human equality, which he in turn grounded in Scriptures: "Equality of all men is not due to man's innocence or virtue. Equality of man is due to *God's love and commitment to all men*" (para. 53). He further tied this equality to the creation of all men in the image of God, "a likeness representing the King of kings" (para. 62). Noting that the prophets were particularly solicitous of the poor, Heschel quoted Proverbs

14:31: "He who oppresses a poor man insults his Maker; But he who is kind to the needy honors Him."

Cautioning against despair, Heschel noted both that "*the Negro problem is God's gift to America*, the test of our integrity, a magnificent spiritual opportunity," and that "what we must do is set an example, not merely to acknowledge the Negro but to welcome him, not grudgingly but joyously, to take delight in enabling him to enjoy what is due to him" (paras. 72 and 79).

Heschel further cited the manner in which Joseph emerged from slavery in Egypt in order to further God's purpose of freeing his people, while echoing the call for righteousness in Amos 5:25. As he explained, "Righteousness as a mere tributary, feeding the immense stream of human interests, is easily exhausted and more easily abused. But righteousness is not a trickle; it is God's power in the world, a torrent, an impetuous drive, full of grandeur and majesty. The surge is choked, the sweep is blocked. Yet the mighty stream will break all dikes" (para. 90).

See also Judaism; King, Martin Luther, Jr.; Segregation and Anti-miscegenation Laws

For Reference and Further Reading

Held, Shai. 2013. *Abraham Joshua Herschel: The Call of Transcendence*. Indianapolis: Indiana University Press.
Heschel, Abraham Joshua. 1955. *God in Search of Man*. New York: Harper Torchbooks.
Heschel, Abraham Joshua. 1963. "Religion and Race." Voices of Democracy. January 14. https://voicesofdemocracy.umd.edu/heschel-religion-and-race-speech-text/.
Lipton, Diana. 2008. "Abraham Joshua Heschel: His Place in a Biblical Chain of Tradition." *European Judaism: A Journal for the New Europe* 41 (Spring): 25–35.

Hooker, Thomas

Sometimes it is difficult to separate theological and political language. Such is the case with Thomas Hooker (1586–1647). Hooker was one of the most gifted, and evangelically minded, Puritan pastors who came to America from England, where he was educated at Cambridge. Although historians continue to debate the degree to which he agreed or disagreed with the leading light of Massachusetts, in 1636, he led the journey from this colony to the settlement in Connecticut, taking much of his congregation with him, in a scene depicted in Frederic Edwin Church's painting entitled *Hooker and Company Journeying through the Wilderness from Plymouth to Hartford, in 1636*.

In 1860, a manuscript was discovered with outlines of some of Hooker's sermons. These include a sermon that he delivered in 1638 on the book of Deuteronomy focusing on Chapter 1:13, in which Moses was advised to "take you wise men, and understanding, and known among your tribes, and I will make them rulers over you." The outline indicated that Hooker stressed "that the choice of public magistrates belongs unto the people by Gods own allowance"; "that the privilege of election which belongs to the people it must not be exercised according to their humors but according to the blessed will and law of God"; that "they who have power to appoint officers and magistrates it is in their power also to set the bounds and limits of the power and places unto which they call themselves"; and that "the foundation of authority is laid 1stly in the free consent of the people" (cited in Besso 2012, 200).

The fact that Hooker was giving this sermon about the time that his colony was establishing the Fundamental Orders of Connecticut further suggested that Hooker might have been attempting to provide guidelines for that document, which some have hailed as the first such written constitution in America. Michael Besso (2012) has argued that this tie may be more tenuous than previously thought and that Hooker may have been far more interested in the governance of the church than in the governance of the commonwealth as a whole. The government of Connecticut was actually more theocratic than that of a number of its neighbors (especially in Roger Williams's neighboring Rhode Island), and Hooker may have been as interested in establishing the people's obligations to obey their magistrates as in their power to elect or depose them.

However this debate is ultimately resolved, it seems clear that Hooker, and other Puritans, recognized the need to divide authority within government, much as they divided power among various congregations of believers. They believed that magistrates were ordained by, and accountable to, God as well as to the people whom they served. As individuals who had high regard for the law, and especially the Ten Commandments, which they often tried to enact, they stressed the kinds of civic virtues that provided a sound foundation for future governments (Ahlstrom 1963).

See also Covenants, Compacts, Contracts, and Constitutions; Puritans; Ten Commandments

For Reference and Further Reading

Ahlstrom, Sydney E. 1963. "Thomas Hooker: Puritanism and Democratic Citizenship: A Preliminary Inquiry into Some Relationships of Religion and American Civic Responsibility." *Church History* 32 (December): 415–31.

Besso, Michael. 2012. "Thomas Hooker and His May 1638 Sermon." *Early American Studies* 10 (Winter): 194–225.

Miller, Perry Gilbert. 1931. "Thomas Hooker and the Democracy of Early Connecticut." *New England Quarterly* 4 (October): 663–712.

Huckabee, Mike

Mike Huckabee (b. 1955) is a former Arkansas governor, who (like Bill Clinton) was born in Hope, Arkansas, and educated at Ouachita Baptist University. He spent a year at Southwestern Baptist Theological Seminary before working with televangelist James Robison, becoming an ordained Baptist minister and leading congregations in Pine Bluff and Texarkana before entering politics. As a state governor, Huckabee gained a reputation as a populist who was willing to raise taxes for public projects.

In 2008 Huckabee launched a bid for the Republican nomination for the presidency and came in first in the Iowa caucus after outlining a platform of "Faith, Family, Freedom" (Chafets 2007) and running an advertisement entitled "Believe," in which he presented himself as a "Christian leader" (Medhurst 2009, 225). One reporter who followed Huckabee in his 2008 campaign observed that many members of his audience were unfamiliar with his biblical references and that it was almost as though he were speaking "a separate dialect" (Hagerty 2008).

Huckabee was not as successful in other state contests after largely abandoning his earlier populism for more traditional conservative value-laden issues like opposition to same-sex marriage, abortion, and immigration. Nor did he succeed in capturing the 2016 Republican nomination. A reporter observed that in this campaign, Huckabee used biblical arguments to oppose same-sex marriage, oppose the minimum wage (his somewhat quixotic interpretation of Jesus's parable in Matthew 20:1–16), favor strict governmental controls on immigration, suggest that creationism should be taught in public schools, and claim that if Jesus had opposed the death penalty, he surely would have said so while he was being crucified (Jenkin 2015).

One of Huckabee's more fascinating comments with respect to his support of a human rights amendment in the 2008 campaign occurred when he spoke to a group of pastors. He told them that "I believe it's a lot easier to change the Constitution than it would be to change the word of the living God, and that's what we need to do is to amend the Constitution so it's God's standards rather than to try to change God's standards" (Medhurst 2009, 229).

Huckabee takes a high and fairly literal view of the Bible. He thus says that "I believe the Bible is exactly what it is. It's the word of revelation to us from God himself. I don't fully comprehend and understand it all, because the Bible is a revelation of an infinite god, and no finite person is ever going to fully understand it. If they do, their god is too small" (Winder 2019, 91). He says that his favorite verse is 2 Corinthians 12:9, which focuses on the sufficiency of the power of Christ within the believer (90). However, he believes that one aspect of faith is that it teaches that all human beings are frail and all need redemption (91). After being pressed by journalist Anderson Cooper about evading a question during a debate among Republican candidates in 2007 at St. Petersburg, Florida, as to what Jesus would do with respect to the death penalty, Huckabee got applause by saying, "Jesus was too smart to ever run for public office, Anderson. That's what Jesus would do" (CNN 2007).

Huckabee has a laid-back avuncular personality that is evident on his eponymous television show on the Fox channel, in which he mixes interviews with playing on his own bass guitar. His daughter Sarah served for a time as President Donald Trump's press secretary.

See also Baptists; Electioneering; Evangelicals; Ten Commandments

For Reference and Further Reading

Chafets, Zev. 2007. "The Huckabee Factor." *New York Times Magazine*. December 12.

CNN. 2007. "Part I: CNN/YouTube Republican Presidential Debate Transcript." https://www.cnn.com/2007/POLITICS/11/28/debate.transcript/index.html.

Hagerty, Barbara Bradley. 2008. "Understanding the Gospel according to Huckabee." NPR. February 8. https://www.npr.org/templates/story/story.php?storyid=18821021.

Jenkins, Jack. 2015. "Six Times Mike Huckabee Used Bad Theology to Support His Policies." ThinkProgress. May 5. https://thinkprogress.org/six-times-mike-huckabee-used-bad-theology-to-support-his-policies-bc8fb629a261/.

Medhurst, Martin J. 2009. "Evangelical Christian Faith and Political Action: Mike Huckabee and the 2008 Republican Presidential Nomination." *Journal of Communication and Religion* 32 (November): 199–239.
Winder, Mike. 2019. *Favorite Scriptures of 100 American Leaders*. Springville, UT: Plain Sight.

Hutchinson, Anne

One of the most publicized trials in early America was the trial of Mrs. Anne Hutchinson (1591–1643) in November 1637. Hutchinson, who was born in England, had come to America in part because she missed the dynamic preaching of John Cotton (1585–1652), who had preceded her, to the Massachusetts Bay Colony.

In time, she began holding very popular Bible studies in her house, in which she apparently expressed the view that whereas Cotton, and her husband's brother-in-law John Wheelwright, was preaching a covenant of grace (Protestants typically emphasized that one secured salvation through God's grace rather than by one's good works), others were preaching a covenant of works. In contrast to the latter, Hutchinson did not believe that outward works could in any way reveal whether an individual had been elected by God unto salvation or not. Opponents thus claimed that she was an antinominalist (one who opposed all laws), which they often associated with licentious living.

Governor John Winthrop thus called Hutchinson before a court. Although she would be convicted and banished from the colony (later to be killed with most of the rest of her family by Native American Indians), she is today recognized for the stance that she took on behalf of conscience, for her insistence that the court follow due process, and for what some regard as a type of feminism. Prior to the trial, Hutchinson had abstained from signing any petitions or engaging in public behavior that would clearly identify her with the antinomians. Clearly unintimidated by the setting, she demanded that the court specify the specific charges against her, questioned the use of evidence from private conversations that she had with members of the clergy, asked that those testifying against her do so under oath (it was thought that misstating facts in such a situation could lead to hell fire), and portrayed herself as the intellectual equal of the men who were prosecuting her.

In addition to citing conscience, Hutchinson showed equal mastery of Scripture with her accusers. When Winthrop accused her of disobeying the fifth commandment by dishonoring her parents, she countered that she had an equal duty to fear the Lord. Moreover, citing Titus 2:3–5, she pointed to the duty of elder women to instruct younger ones. Pointing out her own Separatist credentials, she quoted the Scripture in 1 John 4:2 that "he that denies Jesus Christ to be come in the flesh is antichrist," cited another passage from Hebrews 9, and said that it was important to separate the message of "my beloved" (Jesus) from that of Moses or others.

Asked how she knew that she was hearing the voice of Jesus, she responded that she did so in the same way that Abraham knew that God was asking him to violate the sixth commandment by offering his son as a sacrifice, that is, "by an immediate revelation" ("Transcript" 1637). She further cited Jeremiah 46:27–28 to establish her belief that God would remain with her and that her primary fear (Matthew 10:28) was not of those who could kill the body but of Christ, who controlled both body and soul. She argued that God could deliver her just as He had delivered Daniel from the lion's den. Hutchinson's appeal to direct revelation threatened to undermine established clerical authorities and arguably even Scripture itself. Quakers, who were unwelcome in the colony, had made similar claims (McGunigal 2016, 163), which Puritans often associated with the fanatical "Anabaptists," or "familialists," who had taken over the city of Munster, Germany, in 1534 (McKenna 2007, 17).

After a Mr. Harlakenden, who was an assistant to the court, said that "I may read scripture and the most glorious hypocrite may read them and yet go down to hell" ("Transcript" 1637), the court ruled that she was "unfit for society" and sent her to prison until she and her family could be banished from the colony.

The trial's verdict appears to have been a forgone conclusion, more like an ecclesiastical trial than a trial for genuine criminal offenses, but it took place in a colony where the congregational church was the established church, where only church members could participate in politics, and where unity was considered to be extremely important. Given this context, John Winthrop continues to have his defenders (Morgan 1958).

See also Cotton, John; Puritans; Model of Christian Charity (Winthrop)

For Reference and Further Reading

McGunigal, Lisa. 2016. "The Criminal Trial of Anne Hutchinson: Ritual, Religion, and Law." *Mosaic: An Interdisciplinary Critical Journal* 49 (June): 149–66.

McKenna, George. 2007. *The Puritan Narrative*. New Haven, CT: Yale University Press.

Morgan, Edmund S. 1958. *The Puritan Dilemma: The Story of John Winthrop*. Boston: Little, Brown.

Pearl, Valerie, and Morris Pearl. 1990. "Governor John Winthrop on the Birth of the Antinomians' 'Monster': The Earliest Reports to Reach England and the Making of a Myth." *Proceedings of the Massachusetts Historical Society*, 3rd Series 102: 21–37.

"Transcript of the Trial of Anne Hutchinson." 1637. http://bcs.bedfordstmartins.com/WebPub/history/mckayunderstanding1e/0312668872/Primary_Documents/US_History/Transcript%20of%20the%20Trial%20of%20Anne%20Hutchinson.pdf.

Withington, Ann Fairfax, and Jack Schwartz. 1978. "The Political Trial of Anne Hutchinson." *New England Quarterly* 51 (June): 226–40.

• I •

Immigration

Few issues have roiled Americans in recent years as the issue of immigration. Indeed, Donald Trump began his 2016 presidential campaign with the charge that America was being overrun with aliens, whom he linked to violent criminal behavior (Vile 2016, 248–49). During crackdowns on immigration, particularly from Latin America, under Trump's tenure, thousands of children have been forcibly separated from their parents and held in detention camps along the border.

Ironically, America is often described as a nation of immigrants, and, whereas the British considered English citizenship to be a lifelong status, the adoption of the U.S. Constitution considered all persons then living in the United States as American citizens eligible to run for even the office of the presidency. Early American laws encouraged immigrants to a nation where land was in great supply and laborers were often needed. The Alien Act of 1798, a partisan measure adopted by Federalists who sought to limit the time required for immigrants to become citizens, was widely criticized and repealed. Only later in the nineteenth century was immigration restricted, often with a view of the danger of being swamped by Chinese or Japanese, whose views were considered to be alien, and whose race differed from the majority of American whites. Even then, America considered itself a haven for individuals fleeing persecution and seeking better lives for themselves. Such sentiment is reflected in a poem composed by Emma Lazarus, which is inscribed on a plaque at the base of the Statue of Liberty:

> "Keep ancient lands, your storied pomp!" cries she
> With silent lips, "Give me your tired, your poor,
> Your huddled masses yearning to breathe free,
> The wretched refuse of your teeming shore.
> Send these, the homeless, tempest-tost to me,
> I lift my lamp beside the golden door!" (Vile 2016, 111)

Still, through much of the early twentieth century, racial quotas severely limited individuals admitted into the country, including Jews who were fleeing persecution in Nazi Germany and nations under its control (Vile 2016). The terrorist attacks against the United States of September 11, 2001, as well as reports of illegal smuggling of drugs and the immigration of some gang members, undoubtedly contributed to a sense that immigration was getting out of hand. Although farms and industries often profited from employing immigrants, typically in jobs that were unappealing to U.S. citizens, border states often bore financial burdens in providing educational, medical, and other services to immigrants. Citizens of lower socioeconomic status were often much more likely to perceive immigrants as threatening their jobs than others.

The Bible has much to say about immigrants and the treatment of immigrants, without therefore necessarily providing a template for modern policies. While one might question whether it is proper to consider Adam and Eve to have been "refugees" from the Garden of Eden (Romero 2010, 321), there is little doubt that the children of Israel first came to Egypt as immigrants fleeing famine and that when they returned to Israel, they had to cope with foreigners in their own midst.

A contemporary study says that "while the Hebrew Bible has but one commandment to love the neighbor, it includes thirty-six commands to love the stranger" (McCormick and McCormick 2006, 857). Professor Jennifer Lee Koh has, however, observed that some commentators have sought to limit the scope of these passages by suggesting that they apply only "to resident aliens or permanent residents" who are legally present (2017, 233).

The Old Testament not only commanded hospitality to strangers and aliens but also offered at least two justifications. One such rationale, which McCormick and McCormick trace to Genesis 18–19, Joshua 2–6, and 1 and 2 Kings, "suggests that the stranger could be God or an agent of God, and that life-saving hospitality will be rewarded with a comparable gift of life" (2006, 863). Perhaps even more compellingly, "Another set of texts, found in Exodus, Leviticus, Deuteronomy and the Prophets, reminds the Hebrews of God's hospitality to them in Egypt and the wilderness and demands a similar hospitality to the alien in their midst" (863). Biblical examples of hospitality include the reception of strangers by Abraham and Sarah, Lot's offer of hospitality to visiting strangers in Sodom, Joshua's protection of Rahab, who had harbored two Jewish spies in Jericho, and widows who protected the prophets Elijah and Elisha (863–65).

Jesus and his family fled during his early childhood to Egypt, while Jesus's parable of the last judgment in Matthew 25:31–46 suggests that he will separate individuals (sheep and goats) based in part on whether, when they encountered strangers, they were willing to give them shelter. Jesus reiterated this theme in the Parable of the Good Samaritan (Luke 10:30–37), where he lauds a Samaritan, who was not considered to be a full citizen, for aiding a crime victim. Such passages suggest that proposed laws that would penalize those who give aid to immigrants would be especially odious, putting citizens in the situation that some found themselves in during the nineteenth-century passage of fugitive slave laws.

The obligation of individual Americans to those in need does not, of course, mean that a nation does not have the right to protect itself against immediate threats of terrorism and other forms of crime or against depleting its own resources to a degree that it cannot meet the needs of its own citizens. It seems paradoxical, but, especially in the Trump administration, many evangelical Christians have been among the most vocal supporters for extending the border wall between the United States and Mexico and strengthening penalties against illegal immigrants (Burton 2018). America is believed to have somewhere between ten million and twelve million undocumented persons (or illegal aliens), many of whom evaded somewhat legal methods of entry, and while such entry is still a civil, rather than a criminal, offense, there are those who fear that providing full-scale amnesty for such individuals will erode respect for law and effectively reward those who acted illegally (Munsil 2012). Former attorney general Jeff Sessions was among those who cited Romans 13 as an argument for punishing those who violated U.S. immigration laws. This argument is not necessarily as compelling for children who were brought to the United States by their parents and have been the subject of the proposed DREAM Act, which, if adopted, would provide citizenship to those who had not committed criminal offenses.

One of the most systematic attempts to address immigrants from a biblical perspective emerged from a group formed in June 2012 called the Evangelical Immigration Table. It included such individuals as Leith Anderson, the president of the National Association of Evangelicals; Russell Moore, the president of the Ethics and Religious Liberty Commission of the Southern Baptist Convention; and Edgar Sandoval, the president of World Vision United States. In 2019, this group published an e-book that is available online. The publication notes the number of times that the Old Testament commanded individuals to give special attention to, and provide protection for, "the foreigner, the fatherless, and the widow" (Deuteronomy 24:19–21), a plea that is repeated in the prophets (Evangelical Immigration Table 2019, 3–4).

Recognizing that biblical principles are often difficult to translate directly into public policies, this report identified six key principles that should be applied to this issue. Such a solution:

- *Respects the God-given dignity of every person*
- *Protects the unity of the immediate family*
- *Respects the rule of law*
- *Guarantees secure national borders*
- *Ensures fairness to taxpayers*
- *Establishes a path toward legal status and/or citizenship for those who qualify and who wish to become permanent residents.* (Evangelical Immigration Table 2019, 13)

One fascinating aspect of this report was its conclusion that about 16 percent of U.S. evangelical Christians were either immigrants or the children of immigrants (2019, 6). It further noted that the presence of immigrants gave Christians the opportunity to fulfill the Jesus's Great Commission in Matthew 28:19 to "go and make disciples of all nations" (8).

See also Citizenship; Sessions, Jeff

For Reference and Further Reading

Burton, Tara Isabella. 2018. "The Bible Says to Welcome Immigrants. So Why Don't White Evangelicals?" Vox. October 30. https://www.vox.com/2018/10/30/18035336/white-evangelicals-immigration-nationalism-christianity-refugee-honduras-migrant.

Carroll, M. Daniel. 2013. *Christians at the Border: Immigration, the Church, and the Bible*. Grand Rapids, MI: Brazos Press.

Evangelical Immigration Table. 2019. *Thinking Biblically about Immigrants and Immigration Reform*. E-book.

Koh, Jennifer Lee. 2017. "Agape, Grace, and Immigration Law: An Evangelical Perspective." *Agape, Justice, and Law: How Might Christian Love Shape Law?*, ed. Robert F. Cochran Jr. and Zacharay R. Calo. New York: Cambridge University Press, pp. 228–45.

McCormick, Elizabeth, and Patrick McCormick. 2006. "Hospitality: How a Biblical Virtue Could Transform United States Immigration Policy." *University of Detroit Mercy Law Review* 83: 857–900.
Munsil, Len. 2012. "Justice and Compassion: Applying Biblical Truth to the Problem of Illegal Immigration." *Regent Journal of International Law* 9: 11–18.
Romero, Victor C. 2010. "Christian Realism and Immigration Reform." *University of St. Thomas Law Review* 7: 310–39.
Spencer, Aída Besançon. 1998. "Being a Stranger in a Time of Xenophobia." *Theology Today* 54 (January): 464–69.
Vile, John R., ed. 2016. *American Immigration and Citizenship: A Documentary History.* Lanham, MD: Rowman & Littlefield.

Intelligent Design

See Creationism and Evolution

Iran–Contra Affair

The United States has been at loggerheads with the Iranian government since the Shah left and was replaced by the radical Islamic cleric Ayatollah Khomeini in 1979. After he came to power, the Iranian Revolutionary Guards captured fifty-two Americans and held them hostage during the last 444 days of the Carter administration.

During this time, the U.S. Congress had barred armed sale to Iran. It had also banned aid to the Contra rebels who were seeking to overthrow the left-leaning regime of Daniel Ortega in Nicaragua.

Seeking to avoid both restrictions, the Reagan administration began secret backdoor negotiations to sell arms to Iran in exchange for money that the administration then used to fund the Contra rebels. During the course of these negotiations, Marine Lt. Col. Oliver L. North, a National Security Council aide, took a trip to Iran. In order to curry good will, he brought a cake with a brass key symbolizing the United States' willingness to reopen U.S.-Iranian relations and a Bible that President Reagan had signed to show the common bond among Jews, Christians, and Muslims.

On October 3, 1986, Reagan signed the Bible as follows: "And the Scripture, foreseeing that God would justify the Gentiles by faith, preached the Gospel beforehand to Abraham, saying, 'All the nations shall be blessed in you.' Galatians 3:8" (Associated Press 1987). Neither the cake nor the Bible resulted in improving U.S.-Iranian relations, although subsequent disclosures of the backdoor negotiations led to a lengthy congressional investigation and a report, which suggested that North's behavior was inappropriate and that, if the president did not know about his activities, he should have (Banks 1988). After the report was released, North suggested that they should read Jesus's eighth beatitude, which says, "Blessed are they which are persecuted for righteousness' sake: for theirs is the kingdom of heaven" (Associated Press 1987). North was convicted of violating the law, but his conviction was overturned on a technicality.

North, who converted to Christianity while serving in the armed forces, ran unsuccessfully for governor of Virginia, but he later served as president of the National Rifle Association.

See also Carter, Jimmy; Reagan, Ronald

For Reference and Further Reading

Associated Press. 1987. "The White House Crisis: North Cites Bible Verse in Response to Criticism." *New York Times*. February 28.

Banks, William C. 1988. "While Congress Slept: The Iran-Contra Affair and Institutional Responsibility for Covert Operations." *Syracuse Journal of International Law and Commerce* 14 (Spring): 291–362.

Bill, James A. 1994. "Chocolate-Cake Diplomacy and Colonel Oliver North." *Christian Science Monitor*. October 18.

• J •

Jackson, Jesse

Jesse Jackson (b. 1941) is an African American civil rights leader and Baptist preacher who worked with Dr. Martin Luther King Jr. and who ran for the Democratic national presidential nomination in 1984 and 1988. He was also the District of Columbia's shadow senator from 1991 to 1997.

Jackson was born out of wedlock and into poverty in Greenville, South Carolina (his original last name was Burns). After initially attending the University of Illinois on a football scholarship, Jackson transferred to North Carolina A&T University during which time he was among those who participated in a sit-in at the Greenville Public Library. He subsequently attended the Chicago Theological Seminary before becoming ordained and going into full-time civil rights work.

Jackson was known for his work in Chicago with Operation Breadbasket, which was sponsored by the Southern Christian Leadership Conference. In 1971, he organized People United to Save Humanity, which was also known as Operation PUSH and is often called Rainbow/PUSH. Individuals who have worked on his campaigns attest to his daily Bible readings and to his ability to muster Bible verses in public settings (Easter n.d.). Jackson emphasizes the call in Luke 4:18 "to bind up the bounds of the brokenhearted, to proclaim freedom to the captives," but suggests that God is not limited to communication through Scripture: "God is older than Genesis, and he did not stop with Revelation. The Bible is a holy book but not the only book of God. God is not book-challenged. God cannot be omnipotent, omnipresent, and omniscient and be limited to 5,000 years of biblical history. He is much bigger than that" (Gilbreath 2002).

Jackson is a dynamic speaker who has been likened to a biblical prophet. As such a prophet, he has arguably been better at articulating a vision than in implementing policies. Whereas others extolled the promise of America as a city upon a hill, Jackson has more frequently pointed to the failure of America to achieve its ideals, much in the tradition of so-called jeremiads. One scholar has explained that "as a prophet he can appeal to the ideals of the society, but as a black American he is a tangible reproach and a reminder that the ideal has never been the reality. Unlike biblical prophets who are able to point to moments in the past when a proper relationship to God and a just and caring relationship between members of the society existed, Jackson cannot recall Americans to moments in the past where his prophetic vision was a reality" (McTighe 1990, 596).

Jackson's speech before the Democratic National Convention in 1988 began with praise and honor to God and a call to find "common ground." In one of his most notable analogies, drawn from Isaiah 11:6, Jackson said that just as the Bible described lions and lambs lying down together, so too both lions and lambs could find common ground in wanting to avoid having the forest burn or be subject to other environmental catastrophes. He further described Jesus's appeal in the Garden of Gethsemane, "Not My will, but Thine be done," as "his way of saying that there's a higher good beyond personal comfort or position" (Jackson 1988).

Jackson advocated liberal progressive policies that were particularly aimed at issues of jobs, health care, and other social services. His Rainbow Coalition was designed to emphasize inclusion as was the image he used in his 1988 of a blanket that his grandmother wove together from many patches. Like Dr. King, Jackson attempted to emphasize what he thought was morally right. In his 1988 speech, Jackson observed, in an apparent unstated reference to Romans 5:4, that "suffering breeds character, character breeds faith. In the end faith will not disappoint." Soon after, he returned to one of his signature themes, which is biblically based, and which he often tied to African American empowerment and self-worth, to "Keep hope alive."

See also Baptists; King, Martin Luther, Jr.; Prophets and Jeremiads

For Reference and Further Reading

Easter, Eric. n.d. "Jesse and the Bible." The Pilgrimage of Jesse Jackson. https://www.pbs.org/wgbh/pages/frontline/jesse/impressions/bible.html.

Gilbreath, Edward. 2002. "Still Somebody: Despite an Embarrassing Scandal and Widespread Irritation with His Methods, Jesse Jackson Continues to Be an Influential Voice in the Church. Should Evangelicals Listen?" Christianity Today. February 4.

Howard-Pitney, David. 1986. "The Enduring Black Jeremiad: The American Jeremiad and Black Protests Rhetoric, from Frederick Douglass to W.E.B. Du Bois, 1841–1919." *American Quarterly* 38(3): 481–92.

Jackson, Jesse. 1988. "Address to the Democratic National Convention." July 19. https://americanrhetoric.com/speeches/jessejackson1988dnc.htm.

McTighe, Michael J. 1990. "Jesse Jackson and the Dilemma of a Prophet in Politics." *Journal of Church and State* 32 (Summer): 585–607.

Jackson, Thomas (Stonewall)

Few generals of the Civil War were more successful than Thomas (Stonewall) Jackson (1824–1863), whose military campaigns in the Shenandoah Valley of Virginia are still studied by military strategists. After a childhood in which he lost both parents and a number of siblings at an early age, Jackson secured an appointment at West Point, where he overcame his poor education and made rapid advancement during the Mexican-American War from 1846 to 1848.

He subsequently taught at the Virginia Military Institute, suffered the loss of a wife and child (this wife and another were both daughters of Presbyterian ministers), and became increasingly religious, eventually identifying with the Presbyterian Church, in which he became a deacon, even though he let it be known that he did not agree with its doctrine of predestination. Jackson avoided alcohol and tobacco and strictly observed the Sabbath (although he sometimes fought battles on the Sabbath during the Civil War). He established a Sunday school class for African American children in which he taught from the Bible and is, somewhat incongruously, celebrated by a stained glass African American church in Roanoke, Virginia ("Jackson's 'Colored Sunday School' Class"). He was known to enjoy theological arguments, and as a man of faith and prayer.

As a man who had overcome many adversities, Jackson led an extremely well-disciplined life, and expected similar behavior from his subordinates. Although he joined the forces of his home state of Virginia during the Civil War, he offered little apology for slavery, but seemed simply to accept it as God's will. Similarly, although he prayed constantly for military victory, he always prayed that such victories would be in accord with God's will. He was fond of the saying that "duty is ours; consequences are God's" (Wilkins and Severance 2003, 75). Confident that he was safe whenever he was doing God's will, Jackson exhibited little external fear, and had a reputation for fighting by the Old Testament while living by the New (Francis 1992).

During the Civil War, Jackson pleaded with churches to send chaplains to minister to troops, and urged them to avoid strictly denominational doctrines (Dwyer 2003, 67). He appears to have taken inspiration from the story of Joshua, the biblical judge who succeeded Moses and helped conquer the Promised Land, and has been likened to the English general Oliver Cromwell. He arguably shared a fatalistic view of God's providence that was similar to that of Abraham Lincoln.

Jackson died from complications of an amputation of his left arm as a result of friendly fire after a major victory at Chancellorsville, while stoically enduring the pain and having his wish fulfilled of dying on a Sunday. His last words were, "Let us cross over the river and rest in the shade of the trees" (Robertson n.d.). The most common verse cited at his memorial services was 2 Timothy 4:7: "I have fought a good fight, I have finished my course, I have kept the faith." Jackson's own favorite was Romans 8:28: "And we know that all things work together for good to them that love God, to them who are the called according to his purpose" (Rumburg 1993). His favorite songs included "Amazing Grace" and "There Is a Fountain Filled with Blood" (Francis 1992, 34–35).

An emphasis on Jackson's piety fit in well with "the religion of the 'Lost Cause,'" which interpreted Southern suffering as part of a higher heavenly cause. The Confederacy chose the date of his death (May 10) as the Confederate Memorial Day (Stout n.d.). Chaplains seeking to explain Jackson's untimely death sometimes compared it to that of the biblical Moses, who was able to view but not enter the Promised Land (Nicholas-Belt and Belt 2011, 28).

See also Confederate States of America; Moses as Political Archetype

For Reference and Further Reading

Dwyer, John J. 2003. "Standing Like a Stone Wall." *Faith in God and Generals: An Anthology of Faith, Hope, and Love in the American Civil War*, compiled by Ted Baehr and Susan Wales. Nashville, TN: Broadman & Holman, pp. 65–72.

Francis, Andre L. 1992. "Thomas Jonathan 'Stonewall' Jackson 'Fought by the Old Testament, Lived by the New.'" USAWC Military Studies Program Paper. https://apps.dtic.mil/dtic/tr/fulltext/u2/a250823.pdf.

"Jackson's 'Colored Sunday School' Class." 2006. *Washington Times*. May 5.

Nichols-Belt, Tracy, with Gordon T. Belt. 2011. *Onward Christian Soldiers: Religion and the Army of Tennessee in the Civil War*. Charleston, SC: History Press.

Robertson, James I., Jr. n.d. "'Stonewall Jackson: Christian Soldier." Essential Civil War Curriculum. https://www.essentialcivilwarcurriculum.com/stonewall-jackson-christian-soldier.html.
Rumburg, H. Rondel. 1993. *Stonewall Jackson's Verse*. Spout Spring, VA: Society for Biblical and Southern Studies.
Stout, Harry S. n.d. "Religion in the Civil War: The Southern Perspective." TeacherServe. https://nationalhumanitiescenter.org/tserve/nineteen/nkeyinfo/cwsouth.htm.
Wilkins, Steven, and Diana L. Severance. 2003. "A Man of Prayer: Stonewall Jackson." *Faith in God and Generals: An Anthology of Faith, Hope, and Love in the American Civil War*, compiled by Ted Baehr and Susan Wales. Nashville, TN: Broadman & Holman, pp. 72–75.

Jay, John

John Jay (1745–1829) of New York was one of America's Founding Fathers. A descendant of French Protestant Huguenots, Jay was raised in an orthodox Calvinistic family and believed strongly in God's Providence, particularly with respect to the establishment of America. He studied at King's College (today's Columbia) before becoming a lawyer. A delegate to both the First and Second Continental Congresses, who sought peace with Britain but supported the Revolution when it came, Jay went on to serve as a U.S. minister to Spain, as the secretary of foreign affairs under the Articles of Confederation, as a proponent of the new Constitution who contributed a few essays to *The Federalist*, as the first chief justice of the United States, and as the second governor of New York. In retirement he was first vice president and then president of the American Bible Society (ABS).

Jay was a strong believer in God's providential role in establishing America. Writing to Jedidiah Morse in 1806, Jay said, "A proper history of the United States would have much to recommend it: in some respects it would be singular, or unlike all others; it would develop the great plan of Providence, for causing this extensive part of our world to be discovered, and these 'uttermost parts of the earth' to be gradually filled with civilized and Christian people" (quoted in Fea 2016, 235). Jonathan Den Hartog has said that during his life, Jay respectively emphasized republicanism, federalism, and voluntarism (2009, 146).

Jay expressed his republicanism in his "Address of the Convention of the Representatives of the State of New York to Their Constituents," which was published in December 1776. His speech shows great similarity to the thought of the early Pilgrims. Giving a providential interpretation to U.S. history, he observed that "under the auspices and direction of Divine Providence, your forefathers removed to the wilds and wilderness of America." Acknowledging that the Bible had portrayed the oppression of the Jews by Egypt and other tyrants as punishment for their sins, Jay argued that "no virtuous people were ever oppressed." He salted his address with numerous biblical allusions. These included descriptions of how, for many years, "every man sat under his own vine and his own fig-tree" (1 Kings 4:25; Zechariah 3:10; and Micah 4:4); references to the British king's desire that Americans "should be hewers of wood and drawers of water" (Joshua 9:23); allusions to "the flesh-pots of Egypt" (Exodus 16:3); and the image that he drew from the biblical story of Jacob and Esau in Genesis 25 of selling the American "birthright . . . for a message of pottage."

Calling upon fellow citizens to rouse themselves to action, Jay opined that "divine Providence will not permit this Western World to be involved in the horrours of slavery." Jay further associated American victory with the task of world evangelism: "Consider that, from the earliest ages of the world, Religion, Liberty and Empire, have been bounding their course toward the setting sun. The Holy Gospels are yet to be preached to those western regions, and we have the highest reason to believe that the Almighty will not suffer Slavery and the Gospel to go hand in hand!" Den Hartog observes that Jay's early view of the relation between religion and politics was both "particularist and Protestant" (2009, 155), thus noting that Jay initially questioned whether it was possible to select a chaplain to open proceedings in prayer at the Continental Congress; strongly opposed the Quebec Act, which had recognized Roman Catholicism in Canada; and opposed citizenship for Roman Catholics.

As a Federalist, Jay published an address urging adoption of the Constitution as an alternative to "Licentiousness, disorder, and confusion." In Federalist No. 2, Jay observed, "Providence has been pleased to give this one connected country to one united people—a people descended from the same ancestors, speaking the same language, professing the same religion, attached to the same principles of government, very similar in their manners and customs, and who, by their joint counsels, arms, and efforts, fighting side by side throughout a long and bloody war, have nobly established their general liberty and independence" (1961, 38).

In the early republic, Jay became increasingly concerned with the rise of factionalism and with the influence of infidelity, which he connected to the French Revolution and to the influence of the Bavarian Illuminati (Den Hartog 2009, 161). As governor of New York, Jay issued a Thanksgiving Day proclamation, which closely resembled that of the New England states. He supported legislation to require observation of the Sabbath and eventually succeeded in getting support for a law that provided for the gradual abolition of slavery within the state (Den Hartog 2009, 164). As he aged, Jay shunned the theater and other popular amusements that he thought were ungodly.

Jay led his household in the reading of a chapter from Scripture each day and in prayer and responded to the death of his wife by reading from 1 Corinthians 15 about the hope of the resurrection. In his later years, during which he focused on voluntarist activities, Jay was a member of the American Board of Commissioners of Foreign Missions, supported the American Society for Educating Pious Youth for the Gospel Ministry, and took an active role in the ABS (164–65). Jay tied the spread of the Scripture to the fulfillment of biblical prophecies, which increasingly occupied his attention. He lauded the work of the ABS as combatting those who "by artfully and diligently encouraging defection from Scripture, and from Scripture doctrines . . . gradually introduced and spread that contempt for both, which in the last century was publicly displayed in impious acts of profaneness, and in dreadful acts of ferocity" (quoted in Den Hartog 2009, 165). Urging interdenominational cooperation, Jay argued that the increased distribution of the Bible "has a direct tendency to facilitate the progress of the Gospel throughout the world. That it will proceed, and in due time be accomplished, there can be no doubt" (Stahr 2005, 380).

See also American Bible Society; Puritans

For Reference and Further Reading

Den Hartog, Jonathan. 2009. "John Jay and the 'Great Plan of Providence.'" *Forgotten Founders on Religion and Public Life*, ed. Daniel L. Dreisbach, Mark David Hall, and Jeffry H. Morrison. Notre Dame, ID: University of Notre Dame Press, pp. 145–70.

Den Hartog, Jonathan J. 2015. *Patriotism and Piety: Federalist Politics and the Religious Struggle in the New American Nation*. Charlottesville: University of Virginia Press.

Fea, John. 2016. *Was America Founded as a Christian Nation?: An Historical Introduction*, rev. ed. Louisville, KY: Westminster John Knox Press.

Hamilton, Alexander, James Madison, and John Jay. *The Federalist Papers*. New York: 1961.

Jay, John. [1776]. "Address of the Convention of the Representatives of the State of New York to Their Constituents." https://johnjaybio.wordpress.com/personal-life/the-jay-court/address-of-the-convention-of-the-representatives-of-the-state-of-new-york-to-their-constituents/.

Jay, John. [1788]. *An Address to the People of the State of New-York on the Subject of the Constitution, Agreed upon at Philadelphia, the 17th of September 1987*. New York: Samuel Loudon. Online Library of Liberty. https://oll.libertyfund.org/pages/1787-jay-address-to-the-people-of-n-y-pamphlet.

Stahr, Walter. 2005. *John Jay: Founding Father*. New York: Hambleton and London.

Jefferson Bible

Thomas Jefferson (1743–1826) was one of America's greatest Founding Fathers. Educated at the College of William and Mary where he continued studying law under George Wythe, Jefferson was elected to the Virginia House of Burgesses where he pushed for independence. Subsequently elected to the Second Continental Congress, Jefferson was the chief author of the Declaration of Independence, where he referred to "nature and nature's God"; members of Congress added further references to the Deity. He subsequently served as governor of Virginia and as a minister to France, where he was residing when the Constitutional Convention met in Philadelphia in 1787. Jefferson had worked assiduously to liberalize the laws of Virginia and, with Madison, was able to disestablish the Episcopal Church.

President George Washington appointed Jefferson as the nation's first secretary of state. In this position, he came into almost constant conflict with Alexander Hamilton, the secretary of the Treasury, largely because he thought Hamilton's plans for the national government, including the establishment of a national bank, were too grandiose and favored greater state control. Jefferson was also more favorably disposed to the ideas of the French Revolution, while Hamilton had greater admiration for the government of England. Jefferson also envisioned America as a largely agrarian nation, whereas Hamilton saw its future as commercial. Jefferson eventually resigned his post and, with his close friend James Madison, began building the Democratic-Republican, or Jeffersonian, Party.

Although the rival Federalists won the presidency in 1796, Jefferson came in second in the Electoral College and, consistent with the Constitution of the time, became vice president under his rival John Adams, in whose administration the Sedition Act was adopted, which made it a crime to criticize the government or its officials. In the next election, however, Jefferson was elected president, and he chose James Madison as his secretary of state. During Jefferson's presidency, the nation engaged in war with the Barbary pirates and purchased the Louisiana Territory but was unable to resolve issues with Britain that led to war in the Madison administration that followed.

Jefferson was one of the most urbane and religiously heterodox of the Founding Fathers, and, although he kept his opinions about religion relatively close to his chest, opponents constantly labeled him as a Deist or even an atheist. The rhetoric became so heated in his presidential campaigns that some feared that if Jefferson were elected, he would take their Bibles. Both Jefferson and Madison, however, often found support among Baptists and other evangelicals who remained worried about the power of existing religious establishments and who had encouraged Madison to propose a Bill of Rights with protection for the free exercise of religion in exchange for their support of ratification of the Constitution.

One of the great contradictions of Jefferson's life was the fact that, while he had stated in the Declaration of Independence that all men were created equal, he owned a considerable number of slaves, who worked his plantations at Monticello and at Poplar Forest. Most historians now believe that he fathered a number of children by one of these slaves (Sally Hemmings, his wife's half-sister), who were among the few that he freed prior to his death on July 4, 1826, the fiftieth anniversary of the adoption of the Declaration of Independence.

Jefferson was a strong believer in the power of human reason and an avowed enemy to what he considered to be priest craft. One of three achievements that he asked to be included on his tomb was the founding of the University of Virginia; the other two were the writing of the Declaration of Independence and the Virginia Statute of Religious Freedom. Jefferson professed great admiration for the life and teachings of Jesus but believed that they had been corrupted by unlearned disciples whom he believed misremembered his words; by St. Paul, whom he believed had brought back more particularistic tenets of Judaism; and by church leaders who subsequently attempted to use his teachings for their own purposes. Thus, twice during his life, Jefferson attempted to separate what he believed to have been Jesus's original teachings from the encrustations that he believed that others had added.

Jefferson's first attempt in 1804 was entitled *The Philosophy of Jesus of Nazareth*, at which time he was corresponding with Joseph Priestly (1733–1804), a scientist and Unitarian minister, whom he was hoping would finish the project. Although it is known that Jefferson sought to put together a text of the gospels that excluded miracles and other materials that Jefferson did not believe were original, the text has been lost. What is known about the text thus largely comes from Jefferson's correspondence and a surviving title page.

Jefferson explained this project in a letter that he wrote to John Adams on October 13, 1813:

> We must reduce our volume to the simple evangelists, select, even from them, the very words only of Jesus, paring off the amphiboligisms into which they have been led, by forgetting often, or not understanding what had fallen from him, by giving their own misconceptions as his dicta, and expressing unintelligibly for others what they had not understood themselves. There will be found remaining the most sublime and benevolent code of morals which has ever been offered to man. I have performed this operation for my own use, by cutting verse by verse out of the printed book, and by arranging the matter which is evidently his, and which is as distinguishable as diamonds in a dunghill. The result is an octavo of forty-six pages, of pure and unsophisticated doctrines, such as were professed and acted on by the unlettered Apostles, the Apostolic Fathers, and the Christians of the first century. (Church 1989, 17)

One of the more fascinating aspects of the surviving title page is that Jefferson described it as "an abridgment of the New Testament for the use of the Indians, unembarrassed with matters of fact or faith beyond the level of their comprehension" (Church 1989, 19). The general consensus appears to be that the reference to Indians was ironic, and that it was intended as a reference to his enemies, the Federalists, who had done so much to malign him for his religious views (19).

Whatever became of Jefferson's first rewrite, the project continued to interest him, and he began to revisit it sometime in 1819. Jefferson's opinion remained heterodox and differed in some respects from what he believed to be the views of Jesus, with whom, however, he continued to identify. Writing about his renewed project to Van der Kemp, Jefferson thus observed,

> While this syllabus is meant to place the character of Jesus in its true and high light, as no imposter Himself, but a great Reformer of the Hebrew code of religion, it is not to be understood that I am with Him in all His doctrines. I am a Materialist; He takes the side of Spiritualism. He preaches the efficacy of repentance towards forgiveness of sin; I require a counterpoise of good works to redeem it, etc., etc. It is the innocence of His character, the purity and sublimity, of his moral precepts, the eloquence of His inculcations, the beauty of the apologues in which He conveys them, that I so much admire; sometimes, indeed, needing indulgence to eastern hyperbolism. (Church 1989, 27–28)

Jefferson continued by observing that "I find many passages of fine imagination, correct morality, and of the most lovely benevolence; and others, again, of so much ignorance, so much absurdity, so much untruth, charlatanism and imposture, as to pronounce it impossible that such contradictions should have proceeded from the same Being. I separate, therefore, the gold from the dross; restore to Him the former, and leave the latter to the stupidity of some, and roguery of others of His disciples" (Church 1989, 28).

Jefferson's Bible has four columns, which respectively present the texts in Greek, Latin, French, and English. Professor Charles Mabee points out that Jefferson's Bible consists essentially of three parts, which Mabee describes as "The Advent of Jesus and His Message," "The Message in Conflict with Jewish Religion," and "The Message of the End Time" (1979, 477). Consistent with his own rationalism, Jefferson omits the account of Jesus's virgin birth, his miracles, and his resurrection. The last words of his Bible thus end with John 19:42 and Matthew 27:60: "There they laid Jesus. And rolled a great stone to the door of the sepulcher, and departed" (Jefferson [ca. 1820] 1989, 147).

David Barton, who is the central force behind *The Founders' Bible*, and others have tried to defend Jefferson as a fairly orthodox Christian, but while identifying as a Christian, Jefferson provided his own explanation of the term in a letter to his friend Benjamin Rush. In that letter, Jefferson observed that "I am a Christian, in the only sense he wished any one to be; sincerely attached to his doctrines, in preference to all others; ascribing to himself every human excellence; and believing he never claimed any other" (Church 1989, 30). Jaroslav Pelikan, the noted church historian, observed that Jefferson was not the first or last to attempt to rewrite the Bible. In Pelikan's judgment, "Jefferson was not engaging in a 'quest for this historical Jesus' primarily as an exercise in historical investigation, any more than were most of the others who participated in that quest during the nineteenth and twentieth centuries. He wanted to find the essence of true religion in the Gospels, an essence whose basic content he had already formulated for himself with considerable simplicity and clarity" (Pelikan 1989, 153).

In 1902, Rep. John F. Lacey of Iowa proposed that every member of Congress should receive a copy of the Jefferson Bible, and, after the Government Printing Office began producing the Bibles two years later, every member received a copy from 1905 through the early 1950s (Nutt n.d.).

See also Alternate Scriptures; Declaration of Independence; Deism; *Founders' Bible*; Madison, James

For Reference and Further Reading

Church, F. Forrester. 1989. "The Gospel according to Thomas Jefferson." In Thomas Jefferson. *The Jefferson Bible: The Life and Morals of Jesus of Nazareth*. Boston: Beacon Press, pp. 1–32.

Coulter, Michael, and Warren Throckmorton. 2013. "David Barton Is Wrong." World. Faith & Religion. January 22. https://world.wng.org/2013/01/david_barton_is_wrong.

Goodspeed, Edgar J. 1947. "Thomas Jefferson and the Bible." *Harvard Theological Review* 40 (January): 71–76.

Jefferson, Thomas. [ca. 1820] 1989. *The Jefferson Bible: The Life and Morals of Jesus of Nazareth*. Boston: Beacon Press.

Mabee, Charles. 1979. "Thomas Jefferson's Anti-Clerical Bible." *Historical Magazine of the Protestant Episcopal Church* 48 (December): 473–81.

Nutt, Cullen. n.d. "The Gospel According to Jefferson." *Wilson Quarterly*. http ://archive.wilsonquarterly.com/web-exclusive/gospel-according-jefferson.

Pelikan, Jaroslav. 1989. "Jefferson and His Contemporaries." In Thomas Jefferson. *The Jefferson Bible: The Life and Morals of Jesus of Nazareth*. Boston: Beacon Press, pp. 149–67.

Zastoupil, Lynn. 2009. "'Notorious and Convicted Mutilators': Rammohun Roy, Thomas Jefferson, and the Bible." *Journal of World History* 20 (September): 399–434.

Jehovah's Witnesses

It is doubtful whether any religious group has been the subject of more constitutional rulings in the twentieth century than the Jehovah's Witnesses. Founded by

Charles Taze Russell (1852–1916) in the 1870s, the movement was an offshoot of the Millerite and Adventist movements that stressed the imminent return of Christ to earth. Russell founded the Watch Tower Society in 1881, and its long-time headquarters in Brooklyn, New York (which have since moved to Wallkill, New York), included the parsonage where the famed preacher Henry Ward Beecher once lived (Abrahams 1977, 68). Russell supported Zionism as well as such reform measures as converting to the silver standard, the single tax, inheritance taxes, and land reform (63).

Russell believed that other Christian denominations, especially Roman Catholicism, had been corrupted with pagan influences, and he departed in a number of significant ways from them. Thus, the denomination is non-Trinitarian, it does not celebrate birthdays or Christian holidays, it routinely uses the word Jehovah for God, it does not accept the cross as a symbol (members believe that Jesus was crucified on a stake), and, although it runs a massive publishing operation that supplies materials for its members who are expected to engage in door-to-door evangelism, it rarely engages with other Christian denominations, except for the purpose of proselytizing (Gilmour 2017, 647). One of the unique features of the Witnesses is that since 1961, they have had their own New World Translation (NWT) of the Holy Scriptures, although it contains no information about its translators.

The Witnesses are organized hierarchically, and they retain their belief in the soon return of Christ to earth. Tying events in biblical prophecy to events in their own history, Witnesses believe that the last days began in 1914, that Christ began selecting 144,000 individuals who would rule with him in heaven in 1919, and that the seven trumpets described in Revelation 8:1–9 related to events at Witness Conventions between 1922 and 1928 (Gilmour 2017, 649). In addition to the 144,000 individuals who will rule with God in heaven, Witnesses believe that others will live on a restored earth.

Citing the teaching in John 15:19 that the righteous have "no part of the world" (Knox 2013, 1091), Witnesses take a critical attitude toward most earthly governments and do not therefore think that it is appropriate to vote. On the basis of Romans 13:1, they do advocate obeying laws that do not conflict with the laws of God, and although they believe that the battles of the Israelites described in the Old Testament against their enemies were just wars, they seek exemption from military service for their members, all of whom they consider to be ministers (Knox 2013, 1100). Witnesses currently leave the decision as to whether members should volunteer for alternate civilian service up to them ("Flag Salute"); they believe that paying taxes accords with Jesus's injunction in Matthew 22:21 to "pay back, therefore, Caesar's things to Caesar, but God's things to God" (NWT). In accord with 1 Timothy 2:2, they also believe in praying for public leaders ("Flag Salute").

Door-to-door distribution of religious literature has frequently brought the Witnesses into conflict with local permitting regulations; their refusal to salute the American flag, which they consider to be a form of idolatry forbidden by the Ten Commandments, has brought them into conflict with school authorities; and their belief that Scriptures like Genesis 9:3–4; Leviticus 17:13–14; Acts 15:28 and 21:25, which prohibit the eating of blood, also apply to blood transfusions have all brought them into conflict with secular authorities both in the United States and elsewhere. For many years, Witnesses were represented before the U.S. Supreme Court by Hayden C. Covington (1911–1978), who won a large majority of his cases (Vile 2001).

Two flag-salute cases were among the most dramatic. After contesting the expulsion from public schools for not saluting the flag, the Witnesses lost in *Minersville School District v. Gobitis* (1940) and faced mob action from groups across the nation who considered their actions to be un-American. They subsequently won a reversal in *West Virginia State Board of Education v. Barnette* (1943), in one of the court's most articulate defenses of First Amendment freedoms.

Decisions in *Lovell v. City of Griffin* (1938) further upheld their rights to distribute religious literature door-to-door as did a later decision in *Cantwell v. Connecticut* (1940). A decision in *Chaplinsky v. New Hampshire* (1942), which is still something of a constitutional outlier, did, however, rule that a Jehovah's Witness who referred to a city marshal as a "racketeer" and a "Fascist" could be prosecuted for uttering so-called fighting words. In *Dickinson v. United States* (1953), Witnesses won exemptions from the military draft for those who were devoting themselves to preaching.

See also Roman Catholics; U.S. Flag

For Reference and Further Reading

Abrahams, Edward H. 1977. "The Pain of the Millennium: Charles Taze Russell and the Jehovah's Witnesses 1879–1916." *American Studies* 18 (Spring): 57–70.

Cantwell v. Connecticut, 310 U.S. 296 (1940).

Chaplinsky v. New Hampshire, 315 U.S. 568 (1942).

Dickerson v. United States, 346 U.S. 389 (1953).

"Flag Salute, Voting, and Civilian Services." JW.org. https://www.jw.org/en/publications/books/gods-love/flag-salute-voting-civilian-service/.

Gilmour, Michael J. 2017. "The Bible and Jehovah's Witnesses." *The Oxford Handbook of the Bible in America*, ed. Paul C. Gutjahr. New York: Oxford University Press, pp. 645–60.

Knox, Zoe. 2013. "Jehovah's Witnesses as Un-Americans? Scriptural Injunctions, Civil Liberties, and Patriotism." *Journal of American Studies* 47 (November): 1081–108.

Lawson, Ronald. 1995. "Sect-State Relations: Accounting for the Differing Trajectories of Seventh-Day Adventists and Jehovah's Witnesses." *Sociology of Religion* 56 (Winter): 351–77.

Lovell v. City of Griffin, 328 U.S. 303 (1938).

Minersville School District v. Gobitis, 310 U.S. 586 (1940).

Newton, Merlin Owen. 1995. *Armed with the Constitution: Jehovah's Witnesses in Alabama and the U.S. Supreme Court, 1939–1946*. Tuscaloosa: University of Alabama Press.

Peters, Shawn Francis. 2000. *Judging Jehovah's Witnesses: Religious Persecution and the Dawn of the Rights Revolution*. Lawrence: University Press of Kansas.

Schur, Morris J. 1964. "The Theology of the Jehovah's Witnesses and Its Conflict with Earthly Governments." *Western Political Quarterly* 17 (September): 101–3.

Vile, John R. 2001. "Covington, Hayden C." *Great American Lawyers*, ed. John R. Vile. 2 vols. Santa Barbara, CA: ABC-CLIO. I, pp. 134–40.

West Virginia State Board of Education v. Barnette, 319 U.S. 624 (1943).

Jeremiads

See Prophets and Jeremiads

Jesus

There is no more central figure in Christianity than that of Jesus. Christians believe He was the Son of God and seek to follow his teachings. They believe that the Hebrew Scriptures embodied in their Old Testament point typologically and through prophecy to Jesus. Matthew, Mark, Luke, and John, the first four books of the New Testament, which are known as the gospels, describe the life of Jesus. The remaining books and letters of the New Testament are an attempt to describe the early church and to work out doctrines related to Jesus and to Christian living, and the church that Jesus founded (in all its iterations) seeks to perpetuate his teachings and his worship.

In orthodox Christian theology, Jesus was both God and man. Sent by his father with whom he and the Holy Spirit were one, he was incarnate as a human born to Mary, lived a perfect life of obedience and submission to his father, was crucified, died, buried, and rose again, and ascended to his father in heaven. The New Testament further teaches that he will one day return, judge the world with justice, and rule forever in heaven and, some believe, for a millennium, on earth.

For Christians, Jesus was the Christ, the promised Messiah, who willingly and obediently sacrificed his life on the cross to atone for the sins of his people. Because he specifically proclaimed, however, that his kingdom was not of this world (John 18:36), there are many different ways of applying the teachings of Jesus to politics, and they often vary by denomination, by race, by region, and by time period. Moreover, some individuals like John Adams and Thomas Jefferson admired Jesus as a teacher of morality without believing that he was therefore divine. The Church of Jesus Christ of Latter-Day Saints would later teach that Jesus had appeared in America prior to its settlement by Europeans and that there were additional revelations about him outside of the Bible. Although Jesus has been generally portrayed as white, some African Americans have portrayed him as black.

Puritans often focused as much on the Old Testament as on the New in part because the former had more direct application to law and in part because they conceived of themselves as members of a New Israel who, like their spiritual forbears, had crossed the sea and were settling in a wilderness. In part because of the Second Great Awakening and its emphasis on the work of the Holy Spirit, nineteenth-century Americans placed greater emphasis on the New Testament and on Jesus (Shalev 2013, 152).

One of the most popular novels of the late nineteenth and the early twentieth centuries was a book by Charles Shelton entitled *In His Steps: What Would Jesus Do.* The book is the story of a pastor who inspires his congregation to act for a year in the way that they think Jesus would act. Individuals end up engaging in a variety of social reforms including helping the poor, battling intoxication, and fighting against white slavery, which are typical of those advocated during the heyday of the Social Gospel. In contemporary America, it is still not uncommon for young people to wear bracelets with "WWJD" (What Would Jesus Do) as reminders to follow in Jesus's footsteps, especially with respect to personal behavior (Smith 2015).

One of the greatest symbols of Jesus is the cross, which has become a common item of jewelry. It symbolizes the manner in which Jesus purchased salvation through his death and subsequent resurrection. William Jennings Bryan used the image of a golden cross in running for U.S. president in 1896. In an odd twist, the Ku Klux Klan used the image of a burning cross as a symbol of racial purity. African Americans, in turn, often understood lynchings as a type of African American cross that tied them closer to Jesus's own sufferings (Cone 2011, 1–29).

Because Christians believe that Jesus was the perfect Son of God, it may seem blasphemous to compare American leaders to them, so it has been less common to liken such leaders to Jesus than to other more flawed biblical archetypes like Abraham, Moses, Joshua, Esther, and others. There have been times, however, as when Abraham Lincoln was assassinated on Good Friday or where African Americans were suffering under the lash, where comparisons have been made between particular events in the life of an American leader or group of people and those of Jesus. A number of preachers likened the sufferings of Socialist Eugene Debs, who had been imprisoned for a speech opposing World War I, to Christ (Dorn 2003, 305).

During a debate among Republican hopefuls during the 2000 presidential campaign, George W. Bush surprised the audience when he said that Jesus was his favorite political philosopher (Goodstein 2000), but other politicians have also cited Jesus's teachings as support for their policies. Numerous politicians have referenced Jesus's Sermon on the Mount in Matthew 5–7, which contains the Golden Rule (Matthew 7:12), or his admonition in Matthew 25:35–40 to take care of those in need. Jesus claimed that he had come to fulfill the law and the prophets. Asked which commandment was the greatest, he said, "Thou shall love the Lord thy God with all thy heart, and with all thy soul, and with all thy mind" and added that "the second is like unto it, Thou shalt love thy neighbor as thyself" (Matthew 22:37, 39).

Dr. Martin Luther King Jr., derived his model of civil activism by combining his understanding of Jesus's ethics with the civil disobedience of Mahatma Gandhi (Blum 2011, 29). One difficulty of interpreting and applying the teachings of Jesus to politics is that he often spoke in parables and engaged in little direct political action. It is not always easy to decide whether rules for personal ethics, like those that Jesus articulated in his Sermon on the Mount, can be applied in national, to say nothing of international, politics.

There are, however, numerous editions of the Bible that highlight the words attributed to Jesus in red, thus suggesting that they may have higher priority over others. One evangelical commentator thus titled his guide to faith and politics as a call to Red Letter Christians, who would prioritize issues of social justice that Jesus highlighted (Compolo 2008, 21–29).

In his classic work *Christ and Culture,* theologian H. Richard Niebuhr outlined five different approaches for understanding how Jesus related to culture, which would include both law and politics. He characterized these approaches as follows: Christ against Culture, as when, as with the early church, Christians were a distinct minority; the Christ of Culture, as in repeated refrains that America is a "Christian" nation; Christ above Culture, a view that seeks to prevent the culture from co-opting Jesus to its purposes; Christ and Culture in Paradox, which emphasizes the difficulties of living Christ like in an imperfect world; and Christ Transforming Culture, which emphasizes the role of Christ within time.

See also Bryan, William Jennings; Jefferson Bible; King, Martin Luther, Jr.; Lincoln, Abraham; Lynchings

For Reference and Further Reading

Blum, Edward J. 2011. "'Look Baby, We Got Jesus on Our Flag': Robust Democracy and Religious Debate from the Era of Slavery to the Age of Obama." *Annals of the American Academy of Political and Social Science* 634 (September): 17–37.

Blum, Edward J., and Paul Harvey. 2014. *The Color of Christ: The Son of God and the Saga of Race in America*. Chapel Hill: University of North Carolina Press.

Compolo, Tony. 2008. *Red Letter Christians: A Citizen's Guide to Faith and Politics*. Ventura, CA: Regal.

Cone, James H. 2011. *The Cross and the Lynching Tree*. Maryknoll, NY: Orbis Books.

Dorn, Jacob H. 2003. "'In Spiritual Communion': Eugene V. Debs and the Social Christians." *Journal of the Gilded Age and the Progressive Era* 2 (July): 303–25.

Goodstein, Laurie. 2000. "The 2000 Campaign: The Philosophy; Conservative Church Leaders Find a Pillar in Bush." *New York Times*. January 23.

Harvey, Paul. 2018. *Moses, Jesus, and the Trickster in the Evangelical South*. Athens: University of Georgia Press.

Hetzel, Peter Goodwin. 2009. *Jesus and Justice: Evangelicals, Race, and American Politics*. New Haven, CT: Yale University Press.

Mattson, Stephen. 2017. "Christ, Not America, First." *Sojourners*. February 6. https://sojo.net/articles/christ-not-america-first. Accessed May 27, 2019.

Niebuhr, H. Richard. 1951. *Christ and Culture*. New York: Harper & Row.

Prothero, Stephen. 2003. *American Jesus: How the Son of God Became a National Icon*. New York: Farrar, Straus and Giroux.

Shalev, Eran. 2013. *American Zion: The Old Testament as a Political Text from the Revolution to the Civil War*. New Haven, CT: Yale University Press.

Smith, Erin A. 2015. *What Would Jesus Read? Popular Religious Books and Everyday Life in Twentieth-Century America*. Chapel Hill: North Carolina Press.

Stassen, Glen H. 2003. "It Is Time to Take Jesus Back: In Celebration of the Fiftieth Anniversary of H. Richard Niebuhr's 'Christ and Culture.'" *Journal of the Society of Christian Ethics* 23 (Spring/Summer): 133–43.

Yoder, John Howard. 1994. *The Politics of Jesus*. Grand Rapids, MI: Wm. B. Eerdmans.

Jezebel as Political Archetype

Just as the Bible provides models of good rulers and generals like Moses, David, and Joshua, so too biblical figures can serve as warnings against ungodly behavior. Probably no pair of royal rulers was more maligned in the Old Testament than King Ahab and Jezebel, whose stories are told in 1 and 2 Kings. Identified as the most wicked king of Israel, Ahab was portrayed as being led astray largely by Jezebel, the daughter of Ithobaal I of Sidon, who was a worshiper of Baal, a fertility god often associated with child sacrifice. She vowed to kill the prophet Elijah after he ordered the prophets of Baal killed after a dramatic showdown on Mt. Carmel. In a story related in 1 Kings 21:1–16, she also arranged to frame and execute Naboth, a private citizen, so that Ahab could take his prized vineyard. Outliving her husband, her son Jehoram ruled in his stead. After Jehu killed him, Jezebel dressed to greet him and was thrown out of a window and buried, after which dogs dug up her body and ate it, in fulfillment of the words of Elijah.

As a wicked foreign idol worshipper, Jezebel is a convenient symbol for individuals, especially women, who appear to have overstepped their boundaries. Because American women did not gain nation-wide suffrage until the adoption of the Nineteenth Amendment in 1920, and they still occupy far fewer political offices than men, there have been fewer occasions when the parallel could be drawn, but when they have been they can be quite insulting.

The first such example comes from the time of the Puritans when Anne Hutchinson was prosecuted for alleged antinominalism, or the doctrine that one could disregard law and Scripture on the basis of direct revelation. After she was convicted of heresy and ordered to leave the colony, John Winthrop and other Pilgrims later used the miscarriage of one of her followers (Pearl and Pearl 1990) and the massacre of Hutchinson and her family by Native American Indians—much as Old Testament prophets had used the fact that the dogs had licked up Jezebel's blood—as a sign of her ungodliness (Winship 2002).

There is a long history of classifying African American women with Jezebel and portraying them as sexually seductive and aggressive. This is but one of many sad legacies of American slavery in which slaves were considered as property and had little choice but to submit to the will of their masters. Sociologist David Pilgrim (2002) observes that no white male was convicted of rape or attempted rape of an African American woman from the end of the Civil War until the mid-1960s, during which time many black men were lynched for such offenses, or alleged offenses, against white women.

The name Jezebel is sometimes associated not so much with an individual as with a city and its culture. A number of U.S. cities, most notably New Orleans and Las Vegas, have sometimes been called "sin cities." A movie starring Bette Davis titled *Jezebel*, after its leading figure, describes a yellow fever epidemic that took place in 1853 in New Orleans. Much as later happened when the hurricane Katrina hit the city in 2005, the city itself was identified with Jezebel and blamed for its lack of preparation for the ills that beset it (Bibler 2008).

In more recent times, critics of Hillary Clinton have sometimes compared her to Jezebel. Jonathan Cahn, the leader of a congregation of Messianic Jews, thus authored a book entitled *The Paradigm* (2017) in which he drew this parallel, largely based on the fact that she supported the right to abortion just as the followers of Baal believed in child sacrifice. His book lays out an elaborate paradigm in which he compares Bill Clinton to Ahab, compares Barack Obama to Ahab's successor, and portrays Trump as a flawed ruler who nonetheless seeks to restore morality. John L. Harmer, who once served as Ronald Reagan's lieutenant governor, has written a similar account in the form of a novel (2016).

Sometimes the term "Jezebel" is used not so much for a particular figure as to epitomize a culture that has abandoned the true God. Patterned closely after the ancient jeremiad, a description of a recent book by Michael L. Brown entitled *Jezebel's War with America: The Plan to Destroy Our Country and What We Can Do to Turn the Tide* thus reads as follows: "In twenty-first century America, Jezebel is not a person. But it's as if the spirit of Jezebel is alive again today. The influence of the same demonic force is being felt in the massive increase of pornography and sexual temptation, the militant spirit of abortion, the rise of radical feminism, and, most importantly, in the attempt to silence prophetic voices. Just as Jezebel clashed with strong men almost three thousand years ago, the demonic spirit of Jezebel is powerful in America and it is going after the church" (Amazon.com).

See also Hutchinson, Anne; Natural Disasters; Prophets and Jeremiads

For Reference and Further Reading

Bibler, Michael P. 2008. "Always the Tragic Jezebel: New Orleans, Katrina, and the Layered Discourse of a Doomed Southern City." *Southern Cultures* 14 (Summer): 6–27.

Brown, Michael L. *Jezebel's War with America: The Plot to Destroy Our Country and What We Can Do to Turn the Tide*. https://www.amazon.com/Jezebels-War-America-Destory-Country/dp/1629996661.

Cahn, Jonathan. 2017. *The Paradigm*. Lake Mary, FL: FrontLine.

Harmer, John L. 2016. *Jezebel, Willie, and the Voice*. Rochester, NY: Legends Library.

Pearl, Valerie, and Morris Pearl. 1990. "Governor John Winthrop on the Birth of the Antinomians' 'Monster': The Earliest Reports to Reach England and the Making of a Myth." *Proceedings of the Massachusetts Historical Society*, 3rd Series 102: 21–37.

Pilgrim, David. 2002 [edited in 2012]. "The Jezebel Stereotype." Ferris State University Jim Crow Museum of Racist Memorabilia. https://www.ferris.edu/HTMLS/news/jimcrow/jezebel/index.htm.

Winship, Michael P. 2002. *Making Heretics: Militant Protestantism and Free Grace in Massachusetts, 1636–1641*. Princeton, NJ: Princeton University Press.

Jones, Absalom

Absalom Jones (1746–1818) was an African American clergyman in Philadelphia who had been raised as a slave but bought his freedom and became a leading citizen of Philadelphia. Initially a Methodist, Jones left that church after it forced its African American members to sit in the balcony, and he subsequently created the first black Episcopal congregation, in which he was ordained as a priest.

In the 1790s, Jones and other African Americans stayed behind with Dr. Benjamin Rush during the yellow fever epidemics to care for the sick and bury the dead. Jones sought through this and other acts of public works to raise his race in popular favor at a time when free blacks were still subject to legal discrimination. Contrasting those who emphasized the pillar of clouds that led the Israelites through the wilderness to the Promised Land, Professor Herbert Robinson Marbury has described Jones as such a man rather than those who took a more oppositional pillar of fire approach (2015, 16–30).

Jones's most famous sermon was probably the Thanksgiving Sermon that he delivered at the St. Thomas African Episcopal Church in Philadelphia on January

1, 1808. The sermon was based on the text of Exodus 3:7–8: "And the Lord said, I have surely seen the affliction of my people which are in Egypt, and have heard their cry by reason of their task-masters; for I know their sorrows; and I am come down to deliver them out of the hands of the Egyptians."

Jones preached this sermon to commemorate the adoption (made possible by a provision in the U.S. Constitution that had been written in 1787) of a congressional law abolishing the international slave trade. Recognizing that this law did not mark the end of slavery, Jones chose the biblical text in which God had appeared to Moses from a burning bush and revealed his plans to free His people from their bondage in Egypt.

In the opening paragraph, Jones therefore described the afflictions that the Israelites had suffered during their slavery in Egypt, including the attempt to kill newborn males. Although it seemed that "all was misery; all was grief; all was despair," God told Moses that He had not forgotten his people and was "not indifferent to their suffering" (Jones 1808, 8). Moreover, this was "not the only instance, in which it has pleased God to appear in behalf of oppressed and distressed nations, as the deliverer of the innocent, and of those who call upon his name" (9). Just as God had observed the oppression of the Hebrew people, so too he had seen men kidnapped and sold as chattels in Africa, and in American slave markets, deprived of Sabbath rest, tortured by their masters, and denied religious instruction, and he had intervened when the U.S. Congress and the British Parliament both agreed to end the international slave trade. This intervention required the people to sing of their deliverance like the angels who had announced the birth of Christ.

Jones further urged that this blessing should be accompanied by five duties that went beyond mere ritual religious observances. First, the people should express their gratitude to God. Second, they should join in "prayer to Almighty God, for the completion of his begun goodness to our brethren in Africa" (15). This would include favoring them "with the means of acquiring such parts of human knowledge, as will enable them to read the holy scriptures, and understand the doctrines of the Christian religion, whereby they may become, even while they are the slaves of men, the freemen of the Lord" (16).

Third, Jones argued that his people should "remember the rock whence we were hewn, and the pit whence we were digged [a reference to Isaiah 51:1]" (17). Jones clearly hoped that the exercise of godly virtues on the part of African Americans would lead to future freedoms: "Let us be sober minded, humble, peaceable, temperate in our meats and drinks, frugal in our apparel and in the furniture of our houses, industrious in our occupations, just in all our dealings, and ever ready to honour all men" (17). Jones raised the possibility that African American missionaries might one day return to Africa as missionaries of the gospel. He further suggested that "a Joseph may arise" among the African nations "who shall be the instrument of feeding the African nations with the bread of life, and of saving them, not from earthly bondage, but from the more galling yoke of sin and Satan" (18).

Fourth, Jones urged his compatriots to "be grateful to our benefactors" (18) by which he appears to mean those who worked for the abolition of the slave trade. Fifth, he called for setting aside a day each year to commemorate the end of the slave trade.

Although Jones's entire speech was based on and quoted Scriptures, the last paragraph employed the most. Jones quoted from, without specifically citing, Paul's statement in Acts 17:26, that God "hast made of one blood all nations of men" (19). He cited prophetic references to the time when the knowledge of God will "cover the earth, as the water cover the sea [Habakkuk 2:14]" (20). He cited the prophecy of Isaiah 11:6 in which tame and wild animals would live together in peace and in which "instead of the brier, shall come up the myrtle tree [55:13]" (20).

Jones further evoked God's blessings upon the U.S. president and, perhaps with a view toward continuing tensions with Britain and France, prayed for deliverance "from the calamities of war" (21).

See also Rush, Benjamin; Slavery

For Reference and Further Reading

Jones, Absalom. 1808. "A Thanksgiving Sermon, Preached January 1, 1808, in St. Thomas's, or the African Episcopal, Church, Philadelphia: On Account of the Abolition of the African Slave Trade, on That Day, by the Congress of the United States." Philadelphia: Fry and Kammerer. Accessed at anglicanhistory.org/usa/ajones/thanksgiving1808.html.

Lammers, Anne C. 1982. "The Rev. Absalom Jones and the Episcopal Church: Christian Theology and Black Consciousness in a New Alliance." *Historical Magazine of the Protestant Episcopal Church* 51 (June): 159–84.

Marbury, Herbert Robinson. 2015. *Pillars of Cloud and Fire: The Politics of Exodus in African-American Biblical Interpretation.* New York: New York University Press.

Judaism

The idea of a holy book is hardly unique to Christians. Indeed, the Old Testament, composed of ancient Hebrew Scriptures, constitutes more than half of the books of the Christian Bible. Moreover, because this part of the Christian Bible focuses more specifically on a nation than on a church, it arguably contains more relevant precedents for law and politics. Puritan settlers in America often viewed themselves as the New Israel crossing the sea into the wilderness. The Church of Jesus Christ of Latter-Day Saints viewed Native American Indians as members of the lost tribes of Israel. African American slaves often viewed their quest for freedom in terms as parallel to the Jewish quest for freedom from Egypt.

The first Jews known to have settled in America settled in New Amsterdam, which is today's New York, and they brought a Torah, a scroll containing the first five books of the Bible, known as the Pentateuch, with them (Sarna 2017, 505). American Jews continue to revere this and other ancient books. In contrast to many of their European counterparts, American Jews put far more emphasis on them than on the Talmud, which consists of a much larger mass of rabbinic commentary but which was not even published in the United States until 1919 (506). Many European Jews remain ambivalent toward their Bible in part because Christian identification with it has made it more suspect than the Talmud (Greenspahn 2007, 14).

Jews may be defined by ethnicity, by culture, or by religion. Jews have a shared history with other Jews even if they might not believe the same. Just as Protestants have divided into many denominations, so too American Jews are divided into three main groups. Orthodox Jews hew the most closely to the Bible, taking a strict view of the Jewish law including prohibitions on the eating of certain foods and the keeping of the Sabbath, which is required by the Ten Commandments. Reformed Jews put greater stress on "the *moral* laws of the Bible" and on ceremonies that they believe "elevate and sanctify" their lives (Kertzer 1975, 147). Conservative Jews generally fall somewhere between the two groups, believing that the first is too strict and the latter breaks too sharply with the past. There are, or course, Jews, often designated Messianic Jews, who have converted to Christianity, just as there are Christians who have converted to Judaism.

Historian Jonathan Sarna has observed that the Bible has "served both as a bridge and as a boundary marker between Jews and Christians in America. It linked the two great faiths around commonly cherished biblical teachings. And it demarcated differences over what the term 'Bible' comprehends, and how the Bible's sacred words should be understood" (Sarna 2017, 506). While Jews, Christians, and Muslims all are monotheistic religions, and are often linked together in a Judeo-Christian or Judeo-Christian-Muslim tradition (Silk 1984), only Christians believe specifically in the doctrine of the Trinity.

Jews who could not read Hebrew often depended on English translations and especially the King James Version. It, however, divides the books differently than do the Jews and, when accompanied by commentary, often attempts to interpret Old Testament passages as typologies of events in the New, and understands references to the Messiah to refer specifically to Jesus. In 1853, Isaac Leeser of Philadelphia published the first Jewish version of the Hebrew Scriptures in England, in what has been called "a Declaration of Religious Independence" (Sarna 2017, 507), and Jews have published a number of additional translations since then.

The U.S. Constitution prohibited religious tests for public office, while the First Amendment later prohibited the establishment of a national religion and guaranteed its free exercise. Soon after he became president, George Washington penned a letter to Moses Seixas, of a Hebrew Congregation in Newport, Rhode Island, who had congratulated him on his election to the presidency. Affirming that the new government "gives to bigotry no sanction, to persecution no assistance," Washington expressed his hope that "the children of the Stock of Abraham, who dwell in this land, [may] continue to merit and enjoy the good will of the other Inhabitants" (Vile 2015, 325). Utilizing analogies from the Old Testament, he further hoped that "every one shall sit in safety under his own vine and fig-tree, and there shall be none to make him afraid. May the father of all mercies scatter light and not darkness in our paths, and make us all in our several vocations useful here, and in his own due time and way everlastingly happy" (325).

Although twentieth-century Jews have generally voted Democratic, their political views have often varied according to the section of the nation where they settled. Antebellum northern and southern Jews thus often divided over the issue of slavery. Judah P. Benjamin (1811–1844) of New Orleans held a number of important cabinet posts in the Confederacy. There were, however, exceptions, as when Rabbi Morris Raphall (1798–1868), an Orthodox Jew from New York, argued that slavery was approved by the Bible (Sarna 2017, 506).

Even though the Constitution granted religious freedom to all, Jews often joined other European immigrants who came to the United States from Russia and other nations during the nineteenth century and were sometimes subject to anti-Semitism (members of the Ku Klux Klan opposed Jews and Catholics as well as African Americans). This discrimination is one reason that Jewish leaders often joined those of other faiths in seeking civil rights reforms in the United States in the 1950s and 1960s. Many American Jews, including Supreme Court justice Louis Brandeis (one of a number of Jews who have so served), supported Zionism, the movement to create a Jewish state in Palestine, although many preferred to stay within the United States. The United States recognized Israel in 1948, shortly after it declared its independence. America had very restrictive immigration policies in place during the Holocaust, which limited the number of Jews who could come to America, although some who did—the physicist Albert Einstein in particular—made major contributions to the war effort.

American Jews have often resisted blue laws, which require the closing of certain businesses on Sunday. Orthodox Jews whose convictions lead them to close their businesses on Saturday thus have to close two days a week. Like Roman Catholics, and some groups of fundamentalists, some Jews have created their own schools so that they can combine an education in secular subjects with one in the tenets of their own religion.

American Christians remain divided over American policies toward Israel, with some believing that the promises of land recorded within the Old Testament remain valid, and others believing that such promises were more spiritual in nature and/or that the church has essentially taken on the role of the ancient nation. President Jimmy Carter viewed his Christian faith as an impetus to seek peace in the Middle East, while President Donald Trump has gained approval among evangelical Christians for his strong opposition to Iran, which is an enemy of Israel, and for moving the U.S. Embassy from Tel Aviv to Jerusalem.

See also Carter, Jimmy; Church of Jesus Christ of Latter-Day Saints; Leeser, Isaac; Political Hebraism; Puritans; Slavery; Ten Commandments; Trump, Donald J.; Zionism

For Reference and Further Reading

Greenspahn, Frederick E. 2007. "Jewish Ambivalence towards the bible." *Hebrew Studies* 48: 7–21.

Kertzer, Morris N. 1975. "What Is a Jew?" *Religions of America: Ferment and Faith in an Age of Crisis*, ed. Leo Rosten. New York: Simon & Schuster, pp. 142–55.

Sarna, Jonathan D. 2017. "The Bible and Judaism in America." *The Oxford Handbook of the Bible in America*, ed. Paul C. Gutjahr. New York: Oxford University Press, pp. 505–16.

Silk, Mark. 1984. "Notes on the Judeo-Christian Tradition in America." *American Quarterly* 36 (Spring): 65–85.

Vile, John R., ed. 2015. *Founding Documents of America: Documents Decoded*. Santa Barbara, CA: ABC-CLIO.

Judgment

One pervasive theme of the Bible is God's justice, which can in turn be associated with judgment. The Bible suggests that God sent a great flood to wipe out human wickedness, that he destroyed the cities of Sodom and Gomorrah for godless behavior, and that he allowed the Jews to be carried into captivity by foreign foes for their unfaithfulness. The biblical book of Revelation also describes a coming judgment at the end of human history. By the same token, the book of Jonah suggests that a nation might avert judgment through repentance just as much of the Bible suggests that individuals can also do.

Biblical portrayals of heaven and hell accentuate the manner in which earthly deeds may result in eternal rewards and punishments. Many American statesmen, even those who are not otherwise associated with orthodox Christianity, have argued that a belief in eternal rewards and punishments leads to better citizens. Requiring individuals to swear to tell the truth in legal proceedings (as well as in taking oaths of office) is designed to insure such veracity and is usually done with one hand on the Bible.

In John Winthrop's famous speech entitled "A Model of Christian Charity," he drew from the Sermon on the Mount in likening the Massachusetts Bay Colony to a city upon a hill that cannot be hid. He observed, "The eies of all people are upon us. Soe that if wee shall deale falsely with our God in this worke wee hue undertaken, and so cause him to withdrawe his present help from us, wee shall be made a story and a by-word through the world" (Winthrop 1630, 47).

Ministers typically stress the need for individual salvation, drawing from such verses as Hebrews 9:27: "And as it is appointed unto men once to die, but after this the judgment." In his famous sermon "Sinners in the Hand of an Angry God," Jonathan Edwards portrayed human beings as being like spiders suspended over the pit of hell, who could at any times fall into eternal punishment unless they repented and asked for God's mercy. Like other Puritans, however, Edwards was convinced that God could also punish nations for their misdeeds, especially those like New Englanders, whom he believed had entered (like ancient Israel) into a direct covenant with God. He and his successors were well known for their jeremiads, in which they interpreted natural disasters as signs of God's wrath and argued that further destruction was imminent if the people did not repent. David Barton, who attempts to apply Scripture to contemporary politics, thus cited Obadiah 1:15, which affirms, "For the day of the LORD draws near on all the nations. As you have done, it will be done to you. Your dealings will return on your own head" (2012, 1340).

George Mason uttered one of the more provocative statements about judgment at the Constitutional Convention of 1787. Noting that slaves "bring the judgment of heaven on a Country," he explained that "as nations cannot be rewarded or punished in the next world, so they must in this. By an inevitable chain of causes and effects, Providence punishes national sins by national calamities" (Farrand 1966, II: 370). Perhaps with this speech in mind, in later arguing against ratification of the Constitution, Martin Luther of Maryland observed, "It was said, it ought to be considered that national *crimes* can only be, *and frequently are punished* in this world, by national punishments; and that the *continuance* of the slave trade, and thus giving it a national sanction, and encouragement, ought to be considered as *justly exposing* us to the *displeasure* and *vengeance of Him*, who is equally Lord of all, and who views with equal eye the poor *African slave* and his *American Master*" (Farrand 1966, III: 211). Writing about slavery in his "Notes on the State of Virginia," Thomas Jefferson observed in his answer to the eighteenth query that "I tremble for my country when I reflect that God is just—that His justice cannot sleep forever" (Jefferson 1781). Theodore Frelinghuysen and Henry Warner observed, "Nations die, but rise not again; and as there are no judgments for them beyond the grave, they have their deserts, for good or for evil, in this life; nor of this did any nations ever yet come finally short. Temporal prosperity in various forms, and temporal misfortune and misery no less various, these are the sanctions of a nation's duty" (1838, 145).

Abolitionists stressed this theme in the years leading up to the Civil War and emancipation, and Abraham Lincoln noted in his second inaugural address that "if God wills that it [the Civil War] continue until all the wealth piled by the bondsman's two hundred and fifty years of unrequited toil shall be sunk, and until every drop of blood drawn with the lash shall be paid by another drawn with the sword, as was said three thousand years ago, so still it must be said 'the judgments of the Lord are true and righteous altogether'" (Vile 2018, 132). Others have anticipated that God might judge the nation for a variety of other social ills. In arguing against the Jacksonian policy of Native American removal, Jeremiah Evarts, writing under the name "William Penn," thus observed, "The Great Arbiter of Nations never fails to take cognizance of national delinquencies. No sophistry can elude his scrutiny; no array of plausible arguments, or of smooth but hollow professions, can bias his judgment; and he has at his disposal most abundant means of executing his decisions" (1829, 6). More recently, David Barton, a conservative, suggests that "there are many policies that the Bible makes clear are of direct concern to God—the shedding of innocent blood by taking the lives of the unborn, the rejection of heterosexual marriage as God established it, prohibiting citizens from acknowledging God in public, the taking of private property by government, etc." (2012, 1345). In more extreme fashion, members of the Westboro Baptist Church, who are known for political protests at military funerals, link such deaths to America's failure to oppose homosexuality (Barrett-Fox 2016, 142).

Jerry Falwell and Pat Robertson were widely criticized when they suggested that the terrorist attacks of 9/11 might be an evidence of God's judgment on the agenda "of the pagans, and the abortionists, and the feminists, and the gays and lesbians" (Moyers 2006, 449), while Muslim terrorists believed that some policies that Americans on the right condemned might indeed warrant such judgments. Billy Graham published an article in 2012 suggesting that "our sins are beginning to catch up with us." He specifically cited God's promise of blessings and his threat of punishments to the Jews in Deuteronomy 18:65–66. He pointed to the evils of secularism, materialism, and the rise of divorce and pornography, and asked, "What would happen today if the Bible were the supreme authority in the United States? If every individual in America would accept Christ as Savior and begin to live up to the terms of the Sermon on the Mount?" He answered with, "Jesus Christ could solve the problems that the nation faces—the race problem, the crime problem, the home problem, the international problems. He can also lift the burdens that we have as individuals; He can reach the problems down in the innermost recesses of our own souls" (2012).

In another letter that Graham posted in 2012, Graham told of a time when his wife turned to him after reading a book he was writing and said, "If God doesn't punish America, He'll have to apologize to Sodom and Gomorrah"; Graham went on specifically to point both to the large number of abortions in the United States and to the fact that "self-centered indulgence, pride, and a lack of shame over sin are now emblems of the American lifestyle" (Piatt 2012). Although acknowledging much of what Graham said to be true, a Christian author observed that slavery had been eliminated, that medical advances had extended human life, and that advances were being made against "sexual oppression and abuse"; he thus asked, "Is it really worse now than ever before?" (Piatt 2012).

Americans have often taken consolation in the fact that their government is not overly hostile to God, as were nations ruled by communism, and in 1954, Congress specifically added the words "under God" to the pledge to the American flag as a way of highlighting this distinction. Many undoubtedly viewed the fall of the Iron Curtain in 1989 as a sign that God had finally judged such nations for their impiety.

Many Christians who have supported the nation of Israel quote Genesis 12:3 to support the idea that God will bless those who bless the descendants of Abraham and curse those who do not. For them, support for Israel thus literally becomes a matter of American national security.

See also Covenants, Compacts, Contracts, and Constitutions; Edwards, Jonathan; Evarts, Jeremiah; Graham, Billy; Heaven and Hell; Natural Disasters; Prophets and Jeremiads; Slavery; Zionism

For Reference and Further Reading

Barrett-Fox, Rebecca. 2016. *God Hates: Westboro Baptist Church, American Nationalism, and the Religious Right*. Lawrence: University Press of Kansas.

Barton, David. 2012. "Judgment of Nations: A Sobering Reality." *The Founders' Bible*. Newbury Park, CA: Shiloh Road, pp. 1340–50.

[Evarts, Jeremiah]. 1829. *Essays on the Present Crisis in the Condition of the American Indians First Published in the National Intelligencer, under the Signature of William Penn*. Boston: Perkins & Marvin.

Farrand, Max, ed. 1966. *The Records of the Federal Convention of 1787*. 4 vols. New Haven, CT: Yale University Press.

Frelinghuysen, Theodore, and Henry Whiting Warner. 1838. *An Inquiry into the Moral and Religious Character of the American Government*. New York: Wiley and Putnam.

Graham, Billy. 2012. "America under Judgment?" *Decision*. November 11. https://billygraham.org/decision-magazine/november-2012/america-under-judgment/.

Jefferson, Thomas. 1981. "Notes on the State of Virginia." Teaching American History. https://teachingamericanhistory.org/library/document/notes-on-the-state-of-virginia-query-xviii-manners/.

Moyers, Bill. 2006. "9/11 and God's Sport." *CrossCurrents* 55 (Winter): 442–55.

Piatt, Christian. 2012. "Billy Graham: Punish America or Apologize to Sodom & Gomorrah." *Sojourners*. June 30. https://sojo.net/articles/billy-graham-punish-america-or-apologize-sodom-gomorrah.

Vile, John R., ed. 2018. *The Civil War and Reconstruction Eras: Documents Decoded.* Santa Barbara, CA: ABC-CLIO.
Winthrop, John. 1630. "A Model of Christian Charity." Collections of the Massachusetts Historical Society (Boston, 1838), 3rd series 7: 31–48. Hanover Historical Texts Collection. https://history.hanover.edu/texts/winthmod.html.

Judicial References

Just as articles in law journals are filled with numerous footnotes, often to non-legal sources, so too judges and justices in the United States often cite extrajudicial sources and sometimes quote from the Bible. Steven Green has observed that a book entitled *The Doctor and Student*, which a barrister, Christopher St. Germain, published in England in the 1530s, was responsible for "the rise in legal biblicism during the sixteenth century; following its publication, citations and references to the bible in reported decisions increased significantly. By the seventeenth century it was not uncommon for judges and commentators to look directly to the bible for authority" (1999–2000, 533). He says this practice was furthered by Sir Henry Finch's publication in 1627 of a treatise entitled *Law or a Discourse Thereof*, which claimed that all kinds of laws, including the common law, were founded in common law (533).

In an article that is highly critical of the continuation of the practice of quoting Scripture in American courts, Sanja Zgonjanin observes that it was more characteristic of twentieth-century decisions than in the previous century (2005, 34), although it is possible that what she is observing is simply the fact that modern judges may find it more necessary to cite chapter and verse to a less biblically literate audience than their predecessors.

Zgonjanin is particularly concerned about the times that judges and justices quote from the Bible in criminal sentencing, as when a trial judge cited Jesus's words of warning to those who would harm children in Matthew 18:5–6, in sentencing an individual who had raped a minor (43). Zgonjanin observes that appeals in such cases are often based on whether appellate judges believe the trial judges used the Bible as one source among many or as the definitive source, often suggesting that they did the former in cases of doubt. At other times, appeals courts suggest that passages, such as Proverbs 28:1, which state that "the guilty flee when no man pursueth while the righteous stand bold as a lion," may be dismissed as mere metaphors that have entered common language (51).

Judge Roy Moore of Alabama, who was eventually impeached and removed from judicial office for his attempts to display a large monument to the Ten Commandments in the court house, often cited Scripture to denounce homosexual conduct and as a justification in settling child custody cases (53–54). Other courts used biblical references in order to explain the background of legal concepts. Judges thus commonly cite Exodus 21:28 ("If an ox gore a man or a woman, and they die, he shall be stone and his flesh shall not be eaten") as a way of explaining the legal concept of forfeiture (55). Others have used biblical passages to uphold modern laws against slander. In the case of *Payne v. Tennessee*, which involved the legitimacy of victim-impact statements, Chief Justice William Rehnquist cited the provision in Exodus 21:22–23, providing "an eye for an eye, a tooth for a tooth," in explaining how legal doctrine had developed over time (57). Justice Antonin Scalia joined an opinion by Justice Clarence Thomas quoting Genesis 1:9–10 (God separating the land from the sea) in the Supreme Court's decision in *Jerome B. Grubert, Inc. v. Great Lakes Dredge & Dock Co.*, 513 U.S. 427, 549–50 (1995) dealing with admiralty jurisdiction (cited in Happy and Menefee 1997, 135). Other judges and justices have used the Bible to explain the derivation of words. Many judges have apparently cited the biblical principle stated in Matthew 6:24 that "no man can serve two masters" to explain the rule limiting dual representation by attorneys (Zgonjanin 2005, 61).

After outlining numerous decisions from medieval times, through English law to the present, Happy and Menefee believe the time has come for the development of either a *Lawyer's Bible* or Hornbook providing judicial references to Bible verses, and they illustrate how this might be done by annotating the first chapter of Genesis (1997, 141–48). Basing court decisions on Holy Writ rather than on the Constitution and the law of the land would clearly violate the establishment clause of the First Amendment, but excluding references to biblical wisdom at a time when judges routinely refer to both classic and contemporary works dealing with justice would seem to be unnecessary. Judges should, of course, exercise extreme caution when suggesting that the Bible, rather than the Constitution and laws adopted in accord with its principles, mandate a particular sentence or outcome.

See also Criminal Law; Moore, Roy; Ten Commandments; Torts

For Reference and Further Reading

Green, Steven K. 1999–2000. "The Fount of Everything Just and Right? The Ten Commandments as a Source of American Law." *Journal of Law and Religion* 14(2): 525–58.

Happy, J. Nelson, and Samuel Pyeatt Menefee. 1997. "Genesis! Scriptural Citation and the *Lawyer's Bible* Project." *Regent University Law Review* 9: 89–148.

Hudson, David L., Jr. 2005. "The Bible Tells Them So." *ABA Journal*. July. www.abajournal.com/magazine/article/the_bible_tells_them_so. Accessed April 28, 2019.

Zgonjanin, Sanja. 2005. "Quoting the Bible: The Use of Religious References in Judicial Decision-Making." *City University of New York Law Review* 9 (Winter): 31–91.

• K •

Kasich, John

John Kasich (b. 1952) is an Ohio politician who graduated from Ohio State University and has served as a member of the Ohio Senate, of the U.S. House of Representatives (where he chaired the House Budget Committee from 1995 to 2001), and as governor of Ohio from 2011 to 2019. He unsuccessfully sought the Republican nomination in 2000 and again in 2016. Although Kasich refused to follow the example of a number of Republican rivals and trade barbs with Donald J. Trump, who won the nomination, Kasich refused to attend the 2016 Republican National Nominating Convention even though it was held in his home state.

Raised a Roman Catholic, Kasich has since joined the Anglican Church of St. Augustine in Westerville, Ohio, which is part of the Anglican Church in North America that split from the Episcopal Church when that church elected an openly gay bishop (Preble 2016). In 2010, Kasich published a book detailing the fact that he had for the past twenty years been part of a men's Bible group in Ohio that met twice a month with some direction from a local Methodist minister. Admitting that "I don't find God in ritual and worship" (Kasich 2010, 6), Kasich says that the Bible study has had a major impact on his life. Referring to his Bible group, he says,

> We all believe the Bible is inspired. It's the word of God, rendered by man. We don't agree on everything, even as we've come to a kind of shared view. We all get that the stories of the Old and New Testaments are contextual; in other words, you need to understand each chapter in the context of its time. Some of the stories are historical; some are allegorical. (2010, 20)

The primary biblical passages that Kasich discusses are passages in Romans that point to the insufficiency of achieving salvation through mere obedience to the law. Kasich says that Paul "calls for a new approach. Faith in Christ. It was a revolutionary thought at the time to suggest that the law is not the point. The effort is the point. The best intentions. The pureness of our hearts" (135). Kasich presented an outline of Romans 12 while stating his belief that "Jesus really was the son of God who rose from the dead" (136–37).

Kasich presents the necessity for faith as a primary message of the Bible. Calling faith "a liberating thing" and a "liberating principle," Kasich argues that faith is the primary way to be "plugged in" to God (127). Although he does not appear specifically to mention the chapter, many of the biblical examples of faith that he cites—Abraham, Noah, David, and others—are among those catalogued in Hebrews 11.

In a chapter that focuses on grace and truth, Kasich likened the Bible to the Magna Carta. He argued that America's founders "were in no way frightened or put off by religion. They weren't frightened or put off by the word or the power of God" (196). He further observed,

> The values that run through the Old Testament are essentially the same values this country was founded on: honesty, humility, faith, personal responsibility, accountability, being a good friend and neighbor, trusting in our fellow man, and so on. It's the Judeo-Christian ethic, in full force, although quite a few of our guys [in the Bible study] think the New Testament offers a better, richer, more compassionate template for living. (2010, 196)

Other major themes that Kasich identifies in the Bible are the value of forgiveness, the dangers of vanity, the importance of integrity and generosity, proper use of ambition, the need for justice, and admonitions against greed (205–13). According to a recent book, Kasich's favorite Bible passage is Matthew 7:4–5, the New American Standard version of which has Jesus asking, "Or how can you say to your brother, 'Let me take the speck out of your eye,' and behold, the log is in your own eye? You hypocrite, first take the log out of your own eye, and then you will see clearly to take the speck out of your brother's eye" (Winder 2019, 107).

Although Kasich is a right-wing Republican, his understanding of the gospel has led him to emphasize a different set of issues than some fellow partisans. Preble (2016) observed that Kasich supported the Affordable Care Act and the expansion of Medicaid in Ohio, and once told a state legislature that "when you die and get to the meeting with St. Peter, he's probably not going to ask you much about what you did about keeping government small. But he is going to ask you what you did for the poor. You better have a good answer." Preble further notes that he "has tried to move the conversation away from the saber-rattling over divisive issues such as immigration and ISIS" in preference "to issues such a job creation, national defense and 'healing the divisions between the races,'" which Preble believes are tied to his religious faith.

Although some Republicans had hoped that Kasich might challenge Trump's renomination, he instead published a book entitled *It's Up to Us* and is working for the CNN News Network.

See also Trump, Donald J.

For Reference and Further Reading

Kasich, John. 2010. *Every Other Monday: Twenty Years of Life, Lunch, Faith, and Friendship*. New York: Atria.

Preble, Peter-Michael. 2016. "The Faith of John Kasich." HuffPost. March 10 [updated March 11, 2017]. https://www.huffpost.com/entry/the-faith-of-john-kasich_b_9413406.

Turner, Laura. 2016. "How Kasich's Religion Is Hurting Him with Conservatives." *Politico*. March 15. https://www.politico.com/magazine/story/2016/03/john-kasich-2016-religion-213735.

Winder, Mike. 2019. *Favorite Scriptures of 100 American Leaders*. Springville, UT: Plain Sight.

Kennedy, John F.

John F. Kennedy (1917–1963), who was born to a prominent family in Massachusetts, graduated from Harvard University and commanded patrol torpedo boats during World War II. He served in the U.S. House of Representatives and the U.S. Senate before winning the Democrat nomination for president in 1960 and defeating Richard M. Nixon to become the thirty-fifth president of the United States. He was elected partly amid fears of a "missile gap" between the United States and the Soviet Union and dealt during his presidency with the Soviet installation of nuclear missiles in Cuba just 90 miles from the U.S. coast. Kennedy was a charismatic figure. He gave impetus to America's quest to be the first to reach the moon, took some steps toward civil rights reform (which his successor Lyndon Johnson furthered in his name), helped establish the Peace Corps, and engaged in other policy initiatives before being assassinated in Dallas, Texas, in 1963.

Kennedy is known as the first individual who identified as a Roman Catholic to be elected as president (Democrat Al Smith had run unsuccessfully for the office in 1928), and his religious affiliation was a major issue during his presidential campaign. After an organization of Protestant clergymen called the National Conference of Citizens for Religious Freedom, which was unofficially headed by Rev. Norman Vincent Peale, again raised the question as to whether a Roman Catholic would be able to govern free from the control of the church, which was both a political and a religious organization (Massa 1997, 309–10), Kennedy delivered a speech on the subject. Such concerns dated back to the Protestant Reformation's identification of the Catholic Church as the Great Whore of Babylon as portrayed in the book of Revelation and had been reflected in such books as Paul Blanchard's 1949 *American Freedom and Catholic Power*.

One of the ironies of this concern is that Kennedy's own personal religious commitment was often questioned and did not appear to be reflected in his own private life, which was tainted by profanity, extra-marital affairs, and deceit (Smith 2006, 264). James Wolfe observed that "Kennedy's fidelity to his church seemed to be one of identification, affiliation, and ritual observance rather than one of thought or worldly action" (quoted in Smith 2006, 263). Jacqueline Kennedy once observed that "I think it's so unfair of people to be against Jack because he is a Catholic. He's such a poor Catholic" (quoted in Holmes 2012, 74).

In a speech to the Greater Houston Ministerial Association that Kennedy delivered on September 12, 1960, he sought to allay such fears, which he did by showing strong support for the doctrine of the separation of church and state. Kennedy announced that "I believe in an America that is officially neither Catholic, Protestant, nor Jewish; where no public official either requests or accepts instructions on public policy from the Pope, the National Council of Churches or any other ecclesiastical sources." He pointed out that American history had revealed prejudice similar to that which he was experiencing against Jews, Quakers, Unitarians, and Baptists.

For better or worse, Kennedy sought to allay fears in part by privatizing his own faith. He thus stated that "I believe in a president whose religious views are his own private affair, neither imposed by him upon the nation, or imposed by the nation upon him as a condition to holding that office." He further pointed out that "contrary to common newspaper usage, I am not the Catholic candidate for president. I am the Democratic Party's candidate for president, who happens also to be a Catholic. I do not speak for my church on public matters, and the church does not speak for me." He ended by noting that the presidential oath, like that which he had taken when joining the military and entering Congress, called upon him not to uphold a church but to support the U.S. Constitution.

In a farewell speech that Kennedy gave to his Massachusetts constituents on January 9, 1961, he referred to his state's past with a reference to one of its founders and his evocation of Scripture from the Sermon on the Mount: "But I have been guided by the standard John Winthrop set before his shipmates on the flagship *Arbella* three hundred and thirty-one years ago, as they, too, faced the task of building a new government on a perilous frontier." "We must consider," he said, "that we shall be as a city upon a hill—the eyes of all people are upon us." In a paraphrase of Luke 12:48, Kennedy further observed that "for of those to whom much is given, much is required." He went on to extol the virtues of courage, judgment, integrity, and dedication and ended, in an apparent reference to the Lord's Prayer, by observing that "aware that on earth His will is worked by men, I ask for your help and your prayers, as I embark on this new and solemn journey."

Kennedy quoted the Bible frequently (Smith 2006, 263; Massa 1997, 298). His inaugural address is best known for the statement that "we shall pay any price, bear any burden, meet any hardship, support any friend, oppose any foe to assure the survival and the success of liberty" and for the equally compelling "ask not what your country can do for you—ask what you can do for your country." In this same address, however, he also quoted, without citing, Isaiah 58:6 about the need to "undo the heavy burdens . . . let the oppressed go free." He also quoted from Romans 12:12 about the need to continue "rejoicing in hope, patient in tribulation," and ended by stating that "here on earth God's work must truly be our own." Kennedy took his oath upon a closed family Bible. He later confided to Congressman Tip O'Neill that as he was taking his oath, he was distracted by his amazement that George Kara, a Boston businessman, had managed to get a seat behind his family (Smith 2006, 263).

Some of Kennedy's most poignant references to the Bible are found at the end of the speech that he had prepared to deliver at the Trade Mart in Dallas, Texas, on November 22, 1963, the day that he was assassinated. In a reference to watchmen that is taken from Ezekiel 33, and to the angels' announcement of Jesus's birth in Luke 2:14, Kennedy had written,

> We in this country, in this generation, are—by destiny rather than choice—the watchmen on the walls of world freedom. We ask, therefore, that we may be worthy of our power and responsibility, that we may exercise our strength with wisdom and restraint, and that we may achieve in our time and for all time the ancient vision of "peace on earth, good will toward men." That must always be our goal, and the righteousness of our cause must always underlie our strength. For as was written long ago: "except the Lord keep the city, the watchman waketh but in vain."

Kennedy's assassination was a traumatizing event for the nation. Smith observes that many eulogists "judged Kennedy's death to be vicarious" (2006, 288). Many members of the clergy quoted John 15:13, "Greater love hath no man than this, that a man lay down his life for his friends."

See also City upon a Hill; Roman Catholics

For Reference and Further Reading

Holmes, David. 2012. *The Faiths of the Postwar Presidents: From Truman to Obama.* Athens: University of Georgia Press.
Kennedy, John F. 1960. "Transcript: JFK's Speech on His Religion." NPR. September 12 [posted online on December 5, 2007]. https://www.npr.org/templates/story/story.php?storyId=16920600.
Kennedy, John F. 1961. "'City upon a Hill' Speech." UVA, Miller Center. January 9. https://millercenter.org/the-presidency/presidential-speeches/january-9-1961-city-upon-hill-speech.
Kennedy, John F. 1961, "Transcript of President John F. Kennedy's Inaugural Address (1961)." January 20. https://www.ourdocuments.gov/doc.php?flash=false&doc=91&page=transcript.
Kennedy, John F. 1963. "Remarks Prepared for Delivery at the Trade Mart in Dallas, TX." John F. Kennedy Presidential Library and Museum. November 22. https://www.jfklibrary.org/archives/other-resources/john-f-kennedy-speeches/dallas-tx-trade-mart-undelivered-19631122.
Massa, Mark S. 1997. "A Catholic for President?: John F. Kennedy and the 'Secular' Theology of the Houston Speech, 1960." *Journal of Church and State* 39 (Spring): 197–317.
Smith, Gary Scott. 2006. *Faith and the Presidency: From George Washington to George W. Bush.* New York: Oxford University Press.

Keteltas, Abraham

Abraham Keteltas (1732–1798) was a Presbyterian minister who served in the Provincial Congress that helped establish New York's first constitution. On October 5, 1777, he preached a sermon in Newburyport, Massachusetts, that was soon thereafter published and that presented the American Revolution as a cause that God favored.

His primary text, taken from Psalm 74:12, was "Arise O GOD! Plead thine own cause." The sermon itself was infused with multiple Scriptures from both the Old and New Testaments. After examining the cause of God, which Keteltas identified with truth and justice, Keteltas proceeded to describe how God pled his cause through his word, his spirit, and his providence (Sandoz 1991, 589). Examples began with God pleading the case of Abel against Cain and continued through God's saving Lot from Sodom, Joseph from his brothers, and the Israelites from the kings of Babylon and Persia (Sandoz 1991, 590–91).

The application of the Scripture was arguably even more important. Having surveyed God's past work, Keteltas concluded that "I think we have reason to conclude that the cause of this American continent, against the measures of a cruel, bloody, and vindictive ministry, is the cause of God. We are contending for the rights of mankind, for the welfare of millions now living, and for the happiness of millions yet unborn" (595). He further opined, with almost millennial expectations, that "if the principles on which the present civil war is carried on by the American colonies, against the British arms, were universally adopted and practiced upon by mankind, they would turn a vale of tears, into a paradise of God" (595). Keteltas observed that the principles for which America was fighting were akin to those for which the British had themselves fought when they beheaded Charles I, deposed James II, and otherwise opposed tyranny. He equated the justice of the American cause to that of the prophet Elijah against King Ahab and Queen Jezebel after they falsely accused Naboth and seized his vineyard and for which God had punished them severely (598–99). He further pointed to British war atrocities that had invaded "the lives, liberties, and properties of the inhabitants of these colonies" (601). In an ironic passage, he included the accusation that "our negroes who have been nourished and brought up by us, and the savages of the wilderness, for whose temporal and eternal welfare we have labored, have been instigated to mangle, scalp, and murder us" (599).

Keteltas had little question as to where justice lay:

> Be therefore of good courage; it is a glorious cause: It is the cause of truth, against error and falsehood, the cause of righteousness against iniquity, the cause of the oppressed against the oppressor; the cause of the pure and undefiled religion, against bigotry, superstition, & human inventions. It is the cause of the reformation, against popery; of liberty, against arbitrary power; of benevolence, against barbarity, and of virtue against vice. It is the cause of justice and integrity, against bribery, venality, and corruption. In short, it is the cause of heaven against hell. (Sandoz 1991, 603)

His sermon thus shows how Scripture can be used both to rally countrymen and to assure them of victory when they perceive their cause as being just.

See also Revolutionary War

For Reference and Further Reading

Sandoz, Ellis, ed. 1991. *Political Sermons of the American Founding Era, 1730–1805*. Indianapolis, IN: Liberty Fund. [Keteltas's sermon was originally published in Newburyport, Massachusetts, by John Mycall for Edmund Sawyer in 1777 and is found on pages 579–605.]

King James Version of the Bible

One of the great ironies of American history is that its longest used and favorite Bible is named after the king (James I of England and James VI) of England (1566–1625), under whose reign it was commissioned (1604) and later printed (1611). Although he was the son of a Catholic mother (Queen Mary of Scots, who had been executed under the reign of Elizabeth I), James had been educated as a Calvinist and was one of the more articulate defenders of the divine right of kings, which the American colonies would later repudiate, in part through the circulation of Thomas Paine's *Common Sense* on the eve of the American Revolution.

As he came to power in England in 1603, James headed a church in which more traditional high church elements, which sought to preserve many of the outward forms of the Roman Catholic faith, under which it had been nurtured, were increasingly contested by more Reformation-orientated Protestants who sought to purify the church from what they considered to be departures from the church as outlined in the New Testament. King James presided over a meeting at Hampton Court in 1604 in which those supporting a more formal church won on most issues but in which the king gave his assent to a new translation of the Bible. Because Protestants believed the authority of the Bible was superior to that of the pope or other clerical interpreters, they generally wanted it translated into the vernacular language of the people, while Catholics were generally satisfied with the Latin Vulgate translation of the Bible, which was, because of its language, chiefly accessible to men of education who could explain it in light of church teachings.

Even before the Protestant Reformation, John Wycliffe (1330–1384), a professor at Oxford, had accompanied his questioning of papal claims by inspiriting his students to translate the Bible from Latin into English. Although Wycliffe's body was later exhumed and burned for what church authorities considered to be heretical views, the hand-produced translations published under his name appear to have been fairly widespread (Ferrell 2008, 65).

The invention of moveable type brought about another translation into English by William Tyndale (1494–1536), the New Testament of which he had translated directly from Greek. He was executed for his efforts in Belgium in 1536, but one of his assistants, Miles Coverdale (1488–1568), managed to complete his project, which was recognized by King Henry VIII, who founded the Anglican Church. Indeed, the title page of this so-called Great Bible pictured the king handing out copies to church bishops, under whose authority the king hoped that it would be interpreted, each uttering the words "Vivat Rex," meaning "God Save the King" (Ferrell 2008, 76–77).

In time, this Bible was largely supplanted by the so-called Geneva Bible, which was named after the Swiss city in which it was printed largely under the auspices of William Whittington, a Puritan who had fled English persecution under Queen Mary (Ferrell 2008, 80). Its most notable feature was that it was divided into chapters and verses, which made references to it easier; was illustrated; and contained running commentary in the margins. It became a particular thorn in the side of English monarchs because many of the comments pointed to the foibles of Hebrew kings and endorsed civil disobedience and, in appropriate circumstances, even regicide (Ferrell 2008, 82). One scholar observes, "The Geneva was, in short, a book that today undoubtedly would be titled *The Bible for Dummies*. This multitude of 'helps,' along with its compact size, made it the first Bible designed to assist the common English reader, which in turn made it popular on an unprecedented scale. Its very user-friendliness ensured, however, that religious radicalism would be indelibly associated with individual, private biblical accessibility in the future" (Ferrell 2008, 83). Queen Elizabeth I encouraged the publication of a "Great Bible," or "Bishops' Bible," which never proved as popular as its Geneva predecessor, which continued to outsell it.

One of King James's chief ends in authorizing yet another translation was to eliminate the anti-monarchical and anticlerical commentary in the Geneva Bible. Ironically, one of the chief Roman Catholic objections to the King James Bible was that it was lacking accompanying commentary that would explain how its leaders thought it should be interpreted. Another irony is that, while many Puritans, including those who settled in America, initially preferred the Geneva Bible, they too came to accept the King James Version. Later, the

American Bible Society and other organizations formed to distribute Bibles generally sought to avoid interdenominational doctrinal disputes by sticking to Bibles without accompanying commentary. Throughout the nineteenth century, it was common for the King James Bible to be read without commentary in public schools, without due regard to the fact that Roman Catholic children were used to hearing from an alternate translation receiving specific instruction as to its meaning by church authorities.

The King James Version of the Bible was the work of forty-seven of Britain's top biblical and linguistic scholars from Oxford, Cambridge, and Westminster, many of whom had come to England from Europe as a result of the religious wars between Catholics and Protestants. Groups of scholars were assigned different portions of Scripture. Their task was not so much to come up with a new translation as to correct any translation errors in existing English translations, most notably the Geneva Bible (Daniell 2003, 440).

Some of the language of the King James Version was thus already somewhat dated when it was translated, but this was done in part on the theory—perhaps somewhat in conflict with the idea of translating the Bible into the English vernacular—that more elevated language was particularly appropriate for Scripture. As one scholar has observed, "In the earlier years of the seventeenth century, the weight of high Anglican politic was heavily on the side of creating, as it was thought, a worshipful distance" (Daniell 2003, 442).

Although there have been a plethora of subsequent English translations, the dignity of the language of the King James Bible makes it a continuing favorite, so much so that some traditional Anglican congregations as well as a number of contemporary fundamentalists and members of the Church of Jesus Christ of Latter-Day Saints reverence it almost as they might had it been in the original language. Most politicians who have quoted the Bible in American history have chosen to quote from the familiar cadence of the King James Version.

Language can sometimes take unusual twists and turns. John Pahl has argued that some of the majestic language in the King James Version of the Bible, including its references to the "king of kings," "glory," and "sacrifice," has encouraged Americans to think of themselves in exalted terms and to justify themselves with the majesty of a nation destined to do great things, even if it might often involve the sacrifice not only of its own citizens but also of those it is attempting to liberate (2013, 414–15).

See also American Bible Society; Church of Jesus Christ of Latter-Day Saints; *Common Sense* (Thomas Paine); Fundamentalists; Geneva Bible; Puritans; Roman Catholics

For Reference and Further Reading

Daniell, David. 2003. *The Bible in English: Its History and Influence*. New Haven, CT: Yale University Press.

Ferrell, Lori Anne. 2008. *The Bible and the People*. New Haven, CT: Yale University Press.

Hallidan, C. P. 2010. *The Authorized Version: A Wonderful and Unfinished History*. London, England: Trinitarian Bible Society.

Levy, Joel J. 2017. "How the King James Bible Came to Be." *Time*. June 19. https://time.com/4821911/king-james-bible-history/.

Pahl, Jon. 2013. "America's King of Kings: The King James Bible and American Civil Religion." *The King James Version at 400*, ed. David G. Burke, John F. Kutsko, and Philip H. Towner. Atlanta, GA: Society of Biblical Literature, pp. 413–44.
Pruitt, Sarah. 2019. "Why the King James Bible of 1611 Remains the Most Popular Translation in History." History.com. March 22 [updated April 16, 2019]. https://www.history.com/news/king-james-bible-most-popular.

King, Martin Luther, Jr.

Dr. Martin Luther King Jr. (1929–1968) was such an important civil rights leader that, since 1986, he has been commemorated by an annual holiday. A third-generation Baptist pastor who was born and raised in Atlanta, Georgia, both he and his father's original names of Michael were changed in 1934 to honor the great German reformer.

King attended the historically black Morehouse College, from which he graduated at the age of nineteen, attended the Crozer Theological Seminary in Pennsylvania, and later earned a PhD from Boston University. His initial beliefs in the power of good will appear to have been tempered by his awareness of the reality of sin, which he seems to have taken in part from the thought of Reinhold Niebuhr (Shulman 2008, 101). By the time he earned his PhD, he had begun preaching at the Dexter Avenue Baptist Church in Montgomery, Alabama.

In 1954, the U.S. Supreme Court ruled in *Brown v. Board of Education* that the system of racial segregation must end, but whites strongly resisted this decision. After Rosa Parks refused to give up her place at the front of a bus in 1955, King helped lead a boycott of the city bus system that, with his great rhetorical abilities, propelled him to leadership in the civil rights movement.

He subsequently helped found the Southern Christian Leadership Conference, which, drawing from the philosophy of Mahatma Gandhi, he steered toward nonviolent action on behalf of civil rights. When he was arrested and imprisoned for leading a demonstration without a permit in Birmingham, Alabama, King wrote an important letter responding to criticism by local clergymen who felt that he was simply stirring up trouble. In responding, King indicated that the laws of God were superior to those of man and that it was sometimes necessary for Christians to obey the former over the latter. King had elsewhere rejected the idea that a materialist philosophy like communism could ever meet the aspirations of African Americans.

King's most successful march was his March on Washington for Jobs and Freedom in August 1963. In his "I Have a Dream" speech, he attempted to combine the biblical ideal of human brotherhood with the affirmation of the Declaration of Independence and other founding documents of human equality of rights. The speech gained much of its resonance from King's conviction, expressed in an early sermon, that "God has planted in the fiber of the universe certain eternal laws which forever confront every man. They are absolute and not relative. There is an eternal and absolute distinction between right and wrong" (Shulman 2008, 102). The following year, he was awarded the Nobel Peace Prize, at a time when the Civil Rights Act of 1964 sought to outlaw racial discrimination, while the Voting Rights Act of 1965 sought to expand voting rights.

As King began to address wider issues of social justice, he was increasingly critical of America's war efforts in Vietnam. While supporting a sanitary workers' strike in Memphis, he was assassinated in 1968. The previous evening, he had given a speech in which, likening himself to Moses, he proclaimed that, like Moses, he might not himself make it to the Promised Land, but he had been given a vision of it.

King's thought embodies a number of strands, many of which tie directly to the Bible. He was, of course, a member of the African American church, with deep roots in Scripture. King put particular emphasis on Old Testament prophets, who were often calling their societies to task for their injustices and inequities. As indicated above, he identified closely with Moses in attempting to lead his people from oppression to equality. Although it is not clear that he believed that Jesus was the Son of God in a traditional orthodox sense or that he literally rose from the dead (Hartnell 2011, 109–10), King identified closely with Jesus's Sermon on the Mount and with his emphasis on the importance of agape love in building a beloved community. King put particular emphasis on Jesus's proclamation at the beginning of his ministry as recorded in Luke 4:18, in which he alluded to the Year of Jubilee: "The Spirit of the Lord is upon me because he has anointed me; he has sent me to announce good news to the poor, to proclaim release for prisoners and recovery of sight for the blind: to let the broken victims go free, to proclaim the year of the Lord's favor" (Hartnell 2011, 58).

Peter Heltzel says that "King's Christology is best understood as a theology of the cross" (2009, 47). He observes that King attempted to call "white North American Christians to confront their theologies of triumph and embrace a theology of the cross"; in so doing he was attempting to call them " back to the Gospels, back to their Savior, and back to the call to love thy neighbor" (47).

See also Civil Disobedience; Communism and Anti-Communism; Declaration of Independence; Jesus; Moses as Political Archetype; Niebuhr, Reinhold

For Reference and Further Reading

Garrow, David. 2004. *Bearing the Cross: Martin Luther King, Jr., and the Southern Christian Leadership Conference*. New York: William Morrow Paperbacks.

Hartnell, Anna. 2011. *Rewriting Exodus: American Futures from Du Bois to Obama*. Minneapolis, MN: Pluto Press.

Heltzel, Peter Goodwin. 2009. *Jesus and Justice: Evangelicals, Race, and American Politics*. New Haven, CT: Yale University Press.

Reider, Jonathan. 2013. *Gospel of Freedom: Martin Luther King, Jr.'s Letter from Birmingham Jail and the Struggle That Changed a Nation*. New York: Bloomsbury Press.

Shulman, George. 2008. *American Prophecy: Race and Redemption in American Political Culture*. Minneapolis: University of Minnesota Press.

Koop, C. Everett

Dr. C. Everett Koop (1916–2013) was probably the most recognized and most consequential individual ever to serve as U.S. surgeon general. President Ronald Reagan appointed him to this post in which he served throughout his administration.

A graduate of Dartmouth College and of Cornell Medical School, Koop spent most of his working life as surgeon in chief of the Children's Hospital in Philadelphia, where he pioneered operations to correct birth defects and separate conjoined twins and edited the *Journal of Pediatric Surgery*. This led to his opposition to refusing care to children with such congenital defects.

Through the ministry of the Tenth Presbyterian Church of Philadelphia, which was pastored by James Montgomery Boice, Koop became an evangelical Christian after the birth of his third child and was a Presbyterian elder and long-time president of the Evangelical Association. He observed, "As an evangelical Christian, I attempted to evaluate everything in the light of Scripture, and in the Bible I found my guide for faith and conduct, always tempered by God's grace and forgiveness" (quoted in Bergman 2011). Koop lost a son in a climbing accident, but accepted this as God's will.

Prior to his appointment as surgeon general, Koop had joined with theologian Francis Schaeffer in opposing abortion (Schaeffer and Koop 1979), which was also one of President Reagan's positions. In a letter, Koop observed that "in Psalm 139 David writes about God's role in his own life before birth: For you created my inmost being; you knit me together in my mother's womb. I praise you because I am fearfully and wonderfully made" (quoted in Bergman 2011). Koop took a literalistic view of Genesis and was an opponent of evolution and of secular humanism. He explained,

> Unlike the evolutionary concept of an impersonal beginning plus time plus chance, the Bible gives an account of man's origin as a finite person made in God's image, that is, like God. We see then how man can have personality and dignity and value. Our uniqueness is guaranteed, something which is impossible in the materialistic system. If there is no qualitative distinction between man and other organic life (animals and plants), why should we feel greater concern over the death of a human being than over the death of a laboratory rat? Is man in the end any higher? (Bergman 2011)

Lauded by conservatives for his strong stance against abortion, and feared by liberals both for this and for his general moralism, Koop reintroduced the practice of wearing a military uniform as surgeon general and put his job as the nation's chief doctor over his prior anti-abortion advocacy. As surgeon general, he led a strong campaign against smoking and played a major role in spreading information to combat AIDS, despite his view that the Bible condemned homosexual behavior. Nancy Mahon, the global executive director of the MAC AIDS Fund, thus observed that he took "a very Mother Teresa approach," and that "he was first and foremost a doctor. He didn't allow any of the politics or hysteria change or mute his focus" (Andriote 2013).

Noting how Koop would almost never cancel a speaking engagement, even when called to testify before Congress, Georgetown University law professor Tim Westmorland observed that he "was quite possibly the most principled person I've ever met in my life" (quoted in Andriote 2013). In this same spirit, however, he responded to critics who opposed his explicit treatment of AIDS by saying, "I'm the nation's doctor, not the nation's chaplain" (quoted in Andriote 2013).

See also Abortion; Creationism and Evolution; Schaeffer, Francis

For Reference and Further Reading

Andriote, John Manuel. 2013. "Doctor, Not Chaplain: How a Deeply Religious Surgeon General Taught a Nation about HIV." *The Atlantic*. March 4. https://www.theatlantic.com/health/archive/2013/03/doctor-not-chaplain-how-a-deeply-religious-surgeon-general-taught-a-nation-about-hiv/273665/.

Bergman, Jerry. 2011. "C. Everett Koop—Christian and Darwin Doubter." *Journal of Creation* 25 (December): 63–67. https://creation.com/everett-koop-darwin-doubter.

Noble, Holcomb B. 2013. "C. Everett Koop, Forceful U.S. Surgeon General, Dies at 96." *New York Times*. February 25.

Schaeffer, Francis A., and C. Everett Koop. 1979. *Whatever Happened to the Human Race?* Tappan: Fleming H. Revell.

Koresh, David

Scholars continue to debate what separates a "cult" from a "denomination" or "church." Some scholars have indeed argued that cults often emerge as reactions to over accommodation by established churches or denominations with secular culture and later themselves either die or assume many of the institutional forms against which they revolted (Lawson 1995). Leaders who split from existing Christian denominations often do so as a result of Bible studies that lead them to believe that the church has strayed from its original foundations. In the early nineteenth century, the Restorationist movement led to the establishment of a number of such denominations, which typically stressed one or another aspect of either Old Testament law or the early church.

Sometimes such renewed attention to particular portions of ancient Scripture is accompanied by additional prophetic revelations. Thus, the Church of Jesus Christ of Latter-Day Saints grew in part from additional revelations that Joseph Smith claimed to have received from the angel Maroni. So, too, Ellen White was recognized by Seventh-Day Adventists as a prophet whose works led to deeper understandings of the Scripture, and members of the Christian Science faith regard Mary Baker Eddy's writings as additional revelations essential to understanding original Scriptures.

Vernon Wayne Howell (1959–1993) appears to have regarded himself in a similar prophetic role. After being excommunicated from a local Seventh-Day Adventist church, he joined a group of Branch Davidians under the leadership of Lois Roden and gradually took over her role with the claim to continuing revelations (Corrigan and Neal 2010, 217). In 1990, he took the name of David Koresh, based on the name of Israel's greatest king and Cyrus, which is Koresh in Hebrew (217).

Koresh gathered followers together in a compound in Waco, Texas, where he taught his understandings of the Bible with particular emphasis on the Old Testament prophets and the New Testament book of Revelation. In time, he began to make messianic claims about himself. He also took a number of wives, some of whom were under the legal age of consent, and claimed access to the wives of members. Members who left the group circulated additional rumors about his collection of guns, his abuse of children, and his desire, which he denied, of creating a mass suicide similar to the one conducted by close to a thousand followers of Jim Jones in Jonestown, Guyana, on November 18, 1978.

In time, such reports led agents of the Bureau of Alcohol, Tobacco, and Firearms to approach the compound. After gunfire left both agents and Branch Davidians dead, a long siege ensued. The government, partly fearing mass suicide, ultimately stormed the compound, which burned, killing most members of the group. There is still dispute as to whether Koresh gave an order to burn the compound or whether it burned as a result of tear gas or as agents toppled lanterns. In either event, Corrigan and Neal (2010) believe that the incident might have ended without bloodshed if governmental agents had not been blinded with the label of "cult," if they had taken Koresh's arguments from Scripture more seriously, and if they could have believed Koresh's claims that he and his followers would emerge after he had written an essay on the meaning of the seven seals described in the book of Revelation.

Although agents considered this claim to be a stalling tactic, Koresh had, in fact, been working on such an account, which is available online. The most notable aspect of this writing is that it is suffused with Scripture, almost all from the prophets and the book of Revelation. In interpreting this document, Phillip Arnold and James Tabor believe that it shows that although Koresh did not consider himself, like Jesus, to be coequal with God, he did believe that he would be the Lamb described in Revelation 5:5 as being the one worthy to open to the seals, to ride a white horse, and to play a role similar to the one that Cyrus had played in the Old Testament. Koresh appeared to equate the government's actions against him as a form of persecution, similar to that which Jesus (who was also thirty-three at the time of his death) had faced.

See also Alternate Scriptures; Cyrus as Political Archetype; Polygamy; Violence

For Reference and Further Reading

Agne, Robert R., and Karen Tracy. "Bible Babble': Naming the Interactional Trouble at Waco." *Discourse Studies* 2 (August): 269–94.

Corrigan, John, and Lynn S. Neal. 2010. *Religious Intolerance in America*. Chapel Hill: University of North Carolina Press.

Koresh, David. 1994. "The David Koresh Manuscript: Exposition of the Seven Seals." © Phillip Arnold and James Tabor. http ://ccat.sas.upenn.edu/gopher/text/religion/koresh/Koresh%20Seals.

Lawson, Ronald. 1995. "Sect-State Relations: Accounting for the Differing Trajectories of Seventh-Day Adventists and Jehovah's Witnesses." *Sociology of Religion* 56 (Winter) 351–77.

• L •

Land Ownership

Puritans described America both as the Garden of Eden or a New Jerusalem and as a wilderness. Neither picture was completely accurate.

For the most part, the English settlement of North America followed the Spanish conquest of Latin America, which itself had been initiated by its discovery by Christopher Columbus, who saw his discovery as the fulfillment of biblical prophecy. The Spanish apparently based their own policies, requiring natives either to covert or be subjugated, on the Islamic resurrection of scriptures from Deuteronomy 20:10–16, which had to do with the Jewish conquest of Canaan. According to this passage, the Israelites were either to allow a town they approached to surrender and become slaves or to war against it, killing its inhabitants and taking their possessions as booty (Newman 2016, 131).

American Puritans, like Spanish conquistadors to the South, understand themselves to be part of a New Israel. After practically wiping out the Pequot Indians in 1637–1638, soldiers petitioned Governor Winthrop asking for their share of booty, which included enslaving some of those they had captured (Newman 2016, 133).

When they came to America, the Puritans relied heavily on Genesis 1:28, in which, after blessing Adam and Eve, God told them, "Be fruitful and multiply, and fill the earth and subdue it; and have dominion over the fish of the sea and over the birds of the air and over every living thing that moves upon the earth." This passage had, in turn, been linked in English history to the notion that, to become private property, land had to be enclosed or improved upon, and was associated with the philosophy of John Locke, who had proclaimed that "as much Land as a Man Tills, Plants, Improves, Cultivates, and can use the Product of, so much is his Property" (quoted in Newman 2016, 136). In time, this allowed judges to distinguish Native American Indians' "possession and occupancy" of the land from ownership by Europeans who settled and improved it.

Newman points out that Canadians to the north followed similar legal understandings. (137).

See also America as New Israel; Columbus, Christopher; Manifest Destiny; Model of Christian Charity (Winthrop); Native American Indians; Puritans; Slavery

For Reference and Further Reading

Charles, Mark, and Soong-Chan Rah. 2019. *Unsettling Truths: The Ongoing, Dehumanizing Legacy of the Doctrine of Discovery*. Downers Grove, IL: InterVarsity Press.

Newman, Judith H. 2016. "Tracing the Use of the Bible in Colonial Land Claims in North America." *The Bible in Political Debate: What Does It Really Say?*, ed. Frances Flannery and Rodney A. Werline. New York: Bloomsbury T&T Clark, pp. 127–40.

Leeser, Isaac

Isaac Leeser (1806–1868) was one of the most influential American Jews of the nineteenth century. Born and educated in Westphalia, Germany, he immigrated to Richmond, Virginia, in 1824. Four years later, he moved to Philadelphia, where he served as a *chazzan* (reader) for Philadelphia's Mikveh Israel congregation, later serving a newly formed congregation, Beth El Emeth (Seller 1968a, 231).

Leeser was a leading figure in Philadelphia, founding numerous organizations, some of which remain to this day. He sought to bring practices from American Protestantism into Jewish worship, including the idea of preaching, and his speeches and sermons, which were compiled into his *Discourses on the Jewish Religion*, eventually filled ten volumes (Sussman 1985, 163). He served as the long-time editor of a monthly journal entitled the *Occident*, which was especially notable for containing a friendly dialogue with Protestant clergymen on doctrinal issues (Seller 1968a). He also served as a chaplain for wounded soldiers in Philadelphia during the Civil War. He sought to see that rabbis were commissioned as chaplains during the war, fought against state laws barring Jews from public office, opposed blue laws requiring businesses to close down on Sundays, and fought against laws requiring religious instruction and Bible reading in public schools.

Leeser's central contribution to Jewish American life was his translation of the Hebrew Bible into English, which he completed in 1853–1854. One fascinating aspect of his work is that he believed that God was looking over his own work as a translator to assure its accuracy (Sussman 1985, 172). He was familiar with a wide variety of previous translations, including the Mendelssohn Bible, which had been published in German from 1783 to 1791. Leeser published a revised edition of his own Bible in 1856, publishing it in a smaller, more accessible version, and choosing to put greater distance between it and the dominant King James Version. It remained the dominate Bible among American Jews until the Jewish Publication Society edition of another version in 1917, which has, in turn, been subsequently succeeded by another entitled the Tanakh—the Hebrew acronym for the three grand divisions known as the Torah, or Pentateuch; the Nevi'im, or Prophets; and the Ketuvim, or Writings (Levitt 2011, 83). In 2018, Paul V. Mankowski further published a three-volume translation of the Hebrew Bible with commentary.

Like his American evangelical counterparts, Leeser held a deep conviction that the Bible was the word of God. Indeed, Lance Sussman says that he considered it to be "the only source of religious truth" (1985, 170). In his final sermon of 1847, Leeser listed five basic dogmas that the Bible had revealed. These included "the existence of God, including his unity, eternity, unchangeability, incorporeality, and sole claim to worship"; "the existence of revelation" with particular confidence in "the truth of the prophets, especially the great teacher of Israel, Moses"; the "existence of rewards and punishments"; the coming of a messenger who will bring true knowledge of God; and "the resurrection of the dead, embracing the spiritual perfection of all the intelligent beings that ever emanated from the creative hand of God" (170).

Leeser also believed that the land of Palestine would be restored to the Jewish people, and, although he never visited, he sought to promote economic development there (Seller 1968b). In the meantime, however, he encouraged German Jews to assimilate into America by learning English (one reason he chose to translate Scripture into English rather than German), by celebrating American holidays such as Thanksgiving, and by participating in public affairs.

See also Judaism; King James Version of the Bible; Zionism

For Reference and Further Reading

Alter, Robert. *The Hebrew Bible: A Translation with Commentary*. 3 vols. New York: W. W. Norton.

Levitt, Laura S. 2011. "Beyond a Shared Inheritance: American Jews Reclaim the Hebrew Bible." *The Calling of the Nations: Exegesis, Ethnography, and Empire in a Biblical-Historic Present*, ed. Mark Vessey, Sharon V. Betcher, Robert A. Daum, and Harry O. Maier. Toronto: University of Toronto Press, pp. 83–101.

Seller, Maxine S. 1968a. "Isaac Leeser: A Jewish-Christian Dialogue in Antebellum Philadelphia." *Pennsylvania History: A Journal of Mid-Atlantic Studies* 35 (July): 231–42.

Seller, Maxine S. 1968b. "Isaac Leeser's Views on the Restoration of a Jewish Palestine." *American Jewish Historical Quarterly* 58 (September): 118–35.

Sussman, Lance J. 1985. "Another Look at Isaac Leeser and the First Jewish Translation of the Bible in the United States." *Modern Judaism* 5 (May): 159–90.

Leland, John

John Leland (1754–1841) was a Baptist preacher who was one of the primary proponents of freedom of conscience in early America. Born in Massachusetts, he spent quite a number of years in Virginia before returning as a pastor to his native state.

In Virginia, Leland lent strong support to the disestablishment of the Episcopal Church. He is believed to have met with James Madison to help persuade him to support the addition of a bill of rights to the U.S. Constitution that would provide for freedom of conscience, and in his later years he worked to disestablish the Congregational churches in Connecticut and Massachusetts.

Although he himself was a life-long evangelist, he was skeptical that the establishment of Bible societies, missionary societies, and related organizations would advance the gospel as much as calls by the Holy Spirit to individual action.

In part because of Jefferson's and Madison's support for religious freedom, Leland became a strong Democratic-Republican, even in the wake of accusations that Jefferson was a Deist rather than a Christian. On January 2, 1802, Leland arrived at the White House from Massachusetts to present Jefferson with a large Cheshire cheese, which was reportedly made from the milk of nine hundred Democratic-Republican cows. Soon thereafter, Leland gave a speech to the Congress based on Matthew 12:42 observing, in obvious reference to President Jefferson, that the Queen of Sheba would condemn the generation that rejected Jesus, for "she came from the uttermost parts of the earth to hear the wisdom of Solomon; and, behold, a greater than Solomon is here."

On July 5 of that year, Leland delivered an oration to celebrate Independence Day. In his opening paragraphs, he ranked the American Revolution with "the creation of the world, the deluge of the earth, the deliverance of Israel from Egypt, the founding of Rome, the birth of Christ, the flights of Mahomet, and other important events" (Leland 1802). Reviewing the history of the Revolution, Leland pointed to events that appeared to show that Providence had intervened on behalf of the American cause. In obvious reference to words that Jesus spoke (of himself) in Matthew 22:30, Leland observed that "when equitable laws are administered by a magistrate, in whom the people place confidence, their yoke is easy and their burden is light." He contrasted such burdens to those that Rehoboam had attempted to levy through taxes when he tried to gain Solomon's throne.

Noting claims for the necessity of energy in government that Federalists often advocated, Leland observed, "Those who are always contending for the energy of government, generally have some office under that government, either in their own hands or the hands of their friends, which makes the government a profit to them, rather than a burden; and they wish that profit to be secured by energetic laws." He further observed that "I would as soon give my vote to a wolf to be a shepherd, as to a man, who is always contending for the energy of government, to be a ruler."

Leland believed that "state-established religion . . . is spiritual tyranny—the worst of despotism. It is turnpiking the way to heaven by human law, in order to establish ministerial gates to collect toll. It converts religion into a principle of state policy, and the gospel into merchandise." Leland hoped for the day when heaven might "move on the minds of their masters, and open a way in Providence to bring them out of bondage, with the consent of their masters, and consistent with good policy." Expressing similar concern over the tyranny he associated with religious establishments, Leland likewise drew a comparison to the Egyptian Pharaoh. Just as Pharaoh has spoken to Moses, "Go ye and serve the Lord, but let your flocks and herds be staid" (Exodus 10:24), so the leaders of Massachusetts said, "Go ye and serve the Lord, but pay for building the parish meetinghouse, and the salary of the teacher of piety, morality and religion." As his speech ended, Leland proposed numerous toasts, almost all of which were in support of Democratic-Republican policies.

In 1802, Leland also published a pamphlet in which he opposed the Connecticut practice of requiring everyone either to contribute to the support of ministers or to get a special exemption by specifying another church to which they were giving. In this essay, Leland argued that government by contract was superior to that of monarchy or aristocracy, which he associated with established churches. Much like Roger Williams had argued before him, Leland believed that such arrangements corrupted the church. Because he believed that one's relationship to God was a matter of private conscience, he argued that "government has no more to do with the religious opinions of men than it has with the principles of the mathematics" (Leland 1802 in Sandoz 1991, 1089).

Although this pamphlet did not, as one might expect sermons to do, work from a single text, he wove a number of scriptural themes into his work. At one point, probably drawing from 1 Corinthians 1:27 and Matthew 11:25, he rhetorically asked, "Has God chosen many of the wise and learned? Has he not hidden the mystery of gospel truth from them and revealed it to babes?" (Leland 1802 in Sandoz 1991, 1090). Perhaps drawing from Scottish Common Sense philosophy, Leland again asked, "Is not the vision written so plain that he that runs may read it. Do not those who understand the original languages which the bible was written in differ as much in judgment as others? Are the identical copies of Matthew, Mark, Luke and John together with the epistles, in every university, and in the hands of every master of arts?" (Leland 1802 in Sandoz 1991, 1090).

Leland noted that "Mahomet called in the use of law and sword to convert people to his religion; but Jesus did not, does not" (Leland 1802 in Sandoz 1991, 1095). Leland further associated the conversion of the virgin bride of Christ (the church) into a harlot, with the church's association with the state and the establishment of the papacy. Recognizing, however, that the establishment clause of the First Amendment only limited actions of the national government, Leland knew that if the people of Connecticut wanted to disestablish their church, they had to do it on their own (Leland 1802 in Sandoz 1991, 1098).

See also Jefferson Bible; Madison, James; Sunday Mail Delivery; Williams, Roger

For Reference and Further Reading

Butterfield, L. H. 1952. "Elder John Leland, Jeffersonian Itinerant." *American Antiquarian Society* 62: 156–242.

Dreisbach, Daniel L. 2001. "Mr. Jefferson, a Mammoth Cheese, and the 'Wall of Separation between Church and State': A Bicentennial Commemoration." *Journal of Church and State* 43 (Autumn): 725–45.

Leland, John. July 5, 1802. "An Oration Delivered at Cheshire." Writings of Elder John Leland, pp. 201–11. http ://www.paradisepbc.org/Articles/John%20Leland/Writings%20of%20Elder%20John%20Leland.pdf.

Leland, John. 1802. *The Connecticut Dissenters' Strong Box.* New London, CT: Charles Holt. Printed in Sandoz, Ellis, ed. *Political Sermons of the American Founding Era, 1730-1805.* Indianapolis: Liberty Fund, pp. 1081–99.

Liberty Bell

The Liberty Bell was commissioned by a legislature in which Quakers dominated. Its inscription immortalizes some of the words of Leviticus 25:10 as found in the King James Version of the Bible.

Leviticus is the third book of the Torah (the first five books of the law in Hebrew Scriptures, which are often attributed to Moses) and of the Christian Old Testament, which details laws related to priests and Levites. The passage, which quotes words that the prophet Moses received on Mount Sinai, where he also received the Ten Commandments, is an elaboration upon the fourth commandment, which required the Jews to "remember the Sabbath day, and keep it holy" (Exodus 20:8).

Leviticus 25:8–11 thus says,

> And thou shalt number seven sabbaths of years unto thee, seven times seven years; and the space of the seventh Sabbaths of years shall be unto thee forty and nine years. Then shalt thou cause the trumpet of the jubilee to sound on the tenth day of the seventh month, in the day of atonement shall ye make the trumpet sound throughout all your land. And ye shall hallow the fiftieth year, and proclaim liberty throughout all the land unto all the inhabitants thereof: it shall be a jubilee unto you; and ye shall return every man unto his possession, and ye shall return every man unto his family. A jubilee shall that fiftieth year be unto you: ye shall not sow, neither reap that which growth of itself in it, nor gather the grapes in it of thy vine undressed.

In addition to setting aside the Sabbath day for rest and worship, this passage indicated that the people were also obligated to set aside every fiftieth year—some (see Bergsma, 2005) think forty-ninth—as its own Sabbath. During this year, for which the people were to prepare in advance, they would give the land itself a rest by not sowing or cultivating it. In addition to allowing the land to lie fallow for a year, this year was to be one where tribal lands that had been sold or forfeited to individuals outside the tribe would be returned, debts would be forgiven, and those who had been held in slavery would be freed. Despite this clear command, it is not clear that the year was ever implemented (Chase 1990, 134), perhaps highlighting America's own later gap between aspirations and practice.

An extensive collection of sermons from the American founding period cites two sermons from Leviticus 25. The first is from verses 14–17 and the second from verses 44–46 (Sandoz 1991, 589, 1050). Somewhat ironically, although the first passage references the Year of Jubilee, the latter passage was actually used to justify slavery of foreigners, especially the Gibeonites.

The passage in Leviticus 25 is often tied to a corresponding passage in the opening verses of Isaiah 61. The first two verses of this passage, which Luke 4:16–21 records Jesus reading in a synagogue at the start of his ministry (Monshouwer 1991), say, "The Spirit of the Lord God is upon me; because the LORD hath anointed me to preach good tidings unto the meek; he hath sent me to bind up the brokenhearted, to proclaim liberty to the captives, and the opening of the prison to them that are bound; To proclaim the accepted year of the LORD, and the day of vengeance of our God; to Comfort all that mourn."

Given the role of the family of Isaac Norris in the reception of Penn's Charter Privileges of 1701, a predecessor to subsequent written constitutions, many scholars believe that, in addition to the more practical function of being heard throughout the city, the bell may have been commissioned to mark the fiftieth anniversary, or Jubilee, of this event. However, the bells ended up being dated 1752 and 1753, their dates of manufacture rather than the year in which they were commissioned.

This use of Jubilee may, over times, have melded with others. The Liberty Bell was thus rung on the fiftieth anniversary, or Jubilee, of the adoption of the Declaration of Independence and again on news of the death that day of John Adams and Thomas Jefferson. Just as the Jewish Jubilee was to mark freedom for the captive, so too the Liberty Bell rose to prominence as part of the campaign by abolitionists against American slavery.

Consistent with colonial practice, the Jubilee Year was announced by a bell rather than by a trumpet or ram's horn—one nineteenth-century source, perhaps trying to bridge this gap, observed that the bell was "the trumpet that told the Britishers a tale of vengeance!" (Watson 1852, 16). Further consistent with the Christian emphasis on the need for evangelism, liberty would not only be practiced but also "proclaimed" throughout the land. In what would arguably be an exegetical basis for applying the admonition to American slaves and later to the women's suffrage movement (and even to resident aliens), the proclamation was to be proclaimed not only throughout "all the land" but also to "all the inhabitants thereof" rather than simply to those who would have been recognized as equal citizens.

Malcolm Chase observed that in England, the idea of the Jubilee, especially among Methodists, was "closely associated with ideas of spiritual renewal, religious liberty and the Second Coming" (1990, 137). Within America, Quakers were especially associated with religious liberty, which was a hallmark of the colony. In 1857, George B. Cheever authored a book titled *God against Slavery and the Freedom and Duty of the Pulpit to Rebuke It, as a Sin against God*, in which he based a good bit of his argument on Leviticus 25 (Kramer 1975, 86).

In 1873, John Shoemaker, who was chair of the Philadelphia Centennial Committee, tied the Liberty Bell to the Year of Jubilee. He thus observed,

> This is true, there appears to have been no first jubilee to all the inhabitants on our fiftieth anniversary—too many millions of our inhabitants were then in slavery—we then could not fully carry out the text and proclaim liberty to all. But now upon the second fiftieth year we are able to do so. Cracked and shattered as the bell may be the base upon which that motto is cast remains firm and solid, and shaken as has our country been with the din of battle and bloody strife, that principle remains pure and perfect for all time to come and the whole text, Liberty Jubilee, will be literally carried out in 1876. "Liberty can now be proclaimed throu all the land to all inhabitants thereof." (quoted in Paige 1988, 85)

In remarks at bicentennial celebrations in Philadelphia on July 4, 1976, after observing that he was standing in front of "the great bronze bell that joyously rang out the news of the birth of our Nation from the steeple of the State House," President Gerald R. Ford observed that although "it was never intended to be a church bell," it contained a Bible verse from the book of Leviticus that "refers to the ancient Jewish year of Jubilee" during which "the land and the equality of persons that prevailed when the children of Israel entered the land of promise" were restored. Further noting that "our Founding Fathers knew their Bibles as well as their Blackstone [a noted British judge and writer of treatises]," Ford said, "They boldly reversed the age-old political theory that kings derive their powers from God and asserted that both powers and unalienable rights belong to the people as direct endowments from their Creator."

The biblical inscription from Leviticus on the Liberty Bell, like the inscription "In God We Trust" on U.S. coins, the words "one nation, under God" in the pledge to the U.S. flag, and such song lyrics as "God bless America" are examples of civil religion that mix secular and sacred symbolism.

In 1926, the Union of Jewish Orthodox Congregations erected a replica of the Liberty Bell in New York City in which the biblical inscription ("Proclaim Liberty . . .") was spelled out in Hebrew as "U grathem Dror Ba aretz Lihal Yoshvah" (Paige 1988, 95).

In 2016, the Museum of the Bible installed what it called "an exact replica of the Liberty Bell" as its first exhibit. Commissioned in 2003 by the Providence Forum to recognize the three hundredth anniversary of William Penn's Charter of Liberties (which was actually given in 1701) and cast by the same Whitechapel Foundry that cast the original, the replica, which is called "The Spirit of Liberty," is 3,200 pounds, which is actually more than 1,000 pounds heavier than the original ("Museum of the Bible"). Guests were permitted to ring the bell, which peals out an E flat, which is symbolically mounted from wood from what is believed to be the last Liberty Tree, which came from Annapolis, Maryland.

See also Moses as Political Archetype; Quakers; Slavery; Ten Commandments

For Reference and Further Reading

Bergsma, John S. 2005. "Once Again, the Jubilee, Every 49 or 50 years?" *Vetus Testamentum* 55 (January): 121–25.

Chase, Malcolm. 1990. "From Millennium to Anniversary: The Concept of Jubilee in Late Eighteenth- and Nineteenth-Century England." *Past & Present* 129 (November): 132–47.

Ford, Gerald R. July 4, 1976. "Remarks of Gerald R. Ford in Philadelphia, Pennsylvania (Bicentennial Celebration)." Gerald R. Ford Presidential Library and Museum. https://www.fordlibrarymuseum.gov/library/speeches/760645.asp.

Kramer, Justin. 1975. *Cast in America*. Los Angeles, CA: Justin Kramer.

Monshouwer, D. 1991. "The Reading of the Prophet in the Synagogue at Nazareth." *Biblica* 72: 90–99.

"Museum of the Bible Installs First Exhibit Item: An Exact Replica of the Liberty Bell." Press Release. https://www.charismanews.com/us/59303-museum-of-the-bible-installs-first-exhibit.

Paige, John C. 1988. *The Liberty Bell of Independence National Historical Park: A Special History Study*, ed. David C. Kimball. Denver, CO: Denver Service Center, National Park Service, Department of the Interior.

Sandoz, Ellis, ed. 1991. *Political Sermons of the American Founding Era, 1730–1805*. Indianapolis, IN: Liberty Fund.

Vile, John R. 2019. *The Liberty Bell and Its Legacy: An Encyclopedia of an American Icon in U.S. History and Culture*. Santa Barbara, CA: ABC-CLIO.

Watson, Henry C. 1852. *The Old Bell of Independence; Or, Philadelphia in 1776*. Philadelphia: Lindsay and Blakiston.

Lieberman, Joseph

Joe Lieberman (b. 1942) of Connecticut earned his undergraduate and law degrees at Yale University, served for six years as the state's attorney general, and served from 1989 to 2013 in the U.S. Senate, first as a Democrat and later as an independent. Lieberman is an observant Jew who may be best known for having been the vice presidential candidate on the ticket with Al Gore in 2000 that received the most number of popular votes but lost in the Electoral College. Lieberman believes that his own opportunity to run as a Jew opened the way for Barack Obama (an African American) and others to run for office as well. In a speech that Lieberman gave at Brigham Young University, he thus cited Jesse Jackson as saying, "Each time a barrier falls for one person, the doors of opportunity open wider for every other American" (Lieberman 2011a).

Throughout his career, Lieberman has been a strong supporter of the state of Israel and has talked to audiences about his faith. In a speech that he gave to Christians United for Israel (CUFI), he introduced himself by saying, "I am your brother Joseph," said that pastor John Hagee reminded him of Miriam and Moses, and emphasized their common belief in God and the Bible. He further said that Israel needed to be prepared for war with Iran much in the way that Jacob had prepared to meet his estranged brother Esau (Gedalyahu 2008).

He notes that the Puritans who settled England, like fellow Jews, put strong emphasis on the law of Moses, and he believes that the principle of equality that the Declaration of Independence articulates is similar to the biblical principle that all human beings are created in the image of God.

In recent years, Lieberman has put particular emphasis on the importance of keeping the Sabbath, and he has written a book on the subject (Lieberman 2011b). More recently, he has written a book of essays in conjunction with Rabbi Ari D. Kahn, which are suitable for reading during the forty-nine days between the celebration of the Jewish Passover, commemorating deliverance from Egypt and Shavuot, which commemorates the giving of the Ten Commandments, and largely focusing on Hebrew Scriptures. He observes that God did not secure freedom for the Israelites simply so they could "be free in the desert, but, consistent with Exodus 5:1, so that the people could serve him" (Lieberman 2018, 6). Lieberman further believes that "the freedom God granted on Passover will inevitably lead to chaos, violence, and immorality without the law and the values God presented on Shavuot" (xiv). He favorably cited the teaching of Hillel in Shabbat 31a, that the law could be summarized by the command, "That which is despicable to you, do not do to your fellow. This is the entire Torah; the rest is commentary. Go and learn," which he further identifies as the "Golden Rule" (13–14).

Lieberman's essays reflect on a number of topics. For example, citing Genesis 15:16, in which God proclaims to Abraham that "the iniquity of the Emorites is not yet full," Lieberman observes that "Abraham's descendants could inherit the land only when the current inhabitants forfeited their right to it" (34). He approvingly cites Pope Benedict XVI as saying, "When every man lives without law, every man lives without freedom" (38). He argues that "commitment to the rule of law unifies a nation" (43).

Lieberman lauds the Ten Commandments as the first system of law that "came from God" (58), and he devotes separate chapters in his book to each of the Ten Commandments. At one point he notes with pride that he took his oath of office on a Hebrew Bible that was given to him by his father, who had received it, like other Jews, when he enlisted to fight during World War II. At another point he compares interpreting the U.S. Constitution to interpreting the Bible, comparing the development of the constitutional right to privacy to the manner in which rabbis were not permitted to add to commandments but they could "interpret and apply them to emerging realities" (101). Citing Isaiah 1:15–17 and 1 Samuel 15:22, Lieberman further stressed that it was better to obey God than to engage in offerings and sacrifices (104).

Lieberman recounts the time that he prepared a talk before the National Prayer Breakfast for Senator Abraham Ribicoff, in which he argued that the God of the Old Testament was a God of love rather than of vengeance, who like a "loving father . . . sets standards of behavior for His children and chastises them when they fail to meet those standards" (131). He further cites an interpretation of the biblical book of Ruth as "an allegory for acceptance of the Ten Commandments and Torah by the Israelites as Sinai, and the fulfillment of the covenant between Abraham and God" (147).

See also Constitutional Interpretation; Declaration of Independence; Hagee, John; Judaism; Moses as Political Archetype; Puritans; Ten Commandments; U.S. Constitution; Zionism

For Reference and Further Reading

Gedalyahu, Tzvi Ben. 2008. "Bible-Thumping Joe Lieberman Connects Esau with Iran." Israel National News. July 29. www.israelnationalnews.com/News/News.aspx/126988.

Lieberman, Joseph. 2011a. "Faith and the Public Square." October 25. https://speeches.byu.edu/talks/joseph-lieberman/faith-and-the-public-square.

Lieberman, Joe. 2011b. *The Gift of Rest: Rediscovering the Beauty of the Sabbath*. New York: Howard Books.

Lieberman, Joe, with Ari D. Kahn. 2018. *With Liberty and Justice: The Fifty-Day Journey from Egypt to Sinai*. New Milford, CT: Maggid Books and OU Press.

Lincoln, Abraham

Probably no individual who became U.S. president infused his speeches with more biblical references than did Abraham Lincoln (1809–1865). Indeed, Elton Trueblood observed that in Lincoln's "First Lecture on Discoveries and Inventions," he included thirty-four separate references to the Bible (1973, 59). Born in a log cabin in Kentucky, Lincoln's sparsely furnished home included copies of John Bunyan's *Pilgrim's Progress*, *Aesop's Fables*, and the Bible (Huhn 2011, 1).

Lincoln went on to study and practice law, serve in Congress (where he opposed U.S. entry into the Mexican War), debate Stephen Douglas for a Senate seat from Illinois, and be selected as the sixteenth president of the United States. His election led to the secession of eleven southern states, and Lincoln's resolve that the Union was perpetual led him to lead America's bloodiest War (1861–1865), shortly after the successful conclusion of which he was assassinated by John Wilkes Booth and succeeded by Andrew Johnson.

As a young man living in New Salem, Illinois, Lincoln appears to have been influenced by reading the skeptical works of Thomas Paine and the French philosopher Constantin Volney (1757–1820) and to have developed a reputation for infidelity. It appears that he even wrote a short book on the subject that a friend burned rather than have it become an issue in his political campaigns (Mansfield

2012, 42). In running for Congress in 1843, Lincoln felt it necessary to issue a denial:

> A Charge having got into circulation in some of the neighborhoods of this District, in substance that I am an open scoffer at Christianity, I have by the advice of some friends concluded to notice the subject in this form. That I am not a member of any Christian Church, is true, but I have never denied the truth of the Scripture; and I have never spoken with intentional disrespect of religion in general, or of any denomination of Christians in particular. It is true that in early life I was inclined to believe in what I understand is called the "Doctrine of necessity"—that is, that the human mind is impelled to action, or held in rest by some power, over which the mind itself has no control. (Mansfield 2012, 64–65)

In addition to periods of melancholia, Lincoln and his wife went through periods of deep depression after the deaths (at different times) of two of their sons. Some accounts suggest that these periods were eased in part by Lincoln's belief that his sons might still be alive in heaven.

Lincoln regularly attended church without ever becoming a member. This may have stemmed in part from Lincoln's detestation of hypocrisy and on what he considered to be excessive focus on denominational distinctions. In a conversation with Henry Rankin in 1846, Lincoln was reported to have said that "I cannot without mental reservations assent to long and complicated creeds and catechisms. If the church would ask simply for assent to the Savior's statements of the substance of the law: 'Thou shalt love the Lord thy God with all they heart, and with all they soul, and with all thy might, and thy neighbor as thyself' [Matthew 22:37, 39], that church would I gladly unite with" (Mansfield 2012, 69). Lincoln appears to have been impressed by *The Christian's Defense*, a work of Christian apologetics written by Rev. James Smith of the Springfield First Presbyterian Church. He is known to have kept a Bible on his desk and at a table near his sofa and to have carried a New Testament (127). When presented with a Bible by the "Loyal Colored People of Baltimore," he said, "In regard to this Great book, I have but to say, it is the best gift God has given to man. All the good the Savior gave to the world was communicated through this book. But for it we could not know right from wrong. All things most desirable for man's welfare, here and hereafter, are to be found portrayed in it" (151).

This book includes essays that focus on biblical references in three of Lincoln's most notable addresses. These are the "House Divided" Speech that he gave to the Illinois Republican Convention in 1858, his famed Gettysburg Address of 1863, and his second inaugural address in 1865. Far from being exhaustive, these speeches are but indications of Lincoln's wider rhetoric.

In addition to these three speeches, Wilson Huhn examines four other instances where Lincoln's understanding of the Bible played a prominent role. In responding in Peoria, Illinois, to a speech that Senator Stephen Douglas gave defending the Kansas–Nebraska Act, which overturned the Missouri Compromise and provided for popular sovereignty whereby territories would decide whether or not they wanted to establish slavery, Lincoln drew from Luke 6:45 to say, "It still will be the abundance of man's heart, that slavery extension is wrong; and out of the abundance of his heart, his mouth will continue to speak" (Huhn 2011, 9).

In a speech in Chicago on July 10, 1858, Lincoln built a speech around the words from the Declaration of Independence declaring that "all men are created equal," through which he sought to interpret the U.S. Constitution in an expansive fashion. In so doing, Lincoln relied heavily on Matthew 5:58, reversing the order of the phrases, to say, "As your Father in Heaven is perfect, be ye also perfect" (Huhn 2011, 14).

Lincoln pursued a similar theme in a speech at Lewistown, Illinois, on August 17, 1858. Referring again to the principles of the Declaration of Independence, Lincoln encouraged his audience to "return to the fountain whose waters spring close by the blood of the Revolution" (Huhn 2011, 15). Huhn traces this imagery to the Song of Songs 4:15; Jeremiah 2:13; Isaiah 58:11; and Revelation 7:13–14 (2011, 16).

Likewise, in early 1861, Lincoln left a fragment meditating on the relationship between the Declaration of Independence and the Constitution. Citing Proverbs 25:11, Lincoln observed that "the assertion of that *principle* [liberty to all within the Declaration of Independence], *at that time,* was the word, *'fitly spoken'* which has proved an 'apple of gold' to us. The *Union,* and the *Constitution,* are the *picture* of *silver,* subsequently framed around it. The picture was made, not to *conceal,* or *destroy* the apple; but to *adorn,* and *preserve* it. The *picture* was made *for* the apple—*not* the apple for the picture" (quoted in Huhn 2011, 20). In Huhn's reading, Lincoln thus identifies the Declaration of Independence with "the Word of God, the Bible," and the existing American government as "the Church, the vessel carrying the word." Quoting Trueblood, Huhn thus argues that Lincoln's religion "was centered far more in the Bible than in the Church" (21).

In summarizing Lincoln's approach to the Bible, Huhn concludes that Lincoln "read the Bible daily but he did not interpret it literally." Instead of merely dropping "isolated biblical quotations into his speeches and letters to convey an impression of religiosity," he evoked "myriad associations with the biblical contexts from which the quotations are taken. It is not the words themselves but the meaning behind the words that he seeks to convey" (36–37).

The King James Version of the Bible on which Lincoln took his presidential oath of office has since been used in the inaugurations of Barack Obama and Donald Trump.

See also Declaration of Independence; Lincoln, Abraham (Gettysburg Address); Lincoln, Abraham (House Divided Speech); Lincoln, Abraham (Second Inaugural Address); Lincoln Inaugural Bible; Presidential Inaugural Bibles

For Reference and Further Reading

Huhn, Wilson. 2011. "A Higher Law: Abraham Lincoln's Use of Biblical Imagery." Rutgers Journal of Law and Religion, forthcoming; U of Akron Legal Studies Research Paper No. 11-1. Available at SSRN: https://ssrn.com/abstract=17482, 38pp.

Mansfield, Stephen. 2012. *Lincoln's Battle with God: A President's Struggle with Faith and What It Meant for America.* Nashville, TN: Thomas Nelson.

Trueblood, Elton. 1973. *Abraham Lincoln: Theologian of American Anguish.* New York: HarperOne.

Lincoln, Abraham (Gettysburg Address)

Probably no speech is better known than the 272-word speech that President Abraham Lincoln delivered at the dedication of a national cemetery at Gettysburg, Pennsylvania, on November 19, 1863. On July 2 of that year, Union forces had beaten back an attack by Confederate forces under General Robert E. Lee, whose army had penetrated farther north than any previous general, but the battle had been costly on both sides, and Lincoln sought to make sense of the sacrifice and its larger meaning for the Union.

Lincoln's second inaugural address in 1865 would show that he had one of the most profound understandings of Scripture of any U.S. president. Although Lincoln did not quote a single Scripture in his Gettysburg Address, his speech masterfully embodied both the cadence of the King James Version of the Bible and the Book of Common Prayer while employing language that evoked specific scriptural passages.

Lincoln's opening paragraph somewhat anachronistically referred to the nation's birth "four score and seven years ago," which would indicate that the nation had already exceeded the years ("three score and ten") that Psalm 90:10 had allocated to a typical man. Huhn (2011) notes that other biblical references with the word "fourscore" had applied to Abram (Genesis 16:16) , Moses (Exodus 7:7), Barzilla (2 Samuel 19:32), and Caleb (Joshua 14:10–11). These words indicated that Lincoln dated the nation's birth to the Declaration of Independence, with its "proposition that all men are created equal," rather than to the U.S. Constitution, with its more ambiguous response to the issue of slavery.

Lincoln's reference to "our fathers" further evoked Old Testament patriarchs, including his own biblical namesake, who was recognized as both the father of the Jews (through Jacob) and the Arabs (through Ishmael), or perhaps Jacob and Esau (the twin sons of Isaac). This reference may have reminded listeners of the opening "Our Father" of the Lord's Prayer while Lincoln's reference to hallowing the ground of the battlefield may further have evoked the phrase "hallowed be thy name" (Dreisbach 2013). The words "brought forth" evoked the creation story in Genesis 1:12, 21; Moses's liberation of the Israelites from their bondage in Israel in the book of Exodus, which was tied to numerous anti-slavery narratives of the period; and the birth of Jesus to Mary (Dreisbach 2013).

The Bible associates the death of Jesus with the salvation of his people—a theme also reflected in "The Battle Hymn of the Republic." So too, in the second paragraph of his address, Lincoln referred to "those who here gave their lives that that nation might live." One of the best known summaries of the sacrificial work of Jesus is incorporated in John 3:16, which says that God sent His Son so that all who believe in Him "shall not perish but have everlasting life." This biblical chapter is also tied to the need for a "new birth" or conversion. Again, without quoting directly from this passage, Lincoln concludes his speech with the hope that "government of the people, by the people, for the people, shall not perish from the earth." This terminology is also close to that of Job 18:17 and Jeremiah 10:11.

One might find further parallels to the book of James—with its emphasis on how works confirm one faith—with Lincoln's sentiments, as expressed in his third paragraph, that "we can not consecrate—we can not hallow—this ground," but that "the brave men, living and dead, who struggled here" have already done so.

Daniel Dreisbach (2017) has observed that "Lincoln's invocation of the unmistakable gospel themes of conception, birth, death, and rebirth, and, in particular, equating the sacrificial shed blood of Union soldiers with Christ's atoning death at Calvary, has struck some critics as verging on blasphemy." By contrast, Dreisbach views Lincoln's second inaugural address as "a sincere meditation on the will and ways of God in a partisan conflict in which both sides pray to the same God and solicit the same God's assistance."

See also Battle Hymn of the Republic; Lincoln, Abraham (Second Inaugural Address)

For Reference and Further Reading

Boritt, Gabor. 2006. *The Gettysburg Gospel: The Lincoln Speech That Nobody Knows.* New York: Simon & Schuster.

Brown, Matthew. 2013. "Gettysburg Address Laced with Religious Language and Meaning." Deseret News. November 19. https://www.deseretnews.com/article/865590845/Gettysburg-Address-laced-with-religious-language-and-meaning.html.

Dreisbach, Daniel. 2013. "The Sacred Sounds of Lincoln's Gettysburg Address." Law & Liberty November 19. https://www.lawliberty.org/2013/11/19/the-sacred-sounds-of-lincolns-gettysburg-address/.

Dreisbach, Daniel L. 2017. "The Promises and Perils of Using the Bible in Political Discourse." February. www.bibleinterp.com/articles/2017/02/dre418022.shtml.

Elmore, A. E. *Lincoln's Gettysburg Address: Echoes of the Bible and the Book of Common Prayer.* Carbondale: Southern Illinois University Press.

Huhn, Wilson. 2011. "A Higher Law: Abraham Lincoln's Use of Biblical Imagery." Rutgers Journal of Law and Religion, forthcoming; U of Akron Legal Studies Research Paper No. 11-1. Available at SSRN: https://ssrn.com/abstract=17482, 38pp.

Smith, Peter. 2013. "President Lincoln's Gettysburg Address Had Biblical Cadence." *Pittsburgh Post-Gazette.* November 18. https://www.post-gazette.com/Gettysburg-Stories/2013/11/19/Address-had-biblical-cadence/stories/201311190063. Accessed March 29, 2019.

Wills, Garry. 2006. *Lincoln at Gettysburg: The Words that Remade America.* New York: Simon & Schuster.

Lincoln, Abraham (House Divided Speech)

When he delivered his speech to the Illinois Republican Convention on June 16, 1858, Lincoln appropriated and extended on a biblical analogy from the teachings of Jesus in Mark 3:25, and other gospel references (some of which refer instead to a "kingdom"), which admonished that "if a house be divided against itself, that house cannot stand."

Theodore Parker (1810–1860) had on July 2, 1854, delivered a "Sermon Preached on the Dangers which Threaten the Rights of Man in America," which he published not long after (Elmore 2009, 3) and which had mentioned this analogy, but Lincoln refined and extended on it.

Arguing that he did not believe the U.S. government could "endure, permanently half slave and half free," Lincoln portrayed the nation split between those like him who wanted to stop the further spread of slavery and those, like his opponent Stephen Douglas, who were either indifferent about its spread or, like those in the South, who were actively promoting its spread.

Whereas the analogy was but one of many that Parker employed, Lincoln continued to weave the analogy throughout his speech, noting that those favoring the expansion of slavery appeared to be working in tandem to build a solid house for slavery. Whereas Parker had questioned whether "it is possible for the Anglo-Saxons of America to remain as one nation for a great many years," Lincoln had stated that "I do not expect the Union to be *dissolved*—I do not expect the house to *fall*—but I *do* expect it will cease to be divided" (Elmore 2009, 5–6).

As president, Lincoln insisted that the Union was perpetual, and that he was sworn to uphold it. The war that he waged to preserve the Union ultimately ended with the abolition of involuntary servitude, which had been the central issue of division.

In addition to using the analogy from the Bible, Lincoln accused proponents of slavery of working together to hide their designs from the people, which he likened to "the cautious *patting* and *petting* of a spirited horse, preparatory to mounting him, when it is dreaded that he may give the rider a fall."

See also Civil War; Lincoln, Abraham; Slavery

For Reference and Further Reading

Elmore, A. E. 2009. *Lincoln's Gettysburg Address: Echoes of the Bible and Book of Common Prayer*. Carbondale: Southern Illinois University Press.

Lincoln, Abraham. 1858. "House Divided Speech." June 16. www.abrahamlincolnonline.org/lincoln/speeches/house.htm.

Lincoln, Abraham (Second Inaugural Address)

Although Lincoln's Gettysburg Address may be better known, his second inaugural address, which he delivered on March 4, 1865, is arguably more theologically profound. C. Clifton Black believes that this address, along with George Washington's Farewell Address, were examples of an *Abschiedrede*, or what he describes as "a patriarch's farewell to his heirs on the eve of his death" similar to those of Jacob, Moses, Socrates, Jesus, and Paul (2014, 172). Although the speech was Lincoln's last major one, unlike his predecessors, he did not deliver it anticipating that it would likely be his last.

In the beginning of his speech, Lincoln observed that Union forces had made gains during his first administration, but tempered his "high hope for the future," by indicating that "no prediction in regard to it is ventured" (Vile 2018, 131). As Lincoln looked backward, his tone was almost fatalistic: "Both parties deprecated war, but one of them would make war rather than let the nation survive, and the other would accept war rather than let it perish, and the war came" (131).

Tying the coming of war specifically to differences between the North and the South over slavery, Lincoln observed that "both read the same Bible and pray to the same God, and each invokes His aid against the other" (132). Thereafter, Lincoln devoted eighty-five of the speech's approximately seven hundred words to Scripture (about 12 percent of his total speech) in what Black describes as "quotations, allusions, or conflations of Scripture that Lincoln's listeners surely recognized" (2014, 180). Black proceeds to delineate nine such references in a useful chart in which he compares the words of Lincoln side by side with those of Scripture.

Prior to assuming the presidency, in speaking of slavery Lincoln had drawn imagery from Revelation 16 in noting that, as war approached, it seemed "as if God had borne with this thing until the very teachers of religion had come to defend it from the Bible to claim for it a divine character and sanction; and now the cup of iniquity is full, and the vials of wrath will be poured out" (McQueen 2018, 4). In noting in his second inaugural address that "it may seem strange that any men should dare to ask a just God's assistance in wringing their bread from the sweat of other men's faces" (Black 2014, 181) Lincoln echoed Genesis 3:19, the curse upon Adam and Eve for their sins, that "in the sweat of thy face shall thou eat bread" (181). In immediately warning "let us judge not, that we be not judged," Lincoln in turn echoed the words of Jesus in Matthew 7:1 (181).

After noting that God could not answer the prayers of both North and South against one another, Lincoln noted that God had answered neither side fully and that "The Almighty has His own purposes" (Vile 2018, 132). In so doing, he echoed the words of the prophet Jeremiah, in 49:20: "Therefore hear the counsel of the LORD . . . and his purposes" (Black 2014, 181).

Lincoln then quoted Scriptures almost word for word (the quotation is within quotation marks in printed versions of his speech) in Matthew 18:7, in which Jesus warned against those who were stumbling blocks. Lincoln thus says, "Woe unto the world because of offenses! For it must needs be that offenses come: but woe to that many by whom the offense cometh" (Black 2014, 181). More generally, the term "woe" was used throughout the Bible to denote impending judgment or catastrophe, especially against those who had done evil.

Lincoln continued by hypothesizing that slavery may be such an offense, "which in the providence of God, must needs come, but which, having continued through His appointed time, He now wills to remove, and that He gives to both North and South this terrible war as the woe due to those by whom the offense came" (Vile 2018, 132). Black observes that what Lincoln calls "His appointed time" closely resembles Habakkuk's "yet for an appointed time" in Habakkuk 2:3. As Lincoln observes that believers could discern no departure "from those divine attributes which the believers in a living God always ascribe to Him," Black notes that the phrase "the living God is among you" is found in Joshua 3:10 (2014, 181).

As he continued his reflection on God's will, Lincoln observed, "Yet, if God wills that it continue until all the wealth piled by the bondsman's two hundred and fifty years of unrequited toil shall be sunk, and until every drop of blood drawn with the lash shall be paid by another drawn with the sword, as was said three thousand years ago, so still it must be said 'the judgments of the Lord are true and righteous altogether'" (Vile 2018, 132). Although the latter phrase might seem more reminiscent of God's judgment against Egypt for enslaving the people of Israel, it is, in fact, another word-for-word quotation, this time from Psalm 19:9 (Black 2014, 181).

In his final sentence, Lincoln pointed the way forward: "With malice toward none, with charity for all, with firmness in the right as God gives us to see the right, let us strive to finish the work we are in, to bind up the nation's wounds, to care for him who shall have borne the battle and for his widow and his orphan, to do all which may achieve and cherish a just and lasting peace among ourselves and with all nations" (Vile 2018, 132). Black observes that this passage resembles Deuteronomy 14:29 (2014, 181), although this is but one of many biblical passages that admonish the people to care for orphans and widows.

Black believes that Lincoln's speech was the product of deep theological reflection, and cites his "Meditation on the Divine Will," which he dated September 1862, as well as a letter to a Tennessee woman's request for the release of her husband, which he authored about December 6, 1864. After she informed Lincoln that her husband was a religious man, Lincoln had observed that "I am not much of a judge of religion, but . . . in my opinion, the religion that sets men to rebel and fight against their government, because, as they think, that government does not sufficiently help some men to eat their bread in the sweat of other men's faces, is not the sort of religion upon which people can get to heaven" (Black 2014, 182–83).

See also Lincoln, Abraham; Moses as Political Archetype; Slavery

For Reference and Further Reading

Black, C. Clifton. 2014. *Reading Scripture with the Saints.* Cambridge: Lutterworth Press.

McQueen, Alison. 2018. *Political Realism in Apocalyptic Times.* New York: Cambridge University Press.

Tanner, John S. "The King James Bible in America: Pilgrim, Prophet, President, Preacher." *Brigham Young University Studies* 50(3): 4–24.

Vile, John R., ed. 2018. *The Civil War and Reconstruction Eras: Documents Decoded.* Santa Barbara, CA: ABC-CLIO.

White, Ronald C., Jr. 2002. *Lincoln's Greatest Speech: The Second Inaugural.* New York: Simon & Schuster.

Lincoln Inaugural Bible

Among inaugural Bibles other than the one that was used for George Washington's first inauguration, probably none is more revered than the Bible that President Abraham Lincoln used for his 1861 inauguration. As a lawyer, Lincoln would undoubtedly have seen many people swear on a Bible in the courtroom. If Lincoln opened the Bible to a particular passage during his swearing in, it does not appear to have been recorded.

Lincoln's relatively small volume is, like Washington's inaugural Bible, a King James Version. Lincoln's own possessions had not yet arrived by train from Illinois, so the Bible that he used was supplied by William Thomas Carroll, the clerk of the U.S. Supreme Court, who had also supplied a different copy for the previous inauguration of James Buchanan (Gilgoff 2008). It was published in 1853 by the Oxford University Press, was eventually donated by Carroll and his wife, Sally, to the Lincoln family, and remained with them until they donated it to the Library of Congress.

The Bible that Lincoln used at his second inauguration has not been located, but he had marked three biblical passages. They were Matthew 7:1: "Judge not, that ye be not judged"; Matthew 18:7: "Woe unto the world because of offences! For it must needs be that offences come; but woe to that many by whom the offense cometh!"; and Revelation 16:7: "And I heard another out of the altar say, Even so, Lord God Almighty, true and righteous are thy judgments," and played a major part in his inaugural address (cited by Winder 2019, 123).

In 2009, President Barack Obama used the Bible, which is signed and sealed by William Thomas Carroll attesting that it was used for Lincoln's oath. Obama chose to use the Bible because of Lincoln's issuance of the Emancipation Proclamation and other orders that led to the abolition of involuntary servitude in the Thirteenth Amendment in 1865 (Campbell 2010, 205). The Library of Congress included the Bible in an exhibit entitled "With Malice toward None" in honor of Lincoln's two hundredth birthday on February 12, 2009 (Raymond 2009).

At his second inauguration, Obama used both the Lincoln Bible and Dr. Martin Luther King Jr.'s "traveling Bible," another King James Version that King had owned since the time he gave his first sermons in 1954. At a private swearing-in on Sunday, January 20, Obama swore on his wife's family Bible while Vice President Joe Biden took his oath on a Bible with a Celtic cross that had been in his family for 120 years (Associated Press 2013).

Trump used this Bible again at his inauguration in 2017, along with a personal Bible that his mother gave him when he graduated from church school at the First Presbyterian Church on June 12, 1955; it was a Revised Standard Version that Thomas Nelson and Sons had published in New York in 1953 (NCC Staff 2017).

In 2019, the family of Rev. Noyes W. Miner, a Baptist minister who had lived across the street from Lincoln in Springfield, Illinois, presented another Bible to the Lincoln Presidential Library and Museum in Springfield, where the Bible, which had largely been lost to history, has been displayed for the first time. One of only six Bibles known to have been owned by Lincoln, the 14 ½ × 11 5/8 inch Bible had been presented to Lincoln in Philadelphia in 1864 when he made a trip there to raise money for wounded soldiers. Its cover read "Presented to Abraham Lincoln, President of the United States, by the Ladies of the Citizens Volunteer Hospital of Philadelphia" and was inscribed with the words "Faith," "Hope," and "Charity" from 1 Corinthians 13:13. The back cover of the Bible, which Mrs. Lincoln had presented to Miner, was further inscribed "Mrs. Abraham Lincoln to N.W. Miner, D.D., Oct. 15, 1872" (Baker 2019).

See also Lincoln, Abraham (Second Inaugural Address); Obama, Barack; Trump, Donald J.; Washington Inaugural Bible

For Reference and Further Reading

Associated Press. 2013. "Obama to Use 2 Bibles When He Takes Oath of Office." Fox News. January 10 [updated December 20, 2015]. https://www.foxnews.com/politics/obama-to-use-2-bibles-when-he-takes-oath-of-office.

Baker, Peter. 2019. "A New Lincoln Bible, from a Mantel to a Presidential Library." *New York Times*. June 19.

Campbell, Gordon. 2010. *Bible: The Story of the King James Version 1611–2011.* New York Oxford University Press.
Gilgoff, Dan. 2008. "The Story behind the Lincoln Bible at Obama's Inauguration." U.S. News. December 23. https://www.usnews.com/news/blogs/god-and-country/2008/12/23/the-story-behind-the-lincoln-bible-at-obamas-inauguration.
NCC Staff. 2017. "How Presidents Use Bibles at Inaugurations." Constitutional Daily. January 20. https://constitutioncenter.org/blog/how-presidents-use-bibles-at-inaugurations/. Accessed March 21, 2019.
Raymond, Matt. 2009. "The Lincoln Inaugural Bible, Chapter and Verse." Library of Congress Blog. January 14. https://blogs.loc.gov/loc/2009/01/the-lincoln-inaugural-bible-chapter-and-verse/.
Winder, Mike. 2019. *Favorite Scriptures of 100 American Leaders.* Springville, UT: Plain Sight.

Lynchings

One of the bitter legacies of American slavery and racism was the rise of mob violence in the wake of the Reconstruction period (1865–1877). The Equal Justice Initiative has thus documented close to four thousand lynchings in twelve southern states between 1877 and 1950 (Bouie 2015). These victims have been recently memorialized in the National Memorial for Peace and Justice that has been established in Montgomery, Alabama.

Although it seems odd to discuss such perversions of justice and due process on a book that focuses on the Bible in American politics and law, many scholars have linked the practice, which often involved the public burning or hanging of the bodies of alleged criminals and the collection of body parts of the victims as souvenirs, to religious rituals, "laded with Christian symbolism and significance" involving the need for blood sacrifice to restore community purity (Bouie 2015). Tying the practice to Deuteronomy 21, Ida Jones observed that verse 23 indicated that "he that is hanged is accursed of God" and observed that "those who see a man thus hanging between heaven and earth, will conclude him abandoned of both, and unworthy of either" (Jones 2002–2003, 51). Civil rights activist Ida B. Wells (1862–1931) observed that white mobs often justified lynching as a way of stopping those who were attempting to provoke riots, as a way of expressing their patriotism, and as a way of protecting white women against sexual attacks (Jones 2002–2003, 49). She further traced such brutality to making a religion of southern history and to the mentality of the lost cause, a phenomenon evident in the Ku Klux Klan and the prominence within its ceremonies of a burning cross.

In addition to violating the biblical command against murder, lynching was inimical to the whole idea of the rule of law. Citing other scholars, Ashraf Rushdy notes that some have "offered a cogent interpretation of lynching as an avatar of Christian ritual sacrifice" (2012, 131). He further noted, however, that "white lynch mobs celebrating in such 'dramatic and public fashion' this act of human sacrifice seemed unaware, and would have been horrified to discover, that in their act 'the Christ had become black'" (131). Moreover, African Americans often associated the lynchings with Jesus's own death on the cross, sometime expressing the hope, as did the mother of Emmett Till, who was lynched in 1955 for allegedly whistling at a white woman and saying "bye baby" to her, that his own death would not be in vain but would awaken others to the evils of racism (Cone 2013, 68–69).

In 1903, Rev. Robert Elwood (1873–1949), who was pastor of the Oliver Presbyterian Church in Wilmington, Delaware, with a reputation as an advocate of progressive political reform and anti-corruption, preached a sermon entitled "Should the Murderer of Miss Bishop Be Lynched?" that stirred a mob to lynch George White, an African American linked by circumstantial evidence to the brutal assault of eighteen-year-old Helen Bishop, who had died from her injuries. Drawing from both the need for a speedy trial as outlined in the Sixth Amendment to the U.S. Constitution and from the Bible, Elwood argued that there was no time for delay. Describing White as "a man with the heart of a beast, with the desires of a fiend, who gave vent to the bestiality and executed this damnable crime," Elwood cited 1 Corinthians 13:9 for the need to "put away from among yourselves that wicked person" (Downey 2001, 137). Citing the prophet Nathan's confrontation with King David after David had committed adultery with the wife of Uriah and had him put in harm's way, Elwood told the crowd, "Let me say to you with a full realization of the responsibility of my words, even as Nathan said to King David of old, after his soldiers had killed Uriah, 'Thou are the man!' So I would say to you, 'The responsibility for lynching would be yours for delaying the execution of the law' " (138). His sermon did not apparently mention Romans 12:10, which advises that vengeance belongs to God.

The next day, a mob gathered at the jail, extracted White, who gave a public confession, shackled him, and lit a fire under him. When he tried to escape, a member of the crowd cut off his right leg while another hit him over the head. After he was burned, several discharged their guns into his body, while others collected souvenirs, with a local physician later displaying his skull and right foot in the window of a local saloon (Downey 2013, 241–42).

Although Elwood faced church discipline, which largely resulted in a mild rebuke (Downey 2001, 145), he became a popular public speaker and moved to a larger congregation. He was eventually dismissed for inappropriate correspondence with a teenage girl, although he died as a minister in good standing at another church (Downey 2013, 252).

Another Wilmington minister, Montrose Thornton, of the local Bethel A.M.E. Church, portrayed the lynching as a complete breakdown of democracy and decency and began his own state-wide campaign against similar injustices (Downey 2013, 247). Reversing the image that Elwood had drawn of George White, Thornton described the white man as "a heathen, a fiend, a monstrosity before God, and is equal to any act in the category of crime" (quoted in Downey 2013, 248). He too moved onto larger congregations as a result of his stance in this case.

See also Segregation and Anti-miscegenation Laws; Slavery; Ten Commandments

For Reference and Further Reading

Bouie, Jamelle. 2015. "Christian Soldiers." *Slate*. February 20. https://slate.com/news-and-politics/2015/02/jim-crow-souths-lynching-of-blacks-and-christianity-the-terror-inflicted-by-whites-was-considered-a-religious-ritual.html.

Cone, James H. 2013. *The Cross and the Lynching Tree*. Maryknoll, NY: Orbis Books.
Downey, Dennis B. 2001. "The Lord's Messenger: Racial Lynching and the Church Trial of Robert Elwood." *Journal of Presbyterian History* 79 (Summer): 135–49.
Downey, Dennis B. 2013. "The 'Delaware Horror': Two Ministers, a Lynching, and the Crisis of Democracy." *Lynching beyond Dixie: American Mob Violence outside the South*, ed. Michael J. Pfeifer. Champaign: University of Illinois Press, pp. 237–60.
Jones, Ida E. 2002–2003. "Contacts without Fellowship: Lynching, the Bible and the Christian Community." *Black History Bulletin* 65–66 (January–December): 48–55.
Rushdy, Ashraf H. A. 2012. *American Lynching*. New Haven, CT: Yale University Press.

• M •

Madison, James

James Madison (1751–1836) was one of America's most influential founders. He was born on a plantation in Virginia to a devout mother and a father who served as a vestryman for an Anglican church. Madison, like many other of America's Founding Fathers, was educated at the College of New Jersey (today's Princeton), where he studied under John Witherspoon, who was the only clergyman to sign the Declaration of Independence.

After returning home, Madison thought both about becoming a minister and about going into law but was caught up in the fervor that surrounded the American Revolution. He was also deeply troubled to find that the established church in Virginia had imprisoned Baptist ministers for preaching without a license. Throughout his life, he was an ardent advocate of the free exercise of religion. He was able to put these beliefs into action when, as a member of the committee to draw up the Virginia Declaration of Rights, he was able to change the language so that it not only granted "toleration" to other religious faiths but actually protected their "free exercise."

After serving on the governor's council during the Revolutionary War, Madison served in the state legislature, where he eventually succeeded in gaining approval for Jefferson's Statute for Religious Freedom, which disestablished the state church. Madison authored his "Memorial and Remonstrance" in defense of this act, arguing that men were accountable to God prior to entering the social contract and that government thus had no control over religious beliefs (Brann 2018). He was also elected to Congress where he became convinced that the powers of the government under the Articles of Confederation were inadequate to protect the people's liberty.

Madison was one of the delegates who attended the Annapolis Convention, which discussed trade matters and was used as a springboard to call for a convention to discuss the wider problems of government under the Articles. Prior to the Convention, Madison had engaged in extensive study of the problems that had led to the demise of earlier confederacies and had written out his thoughts in two essays.

Madison was a leading delegate from Virginia to the Constitutional Convention, where he was largely responsible for drafting the Virginia Plan, which dominated the early weeks of discussion. It called for replacing the government of the Articles with a government consisting of three branches, including a bicameral Congress apportioned on state population, with greater powers over taxation and commerce. Although he was not the official secretary, Madison's notes of the deliberations were the most complete and continue to serve as a way of understanding the central issues that the Convention faced. Many of Madison's ideas were modified during the course of the Convention, but although he was somewhat disappointed with the outcome, he joined Alexander Hamilton and John Jay in defending the new document in a series of essays known as *The Federalist* and was a leading figure at the Virginia Ratifying Convention.

One of the key points of opposition to the Constitution was that it lacked a bill of rights, which was among the critiques of Madison's close friend, Thomas Jefferson. Although Madison was not initially convinced of the necessity of such a bill, he agreed to support it to allay popular concerns. As a member of the first House of Representatives, Madison took the lead in introducing such a bill that included today's First Amendment, which both prohibited Congress from establishing a religion and guaranteed its free exercise.

With Jefferson, Madison was one of the founders of the Democratic-Republican Party, whose members were concerned that their Federalist rivals were exceeding the bounds of the new Constitution and were limiting civil rights and liberties in the process, as in the Alien and Sedition Acts of 1798. When Jefferson was elected president in 1801, he selected Madison to serve as his secretary of state. When Jefferson left office after two terms, Madison succeeded him. He was president during the War of 1812, which involved a number of military defeats and the British burning of the White House prior to final victories and a treaty that essentially restored the status quo ante, but Madison left office without having used the war to limit civil liberties.

Toward the end of his life (he was the last of the fifty-five delegates who attended the Constitutional Convention to die), Madison, who had retired to his Virginia home Montpelier, became increasingly concerned about sectionalism. In a document entitled "Advice to My Country," which was published in the *National Intelligencer* in 1850, Madison drew from both classical literature and the story of the fall of man as recorded in the biblical book of Genesis when he recorded, "The advice nearest to my heart and deepest in my convictions is that the Union of the States be cherished & perpetuated. Let the open enemy to it be regarded as a Pandora with her box opened, and the disguised one, as the Serpent creeping with his deadly wiles into Paradise" (Meyers 1973, 567). The latter image also corresponded to the idea, implicit in Puritan thought, that America would be a garden established as an errand in the wilderness.

Madison kept his religious views fairly close to his vest, and scholars continue to debate how much he kept of his Anglican upbringing and how close he came to the Deism or Unitarianism of his friend Thomas Jefferson. What seems most clear is that religious freedom remained a polestar for Madison throughout his career.

One impetus for Madison's defense of religious liberty may well have been his understanding of the difficulty of interpreting Scripture and his knowledge of how differing religious interpretations of Scriptures had led to religious persecution not only in Europe but also within his home state. In Federalist No. 37, in which Madison examined the difficulties that faced the Constitutional Convention in balancing "stability" and "energy" in the new government, he pointed to the difficulties in devising and interpreting laws. He observed that "however accurately objects may be discriminated in themselves, and however accurately the discrimination may be considered, the definition of them may be rendered inaccurate by the inaccuracy of the terms in which it is delivered" (Hamilton, Madison, and Jay [1788] 1961, 229). He further observed, "When the

Almighty himself condescends to address mankind in their own language, his meaning, luminous as it must be, is rendered dim and doubtful by the cloudy medium through which it is communicated" (229).

Madison's solution, largely embodied in the U.S. Constitution, was to refine public passions through a system of representative government based on separation of powers, checks and balances, and, ultimately, a bill of rights. Although Madison rarely used Scriptures in public discourse (perhaps because he largely wanted to insulate politics from sectarian conflict), his writings suggest that his view of government stemmed from a view of human nature that would have been similar to those taught at Princeton, which was a Presbyterian stronghold. After stating in Federalist No. 51 that "ambition must be made to counteract ambition" and that "the interest of the man must be connected with the constitutional rights of the place," Madison went on to say,

> It may be a reflection on human nature that such devices should be necessary to control the abuses of government. But what is government itself but the greatest of all reflections on human nature? If men were angels, no government would be necessary. If angels were to govern men, neither external nor internal controls on government would be necessary. In framing a government which is to be administered by men over men, the great difficulty lies in this: you must first enable the government to control the government; and in the next place oblige it to control itself. ([1788] 1961, 322)

Madison's view of human nature was not, however, completely bleak. In Federalist No. 55, he thus observed, "As there is a degree of depravity in mankind which requires a certain degree of circumspection and distrust, so there are other qualities in human nature which justify a certain portion of esteem and confidence. Republican government presupposes the existence of these qualities in a higher degree than any other form" (346).

Although he issued calls for prayer and thanksgiving during his presidency, which were arguably in conflict with his support for separation of church and state, Madison justified this on the basis that he had received a specific request to do so from Congress (Fleet 1946, 562). After he retired, Madison questioned whether it was appropriate for the government to supply chaplains either in Congress or in the military, believing that this was the task of individual denominations (Grunes 2008).

See also Constitutional Convention of 1787; Days of Humiliation, Fasting, and Thanksgiving; First Amendment; Jefferson Bible; U.S. Constitution; Witherspoon, John

For Reference and Further Reading

Brann, Eva. 2018. "Madison's 'Memorial and Remonstrance': A Jewel of Republican Rhetoric." The Imaginative Conservative. October 29. https://theimaginativeconservative.org/2018/10/madison-memorial-and-remonstrance-republican-rhetoric-90-eva-brann.html.

Fleet, Elizabeth. 1946. "Madison's 'Detached Memoranda,'" *William and Mary Quarterly* 3 (October): 534–68.

Franck, Matthew J. 2016. "Christianity and Freedom in the American Founding." *Christianity and Freedom*, Vol. I: *Historical Perspectives*, ed. Timothy Samuel Shah and Allen D. Hertzke. New York: Cambridge University Press, pp. 264–89.

Grunes, Rodney A. 2008. "James Madison and Religious Freedom." *James Madison, Philosopher, Founder, and Statesman*, ed. John R. Vile, William D. Pederson, and Frank J. Williams. Athens: Ohio University Press, pp. 105–32.
Hamilton, Alexander, James Madison, and John Jay. [1788] 1961. *The Federalist Papers*. New York: New American Library.
Meyers, Marvin, ed. 1973. *The Mind of the Founder: Sources of the Political Thought of James Madison*. Indianapolis, IN: Bobbs-Merrill.
Munoz, Vincent Phillip. 2003. "James Madison's Principle of Religious Liberty." *American Political Science Review* 97 (February): 17–32.
Loconte, Joseph. 2003. "Faith and the Founding: The Influence of Religion on the Politics of James Madison." *Journal of Church and State* 45 (Autumn): 699–715.

Manhattan Declaration: A Call of Christian Conscience

Most Christians identify either as Roman Catholics, Orthodox, or Protestants, and each of these groups has its own divisions, with denominationalism being particularly strong among Protestants, some of whom are nontrinitarian. Each has its own approach to Scripture and how to balance Scripture with tradition, natural law teachings, and history, especially with respect to political issues.

In September 2009, representatives of the three major Christian groups signed a joint declaration, known as the Manhattan Declaration, which was coauthored by Chuck Colson, an evangelical; Dr. Timothy George at the Beeson Divinity School at Samford University; and Dr. Robert George, a Roman Catholic teaching at Princeton University (Stonestreet and Carlson 2019). It was signed by 148 religious leaders and addressed three central issues, and represented a judicious blend of scriptural and extra-scriptural citations.

The preamble observed that "Christians are heirs of a 2,000-year-tradition of proclaiming God's word, seeking justice in our societies, resisting tyranny, and reaching out with compassion to the poor, oppressed and suffering" (2009). It recounted how Christians had rescued abandoned children from Roman trash heaps, preserved the Bible and Western literature and art, combatted the slave trade, supported women's suffrage, battled human trafficking, and provided compassionate care to individuals afflicted with AIDS. It further affirmed three major affirmations related to contemporary public policy: "1) the profound, inherent, and equal dignity of every human being as a creature fashioned in the very image of God, possessing inherent rights of equal dignity and life; 2) marriage as a conjugal union of man and woman, ordained by God from the creation and historically understood by believers and non-believers alike, to be the most basic institution of society and; 3) religious liberty, which is grounded in the character of God, the example of Christ, and the inherent freedom and dignity of human beings created in the divine image".

The affirmation of life began with quotations from Genesis 1:27, affirming the creation of human beings in the image of God, and John 10:10, which refereed to abundant life. Citing Pope John Paul II's concern that permissive abortion, human embryo research, assisted suicide, and voluntary euthanasia were leading to "the culture of death," the Declaration said that "we defend and speak for the unborn, the disabled, and the dependent. What the Bible and the light of reason make clear, we must make clear."

The defense of heterosexual marriage began with the reference in Genesis 2:23–24 to one-flesh relationships and to Ephesians 5:32–33 likening this relationship to that of Christ and his church. Recognizing that the church itself had acquiesced in permissive divorce laws and in the increasing number of out-of-wedlock births, the Declaration recognized calls for same-sex and multiple-partner relationships as "a symptom, rather than the cause, of the erosion of the marriage culture." It further recognized that "there are those who are disposed towards homosexual and polyamorous conduct and relationships, just as there are those who are disposed towards other forms of immoral conduct."

Responding to the argument that recognition of same-sex marriages posed no harm to others, the Declaration asserted that, by failing to recognize marriage as "an objective reality, 'a covenantal union of husband and wife,'" the law would undermine religious liberty, lead to teachings in public schools to which parents objected and damage the "critical pedagogical function" of the law.

The final section on religious liberty began with a reference to Isaiah 61:1, which speaks of "freedom for the captives and release from darkness for the prisoners," and Matthew 22:21, which details the obligations to God and Caesar. It also referenced the apocryphal Epistle to Diognetus 7:3–4, an early apologetic writing, denying that God secured belief through compulsion. This section was especially concerned with "the effort to weaken or eliminate conscience clauses, and therefore to compel pro-life institutions (including religiously affiliated hospitals and clinics), and pro-life physicians, surgeons, nurses, and other health care professionals, to refer for abortions and, in certain cases, even to perform or participate in abortions."

After stating that "as Christians, we take seriously the biblical admonition to respect and obey those in authority. We believe in law and the rule of law. We recognize the duty to comply with laws whether we happen to like them or not, unless the laws are gravely unjust or require those subject to them to do something unjust or otherwise immoral," the Declaration proceeded to cite Peter and John's refusal in Acts 4 to put the laws of man over God. It also cited the argument by Dr. Martin Luther King Jr. for civil disobedience in his Letter from a Birmingham Jail. It ended by observing that "we will fully and ungrudgingly render to Caesar what is Caesar's. But under no circumstances will we render to Caesar what is God's."

See also Abortion; Civil Disobedience; Colson, Chuck; Same-Sex Marriage

For Reference and Further Reading

"Manhattan Declaration: A Call of Christina Conscience." 2009. *First Things*. November 20. https://www.firstthings.com/web-exclusives/2009/11/manhattan-declaration-a-call-of-christian-conscience.

Stonestreet, John, and David Carlson. 2019. "The Manhattan Declaration 10 Years On." *Christian Post*. May 10. https://www.christianpost.com/voice/the-manhattan-declaration-10-years-on.html.

Manifest Destiny

The idea that European settlers in America were destined to expand from coast to coast is embodied in the idea of manifest destiny, which originated in an article published by journalist John O'Sullivan (1815–1895) in an issue of the *United States*

Magazine and Democratic Review in 1845. There he had argued that "Providence" had given the West to Americans "for the development of the great experiment of liberty and federated self-government entrusted to us" (Baigell 1990, 6).

The idea has, in turn, been linked to a number of themes and texts. Puritans who came to America saw themselves as members of a New Israel, who, like biblical Jews, were entering a Promised Land, or Canaan, which God had reserved for them, just as God had earlier entrusted Adam and Noah with dominion over the earth.

European doctrines of discovery, which Chief Justice John Marshall recognized in the case of *Johnson v. McIntosh* (1823), further vested ownership of new lands to those who discovered them. The pope actually issued a papal bull in 1493 purporting to divide South America between Spain and Portugal, both Catholic nations (McSloy 1996, 42). While Protestant nations hardly heeded this division, they took a similar view of their own authority to assert ownership when claiming new territory. Settlers could claim ownership of lands that Native Americans used for hunting grounds by bringing them under cultivation and thus increasing their inherent value.

In laying out America's claim to the Oregon Territory in 1846, then congressman John Quincy Adams actually read Genesis 1:28 ("God blessed them [Adam and Eve] and God said to them: Be fertile and increase, fill the earth and master it; rule the fish of the sea, the birds of the sky, and all the living things that creep on earth") into the congressional record (Baigell 1990, 8).

In addition to ideas of cultivation, the doctrine of manifest destiny was often based on conceptions of white racial superiority. In time, this doctrine, which had been applied to the white conquest of the American West, was further applied to U.S. rule over Mexicans in the Southwest as well as over Hawaii and the Philippines. By this point, racial distinctions had been elevated to the point where some Americans had come to deny the hitherto understood biblical principle, seemingly affirmed in Acts 17:26, that Adam and Eve had parented the entire human race and that all were therefore of one blood (Baigell 1990, 9).

See also Adams, John Quincy; Colonization; Native Americans; Puritans

For Reference and Further Reading

Baigell, Matthew. 1990. "Territory, Race, Religion: Images of Manifest Destiny." *Smithsonian Studies in American Art* 4 (Summer–Autumn): 2–21.

Johnson v. McIntosh 21 U.S. (Wheat) 543 (1823).

McSloy, Steven Paul. 1996. "'Because the Bible Tells Me So': Manifest Destiny and American Indians." *Saint Thomas Law Review* 9: 37–47.

Mann, Horace

Horace Mann (1796–1859) was arguably America's most influential educator. Born in Massachusetts, Mann was tutored by his mother and sisters as well as being subjected to the teaching of Rev. Nathaniel Emmons, a strict Calvinist minister, whose teaching Mann described as follows:

> He expounded all the doctrines of total depravity, election and reprobation, and not only the eternity, but the extremity, of hell-torments, unflinchingly and in

> their most terrible significance, while he rarely if ever descanted upon the joys of heaven, and never, to my recollection upon the essential and necessary happiness of a virtuous life. (Finkelstein 1990, 10)

Mann's childhood was marred by the death of his father and of his brother, with Pastor Emmons suggesting that God had punished the latter for swimming on the Sabbath. After being subject to what one scholar describes as "guilt, depression, loneliness, self-torment, and seven hallucinations" (Finkelstein 1990, 10), Mann experienced a kind of reverse conversion in which he embraced "Christian teachings emphasizing individual responsibility, charity, [and] a loving and gentle God" (13). In time, he would identify himself as a Unitarian. Mann rejected the idea of original sin and believed that a proper education in moral values was essential for good citizenship.

Mann attended both Brown University in Rhode Island and the Litchfield School of Law in Connecticut. He was elected to the Massachusetts state legislature, but made his greatest impact as secretary of the Massachusetts Board of Education that was established in 1837. In this role, he pushed for universal public education, which Massachusetts was the first to establish in 1852. Pushing for common standards for teacher education, Mann envisioned public schools as nurturers of nationalism, which he thought was particularly important for immigrants, who might not otherwise understand American ideals. Mann continued the practice of Bible reading in schools, which had been pervasive in a state which did not abolish its established congregational church until 1833, but prohibited teachers from commenting on the readings, thus attempting to assure that they were Christian but nonsectarian, which, for orthodox believers, appeared to omit the Bible's central teachings.

Mann's support for reading the Bible in public schools without comment did not satisfy most Roman Catholics, who not only had their own version of Scripture but also believed that the Bible should be interpreted through church doctrine. Moreover, long after the U.S. Supreme Court has declared devotional readings to be unconstitutional, the idea that public schools can be neutral with respect to either religion on the Bible strikes some advocates of contemporary home or Christian schooling as an impossible ideal (Garris n.d.).

Mann, who opposed the spread of slavery to the U.S. territories, was elected to Congress to fill the seat vacated by John Quincy Adams's death and served from 1848 to 1853. At his death, Mann was serving as president of Antioch College in Ohio.

See also Abington v. Schempp (1963); Roman Catholics

For Reference and Further Reading

Andress, J. Mace. 1912. "The Last Vestige of Puritanism in the Public Schools of Massachusetts." *School Review* 20 (March): 161–69.

Finkelstein, Barbara. 1990. "Perfecting Childhood: Horace Mann and the Origins of Public Education in the United States." *Biography* 12 (Winter): 6–20.

Garris, Zachary. n.d. "Horace Mann's Utopian Vision for Public Education." Teach Diligently. http://teachdiligently.com/articles/horace-mann-utopian-vision-for-public-education.

Moore, R. Laurence. 2000. "Bible Reading and Nonsectarian Schooling: The Failure of Religious Instruction in Nineteenth-Century Public Education." *Journal of American History* 86 (March): 1581–99.
Peterson, Paul E. 2010. *Saving Schools: From Horace Mann to Virtual Learning.* Cambridge, MA: Harvard University Press.

Marshall, Peter

Peter Marshall (1902–1949) was a Scottish-born Presbyterian minister who immigrated to the United States in 1927 and graduated from the Columbia Theological Seminary in Decatur, Georgia. He pastored a number of high-profile churches, including in New York Avenue Presbyterian Church in Washington, DC, before being named chaplain of the Senate. He is perhaps best known as a result of a biography that his wife wrote in 1951 entitled *A Man Called Peter*, which was later made into a movie.

Professor Frederick Hale notes that Marshall was an absolutist who stated that "the Bible is the supreme law of right and wrong, and the church is the arbiter" (2017, 21). Hale observes that Marshall spent the early years of his ministry at the New York Avenue church in attempts to persuade his audience to forsake its isolationism and to recognize the threat that Adolph Hitler posed not only to Europe and Britain but also to the United States. Once America entered the war, he increasingly delivered jeremiads urging the nation to repent of its sins (Hale 2017, 29). Marshall believed that America had a providential destiny, quoting 2 Chronicles 7:14: "If my people, which are called by my name, shall humble themselves, and pray, and seek my face, and turn from their wicked ways; then will I hear from heaven, and will forgive their sin, and will heal their land." Although he thus supported President Roosevelt's proclamation of a Day of Prayer, Marshall criticized him for not also calling for national repentance (24). Marshall was concerned both about American racial injustices and about what he believed to be the disparity between the rich and the poor.

Although Marshall favored religious freedom, perhaps because he came from a country with a state church, his criticisms often focused on the failure of public schools and other institutions to teach the Bible. He saw increasing divorce rates, decreased respect for Sunday, and increased materialism as signs of America's moral decline. He ended one sermon by pointing to Proverbs 14:34, "Righteousness exalteth a nation," and praised former president Woodrow Wilson for applying Christian principles to international relations (28).

See also American Exceptionalism; Prophets and Jeremiads; Wilson, Woodrow

For Reference and Further Reading

Hale, Frederick. 2017. "Fighting the Good Fight from the 'Church of the Presidents': Peter Marshall's Homiletics during the Second World War." *Journal of Presbyterian History* 95 (Spring/Summer): 18–31.

Massachusetts Body of Liberties

When they immigrated from England and Holland, American Puritans brought with them a strong tradition of congregationalism, which assured the independence of individual churches. They also brought with them a strong tradition of republicanism that disdained the power of monarchs, bishops, or the pope to make decisions related to spiritual matters. Puritans had a deep sense of their own rights under the British common law as articulated in such documents as the Magna Carta (1215) and the English Bill of Rights (1689).

Much of this understanding was codified in the Massachusetts Body of Liberties of 1641, which is largely attributed to Nathaniel Ward. Article I of this document proclaimed,

> No mans life shall be taken away, no mans honour or good name shall be stayned, no mans person shall be arrested, restrained, banished, dismembered, nor any ways punished, no man shall be deprived of his wife or children, no mans goods or estaite shall be taken away from him, nor any way indammaged under colour of law or Countenance of Authoritie, unlesse it be by virtue or equitie of some expresse law of the Country warranting the same, established by a generall Court and sufficiently published, or in case of the defect of a law in any parteculer case by the word of God.

In addition to incorporating numerous procedural protections, the code is noted for having specific sections dealing with the "Liberties of Women," the "Liberties of Children," the "Liberties of Servants," the "Liberties of Forreiners and Strangers," and even protections for animals.

Capital punishment had been widespread in England for a variety of offenses. Section 94 of the Body of Liberties specifically outlined twelve capital offenses, each with appropriate scriptural citations from the books of Exodus, Leviticus, Numbers, and Deuteronomy. They respectively involved idolatry, witchcraft, blasphemy, murder, crimes of passion, poisonings, bestiality, homosexual relations, adultery, manstealing, and bearing false witness. Although it included no scriptural citation, the law also made insurrection or rebellion a capital offense.

Aside from capital penalties, there were many in Massachusetts who thought that the magistrates were reserving too much discretion in their sentencing, and the Body of Liberties was followed by another document, the Laws and Liberties of 1648, which was designed to correct this perceived defect (Cahn 1989).

See also Capital Punishment; Puritans

For Reference and Further Reading

Cahn, Mark D. 1989. "Punishment, Discretion, and the Codification of Prescribed Penalties in Colonial Massachusetts." *American Journal of Legal History* 33 (April): 107–36.

"The Massachusetts Body of Liberties (1641)." https://history.hanover.edu/texts/masslib.html.

Mather, Cotton

Cotton Mather (1663–1728) was a member of one of the most prominent families in New England, being the son of Increase Mather, who was president of Harvard, and the grandson of John Cotton, another Massachusetts cleric.

Mather was the author of more than four hundred works, including a commentary on the Bible consisting of 4,500 manuscript pages (Van Engen 2017, 424), which has only recently been published. Mather did much to identify the cause of New England with that of Christianity, describing the settlers as the founders of a New Israel who had made a successful errand in the wilderness where they had overcome the influence of the Devil, which Mather often associated with the paganism of Native American Indians.

Aware of contemporary biblical criticism, Mather made an effort to show the compatibility of Scripture with the science of his day. He authored the *Magnalia Christi Americana*, which explained New England's history, as well as his Bible commentary.

Mather's work on witchcraft may have contributed to the panic of the Salem witch trials, which resulted in 1692 in the executions of nineteen people and two dogs! Ironically, he viewed the perceived outbreak of witchcraft, which was a capital offense in ancient Israel, as a sign that Satan was doing his best to thwart the progress of Christianity in the region. Although he expressed some reservations about the use of spectral evidence (visions that could only be seen by those making the accusations), he arguably did not express them with sufficient clarity to avert the executions that followed. Whereas Increase Mather expressed the view that "I would rather judge a witch to be an honest woman than judge an honest woman as a witch," Cotton was more concerned about letting witches go free (Schiff 2015).

On a much more positive note, Mather was a strong advocate of education and of inoculation for smallpox.

Some modern scholars have perceived Mather's hermeneutics, like those of Jonathan Edwards, as a precursor to that of modern American evangelical thought (Van Engen 2017, 435). An entry in his diary designed to answer the question of "Why do I believe the Scriptures to be the Word of God?" described his encounter with the book in his study:

> I took into my hands the Bible . . . and presenting myself with it, on knees before the Lord, I professed unto Him, that I did embrace the precious book, as His Word; resolving ever therefore to credit all the revelations of it: that I would love it, prize it, converse with it, as His: that I would be so awed by the promises, and threatenings and histories of it, as to study a conformity unto the precepts of it, while I have my being. So I blessed Him, for His vouchsafing of this invaluable Word unto me. (Kennedy, 2015, 5)

See also Edwards, Jonathan; Evangelicals; Puritans; Satan

For Reference and Further Reading

Bercovitch, Scvan. 1966. "New England Epic: Cotton Mather's Magnalia Christi Americana." *ELH* 33 (September): 337–50.

"Cotton Mather." United States History. https://www.u-s-history.com/pages/h1168.html.

Kennedy, Rick. 2015. *The First American Evangelical: A Short Life of Cotton Mather*. Grand Rapids, MI: William B. Eerdmans.

Lowance, Mason I., Jr. 1969. "Typology and the New England Way: Cotton Mather and the Exegesis of Biblical Types." *Early American Literature* 4 (Spring): 15–37.

Schiff, Stacy. 2015. "The Witches of Salem: Diabolical Doings in a Puritan village." *New Yorker*. August 31. https://www.newyorker.com/magazine/2015/09\07/the-witches-of-salem.
Van Engen, Abram. 2017. "Review: A Medieval Puritan Welcomes the Early American Enlightenment: What Bible Commentaries Can Offer Postsecular and Literacy Studies." *Early American Literature* 52(2): 423–42.

Mayflower Compact

Of all the concepts that the Pilgrims brought with them to America, few were more prominent than the idea of covenants between God and his people, and among the people themselves. Theologians of the day believed that God had entered into such agreements with Adam, with Noah, with Abraham, with the people of Israel through the giving of the Ten Commandments to Moses, and with David. Christians divide Scriptures into the Old and New Testaments, or covenants, which they believe represent God's respective dealings with the Jews and with Christians. Sometimes individuals, like David and Jonathan, entered into covenants with one another.

Although it goes by a different, albeit related, name, the Mayflower Compact (also known as the Plymouth Combination) is an example of a covenant which both Pilgrims and non-Pilgrim settlers agreed to in 1620 before disembarking from the *Mayflower*, on rules that would govern them. In this context, Donald Lutz observes that "a compact was" an agreement between a large group of people creating a new community based upon their own consent (1988, 17). As the colonies became more secularized, such covenants, or compacts, were (as in the writings of the British social contract philosophers, Thomas Hobbes and John Locke) called contracts.

The Mayflower Compact began with the words, "In the name of God, Amen." Acknowledging the rule of King James I "by the grace of God," and as a "defender of the faith," the signers acknowledged that they had undertaken "for the glory of God, and the advancement of the Christian faith, and honour of our king and country, a voyage to plant the first colony in the Northerne parts of Virginia." They entered in a "covenant and combine ourselves together into a civill body politick, for our better ordering and preservation, and furtherance of the ends aforesaid." They further vested this new body politics with the power "to enacte, constitute, and frame such just and equall laws, ordinances, acts, constitutions and offices, from time to time, as shall be thought most meete and convenient for the generall good of the Colonie unto which we promise all due submission and obedience." In a form that would later be repeated in other American founding documents, the Compact ended with the date and with signatures.

Lutz believes that the Mayflower Compact was a prelude to future state constitutions.

See also Covenants, Compacts, Contracts, and Constitutions; Puritans

For Reference and Further Reading

Kendall, Willmoore, and George W. Carey. 1970. *The Basic Symbols of the American Political Tradition*. Baton Rouge: Louisiana State University Press.

Lutz, Donald S. 1980. "From Covenant to Constitution in American Political Thought." *Publius* 10 (Fall):101–34.
Lutz, Donald S. 1998. *The Origins of American Constitutionalism*. Baton Rouge: Louisiana State University Press.

Mayhew, Jonathan

Although most American settlers brought their allegiance to the British king to America, long before Thomas Paine questioned the institution of kingship in his *Common Sense*, Puritans sometimes expressed skepticism of claims of divine right that were similar to their skepticism of the power of the Catholic pope or British bishops. In 1750, Rev. Jonathan Mayhew (1720–1766), a Congregationalist minister from the West Church in Boston, published a sermon in which he questioned the practice, proclaimed by Charles II, of annually honoring his father, whom the king described as a martyred saint, on the anniversary of his execution.

Acknowledging in his preface the concern that clerics might be "preaching politics, instead of CHRIST," Mayhew thought that it was as appropriate for him to explicate scriptural passages related "to civil government" as well as others. Expressing sentiments similar to those that Thomas Jefferson would use in one of his last letters explaining the Declaration of Independence, Mayhew observed that "people have no security against being unmercifully priest-ridden, but by keeping all imperious BISHOPS, and other CLERGY-MEN who love to 'lord it over God's heritage,' from getting their foot into the stirrup at all" (1750, vii).

Mayhew's text was Romans 13:1–8. In the first verse of this passage, Paul had admonished, "Let every soul be subject unto the higher powers. For there is no power but of God: the powers that be, are ordained of God." This and succeeding verses would appear to require Christians to join the mandated celebration in honor of Charles I and to give unlimited obedience to the king.

Mayhew believed, however, that Paul had directed this passage to converts from Judaism (Mayhew relies largely on stereotypes) and to converted pagans, who had been accustomed to think that the law did not apply to them (1750, 3). Christians should be willing to subject themselves to rulers who were governing on behalf of the common good, but there was still an issue with respect to "the *extent* of that subjection *to the higher powers*, which is here enjoined as a duty upon all Christians" (12), and he devoted most of the rest of his discourse to showing that Paul was not arguing that such obedience should be unlimited.

In making his argument, Mayhew observed that many Scriptures that appear on their face to make general commands have been reasonably interpreted to allow for exceptions. He thus observed that while Ephesians 6 urges children to obey their parents, servants their masters, and wives their husbands, few would expect them to do so if such commands violated ordinances of God or put them in danger. Just as one would refuse obedience to parents, masters, and husbands who violated their own duties, so too Paul was "not in favor of submission to all who bear the *title* of rulers, in common; but only those who *actually* perform the duty of rulers, by exercising a reasonable and just authority, for the good of human society" (20). Extending the analogy, perhaps with prelates of the Church of England in mind, Mayhew asked whether it would be appropriate to honor pastors who refused to preach or take care of their flocks other than to secure their money (21–22). Like leaders of the church, "rulers have no authority from God to do mischief. They are not God's ordinance, or God's ministers, in any other sense than as it is by his permission and providence, that they are exalted to bear rule" and as they duly exercise their authority (23). Those who fail in their tasks are not ministers of God but of Satan, who should be accordingly resisted.

Mayhew thought it was especially important to resist tyrants. Moreover, he observed that although Paul "does not concern himself with the different forms of government," his admonition was not an admonition to obey monarchical governments only but should also apply in republics (32).

As to when it was proper to disobey governmental commands, Mayhew observed, "A PEOPLE, really oppressed to a great degree by their sovereign, cannot well be insensible when they are so oppressed" (38), and he devoted considerable efforts to showing that Charles I had been such an oppressive ruler by ruling tyrannically, marrying a Catholic, disregarding the English constitution, authorizing a book that would have favored the playing of sports on the Sabbath, encouraging papists, and the like. Moreover, the resistance that was mounted against him was the work not of "a private *junto*" or "a small seditious *party*" but of the duly elected parliament (44). Their actions did not constitute a "*rebellion*" but "a most righteous and glorious stand, made in defence of the natural and legal rights of the people, against the unnatural and illegal encroachments of arbitrary power" (44). As to the king's execution, "he had, in fact, *unkinged* himself long before, and had forfeited his title to the allegiance of the people" (47).

Mayhew wondered how the clergy of the Episcopal Church could continue to refer to such a man as "a *great Saint* and a *Martyr*" (49). Mayhew suggested, "That church must be but *poorly stocked* with saints and martyrs, which is forced to adopt such enormous sinners into her *kalendar*, in order to swell the number" (50–51). Mayhew further observed that even had their forefathers participated in the killing of a just king, it was unfair to impute this to their successors, the doctrine of original sin notwithstanding (54).

Concluding that government is sacred and that "it is our happiness to live under the government of a PRINCE who is satisfied with ruling according to law; as every other *good prince* will" (55), Mayhew warned against using liberty "*for a close of maliciousness*" or aiming "at *popularity* under the disguise of *patriotism*" (55).

Focusing particularly on Mayhew's use of New Testament Scriptures, James P. Byrd cites Mayhew's work as an example of what he calls "pre-revolutionary apostolic patriotism" (2013, 123) and notes that Revolutionary War patriots often had to face similar arguments for obedience to the king from their Tory counterparts.

See also Civil Disobedience; *Common Sense* (Thomas Paine); Revolutionary War

For Reference and Further Reading

Byrd, James P. 2013. *Sacred Scripture, Sacred War: The Bible and the American Revolution*. New York: Oxford University Press.

Fea, John. 2014. "Does America Have a Biblical Heritage?" *The Bible in the Public Square: Its Enduring Influence in American Life*, ed. Mark A. Chancey, Carol Meyers, and Eric M. Meyers. Atlanta, GA: Society of Biblical Literature, pp. 65–79.

Mayhew, Jonathan. 1750. *A Discourse Concerning Unlimited Submission and Obedience to the Higher Powers: With Some Reflections on the Resistance Made to King Charles I. And on the Anniversary of His Death: In Which the Mysterious Doctrine of That Prince's Saintship and Martyrdom Is Unriddled.* University of Nebraska-Lincoln. Digital Commons. Accessed at https://digitalcommons.unl.edu/etas/44.

McKinley, William

William McKinley (1843–1901), who was first elected to the presidency in 1896, and again in 1900, appears to have been among the most devout men who ever served in that office. A veteran of the Civil War, where he reached the rank of Brevet Major in the Ohio infantry, McKinley practiced law before serving in the U.S. House of Representatives from 1877 to 1884 and again from 1885 to 1891, after which he served as governor of Ohio before being elected president.

McKinley had a conversion experience in a meeting at a Methodist Church in 1856 and later proclaimed that "I am a Methodist and nothing but a Methodist—a Christian and nothing but a Christian" (quoted in Smith 2015, 160). He would maintain his Methodist faith throughout his life, avoided habits like drinking or swearing, and was a regular churchgoer who read the Bible regularly. McKinley linked his own service to his country with his service to God, noting in a diary during the Civil War that if he were to die, "I fell not only as a soldier of my Country, but also as a Soldier of Jesus Christ" (Smith 2015, 161). He called the Bible "God's great love story to man," and said that "the more profoundly we study this wonderful book, and the more clearly we observe its divine precepts, the better citizens we will become and the higher will be our destiny as a nation" (quoted in Smith 2015, 161, from tract by American Bible Society). McKinley's mother often expressed regret that her son had become president "when he could have had such a useful and brilliant career in the church" (Smith 2015, 194).

The opening paragraph of his first presidential inaugural address (1897) evoked "the guidance of Almighty God" and observed that "our faith teaches that there is no safer reliance than upon the God of our fathers, who has so singularly favored the American people in every national trial, and who will not forsake us so long as we obey His commandments and walk humbly in His footsteps." This sentiment was likely taken from Micah 6:8, which reads, "What does the Lord require of thee, but to do justly, and to love mercy, and to walk humbly with thy God?" The specific verse to which McKinley opened the Bible on which he took his oath—a Bible that had been given to him by the bishops of the African Methodist Episcopal Church (Winder 2019, 137)—was 2 Chronicles 1:10: "Give me now wisdom and knowledge . . . for who can judge this thy people, that is so great." At his second presidential inaugural address, he opened it to Proverbs 16:21–22: "The wise in heart shall be called prudent. . . . Understanding is a wellspring of life unto him that hath it" (Smith 2015, 162).

During McKinley's presidency, the United States went to war with Spain, largely over Spain's mistreatment of the Cuban people. At the end of the war, America acquired both Cuba and the Philippines. McKinley's decision to rule the latter as a colony, which included suppressing a homegrown revolutionary movement, was highly controversial. Indeed, William Jennings Bryan, whom McKinley had defeated in 1896, and whom he would run against again in 1900, observed, "The commandment, 'Go ye into all the world and preach the gospel to every creature' [Jesus's Great Commission in Mark 16:15 and Matthew 18:19–20], has no Gatling gun attachment. Love, not force, was the weapon of the Nazarene" (quoted in Smith 2015, 166).

McKinley's biographer reported that McKinley had explained his decision to keep control of the Philippines to a visiting group of five members of the Methodist General Missionary Committee who visited the White House. He was reported to have said that after praying to God for guidance, he had decided that it was America's responsibility to "educate the Filipinos, and uplift and civilize and Christianize them, and by God's grace do the very best we could by them, as our fellow-men for whom Christ also died" (reported in Smith 2015, 183). Although many scholars have viewed this explanation as a simple cover for McKinley's desire to acquire a naval base that would help with American trade to China and other countries in that region, while still others have expressed doubt over this account, it certainly appears to have reflected McKinley's view that God had a special destiny for America. Smith observes that "McKinley was a product of the Victorian generation who believed in Anglo-Saxon superiority, honor, and the duty to uplift the downtrodden and to civilize and Christianize 'inferior peoples.' Lacking modern sensibilities about multiculturalism and appreciation of different cultural traditions, McKinley and his advisers genuinely believed that by administering the archipelago they were helping the Filipino people" (187). One irony of this belief was the fact that the large majority of the Filipino people were professing Roman Catholics.

McKinley's reputation stems in part from his assassination at the Pan-American Exposition in Buffalo, New York, where, after being shot, he prevented a crowd from beating his assassin to death by saying, "Let no one hurt him; may God forgive him." In the succeeding days, many Americans likened these words to those of Jesus on the cross in Luke 23:34 (Smith 2015, 189). After his death, many compared McKinley's death to that of Jesus, and there were numerous commemorative items that were issued with McKinley's picture or profile and McKinley's reputed last words, which seemed to echo the Lord's Prayer, "It is God's way. His will, not ours, be done" (189). Among his eulogies was one by an Episcopal priest who observed that Washington was "the liberator of the colonies; Lincoln the emancipator of the slaves; [and] McKinley the deliverer of oppressed and dying Cuba" (192).

Advocates of the social gospel were among those who believed that American imperialism would further the cause of Christ on earth. It is not surprising that a man who stated that "piety and patriotism go well together" and that "love of flag, love of country are not inconsistent with our religious faith" should sometimes fail to "distinguish between love of God and love of the United States, between biblical teachings and American aims" (194).

See also America as New Israel; Bryan, William Jennings; Colonialism; Presidential Inaugural Verses; Social Gospel; What Doth the Lord Require? (Micah 6:8)

For Reference and Further Reading

McKinley, William. 1897. "First Inaugural Address of William McKinley." The Avalon Project. March 4. https://avalon.law.yale.edu/19th_century/mckin1.asp.

Smith, Gary Scott. 2015. *Religion in the Oval Office: The Religious Lives of American Presidents*. New York: Oxford University Press.

Winder, Mike. 2019. *Favorite Scriptures of 100 American Leaders*. Springville, UT: Plain Sight.

Mennonites

Mennonites (some of whom call themselves Amish) are, like Quakers, Brethren, and Jehovah's Witnesses, pacifists. Like the latter, they also believe that saluting the U.S. flag is a form of idolatry forbidden by the Ten Commandments, and most refrain from voting.

The movement originated in Europe, chiefly Germany and Holland, among Anabaptists who opposed child baptism. Their name comes from Menno Simmons (1496–1561), a Roman Catholic priest whom they followed in opposition both to the Roman Catholic Church and mainline Protestantism. They first settled in Germantown, Pennsylvania, in the mid-1600s. Often characterized by their plain dress and/or by their refusal to allow electricity and other forms of modern technology in their homes or to drive motorized vehicles, they often rely on John 17:16, 18, where in a prayer describing his disciples, Jesus pronounced, "They are not of the world, even as I am not of the world. As thou has sent me into the world, even so have I sent them into the world" (Huxman and Biesecker-Mast 2004, 539). Mennonite women typically wear a covering on their heads.

Mennonites take seriously Jesus's admonition in his Sermon on the Mount in Matthew 5:39 not to resist evil. They value the admonition in Matthew 23:12, which states that "whosoever shall exalt himself shall be abased, and he that shall humble himself shall be exalted." Largely as a result, they have sought alternate humanitarian service in place of military service and even showed up to boot camp in World War I and then asked for exemption from combat service (Huxman and Biesecker-Mast 2004, 545). In one of their most cherished stories, first reported in *Martyrs Mirror*, authored by Thieleman van Braght in 1695, they recount how Dirk Willems, a Mennonite being pursued by his enemies across an ice-covered pond, stopped to rescue his pursuer from drowning even though it meant that Willems would be executed (546). This was consistent with the biblical injunction in the Sermon on the Mount (Matthew 5:44) to "love your enemies, and pray for those who persecute you, that you may be sons of your Father in heaven."

Another story, designed to highlight how Mennonites remain patriotic even while opposing U.S. military ventures, a Mennonite minister accedes to the request of a mob outside his house to raise the American flag during World War I and, after asking that they join him in singing "America," shows that he is the only one there who knows the words to all of its verses (547–48).

In *Wisconsin v. Yoder* (1972), a group of Amish parents won the right to take their children out of public schools after the eighth grade, but in *United States v. Lee* (1982), the court denied them the right of exempting their employees from the Social Security System.

See also Jehovah's Witnesses; Quakers

For Reference and Further Reading

Huxman, Susan, and Gerald Biesecker-Mast. 2004. "In the World but Not of it: Mennonite Traditions as Resources for Rhetorical Invention." *Rhetoric and Public Affairs* 7 (Winter): 539–54.

Ottoson, Robin Deich. 2010. "The Battle over the Flag: Protest, Community Opposition, and Silence in the Mennonite Colleges in Kansas during the Vietnam War." *Journal of Church and State* 52 (Autumn): 686–711.

United States v. Lee, 455 U.S. 252 (1982).

Wisconsin v. Yoder, 406 U.S. 205 (1972).

Military

Printers often design special editions of the Bible for different demographic groups. There are Bibles for students, Bibles for children, Bibles for women, Bibles for men, and the like. It is not surprising that a number of publishers and a number of groups targeting the military have designed special Bibles for them as well. There are, of course, some pacifist denominations such as Mennonites, Jehovah's Witnesses, and Quakers who believe the Bible requires their members to refrain from military participation.

Edward Waggoner's study of military Bibles indicates that they "draw from especially powerful symbols, images, concepts, and language"; that they "show a particularly close fit between symbols, images, concepts, and language 'inside' the covers of the text and those 'outside' it"; and that they "suggest some distinctive views about divine providence, atonement, God's identity, and human transformation" (2017, 334–35). Waggoner thus notes that many such Bibles have camouflaged covers, that many feature introductions from military personnel, and that many attempt to identify with members of the armed services by comparing their own sacrifices to those of Jesus or other biblical figures. He also observes that "military editions of the Bible offer narratives in which divine, national military, and individual histories align" (336). Focusing specifically on Biblica, which is one of the largest producers and distributors of such military Bibles, he says that its "version of the history of salvation is quasi-imperial, military, nation-building-or-restoring, justice-bringing story" (337).

Waggoner further notes that, as many liberal denominations became disaffected with the military, more conservative chaplains, often sympathetic to the religious right, enlisted. This has led to charges that some were proselytizing rather than simply meeting the spiritual needs of troops.

Waggoner points out that Bible societies, and sometimes the U.S. government itself, have sought to enlist members of the military to serve as colporteurs to lands in which American forces were fighting. He traces this back to the war with Mexico from 1846 to 1848, to the American occupation of the Philippines after the Spanish-American War, and to attempts (supported by General Douglas MacArthur) to distribute Bibles in Japan after World War II and still later in Korea. Such efforts were sometimes counterproductive, as when soldiers were given Scriptures to pass out in Muslim countries, and led the U.S. military in at least one highly controversial case in Afghanistan, to burn such Bibles (Starnes

2012). In another incident, American commanders apologized and pulled a U.S. sniper from Baghdad in 2008 after he used a Koran for target practice (Zavis 2008). The U.S. military, which led the way in racial desegregation, is, of course, open to Muslims, although there are relatively few imams who serve as chaplains (Sandhoff 2017, 38).

See also Bible Burnings; Jehovah's Witnesses; Quakers

For Reference and Further Reading

Sandhoff, Michelle. 2017. *Service in a Time of Suspicion: Experiences of Muslims Serving in the U.S. Military Post-9/11*. Iowa City: University of Iowa Press.

Starnes, Todd. 2012. "The Day the US Military Burned the Bible in Afghanistan." Fox News. March 2. https://www.foxnews.com/opinion/the-day-the-us-military-burned-the-bible-in-afghanistan.

Waggoner, Edward. 2017. "The Bible and the Military." *The Oxford Handbook of the Bible in America*, ed. Paul C. Gutjahr. New York: Oxford University Press, pp. 333–45.

Zavis, Alexandra 2008. "U.S. Sniper Pulled from Iraq for Using Quran as a Target." *Baltimore Sun*. May 16. https://www.baltimoresun.com/news/bs-xpm-2008-05-19-0805190113-story.html.

Model of Christian Charity (Winthrop)

One of the speeches that has been used not only to epitomize American Puritan thought but also as the source of a metaphor to inspire later Americans is John Winthrop's essay (usually described as a sermon) from 1630 entitled "A Model of Christian Charity." He probably either delivered this aboard the ship *Arbella* or possibly circulated it in written form (Rodgers 2018, 27–28). It may also have been given prior to the trip to a group that included not only the Puritans who were headed to America but also those who remained behind (Dawson 1998). It was designed to prepare Pilgrims heading to America for their anticipated life on a new continent where they hoped to find religious freedom for themselves while establishing their own Christian commonwealth.

Winthrop (1588–1649) was a Trinity College–educated lawyer who would serve for many years as the governor of the Massachusetts Bay Colony. Although his sermon is today regarded as a foundational text not only for explaining Puritanism but also for explaining what is unique about America, the manuscript does not appear to have been widely circulated at the time that it was printed. It was not rediscovered until 1838, when antiquarian George Folsom found it in the collections of the New York Historical Society (Van Engen 2013, 285). Moreover, the manuscript was not in Winthrop's handwriting and may or may not be complete.

One of the frustrating aspects of this text is that even shortened editions of the speech omit many of the Bible citations. Indeed, in presenting his own masterful analysis of the speech, Abram Van Engen observed that "despite all the attention it has received, 'Christian Charitie' has never been analyzed for its many biblical quotations, citations, echoes, parallels, paraphrases, and inferences—especially the Pauline models that form the basis of Winthrop's text. Apart from studying its most famous phrase—'we shall be as a city upon a hill'—no article or book has yet investigated which biblical passages ground the sermon, which

Bible Winthrop used, or how such details affect its meaning" (Van Engen 2013, 546). Moreover, Van Engen makes a powerful argument that suggests both that the sermon may be missing its first page, which he believes to have referenced Galatians 5:13, and that the Bible to which Winthrop would have referred would not have been the more commonly quoted King James Version but the Geneva Bible, which contained notes and numerous cross references, and which read, "For brethren, ye have been called unto liberty: only use not your liberty as an occasion unto the flesh, but by love serve one another." Van Engen also believes that the individual who copied the manuscript incorrectly copied the chapter and verse numbers of a number of the biblical passages.

The extant text, which, as noted above, may be missing a page, begins with the observation that "GOD Almighty in his most holy and wise providence, hath soe disposed of the condition of mankind, as in all times some must be rich, some poore, some high and eminent in power and dignitie; others mean and in submission" (Winthrop 1630, 33). Winthrop cites such divisions as a way for God to demonstrate his greatness, to display the work of his spirit and so that man might be "knit more nearly together in the Bonds of brotherly affection" (34). Citing Ezekiel 16:17 and Proverbs 3:9, which call upon individuals to honor God with possessions and service, Winthrop proceeded, probably with Micah 6:8 in mind, to say that "there are two rules whereby we are to walk one towards another: Justice and Mercy" (34). He further tied these to the biblical injunction to love one's neighbor and to the biblical Golden Rule, which he illustrated through biblical examples while observing, in an apparent reference to Galatians 6:10, that we should "doe good to all, especially to the household of faith" (35). In opposition to the mere law of nature, Winthrop observed that Matthew 5:44 (from the Sermon on the Mount) further urges Christians to do good even to their enemies (35).

Winthrop urged that Christians should show mercy through giving, lending, and forgiving—chiefly a reference to debts. They should give to one another abundantly. This was in obedience to the advice in Ecclesiastes 11:1 to cast one's bread upon the water and in line with such New Testament Scriptures as Matthew 6[incorrectly listed as 16]:19, urging disciples to lay up treasures in heaven; Matthew 6:21, which Winthrop does not cite by chapter and verse, which states that "where the treasure is there will ye heart be allsoe"; and with admonitions from 1 John 3:17 about the obligation to help brothers in need (36).

When lending, the Pilgrims should follow Deuteronomy 15:2 and 7, Matthew 5:42, and the Golden Rule in lending to those in genuine need even if it might result in financial loss. Such liberality would be particularly important within a "community of peril" (38). Winthrop illustrated with a plethora of passages from both the Old and New Testaments. As he proceeded, he noted that "love is the bond of perfection" (40), and he cited numerous New Testament passages, such as 1 Corinthians 12, which liken the church to the body of Christ, which is held together through the ligaments of love. He illustrated the unity of love by citing Ezekiel's description in his 39th chapter of the coming together of dry bones as well as the examples of Adam and Eve in the Garden of Eden, David and Jonathan, and Ruth and Naomi and by citing Paul's exhortation to love in 1 Corinthians 13.

Having expounded Scripture, Winthrop proceeded, as was common in Puritan sermons, to apply it, with respect to persons, the work, the end, and the means. His address is to "a company professing ourselves fellow members of Christ" who were "knit together by this bond of love" (44). As to the work at hand, it focused on seeking out "a place of cohabitation and Consorteshipp under a due forme of Government both civill and ecclesiasticall" (45). The end was "to improve our lives to doe more service to the Lord and worke out our Salvation under the power and purity of his holy ordinances" (45). Because such ends were so "extraordinary," the means must be tailored to them; "That which the most in theire churches mainetaine as truthe in profession onely, wee must bring into familiar and constant practice; as this duty of loue, wee must loue brotherly without dissimulation, wee must loue one another with a pure hearte fervently. Wee must beare one anothers burthens. We must not looke onely on our owne things, but allsoe on the things of our brethren" (45). By doing so, the Pilgrims will stimulate jealousy among the English church to bring them back to a truer worship. Because of the Puritan covenant (which Winthrop likens to a marriage) with God, Puritans had a special commission, which, in light of later Puritan–Native American conflicts, Winthrop somewhat forebodingly likened to Saul's commission to destroy the Amalekites (46).

Warning that if the Pilgrims forgot their mission and failed to live up to the covenant, "the Lord will surely breake out in wrathe against us," he argued that "the only way to avoyde this shipwracke [which was a particularly appropriate analogy if the message were given or circulated at sea], and to provide for our posterity, is to follow the counsel of Micah, to doe justly, to love mercy, to walk humbly with our God" (46). If Pilgrims did so, "wee shall finde that the God of Israell is among us, when ten of us shall be able to resist a thousand of our enemies; when hee shall make us a prayse and glory that men shall say of succeeding plantations, 'the Lord make it likely [like] that of New England' " (47).

This is the point, stressed in most subsequent analyses, where Winthrop, drawing from Jesus's analogy in his Sermon on the Mount, said, "For wee must consider that wee shall be as a city upon a hill. The eies of all people are upon us. Soe that if wee shall deale falsely with our God in this worke wee haue undertaken, and so cause him to withdrawe his present help from us, wee shall be made a story and a by-word through the world" (47). One fascinating aspect of this part of the speech is that Winthrop's reference to the eyes of God is similar to a letter to Queen Elizabeth in the Geneva Bible that said that "the eyes of all that feare God in all places beholde your countreyes as an example to all that believe" (quoted in Van Engen 2013, 576). Far from being the proclamation of triumphalism that it is sometimes interpreted to be, Winthrop's words arguably come closer to a warning that being God's New Israel carried special obligations with it and that their conduct would thus either glorify or bring reproach upon the name of God.

Winthrop ended his discourse by citing Moses's farewell in Deuteronomy 30:19 setting forth a choice between "life and good" or "death and evill" (1630, 47).

After years of faithful government service, in 1645 Winthrop was tried before the general court for refusing, as a magistrate, to confirm the election of a militia captain by the town of Hingham. After being acquitted, he delivered a "little speech," which affirmed that he remained committed to rule by an aristocracy. Believing that he had kept his "covenant" with those who had elected him, Winthrop distinguished between the "natural" liberty that men had in common with animals and which "makes men grow more evil, and in time to be worse than brute beasts" and the "civil or federal" liberty that they possessed within society (Mason and Baker 1985, 63). He observed that the liberty that is "maintained and exercised in a way of subjection to authority" and which "is of the same king of liberty wherewith Christ hath made us free [a close paraphrase of Galatians 5:1]" is similar to the manner in which women should be subject to their husbands (Mason and Baker 1985, 63). Magistrates should be willing to listen to their constituents, but it was the duty of citizens to uphold "the honor and power of authority amongst you" (54).

See also City upon a Hill; Covenants, Compacts, Contracts, and Constitutions; Geneva Bible; Puritans; Violence; What Doth the Lord Require? (Micah 6:8)

For Reference and Further Reading

Dawson, Hugh J. 1998. "'Christian Charity' as Colonial Discourse: Rereading Winthrop's Sermon in Its English Context." *Early American Literature* 33(2): 117–48.

Mason, Alpheus, and Gordon E. Baker. 1985. *Free Government in the Making: Readings in American Political Thought*. 4th ed. New York: Oxford University Press.

Miller, Perry. 1953. "Errand into the Wilderness." *William and Mary Quarterly* 10 (January): 3–32.

Morgan, Edmund S. 1958. *The Puritan Dilemma: The Story of John Winthrop*. Boston: Little, Brown.

Rodgers, Daniel T. 2018. *As a City on a Hill: The Story of America's Most Famous Lay Sermon*. Princeton, NJ: Princeton University Press.

Schaar, John H. 1991. "Liberty/Authority/Community in the Political Thought of John Winthrop." *Political Theory* 19 (November): 493–518.

Van Engen, Abram C. 2013. "Origins and Last Farewells: Bible Wars, Textual Form, and the Making of American History." *New England Quarterly* 86 (December): 543–92.

Winthrop, John. 1630. "A Modell of Christian Charity." Collections of the Massachusetts Historical Society (Boston, 1838), 3rd series 7: 31–48. Hanover Historical Texts Collection. https://history.hanover.edu/texts/winthmod.html.

Moore, Roy S.

The Ten Commandments, like Moses who promulgated them, have served as an important symbol throughout much of American history. Relying on the First and Fourteenth Amendments to the U.S. Constitution, and especially the establishment clause, the U.S. Supreme Court has issued a number of decisions in which it has limited the display of these commandments on public property, especially in public schools or in isolation from other monuments.

Because of their symbolic value, however, such displays have often served as a rallying point for those who believe that their free exercise rights are greater than any dangers of religious establishment and by those who believe there is nothing wrong with acknowledging what they consider to be part of the nation's common spiritual heritage. One such individual is Roy S. Moore (b. 1947). A 1969 graduate of the U.S. Military Academy of West Point and of the University of Alabama School of Law, Moore gained a reputation as judge on the Sixteenth Judicial Circuit in Etowah County, Alabama, for displaying what John Pottenger describes as "a hand-carved, wooden plaque of the Decalogue in his courtroom" and for beginning each day with a Christian prayer (2007, 16). Moore said that "I consider it my duty to acknowledge God. To take down the Ten Commandments would be a violation of that duty. To stop prayer would be a violation of that duty. I will not take down the Ten Commandments. I will not stop prayer" (quoted in Pottenger 2007, 16). Congress adopted a resolution supporting this display, and challenges to this practice were eventually dismissed on technical grounds. In 2000, voters in Alabama selected Moore as chief justice of the state supreme court.

As the individual responsible for the Alabama Judicial Building, Moore placed a massive granite monument that he had commissioned and paid for in the rotunda of the court, associating the display with the idea that individuals are bound by a higher law. A federal district judge and a federal appellate court ruled that this was unconstitutional and found Judge Moore in contempt. The Alabama Court of the Judiciary subsequently removed Moore from office, and his attempt at reinstatement failed before another judicial panel (Pottenger 2007, 18–19). In 2012, however, the voters reelected Moore to the Alabama Supreme Court, although he was again ousted after urging fellow state judges to resist the U.S. Supreme Court decision in *Obergefell v. Hodges* (2015) permitting same-sex marriage, which Moore had likened to bestiality (Chason 2017).

Moore was lauded by some evangelical leaders who were sympathetic to his stance and appreciated his courage, and in 2017 Republicans nominated him as their candidate for the U.S. Senate seat that had been vacated by Jeff Sessions, who had resigned to become the attorney general of the United States. During a campaign against Democrat Doug Jones, however, Moore was faced with allegations that he had inappropriately pursued teenage girls, and he lost the election and has not been renominated for other state-wide offices.

In 2020, Moore ran unsuccessfully for the Republican senatorial nomination to oppose Jones.

See also Congressional Resolution on the Ten Commandments (1997); Sessions, Jeff; Ten Commandments

For Reference and Further Reading

Chason, Rachel. 2017. "A Short History of Roy Moore's Controversial Interpretations of the Bible." *Washington Post*. September 27. https://www.washingtonpost.com/news/acts-of-faith/wp/2017/09/27/a-short-history-of-roy-moores-controversial-interpretations-of-the-bible/.

Cillizza, Chris. 2019. "Roy Moore Is a Living, Breathing Republican Nightmare." CNN. May 29. https://www.cnn.com/2019/05/29/politics/roy-moore-doug-jones-donald-trump/index.html.

Davis, Derek H. 1997. "Editorial: Religion and the Abuse of Judicial Power." *Journal of Church and State* 39 (Spring): 203–14.

Pottenger, John R. 2007. *Reaping the Whirlwind: Liberal Democracy and the Religious Axis*. Washington, DC: Georgetown University Press.

Moses as Political Archetype

Americans sometimes look to biblical sources for suitable political archetypes. One of the most prominent biblical leaders, known to Christians, Jews, and Muslims, is that of Moses. According to the biblical story outlined in the book of Exodus, the opening chapters of which were omitted from the so-called Slave Bible, is that of Moses. Born at a time when Pharaoh had ordered all Hebrew boys to be slaughtered, his mother put him in a basket in the Nile, where Pharaoh's daughter found him, took pity upon him, and raised her as her own son in the courts of Pharaoh.

When Moses came of age and realized his heritage, he killed an Egyptian taskmaster and subsequently fled from Pharaoh. He became a shepherd before encountering God in a burning bush, reluctantly accepting God's command for him to tell Pharaoh to let the children of Israel go, bringing down ten plagues upon the Egyptians until they relented, and then leading his people across the Red (or Reed) Sea, where they spent forty years in the wilderness before reaching the Promised Land of Canaan. During this time, Moses ascended Mount Sinai where God revealed the Ten Commandments to him. The first five books of the Bible are often called the books of Moses and have traditionally been attributed to him.

In a fairly comprehensive treatment of the image of Moses throughout American history, Bruce Feiler documents how the story of Moses is a pervasive theme in U.S. history. Feiler observes that the Pilgrims believed that they were following in Moses's spiritual footsteps when they crossed the Atlantic and settled in a wilderness; the Geneva Bible, which many of them used, featured a depiction of the Jews crossing the Red Sea on its title page. When Pennsylvanians chose to celebrate their own fiftieth anniversary, they chose the words of Moses in Leviticus 25:10 to articulate their desire for freedom. Both Benjamin Franklin and Thomas Jefferson suggested using symbols that included Moses on the Great Seal of the United States.

Although other images were certainly used (e.g., Cincinnatus, Joshua, and Gideon), George Washington was often likened to Moses leading a people out of British slavery (Hay 1969). In time, African Americans incorporated the story of Moses in songs designed to inspire hope of liberation. Harriet Tubman, who worked with the Underground Railroad to bring slaves to freedom, was likened to a female Moses about the same time the nation was portraying Daniel Boone as an American Moses helping to settle the American wilderness. After Abraham Lincoln issued his Emancipation Proclamation and then worked for the adoption of constitutional amendments to free the slaves and protect their rights, he too was likened to Moses (as well as Jesus). In proclaiming the abolition of slavery in Tennessee, where Lincoln had named him military governor, Andrew Johnson, who would succeed Lincoln to the presidency, proclaimed to African Americans that "he would 'be your Moses' and lead them 'through the Red Sea of war and bondage, to a fairer future of liberty and peace'" (Bowman 2019, 152). Ironically, during the Civil War, some Southerners reversed the imagery and portrayed Lincoln as the Pharaoh who would not let the people go and Jefferson Davis, the Confederate president, as the Moses who was leading them away (Daniell 2003, 718).

Many immigrants, especially Jews, who came to America saw their passage, as had the pilgrims before them, as another crossing of the sea to freedom. For many the Statue of Liberty, which held a tablet much like those that Moses brought down from Sinai, and the Ten Commandments continued to have a special place in American thinking, with Cecil B. DeMille later viewing his classic movie, *The Ten Commandments* (1956), as a way of reaffirming American values against rival communist nations.

Figures of Moses are displayed prominently at the U.S. Supreme Court and other governmental sites. Controversies continue to arise about public displays of the Ten Commandments and the appropriateness of such displays in public schools.

In the 1960s, Dr. Martin Luther King Jr.'s followers often likened him to Moses. As he prophetically indicated in his speech, like Moses, King never entered into the Promised Land of equal rights, but he had been in the vanguard of those who had sought to ring in equal rights for all, drawing deeply on the words of the Liberty Bell as embodied in "America" in the process.

In recent years, Moses has been used to describe such diverse figures as Betty Friedan of the feminist movement, Harvey Milk of the LBGTQ movement, and even contemporary presidents (Feiler 2009, 177–78). George W. Bush says that the story of Moses was an important part of his own call to politics (Siker n.d.), and it seems likely he will not be the last to be so influenced.

Feiler observes that part of the attraction of Moses is that he was a flawed figure who recognized the need to balance both liberty and law. Shalom Carmy observes that it is important to remember that the Bible depicts Moses more as a prophet, or religious, than as "a royal" or political figure; he likens him to "a legislator-ruler" (2010, 79).

In addition to serving as an archetype, the laws of Moses, and particularly the Ten Commandments, were especially influential in the laws of the early New England colonies. In the late nineteenth century, Henry George, the author of *Progress and Poverty*, who advocated a single tax on land, further lauded Moses for specifying widespread distribution of property in Canaan, for providing for a Sabbath, which would provide rest for members of all classes, and for the Year of Jubilee, which would forgive debts and free slaves every fiftieth year.

See also Geneva Bible; George, Henry; Great Seal of the United States; Liberty Bell; Lincoln, Abraham; Statue of Liberty; Ten Commandments

For Reference and Further Reading

Bowman, Frank O., III. 2019. *High Crimes and Misdemeanors: A History of Impeachment for the Age of Trump*. New York: Cambridge University Press.

Callahan, Allen Dwight. 2006. *The Talking Bible: African Americans and the Bible*. New York: Oxford University Press.

Carmy, Shalom. 2010. "Personal Ethics, Public Virtue, and Political Legitimacy in Biblical Kings and American Presidents." *Presidential Studies Quarterly* 40 (March): 76–89.

Daniell, David. 2003. *The Bible in English: Its History and Influence*. New Haven, CT: Yale University Press.

Feiler, Bruce. 2009. *America's Prophet: Moses and the American Story*. New York: William Morrow.
Hay, Robert P. 1969. "George Washington: American Moses." *American Quarterly* 21 (Winter): 780–91.
Siker, Jeffrey S. n.d. "President Bush, Biblical Faith, and the Politics of Religion." SBL Forum, n.p. http://sbl-site.org/Article.aspx?ArticleID=151. Accessed April 1, 2019.
Walzer, Michael. 1985. *Exodus and Revolution*. New York: Basic Books.
Wildavsky, Aaron. 1984. *The Nursing Father: Moses as a Political Leader*. Tuscaloosa: University of Alabama Press.

Muhammad, Elijah

Elijah Muhammad (1934–1975) was a leader of a black nationalist movement called the Nation of Islam (NOI), and influenced Malcolm X, Louis Farrakhan, and Muhammad Ali. Muhammad, whose original name was Elijah Robert Poole, became a Muslim after hearing a speech by Wallace Fard Muhammad, whom he later identified as Allah, while designating himself as Fard's prophet. He was succeeded as head of the NOI by his son Warith Deen Mohammed.

In his *Message to the Blackman in America*, Muhammad argued that the Jewish and Christian Bible had been corrupted, and that their Bible was inferior to the Holy Koran, which he believed God had dictated directly to the Prophet Muhammad rather than filtering through messengers. Muhammad associated the Jewish and Christian Bible with white people, whom he considered to be devils (noting, in the process, that if [as some believed] blacks were the sons of Noah's son Ham, then the flood had destroyed whites). Muhammad also made a point of how the most prominent version of the Bible in English was dedicated to an English king.

Although he sought commonalities between the Christian and Muslim holy books, Muhammad took great exception to the biblical story of redemption: "Jesus, a righteous man, had to be murdered to pay the price of the sin of the murderer (Adam) in order to free the people who were under a death penalty for the sin of Adam—while yet the Book teaches that God is a just God. No common father of a son would like to kill his own son for the wrong of a man who lived 4,000 years before his son was born" (Muhammad 1973, 91). He further questioned how the sacrifice of Jesus could have been effective, if God had redeemed him from the dead.

Muhammad decided that the God of whites in the Bible and the God of blacks in the Koran were not the same God (94). He continued,

> The Bible is the graveyard of my poor people (the so-called Negroes) and I would like to dwell upon this book until I am sure that they understand that it is not quite as holy as they thought it was. I don't mean to say that there is no truth in it; certainly there is plenty of truth, if understood. Will you accept the understanding of it? The Bible charges all of its Great Prophets with evil, it makes God guilty of an act of adultery by charging Him with being the father of Mary's baby (Jesus), again it charges Noah and Lot with drunkenness, and Lot with getting children by his daughter. What a Poison Book. (1973, 95)

Muhammad went on to argue that the stories of the Lost Sheep and the Prodigal Son found in Luke 15 should be applied to American Negroes (95–96).

Muhammad further questioned the biblical injunctions in Luke 6:17–29 to love one's enemies and turn the other cheek, observing that "the slave-masters couldn't have found a better teaching for their protection against the slaves' possible dissatisfaction with their master's brutal treatment" (96). He argued that the Pharaoh of Egypt had "feared that Moses would teach this people the true religion, Islam!" while further suggesting that "both the present Bible and Holy Qur-an must soon give way to that Holy Book which no man as yet but Allah has seen" (97). At the end of Muhammad's book, he included "A Guide to Understanding the Bible," and a "Guide to Understanding the Holy Qur-an," both of which have extensive references to chapters and verses of the respective texts (349–55).

Although Elijah Muhammad identified himself as a Muslim, there is continuing dispute as to whether this identification is accurate (Berg 2009). There are certainly numerous differences between Elijah Muhammad's understandings and those of traditional Islam, most notably the former's stark distinctions between whites and blacks.

See also Alternate Scriptures, Slavery

For Reference and Further Reading

Berg, Herbert. 2009. *Elijah Muhammad and Islam*. New York: NYU Press.

Callahan, Allen Dwight. 2006. *The Talking Book: African Americans and the Bible*. New Haven, CT: Yale University Press.

Muhammad, Elijah. 1973. *Message to the Blackman in America*. Phoenix, AZ: Secretarius Memps.

Muhlenberg, Peter

Anglican ministers faced a special challenge during the Revolutionary War, because their position as members of the official Church of England required their loyalty to the British monarchy. Although Peter Muhlenberg (1746–1807) was raised by Lutheran missionaries in Pennsylvania, attended the Academy of Philadelphia, and studied theology under his father, he was ordained as an Anglican in England before he took a job at a church in Woodstock, Virginia. He served in the House of Burgesses and the First Virginia Convention during his pastorate.

Muhlenberg is best known for a story apparently first told in any detail by his grandnephew, Henry Augustus Muhlenberg, in 1849. According to the account, having told his congregation that he was going to give a farewell sermon, he preached from Ecclesiastes 3 (which details how "To everything there is a season"). After proclaiming that this was a season for war, he removed his clerical garb to reveal his military uniform, persuading many of his congregation to enlist with him. This story was further immortalized in a poem by Thomas Buchanan Read first published in 1862 in *The Wagoner of the Alleghenies: A Poem of the Days of Seventy-Six,* and later published in McGuffey Readers. In 1889, Pennsylvania donated a statue of Muhlenberg taking off his clerical garb to the U.S. Capitol Building, and there are additional statues on Connecticut Avenue in Washington, DC, and in front of the Shenandoah County Courthouse in Woodstock, Virginia. The best current evidence, however, some of which was discussed in a segment of PBS's History Detectives, indicates that while Muhlenberg had given up his church in order to serve in the military, this particular version of events probably never occurred (Rodda 2007).

Muhlenberg did, however, have an impressive military career, involving service in a number of important battles and campaigns where he and his men were recognized for their bravery and discipline (Horn 2015). Moreover, Muhlenberg continued with impressive service, which included being the vice president of Pennsylvania, a member of the U.S. House of Representatives, a U.S. senator, the supervisor of revenue for Pennsylvania, and the customs director for the port of Philadelphia.

See also Revolutionary War

For Reference and Further Reading

Horn, Joshua. 2015. "Peter Muhlenberg: The Pastor Turned Soldier." *Journal of the American Revolution*. November 9. https://allthingsliberty.com/2015/11/peter-muhlenberg-the-pastor-turned-soldier/.

Rightmyer, Thomas Nelson. 1961. "The Holy Orders of Peter Muhlenberg." *Historical Magazine of the Protestant Episcopal Church* 30 (September): 183–97.

Rodda, Chris. 2007. "PBS Show Gets It Right with the Story of Peter Muhlenberg's Robe." Talk to Action. August 4. www.talk2action.org/story/2007/8/4/201559/9741.

• N •

Nation, Carry A.

Carry A. Nation (1846–1911) is probably better known for carrying a Bible and a hatchet than quoting from the former, but her own writing and speeches referred frequently to the Bible, and her opposition to alcoholic beverages was grounded in biblical condemnations of drunkenness.

Born in Kentucky, she endured a difficult childhood in which family slaves gave her more attention than her parents. She married Charles Gloyd in 1867 only to find that her parents had been correct in identifying him as a hopeless alcoholic, who died only months after the birth of their only child. Although she remarried David Nation, who was a journalist, a lawyer, and a pastor, in 1874, this marriage fared little better, and eventually ended in divorce on the grounds that Carry had deserted him for her anti-prohibition crusade. Carry continued to keep her second husband's name, noting that "C.A.N. are the initials of my name, then C. (see) A Nation! And all together Carry A. Nation! This is no accident but Providence. This does not mean that I will carry a nation, but that the roused heart and conscience will, as I am the roused heart and conscience of the people in operation" (Nation 1908, 129).

Although baptized as a member of the Disciples of Christ (sometimes pejoratively known as Campbellites), she received the "baptism of the Holy Ghost" at a Methodist revival, she dressed as a Quaker, and she included Catholicism and the Salvation Army among her influences (Carver 1999, 36). Her autobiography makes many references to the Bible, although she admits that "I often had doubts as to whether the Bible was the work of God or man" (Nation 1908, 56). She obviously regarded it highly: "I wanted to believe the Bible the Word of God. I early saw that to close the Bible was to shut out all knowledge of the purpose of life. Without its revelations one does not know why we are born, why we live, or where we go after death. We can see the purpose of all nature, but not of this life of ours, and God had, by revelation, to make this known" (Nation 1908, 56). She further explained that she largely took the Bible on faith:

> I do not believe the Bible because I understand it; for there are few things of revelation that I do understand. Creation is a mystery, still we know everything had a beginning. I do not know how things grow out of the earth. Why they are green. Why grass makes wool on a sheep and hair on a cow, but I know these are facts. I cannot understand how the blood of Jesus Christ cleanses from sin, neither do I understand that greatest of all mysteries, the new birth, but nothing is more positively a fact in my experience. (Nation 1908, 56)

After moving to Medicine Lodge, Kansas, Nation founded a chapter of the Women's Christian Temperance Union and began walking into saloons with a Bible where (imitating Moses's smashing of the Ten Commandments and Jesus's cleansing of the temple) she would throw stones and bricks at the mirrors and bottles of alcohol. A hatchet that a supporter gave her subsequently became her most prominent symbol, and she subsequently sold pewter pins in the shape of a hatchet to raise money for her cause as she appeared not only at saloons but also on vaudeville stages, on college campuses, at chautauquas, and at other events.

Nation was an imposing woman who was six feet tall, and had a knack for capturing attention and derision from those who questioned her apparent defiance of contemporary sexual roles; she often referred to herself as a biblical Deborah, after the Old Testament judge who had led an army against Israel's enemies. A scholar observes that "she was jailed more than thirty times in states from Maine to California; she was beaten with a broom, horsewhipped in the street, bombed with raw eggs, kicked into the gutter, beaten by a band of prostitutes hired especially for the purpose, knocked on the head with chairs, and hit so hard one time that she swallowed a false tooth. Twice she barely escaped a 'necktie party' (that is, a lynch mob)" Carver 1999, 39).

Nation collapsed while lecturing in 1911 and died soon after. Her tombstone reads, "Faithful to the Cause of Prohibition. She Hath Done What She Could."

See also Temperance Movement

For Reference and Further Reading

Blakemore, Erin. 2018. "Activist Carry Nation Used a Hatchet to Smash Booze Bottles before Prohibition." History.com. December 10. https://www.history.com/news/carry-nation-temperance-prohibition-alcohol.

Carver, Frances Grace. 1999. "With Bible in One Hand and Battle-Axe in the Other: Carry A. Nation as Religious Performer and Self-Promoter." *Religion and American Culture: A Journal of Interpretation* 9 (Winter): 31–65.

Nation, Carry A. 1908. *The Use and Need of the Life of Carry A. Nation*. Topeka, KS: F.M. Steves & Sons, 1909.

National Association of Evangelicals (For the Health of the Nation)

If members of any group might be expected to base their position on biblical principles, it might be the National Association of Evangelicals (NAE). Founded in 1942 as "a response to theological liberalism and rising fundamentalism" (NAE 2018, 5) as well as from the belief that radio and television programming was being disproportionally allocated to more liberal mainline Protestant denominations (Matthews 1992, 39–47), this organization represents forty-five thousand churches from forty denominations, which are generally united by their high view of Scriptures, their belief in the necessity for conversion (hence members often refer to themselves as "born-again" Christians), and their belief in the need for personal evangelism.

Although there have been evangelical components of religion throughout American history, they came to prominence in 1976 when Jimmy Carter identified himself as an evangelical Christian, although many who shared this identity subsequently preferred the more conservative political policies of Ronald Reagan. Since then, significantly more Republicans than Democrats have identified themselves as evangelicals. In contrast to earlier periods in history, such evangelicals have often allied themselves with Roman Catholics on such issues as opposition to abortion and to same-sex marriage.

In 2004, the NAE issued a report entitled "For the Health of the Nation," which Jacques Berlinerblau has described as "nothing less than a full-blown party platform" (2008, 14). The most recent version of this document presents an introduction, a discussion of the basis for Christian engagement, another on the methods for doing so, one on the structure and public life, and eight principles of Christian Political Engagement.

The discussion of "The Basis for Christian Engagement" begins with a reference to Genesis 27–28 of God's creation of "our first parents in his image" and his vesting them with "dominion over the earth" (NAE 2018, 8). This section continues with reference to ten other Scriptures, all but one from the New Testament.

In discussing "The Method for Christian Civic Engagement," this report attempts to ground its approach in Scripture. Noting that "every political judgment requires both a normative vision and factual analysis," the report says that "as Christians committed to the full authority of Scripture, our normative vision must flow from the Bible and from the moral order that God has embedded in his creation" (12). While further seeking "to submit to the authority of Scripture in every area of life," the report recognizes that "many contemporary political decisions . . . deal with complex sociological or technological issues not explicitly discussed in the Bible" (12). It further recognized "that biblical faith is vastly larger and richer than every limited, inevitably imperfect political agenda and that commitment to the lordship of Christ and his one Body far transcends all political commitments" (15).

The section of the report on "The Structures of Political Life" stresses the need for organizational structures and for spiritual leaders. It endorses "representative democracy," and "a constitutional order" (18), that "preserves the God-ordained responsibilities of society's other institutions" (19).

The first of eight principles that the report outlines is the need to protect religious freedom and liberty of conscience. Indeed, the opening sentence of this section lists five separate Scriptures, all from the New Testament, demonstrating that God ordained "the two coexisting institutions of church and state as distinct from the other with each occupying its own center of authority under a sovereign God" (21). Advocating "gospel pluralism," this section argues that the First Amendment does "not shield individuals from exposure to the religious views of nongovernmental speakers" while tax exemptions from religious organizations do "not establish religion by leaving it alone" (21–22). It takes a similar position with respect to governmental aid focused through both religious and nonreligious organizations and points out that the government should also seek to promote religious freedom abroad.

In addressing "Safeguarding the Nature and Sanctity of Human Life," the report links concern for the unborn, supported by a reference to Psalm 139:13, with "the very young, the aged, those living in poverty, the chronically or terminally ill, those with disabilities and those with genetic diseases" (25). It opposes research on embryonic stem cells, euthanasia, and "genetic modifications and biotechnologies that treat the human body as a commodity" (26).

The section of the report addressing "Strengthening Marriages, Families and Children" has twelve references to Scripture in the first two paragraphs. It further defines marriage "as a lifetime covenantal relationship between one man and one woman" and as "a normative biblical symbol of God's relationship with his people" (29).

The succeeding section on "Seeking Justice and Compassion for the Poor and Vulnerable" is also replete with many scriptural references to both the Old and New Testaments. It indicates that "immigration policies should prioritize family unity and avoid separating families by deportation or detention" (34).

The section on "Pursuing Racial Justice and Reconciliation" is based on the biblical recognition of the dignity of all individuals. It rejects racism and white supremacy and calls upon Christians to be "ambassadors of reconciliation" (42).

Interestingly, the only principle that does not include any scriptural citations is that on "Promoting Just Peace and Restraining Violence." It does reference "classical just war principles, which are designed to clarify the limited conditions under which military action is justifiable" (45). Specifically addressing the issue of nuclear weapons, the report supports "a no first use policy, a continuing ban on nuclear testing, removing nuclear weapons from hair trigger alert status, efforts to secure mutual reductions in current nuclear stockpiles, and ongoing dialogue on the effects of possession and threatened use of nuclear weapons" (47).

The section on "Caring for God's Creation" includes references to a number of Scriptures related to the environment. It further identifies climate change as "a threat multiplier" that "increases the harm from desertification, pollution and other damage to creation" (49).

The report ends with a commitment to political activity that reflects "honesty, civility and respect for opponents" and to "regular prayer for those who govern" (53).

See also Abortion; Carter, Jimmy; Climate Change; Evangelicals; Immigration; Same-Sex Marriage; Manhattan Declaration: A Call of Christian Conscience; Violence

For Reference and Further Reading

Berlinerblau, Jacques. 2008. *Thumpin' It: The Use and Abuse of the Bible in Today's Presidential Politics*. Louisville, KY: Westminster John Knox Press.

Heltzel, Peter Goodwin. 2009. *Jesus and Justice: Evangelicals, Race, and American Politics*. New Haven, CT: Yale University Press.

Matthews, Arthur H. 1992. *Standing Up, Standing Together: The Emergence of the National Association of Evangelicals*. Carol Stream, IL: National Association of Evangelicals.

National Association of Evangelicals (NAE). 2018. *For the Health of the Nation: An Evangelical Call to Civic Responsibility*. https://www.nae.net/for-the-health-of-the-nation/.

National Bible Week

Since colonial times, governments have designated certain days as days of fasting, prayer, and/or thanksgiving. In 1983, President Ronald Reagan proclaimed the year to be the "Year of the Bible." Years before, in 1941, President Franklin D.

Roosevelt had proclaimed the week of Thanksgiving to be National Bible Week, and each subsequent president has followed his lead.

Much as television stations once ended the broadcast day by playing the national anthem, at the time of Roosevelt's original proclamation, the National Bible Association read Bible passages between radio broadcasts ("National Bible Week").

In recent years, presidents have followed a law that Congress adopted in 1988 asking the president to declare the first Thursday in May to be a "National Day of Prayer." In his 2019 Proclamation, President Trump cited the prayer that Franklin D. Roosevelt delivered on D-day and expressed the wish that "each of us, according to our own faiths, call upon God for His guidance and express our gratitude for the love and grace He bestows on us and our country."

While many churches and religious organizations apparently observe this week, such presidential proclamations do not require anyone to do anything. Indeed, the author of an article on the Secular Web declares that of all best sellers, the Bible is "the only one that, for the most part, is not read" (Murphy 1997). It is apparently common for members of Congress to commemorate the event. In 2016, members of the House of Representatives participated in an hour-long meeting in which members recited verses from the Bible and explained the role that they had played in their lives (Petersen 2016).

See also Days of Humiliation, Fasting, and Thanksgiving; Year of the Bible

For Reference and Further Reading

McIntyre, Dean. 2007. "National Bible Week and the Hymnal." Discipleship Ministries. November 2. https://www.umcdiscipleship.org/resources/national-bible-week-and-the-hymnal.

Murphy, John Patrick Michael. 1997. "National Bible Week (1997)." The Secular Web. https://infidels.org/library/modern/john_murphy/bibleweek.html.

Petersen, Jonathan. 2016. "Bible Honored in US House of Representatives." BibleGateway. November 16. https://www.biblegateway.com/blog/2016/11/bible-honored-in-us-house-of-representatives/.

Trump, Donald J. 2019 "Presidential Proclamation on National Day of Prayer, 2019." April 30. https://www.whitehouse.gov/presidential-actions/presidential-proclamation-national-day-prayer-2019/

National Prayer Breakfast

Each year since 1953, there has been a National Prayer Breakfast to which American leaders have been invited. President Dwight D. Eisenhower spoke at the first event, and sitting presidents have spoken every consecutive year since 1961. The president typically arrives an hour or so in advance and often meets with prominent foreign leaders and other noteworthy attendees before the meeting, with some apparently mistakenly believing that Congress or the federal government is the sponsor (Lindsay 2006, 394–95).

The event grew out of a prayer movement begun by Abraham Vereide (1886–1969), of Goodwill Industries, on the West Coast and followed the formation of prayer and Bible groups in both the U.S. House of Representatives and Senate (Peterson 2017, 214). Douglas Coe (1928–2017) (who has been described as a "stealth Billy Graham"; Lindsay 2006, 393) and Rev. Dr. Richard Halverson (1916–1995), a former chaplain in the U.S. Senate, have also been mainstays of this event. The breakfasts are sponsored by the Fellowship Foundation, which is a successor to the National Committee for Christian Leadership (NCCL), and which prefers to do most of its work in private (Lindsay 2006, 391).

In an analysis of presidential remarks at these events, Jonathan Peterson discovered that the speeches have become increasingly long and increasingly less complex. Bill Clinton and Barack Obama have quoted the most Bible verse and Presidents Eisenhower, Nixon, and the first Bush the least. Unfortunately, Peterson did not specifically identify the Scriptures used, although those interested can find them by accessing individual presidential speeches. Presidents made considerably more references to God, to prayer, and to faith. Both Presidents Clinton and Obama have referenced the Koran.

See also Hatfield, Mark

For Reference and Further Reading

Lindsay, Michael. 2006. "Is the National Prayer Breakfast Surrounded by a 'Christian Mafia'? Religious Publicity and Secrecy within the Corridors of Power." *Journal of the American Academy of Religion* 74 (June): 390–419.

"National Bible Week—Week of Thanskgiving." 2020. National Day Calendar. https://nationaldaycalendar.com/national-bible-week-week-of-thanksgiving/

Peterson, Jonathan R. 2017. "The Religious Content of the President' Remarks at the National Prayer Breakfast, 1953–2016." *Congress & the Presidency* 44(2): 212–34.

Native American Indians

Although Pilgrims and other American settlers often portrayed America as a wilderness, it was actually populated by Native Americans, many of whom, however, fell prey to European diseases against which they had little or no immunity. Although some European settlers speculated as to whether natives might be the so-called lost tribes of Israel (Corrigan and Neal 2010, 126), when they proved relatively difficult to convert to Christianity, it was more common to think of them either as Canaanites (the inhabitants of the land which the Bible said that God had given to the Jews) who were impeding the creation of a New Israel on the part of Europeans or as Amalekites, a tribe that had harassed the Israelites in the wilderness and whom prophets had told them to destroy. More generally, European settlers considered themselves to be civilized Christians, and they looked upon Native Americans as uncivilized pagans.

These differences, as well as settlers' incursion on Native American lands, almost inevitably led to conflicts, which some groups handled better than others. In a story that has often been celebrated, in Virginia, John Rolfe married Pocahontas, the daughter of a Native American chief who was alleged to have saved the life of explorer John Smith, and she was baptized and accepted into the Anglican Church (Snyder 2015). American folk painter Edward Hicks (1780–1849) was known for depictions of a peaceable kingdom similar to biblical portrayals of a millennium in which Christ ruled where American carnivores, herbivores, and children played peacefully together in the foreground as William Penn (a Quaker pacifist) came to an amiable agreement with Native Americans in the background. The reality was often quite different, with settlers and Native Americans almost always viewing one another with suspicions, which were furthered by concerns that they might be allied with America's French or Spanish rivals.

English, French, and Spanish explorers had often been accompanied by pastors and priests who considered it part of their mission to convert the natives. Indeed, the first Bible ever published in America was the Bible that John Eliot translated into the Wôpanâak language, which was printed in Cambridge, Massachusetts (Fisher 2017, 48–49). However, this mission was frequently subservient to that of settling lands and seeking wealth. Moreover, Native American proclivities, either to mix Christian teachings with their own or to reject Christianity altogether, were often taken to be a sign that they were among those whom God have given settlers the right to exterminate. Some of the most shocking accounts of violence in America are those by Puritans that describe the "laughter" and "singing" of their troops as they burned Native American families in their wigwams (Juster 2016, 119). Settlers sometimes described such massacres as "sacrifices" to God (Corrigan and Neal 2010, 135).

It is not always possible to ascertain the sincerity of their beliefs. On some occasions, however, Native Americans, especially those who had converted to Christianity, were able to cite the words of Ephesians 2:19 that "now therefore ye are no more strangers and foreigners, but fellow citizens with the saints, and of the household of God," or of Acts 17:26 claiming that all nations were of one blood, in order to pursue their claims in colonial courts (Eden 2014, 37, 43).

As American settlements in the East expanded, they pushed Native Americans to the West, and fighting continued through the end of the nineteenth century. Many Native Americans were moved to reservations, and, at times, their children were taken away to receive Christian educations.

Native Americans continue to attempt to safeguard sacred sites, bones dug up in archeological explorations, and native languages. In a recent incident, it took many years for a group of Mohicans in Wisconsin to recover a Bible and a communion set from a museum in Stockbridge, Massachusetts, that had exhibited them after they had been stolen from the tribe (Miron 2018).

See also Penn, William; Puritans; Violence

For Reference and Further Reading

Corrigan, John. 2011. "Amalek and the Rhetoric of Extermination." *The First Prejudice: Religious Tolerance and Intolerance in Early America*, ed. Chris Beneke and Christopher S. Grenda. Philadelphia: University of Pennsylvania Press, pp. 53–72.

Corrigan, John, and Lynn S. Neal. 2010. *Religious Intolerance in America: A Documentary History*. Chapel Hill: University of North Carolina Press.

Eden, Jason. 2014. "'Therefore Ye Are No More Strangers and Foreigners': Indians, Christianity, and Political Engagement in Colonial Plimouth and on Martha's Vineyard." *American Indian Quarterly* 38 (Winter): 36–59.

Fisher, Linford D. 2017. "The Bible and Indigenous Language Translations in the Americas." *The Oxford Handbook of the Bible in America*, ed. Paul C. Gutjahr. New York: Oxford University Press, pp. 39–59.

Juster, Susan. 2016. *Sacred Violence in Early America*. Philadelphia: University of Pennsylvania Press.

Miron, Rose. "Fighting for the Tribal Bible: Mohican Politics of Self-Representation in Public History." *Native American and Indigenous Studies* 5 (Fall): 91–122.
Snyder, Holward A. 2015. *Jesus and Pocahontas: Gospel, Mission, and National Myth.* Cambridge: Lutterworth Press.

Natural Disasters

Public responses to natural disasters are often viewed as measures of their leaders' concern and governmental effectiveness. In providing such aid, governments sometimes rely on agencies such as the Salvation Army and Red Cross with religious roots. Governments may in turn promote policies that lead to moral hazard when they provide overly generous insurance benefits that encourage people to build in flood or other hazardous zones or when individuals fail to take other preventive actions because they expect governments to pay for any damages.

Throughout much of world history, people have attributed natural disasters to God's wrath. The book of Genesis describes God as wiping out the cities of Sodom and Gomorrah with fire and brimstone for their wickedness. In the book of Exodus, Moses calls down plagues on the Egyptians until the Pharaoh finally relents after God strikes down each firstborn, exempting only the Israelites who put blood over their doorposts. In the book of Jonah, God first warns the city of Nineveh of impending doom, only to spare it after its inhabitants repent. The Old Testament further describes God's power in conjunction with earthquakes, storms, and other natural phenomena, and sometimes, as in Psalm 18:7, it identifies earthquakes as messages from God. The New Testament book of Revelation associates the end times with various wars, diseases, and other disasters, often symbolized by the Four Horsemen of the Apocalypse in Chapter 6 and the seven vials (or bowls) of plagues in Chapter 16.

Historically, natural disasters have prompted theological and philosophical speculation. Perhaps most notably, the destructive earthquake in Lisbon, Portugal, in 1755 resulted in speculation by English evangelist John Wesley (1703–1791) that God was punishing the city for the inquisition against Protestants, and by Voltaire's novel *Candide*, in which he mocked those, following the German philosopher Gottfried Leibnitz (1646–1716), who thought that the current world was the best possible world (Chester n.d., 9 and 15).

Professor Lauri Coleman observes that early Americans often drew from a set of beliefs that she describes as "supernatural rationalism" to explain such disasters (2009, 234). This view understood that God could act through nature to send warnings to people. Thus, droughts and other natural disasters often prompted public calls for prayer and thanksgiving. Preachers routinely used such disasters either to emphasize the precariousness of human existence, and hence the need for individuals to get right with God before it was too late, or as signs of the end time. Such events could thus heighten millennial expectations.

Americans, however, did not interpret all natural disasters as God's punishment. Writing in 1834, lexicographer Noah Webster thus observed that most human sufferings are the result of either physical or moral evils. Addressing the former, he observed that "physical events, such as diseases, storms, famine and earthquakes, are often unavoidable, and in that case are to be borne with resignation to the divine will" (Webster 1834, 173). By contrast, he believed that most moral evils were the result of sin and that "sin is the procuring cause of almost all the sufferings of mankind" (Webster 1834, 173).

After terrorists attacked the United States on September 11, 2001, Rev. Jerry Falwell was among those who explained that God was punishing the United States for its tolerance of homosexuality and other perceived moral evils (Goodstein 2001). Rev. Pat Robertson, who had made similar accusations, generated considerable attention and some ridicule when he claimed that his prayers and those of his followers had helped avert the landfall of a hurricane (Pierre 2018).

David Chester of the University of Liverpool has observed that in recent years, "Christian belief has neither inhibited more practical measures being taken to reduce hazard exposure, nor has it prevented people accepting help from the civil authorities" (Chester n.d., 18). He further observes, "Virtually every community in a country with a Christian history has a church, which is not only a religious focus but a social one, with clergy acting as a useful 'resource' in identifying victims and providing counselling, relief and leadership" (Chester n.d., 18). Historically, Christian publications, especially the *Christian Herald* in the nineteenth century, took the lead in publishing stories, often in graphic detail, designed to elicit help from Christians in relieving human suffering both at home and abroad (Curtis 2019).

In recent years, scientists have expressed increasing concern that the increased burning of fossil fuels has led to global warming, which has accentuated the power of natural disasters. Such reports have been phrased in increasingly apocalyptic language and arguably resemble earlier jeremiads that pastors once delivered about moral failings (Lilly 2016).

See also Climate Change; Falwell, Jerry; Four Horsemen of the Apocalypse; Prophets and Jeremiads; Robertson, Pat; Salvation Army

For Reference and Further Reading

Chester, David K. n.d. "Natural Disasters and Christian Theology." https://faraday-institute.org/resources/FAR268%20Chester.pdf.

Coleman, Lauri Bauer. 2009. "'Rain Down Righteousness': Interpretations of Natural Events in Mid-Eighteenth-Century Boston." *Remaking Boston: An Environmental History of the City and Its Surroundings*, ed. Anthony N. Penna and Conrad Edick Wright. Pittsburg, PA: University of Pittsburg Press, pp. 233–58.

Curtis, Heather D. 2019. *Holy Humanitarians: American Evangelicals and Global Aid.* Cambridge, MA: Harvard University Press.

Goodstein, Laurie. 2001. "Falwell: Blame Abortionists, Feminists and Gays." *Guardian.* September 19. https://www.theguardian.com/world/2001/sep/19/september11.usa9.

Lilly, Ingrid Esther. 2016. "The Planet's Apocalypse: The Rhetoric of Climate Change." *Apocalypses in Context: Apocalyptic Currents through History*, ed. Kelly J. Murphy and Justine Jeffcoat Scheedtler. Minneapolis, MN: Augsburg Fortress, pp. 359–79.

Pierre, Joe. 2018. "Hurricanes, Homosexuality, and Belief in the Hand of God." *Psychology Today.* September 13. https://www.psychologytoday.com/us/blog/psych-unseen/201809/hurricanes-homosexuality-and-belief-in-the-hand-god.

Vile, John R., ed. 2018. *Governmental Responses to Natural Disasters in the U.S.* Clark, NJ: Talbot.
Webster, Noah. 1834. *Value of the Bible and Excellence of the Christian Religion: For the Use of Families and Schools.* New Haven, CT: Durrie & Peck.

Natural Law

Although Jews and Christians may differ both among themselves and with one another about how the Bible should be interpreted and about which biblical laws are designed to be enforced by governments, they generally agree that Scriptures are the revealed word of God. Because not everyone is a Jewish believer or a Christian, simply quoting from the Bible may often prove unconvincing in political debates, even if it involves quoting directly from the Ten Commandments. It is therefore common to seek to appeal to wider moral principles, which are often classified under the heading of natural law.

St. Thomas Aquinas (1225–1274) delineated the classic Christian position on laws before the Christian church was divided into Catholic and Protestant believers. He outlined four types of law. Aquinas used the term "eternal law" to describe the mind of God. Divine law is that part of God's mind which he had shared chiefly through divine revelation, as in the Bible. Human law, which may overlap or be in opposition to the law of God, is the law of particular forms of government. Natural law is that part of eternal law which human beings, as individuals created in the image of God, are able to ascertain through the use of reason. Though such reason, they may be able to ascertain that certain human laws fall short and require correction. Through sheer reason, humans might not, apart from divine law or revelation, be able to ascertain that they should honor the Sabbath or even that they should not bow down to graven images, but rational reflection might demonstrate the wisdom of securing civil peace by not committing murder, theft, or bearing false witness.

In his law lectures at the College of Philadelphia, future Supreme Court justice James Wilson (1742–1798) described law much as Aquinas had done when he divided the subject into "law eternal," "law celestial," laws of physical nature, and laws governing human morality. He further observed that "his law, natural or revealed, made for men or for nations, flows from the same divine source: it is the law of God" (Wilson 1790).

Much modern Roman Catholic social thinking is based on the idea of natural law, but law professor Robert Cochran has observed that Protestants sometimes cite Romans 2:15, which portrays those without the Bible as still having a law "written on their hearts." Protestants often describe this as a gift of "common grace" that God gives to all; the doctrine is similar to the idea, dominant in Scottish Common Sense philosophy, that all human beings have a conscience or "moral sense" by which they can judge right from wrong (Cochran 2007, 302). Cochran further notes that Roman Catholics often combine the idea of natural law with "subsidiarity," granting the importance of institutions between individuals and national governments, which is similar to what Protestants sometimes call "sphere sovereignty," a term coined by a Dutch theologian and statesman named Abraham Kuyper (1837–1920) (Cochran 2007, 298).

As an international lawyer, John Foster Dulles (1888–1959), President Eisenhower's secretary of state, whose father was a Presbyterian minister and later a professor at Auburn Theological Seminary, participated in a number of international conferences prior to World War II in which he stressed the need to incorporate the unifying principles he found in his belief in Jesus Christ and the moral law into international law. John Mulder notes that Dulles would base his own policies as secretary of state on the principles that "there is a God; there is a moral law which is created by God and which many can know and must uphold; and individuals are created by God and given 'a spiritual dignity and worth which others should respect' " (1971, 163; also see Toulouse 1985).

American founders often appealed, as in the Declaration of Independence, to the idea of natural rights rather than to natural law, but the two are related. Notably, the Declaration of Independence specifically said that human beings are "endowed by their Creator" with the rights of "life, liberty, and the pursuit of happiness."

Although natural law principles thus arise from outside Scriptures, they must not be incompatible with them. The difficulty of natural law, and similar forms of thinking, is twofold. First, individuals often disagree vehemently on matters of right and wrong, or emphasize different aspects. Thus, one individual might believe it to be relatively self-evident that humans become human at the point of conception and thus should have rights of personhood from that point forward, while another individual might believe that a woman has an equal freedom over her own body that encompasses the right to terminate such a pregnancy. It is possible for individuals to argue that homosexual relations are unnatural because they cannot produce progeny or to argue that voluntary decisions relative to such personal intimate conduct should not be the concern of government. Second, deciding that natural law principles exist does not determine which specific agency or agencies within government have the right to enforce them. In some cases, the ideas of subsidiarity and/or sphere sovereignty might suggest that these decisions should be made by families or states rather than by the national government.

Natural law principles are often evoked by those who believe that existing governmental policies are immoral. Dr. Martin Luther King Jr. thus argued for civil disobedience against Jim Crow laws because he thought such laws were an affront to equal rights even before the Supreme Court had invalidated them in *Brown v. Board of Education* (1954). Advocates for women's rights argued that laws denying women equal protection, while ensconced in both law and judicial precedents, were still unjust. In recent years, individuals have argued that governmental policies toward immigrants were similarly unjust.

Just as many individuals argue that governments, at a minimum, need not require behaviors that the Bible forbids, so too many believe that, in the least, governmental policies should not violate fundamental norms of justice, whether they identify such laws as "natural laws" or use some other term for them. Somewhat complicating the picture still further is that the U.S. Constitution is often regarded as a type of "higher law" (Corwin 1965), which is supreme over all other laws, perhaps with the exception of the natural law itself.

In a speech that he delivered at Notre Dame University on October 21, 2019, Donald Trump's attorney general William Barr, who is a Roman Catholic, argued that freedom is only possible for a people who exercise self-control and who follow Scripture and natural law principles. He argued that "progressives" have joined "secularists" in "the campaign to destroy the traditional moral order," which he largely associated with governmental failure to uphold laws "that reflect traditional moral norms." As examples, he cited legislation liberalizing abortion laws, permitting euthanasia, and secular curricula that were contrary to traditional moral values.

See also Civil Disobedience; Declaration of Independence; King, Martin Luther, Jr.; Roman Catholics; Ten Commandments

For Reference and Further Reading

Barr, William P. 2019. "Attorney General William P. Barr Delivers Remarks to the Law School and the de Nicola Center for Ethics and Culture at the University of Notre Dame." United States Department of Justice. October 11. https://www.justice.gov/opa/speech/attorney-general-william-p-barr-delivers-remarks-law-school-and-de-nicola-center-ethics.

Budziszewski, J. 1997. *Written on the Heart: The Case for Natural Law.* Downers Grove, IL: InterVarsity Press.

Cochran, Robert F., Jr. 2007. "Catholic and Evangelical Supreme Court Justices: A Theological Analysis." *University of Saint Thomas Law Journal* 4: 296–311.

Corwin, Edward S. 1965. *The "Higher Law" Background of American Constitutional Law.* Ithaca, NY: Cornell University Press.

Finnis, John. 2011. *Natural Law and Natural Rights,* 2nd ed. New York: Oxford University Press.

Mulder, John M. 1971. "The Moral World of John Foster Dulles: A Presbyterian Layman and International Affairs." *Journal of Presbyterian History* 49 (Summer): 157–82.

Toulouse, Mark G. 1985. "The Development of a Cold Warrior: John Foster Dulles and the Soviet Union, 1945–1952." *American Presbyterians* 63 (Fall): 309–22.

Wilson, James. 1790. "Lectures on Law." *Collected Works of James Wilson,* Vol. I, ed. Mark David Hall and Kermit L. Hall. Indianapolis, IN: Liberty Fund, 2007, Chapter II. Natural Law, Natural Rights, and American Constitutionalism. http ://www.nlnrac.org/node/241.

New Haven Constitution of 1639

In founding a government for New Haven, Connecticut, Pilgrims drew upon the thoughts of Rev. John Davenport (1597–1670), which were expressed in a work entitled *A Discourse about Civil Government in a New Plantation Whose Design Is Religion.* They met in an assembly on June 4, 1639, to discuss the foundation both of a civil constitution and of a church for the area. Ultimately, they were asked to answer six queries, five of which were directed toward the establishment of the government, and the sixth of which related to the church. Each proposition was twice affirmed by a show of hands, perhaps much in the manner in which they might have imagined ancient Israelites agreeing to a covenant with God. The notes of the meeting indicate that a key objective was to seek the mind of God on the subject.

The first query asked, "WHETHER the scriptures do hold forth a perfect rule for the direction and government of all men in all duties which they are to perform to GOD and man, as well in families and commonwealth, as in matters of the church?" ("Fundamental Agreement" 1639). They agreed unanimously to this proposition.

In a second action, the assembly members reaffirmed their adherence to the "plantation covenant," or civil covenant, to which it had earlier agreed but a copy of which no longer exists (Weir 2005, 91), and which they distinguished from "a church covenant." The civil covenant was affirmed as dealing with the "civil order, as choice of magistrates and officers, making and repealing laws, dividing allotments of inheritance, and all things of like nature," by which "we would all of us be ordered by those rules which the scripture holds forth to US" ("Fundamental Agreement" 1639).

In a third action, the assembly recognized free planters who were willing to be considered for church membership. In a fourth action, the people further agreed to be "bound to establish such civil order as might best conduce to the securing of the purity and peace of the ordinance [matters relating to the church] to themselves and their posterity according to GOD" ("Fundamental Agreement" 1639).

In instructing the assembly, Davenport then recommended that the individuals chosen to lead such government should follow the qualifications established in Exodus 18:2, Deuteronomy 1:13 and 17:15, and 1 Corinthians 6:1–7. The first nondescript verse referenced Moses's father-in-law Jethro, who had advised him on judicial administration; the second referred to "wise men" who were well known by the compatriots and one of them; and the third advised church members to solve their own disputes rather than taking them to secular authorities. In its fifth action, the assembly then voted to restrict civil leaders to those who would be members of the church. They did this to assure that such men would be God-fearing. Although this was approved after the vote was taken, some members indicated their belief that the people should be able to take such power in their own hands "if things were not orderly carried" ("Fundamental Agreement" 1639).

In its final action, the assembly voted to choose twelve men (who would in turn choose seven of their members) to form the first church.

In the process of distinguishing civil government from the government of the church, the colony thus managed to link the two by requiring that members of the former be members of the latter.

See also Covenants, Compacts, Contracts, and Constitutions; Fundamental Orders of Connecticut; Pilgrims

For Reference and Further Reading

Davenport, John [Work incorrectly attributed to John Cotton]. 1643. *A Discourse about Civil Government in a New Plantation Whose Design Is Religion*. Cambridge: Samuel Green and Marmaduke Johnson. Evans Early American Imprint Collection. University of Michigan. https://quod.lib.umich.edu/cgi/t/text/text-idx?c=evans;cc=evans;rgn=main;view=text;idno=N00042.0001.001.

"Fundamental Agreement, or Original Constitution of the Colony of New Haven." June 4, 1639. The Avalon Project, Yale Law School. https://avalon.law.yale.edu/17th_century/ct01.asp.

Weir, David A. 2005. *Early New England: A Covenanted Society*. Grand Rapids, MI: William B. Eerdmans.

New York School Controversy, 1840–1842

There were a number of controversies in the nineteenth century over the role of the Bible in public schools. A controversy that arose in Philadelphia in 1844 contributed to rioting that resulted in the loss of life and the burning of churches. In 1869, there was a similar dispute in Cincinnati that barely avoided violence. The controversy in New York City preceded both of these.

In each case, however, the controversies revolved around similar issues. In New York City, "public" schools were actually operated by the Public School Society , which has been described as "a Quaker-oriented philanthropy designed originally 'for the establishment of a free school for the education of poor children who do not belong to, or are not provided for by, any religious society'" (McCadden 1964, 188). The problem with such an arrangement in New York, as in other cities, was that these schools conveyed a type of generic Protestantism that included daily readings from the King James Version of the Bible. Because Roman Catholics generally objected both to this translation and to the idea of reading from a Bible without accompanying notes that conveyed the church's interpretation of the text, and because they found that a number of textbooks had a strong anti-Catholic bias, many withheld their children from the schools, and there were not enough Catholic parochial schools to accommodate them.

New York archbishop John Joseph Hughes (1797–1864) and other Catholics objected to this arrangement. A Catholic priest, commenting on "the *sectarian* character of the public schools," observed that:

> The Holy Scriptures are read every day, with the restriction that no specific tenets are to be inculcated. Here, sir, we find the great demarcating principle between the Catholic Church and the sectaries introduced *silently*. The Catholic Church tells her children that they must be taught their religion by AUTHORITY. The sects say, read the Bible; the children are allowed to judge for themselves. The Protestant principle is therefore acted upon, silently inculcated, and the schools are sectarian. (McCadden 1964, 194–95).

After continued conflict over this issue, the public schools made some attempts to expunge texts of anti-Catholic sentiments. Governor William Seward, who, in addition to any desire he might have had to secure support from Roman Catholic voters, was deeply interested in seeing that all children were educated (Lannie 1966), supported plans whereby Catholics would attend schools taught only by other Catholics or whereby the two systems would merge, with neither containing Bible readings or doctrinal instruction. Absent this, Roman Catholics pushed for state support for their own schools.

All these plans encountered serious opposition with directors of the Public School Society continuing to insist that there was nothing sectarian about reading the Bible. As Theodore Sedgwick, one of its members, observed,

> If the whole Bible cannot be used, cannot such extracts from it be compiled as will satisfy all parties? . . . On one point surely we of the Protestant faith cannot claim any superiority. In the *moral teaching* of the two versions, there is no considerable difference. . . . The great moral precepts (I speak now of the teaching of

> Our Saviour) are the same. How can it be otherwise? We are all Christians; either Bible is the code of Christ. (McCadden 1964, 201)

Others also argued that any public support for Roman Catholic schools would violate the doctrine of separation of church and state, which was associated with the establishment clause of the First Amendment. Although the schools were not merged and no public funds were shared with Catholic schools, the dispute did result in the creation of an elected school board that worked to limit the growth of schools under the authority of the Public School Society and to assure that school curricula were less offensive to Roman Catholics (Pratt 1961, 362).

Twentieth-century Supreme Court decisions, most notably *Abington v. Schempp* (1963), have further restricted devotional Bible readings in public schools.

See also Abington v. Schempp (1963); Cincinnati Bible War of 1869; King James Version of the Bible; Philadelphia Bible Riots of 1844; Roman Catholics

For Reference and Further Reading

Lannie, Vincent Peter. 1966. "William Seward and the New York School Controversy. 1840–1842: A Problem in Historical Motivation." *History of Education Quarterly* 6 (Spring): 52–71.

McCadden, Joseph J. 1964. "Bishop Hughes versus the Public School Society of New York." *Catholic Historical Review* 50 (July): 188–207.

Pratt, John W. 1961. "Governor Seward and the New York City School Controversy, 1840–1842: A Milestone in the Advance of Nonsectarian Public Education." *New York History* 42 (October): 351–64.

Niebuhr, Reinhold

Reinhold Niebuhr (1892–1971) was a prominent theologian who is perhaps best known for interjecting a strong dose of realism into American theological liberalism. The son of a pastor, Niebuhr was educated at Eden Theological Seminary and Yale Divinity School, and he began preaching at the Bethel Evangelical Church in Detroit, where he expressed sympathy with the concerns of labor and joined the Socialist Party then headed by Norman Thomas. He spent most of his life as a professor at New York's Union Theological Seminary and was a prolific writer who frequently contributed to the *Christian Century* and a variety of newspapers and magazines. He helped found both *Christianity and Society* and *Christianity and Crisis* (Finstuen 2009, 104). Niebuhr is sometimes associated with the neo-orthodox theology of the Swiss Reformed theologian Karl Barth (1886–1968) and was known for distinguishing between "taking the Bible seriously and taking it literally" (Schlesinger 2005).

At a time when many advocates of the social gospel and other postmillennialists were foreseeing a time of unlimited progress, Niebuhr resurrected the Christian doctrine of "original sin," which suggested that people were self-centered and that they rarely achieved the level of agape love that Jesus embodied. Moreover, as the title of one of his most famous books, *Moral Man and Immoral Society*, suggested, Niebuhr believed that people behaved even more badly in groups than they did as individuals.

Niebuhr frequently commented on issues of his day. He warned about the American tendency to view itself naïvely as a redeemer nation with higher ideals than other nations. He favored democratic government while realizing that it was flawed. In one of his most famous statements, he said, "Man's capacity for justice makes democracy possible; but man's inclination to injustice makes democracy necessary" (Schlesinger 2005). He is also widely known for composing the Serenity Prayer: "God grant me the serenity to accept the things I cannot change, the courage to change the things I can, and the wisdom to know the difference" (Fackre 2002).

In contrast to many fellow liberal theologians, Niebuhr was an advocate of Zionism, believing that it was important in the wake of World War II to have a homeland that Jews could call their own (Mosley 2013). Although he valued the agape love described by the Bible, Niebuhr believed that justice was the highest practical ideal to which nations should strive. (Thompson 1975, 283).

Although wary of utopian political movements of any time, he affirmed the hope of the Christian resurrection (Fackre 2002). When asked what he believed to be the most important verse in the Bible, he cited Ephesians 4:32: "And be ye kind one to another, tender-hearted, forgiving one another, even as God for Christ's sake hath forgiven you" (Thompson 1975, 282).

Dr. Martin Luther King Jr. was among the individuals who credited Niebuhr with steering him away from what he believed to be an unduly optimistic view of human nature, and King wrote an essay on him (1953–1954?). Presidents Jimmy Carter and Barack Obama have also cited him as an important influence on their own political thought.

See also Carter, Jimmy; King, Martin Luther, Jr.; Obama, Barack; Zionism

For Reference and Further Reading

Fackre, Gabriel. 2002. "Was Reinhold Niebuhr a Christian?" First Things. October. https://www.firstthings.com/article/2002/10/was-reinhold-niebuhr-a-christian.

Finstuen, Andrew S. 2009. *Original Sin and Everyday Protestants: The Theology of Reinhold Niebuhr, Billy Graham, and Paul Tillich in an Age of Anxiety*. Chapel Hill: University of North Carolina Press.

King, Martin Luther, Jr. April 1, 1953 to June 30, 1954?. "The Theology of Reinhold Niebuhr." The Martine Luther King, Jr. Research and Education Institute. https://kinginstitute.stanford.edu/king-papers/documents/theology-reinhold-niebuhr.

Mosley, Carys. 2013. *Nationhood, Providence and Witness: Israel in Modern Theology and Social Theory*. Eugene, OR: Cascade Books.

Schlesinger, Arthur, Jr. 2005. "Forgetting Reinhold Niebuhr." *New York Times*. September 18. https://www.nytimes.com/2005/09/18/books/review/forgetting-reinhold-niebuhr.html.

Thompson, Dennis L. 1975. "The Basic Doctrines and Concepts of Reinhold Niebuhr's Political Thought." *Journal of Church and State* 17 (Spring): 275–99.

• O •

Obama, Barack

Barack Obama (b. 1961) served two terms as president between the presidencies of George W. Bush and Donald J. Trump. Although two other entries in this volume specifically describe Obama's "A Call to Renewal" (a speech that he gave while running for the Senate) and his eulogy for Senator Clementa Pinckney in the aftermath of the massacre at the Emanuel African Methodist Episcopal Church in Charleston, South Carolina, both speeches can be better understood against the wider canvas of Obama's biblical rhetoric.

In an excellent study, Professor Jeffrey S. Siker indicates that Obama and his speechwriter, Jon Favreau, relied on three primary sources for words and stories. They were Abraham Lincoln, Martin Luther King Jr., and Scripture. Obama was the nation's first African American president. He did not grow up in a very religious background, lived in Hawaii and Indonesia during some of his childhood, and had a Muslim father. As the first African American president, it is probably significant that he opened his autobiography entitled *Dreams from My Father* with a quotation from 1 Chronicles 29:15: "For we are strangers before these, and sojourners, as were all our fathers" (Siker 2012, 588).

Obama became interested in Christianity when serving as a community organizer in Chicago and attending the Trinity United Church of Christ, which was pastored by Jeremiah Wright. Its motto was "Unashamedly black and unapologetically Christian" (Siker 2012, 590). Obama was particularly moved by a sermon entitled "The Audacity to Hope," which was based on the story of Hannah, who was grieving over her barrenness as recorded in 1 Samuel 1. In explaining his reaction, Obama wrote, "I imagined the stories of ordinary black people merging with the stories of David and Goliath, Moses and Pharaoh, the Christians in the lion's den, Ezekiel's field of dry bones" (Siker 2012, 591, from Obama's *Dreams from My Father*). Obama is also quite favorably disposed to the thought of the theologian Reinhold Niebuhr, which sometimes tempers his optimism with realism.

Siker says that one of Obama's most frequently repeated biblical phrases, from Genesis 4:9, is based on Cain's question as to whether he was his brother's keeper. In thus nominating John Kerry at the 2004 Democrat National Convention, Obama affirmed, as he would many times later, "I am my brother's keeper, I am my sister's keeper—that makes this country work. It's what allows us to pursue our individual dreams, yet still come together as a single American family" (quoted in Siker 2012, 594).

Another of Obama's favorite images was that of a "Joshua Generation." In thus commemorating "Bloody Sunday" (March 7, 1965) in Selma, Alabama, in 2007, Obama observed, "I'm here because somebody marched. I'm here because you all sacrificed for me. I stand on the shoulders of giants. I thank the Moses generation; but we've got to remember, now, that Joshua still had a job to do.

As great as Moses was, despite all that he did, leading people out of bondage, he didn't cross over the river to see the Promised Land" (Siker 2012, 596). This was the job of Obama's own "Joshua generation." As previous civil rights leaders had fought for civil rights, Obama's generation needed to fight for economic rights, confident that God would be with them as he had been with the generation that preceded them (Siker 2012, 596). In a speech that he delivered in January 2008 entitled "The Great Need of the Hour," Obama further refined this image by describing how Joshua was able to bring down the walls of Jericho by uniting his people. In this speech, he paraphrased Amos 5:25, in saying that if the nation would be united "then perhaps that wall would come tumbling down, and justice would flow like water, and righteousness like a mighty stream" (Siker 2012, 597).

When Obama took his oath of office, he did so on the Lincoln Bible, choosing not to open it to a specific passage. In his 2009 inaugural address, Obama cited Paul's injunction in 1 Corinthians 13:11 to set aside childish things (Smith 2015, 604). In a speech that same year at Georgetown University, Obama drew from Jesus's story about the need to build a house on a solid foundation rather than sand (Smith 2012, 605). A study of presidential remarks at National Prayer Breakfasts indicates that Presidents Obama and Clinton made the most frequent references to the Bible (Peterson 2017, 218–19). Obama received considerable criticism for remarks that he made at the National Prayer Breakfast in 2015, which, while not quoting from Scripture, pointed to the way that he thought Christians, like other religious groups, sometimes distorted religious doctrines:

> So how do we, as a people of faith, reconcile these realities—the profound good, the strength, the tenacity, the compassion and love that can flow from all our faiths, operating alongside those who seek to hijack religion for their own murderous ends? Humanity has been grappling with these questions throughout human history. And lest we get on our high horse and think this is unique to some other place, remember that during the Crusades and the Inquisition, people committed terrible deeds in the name of Christ. In our home country, slavery and Jim Crow all too often was justified in the name of Christ. (Newton 2017, 221–22)

In a less controversial practice, Obama often resorted to Scripture to comfort those who were mourning. After a shooting that included severe injury to Congressman Gabrielle Giffords in Tucson, Arizona, and again at a 2011 commemoration of the 9/11 attacks in New York, Obama cited Psalm 46:4–5:

> There is a river whose streams make glad the city of God,
> The holy place where the Most High dwells,
> God is within her, she will not fall;
> God will help her at break of day. (Smith 2012, 606).

In the former speech, he also quoted from Job 30:26 to acknowledge his awareness of evil and darkness in the world. After the shootings in Aurora, Colorado, in July 2012, Obama cited Revelation 21:4, which says that God "will wipe away every tear from their eyes, and death shall be no more. Neither shall there be mourning, nor crying, nor pain anymore" (Smith 2015, 375). In comforting victims of the Sandy Hook massacre five months later, Obama quoted 2 Corinthians 5:1: "For we know that if the earthly tent we live in is destroyed, we have a building from God, an eternal house in heaven, not built by human hands" (quoted in Smith 2015, 375). U.S. Senate majority leader Mitch McConnell also used Scripture as he referred to the massacre on the Senate floor with a paraphrase of 1 Corinthians 12:12 about the state of our imperfect knowledge of God's plans and from Revelation 21:4 about God one day wiping away all tears (Winder 2019, 132–33).

Despite his Christian professions, throughout his presidency, many individuals continued to believe that Obama was a Muslim. This may have arisen in part from Obama's language of inclusivity, which he likely thought was especially important as the nation became more pluralistic. In contrast to many presidents and other leaders who referred to the United States as a "Christian nation," in Obama's first inaugural address, he specifically identified the nation as one of "Christians and Muslims, Jews and Hindus and nonbelievers" (Smith 2015, 378).

In summarizing his research, Siker finds that "Obama's approach to the Bible is deeply shaped by the traditions of the black church"; that although he is not adverse to citing faith claims, he believes they "must be translated into reasoned discourse"; and that he "appears to approach the Bible first and foremost as a set of wisdom texts grounded in a people's story" (2012, 607). In another study, Elaine Graham observes that Obama drew successfully from a tradition "of religion as a potent source of social capital, or the values and norms that inspire us to force social bonds, to form relationships of trust and outreach" (2009, 157).

See also King, Martin Luther, Jr.; Lincoln Bible; Obama, Barack (A Call to Renewal); Obama, Barack (Eulogy for Senator Clementa Pinckney); Presidential Inaugural Bible Verses; Wright, Jeremy

For Reference and Further Reading

Coe, Kevin, and Sarah Chenoweth. 2013. "Presidents as Priests: Toward a Typology of Christian Discourse in the American Presidency." *Communication Theory* 23 (November): 375–94.

Graham, Elaine. 2009. "A Window on the Soul: Four Politicians on Religion and Public Life." *International Journal of Public Theology* 3: 144–63.

Mansfield, Stephen. 2008. *The Faith of Barack Obama*. Nashville, TN: Thomas Nelson.

Newton, Richard. 2017. "The African American Bible: Bound in a Christian Nation." *Journal of Biblical Literature* 136 (Winter): 221–28.

Peterson, Jonathan. R. 2017. "The Religious Content of the Presidents' Remarks at the National Prayer Breakfast, 1953–2016." *Congress & the Presidency* 44(2): 212–34.

Siker, Jeffrey S. 2012. "President Obama, the Bible, and Political Rhetoric." *Political Theology* 13(5): 586–609.

Smith, Gary Scott. 2015. *Religion in the Oval Office: The Religious Lives of American Presidents*. New York: Oxford University Press.

Winder, Mike. 2019. *Favorite Scriptures of 100 American Leaders*. Springville, UT: Plain Sight.

Obama, Barack (A Call to Renewal)

A website by Hillary Kaell and Marilyn Mellowes identifies a speech that Barack Obama gave on June 28, 2006, as among the works that could be considered to be "American Scripture." Obama gave the speech entitled "A Call to Renewal" at a meeting of a group of progressive evangelical Christians when he was running for the U.S. Senate. The group that he was addressing had put out a "Covenant for a New America," which recommended a number of changes to governmental policies.

Obama's central concern in the speech was to address what he considered to be a widening divide between "religious America and secular America." He was particularly concerned that a senatorial opponent, Alan Keyes, had claimed that Jesus Christ could not vote for Obama. Acknowledging an increasing gap "between those who attend church regularly and those who don't," Obama felt that "conservative leaders have been all too happy to exploit this gap," and "Democrats, for the most part, have taken the bait." By contrast, Obama recognized "that Americans are a religious people," and that religion plays an important part in their lives. Noting that he had not been raised in a particularly religious family, Obama said that as he began work as a community activist in Chicago, he began working with churches who quickly saw "that I knew their Book and that I shared their values and sang their songs." In time, he became drawn to the African American church, because he recognized the role that it had played in social justice.

Without citing chapter or verse, Obama indirectly referred to Jesus's call in Matthew 25:35–36 "to feed the hungry and clothe the naked and challenge powers and principalities." Obama also cited the church's "historical struggles for freedom and the rights of man," and its role "as a source of hope." He associated the church with the recognition that "you are first of this world, not apart from it." Again without citing a specific verse, Obama associated going to church as an acknowledgment that "you need to embrace Christ precisely because you are human and need an ally in this difficult journey." He had done so at the Trinity United Church of Christ in Chicago.

Recognizing that America was a pluralistic society, embracing "evangelicals, Catholics, Protestants, Jews and Muslims alike," he thought it was important for progressives not to abandon the field of religious discourse to those on the right. He noted that Abraham Lincoln had referred in this second inaugural address to "the judgments of the Lord," and that Martin Luther King Jr. had referred in his "I Have a Dream" speech to "all of God's children." Perhaps seeking to temper political expectations, with the recognition of "the imperfections of man," Obama believed that changes in governmental policies often needed to be accompanied by changes in individual hearts and minds, illustrating with reference to racism, gun violence, and sexual misbehavior.

Again quoting from Scripture (Proverbs 22:6) without identifying a specific chapter and verse, he said that "my Bible tells me that if we train a child in the way he should go, when he is old he will not turn from it." Although morality may exist apart from religious faith, there was no need for religious people to "leave their religion at the door before entering into the public sphere." He cited the way that Rick Warren, T. D. Jakes, Jim Wallis, and Tony Campolo "are lifting up the Biblical injunction to help the poor as a means of mobilizing Christians against budget cuts to social programs and growing inequality." He further cited "Baptists like John Leland who didn't want the established churches to impose their views on folks who were getting happy out in the fields and teaching the scripture to slaves." He continued, "Whatever we once were, we are no longer just a Christian nation; we are also a Jewish nation, a Muslim nation, a Buddhist nation, a Hindu nation, and a nation of nonbelievers."

Obama noted that even if the nation expelled all non-Christians, those who remained would still be divided in their interpretations of the Bible:

> Whose Christianity would we teach in the schools? Would we go with James Dobson's, or Al Sharpton's? Which passages of Scripture should guide our public policy? Should we go with Leviticus, which suggests slavery is ok and that eating shellfish is abomination? How about Deuteronomy, which suggests stoning your child if he strays from the faith? Or should we just stick to the Sermon on the Mount—a passage that is so radical it's doubtful that our own Defense Department would survive its application? So before we get carried away, let's read our bibles. Folks haven't been reading their bibles.

After pointing to such divisions, Obama said, "Democracy demands that the religiously motivated translate their concerns into universal, rather than religion-specific, values. It requires that their proposals be subject to argument, and amenable to reason." Recognizing that this could be difficult for evangelicals who believed in "the inerrancy of the Bible," Obama distinguished between the manner in which one conducted one's personal life and what was politically possible.

Pointing to the story of Abraham's willingness to heed God's call to sacrifice his beloved son Isaac (Genesis 22), Obama said that anyone seeing a man about to do this would be obligated to call the police. He observed, "Even those who claim the Bible's inerrancy make distinctions between Scriptural edicts, sensing that some passages—the Ten Commandments, say, or a belief in Christ's divinity—are central to Christian faith, while others are more culturally specific and may be modified to accommodate modern life." It was important to maintain "a sense of proportion," and Obama acknowledged his own "pang of shame" when he recognized that words on his own campaign site had unfairly demonized those who opposed abortion as "right-wing ideologues who want to take away a woman's right to choose."

Obama arguably sometimes fell short of taking his own advice. During his first presidential campaign in 2008, he thus characterized working-class workers in old industrial towns by saying that "they get bitter, they cling to guns or religion or antipathy to people who aren't like them or anti-immigrant sentiment or anti-trade sentiment as a way to explain their frustrations" (quoted in Pilkington 2008). After he became president, he was further criticized for having stayed in a church (which he soon left) where the founding pastor, Rev. Jeremiah A. Wright Jr., had sometimes used inflammatory language against American policy (Powell 2008). By contrast, one of the high watermarks of Obama's presidency may well have been the eulogy that he gave at the College of Charleston for Senator Clementa Pinckney, who had been murdered in a mass shooting at a church in that city.

See also Leland, John; Obama, Barack; Obama, Barack (Eulogy for Senator Clementa Pinckney); Ten Commandments; Wright, Jeremiah, Jr.

For Reference and Further Reading

Kaell, Hillary, and Marilyn Mellowes. 2011. "American Scripture." PBS. October 11. http://www.pbs.org/godinamerica/american-scripture/.

Obama, Barack. 2006. "'Call to Renewal' Keynote Address." June 28. http://obamaspeeches.com/081-Call-to-Renewal-Keynote-Address-Obama-Speech.htm.

Pilkington, Ed. 2008. "Obama Angers Midwest Voters with Guns and Religion Remark." *Guardian*. April 14. https://www.theguardian.com/world/2008/apr/14/barackobama.uselections2008. Accessed March 30, 2019.

Powell, Michael. 2008. "Following Months of Criticism, Obama Quits His Church." *New York Times*. June 1. https://www.nytimes.com/2008/06/01/us/politics/01obama.html. Accessed March 30, 2019.

Obama, Barack (Eulogy for Senator Clementa Pinckney)

In June 2015 a young white gunman walked into the Emanuel African Methodist Episcopal Church in Charleston, South Carolina, and killed nine individuals. One of an increasing number of mass murders, this was particularly shocking because it occurred at a prayer meeting in a church. The church reacted with forgiveness for the gunman, Dylann Roof (who was later sentenced to death), while politicians called for stricter gun control laws and the state governor Nikki Haley joined in a successful effort to remove the Confederate Flag from the grounds of the state capital.

President Barack Obama subsequently came to the College of Charleston to deliver a eulogy for one of the victims, Rev. Clementa Pinckney, a forty-one-year-old state senator. It was one of Obama's most scripturally infused speeches.

Quoting liberally from Hebrews 11, Obama, who had titled his own biography *The Audacity of Hope*, observed that "the Bible calls us to hope. To persevere, and have faith in things not seen." He further said, "They were living by faith when they died. . . . They did not receive the things promised; they only saw them and welcomed them from a distance, admitting that they were foreigners and strangers on Earth."

Describing Rev. Pinckney as another such man of faith, Obama cited him as one who "embodied the idea [associated with the biblical epistle of James] that our Christian faith demands deeds and not just words." Drawing from another biblical passage (Matthew 25:31–46) that he had cited in his 2006 "Call for Renewal," Obama further observed "that to put our faith in action is more than individual salvation, it's about our collective salvation; that to feed the hungry and clothe the naked and house the homeless is not just a call for isolated charity but the imperative of a just society."

As in his earlier speech, Obama praised the African American church for serving as a hub for organizing for racial justice "not just for blacks, not just for Christians, but for every American who cares about the steady expansion of human rights and human dignity in this country; a foundation stone for liberty and justice for all."

Citing, without attributing a Christian poem (later converted into a hymn) that William Cowper authored in 1773, that "God works in mysterious ways," Obama suggested, in a manner reminiscent of Lincoln's musings about God's providence in his second inaugural address, that although the killer did not know it, God was using him. "The alleged killer could have never anticipated the way the families of the fallen would respond when they saw him in court—in the midst of unspeakable grief, with words of forgiveness. He couldn't imagine that."

A central biblical theme reflected particularly strongly throughout much of the New Testament (consider especially Ephesians 2:8–9) is that of God's grace, especially as revealed in the sacrifice of Jesus on the cross. Citing the song "Amazing Grace," which had been penned by John Newton (1725–1807), a one-time slave trader, and first published in 1779, Obama intoned, "According to the Christian tradition, grace is not earned. Grace is not merited. It's not something we deserve. Rather, grace is the free and benevolent favor of God—as manifested in the salvation of sinners and the bestowal of blessings."

Anticipating further unintended consequences from the gunman's actions, Obama observed that the pain of the shooting had helped to uncover "the pain that the Confederate flag stirred in too many of our citizens." He further said, "Removing the flag from this state's capitol would not be an act of political correctness; it would not be an insult to the valor of Confederate soldiers. It would simply be an acknowledgment that the cause for which they fought—the cause of slavery—was wrong—the imposition of Jim Crow after the Civil War, the resistance to civil rights for all people was wrong."

Noting that even gun owners were often sensitive to the evils of gun violence, Obama said that "by making the moral choice to change, we express God's grace. We don't earn grace. We're all sinners. We don't deserve it. But God gives it to us anyway. And we choose how to receive it. It's our decision how to honor it." Recognizing that "there are good people on both sides of these [gun] debates," he also recognized that "whatever solutions we find will necessarily be incomplete." Calling for open hearts, Obama began singing the words to "Amazing Grace." Paraphrasing the song he had just cited, Obama ended by repeating the name of each victim who had died and indicating that each had "found that grace." He ended with his hope: "May grace now lead them home. May God continue to shed His grace on the United States of America."

See also Obama, Barack (A Call to Renewal); Lincoln's Second Inaugural Address

For Reference and Further Reading

Horowitz, Jason, Nick Corasaniti and Ashley Southall. 2015. "Nine Killed in Shooting at Black Church in Charleston." *New York Times*. June 17. https://www.nytimes.com/2015/06/18/us/church-attacked-in-charleston-south-carolina.html.

Obama, Barack. 2015. "Remarks by the President in Eulogy for the Honorable Reverend Clementa Pinckney." June 26. https://obamawhitehouse.archives.gov/the-press-office/2015/06/26/remarks-president-eulogy-honorable-reverend-clementa-pinckney.

Official State Book

In addition to having their own flags, American states are notorious for designating trees, flowers, birds, animals, and other objects as official state symbols.

In recent years, legislators in at least three states, all in the South, have introduced resolutions to make the Bible their official state book. In 2014, Rep. Thomas Carmody of Louisiana withdrew such a proposal after critics charged that it would be like making Christianity the state's official religion, which would violate the establishment clause of the First Amendment. The next year, a similar bill failed to make it out of the committee (Chan 2016). A similar fate befell a bill in a Mississippi state legislative committee in 2015.

The latest such attempt occurred in Tennessee in 2016 but was overridden by the then governor Bill Haslam, who feared that such legislation "trivializes" the "sacred text" (quoted in Chan 2016). There was also concern that the law might conflict with a state constitutional provision.

Carolyn Kellogg observes, "Making a book the official state book doesn't require that people read it, of course, any more than making 'The Tennessee Waltz' the state song would require people [to] sing it" (2015).

See also National Bible Week

For Reference and Further Reading

Chan, Melissa. 2016. "Tennessee Wasn't First State to Attempt to Make the Bible the Official State Book." *Time*. April 20. http://time.com/4301131/bible-state-book-bill-fail/. Accessed April 15, 2019.

Kellogg, Carolyn. 2015. "Tennessee Legislator Wants the Bible to Become Official State Book." *Los Angeles Times*. February 12. https://www.latimes.com/books/jacketcopy/la-et-jc-tennessee-bible-official-state-book-20150212-story.html. Accessed June 15, 2019.

Old Deluder Satan Act (1647)

Modern public schools are sometimes the source of conflict over the degree to which religious instruction should be permitted, but in colonial America, schools were typically viewed as necessary to support citizens who could read and interpret the Bible for themselves. One of the best indications of this is the Old Deluder Satan Act that the colony of Massachusetts adopted in 1647.

The law, which received its name from language in the first line, observed that it was "one chief project of that old deluder, Satan, to keep men from the knowledge of the Scriptures." Without mentioning that denomination by name, the law indicated that Roman Catholics had sought "to keep men from the knowledge of the Scriptures . . . by keeping them in an unknown tongue [Latin]." Similarly "in these latter times," some sought to seek to persuade "from the use of tongues, . . . so that at least the true sense and meaning of the original might be clouded and corrupted with love and false glosses of saint-seeming deceivers; and to the end that learning may not be buried in the grave of our forefathers, in church and commonwealth, the Lord assisting our endeavors." To guard against this, the law went on to require each town with fifty or more households to appoint an instructor to teach children to read and write and to require every town of one hundred families or more to "set up a grammar school, the master thereof being able to instruct youth so far as they may be fitted for the university."

Political science professor David Carleton has observed that this law, which built upon a law adopted five years earlier, not only arguably laid the groundwork for later controversies over the role of schools relative to religious faith but also set up at least four principles. There were "that basic education is a public or community responsibility; that the state can require communities to raise and expend local funds for schools; that day-to-day responsibility for the operation of schools rests at the local level, and that schools are to be organized in levels separating elementary from secondary education" (Carleton 2009).

See also Puritans; Roman Catholics

For Reference and Further Reading

Carleton, David. 2009. "Old Deluder Satan Act of 1647 (1647)" [electronic resource]. The First Amendment Encyclopedia, Middle Tennessee State University. http://www.mtsu.edu/first-amendment/article/1032/old-deluder-satan-act-of-1647. Accessed April 14, 2019.

"The Old Deluder Act (1647)." Constitution Society. https://www.constitution.org/primarysources/deluder.html.

• P •

Patrick, Deval

Deval Patrick (b. 1956) is an African American Democratic politician who grew up in humble circumstances in Chicago and earned his undergraduate and law degrees from Harvard University. He served as assistant attorney for the Civil Rights Division under President Bill Clinton and as governor of Massachusetts from 2007 to 2015. Patrick, who decided to join the field seeking the Democrat nomination for president in late 2019, is a good example of how progressives use the Bible for inspiration.

He discussed his view of the Bible in his autobiography entitled *A Reason to Believe*. Noting that he had gotten most of his respect for religion and the Bible from his grandmother, he observed that "Scripture itself is full of poetry about kindness and magnanimity, about the charge to care about and help your fellow man," which he illustrated by quoting from Micah 6:8 about the need for justice, mercy and humility (2011, 148). He argued that "hating homosexuals and despising illegal immigrants instead of hating poverty and despising homelessness seems to miss the point of a life of faithfulness," which he further illustrated by quoting Jesus's words in Matthew 15:35–40 about feeding the hungry, giving water to the thirsty, taking in the stranger, clothing the naked, and visiting the imprisoned (164).

Patrick described how, in his first race for governor, he faced opposition from some churches over his support for marriage equality, which he had supported before he knew that his daughter was gay. He further indicated that one of his most cherished moments during a primary campaign was a time where he let people working in the hospitality industry in Boston know that he saw and appreciated them (167).

Clearly identifying himself as a Christian, Patrick ended the chapter by observing that "we Christians believe that Christ will return one day. I've thought about what form Christ will take when he does. I'm pretty sure he will not descend in flowing robes or amid spectral choruses. I think there's a good chance he will be the guy in rags, in an out-of-the-way place somewhere, begging, wondering if anyone sees him" (172).

For both of his gubernatorial inaugurations, Patrick took his oath upon the Mendi Bible, which had been given by the Mendi people of Sierra Leone. Their ancestors had been slaves aboard the ship *La Amistad*, whose freedom John Quincy Adams had helped to secure in a case that made its way to the U.S. Supreme Court (Preble n.d.).

See also Adams, John Quincy; Same-Sex Marriage; What Doth the Lord Require? (Micah 6:8)

For Reference and Further Reading

Patrick, Deval. 2011. *A Reason to Believe: Lessons from an Improbable Life*. New York: Broadway.

Preble, Peter M. n.d. "The Mendi Bible." http ://www.frpeterpreble.com/2014/07/mendi-bible.html.

Pence, Mike

Donald J. Trump's vice president, Mike Pence, has a reputation for being among those contemporary politicians who are most likely to quote Scriptures. Pence, a graduate of Hanover College, a former radio host, and an Indiana governor who was raised a Roman Catholic, is now, after a professed conversion experience at a Christian music festival in 1978, an evangelical Christian. President Trump appears to have chosen Pence in part for his evangelical connections.

At a meeting prior to a national breakfast, Pence talked about Jeremiah 29:11, a verse that he displays above his mantle at home. It says, "For I know the plans I have for you, plans to prosper you and not to harm you, plans to give you hope and a future." He also quoted 2 Chronicles 7:14, the verse to which he opened his Bible when taking his oath of office. Directed to Israel, but often applied to the United States, it proclaims, "If my people, who are called by my name, will humble themselves and pray, and seek my face and turn from their wicked ways, then I will hear from heaven, and will forgive their sin and will heal their land" ("Vice President Pence").

Maureen Groppe observes that in addressing mourners after a massacre at a Texas church, Pence reminded the audience that "the Lord is close to the brokenhearted," a reference to Psalm 34:18. Pence is also fond of evoking biblical passages about servant leadership, including Mark 10:44, which he cited in an address to graduates of Grove City College (Groppe 2018). Groppe notes that Pence often refers to the Bible as "the Old Book."

After his second unsuccessful bid for a congressional seat, in which Pence relied heavily on negative campaigning, he ran an article titled "Confessions of a Negative Campaigner." He began the article with a quotation from 1 Timothy 1:15 indicating that Christ had come to save sinners "among whom I am foremost of all" (Coppins 2018).

Although evangelicals particularly appreciate the access that Pence has brought them within the Trump administration, many believe that Trump uses Pence's presence to help mitigate criticisms of his own character. Coppins (2018) says, "Campaign operatives discovered that anytime Trump did something outrageous or embarrassing, they could count on Pence to clean it up." Coppins further observes that his supporters have sometimes compared Pence to Mordecai, the devout Jew who served under the pagan king of Persia who married Esther; to Daniel, who likewise served under the king of Babylon; and even to Joseph, who served in the courts of Pharaoh.

Although Pence is believed to harbor strong presidential ambitions, he has to date publicly subordinated his own ambitions to those of serving the president. He continues to receive criticism for his prior support for gay "conversion therapy," and for supporting businesses that seek to deny certain services to gay customers. Pete Buttigieg, the gay mayor of South Bend, Indiana, who is seeking the Democrat nomination for the presidency, observed that if Pence has "a problem with who I am, your problem is not with me—your quarrel, sir, is with my creator" (Cole 2019). Pence has been quoted as saying, "My family and I have a view of marriage that's informed by our faith. But that doesn't mean that we're—that we're critical of anyone else who has a different point of view" (Peters 2019). Buttigieg has, in turn, been criticized for his belief that Christianity and progressivism are synonymous (Wehner 2019).

See also Buttigieg, Pete; Esther as Political Archetype; Trump, Donald J.

For Reference and Further Reading

Cole, Devan. 2019. "Buttigieg to Pence: 'If You Got a Problem with Who I Am, Your Problem Is Not with Me—Your Quarrel, Sir, Is with My Creator." CNN. April 8. https://www.cnn.com/2019/04/08/politics/pete-buttigieg-mike-pence/index.html.

Coppins, McKay. 2018. "God's Plan for Mike Pence." *The Atlantic*. January/February. https://www.theatlantic.com/magazine/archive/2018/01/gods-plan-for-mike-pence/546569/.

Groppe, Maureen. 2018. "How the Bible Helps Pence Navigate His Role as Trump's Vice President." *USA Today*. January 21. https://www.usatoday.com/story/news/politics/2018/01/21/how-bible-helps-pence-navigate-his-role-trumps-vice-president/1044357001/.

Peters, Jeremy W. 2019. "Pete Buttigieg, Gay and Christian, Challenges Religious Right on Their Own Turf." *New York Times*. April 10. https://www.nytimes.com/2019/04/10/us/politics/pete-buttigieg-sexuality-religion.html.

"Vice President Pence: The Verse above His Mantle." Museum of the Bible. https://www.museumofthebible.org/book/minutes/345.

Wehner, Peter. 2019. "Pete Buttigieg's Very Public Faith Is Challenging Assumptions." *The Atlantic*. April 10. https://www.theatlantic.com/ideas/archive/2019/04/buttigieg-wrong-about-christianity-and-progressivism/586810/.

Penn, William

See Quakers

Pennsylvania Charter of Liberties and Frame of Government (1682)

Although it is common to laud the Puritans for seeking religious liberty, it was a Quaker, William Penn (1644–1714), who actually extended religious freedom in America to those of other faiths.

Nowhere was this clearer than in the Charter of Liberties and Frame of Government that he provided for the colony of Pennsylvania in 1682 and in his accompanying preface.

Penn began his preface, with a reference to the creation stories in the book of Genesis, by observing that "when the great and wise God had made the world, of all its creatures, it pleased him to chuse man his Deputy to rule it: and to fit him for so great a charge and trust, he did not only qualify him with skill and power, but with integrity to use them justly." Although noting that man had been created with "native goodness," he observed that "lust prevailing against duty, made a lamentable breach upon it," requiring the introduction of law (Penn 1682).

Penn proceeded by noting that St. Paul had observed that "The law . . . was added because of transgression" (Galatians 3:10). He further cited Paul's teaching (in 1 Timothy 1:9) "that the law was not made for the righteous man, but for the disobedient and ungodly, for sinners, for unholy and prophane, for murders, for whoremongers, for them that defile themselves with mankind, and for man-stealers, for lyers, for perjured persons." He also cited Paul's admonition (Romans 13:1–3): "Let every soul be subject to the higher powers; for there is no power but of God. The powers that be are ordained of God: whosoever therefore resisteth the power, resisteth the ordinance of God. For rulers are not a terror to good works to evil: wilt thou then not be afraid of the power? Do that which is good, and thou shall have praise of the same," and followed with some additional admonitions from this chapter (Penn 1682).

Penn argued that although laws could not "remove the cause, it crushes the effects of evil" which will continue until "the coming of the blessed *Second Adam*, the Lord from heaven," a concept from 1 Corinthians 15:45 (Penn 1682). In a philosophy that was arguably quite different from that of later American founders who perceived that governmental structures might be arranged to mitigate abusive powers (albeit consistent with some advocates of civil republicanism), Penn expressed the view that "let men be good, and the government cannot be bad; if it be ill, they will cure it. But, if men be bad, let the government be never so good, they will endeavor to warp and spoil it to their turn" (Penn 1682). He further posited that "liberty, without obedience is confusion, and obedience without liberty is slavery" (Penn 1682).

In section xxii of his Frame of Government, Penn further set aside Sunday so that "the business appointed for that day shall be deferred till the next day, unless in case of emergency" (Penn 1682).

In an addendum on the laws that had been agreed to in England, Penn further provided in section xxxiv that all officers of government "shall be such as possess faith in Jesus Christ." Section xxxvii further clarified that whatever beliefs the people might be allowed to profess, government had a responsibility to enforce proper behaviors as a way of averting God's wrath:

> That as a careless and corrupt administration of justice draws the wrath of God upon magistrates, so the wildness and looseness of the people provide the indignation of God against a country: therefore that all such offences against God, as swearing, cursing, lying, prophane talking, drunkenness, drinking of healths, obscene words, incest, sodomy rapes, whoredom, fornication, and other uncleanness (not to be repeated) all treasons, misprisions, murders, duels, felony, seditions, maims, forcible entries, and other violences, to the persons and estates of the inhabitants within this province; all prizes, stage-plays, cards, dice, May-gamers, gamesters, masques, revels, bull-baitings, cock-fightings, bear-baitings, and the like, which excite the people to rudeness, cruelty, looseness, and irreligion, shall be respectively discouraged, and severely punished. (Penn 1682)

See also Judgment; Quakers

For Reference and Further Reading

Hall, Mark David. 2011. "Did America Have a Christian Founding?" June 7. https://www.heritage.org/political-process/report/did-america-have-christian-founding.

Offutt, William M., Jr. 1995. *Of "Good Laws" & "Good Men": Law and Society in the Delaware Valley, 1680–1710.* Urbana: University of Illinois Press.

Penn, William. 1682. "Charter of the Liberties and Frame of Government of Pennsylvania." Online Library of Liberty. https://oll.libertyfund.org/pages/1682-charter-of-the-liberties-and-frame-of-government-of-pennsylvania.

Perry, Rick

Rick Perry (b. 1950) served as secretary of energy under President Trump. As Texas's longest-serving governor, who was then vying unsuccessfully for the 2012 Republican presidential nomination, Perry called a Prayer Rally known as "The Response: A Call to Prayer for a Nation in Crisis" in August 2011, which some twenty thousand to thirty thousand individuals attended. Earlier in the year, he had called a "Prayer for Rain in the State of Texas."

About two years earlier, Perry had been visited by Pastors Tom Schlueter and Bob Long, members of the New Apostolic Reformation, which was founded by C. Peter Wagner (the author of *Apostles Today: Biblical Government for Biblical Power*, 2006). They had informed Perry that God had a special mission for him and for Texas. Forrest Wilder quotes Schlueter as saying that "the government of our nation was basically founded on biblical principles" and affirming that God is "ultimately in charge of our nation" (2011). Members, who believed that a second apostolic age began sometime around 2001, sometimes predict natural disasters or warn that they are coming absent national repentance. They are particularly interested in gaining control of "the 'Seven Mountains' of society: family, religion, arts and entertainment, media, government, education and business" (Wilder 2011).

Although Perry, a Methodist who attended an evangelical church, extended invitations to governors of all fifty states, the only other one who attended was Sam Brownback of Kansas, although Rick Scott of Florida sent a video message. Evangelical leaders James Dobson, Richard Land, and Tony Perkins were among those invited to speak. The event, which included a prayer by Governor Perry for the then president Barack Obama, was endorsed by John Hagee, of the Cornerstone Church, whose endorsement John McCain had rejected in a previous campaign.

Contrasting his approach to what he called the "cite and run," strategies of candidates who quote a verse that aligns with their policies and then move on, a reporter for the *Washington Post* observed that Perry "engaged in extended citation of passages from Joel, Isaiah and Ephesians"; he apparently read from these Scriptures "without comment" (Berlinerblau 2011). Perry's central focus appeared to be from the book of Joel, which is named for an Old Testament prophet. The specific passage from 2:12–17 was as follows:

> "Even now," declares the Lord, "return to me with all your heart, with fasting and weeping and mourning." Rend your heart and not your garments. Return to the Lord your God, for he is gracious and compassionate, slow to anger and abounding in love, and he relents from sending calamity. Who knows? He may turn and have pity and leave behind a blessing—grain offerings and drink offerings for the Lord your God. Blow the trumpet in Zion, declare a holy fast, call a sacred assembly. Gather the people, consecrate the assembly; bring together the elders, gather the children, those nursing at the breast. Let the bridegroom leave his

> room and the bride her chamber. Let the priests, who minister before the Lord, weep between the temple porch and the altar. Let them say, "Spare your people, O Lord. Do not make your inheritance an object of scorn, a byword among the nations. Why should they say among the peoples, 'Where is their God?' "

Wiegel (2011) observes that the crowd interrupted with cheers after the mention of blowing the trumpet in Zion.

See also Days of Humiliation, Fasting, and Thanksgiving; Dobson, James; Hagee, John

For Reference and Further Reading

Berlinerblau, Jacques. 2011. "Piety Is the Policy at Rick Perry's Prayer Rally." *Washington Post*. August 8.

Wiegel, David. 2011. "And God Will Send Rick Perry." *Slate*. August 6. https://slate.com/news-and-politics/2011/08/rick-perry-leads-prayers-for-jobs-becomes-the-great-republican-hope.html.

Wilder, Forrest. 2011. "Rick Perry's Army of God." *Texas Observer*. August 3. https://www.texasobserver.org/rick-perrys-army-of-god/.

Philadelphia Bible Riots of 1844

More than a hundred years before the U.S. Supreme Court banned devotional Bible readings in public schools in *Abington v. Schempp* (1963), events in the city of Philadelphia had shown how the issue could provoke chaos and violence.

In 1834, the Pennsylvania state legislature had adopted a Free School Act that established a state system of public schools. It was common to open the school day with exercises that included the reading of a passage from the King James Version (KJV) of the Bible, which was almost universally used among American Protestants. In 1838, the legislature adopted a law that not only sanctioned this existing custom but that also made the Bible a mandatory read. It thus provided that "the Old and New Testaments, containing the best extant code of morality, in simple, beautiful and pure language, shall be used as a school book for Reading, without comment by the Teacher, but not as a textbook for religious discussion" (Lannie and Diethorn 1968, 48). Although the law did not specify the use of the KJV, in contrast to the Roman Catholic Douay version, it was commonly accepted among all Protestant denominations and was therefore widely considered by Protestants to be nonsectarian. This thus upped the ante for Roman Catholics, and their bishop, Francis Kenrick (1796–1863), who did not think their students should be forced to use it.

Moreover, in April 1842, a teacher was actually fired from a public school for refusing to read from the KJV to her students (Lannie and Diethorn 1968, 54). As some Catholic parents sought to forbid their children from reading the KJV Bible, schools punished or humiliated them (55). Bishop Kenrick pushed back. He noted that he objected "inasmuch as Catholic children are thus led to view as authoritative a version which is rejected by the Church"; he specifically observed "that several books of Divine Scripture are wanting in that version and that the meaning of the original text is not faithfully expressed" (56). He further objected that many schools accompanied readings from the KJV with prayer and/or the singing of a hymn and that "it is not consistent with the laws and discipline of the Catholic Church for her members to unite in religious exercises with those who are not of their communion" (56). He further observed that public schools in Baltimore had provided Catholic school children with their own version of the Bible. Contrary to reports that nativists would later circulate, Kenrick did not oppose Bible reading in schools per se but did advocate allowing Catholic students to use their own version.

The Board of Controllers subsequently adopted a resolution exempting students whose parents objected from mandatory Bible reading and permitting them to bring other Bibles. It practically took back with one hand what it appeared to have given with another, however, when it specified that such other versions be "without note or comment," which excluded the Catholic Duoay version (57–58). Kenrick's efforts to allow Catholic students to use the Duoay version met with strong Protestant resistance. They argued that America was a largely Protestant country, that they had founded the schools, and that they had the right to mandate a nonsectarian Bible, especially given the absence of compulsion. They further associated Roman Catholics with foreigners who were under the authority of a foreign pope. They thus received support from nativist groups, many of whom believed that immigrants were taking their jobs.

Tensions were heightened after a somewhat inaccurate report circulated that a school director had ordered a teacher to stop reading the KJV Bible in school. This mood was reflected in local editorials, including one in the *Episcopal Recorder* that asked, "Are we to yield our personal liberty, our inherited rights, our very Bibles, the special, blessed gift of God to our country, to the will, the ignorance, or the wickedness of these hordes of foreigners, subjects of a foreign despot . . . ? We have yielded to Papists, as citizens, already too much, for vain is their assurance of the separation between their civil and their religious obedience" (67).

The board eventually resolved one issue by permitting Catholic teachers who objected to reading the KJV have another teacher perform this task in their place but still excluding the Duoay version. On May 6, 1844, however, Protestant nativists provocatively gathered and rallied around a U.S. flag in the largely Catholic neighborhood of Kensington and were met by a mob. A bullet killed George Shiffler, an eighteen-year-old Protestant, who became an instant martyr. Nativist crowds that had gathered at Independence Hall subsequently marched back to Kensington and burned St. Augustine's Church and about thirty Catholic houses. During a third day of rioting, mobs burned St. Michael's Church as many Catholics posted signs saying "Native American" on their doors to save them from the torch (75).

Independence Day witnessed renewed tensions as some seventy thousand people showed up for a parade in which many carried banners with such slogans as "Search the Scriptures," "The Bible is our Guide," "Liberty and the Bible," "The Light of the World and the Guide of the Nations," "The Bible is the basis of Education and the safeguard of Liberty," while other banners depicted what Lannie and Diethorn describe as "a child reading the Bible, a figure of Liberty holding an open Bible, a figure of Liberty instructing a child from the Bible, and an American eagle grasping an open Bible in its claws" (82). Only the arrival of troops prevented another tragedy after Protestants saw fearful Catholics bringing weapons into St. Philip's Church in the Southwark neighborhood and threatened to burn it down (84–85).

Concerned about civil peace, Bishop Kenrick largely abandoned efforts to change the status quo in the public schools, although Pope Gregory XVI (1765–1846) probably inadvertently kept the issue in view when he issued a letter in mid-July 1844 in which he renewed opposition to reading Bibles "in the vulgar tongue" that were not church approved and did not contain church commentary (87). Believing the public schools had become enclaves for Protestants, the American Catholic Church sought to provide more parochial schools for their own students.

See also Abington v. Schempp (1963); King James Version of the Bible; Roman Catholics

For Reference and Further Reading

Fessenden, Tracy. 2005. "The Nineteenth-Century Bible Wars and the Separation of Church and State." *Church History* 74 (December): 784–811.

Gebarowski-Shafer, Ellie. 2013. "The Transatlantic Reach of the Catholic 'False Translation' Argument in the School 'Bible Wars.'" *U.S. Catholic Historian* 31 (Summer): 47–76.

Lannie, Vincent P., and Bernard C. Diethorn. 1968. "For the Honor and Glory of God: The Philadelphia Bible Riots of 1844." *History of Education Quarterly* 8 (Spring): 44–106.

Political Engagement

Although some societies are theocracies, where priests, mullahs, or other religious figures exercise control of both secular and religious affairs, the U.S. Constitution does not mention God, the First Amendment disestablished any religion in the United States, and the Constitution has been accordingly described as a "Godless Constitution" (Kramnick and Moore 2005). Unlike some documents, however, it does not attack the Bible, and the First Amendment provides for the "free exercise" of religion.

Like attitudes toward the relation between Christianity and culture in general (Niebuhr 1951), different denominations have approached politics differently than others. Throughout American history, some religious groups, most notably Mennonites (associated with the Anabaptist tradition) and Jehovah's Witnesses, have opposed even such measures of political participation as voting or saluting the U.S. flag, which they consider to be a form of idolatry. These and some other groups, most notably Quakers, have also often opposed participation in military forces, which they believe Scripture forbids. Others, particularly premillennialists, have sometimes put so much emphasis on what they believe to be the imminence of the return of Jesus Christ to earth that it seemed largely futile for their members to invest much effort in a society that was bound for fairly imminent destruction.

At other times, some groups have largely withdrawn from the public square. This happened in part when Roman Catholics formed their own schools in the wake of Protestant religious exercises in public schools in the nineteenth century—something Protestants would do later in the twentieth century in light of

Supreme Court decisions ending such practices. Similarly, many conservative Protestants largely withdrew from the public square and began founding their own Bible colleges and other institutions after what some saw as an embarrassing repudiation of fundamentalist theology in the aftermath of the Scopes Trial in 1925.

Most other religious groups have, however, accepted the idea that political participation and public service are honorable means of fulfilling duties as required in sacred Scriptures. Historically, postmillennialists have thought that bringing religious principles to bear on matters of public policy was a way of hastening the establishment of God's earthly kingdom on earth. Others have simply viewed such work as advancing what they believe to be biblical policies that seek justice, aid the poor, and ensure civil rights and liberties, including the "free exercise" of religion. Bill Bright (1921–2003), who headed Campus Crusade for Christ, viewed praying for leaders, registering to vote, becoming informed, helping to elect godly people, and voting as key Christian duties (Bright 2008).

A recent publication of the Family Research Council, which is specifically addressed to "Bible-believing, gospel-loving Christians" (Closson 2019, 7), notes that many Christians are wary of participating in politics because it is so partisan but point out that politics itself is connected to community (4). It further points to the examples of Joseph and Daniel as public administrators; to prophet Jeremiah's instruction (Jeremiah 29:7) to Jewish exiles in Babylon to seek the warfare of that empire; and to Paul's teaching in Romans 13, which urged obedience to earthly authorities, as indications that voting and other acts of political participation are "an exercise in delegating God-ordained authority" (5, 10). In an essay entitled "Why Should Christians Be Involved in Politics?" a British group, Christians in Politics, further cites Jesus's admonition in the Sermon on the Mount in Matthew 5:13–16 for Christians to be as salt and light in the world, as well as God's commands in Proverbs 31:8 to be a voice to the voiceless, and in Ephesians 4:28 to help those in need. Another of its essays on "Politics in the Bible" provides a helpful thumbnail sketch of how every book in both the Old and New Testaments addresses politics in one way or another.

The specific issues that have engaged religious groups have varied significantly over time and by denominations. Prominent issues in the nineteenth century included opposition to slavery, dueling, concern over Sunday delivery of mails and obscenity, and similar concerns. Desegregation and related issues like lynching were a concern especially prominent in liberal Protestant, Catholic, and Jewish denominations in the mid-twentieth century. Many also opposed Nazism and communism, both of which they thought were inimical to religious ideals. Contemporary evangelical Protestants and Roman Catholics have often put their greatest emphasis on opposition to same-sex marriage and abortion, while more liberal members of both groups have been far more likely to stress issues of social justice like fighting racism, poverty, and the unequal distribution of wealth; equal educational opportunity; opposition to capital punishment; opposition to foreign wars like those in Vietnam and Iraq; and support for women's rights.

Although Article VI of the U.S. Constitution prohibits religious tests as a condition for holding public office, religious identity, or perceived identity, has been an issue in many elections. In the presidential election of 1800, it was common for supporters of Federalist John Adams to identify his Democratic-Republican opponent Thomas Jefferson as an atheist. In 1884, after Samuel Burchard, a Presbyterian minister who supported Republican candidate James G. Blaine, identified the Democratic Party as the party of "rum, Romanism [meaning Roman Catholicism], and rebellion [the Civil War]," the public reacted by electing Democrat Grover Cleveland. John F. Kennedy undoubtedly garnered support from fellow Roman Catholics but was also the subject of sermons by many Protestant ministers who feared that his membership in that church would make him subservient to the pope. Republicans George and Mitt Romney faced questions about their membership in the Church of Jesus Christ of Latter-Day Saints in their quest for the U.S. presidency.

Quite apart from denominational affiliations, many religious groups have urged their members to take character, often tied to perceive godliness, into account when choosing leaders. Psalm 125:3 observed that "the wicked shall not rule the godly, lest the godly be forced to do wrong" (Bright 2008, 8). Proverbs 29:2 says, "With good men in authority the people rejoice; but with the wicked in power, they groan" (16). In the nineteenth century, Noah Webster thus cited the statement in 2 Samuel 23:3, "He that ruleth over men must be just, ruling in the fear of God," to suggest that failure to heed this admonition had led to most of the nation's ills during his own time (1834, 175). He also recognized that it was sometimes difficult for voters to gauge the moral behaviors of office holders with whom they might never be in direct personal contact.

Emphases vary with the times. Many evangelical Christians who expressed great outrage over Bill Clinton's sexual misdeeds have been largely silent over similar allegations (and outrageous personal insults) during the Trump administration, which they perceive to be more sympathetic to their policy positions. Interestingly, while addressing the issues of abortion, same-sex marriage, poverty, and race, the conservative Family Research Council, likely pleased with many of the policies of the Trump administration, did not in its 2019 report even address the issue of morality among leaders in government.

See also Evangelicals; Jehovah's Witnesses; Mennonites; Quakers; Roman Catholics

For Reference and Further Reading

Bright, Bill. 2008. *Your 5 Duties as a Christian Citizen*. Peachtree City, GA: New Life Resources.

Christians in Politics. n.d. "Politics in the Bible." http ://www.christiansinpolitics.org.uk/politics-in-the-bible/.

Christians in Politics. n.d. "Why Should Christians Be Involved in Politics?" http ://www.christiansinpolitics.org.uk/why-should-christians-be-involved-in-politics/.

Closson, David. 2019. *Biblical Principles for Political Engagement: Worldview, Issues, and Voting*. Washington, DC: Family Research Council.

"For the Health of the Nation: An Evangelical Call to Civic Responsibility." 2004. Approved by the National Association of Evangelicals. October 8. http ://www.ricklove.net/wp-content/uploads/2010/04/For_The_Health_Of_The_Nation1.pdf.

Hanson, Paul D. 2010. *Political Engagement as Biblical Mandate*. Cambridge: James Clarke.

Kramnick, Isaac, and R. Laurence Moore. 2005. *The Godless Constitution: A Moral Defense of the Secular State*. New York: W. W. Norton.
Niebuhr, H. Richard. 1951. *Christ and Culture*. New York: Harper & Row.
Webster, Noah. 1834. *Value of the Bible, and Excellence of the Christian Religion: For the Use of Families and Schools*. New Haven, CT: Durrie & Peck.

Political Hebraism

It is common to compare the American political system to classical models of government (kingship/monarchy, aristocracy/oligarchy, democracy/mob rule) or to those of the Enlightenment that embodied such principles as republicanism, separation of powers, and checks and balances. For almost a century, it was also common to compare the U.S. system to the government of the twelve tribes of Israel, especially during the period of the judges that lasted from Joshua through Samuel. Eran Shalev, who is among the most prominent students of this development, refers to this as political Hebraism.

According to Shalev, political Hebraism actually began in Europe, and was especially prominent in the Dutch Republic and in England, whose residents often identified themselves, as American Pilgrims would do after them, as a "second Israel" (2013, 54). The movement was prompted by renewed attention to the Hebrew Scriptures brought about by the Protestant Reformation (Nelson 2010). The philosophy was reflected to varying degrees in the philosophy of James Harrington (1611–1677) and Algernon Sidney (1623–1683), who compared the institutions of the judge, the council, and the people to monarchy, aristocracy, and democracy, which were blended in Britain's own mixed government. The English philosopher John Locke (1632–1704) also relied more heavily on the Old Testament than on the New Testament in formulating his own political philosophy, which was quite influential in America (Leiter 2018).

Americans put even greater emphasis on the manner in which the twelve tribes of Israel (some even stretched this number to thirteen) resembled the thirteen American states. The comparison between the United States and Israel during the time of the judges seemed even more complete when the one-time colonies declared their independence from King George III. Thomas Paine had been among those who had argued in *Common Sense* that the Hebrews had strayed from God's will when they had instituted kingship.

Ultimately, delegates to the Constitutional Convention of 1787 decided that the Congress under the Articles of Confederation was inadequate and that the national government needed to be strengthened, but, significantly, supporters of the new Constitution called themselves Federalists, which was another way of continuing to stress the links between the polity they were advocating and that which was outlined in the Old Testament. Many of those who advocated a stronger government than that under the Articles of Confederation were undoubtedly aware that government under the judges ultimately appeared to have broken down because, in the words of Judges 21:25, "in those days there was no king in Israel; every man did that which was right in his own eyes" (Vile and Foshee, 1988).

Among the more fascinating manifestations of political Hebraism was a fruitless attempt by Mordecai Manuel Noah (1785–1851) to establish what

Shalev describes as a "Jewish biblical government in upstate New York" on Grand Island in the Niagara River near Buffalo, to which he hoped to attract oppressed Jews from around the world (2013, 76–77).

See also Articles of Confederation; City upon a Hill; *Common Sense* (Thomas Paine); Constitutional Convention of 1787; Forms of Government; Puritans

For Reference and Further Reading

Leiter, Yechiel J. M. 2018. *John Locke's Political Philosophy and the Hebrew Bible.* Cambridge: Cambridge University Press.

Nelson, Eric. 2010. *The Hebrew Republic: Jewish Sources and the Transformation of European Political Thought.* Cambridge, MA: Harvard University Press.

Shalev, Eran. 2009. "'A Perfect Republic': The Mosaic Constitution in Revolutionary New England, 1775–1788." *New England Quarterly* (June): 235–63.

Shalev, Eran. 2013. *American Zion: The Old Testament as a Political Text from the Revolution to the Civil War.* New Haven, CT: Yale University Press.

Vile, John R., and Andrew Foshee. 1988. "Domestic Politics in the Book of Judges: The Story of Gibeah." *Journal of Political Science* 16 (Spring): 33–42.

Polygamy

Early American colonists discovered that some Native American Indians had more than one wife, and that they often found justification for this practice in the story of the patriarchs from the Bibles that the colonists had translated for them (Pearsall 2019, 82–114). The issue became far more prominent when, in 1852, the Church of Jesus Christ of Latter-Day Saints (LDS; then more commonly known as the Mormons) confirmed at a missionary conference that this had not only been the practice of Brigham Young and other leading members of the church but that it was now established church doctrine.

Orson Pratt (1811–1881) took the lead in announcing and defending this doctrine. As summarized by David J. Whittaker, the university archivist at Brigham Young University, Pratt offered five arguments, which others, including missionaries, repeated through the year 1884. They asserted that the practice

> was the only way to fulfill the original commandment given to Adam and Eve to "multiply and replenish the earth" [Gen. 1:28]; it allowed individuals to fulfill and take part in the promises made to Abraham and his family; historically the earth's population has believed in polygamy, hence monogamy was the exception, not the rule; since monogamy is unnatural and invites immorality, the acceptance of plural marriage would reform the world morally and socially; and, finally, spirit children of God wait for a "noble parentage" who will train them up in righteousness. (Whittaker 1984, 44)

Whittaker observes that LDS drew from non-LDS sources, including writings by Martin Luther, the leader of the Protestant Reformation, and John Milton, the English poet (1984, 60). Whittaker is further fascinated by the manner in which both justifications for, and criticisms of, polygamy often mirrored those involving slavery. Whittaker thus observed that "(1) both appealed to the idea of popular sovereignty; (2) both slavery and polygamy were defended by biblical proof-texts; (3) both slavery and polygamy recognized and argued for a 'natural place' for blacks and women; and (4) both Southerners and Mormons argued that practical considerations justified their systems" (62).

Political scientist John Kincaid further explores such ties, observing that both slavery and polygamy presented forms of "territorially based multiculturalism" that the rest of the nation considered barbaric and eventually eliminated (2003, 75). The government began legislating against polygamy with the Morrill Anti-Bigamy Act of 1862. The Poland Act of 1874 made it easier to prosecute polygamists. The U.S. Supreme Court upheld this law in *Reynolds v. United States* (1879), where, while acknowledging individuals' First Amendment right to believe what they wanted, asserted that the government still had the power to regulate actions that were considered to be repugnant. The Edmunds Act of 1883 further made "unlawful cohabitation" illegal, and the Edmunds-Tucker Act of 1887 set a limit of $50,000 on property owned by the church (Kincaid 2003, 84–86). Congress blocked Utah's entrance into the Union until 1896, six years after Wilford Woodruff, then LDS president, announced that God had told him that the church should abandon the practice (86).

Although the main LDS church complied with Woodruff's recommendation, some fundamentalist LDS members continue the practice. In 2006, federal agents raided the Fundamentalist Latter-Day Saints' Yearning for Zion Ranch in Eldorado, Texas, run by Warren Jeffers, which resulted in Jeff's imprisonment for bigamy and assaults on underage wives. The government has also imprisoned Tony Alamo, a non-LDS preacher, who advocated polygamy on the basis of Jesus's statement in Matthew 5:17 that he had not come to abolish but to fulfill the law. Alamo had further sought justification for marriage to prepubescent girls in the command in Genesis 1:28 to "be fruitful and multiply" but was convicted under the Mann Act, which, largely aimed at prostitution, prevents the transportation of women across state lines for immoral purposes (Allen 2014, 67).

See also Church of Jesus Christ of Latter-Day Saints; Slavery

For Reference and Further Reading

Allen, Spencer L. 2014. "The Anomaly of Tony Alamo Christian Ministries: A New Testament-Based Call for Christian Polygamy." *Nova Religio: The Journal of Alternative and Emergent Religions* 17 (May): 62–82.

Gordon, Sarah Barringer. 2002. *The Mormon Question: Polygamy and Constitutional Conflict in Nineteenth-Century America*. Chapel Hill: University of North Carolina Press.

Kincaid, John. 2003. "Extinguishing the Twin Relics of Barbaric Multiculturalism—Slavery and Polygamy—from American Federalism." *Publius* 33 (Winter): 75–92.

Pearsall, Sarah M. S. 2019. *Polygamy: An Early American History*. New Haven, CT: Yale University Press.

Reynolds v. United States, 98 U.S. 145 (1879).

Whittaker, David J. 1984. "Early Mormon Polygamy Defenses." *Journal of Mormon History* 11: 43–63.

Pompeo, Mike

On April 26, 2018, Mike Pompeo (b. 1963) became the seventieth U.S. secretary of state. A Republican who attended the military academy at West Point and

In the United States, the fact that certain behavior violates scriptural norms is typically considered to be an insufficient justification, in and of itself, for legal regulations. Indeed, although such laws existed in early American history, it would be rare to find prosecutions of immoral consensual sexual behavior, especially in the aftermath of U.S. Supreme Court decisions, most notably *Lawrence v. Texas* (2003), that ruled that such behavior is protected by constitutional privacy rights.

Although fundamentalist and evangelical literature reflect increased concern about pornographic addictions among their own members, including members of the clergy, they have often highlighted anti-pornography laws as part of their political agenda, typically in conjunction with opposition to homosexuality, abortion, and same-sex marriage (Strub 2010, 179–212). Religious conservatives have established such groups as Citizens for Decency through Law, Jerry Falwell's Moral Majority, Donald Wildmon's National Federation for Decency, and other groups and were particularly on the Meese Commission, which President Reagan appointed to investigate the subject.

After numerous conflicting opinions, opponents of pornography achieved at least a partial victory when in 1973, the U.S. Supreme Court ruled in *Miller v. California* that the First Amendment to the U.S. Constitution did not protect pornographic depictions. The problem, of course, is defining pornography. To this end, the court set for forth a three-part test that asked "(a) whether the average person, applying contemporary community standards, would find the work as a whole appealing to the prurient [lustful] interest; (b) whether the work depicts or describes in a patently offensive way sexual conduct specifically defined by the applicable state law and (c) whether the work as a whole lacks serious literary, artistic, political or scientific value" (Vile 2018, 310–11). The court allowed somewhat lower standards for the distribution of materials showing children engaged in sexual conduct in *New York v. Ferber* (1982) but has generally struck down laws that seek unduly to restrict adult viewing rights under the guise of protecting children.

See also Abortion; Evangelicals; Fundamentalists; Ten Commandments

For Reference and Further Reading

George, Robert P. 2001. *The Clash of Orthodoxies: Law, Religion, and Morality in Crisis.* Wilmington, DE: ISI Books.

Gruden, Wayne. 2010. *Politics according to the Bible: A Comprehensive Resource for Understanding Modern Political Issues in Light of Scripture.* Grand Rapids, MI: Zondervon.

Lawrence v. Texas, 539 U.S. 558 (2003).

Miller v. California, 413 U.S. 15 (1973).

New York v. Ferber, 458 U.S. 747 (1982).

Sherkat, Darren E., and Christopher G. Ellison. 1997. "The Cognitive Structure of a Moral Crusade: Conservative Protestantism and Opposition to Pornography." *Social Forces* 75 (March): 957–80.

Strub, Whitney. 2010. *Perversion for Profit: The Politics of Pornography and the Rise of the New Right.* New York: Columbia University Press.

Vile, John R. 2018. *Essential Supreme Court Decisions: Summaries of Leading Cases in U.S. Constitutional Law*, 17th ed. Lanham, MD: Rowman & Littlefield.

Poverty and Justice Bible

One of the specialty Bibles that is available to American audiences is *The Poverty and Justice Bible*, which is described as a Contemporary English Version and published by the Bible Society in Britain. Its distinctiveness comes from highlighting passages that deal with the two subjects in the title and with a thirty-two-page section in the middle of the Bible entitled "The Core," which shows the centrality of biblical teachings on both subjects, and follows with fifty topics. Each of these lists a word, a "Discover" section featuring a biblical passage highlighting the word, a "Dream" or imagining section, and a "Do" section. The intent of the Bible is to show "how issues of poverty and justice are woven into the fabric of the Bible, and how concern for the poor and the oppressed forms part of the DNA of our faith" (2008, 7).

The eclectic key words include people, book, power, body, grapes, bribes, tree, child, toilet, obedience, stone, weeping, torture, tools, scroll, bubbles, Bible, water, Greek, bandages, wages, pennies, refuge, safe, cows, cash, prison, Sabbath, peace, temple, school, straw, heights, sword, widow, redeemer, talk, house, plague, growth, sex, lions, disease, chains, well, and city. The opening word "people," based on Genesis 1:26–27, focuses on how human beings are made in the image of God (7), while the closing word "city" uses Revelation 21:3–7 to point to the eventual holy city in which "there is no more suffering, no more tears. Death, drying and pain are things of the past" (30).

References to MPs (members of Parliament) (32) and the loo (bathroom) (11) highlight the Bible's British origins, although a "Taking It Further" section near the end suggests World Vision, an evangelical aid group chiefly based in the United States, as a way to join others in fighting poverty and seeking justice (31). One form of poverty that the Bible identifies is that of lack of Bibles in some parts of the world, which is further tied to lack of education and illiteracy.

See also Green Bible

For Reference and Further Reading

The Poverty and Justice Bible. 2008. Swindon: Bible Society. [Note: Page references are to the section in the middle of the text.]

Powell, Adam Clayton, Jr.

Adam Clayton Powell Jr. (1908–1972) followed his father as pastor of the Abyssinian Baptist Church in Harlem, New York. As a mixed-race child, he could sometimes pass for white, and he struggled with his racial identity (Marbury 2015, 141–43). He helped lead a bus boycott in 1941, during which many women began calling him "Mr. Jesus" (Capeci 1979, 722), and went on to serve as one of the most powerful African Americans in Congress from 1945 to 1971. In 1961, he became chair of the Education and Labor Committee and worked to pass some of the nation's most important civil rights laws. Eventually excluded from the House for taking young women with him on out-of-country travel, he won an important decision at the Supreme Court in *Powell v. McCormack* (1969) indicating that a vote to expel him from Congress required a two-thirds majority, rather than a simple majority, but he returned to his seat with diminished powers.

He published his book *Keep the Faith, Baby!* in an attempt to remind constituents of his work on their behalf. It consists of numerous sermons that he delivered, all with introductory scriptural texts and many biblical references, and a number of the specific dates that he gave them. Many focused on biblical stories and doctrines that might be appropriate for any Christian pastor, while others also addressed political issues of the day.

In a sermon entitled "Black Power: A Form of Godly Power," Powell used as one of his texts the Song of Solomon 1:5–6, in which a woman refers to herself as "black, but comely" (Powell 1967, 7). Dropping the names of other African American leaders like A. Philip Randolph, Martin Luther King Jr., and Stokely Carmichael, Powell said that his own notion of black power was "not anti-white" (Powell 1967, 10). He further exhorted, "Instead of 'Burn, baby, burn' [a phrase often associated with urban riots], we should be shouting, 'Learn, baby, learn' and 'Earn, baby, earn'" (11). He further referred to black power as "Godly power" (16).

One sermon, "A Living Book for a Dying World," cited the admonition from Ezekiel 33:1–7 about the need for serving as a watchman on the wall to warn of impending calamities (21). In the sermon, he sought to blow the trumpet against modern materialism, secularism, totalitarianism, and racism (25). A later essay on "The Temptation of Modernity" used Jesus's temptations in the wilderness in Matthew 4:1–10 to warn against "materialism, paternalism and power" and the idea that men can live merely by satisfying physical needs (205).

Powell based a sermon on Harlem on the passage from Joshua 1:1–9 in which Joshua took the reins from Moses and advocated for "courage, strength, and perseverance" (33). A sermon entitled "Minimum Living—Minimum Religion" bemoaned the world's loss of "its sense of discipline" (37).

"The Imperishable Dream," dated January 7, 1962, used the story of the biblical Joseph to encourage members of his congregation to dream, while the next sermon, "What We Must Do about Africa," which was dated April 3, 1960, advocated specific policies to change the apartheid policies in South Africa. Powell included sermons on church anniversaries, Palm Sunday, Easter, Pentecost, Mother's Day, and Christmas. Many of the sermons, including one entitled "'This Thing'—Jesus!," emphasized that Jesus's message was "based on God, goodness, love and nonviolence" (73). Another sermon, "Santa Claus versus Jesus Christ," suggested downplaying the holiday emphasis on materialism and replacing it with a focus on Jesus (99–103). One of Powell's essays, "The Whole Gospel for the Whole World," was based on his church's motto.

A sermon dated July 3, 1960, entitled "Let's Give Up Our Own Prejudices" was based on Galatians 3:28—"There is neither Jew nor Greek, there is neither bond nor free, there is neither male nor female: for ye are all one in Christ Jesus"—to discount prejudice based simply on the fact that a politician was from a particular part of the country (he was specifically attempting to defend Lyndon B. Johnson, who was from the South). The following essay, "A New Frontier of Faith," welcomed the election of President John F. Kennedy as a sign that the nation was overcoming its prejudices against Roman Catholics.

Although Powell was ecumenical, in a sermon from October 2, 1955, "Why I Am a Christian," he favorably compared Christianity to its other alternatives and specifically focused on the inspiration of Christian Scriptures and the Golden Rule (1967, 110). A sermon, "Christ in the Nuclear Age," was designed to show the sufficiency of Jesus for modern times, while a sermon on "Democracy and Religion" pointed to the continuing need for "Christian leadership" (157).

In "Man's Debt to God," Powell observed, "The founding fathers of the First Continental Congress did not bestow upon the American citizen the right to freedom; they merely recorded the fact that his Creator originally endowed him with that inalienable right. Liberty, therefore, is of God, not of man" (145). In the same sermon, he observed that "the authority of truth is absolute. It is by decree of God, not by plebiscite of man. It is a birthright no more than a right; it is a duty" (147).

In a sermon dated December 13, 1953, entitled "Walking under a Cloud," he referred to the impending decision in *Brown v. Board of Education* as "momentous" and argued that God's presence was with African Americans just as it had been with the children of Israel while they wandered through the desert (151).

An essay entitled "The Injustice of Justice," dated May 23, 1960, explained his opposition to capital punishment and supported a constitutional amendment to outlaw it throughout the United States. He believed that it was largely inflicted on the poor and conflicted with the admonition in the Ten Commandments not to kill.

Powell's sermon on "Mother's Day" was fairly conventional. He observed, "The Christian family has a Bible basis. In the Bible the Christian family is a physical, spiritual and emotional unity under God for the enjoyment of the member's perpetuation of the human race, the care and the nurture of children, the happiness of mankind and the transmission of faith" (191).

An essay dated November 29, 1959, entitled "Stop Blaming Everybody Else" cited the passage in Exodus 32:21–23, in which Aaron blamed the people for making an idol, to lambast Senator Joe McCarthy for libeling individuals as communists. In a sermon entitled "The Search for Freedom," Powell used Galatians 5:1 to laud Christian liberty, beginning with the quotation from Leviticus 25:10 on the Liberty Bell (267). In the essay, he lauded the freedoms in the First Amendment as well as Franklin D. Roosevelt's Four Freedoms.

Powell's final essay "The Negro and His Church" cited the passage from Psalm 68:31 about princes coming from Egypt and Ethiopia stretching out hands to God and Jesus's Great Commission in Matthew 28:19 to spread the gospel. In so doing, he said that the chief enemies were not the blatant segregationists but internal divisions, "misleadership," indifference, and "*refusal to use civil rights and divine rights which we already possess*" (291). In so doing, he observed that "the oppression we face as Negroes today is not the first, the worst, or the last crisis" (293).

See also Baptists; Capital Punishment

For Reference and Further Reading

Capeci, Dominic J., Jr. 1979. "From Harlem to Montgomery: The Bus Boycotts and Leadership of Adam Clayton Powell, Jr., and Martin Luther King, Jr." *The Historian* 41 (August): 721–37.

Marbury, Herbert Robinson. 2015. *Pillars of Cloud and Fire: The Politics of Exodus in African American Biblical Interpretation*. New York: New York University Press.
Powell, Adam Clayton. 1967. *Keep the Faith, Baby!* New York: Trident Press.
Powell v. McCormack, 395 U.S. 486 (1969).

Presidential Inaugural Bibles

In addition to being considered to be sacred texts, Bibles are often also regarded as holy objects and are often used by individuals who are taking oaths. Indeed, St. Augustine of Hippo (AD 354–430) recorded that individuals used Gospels to take oaths, and kings and queens have since done so (*Presidential Inaugural Bibles* 1969, 6–7). The U.S. Constitution does not require it, but it is common for presidents to add the words "so help me God" to their inaugural oaths, and, in early years, it was quite common for presidents to kiss the Bible after they took their oaths.

In 1969, the National Cathedral displayed all known presidential inaugural Bibles. They were unable to locate inaugural Bibles from Presidents John Adams through John Tyler or from Zachary Taylor, Millard Fillmore, or Franklin Pierce (*Presidential Inaugural Bibles* 1969, 7). John Quincy Adams noted in his diary that Chief Justice John Marshall had brought a volume on laws on which to take the oath, and Marshall might have done so for the previous presidents as well (*Presidential Inaugural Bibles* 1969, 7).

President Washington, whose Bible has also been used by Presidents Warren G. Harding, Dwight Eisenhower, Jimmy Carter, and George H. W. Bush, was borrowed from the St. John's Masonic Lodge in New York City (Campbell 2010, 205). Grover Cleveland, the first president known to have provided his own Bible, used one that his mother had given to him when he was fifteen (*Presidential Inaugural Bibles* 1969, 7). Theodore Roosevelt, Woodrow Wilson, and Franklin D. Roosevelt all used Bibles that they has used in taking gubernatorial oaths; Franklin D. Roosevelt, John F. Kennedy, Lyndon B. Johnson, and Richard M. Nixon all used family Bibles; and Lyndon Johnson used the same Bible on which he had taken his vice presidential oath (*Presidential Inaugural Bibles* 1969, 8, 48).

Abraham Lincoln used a Bible that was supplied by William Thomas Carroll, the clerk of the U.S. Supreme Court who had previously supplied an identical Bible to James Buchanan (*Presidential Inaugural Bibles* 1969, 24). Barack Obama and Donald Trump later used Lincoln's Bible at their inaugurations. A number of inaugural Bibles have notes either from the Supreme Court clerk or the chief justice certifying that they were used for a particular inauguration. The Bible that President James K. Polk used for his inauguration was presented to his wife by the Marshal of the District of Columbia (*Presidential Inaugural Bibles* 1969, 22).

The inaugural Bible used by William McKinley for his first inauguration had been presented to him by Bishop Benjamin W. Arnett, the president of Wilberforce College. Both the Bible and the box in which it was held were said to have been made completely of products of Ohio, which was McKinley's home state (*Presidential Inaugural Bibles* 1969, 35).

earned a law degree from Harvard Law School, Pompeo had previously served from 2011 to 2017 as a member of the U.S. House of Representatives from Kansas and as director of the Central Intelligence Agency in 2017 and 2018.

Pompeo became a Christian while at West Point and is known to have affirmed his belief in the rapture (based on interpretations of Luke 17:34–35; 1 Corinthians 15:51–53; and 1 Thessalonians 4:16–18), in which, near the end of time, Christ will whisk Christians from the earth so they will not have to endure the Great Tribulation. Pompeo and Vice President Mike Pence are among the most visible evangelical Christians serving in the Trump administration, and both are fond of citing the Bible. Indeed, Pompeo, who is a Presbyterian, keeps an open Bible on his desk. In giving a speech in Cairo, Egypt, in early 2019, he observed that "this trip is especially meaningful to me as an evangelical Christian," and added that "I keep a Bible open on my desk to remind me of God and His Word, and The Truth" (Wright 2019, using capitalization from State Department transcript).

Pompeo has likened President Trump to "a modern-day Esther, poised to defend Israel and save the Jewish people" (Joyce 2019). Pompeo has led in the decision to move the American Embassy in Israel from Tel Aviv to Jerusalem and has supported Israeli annexation of the Golan Heights. He has also taken a strong stance against Iran, which he associates with radical Islamic terrorism. Pompeo has been a strong supporter of religious freedom and worked for the release of an evangelical pastor, Andrew Brunson, held in Turkey as well as for the rights of other religious minorities. He has been criticized for holding a press conference open only to "faith-based" media (Wong 2019).

See also Esther as Political Archetype; Evangelicals; Trump, Donald J.; Zionism

For Reference and Further Reading

Joyce, Kathryn. 2019. "The Christianization of U.S. Foreign Policy." *New Republic*. March 25. https://newrepublic.com/article/153387/christianization-us-foreign-policy/.

Kattan, Victor. 2019. "U.S. Recognition of Golan Heights Annexation: Testament to Our Times." *Journal of Palestine Studies* 48 (Spring): 79–85.

Wong, Edward. 2019. "The Rapture and the Real World: Mike Pompeo Blends Beliefs and Policy." *New York Times*. March 30.

Wright, Robin. 2019. "Pompeo and His Bible Define U.S. Policy in the Middle East." *New Yorker*. January 10. https://www.newyorker.com/news/our-columnists/pompeo-and-his-bible-define-us-policy-in-the-middle-east.

Pornography

The Bible is replete with prohibitions against premarital and extramarital sex, including the prohibition in Exodus 20:14, part of the Ten Commandments, against adultery (Gruden 2010, 238–39). In Matthew 5:27–28, which is part of the Sermon on the Mount, Jesus even equated looking upon a woman with lustful intent with adultery. Adherents to biblical morality typically equate depictions of sexual activity as leading to such lusts and accompanying immoral behavior and, thus, as inappropriate for viewing. Some feminists have further sought to link pornography to the dehumanization and objectification of women and with accompanying violence against them.

The oldest known Bible used, and the only one to be written in a language other than English (Dutch) was the family Bible from 1686 that Franklin D. Roosevelt used for his oaths (*Presidential Inaugural Bibles* 1969, 43). The most elaborate volume was the facsimile of the Latin Vulgate Bible, which had been bought by Independence Missouri Chamber of Commerce and presented to President Harry S. Truman as a memorial to his mother (*Presidential Inaugural Bibles* 1969, 45).

Most of the Bibles used for presidential inaugurals were the King James Version of 1611, but President John F. Kennedy used the Douay-Rheims Version of 1582–1610, which was preferred by most Roman Catholics, while Truman, Eisenhower, and Trump used the American Standard Version of 1901 (*Presidential Inaugural Bibles* 1969, 47).

See also Lincoln Inaugural Bible; Presidential Inaugural Bible Verses; Washington Inaugural Bible

For Reference and Further Reading

Campbell, Gordon. 2010. *Bible: The Story of the King James Version 1611–2011*. New York: Oxford University Press.

NCC Staff. 2017. "How Presidents Use Bibles at Inaugurations." Constitution Daily. January 20. https://constitutioncenter.org/blog/how-presidents-use-bibles-at-inaugurations/.

Presidential Inaugural Bibles: Catalogue of an Exhibition, November 17, 1968 through February 23, 1969. 1969. Washington, DC: Washington Cathedral.

Presidential Inaugural Bible Verses

Although the Constitution does not require the practice, U.S. presidents typically take their inaugural oaths with their right hand raised and their left hand placed on the Bible. It has become increasingly common for presidents to open the Bible to a specific passage, typically in the King James Version. Some have used Bibles—like the Washington or Lincoln Inaugural Bibles—with historic significance, but many have also used family Bibles. Five presidents—Truman, Eisenhower, Nixon, Obama, and Trump—have used two Bibles, while John Quincy Adams swore on a book of law that included the U.S. Constitution (NCC Staff 2017).

The Bible on which George Washington took his oath is said to have been opened either specifically to Genesis 49:13 (perhaps at random) or more generically to Genesis 49 and 50, which might have been designed to focus on the blessings of Jacob, to which he might have thought America was heir (Gajanan 2017). In his second term, Lincoln marked three verses (Matthew 7:1; Matthew 18:7; and Revelation 16:7), which Winder summarizes as being "about judging others, offending others, and God's righteous judgments" (2019, 123).

Historian Jon Meacham has compiled a list twenty-nine such passages, beginning with the inauguration of Martin Van Buren in 1837 and continuing through George W. Bush in 2005. The large majority of these passages are taken from the Hebrew Bible, or Christian Old Testament, perhaps in part to emphasize the Judeo-Christian heritage.

The respective passages are as follows (I have summarized each briefly):

Martin Van Buren, 1837, Proverbs 3:17: the ways of God are of pleasantness and peace;
Ulysses S. Grant, 1872, Isaiah 11:1–3: a rod that grows from the stem of Jesse [Grant's father was named Jesse so this passage likely had special significance to him];
Rutherford B. Hayes, 1877, Psalm 118:11–13: destroying enemies compassed about;
James A. Garfield, 1881, Proverbs 21:1, Psalm 118:11–13: the king's heart is in God's hand;
Chester A. Arthur, 1881, Psalm 31:1–3: trust in God who is a "rock" and "fortress";
Benjamin Harrison, 1889, Psalm 121:1–6: God is helper and creator who will protect;
Grover Cleveland, 1893, Psalm 91:12–16: God's protection;
William McKinley, 1897, 2 Chronicles 1:10: request for God's wisdom;
William McKinley, 1901, Proverbs 16:1, 9: man choses his way but God directs his steps;
Theodore Roosevelt, 1905, James 1:22–23: be doers and not just hearers of the word;
William Howard Taft, 1909, 1 Kings 3:9–11: request to God for discernment in governing;
Woodrow Wilson, 1913, Psalm 119: the blessedness of following the law of God;
Woodrow Wilson, 1917: Psalm 46: God as refuge and strength;
Warren G. Harding, 1921, Micah 6:3: God requires people "to do justly, and to love mercy, and to walk humbly with thy God";
Calvin Coolidge, 1925, John 1: "In the beginning was the Word . . .";
Herbert Hoover, 1929, Proverbs 20:18: "Where there is no vision, the people perish";
Franklin D. Roosevelt, 1933, 1937, 1941, 1945, 1 Corinthians 13: value of "charity" (love);
Harry S. Truman, 1949 (used two Bibles), opened to Matthew 5:3–11: the Sermon on the Mount; and Exodus 20:3–17: The Ten Commandments;
Dwight D. Eisenhower, 1953 (used two Bibles), Psalm 127:1: God must build house; 2 Chronicles 7:14: God's people should "humble themselves, and pray, and seek my face";
Dwight D. Eisenhower, 1957, Psalm 33:12: nation with God as Lord is blessed;
Richard M. Nixon, 1969 and 1973, Isaiah 2:4: turning swords into plowshares [perhaps an indication of his Quaker background];
Gerald R. Ford, 1974, Proverbs 3:5–6: trust in the Lord "and He shall direct thy paths";
Jimmy Carter, 1977, Micah 6:8: God requires justice, mercy, and humility;
Ronald Reagan, 1981 and 1985, 2 Chronicles 7:14: God's people should "humble themselves, and pray, and seek my face";
George H. W. Bush, 1989, Matthew 5: Sermon on the Mount;
Bill Clinton, 1993, Galatians 6:8: sowing to flesh reaps corruption but to the Spirit everlasting life;
Bill Clinton, 1997, Isaiah 58:12: building amid wastes to be "the repairer of the breach, the restorer of paths to dwell in";
George W. Bush, 2005, Isaiah 40:31: those who wait on God shall have strength renewed.

Another examination of presidential references to God in inaugural addresses observes that John Quincy Adams cited "Except the Lord keep the city, the watchman watcheth in Vain" (Psalm 127:1); a number of presidents referred to "the God of our fathers"; Gerald R. Ford cited the Golden Rule (Matthew 7:12); Jimmy Carter specifically referenced the Washington Bible on which he took his oath; and Bill Clinton cited the verse (Galatians 6:9), "And let us not be weary in well-doing, for in due season, we shall reap, if we faint not" (Newcombe 2017).

See also Lincoln Inaugural Bible; Presidential Inaugural Bibles; Washington Inaugural Bible

For Reference and Further Reading

Associated Press. 2013. "Obama to Use 2 Bibles When He Takes Oath of Office." Fox News. January 10 [updated December 20, 2015]. https://www.foxnews.com/politics/obama-to-use-2-bibles-when-he-takes-oath-of-office.

Gajanan, Mahita. 2017. "These Are the Bible Verses Past Presidents Have Turned to on Inauguration Day." *Time*. January 19. http ://time.com/4639596/inauguration-day-presidents-bible-passages/.

Meacham, Jon. 2006. *American Gospels: God, the Founding Fathers, and the Making of a Nation*. New York: Random House.

NCC Staff. 2017. "How Presidents Use Bibles at Inaugurations." Constitution Daily. January 20. https://constitutioncenter.org/blog/how-presidents-use-bibles-at-inaugurations/.

Newcombe, Jerry. 2017. "A List of All the Presidents Who Mentioned God in an Inaugural Address." *Christian Post*. January 20. https://www.christianpost.com/news/a-list-of-all-the-presidents-who-mentioned-god-in-an-inaugural-address.html.

Smith, Christopher. 2004. "Inaugural Bible Verses, and What They Tell Us about Our Presidents." Worlds without End. February 17. http ://www.withoutend.org/inaugural-bible-verses-presidents/.

Winder, Mike. 2019. *Favorite Scriptures of 100 American Leaders*. Springville, UT: Plain Sight.

Property Rights

See Land Ownership

Prophets and Jeremiads

Prophecy, which is often associated with visions, has many different meanings. It is common to refer to individuals in American politics as fulfilling a prophetic role, bearing a prophetic mantel, or serving a prophetic function. A role clearly not limited to politicians or preachers, the role may also be associated with poets, singers, novelists, academicians, and members of various social reform movements. Such leaders are often described as charismatic, that is, blessed with God's special grace or insight (Hanska 2009, 97).

Although the idea of prophets and prophecy is not unique to the Bible—as in Tecumseh's brother, Tenskwatawa, the Shawnee prophet (Kilgore 2016, 98–110)—much of the Old Testament consists of books both by major prophets like Isaiah, Jeremiah, Ezekiel, and Daniel, who wrote relatively large books, and by those like Hosea, Joel, Amos, Obadiah, Jonah, Micah, Naham, Habakkuk,

Zephaniah, Haggai, Zechariah, and Malachi, who wrote shorter ones. Moreover, other biblical books describe such prophets as Samuel (also described as a judge), Elijah, Elisha, and Nathan.

The Bible often distinguishes the role of the prophets, who rarely held public offices but received their authority directly from God, from that of the king, or ruler, and those who seek to mix the two roles sometimes encounter problems (McTighe 1990). Whereas the king was at the apex of formal governmental authority, he was subject to God's law, which was delivered, often by way of rebuke, by prophets. Although it is common for modern Americans, especially those who look to the biblical book of Revelation, to look to prophets to predict the future, a biblical prophet was more typically an individual who brought the word of God to a particular situation, often one that involved wrongdoing. Thus, even though they were anointed by prophets, King Saul could be reprimanded by Samuel, King David by Nathan, and King Ahab by Elijah, for their wrongdoing, just as religious figures in U.S. history sometimes indict sitting leaders and institutions. The Old Testament makes it clear, however, that some prophets prostituted their messages to reassure ruling authorities, and prophets who delivered bad news were often persecuted rather than rewarded for their efforts. Jesus, who assumed his own prophet mantel, reminded his listeners who prided themselves on their Hebrew heritage that their forefathers had often persecuted and even killed the prophets of their day. After condemning Herod, John the Baptist was imprisoned, and his head was delivered to Herod's daughter on a plate!

Professor George Shulman identifies biblical prophets as holding a kind of office, which he believes can be placed in one of four categories. Prophets like Amos were chosen as "*messengers* who *announce* truths their audience is invested in denying" (Shulman 2008, 5). Prophets like Micah were called to bear witness by testifying "*to what they see and stand against it*" (5). Prophets like Amos were called to forestall danger by serving as "*watchmen* who *forewarn*" (5). Prophets like Jeremiah might further play the role of "singers who ask and answer the question, What is the meaning of our suffering?" (6).

Using a somewhat different typology, H. Mark Roelofs says that those who fit what he calls the "prophetic paradigm" (1988, 583) generally had three characteristics. They were typically "men of low estate," they conceived of themselves as messengers of God, and God generally sent them "to confront the people" (583).

Shulman further divides the genre of prophecy into three narrative parts (2008, 6–13). One such part is theodicy, which seeks to explain pending disaster as expressing God's judgment. Just as biblical prophets often portrayed enemy invasions as the instruments of God's justice, so Abraham Lincoln suggested that the havoc inflicted by the Civil War might be God's punishment for American slavery. Two days after the terrorist attacks of September 11, 2001, Rev. Jerry Falwell focused not on foreign enemies but on "the pagans, the abortionists, the feminists, the gays and lesbians who are actively trying to make that an alternate lifestyle, the ACLU, People for the American Way—all of them who have tried to secularize America" (cited in Shulman 2008, 13).

A second form of prophetic narrative, which has been quite prominent in U.S. history, is the jeremiad, in which speakers warn Americans that they are failing to live up to founding principles. John Winthrop had warned that, as a city upon a hill, if the people abandoned their covenant and God punished them, "we shall be made a story and a byword throughout the world" (Vile 2015, 21). Within a generation or two, American Pilgrims were questioning whether they exhibited the love for God that their forefathers had displayed. The jeremiad became especially prominent among abolitionists and continued in distinctive African American forms (Howard-Pitney 1986). Frederick Douglass and Abraham Lincoln justly accused Americans of failing to live up to the ideals of the Declaration of Independence. Such jeremiads were typically accompanied by calls for repentance that could lead to national redemption. Proclamations in early American history that called for Thanksgiving were also accompanied by calls for humiliation, fasting, and repentance.

Finally, the narrative of lamentation, which the Old Testament associated especially with the prophet Jeremiah, depicts the people's present suffering, sometimes with hopes again of eventual redemption. In his speech, "What to the slave in the Fourth of July?," Frederick Douglass cited Psalm 137:1, which described the bitterness of the Israelites in Babylonian exile, to describe the sorrows of his enslaved African American brothers and sisters.

A number of indigenous American religions have been founded by individuals whom their followers consider to be prophets. These include the Church of Jesus Christ of Latter-Day Saints, who regard Joseph Smith as such; Seventh-Day Adventists, who so designate both William Miller and Ellen G. White; and Christian Scientists, who revere Mary Baker Eddy (Bringhurst 2006). The Prophet Muhammad played a major role in the founding of Islam.

See also Church of Jesus Christ of Latter-Day Saints; City upon a Hill; Days of Humiliation, Fasting, and Thanksgiving; Declaration of Independence; Douglass, Frederick; Errand into the Wilderness; Lincoln, Abraham

For Reference and Further Reading

Bringhurst, Newell G. 2006. "Four American Prophets Confront Slavery: Joseph Smith, William Miller, Ellen G. White and Mary Baker Eddy." *John Whitmer Historical Association Journal* 26: 120–41.

Gutterman, David S. 2005. *Prophetic Politics: Christian Social Movements and American Democracy*. Ithaca, NY: Cornell University Press.

Hanska, Jan. 2009. "Prophetic Politics—Leadership Based on the Stories of a Golden Past and a Glorious Future." *Perspectives* 17(2): 93–117.

Howard-Pitney, David. 1986. "The Enduring Black Jeremiad: The American Jeremiad and Black Protests Rhetoric, from Frederick Douglass to W.E.B. Du Bois, 1841–1919." *American Quarterly* 38(3): 481–92.

Kilgore, John Mac. 2016. *Mania for Freedom: American Literatures of Enthusiasms from the Revolution to the Civil War*. Chapel Hill: University of North Carolina Press.

Mathewes, Charles, and Christopher McKnight Nichols, eds. 2008. *Prophesies of Godlessness: Predictions of America's Imminent Secularization from the Puritans to the Present Day*. New York: Oxford University Press.

McTighe, Michael J. 1990. "Jesse Jackson and the Dilemma of a Prophet in Politics." *Journal of Church and State* 32 (Summer): 585–607.

Morone, James A. 2003. *Hellfire Nation: The Politics of Sin in American History*. New Haven, CT: Yale University Press.

Roelofs, H. Mark. 1988. "Hebraic-Biblical Political Thinking." *Polity* 20 (Summer): 572–97.

Shulman, George. 2008. *American Prophecy: Race and Redemption in American Political Culture.* Minneapolis: University of Minnesota Press.
Vile, John R., ed. 2015. *Founding Documents of America: Documents Decoded.* Santa Barbara, CA: ABC-CLIO.

Prosperity Gospel

The rise of what has been called the prosperity gospel is a phenomenon that is not only historically interesting but might also have implications for American politics.

Although not all Pentecostals adhere to the prosperity gospel, the movement largely grew from this movement that emphasizes spiritual signs and wonders including speaking in tongues (glossolalia) and faith healing. The movement has been highlighted by such megachurch ministers as Oral Roberts, Joel Osteen, T. D. Jakes, Kenneth Copeland, Jimmy Swaggart, Jim and Tammy Faye Baker, Creflo Dollar, and others, who often have large television ministries. They have focused on biblical passages that promise generally spiritual blessings and have interpreted them in terms of material health and prosperity.

Such ministers stress that God will reward material gifts to their ministry with concomitant material blessings on those who give. In seeking biblical supports, such ministers often refer to the biblical concept of giving one's "first fruits" and of planting financial "seeds" (Bowler 2013, 98). Perhaps drawing from Jesus's parable of the talents, such ministers often promise tenfold or even hundredfold financial blessings (99). They also cite Malachi 3:10: "Bring ye the titles into the storehouse . . . and prove me now herewith, saith the LORD of hosts, if I will not open you the windows of heaven and pour you out a blessing, that there shall not be room enough to receive it." A favorite verse applying to health is the passage from Isaiah 53:5: "But he was wounded for our transgressions, he was bruised for our iniquities; the chastisement of our peace was upon him; and with his stripes we are healed." Adherents also often draw upon Matthew 18:19, which says "that if two of you shall agree on earth as touching any thing that they shall ask, it shall be done for them of my Father which is in heaven."

Professor Bowler has demonstrated that there are many historical precursors to this movement in the nineteenth and early twentieth centuries in which spiritualists and others emphasized the dominance of the mind over the body. Such predecessors included "hydropathy, Grahamism, Adventism, homeopathy, and the burgeoning faith cure movement" (Bowler 2013, 14). The philosopher William James thus dedicated two of twenty lectures in his *Variety of Religious Experience* to "The Religion of Healthy-Mindedness" (Pendergrass 2017). An early proponent was Essek William Kenyon (1867–1948). In the 1950s, Norman Vincent Peale (1898–1993), of the Marble Collegiate Church in New York City, promoted what his most famous book called *The Power of Positive Thinking.* "He invoked Jesus as Teacher, not Savior, whose instructions on divine flow, source, and energy kept followers 'in tune with the Infinite' " (Bowler 2013, 57).

The prosperity gospel contains little emphasis on sin and guilt, the latter of which proponents believe to be a negative emotion. Its teachings suggest that individuals can succeed through faith and hard work. This undoubtedly encourages many individuals to persevere and succeed who might not otherwise do so, but if health and prosperity are the result of such efforts, then one might conclude that those without either such blessing lack sufficient faith, have somehow brought their problems upon themselves, and do not deserve help from either the church or the government. Followers might well also underestimate institutional issues, like racism or lack of access to equal educational facilities or medical care, that might be holding others back. Joel Osteen's Lakewood Church in Houston, Texas, which holds sixteen thousand people for worship, was criticized during Hurricane Harvey for refusing to provide shelter (Luce 2019). Others noted that the church spent only just over 1 percent of its budget on charitable causes (Luce 2019).

President Donald J. Trump invited Paula White, a proponent of the prosperity gospel, to pray at his inauguration (the first woman to be asked to do so); he later appointed her to advise his Faith and Opportunity Initiative (Peters and Haberman 2019). Moreover, he grew up under the preaching of Norman Vincent Peale. Martyn Percy, dean of the Christ Church College at Oxford, who is not a fan of the prosperity gospel, observes that "Trump's interior religious landscape is a kind of politico-spiritual Ponzi scheme, and his politics flow from this. Opportunism, pragmatism and positivism are the lessons Trump learned from Peale's pulpit" (Percy 2018).

Prosperity gospel pastors and evangelists often flaunt extravagant lifestyles as signs of God's blessings upon them. Journalist Sally Quinn notes that Trump's supporters "admire him for the fact that he has made all of his money and that he has never given up. He's brought himself to the top, and somehow if he can do it—it's like the power of positive thinking—he's telling them they can do it too" (Laidler 2017). Quinn also believes that many of Trump's untruthful statements, like his claim to have had the largest crowds for his inauguration, may be exercises of positive thinking. She believes that he may well think that "if he says it and he thinks positively, maybe it will turn out that it was true" (Laidler 2017).

See also Trump, Donald J.

For Reference and Further Reading

Bowler, Kate. 2013. *Blessed: A History of the American Prosperity Gospel.* New York: Oxford University Press.

Laidler, John. 2017. "Try Hard, Find God, Get Rich." *Harvard Gazette.* October4 24. https://news.harvard.edu/gazette/story/2017/10/the-prosperity-gospel-gains-a-foothold-in-u-s-politics-panel-says/.

Luce, Edward. 2019. "A Preacher for Trump's America: Joel Osteen and the Prosperity Gospel." April 17. https://www.ft.com/content/3990ce66-60a6-11e9-b285-3acd5d43599e.

Pendergrass, Drew. 2017. "The Televangelist-in-Chief: Trump and the Prosperity Gospel." *Harvard Political Review.* November 12. https://www.harvardpolitics.com/culture/tevangelistinchief/.

Percy, Martyn. 2018. "To Know Donald Trump's Faith Is to Understand His Politics." *Guardian.* February 6. https://www.theguardian.com/commentisfree/2018/feb/06/donald-trump-faith-politics-religious-presidency.

Peters, Jeremy W., and Maggie Haberman. 2019. "Paula White, Trump's Personal Pastor, Joins the White House." *New York Times.* October 31.

Posner, Sarah. 2008. *God's Profits: Faith, Fraud, and the Republican Crusade for Values Voters.* Sausalito, CA: PoliPointPress.

Providence

Although the Bible uses the word "providence" fairly sparingly (Acts 24:2), the idea that God exercises his providential care over his people, sometimes directly intervening on their behalves, has a long history, especially in Calvinistic Reformed theology that stresses God's sovereignty (Williams n.d.). Roger Williams even designated his settlement in present-day Rhode Island as the Providence Plantation.

Although the theme is hardly unique to America, it was particularly common in the eighteenth and nineteenth centuries to interpret historical events as the work of God's providence, and some modern writers continue this approach (Marshall and Manuel 1977 and 1986). Even American Deists, who generally looked upon God as a watchmaker who had left world affairs to his creation, sometimes perceived God's work in early American history. A study by historian Robert P. Hay traces such providential thinking by examining Independence Day speeches from 1776 to 1876 and contends that "if not *uniquely* American, the idea of protecting Providence was *characteristic* of American patriotism" (1969, 80). Hay cites speakers who attribute God's supervising intervention in delaying the discovery of the New World until such time as there would be Protestants to settle it; in destroying Native American tribes by disease so that the continent would be open for settlers; in intervening on America's behalf during the American Revolution and providing a wise father-leader in George Washington; in prospering America; in simultaneously taking John Adams and Thomas Jefferson on July 4, 1826; and in using the Civil War to abolish slavery.

Historian Mark Noll further examines the crisis in providential thinking that the Civil War occasioned. He believes that thinking providentially was a product both of biblical teachings "about God's control of the world" and of enlightenment confidence that they could understand such thinking; as he puts it, Americans "were children of the Enlightenment as well as children of God" (Noll 2006, 75). He further points out, as Lincoln noted, that both northerners and southerners expected that God's providence would aid their side. General Thomas "Stonewall" Jackson was among those in the South who had complete confidence that God's will would be done, although fellow general Edward Porter Alexander considered this a defect, believing that "it is customary to say that 'Providence did not intend that we should win.' But Providence did not care a row of pins about it" (87).

Contemporary historians are far less likely than they once were to translate the American experience through the eyes of Providence. The argument arguably persists, however, in the popular mind, in the notion that America is a "city upon a hill" with a special calling; that it is therefore an exceptional nation that fulfilled its manifest destiny in expanding from coast to coast; and that it has special responsibilities to the wider world, which at times have been interpreted to call upon it to take up colonization.

See also American Exceptionalism; City upon a Hill; Colonization; Deists; Jackson, Thomas (Stonewall); Manifest Destiny; Revolutionary War

For Reference and Further Reading

Hay, Robert P. 1969. "Providence and the American Past." *Indiana Magazine of History* 65 (June): 79–101.

Marshall, Peter, and David Manuel. 1977. *The Light and the Glory*. Old Tappan, NJ: Fleming H. Revell.

Marshall, Peter, and David Manuel. 1986. *From Sea to Shining Sea*. Old Tappan, NJ: Fleming H. Revell.

Noll, Mark A. 2006. *The Civil War as a Theological Crisis*. Chapel Hill: University of North Carolina Press.

Williams, Michael J. n.d. "What Is Divine Providence? Is It Biblical?" https://www.whatchristianswanttoknow.com/what-is-divine-providence-is-it-biblical/.

Psalm 137

Psalm 137 has been a recurring text in issues related to American law and politics. It is so well known, so much so that it appeared in the form of a song in the very first season of *Mad Men* and as the only part of *Godspell* that was taken from the Old Testament (Stowe 2014, 137, 143).

The Psalm, sometimes attributed to Jeremiah, describes the children of Israel sitting by the rivers of Babylon where they wept in response to their captor's request to sing the songs of Zion in a strange land. The middle of the psalm says,

> If I forget you, O Jerusalem, let my right hand wither!
> Let my tongue cling to the roof of my mouth, if I do not remember you,
> If I do not set Jerusalem above my highest joy

The concluding verses rejoice at the prospect of eventual vengeance against the captors, even observing (in language that most Christian commentators would later seek to interpret allegorically),

> Happy shall they be who take your little one
> and dash them against the rock!

During the British occupation of Boston that preceded the Revolutionary War, an American composer named William Billings used a paraphrase of the psalm to rail against the British:

> If I forget thee [Boston], yea if I do not remember thee,
> Then let my numbers cease to flow,
> Then be my Muse unkind.
> Then let my Tongue forget to move and ever be confi'd.
> Let horrid Jargon split the Air and rive my nerves asunder.
> Let hateful discord greet my ear as terrible as Thunder.
> Let Harmony be banish'd hence and Consonance depart.
> Let Dissonance erect her throne and reign within my Heart. (quoted in Stowe 2014, 145)

Whereas that poem portrayed Britain as Babylon, in his famous Independence Day speech in 1852, Frederick Douglass portrayed America as the Babylon in which fellow African Americans were called upon to sing and celebrate while many of them remained in captivity. Roland Hayes, an African American classical musician, later performed Antonin Dvorak's setting of Psalm 137 as an encore for an integrated recital that he gave in Washington, DC (Stowe 2014, 146). Clarence L. Franklin (1914–1984), a noted American preacher, later used the psalm as the theme of one of his recorded sermons, while Joseph Lowery, a colleague of Dr. Martin Luther King Jr., titled one of his books *Singing the Lord's Song in a Strange Land* (147–48). Rev. Jeremiah Wright, who served for many years as the pastor to Barack Obama, further cast the United States as Babylon, while pointing out that "Daniel had the audacity to hope," a phrase that Obama later used for the title of one of his books (149).

Outside of the United States, Jews suffering persecution under Nazism often cited these verses during their own tribulations.

See also Douglass, Frederick; Revolutionary War; Wright, Jeremiah

For Reference and Further Reading

Stowe, David W. 2014. "History, Memory, and Forgetting in Psalm 137." *The Bible in the Public Square: Its Enduring Influence in American Life,* ed. Mark Chancey, Carol Meyers, and Eric M. Meyers. Atlanta, GA: Society of Biblical Literature, pp. 137–57.

Puritans

For many Americans, Puritans are the Founders of choice. They are celebrated in the second verse of "America the Beautiful," which stresses how their "stern impassioned stress / A thoroughfare for freedom beat, across the wilderness." Their designation as "Pilgrims" further confirms their association with biblical themes and with John Bunyan's classic book, *Pilgrim's Progress*.

Fleeing England, where they were persecuted, and Holland, where they feared they could no longer maintain their separate identity, many Puritans came to America to create a godly commonwealth that would serve as a "city upon a hill." Some Puritans, who believed that the Reformation marked the beginning of the end of Roman Catholicism, which many identified with the Antichrist, further anticipated that America might play a major role in fulfilling God's purposes at the end of times.

Puritans were dissenting members of the Church of England (the Anglican Church) who retained deep suspicions not only of Catholicism but also of Anglican bishops and English kings. They actively opposed King Charles I (1600–1649) in the British Civil War and had him executed and replaced, for a time, by their leader Oliver Cromwell (1599–1658). Many were prominent in the iconoclast movement, in which they smashed images of the saints, stained glass windows, and other sanctuary embellishments, which they thought to be contrary to a pure faith. During the reign of Elizabeth I (1533–1603) and her successors, Puritans continued to push for stripping many of the "high church" elements that remained.

Puritans were Calvinists who believed that human beings were totally depraved, that God chose some to be saved and others to be damned (so-called double predestination), and that there was nothing that an individual could do to earn salvation. Many believed, however, that good works were a sign of salvation. George McKenna observes that Puritan thought contained two strains that he describes as "spiritists" and "preparationists"; he explains that "both spiritists and preparationists held fast to the Reformed Protestant doctrine that human nature is depraved, human 'works' are futile, and people are saved only by God's free grace, but the preparationists tried to moderate it by leaving some room for human agency in salvation" (McKenna 2007, 20). When Anne Hutchinson challenged this view as suggesting a covenant of works, and expressed her belief that she had received a direct revelation from God, she was expelled from Massachusetts. The Puritans also expelled Roger Williams and Baptists, whose ideas on religious liberty they considered to be too liberal, and they hanged some Quakers, whom they also feared would undermine the unity of the colony.

Drawing heavily from the Old Testament, Puritans believed that the people of God were bound to God, and to one another, through a covenant, as articulated in the Mayflower Compact and similar documents. Puritan pastors frequently accused their congregations of departing from this covenant and thus inviting God's judgment upon themselves.

Puritans were highly educated, in part because of their desire to read Scriptures. They adopted one of the earliest educational laws, "The Old Deluder Satan Act," specifically to assure that their children would continue to have access to this source. They also founded some of America's earliest colleges and universities, including Harvard and Yale. Their theologians, especially Jonathan Edwards, had reputations far beyond the American colonies. Richard Baxter, an English Puritan, had observed that "faith does not relinquish or cast out reason for there is nothing in Religion contrary to it, tho' there are many things that do transcend and must captivate it" (quoted in Degler 1970, 35).

Never anticipating that they would provide the same religious liberty to those outside their faith that they themselves were seeking, Puritans limited political participation to members of the congregational churches. Within such churches, however, there was relative equality. Both in the Fundamental Orders of Connecticut and the Massachusetts Body of Liberties, Puritans sought to embody the Ten Commandments, including capital punishment for numerous offenses, laws upholding the keeping of the Sabbath, and laws against blasphemy. Laws against witchcraft, and the acceptance of spectral evidence, led to the well-publicized Salem witch trials, which resulted in the execution of nearly twenty individuals, who were the victims of gossip and hysteria.

Although some Puritans, including Jonathan Edwards, sought to reach out to Native American Indians, whom some initially believed might be members of the lost tribes of Israel, others eventually concluded that they were sons of Canaan and that, like the Canaanites, God's people were authorized to destroy them. Puritan theology, with its deep suspicion of hierarchy and the belief that it was more important to obey God rather than man, provided fuel for the American Revolution. Samuel Adams was a particularly good example of such motivation.

By the time of the American Revolution, most Puritan congregations were open to those who had been baptized as infants without reporting a direct conversion experience. John Cotton and other Puritan theologians justified child baptism on the basis that it was similar to the Old Testament practice of circumcision, which was also based on the idea of a covenant relationship between God and His people (McKenna 2007, 31–33). Increasing prosperity brought threats of "worldliness and luxury" (39). In time, Massachusetts became the center of Unitarianism, transcendentalism, and other beliefs that departed from the Calvinism of their forbears.

Massachusetts remained the last colony to completely disestablish a church, but much of the enthusiasm for religious reforms and righteous living fueled later movements for the abolition of slavery, women's rights, temperance, and other reforms. The Puritan belief that they were a special people with a special mission has also motivated American foreign-policy making. Although Puritans themselves did not oppose the consumption of alcohol, they have often been associated with the view that Christianity is opposed to fun. The journalist H. L. Mencken once defined Puritanism as "the haunting fear that someone, somewhere, may be happy," and the term "puritanical" is still used to describe those who are morally censorious of others, but these overdrawn stereotypes conceal as much as they reveal (Degler 1970, 30).

See also Adams, Samuel; America as New Israel; City upon a Hill; Cotton, John; Covenants, Compacts, Contracts, and Constitutions; Edwards, Jonathan; Election Day Sermons; Hutchinson, Anne; Massachusetts Body of Liberties; Mather, Cotton; Mayflower Compact; Model of Christian Charity (Winthrop); Native American Indians; Old Deluder Satan Act; Political Hebraism; Prophets and Jeremiads; Quakers; Roman Catholics; Williams, Roger

For Reference and Further Reading

Degler, Carl N. 1970. "Were the Puritans Puritanical?" *Out of Our Past: The Forces That Shaped Modern America*. New York: Harper & Row, pp. 28–37. https://1.cdn.edl.io/hjnC2FdZiWd0CSQ1SDMd2IqwLFSSI2NwaJCKruK8YdopHQLB.pdf.

McKenna, George. 2007. *The Puritan Origins of American Patriotism*. New Haven, CT: Yale University Press.

Miller, Perry. *The New England Mind: The Seventeenth Century*. Cambridge, MA: Belknap Press.

Winship, Michael P. 2006. "Godly Republicanism and the Origins of the Massachusetts Polity." *William and Mary Quarterly*, 3rd Ser. 63 (July): 427–62.

Witte, John. 2010. "Puritan Sources of Enlightenment Liberty." *Religion, the Enlightenment, and the New Global Order*, ed. John M. Owen and J. Judd Owen. New York: Columbia University Press, pp. 140–73.

• Q •

Quakers

The Quakers, or Society of Friends, were founded in England by George Fox (1624–1691) in 1652, with some coming to America within the next five years. Early Quakers were particularly unwelcome among Puritans in New England, where many were deported and some were executed. By contrast, they found refuge in Pennsylvania, which William Penn had founded as a "Holy Experiment" and which provided freedom not only to Quakers but also to Christians of all denominations.

In contrast to mainline Protestants who tended to emphasize the all-sufficiency of Scriptures, Quakers tended to stress the universal possession of an inner voice and the idea of progressive revelation, by which Scriptures could be supplemented by future revelation. Whereas Roman Catholics often emphasized the sacrament of the Eucharist, and most Protestants put primary emphasis on the explication of Scripture in a sermon, Quaker meetings were filled with long periods of silence during which members waited upon a voice from the Holy Spirit. Despite suspicions that William Penn and other Quakers were Socinians who denied the Trinity, this charge appears largely to have been based on some loose language that William Penn and others had used rather than because of their affinity with the group later identified as Unitarians (Buranelli 1959).

Although many Protestants accused Quakers of denying the Bible, the situation is far more complex. William Penn, who founded Pennsylvania, frequently cited Scripture. A study thus observed that the first volume of his papers contains "nine lineal inches of references to specific verses in the Bible" (Bronner 1996, 55). Although there were times in their history when Quakers emphasized private revelation over the Bible, by the nineteenth century, most had returned to their biblical roots and were active with other Protestant denominations in Bible societies (Martin 1996).

Although most Protestants had rejected the hierarchical arrangement of the Catholic Church, they retained the idea of a congregation with a distinct hierarchy of pastors and elders, and to families headed by husbands. Because Quakers believed in the equality of all, they faced one another in group meetings rather than facing forward to listen to a preacher (Hicks 2015), and they allowed women to speak. Quakers were often prosecuted for refusing to duff their hats to authorities. They were known for their plain clothes and for their wide-brimmed hats as well as their opposition to theater performances. They interpreted Scriptures to prohibit the taking of oaths in courtrooms and excommunicated members who married outside the Quaker faith.

Quakers referred to others by the terms "thou" and "thee," which at the time indicated this equality (Pestana 1983, 343). Quakers took a much more conciliatory attitude toward Native American Indians than most other sects

(Edward Hicks's paintings of "The Peaceable Kingdom," in which wild and tame animals live peacefully together, often portray William Penn speaking with Native Americans in the background), and they were among the earliest to express reservations about chattel slavery. Anthony Benezet was among the most prominent early Quaker abolitionists.

In their early years, Quakers often disrupted the services of other denominations to warn of Christ's imminent return and to accuse them of having strayed from the model of the early church. In some cases, women would disrobe or dress in sackcloth and cover themselves with ashes, which, along with their tendency to quake as they waited for God's spirit, led some Puritans to believe that they were witches or were otherwise demon-possessed (Pestana 1983, 337). As was indicated by their treatment of Anne Hutchinson, Puritans were especially unsympathetic to women who claimed divine revelation.

Because most Quakers were pacifists, and their legislators were reluctant to support militias, they were often resented by neighbors who thought that they posed a threat to the defense of the colonies. Even individuals like John Dickinson, who eventually joined the Patriots during the American Revolution, were criticized for having continued efforts to reconcile with Britain as long as they could and for refusing to sign the Declaration of Independence.

In addition to contributing to the idea of human equality, Quakers, who emphasized the important role of human conscience and who had themselves suffered under governments that required greater religious conformity, played a major role in providing for freedom of religious beliefs and in modeling toleration of other religions, especially in Pennsylvania. Perhaps in part because of their view of progressive revelation, the Pennsylvania charters, which provided a model for later American constitutions (Calvert 2009), were among the first to delineate the importance of a formal constitutional amending process (Vile 2015, II: 347–48).

Because of the role that women played within the Society of Friends, many abolitionists and supporters of woman's suffrage later came from Quaker ranks. Quakers were also active in opposing the Vietnam War.

See also Benezet, Anthony; Declaration of Independence; Hutchinson, Anne; Native American Indians; Pacifism; Puritans

For Reference and Further Reading

Bronner, Edwin B. 1996. "William Penn and the Scriptures." *Truth's Bright Embrace: Essays and Poems in Honor of Arthur O. Roberts*. Paper 16. http ://digitalcommons.georgefox.edu/truths_bright/16, pp. 53–59.

Buranelli, Vincent. 1959. "William Penn and the Socinians." *Pennsylvania Magazine of History and Biography* 83 (October): 369–81.

Calvert, Jane E. 2009. *Quaker Constitutionalism and the Political Thought of John Dickinson*. New York: Cambridge University Press.

Hicks, Cindy. 2015. "5 Beliefs That Set Quakers Apart from Other Protestant Christians." Newsmax. April 1. https://www.newsmax.com/fastfeatures/quakers-protestant-beliefs-christians/2018/08/13/id/635855/.

Martin, Roger H. 1996. "Quakers, the Bible and the British and Foreign Bible Society." *Quaker History* 85 (Spring): 13–28.

Pestana, Carla Gardina. 1983. "The City upon a Hill under Siege: The Puritan Perception of the Quaker Threat to Massachusetts Bay, 1656–1661." *New England Quarterly* 56 (September): 323–53.

Plank, Geoffrey. 2017. "Quakers as Political Players in Early America." *William and Mary Quarterly* 74 (January): 35–42.

Vile, John R. 2015. *Encyclopedia of Constitutional Amendments, Proposed Amendments, and Amending Issues, 1789–2015*, 2 vols., 4th ed. Santa Barbara, CA: ABC-CLIO.

• R •

Reagan, Ronald

After President Ronald Reagan (1911–2004) identified communism as the "focus of evil in the modern world" in a speech in Orlando, Florida, on March 8, 1983, to the National Association of Evangelicals (NAE), it quickly became known as his "Evil Empire Speech." The primary author appears to have been Antony Dolan, Reagan's chief speechwriter at the time (Rodgers 2018, 237).

Reagan, a former governor of California who had mounted an unsuccessful attempt to wrest the Republican nomination from Gerald R. Ford in 1976, had been elected to the first of two consecutive terms in 1980. He had replaced Jimmy Carter, who had explicitly run for office as an evangelical Christian but who was not as aligned with the evangelical right on such issues as abortion, prayer in schools, and a strong national defense against communism as was Reagan. In August 1980, while attending a National Affairs Briefing to 2,500 pastors from all over the country, after listening to a fervid sermon by Rev. James Robinson, Reagan thrilled the audience by saying, "I know you can't endorse me, but . . . I want you to know that I endorse you and what you are doing" (FitzGerald 2017, 314). At the time of his 1983 speech before the NAE, the idea of entering into a "nuclear freeze" with the Soviet Union was much discussed. Elaborating on John Winthrop's famous "Model of Christian Charity," Reagan was already known for utilizing the analogy of America as a "shining city on a hill."

Evangelicals pride themselves on their adherence to the Bible, so it is hardly surprising that Reagan incorporated a number of biblical references into his speech. He began by thanking the audience for their prayers, and by noting that "there are a great many God-fearing, dedicated, noble men and women in public life, present company included." He associated such individuals with a love of liberty, which they shared with such Founding Fathers as William Penn, who had observed that "if we will not be governed by God, we must be governed by tyrants."

He proceeded to contrast such views with those of "modern-day secularism," which he believed was "discarding the tried and time-tested values upon which our very civilization is based." He further explained how his administration, while not faulting the "intent" of those who thought otherwise, was resisting efforts to provide birth control devices to children without the consent of their parents. He pointed to the words "In God We Trust," argued for prayer in public schools by rephrasing Moses to say "let our children pray," and lauded legislation designed to protect human life.

Noting that a recent survey had confirmed that a large majority of Americans "expressed a belief in God and a huge majority believed the Ten Commandments had real meaning in their lives," he also cited studies showing that "an overwhelming majority of Americans disapprove of adultery, teenage sex, pornography, abortion, and hard drugs." In words that cheered the hearts of members of his audience, he observed that "America is in the midst of a spiritual awakening and a moral renewal." He further quoted an earlier speaker who had cited the words of Amos 5:25: "Let justice roll down like a river, righteousness like a never-failing stream."

Despite his optimism about the course of U.S. history, Reagan said that "we must never forget that no government schemes are going to perfect men." He specifically referenced the biblical idea of sin: "There is sin and evil in the world, and we're enjoined by Scripture and the Lord Jesus to oppose it with all our might." Noting that the nation was not unfamiliar with its own evils, he took heart in "its capacity for transcending the moral evils of our past."

Reagan proceeded to say that "I know that you've been horrified, as have I, by the resurgence of some hate groups preaching bigotry and prejudice. Use the mighty voice of your pulpits and the powerful standing of your churches to denounce and isolate these hate groups in our midst. The commandment given us is clear and simple: 'Thou shall love thy neighbor as Thyself' [Matthew 22:39]."

Reagan proceeded to contrast belief in God with atheistic communism as he explained why he did not favor a nuclear freeze. Playing on the theme of light and darkness that is common in Scripture, Reagan hoped for "the salvation of all of those who live in that totalitarian darkness," and proceeded to identify Soviet totalitarianism as "the focus of evil in the modern world." Perhaps somewhat softening this message, he further quoted from the author C. S. Lewis, a favorite among evangelical Christians, to warn against "the temptation of pride." As Reagan portrayed the situation, "the real crisis we face today is a spiritual one; at root, it is a test of moral will and faith." Citing Whittaker Chambers (1901–1961), who had exposed Alger Hiss as a Soviet agent, Reagan associated communism with "the second oldest faith, first proclaimed in the Garden of Eden [Genesis 3:5] with the words of temptation, 'Ye shall be as gods.'"

Affirming that "the source of our strength in the quest for human freedom is not material, but spiritual," Reagan quoted from Isaiah 40:29 and 31: "He [God] giveth power to the faithful; and to them that have no might, He increased strength. But they that wait upon the Lord shall renew their strength; they shall mount up with wings as eagles; they shall run, and not be weary."

Citing Thomas Paine to say that "we have it within our power to begin the world over again," Reagan gave these words a spiritual application by saying, "We can do it, doing together what no one church could do by itself."

See also Carter, Jimmy; Communism and Anti-Communism; Evangelicals; *Common Sense* (Thomas Paine); Model of Christian Charity (Winthrop)

For Reference and Further Reading

FitzGerald, Francis. 2017. *The Evangelicals: The Struggle to Shape America*. New York: Simon & Schuster.

Rodgers, Daniel T. 2018. *As a City on a Hill: The Story of America's Most Famous Lay Sermon*. Princeton, NJ: Princeton University Press.

Reagan, Ronald. March 8, 1983. "Evil Empire Speech." https://nationalcenter.org/ReaganEvilEmpire1983.html.

Redeemer Nation

One of the most prominent themes in the Bible is that of redemption. In the Old Testament, God redeemed his people from slavery in Egypt and later from a number of foreign foes and invaders. According to the New Testament, God sent his only Son to redeem those who believe and follow him from the wages of sin. The church was entrusted with this message of salvation, and in the Great Commission, Jesus urged them to spread the news throughout the earth.

It is sometimes easy to conflate the mission of the church with that of a nation, especially when religion was important to the founders of such a nation and when its ideals include the spreading of religious freedom and democracy. Americans still look back on John Winthrop's speech indicating that his colony would be, in language borrowed from Jesus's Sermon on the Mount, a city on a hill that cannot be hid. Jonathan Edwards was among those who believed that it was possible that the settling of America was introducing a new era in human history that would initiate the return of Christ (McDermott 1991).

Winthrop and Edwards both recognized that, in addition to serving as a positive beacon for others, the nation could also serve as a negative example of a nation that forsook its covenant and instead shamed the name of God. In prophetic jeremiads, early Puritan pastors constantly interpreted natural disasters and enemy attacks as God's chastisement on them that required repentance, but with the advent of the American Revolution and the nation's expansion onto the world stage, it became more common to emphasize the nation's destiny (as in expanding to the Pacific Ocean) than its sins.

Even when the nation was divided by Civil War, Americans could view it as a redemptive way of washing away the nation's original sin of slavery, and serving once again as the last best hope of mankind. In the aftermath of the Spanish-American War, Americans could further view foreign imperialism as a way of Christianizing foreign peoples. Americans further interpreted their participation in two world wars, and the Cold War that followed, as a way of saving the world from dictatorship and totalitarianism. Their efforts were not in pursuit of wealth or glory but as a sacrifice made on behalf of freedom for all. There might even be times when, as in Vietnam, a commander might think that he needed to destroy a village in order to save it from communism.

In the Old Testament, individuals sought redemption for sins by sacrificing a perfect animal. The New Testament portrays Jesus, as in John 1:20, as "the Lamb of God, which taketh away the sin of the world." One danger of a nation understanding itself as a redeemer nation is that it might be inclined to overlook its own faults, which have included taking the land of Native Americans, enslaving African Americans, demeaning minority groups, and exploiting the environment.

The English, the Dutch, the Spanish, the Portuguese, and others have also connected their nation's expansion to a wider God-ordained cause—the pope actually divided South America between Spain and Portugal, both of which were Roman Catholic. The classic exposition of America as a redeemer nation focused chiefly on its role in international affairs (Tuveson 1968). However, Professor Wilfred M. McClay has argued that the image also applies to political life, where politicians seek redemption for past mistakes, as if, following the theology of Romans 8, they argue that God can even use such mistakes for a greater good (McClay 2013). President Bill Clinton was among those who have made very public displays of personal contrition. Other politicians like Barack Obama have portrayed their own candidacies for "'hope' and 'change'" as an "agent of national redemption" (McClay 2013).

See also American Exceptionalism; City upon a Hill; Clinton, Bill; Edwards, Jonathan; Prophets and Jeremiads

For Reference and Further Reading

McClay, Wilfred M. 2013. "Still the Redeemer Nation." *Wilson Quarterly* 37(2) (Spring).

McDermott, Gerald R. 1991. "Jonathan Edwards, the City on a Hill, and the Redeemer Nation: A Reappraisal." *American Presbyterian* 69: (Spring): 33–47.

Tuveson, Ernest Lee. 1968. *Redeemer Nation: The Idea of America's Millennial Role.* Chicago: University of Chicago Press.

Reparations for Slavery and Segregation

Although the issue has long been on the back burner, a number of Democratic presidential contenders in 2019 have expressed support for the idea of reparations to descendants of African American slaves who were later the victims of segregationist Jim Crow laws.

One impetus for thinking about this topic was an article published in 2014 by Ta-Nehisi Coates, who was invited to speak in June 2019 before a congressional committee on the subject. Most of his arguments were tied to the idea that American laws and institutions have continued through fairly modern times to disadvantage African Americans and that they are therefore entitled to be made whole. It is fascinating, however, that Coates prefaced his 2014 article with verses from Deuteronomy 15:12–15, which are as follows:

> And if thy brother, a Hebrew man, or a Hebrew woman, be sold unto thee, and serve thee six years; then in the seventh year thou shalt let him go free from thee. And when thou sendeth him out free from thee, thou shalt not let him go away empty: thou shalt furnish him liberally out of thy flock, and out of thy floor, and out of thy winepress: of that wherewith the LORD thy God hath blessed thee thou shalt give unto him. And thou shalt remember that thou wast a bondman in the land of Egypt, and the LORD thy God redeemed thee: therefore I command thee this thing today.

In 1969, civil rights activist James Forman (1928–2005) issued a Black Manifesto in which he demanded $500 million in reparations from predominately white churches. The senior pastor of the Riverside Church in New York City, Rev. Dr. Ernest T. Campbell, provided some scriptural support for the idea of reparations by citing the story of Zacchaeus (Luke 19:1–10), in which a repentant tax collector promised to pay back those whom he had defrauded, and Exodus 22:1, which provided that "if a man steals an ox or a sheep and kills it or sells it, he shall pay five oxen for an ox and four sheep for a sheep. He shall make restitution" (cited in Lechtreck 2012, 49).

Some mainline churches responded by increasing budgets for community outreach. Others objected to the manifesto's Marxist ideology (Smylie 1981, 212), opposed what they believed to be the highhanded manner in which church services had been disrupted, and thought that responding affirmatively was to give in to blackmail. In 2019, students at Georgetown University voluntarily raised student fees by $27.20 a semester to reimburse descendants of slaves that the college sold in 1838 in order to save itself (Desai 2019). Since then, a number of seminaries, including Princeton Theological Seminary, have pledged money for scholarships and other initiatives for African American students (Shanahan 2019).

Abraham Lincoln sometime suggested that the devastation resulting from the Civil War might have been God's way of wiping out all the gains that slave labor had brought to the nation, and those who instituted slavery, and most of those who instituted the system of segregation, are long since gone. Moreover, members of certain immigrant groups who arrived after slavery ended, as well as poor whites, could argue that it would be unfair for them to be taxed to pay such reparations.

See also Lincoln, Abraham; Slavery

For Reference and Further Reading

Coates, Ta-Nehisi. 2014. "The Case for Reparations." *The Atlantic*. June. https://www.theatlantic.com/magazine/archive/2014/06/the-case-for-reparations/361631/.

Desai, Saahil. 2019. "The First Reparations Attempt at an American College Comes from Its Students." *The Atlantic*. April 18. https://www.theatlantic.com/education/archive/2019/04/why-are-georgetown-students-paying-reparations/587443/.

D'Sousa, Dinesh. 2002. *What's So Great about America?* Washington, D.C.: Regnery.

Lechtreck, Elaine Allen. 2012. "'We Are Demanding $500 Million for Reparations': The Black Manifesto, Mainline Religious Denominations, and Black Economic Development." *Journal of African American History* 97 (Winter–Spring): 39–71.

Shanahan, Ed. 2019. "$27 Million for Reparations over Slave Ties Pledged by Seminary." *New York Times*. October 21.

Smylie, James H. 1981. "The Bible, Race and the Changing South." *Journal of Southern Presbyterian History* 49 (Summer): 197–218.

Revolutionary War

The United States declared its independence in 1776, but it took five years before Americans finally defeated the British on the battlefield and another two before the two nations signed a treaty of peace.

Americans had the advantage of fighting for what they believed to be their homes and liberties on their own soil, but they depended heavily on militiamen and other volunteers who generally lacked the discipline of the British forces. Although not all joined the revolutionary cause, American pastors played a vital role in recruiting and inspiring troops and giving them the confidence that they could win.

In a comprehensive book on the subject, historian James P. Byrd points out that pastors had already served this role in various wars (King Philip's War, for example) against Native American Indians and during the French and Indian

War that pitted Britain and its thirteen colonies against the French and their Native American allies, and was sometimes perceived as a war between Roman Catholics and Protestants. Even largely secular writers like Thomas Paine often couched their arguments in biblical language, with Paine arguing from Scripture in his *Common Sense* that God had never intended for the ancient Israelites to institute monarchy. Byrd observes that in September 1775, officers of the Continental Army visited the grave of evangelist George Whitefield (1714–1770) in Newburyport, Massachusetts, which they opened and from which they removed his collar and wristbands for inspiration (2013, 17). The admonition in 2 Samuel 10:12 to "be of good Courage, and let us play the men, for our people, and for the cities of our God" was a popular Scripture, as was Jeremiah 48:10, which observed that "cursed be he that keepeth back his Sword from Blood." After the so-called Boston Massacre, preachers had cited the words of Genesis 3:10 invoking the blood of Abel crying out from the ground to God after his brother Cain murdered him. Other pastors cited the prophet Micah, as "God's 'son of liberty,' against the evil tyrant King Ahaz," whom they compared to George III (Byrd 2013, 35).

One of the most prominent motifs of American Patriot preaching compared George Washington to Moses or Joshua, the Patriots to the children of Israel, and King George III to Pharaoh. The destruction of the Pharaoh in the Red Sea and the explanation in Exodus 15:5 that "the Lord is a man of war" was especially popular as was Deuteronomy 32:43, which advised that God "wilt avenge the blood of his servants, and will render vengeance to his adversaries" (Byrd 2013, 51, 54). One difficulty that this narrative posed was that white Americans were holding African Americans in actual chattel slavery, and that many of them began appropriating this rhetoric, as abolitionists would later do. One advantage of likening Washington to Moses rather than to David was that Washington never ruled as a king, like the one from whom Patriots were declaring their independence.

In attempting to rally those who might be inclined to ride out the conflict without supporting either side, Patriot preachers often referred to the Curse of Meroz, found in Judges 5:23, condemning a city whose members failed to join a war against King Jabin. Such timid behavior was often contrasted with that of Deborah, who had led Jewish forces against Sisera, the captain of Jabin's army (Byrd 2013, 78).

Preachers often also utilized the story of King David, who, as a teen, had killed the giant Goliath with a slingshot, who had presented God as a warrior in the Psalms, but whose legacy as a king (much like that of Britain's George III) had been far more ambiguous.

Because Christians recognized significant differences between the Old Testament and the New, many preachers found it propitious to back up references in the former with those to the latter, and they often turned to the epistles of Peter and Paul for this purpose. A favorite verse was Galatians 5:1, in which Paul spoke of "the liberty wherewith Christ hath made us free." Many Patriots, in turn, had to explain how it was possible to oppose a king in the light of Romans 13, in which Paul had written, "Let every soul be subject unto the higher powers. For there is no power but of God: the powers that be are ordained of God. Whosoever therefore resisteth the power, resisteth the ordinance of

God," and 1 Peter 2:13, in which Peter urged believers to "submit yourselves to every ordinance of man for the Lord's sake, whether to the king as supreme, or to governors, as to those who are sent for the punishment of evildoers and for the praise of those who do good." These same passages were later employed after the war to urge allegiance to the new government.

Patriot pastors also drew from the biblical book of Revelation. They drew both from Chapter 2, in which St. John had commended churches who were willing martyrs for the faith, and from more apocalyptic passages like the description of the woman in the wilderness being fought by the Great Dragon (Satan) in Revelation 12:14–17. Many also drew from the description of the war against the beast in Revelation 13 and the description of Christ as a military figure in Revelation 19. Such passages were particularly important in states like Pennsylvania with large numbers of Quakers and other pacifist religious groups. Byrd finds that relatively few pastors relied on the millennial passages from Revelation during the conflict (2013, 162). Moreover, Valeri (1989) cites a group of New Divinity men or Edwardseans, in the New England states, most notably Joseph Bellamy (1719–1790), Levi Hart (1738–1808), and Jonathan Edwards Jr. (1745–1801), who while eschewing civil millennialism, embraced a Scottish enlightenment brand of natural law and led in biblical criticisms of the British and support for the revolutionary cause.

Professor Gregg Frazer has balanced Byrd's study of Patriot pastors with his own study of loyalist clergy. Especially in interpreting Romans 13 and 1 Peter 2, he found that "as a general rule, the Loyalist preachers appealed more to the Bible and held to a more literal and contextual interpretation of the relevant texts of Scripture than did the Patriot preachers. In addition, Loyalists typically took passages at face value without adding to or subtracting from the text, while Patriot preachers adjusted texts to fit their purpose by adding qualifying language" (Frazer 2018, 36). He illustrated his analysis by examining the sermons of Jonathan Boucher, Charles Inglis, Samuel Seabury, George Micklejohn, and others.

Frazer observes that in addition to Romans 13 and 1 Peter 1, Loyalist ministers often cited the example of Jesus's refusal to approve of rebellion against the Romans or even to call God's power on those who were crucifying him (2018, 58–60). Others cited such diverse Old Testament stories as the Garden of Eden (to show that God established authority and submission), the story of the Gileadites' altar in Joshua 22, and the story that Ahitophel played during the rebellion of Absalom against his father, King David (61–67). Many further associated such rebellion with sinfulness and the price paid by both Britain and America as the consequence of sin (67–76).

Frazer observes that these pastors interpreted the meaning of the word "liberty" in Galatians 5:1 as "liberty from sin and from ceremonial religious law" rather than as "civil liberty" (44). Professor John Berens observed that "Loyalist providential rhetoric is significant because it so closely parallels the providential rhetoric of Patriot spokesmen" (1978, 218). He concluded, "Both sides appealed to an intervening, Old Testament Jehovah for sustenance and support, and utilized strikingly similar images and concepts—the New Israel, the Jeremiad tradition, and ultimately the conviction that Divine Providence was somehow specifically interested in the destiny of America. The Patriots felt a divine command to resistance and revolution, while the Loyalists pursued 'the godlike work of preventing bloodshed in the colonies'" (218–19).

See also Common Sense (Thomas Paine); Curse of Meroz; David as Political Architype; Moses as Political Architype; Quakers; Slavery; Washington, George

For Reference and Further Reading

Bercovitch, Sacvan. 1976. "How the Puritans Won the American Revolution." *Massachusetts Review* 17 (Winter): 597–630.

Berens, John F. 1978. "'A God of Order and Not of Confusion': The American Loyalists and Divine Providence, 1774–1783." *Historical Magazine of the Protestant Episcopal Church* 478 (June): 211–19.

Bonomi, Patricia U. 1996. "'Hippocrates' Twins': Religion and Politics in the American Revolution." *History Teacher* 29 (February): 137–44.

Byrd, James P. 2013. *Sacred Scripture, Sacred War: The Bible and the American Revolution*. New York: Oxford University Press.

Fea, John. 2016. *Was America Founded as a Christian Nation?: A Historical Introduction*, rev. ed. Louisville, KY: Westminster John Knox Press.

Frazer, Gregg L. 2018. *God against the Revolution: The Loyalist Clergy's Case against the American Revolution*. Lawrence: University Press of Kansas.

Hall, David W., ed. 1996. *Election Day Sermons*. Oak Ridge, TN: Kuyper Institute.

Hutson, James H. 1998. *Religion and the Founding of the American Republic*. Washington: Library of Congress.

Perry, William Stevens, and Lawrence L. Brown. 1976. "The Alleged 'Toryism' of the Clergy of the United States at the Breaking Out of the War of the Revolution: An Historical Examination." *Historical Magazine of the Protestant Episcopal Church* 45 (June): 133–44.

Valeri, Mark. 1989. "The New Divinity and the American Revolution." *William and Mary Quarterly* 46 (October): 741–69.

Robertson, Pat

Marion Gordon Robertson (b. 1930), known as Pat, is one of the better-known evangelical figures of the past century. He owns the Christian Broadcasting Network (CBN), where he regularly appears on a talk program known as *The 700 Club*.

Born the son of A. Willis Robertson, a prominent U.S. senator from Virginia, Robertson shares his conservative beliefs. He earned his undergraduate degree at Washington and Lee University, his law degree from Yale, and his Master of Divinity degree from New York Theological Seminary. Robertson was ordained as a Southern Baptist minister but, unlike most of his colleagues, emphasized such charismatic gifts as speaking in tongues and faith healing, which are more common among Pentecostals. He gave up his ordination to the Baptist ministry during his 1988 bid for the Republican nomination for president. Robertson founded Regent University, in Virginia Beach, which is designed in part to prepare Christian journalists and statesmen.

Although he has an avuncular style, Robertson has a way of periodically getting news attention by announcements that are sometimes perceived as bizarre. On one notable occasion, he claimed to have successfully altered the course of a hurricane threatening the East Coast through prayer. After Haiti was struck with such a storm, he claimed that the country was "cursed by one thing after another" since swearing a "pact to the devil," when achieving independence (Brendemuehl 2010).

Robertson has said that "the righteous" are the best qualified to govern, and after winning the precinct-level delegate elections in Michigan, he announced that "the Christians have won!" (Toulouse 1989, 76–77). Robertson further played into the hands of critics who feared religious dogmatism when he said, "*Most Christians deal with absolutes.* If God said it, that settled it. *We cannot compromise or negotiate matters of principle. We deal with eternal issues.* We hold in our hands the keys to the kingdom of heaven. *How can we deal away these things in political bargaining?*" (78).

Like members of the Christian Reconstructionist movement, Robertson believes that "our form of government came directly from the Bible," which he believes has the answers to almost all political questions:

> We must read the Bible, study the Bible, understand the Bible and live the Bible. . . . Our view of God, of man, of salvation, of redemption, of eternal punishment, of eternal rewards, of holy living, of relationships between the sexes, of the sanctity of life, of concern for the poor, of citizenship and government, of reliance on God, of wealth, of duty, of honor, of man's relationship to the environment, of what is pure and what is impure and of what is sacred and what is secular must all be redefined in light of the clear mandate of the Scriptures. (Toulouse 1989, 79)

Professor Mark Toulouse associates Robertson, who is a premillennialist, with what he calls Armageddon theology, which emphasizes a final battle that Robertson has sometimes said he believes will be a nuclear war that pits Russia against Israel and its allies and that wipes out most of the world's population (1989, 80). Drawing from prophecies in Daniel, Ezekiel, and Revelation, which he interpreted through the lens of Luke 21:24 ("And Jerusalem will be trampled underfoot by the Gentiles until the times of the Gentiles be fulfilled"), Robertson believed that the Jewish capture of Jerusalem in 1967 marked a turning point that would usher in what he believed to be decade of destiny in the 1980s (81–82). Indeed, he predicted at one point that the end of the world would occur by 1982 (83).

At times, Robertson indicated that he believed it was his destiny and that of his ministry to bring this about. Thus, in an invitation to followers to become founding members of CBN, Robertson said, "We have been chosen since the foundation of the earth for this day and this time. To help usher in the Second Coming of our Lord Jesus Christ" (97). Like other fundamentalists, Robertson believed that the "beast," usually called the Antichrist, described in Revelation 17:11–12 as having ten horns, would arise out of the European Union. Robertson believed that to retain God's favor, the United States needed to be closely aligned with Israel, which he referred to as "The Key to U.S. Security" (89).

When President Trump announced in October 2019 that he planned to withdraw U.S. forces from northern Syria where they had fought the Islamic State of Iraq and Syria (ISIS) side by side with the Kurds, Robertson said that he was "in danger of losing the mandate of heaven" if he followed through (Behrmann 2019). He subsequently compared the move to Neville Chamberlain's appeasement of Adolph Hitler and predicted that "Russia is going to come against us. Turkey is going to come against us, China is going to come against us. North Korea is going to come against us" (Jensen 2019).

See also Christian Reconstructionism; Evangelicals; Judgment; Natural Disasters

For Reference and Further Reading

Behrmann, Savannah. 2019. "Pat Robertson: Trump Could Risk 'Losing the Mandate of Heaven' with Syria Decision." *USA Today*. October 7. https://www.usatoday.com/story/news/politics/elections/2019/10/07/pat-robertson-trump-losing-mandate-heaven-over-syria-decision/3903941002/.

Brendemuehl, Collin. 2010. "A Biblical Basis for Pat Robertson's Theology." First Things. January 17. https://www.firstthings.com/blogs/firstthoughts/2010/01/a-biblical-basis-for-pat-robertsons-theology.

Green, John C. 1993. "Pat Robertson and the Latest Crusade: Religious Resources and the 1988 Presidential Campaign." *Social Science Quarterly* 74 (March): 157–68.

Jensen, K. Thor. 2019. "Right Wing Evangelical Pat Robertson Says Trump Pulling Out of Syria Like Appeasing Hitler." *Newsweek*. October 24. https://www.newsweek.com/pat-robertson-trump-syria-appeasing-hitler-1467580.

Langenbach, Lisa, and John C. Green. 1992. "Hollow Core: Evangelical Clergy & the 1988 Robertson Campaign." *Polity* 25 (Autumn): 147–58.

Toulouse, Mark G. 1989. "Pat Robertson: Apocalyptic Theology and American Foreign Policy." *Journal of Church and State* 31 (Winter): 73–99.

Roman Catholics

When Columbus discovered the Americas in 1492, whatever internal divisions there might have been, Christians in the West were united in a single church under the authority of a pope in Rome. They believed him to be the successor to the apostle Peter whom Jesus had commissioned as the leader of the early church (Matthew 16:18). In 1054, the church had split, largely over the question of the pope's authority with the Eastern Orthodox Church in Constantinople (today's Istanbul), but this church has never had much influence either in Western Europe or in America.

In 1517, after extensive mediation on Scripture and concern over his own sins, Martin Luther (1483–1546), a German monk, nailed ninety-five theses to a church door in Wittenberg initiating the Protestant Reformation. The Catholic Church had relied on a Latin interpretation of the Bible translated by St. Jerome, and largely inaccessible to individuals without formal educations. One of Luther's signal contributions was his translation of the Bible into German vernacular. Moreover, his study of Scripture, and especially the biblical books of Romans and Ephesians, led him to believe that many Roman Catholic practices, including the selling of indulgences for sinful behavior, priestly celibacy, and a sacramental system that Luther believed to be based on works rather than on faith, were contrary to Scriptures, which he considered to be the chief guide to religious doctrine and personal behavior. Luther sometimes referred to the pope as the Antichrist.

With both Catholics and Protestants viewing one another as heretics, there were intense struggles throughout Europe over which would prevail. Protestants were, in turn, divided into a variety of denominations as John Calvin (1509–1564), Huldrych Zwingli (1484–1531), John Knox (1513–1572), and numerous other reformers applied their own readings of the Bible to both religious and secular affairs. The Thirty Years' War (1618–1648) pitted Catholics and Protestants against one another in Central Europe, and England—whose King Henry VIII had declared his nation's independence from the Roman Church—would be rent by a civil war, largely between Catholics and Protestants, between 1642 and 1651.

When Great Britain established the thirteen original U.S. colonies, it was among the most biblically saturated nations within Europe. Many Protestants owned copies of John Fox's vivid *Book of Martyrs* (first published in 1563), which chronicled numerous acts of Catholic persecution of Protestants. The Bible had been wielded by both sides during the English Civil War. King Henry VIII had confiscated much of the property of the Catholic Church in England. The pope had excommunicated Queen Elizabeth I, and English iconoclasts had gone into cathedrals and smashed statues of the Virgin Mary, Catholic saints, and even of Jesus in the belief that their presence was a form of idolatry forbidden by the Ten Commandments. In 1604, Guy Fawkes (1570–1606) and other Catholics sought to strike back by blowing up the British Parliament while the king was there, and each November 5, the British, and often their American counterparts, have celebrated Guy Fawkes Day as the day that this plot had been foiled.

Puritans had left England largely because of their desire to move the Anglican Church even farther away from Catholic practices. Although some Catholics did come to America, most notably in Maryland, Protestants were a majority in all thirteen of the original colonies, and many had laws limiting Catholic freedoms. Puritans, who also persecuted Baptists, Quakers, and other dissident groups, were especially vehement in their opposition to Catholicism, with many like Jonathan Edwards identifying the Catholic Church with the Great Whore of Babylon described in the biblical book of revelation and others identifying the pope as the "man of sin," or Antichrist, which that book also described. Anti-Catholic sentiment was a factor that led to the conflict with France during the French and Indian War, which led to the English acquisition of Canada.

In the years leading up to the Revolutionary War, in which France joined the United States as an ally, the colonies further opposed the British adoption of the Quebec Act, which recognized the Roman Catholic Church as the official church of Canada. Many Protestants had feared the establishment of either an Anglican or a Roman Catholic episcopacy in America. Samuel Seabury (1729–1796) of Connecticut became the first Episcopal bishop in the United States in 1789, and John Carroll of Maryland (1735–1815) became the first Catholic bishop and archbishop in America in 1790.

American revolutionaries and American Founding Fathers often linked Catholicism to monarchy, as when Thomas Paine identified monarchy in *Common Sense* as the "popery of government." George Washington had to issue a specific order preventing his troops from celebrating Guy Fawkes Day during the American Revolution (Vile 2015, 81–82).

Although many states in the North had established congregational churches and some in the South had established the Episcopal Church (derivative from the Church of England), the First Amendment to the U.S. Constitution had, while guaranteeing the "free exercise" of religion, prohibited an official "establishment" of the same at the national level. By the mid-1830s all the states had eliminated official state support for such denominations. Culturally, however, the nation remained a Protestant stronghold. Protestant emphasis on each individual's direct accountability to God combined with its emphasis on individuals' ability to discern the mind of God through reading Scriptures was furthered by the First and Second Great Awakenings, which showed little regard for existing ecclesiastical hierarchies.

Although there was no established church, American Protestants, like Pilgrims before them, associated the nation's mission with that of advancing God's kingdom. They further shared a common high regard for the King James Version of the Bible, which had first been published in England in 1611 under the reign of King James I as a translation from the Bible's original languages. The American Bible Society later made a point of publishing Bibles without commentary as a way of avoiding internecine disputes among Protestant denominations. Indeed, James I had largely commissioned this Bible because he distrusted both the translation and commentary of the prior Geneva Bible.

By contrast, American Catholics had their own English version of the Bible—the Douay, or Douay-Rheims Bible—the New Testament of which was first published as a translation from the Latin Vulgate in 1582. Although both Catholics and Protestants worshiped a triune God, Protestants tended to perceive of the church as the product of biblical teachings while Catholics stressed the role of the church in compiling, protecting, and interpreting the Bible. The Douay Bible thus contained commentary designed to steer readers into interpretations of the Bible endorsed by the Church. A modern Catholic priest explains, "The mission of Jesus continues through the ministry of the Church that he founded, and he has given the Church the inspiration of the Holy Spirit for guidance in everything. The Revelation of Jesus is thus extended to the apostles and handed on through two means: Sacred Scripture and Tradition" (Bransfield n.d.).

Whereas most of the original inhabitants of the thirteen colonies were either whites from England and northern European nations or slaves imported from Africa, the nineteenth century witnessed waves of immigrants often from Ireland and from southern European nations like Italy, which were predominately Roman Catholic. Their cultures often differed from that of their neighbors, and they were much less likely to join causes like temperance that were dear to many native Protestants. Nativist American groups often saw such immigrants as a threat to their way of life, just as some contemporary Americans view Mexicans and immigrants from other Latin American countries. Such charges seemed partly vindicated when Pope Pius IX (1792–1878) issued a *Syllabus of Errors* in 1864 condemning separation of church and state, and future popes issued similar pronouncements suggesting that the church was superior to civil rulers (Corrigan and Neal 2010, 54).

As public schools spread throughout the United States, Protestants, who viewed the King James Bible as a nonsectarian text, sought to incorporate readings from the Bible, and even use of the Bible as a textbook, into public school classrooms. This led to clashes with Roman Catholics in major cities like Philadelphia, Cincinnati, and Boston, as Catholics sought either to exempt their children from such exercises or to permit them to use their own Bibles. In many of these disputes, Protestants seemed to concede the latter point but required that any such Bibles be without notes, thus effectively excluding to Douay Bible. As a consequence, many Catholics took their children out of public schools and enrolled them in parochial ones. It would not be until *Abington v. Schempp* in 1963 that the U.S. Supreme Court invalidated devotional Bible readings in public school classrooms. In the interim, however, many Protestants falsely charged that Roman Catholics were opposed to the Bible per se.

There were numerous books written in the nineteenth century, often purporting to be from former nuns, who claimed that Catholic monasteries prohibited their members from reading the Bible and alleging that they kept nuns and others in virtual slavery (Yacovazzi 2013). Such stories fueled the burning of a Catholic convent in Charlestown, just outside Boston, in 1834 as well as acts of violence that accompanied the Bible riots in Philadelphia in 1844.

Members of the Know Nothing Party in the 1850s, like the Ku Klux Klan that arose in the wake of the U.S. Civil War, were often virulently anti-Catholic as well as anti-Semitic. Other anti-Catholic groups included the American Protective Association and the League for the Protection of American Institutions (Lanthrop 1894, 564–67). Americans and Mexicans both appear to have been motivated in part by religious animus toward one another during the Mexican-American War from 1846 to 1848 (Guardino 2014). One of the reasons that President William McKinley gave for American rule over the Philippines in the wake of the Spanish-American War in 1898 was to bring the gospel to them, even though the large majority of them were professing Roman Catholics. The candidacies of Democrat Al Smith for the presidency in 1928 and Democrat John F. Kennedy in 1960 both generated fears that they would be beholden to the pope in Rome rather than committed to upholding the U.S. Constitution. As distinguished an individual as Dr. Norman Vincent Peale (1898–1993) of the Marble Collegiate Church in New York City was among those who questioned whether a Catholic president could act independently of the church.

In part because of the reform efforts of the Second Vatican Council from 1962 to 1965, recent years have witnessed a "renewal" of Catholic interest in the Bible (Senior 2017, 521). A New American Bible was published between 1952 and 1970 and was revised again in 1986 and 2010 (524). After years of fear that official representation at the Vatican would erode the separation of church and state in America and approve authoritarianism, President Ronald Reagan finally appointed William Wilson as the first U.S. ambassador to the Vatican on January 10, 1984; presidents before him had appointed unofficial personal representatives (Nutt 2017, 63).

Although American Protestant revivalists fanned anti-Catholic flames in the nineteenth century (Hambrick-Stowe 1996; Waldman 2019, 65–80), conservative Catholics and Protestants have united in the late twentieth and early twenty-first centuries around a number of moral issues. These have included opposition to abortion, pornography, gay marriage, liberal divorce laws, and other measures that they believe to be signs of moral decay. Catholics often seek to apply natural-law thinking to political issues; law professor Robert Cochrane notes that "the analogous evangelical doctrine is common grace" (2007, 298), which was embodied in part in Scottish Common Sense philosophy, which was accepted by a number of key American Founding Fathers.

See also Abington v. Schempp (1963); American Bible Society; Cincinnati Bible War of 1869; Columbus, Christopher; *Common Sense* (Thomas Paine); Edwards, Jonathan; French and Indian War; Geneva Bible; King James Version of the Bible; Natural Law; Philadelphia Bible Riots of 1844; Puritans

For Reference and Further Reading

Bransfield, J. Brian. n.d. "Bible at Core of Catholic Beliefs." United States Conference of Catholic Bishops. http ://www.usccb.org/bible/understanding-the-bible/study-materials/articles/bible-at-core-of-catholic-beliefs.cfm.

Cochrane, Robert F., Jr. 2007. "Catholic and Evangelical Supreme Court Justices: A Theological Analysis." *University of Saint Thomas Law Journal* 4: 296–311.

Corrigan, John, and Lynn S. Neal. 2010. *Religious Intolerance in America: A Documentary History*. Chapel Hill: University of North Carolina Press.

Fessenden, Tracy. 2005. "The Nineteenth-Century Bible Wars and the Separation of Church and State." *Church History* 74 (December): 784–811.

Gebarowski-Shafer, Ellie. 2013. "The Transatlantic Reach of the Catholic 'False Translation' Argument in the School 'Bible Wars.'" *U.S. Catholic Historian* 31 (Summer): 47–76.

Guardino, Peter. 2014. "'In the Name of Civilization and with a Bible in Their Hands:' Religion and the 1846–48 Mexican-American War." *Mexican Studies/Estudios Mexicanos* 30 (Summer): 342–65.

Hambrick-Stowe, Charles E. 1996. "Charles G. Finney and Evangelical Anti-Catholicism." *U.S. Catholic Historian* 24 (Fall): 39–52.

Hill, Christopher. 1993. *The English Bible and the Seventeenth-Century Revolution*. New York: Penguin Books.

Lanthrop, George Parsons. 1894. "Hostility to Roman Catholics." *North American Review* 158 (May): 563–73.

Levinson, Sanford. 1979. "'The Constitution' in American Civil Religion." *Supreme Court Review* 1979: 123–52.

Nutt, Rick. 2017. "United States Diplomatic Representation at the Vatican: The Presbyterian Reaction." *Journal of Presbyterian History* 95 (Fall/Winter): 62–73.

Senior, Donald. 2017. "The Bible and Catholicism." *The Oxford Handbook of the Bible in America*, ed. Paul C. Gutjahr. New York: Oxford University Press, pp. 517–30.

Vile, John R., ed. 2015. *Founding Documents of America: Documents Decoded*. Santa Barbara, CA: ABC-CLIO.

Waldman, Steven. 2019. *Sacred Liberty: America's Long, Bloody, and Ongoing Struggle for Religious Freedom*. New York: HarperOne.

Yacovazzi, Cassandra L. 2013. "'Are You Allowed to Read the Bible in a Convent?': Protestant Perspectives on the Catholic Approach to Scripture in Convent Narratives, 1830–1860." *U.S. Catholic Historian* 31 (Summer): 23–46.

Romney, Mitt

Mitt Romney (b. 1947) is one of the nation's most prominent politicians who is a member of the Church of Jesus Christ of Latter-Day Saints. The son of George Romney, a former governor of Michigan who ran unsuccessfully for the Republican presidential nomination in 1968, he earned his JD-MBA from Harvard University before serving as the CEO of Bain and Company, and later cofounding Bain Capital, a private equity investment firm. Romney led the 2002 U.S. Winter Olympic Committee and served as governor of Massachusetts from 2003 to 2007. In 2012, he ran unsuccessfully as the U.S. Republican nominee for president against Barack Obama. He began a term as a U.S. senator from Utah in January 2019.

Like his father, Romney encountered suspicion among his Republican base as to whether his beliefs as a member of the Church of Jesus Christ of Latter-Day Saints posed a threat to American values. He addressed this concern in a speech that he gave at the George Herbert Walker Bush Library in College Station, Texas, on December 6, 2007. It has often been likened to a similar speech that John F. Kennedy delivered in Texas during his presidential campaign in order to allay concerns about his identification with the Roman Catholic Church (Crosby 2015).

Whereas Kennedy had stressed the importance of the separation of church and state, Romney stressed the manner in which morality and religion serve as religious supports for constitutional government. He provided assurances that "no authorities of my church, or of any other church for that matter, will ever exert influence on presidential decisions" (Romney 2007) while refusing to distance himself from his own faith. As he explained, "That I will not do. I believe in my Mormon faith and endeavor to live by it. My faith is the faith of my fathers—I will be true to them and to my beliefs" (Romney 2007).

In what some critics believed was an undue concession to those who might be attempting to impose a test oath, which the U.S. Constitution prohibits, Romney responded to the question "What do I believe about Jesus Christ?" by saying that "I believe that Jesus Christ is the Son of God and the Savior of mankind" (Romney 2007). He proceeded to identify elements that he admired in a variety of Christian denominations, as well as in Judaism and Islam. Drawing from the title of a book (*The Naked Public Square*) by John Neuhaus that would be familiar to both Protestant and Catholic audiences, Romney said, "The founders proscribed the establishment of a state religion, but they did not countenance the elimination of religion from the public square. We are a nation 'Under God,' and in God, we do indeed trust" (Romney 2007). He further professed that, with other Americans, "we believe that every single human being is a child of God—we are all part of the human family" (Romney 2007). Pointing to his father's participation in marches by Dr. Martin Luther King Jr., Romney expressed admiration for Jesus's words (from Matthew 25:35): "For I was an hungered, and ye gave me meat: I was thirsty, and ye gave me drink: I was a stranger, and ye took me in: naked, and ye clothed me."

Citing the cases of Anne Hutchinson, Roger Williams, and Brigham Young, Romney further lauded the fact that Americans had come to honor religious liberty, which he contrasted to "conversion by conquest: violent Jihad, murder as martyrdom . . . killing Christians, Jews, and Muslims with equal indifference" (Romney 2007). He also cited the manner in which Samuel Adams had, in the First Continental Congress, expressed his willingness to hear a prayer from someone other than a member of his own denomination.

Just days before, Romney and some other candidates had been asked during a CNN Republican debate by a citizen from Dallas, "This question will tell us everything we need to know about you. Do you believe ever word of this book? Specifically, this book I am holding in my hand [a Bible], do you believe this book?" In words close to those that Mike Huckabee gave, Romney said to applause, "I believe the Bible is the word of God, absolutely. And I try . . . I try to live by it as well as I can, but I miss in a lot of ways. But it's a guide for my life and for hundreds of millions, billions of people around the world. I believe in the Bible" (CNN 2007).

Further responding to Anderson Cooper's query, "Does that mean you believe every word?" Romney further elaborated, "You know—yes, I believe it's the word of God, the Bible is the word of God. The Bible is the word of God. I mean, I might interpret the word differently than you interpret the word, but I read the Bible and I believe the Bible is the word of God. I don't disagree with the Bible. I try to live by it" (CNN 2007).

During his campaigns, Romney often cited a book by evangelical pastor Rick Warren entitled *The Purpose-Driven Life*, as when suggesting that there is "something greater in life than just yourself" and that "by virtue of belief in a creator, there's a sense of the worth of each individual" (Luo 2007).

See also Church of Jesus Christ of Latter-Day Saints; Huckabee, Mike; Kennedy, John F.; Roman Catholics

For Reference and Further Reading

CNN. 2007. "Part II: CNN/You Tube Republican presidential debate transcript." November 28. https://www.cnn.com/2007/POLITICS/11/28/debate.transcript.part2/.

Crosby, Richard Benjamin. 2015. "Toward a Practical, Civic Piety: Mitt Romney, Barack Obama, and the Race for National Priest." *Rhetoric and Public Affairs* (Summer): 301–30.

Luo, Michael. 2007. "Gingerly, Romney Seeks Ties to Christian Right." *New York Times*. October 16.

Medhurst, Martin J. 2009. "Mitt Romney: 'Faith in America.' And the Dance of Religion and Politics in American Culture." *Rhetoric and Public Affairs* 12 (Summer): 195–221.

Neuhaus, Richard John. 1988. *The Naked Public Square: Religion and Democracy in America*. Grand Rapids, MI: William B. Eerdmans.

Romney, Mitt. 2007. "Transcript: Mitt Romney's Faith Speech." NPR. December 6. https://www.npr.org/templates/story/storyphp?storyId=16969460.

Roosevelt, Franklin D.

Few situations other that war have been direr than the Great Depression that Franklin D. Roosevelt faced when he delivered his first inaugural address on March 4, 1933. He had worked for some time on the speech with Raymond Moley, a professor for Columbia University, and he delivered it just seventeen days after surviving an assassination attempt in Miami. After confiding to Jim Farley that "I think a thought to God is the right way to start off my administration. A proper attitude toward religion, and belief in God, will in the end be the salvation of all peoples" (Houck and Nocasian 2002, 667), on the morning of his inauguration, Roosevelt had attended services at St. John's Episcopal Church.

Roosevelt designated this inauguration day in biblical terms as "a day of consecration" (Wicker 2017). As he took his oath, the Bible was opened to 1 Corinthians 13, which extolled the virtue of "charity," or agape love. Roosevelt took this, and his subsequent three oaths, on an old Roosevelt family Bible that was printed in Dutch in 1686 and that was opened each time to the same passage (Winder 2019, 169). Although the speech today is known primarily for Roosevelt's admonition that "the only thing we have to fear is fear itself," in his second paragraph Roosevelt appeared to minimize the nation's situation by noting that the "common difficulties . . . concern, thank God, only material things," reminding the audience perhaps of Jesus's statement when facing Satanic temptations in the wilderness, that "man shall not live by bread alone" (Matthew 4:4). Roosevelt later noted that "happiness lies not in the mere possession of money; it lies in the joy of achievement, in the thrill of creative effort." He furthered this theme by indicating in almost a direct quotation from Jesus's words in Matthew 20:28 that "our true destiny is not to be ministered unto but to minister to ourselves and to our fellow men."

Shortly thereafter, Roosevelt observed that "we are stricken by no plague of locusts," a clear reference to one of the plagues that Moses called down on the Pharaoh in the book of Exodus. Roosevelt indicated that he did not believe that God had sent the economic crisis that beset the American people as punishment. He did, however, implicate "the unscrupulous money changers," a fairly generic indictment that would have reminded individuals of Jesus's cleansing of the temple, an event, or events, that is described in each of the four gospels (Matthew 21:12–17; Mark 11:15–19; Luke 19:45–48; and John 2:13–16). Roosevelt furthered this analogy in reiterating that "the money changers have fled from their high seats in the temple of our civilization. We may now restore that temple to the ancient truths."

His most serious indictment, however, was that America's economic leaders "have no vision, and when there is no vision the people perish," which is almost a direct quotation from Proverbs 29:18. Ironically, this was the passage to which Roosevelt's presidential predecessor, Herbert Hoover, had opened his Bible when taking his own oath.

Later in the speech, Roosevelt announced that he would "dedicate this Nation to the policy of the good neighbor—the neighbor who resolutely respects himself and, because he does so, respects the rights of other—the neighbor who respects his obligations and respects the sanctity of his agreements in and with a world of neighbors." Although the reference was to foreign affairs, those familiar with the Bible might well have connected this idea to Jesus's parable of the Good Samaritan in Luke 10:25–37, which Jesus gave in response to the question of "Who is my neighbor?"

Roosevelt concluded his speech by saying, "In this dedication of a Nation we humbly ask the blessing of God. May He protect each and every one of us. May He guide me in the days to come."

In analyzing public reactions to the speech as recorded in letters to the White House, Davis W. Houck and Mihaela Nocasian observe that many of the writers associated Roosevelt with "the sense of Divine Mission and Election" (2002, 664). Some even likened him to Moses, Joshua, or even Jesus as the Savior of the nation in a perilous time (666).

In his acceptance speech at the Democratic National Convention in 1936, Roosevelt further elaborated on how he sought to apply the lessons of 1 Corinthians 13 to U.S. politics. After saying that "we do not see faith, hope and charity as unattainable ideals, but we use them as stout supports of a Nation fighting the fight for freedom in a modern civilization," Roosevelt continued,

> Faith—in the soundness of democracy in the midst of dictatorships.
> Hope—renewed because we know so well the progress we have made.
> Charity—in the true spirit of that grand old word. For charity literally translated from the original means love, the love that understands, that does not merely share the wealth of the giver, but in true sympathy and wisdom helps men to help themselves. (Roosevelt 1936)

See also Moses as Political Archetype; Jesus

For Reference and Further Reading

Houck, Davis W., and Mihaela Nocasian. 2002. "FDR's First Inaugural Address: Text, Context, and Reception." *Rhetoric and Public Affairs* 5 (Winter): 649–78.

LaFontaine, Charles V. 1976. "God and Nation in Selected U.S. Presidential Inaugural Addresses, 1789–1945: Part One." *Journal of Church and State* 18 (Winter): 39–60.

LaFontaine, Charles V. 1976. "God and Nation in Selected U.S. Presidential Inaugural Addresses, 1789–1945: Part Two." *Journal of Church and State* 18 (Autumn): 503–21.

Roosevelt, Franklin D. March 4, 1933. "First Inaugural Address of Franklin D. Roosevelt." http ://avalon.law.yale.edu/20th_century/froos1.asp.

Roosevelt, Franklin D. July 27, 1936. "Acceptance Speech at the Democratic National Convention (1936)." https://teachingamericanhistory.org/library/document/acceptance-speech-at-the-democratic-national-convention-1936/.

Wicker, Christine. 2017. "FDR: When an Appeal to Scripture United a Divided Nation." Baptist News Global. January 31. https://baptistnews.com/article/fdr-when-an-appeal-to-scripture-united-a-divided-nation/#.XJjy8SJKiUk.

Winder, Mike. 2019. *Favorite Scriptures of 100 American Leaders*. Springville, UT: Plain Sight.

Woolverton, John F., and James D. Bratt. 2019. *A Christian and a Democrat: A Religious Biography of Franklin D. Roosevelt*. Grand Rapids, MI: Eerdmans.

Roosevelt, Theodore

President Theodore Roosevelt (1858–1919), who served in the White House from 1901 to 1909, is one of four presidents who is commemorated on Mount Rushmore. A sickly child who grew up under a demanding father, whom he tried to emulate, the young Roosevelt developed his body and grew into a vigorous man who extolled his ability to conquer the elements. Roosevelt served both as New York civil service commissioner and governor, raised troops (the so-called Rough Riders) to fight in Cuba during the Spanish-American War, and won a Nobel Prize as president by brokering peace between Japan and Russia.

A member of the Dutch Reformed Church, who taught Sunday school both in his youth and college years, Roosevelt was well versed in biblical language. In "Christian Citizenship," in December 1900, Roosevelt said, "The Decalogue [Ten Commandments] and the Golden Rule must stand as the foundation of every successful effort to better our social or political life. 'Fear God and walk in his ways' and 'Love thy neighbor as thyself'—when we practice these two precepts, the reign of social and civic righteousness will be close at hand" (quoted in Smith 2006, 129). In a speech commemorating the three hundredth anniversary of the King James Version of the Bible, Roosevelt quoted Aldous Huxley in referring to that version as "the Magna Charta of the poor and the oppressed . . . the most democratic book in the world" (quoted in Noll 2011, 253).

Roosevelt's favorite verses included Romans 12:11: "Not slothful in business, fervent in spirit, serving the Lord." He also liked to quote James 1:22: "Be ye doers of the word and not hearers only" (Smith 2006, 135). He titled his speech to the convention that nominated him for his unsuccessful bid for the presidency under the label of the Progressive, or Bull Moose, Party "A Confession of Faith," and closed with the words (an analogy from the book of Revelation), "We stand at Armageddon and we battle for the Lord!" After leaving the White House he contributed to a Christian magazine entitled *The Outlook*. In 1911, he gave a series of five 90-minute lectures on the role of Christians in modern society (Marschall 2010).

One Roosevelt biographer believes that his faith depended more on self-help than on faith in God. Summarizing Micah 6:8, Roosevelt once said that "to love justice, to be merciful. . . . That is my religion, my faith. To me it sums up all religion, it is all the creed I need" (quoted in Hawley 2008, 14).

Comparing Roosevelt to the evangelical Jimmy Carter, one historian has noted that Carter's favorite hymn was "Amazing Grace," whereas Roosevelt's was "A Mighty Fortress Is My God" (Hughes 1979, 80).

See also Carter, Jimmy; King James Version of the Bible

For Reference and Further Reading

Hawley, Joshua David. 2008. *Theodore Roosevelt: Preacher of Righteousness*. New Haven: Yale University Press.

Hughes, Arthur J. 1979. "'Amazin' Jimmy and a Mighty Fortress Was Our Teddy' Theodore Roosevelt and Jimmy Carter the Religious Link." *Presidential Studies Quarterly* 9 (Winter): 80–83.

Marschall, Rick. 2010. "A True Christian American President." CBN. http ://www1.cbn.com/churchandministry/a-true-christian-american-president.

Noll, Mark A. 2011. "William Jennings Bryan, Theodore Roosevelt, Woodrow Wilson and the King James Version of the Bible." *Theology* 114 (4): 251–59.

Smith, Gary Scott. 2006. *Faith and the Presidency: From George Washington to George W. Bush*. New York: Oxford University Press.

Rush, Benjamin

Benjamin Rush (1745–1813) was one of America's most influential doctors and social reformers whose contributions extended far beyond the field of medicine. Educated at a school run by an uncle, Rev. Samuel Finley, Rush later graduated from the College of New Jersey (today's Princeton) and, after an apprenticeship under Dr. John Redman of Philadelphia, completed a medical degree at the University of Edinburgh in Scotland, where he met many of the nation's leading luminaries. While in Scotland, he helped persuade John Witherspoon to accept the presidency of Princeton, whose graduates would provide major leadership roles in early America.

Active upon his return in the American revolutionary movement, Rush helped Thomas Paine publish *Common Sense* and was elected to the Second Continental Congress where he signed the Declaration of Independence and wrote character sketches of almost all of the delegates (Vile 2019). For a time he served as surgeon general of the middle department of the Continental Army, where he became involved in a dispute with authorities over proper sanitation. Although he left his position and spent most of his later life devoted chiefly to medical practice, Rush retained friendships with many of America's political leaders. A friend of both John Adams and Thomas Jefferson, Rush was largely responsible for their resumption of correspondence during their later years. Rush was a devoted physician to all classes of society and stayed when many other doctors fled Philadelphia to care for those with yellow fever. His primary methods, consisting of bleeding, blistering, and purging, may have sometimes done more harm than good but were among leading prescriptions of his time.

Rush had very high hopes for the American Revolution, and the reforms that he anticipated once monarchy and aristocratic influences were eliminated. As a deeply religious man, Rush shared the hope of many of his Puritan forbears that political reform would prepare the way for the coming kingdom of Christ. In a letter dated December 10, 1778, Rush thus wrote,

> I long to see the image of God restored to the human mind. I long to see virtue and religion supported, and vice and irreligion banished from society by wise and equitable governments. I long to see an asylum prepared for the persecuted and oppressed of all countries, and a door opened for the progress of knowledge, literature, the arts, and the gospel of Jesus Christ to the ends of the earth. And these great events are only to be accomplished by establishing and perpetuating liberty in our country. (Rush 1951, I: 221)

Rush grounded his view of the future in his understanding of the Bible:

> The Bible assures us that the time will come when the kingdoms of this world shall become the kingdoms of our Lord [a reference to Revelation 11:15], and that the knowledge and love of his name shall cover the land as the waters cover the sea [a reference to Habakkuk 2:14], Under the influence of these, and other prophesies, I have abstracted my attention from the operations of human governments, and directed it wholly to that kingdom in which there shall be absolute monarchy with perfect freedom, uncontrouled power, with universal justice, perpetual safety without fleets and armies, unparalleld splendor supported without taxes or a national debt, and general equality of rights without disrespect for superiors. This kingdom I believe will be administered in person by our Saviour upon our globe. How long it may be before he will revisit our earth for that purpose I know not—But one thing with me is certain—that "he that cometh"—"will come [a reference to Hebrews 10:37]." (Woods 1967, 32–33)

As political conflict ensued in the early republic, Rush became increasingly skeptical that political reform alone would succeed. Writing to the lexicographer Noah Webster on July 20, 1798, Rush thus observed,

> I fear all our attempts to produce political happiness by the solitary influence of human reason will be as fruitless as the search for the philosopher's stone. It seems to be reserved to Christianity alone to produce universal, moral, political, and physical happiness. Reason produces, it is true, great and popular truths, but it affords *motives* too feeble to induce mankind to act agreeably to them. Christianity unfolds the same truths and accompanies them with motives, agreeable, powerful, and irresistible. I anticipate nothing but suffering to the human race while the present systems of paganism, deism, and atheism prevail in the world. (Rush 1951, II: 799)

Rush's faith was deeply rooted in the Bible. In a memoir that was first published in 1905, Rush observed that he had never "entertained a doubt of the divine origin of the Bible" (quoted in Vile 2019, 34). In a letter that he wrote to John Adams on January 13, 1809, Rush pointed to "the absurdity of deriving human depravity from any other source than that recorded in the Bible" (1951, II: 994).

Rush helped found Dickinson College and proposed a system of state universities capped by a national one. In 1791, the same year that Congress adopted the First Amendment prohibiting the "establishment" of religion, Rush wrote a letter to Rev. Jeremy Belknap in Boston advocating the use of the Bible as a textbook. He based his arguments on five propositions:

> I. That Christianity is the only true and perfect religion, and that in proportion as mankind adopt its principles, and obey its precepts, they will be wise and happy.
> II. That a better knowledge of this religion is to be acquired by reading the Bible, than in any other way.
> III. That the Bible contains more knowledge necessary to man in his present state, than any other book in the world.
> IV. That knowledge is most durable, and religious instruction most useful, when imparted in early life, [and]
> V. That the Bible, when not read in schools, is seldom read in any subsequent period of life. (Rush 1947, 117)

Rush equated the Bible with truth. He thus noted that "the Bible contains more truths than any other book in the world: so true is the testimony that it bears of God in his works of creation, providence, and redemption, that it is called truth itself, by way of pre-eminence above things that are only simply truth" (Rush 1947, 119). Rush associated scriptural principles with those of republicanism. In a letter to John Adams dated July 21, 1789, Rush thus observed that "republican forms of government are more calculated to promote Christianity than monarchies. The precepts of the Gospel and the maxims of republics in many instances agree with each other" (1951, I: 523). He thus observed that even if the Bible "did not convey a single direction for the attainment of future happiness," it would still be worth teaching because it contains "the greatest portion of that kind of knowledge which is calculated to produce private and public temporal happiness" (1947, 122). Whereas some might interpret the existence of different creeds as a result of its ambiguity, Rush believed that "the opposite systems of the numerous sects of Christians arise chiefly from their being more instructed in catechism, creeds, and confessions of faith, than in the scriptures" (1947, 122). Responding to concerns that children may be unable to absorb scriptural truths, Rush responded,

> Let us not be wiser than our Maker. If moral precepts alone could have reformed mankind, the mission of the Son of God into our world, would have been unnecessary. He came to promulgate a system of *doctrines*, as well as a system of morals. The perfect morality of the gospel rests upon a doctrine, which though often controverted, has never been refuted, I mean the vicarious life and death of the Son of God. This sublime and ineffable doctrine delivers us from the absurd hypotheses of modern philosophers, concerning the foundation of moral obligation, and fixes it upon the eternal and self moving principle of LOVE. It concentrates a whole system of ethics in a single test of scripture. "A new commandment I give unto you, that ye love one another, even as I have loved you" [John 13:34]. (Rush 1947, 125)

Rush observed that it was no more difficult to believe in the virgin birth of Christ than to abide by the doctrine of loving one's enemies (1947, 125). Rush believed that revelations in the Bible further aligned both with "internal revelation, or a moral principle, which God has implanted in the heart of every man," and with the "works of creation" (1947, 127). Rush, who was a strong supporter of the Sunday school movement, further lauded their use of the Bible. Observing the nation's political institutions, Rash lamented that "we waste so much time and money in punishing crimes, and take so little pains to prevent them. We profess to be republicans, and yet we neglect the only means of establishing and perpetuating our republican forms of government, that is, the universal education of our youth in the principles of Christianity, by means of the Bible" (1947, 130).

See also Adams, John; *Common Sense* (Thomas Paine); Jefferson Bible; Sunday School Movement; Witherspoon, John

For Reference and Further Reading

Rush, Benjamin. 1947. *The Selected Writings of Benjamin Rush*, ed. Dagobert D. Runes. New York Philosophical Library.

Rush, Benjamin. 1951. *Letters of Benjamin Rush*, ed. by L. H. Butterfield. 2 vols. Princeton, NJ: Princeton University Press.

Vile, John R. 2019. *A Constellation of Great Men: Exploring the Character Sketches of Dr. Benjamin Rush of Pennsylvania of the Signers of the Declaration of Independence*. Clark, NJ: Talbot.

Woods, John A. 1967. "The Correspondence of Benjamin Rush and Granville Sharp 1773–1809." *Journal of American Studies* 2 (April): 1–38.

Rushdoony, Rousas John

See Christian Reconstructionism

• S •

Salvation Army

The Salvation Army was founded in Great Britain by Rev. William Booth (1829–1912), a Methodist minister sympathetic to the Holiness Church, who began preaching to the poor in London and subsequently widened his ministry to include that of meeting their physical and well as their spiritual needs. An American branch was subsequently founded in the United States in 1880 and is today "the nation's largest charitable organization, faith-based or secular, with assets of $8.76 billion according to the Army's 2010 *Annual Report*" (Davis and Robinson 2012, 113).

The Salvation Army is often identified with the social gospel movement and with postmillennialism, or the view that human actions can bring the Kingdom of God to earth. In contrast to many proponents of this movement, it was founded on, and remains strongly tied to, a literalistic view of the Bible and the ethics that it expounds. Booth thus proclaimed, "We believe that the Scriptures of the Old and New Testaments were given by inspiration of God, and that they only constitute the Divine rule of Christian faith and practice" (115). Moreover, the Salvation Army's website commits itself to opposition to abortion and sexual relationships outside monogamous heterosexual marriages, and other conservative social stances (118–19).

In contrast to some organizations with similar beliefs, however, the Salvation Army rejected laissez-faire economics, social Darwinism, and the distinction between the "worthy" and "unworthy" poor (119). It rests instead on the belief that all are created in God's image and that social and economic structures sometimes perpetuate economic justices, especially for the poor and downtrodden. Although the Salvation Army generally eschews direct political participation, it supported alcoholic prohibition and, from its early days, opposed racial segregation; more recently, it has opposed child pornography (122, 138). It has justified its lobbying efforts on the basis of Proverbs 31:9, which says, "Speak up for the poor and see that they get justice" (139).

The Salvation Army is hierarchically organized, with members, or "adherents," "soldiers," cadets," and "officers" (135). Discipline is strict, and officers who marry are expected to marry fellow officers and can be expelled if they do not do so (135–36). Although the Army accepts some government funding for its social service missions, they constitute only about 14 percent of its annual revenue (140). In recent years, the Salvation Army has been particularly active in disaster relief efforts.

See also Natural Disasters; Social Gospel

For Reference and Further Reading

Davis, Nancy J., and Robert V. Robinson. 2012. *Claiming Society for God: Religious Movements and Social Welfare*. Bloomington: Indiana University Press.

Same-Sex Marriage

The Bible describes the family as one of the fundamental institutions of society, preceding both government and the church. According to the stories of human origins in the book of Genesis, God created both man and woman in his own image, giving them dominion over the animals and initially entrusting them with tending the Garden of Eden. Genesis 2:23–24 credits Adam as saying, "This is now bone of my bones, and flesh of my flesh: she shall be called Woman, because she was taken out of Man. Therefore shall a man leave his father and his mother, and shall cleave unto his wife: and they shall be one flesh." Jesus quoted this with apparent approbation in Matthew 19:4–5 when responding to a question by Jewish leaders about the propriety of divorce, about which Jesus took a harsher attitude than they did.

Although the Old Testament appears less critical of polygamy, which is today generally considered to be improper, there are a number of passages in the Old Testament that are directed against same-sex sexual relations. Leviticus 18:22 thus says, "Thou shalt not lie with mankind, as with womankind: it is abomination." Moreover, Leviticus 20:13 provides that individuals caught in such an act were to be subject to the death penalty. These laws were incorporated into British common law and brought to the American colonies by American Puritans and other immigrants.

In the Roman Catholic tradition, marriage is considered to be a sacrament. Protestant denominations have also typically regarded the marriage relationship as a covenantal relationship similar to that between Christ and the church. Although there are scriptural passages that appear to praise celibacy for those who devote their lives completely to Christian service, marriage has traditionally been viewed as the proper way not only to channel sexual energies and have children but also to train them in both private morality and in civic responsibilities, a sentiment that would have been shared in early America by advocates of civic republicanism.

Although the New Testament chiefly portrays the law as a means of teaching proper behavior rather than as a code to keep in order to attain salvation, it appears to continue the prohibition against same-sex sexual relationships, most notably in Romans 1. Some scholars have argued, however, that Paul was primarily addressing prostitution and pederasty, rather than same-sex orientation as it is understood today (but see Sprinkle 2014).

There are, of course many biblical rules, including those against adultery (extramarital sex) and fornication (premarital sex), that have largely disappeared from the law books and from litigation. Moreover, many scholars now believe that same-sex sexual orientation is more a matter of hereditary or environmental influences than of willful disobedience to God's law. With such doubts, it is difficult to uphold laws that deprive same-sex partners of such protections as hospital visitation rights, the right to file joint-income tax returns, and the right to enter into a marital contract.

Moreover, after police raided a gay bar named Stonewall in Greenwich Village on June 28, 1969, the patrons fought back, bringing issues of LGBTQ (Lesbian, Gay, Bisexual, Transsexual, Queer) rights into focus just four years after the U.S. Supreme Court had recognized a right of privacy involving the use of contraceptives in *Griswold v. Connecticut*. Pointing to a long history of legal disapproval of homosexual relations, however, the Supreme Court upheld laws against homosexual behavior in *Bowers v. Hardwick* in 1986, only to reverse course on due process and privacy grounds in *Lawrence v. Texas* (2003).

Although many opponents of same-sex marriage, who have been especially associated with the Roman Catholic Church and with evangelical groups such as James Dobson's Focus on the Family, continued to fear that it would undermine the institution of marriage, with its obvious civic benefits, others pointed out that the number of out-of-wedlock children had continued to increase long before the introduction of same-sex marriage, as had divorce, as states had liberalized laws (so-called no fault divorce laws) on the subject. Moreover, advocates of same-sex marriage were not arguing against heterosexual marriage but simply asking to be extended the same benefits. As a number of state courts began striking laws against same-sex marriage, a prominent scholar advocated a constitutional amendment prohibiting gay marriage (George 2001), and Congress adopted the Defense of Marriage Act (DOMA) designed to protect prohibitions against same-sex marriages. The U.S. Supreme Court invalidated this law in *United States v. Windsor* (2013). In *Obergefell v. Hodges* (2015), it subsequently ruled that state laws prohibiting same-sex marriages violated equal protection and due process rights.

There is general agreement that eliminating the bar to same-sex marriage will not obligate churches who continue to object to such relationships from refusing to give them church sanction, but many details remain to be worked out (Bold 2009).

See also Covenants, Compacts, Contracts, and Constitutions; Dobson, James; Evangelicals; Polygamy; Roman Catholics

For Reference and Further Reading

Boise, David, and Theodore B. Olson. 2014. *Redeeming the Dream: The Case for Marriage Equality*. New York: Viking.

Bold, Fredric J., Jr. 2009. "Vows to Collide: The Burgeoning Conflict between Religious Institutions and Same-Sex Marriage Antidiscrimination Laws." *University of Pennsylvania Law Review* 148 (December): 179–230.

Bowers v. Hardwick, 478 U.S. 186 (1986).

Burton, Neel. 2017. "Same-Sex Relations in the Bible." *Psychology Today*. November 1. https://www.psychologytoday.com/us/blog/hide-and-seek/201711/same-sex-relations-in-the-bible.

George, Robert P. 2001. "The 28th Amendment: It Is Time to Protect Marriage, and Democracy, in America." *National Review* 443 (July 23): 32–34.

Griswold v. Connecticut, 381 U.S. 479 (1965).

Kaplan, Joshua. 2005. "Unmasking the Federal Marriage Amendment: The Status of Sexuality." *Georgetown Journal of Gender and Law* 6: 105–41.

Lawrence v. Texas, 539 U.S. 558 (2003).

Obergefell v. Hodges, 576 U.S. 644 (2015).

Sprinkle, Preston M. 2014. "Romans 1 and Homosexuality: A Critical Review of James Brownson's 'Bible, Gender, Sexuality." *Bulletin for Biblical Research* 24: 515–28.

Tolbert, Mary Ann. 2006. "Marriage and Friendship in the Christian New Testament: Ancient Resources for Contemporary Same-Sex Unions." *Authorizing Marriage? Canon, Tradition, and Critique in the Blessing of Same-Sex Unions*, ed. Mark D.

Jordan, Megan T. Sweeney, and David M. Mellott. Princeton, NJ: Princeton University Press, pp. 41–51.
United States v. Windsor, 570 U.S. 744 (2013)
Viefhues-Bailey, Ludger H. 2010. *Between a Man and a Woman? Why Conservatives Oppose Same-Sex Marriage*. New York: Columbia University Press.

Sanders, Bernie

At least since Jimmy Carter ran as an evangelical Christian in the election of 1976, members of this group have been an important demographic for political candidates. Often associated with opposition to abortion, same-sex marriage, and pornography, evangelicals have pushed back against Supreme Court decisions that they thought attempted to denude public spaces of religious expression, but have generally favored free enterprise over expansive governmental programs.

One of the most liberal Democrats to run for president in 2016 was independent senator Bernie Sanders (b. 1941) of Vermont, who ultimately came in second to Hillary Clinton in securing the Democrat nomination for president. It was therefore surprising when Sanders accepted an invitation from Liberty University, the school founded by Rev. Jerry Falwell and operated by his son (who was an early supporter of Donald J. Trump and who had invited Ted Cruz to announce his presidential run), to speak to a large student convocation there.

In opening his speech, Sanders indicated that he knew that his views differed on many issues including women's rights and gay rights, but that he thought that it was important for individuals with different political views "to engage in civil discourse—not just to shout at each other or make fun of each other." Recognizing and applauding the fact that Liberty University was a "religious school" that "tries to understand the meaning of morality and the words of the Bible, within the context of a very complicated modern world," Sanders, a largely secular Jew, highlighted two Scriptures that he thought might provide the basis for such common ground.

The first was the Golden Rule in Matthew 7:12, which was part of Jesus's Sermon on the Mount. It admonishes, "So in everything do to others what you would have them do to you, for this sums up the law and the prophets." The second passage from Amos 5:24 expressed the desire to "let justice roll on like a river, righteousness like a never-failing stream."

Sanders devoted the rest of his speech to this theme of justice. Using the line that "there is no justice," Sanders focused on numerous issues that are not generally associated with the evangelical agenda. This included the wealth disparity that he thought benefited the top 1 percent of the people; low minimum wages; high childhood poverty and hunger; the lack of health insurance and the high cost of prescription drugs; the lack of parental leave, which he called "an attack on family values"; high youth unemployment; and high rates of incarceration. He ended with the hope that members of the audience would "have the courage to stand with the poor and working people of our country."

Although the audience was silent throughout much of Sanders's presentations, the media generally complimented the reception that the students provided to a speaker whose views generally differed from their own (Walker 2015; Seitz-Wald 2014).

In his bid for the 2020 Democratic nomination for president, Sanders, who has consistently opposed Trump's travel ban on people from certain Muslim countries and expressed sympathy for Palestinians, has been particularly popular among Muslim Americans (Obeidallah 2019).

See also Falwell, Jerry

For Reference and Further Reading

Obeidallah, Dean. 2019. "The Star of the Annual Muslim Convention Was a Jewish Man from Brooklyn." CNN. September 2. https://www.cnn.com/2019/09/01/opinions/bernie-sanders-muslim-american-support-obeidallah/index.html.

Sanders, Bernie. 2015. "Remarks at the Liberty University Convocation." October 3. https://medium.com/@BernieSanders/remarks-at-the-liberty-university-convocation-4b61c51a4b99. Accessed April 4, 2019. [Note: The transcript is not identical to the recorded speech.]

Seitz-Wald, Alex. 2014. "Bernie Sanders Speaks at Liberty University." MSNBC. September 14 [updated September 14, 2015]. www.msnbc.com/msnbc/bernie-sanders-speaks-liberty-university.

Walker, Andrew T. 2015. "In Welcoming Sanders, Liberty University Shows the Left How to Handle Dissent." *National Review*. September 15. https://www.nationalreview.com/2015/09/bernie-sanders-liberty-university-greeted-warmly/.

Sasse, Ben

U.S. senator Ben Sasse (b. 1972) of Nebraska is perhaps the best-educated member of Congress. He earned a bachelor's degree in government from Harvard, during which he spent a junior year abroad at Oxford, earned a master's degree from St. John's College, and two master's degrees and a PhD in history from Yale. Raised as a Lutheran, Sasse was a member of the Fellowship of Christian Athletes and Campus Crusade, and now describes himself as a "Lutero-Calvinist," and a member of the Presbyterian Church of America (Derrick 2016). He wrote his undergraduate thesis on Martin Luther and the just war tradition, his master's thesis on John Calvin and his view of biblical law, and his dissertation on reactions to the U.S. Supreme Court decisions relative to religious exercises in school.

Sasse held a number of teaching and governmental positions before being appointed in 2009 as president of Midland Lutheran College in his hometown, which he is credited with successfully turning around. He was elected to the U.S. Senate in 2014 and is a member of the Judiciary Committee. A conservative Republican, Sasse describes America's heritage as "glorious . . . because it is an anti-statist tradition. The purpose of American limited government is to make a broader, affirmational claim about human dignity and natural rights. Government doesn't give us rights. We get rights from God via nature, and government is our shared project to secure these rights" (Derrick 2016).

Sasse believes that modern technology has had a very disruptive effect. As a parent who helps homeschool his three children, he is concerned that parents are not teaching their children the virtue of self-reliance, which he links in part to physical labor. In his book *The Vanishing American Adult*, Sasse urges individuals to develop a personal library and recommends a variety of books, which he divides into a number of broad categories that have been especially important to him. Under the category of "God," he observes, "There are certain books of the Bible that every educated person should know, whether or not you believe in a higher power. The first eleven chapters of Genesis alone—that is, before we even get to Abraham—are worthy of a year of sustained reading. Among the Gospels, Matthew is the grittiest, placing Jesus against the background of Jewish history and hopes. And Romans is the systemic theology of the whole Bible" (2017, 232). In this category, he proceeds to recommend books by Luther and Calvin.

An article in *Slate*, which is highly critical of Sasse's conservatism and faults him for being unable to translate his ideas into political practice, nonetheless associates him with "dignity" as well as "duty, thoughtfulness, empiricism, and respect for democratic traditions" (Mathis-Lilley 2017). Sasse did not support Trump's presidential bid, and in a recent book, he decries what he considers to be the increased tribalism in American politics.

On October 4, 2018, Sasse gave an impassioned speech on the Senate floor in which he praised the MeToo movement and bewailed the fact that senators confronted over whether to confirm Brett Kavanaugh after allegations of improper sexual behavior from many years before were faced with the false choice between "whether we love our daughters or we trust our sons." Sasse observed that the media was portraying the Kavanaugh and Ford families as though they were warring Hatfields and McCoys: "We saw people having to grapple with the brokenness, and the sinfulness, of a fallen world—but they were not just grappling with it. They were grappling with the nastiness East of Eden real time, on television as a kind of polititainment art." He further rather presciently faulted the media for "giving more oxygen to the one-man clownshow that is Michael Avennati [the controversial attorney representing women in sexual harassment suits, who has since been indicted]." Describing rape as "an act from the pit of hell," Sasse said that "people—men and women—are created in the image of God—*imago Dei*, as we say in Christianity. Sexuality is a deep and precious gift—it is an intimacy, it is an openness—that is to be shared and given—never taken. Sex is big, not small—and you don't get to decide it for someone else."

Sasse bemoaned the fact that President Trump "is dispositionally unable to restrain his impulse to divide us." Again noting that both men and women are "created with dignity and worth," Sasse accused fellow politicians of being disinterested "in truth." He explained, "They think we're interested in political instrumentality. They think we're interested in exploiting differences and divisions in America because we're addicted to short term power in a city that isn't worthy of much respect."

See also Trump, Donald

For Reference and Further Reading

Derrick, J. C. 2016. "Ben Sasse: A Reformed Reformer." *World Magazine*. October 15. https://world.wng.org/2016/09/ben_sasse_a_reformed_reformer.

Mathis-Lilley, Ben. 2017. "The Wasted Mind of Ben Sasse." *Slate*. July 13. https://slate.com/news-and-politics/2017/07/the-wasted-mind-of-nebraska-sen-ben-sasse.html.

Sasse, Ben. 2017. *The Vanishing American Adult: Our Coming-of-Age Crisis—and How to Rebuild a Culture of Self-Reliance*. New York: St. Martin's Press.

Sasse, Ben. 2018. "One of the Best Speeches You Will Ever Hear from the Senate Floor." Justin Taylor, the Gospel Coalition. October 4. https://www.thegospelcoalition.org/blogs/justin-taylor/one-best-speeches-will-ever-hear-senate-floor/.
Sasse, Ben. 2018. *Them: Why We Hate Each Other—and How to Heal.* New York: St. Martin's Press.

Satan

Scriptures contain numerous references to Satan. He appears in the Garden of Eden in the form of a snake tempting the first couple to sin, as a kind of provocateur in the book of Job where God gives him permission to inflict woes upon a just man, as an outcast from heaven in Isaiah 14:12 (also see Luke 10:18), in the wilderness tempting Jesus in the gospels, in the form of demons whom Jesus cast out during his ministry, and—at the end of times—where he is behind the Antichrist and a false prophet. In Ephesians 6:11, Paul urged believers to "put on the whole armour of God that ye may be able to stand against the wiles of the devil," adding in the next verse that "we wrestle not against flesh and blood, against principalities, against powers, against the rulers of the darkness of this world, against spiritual wickedness in high places." 1 Peter 5:8 refers to "your adversary the devil, as a roaring lion, [who] walketh about, seeking whom he may devour."

Satan, also known as the Devil and by a variety of other names, is an embodiment of evil. Theologians have long dealt with the problems of theodicy, or how to explain evil, especially when it is experienced by godly individuals, and the Devil provides a potential partial answer. Theologians still debate the degree to which the Devil is an actual spiritual entity and the degree to which he serves as a metaphor. Conservative theologians generally take the former view and more liberal theologians the latter.

Historically, Satan, and conceptions of Satan, have played a major role in American culture and politics. He was a major subject in John Milton's (1698–1674) classic poem *Paradise Lost* and in other major works of literature. Historian W. Scott Poole thus notes that "America's Satan is . . . seemingly omnipresent, corrupting Christianity itself, seducing leaders in government and business, building an organization structure of his followers to rival the church, hindering religious revivals, leading a huge army of demonic minions who can possess human beings, causing natural disasters, inspiring the enemies of the United States to acts of violence" (2009, 5). In the popular mind, biblical conceptions of the Devil are often mixed with pagan myths and folklore as in Halloween celebrations and horror movies.

The Salem witch trials were among most obvious examples of such influence. As girls writhed in apparent pain and began accusing individuals of witchcraft, contagion spread throughout the colony and resulted in the execution of almost twenty people. Fear may very well have been exaggerated by recent wars against Native Americans, which had led to atrocities on both sides. Although some had hoped that Native Americans might be the lost tribes of Israel, others had viewed them as individuals who had, following Satan, tried to obliterate knowledge of the true God. There are parallels to this thought in the book of

Mormon, which portrayed Native Americans as descendants of the satanic Lamanites (Poole 2009, 53).

Just as many Americans later associated George III with the Antichrist, so too some of them believed that Satan had directly inspired him to war against the colonists' liberties (22). Ironically, the two Great Awakenings that did so much to influence American political development often portrayed individuals at war with Satan and his demons, who were attempting to keep them from being converted. In "The Dangers of an Unconverted Ministry" (1740), evangelist Gilbert Tennant (1703–1762) even thought that it was possible for Satan to do his work covertly through individuals who were supposed to be preaching the gospel (37).

It was not uncommon to associate one's political enemies with Satanism and/or atheism. New England Federalists were particularly likely to use such adjectives against Thomas Jefferson and the Democratic-Republican opponents in the presidential election of 1800. In the nineteenth century, it became increasingly common for evangelical supporters of temperance to refer to "demon liquor" or "demon rum," which many, in turn, associated with immigrants and with Roman Catholicism (68, 72). In 1870, Dr. Nicholas Francis Cooke wrote a book entitled *Satan in Society* in which he linked Satan to birth control and the women's rights movement (85). Somewhat later, Americans linked Satan to the "savages" of the Philippines who were resisting American occupation in the wake of the Spanish-American War (88).

Apocalyptic literature often connects Satan with the Antichrist and the end of times. Hal Lindsey, who had previously authored *The Late Great Planet Earth*, authored a very popular book in 1976 entitled *Satan Is Alive and Well on Planet Earth*. In the 1980s, Satan was been tied to panics that Satanists were abducting and torturing children (170) or spreading his influence through rock music or role-playing games like Dungeons and Dragons (175, 177).

In recent years, Iranian Muslim leaders have sought to reverse the tables on America's view of itself by referring to the nation as the Great Satan. Radical Islamists often portray American toleration of homosexuality and other lifestyles as signs of satanic corruption. Just as America portrayed communism as a tool of Satan during the Cold War, so too it has, in turn, portrayed its war against terrorism in demonizing terms. Republican presidential candidate John McCain thus received thunderous applause when, in a forum at the Saddleback Church in Orange County, he promised to chase Osama bin Laden "to the gates of hell" (218).

See also Antichrist; Native American Indians; Revolutionary War; Roman Catholicism; Temperance Movement

For Reference and Further Reading

Poole, W. Scott. 2009. *Satan in America: The Devil We Know*. Lanham, MD: Rowman & Littlefield.

Scalia, Antonin

Antonin Scalia (1936–2016) was appointed to the U.S. Supreme Court by President Ronald Reagan and served as an associate justice from 1996 until his death in 2016. Educated at Georgetown University and Harvard Law School, he had previously served in a number of other governmental posts, including that of assistant attorney general for the Office of Legal Counsel and as a judge of the United States Court of Appeals for the District of Columbia. Scalia was strongly committed to the view that the Constitution should be interpreted primarily through its text and through its authors' original intentions rather than on the basis of his own personal predilections, and he often penned strong dissenting opinions.

Scalia was known for his deep commitment to the Roman Catholic faith, and his funeral mass at the Basilica of the National Shrine of the Immaculate Conception in Washington, DC, was delivered by his son Rev. Paul D. Scalia, who put the primary focus on Jesus rather than on his father (Scalia 2019, 215–20). Political scientists continue to speculate on how the composition of the Supreme Court from a body composed almost solely of Protestants to one currently occupied only by Roman Catholics and Jews has influenced modern jurisprudence (Blake 2012).

Scalia's views, articulated nicely in a recent posthumous collection of his speeches, essays, and opinions, indicate that he would be quite skeptical of such interpretative attempts. Moreover, Protestants who read his book will likely appreciate the manner in which he so frequently tied his Catholic beliefs to direct quotations from Scriptures, as well as fairly frequent references to John Bunyan's *Pilgrim's Progress* and various works of C. S. Lewis.

In an opening essay, "Not to the Wise—the Christian as Cretin," Scalia rather joyfully embraced the idea that Christians accept faith as a means of acknowledging Jesus's words that God "didst hide these things from the wise and prudent, and didst reveal them to little ones [Matthew 11:25]" and to St. Paul's acknowledgement that "the natural man does not perceive the things that are of the Spirit of God [1 Corinthians 2:14]" (Scalia 2019, 16). He further compared his own Christian faith in the resurrection and miracles to the moral stance of Sir Thomas More, whom he admired as a patron saint of lawyers, and contrasted his own faith to Thomas Jefferson's attempt to rewrite the Bible in a manner satisfactory to the Age of Reason.

In another essay encouraging Christians to be "different," Scalia linked the manner in which his Roman Catholic convictions differentiated him from others with Scriptures drawn from John 15:18 and John 17:14, in which Jesus predicted that the world would hate his followers because of such differences, and from John 18:36, in which Jesus told Pilate that his kingdom was not of this world. In this same essay, Scalia cited Jesus's conversation with the penitent thief on the cross (Luke 23:39–43) to show how Jesus valued those who stood by him (2019, 32–33).

As a Roman Catholic, Scalia believed that abortion was sinful, but as a justice, he explained in an essay on the importance of Roman Catholic education in character formation, that he dissented in cases applying the court's decision permitting abortion in *Roe v. Wade* (1973), not because he thought it was immoral but because he did not believe that the U.S. Constitution granted the central government power to legislate on the matter one way or another. He provided similar reasons for rejecting the idea either that the United States was a Christian nation or that it could make no distinction between favoring religion and irreligion. He expressed concern about the lack of biblical knowledge that would stir the hearts of many Protestants: "A recent survey found that only about half of the American people could name the first book of the Old Testament; only about one third could say who gave the Sermon on the Mount; and only about a fifth could name a single Old Testament prophet. A nation that used to abound with names like Ezekiel and Zebadiah now presumably thinks that the Beatitudes are a female singing group, and that the Apocrypha is a building in Greece" (47). In two separate essays, Scalia recounted how during his oral examinations in history at Georgetown, a professor led him to the realization that the most important event in human history was the incarnation of Christ (50, 58).

In a speech to Xavier High School in Manhattan, Scalia lauded military training as a means of instilling the virtue of courage and noted how the Bible often spoke positively of Roman soldiers (70–71). In another essay on faith and work, Scalia indicated that the relationship varied from one profession to another and that "there is no such thing as a Catholic hamburger. Unless, of course, it is a perfectly made and perfectly cooked hamburger" (76). Again explaining his decisions on abortion, Scalia likened his role as a judge to that of a cook: "Just as there is no Catholic way to cook a hamburger, so also there is no Catholic way to interpret a text, analyze a historical tradition, or discern the meaning and legitimacy of prior judicial decisions—except, of course, to do those things *honestly* and *perfectly*" (81–82). Scalia did argue that there was no shame in advocating laws, like those against bigamy or against cruelty to animals, that might rest on one's religious judgments.

In a speech to American Catholics in Rome, Scalia lauded the idea of separation of church and state as being consistent with Jesus's admonition (in Matthew 22:21) to "render unto God the things that are God's and unto Caesar the things that are Caesar's" (103–4). Noting how likely it would have been for Caesar, had he had the power to do so, continually to feed the people (as Jesus once fed the five thousand), Scalia observed that Jesus focused on a heavenly kingdom, whereas the central role of government was that of "assuring a safe, just, and prosperous society," which he illustrated with a variety of Scripture passages (Matthew 6:25; Luke 12:27; Matthew 6:23) (105–7). Scalia also quoted extensively from Paul's admonition in Romans 13 to be obedient to secular governments, to which he returned in defending the morality of the death penalty (130).

In a speech largely lauding capitalism over socialism, Scalia reiterated that "government is not meant for saving souls, but for protecting life and property and ensuring the conditions for physical prosperity" (117). He suggested that the chief sin of capitalism was "greed" and that of socialism, the quest for "power." (125).

An essay by Rabbi Meir Soloveichik observes that Scalia appears to have been the only recent justice to have cited the Talmud, which he did in *Caperton v. A.T. Massey Coal Co.* (2009), involving possible limits on monetary damages. In that case, he observed that "a Talmudic maxim instructs with respect to the Scripture: 'Turn it over, and turn it over, for all is therein.' Divinely inspired text may contain the answers to all earthy questions, but the Due Process Clause most assuredly does not" (Scalia 2019, 154).

Speaking at a Marine Corps Prayer Breakfast, Scalia lauded tradition, including invocations of God in public places. He traced such acknowledgements of civil religion through the Declaration of Independence, Thanksgiving and other proclamations, national symbols, "The Battle Hymn of the Republic," and even displays of the Ten Commandments. He further expressed this view when dissenting from the court's decision in *McCreary County v. ACLU* (2004), invalidating the display of the Ten Commandments in public schools. He favorably compared what he believed to be the U.S. Constitution's prohibition against recognizing a particular religion to more anticlerical constitutions in Europe that sought to forbid all such mentions (179–87).

See also Abortion; Battle Hymn of the Republic; Capital Punishment; Constitutional Interpretation; Jefferson Bible; Ten Commandments

For Reference and Further Reading

Blake, William. 2012. "God Save This Honorable Court: Religion as a Source of Judicial Policy Preferences." *Political Research Quarterly* 69 (December): 814–26.

Capteron v. A.T. Massey Coal Co., 556 U.S. 868 (2009).

McCreary County v. American Civil Liberties Union, 545 U.S. 844 (2004).

Scalia, Antonin. 2019. *On Faith: Lessons from an American Believer*, ed. Christopher J. Scalia and Edward Whelan. New York: Crown Forum.

Schaeffer, Francis

Francis Schaeffer (1912–1974) was an influential figure among evangelical Christians who did much to encourage understanding of, and engagement with, modern culture that he believed to be on the path to destruction.

Converted to Christianity at the age of seventeen after reading the Bible from cover to cover, Schaeffer was educated at Hampden-Sydney College. He also attended Westminster Theological Seminary, a conservative offshoot of Princeton Theological Seminary founded by J. Gresham Machen (1881–1937), and Faith Theological Seminary, a further offshoot associated with Rev. Carl McIntyre (1906–2002). Although he went by "Dr.," that degree was honorary. He was influenced by theologian Cornelius Van Til (1895–1987), who had argued that individuals were influenced by their presuppositions, or worldviews, and Schaeffer often dwelt on great biblical themes rather than on the proof texting, which is more often associated with biblical literalists (Worthen 2015, 108–9).

After going as a missionary to Switzerland, where he and his wife, Edith, established L'Abris (The Shelter), the Schaeffers increasingly came into contact with college students who were disillusioned by what they considered to be the meaninglessness of life. Schaeffer's own understanding of modern philosophers, whom he often painted with a broad brush, appears to have been derived more from his conversations with students than from deep readings of the philosophers themselves. Schaeffer was convinced that the answers to life's questions were contained in the Bible, and he was willing to engage students in conversations while offering them hospitality. At a time when many evangelicals considered it to be sinful to go to movie theaters or to read modern works, Schaeffer would discuss modern films and books and explain how they were based on what he considered to be a faulty worldview. Schaeffer had a goatee and wore knee socks typical of Switzerland, which arguably made him stand out from some of his contemporaries.

In 1965, he was invited to the United States to give lectures, some of which were published as *The God Who Is There*, the first of numerous books that he wrote, stressing how God had revealed Himself in time and history as recorded in Scripture. Many of these books were published by the InterVarsity Christian Fellowship, which ministered to college and university students, who were drawn both by Schaeffer's interest in worldviews and by his own openness to philosophical questions with which students were grappling.

Schaeffer put great emphasis on humankind's creation in the image of God, and this emphasis led him in time to develop both a film entitled *How Shall We Then Live?* and a book named *Whatever Happened to the Human Race?*, in which he combined with C. Everett Koop, a future U.S. surgeon general, to decry what he believed to be the logical consequence of secular humanism, including abortion on demand.

In contrast to some contemporary evangelicals, Schaeffer was deeply concerned about racism and was willing to perform interracial marriages, sometimes even against the wishes of their parents (Barrs n.d.). Schaeffer also wrote a book entitled *Pollution and the Death of Man* (1970), in which he gave serious attention to environmental issues. He was particularly concerned that individuals might be willing to give up their liberties in exchange for personal peace and security (Dabbs 2016).

His primary contribution was that of teaching Christians that one way to witness effectively was to understand and grapple with rival philosophies of life that he believed were leading civilization into a dead end.

See also Abortion; Koop, C. Everett

For Reference and Further Reading

Barrs, Jerram. n.d. "Francis Schaeffer: The Man and His Message." Covenant Theological Seminary. https://www.covenantseminary.edu/francis-schaeffer-the-man-and-his-message/.

Carter, Joe. 2012. "Know Your Evangelicals: Francis Schaeffer." The Gospel Coalition. January 24. https://www.thegospelcoalition.org/article/know-your-evangelicals-francis-schaeffer/.

Dabbs, Matt. 2016. "Francis Schaeffer on the Politics of Peace and Affluence." Wineskins. March 29. http://wineskins.org/2016/03/29/francis-schaeffer-on-the-politics-and-peace-and-affluence/.

Schaeffer, Francis A. 1970. *Pollution and the Death of Man: The Christian View of Ecology*. Carol Stream, IL: Tyndale House.

Worthen, Molly. 2015. "The Theological Origins of the Christian Right." *Faithful Republic: Religion and Politics in Modern America*, ed. Andrew Preston, Bruce J. Schulman, and Julian E. Zelizer. Philadelphia: University of Pennsylvania Press, pp. 101–16.

Scopes Trial

One of the most publicized trials of the early twentieth century took place in Dayton, Tennessee, in 1925. After Governor Austin Peay signed a law prohibiting the teaching of evolution in the state's public schools, residents of Dayton, with a clear eye to the publicity that a trial would bring to their town, which is not far from Chattanooga, arranged for a high school teacher by the name of John Scopes to challenge the law.

The case, which was widely viewed as pitting modern science against fundamentalist views of biblical interpretation, was sensationalized when William Jennings Bryan, one of the nation's most gifted populist Democrats, stepped forward to prosecute. This in turn prompted Clarence Darrow, perhaps America's most famous defense attorney, to volunteer for the other side. Darrow and the attorneys on his side (Arthur Garfield Hays, Dudley Field Malone, and Dr. John R. Neal) attempted to portray the case as one involving civil liberties, while Bryan and his attorneys (Attorney General A. T. Stewart, William Jennings Bryan Jr., and Sue K. Hicks) sought to paint the issue as one involving the right of the people to decide on the curriculum for their children.

In the most famous part of the case, fictionalized in the play by Jerome Lawrence and Robert E. Lee entitled *Inherit the Wind*, Darrow was able to call Bryan to the stand. Using his powers of cross-examination, he was able to show both that there were biblical conundrums (like where Cain found his wife) that Bryan could not satisfactorily answer from Scripture and that Bryan himself did not accept a literal six-day interpretation of the Genesis creation story, which suggested that other elements of the story might be more liberally interpreted.

The main design of those bringing the case was to appeal it to a higher court, which required that Scopes be convicted. However, when Darrow essentially conceded that Scopes was guilty of violating the law, the judge fined him $100, and the Tennessee Supreme Court overturned this fine because it decided that the jury rather than the judge should have assessed it. This precluded review of the case by federal courts at a time when many other states were considering, and some adopted, similar laws.

Bryan had prepared a closing statement in which he focused not as much on disagreements with the science of evolution as on its interpretations by social Darwinists, but he was precluded from giving it after Darrow conceded that Scopes was guilty of violating the law. Bryan died five days after the trial, and many fundamentalists largely retreated from national politics in the years immediately following.

In the aftermath of the case, Bryan College was established in Dayton and persists to the day. In the intervening years, a number of other states adopted similar laws. In *Epperson v. Arkansas* (1968), the Supreme Court overturned a similar law making it a criminal offense to teach evolution in public schools, and in *Edwards v. Aguillard* (1987) it overturned a Louisiana law designed to mandate the teaching of creation science alongside evolution.

See also Bryan, William Jennings; Creationism and Evolution; *Edwards v. Aguillard* (1987); *Epperson v. Arkansas* (1968)

For Reference and Further Reading

Cornelius, R. M. 1981. "Their Stage Drew All the World: A New Look at the Scopes Evolution Trial." *Tennessee Historical Quarterly* 40 (Summer): 129–43.

Larson, Edward J. 1997. *Summer for the Gods: The Scopes Trial and America's Continuing Debate over Science and Religion.* Cambridge, MA: Harvard University Press.
Larson, Edward J. 2004. *Evolution: The Remarkable History of a Scientific Theory.* New York: Modern Library.
Linder, Douglas O. 1995–2019. "State v. John Scopes ('The Monkey Trial'): An Account." Famous Trials. https://famous-trials.com/scopesmonkey/2127-home.
Szasz, Ferenc M. 1971. "The Scopes Trial in Perspective." *Tennessee Historical Quarterly* 30 (Fall): 288–98.

Segregation and Anti-miscegenation Laws

Debates in the eighteenth and nineteenth centuries over the morality of slavery were often based on the Bible. Such argumentation continued into the twentieth century with respect to racial intermarriage and segregation, although the biblical arguments do not seem to have been as prominent. The policy of legally separating whites and blacks, known as Jim Crow laws, was officially sanctioned by the U.S. Supreme Court in *Plessy v. Ferguson* (1896) and continued in many areas years beyond the decision in *Brown v. Board of Education* (1954), which declared that this policy violated the equal protection clause of the Fourteenth Amendment.

A study by historian David Chappell of the religious ideas of the segregationists says that many of the arguments that segregationists advanced from the Bible were more negative than positive. Medford Evans, a Methodist layperson, after citing Paul's words in Galatians 3:26–28 that God had erased distinctions between Jews and Greeks, bond and free, male and female, thus observed that St. Paul had left other distinctions in place, and that the Bible did not mandate desegregation (Chappell 1998, 241).

On a more positive note, Rev. G. T. Gillespie, the president emeritus of Bellhaven College in Jackson, Mississippi, pointed to examples of mandated biblical separations. They included the following: the separation of Cain from the rest of mankind in Genesis 4:11–26; the divisions of Noah's sons to different regions in Genesis 9:18–19; the confusion of tongues at the Tower of Babel in Genesis 11:19 (which had limited applicability since whites and blacks in America both spoke English); the calling of Abraham from his kinfolk in Genesis 12–25; Mosaic condemnations of marriages with pagans in Leviticus 19:19; and Ezra's condemnations of such marriages in Ezra 9–10 (Chappell 1998, 245–47).

Chappell notes that most white churches either supported the Supreme Court's decision in *Brown v. Board of Education* or chose (like many of their African American church counterparts that Martin Luther King Jr. often condemned) to remain largely silent on the subject. Evangelist Billy Graham was among those who integrated his crusades. Some who argued for segregation used Acts 17:26 to indicate that while God had made all nations of one blood, He had also separated the races (Smylie 1981, 204). Others preferred to refer to eugenics or to suggest that those favoring integration were communist dupes.

One lingering fear among many opponents of desegregation, whose ideas rested on a sense of white superiority, which are not found in the Bible, was that it would lead to racial mixing that would dilute the strength of the Anglo-Saxon race.

It was not until the *Loving v. Virginia* case in 1967 that the U.S. Supreme Court finally outlawed miscegenation laws that prohibited interracial marriages between whites and blacks. Indeed, the trial judge in that case had proclaimed, "Almighty God created the races white, black, yellow, malay and red, and he placed them on separate continents. And but for the interference with his arrangement there would be no cause for such marriages. The fact that he separated the races shows that he did not intend for the races to mix" (*Loving v. Virginia* 1967, 3).

Henry Thompson of the New York Theological Seminary observed that miscegenation laws sometimes protected white males against paternity suits (1971, 104). Thompson observed that 1 Kings 11 spoke negatively against intermarriage with foreign wives, as did Exodus 34:16, and Deuteronomy 7:4, while Numbers 31:18 and Deuteronomy 21:11–13 provided for marriages to women captured in war (104). The Bible seems to condone the marriage of Joseph to an Egyptian woman in Genesis 41:45 and of Moses to a Cushite, whom Thompson believes to have been black, in Numbers 12:1 (104). Jesus himself is said to have descended from interracial marriages between Judah and a Canaanite woman and between Rahab of Jericho and an Israelite, while Esther married the king of Persia (104, 106). Thompson further believes that the reference in Acts 13:1 to "Symeon who was called Niger" in the church of Antioch was to him being black and concluded that there was greater warrant in Scripture for interracial marriage than for marriages between believers and nonbelievers of the same race (106).

Much of the opposition to racial segregation was led by African American ministers like Martin Luther King Jr., Jesse Jackson, and others who viewed their struggle as being similar to that of Moses. After rioting at Ole Miss over desegregation, a group of white Methodist ministers in the state issued a statement on January 2, 1963, called "Born of Conviction." In this statement, they affirmed "freedom of the pulpit"; faith in the 1960 Methodist discipline, which had proclaimed that "Our Lord Jesus Christ teaches that all men are brothers. He permits no discrimination because of race, color, or creed. 'In Christ Jesus you are all sons of God, through faith . . .' (Galatians 3:26)"; and the importance of public education, while renouncing their opposition to communism (opponents often labeled those who favored desegregation as communists). In further citing a statement opposing communism by the Methodist Council of Bishops, the document cited the words of the Lord's Prayer, "Thy Kingdom come, Thy will be done on earth as it is in Heaven," and portrayed Christ as championing "justice, mercy, freedom, brotherhood and peace" (1963).

See also Jackson, Jesse; King, Martin Luther, Jr.; Moses as Political Archetype; Slavery

For Reference and Further Reading

"Born of Conviction." 1963. The Mississippi Methodist Advocate. January 2. https://www.seedbed.com/wp-content/uploads/2014/01/BoC-text2.pdf.

Brown v. Board of Education, 347 U.S. 483 (1954).

Chappell, David L. 1998. "Religious Ideas of the Segregationists." *Journal of American Studies* 32 (August): 237–62.

Loving v. Virginia, 388 U.S. 1 (1967).

Plessy v. Ferguson, 163 U.S. 537 (1896).

Reiff, Joseph T. 2013. "'Born of Conviction': White Mississippians Argue Civil Rights in 1963." *The Civil Rights Movement in Mississippi*, ed. Ted Ownby. Jackson: University Press of Mississippi, pp. 157–79.
Smylie, James H. 1981. "The Bible, Race and the Changing South." *Journal of Southern Presbyterian History* 49 (Summer): 197–218.
Thompson, Henry O. 1971. "Interracial Marriage and the Bible." *Negro History Bulletin* 34 (May): 103–6.

Sessions, Jeff

One of the hot-button issues that appears to have propelled President Donald Trump to electoral victory was the issue of illegal immigration, especially from America's southern border with Mexico. Trump promised to solve the problem by enacting a zero tolerance policy, lengthening the border wall, and requiring Mexico to pay for it.

As part of this policy, his administration began separating entering illegal aliens who were apprehended from their children. This policy came under intense criticism, including from religious leaders. Evangelist Franklin Graham called the policy "disgraceful," while the Southern Baptist Convention adopted a resolution calling for an immigration policy that maintained "the priority of family unity" (quoted in Miller and Shimron 2018).

Trump's attorney general Jeff Sessions, one of Trump's earliest presidential supporters, subsequently defended this policy by quoting Scriptures: "I would cite you to the Apostle Paul and his clear and wise command in Romans 13, to obey the laws of government because God has ordained them for the purpose of order. Orderly and lawful processes are good in themselves and protect the weak and lawful" (Miller and Shimron 2018). White House spokesperson Sarah Sanders subsequently added that "it's very biblical to enforce the law" (Sessions 2018).

Numerous respondents questioned Sessions's use of Scripture, including Johnnie Moore, one of Trump's unofficial evangelical advisors who warned against "proof texting" (Miler and Shimron 2018). Others pointed out that American loyalists had cited Romans 13 during the Revolutionary War to justify continuing allegiance to King George III, others had used it in the years prior to the Civil War to justify fugitive slave laws, and even Dr. Martin Luther King Jr. had to address concerns that he was disobeying this scripture when he was jailed for civil disobedience.

Candida R. Moss (2018) noted that Paul's admonition to obey the law needed to be balanced against the command in Exodus 23:9 that "you shall not oppress a stranger, for you know the feelings of the stranger, having yourselves been Strangers in Egypt." She further observed that the story of Sodom and Gomorrah in Genesis 18–19 warned against inhospitality to strangers and that separating families seemed particularly inconsistent with biblical admonitions in Psalm 68:5, James 1:27, and Matthew 19:14 to protect orphans and children.

See also Immigration; Trump, Donald J.

For Reference and Further Reading

BBC. 2018. "US Attorney General Quotes Bible to Defend Separating Families." June 15. https://www.bbc.com/news/world-us-canada-44499048.

Miller, Emily McFarlan, and Yonat Shimron. 2018. "Why Is Jeff Sessions Quoting Romans 13 and Why Is the Bible Verse So Often Invoked?" Religion News Service. June 16. https://www.usatoday.com/story/news/2018/06/16/jeff-sessions-bible-romans-13-trump-immigration-policy/707749002/.
Moss, Candida. 2018. "Theologian: Jeff Sessions Misreads the Bible to Justify Separating Families." CNN. June 15. https://www.cnn.com/2018/06/15/opinions/jeff-sessions-misreads-bible-to-justify-separating-families-moss/index.html.
Sessions, Jeff. 2018. "Attorney General Sessions Addresses Recent Criticisms of Zero Tolerance by Church Leaders." U.S. Department of Justice. June 14. https://www.justice.gov/opa/speech/attorney-general-sessions-addresses-recent-criticisms-zero-tolerance-church-leaders.

Sewall, Samuel

Samuel Sewall (1652–1730) may be best known as the only judge in the Salem witch trials who later publicly apologized for his role. Born in England but educated at Harvard where he earned both an undergraduate and a master's degree, Sewall married the daughter of a wealthy Boston merchant and worked in his father-in-law's firm. He later served for twenty-five years as an associate justice and for eleven years as the chief justice of the superior court, where he earned a reputation for probity and fairness.

Sewall wrote one of the earliest known American arguments against slavery. His tract appears to have been inspired in part by the rising number of slaves in Boston and what he referred to as "the Uneasiness of them under their Slavery" (Sewall 1770, 1). Both the title of his work and his arguments were solidly grounded in his understanding of the Bible.

Sewall began with the proposition that "forasmuch as Liberty is in real value next to Life: None ought to part with it themselves, or deprive others of it, but upon most mature Considerations" (1). Almost immediately, he cited Psalm 115:16 to show that God had given the earth to all the sons of Adam and Acts 17:26, 27, and 29 to show that God had made all men of one blood.

In Genesis, Joseph's brothers had sold him into slavery, but Sewall argued that they had no more right to do so than Potiphar's wife had to claim rights to his sexual services. He supplemented this argument with the exhortation in Exodus 12:16 against manstealing and selling.

Although he opposed slavery, Sewall shared contemporary racial prejudices. He noted that one obstacle to freeing current slaves was that "they can seldom use their freedom well"; he further observed that "there is such a disparity in their Conditions, Color & Hair, that they can never embody with us, and grow up into orderly Families, to the People of the Land: but still remain in our Body Politick as a kind of extra-vasant Blood" (2). He further noted that they would not make suitable husbands for white women, while deploring the fact that because owners sometimes prevented them from marrying other slaves, many were led into fornication. Quoting a passage from Matthew 19:6, which is often used at weddings, Sewall observed that in taking slaves from Africa, traders were improperly tearing them asunder from their families (2).

Sewall then addressed four arguments commonly used to justify slavery. Citing the argument that Africans were sons of Ham, who had been cursed by

Noah for his sins, Sewall argued that it was dangerous to serve unbidden as "an Executioner of the Vindictive Wrath of God; the extent and duration of which is to us uncertain" (2). He further suggested that the inhabitants of Africa might actually be the sons of Cush, as described in Jeremiah 12:23.

As to the argument that slaves might profit from being brought from a pagan land to one where the gospel was preached, Sewall observed, "Evil must not be done, that good may come of it" (3). He further questioned whether the wars by which slaves were captured could be designated as just, noting that keeping slaves violated the Golden Rule announced in Matthew 7:12. Finally, Sewall sought to undermine justifications based on Abraham's possession of slaves by observing that the circumstances of such slavery were otherwise unknown and by pointing to passages in Leviticus 25:39 and 46, Jeremiah 34:8–22, and Deuteronomy 15:18, in which "the *Israelites* were strictly forbidden the buying, or selling one another for Slaves" (3). Further appealing to the principles of the New Testament, Sewall observed that "Our Blessed Saviour has altered the Measures of the Ancient Love-Song, and set it to a most Excellent New Tune" (3), which he associated with Matthew 5:43–44 and John 13:34, the latter of which commands Christians to love one another.

Sewall's arguments were answered by John Saffin, who had particular interests in one of his own slaves who had sought to escape. In "A Brief and Candidate Answer to a Late Printed Sheet, Entitled, The Selling of Joseph . . ." (Boston, 1701), Saffin accused Sewall of seeking to overturn the natural order of things that God has ordained, which he likened to the variety of functions that Paul described in 1 Corinthians 12:13–26 within the church (Towner 1964, 48). Saffin further distinguished between stealing slaves and buying them, and pointed out that Leviticus 15:24 had permitted the Israelites to enslave heathen (49).

Sewall later argued against a law making intermarriage between whites and Native Americans or African Americans criminal, which he mitigated without preventing; Sewall thus succeeded in inserting a provision that legitimized slave marriages (Peterson 2002, 10). When arguments later arose over whether Christian slave owners were obligated to free slaves who accepted the gospel, Cotton Mather weighed in by arguing instead that their Christianity should make them better slaves (Towner 1964, 51), largely resolving the arguments in favor of slavery until the later emergence of the abolitionist movement.

See also Curses on Cain, Ham, and the Canaanites; Puritans; Segregation and Anti-miscegenation Laws; Slavery

For Reference and Further Reading

Peterson, Mark A. 2002. "The Selling of Joseph: Bostonians, Antislavery, and the Protestant International, 1689–1733." *Massachusetts Historical Review* 4 (Race and Slavery): 1–22.

Sewall, Samuel. 1770. "The Selling of Joseph a Memorial (1700)." University of Nebraska-Lincoln. https://digitalcommons.unl.edu/cgi/viewcontent.cgi?article=1026&context=etas.

Towner, Lawrence W. 1964. "The Sewall-Saffin Dialogue on Slavery." *William and Mary Quarterly* 21 (January): 40–52.

Vile, John R. 2007. "Samuel Sewall: Defender of the Rule of Law?" *Noble Purposes: Nine Champions of the Rule of Law*, ed. by Norman Gross. Athens: Ohio University Press, pp. 3–16.

Sherman, Roger

Roger Sherman (1721–1793) was a Connecticut statesman who was one of America's most influential Founding Fathers. Born in Massachusetts, as a youth, Sherman sat under the preaching of, and may have been taught by, Samuel Dunbar, a student of Cotton Mather. Later, Sherman was in the congregation of Jonathan Edwards Jr. and strongly defended him even as congregational membership dwindled.

Serving in his early life as a cobbler, Sherman went to on publish almanacs from 1750 to 1761. During this time, he was admitted to the bar, served in the Connecticut legislature, became a judge, was the treasurer of Yale, a mayor of New Haven, and a delegate to the Continental Congresses (Vile 2016, II: 790–91). In his role as a delegate, he served on the Committee responsible for writing the Declaration of Independence. He signed this document, the Articles of Confederation, and the U.S. Constitution, while participating in congressional debates on the Bill of Rights.

Sherman did some of his most influential work at the Constitutional Convention of 1787, often going toe to toe with James Madison and other delegates (Robertson 2005). He was a major figure in the adoption of the Connecticut Compromise, which helped guarantee continuing equality for small states in the Senate in exchange for representation based on population in the House of Representatives.

Sherman was among those who were on record as supporting Benjamin Franklin's proposal that the Convention should begin each day with prayer. Sherman was influential in seeing that the Bill of Rights was attached to the end of the U.S. Constitution rather than having amendments incorporated within existing parts of the document.

Sherman came out of Reformed congregational tradition and appears to have been orthodox in his thought, often carrying out discussions with preachers and theologians of his day. In arguing for the necessity of individuals who had been baptized as infants to make a public profession of faith upon becoming adults, Sherman favorably cited arguments by the English Puritan Richard Baxter (1615–1691) but added that "I do not think that his, or any other man's opinion is of any authority in the case, unless supported by the word of God" (Hall 2013, 38). Sherman riled some members of the Continental Congress when, in 1774, he voted against sending out supplies on a Sunday (Hall 2013, 39). Benjamin Rush observed that, relying on Jeremiah 12:23, Sherman's response to the patriot's military defeat on Long Island was to respond, "Truly in vain is salvation hoped for from the hills, and from the multitude of mountains" (Hall 2013, 40).

See also Articles of Confederation; Constitutional Convention of 1787; Declaration of Independence; U.S. Constitution

For Reference and Further Reading

Boyd, Julian. 1932. "Roger Sherman: Portrait of a Cordwainer Statesman." *New England Quarterly* 5: 221–36.

Hall, Mark David, 2013. *Roger Sherman and the Creation of the American Republic.* New York: Oxford University Press.

Robertson, David Brian. 2005. "Madison's Opponents and Constitutional Design." *American Political Science Review* 99 (May): 225–33.

Vile, John R. 2016. *The Constitutional Convention of 17878: A Comprehensive Encyclopedia of America's Founding,* 2 vols., rev. 2nd ed. Clark, NJ: Talbot.

Sherwood, Samuel

One obstacle to the idea of revolution among many Christians is the idea, derived in part from Romans 13, that they should be obedient to governing authorities. One way of combatting this view was to suggest, as Thomas Paine did in publishing *Common Sense* in January 1776, that God had never intended for the world to be divided into kings and subjects. Another was to suggest that King George III represented satanic forces.

This was essentially the route that Samuel Sherwood of Connecticut took in a fast-day sermon that he delivered on January 17, 1776, just a week after Paine published his work. It became what Bruce Feiler describes as "the year's second best-selling publication" (2009, 35).

Sherwood drew his text from Revelation 7:14–17, which describes a persecuted woman. Sherwood interpreted her as a symbol of the church, being carried by an eagle to the wilderness, and being attacked by a great serpent, whom he interpreted as Satan and his minions, who tried to drown her and make war upon her and her seed who remained faithful to God.

From the time of Martin Luther and the Reformation, Protestants had often identified the Great Whore of Babylon as the papacy, through which they thought that Satan had oppressed humankind. Sherwood thus observed that he agreed with "all judicious commentators and expositors that have written on the subject, that popery, or the reign and kingdom of the man of sin, the old serpent, the dragon, its rise and progress, and its downfall and overthrow, is the greatest, the most essential, and the most striking part of this revelation of St. John" (1776, 498). This imagery was similar to that which the prophets had also used against the Pharaoh of Israel.

Sherwood argued that the focus of prior Protestant commentators on the papacy had been too narrow. He thought that God's wrath was directed not only on that institution but also against other schemes "of anti-christian tyranny, as having such an extensive and universal spread over the earth" (502).

Whereas previous interpreters had seen the wilderness as a place of suffering, Sherwood saw the American wilderness as a place of refuge for the church, where God had exercised his providential powers, in what might today be labeled the idea of American exceptionalism:

> The providences of God in first planting his church in this, then howling wilderness, and in delivering and preserving of it to this day, are in a manner

> unequalled, and marvelous; and are reckoned among the most glorious events that are to be found in history, in these latter ages of the world. And there are doubtless yet more glorious events in the womb of providence, which the present commotion thro' the nation and land may (however unlikely in the view of some) be the means of bringing to pass. (1776, 503)

Even though those who fled to America seeking religious freedom continued to be harassed by the mother country, God was just as capable of delivering this people who had settled in the wilderness as he was capable of delivering the children of Israel from the oppression of the Egyptians. Quoting from, but not specifically citing, Isaiah 40:31, Sherwood thus noted that "they that wait on the Lord, shall renew their strength; they shall mount up with wings, as eagles; they shall run, and not be weary, they shall walk and not faint" (507). Sherwood further highlighted what he believed to be America's special destiny: "The American quarter of the globe seemed to be reserved in providence, as a fixed and settled habitation for God's church, where she might have property of her own, and the right of rule and government, so as not to be controul'd and oppres'd in her civil and religious liberties, by the tyrannical and persecuting powers of the earth, represented by the great red dragon" (508). The wilderness itself had swallowed up the waters of trials that Britain had inflicted by producing bountiful crops and providing safety, even as the British had agreed in the Quebec Act to allow Catholicism to flourish in Canada (514).

The godly remnant in America might find help not only among the godly whom they had left behind in Great Britain but also from nations, especially France, that, although once used by the beast to persecute true Protestant believers, might even yet come to their defense. Having allowed liberty to flourish in America, "it is not likely nor probable, that God will revoke the grant he has made of this land to his church," nor is it "probable, that a persecuting, oppressive and tyrannical power, will ever be permitted to rear its head and horns in it, notwithstanding its present violent assaults and struggles. Liberty has been planted here; and the more it is attacked, the more it grows and flourishes" (524).

Professor Stein observes that this speech and publication "undoubtedly strengthened the determination of those who were sympathetic toward open rebellion" (1975, 221). He further believes that they likely helped in removing remaining public reservations about an open break with England. He notes that "Sherwood's apocalyptic rationale for revolution . . . tapped directly into the wellsprings of the day, drawing upon ideas deep within the Protestant mentality" (222).

George Huntston Williams (1959) of the Harvard Divinity School has observed that the juxtaposition of images of paradise and of wilderness have been pervasive in Christian history. In addition to being prominent in Puritan thought, the images were later employed by those who settled the West, by Joseph Smith and the Church of Jesus Christ of Latter-Day Saints, and in African American folk songs.

See also Common Sense (Thomas Paine); Revolutionary War

For Reference and Further Reading

Fea, John. 2014. "Does America Have a Biblical Heritage?" *The Bible in the Public Square: Its Enduring Influence in American Life*, ed. Mark A. Chancey, Carol Meyers, and Eric M. Meyers. Atlanta, GA: Society of Biblical Literature, pp. 65–79.

Feiler, Bruce. 2009. *America's Prophet: Moses and the American Story*. New York: William Morrow.

Sherwood, Samuel. 1776. *The Church's Flight into the Wilderness: An Address on the Times. Containing Some Very Interesting and Important Observations on Scripture Prophesies: Shewing That Sundry of Them Plainly Related to Great-Britain and the American Colonies; and Are Fulfilling in the Present Day*. New York: S. Loudon. Found in Sandoz, Ellis, ed. 1991. *Political Sermons of the Founding Era, 1730–1804*. Indianapolis, IN: Liberty Fund, pp. 495–527.

Stein, Stephen J. 1975. "An Apocalyptic Rationale for the American Revolution." *Early American Literature* 9 (Winter): 211–25.

Williams, George Huntston. 1959. "The Wilderness and Paradise in the History of the Church." *Church History* 28 (March): 3–24.

Slavery

Often identified as America's "original sin," slavery, which had been practiced by numerous other civilizations, began in North America when ships brought Africans to Jamestown in 1619. It continued, mostly in the southern states, until the end of the Civil War and the ratification of the Thirteenth Amendment in 1865.

The Quakers were among the first religious groups to express opposition to slavery, but positions on the morality of slavery varied chiefly on the basis of geography. In time, most major Protestant denominations split into northern anti-slavery and southern pro-slavery wings. Although churches, often aided by revivals, provided the central passion for the fight against slavery, the statements in the Declaration of Independence and other founding documents declaring that all men were created equal and were equally entitled to the rights of life, liberty, and happiness also played a key role, with slavery exposing republican institutions to the charge of hypocrisy.

This book contains numerous summaries of individual speeches and debates that sought to ground their support or opposition to slavery on biblical grounds, so this essay will concentrate on some of the key arguments from both sides. It is important to remember, however, that not everyone thought that biblical arguments were especially useful, and even those who cited biblical arguments often backed them up with arguments from expedience, tradition, racism, and other sources. William Lloyd Garrison, the editor of *The Liberator* who called for immediate emancipation regardless of the consequences, was on record as saying that the issue was not a biblical issue since "nothing in regard to controversial matters had ever been settled by the Bible" (cited in Harrill 2000, 159). One of his supporters, Henry C. Wright, who authored a book entitled *The Errors of the Bible Demonstrated by the Truths of Nature: Or Man's Only Infallible Rule of Faith and Practice*, actually introduced a resolution at the annual meeting of the American Anti-Slavery Society, meeting in Boston in 1850, that "resolved, That if the Bible sanctions slavery, and is thus opposed to the self-evident truth that 'all men are created equal, and have an inalienable right to liberty,' the Bible is a self-evident falsehood, and ought to be, and ere long be, regarded as the enemy of Nature and Nature's God, and the progress of the human race in liberty, justice and goodness" (cited in Harrill 2000, 159). Some slave advocates took similar positions. Thus, William Harper argued that slavery was "a civil institution with which religion has no concern" (quoted in Morrow 1961, 90).

Those who did use the Bible to argue against slavery often suggested that passages from the Old Testament that endorsed slavery were special dispensations given to the Israelites over Canaanites that no longer applied. Many also sought to argue that the term "servant" or "slave" as used in the Old Testament was referring to a different type of institution than that which remained in the American South. Some also attempted to argue that Jesus had never spoken out against slavery because the institution did not exist in the Israel of his day (Harrill 2000, 151). Some also argued that Paul and other apostles had declined to condemn slavery so as to avoid a revolution that might jeopardize the early church.

In reviewing anti-slavery arguments from the New Testament, Professor J. Albert Harrill notes that abolitionists typically elevated general biblical principles over specific verses that appeared to approve of slavery. Abolitionists put special emphasis on the Golden Rule (Matthew 7:12 and Luke 6:31) and combined it with the Whig faith in human progress to argue that God intended for this principle, like a secretly growing seed, to result in the eventual abolition of slavery (Harrill 2000, 154). Some also focused on 1 Timothy 1:10, which had classified "menstealers" along with other moral reprobates (157). In a hermeneutical position that worried many believers, some anti-slavery opponents also appealed to what Harrill calls "the hermeneutics of moral intuition" whereby they argued that "the moral norms of the Bible were conditioned by the social arrangements and cultural assumptions of a particular age and people" (157).

African American opponents of slavery, whose views were often expressed through the medium of folk songs, put particular emphasis on the story of Moses delivering the Israelites from Egypt and portrayed Jesus himself as the "suffering servant" who had come to free his people not only from their personal sins but also from slavery (162). Some African Americans were particularly fond of images in Revelation that portrayed Jesus as coming in judgment, while Denmark Vesey and Nat Turner (as well as John Brown) sought to use the Bible to justify violent rebellion.

According to historian Mark Noll, defenders of slavery were much more likely to cite specific chapters and verses of the Bible rather than referring to more abstract principles. Their favorite passages included Genesis 9:25–27, in which Noah cursed Canaan, the son of Ham, and says that he would serve his brothers. This passage was often combined with arguments that the descendants of Ham were cursed with blackness (Haynes 2002). Proponents of slavery also cited the following: Genesis 17:12, which indicated that Abraham's household included slaves; Deuteronomy 20:10–11, which approved Israel's enslavement of its enemies; 1 Corinthians 7:21, which encouraged slaves to accept their status; Romans 12:1, 7, which urged conformity to earthly leaders; and Colossians 3:22 and 4:1, and 1 Timothy 6:1–2, which encouraged slaves to obey their masters. Slave proponents also cited the fact that, while Jesus repudiated both polygamy and most divorces, both of which had been accepted in the Old Testament, the Bible does not record him speaking specifically against slavery (Noll 2006, 34–35).

Noll believes that those using the Bible to uphold slavery had the rhetorical advantage in nineteenth-century America because they were appealing to more plain reading and commonsense understandings of Scripture that appealed to democratic instincts that did not seem to be "religiously dangerous" (2006, 49). Episcopal bishop John Henry Hopkins (1792–1868) of Vermont thus wrote an anti-abolitionist pamphlet arguing that although his personal sentiments were against slavery, he felt compelled by Scriptures to accept it.

Still, there were many parts of Scripture that slave opponents feared. Thus, in 1807, British missionaries began using a Bible, published in London and now known as the Slave Bible, entitled *Parts of the Holy Bible, Selected for the Use of the Negro Slaves, in the British West-India Islands*. The subject of a display by Fisk University in the Museum of the Bible in 2018 and 2019, this Bible may have been a reaction to the Haitian Revolution in 1804 (Little 2018). The version omitted most of the Old Testament including the book of Exodus, which tells of the Israelites' liberation from Egypt; the book of Jeremiah, which leveled condemnation of those who oppressed others; and the book of Galatians, where, in 3:18, Paul observed that "there is neither Jew nor Gentile, neither slave nor free, nor is there male and female, for you are all one in Christ Jesus" (Law 2019). Not surprisingly, the Bible did included Paul's admonition in Ephesians 6:5: "Slaves, obey your earthly masters with respect and fear, and with sincerity of heart, just as you would obey Christ."

Most southern states further refused to allow the distribution of Bibles to slaves by the American Bible Society and similar groups in part because these states had laws designed to prevent slave literacy. The American Anti-Slavery Society, and later the American and Foreign Anti-Slavery Society, sought to highlight this issue by raising money for such Bible distribution (McKivigan 1982, 62).

Although there were certainly people in the North who resisted attempts to interpret the Bible as calling for immediate emancipation just as there were Southern proponents of slavery who recognized that the institution contained many injustices, states ultimately split in the Civil War on the basis of geography rather than religion. Proponents on both sides believed that their cause was just and would be favored by God.

One fascinating product of the slavery/anti-slavery debate was a book published by Parker Pillsbury in 1883, entitled *Acts of the Anti-Slavery Apostles*, a clear reference to the fifth book of the New Testament. Pillsbury prefaced this history with the words from Acts 8:4: "AND THEY WENT EVERYWHERE PREACHING THE WORD."

Even though the Civil War resulted in the adoption of the Thirteenth Amendment (1865), which eliminated involuntary servitude; the Fourteenth Amendment (1868), which extended rights of due process and equal protection to all persons born or naturalized in the United States; and the Fifteenth Amendment (1870), which prohibited discrimination on the basis of race, both the Fourteenth and Fifteenth Amendments were widely violated until the Supreme Court decision in *Brown v. Board of Education* in 1954, which invalidated the system of Jim Crow segregation that the Court had approved in *Plessy v. Ferguson* in 1896.

Many of the arguments against discriminatory treatment that were aroused by the civil rights movement that this decision and other social developments initiated were based on the same Scriptures as earlier arguments about slavery. Whereas proponents of segregation tended to view such segregation as sanctioned by God's division of the world into nations, with separate peoples, proponents of desegregation tended to stress that God had created all people from one blood. Much of the impetus for reform came from Christian pastors who were willing to disobey discriminatory laws in pursuit of what they considered to be biblical justice. Dr. Martin Luther King Jr. and Rev. Jesse Jackson were among the leaders of this movement.

See also Civil Disobedience; Civil War; Confederate States of America; Curses on Cain, Ham, and the Canaanites; Lynchings; Segregation and Anti-miscegenation Laws; Turner, Nat; Vesey, Denmark

For Reference and Further Reading

Giles, Kevin. 1994. "The Biblical Argument for Slavery: Can the Bible Mislead? A Case Study in Hermeneutics." *Evangelical Quart*erly 661: 3–17.

Harrill, J. Albert. 2000. "The Use of the New Testament in the American Slave Controversy: A Case History in the Hermeneutical Tension between Biblical Criticism and Christian Moral Debate." *Religion and American Culture: A Journal of Interpretation* 10 (Summer): 149–86.

Haynes, Stephen R. 2002. *Noah's Curse: The Biblical Justification for American Slavery.* New York: Oxford University Press.

Hopkins, John H. [1863]. *Bible View of Slavery*. Philadelphia: Publisher unknown. https://ia902308.us.archive.org/33/items/bibleviewofslave00hopk/bibleviewofslave00hopk.pdf.

Law, Jeannie. 2019. "'Slave Bible' on Display at Museum of the Bible; Edition Removes Chapters to Uphold Slavery." *Christian Post*. April 26. https://www.christianpost.com/news/slave-bible-on-display-at-museum-of-the-bible-edition-removes-chapters-to-uphold-slavery.html.

Little, Becky. 2018. "Why Bibles Given to Slaves Omitted Most of the Old Testament." History. December 22 [updated April 3, 2019]. https://www.history.com/news/slave-bible-redacted-old-testament.

McKivigan, John R. 1982. "The Gospel Will Burst the Bonds of the Slave: The Abolitionists Bibles for Slaves Campaign." *Negro History Bulletin* 45 (July–August–September): 62–64.

Morrow, Ralph E. 1961. "The Proslavery Argument Revisited." *Mississippi Valley Historical Review* 48 (June): 79–94.

Noll, Mark A. 2006. *The Civil War as a Theological Crisis*. Chapel Hill: University of North Carolina Press.

Pillsbury, Parker. 1883. *Acts of the Anti-Slavery Apostles*. Concord, NH: Clague, Wegman, Schlicht.

Swartley, Willard M. 1983. *Slavery, Sabbath, War and Women: Case Studies in Biblical Interpretation*. Scottdale, PA: Herald Press.

Smith, Joseph

Joseph Smith (1805–1844) is best known as the founder of the Church of Jesus Christ of Latter-Day Saints (LDS), whose members are more commonly known as Mormons. Raised in New York, Smith published the book of Mormon at the age of twenty-four. Expressing veneration for Christian Scriptures, Smith nonetheless believed that they were incomplete and that the revelation he had translated from golden plates of a past civilization of Jews who had settled in America was a necessary supplement to them (Barlow 1989).

He and his group of followers had respectively moved from New York to Kirtland, Ohio, to Jackson County, Missouri, to Commerce, Illinois, which they renamed Nauvoo, and where Smith became the mayor and exercised considerable power in that city. Disappointed by the candidates of the major political parties, Smith sought to get them to give a pledge of protection for LDS members, and when they refused to do so, supporters nominated him for president and he issued a platform outlining his "View of the Powers and Policy of the Government of the United States."

In the opening paragraph, Smith indicated that "my cogitations like Daniel's [the biblical prophet] have for a long time troubled me." Specifically, he believed that the nation was failing to heed the proclamation of equality within the Declaration of Independence. He further cited the biblical principle (in Acts 17:26) that "God hath made of one blood all nations of men, for to dwell on all the face of the earth," and the preamble of the Constitution of the United States.

Smith's platform looked back to American framers, beginning with Benjamin Franklin, and then quoting each of the first seven presidents, with the aim of showing the importance of religious toleration and national unity. In discussing President James Monroe, Smith cited the biblical proverb (from Proverbs 14:34) that "righteousness exalteth a nation, but sin is a reproach to any people."

As Smith viewed the situation, politics had degenerated under Martin Van Buren, and John Tyler. It was time for the people to "turn unto the Lord and live; and reform this nation." He proposed six specific reforms. He favored reducing membership in Congress by about half, with each state retaining its two senators and two members for each million of population. He also largely favored emptying American prisons, replacing incarceration with work requirements and heeding Jesus's injunction to the woman caught in adultery (John 8:11) to "*go thy way and sin no more*." He favored turning prisons into "seminaries of learning, where intelligence, like the angels of heaven, would banish such fragments of barbarism."

Although Smith had disfavored abolitionist calls for immediate emancipation, he favored abolishing slavery by 1850, which he thought could be accomplished by using the sale of western lands to purchase their freedoms. He also favored discontinuing court marshals for men who deserted from the military believing that appeals to their honor would be more effective.

Smith favored reestablishing a national bank with branches within each of the states. Undoubtedly reflecting the persecution that he and his people had suffered, he further favored giving the president "full power to send an army to suppress mobs" with or without gubernatorial permission. He further favored sending those who repented of such rebellions, like the Good Samaritan's "to preach the gospel to the destitute." Smith favored continuing western expansion by giving "the right hand of fellowship" to Texas, Canada, and Mexico to join the Union.

The nation has seen its share of "democratic presidents: whig presidents; [and] a pseudo democratic whig president." It was now time for *"a president of the United States,"* rather than for someone like Nebuchadnezzar who gloried in his own pride. The conclusion of his platform also contained the most allusions to Scripture: "God, who once cleansed the violence of the earth with a flood; whose Son laid down his life for the salvation of all his father gave him out of the world; and who has promised that he will come and purify the world again with fire in the last days, should be supplicated by me for the good of all people. With the highest esteem, I am a friend of virtue, and of the people."

Unfortunately for Smith, he became involved in an attempt to close down a critical newspaper that had resulted in a riot in Carthage, Illinois. Although acquitted of the charge in Nauvoo, he was taken into custody in Carthage, where, after sitting in jail for two days, he was shot and killed by a mob as he tried to escape through a window (Wood 1998, 190). Wood notes that in addition to other deviations from traditional Protestant orthodoxy, Smith's own advocacy of plural marriage had begun to undermine his platform. His followers moved to Utah, where they established their temple but were not admitted to statehood until their leaders renounced polygamy.

Michigan governor George Romney, a Mormon, unsuccessfully sought the Republican nomination for the presidency in 1968. His son, Mitt Romney, a former governor of Massachusetts, won the nomination in 2012 but was defeated by Barack Obama and was subsequently elected by voters from Utah as a U.S. senator.

See also Alternate Scriptures; Church of Jesus Christ of Latter-Day Saints; Declaration of Independence; Polygamy; Slavery

For Reference and Further Reading

Barlow, Philip L. 1989. "Before Mormonism: Joseph Smith's Use of the Bible, 1820–1829." *Journal of the American Academy of Religion.* 57 (Winter): 739–71.

Bushman, Richard Lyman. 2016. "Joseph Smith's Presidential Ambitions." *Mormonism and American Politics*, ed. Randall Balmer and Jana Riess. New York: Columbia University Press, pp. 3–13.

Smith, Joseph. 1844. "Of the Powers and Policy of the Government of the United States." Nauvoo, IL: John Taylor. Accessed at https://www.josephsmithpapers.org/transcript/general-smiths-views-of-the-power-and-policy-of-the-government-of-the-unite-states-7-february-1844?.

Wood, Timothy L. 1998. "The Prophet and the Presidency: Mormonism and Politics in Joseph Smith's 1844 Presidential Campaign." *Journal of the Illinois State Historical Society* 93 (Summer): 167–93.

Smith, Julia E. (Bible Translation)

One of the more obscure translations of the Bible, which was published in 1876, was the first English translation ever to be published by a woman and was motivated by a political dispute involving taxation and woman's suffrage.

The author was Julia Evelina Smith (1792–1886), whose original name was Juliette Abelinda. She was the fourth of five daughters (the others were Hancy Zephina, Cyrinthia Lucretia, Laurilla Aleroya, and Abby Hadassah) of Zephaniah

Holister Smith, a Yale graduate who had begun as a pastor but became an attorney, and Hannah Hadassah Hickok, who was herself quite linguistically gifted. They owned a farm in Glastonbury, Connecticut. Julia had learned French (which she taught for a time), Latin, and Greek and kept a diary in French for more than thirty years (Housley 1988, 558).

Julia appears to have been stimulated to translate the Bible as a result of the prophecies by William Miller (1782–1849) that Jesus would return to earth on October 23, 1843. Seeking to examine Scriptures for herself, she was encouraged to learn Hebrew by Samuel Jarvis, an Episcopal minister from nearby Middletown, Connecticut, who had previously taught at Trinity College and apparently loaned her some books on the subject from his massive library. He had assured her that "it was a simple language, and easily learned, there being but one book in the world, of pure Hebrew, which was the Bible" (Stern 1977, 25), and partly as a result, she never felt it necessary to confer with other students of Hebrew on her translation.

Smith recorded that from 1847 to 1855 she wrote the Bible out five times, "twice from the Greek, twice from the Hebrew, and once from the Latin—the Vulgate" (Stern 1977, 25), initially with little thought of publishing the result. Their village's decision to raise taxes on the sisters' land (all of whom had remained unmarried), which they resisted under the principle of "no taxation without representation," only to have some of their cows and land sold out from under them, led to Julia's decision to print a thousand copies for which she paid a Hartford publisher, the American Publishing Company, $2,500. She made the decision largely in order to demonstrate that women had equal intellectual endowments with men and therefore deserved the right to vote.

The book was titled *The Holy Bible: Containing the Old and New Testaments; Translated Literally from the Original Tongues*. This translation was sometimes somewhat mockingly dubbed the "Alderney Edition" after the Alderney cows on the Smith farm (two of whom were dubbed Taxey and Votey), who played such a role in contemporary journalistic accounts of the work. In 1879, Julia married a retired judge named Amos Andrew Parker of Fitzwilliam, New Hampshire, and continued her advocacy for woman's suffrage.

Smith's attempt to provide a literal word-for-word translation has been critiqued as being so "mechanical" that it resulted in "much nonsense and in some passages almost complete mistranslation" (Metzger 2001, 97) and as being "neither as readable nor as understandable as the King James Version" (Housley 1988, 564). Nonetheless, the Revising Committee of Elizabeth Cady Stanton's feminist *Woman's Bible* used the volume as its own "ultimate authority" (568).

See also King James Version of the Bible; *Woman's Bible* (Stanton)

For Reference and Further Reading

Housley, Kathleen. 1988. "'The Letter Kills but the Spirit Gives Life': Julia Smith's Translation of the Bible." *New England Quarterly* 61 (December): 555–68.

Metzger, Bruce M. 2001. *The Bible in Translation: Ancient and English Versions*. Grand Rapids, MI: Baker Academic.

Stern, Madeleine B. 1977. "The First Feminist Bible: The 'Alderney' Edition, 1876." *Quarterly Journal of the Library of Congress* 34 (January): 23–31.

Snake-Handling

One of the more bizarre manifestations of biblical interpretation is found in the practice, largely limited to southern states, of snake-handling.

The practice is justified by Mark 16:17–18, in which, after delivering the Great Commission to spread the gospel, Jesus says, "In my name shall they cast out devils; they shall speak with new tongues; They shall take up serpents; and if they drink any deadly thing, it shall not hurt them; they shall lay hands on the sick, and they shall recover." Luke 10:19 further quotes Jesus as saying, "I have unto you power to tread on serpents and scorpions, and over all the power of the enemy: and nothing shall by any means hurt you." The large majority of individuals who oppose the practice are likely to see snake-handling as a way of improperly testing God contrary to Matthew 4:7.

Marsha Maguire had traced the history of the practice to influences of "the Holiness, Pentecostal, and Fundamentalist movements" (1981, 168). These movements stressed the value of a "second blessing" in the process of personal sanctification, which was often attested to by speaking in tongues and other perceived manifestations of the Holy Spirit. It should be noted, however, that the practice has received far greater attention than it arguably warranted by the limited extent of its practice. James Hudnut-Beumler observes that although there are about three million Pentecostal believers in tens of thousands of churches throughout the South, "only about forty churches with roughly one thousand total adherents pick up snakes" (2018, 63).

The actual practice of passing out venomous snakes during religious meetings (sometimes also combined with drinking poison) probably dated back to the actions of George Went Hensley, active in both the Holiness and Pentecostal movements, in Sale Creek, Tennessee, in 1909. Another possibility is that it was originated by A. J. Tobbleson in Cherokee, North Carolina, in 1903 (Maguire 1981, 171–72). The practice is seen as a means of obedience to what is perceived to be the teachings of Christ, a test of faith, and a demonstration of God's power.

As might be expected, from time to time, individuals die from this activity, which states have accordingly attempted to regulate. Drawing from the dichotomy between religious belief—which is arguably absolute—and religious practice—which is not—courts have upheld anti-snake-handling laws on the basis of the obvious threat that it may pose. Practitioners believe that their perceived obligation to God is greater than that to the states, and jurors are often disinclined to indict or convict individuals for what they believe is their faith.

See also Criminal Laws

For Reference and Further Reading

Covington, Dennis. 1994. *Salvation on Sand Mountain: Snake Handling and Redemption in Southern Appalachia*. Reading, MA: Addison-Wesley.

Hudnut-Beumler, James. 2018. *Strangers and Friends at the Welcome Table: Contemporary Christianities in the American South*. Chapel Hill: University of North Carolina Press.

La Barre, Weston. 1969. *They Shall Take Up Serpents: Psychology of the Southern Snake-Handling Cult*. New York: Schocken Books.

Maguire, Marsha. 1981. "Confirming the Word: Snake-Handling Sects in Southern Appalachia." *Quarterly Journal of the Library of Congress*. 38 (Summer): 166–79.

Social Gospel

Christians were often at the forefront of such nineteenth-century reform movements as abolitionism, women's rights, prohibition, the fight against white slavery (prostitution), and other causes, many of which merged with causes espoused by the American Progressive movement in the period roughly from 1890 to 1920. Faced with rising immigration, which was often associated with the rise of big-city bosses, and industrialization, in which many workers were exposed to health and safety issues in large factories, Progressives emphasized political and social reform. They were strong advocates of direct democracy as expressed in primary elections, the initiative, the recall, and the referendum as well as in the movement for national alcoholic prohibition. Many were also convinced of the importance of "scientific management" by nonpartisan experts (McDougall 2019, 119).

In 1908, the Methodist Episcopal Church adopted a Social Creed, which enunciated twelve principles that this church, a predecessor to today's United Methodist Church, believed stemmed from their own biblically based principles, although the creed itself did not specifically refer to Scripture, except to say that its principles stemmed from "the Golden Rule and the mind of Christ as the supreme law of society and the sure remedy for all social ills" (1908). Moreover, one of the points, one day free from labor a week for each week, was clearly patterned on one of the Ten Commandments. Later that year, the Federal Council of Churches accepted a somewhat larger version (fourteen points) of this creed. Key provisions included rights to labor arbitration, protection against dangerous factory conditions, abolition of child labor, protections for women laborers, a limitation on working hours, a "living wage," provisions for people in old age, and "the abatement of poverty" (1908).

Although some advocates of the social gospel opposed imperialism, others associated the American colonization in the wake of the Spanish-American War with the spread of Christianity and the Kingdom of God. Josiah Strong (1847–1916) was among those who favored what Walter McDougall has described as "democratic world evangelism" (2019, 122). Pastor L. B. Hartman said that "without the least consciousness of presumption or extravagance we recognize our republic as the politico-religious handmaid of Providence in the aggressive civilization of the world" (McDougall 2019, 123).

Many of the leading advocates of the social gospel movement were postmillennialists who believed that Christian action was the way of bringing God's kingdom to earth. A leading Methodist in this struggle was Harry Ward (1873–1966), who embraced Christian socialism and was ambiguous about whether this could be brought about short of violent revolution (Rossinow 2005). Walter Rauschenbusch (1861–1918), a Baptist pastor who authored *Christianity and the Social Crisis* and *A Theology for the Social Gospel* in 1917, was a leading spokesman for the movement and may have put greater emphasis on the need for personal, as well as social, regeneration than is generally recognized (Bowman 2007). Norman Thomas (1884–1968), who would later become a socialist and carry its banner in a number of presidential elections, was deeply influenced by the social gospel movement during his days at Union Theological Seminary

(Duram 1974). In time, the outbreak of World War I in 1914 and the Bolshevik Revolution in Russia in 1917 led to increased skepticism about the capacity of religious groups to bring about such social changes.

Moreover, more conservative Protestants began to question the biblical foundations of the social gospel movement. A number of Presbyterian denominations thus issued a "United Declaration of Christian Faith and Social Service" in 1914, which put far less faith in human progress and greater emphasis on traditional views of the fall of man and the need for individual repentance (Smith 1992, 97). Professor William B. Greene Jr. (1854–1928) of Princeton Theological Seminary thus said that the church needed to pay less attention to Jesus as a social reformer and more on his role in atoning for sin and redeeming individuals from it (99). Greene authored an article, "The Bible as the Textbook in Sociology," to the *Princeton Theological Review* of 1914, in which he argued that "the Bible was as 'truly the authority in sociology' as it was in 'dogmatics and ethics'" (103). In time, Reinhold Neibuhr criticized the movement for being over optimistic about human nature and human behavior (Currie 2004, 14–15).

Although the Progressive movement passed, many of its proposals were incorporated into Franklin D. Roosevelt's New Deal programs. Theological conservatives still tend to favor private action over governmental mandates (sometimes accepting governmental support of such private initiatives) and are more likely to seek reforms through laissez-faire economics than through more socialistic approaches.

See also Roosevelt, Franklin D.; Salvation Army

For Reference and Further Reading

Bowman, Matthew. 2007. "Sin, Spirituality, and Primitivism: The Theologies of the American Social Gospel, 1885–1917." *Religion and American Culture: A Journal of Interpretation* 17 (Winter): 95–126.

Currie, Chuck. 2004. "Walter Rauschenbusch and the Social Gospel." *Theologians* (Fall): 1–22. https://chuckcurrie.blogs.com/chuck_currie/files/walter_rauschenbusch_and_the_social_gospel.pdf.

Duram, James C. 1974. "In Defense of Conscience: Norman Thomas as an Exponent of Christian Pacifism during World War I." *Journal of Presbyterian History* 52 (Spring): 19–32.

McDougall, Walter A. 2019. *The Tragedy of U.S. Foreign Policy: How America's Civil Religion Betrayed the National Interest*. New Haven, CT: Yale University Press.

Methodist Episcopal Church. 1908. "The 1908 Social Creed of the Methodist Episcopal Church." Church & Society. https://www.umcjustice.org/who-we-are/social-principles-and-resolutions/the-1908-social-creed-of-the-methodist-episcopal-church.

National Council of Churches. 1908. "The Social Creed of the Churches." December 4. https://nationalcouncilofchurches.us/common-witness/1908/social-creed.php.

Rauschenbusch, Walter. 1907. *Christianity and the Social Crisis*. New York: Hodder & Stoughton.

Rossinow, Doug. 2005. "The Radicalization of the Social Gospel: Harry F. Ward and the Search for a New Social Order, 1898–1936." *Religion and American Culture: A Journal of Interpretation* 15 (Winter): 63–106.

Smith, Gary Scott. 1992. "Conservative Presbyterians: The Gospel, Social Reform, and the Church in the Progressive Ear." *American Presbyterians* 70 (Summer): 93–110.

Sojourner Truth

Born into slavery in New York, Isabella Baumfree (1797–1883) learned the fundamentals of Christianity from her mother, including the Lord's Prayer and the importance of forgiveness. After Baumfree escaped from slavery (after which a couple bought her freedom), she changed her name to Sojourner Truth, a testimony to the lingering influence of Christianity in her life and her own conversion.

Never learning to read, Sojourner had to pick up what she learned from the Bible from readings and expositions of others. For a time, she joined a group led by Elijah Pierson (1786–1834), who called himself Elijah the Tisbite, and Robert Matthew (1778–1841), who called himself Matthias (Krass 1988, 49–55). The group was involved in controversy, and she left it, albeit not before being called a witch, for which she was able to win a libel judgment.

A tall and well-built woman who had done field work, Sojourner became a powerful speaker on behalf of both abolitionism and women's rights who dictated her own narrative, which she sold to meet her expenses. None of her speeches is better known that the speech she gave at a women's rights convention at the Old Stone Church in Akron, Ohio, entitled "Ain't I a Woman." It was not, however, published until 1863, and can thus be found in a number of versions.

Most versions of the speech indicate that Truth's presence was not altogether welcome at the convention, in which men had largely dominated. One pastor had apparently sought to prove women's physical delicacy by describing how men helped them into carriages. To this, she reputedly replied in her speech, "Nobody every helps me into carriages, or over mud-puddles, or gives me any best place! And ain't I a woman?" She further told of raising children who were sold to other masters and crying where "none but Jesus heard me."

As to claims that African Americans and women might not have the same intellectual capacities as men, she asked, "What's that got to do with women's rights or negroes' rights? If my cup won't hold but a pint, and yours holds a quart, wouldn't you be mean not to let me have my little half measure full?"

As to arguments that clergymen had based on the fact that Jesus had been a man, she responded, "Where did your Christ come from? Where did your Christ come from? From God and a woman! Man had nothing to do with Him."

Further turning the tables on those who used the book of Genesis to blame women for the introduction of sin into the world, Truth observed, "If the first woman God ever made was strong enough to turn the world upside down all alone, these women together ought to be able to turn it back, and get it right side up again. And now they is asking to do it, the men better let them."

In many ways, Truth's interpretations of Scripture resembled those of Elizabeth Cady Stanton, who would publish the *Woman's Bible*.

See also Slavery; *Woman's Bible* (Stanton)

For Reference and Further Reading

Krass, Peter. 1988. *Sojourner Truth*. New York: Chelsea House.

Truth, Sojourner. [1851]. "Sojourner Truth: Ain't I a Woman." National Park Service. https://www.nps.gov/articles/sojourner-truth.htm.

Washington, Margaret. 2009. *Sojourner Truth's America*. Urbana: University of Illinois Press.

Space Program

The U.S. space program remains, to this date, the only one that has successfully launched men to the moon and brought them back again. Throughout its history, the National Aeronautics and Space Administration (NASA) program has depended upon public support and congressional funding. In the course of its history, NASA has variously appealed to nationalism, to romanticism, and to pragmatism in touting its programs (Byrnes 1994, 3). All of these aims might be further tied to the idea that America has a manifest destiny not only in the Western hemisphere but also in the heavens themselves; the names for various space endeavors, Mercury, Gemini, and Apollo, although they were not biblical, were references to ancient gods. Professor Charles Wilson has suggested that "the new American mission was scientific, and the world still looked up, not at a city on a hill, but at an American on the moon" (Wilson 1984, 312).

There was an important Cold War dimension to the American space program, which was designed to show the superiority of American science and ingenuity over that of the Soviet Union, which was a communistic atheistic power. Moreover, long after most theologians had denied "the special reality of heaven," Soviet cosmonauts had gleefully reported that in their own orbits in space they neither encountered God nor angels (Oliver 2013, 118), while some religious leaders had warned of the dangers of human pride in science, which they sometimes associated with the Tower of Babel, with the fate of Nebuchadnezzar, and with hubris (118). Although Billy Graham chided Nixon for omitting Christ's abode on earth, President Richard M. Nixon heralded the flight of Apollo 11 by observing that "this is the greatest week in the history of the world since the Creation" (quoted in Wilson 1984, 215).

The very idea of space evokes the idea of the heavens, which are traditionally understood to be the abode of God. There is, however, widespread belief in the idea that science and religion might be rival, as opposed to complementary, ways of understanding the world. Some considered it unnecessary to invest money in a program designed in part to explain the origins of the universe, which many thought was already adequately expressed in Scripture. From a more liberal, or prophetic, theological perspective, some critics suggested that it would be more productive to invest the money that went into the space program into social programs (Wilson 1984, 211). After men landed on the moon, it was common for politicians to claim that if the nation could do that, it could launch other successful social endeavors like conquering poverty or hunger. By contrast, German-born Wernher Von Braun (1912–1977), who supervised American missile research, often tied the space program to the exploration of God's universe, and even suggested that God may have sent his Son to other worlds in the universe to proclaim the good news of the gospel to them (Wilson 1984, 217).

Perhaps as a way of muting criticism by some clerics that it was inappropriate to be launching a space flight during the Christmas holiday, the crew of Apollo 8, which was tasked with the first manned orbital trip around the moon, not only attended church on the Sunday before their launch but also read from the creation story in the King James Version of Genesis 1:1–10 as the nation watched with an image of earth as viewed from space in the background. The reading, which took place on Christmas Eve of 1968, was begun by Bill Anders, a Catholic, and followed by readings from James Lovell and Commander Frank Borman, the latter of whom was a lay reader in the Episcopal Church (Wilson 1984, 220). Despite protests from Madalyn Murray O'Hair, who objected on behalf of atheists and members of non-Christian faiths, the readings sparked more than eight million letters and petitions from citizens arguing for the right of religious free exercise in space (Oliver 2013, 117) and brought high praise from religious leaders as diverse as Billy Graham, the New York Board of Rabbis, and Pope Paul VI (Wilson 1984, 220–21). A U.S. commemorative stamp of the Apollo 8 flight subsequently pictured the earth as viewed from the moon with the caption against the heavens, "In the beginning God . . ."

In July 11, 1969, Apollo 11 reached the moon. Astronauts were wearing a patch of an eagle with an olive branch in its mouth, a symbol originating in the branch that a dove brought to Noah's Ark after the great flood as described in Genesis 8:11 (Wilson 1984, 222). Presbyterian elder Edwin "Buzz" Aldrin celebrated communion aboard the spacecraft and recalled the words of Psalm 8:3–4: "When I consider the heavens, the works of Thy fingers, the moon and the stars which Thou hast ordained, what is man that Thou are mindful of him?" (Wilson 1984, 224). As he watched the Apollo 11 landing, Pope Paul VI responded, "Glory to God in the highest and peace on earth to men of good will. We, humble representatives of that Christ, who, coming among us from the abyss of divinity, has made to resound in the heavens this blessed void, today we make an echo, repeating it in celebration on the part of the whole terrestrial globe, with no more unsurpassable bounds of human existence, but openness to this expanse of endless space and a new destiny" (Wilson 1984, 224).

Although the astronauts planted an American flag on the moon, they had come not only as representatives of America but as representatives of the human race.

When the space shuttle *Challenger* exploded in 1986, killing all seven members of the crew, President Ronald Reagan delivered one of his most memorable speeches. He ended by noting their final goodbyes and quoted John Gillespie Magee Jr.'s poem "High Flight" in observing that they had "'slipped the surly bonds of earth' to 'touch the face of God'" (Reagan 1986).

See also Manifest Destiny

For Reference and Further Reading

Byrnes, Mark E. 1994. *Politics and Space: Image Making by NASA*. Westport, CT: Praeger.

Oliver, Kendrick. 2013. "The Apollo 8 Genesis Reading and Religion in the Space Age." *Astropolitics: The International Journal of Space Politics & Policy*. 11(1–2): 116–21.

Reagan, Ronald. 1986. "President Reagan's Remarks Following the Loss of the Space Shuttle Challenger and Her Crew." NASA. January 28. https://www.nasa.gov/audience/formedia/speeches/reagan_challenger.html.

Wilson, Charles Reagan. 1984. "American Heavens: Apollo and the Civil Religion." *Journal of Church and State* 26 (Spring): 209–26.

Stephens, Alexander H.

Alexander H. Stephens (1812–1883), a lawyer who had served both as a member of Georgia state legislature and of the U.S. House of Representatives, was the vice president of the Confederate States of America. In this capacity, he gave a speech in which he unequivocally counterpoised the philosophy of this new government, and its constitution, with the philosophy that Thomas Jefferson had articulated in the Declaration of Independence, where he and the Second Continental Congress had claimed that "all men are created equal."

Stephens's Cornerstone speech rested firmly upon a central biblical analogy and was supported by a number of others. In Matthew 7:24–27, Jesus had told the story of two men, one wise and one foolish. The first, who was wise, built his house upon the firm foundation of a rock that was able to withstand the rain, the flood, and the wind. The second, who was foolish, built his house on the sand, and it was destroyed.

Stephens identified the unstable sand upon which the northern Union was built as the principle of "the equality of races." By contrast, "our new government is founded upon exactly the opposite idea; its foundations are laid, its corner-stone rests, upon the great truth that the negro is not equal to the white man; that slavery—subordination to the superior race—is his natural and normal condition" (Stephens 1861). Stephens specifically linked this principle to that of Creation. Because God had created races unequal, no government could prosper that was built on the principle of treating them as equals. Stephens distinguished the enslaving of inferior races to "serfdom of certain classes of the same race," which he acknowledged to be "in violation of the laws of nature." Although he did not cite chapter and verse, Stephens rested his belief on African American inequality on "the curse against Canaan." Drawing from 1 Corinthians 15:39–41, he also observed that "for His own purposes, He has made one race to differ from another, as He has made 'one star to differ from another star in glory.'"

Noting that the Confederacy was founded on racial inequality, he went on to describe this principle as its very cornerstone. In what is often considered to be a prophecy of the Messiah, Psalm 118:22 had said that "the stone which the builders rejected has become the chief cornerstone." In apparent reference to himself, Jesus had further cited this psalm in Matthew 21:42. When, however, Stephens said that "this stone which was rejected by the first builders 'is become the chief of the corner' the real 'corner-stone' in our new edifice," he was referring not to the Messiah but to the principle of racial inequality, which he associated with "the eternal principles of truth."

Stephens further regarded the South's mission as that of Christianizing and civilizing slaves: "We hear much of the civilization and Christianization of the barbarous tribes of Africa. In my judgment, those ends will never be attained, but by first teaching them the lesson taught to Adam [Genesis 3:19], that 'in the sweat of his brow he should eat his bread,' and teaching them to work, and feed, and clothe themselves."

Henry Ward Beecher (1813–1887), one of the nation's best-known preachers who believed strongly in the legal equality of all men, pointed to the audacity of this statement when, after quoting Stephens's proclamation that slavery was to be the chief cornerstone of the Confederacy, Beecher observed,

> These words, you will remember, were spoken of the Lord Jesus Christ, when he was set at naught and rejected by the Jews, his countrymen; and this Vice-President of the so- called Confederate States of America does not hesitate to declare that slavery stands, in their new system, in the place that the Lord Jesus Christ holds in the Christian system! It is the soul and centre of it. It is the foundation and corner-stone. (Beecher 1863, 179).

Beecher further cited a southern clergyman, Dr. Smyth (probably Thomas Smyth), as referring to "that *Atheistic Red Republican doctrine of the Declaration of Independence!*" (179).

The eventual outcome of the Civil War suggested that it was ultimately the Confederacy rather than the Union that was built upon the sand and that the rock of American republicanism remained the principles of the Declaration of Independence, which would be further incorporated in the Constitution in the equal protection clause of the Fourteenth Amendment, which was ratified in 1868. As for Stephens, he served during the last year of his life as governor of a post-Reconstruction Georgia.

See also Confederate States of America; Declaration of Independence; Segregation and Anti-miscegenation Laws; Slavery

For Reference and Further Reading

Beecher, Henry Ward. 1863. *Freedom and War. Discourses on Topics Suggested by the Times*. Boston: Ticknor and Fields.

Stephens, Alexander H. March 21, 1861. "Cornerstone Speech." American Rhetoric Online Speech Bank. https://americanrhetoric.com/speeches/alexanderstephenscornerstone.htm.

Stewart, Maria W.

Maria W. Stewart (1803–1879) is believed to be the first African American woman to give a political speech to an audience consisting of both men and women. Born in Hartford, Connecticut, as a free woman, Stewart became a servant to a minister's family when her parents died when she was five. She later partly made up for a lack of formal education by attending Sabbath school. In 1826, she married James W. Stewart, a shipping agent in Boston who had served in the War of 1812, but he died in 1829, and she appears to have been cheated, as many African Americans were at the time, out of her property, though in time she was able to collect a pension because of her husband's military service.

In 1830, Stewart had a conversion experience, and in 1831 she was baptized. She began her own speaking career shortly after the death of the provocative abolitionist David Walker, whom she believed might have been poisoned, but whom she much admired and may have sought to emulate.

Although she rarely appears to have cited chapters and verses, Stewart's speeches were infused with Scriptures. Even editions of her work that include citations often miss many of her references, which are often combined with references to American ideals as expressed in the Declaration of Independence and other republican documents (Cooper 2011, 96).

On October 8, 1831, Stewart published an essay entitled "Religion and the Pure Principles of Morality, the Sure Foundation on Which We Must Build" in the abolitionist publication *The Liberator*, edited by William Lloyd Garrison, with whom she was friends. Providing minimal details about her own life and conversion, Stewart expressed her desire to sacrifice her life if necessary to proclaim God's message. Exhorting fellow African Americans to speak out, she observed, "This is the land of freedom. The press is at liberty. Every man has a right to express his opinion" (Stewart 1987, 29). Moreover, God had fashioned all human beings "in his own glorious image, and hath bestowed upon you reason and strong powers of intellect" while the Constitution had "made all men free and equal" (29).

One of Stewart's favorite biblical books was that of Jeremiah, the weeping prophet, whose name has become synonymous with speeches designed to point out people's sins and call them to repentance, in hopes of receiving God's renewed favor. The jeremiad was a form at which Stewart excelled. Citing Jeremiah 9:1, Stewart exclaimed, "O that my head were waters, and mine eyes a fountain of tears that I might weep day and night for the transgressions of the daughters of my people" (30). Her call was for fellow African Americans to burst "the chains of slavery and ignorance" and "become united as one, and cultivate among ourselves the pure principles of piety, morality and virtue" (30). She accused her audience of moral indifference and of "following the vain bubbles of life" rather than godliness (32). Quoting Proverbs 14:34, she further noted that "righteousness exalteth a nation, but sin is a reproach to any people" (35). If whites were unwilling to provide suitable schools, then African Americans should build their own, an education that should include women whose "minds and talents" have heretofore been buried "beneath a load of iron pots and kettles" (38). White Americans had advanced through "head-work," and it was time for African Americans to do the same (38).

Just as white Americans had declared their independence from British oppression, so too should African Americans: "why should man any longer deprive his fellow-man of equal rights and privileges? Oh, the cloud that hangs over thee, for thy cruel wrongs and injuries to the fallen sons of Africa. The blood of her murdered ones cries to heaven for vengeance against thee [a reference to the blood of Abel crying out against Cain in Genesis 4]" (39). It was time for African Americans, many of whom had white blood in their veins, to proclaim the same love of liberty as the children of Israel and as earlier American revolutionaries. Announcing that 'WE CLAIM OUR RIGHTS," Stewart nonetheless veered from calling for direct violence, using an allusion to Jesus's parable of Lazarus and the rich man, as well as Paul's admonition in Romans 12:19 that "vengeance is Mine, I will repay, saith the Lord," to suggest that God would take up the cause of a people who stood up for themselves (40).

Stewart further explained her call in a lecture that she delivered at Franklin Hall in Boston on September 21, 1832. Beginning with the words uttered by four lepers outside the gates of a city in 2 Kings 7:3, "Why sit ye here and die?" she said that she heard a void asking, "Who shall go forward, and take off the reproach that is cast upon the people of color? Shall it be a woman?" Her answer was, "If it is thy will, be it even so, Lord Jesus!" (45). She addressed her remarks, however, not to southern slaves but to northern freemen.

Arguing that it was difficult for those in slavery to lift themselves from ignorance and bondage, she observed that they nonetheless possessed soul with high aspirations, and although it might cost her to proclaim this news "I am a true born American; your blood flows in my veins, and your spirit fires my breast" (46). Citing one of her favorite verses, Psalm 68:31, Stewart observed "that Ethiopia shall stretch forth her hands unto God," but that this would be better facilitated if whites intent on recolonizing blacks, whom they considered to be lazy, to Africa would instead help educate them (47). She likened the need for African Americans to elevate themselves to the decision of Pilgrims and later American Patriots to seek freedom from Great Britain (49).

In another address before the African American Female Intelligence Society of America, Stewart resumed the jeremiad motif to compare the wickedness of Americans to that of Sodom and Gomorrah (51) while linking "the cause of God" and "the cause of freedom" (52). She charged that Native Americans had been more united than African Americans and particularly called for fellow women to join the cause.

In another address, which Stewart delivered at the African Masonic Hall on February 27, 1833, she began by stating that "African rights and liberty is a subject that ought to fire the breast of every free man of color in these United States, and excite in his bosom a lively, deep, decided and heart-felt interest" (56). Without specifying what the sins were, she said that despite Africa's former glories, God had brought judgment upon her people, that only renewed piety and efforts could restore the former glory. She was particularly critical of fellow African Americans who spent their time in gambling and dancing rather than fighting "for the cause of God and the rights of men" (60). To this end, she advocated for temperance societies, for the creation of educational institutions, and for the abolishment of slavery in the District of Columbia. Using imagery from the book of Revelation, Stewart proclaimed that "like the great city of Babylon," America had become "a seller of slaves and the souls of men" who "has made the Africans drunk with the wine of her fornication" (63), and they needed to respond appropriately.

In a farewell address to her friends in Boston on September 21, 1833, before leaving for New York, Stewart seemed to anticipate Sojourner Truth's greatest speech when Stewart asked, "What if I am a woman; is not the God of ancient times the God of these modern days?" (68). She cited the biblical examples of Deborah, Esther, and Mary Magdalene to counter Paul's teaching that called for women to be submissive (68). Pointing to the need for women to rise up, she observed that "it is not the color of the skin that makes the man or the woman, but the principle formed in the soul" (70). It was time for others to apply themselves to virtuous accomplishment of the tasks at hand, which even if not fully accomplished in this life, would lead to eternal rewards.

See also Abolitionists; Declaration of Independence; Prophets and Jeremiads; Slavery; Sojourner Truth; Walker, David

For Reference and Further Reading

Bassard, Katherine Clay. 2010. *Transforming Scriptures: African American Women Writers and the Bible*. Athens: University of Georgia Press.

Cooper, Valerie C. 2011. *Word, Like Fire: Maria Stewart, the Bible, and the Rights of African Americans*. Charlottesville: University of Virginia Press.

Pelletier, Kevin. *Apocalyptic Sentimentalism: Love and Fear in U.S. Antebellum Literature*. Athens: University of Georgia Press.

Stewart, Maria W. 1987. *Maria W. Stewart, America's First Black Woman Political Writer: Essays and Speeches*, ed. and introduced by Marilyn Richardson. Bloomington: Indiana University Press.

Stiles, Ezra

Sermons delivered after the election of governors and other officials were standard fare throughout colonial and early U.S. history. One of the better known of these was delivered by Ezra Stiles (1727–1795) in 1783 on the reelection of Governor Jonathan Trumbull. Stiles was a long-time pastor of Newport, Rhode Island; a friend of Benjamin Franklin; the recipient of a Doctor of Divinity degree from the University of Edinburgh; the president of Yale University; and a scholar who had mastered Hebrew (Chiel 1971).

The date of the sermon is important because it marks the year that the United States signed the Treaty of Paris, formally ending the Revolutionary War when the nation was still governed by the Articles of Confederation, which had vested primary sovereignty within the states. America's victory in the war appeared to be a mark of divine favor that marked the nation out for a still greater future. Stiles appeared to transfer many of the hopes that the Pilgrim colonists had brought with them to the nation as a whole, believing that the spread of liberty might even facilitate the eventual millennial reign of Christ on earth.

Stiles chose as his text Deuteronomy 26:19: "And to make thee high above all nations, which he hath made in praise, and in name, and in honor; and that you mayest be an holy people unto the Lord thy God." Stiles identified his topic as that of "the political welfare of God's American Israel; and as allusively prophetic of the future prosperity and splendor of the United States" (1783, 7). Stiles attempted first to explain why the United States might come to fulfill this role, and how such rule would be imperfect without "the diffusion of virtue among the people" (7).

Believing that "dominion is founded in property," Stiles lauded the American distribution of property, which led to industry. Perhaps drawing from the English philosopher John Locke (1632–1704), Stiles pointed out that European settlers were making much better use of the land than had Native American Indians, increasing its value from ten- to a thousandfold (8–9). Largely believing Native American numbers on the continent to be small, Stiles considered the land to be open "for the reception of a new enlargement of Japhet" (9), a reference to one of the sons of Noah who was widely believed to be the progenitors of Europeans. In another rhetorical move that would have justified war against Native Americans (and that might foreshadow later revelations to Joseph Smith), Stiles observed that "I rather consider the American *Indians* as *Canaanites* of the expulsion of

Joshua"—indeed Stiles pursues the tangent that Native Americans came from Asia, whose progenitors may have been the Canaanites (10). One cause for Stile's optimism over the eventual triumph of the sons of Japhet was his belief that "the Indians, as well as the million Africans in America, are decreasing as rapidly," which seemed to portent the eventual end of slavery (14).

People require civil government, and the republican government of America, which provided both civil and religious freedom, was superior to others. Stiles believed that this republic was actually a "DEMOCRATICAL ARISTOCRACY, standing upon the annual elections of the people, and revocable at pleasure" (21). Much as James Madison would later argue in Federalist No. 10, Stiles argued that the people originate power, there are too many of them to assemble together, so they "represent themselves by delegation" (21). He further lauded such state constitutional provisions as bicameralism, including provision of a Senate, annual elections, and, in a reference to the Articles of Confederation, "the *amphictyonhic council* of the GNERAL CONGRESS" (23).

With relatively little reference to Scripture, Stiles went on to laud the union symbolized by the U.S. flag, the system of "LAW AND JURISPRUDENCE founded in *justice*, equity, and public right," independent judges, and taxation with representation (24–25). Perhaps with an eye to Congressional weakness in this area, he also pointed to the need for more widespread commerce. He also advocated continuation of American militia and constant "vigilance against corruption" (33), a theme that republicans often shared with Christians. Stiles also advocated the cultivation of education, favoring a system where "all should be taught to read the scriptures" and where libraries and colleges would flourish (34).

Believing that the American vine (a symbol that was often used in the Old Testament to refer to Israel) would likely continue to flourish, Stiles observed that "liberty, civil and religious, has sweet and attractive charms. The enjoyment of this, with property, has filled the English settlers in America with a most amazing spirit, which has operated, and still will operate with great energy" (35).

Just as Israel had seen signs of God's providence, so too "we live in an age of wonders: we have lived an age in a few years: we have seen more wonders accomplished in *eight* years, than are usually unfolded in a century" (36). Somewhat departing from more common descriptions of George Washington as a Moses, Stiles referred to him as "this American JOSHUA" (37, see also p. 42 for even more effusive praise) whose military victories confirmed God's favor upon him and the nation. Stiles went on to extol other Founding Fathers, correctly identifying Thomas Jefferson as the chief author of the Declaration of Independence (46).

Utilizing a further biblical analogy, Stiles likened Great Britain to Rehoboam, the son of Solomon who treated his people harshly and lost ten tribes (49). God was likely working through the land to spread "American ideas of toleration and religious liberty" (52) especially through the dissemination of the King James Bible. Noting that it had not been altered in 180 years, he observed that "it may have been designed by providence for the future perusal of more millions of the human race than ever were able to read one book, and for their use to the millennial ages" (52).

Lauding religious diversity in a way that his Puritan forbears could not likely have imagined, Stiles celebrated the way that Congregationalists, Presbyterians, and other denominations lived in "friendly cohabitation," likening America to the biblical Joseph whose own betrayal into the hands of the Egyptians eventually brought blessings to his people (55). He speculated that it might be up to America to "restore the church to its primitive purity" (56). If so, this would fulfill a number of biblical prophecies that Stiles linked to "the annihilation of the pontificate, the reassembling of the jews, and the fulness of the gentiles" (56). Using another analogy that others before him had used of a woman who fled into the wilderness from a dragon as described in Revelation 12, Stiles observed, "It may have been of the Lord, that Christianity is to be found in such great purity, in this church exiled into the wilderness of America: and that its purest body should be evidently advancing forward, by an augmented natural increase and spiritual edification, into a singular superiority—with the ultimate subserviency to the glory of God in converting the world" (57). Noting his own concern over "our laodiceanism [lukewarmness found in one of the churches to which the book of Revelation was directed], deficient morals and incidental errors," Stiles still speculated that "the *collective system of evangelical doctrines*, the *instituted ordinances*, and the true ecclesiastical polity [which he especially associated with the Presbyterian and congregational churches], may be found here in a great degree of purity" (58).

Further defending American churches against charges that their pastors were not part of the apostolic line of ordination, Stiles said that he expected great things to be accomplished in the next seven or eight hundred years that he anticipated prior to Christ's earthly millennial reign after "filling the whole earth with the knowledge of the glory of the Lord" (68). Returning to his key text, he observed that "thus the American republic, by illuminating the world with TRUTH and LIBERTY, would be exalted and made high among the nations in praise, and in name, and in honor" (69).

For this to happen, Americans must show themselves to "be an holy people unto the Lord thy God." He went on to argue that holy Christian statesmen would (like the biblical Daniel) be better public servants than Deists or atheists. The best republic would be a "Christian republic" (79), because Christian virtues, being outlined in revelation, are superior to those attained through mere reason (80). In his penultimate paragraph, he concluded that "the United States are under peculiar obligations to become a holy people unto the Lord our God, on account of the late eminent deliverance, salvation, peace, and glory, with which he hath now crowned our new sovereignty" (87).

See also Articles of Confederation; Curses on Cain, Ham, and the Canaanites; Election Day Sermons; Puritans

For Reference and Further Reading

Chiel, Arthur A. 1971. "Ezra Stiles—the Education of an 'Hebrician.'" *American Jewish Historical Quarterly* 60 (March): 235–41.

Stiles, Ezra. 1783. The United States Elevated to Glory and Honor, ed. Reiner Smolinski. DigitalCommons@University of Nebraska-Lincoln. http://digitalcommons.unl.edu/etas/41.

Stone v. Graham (1980)

In *Stone v. Graham*, the U.S. Supreme Court issued a per curiam opinion (unsigned opinion on behalf of the majority) in which it struck down a Kentucky law that had required the posting of the Ten Commandments in each public school classroom in the state as violating the First and Fourteenth Amendments to the U.S. Constitution. Each posting was to be 16 inches wide and 20 inches long and was to be financed by private funding. Each required a notation that said, "The secular application of the Ten Commandments is clearly seen in its adoption as the fundamental legal code of Western Civilization and the Common Law of the United States" (*Stone v. Graham* 1980, 40, n. 1). A state trial court found that the law thus had a secular legislative purpose, a finding that an equally divided Kentucky Supreme Court had affirmed.

In striking down the law, the U.S. Supreme Court evoked the so-called Lemon Test, from *Lemon v. Kurtzman* (1971), requiring a "secular legislative purpose," a "principal or primary effect . . . that neither advances nor inhibits religion," and a prohibition against "an excessive government entanglement with religion" (*Stone v. Graham* 1980, 40). In this case, the court decided that the law failed the first prong of the test calling for a secular legislative purpose. Acknowledging that the notation that the court required presented an "avowed" secular purpose, the court indicated that its decision in *Abington v. Schempp* (1963) had rejected a similar avowed purpose for devotional Bible readings in school, and that "the pre-eminent purpose for posting the Ten Commandments on schoolroom walls is plainly religious in nature" (41). Quoting both from Exodus 20 and Deuteronomy 5, the court observed that "the Commandments do not confine themselves to arguably secular matters, such as honoring one's parents, killing or murder, adultery, stealing, false witness, and covetousness," but that "the first part of the Commandments concerns the religious duties of believers; worshipping the Lord God alone, avoiding idolatry, not using the Lord's name in vain, and observing the Sabbath Day" (42). The majority further noted that this was not an example, permitted in *Abington v. Schempp*, in which "the Bible may constitutionally be used in an appropriate study of history, civilization, ethics, comparative religion, or the like," but that if the posting were to have any effect, "it will be to induce the schoolchildren to read, meditate upon, perhaps to venerate and obey, the Commandments" (42). Although this might be desirable "as a matter of private devotion, it is not a permissible state objective under the Establishment Clause" (42). Moreover, although the displays were to be privately financed, "the mere posting of the copies under the auspices of the legislature provides the 'official support of the State'" (42). The First Amendment prohibits even "relative minor encroachments on the First Amendment" (42).

Chief Justice Warren Burger and Justice Harry Blackmun would have preferred to give the case fuller consideration. Justice Potter Stewart wrote a one-sentence dissent, while Justice William Rehnquist wrote a more extensive one. Rehnquist relied on the judgment both of the state legislature and of the lower courts that the law had a clear secular purpose, and observed, "The fact that the asserted secular purpose may overlap with what some may see as a religious objective does not render it unconstitutional" (44). Rehnquist would accept the legislative judgment that the Ten Commandments "had a significant impact on the development of secular legal codes of the Western World" (45). He observed that "the Establishment Clause does not require that the public sector be insulated from all things which may have a religious significance or origin," especially given that "religion has been closely identified with our history and government" (45–46).

Although the court did not focus on the point, the fact that Kentucky had chosen to post the Commandments in public schools, where the audience would likely be more impressionable, as well as future cases such as *Van Orden v. Perry* (2005), suggests that this case may or may not apply to monuments to the Ten Commandments in public settings. In *McCreary v. American Civil Liberties Union* (2005), however, the U.S. Supreme Court upheld a preliminary injunction against attempts to post the Ten Commandments in Kentucky courthouses along with other secular documents in part because it believed that two previous attempts, the first of which would have posted the Ten Commandments alone, violated the First Amendment because they were motivated by a religious rather than a secular legislative purpose.

See also Abington v. Schempp (1963); Ten Commandments; *Van Orden v. Perry* (2005)

For Reference and Further Reading

Abington v. Schempp, 374 U.S. 203 (1963).
Bartlett, Gregory M. 2003. "Displaying the Ten Commandments on Public Property: The Kentucky Experience: Wasn't It Written in Stone?" *Northern Kentucky Law Review* 30: 163–87.
Lemon v. Kurtzman, 403 U.S. 602 (1971).
McCreary County v. American Civil Liberties Union, 545 U.S. 844 (2005).
Stone v. Graham, 449 U.S. 39 (1980).
Van Orden v. Perry, 545 U.S. 677 (2005).

Stowe, Harriett Beecher

Harriet Beecher Stowe (1811–1989) was the daughter of Lyman Beecher, one of the most influential Calvinist ministers of the day. She was also the sister of Henry Ward Beecher and other male siblings who were also influential preachers.

A graduate of the Hartford Female Seminary, Stowe moved to Ohio when her father became president of Lane Theological Seminary, and she married Calvin Ellis Stowe, who was a professor there. Although it was not her first literary endeavor, Stowe is best known for authoring *Uncle Tom's Cabin: Life among the Lowly*, a novel originally serialized in *The National Era* newspaper from 1851 to 1852. It described the horrors of slavery and took particular aim at the evils of the fugitive slave law, which she believed conflicted with higher law and thus a subject for legitimate civil disobedience.

At a time when denominations and regions were split over the morality of slavery and its compatibility with the Bible, Stowe, probably influenced by the loss of one of her own children to cholera and a vision of a dying slave that she experienced during a church service, moved discourse from a discussion of biblical texts to sympathetic portrayals of the effect that the institution was having on family life. The novel was soaked in biblical references and biblical imagery. At one point, a slave named George responds to someone who tells him that he had the same obligation to return to his master as the biblical Hagar had to return to Abraham and Onesimus to Philemon by saying, "To quote Bible to a fellow in my circumstances, is enough to make him give it up altogether. I appeal to God Almighty;—I'm willing to go with the case to Him, and ask Him if I do wrong to seek my freedom" (Smylie 1995, 169). At another time, one of her characters quotes Psalm 73 for the proposition that the wicked sometimes prosper while the righteous suffer.

The subtitle of Stowe's novel was designed to highlight Jesus's words in Matthew 25:31–46 about his identification with the oppressed (Smylie 1995, 167). She highlights this theme when one of the figures in the novel, Senator John Bird, decides to help a fugitive slave contrary to a law that he had himself sponsored. In similar fashion, Stowe highlighted Jesus's teaching about giving a cup of cold water in Mark 9:41 and Matthew 10:42.

Although Stowe was familiar with the higher criticism of biblical texts (Smith 2018), her novel showed the influence of Romanticism and Wesleyan perfectionism (Hill n.d.) and emphasized a childlike reading of Scripture consistent with Jesus's blessing of children in Mark 10:13 (Smylie 1995, 170). At another point, she cited Ecclesiastes 4:1–2 in describing the horrors of the slave plantation.

Stowe describes Tom, the hero of the novel, who is beaten to death by his master, like Jesus, as a man of sorrows whose dying words assert with Romans 8:28 that even death cannot separate him from God's love. At another point, when a master frees his slaves, they respond by singing a Methodist hymn, "The Year of Jubilee Is Come," which refers to the fiftieth year described in the Old Testament where debts would be forgiven and slaves freed.

See also Civil Disobedience; Jesus; Slavery

For Reference and Further Reading

Hedrick, Joan D. 1988. "'Peaceable Fruits': The Ministry of Harriet Beecher Stowe." *American Quarterly* 40 (September): 307–32.

Hill, Patricia R. n.d. "*Uncle Tom's Cabin* as a Religious Text." utc.iath.virginia.edu/interpret/exhibits/hill/hill.html.

Koester, Nancy. 2011. "Harriet Beecher Stowe on the Christian Life." *Journal of Lutheran Ethics*. March 1. https://www.elca.org/JLE/Articles/233.

Smith, Gail K. 2018. *Above the American Renaissance: David S. Reynolds and the Spiritual Imagination in American Literary Studies*. Amherst: University of Massachusetts Press.

Smylie, James H. 1995. "'Uncle Tom's Cabin' Revisited: The Bible, the Romantic Imagination, and the Sympathies of Christ." *American Presbyterians* 73 (Fall): 165–76.

Stringfellow, Thornton

Thornton Stringfellow (1788–1869) was a prominent Virginia slave owner and Baptist minister, who ministered to both blacks and whites. As a social reformer he is primarily known for his biblically based defense of the institution of slavery, which he identified with his native South, but in addition to advocating the formation of the Southern Baptist Convention, he was also active in the Sunday school movement, the foreign missions movement, and the temperance movement (Faust 1977). Much to his surprise and chagrin, after Union troops invaded his plantation, his slaves deserted him.

In 1841, Stringfellow advanced arguments, originally published in the *Religious Herald*, designed to show that the Bible approved of slavery, and his defense was one of the most comprehensive available. He divided his main text into four sections. They respectively sought to show that the institution had been practiced by patriarchs, whom the Scriptures had lauded; that the Mosaic law had provided further sanction of the institution; that Jesus and his apostles had approved of the institution; and that it was merciful.

In arguing that the institution dated back to the time of biblical patriarchs, Stringfellow argued that the Hebrew word that had been translated as "servant" referred to individuals who were owned by others rather than simply to those who were hired by them. He also relied on the idea that slaves were the descendants of Canaan, who had been cured by Noah (Stringfellow 1841, 2). He further identified Abraham, Joseph, Isaac, Job, and others as slaveholders whom God had commended.

In arguing that the laws that God had given to Moses approved of slavery, he associated this right with "the right to govern, by a severity which knows no bounds but the master's discretion" (8). He cited Leviticus 25:44–45 to show that the Jews were permitted to purchase slaves from those around them (8), and Exodus 21:11–12 to show that "the slave is the *master's money*" (9). Further citing Exodus 21:2–4, he indicated that the Mosaic law permitted a slaveholder to separate family members, observing that "the *preference* is given of God to *enslaving the father* rather than *freeing the mother and children*" (9). He compared the mark on the ear of a servant who decided to stay in bondage with his family with similar marks on cattle (9).

Turning to the time of Jesus, Stringfellow observed that Jesus had mandated the same law as Leviticus 19:18 that "thou shalt love thy neighbor as thyself" but that this mandate was never intended to "level all inequalities in human condition" (10). He then proceeded to look at passages in Ephesians; Colossians; 1 Corinthians 7:17, 20, 24; and 1 Peter 2: 13, 15, 18, intended to show that the apostles did not identify slavery as a moral evil or require believers to free their slaves. He cited Romans 13:1–10 to show the obligation to obey existing laws, and related passages from Titus 1:16, 1:1–10, 3:3, and 1 Timothy 6:1–2, all designed to show that the apostles essentially left the system of slavery, which was widespread in the Roman empire, as it was. He further observed that conquerors had enslaved their enemies rather than killing them.

This led into Stringfellow's fourth argument that "the institution of slavery is full of mercy" (16). Through slavery, God had saved "millions of Ham's descendants" from "eternal ruin" (16). By contrast, by acting as busybodies in violation of 1 Peter 4:15–16, Northerner abolitionists had caused great harm:

> Our citizens have been murdered—our property has been stolen . . . our lives have been put in jeopardy—our characters traduced—and attempts made to force political slavery upon us in the place of domestic, by strangers who have no right to

> meddle with our matters. Instead of mediating generous things to our slaves, as a return for Gospel subordination, we have to put on our armor to suppress a rebellious spirit, engendered by 'false doctrine,' propagated by men 'of corrupt minds, and destitute of the truth,' who teach them that the gain of freedom to the slave, is the only proof of godliness in the master. (Stringfellow 1841, 17)

To show that some dialogue continued with Northern brethren on the subject, Stringfellow proceeded to examine biblical passages supplied by a Northern abolitionists that he believed to have opposed slavery. They included twelve passages, the first of which was Acts 17:26 stating that God has "made of one blood all nations," which Stringfellow argued had not prevented slavery in the Bible. He attempted to refute the argument from Matthew 12:12 noting that man was better than a sheep by indicating that slaves sold for more (18).

One of the more fascinating arguments stemmed from arguments drawn from Thomas Jefferson that slavery was inconsistent with God's character because "all men are born free and equal" (22). Pointing to Jefferson's suspect relationship with the Bible, Stringfellow responded, "Now, I say let him throw away his Bible as Mr. Jefferson did his, and then they will be fit companions. But never disgrace the Bible by making Mr. Jefferson its expounder, nor Mr. Jefferson by deriving his sentiments from it. Mr. Jefferson did not bow to the authority of the Bible, and on this subject I do not bow to him. How can any man, who believes the Bible, admit for a moment that God intended to teach mankind by the Bible, that all are born free and equal?" (22). Stringfellow further identified Northern abolitionists as men "who have more zeal than knowledge on this subject" and classified their actions as "seditious" (23).

Responding to yet another set of arguments from another correspondent who said that if slavery were accepted, so too would be polygamy and divorce, Stringfellow denied that the Bible had ever approved of the former and observed that Jesus has strictly limited the latter in a way that he had not limited slavery (18).

See also Abolitionists; Curses on Cain, Haim, and the Canaanites; Jefferson Bible; Slavery

For Reference and Further Reading

Faust, Drew Gilpin. 1977. "Evangelicalism and the Meaning of the Proslavery Argument: The Reverend Thornton Stringfellow of Virginia." *The Virginia Magazine of History and Biography* 84 (January): 3–17.

Noll, Mark A. 2008. *God and Race in American Politics*. Princeton, NJ: Princeton University Press.

Stringfellow, Thornton. 1841. *A Brief Examination of Scripture Testimony on the Institution of Slavery*. Locust Grove, VA: Library of Congress. https://cdn.loc.gov/service/rbc/rbaapc/28100/28100.pdf.

Sunday, Billy

Billy Sunday (1862–1935) was one of the most colorful evangelists in U.S. history. Born to an impoverished family in Iowa, his father died of pneumonia while serving in the Union Army. Sunday escaped this poverty by playing professional baseball before being converted to Christianity at the Pacific Garden Mission in Chicago, after which he felt called to preach.

On the flyleaf of his Bible, Sunday wrote,

> I entered through the portico of Genesis and walked down through the Old Testament's art gallery, where I saw the portraits of Joseph, Jacob, Daniel, Moses, Isaiah, Solomon and David hanging on the wall; I entered the music room of the Psalms and the Spirit of God struck the keyboard of my nature until it seemed to me that every reed and pipe in God's great organ of nature responded to the harp of David, and the charm of King Solomon in his moods. I walked into the business house of Proverbs. (Sunday 1970, 23)

He continued in a similar vein to the gospels and the church before "I walked into the throne room and . . . I saw One standing there, fair as the morning, Jesus Christ, the Son of God" (23).

Sunday interpreted the Bible literally, and viewed those who interpreted it more liberally with contempt, often using coarse language that shocked high society. Despite this, he had many friends among the leaders of industry who often supported his evangelistic crusades.

Although he suggested that the main path to reform was personal conversion, in contrast to some evangelists, Sunday was a strong advocate for reform. Distaining big government, socialism, and communism, which he tended to group together, he favored women's suffrage, sought to end child labor, advocated sex education in the schools (which he thought would lead to better morality), was one of the nation's strongest proponents of national alcoholic prohibition, and supported movements in a number of states for prohibition. Classifying the discovery of America as one of the four greatest events in world history (Giffin 1973, 218), Giffin observes that Sunday "believed that Americans were God's chosen people, and that anyone not clearly bearing the traces of 'pure Americanism' ought to be either converted or outlawed. 'America is not a country for a dissenter to live in,' Billy affirmed. Such 'slag and scum' ought to be 'skimmed off'" (218).

Sunday put great emphasis on traditional gender roles. He stressed the importance of motherhood, linking "home, church, and state closely together as key social institutions" (Gutterman 2005, 57). Similarly, he typically linked American social ills "squarely with the faults of personal behavior" (58), often advising those who were unemployed to leave cities and return to farms (56).

When America entered World War I, Sunday turned many of his services into calls to join the U.S. military and to invest in liberty bonds. Likely associating the German enemy both with brewing and with leading philosophical movements that he opposed, Sunday appealed to the U.S. flag and portrayed the Germans as barbarians (Firstenberger 2005, 61). Delivering a prayer on the floor of Congress on January 10, 1918, Sunday thus said,

> Thou knowest, O Lord, that we are in a life-and-death struggle with one of the most infamous, vile, greedy, avaricious, blood-thirsty, sensual and vicious nations that has ever disgraced the pages of history. . . . We pray Thee that Thou wilt make bare thy mighty arm and beat back that great pack of hungry, wolfish

> Huns whose fangs drip with blood and gore. We pray Thee that the stars in their courses and the winds and waves may fight against them. (Gutterman 2005, 65)

Sunday was a consummate entertainer and performer, and he appeared to epitomize the idea of the manly Christian, or "muscular Christianity," which he believed Scriptures celebrated (Gutterman 2005, 62–64). A commentator observes that Sunday said that "you never become a man until you become a Christian" and that his "plea for sinners to accept Jesus as their Savior or for Christians to rededicate their lives to God was a challenge to the males in his audience to be men" (Martin 1996, 817). His services often highlighted hymns like "Onward Christian Soldiers" and the "Battle Hymn of the Republic," and his imagery often "turned to metaphors of warfare to depict the struggles of the righteous" (817).

See also America as God's New Israel; Temperance Movement

For Reference and Further Reading

Firstenberger, W. A. 2005. *In Rare Form: A Pictorial History of Baseball Evangelist Billy Sunday*. Iowa City: University of Iowa Press.
Giffin, Frederick C. 1973. "Billy Sunday: The Evangelist as 'Patriot.'" *Social Science* 48 (Autumn): 216–21.
Gutterman, David S. 2005. *Prophetic Politics: Christian Social Movements and American Democracy*. Ithaca, NY: Cornell University Press.
Martin, Robert F. 1996. "Billy Sunday and Christian Manliness." *The Historian*. 58 (Summer): 811–23.
Sunday, Billy. 1970. *Billy Sunday Speaks*, ed. David Gullen. New York: Chelsea House.

Sunday Closing Laws

The fourth of the Ten Commandments, found in Exodus 20:8–11, admonishes readers to "remember the Sabbath day to keep it holy" and forbids most work on that day. Indeed, the book of Genesis reports that God Himself rested on the seventh day, after six days of creation.

In time, most Christians began worshipping and resting on Sundays (the day of Jesus's resurrection) rather than Saturday, and, for them, this became their Sabbath. Muslims, in turn, set aside Friday for these functions.

Most early American colonists were members of Christian denominations, and most colonies adopted laws either requiring worship on Sundays or limiting the business and recreational activities, including travel other than for emergency or ministry purposes. Most governmental offices at both state and national levels remain closed in the United States. In the nineteenth century, controversies emerged over whether mails should be transported and/or delivered on Sundays, with employees whose convictions forbade them from working on Sundays claiming that this interfered with their free exercise rights under the First Amendment.

Remnants of such laws, often called blue laws, remain in many states and have been challenged in court. In perhaps the leading contemporary case on the subject, the U.S. Supreme Court decided in *McGowan v. Maryland* (1961) that such laws fell short of establishing a religion in violation of the First and

Fourteenth Amendments, because they had a clear secular legislative purpose, a standard that was to become one of three prongs of the so-called Lemon Test established in *Lemon v. Kurtzman* in 1971. Although acknowledging that such laws, which dated back to English monarchs, were originally designed to encourage attendance at worship and to honor the Christian Sabbath, the court found that modern laws were designed to assure that employees would have at least one day free from manual labor and could spend time with their families. The court further noted that the First Amendment "does not ban federal or state regulation of conduct whose reason or effect merely happens to coincide or harmonize with the tenets of some or all religions" and cited laws against murder and polygamy as examples (McGowan 1961, 442).

Most states have relaxed such laws, and many are a hodgepodge of exemptions and exceptions, but, as of now, they remain constitutional.

See also Sunday Mail Delivery; Ten Commandments

For Reference and Further Reading

Leband, David, and Deborah Hendry Heinbuch. 1987. *Blue Laws: The History, Politics and Economics of Sunday Closing laws*. Lanham, MD: Lexington Books.
Lemon v. Kurtzman, 403 U.S. 602 (1971).
McGowan v. Maryland, 366 U.S. 420 (1961).

Sunday Mail Delivery

In 1810, Congress mandated that post offices that received mail should be open at least one hour for delivery on that day, a policy that it reenacted in 1825 (Rohrer 1987, 53–54). Both enactments sparked movements, largely led by evangelical Christians, to revoke this order, and counter movements, which portrayed this opposition as an attempt to "establish" a national religion in the United States.

Sunday is, of course, the Christian version of the Sabbath, which is a day for worship and rest, as outlined in the fourth commandment, and was taken very seriously especially in the New England states, many of which had local prohibitions against operating businesses or travel on this day. Many individuals from this Puritan Protestant background considered the Sabbath to be a covenantal obligation that Christians had with God; moreover, some feared that God might bring judgment on the nation that ignored the Sabbath (West 1996, 141). Tapping into republican ideology, many also argued that the Sabbath was an incubator for private virtue, providing not only the opportunity for moral instruction but also giving families time together (141). Perhaps most importantly, however, proponents of repealing Sunday mail saw the regulation as one that interfered with the religious rights of those who faced the decision as to whether to violate their consciences or to work on the Sabbath (143). For them, the regulation was a type of religious test, forbidden by the Constitution, in that it effectively weeded out those who believed it was their religious obligation to abstain from work on the Sabbath (145).

Some individuals opposed the law as a federal interference with state and local laws, which they considered to violate the Tenth Amendment. One scholar has observed that, when Congress adopted the 1810 law, in many communities it became "the only local institution impervious to local control" (John 1990, 528). This situation was highlighted when authorities in Princeton, New Jersey, stopped a wagon on the Sabbath, only to find at day's end that the owner was carrying mail (551). Others argued that there was no commercial necessity for the change (West 1996, 145). This argument was reinforced by the argument that most other governmental offices were already closed on Sundays.

At a time when evangelicals were increasingly becoming active in the anti-slavery, anti-dueling, and temperance movements, however, what evangelicals regarded as a defense of their members' right to conscience was viewed by some as an attempt to enforce their morality upon others (Schlereth 2007). Many were particularly concerned when Ezra Stiles Ely, a Presbyterian Minister, argued in *The Duty of Christian Freemen to Elect Christian Rulers*, which he published in 1827, that evangelical Protestants should band together to elect fellow Protestants to public offices. Moreover, some within evangelical ranks (particularly some groups of Baptists and Disciples of Christ) feared even the slightest step toward religious establishments. Seventh-Day Baptists, or Adventists as they came to be called, believed that the appropriate day of rest was Saturday rather than Sunday, and they likewise approved of the laws mandating Sunday mail service. Professor Richard John thus observes that "to a far greater extent than most historians have acknowledged, the Sabbatarianism controversy may well have been less of a struggle pitting liberals against conservatives, evangelicals against anti-evangelicals, or promoters against opponents of social control, than a debate among evangelicals over the proper relationship of church and state" (1990, 555).

Although those opposed to Sunday mail delivery lost both attempts to roll back congressional legislation, they might be said to have lost this battle by winning the larger war on two fronts. First, they reinforced existing laws relative to other Sabbath Day regulations and reinforced the public perception that the Sabbath was a day for rest and worship. More importantly, the railroad and the telegraph both lessened the need for seven-day delivery of the mail, and after the Post Office first saved money by restricting railroad transport to six days, by 1912, Congress had closed down post offices on Sundays for good (John 1990, 563–64).

See also Ely, Ezra Stiles; Sunday Closing Laws; Ten Commandments

For Reference and Further Reading

John, Richard R. 1990. "Taking Sabbatarianism Seriously: The Postal System, the Sabbath, and the Transformation of American Political Culture." *Journal of the Early Republic* 10 (Winter): 517–67.

Rand, Lizabeth A. 2014. "A Rhetoric of Opposition: The Seventh-Day Adventist Church and the Sabbath Tradition." *Renovating Rhetoric in Christian Tradition*, ed. Elizabeth Vander Lei, Thomas Amorose, Beth Daniell, and Anne Ruggless Gere. Pittsburgh: University of Pittsburgh Press, pp. 17–27.

Rohrer, James R. 1987. "Sunday Mails and the Church-State Theme in Jacksonian America." *Journal of the Early Republic* 7 (Spring): 53–74.

Schlereth, Eric R. 2007. "Fits of Political Religion: Stalking Infidelity and the Politics of Moral Reform in Antebellum America." *Early American Studies* 5 (Fall): 288–323.

West, John G., Jr. 1996. *The Politics of Reason and Revelation: Religion and Civic Life in the New Nation*. Lawrence: University Press of Kansas.

Sunday School Movement

One of the primary ways in which many Americans have become familiar with the Bible is through instruction they received (typically beginning in their youth) through Sunday school classes, often preceding regular worship services where the general focus is often a sermon or homily. Inspired by a similar movement in Great Britain, such schools first appeared in Philadelphia in 1791 (Dr. Benjamin Rush was an early supporter) under sponsorship of the First Day Society. They were originally directed toward teaching reading and other basic skills to children of the working poor prior to the availability of universal public education (Boylan 1988, 6–7). As states adopted such public education, however, the first day schools were largely replaced by evangelical Sunday schools that were open alike to the poor and to the children of church members and that were increasingly concerned not only with teaching basic biblical truths but also with emphasizing denominational distinctives.

The movement was particularly important because Sunday schools became a means of inculcating virtues that were not only prized by churches but that were also believed to be essential to republican citizenship. Ann Boylan has observed that "millions of children imbibed a shared Protestant nationalism as part of the standard curriculum in both common and Sunday schools" (1988, 3). She further noted that "the Sunday school first became an American institution because it promised to fulfill the broad millennial expectations of evangelical reformers" (4).

The year 1824 marked the establishment of the American Sunday School Union, which sent missionaries throughout the United States to spread acceptance of the movement. Although the Union was interdenominational, in the course of time, individual denominations produced their own materials to emphasize specific doctrines. The movement faced particular difficulties during the antebellum period as denominations split into Northern and Southern wings, with the former openly condemning slavery as a violation of biblical norms and the latter taking offense at such interpretations.

Sunday schools often stressed not only moral behaviors that were conducive to republican citizenship but also the need for personal conversion. Tensions remained, however, between the Calvinistic understanding that children were born into condemnation and were damned unless they were converted (or baptized) and more liberal believers who thought either that children were guiltless prior to an age of accountability when they could distinguish between right and wrong or who thought that through long-term teaching and nurture, children might simply grow into an adequate understanding of the faith (Boylan 1988, 148).

Sunday schools often adapted their teaching techniques to changing understandings of childhood development. In time, Sunday schools may have had as much influence overseas as at home. Domestically, "Sunday school leaders explicitly promoted the notion that the fate of the republic depended upon the triumph of evangelical ideals and institutions" (169). Perhaps as importantly, "when American missionaries in the late nineteenth century headed for foreign lands, they took the Sunday school with them. If the central symbols of

British efforts to bring their brand of enlightenment and civilization to the world were the army officer and the bureaucrat, American 'civilizers' were more likely to be missionaries bearing Bibles and Sunday school books" (169).

See also Evangelicals; Rush, Benjamin; Slavery

For Reference and Further Reading

Boylan Anne M. 1988. *Sunday School: The Formation of an American Institution, 1790–1880*. New Haven, CT: Yale University Press.

Swords into Plowshares

International organizations are designed to create a meeting place where nations can peacefully resolve their disputes. Although the United States did not participate in the League of Nations, which Woodrow Wilson had helped to establish after World War I, American leaders took the lead in establishing the United Nations in San Francisco on October 24, 1945.

Its charter provided in Article 2 (4) that "all members shall refrain in their international relations from the threat or use of force against the territorial integrity or political independence of any state, or in any other manner inconsistent with the Purposes of the United Nations." Somewhat fortuitously, when the United Nations moved to its headquarters in New York City in 1952, it was located across from a wall built in 1948 beside some steps to a housing development on which words from Isaiah 2:4 were inscribed on all capital letters: "They shall beat their swords into plowshares and their spears into pruning hooks; nation shall not lift up sword against nation, neither shall they learn war any more."

It was not until September 1975, when the wall became part of a park dedicated to Ralph Bunche (1904–1971), that a reference to Isaiah 2:4 was added (the same quotation is also found in Micah 4:3), after a citizen lobbied for ten years to include the reference (Louth 2013). The wall is accordingly referred to as the Isaiah Wall. Bunche had been a political scientist, civil rights proponent, and diplomat, who in 1950 became the first African American to receive the Nobel Peace Prize after securing a cease-fire between Israel and Palestine. The verse from Isaiah was his favorite.

Close by is a garden at the United Nations, which contains a sculpture of a man with a hammer striking a sword called "Let Us Beat Our Swords into Plowshares." It had been designed by Yevgeny Vuchetich (1908–1974) of the Soviet Union for the 1958 World's Fair in Brussels, Belgium, which had highlighted the "atoms for peace" agenda. Yevgeny is also known for a statute "The Motherland Calls," commemorating the Heroes of the Battle of Stalingrad in which a woman lifts a huge sword in her right hand. The steps in front of the Isaiah Wall are now designated as the Sharansky Steps to honor Natan Sharansky (b. 1948), who was a Soviet dissident, who immigrated to Israel.

The words on the wall symbolize the hope of Hebrew prophets for peace and justice, which some Christians associate with a millennial (thousand-year) reign of Christ on earth. Similar hopes are captured in early American folk paintings by Edward Hicks (1780–1849), a Quaker, who painted numerous scenes of "A Peaceable Kingdom," based on Isaiah 11:6–8, in which children are portrayed as peacefully coexisting with both carnivores and herbivores often with a picture of William Penn and Native Americans in the background.

Just as prophets often mixed portrayals of future blessings with condemnations of current injustices, New York City mayor Ed Koch (1924–2013) became so enraged at resolutions by the United Nations against Israel that he threatened in 1982 to add a reference on the wall to "hypocrisy, immorality, and cowardice" (Haberman 1982).

See also Violence; Wilson, Woodrow

For Reference and Further Reading

Haberman, Clyde 1982. "Koch, Angry at U.N., Would Alter Isaiah Wall." *New York Times*. February 10.

Kruger, Thomas. 2007. "'They Shall Beat Their Swords into Plowshares': A Vision of Peace through Justice and Its Background in the Hebrew Bible." *War and Peace in the Ancient World*, ed. Kurt A. Raaflaub. Malden, MA: Blackwell, pp. 161–71.

Louth, John. 2013. "Isaiah's Echo: Progress, Prophecy, and the UN Charter." EJIL:Talk! March 27. https://www.ejiltalk.org/isaiahs-echo-progress-prophecy-and-the-un-charter/.

• T •

Tax Exemption for Bible Materials

In 1818, Samuel Bayard (1767–1840) petitioned Congress on behalf of the American Bible Society (ABS) asking for a tariff exemption on foreign paper and stereotype plates purchased abroad for the production of Bibles. Bayard also asked for franking (free mailing) privileges for officers of the Society.

Bayard argued that the ABS was entitled to such an exemption because its work was devoted to shaping the "national character" in a positive direction. He further argued that the Society's work was serving the public good in much the same way as were flyers advocating vaccinations, which had received an earlier tax exemption. In his words, promoting religion and morals, "and the consequent improvement of society, is no less important in a national view" (Few 2016, 24). Drawing from John 6:27, he also contrasted governmental efforts to promote jobs through investments that would purchase "the bread that perishes" with ABS efforts to provide the "Bread of Life" (Few 2016, 25).

Bayard argued that the establishment clause of the First Amendment had not intended to prohibit indirect support for interdenominational groups like the ABS but that taxes imposed would limit the free exercise of religion by diverting money that could otherwise be used to produce the Bibles themselves.

Even though Congress did not act on this petition, it provides insight into the way the ABS and other benevolent organizations associated their work, and Protestantism in general, with American nationalism (Few 2016, 26).

Reacting to President Trump's threat to place a 25 percent tariff on all goods coming to the United States from China, HarperCollins Christian Publishing pointed out that more than three-quarters of its expenses in publishing Bibles were expended in China. It requested that such Bibles be exempted from any such tariffs, which they argued would shift an "unfair burden on Bible readers, churches, ministries and outreach organizations" (quoted in Egan 2019). Altogether 8.1 million Bibles, many of which were printed in China, were sold in the United States in 2018 (Egan 2019).

See also American Bible Society; First Amendment; Trump, Donald J.

For Reference and Further Reading

Egan, Matt. 2019. "The Bible Could Be a Victim in Trump's Trade War." CNN. July 9. https://www.cnn.com/2019/07/09/business/bible-tariff-china-trade-war-trnd/index.html.

Few, John. 2016. *The Bible Cause: A History of the American Bible Society*. New York: Oxford University Press.

Temperance Movement

The temperance movement was one of the most powerful reform movements during the nineteenth and early twentieth centuries. After succeeding in outlawing alcohol in many states, the movement ultimately led to the adoption of the Eighteenth Amendment in 1913, an amendment later repealed by the Twenty-First Amendment in 1933. Women, especially those in the Women's Christian Temperance Union (WCTU), which was founded in 1874, played an important role in this movement, as did members of the more politically oriented Anti-Saloon League (founded in 1893), many of whom associated the evils of alcohol with waves of immigrants, many of whom were Roman Catholics, coming into the United States from Ireland and southern Europe.

Biblical interpretations played a key role in the development of the prohibition movement. Puritans like Increase Mather had called drink "a good creature of God" although he opposed indulging in excess (Merrill 1988, 147). In time, the American Temperance Society, which was founded in 1826, distinguished between fermented drinks like wine that were available in the Bible and that it thought were therefore permissible, and distilled beverages, which were not available in biblical times, had higher alcohol levels, and thus were not permissible (147).

By the time of the founding of the American Temperance Union in 1836, leaders required a pledge of their members for "total abstinence from all intoxicating liquor" (Merrill 1988, 148). Religious supporters of prohibition were often troubled by biblical passages indicating that Jesus had drunk, and had even converted water into, wine. Some said he did so because he lacked modern scientific knowledge about the dire effects of intoxication (150). In time, the more common view among advocates of temperance was the so-called two-wine theory. It was occasioned by the publication of Moses Stuart's *Essay on the Prize-Question, Whether the Use of Distilled Liquors, or Traffic in Them, Is Compatible at the Present Time, with Making a Profession of Christianity* and further refined by George Duffield, who argued that the Bible actually distinguished between intoxicating wine and grape juice (153–54).

Modern scholars have not been particularly impressed by these distinctions, which seemed more designed to align biblical interpretation with prohibition than prohibition with strict biblical interpretation. After dentist Thomas Bramwell Welch discovered a way in 1869 to make unfermented grape juice through a process discovered by Louis Pasteur, Baptists, Methodists, and other evangelical denominations began substituting it for wine during communion (Peck 2009, 180), whereas Lutherans, Roman Catholics, and Episcopalians continued to use wine. Professor Garrett Peck observed that the attitude toward drinking alcohol among modern American denominations tends to cover "the full spectrum: acceptance, ambivalence, or abstinence" (2009, 181).

Individual believers sometimes remain conflicted about what the Bible teaches. Peck quotes a woman who called into the *Ellen DeGeneres Show* to say, "I love Jesus, but I drink a little" (179). Whatever views religious believers and the denominations to which they belong take with regard to personal behavior, experience under the Eighteenth Amendment led many Americans to conclude that legalized prohibition produced as many problems as it attempted to solve. The law was met with widespread evasion that undermined respect for the rule of law as well as the employment of police practices that were at odds with privacy and due process. States still retain power over the sale of alcohol, and some areas of the country remain officially dry as a result of such regulations.

In a development that bears some similarities to the repeal of national alcoholic prohibition, a number of states have legalized marijuana (sometimes for recreational as well as personal use) in recent years just as others continue to view any sale or consumption of such drugs as a felony.

See also Jesus

For Reference and Further Reading

Haupt, Paul. 1917. "Alcohol in the Bible." *Journal of Biblical Literature* 36(1/2): 75–83.

Merrill, John L. 1988. "The Bible and the American Temperance Movement: Text, Context, and Pretext." *Harvard Theological Review* 82 (April): 145–70.

Peck, Garrett. 2009. *The Prohibition Hangover: Alcohol in America from Demon Rum to Cult Cabernet*. New Brunswick, NJ: Rutgers University Press.

Volk, Kyle G. 2014. *Moral Minorities and the Making of American Democracy*. New York: Oxford University Press.

Ten Commandments

The Ten Commandments, or Decalogue (Ten Words), constitute one of the most ubiquitous portions of Scripture in American life and politics. According to Exodus 20, the Commandments were written by God and presented to Moses on Mount Sinai during the years that he was leading the children of Israel in the wilderness on the journey from Egypt to the land of Canaan. Scripture further records that when Moses descended from the mountain and saw his people engaged in inappropriate conduct, he smashed the stones, which God later replaced.

The Ten Commandments are similar to ancient suzerainty covenants, and thus begin with an identification of the lead party, namely God. He identifies himself as "the LORD thy God, which have brought thee out of the land of Egypt, out of the house of bondage" (Exodus 20:2). As long as the people pledged to adhere to the Commandments, they would be God's people, and He would be their God.

Puritans and many of their American successors would later appropriate the idea that they were God's chosen people who had crossed the Atlantic Ocean (the biblical Red Sea) in order to settle in a New Canaan, or New Jerusalem, which would, as John Winthrop proclaimed, be like the city on the hill about which Jesus had spoken in the Sermon on the Mount. Puritans attempted to pattern some of their early laws around the Ten Commandments and related biblical injunctions, sometimes citing chapter and verse for individual laws and penalties. Although the Ten Commandments appeared to have played little direct role in the formation of state constitutions and early state laws, it was common for nineteenth-century thinkers to understand laws as having such a foundation. In a lecture published in 1852, pastor Lyman Beecher wrote that "our own republic, in its constitution and laws, is of heavenly origin. It was not borrowed from Greece or Rome, but from the Bible. . . . It was God, that gave the elementary principles to our forefathers, as the 'pillar of fire by night, and the clouds by day,' for their guidance" (quoted in Green 1999–2000, 549).

In 1860, David Wyrick of Newark, Ohio, professed to have found an ancient Hebrew version of the Ten Commandments in a Native American Indian burial ground, which further led many Americans to believe that America was the new promised land (Joselit 2017, 9–29). Cecil B. DeMillle's hit movie *The Ten Commandments* (1956), in which in a final scene, Moses repeats the words inscribed on the Liberty Bell and raises his arm in what appears to be an imitation of the Statue of Liberty, did much to further this identification in the American mind.

Whereas Protestants, Catholics, and Jews all claim the Ten Commandments, they number them differently. Jenna Joselit thus observes,

> For the Jews, the first commandment of the lot was "I am the Lord thy God who brought you out of Egypt, the house of bondage." While not disavowing the historicity of that assertion, neither Protestants nor Catholics acknowledged its status as a commandment. For them, it figured more as a preamble. Another difference: among Protestants and Jews, the second commandment prohibited graven images; the Catholics had no such commandment [others say they combine this within the commandment that preceded]. And a third: the Catholic version of the Ten Commandments contained two separate interdictions against coveting; the Protestant and Jewish versions had only one. (2017, 36)

When the Fraternal Order of Eagles placed granite statues of the Ten Commandments in major cities and towns throughout the United States in the late 1950s, they sought to minimize such discrepancies in part by leaving off the numbers (Joselit 2017, 37). The monuments included depictions of the American Eagle clutching an American flag under the eye of God as depicted on the Great Seal of the United States (which some might think to be a violation of the prohibition against "graven images") as well as two six-pointed stars representing Judaism and a symbol of two Greek letters (chi and rho) that are the first two letters for Christ (Coogan 2014, 5).

Puritans attempted to pattern many of their own laws around the Ten Commandments, and surrounding Old Testament texts, although they also brought with them English common law, which they in turn sought to adapt to American circumstances. In the late 1800s Charles Alters, a populist politician from Kansas, stirred up controversy in an unsuccessful attempt to incorporate the Commandments into Kansas laws with appropriate penalties (Joselit 2017, 53). Although law professor Mark Osler (2007) (who probably should have included laws against perjury, which is a form of false witness) argues that the only American laws that are directly parallel to the Ten Commandments are those dealing with murder and theft and that the enforcement of others are limited by provisions in the Bill of Rights, others have argued that many laws originate in one or more of the commandments (Federer 2003). Moreover, many politicians have continued to assert that the Commandments remain at the base of the American legal system, and in 1997 Congress adopted a resolution not only repeating this assertion but also proclaiming that replicas of the Ten Commandments should continue to be displayed in public places.

Controversies continue about the degree to which displays of the Ten Commandments on public property conflict or comply with the prohibition against the establishment of religion within the First Amendment to the U.S. Constitution. There is general agreement that the Ten Commandments fall logically into two parts, with the first set of commandments relating primarily to the relationship of human beings to God (no idolatry, no images, no taking the name of God in vain, keeping the Sabbath) and the second half (prohibitions against actions often identified with natural law principles that are accessible through human reason) dealing with their relationship with one another. When asked which of the commandments was greatest, Mark 12:29–31 reports that Jesus said, "The first of all the commandments is, Hear, O Israel, The Lord our God is one Lord: And thou shalt love the Lord thy God with all thy heart, and with all thy soul, and with all thy mind, and with all thy strength: this is the first commandment. And the second is like, namely this, Thou shalt love thy neighbor as thyself." The first part of the commandments are thus particularly susceptible to the idea that they serve either to given undue preference to religion over irreligion or to one set of beliefs about God over others (as, e.g., monotheism over polytheism).

In *Stone v. Graham* (1980), the Supreme Court invalidated a Kentucky law that required the posting of the Ten Commandments in every public classroom in the state, and in *McCreary County v. American Civil Liberties Union* (2005), it found that similar displays in state courthouses, even though surrounded by other seminal documents, violated the secular purpose prong of the Lemon Tests. In *Van Orden v. Perry* (2005), however, the Court upheld the continuing presence of a monument presented years before by the Fraternal Order of Eagles in a public park that contained other monuments. Judge Roy Moore of Alabama stirred considerable controversy when he installed a 5,280-pound monument of the Ten Commandments in the lobby of the judicial building that housed the state supreme court and was later removed from office for failing to comply with an order to remove it.

Still, it is important to distinguish the role of the Ten Commandments as part of American law and their wider role in American culture. Mark Osler observes, "That the Commandments are not a fundamental part of American law does not imply that they are anything less than a fundamental part of American society. Because the Commandments are common to so many of our faiths, they are more than a guide to personal morality, they are a glue that holds us together, with or without the law being mustered in their support" (2007, 695).

See also Congressional Resolution on the Ten Commandments (1997); *McCreary County v. American Civil Liberties Union* (2005); Lieberman, Joseph; Moore, Roy; Moses as Political Archetype; *Stone v. Graham* (1980); *Van Orden v. Perry* (2005)

For Reference and Further Reading

Coogan, Michael. 2014. *The Ten Commandments: A Short History of an Ancient Text.* New Haven, CT: Yale University Press.

Federer, William J. 2003. *The Ten Commandments and their Influence on American Law.* St. Louis, MO: Amerisearch.

Green, Steven K. 1999–2000. "The Fount of Everything Just and Right? The Ten Commandments as a Source of American Law." *Journal of Law and Religion* 14(2): 525–58.

Joselit, Jenna Weissman. 2017. *Set in Stone: America's Embrace of the Ten Commandments.* New York: Oxford University Press.

Lieberman, Joe, with Ari D. Kahn. 2018. *With Liberty and Justice: The Fifty-Day Journey from Egypt to Sinai.* New Milford, CT: Maggid Books and OU Press.

Mott, Kenneth F. n.d. "Ten Commandments." The First Amendment Encyclopedia. https://mtsu.edu/first-amendment/article/974/ten-commandments. Accessed May 9, 2019.
Osler, Mark. 2007. "Aseret Had'Varim in Tension: The Ten Commandments and the Bill of Rights." *Journal of Church and State* 49 (Autumn): 683–96.
Pottenger, John R. 2007. *Reaping the Whirlwind: Liberal Democracy and the Religious Axis*. Washington, DC: Georgetown University Press.

Thanksgiving and Fast Days

See Days of Humiliation, Fasting, and Thanksgiving

Thomson, Charles

Charles Thomson (1729–1824) may have been one of the most important civilian governmental functionaries during the First and Second Continental Congresses and the Articles of Confederation, during which time he served as the congressional secretary. Born in Ireland, he came to America as a ten-year-old whose sole surviving parent died on the journey and was buried at sea. After facing the unwelcome prospect of being apprenticed to a blacksmith, Thomson fled and encountered a woman who, upon asking him what he wanted to be, found that he wanted to be a scholar. She subsequently provided for his education in an academy near Philadelphia that was run by Dr. Francis Alison, where Thomson learned Latin and Greek, after which he was appointed to teach these subjects at another academy.

After teaching for several years and marrying into wealth, he became a successful importer and advocate of the revolutionary cause. In his diary, John Adams thus described him as "the Sam Adams of Philadelphia, the life of the cause of liberty, they say" (Grobel 1943, 146). In his sixteen consecutive years of service as congressional secretary, Thomson played a role that historian Fred Rolater (1977) has likened to that of "prime minister." Although it was later signed by others, the initial Declaration of Independence went into effect when signed only by John Hancock and Thomson. As secretary, Thomson not only kept track of votes but also corresponded with foreign diplomats, helped design the Great Seal of the United States, issued letters of marque and reprisal, collected state constitutions and other documents, and oversaw treaties with Native Americans and foreign countries (Rolater 1977). He took a special interest in the Delaware Indians, who dubbed him with a name meaning "man who tells the truth" (Lyons 1939, 214). A former president of Princeton said that it was common to say that a statement was "as true as if Charles Thomson's name was to it" (214).

Although Thomson had argued on behalf of the new Constitution, he was not retained in his congressional office in the new office, in part perhaps because many regarded him (at the age of sixty) as too old to continue such duties. Over the next thirty-five years, however, he perfected and published a translation that he had begun of the Greek Septuagint, the Old Testament version that many New Testament figures, included Jesus, had quoted, into English. This, and the accompanying translation of the New Testament (also from Greek), was, indeed, the first such translation published in the English language. Thomas relied for editing upon Ebenezer Hazard, a former postmaster general of the United States (Hendricks 1979, 175–76). His Bible was published in four volumes by Jane Aitken, a Philadelphia printer who was the daughter of Robert Aitken, who had published the first English Bible in America.

Although scholars have generally lauded his work, Thomson's Bible, which was published in 1808, sold less than a thousand copies. This may have stemmed, in part, from his failure to include a preface describing his own method of translation or highlighting its unique features. Although he did allow himself to be identified as "Late Secretary to the Congress of the United States," he asked that his name not be followed by the title "Esq.," and observed in his correspondence that "Prefaces, Introductions and dedications, I know, are common. But of what use are they? Examine them; and what are they but sprouts or fruits of vanity and vain attempts to hide it. Or sly arts to obtain the applause which the author thinks himself intitled [*sic*] to?" (Clark 1955, 244, 247).

Recognizing his ties to the Presbyterian Church—Thomson also had ties to Quakers and Baptists—J. Ramsey Michaels describes Thomson as a "believing rationalist" (2011, 357). He further associates him with "the Baconian style of theology," which was "fined-tuned by the Scottish Common Sense Realism of the eighteenth century and common to Deists and orthodox Christians alike" (357). Quoting a fellow scholar, Michaels classifies Thomson as a practitioner of "evidential Christianity," which believed "that Christian theology was rational" (357). Michaels observes that one way that Thomson's experience in politics may have influenced his translation was his predilection for translating some of Paul's letters "in the form of dialogues between Paul and those he imagines rhetorically as his interlocutors" (361). Thomson indicated in his correspondence that, in translating the Bible, he was "attached to no system nor peculiar tenets of any sect or party. I have sought for truth with the utmost ingenuity" (Clark, 1955, 239). Thomson also published *A Synopsis of the Four Evangelists* in 1815.

See also Aitken Bible; Articles of Confederation; Declaration of Independence; Great Seal of the United States; Revolutionary War

For Reference and Further Reading

Clark, Paul Odell. 1955. "Letters of Charles Thomson on the Translation of the Bible." *Journal of the Presbyterian Historical Society* 33 (December): 239–56.

Clark, Paul Odell. 1956. "Letters of Charles Thomson on the Translation of the Bible (Concluded)." *Journal of the Presbyterian Historical Society* 34 (June): 112–23.

Grobel, Kendrick. 1943. "Charles Thomson, First American N.T. Translator: An Appraisal." *Journal of Bible and Religion* 11 (August): 145–51.

Hendricks, J. Edwin. 1979. *Charles Thomson and the Making of a New Nation, 1729–1824*. Cranbury, NJ: Associated University Presses.

Lyons, John F. 1939. "Thomson's Bible." *Journal of the Department of History* 18 (March): 211–20.

Michaels, J. Ramsey, 2011. "Charles Thomson and the First American New Testament." *Harvard Theological Review* 104 (July): 349–65.

Rolater, Fred S. 1977. "Charles Thomson, 'Prime Minister' of the United States." *Pennsylvania Magazine of History and Biography* 101 (July): 322–48.

Schlenther, Boyd Stanley. 1990. *Charles Thomson: A Patriot's Pursuit*. Newark: University of Delaware Press.

Tort Law

In law, a tort is a private or civil wrong, other than one involving a breach of contract. For a tort to occur, an individual or individuals must show that there was a duty to be performed, that this duty was breached (typically through negligence), and that this breach resulted in damages, which may be either compensatory (to make up for actual losses) or punitive (to deter future violations). In American law, torts are distinguished from criminal actions, which are prosecuted by the state rather than by private parties.

Many ancient law codes, including the Mosaic Law, described tortious situations that undoubtedly served as models for English common law and for modern American tort law. One lawyer cites four biblical examples that are similar to modern civil liability statutes. They respectively involve the following:

> Digging a pit but failing to cover it (EX. 21:33–34);
> Allowing animals to trespass on to the property of another and do harm (Ex. 22:5);
> Kindling a fire but negligently allowing it to get out of control and harm a neighbor's property (Ex. 22:6); and
> Building a flat roof on which people foreseeably would spend time, but failing to construct protective parapets to prevent their falling off the sides (Deut. 22:8). (Fudge 2006)

This author further points out that the Law of Moses recognized "degrees of negligence," depending on the foreseeability of an injury, and that it provided for both compensatory and punitive damages. Thus, someone who stole an animal and sold it was required to reimburse the owner four- or fivefold, whereas if the thief still had the animal, he was only required to pay double.

Exodus 21:28–32 distinguished the liability that was required when an ox gored an individual to death, based largely upon whether the owner knew that the ox had such a propensity and had sought to guard against it versus cases where this was a first-time event (Methvin 2006, 22).

The Law of Moses clearly valued human life over both animal life and property and was generally reluctant to put a monetary value on human life. This emphasis persisted for a long time in both English and American law (Finkelstein 1973).

The New Testament principle of agape love called upon Christians to go beyond typical duties of care in meeting the needs of others, but such supererogation might not fit readily into a secular legal system (Moreland 2017, 207).

See also Moses as Political Archetype; Ten Commandments

For Reference and Further Reading

Finkelstein, Jacob J. 1973. "The Goring Ox: Some Historical Perspectives on Deodands, Forfeitures, Wrongful Death and the Western Notion of Sovereignty." *Temple Law Quarterly* 46 (Winter): 169–290.

Fudge, Edward. 2006. "The Law of Moses and Modern Tort Law." https://edwardfudge.com/writte-nministry-articles-2/the-law-of-moses-and-modern-tort-law/. Accessed May 23, 2019.

Gaffney, Edward McGlynn, Jr. 1986. "Biblical Law and the First Year Curriculum of American Legal Education." *Journal of Law and Religion* 4(1): 63–95.
Methvin, Thomas J. 2006. "Trial Lawyers and the Biblical Basis for What We Do." *Alabama Association for Justice Journal* 26: 21–27.
Moreland, Michael P. 2017. "Justice, Love, and Duties of Care in Tort Law." *Agape, Justice, and Law: How Might Christian Love Shape Law?*, ed. by Robert F. Cochran Jr. and Zachary R. Calo. New York: Cambridge University Press, pp. 188–208.
Titus, Herbert W. 2008. "The Bible and American Law." *Liberty University Law Review* 2: 305–27.

Truman, Harry S.

Harry S. Truman (1884–1972), who was frequently criticized for drinking, playing cards, and using profanity, was one of the more biblically literate presidents. Even though he never attended college, he reported that the Bible was among the books that inspired him as a youth, and that he had read through both the Bible and accompanying materials in the family's Bible at least twice before he reached the age of twelve (Truman 1934). Truman was baptized at the age of eighteen by a Baptist preacher, and he frequently referred to the Bible during his political career, which began as a country judge, included service in the U.S. Senate, a brief vice presidency during which he succeeded Franklin D. Roosevelt, and almost two full terms as president.

In describing his life prior to running for the Senate, Truman recounted his service as a Captain during World War I, falling in love and marrying his childhood sweetheart, and a number of financial reverses. Then, he added, "And now I am a candidate for the United States Senate. If the Almighty God decides that I go there I am going to pray as King Solomon did for wisdom to do the job" (1934). As he hastily took the oath after the death of Roosevelt, Truman swore upon a Bible that had been used in previous inaugurations. At his presidential inauguration in 1948, Truman brought two Bibles, the one that he had used on first assuming the presidential office, which was opened to the Sermon on the Mount as recorded in Matthew 5, and the other a facsimile copy of the first volume of the Gutenberg Bible, which the Chamber of Commerce of Independence, Missouri, had purchased as a memorial to Truman's mother. It was opened to the Ten Commandments in Exodus 20 and is today displayed at the Truman Library and Museum in Independence, Missouri (Stillwell 2018).

These were the two Scriptures that Truman mentioned most frequently during his political career, during which he "employed hundreds of biblical quotations and allusions, persistently preached morality, denounced communist atheism, and exuded postmillennial optimism that humans, empowered by God, could create a better world" (Smith 2015, 259). Truman was fond of quoting the Hebrew prophets and cited Micah in a statement that he wrote for the American Bible Society in 1948. In a belief that was sometimes criticized as naïve, Truman believed that foreign policy could be conducted according to the biblical Golden Rule (Smith 2015, 243), and he apparently dubbed his "Good Neighbor Policy" in South America on the basis of Jesus's story of the Good Samaritan. Truman prized an illuminated print of the Ten Commandments that the Fraternal Order of Eagles gave to him, believed that the following the Commandments was key to an ethical life, and said that the U.S. government was "patterned to some extent from the law presented to Moses on Mount Sinai" (Joselit 2017, 45).

When Roosevelt died, Truman became president while World War II was still raging, and he made the decision to drop the first two atomic bombs on Japan to end the war. Soon thereafter, he confronted a world that was divided between democratic and communist powers. He devised the Truman Doctrine, which pledged American military assistance to countries fighting communist aggression; directed the Berlin air lift in response to a Soviet blockade; supported the Marshall Plan to rebuild Europe and the United Nations; and sent U.S. troops under UN auspices to repel the North Korean invasion of South Korea.

Although many of these decisions had the support of Secretary of State George Marshall and other advisors, Truman went against their advice in recognizing the new nation of Israel in 1948, and he appears to have done so largely for humanitarian reasons and despite potential geopolitical costs—including the possibility of alienating the oil-producing Arab nations of the region. Truman appears to have been influenced by Scriptures in the Old Testament, including Deuteronomy 1:8, which White House counsel Clark Clifford had quoted to him (Mead 2008, 28), in which God is recorded as saying, "Behold, I have set the land before you: go in and possess the land which the Lord sware unto your fathers, Abraham, Isaac, and Jacob, to give unto them and to their seed after them." Israel's first president subsequently said that Truman had been born to restore the Jews to their homeland, and likened him to the biblical King Cyrus, as described in Ezra 1, who had allowed Jews to return from Babylon to their homeland (Benson 1994, 21). In 1953, after an army buddy Eddie Jacobson introduced Truman to a group of Jewish dignitaries at the Jewish Theological Seminary in New York, as "the man who helped created the State of Israel," Truman responded, "What do you mean, 'helped to create'? I am Cyrus. I am Cyrus" (Merkley n.d.).

Even though they were both Baptists, Truman was one of the few presidents of his era who did not look with favor on evangelist Billy Graham, whom he thought was making personal capital out of a meeting they had in the White House (Smith 2015, 245). Truman remained wary of religious pretentions and apparently sought the counsel of fundamentalist pastor J. Frank Norris with respect to the issue of Israel (254).

Truman was among those presidents who believed that God had given America a special mission, and he sometimes pictured the world in very black-and-white terms in which Christian America and its allies were allied on one side against totalitarian communism on the other. Leaving office in 1953 with a very low public approval rating, Truman is now widely respected for meeting the challenges that his accidental presidency inherited with hope and integrity and with laying the groundwork for American foreign policy up to the demise of the Soviet Union. On a more negative side, in 1963, Truman, when asked whether integration might lead to interracial marriage, responded, "I hope not. I don't believe in it. The Lord created it that way. You read your Bible and you'll find out" (Liberty and Power 2004).

See also Baptists; Cyrus as Political Archetype; Graham, Billy; Presidential Inaugural Bible Verses; What Doth the Lord Require (Micah 6:8); Zionism

For Reference and Further Reading

Benson, Michael T. 1994. "Harry S. Truman as a Modern Cyrus." *Brigham Young University Studies*. 34(1): 7–27.

Joselit, Jenna Weissman. 2017. *Set in Stone: America's Embrace of the Ten Commandments*. New York: Oxford University Press.

Mead, Walter Russell. 2008. "The New Israel and the Old: Why Gentile Americans Back the Jewish State." *Foreign Affairs* 87 (July–August): 28–46.

Merkley, Paul Charles. n.d. "I Am Cyrus." *Christianity Today*. https://www.christianitytoday.com/history/issues/issue-99/i-am-cyrus.html.

Smith, Gary Scott. 2015. *Religion in the Oval Office: The Religious Lives of American Presidents*. New York: Oxford University Press.

Stillwell, Ted W. 2018. "Truman's White House Bibles." *The Examiner* (Jackson County Missouri). January 30. https://www.examiner.net/news/20180130/trumans-white-house-bibles. Accessed April 28, 2019.

Truman, Harry S. 1934. "Longhand Note by Harry S. Truman, May 14, 1934. President's Secretary's Files—Longhand Notes." Truman Library & Museum. May 14. https://www.trumanlibrary.gov/library/research-files/longhand-note-harry-s-truman?documentid=6&pagenumber=1. Accessed April 28, 2019.

Liberty and Power. 2004. "Truman's Opposition to Interracial Marriage." History News Network, citing *Chicago Daily Defender*, September 12, 1963. https://historynewsnetwork.org/blog/6173. Accessed April 28, 2019.

Trump, Donald J.

Many opponents of President Donald Trump expressed surprise when Michele Bachmann, a former member of the U.S. House of Representatives from Minnesota, appeared on a Christian radio show called "Understanding These Times" and said that Trump was "highly biblical, and I would say to your listeners, we will in all likelihood never see a more godly, biblical president again in our lifetime" (quoted in Cillizza 2019). Relatively early in his first presidential campaign, Trump had received the endorsement of Jerry Falwell Jr., the son of the televangelist and the president of Liberty University (Robies and Rutenberg 2019). In addition to what they considered to be questionable policies (like separating members of immigrant families and bullying political opponents), Trump critics pointed out that he had been twice divorced and that he had been accused of inappropriate sexual relations including sexual harassment and hush money payments to conceal them.

Somewhat distinguishing Trump the man from Trump the politician, evangelist Franklin Graham (son of Billy) had earlier said that "I never said he was the best example of the Christian faith. He defends the faith. And I appreciate that very much" (Cillizza 2019). Robert Jeffress, who heads a large Dallas Baptist church, says, "I want the meanest, toughest SOB I can find to protect this nation," a sentiment echoed by Tony Perkins of the Family Research Council (Wehner 2019, 84–85).

After Graham called upon churches to pray to protect Trump against his "enemies" in their services on June 2, 2019, a number of evangelical critics accused Graham of seeking to weaponize prayer. Warren Throckmorton, a psychology professor at the evangelical Grove City College, observed, "Nothing in the call to prayer calls Trump to repentance for his many lies, for his support for ruthless dictators around the world, for his obstructions of reasonable congressional oversight, or for the authorization of cruel treatment of asylum seekers at the border" (Burke 2019). Other Trump defenders have likened him to the pagan King Cyrus who helped restore Jews to their homeland. The book entitled *The Faith of Donald J. Trump* tells the story of Lance Wallnau, a Dallas businessman who prophesied in 2015 that Trump would be president. Wallnau recounted that he heard a voice that said, "The next President of the United States will be the forty-fifth president, and he will be an Isaiah 45 president" (Howe 2019, 52). Turning to this chapter, he recognized that it portrayed King Cyrus as God's anointed.

Trump often identifies himself with Norman Vincent Peale, the pastor of the Marble Collegiate Church in New York where he and Ivana Zelníčková were married, and he appears to identify with proponents of the so-called prosperity gospel that interprets earthly riches as a sign of God's blessings (Percy 2018). Trump frequently tells audiences that the Bible is his favorite book, followed by his own *Art of the Deal*. In a film entitled *American Heretics: The Politics of the Gospel*, Rev. Robin R. Meyers of Oklahoma City's Mayflower Congregational Church of Christ suggests that Trump may appeal to those who believe he is similar to the God of the Old Testament, who is sometimes portrayed as "angry, unforgiving and vengeful" (as described by Schager, 2019).

Chris Cillizza observes that evangelicals and others who laud Trump as a biblical president are following Graham in identifying policies with which they agree rather than identifying with Trump's personal faith. Many thus laud Trump for conservative judicial appointees whom they hope will tighten abortion laws, with his recognition of Jerusalem as the capital of Israel and his support for Israeli prime minister Benjamin Netanyahu, for his ban on transgender individuals in the military, and perhaps even for his strong stand against illegal immigration.

Trump has compared the Bible to a great movie, as in an interview with David Brody (2015) when Trump said, "I don't like to use this analogy, but like a great movie, a great, incredible movie. You'll see it once it will be good. You'll see it again. You can see it 20 times and every time you'll appreciate it more. The Bible is the most special thing." Trump's own knowledge of Scripture seems relatively shallow. At an appearance at Liberty University in January 2016, he evoked laughter from his audience when, in an otherwise appropriate verse for the audience, he referred to "Two Corinthians, 3:17" ("Now the Lord is that Spirit: and where the Spirit of the Lord is, there is Liberty") rather than "Second Corinthians." At a 2015 forum, he suggested that instead of asking God for forgiveness, "I just go on and try to do a better job from there"; he described taking communion as have a little drink of wine and "my little cracker," and he put cash on the communion plate (Cillizza 2019). Trump once identified his favorite verse as the reference to an "eye for an eye" in Exodus 21:24, but this is a concept that Jesus specifically repudiated in his Sermon on the Mount in Matthew 5:38–39 (Morton 2016; Kristof 2019).

At his inauguration, Trump took his oath on a Revised Standard Version of the Bible that his mother had given him when he was twelve. It is now on display at the Museum of the Bible in Washington, DC. During his inaugural address,

Trump paraphrased Psalm 133:1 when he intoned that "how good and pleasant it is when God's people live together in unity"; identifying America with ancient Israel, he further said, "When America is unified, America is totally unstoppable . . . and most importantly, we will be protected by God" (O'Neil 2017).

As president, Trump encountered some controversy when he signed the covers of the Bibles of people who had been adversely affected by a tornado in Alabama. In July 2019, a Catholic priest, Percival D'Silva, told his congregation that Trump should quit after Trump had told women of color in the U.S. House of Representatives that they should go back from where they came (Giacomo 2019).

Ralph Reed, who founded the Faith and Freedom Coalition, stirred controversy when he announced that Regnery would be publishing a book entitled *For God and Country: The Christian Case for Trump*, in which he would be arguing that Christians had a duty to reelect Trump. The original title, taken from Chapter 22 of the gospel of Matthew, was apparently originally titled *Render to God and Trump* (Orr 2019).

In the meantime, a satirical blogger claimed to have found a MAGA ("Make America Great Again") translation of the Bible with a Book of 2 Republicans and a Gospel According to Don. Chapter 23:4 of the Gospel of Don is quoted as saying, "For Caucasian God did not so love the world, He so loved America—so much so, that he sent White Jesus to build walls, take away health insurance, ignore climate change, vilify sexual assault survivors, and make the one percent richer" (Pavlovitz 2019).

See also Bible Signings; Cyrus as Political Archetype; Evangelicals; Falwell, Jerry; Graham, Billy; Prosperity Gospel

For Reference and Further Reading

Balmer, Randall. 2019. "God Is on Team Trump? Let's Just Take a Quick Check with the Bible." *Los Angeles Times*. February 4. https://www.latimes.com/opinion/op-ed/la-oe-balmer-god-and-trump-20190204-story.html. Accessed April 16, 2019.

Brody, David. 2015. "Brody File Video Exclusive: Donald Trump Talks about the Bible and Book of Proverbs." CBN News. September 16. https://www1.cbn.com/thebrodyfile/archive/2015/09/16/brody-file-video-exclusive-donald-trump-talks-about-the-bible.

Burke, Daniel. 2019. "Franklin Graham Wants the Nation to Pray for Trump on Sunday. But Other Christians Call It Propaganda." CNN. May 31. https://www.cnn.com/2019/05/30/us/franklin-graham-trump-day-of-prayer/index.html.

Cillizza, Chris. 2019. "Michelle Bachmann Claimed That Donald Trump Is 'Highly Biblical.' So . . ." CNN. April 16. https://www.cnn.com/2019/04/16/politics/michele-bachman-donald-trump-bible-religious/index.html.

Giacomo, Carol. 2019. "For Spewing Hate, Trump Should Quit, a Priest Tells Parishioners." *New York Times*. July 24.

Howe, Ben. 2019. *The Immoral Majority: Why Evangelicals Chose Political Power over Christian Values*. New York: Broadside Books.

Jen, Joanna Tice. 2019. "'Be Joyful Always!': Twenty-First-Century Evangelical Conceptions of Happiness and Trumpist Politics." *Regimes of Happiness: Comparative and Historical Studies*, ed. Yuri Contrerar-Vejar, Joanna Tice Jen, and Bryan S. Turner. New York: Anthem Press, pp. 93–110.

Kristof, Nicholas. 2019. "We're Less and Less a Christian Nation, and I Blame Some Blowhards." *New York Times*. October 26.

Liftin, Duane. 2019. "The Lost Genius of the American Settlement." Christianity Today. September 30. https://www.christianitytoday.com/ct/2019/september-web-only/subverting-american-settlement.html.

Morton, Victor. 2016. "Donald Trump's Favorite Bible Verse Is One Jesus Specifically Repudiated." *Washington Times*. April 14. https://www.washingtontimes.com/news/2016/apr/14/donald-trump-favorite-bible-verse-one-jesus-specif/.

Murphy-Gill, Meghan. 2017. "The Faith of Donald Trump." U.S. Catholic. January 19. https://www.uscatholic.org/articles/201701/faith-donald-trump-30910.

O'Neil, Tyler. 2017. "Trump Adds to Scripture in Inaugural Speech." PJ Media. January 20. https://pjmedia.com/faith/2017/01/20/trump-adds-to-scripture-in-inaugural-speech/.

Orr, Gabby. 2019. "'Render to God and Trump': Ralph Reed Calls for 2020 Obedience to Trump." *Politico*. October 9. https://www.politico.com/news/2019/10/09/ralph-reed-trump-book-040920.

Pavlovitz, John. 2019. "The MAGA Bible: A Political Translation of God's Word for a Corrupted Faith." *Milwaukee Independent*. September 22. http ://www.milwaukeeindependent.com/john-pavlovitz/maga-bible-political-translation-gods-word-corrupted-faith/.

Percy, Martyn. 2018. "To Know Donald Trump's Faith Is to Understand His Politics." *Guardian*. February 6. https://www.theguardian.com/commentisfree/2018/feb/06/donald-trump-faith-politics-religious-presidency.

Posner, Sarah. 2017. "Amazing Disgrace." *New Republic*. March 20. https://newrepublic.com/article/140961/amazing-disgrace-donald-trump-hijacked-religious-right.

Robles, Frances, and Jim Rutenberg. 2019. "The Evangelical, the 'Pool Boy,' the Comedian and Michael Cohen." *New York Times*. June 18.

Schager, Nick. 2019. "A More Righteous Path: The Pro-Immigrant Bible-Belt Preachers Standing Up to Trump's Xenophobia." Daily Beast. July 13. https://www.thedailybeast.com/american-heretics-the-pro-immigrant-bible-belt-preachers-standing-up-to-trumps-xenophobia.

Wehner, Peter. 2019. *The Death of Politics: How to Heal Our Frayed Republic after Trump*. New York: HarperOne.

Turner, Nat

In 1831, at a time when many Southern clerics and intellectuals were quoting the Bible to uphold the institution of slavery in the United States, a slave named Nat Turner from Southampton County, Virginia, used the Bible to justify a bloody slave uprising that resulted in the death of fifty-seven whites and as many as two hundred blacks, including Turner, who was hanged (Santoro 2008, 115). The revolt was particularly known for its destruction of all the whites they encountered, including women and children.

Prior to Turner's execution, Thomas R. Gray, an attorney, interviewed him and subsequently published an account of the interview that was widely circulated and has been somewhat immortalized in a contemporary novel by William Styron entitled *The Confessions of Nat Turner*. Anthony Santoro has published an extensive review of Gray's interview, with special attention to Turner's biblical interpretations. Turner's most direct biblical exhortations centered on Matthew 6:33 (Turner did not cite chapter and verse), which admonished, "Seek ye [first] the kingdom of Heaven and all [these] things shall be added unto you" (Gray 1831, 9). He also paraphrased (again without chapter and verse) the exhortation in Luke 12:47 that the "servant, which knew his lord's will and prepared not himself, neither did according to his will, shall be beaten with many stripes" (10). Turner used many other biblical analogies such as the shed blood of Christ, the loosening of the Serpent, Jesus's maxim that the last shall be first and the first shall be last, and reference to apocalyptic signs in the heavens (10–11).

In his analysis of this narrative, Santoro observes that Turner sought to place himself in the biblical prophetic tradition by telling of his accounts as a child of events that happened before his own birth. Santoro believes that Turner also tapped into the "biblical holy war tradition" that is especially evident in the biblical book of Judges, the need to strike terror in his enemies, and his belief that the rebellion was guided by God, which views Turner variously culled from Joshua, Ezekiel, and other biblical prophets (2008, 123). Santoro further believes that Turner's millennial vision was "derived from Isaiah, Revelation, Luke, and Mark" (131). Santoro thinks that Turner showed particular creativity in utilizing the passage from Luke 12, which was typically used to justify the use of force against rebellious slaves, as justification for a slave revolt (133).

Although Turner revealed in his interview that he had returned to his master after fleeing from him, he downplayed the fact that his master had sold his wife to another while emphasizing the role he had played in baptizing a white man, which he might well have thought was a biblical sign of the end of an age (137). Turner apparently thought that his own execution would help provide redemption for his people in the same manner as Christians believed that Jesus's death had redeemed those who followed him (142).

The savagery of Turner's revolt arguably made him a far less sympathetic figure than John Brown (who had participated in savagery of his own while in Kansas), whose attack at Harper's Ferry on the eve of the Civil War was a major catalyst to that conflict.

See also Brown, John; Slavery; Vesey, Denmark

For Reference and Further Reading

Blum, Edward J. 2011. "'Look Baby, We Got Jesus on Our Flag': Robust Democracy and Religious Debate from the Era of Slavery to the Age of Obama." *Annals of the American Academy of Political and Social Science* 634 (September): 17–37.

Gray, Thomas R. 1831. *The Confessions of Nat Turner, the Leader of the Late Insurrection in Southampton, VA*. Baltimore: Thomas R. Gray. Found at University of Nebraska DigitalCommons at https://digitalcommons.unl.edu/etas/15.

Santoro, Anthony. 2008. "The Prophet in His Own Words: Nat Turner's Biblical Construction." *Virginia Magazine of History and Biography* 116(2): 114–49.

• U •

Under God

Few phrases have been probably cited more frequently to show that America is a religious nation than the words "under God" in the Pledge of Allegiance to the American flag. Fewer may know that Congress did not adopt, and President Dwight D. Eisenhower did not sign, this measure until 1954. The original salute, which had undergone a number of small changes, had been formulated by a former Baptist preacher named Francis J. Bellamy (1855–1931) to commemorate the four hundredth anniversary of Columbus's discovery of America. The pledge was viewed as a way of inculcating American values in all children, but especially the children of immigrants.

The chief impetus for this change appears to have been a sermon that Dr. George M. Docherty (1911–2008), who had been born in Scotland and educated at Glasgow University before coming to the United States in 1950, preached on February 7, 1954, at the New York Avenue Presbyterian Church in Washington, DC, that Abraham Lincoln had attended. President Eisenhower was in the audience, for the sermon that commemorated Lincoln's birth.

The published sermon does not begin with a Scripture verse but with a story about how Sparta was secure not by building a wall but through its citizen soldiers. In exploring the nature of freedom, Docherty described a wide variety of experiences that individuals associated with the "American way of life" and concluded that this life had been made possible by the Pilgrims who "wished to live the pure and noble life purged of all idolatry and enslavement of the mind, even by the church." This was followed by fairly generic references to both the Old and New Testaments: "These fundamental concepts of life had been given to the world from Sinai, where the moral law was graven upon tables of stone, symbolizing the universal application to all men; and they came from the New Testament, where they heard in the words of Jesus of Nazareth the living Word of God for the world."

Docherty linked this to Lincoln's belief in divine providence. "Wherefore, he claims that it is under God that this Nation shall know a new birth of freedom. And by implication, it is under God that 'government of the people, by the people, and for the people shall not perish from the earth.'" As an immigrant, Docherty had listened intently as his children came home from school and described the pledge to the flag. As he listened he observed that as "noble" as the words were, "there was something missing in this pledge, and that which was missing was the characteristic and definitive factor in the American way of life. Indeed, apart from the mention of the phrase, the United States of America, this could be a pledge of any republic." He illustrated by telling how Russia also claimed to be indivisible, to have liberty, to be just, and to be democratic.

Pointing back to Lincoln's Gettysburg Address, Docherty highlighted the absence of the words "under God," which he further associated with the references to God within the Declaration of Independence. By contrast, he believed "that two world convulsions shattered the illusion that you can build a nation on human ideas without a fundamental belief in God's providence." Docherty further argued that the Cold War was "a theological war." Rather than a fight between two philosophies or two rival views of economics, "it is a fight for the freedom of the human personality." As he further explained, "It is the view of man as it comes down to us from Judeo-Christian civilization in mortal combat against modern, secularized, godless humanity."

Anticipating objections that such an addition would violate the establishment clause of the First Amendment, Docherty distinguished the words "under God" from "under the church," which would require identifying one church over another. Moreover, he distinguished "under God," from "under Jesus Christ" or "under the King of Kings," pointing to the words at the base of the Statue of Liberty and observing that "there is no religious examination on entering the United States of America—no persecution because a man's faith differs even from the Christian religion."

Expressing his view that atheists, some of whom he acknowledged to be good citizens, were "spiritual parasites," because they live "upon the life force of another organism without contributing to the life of the other," Docherty observed that "he cannot deny the Christian revelation and logically live by the Christian ethic." The nation acknowledges this link by engraving the words "In God We Trust" on coins, in opening sessions of Congress with prayer, by having presidents take their oaths "upon the Holy Bible," and by asking naturalized citizens to take their oath with the words "so help me God." Saying that the American way of life "sees man, not as the ultimate outcome of a mysterious concatenation of evolutionary process, but a sentient being created by God and seeking to know His will, and 'Whose soul is restless till he rest in God.'"

Adapting, without citing, Galatians 3:28, Docherty observed, "In this land, there is neither Jew nor Greek, neither bond nor free, neither male nor female, for we are one nation indivisible under God, and humbly as God has given us the light we seek liberty and justice for all."

See also Declaration of Independence; First Amendment; Lincoln, Abraham (Gettysburg Address); Puritans; U.S. Flag

For Reference and Further Reading

Canipe, Lee. 2003. "Under God and Anti-Communist: How the Pledge of Allegiance Got Religion in Cold War America." *Journal of Church and State* 45 (Spring): 305–23.

Docherty, George M. 1954. "Under God." February 7. http://www.christianheritagemins.org/articles/UNDER%20GOD.pdf. Accessed April 15, 2019.

Kao, Grace Y. 2007. "'One Nation Under God' or Taking the Lord's Name in Vain?: Christian Reflections on the Pledge of Allegiance." *Journal of the Society of Christian Ethics* 27 (Spring/Summer): 183–204.

Smith, Whitney. 2009. "'One Nation Under God': The Crusade to Capture the American Flag." *Proceedings: The XIX International Congress of Vexillology.* U.K. Flag Institute, York, July 23–27, 2001, pp. 67–74.

Updegraph v. Commonwealth (1824)

Even after most states had disestablished religion, a number of cases in early American history were explicitly based on the premise that the common law incorporated Christian principles, although most of the decisions actually rested on narrower concerns like breach of the peace (Banner 1998). One such case, which was decided by the Pennsylvania Supreme Court, confirms this view.

In the case, Abner Updegraph was indicted and convicted of blasphemy for violating a law adopted in 1700 that provided "that whosoever shall willfully, premeditatedly and despitefully blaspheme, and speak loosely and profanely of Almighty God, Christ Jesus, the Holy Spirit, or the Scripture of Truth" should be fined. The state accused Updegraph of having "in the presence and hearing of several persons, unlawfully, wickedly, and premeditatedly, despitefully and blasphemously," said "among other things, in substance, as follows: 'that the Holy Scriptures were a mere fable, that they were a contradiction, and that although they contained a number of good things, yet they contained a great many lies'" (1824, 398).

Refusing to accept the explanation that Updegraph may have uttered these words before a debating society, Justice Duncan said that he could not acknowledge such a defense and that if there is a society "in which so serious a subject is treated with so much levity, indecency and scurrility, existing in this city, I am sorry to hear, for it would prove a nursery of vice, a school of preparation to qualify young men for the gallows, and young women for the brothel and there is not a skeptic of decent manners and good morals, who would not consider such debating clubs as a common nuisance and disgrace to the city" (399). If the state law disestablishing religion were understood to have permitted such breaches of the peace, then "all the laws which have Christianity for their objects . . . would be carried away at one fell swoop—the act against cursing and swearing, and breach of the Lord's day; the act forbidding incestuous marriages, perjury by taking a false oath upon the book, fornication and adultery *et peccatum illud horrible non nominandum inter Christianos* [bestiality and sodomy]—for all these are founded in Christianity" (399). Duncan proceeded to review both English and colonial history to show that blasphemy had long been an offence. At one point, he observed, "If Christianity was abolished, all false oaths, all tests by oath, in the common form, by the book, would cease to be indictable as perjury; the indictment must state the oath to be on the holy Evangelists of almighty God; the accused, on his trial, might argue that the book by which he was sworn, so far from being holy writ, was a pack of lies, containing as little truth as Robinson Crusoe. And is every jury in the box to decide as a fact whether the scriptures are of divine origin?" (403). With a view back to the French Revolution, Justice Duncan argued that if blasphemy were to be permitted, "impiety and profanity must reach their acme with impunity, and every debating club might dedicate the club-room to the worship of the Goddess of Reason, and adore the deity in the person of a naked prostitute" (404).

Rejecting the argument that judgments against blasphemy should be left solely to God, Justice Duncan noted that the Supreme Court of New York "solemnly determined, that Christianity was part of the law of the land, and that to revile the Holy Scriptures was an indictable offence" (405). The state provided relatively mild punishments for such offenses to preserve public order. Without protections against publications that deny "the being and providence of God," or that engage in "contumelious reproaches of Jesus Christ; profane and malevolent scoffing at the scriptures, or exposing any part of them to contempt and ridicule," or "certain immoralities tending to subvert all religion and morality . . . no free government can long exist. It is liberty run mad" (406).

Arguing that "no free government now exists in the world, unless where Christianity is acknowledged, and is the religion of the country," Duncan described it as creating "the purest system of morality" in existence (407). Acknowledging that Pennsylvania law "secures liberty of conscience and freedom of religious worship to all," Duncan said that "it is not necessary to maintain that any man should have the right publicly to vilify the religion of his neighbors and of the country . . . not to force conscience by punishment, but to preserve the peace of the country by an outward respect to the religion of the country" (408).

Having thus established the right to punish such blasphemy, the court, in a somewhat anticlimactic twist, determined that the indictment had been improperly worded and that the judgment therefore had to be reversed.

People v. Ruggles (1811) and *Commonwealth v. Kneeland* (1838) are other nineteenth-century state cases that asserted that blasphemy was an offense under the common law. In 1952, however, the U.S. Supreme Court decided in *Burstyn v. Wilson* that such laws violated the First Amendment.

See also Vidal v. Girard's Executor (1844)

For Reference and Further Reading

Banner, Stuart. 1998. "When Christianity Was Part of the Common Law." *Law and History Review* 16 (Spring): 27–62.

Burstyn v. Wilson, 343 U.S. 495 (1952).

Commonwealth v. Kneeland, 37 Mass. 206 (1838).

People v. Ruggles, 8 Johns. R. 290 (NY 1811).

Updegraph v. Commonwealth, 11 Serg. & Rawle 394 (PA 1824).

U.S. Constitution

The text of the U.S. Constitution does not, like the Declaration of Independence, refer in any manner to God (a "mistake" that the Confederate Constitution later attempted to correct), and it does not quote directly from the Bible. This has led some commentators to refer to it as "The Godless Constitution" (Kramnick and Moore, 1996). The Constitution does not, however, express anti-religious or anti-biblical sentiments, although a provision in Article VI of the document does prohibit any "religious Test . . . as a Qualification to any Office or public Trust under the United States." When taking the oath of office, the Constitution, in deference to Quakers, allows individuals to "affirm" instead of swear, and, likely in light of widespread Christian practice, the document does not include Sundays in the number of days during which a president has to veto a bill.

Even though the Constitution does not mention God, many still believe that it created a "Christian nation," and for much of its history, it has certainly governed a nation a majority of whose citizens would have so identified themselves. Some individuals have made elaborate claims for biblical influences. In a sermon in 1833, Jasper Adams of South Carolina (1793–1841) argued that the attestation clause, which referred to "the unanimous consent of the States present, the seventeenth day of September, in the year of our Lord, 1787, and of the independence of the United States of America, the twelfth," contains "a distinct recognition of the authority of Christ, and of course, of his religion by the people of the United States" (Dreisbach 1996, 63). Professor John Fea observes that David Barton of the WallBuilders "believes that virtually everything in the United States Constitution is based directly upon a biblical concept" (2014, 66; see also Gilbert 1936).

More commonly, it is possible to point to a number of biblical suppositions, at least as commonly understood at the time it was written (see Sherwood 2008), that may underlie the document. Although some of the founders clearly hoped for progress, and believed that republican institutions improved on those of the past, many also appear to have shared the Puritans' distrust about human nature, based on the corrupting influence of sin. One of the clearest statements of this philosophy is found in James Madison's statement in Federalist No. 51:

> Ambition must be made to counteract ambition. The interest of the man must be connected with the constitutional rights of the place. It may be a reflection on human nature that such devices should be necessary to control the abuses of government. But what is government itself but the greatest of all reflections on human nature? If men were angels, no government would be necessary. In forming a government which is to be administered by men over men, the great difficulty lies in this: you must first enable the government to control the governed; and in the next place oblige it to control itself. (Hamilton, Madison, and Jay 1961, 322)

Such an attitude was arguably the basis for the separation of powers among the legislative, executive, and judicial branches, as well as bicameralism (the division of Congress into two houses), federalism (shared powers between the national and state governments), and similar measures. There are additional parallels between American federalism and the government among the twelve tribes of Israel (Shalev 2013) as well as the American hierarchical system of courts and the arrangements that Moses made on the advice of his father-in-law (Exodus 18:17–22) to settle disputes that did not require his intervention.

The whole idea of a constitution is that of establishing a functioning rule of law, which reflects laws such as those that Moses gave to the people of Israel under God's direction, especially those within the second part of the Decalogue, which deal specifically with the relations of individuals to one another. The idea that the Constitution is a form of "higher law" (what Article VI of the Constitution calls "the supreme law of the land") is also consistent with the notion that certain laws like the Ten Commandments are of higher status than the laws that are merely designed to explicate and enforce them.

Although the goals of the Constitution as articulated in the preamble are directed to this-worldly concerns, the emphases on justice, welfare, and liberty are arguably biblical themes. The last is reflected in the Scripture from Leviticus 25:10 on the Liberty Bell (Zlotowitz 1988, 328–29).

Many proponents of the free exercise of religion, which is delineated in the First Amendment to the U.S. Constitution, based their own arguments on what they considered to be biblical principles, most notably those that spoke to the accountability of individuals directly to God.

Just as other institutional restraints pointed to the sinfulness of human nature, so too the equal protection clause of the Fourteenth Amendment arguably points to the common humanity that all men share being, as Paul would tell the Athenians in Acts 17:26, "of one blood."

Historically, it is also possible to trace other individual constitutional provisions to biblical origins. The provision in Article III, Section 3, requiring the testimony of two witnesses for conviction of treason is similar to a comparative provision in Deuteronomy 17:6 for capital crimes and the provisions in the Sixth Amendment for the right to a speedy trial and the right to confront witnesses to provisions within the Mosaic code (Zlotowitz 1988, 331–32).

Although its proponents made many arguments on its behalf from Scripture, there is consensus that the Eighteenth Amendment providing for national alcoholic prohibition—the only such amendment ever to be repealed (by the Twenty-First Amendment)—exceeded the actual language of Scripture, which tended to be phrased in terms of admonitions against drunkenness rather than against alcohol itself. It further bears witness to the dangers of making the law of the land too prescriptive over personal moral behaviors.

See also Christian Amendment; Criminal Law: Political Hebraism; Ten Commandments; U.S. Constitutional Convention of 1787

For Reference and Further Reading

Dreisbach, Daniel L., ed. 1996. *Religion and Politics in the Early Republic: Jasper Adams and the Church-State Debate.* Lexington: University Press of Kentucky.

Fea, John. 2014. "Does America Have a Biblical Heritage?" *The Bible in the Public Square: Its Enduring Influence in American Life*, ed. Mark A. Chancey, Carol Meyers, Eric M. Meyers. Atlanta, GA: Society of Biblical Literature, pp. 65–79.

Gilbert, Dan. 1936. *The Biblical Basis of the Constitution.* San Diego, CA: Danielle Publishers.

Hamilton, Alexander, James Madison, and John Jay. [1788] 1961. *The Federalist Papers.* New York: New American Library.

Hutchinson, John A. 1947. "Biblical Foundations of Democracy." *Journal of Bible and Religion* 14 (January): 34–37.

Kramnick, Isaac, and R. Laurence Moore. 1996. *The Godless Constitution: The Case against Religious Correctness.* New York: W. W. Norton.

Shalev, Eran. 2013. *American Zion: The Old Testament as a Political Text from the Revolution to the Civil War.* New Haven, CT: Yale University Press.

Sherwood, Yvonne. 2008. "The God of Abraham and Exceptional States, or the Early Modern Rise of the Whig/Liberal Bible." *Journal of the American Academy of Religion* 76 (June): 312–43.

Zlotowitz, Bernard M. 1988. "The Biblical and Rabbinic Underpinnings of the Constitution." *Judaism* 37 (Summer): 328–34.

U.S. Constitutional Convention of 1787

The U.S. Constitution was formulated as an alternative to the Articles of Confederation at a Convention that met in Philadelphia from May through September 1787. Of the 55 representatives who attended from twelve states, 39 of 42 remaining delegates signed the Constitution and sent it to the states for ratification. James Madison and other delegates kept notes of almost every day of the convention, although it is possible that Madison, who generally tried to keep sectarian issues out of public debates, may have downplayed some references, as is evident by comparing his notes about slavery to a description of the same debates offered by Luther Martin of Maryland (Vile 2016, I: 61–62).

Pennsylvania's Benjamin Franklin is reported to have made more biblical references than any other delegates. These included comparing the Egyptian Pharaoh who had kept the children of Israel in bondage to a typical monarch (Farrand 1966, I: 60) and three biblical references when proposing that the Convention should begin each day with prayer. They also included a reference to Matthew 10:20 about the need for God to build a strong house, a reference to the tower of Babel, and a biblical admonition against covetousness (Vile 2016, I: 60).

Gouverneur Morris, also representing Pennsylvania, referred to the biblical King Rehoboam, who did not listen very well to his people (Farrand 1966, I: 113). He also referenced the distinction between the creature and his creator, the tendency of demagogues to bribe people with "loaves and fishes," and "the curse of heaven" on states that had slavery (Farrand 1966, I: 552, I: 513, II: 221).

George Read of Delaware cited an analogy by Jesus from Matthew 9:16 about "putting new cloth on an old garment" (Farrand 1966, I: 137). He also likened the congressional power to print money to "the mark of the Beast in Revelation" (Farrand 1966, II: 310).

Both James Wilson of Pennsylvania and Luther Martin of Maryland referred to Solomon. Wilson compared the debate over state representation to that of the dispute that Solomon had to judge between two women claiming the same baby, and Martin focused on the mother's tenderness in this case (Farrand 1966, I: 137, I: 348).

In an analogy that Abraham Lincoln later employed, General Charles Cotesworth Pinckney referred to a kingdom divided against itself when talking about state and federal offices (Farrand 1966, I: 366). In a speech that he prepared for the Convention, John Dickinson of Delaware quoted Paul's admonition in 1 Corinthians 6:12 that "all things to thee are lawful but not convenient" (Hutson 1987, 137), made a further reference to Reuben talking with his brothers about selling Joseph into slavery (Hutson 1987, 139), and cited the word "Shibboleth" drawn from Judges 12:6 (Farrand 1966, II: 278). Elbridge Gerry further referred to the mark of Cain, which was taken from Genesis 4:5 (Farrand 1966, II: 332).

In condemning the further importation of slaves, Virginia's George Mason referred to such an evil as bringing "the judgment of heaven on a Country" (Farrand 1966, II: 370), which, because nations do not have souls, would be inflicted in their lifetimes.

A number of delegates and commentators later referred to the Convention's ability to craft a new constitution as a virtual "miracle" (Vile, 2016, I: 62). George Read referred to the divisiveness of religious creeds (Farrand 1966, I: 582), while James Madison, who was an advocate of strict separation of church and state, warned of religious "persecution & oppression" (Farrand 1966, I: 135) and joined South Carolina's Charles Pinckney in proposing that "no preferences or distinctions should be allowed on account of religion" (Farrand 1966, II: 616).

Franklin observed how both the Roman Catholic and Anglican Churches considered themselves infallible (Farrand 1966, II: 642).

See also Franklin, Benjamin; Madison, James; Judgment; Slavery

For Reference and Further Reading

Farrand, Max, ed. 1966. *The Records of the Federal Convention of 1787.* 4 vols. New Haven, CT: Yale University Press.

Hall, Mark David. 2011. "Did America Have a Christian Founding?" Heritage Foundation. June 7. https://www.heritage.org/political-process/report/did-america-have-christian-founding.

Hutson, James H., ed. 1987. *Supplement to Max Farrand's The Records of the Federal Convention of 1787.* New Haven, CT: Yale University Press.

Vile, John R. 2016. *The Constitutional Convention of 1787: A Comprehensive Encyclopedia of America's Founding*, rev. 2nd ed., 2 vols. Clark, NJ: Talbot.

U.S. Flag

In addition to serving as a source of inspiration and spiritual instruction, the Bible is often a unifying symbol for groups of religious believers. It has also sometimes been viewed much like a totem or good luck charm with semimagical powers that protect and ward off evil.

Professor David Morgan has made a persuasive argument that the disestablishment of religion in America and the rise of the public schools as the main instrument for the socialization of children were accompanied by "the sacralization of the American flag in the quest for a compelling icon of national identity" (2014, 111). During the Civil War, Union soldiers were given miniature flags that became known as Bible flags because they were small enough to carry in the Bibles that they took with them into battle (Leepson 2018, 10).

As the flag became more ubiquitous and the religious diversity of Americans became even more pronounced, the flag was accompanied by a salute (that, in 1954, was altered to include the words "under God"), by the adoption of a national anthem that was named after and celebrated it, and by a fairly complex code of flag etiquette. Historians often point to the last two decades of the nineteenth century as the development of the "cult of the flag," which may have reached its apotheosis with the publication of William Guthrie's *The Religion of Old Glory* in 1919 (Vile 2018, 138).

More than forty years earlier, Henry Ward Beecher, one of America's most popular preachers, had connected the flag to Scriptures in his book *Freedom and War*. He led off a chapter on the flag with Psalm 9:4: "Thou hast given a banner to them that fear thee, that it may be displayed because of the truth." Connecting the flag to liberty, Beecher observed that "the stars upon it were to the pining nations like the bright morning stars of God, and the stripes upon it were beams of morning light" (1863, 112). Connecting the flag to the prophecies of a Messiah in Isaiah 9:2 and Matthew 4:16, Beecher observed that "the people which sat in darkness saw a great light; and to them which sat in the region and shadow of death light is sprung up" (113). Beecher proclaimed that the flag "is not a painted rag. It is a whole national history. It is the Constitution. It is the government. It is the free people that stand in the government on the Constitution" (123).

In the twentieth century, it became increasingly common to display American flags, often with newly designed Christian flags, at the front of churches. Some Puritans had objected to the display of the British flag because of their opposition to what they considered to be idolatrous symbols, including crosses. Notably, the only object that the flag code specifies may be placed on an American flag is a Bible or other holy book.

See also Beecher, Henry Ward; Under God

For Reference and Further Reading

Beecher, Henry Ward. 1863. *Freedom and War. Discourses on Topics Suggested by the Times*. Boston: Ticknor and Fields.

Leepson, Marc. 2018. "Flag Etiquette." In John R. Vile, *The American Flag: An Encyclopedia of the Stars and Stripes in U.S. History, Culture, and Law*. Santa Barbara, CA: ABC-CLIO, pp. 10–18.

Morgan, David. 2014. "The Image of the Protestant Bible in America." *The Bible in the Public Square: Its Enduring Influence on American Life*, ed. Mark A. Chancey, Carol Meyers, and Eric M. Meyers. Atlanta, GA: Society of Biblical Literature, pp. 93–119.

Vile, John R. 2018. *The American Flag: An Encyclopedia of the Stars and Stripes in U.S. History, Culture, and Law*. Santa Barbara, CA: ABC-CLIO.

• V •

Van Orden v. Perry (2005)

The Ten Commandments, which Exodus 20 describes God as giving to Moses on Mount Sinai, are among the highlights of Jewish history, but their displays on public property can sometimes raise questions as to whether they violate the establishment clause of the First Amendment. *Van Orden v. Perry*, which the U.S. Supreme Court decided in 2005, is one such case.

Thomas David Van Orden was a lawyer who questioned the constitutional propriety of a granite monument measuring 6 feet high and 3 ½ feet wide with a number of symbols and the text of the Commandments on the grounds of the Texas state capital. The Fraternal Order of Eagles had donated this monument in 1961 as part of a campaign initiated by E. J. Ruegemer, a Minnesota juvenile court judge, who hoped that disseminating the words of the Commandments might reduce juvenile delinquency; Cecil B. DeMille, who produced a movie on the Commandments, also had a hand in the efforts.

Lower courts had upheld the display, which was one of seventeen monuments and twenty-one historical markers in the 22-acre grounds, on the basis that it was a passive monument with the secular purpose of recognizing the work of the Eagles in reducing juvenile delinquency. The Supreme Court's plurality decision was authored by Chief Justice William Rehnquist and accepted by Antonin Scalia, Anthony Kennedy, and Clarence Thomas.

Observing that establishment clause cases were Janus-like, in pointing both toward the role that religion had played in U.S. history and forward to concerns that governmental intervention might undermine religious freedom, Rehnquist pointed to past decisions in which the court had recognized that "our institutions presuppose a Supreme Being, yet these institutions must not press religious observances upon their Citizens" (2005, 683). Although the court had often applied the Lemon Test, which required laws to have a secular legislative purpose, neither to inhibit nor to advance religion, and to avoid excessive entanglement with religion, Rehnquist did not think this precedent was "useful in dealing with the sort of passive monument that Texas has erected on its Capitol grounds" (686). After referencing early presidential Thanksgiving Day proclamations, and observing that the Supreme Court had in *McGowan v. Maryland* (1961) upheld a Sunday closing law, even though it derived in part from one of the commandments, Rehnquist went on to give a detailed description of numerous depictions of Moses and the Commandments in the nation's capital including the Supreme Court:

> Since 1936, Moses has stood, holding two tablets that reveal portions of the Ten Commandments written in Hebrew, among other lawgivers in the south frieze. Representations of the Ten Commandments adorn the metal gates lining the north and south sides of the Courtroom as well as the doors leading into the

> Courtroom. Moses also sits on the exterior east façade of the building holding the Ten Commandments tablets.
> Similar acknowledgements can be seen throughout a visitor's tour of our Nation's Capital. For example, a large statue of Moses holding the Ten Commandments, alongside a statue of the apostle Paul, has overlooked the rotunda of the Library of Congress' Jefferson Building since 1897. And the Jefferson Buildings' Great Reading Room contains a sculpture of a woman beside the Ten Commandments with a quote above her from the Old Testament (Micah 6:8). A medallion with two tablets depicting the Ten Commandments decorates the floor of the National Archives. Inside the Department of Justice, a statue entitled "The Spirit of Law" has two tablets representing the Ten Commandments lying at its feet. In front of the Ronald Reagan Building is another sculpture that includes a depiction of the Ten Commandments. So too a 24-foot-tall sculpture, depicting, among other things, the Ten Commandments and a cross, stands outside the federal courthouse that houses both the Court of Appeals and the District Court for the District of Columbia. Moses is also prominently featured in the Chamber of the United States House of Representatives. (2005, 688)

Acknowledging that "the Ten Commandments are religious" and have "religious significance," Rehnquist also observed that Moses "was a lawgiver as well as a religious leader. And the Ten Commandments have an undeniable historical meaning" (690). Rehnquist further distinguished this case from those, like *Stone v. Graham* (1980), that had invalidated similar displays in public schools. Not only were such students more impressionable, but they were forced to attend schools, whereas no one was forced to pass by the Texas landmark.

In a brief concurring opinion, Justice Antonin Scalia said that there was nothing unconstitutional about a state favoring nonsectarian religion, while Justice Clarence Thomas argued both that the court should never have applied the establishment clause to the states and that the clause was only designed to prohibit "actual legal coercion" (693). In a separate concurrence, which provided the critical fifth vote, Justice Stephen Breyer distinguished separation of church and state from "mutual hostility and suspicion" (700). Recounting the history of the Eagles' donation, he believed that, in context, the monument "conveys a predominantly secular message" and had not been challenged during the first forty years, suggesting that it had not evoked hostility (702).

Justice John Paul Stevens authored a dissenting opinion joined by Justice Ruth Bader Ginsburg. It began with the words on the monument and questioned how, if at all, they related, like other monuments in the vicinity, to the founding of Texas. He believed that the establishment clause "has created a strong presumption against the display of religious symbols on public property" (708) and suggested that Rehnquist's compilation of religious symbols was of "marginal relevance" since none of them "includes the full text of the Commandments," and all were "exhibited in different settings" (712). However laudable it was to seek to combat juvenile delinquency, "achieving that goal through biblical teachings injects a religious purpose into an otherwise secular endeavor" (714). The character of this message was manifested by the fact that the monument had highlighted the words "I AM the LORD thy God" in large letters (717). Catholics and Protestants differed on the wording of the Commandments, which were not part of the sacred Scriptures of Buddhists, Hindus, and other Americans. Moreover, a monument with such language on the grounds of a state capital was much different from a political speech (like inaugural addresses) in which listeners would understand that the language reflected the thoughts of the speaker rather than official U.S. policies.

Justice Sandra Day O'Connor authored a separate dissent joined by Stevens and Ginsburg, arguing that the display violated the principle of religious neutrality. Further seeking to discount the numerous examples to which Rehnquist had alluded, O'Connor observed that none of these highlighted the text of the Commandments in the same manner and that many of the examples he cited were "mixed with symbols of moral and intellectual abstractions like Equity and Authority" (740). Nor did she think that earlier decisions relating to school displays were intended to be necessarily limited to classrooms. She also suggested that others may have refused to challenge the monument not because they were unoffended but because they lacked the financial means or feared "the risk of social ostracism" (747).

See also McGowan v. Maryland; Moses as Political Archetype; *Stone v. Graham*; Ten Commandments

For Reference and Further Reading

Coogan, Michael. 2014. *The Ten Commandments: A Short History of an Ancient Text.* New Haven, CT: Yale University Press.
McGowan v. Maryland, 366 U.S. 420 (1961).
Stone v. Graham, 449 U.S. 39 (1980).
Van Orden v. Perry, 545 U.S. 677 (2005).

Vesey, Denmark

Denmark Vesey (ca. 1767–1822) was a skilled African American carpenter who won a lottery and was able to purchase his freedom but not that of his wife and children. He was charged and hanged for his alleged attempt to launch a slave rebellion in Charleston, South Carolina, in June 1822, in which he had encouraged slaves to slaughter their masters and their families. Although nipped in the bud, the prospect of such a revolt spread fear throughout the South and led to even more restrictive laws against instructing slaves to read or write, even in Sunday schools.

Scholars continue to debate the degree to which Vesey had simply been letting off hot air and the degree to which he and his compatriots had an organized plan in place for what might have been the largest such slave revolt in Southern history, and the alleged ringleaders fairly stoically resisted attempts to get them to expose alleged coconspirators (Wiener 2002). Slave suspects were likely subject to torture, and laws limited the admissibility of their testimony in judicial proceedings.

The contemporary official report of the judicial proceedings that resulted in numerous executions suggested that Vesey had two favorite scriptural passages, both of which were taken from Old Testament visions of a holy war. Zechariah 14:1–3 thus described the destruction of Jerusalem, which would include the ravishing of women, and the death and captivity of the population as a whole.

Joshua 6:21 further described how Joshua and his men killed all the inhabitants of the city of Jericho excepting Rahab, who had aided Jewish spies, and her family members (Higginson 1861). Vesey also quoted from biblical passages such as Exodus 1:23–25, involving the plight of the children of Israel as they served as slaves in Egypt (Schipper 2019, 27). He may have received additional inspiration from the story of the campaign that the biblical Judge Samson led against the Philistines in Judges 13–16 (Schipper 2019, 28); from descriptions of the destruction of Heshbon and Bashan as described in Deuteronomy 3:3–7; and from similar descriptions of the destruction of Midian in Numbers 31:7–18 (Schipper 2019, 33).

Contrasting Vesey's apparent use of Scripture against those of Absalom Jones, Professor Jeremy Schipper, who is working on a book entitled *Denmark Vesey's Bible*, has suggested that Vesey used the Bible not simply "as an endorsement of liberation from slavery as Jones's 'Thanksgiving Sermon' does" but that "they imply that Vesey also used them as a justification for the violent methods that he and his associates intended to use during the insurrection" (Schipper 2019, 30).

Noting that many of the Scriptures that Vesey apparently cited involved Canaanites (those inhabiting the land of Israel prior to the time of Joshua), Schipper has argued that Vesey may have regarded American whites (much as Puritans had once viewed Native Americans) as analogous to such Canaanites, who were to be slaughtered without mercy (2019, 35). Schipper believes that this argument might, in turn, have further spurred slavery apologists to attempt to turn the tables by portraying descendants of Noah's son, Ham, as blacks who bore slavery as a result of a biblical curse (36–37).

In 1831, Nat Turner, who also claimed religious inspiration, launched a slave revolt in Southampton County, Virginia, which led to still greater Southern fears and increasingly repressive legislation. John Brown's raid at Harper's Ferry, Virginia (now West Virginia), played a role in increasing the tensions that led to the Civil War.

See also Brown, John; Curses on Cain, Ham, and the Canaanites; Slavery; Jones, Absalom; Turner, Nat

For Reference and Further Reading

Higginson, Thomas Wentworth. 1861. "The Story of Denmark Vesey." *The Atlantic*. June. https://www.theatlantic.com/magazine/archive/1861/06/denmark-vessey/396239/.

Robertson, David. 1999. *Denmark Vesey: The Buried Story of America's Largest Slave Rebellion and the Man Who Led It*. New York: Alfred A. Knopf.

Schipper, Jeremy. 2019. "'Misconstruction of the Sacred Page': On Denmark Vesey's Biblical Interpretations." *Journal of Biblical Literature* 128(1): 23–38.

Wiener, Jon. 2002. "Denmark Vesey: A New Verdict." *The Nation*. February 21. https://www.thenation.com/article/denmark-vesey-new-verdict/.

Vidal v. Girard's Executors (1844)

Since the Supreme Court's decision in *Abington v. Schempp* (1963), devotional readings of the Bible have been prohibited in public schools under the establishment clause of the First Amendment as applied to the states through the due process clause of the Fourteenth Amendment, but it was not always so.

In 1844, John Girard, a wealthy man who had died childless, bequeathed his money to establish a school to teach white orphans in Philadelphia. In his will, he stipulated that "no ecclesiastic, missionary, or minister of any sect whatsoever, shall ever hold or exercise any station or duty whatever in the said college; nor shall any such person ever be admitted for any purpose, or as a visitor, within the premises appropriated to the purposes of the said college" (1844, 133). He further specified, "In making this restriction, I do not mean to cast any reflection upon any sect or person whatsoever; but, as there is such a multitude of sects, and such a diversity of opinion amongst them, I desire to keep the tender minds of the orphans, who are to derive advantage from this bequest, free from the excitement which clashing doctrines and sectarian controversy are so apt to produce" (133). Moreover, he had expressed his desire that "all the instructors and teachers in the college shall take pains to instill into the minds of the scholars the purest principles of morality, so that, on their entrance into active life, they may, from inclination and habit, evince benevolence towards their fellow-creatures, and a love of truth, sobriety, and industry, adopting at the same time such religious tenets as their matured reason may enable them to prefer" (133).

Francois Vidal and others had challenged this bequest on the basis that the exclusion of religious instructors and, by implication, instruction in the Christian religion were inconsistent with the state constitution. The decision was rendered by Justice Joseph Story (1779–1845), an esteemed justice and constitutional commentator, who had elsewhere argued that American common law included Christian principles. In this decision, in which he upheld the validity of Girard's will, Story relied on an early state case in *Updegraph v. Commonwealth* (1824), for the principle that "although Christianity be a part of the common law of the state, yet it is so in this qualified sense, that its divine origin and truth are admitted, and therefore it is not to be maliciously and openly reviled and blasphemed against, to the annoyance of believers or the injury of the public" (198).

Interpreting Girard's instructions so as to save them from constitutional defect, Story interpreted his will neither as excluding the teaching of Christianity nor the reading of the Bible but simply as leaving such instruction to laymen rather than to representatives of particular denominations. Believing that teachers could provide moral guidance both through example and through teaching, Story rhetorically asked, "Why may not the Bible, and especially the New Testament, without note or comment, be read and taught as a divine revelation in the college—its general principles expounded, its evidence explained, and its glorious principles of morality inculcated? What is there to prevent a work, not sectarian, upon the general evidences of Christianity, from being read and taught in the college by lay-teachers?" (200).

Further denying that Girard had intended to exclude such moral instruction, Story asked, "Where can the purest principles of morality be learned so clearly or so perfectly as from the New Testament? Where are benevolence, the love of truth, sobriety and industry, so powerfully and irresistibly inculcated as in the sacred volume?" (200). He concluded that "there is nothing in the devise establishing the college, or in the regulations and restrictions contained therein, which are inconsistent with the Christian religion, or are opposed to any known policy of the state of Pennsylvania" (201).

See also Abington v. Schempp (1963); *Updegraph v. Commonwealth* (1824)

For Reference and Further Reading

Banner, Stuart. 1998. "When Christianity Was Part of the Common Law." *Law and History Review* 16 (Spring): 27–62.
Updegraph v. Commonwealth, 11 Serg. & Rawle 394 (PA 1824).
Vidal v. Girard's Executors, 43 U.S. 127 (1844).

Vine and Fig Tree

See Washington, George

Violence

The first mentions of violence in the Bible, described in Genesis 4, was Cain's murder of his brother Abel, which occurred after mankind had sinned and God had expelled them from the Garden of Eden. Isaiah 9:6, which Christians understand as a prophecy of Jesus, the Messiah, refers to Him as a "Prince of Peace." In his Sermon on the Mount, Jesus further blessed "peacemakers" and said that "they shall be called the children of God" (Matthew 5:9).

However, in a number of places, the biblical book of Revelation portrays Christ as a warrior who will come to judge the world. Moreover, in addition to containing numerous descriptions of violence, the Old Testament portrays numerous battles in which God is said to have instructed the Israelites to exterminate their enemies.

These include the command in Deuteronomy 20 utterly to destroy the inhabitants of Canaan and later accounts of such actions in the book of Joshua, which records the Jews' conquest of the land. Judges 20:23 had similarly described the slaughter of the members of the tribe of Benjamin during the tumultuous period of the judges. Chapter 15 of 1 Samuel further described the eradication of the Amalekites (Samuel hacked King Agag to pieces after King Saul disobediently had sought to spare his life), a wandering tribe that harassed the children of Israel as they wandered in the wilderness and whose very memory they were instructed to blot out. Although the respective contexts vary significantly, Psalm 137 pronounces as "happy" the one who "taketh and dasheth thy little ones against the stones"; Jeremiah 48:10 pronounced a curse on "he that keepeth back his sword from blood"; and Ezekiel 9:6 says to "slay utterly old and young, both maids and little children, and women."

Although some philosophers and theologians had sought to counter arguments by Deists that such accounts demonstrated that the Old Testament did not rise to the moral level of enlightenment thinking, others had sought to justify Jewish actions as obeying God's mandate to punish a wicked people by arguing that such a mandate by God to the Israelites did not serve as a justification for modern nations to do the same (Ilany 2012; Ilany 2018). Although there were groups like Quakers and Mennonites who believed that their beliefs required them to be pacifists, most Christian denominations, consistent with the thought advanced by St. Augustine, were convinced that it was appropriate for them to fight in just wars, which were largely considered to be defensive wars that responded proportionately to provocations.

In the Middle Ages, Europe witnessed a number of crusades, or so-called holy wars, in which Christian warriors committed mayhem while trying to free Jerusalem from Muslims, whom they considered to be infidels. This violence by professing Christians against non-Christians was in turn followed after the Reformation by bloody wars between Roman Catholics and Protestants and of differing sects of Protestants against one another. The English and German civil wars were especially bloody and were often justified in the language of holy war.

Tragically, European Christian encounters with Native American Indians continued this bloody heritage. Spanish conquistadors in Central and South America, who were often accompanied by Catholic priests, believed that they were on a holy mission, which included the right to exterminate natives (some of whom engaged in cannibalism and human sacrifice) who refused to convert to their religion (Canizares-Esguerra 2009). English settlers in North America often fancied themselves as a New Israel, crossing the ocean like ancient Jews had crossed the Red Sea, and coming to bring civilization to the wilderness where they would serve as a city on a hill.

For settlers who identified themselves as part of a New Israel, it was not a big stretch to view the Native Americans as Canaanites or Amalekites who were subject to God's judgment. Somewhat ironically, Puritans and others, including later members of the Church of Jesus Christ of Latter-Day Saints, sometimes also identified the Native Americans as being remnants of the lost tribes of Israel (Corrigan 2011, 66). Under English conceptions of property, epitomized in the philosophy of John Locke, uncultivated land was practically useless, and individuals only earned the right to it by mixing their labor with it.

Not surprisingly, these rival cultures were often at war with one another. Native Americans sometimes received support, or were perceived as receiving such support, from European enemies of Britain like France and Spain where Catholics predominated (Corrigan 2011, 64). During the French and Indian War, British colonists began characterizing their French Catholic enemies as Amalekites (Corrigan 2011, 72).

Puritan Captain John Mason led the raid that resulted in the burning of a Native American village at Mystic, Connecticut, in 1637 that killed about five hundred people including women and children. He described giving the order "WE MUST BURN THEM, and immediately stepping into the Wigwam, brought out a Fire-brand, and putting it into the Matts with which they were covered, set the Wigwams on Fire. Thus was God seen in the Mount, crushing his enemies and the enemies of his people . . . burning them up in the Fire of his wrath and dunging the Ground with their Flesh: It was the LORDS DOINGS, and it is marvelous to our Eyes" (Juster 2016, 53). In a reference to Psalm 126, Mason further described the feelings of his men by saying, "Then was our Mouth filled with Laughter, and our Tongue with Singing; thus we may say the Lord hath done great things for us among the Heathen, whereof we are glad. Praise ye the Lord!" (119). In his history *Of Plymouth Plantation*, William Bradford would later comment that "it was a fearful sight to see them thus frying in the fire and the streams of blood quenching the same, and horrible was the stink and scent thereof; but the victory seemed a sweet sacrifice" (Juster 2016, 53). Puritans further described their own fallen soldiers as martyrs to the cause of Christ (Corrigan 2011, 69).

From 1675 to 1678 Puritans engaged in a war with the Wampanoag led by Metacomet, or King Philip, that, in terms of percentages of participants who died (about four thousand were killed), was the most violent in American history (Simon 2016). As in earlier conflicts, Christian Puritans and pagan Native Americans mimicked one another in their levels of violence, and each evoked their respective religions. In a history of the American West, Theodore Roosevelt thus observed, "Many of the best of the backwoodsmen were Bible-readers, but they were brought up in a creed that made much of the Old Testament, and laid slight stress on pity, truth, or mercy. They looked at their foes as the Hebrew prophets looked at the enemies of Israel. What were the abominations because of which the Canaanites were destroyed before Joshua, when compared with the abominations of the red savages whose land they, another chosen people, should in their turn inhabit?" (Mead 2008, 37).

Ideas of Anglo-Saxon racial superiority persisted through the nineteenth century. The doctrine of manifest destiny justified the displacement of Native Americans, through violence when necessary, in the European settling of the American West, and anti-Catholic protests sometimes resulted in bloody riots. The United States further used such racial justifications in quelling indigenous independence movements in the Philippines, which it gained from Spain in the Spanish-American War.

Early American treatment of Native Americans was perilously close to later genocides and attempts at racial cleansings, which, as the twentieth century has revealed, may be entwined with, but hardly require, religious justifications. Any discussion of the subject of violence and the Bible must always recognize that it is often difficult to tease out biblical *motivations* for, or *commands* to commit, violence as opposed to biblical *pretexts* or *rationalizations* for it.

The debate over gun violence in the United States continues to pit those who favor greater regulation of gun sales and those who emphasize individual right of self-defense, which they associate with the Second Amendment. Some on the individual-rights side have argued that the Bible supports their position. Joel McDurmon, a biblical Reconstructionist, thus published an article entitled "Bring Your Pieces to Church," in which he provocatively argued,

> Christians should be aware that the use of force in preservation of life is a biblical doctrine (Ex.22:2–3; Prov. 24:10–12; Est. 8–9; Neh. 4; cp. John 15:13–14). Likewise those who possessed weapons in Scripture are often said to be well skilled in the use of them (Judg. 20:15–16; 1 Chron. 12:1–2, 21–22). We can only surmise that 1) God gave them talent in this regard, and that 2) they engaged in target practice

> regularly. Further, under biblical law, to be disarmed was to be enslaved and led to a disruption of the economic order due to government regulations and monopolies (1 Sam 13:19–22). (Posner and Ingersoll 2010, 121)

See also America as New Israel; City upon a Hill; Colonization; French and Indian War; Manifest Destiny; Mennonites; Native American Indians; Puritans; Quakers; Roman Catholics

For Reference and Further Reading

Canizares-Esguerra, Jorge. 2009. *Soundings in Atlantic History*. Cambridge, MA: Harvard University Press.

Collins, John J. 2004. *Does the Bible Justify Violence?* Minneapolis, MN: Fortress Press.

Corrigan, John. 2011. "Amalek and the Rhetoric of Extermination." *The First Prejudice: Religious Tolerance and Intolerance in Early America*, ed. Christ Beneke and Christopher S. Grenda. Philadelphia: University of Pennsylvania Press, pp. 53–72.

Ilany, Ofri. 2012. "From Divine Commandment to Political Act: The Eighteenth-Century Polemic on the Extermination of the Canaanites." *Journal of the History of Ideas* 73 (July): 437–61.

Ilany, Ofri. 2018. *In Search of the Hebrew People: Bible and Nation in the German Enlightenment*. Indianapolis: Indiana University Press.

Juster, Susan. 2016. *Sacred Violence in Early America*. Philadelphia: University of Pennsylvania Press.

Lytton, Timothy D. 2002–2003. "'Shall Not the Judge of the Earth Deal Justly': Accountability, Compassion, and Judicial Authority in the Biblical Story of Sodom and Gomorrah." *Journal of Law and Religion* 18: 31–55.

Mead, Walter Russell. 2008. "The New Israel and the Old: Why Gentile Americans Back the Jewish State." *Foreign Affairs* 87 (July–August): 28–46.

Posner, Sarah, and Julie Ingersoll. 2010. "Gun Ownership: 'An Obligation to God,'" *At the Tea Party: The Wing Nuts, Whack Jobs, and White-Whiteness of the New Republican Right...and Why We Should Take It Seriously*, ed. Laura Flanders. New York: OR Books, pp. 117–24.

Scholz, Susanne, and Pablo R. Andinach, eds. *La Violencia and the Hebrew Bible: The Politics and Histories of Biblical Hermeneutics on the American Continent*. Atlanta, GA: Society of Biblical Literature.

Simon, Ed. 2016. "The Remembrance of Amalek." *The Revealer: A Review of Religion & Media*. March 22. https://therevealer.org/the-remembrance-of-amalek/.

Stevens, Paul. 1993. "'Leviticus Thinking' and the Rhetoric of Early Modern Colonialism." *Criticism* 35 (Summer): 441–61.

• W •

Walker, David

David Walker (1796–1830) was a prominent African American abolitionist who published three different editions of his *Walker's Appeal, in Four Articles; Together with a Preamble, to the Coloured Citizens of the World, but in Particular, and Very Expressly, to Those of the United States of America*, from 1829 to 1830.

Born a free black in North Carolina, Walker moved to Charleston, South Carolina, and later to Boston where he found a community of fellow blacks in Beacon Hill. From this venue, Walker published his appeal, which he tried to have smuggled into the South, whose leaders did their best to suppress it. In contrast to works that had depended on God to end slavery, Walker called upon the enslaved to assert their natural and God-given rights to freedom, much as though he were a biblical prophet calling down woe upon the nation in the process. Walker's appeal was thoroughly soaked in Scriptures, especially those related to Joseph and Moses, albeit in sometimes counterintuitive ways, as when he argued that the Egyptians had been far more benevolent than their Christian successors. Walker's work was also unique in seeking directly to counter the arguments that Thomas Jefferson had made for racial inferiority in his *Notes on the State of Virginia*, and for contrasting the words of Jefferson's Declaration of Independence against the reasoning from Jefferson's book.

In Walker's preamble, he described African Americans as "the most degraded, wretched, and abject set of beings that ever lived since the world began" (1830, 3). Such a situation was especially intolerable in "*this Republican Land of Liberty*" (5). Moreover, given that God was both just and merciful, there was no way that this situation could be allowed to continue. Echoing Patrick Henry, or perhaps, more directly, the words of Jeremiah 6:14, Walker observed that calls for "Peace!—Peace!" were out of place in such circumstances. As he rhetorically asked, "If God gives you peace and tranquility, and suffers you thus to go on afflicting us, and our children, who have never given you the least provocation—would he be to us a *God of justice*" (8).

Walker divided his appeal into four articles, the first of which was labeled, "Our Wretchedness in Consequence of Slavery" (9). Perhaps seeking to echo the words of the resolution for independence that Richard Henry Lee had introduced at the Second Continental Congress and which had been included in the Declaration of Independence, Walker pointed out that African Americans were "called *men*, and of course are, and ought to be free" (9). Despite biblical condemnation of the Egyptians, they permitted non-native men like Joseph and Moses to rise to positions of authority, and even permitted intermarriage—a privilege, however, for which Walker said he would "not give a pinch of snuff" (11). Moreover, Egyptians never insulted the Israelites, as Jefferson had insulted African Americans in suggesting that they mated with monkeys or orangutans (12). Nor did the Egyptians see a different skin color as being an "unfortunate" condition as Jefferson had done (14–15). The key fact was that African Americans were men, entitled to natural rights, and obliged to no master other than Jesus Christ (20). Moreover, if the world were ever to become Christianized, it would not be the result of white hypocrites but as a result of African Americans themselves (21).

In his second article, Walker described "Our Wretchedness in Consequence of Ignorance" (22). Seeking to rebut the idea that African Americans were descendants of Noah's son, Ham, and thus cursed with their blackness, Walker pointed to Africans like Hannibal who had been great in their day. He had particular scorn for African Americans who worked with whites to help return fugitive slaves to their owners, and he continued to treat Jefferson's ideas about black racial inferiority with scorn. Walker expressed further concern that even African American children who attended school were not taught English grammar and other subjects that their white peers were taught.

Whereas the gospel of Christ was supposed to be liberating, Walker's Article III pointed to "Our Wretchedness in Consequence of the Preachers of the Religion of Jesus Christ" (39). Observing that "pure and undefiled religion [a reference to James 1:27], such as was preached by Jesus Christ and his apostles, is hard to be found in all the earth" (39–40), he observed that slave masters sometimes beat slaves whom they found praying. This was in direct contravention to Peter's statement when sharing the gospel with the Roman centurion Cornelius in Acts 14:25–27, that God "has no respect to persons, but in every nation he that feareth God and worketh righteousness is accepted with him" (42). Walker further contrasted the treatment that masters meted out to their slaves with Jesus's admonition in the Golden Rule. He ridiculed preachers who used the Bible to tell slaves that they "must be obedient to their masters—must do their duty to their masters or be whipped—the whip was made for the backs of fools" (44).

Utilizing the role of the prophet, Walker proclaimed that "unless you speedily alter your course, you and your Country are gone!!!!! For God Almighty will tear up the very face of the earth!!!" (45). Walker cited Revelation 22:11: "He that is unjust, let him be unjust still:—and he which is filthy, let him be filthy still: and he that is righteous, let him be righteous still: and he that is holy, let him be holy still," presumably in preparation for God's judgment (45). Professing that "we would not wish to see them destroyed notwithstanding, they have and do now treat us more cruel than any people have treated another" (46), he rhetorically asked, "How can the preachers and people of America believe the Bible?" He observed that, in the Great Commission of Matthew 28:18–20, Jesus had instructed disciples to go out and teach and baptize all nations, which would include those in Africa (47).

In his fourth and final article, Walker discussed "Our Wretchedness in Consequence of the Colonizing Plan" (49). Here he poured ridicule on plans advocated by Senator Henry Clay and others to settle free blacks in Liberia where they could no long inspire those who were enslaved with their doctrines. Pointing out that slaves had invested as much of their lives and blood in America as had others, no one had the right to send them away from their new homes.

Walker observed that the barbarities of American slaveholders was just as evil, and deserving of judgment, as the conduct of men in Noah's day who were destroyed by the great flood and by those who live in Sodom and Gomorrah at the time of God's judgment on these cities (60). Quoting from Bishop Richard Allen of the African Methodist Episcopal Church in the United States, Walker observed, "This land which we have watered with our *tears* and our blood, is now our *mother country*, and we are well satisfied to stay where wisdom abounds and the gospel is free" (65).

Further ridiculing the notion that blacks (who were equally sons of Noah as were whites) could somehow bear the Curse of Cain (69), Walker observed that all were equally made in God's image. African Americans needed to awake from their lethargy, knowing that Jesus himself (in Matthew 18:6) had condemned those who had offended any of his children (75).

Walker still held out the hope that God desired to save America from destruction, but he argued that this would only occur when they began treating all men equally. Without such repentance, "I call God, I call Angels, I call men to witness, that the destruction of the Americans is at hand, and will be speedily consummated unless they repent" (80).

Walker included an extensive quotation from the Declaration of Independence, and urged his readers to "compare your own language above . . . with your cruelties and murders" (85). He further cited the language of the Declaration as to both the "right" and the "duty" to throw off such oppression (85). He ended with words from a hymn that was based on Psalm 10 (Meacham and McGraw 2019, 53).

Herbert Marbury contrasts Walker's challenging "pillar of fire" approach to Absalom Jones's "pillar of cloud" approach to seeking white supporters (2015, 16–48). Walker's erudition matched his passion and arguably interpreted the philosophy of the Declaration of Independence in a republican fashion. However, it probably did as much to raise fears of African American uprisings among whites as it did to inspire slave uprisings and undoubtedly reinforced the views of Southern whites that Northern abolitionists were fanatics who were more interested in claiming and preserving moral high ground than in seeking reasonable solutions to the slavery issue.

See also Curses on Cain, Ham, and the Canaanites; Declaration of Independence; Jefferson Bible; Jones, Absalom; Moses as Political Archetype

For Reference and Further Reading

Marbury, Herbert Robinson. 2015. *Pillars of Cloud and Fire: The Politics of Exodus in African American Biblical Interpretation*. New York: New York University Press.

Meacham, Jon, and Tim McGraw. 2019. *Songs of America: Patriotism, Protest, and the Music That Made a Nation*. New York: Random House.

Walker, David. 1830. *Walker's Appeal in Four Articles: Together with a Preamble, to the Coloured Citizens of the World, but in Particular, and Very Expressly, to Those of the United States of America*, 3rd ed. Boston: David Walker. Accessed at https://docsouth.unc.edu/nc/walker/walker.html.

Wallace, Henry A.

Henry Agard Wallace (1888–1965) was an Iowa journalist who served as secretary of state, vice president, and secretary of commerce under Franklin D.

Roosevelt and ran unsuccessfully for president under the Progressive Party label in 1948 (Peterson 1948). Often considered to be one of the chief proponents and philosophers of Roosevelt's New Deal policies, Wallace was a strong advocate of the Agricultural Adjustment Act of 1934, which called for reducing agricultural production, setting a floor for commodity prices, and promoting cooperation among farmers (Schapsmeier and Schapsmeier 1979, 528). He was highly influenced by Walter Rauschenburch, one of the founders of the Social Gospel movement, and by sociologist Thorstein Veblen.

Wallace delivered the Alden-Tuthill Lectures before the Chicago Theological Seminary in 1934. They were published as a book that also included a talk that Wallace had given to the Federal Council of Churches in December 1933. In this book, Wallace indicated that he had grown up in the United Presbyterian Church, the denomination in which his grandfather had been a preacher, but finding that the intellectualism of both Presbyterians and Roman Catholics was off putting, he had begun attending an Episcopalian parish (1934, 47).

The opening chapter of the book discussed "The Spiritual Adventure of the Prophets." Crediting the Hebrew prophets as "the first people in recorded history to cry out in a loud clear voice concerning the problems of human justice" (1934, 18), he observed that it had taken leaders like David and Solomon to govern the Jews and Canaanites, but that the rural southern kingdom, whose philosophy was best articulated by the prophets, had afterwards split from the commercial north. He further believed "that the Biblical record is heavily loaded on the side of the Progressive Independents" (22). Wallace focused at length on the manner in which the prophets Elijah, Amos, Micah, and Jeremiah had railed against those who misused their power and wealth to oppress farmers and others with limited means. He believed that "the stage is being set for a social battle astonishingly similar to that which raged in Judah and Israel from the time of Solomon until Judah went into captivity" (36).

In his second lecture, Wallace discussed "The Spiritual Adventure of the Reformers." In the lecture, he focused on the way that Martin Luther, John Calvin, and John Knox had also opposed existing authorities while preparing the way for the "rugged individualism" that had been so important in America's political and economic development (42). Wallace observed, "To battle entrenched authority of this sort the reformers rationalized their inner certainty of righteousness by erecting a formidable logic based on the infallibility of the Bible" (70–71). Whereas the prophets had foreseen "the eventual triumph of the Lord of Peace," "the battle of the reformers brought no such vision but it did result in the generation of tremendous material power which expressed itself first in the creation of democratic institutions and secondly in science and the production of great capitalistic wealth" (71). He then asked whether "it is possible that the world is finally ready for the realization of the teachings of Jesus, the appreciation of the Sermon on the Mount, the bringing of the kingdom of heaven to earth" (71).

In addressing "The Great Spiritual Adventure of the Age" in his next chapter, Wallace began by describing the Great Seal of the United States, translating "Annuit Coeptis" as "He hath prospered our beginnings," and "Novus Ordo Seclorum" as the "new order of the ages," which Wallace believed might have been a reference to Isaiah's vision of a time of peace when people would come to the mountain of the Lord (78). In an obvious reference to Psalm 118:22, Wallace reared that "if we reject the stone, I have no doubt that in due process of time it [national leadership] will pass to some other nation" (79). Quoting, but not citing, Psalm 127:1, Wallace observed that "except the Lord build the house, their labor is but loss that built it" (80). Accepting the links that the English economist R. H. Tawney (1880–1962) and the German sociologist Max Weber (1864–1920) had drawn between the Protestant work ethic and capitalism, Wallace believed that it was time to reject "the doctrine of the simple life with regular, long, hard hours of work with simple tools" (84) and recognize the importance of updating "our social machinery," which will involve a change in "human hearts and human wills" (94). Instead of individuals striving for their own personal economic security, people must work together for the common good with recognition of "the fatherhood of God and the brotherhood of man" (104). Religions have been "defaced by the materialists and those fundamentalists who hold strictly to dry, literal, logistic, textual interpretations" rather than "for seeing that inner truth given tangible manifestation in terms of the machinery of human relationships" (105). The Kingdom of God need not be a merely transcendent (otherworldly) concept but one that is imminent (present) within the world.

In his final chapter on "Statesmanship and Religion," Wallace identified "the problem of statesmanship" as that of molding "a policy leading toward a higher state for humanity, and to stick by that policy and make it seem desirable to the people in spite of short-time political pressure to the contrary" (115). Describing Isaiah, Jeremiah, and Micah as such statesmen, Wallace cited Jesus's commands to love God and others (117): "To enter the kingdom of heaven brought to earth and expressed in terms of rich material life it will be necessary to have a reformation even greater than that of Luther and Calvin" (120). As the economy has failed, capitalists "have been merely blowing bubbles" (124). In an apparent allusion to Romans 3:23, Wallace observed that "we have all sinned in one way or another and we are all sick and sore at heart as we look at the misery of so many millions of people" (125). The "dry bones" (a reference to Ezekiel 37) of "economic man" must give way to "the flesh, and blood and spirit of the religious and the artistic man" (127). Men must reach a "higher law of cooperation" (131) that reflects the vision of Isaiah and Jesus. Nationalism must give way to internationalism, tariffs must be lowered, and farmers must be willing to produce less in order to earn more. "We are no longer faced with the problems of material scarcity. It no longer suffices, therefore, to strengthen the spiritual powers of the individual with the simple doctrine of the Psalms of David. The time has come now for the striking of a more universal note" (138).

Scholars Edward and Frederick Schapsmeier note that "orthodox clergymen rejected his socially oriented theology and fundamentalists denounced him outright" (1970, 185). President Herbert Hoover also believed that Wallace's philosophy and the New Deal subverted the American ideal of self-reliance (186).

Ezra Benson, one of Council of Twelve of the Church of Jesus Christ of Latter-Day Saints, who became secretary of agriculture of President Eisenhower, and embodied many of the moral values of "individualism, self-reliance and competition" that Wallace had downplayed, later sought to undo the agricultural policies that Wallace had implemented (Schapsmeier and Schapsmeier 1979, 532).

See also Great Seal of the United States; Social Gospel Movement

For Reference and Further Reading

Peterson, Osler L. 1948. "Henry Wallace: A Divided Mind." *The Atlantic*. August. https://www.theatlantic.com/magazine/archive/1948/08/henry-wallace-a-divided-mind/306029/. Accessed May 8, 2019.

Schapsmeier, Edward L., and Frederick H. Schapsmeier. 1970. "Henry A. Wallace: New Deal Philosopher." *The Historian* 32 (February): 177–90.

Schapsmeier, Edward L., and Frederick H. Schapsmeier. 1979. "Religion and Reform: A Case Study of Henry A. Wallace and Ezra Taft Benson." *Journal of Church and State* 21 (Autumn): 525–35.

Wallace, Henry A. 1934. *Statesmanship and Religion*. New York: Round Table Press.

Ward, Nathaniel

Although Pilgrims are often lauded for coming to America to exercise religious liberty, the liberty that they initially advocated was a liberty to believe and practice Puritan tenets. They sometimes hanged Quakers and drove Roger Williams from their midst. One of the most literary works by early American Pilgrims on political matters was a work written by attorney Nathanial Ward, the primary author of the Massachusetts Body of Liberties of 1641, entitled *The Simple Cobler of Aggawam in America*, which sought to justify such an approach. As the title suggests, the work was written under the pseudonym of Theodore de la Guard, who was purportedly a simple cobbler.

The work was divided into three parts. The first, which is the primary subject of this essay, expressed Ward's concern about the doctrine that governments should provide for religious toleration. The second focused on women's fashions (of which he was highly critical), and the third discussed contemporary controversies within England.

Like many other Puritan publications of its day, this work made many references to Scripture, including its opening paragraph, which refers to apocalyptic images from Job 9:6–7 and Acts 1:19–20. Ward was committed to defending the reputations of colonists in America:

> Wee have beene reputed a Colluvies of wild Opinionists, swarmed into a remote wilderness to find elbow-roome for our phanatick Doctrines and practices: I trust our diligence past, and constant fedulity against such persons and courses, will plead better things for u. I dare take upon me, to bee the Herauld of New-Engalnd so farre, as to proclaime to the world, in the name of our Colony, that all Familists, Antinomians, Anabaptists, and other Enthusiasts shall have free Liberty to keepe away from us, and such as will come to be gone as fast as they can, the sooner the better (1647, 3; *f*'s changed to *s*'s where appropriate)

Opposing a law in a "West-Indian Island" that provided for such heresies, Ward distinguished between "tolerations in things tolerable, exquisitely drawn out by the lines of the Scripture," and "irregular dispensations, dealt forth by the facilities of men," which are "the redoubts of Schisme, the perilious irritaments of carnall and spirituall enmity" (1647, 4–5). Ward argued that "if the whole Creature should conspire to doe the Creator a mischief, or offer him an insolency, it would be in nothing more, than in erecting untruths against his Truth, or by sophisticating his Truths with humane medleys: the removing of some one jota in Scripture, may draw out all the life, and traverse all the Truth of the whole Bible: but to authorize an untruth, by a Toleration of State, is to build a Sconce against the walls of heaven, to batter God out of his Chaire" (5–6).

Notable for his language, Ward argued that "he that is willing to tolerate any unfound Opinion, that his own may also be tolerated, though never so found, will for a need hang Gods Bible at the Devills girdle" (8). Ward opposed toleration not only in America but also in England. He observed "that if the State of *England* shall either willingly Tolerate, or weakly connive as such Courses, the Church of that Kingdome will sooner become the Devils dancing-Schoole, then [than] Gods Temple: The Civill State a Beare-garden, then an Exchange: The whole Realme a Pais base then an *England*" (9). To engage in general toleration would be to replace the teaching of Paul with "an English Pantheon" where all doctrines were regarded as equal (12). He proceeded to attack Anabaptists who opposed child baptism.

Noting that the gospel had thrived in England, Ward expressed the hope that the Pilgrims might one day return. He cited Jeremiah 2:12 and 22:10, which he summarized as teaching "that no man ought to forsake his owne country, but upon extraordinary cause, and when that cause ceaseth, he is bound in conscience to returne if he can: We are looking to him who hath our hopes and seasons in his only wise hand" (24).

Ward was also known for his jeremiads, or lamentations, over the course of other political developments (Egan 1978).

See also Massachusetts Body of Liberties; Pilgrims; Prophets and Jeremiads

For Reference and Further Reading

Arner, Robert D. 1971. "'The Simple Cobler of Aggawam': Nathaniel Ward and the Rhetoric of Satire." *Early American Literature* 4 (Winter): 3–16.

Egan, James. 1978. "'This Is a Lamentation and Shall Be for a Lamentation': Nathaniel Ward and the Rhetoric of the Jeremiad." *Proceedings of the American Philosophical Society* 122 (December 18): 400–10.

Mason, Alpheus Thomas, and Gordon E. Baker. 1985. *Free Government in the Making: Readings in American Political Thought*, 4th ed. New York: Oxford University Press.

[Ward, Nathaniel] de la Guard, Theodore. 1647. *The Simple Cobler of Aggawam in America*, 4th ed. London: Printed by J. D. & R. I. for Stephen Eawred, at the signe of the Bible in Popes Head-Alley.

Washington, Booker T.

Booker T. Washington (1856–1914), who was born into slavery, rose to become the president of Tuskegee Institute in Tuskegee, Alabama, and one of the most influential African American leaders of his day. He described his life in his best-selling autobiography published in 1901, entitled *Up from Slavery*.

Educated at the Hampton Normal and Agricultural Institute, and for a time at Wayland Seminary, Washington was extremely grateful for both his freedom and his education, and he encouraged fellow African Americans to lift themselves up by their own bootstraps. Perhaps best known for his speech at the

Atlanta Exposition of 1895, Washington seemed to prepare the way for the doctrine of separate but equal that the U.S. Supreme Court would announce the next year in *Plessy v. Ferguson*, where it upheld segregationist Jim Crow laws. In that speech, Washington said that "the agitation of questions of social equality is the extremest folly, and that progress in the enjoyment of all the privileges that will come to us must be the result of severe and constant struggle rather than of artificial forcing. No race that has anything to contribute to the markets of the world is long in any degree ostracized" (quoted in Mason and Baker 1985, 569). Noting that many southerners were beginning to look for foreign workers, he encouraged them to "cast down your bucket where you are": "Cast it down among the eight millions of Negroes whose habits you know, whose fidelity and love you have tested in days when to have proved treacherous meant the ruin of your firesides. Cast down your bucket among these people who have, without strikes and labour wars, tilled your fields, cleared your forests, builded your railroads and cities, and brought forth treasures from the bowels of the earth, and helped make possible this magnificent representation of the progress of the South" (568). Booker's deferential approach to the prejudices of his day brought him both recognition by prominent white leaders and criticism from individuals like the African American intellectual W. E. B. DuBois (1868–1963), who believed that his approach was too obsequious to the dominant white culture.

Washington frequently commended the Bible, as in a speech entitled "The Place of the Bible in the Uplifting of the Negro Race," which he gave to a packed house in a Memorial Hall in Columbus, Ohio, on May 24, 1900. In this speech, he said that "the men doing the vital things of life are those who read the Bible and are Christians and not ashamed to let the world know it" (Washington 1900, V: 544). Observing that only one of the many graduates of Tuskegee Institute had been sentenced to the penitentiary, even as he arguably appealed to existing racial stereotypes, Washington associated the Bible with industry and civilization:

> Just remember that the negro came out of Africa a few centuries ago, half naked, with rings in his nose and ears and chains upon his ankles and wrists. He came out of that, clothed according to civilized customs with a hammer and saw in his hands and a Bible in his hands. No man can read the Bible and be lazy. Christianity increases a man's wants, and therefore increases his capacity for labor. The negro doesn't run from the Bible either. (Washington 1900, V: 544).

Washington advocated what he called a "gospel of service" and employed messianic imagery in comparing the birth of Tuskegee Institute to that of Jesus, the tasks of building the institution to that of the task of the Israelites in Egypt, their quest as reaching the Promised Land, and their role as suffering servants to identify with the humble qualities of Jesus (Howard-Pitney 2005, 63). Washington was sometimes portrayed as a Moses figure, who was helping his people rise through economic self-help (67).

A study of Washington's faith suggests that it was similar to that of Thomas Jefferson and other American Founding Fathers in being extremely pragmatic, putting far less emphasis on future rewards or punishments and far more on earthly behaviors and success. Washington used the Bible to emphasize such values as "hard work, hygiene, thrift, and self-denial" that are typically identified with what German sociologist Max Weber (1864–1920) would later identify as the Protestant work ethic (Reavis 2015, 53). In a speech that he gave to the American Methodist Episcopal Conference in Charlotte, North Carolina, he observed, "The Negro workman with the spirit of Christ in his head and heart wants land, wants a good house, wants another house, wants decent furniture, wants a newspaper or magazine" (quoted in Reavis 2015, 54).

Although Washington rarely critiqued whites, he did criticize what he believed to be the low bar that African Americans set for their pastors. In urging the church to adopt contemporary white standards, Washington said, "Mine is not a selfish plea to the church. I want to see the Negro saved for his own sake, and I want to see the Negro saved in order that the white race which surrounds him may be saved" (Reavis 2015, 60).

There may be ties to Washington's thinking and the modern prosperity gospel, which emphasizes wealth as a sign of God's favor, that is associated with such pastors as Creflo Dollar, T. D. Jakes, and Joel Osteen (Lee 2007).

See also Jefferson Bible; Moses as Political Archetype; Prosperity Gospel; Segregation and Anti-miscegenation Laws; Slavery

For Reference and Further Reading

Howard-Pitney, David. 2005. *The African American Jeremiad: Appeals for Justice in America*, rev. ed. Philadelphia, PA: Temple University Press.

Lee, Shayne. 2007. "Prosperity Theology: T.D. Jakes and the Gospel of the Almighty Dollar." *CrossCurrents* 57 (Summer): 227–36.

Mason, Alpheus Thomas, and Gordon E. Baker. 1985. *Free Government in the Making: Readings in American Political Thought*, 4th ed. New York: Oxford University Press.

Reavis, Jonathan. 2015. "To See the Negro Saved: The Religious Pragmatism of Booker T. Washington." *Lucerna* 10: 49–62. Accessed at https://mospace.umsystem.edu/xmlui/bitstream/handle/10355/48993/Lucerna%202016%20Volume%2010%20-%208-Reavis.pdf?sequence=1&isAllowed=y.

Washington, Booker T. 1900. "An Account of a Speech in Columbus, Ohio." *The Booker T. Washington Papers Collection*, 14 vols., ed. Louis R. Harlan and Raymond W. Smock. Champagne: University of Illinois Press, V: *1899–1900*, pp. 541–44.

Washington, George

George Washington (1732–1799) was the leader of American forces during the Revolutionary War, president of the Constitutional Convention of 1787, and America's first president. Although he was a member of an Anglican church, scholars continue to argue about the content and depth of his religious sentiments. There is little doubt that many Americans considered him to have played a role similar to that which Moses had played in leading the Israelites out of the land of Egypt or that Joshua had played in conquering the land of Canaan. Moreover, it is clear that Washington himself exhibited a high degree of religious toleration.

Washington also exhibited considerable faith in God's providential protection not only of himself but also of the American nation (Fea 2016, 175–77). Writing to his brother during the French and Indian War, Washington thus observed that "by the all-powerful dispensation of Providence, I have been protected beyond all human probability; I had 4 bullets through my coat, and two horses shot under me yet escaped unhurt although death was leveling my companions on every side of me" (Hall 2019, 11).

Washington's wife, Martha, was known to read the Bible regularly, and Professor Daniel Dreisbach observes that he regularly employed a variety of biblical images, many of which contemporary scholars have missed because he typically did not include citations to chapters and verses. Such citations included the following:

> 'forbidden fruit' (Genesis 3), 'fat of the land' (Genesis 45:18); 'seven times seven years' (Leviticus 25:8), 'thorn in our side' (Numbers 33:55; Judges 2:3; see also 2 Corinthians 12:7), 'first fruit' (Deuteronomy 26:2), 'sleep with my Fathers' (Deuteronomy 31:16; 2 Samuel 7:12; 1 Kings 1:21), 'neither sleep nor slumber' (Psalm 121:4; Isaiah 5:27), 'like sheep, to the Slaughter' (Psalm 44:22; Acts 8:32; Romans 8:36), 'engraved on every man's heart' (see Jeremiah 17:1; Jeremiah 31:33; Romans 2:15), 'separating the Wheat from the Tares' (Matthew 13:25ff), 'a mill-stone hung to your neck' (Matthew 18:6; Mark 9:42; Luke 17:2); 'wars and rumors of wars' (Matthew 24:6; Mark 13:7), 'good and faithful servant' (Matthew 25:21, 23), 'take up my bed and walk' (Mark 2:9; John 5:8– 12), 'widow's mite' (Mark 12:42; Luke 21:2–3), *'the scales are ready to drop from the eyes'* (Acts 9:18), and 'Throne of Grace' (Hebrews 4:16). (Dreisbach 2014, 154–55)

In composing a circular letter to the states on June 8, 1783, Washington observed that citizens should "felicitate ourselves on the lot which Providence has assigned us, whether we view it in a natural, a political or a moral point of light" (Vile 2015, 127). Further arguing that "Heaven has crowned all its other blessings, by giving a fairer opportunity for political happiness, than any other Nation has ever been favored with," Washington proceeded to outline such blessings, including "above all, the pure and benign light or Revelation," which he said "has a meliorating influence on mankind and increased the blessings of Society" (128).

In a letter that he wrote to a Jewish Congregation in Savannah, Georgia, that had complemented him after he became president, after rejoicing in the "spirit of liberality and philanthropy" that he found to be prevailing in the world, Washington tied the God who had delivered the Jews out of Egypt with the one who had smiled upon America. He thus expressed the wish that "the same wonder-working Deity, who long since delivered the Hebrews from their Egyptian Oppressors planted them in the promised land—whose providential agency has lately been conspicuous in establishing these United States as an independent nation—still continue to water them with the dews of Heaven and to make the inhabitants of every denomination participate in the temporal and spiritual blessings of that people whose God is Jehovah" (Washington 1790).

The image of the vine and fig tree was one of Washington's favorites, appearing in no less than fifty of his letters. This analogy is found in at least three passages within Hebrew Scriptures (Micah 4:4; 1 Kings 4:25; and Zechariah 3:10). Washington appears to have been most familiar with the passage from the book of Micah in which the prophet had presented his vision of a New Jerusalem, in which God would administer perfect justice.

Dreisbach observes that Washington, who frequently professed his preference for private life over public service, often associated his own house at Mount Vernon with this image. Dreisbach further argues that the image was designed to evoke the contentment that came from freedom from want and the joys of hospitality; the freedom from fear that was brought about by peace; and, in an American variation on the biblical theme, the joys of freedom of religion (2007, 309–22).

Shortly after Washington became the first president of the United States, Moses Seixas, the warden of a Jewish congregation in Newport, Rhode Island, sent a letter to Washington expressing the esteem of the "children of the stock of Abraham" and their gratitude for a Constitution that provided for their civil liberties. Seixas believed that this work was "the work of the Great God, who ruleth in the Armies of Heaven, and among the Inhabitants of the Earth, doing whatever seemeth him good" (Vile 2015, 323). Referring to the biblical judge who followed Moses, Seixas further expressed the hope that "when, like Joshua full of days and full of honour, you are gathered to your Fathers, may you be admitted into the Heavenly Paradise to partake of the water of life, and the tree of immortality" (323).

In responding, Washington observed that in granting the free exercise of religion, the Constitution went beyond mere toleration. As he explained that "happily the Government of the United States, which gives to bigotry no sanction, to persecution no assistance, requires only that they who live under its protection shall demean themselves as good citizens, in giving it on all occasions their effectual support" (324).

As he came to the end of his letter, Washington expressed the hope that "the children of the Stock of Abraham, who dwell in this land," would "continue to merit and enjoy the good will of the other Inhabitants; while every one shall sit in safety under his own vine and fig-tree, and there shall be none to make him afraid" (325). Further referring to God as "the father of all mercies," a title with firm biblical foundations, Washington further used biblical language to express the hope that God might "scatter light and not darkness in our paths, and make us all in our several vocations useful here, and in his own due time and way everlastingly happy" (325).

In Washington's Farewell Address to the nation, perhaps out of concern for some of the doctrines that had emerged during the French Revolution, Washington argued for the importance of religion and morality:

> Of all the dispositions and habits which lead to political prosperity, religion and morality are indispensable supports. In vain would that man claim the tribute of patriotism, who should labor to subvert these great pillars of human happiness, these firmest props of the duties of men and citizens. The mere politicians, equally with the pious man, ought to respect and to cherish them. A volume could not trace all their connections with private and public felicity. Let it simply be asked: Where is the security for property, for reputation, for life, if the sense of religious obligation desert the oaths which are the instruments of investigation in courts of justice? And let us with caution indulge the supposition that morality can be maintained without religion. Whatever may be conceded to the influence of refined education on minds of peculiar structure, reason and

> experience both forbid us to expect that national morality can prevail in exclusion of religious principle. (Vile 2016, 93)

In later years, Justice David J. Brewer (1837–1910) used the vine and fig tree in a speech that he gave at Yale University entitled "The Protection of Private Property from Public Attack." In the speech, he observed, "In the picture drawn by the prophet of millennial days, it is affirmed that, 'They shall sit every man under his vine and under his fig tree, and none shall make them afraid: for the mouth of the Lord of hosts hath spoken it.' If we would continue this government into millennial times, it must be built upon this foundation" (quoted in Przbyszewski 2000, 231).

See also Brewer, David J.; Gideon as Political Archetype; Judaism; Moses as Political Archetype; Providence

For Reference and Further Reading

Dreisbach, Daniel L. 2014. "The Bible and the Political Culture of the American Founding." *Faith and the Founders of the American Republic*, ed. Daniel L. Dreisbach and Mark David Hall. New York: Oxford University Press, pp. 133–73.

Dreisbach, Daniel L. 2007. "The 'Vine and Fig Tree' in George Washington's Letters: Reflections on a Biblical Motif in the Literature of the American Founding Era." *Anglican and Episcopal History* 76 (September): 299–326.

Fea, John. 2016. *Was America Founded as a Christian Nation?: An Historical Introduction*, rev. ed. Louisville, KY: Westminster John Knox Press.

Hall, Mark David. 2019. *Did America Have a Christian Founding?: Separating Modern Myth from Historical Truth*. Nashville, TN: Nelson Books.

Przbyszewski, Linda. 2000. "The Religion of a Jurist: Justice David J. Brewer and the Christian Nation." *Journal of Supreme Court History* 25 (November): 228–42.

Vile, John R., ed. 2015. *Founding Documents of America: Documents Decoded*. Santa Barbara, CA: ABC-CLIO.

Vile, John R., ed. 2016. *The Early Republic: Documents Decoded*. Santa Barbara, CA: ABC-CLIO.

Washington, George. 1790. "From George Washington to the Savannah, Ga., Hebrew Congregation 14 June 1790." Founders Online. https://founders.archives.gov/documents/Washington/05-05-02-0279.

Washington Inaugural Bible

Bibles that are associated with famous statesmen often take on a special significance. This is certainly true of the Bible on which George Washington took the oath of office when he became the first president of the United States of America on April 30, 1789. Although there is continuing dispute as to whether Washington spoke the words "so help me God," which are not specifically required in the U.S. Constitution, when he took his oath, the fact that he took an oath on the Bible certainly indicates that he was not breaking with popular reverence for the document during this inauguration.

As Washington prepared for his inauguration, no one had apparently brought a Bible for the ceremony, but Robert R. Livingston, the New York chancellor, accordingly sent General Jacob Morton, the parade marshal, to the Lodge Room of St. John's Lodge #1, which was nearby, and he retrieved one from there. Bruce Feiler has suggested that "Washington may have been playing a clever game"; by using a Bible from a nondenominational organization like the Masons, he would not have had to give precedent to any of the twenty-three churches in New York (2009, 80).

The Bible had been presented to the lodge by Jonathan Hampton on November 28, 1770, after the previous lodge burned and at a time when the colonies still recognized the authority of King George III. The gold lettering on the cover was: "God shall establish; St. John's Lodge constituted 5757; Burnt down 8th March, 5770. Rebuilt and opened November 18th, 5770. Officers then presiding: Jonathan Hampton, Master: William Butler, Senior Warden: Isaac Heron, Junior Warden" ("George Washington Inaugural Bible"). The Bible was a King James Version, in this case a 1767 edition printed in London by Mark Baskett, who was the king's printer (Campbell 2010, 204). The Bible contained the Apocrypha as well as "historical, astronomical and legal data of the day," including steel engravings by the English artist John Stuart.

The Bible was apparently opened to Genesis 49 and 50. One writer says that it was opened at random to Genesis 49:13, which says that "Zebulun shall dwell at the haven of the sea; and he shall be for an haven of ships; and his border shall be unto Zidon" (Gajanan 2017), but it is possible that the focus was on the blessing and death of Jacob ("George Washington Inaugural Bible"). That would have confirmed the idea that the people of America, like those of Israel, were divinely blessed. Indeed, historian Carl Richard says that "in this way, Washington designated the United States the new Israel" (2016, 141). The freemasons continue to own this Bible, which they consider to be among their greatest treasures.

The Bible contained a page with the following insert:

> On this sacred volume, on the 30th day of April, A.L. 5789, in the city of New York, was administered to George Washington, the first president of the United States of America, the oath to support the Constitution of the United States. This important ceremony was performed by the Most Worshipful Grand Master of free and Accepted Masons of the State of New York, the Honorable Robert R. Livingston, Chancellor of the State.
> Fame stretched her wings and with her trumpet blew.
> Great Washington is near. What praise is due?
> What title shall he have? She paused, and said
> "Not one—his name alone strikes every title dead." ("George Washington Inaugural Bible")

The Bible continued to have a storied history. It was used for Masonic cornerstone ceremonies as well as the centennials of the Capitol Building, the White House, and the Statue of Liberty. It was also used at Washington's funeral, the 1992 launching of the USS *George Washington*, and the funerals of presidents Andrew Jackson, Zachary Taylor, and Abraham Lincoln (Campbell 2010, 204). Presidents Warren Harding, Dwight Eisenhower, Jimmy Carter, and George H. W. Bush also used the Bible on the occasions of their own oaths of office (205). President George W. Bush had planned to use the Bible at his inauguration but was prevented from doing so by inclement weather ("Washington Bible"). Although it occasionally travels elsewhere, the Bible is on permanent display at the Federal Hall National Memorial in New York City, the site of Washington's original inauguration (205).

At the time of the terrorist attack on the World Trade Center's Twin Towers in 2001, the Masons had loaned the Bible for an exhibition at nearby Fraunces Tavern Museum, but it was not damaged in the attack. Masons prohibit the transport of the Bible by air, limiting it to travel by land, and in the company of three lodge members ("Washington Bible").

Washington owned a number of personal Bibles. These included "a three-volume, hand-autographed Bible," which is in the Rare Book Collection of the Library of Congress (Millard 1991). The archives of Washington's house Mount Vernon further contain a Washington family Bible, which recorded Washington's birth; the Book of Common Prayer, signed by Martha Washington; a 1760 concordance to Scriptures; and Marsha Washington's own autographed family Bible (Millard 1991). Washington also purchased a large leather-bound Bible and Psalter for the Pohick Church in Lorton, Virginia, and, in his will, he bequeathed a three-volume Bible "to the Reverend, now Bryan, Lord Fairfax," which Washington had received from "the Right Reverend Thomas Wilson, Bishop of Sodor and Man" (Millard 1991).

See also Presidential Inaugural Bibles; Presidential Inaugural Bible Verses; Washington, George

For Reference and Further Reading

Campbell, Gordon. 2010. *Bible: The Story of the King James Version 1611–2011*. New York: Oxford University Press.

Feiler, Bruce. 2009. *America's Prophet: Moses and the American Story*. New York: William Morrow.

Gajanan, Mahita. 2017. "These Are the Bible Verses Past Presidents Have Turned to on Inauguration Day." *Time*. January 19. http ://time.com/4639596/inauguration-day-presidents-bible-passages/.

"George Washington Inaugural Bible." http ://www.stjohns1.org/portal/gwib. Accessed March 17, 2019.

Millard, Catherine. 1991. "The Truth about George Washington's Presidential Inaugural Bible." From *The Rewriting of America's History*. http ://www.christianheritagemins.org/articles/The%20Truth%20about%20Washington's%20Inaugural%20Bible.pdf.

Richard, Carl J. 2016. *The Founders and the Bible*. Lanham, MD: Rowman & Littlefield.

"Washington Bible." http ://www.masonicinfo.com/washington_bible.htm. Accessed March 17, 2019.

Webster, Noah

Noah Webster (1748–1843) was America's greatest lexicographer. Born in Connecticut, Webster was educated at Yale and studied law for a time under Oliver Ellsworth. In 1785, he wrote *Sketches of American Policy* and supported adoption of the U.S. Constitution. He subsequently wrote for a Federalist newspaper and served in the Connecticut House of Representatives, but his primary contributions were literary and scholarly. By creating a standard language, he helped unify the American nation.

Although he is best known for publishing his massive *Dictionary of the American Language*, in which he attempted to standardize American spellings and make American English distinct from its British origins, he wrote two works that were specifically tied to the Bible. Unfortunately, neither remains particularly well known today.

The first, which he published in 1833, was a revised edition of the dominant King James Version of the Bible. Warfel has described Webster's central goals as those of correcting "those faults which impaired its beauty, obscured its sense, or offended feelings of decency" (1934, 579). In the words of historian Jill Lepore, "Webster considered the King James ungrammatical, obsolete, and filthy" (2011). Although Webster's desire to update anachronistic language remains a worthy goal, many of his other suggested changes seem anachronistic or prudish. Thus, Webster sought to substitute the word "shuns" for "eschews"; eliminate the prepositions "wherein, therein, whereon" and "thereon"; substitute the word "nursed" for "suck" and the word "limbs" for "legs"; and to eliminate such expressions as "three score and ten," which he chose simply to render as "70" (Lepore 2011).

Noah's second contribution was his publication in 1834 of a book entitled *Value of the Bible and Excellence of the Christian Religion: For the Use of Families and Schools*. Although Webster, who had undergone a conversion experience in 1808, had long revered the Scriptures, he had omitted scriptural readings from his texts lest children would treat them cavalierly (Vile 2008, xix). By contrast, this book provided commentary to accompany readings from both designated chapters of the Old and New Testaments.

In his discussion of Genesis, Webster emphasized the dignity of man. He thus noted that "the form of man is erect and dignified; his body and limbs are equally distinguished for strength, for beauty and for convenient action" (1834, 23). Webster devoted considerable attention to explaining the Ten Commandments, not once but twice, covering each commandment individually (68–75, 156–70). He observed that "they are the basis of the whole moral law, which is binding upon us and upon the whole world of mankind," further quoting Christ's summary of the law in Matthew 22:40 as requiring love for God and fellow human beings (75).

After observing modern skepticism about miracles, Webster offered a defense: "But we may rationally suppose God always employs the means necessary to accomplish his purposes, whether the means are common or unusual; and it is no more improbable that he should by miracles save Israel, the nation which he intended to be the depositaries of his laws, than that he should make man at first by a direct act of his own power, independent of other means" (82). He later argued that "the miracles of Christ are among the most convincing evidences of his divine mission and almighty power" (142).

Skipping a discussion of the book of Judges, Webster simply observed, "Having no settled form of government, no king, and no regular mode of appointing or choosing a chief magistrate, they depended on judges or distinguished men, who were occasionally raised up by providence for their deliverance" (85). Somewhat later, he observed, "It is the neglect of this divine precept [for rulers to govern justly], that is, the wickedness of rulers, and the depravity of men who elect wicked rulers, which in every age, have filled the world with violence, and which have brought, and still bring war, oppression and misery upon the human race" (97). In discussing the fate of the Jews, Webster further noted that "at last, God executed judgment upon the nation by the captivity of the king and most of the people, and putting an end to the state. Such or similar has been the fate of all corrupt nations; and such will be *our* fate, if we neglect the worship and service of God. God's moral government requires that men and nations, renouncing his authority, should meet with exemplary punishment" (109).

Webster interpreted the book of Daniel as predicting the rise of Rome, the coming of Christ, as well as the destruction of the Jewish temple in Jerusalem (119). As he began his discussion of the gospel of Matthew, Webster further described "the most important event that has ever taken place in the world since the creation" as "the birth of the Son of God, who was sent to repair the ruins of the Apostasy, and to redeem mankind from the penalties denounced against their disobedience" (125). Webster had similar high praise for the Christian religion:

> It has banished idolatry and pagan superstition from many countries; it has civilized and softened the manners of nations; it has mitigated the cruelties of war; it has inspired a spirit of peace; it has raised the female part of our species from degradation and slavery; it has founded charitable institutions to alleviate the sufferings of the poor; it has introduced the true principles of civil liberty; it has begun to arrest the barbarous practice of enslaving our fellow men; it has changed or is changing the character of the whole world. (1834, 151)

Webster had a similarly high view of Scripture. He thus observed that "the first and most essential advantage of the religion of the bible, is, that it proceeds from God himself by revelation" (152).

After presenting the Ten Commandments for a second time, Webster applied them to a number of issues. These included the following: temperance (he recommending drinking water over alcohol), war (which should be defensive only), and dueling and slavery (both of which he wanted to abolish) (170–72).

Webster's discussion of forms of government indicated some disillusionment: "Numerous forms have been tried; monarchy, aristocracy and democracy. After all their efforts, a perfect government has not yet been found. In the best form hitherto devised, defects have been discovered, which have frustrated the hopes of the founders" (174). Seeking the source of such frustrations, Webster observed that "men have not obeyed God's precepts" (174). Seeking a remedy, especially applicable to republican governments, Webster cited the admonition in 2 Samuel 23:3 that "he that ruleth over men must be just, ruling in the fear of God" (175). When voters chose "bad men," it was generally their own "fault" (175). They should give greater attention to character than to political party identification: "as surely as there is a God in heaven, who exercises a moral government over the affairs of this world, so certainly will the neglect of the divine command, in the choice of rulers, be followed by bad laws and a bad administration; by laws unjust or partial, by corruption, tyranny, impunity of crimes, waste of public money, and a thousand other evils" (175–76).

As he ended his book, Webster reiterated the reliability of Scripture, human dignity (which consisted in following the Bible), and the need for human beings to avoid idleness and work together with God. Recognizing the importance of distinguishing "the real religion taught by Christ and his apostles, from those systems which interested men have established," Webster observed that "we find the true religion of Christ in the Bible only," which is incorporated "in two short phrases, *love to God*, and *love to men*" (180).

See also King James Version of the Bible; Slavery; Ten Commandments

For Reference and Further Reading

Kendall, Joshua. 2010. *The Forgotten Founding Father: Noah Webster's Obsession and the Creation of an American Culture*. New York: Berkeley Books.

Lepore, Jill. 2011. "An American King: Noah Webster's Holy Bible." *New Yorker*. September 28. https://www.newyorker.com/books/page-turner/an-american-king-noah-websters-holy-bible.

Unger, Harlow Giles. 1998. *The Life and Times of an American Patriot*. New York: John Wiley & Sons.

Vile, John R. 2008. "Noah Webster: Proposing and Promoting Stronger National Union through the Power of the English Language." Introduction to Webster, Noah. *Sketches of American Policy*. Clark, NJ: Lawbook Exchange, pp. iii–xix, xix.

Warfel, Harry R. 1934. "The Centenary of Noah Webster's Bible." *New England Quarterly* 7 (September): 578–82.

Webster, Noah. [1785] 2008. *Sketches of American Policy*. Introduction by John R. Vile. Clark, NJ: Lawbook Exchange.

Webster, Noah. 1834. *Value of the Bible, and Excellence of the Christian Religion: For the Use of Families and Schools*. New Haven: Durrie & Peck.

Weld, Theodore Dwight

In the years leading up to the Civil War, proponents and opponents of slavery thought it was very important to find scriptural support for their positions. Although, as Abraham Lincoln would later note, both Northerners and Southerners read the same Bible, they often came to radically different conclusions about an institution that had almost disappeared from the North but was flourishing in the South.

One of the individuals who argued against slavery was Theodore Dwight Weld (1803–1895). Born in Connecticut, Weld was a well-known lecturer who was strongly influenced by evangelist Charles Finney (1792–1875). Weld had a hand in the founding of Lane Theological Seminary in Cincinnati and eventually was employed by the American Anti-Slavery Society. He married Angelina Grimke and, in 1839, coauthored, with her and her sister Sarah, *American Slavery as It Is: Testimony of a Thousand Witnesses*, which became a kind of anti-slavery sourcebook.

In 1837, Weld authored *The Bible against Slavery*, which went into subsequent editions. He began with a clever analogy by likening slavery to an unclean spirit seeking shelter in the Bible (Weld 1838, 2). He quickly moved to explain that slavery was not the mere deprivation of such privileges as suffrage but was the actual process of reducing human beings into "ARTICLES OF PROPERTY—making free agents, chattels—converting *persons*, into *things*—sinking immortality, into *merchandise*" (8).

Defined as such, Weld was confident that slavery violated two of the Ten Commandments, namely the commandment against theft and that against coveting. Moreover, it was also in direct violation of the law in Exodus 21:16 that provided that "he that stealeth a man and selleth him, or if he be found in his hand, he shall surely be put to death." He further argued that to treat human beings as slaves was to erase the boundary that the Bible had established between human beings and beasts while indicating that the former were specifically created in God's image. He reaffirmed this by citing Leviticus 24: 17, 18, and 21, which provided the death penalty for individuals who killed other human beings (16).

Pro-slavery apologists sought to give biblical sanction to slavery by showing that it had existed in the Old Testament, but Weld devoted much of his argument to indicating that those whom the Bible had designated as slaves had actually sold their labor to their employers rather than being owned by them. He further sought to show that those whom the Old Testament designated as servants (including the Jews living in Egypt) owned their own property, were guarded by the laws, and received wages. Perhaps most importantly, they were not treated as mere items of property. Although some slave apologists had portrayed the Gibeonites as slaves, Weld argued that they were more like a separate people who were allowed to live in their own cities and give the Israelites tribute.

After thus contrasting American slavery to the institutions of the Bible, Weld sought to answer some objections. He thus answered arguments that slavery was justified by Noah's prophecy against Canaan. Weld made many arguments, but his most salient one was to deny that Africans were descendants of Canaan. He thus observed that "a prophecy of evil to one people, is quoted to justify its infliction on another" (Weld 1838, 47).

Weld next sought to argue against an interpretation of Exodus 21:21–22, which appeared to equate a slave with money, after absolving a man from murder if his servant did not immediately die after he disciplined him. Weld argued that the intent of this passage was not to equate individuals with money but to distinguish intentional murder from mere manslaughter (49).

In answering a third objection, Weld sought to refute an interpretation from Leviticus 25:44–46, which slave advocates had used to justify the Jews in enslaving heathen nations around them. Disputing in part the meaning of the word "bondsmen," Weld observed, "As the caprices of King James's translators were not inspired, we need stand in no special awe of them" (53).

The fourth objection to which Weld responded dealt with Leviticus 25:39–40, which seemed to distinguish those who could sell themselves into slavery from those who could not (57). Circling back to an earlier argument, Weld further argued that the Israelites had been commanded to kill the Canaanites, not to enslave them (79).

See also Curses on Cain, Ham, and the Canaanites; Grimke, Angelina; Lincoln, Abraham (Second Inaugural Address); Slavery; Ten Commandments

For Reference and Further Reading

Hempton, David. 2008. *Evangelical Disenchantment: Nine Portraits of Faith and Doubt.* New Haven, CT: Yale University Press.

Noll, Mark A. 2008. *God and Race in American Politics: A Short History*. Princeton, NJ: Princeton University Press.
Weld, Theodore Dwight. 1838. *The Bible against Slavery: An Inquiry into the Patriarchal and Mosaic Systems on the Subject of Human Rights*, 3rd ed. New York: American Anti-Slavery Society.

What Doth the Lord Require? (Micah 6:8)

Presidents Warren G. Harding and Jimmy Carter both opened their Bibles to Micah 6:8 when taking their presidential oaths of office, and William McKinley appears to have had this verse in mind when he gave his first presidential inaugural address. After asking "what does the LORD require of thee," the verse answered, "To do justly, and to love mercy, and to walk humbly with thy God." Professor Daniel L. Dreisbach has further noted that it was a favorite among America's Founding Fathers.

As Dreisbach explains, the context of this verse is a dramatic courtroom scene in which God accuses the people of Israel of breaching their covenant with God. Acting as a prosecutor, God pleads his own case, demonstrating the good that he has done for the nation and its own failure to reciprocate by following Him. After the people ask what they can do, Micah responds with his threefold answer.

Dreisbach examines two major American founding documents that highlight this passage. One is John Winthrop's sermon "A Model of Christian Charity," which he delivered in 1730. Another is George Washington's Circular Letter to the States that he composed in 1783 as he was resigning his commission as commander in chief and retiring to private life.

Washington's final paragraph, which references without citing the specific chapter and verse in Micah, is the most pious:

> I now make it my earnest prayer, that God would have you, and the State over which you preside, in his holy protection, that he would incline the hearts of the Citizens to cultivate a spirit of subordination and obedience to Government, to entertain a brotherly affection and love for one another, for their fellow Citizens of the United States at large, and particularly for their brethren who have served in the Field, and finally, that he would most graciously be pleased to dispose us all, to do Justice, to love mercy, and to demean ourselves with that Charity, humility and pacific temper of mind, which were the Characteristicks of the Divine Author of our blessed Religion, and without an humble imitation of whose example in these things, we can never hope to be a happy Nation.

Dreisbach observes that Washington effectively Christianized the text by his reference to "the Divine Author of our blessed Religion" (an apparent reference to Jesus) but that Washington does not so much stress the necessity for "*belief* in Christ" as for "the *imitation* of Christ" (Dreisbach 2009, 94).

In addition to these two main references, Dreisbach cites letters of John Adams and sermons that also cite the passage. Perhaps his most interesting conclusion is that while contemporary Americans are most likely to read the verse as "a manual for the moral and ethical conduct of individuals . . . many founders recognized in this passage a call to *national* virtue" (97). Dreisbach further notes,

"There was a consensus among the founders that both individual and collective righteousness was a prerequisite for Divine favor and vital to the success of the American political experiment in self-government" (97).

See also McKinley, William; Model of Christian Charity (Winthrop); Washington, George

For Reference and Further Reading

Dreisbach, Daniel L. 2009. "Micah 6:8 in the Literature of the American Founding Era: A Note on Religion and Rhetoric." *Rhetoric and Public Affairs* 12 (Spring): 91–105.

Washington, George. June 8, 1783. "Washington's Circular Letter of Farewell to the Army, June 8, 1783." Library of Congress. http://www.loc.gov/teachers/classroommaterials/presentationsandactivities/presentations/timeline/amrev/peace/circular.html.

Williams, Elisha

Elisha Williams (1694–1755) was a congregational minister, Connecticut state legislator, and jurist who graduated from Harvard and later served as a rector of Yale. In 1741, he anonymously published a work in Boston entitled *The Essential Rights and Liberties of Protestants*, which, in attacking a recent Connecticut law that allowed civil authorities to prevent what they considered to be schismatic pastors from preaching in their jurisdictions, laid out a strong case for religious freedom. The law was the result of the divisions that the First Great Awakening had brought about between the Old Side and New Side Presbyterians, the former of whom continued to plead for decorum and order and the latter of whom put greater emphasis on visible works of the spirit in revival meetings.

Williams may well have relied in part on the view of the English philosopher John Locke (1632–1704) on toleration, which was also predicated in part on Scriptures. Williams believed that "the *End* of civil Government" was "the greater Security of Enjoyment of what belongs to every one, and *this Right of private judgment*, and *worshipping* GOD according to their *Consciences*," was "the *natural and unalienable Right* of *Every Man*, what Men by entering into civil Society neither did, nor could give up into the Hands of the Community" ([1742] 1967, 324).

Citing biblical images (in Numbers 11:12 and Acts 13:18) of Moses as a "nursing father," Williams argued that the civil magistrate had a similar role to play with respect to the church. Drawing from Protestant interpretations of the book of Revelation and from the biblical indictment in Ezekiel 34:2 of religious leaders who instead of caring for their flock decided to feast on them, Williams accused the magistrates of doing the same. In orthodox Protestant fashion, Williams argued that the church had no "other Rule of Faith and Practice in Religion, besides the *Bible*" (326). Williams believed that "*this natural Right of private Judgment in Matters of Religion*" was essential in order "that the sacred *Scriptures only may become the Rule to all Men in all religious Matters, as they ought to be*" (326). Each individual had the right to determine what to believe and how to worship.

Individuals thus had the right of "judging the Doctrines taught them by the sacred Scriptures" (328), and of replacing ministers whom they did not believe interpreted Scripture correctly. The majority of each congregation had the right to exercise this authority, but, consistent with the Golden Rule in Matthew 7:12, a minority within a congregation also had the right to establish another congregation with another pastor if they so chose.

Williams continually referred to the idea of "Christian Liberty" (331). He further suggested that this right was granted by the British Act of Toleration, which applied to Connecticut through its charter. Despite the title of his essay, Williams suggested that rights extended not only to Protestants but also to Catholics and even pagans (337). In rhetoric similar to that which colonists would use in the years leading up to the Revolutionary War, Williams argued that rights like those articulated in the Magna Carta "depend not on the Will of the Prince, or the Will of the Legislature; but they are the inherent natural *Rights of Englishmen*: secured and confirmed they may be by the Legislature, but not derived from nor dependent on their Will" (338–39).

Williams portrayed the right of individuals to settle on their own ministers as based on the principle *"that CHRIST will be King in his own Kingdom"* (329). Williams's writing is important because it demonstrates that ideas of religious freedom advocated by Roger Williams and others who were initially considered to be heretics were becoming more mainstream, and that New Englanders were increasingly associating the Bible not only with a set of religious beliefs but also with the idea of religious freedom that would later find expression in the writings of James Madison, Thomas Jefferson, and others.

See also Madison, James; Puritans; Williams, Roger

For Reference and Further Reading

Williams, Elisha. [1742] 1967. *The Essential Rights and Liberties of Protestants. As Found in the Great Awakening: Documents Illustrating the Crisis and Its Consequence*, ed. Alan Heimert and Perry Miller. Indianapolis: Bobbs-Merrill.

Williams, Roger

Roger Williams (1603–1683) was a theologian who had been educated at Cambridge University and immigrated to America. He split from the Puritans of Massachusetts in advocating religious freedom and separation of church and state and went on to found the colonies of Rhode Island and Providence Plantation. The founder of the first Baptist Church in America in Providence, Williams found it difficult to remain attached to any single denomination.

Williams's most famous work is his book *The Bloudy Tenent of Persecution for Cause of Conscience*, which was printed in London in 1644 when Williams was seeking a charter for Rhode Island. The book consists of a fairly discursive conversation between personifications of Peace and Truth, is suffused throughout with Scripture, and includes a response by John Cotton on behalf of the established Puritan Church in Massachusetts.

An early chapter outlines Williams's central arguments from the Bible in addressing the issue of "whether persecution for cause of conscience be not against the doctrine of Jesus Christ, the king of kings" and begins with five main points (2001, 11). Citing Matthew 13:30, 38 as his first Scripture, Williams referred to Jesus's instructions to allow the tares (weeds) to grow among wheat until the final harvest at the end of the world, and Williams recurred to this analogy throughout the book (11). In a more obtuse analogy, Williams cited Matthew 14:14 for the principle that the blind will lead one another into the ditch—apparently without the necessity of state help (11–12). In a third argument, Williams cited Jesus's rebuke to disciples who wanted to call down fire on Samaritans by citing his admonition in Luke 9:54–55 that "the Son of man is not come to destroy men's lives, but to save them" (12). Williams's fourth scriptural support was from 2 Timothy 1:24–26, where Paul urged fellow Christians to be gentle to all men, while Williams's fifth cited prophetic passages from Isaiah 2:4 and Micah 4:3–4 about how God will break swords into ploughshares and 2 Corinthians 10:4 about how the weapons for conversion are spiritual rather than physical (12).

After citing such scriptural authorities, Williams then proceeded to cite others. William thus cited a passage from the early Christian apologist Tertullian (AD 155–220)—which Thomas Jefferson later echoed—when he observed that "another man's religion and belief neither hurts nor profits anyone, neither beseems it any religion to compel another to be of their religion, which willingly and freely should be embraced, and not by constraint" (15).

One of Williams's central distinctions was between what he called the "garden" of the church from the "wilderness" of the world. He did not believe that civil authorities had the right to enforce the Ten Commandments, except in cases like murder or theft, where breaking the commandments resulted in direct harm to others. Unlike fellow Puritans, Williams did not believe that the New England colonies, and their church, inherited the mantle of the Israelites to conquer the surrounding Canaanites, or Native American Indians (67, 200), with whom Williams attempted to cultivate friendship.

Baptists and other dissenting churches eventually worked with statesmen like Thomas Jefferson and James Madison to disestablish churches within America, and Jefferson became one of the strongest proponents for the doctrine of separation of church and state.

See also Baptists; Cotton, John; Jefferson Bible; Native American Indians; Puritans; Ten Commandments

For Reference and Further Reading

Williams, Roger. [1644] 2001. *The Bloudy Tenent of Persecution for Cause of Conscience*, ed. Richard Groves. Macon, GA: Mercer University Press.

Wilson, Woodrow

The only president ever to have earned a PhD (from Johns Hopkins), Woodrow Wilson (1856–1924) was president of Princeton and governor of New Jersey prior to winning the presidency in the elections of 1912 and 1916. Widely known for his idealism, he was the son of a Presbyterian pastor and of a mother who also descended from pastors. Wilson's father, a founding member of the Presbyterian Church of the United States (PCUS), had authored a sermon entitled the "Mutual Relations of Masters and Slaves as Taught in the Bible" (Morton 2008), and his

distinguish between right and wrong not only in personal relations but also in government (Fea 2016, 239).

Even though he was a clergyman, Witherspoon was deeply involved in political affairs. In addition to a number of state offices, Witherspoon was a member of the Continental Congress and a signer of the Declaration of Independence. During his tenure, Princeton was a nursery of patriots, educating twelve members of the Continental Congress, five delegates to the U.S. Constitutional Convention, a president (James Madison), a vice president (Aaron Burr), and numerous other leaders (Morrison 1999, 553). Witherspoon led efforts to ally Presbyterians and Congregationalists in common causes, especially opposing the establishing of an Episcopal bishop in America. Although he favored government support of religion in general, he opposed support for individual denominations and favored civil and religious liberty.

Witherspoon delivered his first sermon in which he specifically addressed political issues on May 17, 1776, before the signing of the Declaration of Independence. This sermon, which appears to have been widely circulated, was entitled "The Dominion of Providence over the Passions of Men." Witherspoon's main text, which he supplemented with many other scriptural references, was Psalm 76:10: "Surely the Wrath of Man shall praise thee; the remainder of Wrath shall thou restrain," which was apparently written in order to celebrate the failure of the Assyrian king to capture Jerusalem during the time of Hezekiah.

James Smylie has argued that one of Witherspoon's main contributions to the political thought of James Madison was that of emphasizing the corruption of human nature and the need to corral it through such institutional restraints as checks and balances and separation of powers. In his first sermon on public affairs, Witherspoon thus pointed to "the corruption of our nature, which is the foundation stone of the doctrine of redemption" (1990, 128). Among the scriptural proofs that he cited were James 4:1, which attributed conflicts to human lusts. With a clear reference to the book of Genesis, Witherspoon observed that "men of lax and corrupt principles take great delight in speaking to the praise of human nature and extolling its dignity without distinguishing what it was, at its first creation, from what it is in its present fallen state"; moreover, in a footnote, he further criticized Thomas Paine's attack on the doctrine of original sin in *Common Sense* (130).

Witherspoon argued that the calamity of war was a way both for God to reveal his wrath against sin and a way of reminding men of the precariousness of their position and the need for repentance. Drawing from both Esther and the crucifixion of Jesus, Witherspoon argued that God could confound the designs of the wicked through His providential guidance, a point that he further illustrated with examples from early Christian history, the history of the Reformation, and English history. Moreover, God had already shown his Providence in the New World. Although driven by persecution from England, "Some of the American settlements, particularly those in New England, were chiefly made by them; and as they carried the knowledge of Christ to the dark places of the earth, so they continue themselves in as great a degree of purity, of faith, and strictness of practice, or rather a greater than is found in any protestant church now in the world" (136).

Following this exposition of God's providence, Witherspoon proceeded, in typical Puritan fashion, to provide a contemporary application. Not surprisingly, his first advice was for sinners to repent before falling possible victim to God's wrath. Second, he urged his listeners to praise God for the providence by which he had already confounded enemy councils and brought American victory from possible defeat. In so doing, however, he cautioned against excessive pride, such as that which Goliath had displayed against David in 1 Samuel 14:42–45 before David slew him. Witherspoon said, "If your cause is just, you may look with confidence to the Lord and entreat him to plead it as his own" (140). He further believed that the cause of the colonies in resisting oppression was just: "I am satisfied that the confederacy of the colonies has not been the effect of pride, resentment, or sedition, but of a deep and general conviction that our civil and religious liberties, and consequently in a great measure the temporal and eternal happiness of us and our posterity, depended on the issue" (140). He observed that "there is not a single instance in history in which civil liberty was lost, and religious liberty preserved entire" (140–41). He added that "if to the justice of your cause, and the purity of your principles, you add prudence in your conduct, there will be the greatest reason to hope, by the blessing of God, for prosperity and success" (143). Although Witherspoon believed the issue was in God's hands, he said that "I would neither have you to trust in an arm of flesh, nor sit with folded hands and expect that miracles should be wrought in your defense; this is a sin which is in Scripture styled tempting God" (143).

To aid the cause, it was important for the American people to cultivate "the public interest of religion, or in other words, zeal for the glory of God and the good of others" (144). This did not require the imposition of one religious view over another: "I do not wish you to oppose anybody's religion, but everybody's wickedness" (144). The people should further cultivate "habits of industry" (146) and frugality. Witherspoon ended with the hope that "God grant that in America true religion and civil liberty may be inseparable and that the unjust attempts to destroy the one, may in the issue tend to the support and establishment of both" (14).

As a member of Congress, Witherspoon drafted a Fast Day Proclamation for December 11, 1776, and the Thanksgiving Day Proclamations of October 26, 1781, and October 11, 1782, in which he reiterated his emphasis on God's divine providence in granting Americans the victory in their war for independence (Morrison 1999, 570–73). Witherspoon was also a member of the congressional committee that endorsed the publication of the so-called Aitken Bible during the Revolutionary War. When Isaac Collins prepared an American edition of the King James Bible in 1791, Witherspoon wrote a brief preface to replace the English dedication to King James I, which Witherspoon thought was "wholly unnecessary for the purposes of edification" and "improper" for a republican audience (Dreisbach 2014, 146).

See also Aitken Bible; *Common Sense* (Thomas Paine); Days of Humiliation, Fasting, and Thanksgiving; King James Version of the Bible; Providence; Revolutionary War

For Reference and Further Reading

Dreisbach, Daniel L. 2014. "The Bible and the Political Culture of the American Founding." *Faith and the Founders of the American Republic*, ed. Daniel L. Dreisbach and Mark David Hall. New York: Oxford University Press, pp. 144–73.

Fea, John. 2016. *Was American Founded as a Christian Nation?: An Historical Introduction*, rev. ed. Louisville, KY: Westminster John Knox Press.
Mailer, Gideon. 2017. *John Witherspoon's American Revolution: Enlightenment and Religion from the Creation of Britain to the Founding of the United States*. Chapel Hill: University of North Carolina Press.
Morrison, Jeffry Hays. 1999. "John Witherspoon and 'The Public Interest of Religion.'" *Journal of Church and State* 41 (Summer): 551–73.
Noll, Mark A. 1989. *Princeton and the Republic, 1768–1822: The Search for a Christian Enlightenment in the Era of Samuel Stanhope Smith*. Princeton, NJ: Princeton University Press.
Smylie, James H. 1995. "Madison and Witherspoon: Theological Roots of American Political Thought." *American Presbyterians* 73 (Fall): 155–64.
Witherspoon, John. 1990. "The Dominion of Providence over the Passions of Men." *The Selected Writings of John Witherspoon*, ed. Thomas Miller. Carbondale: Southern Illinois University Press, pp. 126–47.

Woman's Bible (Stanton)

One of the more controversial attempts to alter biblical interpretation for political purposes was the effort by feminist Elizabeth Cady Stanton (1815–1902) to provide commentary on all biblical passages dealing with women from a nineteenth-century feminist perspective. Stanton was a long-time abolitionist who with Lucretia Mott had helped organize the historical Seneca Falls Women's Rights Convention in 1848, which had called for women's suffrage, which at the time was quite a radical idea. She was also an advocate for such diverse causes as "coeducation, girls' sports, job training, equal wages, labor unions, birth control, cooperative nurseries and kitchens, property rights for wives, child custody rights for mothers, and reform of divorce laws" (Griffith 1984, xiv).

Stanton explained her impetus for writing the *Woman's Bible* in *Eighty Years and More*: "I had long heard so many conflicting opinions about the Bible—some saying it taught woman's emancipation and some her subjection—that, during this visit of my children, the thought came to me that it would be well to collect every biblical reference to women in one small compact volume, and see which side the balance of influence really was" (quoted in Mace 2009, 9). Staunton initially intended to form committees of women who were scholars of ancient languages and of the Bible, but most of the individuals she contacted decided not to participate, and ultimately most of the commentary was her own (Mace 2009, 9–10). Stanton's procedure was similar to the one that Jefferson had used to compose his own Bible. Commentators were instructed to cut out portions of the Bible dealing with women, and then include their own commentaries underneath.

Stanton ultimately published two volumes, the first in 1895 and the second in 1898. The first included commentary on the first five books of the Old Testament, while the second added commentary on other books in the Old Testament as well as the New (Mace 2009, 10). Although the overall view that Stanton presented was that the Bible had been adverse to women's rights, there were times where she or her contributors attributed this view to mistranslation and to the chauvinism of prior biblical commentators. In analyzing the story of Noah and the ark in Genesis 6 and whether it was proper to use the word "obey" or "defer" for women's role, one commentator thus observed that "our translators were not inspired, and that we have strong presumptive proof that prejudice of education was in some instances stronger than grammatic context, in translating these contested points" (Stanton 1895, 28).

From the very beginning of her commentary, Stanton departed from orthodox Christianity. Thus in explaining Genesis 1:25–28, Stanton observed,

> Here is the sacred historian's first account of the advent of woman; a simultaneous creation of both sexes, in the image of God. It is evident from the language that there was consultation in the Godhead, and that the masculine and feminine elements were equally represented. Scott in his commentaries says, "this consultation of the Gods is the origin of the doctrine of the trinity." But instead of three male personages, as generally represented, a Heavenly Father, Mother, and Son would seem more rational. (Stanton 1895, 4)

Moreover, shortly thereafter, she observed that "the crowning glory was realized when man and woman were evolved on the sixth day, the masculine and feminine forces in the image of God, that must have existed eternally, in all forms of matter and mind" (Stanton 1895, 5).

Commenting on the story of Rebekah waiting on Isaac's servant at the well in Genesis 24, Stanton suggested that modern Rebekahs "would have promptly summoned the spectators to share their labors, even at the risk of sacrificing a desirable matrimonial alliance. The virtue of self-sacrifice has its wise limitations. Though it is most commendable to serve our fellow-beings, yet woman's first duty is to herself, to develop all her own powers and possibilities, that she may better guide and serve the next generation" (39).

In discussing the story of Jacob and Laban in Genesis 29 and 31, Stanton observed that men had, as during the Civil War, tended to make God in their own image, as either favoring or disfavoring slavery (51). Citing her own campaign for woman's suffrage, Stanton then arguably sought to do what she had accused the men of doing by crafting the Bible in her own image:

> If the Jewish account is true, then the God of the Hebrews falls short of the Christian ideal of a good, true manhood, and the Christian ideal as set forth in the New Testament falls short of our ideal of the Heavenly Father to-day. We have no fault to find with the Bible as a mere history of an ignorant, undeveloped people, but when special inspiration is claimed for the historian, we must judge of its merits by the moral standards of to-day, and the refinement of the writer by the questionable language in which he clothes his descriptions. (Stanton 1895, 52)

Fairly soon after, she observes, "We need an expurgated edition of most of the books called holy before they are fit to place in the hands of the rising generation" (52). Responding to some committee members who urged her to "be more reverent in criticizing the 'Word of God,'" Stanton rhetorically asked, "Does any one at this stage of civilization think the Bible was written by the finger of God, that the Old and New Testaments emanated from the highest divine thought in the universe?" (52).

Such frank statements of her own views led other suffragists to distance themselves from her, explaining in part why they often preferred to celebrate Susan B. Anthony as the main figure in the movement. After one cleric said that the *Woman's Bible* was the work of women and the devil, Stanton replied, "This is a great mistake. His Satanic Majesty was not invited to join the Revising Committee, which consists of women alone" (quoted in Marshall 2017, 31). Stanton's book was out of print until the 1970s, after which some modern feminists turned to Stanton in an attempt better to understand their own history.

See also Alternate Scriptures; Jefferson Bible

For Reference and Further Reading

Griffith, Elizabeth. 1984. *In Her Own Right: The Life of Elizabeth Cady Stanton*. New York: Oxford University Press.

Mace, Emily R. 2009. "2009 Elisabeth Schussler Fiorenza New Scholar Award Winner: Feminist Forerunners and a Usable Past: A Historiography of Elizabeth Cady Stanton's The Woman's Bible. *Journal of Feminist Studies in Religion* 25 (Fall): 5–23.

Marshall, Jill E. 2017. "The Recovery of Paul's Female Colleagues in Nineteenth-Century Feminist Biblical Interpretation." *Journal of Feminist Studies in Religion* 33 (Fall): 21–36.

Stanton, Elizabeth Cady. [1895]. *The Woman's Bible*. Lexington, KY: n.p.

Wright, Jeremiah

Although perceived faith in God can be an asset for politicians who often seek to identify themselves with popular preachers or evangelists like Billy Graham, association with members of the clergy who are perceived to be outside the biblical mainstream can also prove to be embarrassing. Nowhere was this clearer than when controversy erupted over a sermon that Jeremiah Wright (b. 1941), the pastor of Trinity United Church of Christ in Chicago where Barack Obama had attended, released in March 2008. By May, Obama had moved his church membership.

Wright had first delivered the sermon in question on Palm Sunday on April 13, 2003. He had chosen the text from Luke 19:37–44, which described Jesus's joyful entry into Jerusalem the Sunday before he was crucified. Curiously, Wright began with a shorter text from John 11:35 indicating that Jesus had wept both at the funeral of Lazarus and over Jerusalem on Palm Sunday because the people had not understood his message of peace.

Taking his audience back to the time of the Romans, Wright observed that they had the political and military power, and that the people not only wanted to regain self-rule, but they also wanted revenge. In Wright's view, however, which obviously referenced events within the Bush administration, the Jews were mistaken in thinking that peace could be brought about by military force, by "regime change," or by colonization. Their central problem was that they "were confusing God and Government." He likened this mistake to Muslim "jihad," to Christian "crusades," and to terms like "collateral damage," "friendly fire," and "shock and awe."

In language that arguably equated American responses to the terrorist actions of 9/11, Wright claimed, "We cannot see how what we are doing is the same

Al-Qaida is doing under a different colour flag, calling on the same of a different God to sanction and approve our murder and our mayhem!" Wright used Jesus's example from Matthew 7:3–5 of seeing the speck in others' eyes while missing the logs in one's own. He went on to castigate Americans for using the theme of the "Promised Land" to take land from Native American Indians, for using the Bible to justify slavery, for counting slaves as three-fifths of a person, for justifying segregation, for using an inordinate amount of the earth's resources, for thinking Americans had a right to oil in foreign countries, and for denying equal rights to women.

Wright proceeded to illustrate how governments lie. He not only pointed to such examples as false reports on the Gulf of Tonkin attack and the Tuskegee experiment on African Americans with syphilis, but he also bought into the theory that America knew beforehand about the Japanese attack on Pearl Harbor. He anchored this part of his sermon on Numbers 23:10, which stated that "God is not Man that he should lie."

Wright also argued that governments change. The Israelites escaped from the clutches of Pharaoh, God executed judgment on Belshazzar (Daniel 5), Lincoln helped adopt the postbellum amendments, and President Truman desegregated the U.S. military. Although governments change, Malachi 3:6 indicated that God does not. Wright repeated the lines of the hymn "Great Is Thy Faithfulness."

Wright's next point was that "governments fail." He cited the governments of Rome, Britain, Japan, and Germany before noting that the U.S. government had also failed, as in mistreating Native American Indians, individuals of Japanese descent during World War II, and African Americans. After alleging that "the government gives them drugs, builds bigger prisons, passes a three-strike law, and then wants us to sing 'God Bless America,'" Wright got to the most controversial part of his sermon. People should not be singing "God Bless America" but "God Damn America": "That's in the Bible, for killing innocent people. God Damn America for treating her citizens as less than human. God Damn America as long as she keeps trying to act like she is God and she is supreme!"

Comparing the few high-profile wealthy African Americans like television personality Oprah Winfrey and golfer Tiger Woods to the millions who were poor and unemployed, Wright pointed out that the Bible contained both blessings and cursings and asked members of the congregation to turn to one another and say, "Forgive him for the 'God Damn,' that's in the bible Lord.' Blessings and cursing is in the Bible."

Wright ended on a more uplifting note by noting, in a paraphrase of many Scriptures, that "God never fails." Wright tied this to a paraphrase of Philippians 4:13 that "you are more than a conqueror, through Christ you can do all things, through Christ who strengths you." He further tied this affirmation with God's victory over death in raising Jesus from the dead.

As criticism mounted over Wright's speech, he argued that critics were not attacking him but the black church in America. In a speech and a question and answer session at the National Press Club, he tied his own remarks to Black Liberation Theology (relying especially on Isaiah 61 and Luke 4), which he further tied to the themes of transformation and reconciliation. Attempting to defend earlier statements after the 9/11 terrorist attacks that "America's chickens are coming home to roost," he backed them up with Galatians 6:7, "Be not deceived. God is not mocked. For whatsoever you sow, that you also shall reap," as well as with the Golden Rule. He further refused to attack black Muslim leader Louis Farrakhan and sought to excuse Obama for distancing himself by noting that that was what politicians had to do. Although he exhibited some humor, he arguably further lost credibility by suggesting that the government was using the HIV virus against people of color and by attributing his criticisms to faulty media reporting.

Defenders insisted that Wright fell well within the African American jeremiadic tradition. Such a tradition generally consists of citing a promise, showing how an individual or nation has failed to meet that promise, and then delivering a prophecy about how that promise will be fulfilled (Bell 2009, 337; Walker and Smithers 2009).

See also Obama, Barack; Prophets and Jeremiads

For Reference and Further Reading

Ambinder, Marc. 2008. "The Full Wright Transcript." *The Atlantic*. April 28. https://www.theatlantic.com/politics/archive/2008/04/the-full-wright-transcript/52865/. Accessed April 15, 2019.

Bell, Bernard W. 2009. "President Barack Obama, the Rev. Dr. Jeremiah Wright, and the African American Jeremiadic Tradition." *Massachusetts Review* 50 (Autumn): 332–43.

Walker, Clarence E., and Gregory D. Smithers. 2009. *The Preacher and the Politician: Jeremiah Wright, Barack Obama, and Race in America*. Charlottesville: University of Virginia Press.

Wright, Jeremiah. 2003. "God Damn America." April 13. http://forums.sluggy.com/viewtopic.php?p=315691&sid=4b3e97ace4ee8cee02bd6850e52f50b7. Accessed April 15, 2019.

• Y •

Year of the Bible

In an idea apparently inspired by Bill Bright (1921–2003), the founder of Campus Crusade for Christ, on October 4, 1982, Congress adopted a joint resolution authorizing President Ronald Reagan to proclaim the next year as the "Year of the Bible."

Identifying the Bible as "the Word of God," the congressional resolution argued that the book "has made a unique contribution in shaping the United States as a distinctive and blessed nation and people." It went on to credit the Bible with serving as the source of religious conviction for those who settled the nation and for inspiring "concepts of civil government that are contained in our Declaration of Independence and the Constitution of the United States." It pointed to commendations that American presidents had made with respect to the Bible and the value "of voluntarily applying the Scriptures in the lives of individuals, families, and societies." It further observed that the nation faced great challenges and "that renewing our knowledge of and faith in God through Holy Scripture can strengthen us as a nation and a people."

President Reagan issued his own proclamation on February 3, 1983, while elaborating on many of the points in the congressional resolution. Reagan highlighted how the Bible, which he specifically identified as consisting of both "the Old and New Testaments," had inspired early American settlers and helped "forge a sense of common purpose . . . which laid the foundation for the spirit of nationhood that was to develop in later decades." He associated the Bible with belief "in the inalienable rights of the individual," which he believed had also been manifest in English common law.

Reagan said that "the Bible's emphasis on compassion and love for our neighbor has inspired institutional and governmental expressions of benevolent outreach such as private charity, the establishment of schools and hospitals, and the abolition of slavery." Citing other presidential acknowledgements of the importance of the Bible, Reagan argued that as the nation faced further tests, "we will need resources of spirit even more than resources of technology, education and armaments."

Although the proclamation appeared to carry no penalties, Reagan used it to "encourage all citizens, each in his or her own way, to reexamine and rediscover its priceless and timeless message."

Later that year, the American Civil Liberties Union (ACLU) sought a declaration that the law was an unconstitutional violation of the establishment clause of the First Amendment in that it recognized a specific holy book in a way that "essentially recognizes Christianity as the official religion of the United States." The ACLU likened the proclamation to telling non-Christians that they had to sit at the back of the bus.

Congress proposed a similar resolution to designate another year of the Bible for 2009, in language that was arguably even more expansive than the earlier one. The resolution claimed that "the Bible has been a cornerstone in the development of Western civilization, influencing the nations in the areas of history, law, politics, culture, music, literature, art, drama, and especially moral philosophy," but President Obama did not issue such a declaration.

A resolution similar to the congressional resolution passed by the Pennsylvania House of Representatives declaring 2012 to be the Year of the Bible for that state encountered opposition (Fea 2014, 65), but Kentucky governor Matt Bevin declared both 2016 and 2017 to be the Years of the Bible in his state.

See also First Amendment; Reagan, Ronald; Ten Commandments

For Reference and Further Reading

"Civil Liberties Union Calls Reagan's 'Year of the Bible' Illegal." 1983. *New York Times.* November 25. https://www.nytimes.com/1983/11/25/us/civil-liberties-union-calls-reagan-s-year-of-the-bible-illeagal.html. Accessed April 7, 2019.

Fea, John. 2014. "Does America Have a Biblical Heritage?" *The Bible in the Public Square: Its Enduring Influence in American Life*, ed. Mark A. Chancey, Carol Meyers, and Eric M. Meyers. Atlanta, GA: Society of Biblical Literature, pp. 65–79.

"Public Law 97–280 OCT. 4, 1982." National Liberty Alliance. https://www.nationallibertyalliance.org/sites/default/files/public_law_97-280_oct._4_1982_0.pdf. Accessed April 7, 2019.

"Year of the Bible." https://www.allabouthistory.org/year-of-the-bible.htm. Accessed April 7, 2019.

• Z •

Zionism

The movement encouraging Jews throughout the world to return to their homeland in Israel was largely led by Theodor Hertzl (1860–1904) of Hungary, which was then part of the Austrian Empire. In 1917, the British adopted the Balfour Declaration—named after James Balfour (1848–1930), the British foreign secretary—indicating their support for a national home for the Jewish people in an area that was at the time part of the Ottoman Empire. The movement received an impetus after Nazi atrocities against the Jews during World War II suggested that many Jews were otherwise unsafe in majority Gentile nations.

The Jewish state was officially founded by Jewish settlers in 1948 and almost immediately endorsed by President Harry Truman but left a legacy of bitterness among the displaced Palestinians who also regarded this area as their own home. The 1967 war, in which Israel captured the Golan Heights and other territories, suggested that Israel, which was one of the few democracies in the area and which had received American aid, had come into its own as a military power. In part motivated by his own evangelical beliefs, President Jimmy Carter attempted to negotiate peace between Israel and Egypt in the so-called Camp David Accords, and American evangelicals are among the strongest supporters of the state of Israel over its Arab enemies.

The explorer Christopher Columbus had been among those who believed that he could hasten the return of Christ if he could lead a movement to recapture Israel from the Turks. Even though they were Gentiles, early American Puritans regarded themselves as a New Israel, which, like the ancient Israelites, had crossed the sea to set up a city on a hill amid a wilderness thinly populated by Native Americans, who were often regarded as Canaanites whom it was appropriate to dispossess from the land. Such beliefs were consistent with those of the Puritan forbears in England, including Oliver Cromwell, who had attempted to pattern his own New Model Army on Old Testament models (Pieterse 1991, 81). In the 1840s, members of the British Israelite movement believed that the British people originated in the ten lost tribes of Israel, which was not dissimilar from the view of the Church of Jesus Christ of Latter-Day Saints that Jews had fled to the Americas where Jesus had also appeared to them.

In the nineteenth century, there was a growing belief among evangelical Christians that biblical prophecies pointed to the reestablishment of a Jewish state, often thought to be accompanied by the reconstruction of the Jewish Temple, as one of the signs of the end times. The year 1868 marked the beginning of a number of Niagara and International Prophetic Conferences in which this idea was developed. It was often combined with the thought of the Brethren Bible teacher John Nelson Darby (1800–1882) of Ireland, who was a leading exponent of dispensationalism, the idea that human history could be divided into different time periods during which God dealt with people in different ways. Drawing from Daniel 9:22–27, which spoke of seventy weeks, Darby believed that the reestablishment of Israel would bring about the end of the "church age" and initiate the last of these weeks (a period of seven years). Prior to this he believed, on the basis of 1 Thessalonians 4:15–17, that Jesus would secretly rapture true believers to save them from the so-called Great Tribulation, during which the Antichrist would reign on Satan's behalf to be eventually defeated by Jesus at the battle of Armageddon and bring in his millennial rule. This view was known as premillennialism.

In 1878, a Chicago real estate developer named William E. Blackstone (1841–1935), who was a friend of evangelist Dwight L. Moody (1837–1899), published a very popular book entitled *Jesus Is Coming*. It popularized the dispensational view, which was in stark contrast both to earlier Puritan views and to the views of contemporary Protestant modernists, that social reform would hasten Christ's return. It pointed instead to signs that the world situation was deteriorating and that very little time remained before Christ would come and establish his millennial kingdom. Hearing of the Russian czar's determination to follow a number of other European nations (including Spain) that had ordered Jews to leave, in 1891 Blackstone authored a memorial, signed by the chief justice of the United States, the Speaker of the House of Representatives, and many other prominent political and economic leaders, asking President Benjamin Harrison to support an international conference to consider setting up a homeland for the Jews. In this petition, he cited Isaiah 49:22, which predicted that the Gentiles "shall bring thy sons in their arms, and thy daughters shall be carried upon their shoulders," and Ezekiel 34, in which God had promised to set up a leader among the Israelites. Even more prescient of future scriptural sources, he cited God's promised blessing to Abraham in Genesis 12:3 that "I will bless them that bless thee," which was also followed by a curse for those who cursed them (Blackstone 1891).

Many reform Jews had come to believe that biblical prophecies should be interpreted spiritually. Thus one rabbi said, "We, the modern Jews, do not wish to be restored to Palestine. We have given up hope in the coming of a political personal Messiah. We say 'the country wherein we live is our Palestine, and the city wherein we dwell is our Jerusalem'" (Mouly and Robertson 1983, 99). In his memorial, Blackstone noted that not all American Jews favored a return to Palestine, which he attributed to the fact that their rabbis "have renounced their belief in ancient Scriptures and openly proclaim that the Jews should amalgamate with the various nations, wherein they are scattered," but he believed that most favored the reestablishment of such a homeland (Blackstone 1891).

In 1906, the Azuza Street Revival in southern California led to a resurgence of Pentecostal Protestantism. Many of these interpreted the renewal of speaking and tongues, faith healing, prophecies, and other miracles with the signs described in Acts 2:17–20, which they believed portended the end of the world (Sutton 2014, 29). Many postmillennial hopes were further shattered by the carnage brought about by World War I and the rise of communism in Russia.

Although the thought of Christ's imminent return might have dulled some reform efforts, it certainly increased the urgency of world evangelism. Moody thus said that "I look on this world as a wrecked vessel. God has given me a life-boat, and said to me, 'Moody, save all you can'" (Sutton 2014, 35). Many fundamentalists further withdrew from the public arena after what many considered to be their drubbing in the Scopes Trial of 1925 involving the teaching of evolution in public schools.

In the meantime, another world war seemed to point to the fulfillment of the Scripture in Matthew 24:3–8, in which Jesus had described "wars and rumors of war" as signs of the last day (Sutton 2014, 42–43). The most prominent U.S. spokesman for Zionism who lent the greatest credibility to the cause, however, was not an evangelical Christian but a secular Jew, Louis Brandeis (1856–1941), who had the distinction of being the first Jew to become a U.S. Supreme Court justice. A proponent of many reform causes who lived an outwardly simple life, he was often likened to such biblical prophets as Daniel and Isaiah and was, indeed, described as "the greatest Jew in the world since Jesus Christ" (Sarna 1994).

Since the establishment of Israel in 1948, evangelical Protestants have been among the strongest supporters of the state of Israel. Billy Graham, Jerry Falwell, Pat Robertson, John Hagee, and other preachers have all publicly supported Israeli policies, even when other liberal Christians complained that they were unfairly treating Palestinians. They have helped create such groups as the Temple Mount Foundation; the International Christian Embassy in Jerusalem (ICEJ); Christians United for Israel (CUFI), which was founded by televangelist John Hagee; and other pro-Israeli organizations. These groups continue to cite Genesis 12:3 for the proposition that God will bless the nations that bless the descendants of Abraham and curse those who curse them. Utilizing an image from Isaiah 62:6, many also refer to themselves as "watchmen" whom God had placed on the walls to protect Israel against modern enemies like Iraq and radical Islamic terrorists (Durbin 2014, 106).

In a study of the views of various denominations' attitudes toward the nation of Israel, scholar F. Michael Perko observed that conservative Protestant Christian Zionists, who tend toward fairly literalistic interpretations of Scripture, often relied on Jesus's words in Luke 21:24 and following verses about Israel being downtrodden "until the times of the Gentiles are fulfilled," for the idea that Christians can hasten this second coming by supporting Israel (2003, 3–4). Perko also identified some conservative Christian Anti-Zionists who believed either that the church had replaced Israel in prophecy or that the land belongs to God rather than to any specific political entity (5–6). More liberal Protestant denominations, who often interpret the Bible through what Perko describes as "the lens of historical/textual criticism" (6), exhibited less consensus, expressing support for the principles of Jewish "self-determination" and the need to provide "a haven for victimized people" (6), but seeking also to uphold Palestinian rights. Roman Catholic thought has exhibited a similar ambiguity.

In an interesting twist, some Palestinian liberation theologians have suggested that the story of the exodus from the oppression of the Pharaohs should be applied equally to Palestinians who have been disposed of their lands as to Jews. Palestinian Anglican priest Naim Ateek has thus argued that the story of Ahab's seizure of Naboth's vineyard in 1 Kings 21, and of the false prophets seeking to curry favor with the king in the following chapter, also supports the Palestinian, rather than the Zionist, cause (Perko 2003, 12).

In yet another twist, historian Paul S. Boyer has observed that one strand of dispensationalism is the belief that Jewish persecutions, including the holocaust, represent "God's 'chastisement' of his chosen but disobedient people" ("Forum" 2011, 17). Dispensationalists have also taught that the Antichrist will engage in a major slaughter of Jews during the Great Tribulation ("Forum" 2011, 17).

See also Church of Jesus Christ of Latter-Day Saints; Columbus, Christopher; Falwell, Jerry; Graham, Billy; Hagee, John; Judaism; Puritans; Truman, Harry S.

For Reference and Further Reading

Blackstone, William E. 1891. "Blackstone Memorial." https://en.wikisource.org/wiki/Blackstone_Memorial.

Chetty, Irvin G. 2014. "The New Apostolic Reformation and Christian Zionism." *Journal for the Study of Religion* 27(2): 297–312.

Durbin, Sean. 2014. "Walking in the Mantle of Esther 'Political' Action as 'Religious Practice.'" *Comprehending Christian Zionism: Perspectives in Comparison.* Minneapolis, MN: Augsburg Fortress, pp. 85–124.

"Forum: American Scriptures." 2011. *Religion and American Culture: A Journal of Interpretation* 21 (Winter): 1–38.

Gunner, Goran, and Smith, Robert O., eds. 2014. *Comprehending Christian Zionism: Perspectives in Comparison.* Minneapolis, MN: Augsburg Fortress.

Mead, Walter Russell. 2008. "The New Israel and the Old: Why Gentile Americans Back the Jewish State." *Foreign Affairs* 87 (July–August): 28–46.

Mouly, Ruth, and Roland Robertson. 1983. "Zionism in American Premillenarian Fundamentalism." *American Journal of Theology & Philosophy* 4 (September): 97–109.

Perko, F. Michael. 2003. "Contemporary American Christian Attitudes to Israel Based on the Scriptures." *Israel Studies* 8 (Summer): 1–17.

Pieterse, Jan Nederveen. 1991. "A History of a Metaphor: Christian Zionism and the Politics of Apocalypse." *Archives de sciences sociales des religion.* 36 (June–September): 75–103.

Sarna, Jonathan D. 1994. "'The Greatest Jew in the World since Jesus Christ': The Jewish Legacy of Louis D. Brandeis." *American Jewish History* 81 (Spring/Summer): 346–64.

Silk, Mark. 1984. "Notes on the Judeo-Christian Tradition in America." *American Quarterly* 36 (Spring): 65–85.

Sutton, Matthew Avery. 2014. *American Apocalypse: A History of Modern Evangelicalism.* Cambridge, MA: Harvard University Press.

Glossary

Apocalypse The end of the world, often the subject of biblical prophecy and its interpretations.

Apocrypha A number of books of the Bible, typically located between the Old and New Testaments, that Protestants do not generally consider to be as inspired as other Scriptures from which they are often omitted.

Archetype A model. Americans have often used biblical figures like Abraham, Moses, and Joshua to describe national political figures.

Calvinists Protestant Christians, especially Presbyterians, who follow the teaching of John Calvin and emphasize the sovereignty of God and his predestination of those who would be eternally saved or damned.

Canaan The biblical promised land of Israel said to be flowing with milk and honey. Puritans regarded America as a new Canaan, which God had reserved for them.

Canonical Included among the list of sacred books of the Bible that are generally recognized. Roman Catholics accept more books as canonical than do most Protestants.

Chosen People A people chosen by God for special purposes, often connected to their faithfulness to their covenant with him. The Old Testament presents the Jews as a chosen people. The New Testament presents Christians as a chosen people. Historically, many have interpreted America as a chosen land.

City upon a Hill An analogy used by Jesus in the Sermon on the Mount, applied by Puritans to the colony of Massachusetts, and subsequently used by some statesmen to refer to the United States.

Covenant An agreement between two people or nations (or between a nation and God), the secular form of which is often called a contract.

Decalogue The Ten Commandments.

Dispensationalism A form of biblical interpretation, largely initiated by John Nelson Darby, that divided God's dealings with human beings into various historic dispensations, which will eventually end in Christ's second coming.

Eisegesis Reading a subjective interpretation into a text, especially the Bible, as in proof texting.

Epistles Letters. A large number of books in the New Testament were originally letters to early Christian churches from apostles like Peter, James, John, and Paul.

Exegesis Explanation or interpretation of texts, especially those of the Bible, as objectively as possible.

Exodus The second book of the Bible, which largely describes the physical exit, or exodus, of the Jews from Egypt, where they were kept in bondage, to the promised land of Canaan.

Evangelicals Individuals across denominations who emphasize the importance of being "born again," consider the Bible as their ultimate authority, and consider

Jesus's death on the cross and resurrection from the dead as redemptive for those who believe on Him.

First Amendment The first of ten amendments to the U.S. Constitution, which, in addition to guaranteeing freedom of speech, press, and peaceable assembly, prohibits an "establishment" of religion and guarantees the "free exercise thereof."

Fundamentalists Those who reacted to modernist interpretations of the Bible by doubling down on traditional Christian teachings, including a belief in miracles. Fundamentalists are often associated with literal interpretations of biblical texts including opposition to the idea that man evolved from lower forms of animals.

Gospels The first four books of the New Testament (Matthew, Mark, Luke, and John) that describe the life of Jesus. The word *gospel* means "good news."

Hebraic Republicanism The idea that the Hebrew Scriptures (the Christian Old Testament) preferred a republican, or kingless, government.

Hermeneutics The interpretation of texts such as literary works, the U.S. Constitution, or the Bible.

Inerrant Without error. Fundamentalists and many evangelical Christians believe that the Bible, at least in its original manuscripts, was without error. This does not, of course, mean that it has been properly translated.

Jeremiad A sermon, typically addressed to a nation, that points to sin and indicates that God is likely to bring judgment in the absence of repentance.

King James Version (1611) An English version of the Bible published under the reign of James I and widely used in the United States, especially through the end of the nineteenth century.

Lemon Test A three-pronged test developed by the U.S. Supreme Court to ascertain infringements of the establishment clause of the First Amendment. It specifies that to avoid conflicting with the establishment clause, laws must have a clear secular legislative purpose, neither advance nor inhibit religion, and avoid excessive entanglement between church and state.

Millennium A thousand-year reign of Christ on earth described in Scripture and which has been interpreted both literally and figuratively.

Monotheism Belief in a single God, which is held by Jews, Christians, and Muslims.

New Testament The twenty-six books that constitute the second part of the Christian Bible and consist chiefly of the four gospels that describe the life of Jesus; the book of Acts, which describes the early church; other books of doctrine and instruction—including letters, or epistles—largely attributed to the apostles; and the book of Revelation, which deals in part with the end times.

Old Testament The first thirty-nine books of the Bible, which deal chiefly with God's dealings with the Jews and which are thus also referred to as Hebrew Scriptures. These include the books of the law, history, psalms, and wisdom literature, as well as the major and minor prophets.

Pacifists Individuals, often motivated by interpretations of Scripture, who oppose participation in war. Quakers and Mennonites within the United States are often pacifists.

Pentateuch The first five books of the Hebrew Bible (the Christian Old Testament), which are often attributed to Moses.

Pilgrim A pilgrim is an individual who journeys to a sacred place. In the American context, the Pilgrims were Calvinists who were disaffected from the English Anglican Church who came to America for greater freedom to practice their religion.

Postmillennialism The view that after the earth is properly reformed, Jesus will return to rule for a thousand years near the end of earthly history.

Premillennialism The view that Jesus will initiate his thousand-year kingdom on earth after earthly rulers prove incapable of bringing about peace.

Promised Land The land of Canaan, which the Bible presents as the land for the Jews, but which has often been interpreted as America—with America itself being interpreted as a New Israel.

Proof Texting The use of one or more isolated passages or verses, typically from the Bible and often out of context, to establish a point.

Providence God's continuing intervention in world affairs. From Puritan times to the present, some individuals have believed that God has exercised his providence in protecting the nation and advancing its ideals.

Protestant Reformation The movement initiated by Martin Luther of Germany in 1517 against perceived excesses of the existing Roman Catholic Church, which eventually resulted in splitting Christendom.

Puritans The group of Calvinists who attempted to "purify" the Church of England against what they perceived to be lingering remnants of Catholicism. Many came to America, where they settled in the New England colonies.

Republicanism A ideology that emphasizes citizen virtue in defending and serving the nation and in choosing wise leaders.

Revelation A revelation is a disclosure, often of divine nature. The last book of the New Testament is called Revelation because it is based on visions attributed to the apostle John, many of which appear to deal with future events.

Secularization The process, evident in many advanced nations, albeit not so much in the United States, of decreasing emphases on spiritual explanations, often associated with enlightenment and/or advances in the natural sciences.

Septuagint The earliest known translation of the Hebrew Old Testament into Greek on which some English translations of the Bible have been based.

Sermon on the Mount A sermon by Jesus recorded in the book of Matthew and containing the beatitudes ("blessed is").

Social Contract An agreement among people to leave a lawless condition to achieve protection for basic rights of life, liberty, and property.

Sola Scriptura A belief, often associated with Martin Luther and the Protestant Reformation, that the Bible alone is a sufficient guide to life.

Tanakh The name for a Hebrew translation of the Bible published in 1985. It is from the Hebrew acronym for three divisions of the Hebrew Bible—the Torah, or Pentateuch; the Nevi'im, or Prophets; and the Ketuvim, or Writings.

Ten Commandments Two tablets that the book of Exodus describes God as having given to Moses on Mount Sinai to help form the Jewish legal system and the basis of both Jewish and Christian ethics. The first part of the

Commandments deal chiefly with humans' relationship to God and the second with their relationships with one another.

Torah The first five books of the Hebrew Bible also known as the books of the law.

Translation The process of converting the original biblical languages (Hebrew, Greek, and Aramaic) into modern languages. Some translators seek word-for-word equivalence wherever possible, while others put greater emphasis on what they believe to be the overall sense of passages.

Typology A form of biblical interpretation, especially common in early American history, that interprets Old Testament stories as types of New Testament truths or which analogizes current communities and events to earlier biblical counterparts, as in likening the Pilgrims to the New Israel or America to either a wilderness or a new Eden.

Vernacular The common language. The Protestant Reformation put great emphasis on translating the Bible into languages like German and English that the common people could understand rather than in Latin, which was only accessible to those who were better educated.

Version Another word for translation. The books of the Bible were originally largely written In Hebrew (Old Testament) and Greek (New Testament) and thus need to be translated for those who are unable to read these languages in their original.

Vulgate A Latin translation of the Bible by St. Jerome, which the Catholic Church long used as the basis for translations into other national languages.

Wilderness A largely uninhabited, often fruitless land, through which the children of Israel wandered after leaving Egypt but before entering the land of Canaan. Pilgrims initially looked upon their immigration to America as an "errand in the wilderness."

Wisdom Literature A collective term used to refer to the biblical books of Job, Proverbs, Ecclesiastes, Song of Songs, Wisdom of Solomon (part of Roman Catholic Apocrypha), and Ecclesiasticus.

Zion The name of a hill outside of Jerusalem that is also used as a synonym for the city or the land of Israel as a whole. Early American Pilgrims sometimes viewed their objective as that of creating a new Zion in the wilderness.

Bibliography

Articles and Chapters

"Abortion in the Bible." 1980. *Social Sciences* 55 (Autumn): 221.

Abrahams, Edward H. 1977. "The Pain of the Millennium: Charles Taze Russell and the Jehovah's Witnesses 1879–1916." *American Studies* 18 (Spring): 57–70.

Adair, Douglass, and Marvin Harvey. 1955. "Was Alexander Hamilton a Christian Statesman?" *William and Mary Quarterly* 12 (April): 308–29.

Adams, Samuel. 1776. "'American Independence' Samuel Adams Speech – August 1, 1776." August 1. http://www.revolutionary-war-and-beyond.com/american-independence-speech-by-samuel-adams-august-1-1776.html.

Agne, Robert R., and Karen Tracy. "Bible Babble': Naming the Interactional Trouble at Waco." *Discourse Studies* 2 (August): 269–94.

Ahlstrom, Sydney E. 1963. "Thomas Hooker: Puritanism and Democratic Citizenship: A Preliminary Inquiry into Some Relationships of Religion and American Civic Responsibility." *Church History* 32 (December): 415–31.

Ahlstrom, Sydney E. 1976. "The Religious Dimension of American Aspiration." *Review of Politics* 38 (July): 332–42.

"Aitken's Bible Endorsed by Congress." Free Republic. www.freerepublic.com/focus/f-news/2722475/posts.

Albala, Ken. 2015. "The Other Side of Thanksgiving: Fasting." *San Francisco Chronicle*. November 20. https://www.sfchronicle.com/opinion/article/The-other-side-of-Thanksgiving-fasting-6644328.php.

Allen, Barbara. 2000. "Martin Luther King's Civil Disobedience and the American Covenant Tradition." *Publius* 30 (Autumn): 71–113.

Allen, Spencer L. 2014. "The Anomaly of Tony Alamo Christian Ministries: A New Testament-Based Call for Christian Polygamy." *Nova Religio: The Journal of Alternative and Emergent Religions* 17 (May): 62–82.

Alvis, John. 1998. "Milton and the Declaration of Independence." *Interpretation* 24 (Spring): 367–405.

Ambrosino, Brandon. 2019. "Someone's Gotta Tell the Freakin' Truth': Jerry Falwell's Aides Break Their Silence." *Politico*. September 9. https://www.politico.com/magazine/story/2019/09/09/jerry-falwell-liberty-university-loans-227914.

Amos, Owen. 2018. "Inside the White House Bible Study Group." BBC. April 8. https://www.bbc.com/news/world-us-canada-43534724.

Anderson, George Pomeroy. 1937. "Who Wrote 'Ethan Allen's Bible'?" *New England Quarterly* 10 (December): 685–96.

Andress, J. Mace. 1912. "The Last Vestige of Puritanism in the Public Schools of Massachusetts." *School Review* 20 (March): 161–69.

Andriote, John Manuel. 2013. "Doctor, Not Chaplain: How a Deeply Religious Surgeon General Taught a Nation about HIV." *The Atlantic*. March 4. https://www.theatlantic.com/health/archive/2013/03/doctor-not-chaplain-how-a-deeply-religious-surgeon-general-taught-a-nation-about-hiv/273665/.

AP [Associated Press]. 1987. "The White House Crisis: North Cites Bible Verse in Response to Criticism." *New York Times*. February 28.

Apess, William. 1833. "An Indian's Looking-Glass for the White Man." University of Houston Clear Lake. http://coursesite.uhcl.edu/HSH/Whitec/texts/Amerind/

apesslkggls.htm. [Note: Because this text leaves out many of Apess's references to the Bible, I have supplemented it with https://www.youtube.com/watch?y=NiY5ef4hWTO.]

Apess, William. 1836. "Eulogy on King Philip." Voices of Democracy: The U.S. Oratory Project. https://voicesofdemocracy.umd.edu/apess-eulogy-speech-text/.

Arner, Robert D. 1971. "'The Simple Cobler of Aggawam': Nathaniel Ward and the Rhetoric of Satire." *Early American Literature* 4 (Winter): 3–16.

Ariel, Yaakov. 2014. "Biblical Imagery, the End Times, and Political Acton: The Roots of Christian Support for Zionism and Israel." *The Bible in the Public Square: Its Enduring Influence in American Life*, ed. Mark A. Chancey, Carol Meyers, and Eric M. Meyers. Atlanta, GA: Society of Biblical Literature, pp. 37–62.

"Articles, Laws, and Orders, Divine, Politic, and Martial for the Colony in Virginia." 1611. Teaching American History. https://teachingamericanhistory.org/library/document/articles-laws-and-orders-divine-politic-and-martial-for-the-colony-in-virginia/.

Associated Press. 2009. "Conservative Bible Project Aims to Rewrite Scripture to Counter Perceived Liberal Bias." December 4. https://www.nydailynews.com/life-style/conservative-bible-project-aims-rewrite-scripture-counter-perceived-liberal-bias-article-1.431955.

Associated Press. 2013. "Obama to Use 2 Bibles When He Takes Oath of Office." January 10 [updated December 20, 2015]. Fox News. https://www.foxnews.com/politics/obama-to-use-2-bibles-when-he-takes-oath-of-office.

Avis, P. D. L. 1975. "Moses and the Magistrate: A Study in the Rise of Protestant Legalism." *Journal of Ecclesiastical History* 26 (April): 149–72.

Backus, Isaac. 1773. *An Appeal to the Public for Religions Liberty, Against the Oppressions of the Present Day.* Boston: John Boyle. Reprinted in Sandoz, Ellis, ed. 1991. *Political Sermons of the Founding Era, 1730–1804*. Indianapolis: Liberty Fund, pp. 327–68.

Baigell, Matthew. 1990. "Territory, Race, Religion: Images of Manifest Destiny." *Smithsonian Studies in American Art* 4 (Summer–Autumn): 2–21.

Baker, Peter. 2019. "A New Lincoln Bible, From a Mantel to a Presidential Library." *New York Times*. June 19.

Balmer, Randall. 2019. "God Is on Team Trump? Let's Just Take a Quick Check with the Bible." *Los Angeles Times*. February 4. https://www.latimes.com/opinion/op-ed/la-oe-balmer-god-and-trump-20190204-story.html.

Banks, John. 2019. "Visiting Jimmy Carter's Sunday School Class Has Become an American Pilgrimage." *Dallas News*. February 17. https://www.dallasnews.com/opinion/commentary/2019/02/17/visiting-jimmy-carters-sunday-school-class-become-american-pilgrimage.

Banks, William C. 1988. "While Congress Slept: The Iran-Contra Affair and Institutional Responsibility for Covert Operations." *Syracuse Journal of International Law and Commerce* 14 (Spring): 291–362.

Banner, Stuart. 1998. "When Christianity Was Part of the Common Law." *Law and History Review* 16 (Spring): 27–62.

Banwart, Doug. 2013. "Jerry Falwell, the Rise of the Moral Majority, and the 1980 Election." *Western Illinois Historical Review* 5 (Spring): 133–57.

Barillas, Martin M. 2019. "U.S. Legislator Persecuted for Praying to Jesus before Swearing In of Muslim." LifeSite News. March 27. https://www.lifesitenews.com/news/u.s.-legislator-prays-to-jesus-before-swearing-in-of-muslim-and-is-accused-of-islamophobia.

Barka, Mokhtar Ben. 2011. "The Christian Nation Debate and the U.S. Supreme Court." *European Journal of American Studies*." Special Issue: Oslo Conference. https://journals.openedition.org/ejas/8882.

Barlow, Philip L. 1989. "Before Mormonism: Joseph Smith's Use of the Bible, 1820–1829." *Journal of the American Academy of Religion* 57 (Winter): 739–71.

Barlow, Philip L. 1990. "Joseph Smith's Revision of the Bible: Fraudulent, Pathologic, or Prophetic?" *Harvard Theological Review* 83 (January): 45–64.

Barr, William P. 2019. "Attorney General William P. Barr Delivers Remarks to the Law School and the de Nicola Center for Ethics and Culture at the University of Notre Dame. U.S. Department of Justice. October 11. https://www.justice.gov/opa/speech/attorney-general-william-p-barr-delivers-remarks-law-school-and-de-nicola-center-ethics.

Barrs, Jerram. n.d. "Francis Schaeffer: The Man and His Message." Covenant Theological Seminary. https://www.covenantseminary.edu/francis-schaeffer-the-man-and-his-message/.

Bartlett, Gregory M. 2003. "Displaying the Ten Commandments on Public Property: The Kentucky Experience: Wasn't It Written in Stone?" *Northern Kentucky Law Review* 30: 163–87.

Barton, David. 2012. "Judgment of Nations: A Sobering Reality." *The Founders' Bible*. Newbury Park, CA: Shiloh Road, pp. 1340–50.

Bau, Ignatius. 1986. "The Legal Parameters of Sanctuary: Harboring and Alien Smuggling." *In Defense of the Alien* 9: 167–75.

Behrmann, Savannah. 2019. "Pat Robertson: Trump Could Risk 'Losing the Mandate of Heaven' with Syria Decision." *USA Today*. October 7. https://www.usatoday.com/story/news/politics/elections/2019/10/07/pat-robertson-trump-losing-mandate-heaven-over-syria-decision/3903941002/.

Bell, Bernard W. 2009. "President Barack Obama, the Rev. Dr. Jeremiah Wright, and the African American Jeremiadic Tradition." *Massachusetts Review* 50 (Autumn): 332–43.

Benezet, Anthony. 1778. "Serious Considerations on Several Important Subjects." Philadelphia: Joseph Crukshank. https://quod.lib.umich.edu/cgi/t/text/text-idx?c=evans;cc=evans;rgn=main;view=text;idno=N12457.0001.001.

Bennet, James. 1998. "Testing of a President: The President: Tearful Clinton Tells Group of Clerics, 'I Have Sinned.'" *New York Times*. September 12. https://www.nytimes.com/1998/09/12/us/testing-president-president-tearful-clinton-tells-group-clerics-have-sinned.html.

Benson, Michael T. 1994. "Harry S. Truman as a Modern Cyrus." *Brigham Young University Studies* 34(1): 6–27.

Bercovitch, Sacvan. 1966. "New England Epic: Cotton Mather's Magnalia Christi Americana." *ELH* 33 (September): 337–50.

Bercovitch, Sacvan. 1968. "The Typology of America's Mission." *American Quarterly* 30 (Summer): 135–55.

Bercovitch, Sacvan. 1976. "How the Puritans Won the American Revolution." *Massachusetts Review* 17 (Winter): 597–630.

Berens, John F. 1978. "'A God of Order and Not of Confusion': The American Loyalists and Divine Providence, 1774–1783." *Historical Magazine of the Protestant Episcopal Church* 478 (June): 211–19.

Berggren, D. Jason. 2005. "'I Had a Different Way of Governing': The Living Faith of President Carter." *Journal of Church and State* 47 (Winter): 43–61.

Bergman, Jerry. 2011. "C. Everett Koop—Christian and Darwin Doubter." *Journal of Creation* 25 (December): 63–67. https://creation.com/everett-koop-darwin-doubter.

Bergsma, John S. 2005. "Once Again, the Jubilee, Every 49 or 50 Years?" *Vetus Testamentum* 55 (January): 121–25.

Berlinerblau, Jacques. 2011. "Piety Is the Policy at Rick Perry's Prayer Rally." *Washington Post*. August 8.

Berlinerblau, Jacques. 2013. "The Bible in the Presidential Elections of 2012, 2008, 2004, and the Collapse of American Secularism." *Interested Reader: Essays on the Hebrew Bible in Honor of David J.A. Clines*, ed. James K. Aitken, Jeremy M.S. Clines, and Christl M. Maier. Atlanta, GA: Society for Biblical Literature, pp. 197–218.

Besso, Michael. 2012. "Thomas Hooker and His May 1638 Sermon." *Early American Studies* 10 (Winter): 194–225.

Betteridge, Maurice S. 1983. "The Bitter Notes: The Geneva Bible and Its Annotations." *Sixteenth Century Journal* 14 (Spring): 41–62.

Beveridge, Albert J. 1900. "U.S. Senator Albert J. Beveridge Speaks On The Philippine Question, U.S. Senate, Washington, D.C., January 9, 1900." January 9. https://china.usc.edu/us-senator-albert-j-beveridge-speaks-philippine-question-us-senate-washington-dc-january-9-1900.

"Bible Project." American Judicial Alliance. https://ajatoday.com/bible-project.

Bibler, Michael P. 2008. "Always the Tragic Jezebel: New Orleans, Katrina, and the Layered Discourse of a Doomed Southern City." *Southern Cultures* 14 (Summer): 6–27.

"Biblical Reference in Patrick Henry's Speech." Bible and Civil Government. http://bibleandcivilgovernment.com/christian_heritage/patrick_henry_give_me_liberty.php.

Bielo, James. "Materializing the Bible." https://www.materializingthebible.com/.

Bill, James A. 1994. "Chocolate-Cake Diplomacy and Colonel Oliver North." *Christian Science Monitor*. October 18.

"Billy Graham." 2018. Special Issue. *Christianity Today*. https://www.christianitytoday.com/ct/2018/billy-graham.

Bizell, Patricia. 2006. "(Native) American Jeremiad the 'Mixedblood' Rhetoric of William Apess." *American Indian Rhetoric of Survivance: Word Medicine, Word Magic*, ed. Ernest Stromberg. Pittsburg, PA: University of Pittsburgh Press, pp. 34–49.

Blackstone, William E. 1891. "Blackstone Memorial." https://en.wikisource.org/wiki/Blackstone_Memorial.

Blakemore, Erin. 2018. "Activist Carry Nation Used a Hatchet to Smash Booze Bottles before Prohibition." History. December 10. https://www.history.com/news/carry-nation-temperance-prohibition-alcohol.

Blankley, Bethany. 2012. "The Biblical Civil Disobedience Mandate." HuffPost. February 6 [updated April 7, 2012]. https://www.huffpost.com/entry/biblical-civil-disobedience-mandate_b_1249785.

Blau, Joseph L. 1987. "Government or Anarchy? In the Debates on the Constitution." *Transactions of the Charles S. Peirce Society* 23(7) (Fall): 507–19.

Blinka, Daniel D. 2007. "The Roots of the Modern Trial: Greenleaf's Testimony to the Harmony of Christianity, Science, and Law in Antebellum America." *Journal of the Early Republic* 27 (Summer): 293–334.

Blinka, Daniel David. 2019. "Harvard's Evangelist of Evidence: Simon Greenleaf's Christian Common Sense." *Great Christian Jurists in American History*, ed. Daniel L. Dreisbach and Mark David Hall. New York: Cambridge University Press, pp. 161–78.

Blum, Edward J. 2011. "'Look Baby, We Got Jesus on Our Flag': Robust Democracy and Religious Debate from the Era of Slavery to the Age of Obama." *Annals of the American Academy of Political and Social Science* 634 (September): 17–37.

Boel, Bent. 2014. "Bible Smuggling and Human Rights in the Cold War." *Transnational Anti-Communism and the Cold War: Agents, Activities, and Networks*, ed. Luc van Dongen, Stephanie Roulin, and Giles Scott-Smith. New York: Palgrave Macmillan, pp. 263–75.

Boissoneault, Lorraine. 2017. "A Brief History of Book Burning, from the Printing Press to Internet Archives." *Smithsonian*. August 31. https://www.smithsonianmag.com/history/brief-history-book-burning-printing-press-internet-archives-180964697/.

Bold. Fredric J., Jr. 2009. "Vows to Collide: The Burgeoning Conflict between Religious Institutions and Same-Sex Marriage Antidiscrimination Laws." *University of Pennsylvania Law Review* 148 (December): 179–230.

Bonomi, Patricia U. 1996. "'Hippocrates' Twins': Religion and Politics in the American Revolution." *History Teacher* 29 (February): 137–44.

Borden, Morton. 1979. "The Christian Amendment." *Civil War History* 25 (June): 156–67.
"Born of Conviction." 1963. The Mississippi Methodist Advocate. January 2. https://www.seedbed.com/wp-content/uploads/2014/01/BoC-text2.pdf.
Bosco, Ronald A. 1978. "Lectures at the Pillory: The Early American Execution Sermon." *American Quarterly* 30 (Summer): 156–76.
Bost, George H. 1948. "Samuel Davies as President of Princeton." *Journal of the Presbyterian Historical Society* 26 (September): 165–81.
Botting, Eileen Hunt, and Sarah L. Houser. 2006. "'Drawing the Line of Equality': Hannah Mather Crocker on Women's Rights." *American Political Science Review* 100 (May): 265–78.
Bouie, Jamelle. 2015. "Christian Soldiers." *Slate*. February 20. https://slate.com/news-and-politics/2015/02/jim-crow-souths-lynching-of-blacks-and-christianity-the-terror-inflicted-by-whites-was-considered-a-religious-ritual.html.
Bova, Gus. 2018. "Under Trump, Islamophobic Pastor John Hagee's Star Rises Again." *Texas Observer*. August 9. https://www.texasobserver.org/trump-pastor-john-hagee-texas-jerusalem/.
Bowman, Matthew. 2007. "Sin, Spirituality, and Primitivism: The Theologies of the American Social Gospel, 1885–1917." *Religion and American Culture: A Journal of Interpretation* 17 (Winter): 95–126.
Boyd, Julian. 1932. "Roger Sherman: Portrait of a Cordwainer Statesman." *New England Quarterly* 5: 221–36.
Brann, Eva. 2018. "Madison's 'Memorial and Remonstrance': A Jewel of Republican Rhetoric." The Imaginative Conservative. October 29. https://theimaginativeconservative.org/2018/10/madison-memorial-and-remonstrance-republican-rhetoric-90-eva-brann.html.
Bransfield, J. Brian. n.d. "Bible at Core of Catholic Beliefs." United States Conference of Catholic Bishops. http://www.usccb.org/bible/understanding-the-bible/study-materials/articles/bible-at-core-of-catholic-beliefs.cfm.
Brant, Ginny Dent. n.d. "Lessons from Chuck Colson: A Heaven-Bent Transformer of this World." CBN. https://www1.cbn.com/spirituallife/lessons-from-chuck-colson.
Brendemuehl, Collin. 2010. "A Biblical Basis for Pat Robertson's Theology." First Things. January 17. https://www.firstthings.com/blogs/firstthoughts/2010/01/a-biblical-basis-for-pat-robertsons-theology.
Bringhurst, Newell G. 2006. "Four American Prophets Confront Slavery: Joseph Smith, William Miller, Ellen G. White and Mary Baker Eddy." *John Whitmer Historical Association Journal* 26: 120–41.
Brody, David. 2016. "Brody File Video Exclusive: Donald Trump Talks about the Bible and Book of Proverbs." CBN. September 16. https://www1.cbn.com/thebrodyfile/archive/2015/09/16/brody-file-video-exclusive-donald-trump-talks-about-the-bible.
Bronner, Edwin B. 1996. "William Penn and the Scriptures." *Truth's Bright Embrace: Essays and Poems in Honor of Arthur O. Roberts*. Paper 16. http://digitalcommons.georgefox.edu/truths_bright/16, pp. 53–59.
Brooks, Clem, and Jeff Manza. 2004. "A Great Divide? Religion and Political Change in U.S. National Elections, 1972–2000." *Sociological Quarterly* 45 (Summer): 421–50.
Brown, John. 1859. "A Declaration of Liberty by the Representatives of the Slave Population of the United States of America." Digital History. www.digitalhistory.uh.edu/active_learning/explorations/brown/planning3.cfm.
Brown, Matthew. 2013. "Gettysburg Address Laced with Religious Language and Meaning." Deseret News. November 19. https://www.deseretnews.com/article/865590845/Gettysburg-Address-laced-with-religious-language-and-meaning.html.
Bruns, Roger A. 1976. "A Quaker's Antislavery Crusade: Anthony Benezet." *Quaker History* 65 (Autumn): 82–92.

Bryan, William Jennings. 1925. "Text of Closing Statement of William Jennings Bryan at the Trial of John Scopes, Dayton, Tennessee, 1925." http://www2.csudh.edu/oliver/smt310-handouts/wjb-last/wjb-last.htm.

Brydon, G. MacLaren. 1948. "The 'Confederate Prayer Book.'" *Historical Magazine of the Protestant Episcopal Church* 17 (December): 339–44.

Buranelli, Vincent. 1959. "William Penn and the Socinians." *Pennsylvania Magazine of History and Biography* 83 (October): 369–81.

Burke, Daniel. 2013. "How the Antichrist Reflects an Era's Anxieties." The Christian Century. February 7. https://www.christiancentury.org/article/2013-02/how-antichrist-reflects-eras-anxieties.

Burke, Daniel. 2019. "Franklin Graham Wants the Nation to Pray for Trump on Sunday. But Other Christians Call It Propaganda." CNN. May 31. https://www.cnn.com/2019/05/30/us/franklin-graham-trump-day-of-prayer/index.html.

Burke, Daniel. 2019. "How Pete Buttigieg Found God." CNN Politics. August 17. https://www.cnn.com/2019/08/16/politics/pete-buttigieg-religious-journey/index.html.

Burnidge, Cara L. 2013. "The Business of Church and State: Social Christianity in Woodrow Wilson's White House." *Church History* 82 (September): 659–66.

Burton, Neel. 2017. "Same-Sex Relations in the Bible." *Psychology Today*. November 1. https://www.psychologytoday.com/us/blog/hide-and-seek/201711/same-sex-relations-in-the-bible.

Burton, Tara Isabella. 2018. "The Bible Says to Welcome Immigrants. So Why Don't White Evangelicals?" Vox. October 30. https://www.vox.com/2018/10/30/18035336/white-evangelicals-immigration-nationalism-christianity-refugee-honduras-migrant.

Burton, Tara Isabella. 2018. "The Biblical Story the Christian Right Uses to Defend Trump." Vox. March 5. https://www.vox.com/identities/2018/3/5/16796892/trump-cyrus-christian-right-bible-cbn-evangelical-propaganda.

Burton, Tara Isabella. 2018. "Understanding the Fake Historian behind America's Religious Right." Vox. January 25. https://www.vox.com/identities/2018/1/25/16919362/understanding-the-fake-historian-behind-americas-religious-right.

Bushman, Richard Lyman. 2016. "Joseph Smith's Presidential Ambitions." *Mormonism and American Politics*, ed. Randall Balmer and Jana Riess. New York: Columbia University Press, pp. 3–13.

Butterfield, L. H. 1952. "Elder John Leland, Jeffersonian Itinerant." *American Antiquarian Society* 62: 156–242.

Cahn, Mark D. 1989. "Punishment, Discretion, and the Codification of Prescribed Penalties in Colonial Massachusetts." *American Journal of Legal History* 33 (April): 107–36.

Calhoun, Charles W. 1993. "Civil Religion and the Gilded Age Presidency: The Case of Benjamin Harrison." *Presidential Studies Quarterly* 23 (Fall): 651–67.

Callahan, Allen Dwight. 2006. *The Talking Book: African Americans and the Bible*. New Haven, CT: Yale University Press.

Campbell, David E., and J. Quin Monson. "Dry Kindling: A Political Profile of American Mormons." *From Pews to Polling Places: Faith and Politics in the American Religious Mosaic*, ed. J. Matthew Wilson. Washington, DC: Georgetown University Press, pp. 105–29.

Canipe, Lee. 2003. "Under God and Anti-Communist: How the Pledge of Allegiance Got Religion in Cold War America." *Journal of Church and State* 45 (Spring): 305–23.

Cannon, Mark W. 1961. "The Crusades Against the Masons, Catholics, and Mormons: Separate Waves of a Common Current." *Brigham Young University Studies* 3 (Winter): 23–49.

Capeci, Dominic J., Jr. 1979. "From Harlem to Montgomery: The Bus Boycotts and Leadership of Adam Clayton Powell, Jr., and Martin Luther King, Jr." *The Historian* 41 (August): 721–37.
Carlacio, Jami. 2002. "'Ye Knew Your Duty, but Ye Did It Not': The Epistolary Rhetoric of Sarah Grimke." *Rhetorical Review* 21(3): 247–63.
Carlson, Allan C. 2018. "Woodrow Wilson, the Bible, and the End of the Great War." The Hill. November 11. https://thehill.com/opinion/white-house/415973-woodrow-wilson-the-bible-and-the-end-of-the-great-war.
Carmy, Shalom. 2010. "Personal Ethics, Public Virtue, and Political Legitimacy in Biblical Kings and American Presidents." *Presidential Studies Quarterly* 40 (March): 76–89.
Carter, Joe. 2012. "Know Your Evangelicals: Francis Schaeffer." January 24. https://www.thegospelcoalition.org/article/know-your-evangelicals-francis-schaeffer/.
Carter, Joe. 2012. "The 7 Most Popular Contenders for the Title 'Antichrist.'" The Gospel Coalition. November 16. https://www.thegospelcoalition.org/article/the-7-most-popular-contenders-for-the-antichrist/.
Carter, Michael S. 2007. "'Under the Benign Sun of Toleration': Matthew Carey, the Douai Bible, and Catholic Print Culture, 1789–1791." *Journal of the Early Republic* 27 (Fall): 437–69.
Carver, Frances Grace. 1999. "With Bible in One Hand and Battle-Axe in the Other: Carry A. Nation as Religious Performer and Self-Promoter." *Religion and American Culture: A Journal of Interpretation* 9 (Winter): 31–65.
Cathey, Boyd D. 2019. "Abortion, Balaam's Donkey, and President Donald Trump." *Remnant Newspaper*. January 22. https://remnantnewspaper.com/web/index.php/fetzen-fliegen/item/4306-abortion-balaam-s-donkey-and-president-donald-trump.
CBN News. 2017. "Bible Studies at the White House: Who's Inside This Spiritual Awakening?" July 31. https://www1.cbn.com/cbnnews/politics/2017/july/bible-studies-at-the-white-house-whos-at-the-heart-of-this-spiritual-awakening.
Ceaser, James W. 2012. "The Origins and Character of American Exceptionalism." *American Political Thought* 2 (Spring): 3–28.
Chafets, Zev. 2007. "The Huckabee Factor." *New York Times Magazine*. December 12.
Chan, Melissa. 2016. "Tennessee Wasn't First State to Attempt to Make the Bible the Official State Book." *Time*. April 20. http://time.com/4301131/bible-state-book-bill-fail/. Accessed April 15, 2019.
Chappell, David L. 1998. "Religious Ideas of the Segregationists." *Journal of American Studies* 32 (August): 237–62.
Chase, Malcolm. 1990. "From Millennium to Anniversary: The Concept of Jubilee in Late Eighteenth- and Nineteenth-Century England." *Past & Present* 129 (November): 132–47.
Chason, Rachel. 2017. "A Short History of Roy Moore's Controversial Interpretations of the Bible." *Washington Post*. September 27. https://www.washingtonpost.com/news/acts-of-faith/wp/2017/09/27/a-short-history-of-roy-moores-controversial-interpretations-of-the-bible/.
Cheesebrough, David B., and Lawrence W. McBride. 1990. "Sermons as Historical Documents: Henry Ward Beecher and the Civil War." *History Teacher* 23 (May): 275–91.
Chester, David K. n.d. "Natural Disasters and Christian Theology." https://faraday-institute.org/resources/FAR268%20Chester.pdf.
Chetty, Irvin G. 2014. "The New Apostolic Reformation and Christian Zionism." *Journal for the Study of Religion* 27(2): 297–312.
Chiel, Arthur A. 1971. "Ezra Stiles—the Education of an 'Hebrician.'" *American Jewish Historical Quarterly* 60 (March): 235–41.

Chivers, Tom. 2009. "North Carolina Church Plans Halloween Bible Burning." *Telegraph*. October 16. https://www.telegraph.co.uk/news/religion/6346662/North-Carolina-church-plans-Halloween-Bible-burning.html.

Christians in Politics. "Politics in the Bible." http://www.christiansinpolitics.org.uk/politics-in-the-bible/.

Christians in Politics. "Why Should Christians Be Involved in Politics?" http://www.christiansinpolitics.org.uk/why-should-christians-be-involved-in-politics/.

Chua-Eoan, Howard. 2012. "The Watergate Dirty Trickster Who Found God: Charles Colson (1931–2012)." *Time*. April 21.

Church, F. Forrester. 1989. "The Gospel according to Thomas Jefferson." In Jefferson, Thomas. *The Jefferson Bible: The Life and Morals of Jesus of Nazareth*. Boston: Beacon Press, pp. 1–32.

Cillizza, Chris. 2019. "Michelle Bachmann Claimed That Donald Trump Is 'Highly Biblical.' So . . ." CNN. April 16. https://www.cnn.com/2019/04/16/politics/michele-bachman-donald-trump-bible-religious/index.html.

"Civil Liberties Union Calls Reagan's 'Year of the Bible' Illegal." 1983. *New York Times*. November 25. https://www.nytimes.com/1983/11/25/us/civil-liberties-union-calls-reagan-s-year-of-the-bible-illeagal.html.

Clark, Paul Odell. 1955. "Letters of Charles Thomson on the Translation of the Bible." *Journal of the Presbyterian Historical Society* 33 (December): 239–56.

Clark, Paul Odell. 1956. "Letters of Charles Thomson on the Translation of the Bible (Concluded)." *Journal of the Presbyterian Historical Society* 34 (June): 112–23.

Clarkson, Frederick. 2011. "The Rise of Dominionism—Remaking America as a Christian Nation." *Public Eye Magazine*. April 12. www.spaulforrest.com/2011/04/rise-of-dominionism-remaking-america-as.html.

Clinton, Bill. 1992. "In Their Own Words: Transcript of Speech by Clinton Accepting Democratic Nomination." *New York Times*. July 17. https://www.nytimes.com/1992/07/17/their-own-words-transcript-speech-clinton-accepting-democratic-nomination.html.

Clinton, Bill. 1998. "I Have Sinned." History Place Great Speeches Collection. September 11. http://www.historyplace.com/speeches/clinton-sin.htm.

CNN. 2007. "Part I: CNN/YouTube Republican Presidential Debate Transcript." November 28. https://www.cnn.com/2007/POLITICS/11/28/debate.transcript/index.html.

CNN. 2007. "Part II: CNN/YouTube Republican Presidential Debate Transcript." November 28. https://www.cnn.com/2007/POLITICS/11/28/debate.transcript.part2/.

Coates, Ta-Nehisi. 2014. "The Case for Reparations." *The Atlantic*. June. https://www.theatlantic.com/magazine/archive/2014/06/the-case-for-reparations/361631/.

Cochrane, Robert F., Jr. 2007. "Catholic and Evangelical Supreme Court Justices: A Theological Analysis." *University of Saint Thomas Law Journal* 4: 296–311.

Coe, Kevin, and Sarah Chenoweth. 2013. "Presidents as Priests: Toward a Typology of Christian Discourse in the American Presidency." *Communication Theory* 23 (November): 375–94.

Cohen, Charles L. "The 'Liberty or Death' Speech: A Note on Religion and Revolutionary Rhetoric." *William and Mary Quarterly* 38 (October): 702–17.

Cohen, Daniel A. 1988. "In Defense of the Gallows: Justifications of Capital Punishment in New England Execution Sermons, 1674–1825." *American Quarterly* 40 (June): 147–64.

Cole, Devan. 2019. "Buttigieg to Pence: 'If You Got a Problem with Who I Am, Your Problem Is Not with Me—Your Quarrel, Sir, Is with My Creator." CNN. April 8. https://www.cnn.com/2019/04/08/politics/pete-buttigieg-mike-pence/index.html.

Coleman, Lauri Bauer. 2009. "'Rain Down Righteousness': Interpretations of Natural Events in Mid-Eighteenth-Century Boston." *Remaking Boston: An Environmental History of the City and Its Surroundings*, ed. Anthony N. Penna and Conrad Edick Wright. Pittsburgh: University of Pittsburgh Press, pp. 233–58.
Colson, Chuck. 2011. "Making the Case: Don't Quote the Bible?" April 27. https://www.christianheadlines.com/columnists/breakpoint/making-the-case-don-t-quote-the-bible.html.
Concannon, Cavan. 2019. "Every Day Is Already 'Bring Your Bible to School Day.'" Religion & Politics. October 1. https://religionandpolitics.org/2019/10/01/every-day-is-already-bring-your-bible-to-school-day/.
"Conservative Bible Project." Conservapedia. https://www.conservapedia.com/Conservative_Bible_Project.
Coppins, McKay. 2018. "God's Plan for Mike Pence." *The Atlantic*. January/February. https://www.theatlantic.com/magazine/archive/2018/01/gods-plan-for-mike-pence/546569/.
Cornelius, R. M. 1981. "Their Stage Drew All the World: A New Look at the Scopes Evolution Trial." *Tennessee Historical Quarterly* 40 (Summer): 129–43.
Corn-Revere, Robert. 2014. "Bonfires of Insanity: A History of Book Burnings from Nazis to ISIS." Daily Beast. February 28 [updated April 14, 2017]. https://www.thedailybeast.com/bonfires-of-insanity-a-history-of-book-burnings-from-nazis-to-isis.
Corrigan, John. 2011. "Amalek and the Rhetoric of Extermination." *The First Prejudice: Religious Tolerance and Intolerance in Early America*, ed. Christ Beneke and Christopher S. Grenda. Philadelphia: University of Pennsylvania Press, pp. 53–72.
"Cotton Mather." United States History. https://www.u-s-history.com/pages/h1168.html.
Coulter, Michael, and Warren Throckmorton. 2013. "David Barton Is Wrong." World. Faith & Religion. January 22. https://world.wng.org/2013/01/david_barton_is_wrong.
Crosby, Richard Benjamin. 2015. "Toward a Practical, Civic Piety: Mitt Romney, Barack Obama, and the Race for National Priest." *Rhetoric and Public Affairs* (Summer): 301–30.
Currie, Chuck. 2004. "Walter Rauschenbusch and the Social Gospel." *Modern Theologians* (Fall): 1–22. https://chuckcurrie.blogs.com/chuck_currie/files/walter_rauschenbusch_and_the_social_gospel.pdf.
Currie, Chuck. 2011. "The Christian Faith of Senator Mark Hatfield." HuffPost. August 8. https://www.huffpost.com/entry/christian-faith-mark-hatfield_b_921230.
Cushman, Robert Fairchild. 1955. "Holy Bible and the Public Schools." *Cornell Law Review* 40 (Spring): 475–99.
Dabbs, Matt. 2016. "Francis Schaeffer on the Politics of Peace and Affluence." Wineskins. March 29. http://wineskins.org/2016/03/29/francis-schaeffer-on-the-politics-and-peace-and-affluence/.
Dahl, Curtis. 1974. "The Clergyman, the Hussy, and Old Hickory: Ezra Stiles Ely and the Peggy Eaton Affair." *Journal of Presbyterian History* 52 (Summer): 127–55.
Danforth, John. 2017. "Sermon Delivered by Danforth at Harvard Memorial Church: 'Parables, Priorities, and Politics.'" Posted by Debra Kennard. September 27. https://rap.wustl.edu/sermon-delivered-by-danforth-at-harvard-memorial-church-parables-priorities-and-politics/.
Daniel, W. Harrison. 1958. "Bible Publication and Procurement in the Confederacy." *Journal of Southern History* 24 (May): 191–201.
Davenport, John [work incorrectly attributed to John Cotton]. 1643. *A Discourse about Civil Government in a New Plantation Whose Design Is Religion*. Cambridge: Samuel

Green and Marmaduke Johnson. Evans Early American Imprint Collection. University of Michigan. https://quod.lib.umich.edu/cgi/t/text/text-idx?c=evans;cc=evans;rgn=main;view=text;idno=N00042.0001.001.

Davies, Samuel. 1760. "Religion and the Public Spirit. A Valedictory Address to the Senior Class, Delivered in Nassau-Hall, September 21, 1760. The Sunday before the Commencement." Portsmouth, NH: Daniel Fowle. https://quod.lib.umich.edu/e/evans/N07144.0001.001?rgn=main;view=fulltext.

Davis, David Brion. 1957. "The Movement to Abolish Capital Punishment in America, 1787–1861." *American Historical Review* 63 (October): 23–46.

Davis, Derek H. 1994. "Religious Dimensions of the Declaration of Independence: Fact and Fiction." *Journal of Church and State* 36 (Summer): 469–82.

Davis, Derek H. 1997. "Editorial: Religion and the Abuse of Judicial Power." *Journal of Church and State* 39 (Spring): 203–14.

Davis. Derek H. 2006. "President George Bush: America's Pastor in Troubled Times?" Society of Biblical Literature. https://www.sbl-site.org/publications/article.aspx?Articleld=153.

Davis, Jefferson. 1862. "A Veto Message from Jeff. Davis." *New York Times*. October 26. Archives.

Dawson, Hugh J. 1998. "'Christian Charity' as Colonial Discourse: Rereading Winthrop's Sermon in Its English Context." *Early American Literature* 33(2): 117–48.

Deacon, Andrea. 2003. "Navigating 'The Storm, the Whirlwind, and the Earthquake': Re-assessing Frederick Douglass, the Orator." *Rocky Mountain Review of Language and Literature* 47(1): 65–81.

DeCaro, Louis A., Jr. 2007. "John Brown the Abolitionist—a Biographer's Blog." May 6. http://abolitionist-john-brown.blogspot.com/.

Degler, Carl N. 1970. "Were the Puritans Puritanical?" *Out of Our Past: The Forces That Shaped Modern America*. New York: Harper & Row, pp. 28–37. https://1.cdn.edl.io/hjnC2FdZiWd0CSQ1SDMd2IqwLFSSI2NwaJCKruK8YdopHQLB.pdf.

Delaney, Carol. 2006. "Columbus's Ultimate Goal: Jerusalem." *Comparative Studies in Society and History* 48 (April): 260–92.

D'Elia, Donald J. 1974. "Benjamin Rush: Philosopher of the American Revolution." *Transactions of the American Philosophical Society* 64: 1–113.

Demar, Gary. n.d. "Foreword" to Boudinot, Elias. 1802. *The Age of Revelation. Or The Age of Reason Shewn to Be an Age of Infidelity*. Philadelphia: Asbury Dickins. Reprinted by Power Springs, GA: American Vision Press, pp. vii–xiv.

Den Hartog, Jonathan. 2009. "John Jay and the 'Great Plan of Providence.'" *Forgotten Founders on Religion and Public Life*, ed. Daniel L. Dreisbach, Mark David Hall, and Jeffry H. Morrison. Notre Dame, ID: University of Notre Dame Press, pp. 145–70.

Den Hartog, Jonathan. 2014. "Elias Boudinot, Presbyterians, and the Quest for a 'Righteous Republic.'" *Faith and the Founders of the American Republic*, ed. Daniel L. Dreisbach and Mark David Hall. New York: Oxford University Press, pp. 253–76.

Deneen, Patrick K. 2012. "Cities of Man on a Hill." *American Political Thought* 2 (Spring): 29–52.

DePalma, Margaret. 2003. "Religion in the Classroom: The Great Bible Wars in Nineteenth Century Cincinnati." *Ohio Valley History* 3 (Fall): 17–36.

Derrick, J. C. 2016. "Ben Sasse: A Reformed reformer." *World Magazine*. October 15. https://world.wng.org/2016/09/ben_sasse_a_reformed_reformer.

Desai, Saahil. 2019. "The First Reparations Attempt at an American College Comes from Its Students." *The Atlantic*. April 18. https://www.theatlantic.com/education/archive/2019/04/why-are-georgetown-students-paying-reparations/587443/.

Devi, Gayatri. 2014. "Candidates Use the Bible to Justify Their Views. We Must Respond with Reason." *Guardian*. November 5. https://www.theguardian.com/commentisfree/2015/nov/05/candidates-bible-views-noahs-ark-donald-trump-ben-carson.

Dias, Elizabeth. 2019. "'Mormon' No More: Faithful Reflect on Church's Move to Scrap a Moniker." *New York Times*. June 29.

Dicker, Ron. 2019. "Lawmaker's Prayer Mentions Jesus 13 Times before Muslim Colleague Is Sworn In." HuffPost. March 27. https://www.yahoo.com/huffpost/law-maker-apos-prayer-mentions-jesus-113436078.html.

Dickson, Charles Ellis. 1987. "Jeremiads in the New American Republic: The Case of National Fasts in the John Adams Administration." *New England Quarterly* 60 (June): 187–207.

Dillon, Michele. 1995. "Religion and Culture in Tension: The Abortion Discourses of the U.S. Catholic Bishops and the Southern Baptist Convention." *Religion and American Culture: A Journal of Interpretation* 5 (Summer): 159–80.

Docherty, George M. 1954. "Under God." February 7. http://www.christianheritagemins.org/articles/UNDER%20GOD.pdf.

Dorn, Jacob H. 2003. "'In Spiritual Communion': Eugene V. Debs and the Social Christians." *Journal of the Gilded Age and the Progressive Era* 2 (July): 303–25.

Douglass, Frederick. 1852. "What to the Slave Is the Fourth of July?" July 5. TeachingAmericanHistory.org. http://teachingamericanhistory.org/library/document/what-to-the-slave-is-the-fourth-of-july/.

Douthat, Ross. 2019. "The Abortion Mysticism of Pete Buttigieg." *New York Times*. September 17.

Dow, Lorenzo. 1851. "Analects upon Natural, Social, and Moral Philosophy." 7th ed., enlarged, *History of Cosmopolite: Or, The Writings of Rev. Lorenzo Dow: Containing His Experience and Travels, in Europe and America, Up to Near His Fiftieth Year*. N.p.: J.B. Smith, pp. 417–78.

Downey, Dennis B. 2001. "The Lord's Messenger: Racial Lynching and the Church Trial of Robert Elwood." *Journal of Presbyterian History* 79 (Summer): 135–49.

Downey, Dennis B. 2013. "The 'Delaware Horror': Two Ministers, a Lynching, and the Crisis of Democracy." *Lynching Beyond Dixie: American Mob Violence Outside the South*, ed. Michael J. Pfeifer. Champaign: University of Illinois Press, pp. 237–60.

Dreisbach, Daniel L. 1996. "Introduction: A Debate on Religion and Politics in the Early Republic." *Religion and Politics in the Early Republic: Jasper Adams and the Church-State Debate*, ed. Daniel L. Dreisbach. Lexington: University Press of Kentucky, pp. 1–35.

Dreisbach, Daniel L. 2001. "Mr. Jefferson, a Mammoth Cheese, and the 'Wall of Separation Between Church and State': A Bicentennial Commemoration." *Journal of Church and State* 43 (Autumn): 725–45.

Dreisbach, Daniel. 2013. "The Sacred Sounds of Lincoln's Gettysburg Address." Law & Liberty November 19. https://www.lawliberty.org/2013/11/19/the-sacred-sounds-of-lincolns-gettysburg-address/.

Dreisbach, Daniel L. 2014. "The Bible and the Political Culture of the American Founding." *Faith and the Founders of the American Republic*, ed. Daniel L. Dreisbach and Mark David Hall. New York: Oxford University Press, pp. 133–73.

Dreisbach, Daniel L. February 2017. "The Promises and Perils of Using the Bible in Political Discourse." www.bibleinterp.com/articles/2017/02/dre418022.shtml.

Dreisbach, Daniel L. 2019. "Introduction: Christianity and American Law." *Great Christian Jurists in American History*, ed. Daniel L. Dreisbach and Mark David Hall. New York: Cambridge University Press, pp. 1–15.

Dunn, Richard S. 1987. "An Odd Couple: John Winthrop and William Penn." *Proceedings of the Massachusetts Society*, 3rd Series 99: 1–24.

Duram, James C. 1974. "In Defense of Conscience: Norman Thomas as an Exponent of Christian Pacifism During World War I." *Journal of Presbyterian History* 52 (Spring): 19–32.

Durant, Robert F. 2006. "A 'New Covenant' Kept: Core Values, Presidential Communications, and the Paradox of the Clinton Presidency." *Presidential Studies Quarterly* 36 (September): 345–72.

Durbin, Sean. 2014. "Walking in the Mantle of Esther 'Political' Action as 'Religious Practice." *Comprehending Christian Zionism: Perspectives in Comparison*. Minneapolis, MN: Augsburg Fortress, pp. 85–124.

Durocher, Aurele. 1961. "The Social Ideas of Henry George." *American Journal of Economics and Sociology* 20 (October): 497–512.

Dwyer, John J. 2003. "Standing Like a Stone Wall." *Faith in God and Generals: An Anthology of Faith, Hope, and Love in the American Civil War*. Compiled by Ted Baehr and Susan Wales. Nashville, TN: Broadman & Holman, pp. 65–72.

Easter, Eric. "Jesse and the Bible." The Pilgrimage of Jesse Jackson. https://www.pbs.org/wgbh/pages/frontline/jesse/impressions/bible.html.

Eden, Jason. "'Therefore Ye Are No More Strangers and Foreigners': Indians, Christianity, and Political Engagement in Colonial Plimouth and on Martha's Vineyard." *American Indian Quarterly* 38 (Winter): 36–59.

Edmondson, Catie. 2019. "'So Help Me God' No More: Democrats Give House Traditions a Makeover." *New York Times*. May 11.

Edwards, Jonathan. 2015. "Sermon: 'Sin and Wickedness Bring Calamity and Misery' (1729)." *The Other Jonathan Edwards: Selected Writings on Society, Love, and Justice*, ed. Gerald McDermott and Ronald Story. Amherst: University of Massachusetts Press, pp. 35–41.

Eells, Robert J. 1991. "Theodore Frelinghuysen, Voluntaryism and the Pursuit of the Public Good." *American Presbyterians* 69 (Winter): 257–70.

Egan, James. 1978. "'This Is a Lamentation and Shall Be for a Lamentation': Nathaniel Ward and the Rhetoric of the Jeremiad." *Proceedings of the American Philosophical Society* 122 (December 18): 400–10.

Egan, Matt. 2019. "The Bible Could Be a Victim in Trump's Trade War." CNN. July 9. https://www.cnn.com/2019/07/09/business/bible-tariff-china-trade-war-trnd/index.html.

Eggen, Dan. 2001. "Ashcroft's Faith Plays Visible Role at Justice." *Washington Post*. May 14.

Elazar, Daniel J. 1980. "The Political Theory of Covenant: Biblical Origins and Modern Developments." *Publius* 10 (Fall): 3–30.

Elazar, Daniel J. 1992. "Deuteronomy as Israel's Ancient Constitution: Some Preliminary Reflections." *Jewish Political Studies Review* 4 (Spring): 3–39.

Ellison, Christopher G. 1996. "Conservative Protestantism and the Corporal Punishment of Children: Clarifying the Issues." *Journal for the Scientific Study of Religion* 35 (March): 1–16.

Emery, Robert. 2009–2010. "Church and State in the Early Republic: The Covenanters' Radical Critique." *Journal of Law and Religion* 25(2): 487–501.

Englander, Meryl E. 1978. "The Court's Corporal Punishment Mandate to Parents, Local Authorities, and the Profession." *Phi Delta Kappan* 59 (April): 529–32.

Enns, Pete. "Ben Carson and the Bible: Maybe He Should Get a Second Opinion." https://peteenns.com/ben-carson-and-the-bible-maybe-he-should-get-a-second-opinion/.

Erickson, Paul D. 1984. "Daniel Webster's Myth of the Pilgrims." *New England Quarterly* 57 (March): 44–64.

Erzen, Tanya. 2007. "Testimonial Politics: The Christian Right's Faith-Based Approach to Marriage and Imprisonment." *American Quarterly* 59 (September): 991–1015.

Evangelical Climate Initiative. n.d. "Climate Change: An Evangelical Call to Action." https://www.npr.org/documents/2006/feb/evangelical/calltoaction.pdf.

Fabisiak, Thomas. 2009. "The Conservative Bible Project: Looking for Conservative Diamonds in a Liberal Dung-Hill." Rewire News. October 21. http://religiondispatches.org/the-conservative-bible-project-looking-for-conservative-diamonds-in-a-liberal-dung-hill/.

Fackre, Gabriel. 2001. "Was Reinhold Niebuhr a Christian?" First Things. October. https://www.firstthings.com/article/2002/10/was-reinhold-niebuhr-a-christian.

Falls, Thomas B. 1942. "The Carey Bible." *Records of the American Catholic Historical Society of Philadelphia* 53 (June): 111–15.

Faust, Drew Gilpin. 1977. "Evangelicalism and the Meaning of the Proslavery Argument: The Reverend Thornton Stringfellow of Virginia." *Virginia Magazine of History and Biography* 84 (January): 3–17.

Fea, John. 2014. "Does America Have a Biblical Heritage?" *The Bible in the Public Square: Its Enduring Influence in American Life*, ed. Mark A. Chancey, Carol Meyers, and Eric M. Meyers. Atlanta, GA: Society of Biblical Literature, pp. 65–79.

Fessenden, Tracy. 2005. "The Nineteenth-Century Bible Wars and the Separation of Church and State." *Church History* 74 (December): 784–811.

Fielding, Howard Ioan. 1940. "John Adams: Puritan, Deist, Humanist." *Journal of Religion* 20 (January): 33–46.

Finkelstein, Jacob J. 1973. "The Goring Ox: Some Historical Perspectives on Deodands, Forfeitures, Wrongful Death and the Western Notion of Sovereignty." *Temple Law Quarterly* 46 (Winter): 169–290.

Finkelstein, J. J. 1981. "The Ox That Gored." *Transactions of the American Philosophical Society* 71(1): 1–89.

Finn, Nathan A. 2013. "Francis Wayland and Richard Fuller: Debating Slavery with Christian Civility." Andrew Fuller Center for Baptist Studies. May 10. http://andrewfullercenter.org/articles/blog/2013/05/francis-wayland-and-richard-fuller-debating-slavery-with-christian-civility.

Fisher, Linford D. 2017. "The Bible and Indigenous Language Translations in the Americas." *The Oxford Handbook of the Bible in America*, ed. Paul C. Gutjahr. New York: Oxford University Press, pp. 39–59.

Fishwick, Marshall W. 1986. "The Bird, the Bible and the Constitution: Trinitarian America." *Laws of our Fathers: Popular Culture and the U.S. Constitution*, ed. Ray B. Browne and Glenn J. Browne. Bowling Green, OH: Bowling Green State University, pp. 154–66.

Fitzenberger, W. A. 2005. *In Rare Form: A Pictorial History of Baseball Evangelist Billy Sunday*. Iowa City: University of Iowa Press.

"Flag Salute, Voting, and Civilian Services." JW.Org. https://www.jw.org/en/publications/books/gods-love/flag-salute-voting-civilian-service/.

Fleet, Elizabeth. 1946. "Madison's 'Detached Memoranda,'" *William and Mary Quarterly* 3 (October): 534–68.

Flick, Stephen. n.d. "Elias Boudinot: Building America on Christ." Christian Heritage Fellowship. https://christianheritagefellowship.com/elias-boudinot-building-america-on-christ/.

Flowers, Ronald B. 1983. "President Jimmy Carter, Evangelicalism, Church-State Relations, and Civil Religion." *Journal of Church and State* 25 (Winter): 113–32.

"For the Health of the Nation: An Evangelical Call to Civic Responsibility." 2004. Approved by the National Association of Evangelicals. October 8. http://www.ricklove.net/wp-content/uploads/2010/04/For_The_Health_Of_The_Nation1.pdf.

Ford, Gerald R. 1976. "Remarks of Gerald R. Ford in Philadelphia, Pennsylvania (Bicentennial Celebration)." Gerald R. Ford Presidential Library and Museum. July 4. https://www.fordlibrarymuseum.gov/library/speeches/760645.asp.

Forman, John A. 1960. "Lewis Charles Levin: Portrait of an American Demagogue." *American Jewish Archives* (October): 150–94.

"Forum: American Scriptures." 2011. *Religion and American Culture: A Journal of Interpretation* 21 (Winter): 1–38.

Francis, Andre L. 1992. "Thomas Jonathan 'Stonewall' Jackson 'Fought by the Old Testament, Lived by the New.'" USAWC Military Studies Program Paper. https://apps.dtic.mil/dtic/tr/fulltext/u2/a250823.pdf.

Franck, Matthew J. 2016. "Christianity and Freedom in the American Founding." *Christianity and Freedom*, Vol. I: *Historical Perspectives*, ed. Timothy Samuel Shah and Allen D. Hertzke. New York: Cambridge University Press, pp. 264–89.

Freedman, Robert. 2005. "The Religious Right and the Carter Administration." *Historical Journal* 48 (March): 231–60.

French, David. 2019. "Jerry Falwell Jr. Shows How the Advance of Christendom Can Harm Christianity." *National Review*. September 11. https://www.nationalreview.com/2019/09/jerry-falwell-jr-shows-how-the-advance-of-christendom-can-harm-christianity/.

Fudge, Edward. 2006. "The Law of Moses and Modern Tort Law." https://edwardfudge.com/writte-nministry-articles-2/the-law-of-moses-and-modern-tort-law/.

"Fundamental Agreement, or Original Constitution of the Colony of New Haven, June 4, 1639 The Avalon Project, Yale Law School." 1639. https://avalon.law.yale.edu/17th_century/ct01.asp.

Furman, Richard. [December 24, 1822] 1985. "Exposition of the Views of the Baptists Relative to the Coloured Population of the United States in Communication to the Governor of South Carolina." Reprinted in Roberts, James A. 1985. *Richard Furman: Life and Legacy*. Macon, GA: Mercer University Press, pp. 274–86. Accessed at https://glc.yale.edu/exposition-views-baptists-relative-coloured-population.

Gaffney, Edward McGlynn, Jr. 1986. "Biblical Law and the First Year Curriculum of American Legal Education." *Journal of Law and Religion* 4(1): 63–95.

Gaines, William H., Jr. 1950/1951. "The Continental Congress Considers the Publication of a Bible, 1777." *Studies in Bibliography* 3: 274–81.

Gajanan, Mahita. 2017. "These Are the Bible Verses Past Presidents Have Turned to on Inauguration Day." *Time*. January 19. http://time.com/4639596/inauguration-day-presidents-bible-passages/.

Gallagher, Eugene V. 2013. 2013. "Sources, Sects, and Scripture: The Book of Satan in The Satanic Bible." *The Devil's Party: Satanism in Modernity*, ed. Per Faxneld and Jesper A. Peterson. New York: Oxford University Press, pp. 103–22.

Gander, Kashmira. 2018. "White House Bible Study Led by Pastor Who Is Anti-Gay, Anti-Women and Anti-Catholic." *Newsweek*. April 11. https://www.newsweek.com/white-house-bible-group-led-pastor-anti-gay-anti-women-anti-catholic-881860.

Gardner, Catherine Villanueva. 2004. "Heaven-Appointed Educators of Mind: Catharine Beecher and the Moral Power of Women." *Hypatia*. 19 (Spring): 1–16.

Gardner, Robert. 1960. "A Tenth-Hour Apology for Slavery." *Journal of Southern History* 26 (August): 352–67.

Garet, Ronald R. 2009. "With Radiant Countenance: Creation, Redemption, and Revelation." *Michigan State Law Review* 2002: 289–306.

Garfield, James A. 1881. "Inaugural Address." March 4. https://www.bartleby.com/124/pres36.html.
Garnet, Henry Highland. 1843. "An Address to the Slaves of The United States." https://www.blackpast.org/african-american-history/speeches-african-american-history/1843-henry-highland-garnet-address-slaves-united-states/.
Garris, Zachary. n.d. "Horace Mann's Utopian Vision for Public Education." Teach Diligently. http://teachdiligently.com/articles/horace-mann-utopian-vision-for-public-education.
Gass, Nick. 2015. "Ben Carson's 15 Most Controversial Quotes." *Politico*. October 9. https://www.politico.com/story/2015/10/ben-carson-controversial-quotes-214614.
Gebarowski-Shafer, Ellie. 2013. "The Transatlantic Reach of the Catholic 'False Translation' Argument in the School 'Bible Wars.'" *U.S. Catholic Historian* 31 (Summer): 47–76.
Gedalyahu, Tzvi Ben. 2008. "Bible-Thumping Joe Lieberman Connects Esau with Iran." Israel National News. July 29. www.israelnationalnews.com/News/News.aspx/126988.
George, Henry. "Moses." [1878] 1956. Paramount Pictures. Reprinted from New York: Robert Schalkenbach Foundation.
George, Robert P. 2001. "The 28th Amendment: It Is Time to Protect Marriage, and Democracy, in America." *National Review* 443 (July 23): 32–34.
"George Washington Inaugural Bible." n.d. http://www.stjohns1.org/portal/gwib.
Georgini, Sara. 2013. "John Quincy Adams at Prayer." *Church History* 83 (September): 649–58.
Giacomo, Carol. 2019. "For Spewing Hate, Trump Should Quit, a Priest Tells Parishioners." *New York Times*. July 24.
Giffin, Frederick C. 1973. "Billy Sunday: The Evangelist as 'Patriot.'" *Social Science* 48 (Autumn): 216–21.
Gilbreath, Edward. 2002. "Still Somebody: Despite an Embarrassing Scandal and Widespread Irritation with His Methods, Jesse Jackson Continues to Be an Influential Voice in the Church. Should Evangelicals Listen?" *Christianity Today*. February 4. https://.ink.gale.com/apps/doc/A82772011/AONE?u=tel_middleten&sid=AONE&xid=b26637fb.
Giles, Kevin. 1994. "The Biblical Argument for Slavery: Can the Bible Mislead? A Case Study in Hermeneutics." *Evangelical Quarterly* 661: 3–17.
Gilgoff, Dan. 2008. "The Story behind the Lincoln Bible at Obama's Inauguration." U.S. News. December 23. https://www.usnews.com/news/blogs/god-and-country/2008/12/23/the-story-behind-the-lincoln-bible-at-obamas-inauguration. Accessed May 6, 2019.
Gilmore, Michael J. 2017. "The Bible and Jehovah's Witnesses." *The Oxford Handbook of the Bible in America*, ed. Paul C. Gutjahr. New York: Oxford University Press, pp. 645–60.
Gilpin, R. Balkeslee. 2013. "John Brown, Religion and Violent Abolition: 'Choose You This Day Whom You Will Serve.'" HuffPost. January 22. https://www.huffpost.com/entry/john-brown-religion-and-violent-abolition_b_2527903.
Glazener, Nancy. "Benjamin Franklin and the Limits of Secular Civil Society." *American Literature* 80 (June): 203–31.
Glynn, Tom. 2015. *Reading Publics: New York City's Public Libraries, 1754–1711.* New York: Fordham University. [Chapter 4: "The Biblical Library of the American Bible Society: Evangelicalism and the Evangelical Corporation," pp. 101–17.]
"God in the White House." God in America. www.pbs.org/godinamerica/god-in-the-white-house/.
Goldman, Shalom. 2014. "'God's New Israel': American Identification with Israel Ancient and Modern." *The Bible in the Public Square: Its Enduring Influence in American*

Life, ed. Mark A. Chancey, Carol Meyers, and Eric M. Meyers. Atlanta, GA: Society of Biblical Literature, pp. 81–92.

Gomez, Justin. 2019. "Franklin Graham Attacks Pete Buttigieg for Being Gay, Says He Should Repent." ABC News. April 25. https://abcnews.go.com/Politics/franklin-graham-attacks-pete-buttigieg-gay-repent/story?id=62625378&cid=clicksource_4380645_null_twopack_hed. Accessed April 25, 2019.

Goodnight, Ethan. 2017. "William Apess, Pequot Pastor: A Native American Revisioning of Christian Nationalism in the Early Republic." *Religions* 8(18): 17pp. https://www.mdpi.com/2077-1444/8/2/18.

Goodspeed, Edgar J. 1947. "Thomas Jefferson and the Bible." *Harvard Theological Review* 40 (January): 71–76.

Goodstein, Laurie. 2000. "The 2000 Campaign: The Philosophy: Conservative Church Leaders Find a Pillar in Bush." *New York Times*. January 23.

Goodstein, Laurie. 2001. "Ashcroft's Life and Judgments Are Steeped in Faith." *New York Times*. January 14.

Goodstein, Laurie. 2001. "Falwell: Blame Abortionists, Feminists and Gays." *Guardian*. September 19. https://www.theguardian.com/world/2001/sep/19/september11.usa9.

Gordon, James W. 2011. "Religion and the First Justice Harlan: A Case Study in Late Nineteenth Century Presbyterian Constitutionalism." *Marquette Law Review* 85 (Winter): 317–422.

Gouverneur, Joe. 2007. "Underground Evangelism: Missions During the Cold War." *Transformation* 24 (April): 80–86.

Graham, Billy. 2012. "America under Judgment?" Bill Graham Evangelistic Association. November 1. https://billygraham.org/decision-magazine/november-2012/america-under-judgment/.

Graham, Elaine. 2009. "A Window on the Soul: Four Politicians on Religion and Public Life." *International Journal of Public Theology* 3: 144–63.

Granberg-Michaelson, Wes. 2011. "A Tribute to Mark O. Hatfield." *Sojourners*. August 8. https://sojo.net/articles/tribute-mark-o-hatfield.

Green, John C. 1993. "Pat Robertson and the Latest Crusade: Religious Resources and the 1988 Presidential Campaign." *Social Science Quarterly* 74 (March): 157–68.

Green, John C., and James L. Guth. 1991. "The Bible and the Ballot Box: The Shape of Things to Come." *The Bible and the Ballot Box: Religion and Politics in the 1988 Election*, ed. James L. Guth and John C. Green. Boulder: Westview Press, pp. 207–25.

Green, Steven K. 1999–2000. "The Fount of Everything Just and Right? The Ten Commandments as a Source of American Law." *Journal of Law and Religion* 24(2): 525–58.

Greenberg, Kenneth S. 1976. "Revolutionary Ideology and the Proslavery Argument: The Abolition of Slavery in Antebellum South Carolina." *Journal of Southern History* 42 (August): 365–84.

Greenspahn, Frederick E. 2007. "Jewish Ambivalence towards the Bible." *Hebrew Studies* 48: 7–21.

Grey, Thomas C. 1984. "The Constitution as Scripture." *Stanford Law Review* 37: 1–25.

Grimke, Sarah M. 1836. "An Epistle to the Clergy of the Southern States." https://en.wikisource.org/wiki/An_Epistle_to_the_Clergy_of_the_Southern_States.

Grobel, Kendrick. 1943. "Charles Thomson, First American N.T. Translator: An Appraisal." *Journal of Bible and Religion* 11 (August): 145–51.

Gropee, Maureen. 2018. "How the Bible Helps Pence Navigate His Role as Trump's Vice President." *USA Today*. January 21. https://www.usatoday.com/story/news/politics/2018/01/21/how-bible-helps-pence-navigate-his-role-trumps-vice-president/1044357001/.

Grunes, Rodney A. 2008. "James Madison and Religious Freedom." *James Madison, Philosopher, Founder, and Statesman*, ed. John R. Vile, William D. Pederson, and Frank J. Williams. Athens: Ohio University Press, pp. 105–32.

Guardino, Peter. 2014. "'In the Name of Civilization and with a Bible in Their Hands:' Religion and the 1846–48 Mexican-American War." *Mexican Studies/Estudios Mexicanos* 30 (Summer): 342–65.

Gutjahr. Paul C. 2001. "Sacred Texts in the United States." *Book History* 4: 335–70.

Haddock. Vicki. 2002. "Son of a Preacher Man / How John Ashcroft's Religion Shapes His Public Service." SF Gate. August 4. https://www.sfgate.com/opinion/article/Son-of-a-Preacher-Man-How-John-Ashcroft-s-2787948.php.

Hagerty, Barbara Bradley. 2008. "Understanding the Gospel according to Huckabee." NPR. February 8. https://www.npr.org/templates/story/story.php?storyid=18821021.

Hahn, George E. 1982. "Creation-Science and Education." *Phi Delta Kappan* 63 (April): 553–55.

Halcombe, Madeline. 2010. "Judge Who Gave Convicted Murderer Amber Guyger a Bible Is Accused of Bridging the Church-State Divide." CNN. October 4. https://www.cnn.com/2019/10/04/us/guyger-judge-freedom-religion/index.html.

Hale, Frederick. 2017. "Fighting the Good Fight from the 'Church of the Presidents': Peter Marshall's Homiletics during the Second World War." *Journal of Presbyterian History* 95 (Spring/Summer): 18–31.

Hall, David W. 1996. "Introduction: Revolutionary Pulpits." *Election Day Sermons*, ed. David W. Hall. Oak Ridge, TN: Kuyper Institute, pp. 9–26.

Hall, Mark David. 2011. "Did America Have a Christian Founding?" Heritage Foundation. June 7. https://www.heritage.org/political-process/report/did-america-have-christian-founding.

Hambrick-Stowe, Charles E. 1996. "Charles G. Finney and Evangelical Anti-Catholicism." *U.S. Catholic Historian* 24 (Fall): 39–52.

Hanska, Jan. 2009. "Prophetic Politics—Leadership Based on the Stories of a Golden Past and a Glorious Future." *Perspectives* 17(2): 93–117.

Happy, J. Nelson, and Samuel Pyeatt Menefee. 1997. "Genesis! Scriptural Citation and the *Lawyer's Bible* Project." *Regent University Law Review* 9: 89–148.

Harrill, J. Albert. 2000. "The Use of the New Testament in the American Slave Controversy: A Case History in the Hermeneutical Tension between Biblical Criticism and Christian Moral Debate." *Religion and American Culture: A Journal of Interpretation* 10 (Summer): 149–86.

Hatch, Nathan O. 1974. "The Origins of Civil Millennialism in America: New England Clergymen, War with France, and the Revolution." *William and Mary Quarterly* 31 (July): 407–30.

Haupt, Paul. 1917. "Alcohol in the Bible." *Journal of Biblical Literature* 36(1/2): 75–83.

Hay, Robert P. 1969. "George Washington: American Moses." *American Quarterly* 21 (Winter): 780–91.

Hay, Robert P. 1969. "Providence and the American Past." *Indiana Magazine of History* 65 (June): 79–101.

Hayes, Kevin J. 2004. "How Thomas Jefferson Read the Qur'an." *Early American Literature* 39(2): 247–61.

Hayhoe, Katharine. 2019. "Caring about Climate Change Is the Christian Thing to Do." *New York Times*. October 31.

Hedrick, Joan D. 1988. "'Peaceable Fruits': The Ministry of Harriet Beecher Stowe." *American Quarterly* 40 (September): 307–32.

Hefelbower, S.G. 1920. "Deism Historically Defined." *American Journal of Theology* 24 (April): 217–23.

Henry, Patrick. "Give Me Liberty or Give Me Death!" Colonial Williamsburg. https://www.history.org/almanack/life/politics/giveme.cfm.

Herlinger, Chris. 1996. "Clinton Tells Religious Leaders: 'I Have Sinned.'" The Layman. September 18. https://layman.org/news61c4/.

Hertzberg, Benjamin R. 2015. "Daniel, Esther, and the Minority Politics of the Hebrew Bible." *Polity* 47 (July): 397–416.

Heschel, Abraham Joshua. 1963. "Religion and Race." Voices of Democracy. January 14. https://voicesofdemocracy.umd.edu/heschel-religion-and-race-speech-text/.

Hicks, Cindy. 2015. "5 Beliefs That Set Quakers Apart from Other Protestant Christians." Newsmax. April 1. https://www.newsmax.com/fastfeatures/quakers-protestant-beliefs-christians/2018/08/13/id/635855/.

Higgonson, Thomas Wentworth. 1861. "The Story of Denmark Vesey." *The Atlantic*. June. https://www.theatlantic.com/magazine/archive/1861/06/denmark-vesey/396239/.

Hill, Patricia R. n.d. "*Uncle Tom's Cabin* as a Religious Text." utc.iath.virginia.edu/interpret/exhibits/hill/hill.html.

Hirsch, Elizabeth Feist. 1941. "John Cotton and Roger Williams: Their Controversy Concerning Religious Liberty." *Church History* 10 (March): 38–51.

Hogue, William M. 1991. "An Authorized Bible for Americans." *Anglican and Episcopal History* 60 (September): 361–82.

Holland, David. 2017. "The Bible and Mormonism." *The Oxford Handbook of the Bible in America*, ed. Paul C. Gutjahr. New York: Oxford University Press, pp. 611–26.

Horn, Joshua. 2015. "Peter Muhlenberg: The Pastor Turned Soldier." *Journal of the American Revolution*. November 9. https://allthingsliberty.com/2015/11/peter-muhlenberg-the-pastor-turned-soldier/.

Horowitz, Jason, Nick Corasaniti, and Ashley Southall. 2015. "Nine Killed in Shooting at Black Church in Charleston." *New York Times*. June 17. https://www.nytimes.com/2015/06/18/us/church-attacked-in-charleston-south-carolina.html.

Houck, Davis W., and Mihaela Nocasian. 2002. "FDR's First Inaugural Address: Text, Context, and Reception." *Rhetoric and Public Affairs* 5 (Winter): 649–78.

Housley, Kathleen. 1988. "'The Letter Kills but the Spirit Gives Life': Julia Smith's Translation of the Bible." *New England Quarterly* 61 (December): 555–68.

Howard-Pitney, David. 1986. "The Enduring Black Jeremiad: The American Jeremiad and Black Protests Rhetoric, from Frederick Douglass to W.E.B. Du Bois, 1841–1919." *American Quarterly* 38(3): 481–92.

Hudson, David L., Jr. 2005. "The Bible Tells Them So." *ABA Journal*. July. www.abajournal.com/magazine/article/the_bible_tells_them_so.

Huhn, Wilson Ray. 2011. "A Higher Law: Abraham Lincoln's Use of Biblical Imagery." *Rutgers Journal of Law and Religion*, forthcoming; University of Akron Legal Studies Research Paper No. 11-1. Available at SSRN: https://ssrn.com/abstract=17482, 38pp.

Hutchinson, John A. 1947. "Biblical Foundations of Democracy." *Journal of Bible and Religion* 14 (January): 34–37.

Huxman, Susan, and Gerald Biesecker-Mast. 2004. "In the World but Not of It: Mennonite Traditions as Resources for Rhetorical Invention." *Rhetoric and Public Affairs* 7 (Winter): 539–54.

Hyer, Majorie. 1983. "Colson Preaches That Watergate Proves the Bible." *Washington Post*. September 28.

Hylton, J. Gordon. 2998. "David Josiah Brewer and the Christian Constitution." *Marquette Law Review* 82 (Winter): 417–25.

Ilany, Ofri. 2012. "From Divine Commandment to Political Act: The Eighteenth-Century Polemic on the Extermination of the Canaanites." *Journal of the History of Ideas* 73 (July): 437–61.

Ilany, Ofri. 2018. *In Search of the Hebrew People: Bible and Nation in the German Enlightenment*. Indianapolis: Indiana University Press.

Imholt, Robert J. 2013. "The Fast Day Sermons of Timothy Dwight." *Connecticut History Review* 52 (Spring): 75–85.

Inabinet, Brandon. 2007. "Albert J. Beveridge, 'March of the Flag' (16 September 1898)." *Voices of Democracy* 1 (June): 148–64.

Ippel, Henry P. 1980. "Blow the Trumpet, Sanctify the Fast." *Huntington Library Quarterly* 44 (Winter): 43–60.

Jackson, Amanda. 2019. "Muslim and Jewish Holy Books among Many Used to Swear-In Congress." CNN. January 3. https://www.cnn.com/2019/01/03/us/congress-swear-in-religious-books-trnd/index.html.

Jackson, Brian. 2007. "Jonathan Edwards Goes to Hell (House): Fear Appeals in American Evangelism." *Rhetoric Review* 26(1): 42–59.

Jackson, Jesse. 1968. "Address to the Democratic National Convention." July 19. https://americanrhetoric.com/speeches/jessejackson1988dnc.htm.

Jackson, Kent P. 2014. "The Cooperstown Bible." *New York History* 95 (Spring): 243–70.

"Jackson's 'Colored Sunday School' Class." 2006. *Washington Times*. May 5.

Jacobs, Jaap. 2015. "'Hot Pestilential and Unheard-Of Fevers, Illnesses and Torments': Days of Fasting and Prayer in New Netherland." *New York History* 96 (Summer/Fall): 284–300.

Jauhiainen, Peter D. 2001. "'Reasoning Out of the Scriptures': Samuel Hopkins, the Theological Enterprise, and the Deist Threat." *Journal of Presbyterian History* 79 (summer): 119–33.

Jay, John. [1776]. "Address of the Convention of the Representatives of the State of New York to Their Constituents." https://johnjaybio.wordpress.com/personal-life/the-jay-court/address-of-the-convention-of-the-representatives-of-the-state-of-new-york-to-their-constituents/.

Jelen, Ted G. 1992. "The Clergy and Abortion." *Review of Religious Research* 34 (December): 132–51.

Jen, Joanna Tice. 2019. "'Be Joyful Always!': Twenty-First-Century Evangelical Conceptions of Happiness and Trumpist Politics." *Regimes of Happiness: Comparative and Historical Studies*, ed. Yuri Contrerar-Vejar, Joanna Tice Jen, and Bryan S. Turner. New York: Anthem Press, pp. 93–110.

Jenkins, Jack. 2015. Six Times Mike Huckabee Used Bad Theology to Support His Policies." ThinkProgress. May 5. https://thinkprogress.org/six-times-mike-huckabee-used-bad-theology-to-support-his-policies-bc8fb629a261/.

"Jezebel's War with America: The Plot to Destroy Our Country and What We Can Do to Turn the Tide." https://www.amazon.com/Jezebels-War-America-Destory-Country/dp/1629996661.

"John Danforth on Faith, Evangelicals and Politics." NPR Newscast. https://www.npr.org/templates/story/story.php?storyId=103929890.

John, Richard R. 1990. "Taking Sabbatarianism Seriously: The Postal System, the Sabbath, and the Transformation of American Political Culture." *Journal of the Early Republic* 10 (Winter): 517–67.

Johnson, Paul. 1995. "God and the Americans: The City upon a Hill." *Commentary* 99 (January): 25–32.

Jones, Absalom. 1808. "A Thanksgiving Sermon, Preached January 1, 1808, in St. Thomas's, or the African Episcopal, Church, Philadelphia: On Account of the Abolition of the African Slave Trade, on That Day, by the Congress of the United States." Philadelphia: Fry and Kammerer. Accessed at anglicanhistory.org/usa/ajones/thanksgiving1808.html.

Jones, Bob. 2001. "Man of the Law." *World Magazine*. December 22. https://world.wng.org/2001/12/man_of_the_law.

Jones, Ida E. 2002–2003. "Contacts without Fellowship: Lynching, the Bible and the Christian Community." *Black History Bulletin* 65–66 (January–December): 48–55.

Jordan, Winthrop D. 1973. "Familial Politics: Thomas Paine and the Killing of the King, 1776." *Journal of American History* 60 (September): 294–308.

Joyce, Kathryn. 2019. "The Christianization of U.S. Foreign Policy." *New Republic*. March 25. https://newrepublic.com/article/153387/christianization-us-foreign-policy.

Junkkarinen, Marko. 2015. "Reason and Revelation during the Revolutionary Period: Robert Morris' Views on Omnipotence and the Afterlife." *Anglican and Episcopal History* 84 (December): 416–38.

Juzwik, Mary M. 2014. "American Evangelical Biblicism as Literate Practice: A Critical Review." *Reading Research Quarterly* 49 (July/August/September): 335–49.

Kaell, Hillary, and Marilyn Mellowes. 2011. "American Scripture." PBS. October 11. http://www.pbs.org/godinamerica/american-scripture/.

Kammen, Michael. 1980. "From Covenant to Constitution in American Political Thought." *Publius* 10 (Fall): 101–35.

Kao, Grace Y. 2007. "'One Nation under God' or Taking the Lord's Name in Vain?: Christian Reflections on the Pledge of Allegiance." *Journal of the Society of Christian Ethics* 27 (Spring/Summer): 183–204.

Kaplan, Joshua. 2005. "Unmasking the Federal Marriage Amendment: The Status of Sexuality." *Georgetown Journal of Gender and Law* 6: 105–41.

Kattan, Victor. 2019. "U.S. Recognition of Golan Heights Annexation: Testament to Our Times." *Journal of Palestine Studies* 48 (Spring): 79–85.

Kauffman, Gretel. 2016. "Is the Bible a Defense for Corporal Punishment of Children?" Christian Science Monitor. September 1. https://www.csmonitor.com/USA/Justice/2016/0901/Is-the-Bible-a-defense-for-corporal-punishment-of-children.

Kelley, Robert. 1966. "Presbyterianism, Jacksonianism and Grover Cleveland." *American Quarterly* 18 (Winter): 615–36.

Kellogg, Carolyn. 2015. "Tennessee Legislator Wants the Bible to Become Official State Book." *Los Angeles Times*. February 12. https://www.latimes.com/books/jacketcopy/la-et-jc-tennessee-bible-official-state-book-20150212-story.html.

Kellstedt, Lyman A., and Corwin E. Smidt. 1993. "Doctrinal Beliefs and Political Behavior: Views of the Bible." *Rediscovering the Religious Factor in American Politics*, ed. David C. Leege and Lyman A. Kellstedt. Armonk, NY: M. E. Sharpe, pp. 177–98.

Kennedy, John F. 1961. "The City upon a Hill Speech." John F. Kennedy Presidential Library and Museum. January 9. https://www.jfklibrary.org/learn/about-jfk/historic-speeches/the-city-upon-a-hill-speech.

Kennedy, John F. 1961. "'City upon a Hill' Speech." UVA, Miller Center. January 9. https://millercenter.org/the-presidency/presidential-speeches/january-9-1961-city-upon-hill-speech.

Kennedy, John F. 1961. "Transcript of President John F. Kennedy's Inaugural Address (1961)." January 20. https://www.ourdocuments.gov/doc.php?flash=false&doc=91&page=transcript.

Kennedy, John F. 1963. "Remarks Prepared for Delivery at the Trade Mart in Dallas, TX, November 22, 1963." John F. Kennedy Presidential Library and Museum. November 22. https://www.jfklibrary.org/archives/other-resources/john-f-kennedy-speeches/dallas-tx-trade-mart-undelivered-19631122.

Kennedy, John F. 1960. "Transcript: JFK's Speech on His Religion." NPR. September 12 [posted online on December 5, 2007]. https://www.npr.org/templates/story/story.php?storyId=16920600.

Kertzer, Morris N. 1975. "What Is a Jew?" *Religions of America: Ferment and Faith in an Age of Crisis*, ed. Leo Rosten, New York: Simon & Schuster, pp. 142–55.

Kestenbaum, Sam. 2019. "The Curious Mystical Text Behind Marianne Williamson's Presidential Bid." *New York Times*. July 5.

Kestenbaum, Sam. 2019. "#MAGA Church: The Doomsday Prophet Who Says the Bible Predicted Trump." *New York Times*. March 15.

Kilgore, Ed. 2018. "Bible and the Christian Right Agree: Trump Is the New Cyrus the Great." *Intelligencer*. March 5. http://nymag.com/intelligencer/2018/03/bibi-and-the-christian-right-trump-the-new-cyrus-the-great.html.

Kilgore, Ed. 2018. "Is Cory Booker the Candidate of the Christian Left?" *Intelligencer*. December 17. http://nymag.com/intelligencer/2018/12/is-cory-booker-the-candidate-of-the-christian-left.html.

Kincaid, John. 2003. "Extinguishing the Twin Relics of Barbaric Multiculturalism—Slavery and Polygamy: From American Federalism." *Publius* 33 (Winter): 75–92.

Kincheloe, Joe L., and George Staley. 1982. "The Menachem Begin-Jerry Falwell Connection: A Revolution in Fundamentalism." *Journal of Thought* 17 (Summer): 35–39.

King, Martin Luther, Jr. April 1, 1953–June 30, 1954?. "The Theology of Reinhold Niebuhr." Martin Luther King, Jr. Research and Education Institute. https://kinginstitute.stanford.edu/king-papers/documents/theology-reinhold-niebuhr.

King, Martin Luther, Jr. August 1963. "Letter from Birmingham Jail." https://web.cn.edu/kwheeler/documents/Letter_Birmingham_Jail.pdf.

Koester, Nancy. 2011. "Harriet Beecher Stowe on the Christian Life." *Journal of Lutheran Ethics*. March 1. https://www.elca.org/JLE/Articles/233.

Koh, Jennifer Lee. 2017. "Agape, Grace, and Immigration Law: An Evangelical Perspective." *Agape, Justice, and Law: How Might Christian Love Shape Law?*, ed. Robert F. Cochran Jr. and Zacharay R. Calo. New York: Cambridge University Press, pp. 228–45.

Konig, David Thomas. 1982. "'Dale's Laws' and the Non-Common Law Origins of Criminal Justice in Virginia." *American Journal of Legal History* 26 (October): 354–75.

Koresh, David. 1994. "The David Koresh Manuscript: Exposition of the Seven Seals." © Phillip Arnold and James Tabor. http://ccat.sas.upenn.edu/gopher/text/religion/koresh/Koresh%20Seals.

Kristof, Nicholas. 2019. "We're Less and Less a Christian Nation, and I Blame Some Blowhards." *New York Times*. October 26.

LaFontaine, Charles V. 1976. "God and Nation in Selected U.S. Presidential Inaugural Addresses, 1789–1945: Part One." *Journal of Church and State* 18 (Winter): 39–60.

LaFontaine, Charles V. 1976. "God and Nation in Selected U.S. Presidential Inaugural Addresses, 1789–1945: Part Two." *Journal of Church and State* 18 (Autumn): 503–21.

Laidler, John. 2017. "Try Hard, Find God, Get Rich." *Harvard Gazette*. October 24. https://news.harvard.edu/gazette/story/2017/10/the-prosperity-gospel-gains-a-foothold-in-u-s-politics-panel-says/.

Lammers, Anne C. 1982. "The Rev. Absalom Jones and the Episcopal Church: Christian Theology and Black Consciousness in a New Alliance." *Historical Magazine of the Protestant Episcopal Church* 51 (June): 159–84.

Langenbach, Lisa, and John C. Green. 1992. "Hollow Core: Evangelical Clergy & the 1988 Robertson Campaign." *Polity* 25 (Autumn): 147–58.

Lannie, Vincent Peter. 1966. "William Seward and the New York School Controversy. 1840–1842: A Problem in Historical Motivation." *History of Education Quarterly* 6 (Spring): 52–71.

Lannie, Vincent P., and Bernard C. Diethorn. 1968. "For the Honor and Glory of God: The Philadelphia Bible Riots of 1844." *History of Education Quarterly* 8 (Spring): 44–106.

Lanthrop, George Parsons. 1894. "Hostility to Roman Catholics." *North American Review* 158 (May): 563–73.

LaPlante, Eve. 2007. "The Opposite of Thanksgiving." *Boston Globe*. November 18. archive.boston.com/bostonglobe/ideas/articles/2007/11/18/the_opposite_of_thanksgiving.

Larry King Live. 2001. "What Did John Ashcroft Say at Bob Jones University?" CNN.com transcripts. January 12. http://transcripts.cnn.com/TRANSCRIPTS/0101/12/lkl.00.html.

Law, Jeannie. 2019. "'Slave Bible' on Display at Museum of the Bible; Edition Removes Chapters to Uphold Slavery." *Christian Post*. April 26. https://www.christianpost.com/news/slave-bible-on-display-at-museum-of-the-bible-edition-removes-chapters-to-uphold-slavery.html.

Lawrence, W. R. 1956. "Democratic Keynote Talk Assails Nixon as 'Hatchet Man' of G.O.P.; Lays 'Indifference' to President." *New York Times*. August 14.

Lawson, Ronald. 1995. "Sect-State Relations: Accounting for the Differing Trajectories of Seventh-Day Adventists and Jehovah's Witnesses." *Sociology of Religion* 56 (Winter): 351–77.

Lechtreck, Elaine Allen. 2012. "'We Are Demanding $500 Million for Reparations': The Black Manifesto, Mainline Religious Denominations, and Black Economic Development." *Journal of African American History* 97 (Winter–Spring): 39–71.

Lee, Shayne. 2007. "Prosperity Theology: T.D. Jakes and the Gospel of the Almighty Dollar." *CrossCurrents* 57 (Summer): 227–36.

Lee, Umphrey. 1935. "The English Bible and American Public Men." *Christian Education* 19 (October): 18–21.

Leland, John. 1802. "An Oration Delivered at Cheshire." July 5. *Writings of Elder John Leland*, pp. 201–11. http://www.paradisepbc.org/Articles/John%20Leland/Writings%20of%20Elder%20John%20Leland.pdf.

Leonard, Bill J. 1987. "Independent Baptists: From Sectarian Minority to 'Moral Majority.'" *Church History* 56 (December): 504–17.

Levinson, Martin H. 2012. "Indexing the Religious Beliefs of American Founders." *ETC: A Review of General Semantics* 69 (October): 384–93.

Levinson, Sanford. 1979. "'The Constitution' in American Civil Religion." *Supreme Court Review* 1979: 123–51.

Levitt, Laura S. 2011. "Beyond a Shared Inheritance: American Jews Reclaim the Hebrew Bible." *The Calling of the Nations: Exegesis, Ethnography, and Empire in a Biblical-Historic Present*, ed. Mark Vessey, Sharon V. Betcher, Robert A. Daum, and Harry O. Maier. Toronto, Canada: University of Toronto Press, pp. 83–101.

Levy, Joel J. 2017. "How the King James Bible Came to Be." *Time*. June 19. https://time.com/4821911/king-james-bible-history/.

Lieberman, Joseph. 2011. "Faith and the Public Square." October 25. https://speeches.byu.edu/talks/joseph-lieberman/faith-and-the-public-square.

Lilly, Ingrid Esther. 2016. "The Planet's Apocalypse: The Rhetoric of Climate Change." *Apocalypses in Context: Apocalyptic Currents through History*, ed. Kelly J. Murphy and Justine Jeffcoat Scheedtler. Minneapolis, MN: Augsburg Fortress, pp. 359–79.

Lincoln, Abraham. 1858. "House Divided Speech." June 16. www.abrahamlincolnonline.org/lincoln/speeches/house.htm.

Linder, Douglas O. 1995–2019. "State v. John Scopes ('The Monkey Trial'): An Account." Famous Trials. https://famous-trials.com/scopesmonkey/2127-home.

Linder, Robert D. 1996. "Universal Pastor: President Bill Clinton's Civil Religion." *Journal of Church and State* 38 (Autumn): 733–49.

Lindsay, Michael. 2006. "Is the National Prayer Breakfast Surrounded by a 'Christian Mafia'?: Religious Publicity and Secrecy within the Corridors of Power." *Journal of the American Academy of Religion* 74 (June): 390–419.

Lindsey, Donald B., and John Heeren. 1992. "Where the Sacred Meets the Profane: Religion in the Comic Pages." *Review of Religious Research* 34 (September): 73–77.

Lipton, Diana. 2008. "Abraham Joshua Heschel: His Place in a Biblical Chain of Tradition." *European Judaism: A Journal for the New Europe* 41 (Spring): 25–35.

Litfin, Duane. 2019. "The Lost Genius of the American Settlement." *Christianity Today*. September 30. https://www.christianitytoday.com/ct/2019/september-web-only/subverting-american-settlement.html.

Little, Becky. 2019. "Why Bibles Given to Slaves Omitted Most of the Old Testament." History. December 11 [updated April 3, 2019]. https://www.history.com/news/slave-bible-redacted-old-testament.

Loconte, Joseph. 2003. "Faith and the Founding: The Influence of Religion on the Politics of James Madison." *Journal of Church and State* 45 (Autumn): 699–715.

Lowance, Mason I., Jr. 1969. "Typology and the New England Way: Cotton Mather and the Exegesis of Biblical Types." *Early American Literature* 4 (Spring): 15–37.

Luce, Edward. 2019. "A Preacher for Trump's America: Joel Osteen and the Prosperity Gospel." *Financial Times*. April 17. https://www.ft.com/content/3990ce66-60a6-11e9-b285-3acd5d43599e.

Luo, Michael. 2007. "Gingerly, Romney Seeks Ties to Christian Right. *New York Times*. October 16.

Lutz, Donald S. 1980. "From Covenant to Constitution in American Political Thought." *Publius* 10 (Autumn): 101–33.

Lutz, Donald S. 1984. "The Relative Influence of European Writers on Late Eighteenth-Century American Political Thought." *American Political Science Review* 78 (March): 189–97.

Lyons, John F. 1939. "Thomson's Bible." *Journal of the Department of History*. 18 (March): 211–20.

Lytton, Timothy D. 2002–2003. "'Shall Not the Judge of the Earth Deal Justly?': Accountability, Compassion, and Judicial Authority in the Biblical Story of Sodom and Gomorrah." *Journal of Law and Religion* 18: 31–55.

Mabee, Charles. 1979. "Thomas Jefferson's Anti-Clerical Bible." *Historical Magazine of the Protestant Episcopal Church* 48 (December): 473–81.

Mace, Emily R. 2009. "2009 Elisabeth Schussler Fiorenza New Scholar Award Winner: Feminist Forerunners and a Usable Past: A Historiography of Elizabeth Cady Stanton's The Woman's Bible. *Journal of Feminist Studies in Religion* 25 (Fall): 5–23.

Mach, Andrew. 2015. "'The Name of Freeman Is Better than Jesuit': Anti-Catholicism, Republican Ideology, and Cincinnati Political Culture, 1853–1854." *Ohio Valley History* 15 (Winter): 3–21.

Madan, Rafael Alberto. 2008. "The Sign and Seal of Justice." *Ave Maria Law Review* 7: 123–204.

Maguire, Marsha. 1981. "Confirming the Word: Snake-Handling Sects in Southern Appalachia." *Quarterly Journal of the Library of Congress* 38 (Summer): 166–79.

"Manhattan Declaration: A Call of Christina Conscience." 2009. First Things. November 20. https://www.firstthings.com/web-exclusives/2009/11/manhattan-declaration-a-call-of-christian-conscience.

Marshall, Jill E. 2017. "The Recovery of Paul's Female Colleagues in Nineteenth-Century Feminist Biblical Interpretation." *Journal of Feminist Studies in Religion* 33 (Fall): 21–36.

Martin, Robert F. 1996. "Billy Sunday and Christian Manliness." *The Historian* 58 (Summer): 811–23.

Martin, Roger H. 1996. "Quakers, the Bible and the British and Foreign Bible Society." *Quaker History* 85 (Spring): 13–28.

Massa, Mark S. 1997. "A Catholic for President?: John F. Kennedy and the 'Secular' Theology of the Houston Speech, 1960." *Journal of Church and State* 39 (Spring): 197–317.

Mathews, Donald G. 1993. "'Spiritual Warfare': Cultural Fundamentalism and the Equal Rights Amendment." *Religion and American Culture: A Journal of Interpretation* 3 (Summer): 129–54.

Mathis-Lilley, Ben. 2017. "The Wasted Mind of Ben Sasse." *Slate*. July 13. https://slate.com/news-and-politics/2017/07/the-wasted-mind-of-nebraska-sen-ben-sasse.html.

Mattson, Stephen. 2017. "Christ, Not America, First." *Sojourners*. February 6. https://sojo.net/articles/christ-not-america-first.

Mauss, Armand L., and Philip L. Barlow. "Church, Sect, and Scripture: The Protestant Bible and Mormon Sectarian Retrenchment." *Sociological Analysis* 52 (Winter): 397–414.

McCadden, Joseph J. 1964. "Bishop Hughes versus the Public School Society of New York." *Catholic Historical Review* 50 (July): 188–207.

McCammack, Brian. 2007. "Hot Damned America: Evangelicalism and the Climate Change Policy Debate." *American Quarterly* 49 (September): 545–668.

McClay, Wilfred M. 2013. "Still the Redeemer Nation." *Wilson Quarterly* 37(2) (Spring).

McCormick, Elizabeth, and Patrick McCormick. 2006. "Hospitality: How a Biblical Virtue Could Transform United States Immigration Policy." *University of Detroit Mercy Law Review* 83: 857–900.

McDermott, Gerald R. 1991. "Jonathan Edwards, the City on a Hill, and the Redeemer Nation: A Reappraisal." *American Presbyterian* 69: (Spring): 33–47.

Mcdermott, Jennifer. 2019. "Some Cheer, Some Decry Trump's Signing of Bibles." *Tennessean*. March 11, p. 16A.

McGunigal, Lisa. 2016. "The Criminal Trial of Anne Hutchinson: Ritual, Religion, and Law." *Mosaic: An Interdisciplinary Critical Journal* 49 (June): 149–66.

McInerney, Daniel J. 1991. "'A Faith for Freedom': The Political Gospel of Abolition." *Journal of the Early Republic* 11 (Autumn): 371–93.

McIntyre, Dean. 2007. "National Bible Week and the Hymnal." Discipleship Ministries. November 2. https://www.umcdiscipleship.org/resources/national-bible-week-and-the-hymnal.

McKinley, William. 1897. "First Inaugural Address of William McKinley." The Avalon Project. March 4. https://avalon.law.yale.edu/19th_century/mckin1.asp.

McKivigan, John R. 1982. "The Gospel Will Burst the Bonds of the Slave: The Abolitionists Bibles for Slaves Campaign." *Negro History Bulletin* 45 (July–August–September): 62–64, 77.

McNair, Matthew. 2016. "Rhetorical Continuity: Evolution, Creation Science, and Intelligent Design." *First Amendment Studies in Arkansas*. Little Rock: University of Arkansas Press, pp. 223–54.

McSloy, Steven Paul. 1996. "'Because the Bible Tells Me So': Manifest Destiny and American Indians." *Saint Thomas Law Review* 9: 37–47.

McTighe, Michael J. 1990. "Jesse Jackson and the Dilemma of a Prophet in Politics." *Journal of Church and State* 32 (Summer): 585–607.

Mead, Walter Russell. 2008. "The New Israel and the Old: Why Gentile Americans Back the Jewish State." *Foreign Affairs* 87 (July–August): 28–46.

Medhurst, Martin J. 2009. "Evangelical Christian Faith and Political Action: Mike Huckabee and the 2008 Republican Presidential Nomination." *Journal of Communication and Religion* 32 (November): 199–239.

Medhurst, Martin J. 2009. "Mitt Romney, 'Faith in America,' and the Dance of Religion and Politics in American Culture." *Rhetoric and Public Affairs* 12 (Summer): 195–221.

Medina, Jennifer. 2019. "The Yom Kippur Prayer on Cory Booker's Lips." *New York Times*. October 8. https://www.onenewspage.com/n/US/1zkk83f4ch/The-Yom-Kippur-Prayer-on-Cory-Booker.htm.

Merkley, Paul Charles. n.d. "I Am Cyrus." *Christianity Today*. https://www.christianitytoday.com/history/issues/issue-99/i-am-cyrus.html.

Merrill, John L. 1988. "The Bible and the American Temperance Movement: Text, Context, and Pretext." *Harvard Theological Review* 81 (April): 145–70.

Methodist Episcopal Church. 1908. "The 1908 Social Creed of the Methodist Episcopal Church." Church & Society. https://www.umcjustice.org/who-we-are/social-principles-and-resolutions/the-1908-social-creed-of-the-methodist-episcopal-church.

Methvin, Thomas J. 2006. "Trial Lawyers and the Biblical Basis for What We Do." *Alabama Association of Justice Journal* 16: 21–27.

Meyer, Holly. 2019. "Lee's Prayer, Fasting Day Draws Mixed Responses." *Tennessean*. October 8, pp. 1 and 11A.

Michaels, J. Ramsey. 2011. "Charles Thomson and the First American New Testament." *Harvard Theological Review* 104 (July): 349–65.

Millard, Catherine. 1991. "The Truth about George Washington's Presidential Inaugural Bible." From *The Rewriting of America's History*. http://www.christianheritagemins.org/articles/The%20Truth%20about%20Washington's%20Inaugural%20Bible.pdf.

Miller, Emily McFarlan, and Yonat Shimron. 2018. "Why Is Jeff Sessions Quoting Romans 13 and Why Is the Bible Verse So Often Invoked?" Religion News Service. June 16. https://www.usatoday.com/story/news/2018/06/16/jeff-sessions-bible-romans-13-trump-immigration-policy/707749002/.

Miller, Perry. 1953. "Errand into the Wilderness." *William and Mary Quarterly* 10 (January): 3–32.

Miller, Perry. 1955. "The Garden of Eden and the Deacon's Meadow." American Heritage. December. https://www.americanheritage.com/garden-eden-and-deacons-meadow.

Miller, Perry Gilbert. 1931. "Thomas Hooker and the Democracy of Early Connecticut." *New England Quarterly* 4 (October): 663–712.

Miron, Rose. 2018. "Fighting for the Tribal Bible: Mohican Politics of Self-Representation in Public History." *Native American and Indigenous Studies* 5 (Fall): 91–122.

Monshouwer, D. 1991. "The Reading of the Prophet in the Synagogue at Nazareth." *Biblica* 72: 90–99.

Moore, R. Laurence. 2000. "Bible Reading and Nonsectarian Schooling: The Failure of Religious Instruction in Nineteenth-Century Public Education." *Journal of American History* 86 (March): 1581–99.

Moore, Randy. 1999. "Creationism in the United States: IV. The Aftermath of Epperson v. Arkansas." *American Biology Teacher* 61 (January): 10–16.

Moore, Randy, Murray Jensen, and Jay Hatch. 2003. "Twenty Questions: What Have the Courts Said about the Teaching of Evolution and Creationism in Public Schools?" *BioScience* 53 (August): 766–71.

Morais, Herbert M. 1932. "Deism in Revolutionary America (1763–89)." *International Journal of Ethics* 42 (July): 434–53.

Moreland, Michael P. 2017. "Justice, Love, and Duties of Care in Tort Law." *Agape, Justice, and Law: How Might Christian Love Shape Law?*, ed. Robert F. Cochran Jr. and Zachary R. Calo. New York: Cambridge University Press, pp. 188–208.

Morgan, David. 2014. "The Image of the Protestant Bible in America." *The Bible in the Public Square: Its Enduring Influence on American Life*, ed. Mark A. Chancey, Carol Meyers, and Eric M. Meyers. Atlanta, GA: Society of Biblical Literature, pp. 93–119.

Morris, Kenneth R. 1993. "Theological Sources of William Penn's Concept of Religious Toleration." *Journal of Church and State* 35 (Winter): 83–111.

Morrison, Jeffry Hays. 1999. "John Witherspoon and 'The Public Interest of Religion.'" *Journal of Church and State* 41 (Summer): 551–73.

Morrison, Larry R. 1980. "The Religious Defense of American Slavery before 1830." *Journal of Religious Thought* 37: 16–29. https://www.kingscollege.net/gbrodie/The%20religious%20justification%20of%20slavery%20before%201830.pdf.

Morrow, Ralph E. 1961. "The Proslavery Argument Revisited." *Mississippi Valley Historical Review* 48 (June): 79–94.

Morton, Victor. 2016. "Donald Trump's Favorite Bible Verse Is One Jesus Specifically Repudiated." *Washington Times*. April 14. https://www.washingtontimes.com/news/2016/apr/14/donald-trump-favorite-bible-verse-one-jesus-specif/.

Moss, Candida. 2018. "Theologian: Jeff Sessions Misreads the Bible to Justify Separating Families." CNN. June 15. https://www.cnn.com/2018/06/15/opinions/jeff-sessions-misreads-bible-to-justify-separating-families-moss/index.html. Accessed March 29, 2019.

Moss, Candida. 2019. "The Big Problem with 'Biblical Literacy.'" Daily Beast. February 10. https://www.thedailybeast.com/the-big-problem-with-biblical-literacy.

Mouly, Ruth, and Roland Robertson. 1983. "Zionism in American Premillenarian Fundamentalism." *American Journal of Theology & Philosophy* 4 (September): 97–109.

Moyers, Bill. 2006. "9/11 and God's Sport." *CrossCurrents* 55 (Winter): 442–55.

Mulder, John M. 1971. "The Moral World of John Foster Dulles: A Presbyterian Layman and International Affairs." *Journal of Presbyterian History* 49 (Summer): 157–82.

Munoz, Vincent Phillip. 2003. "James Madison's Principle of Religious Liberty." *American Political Science Review* 97 (February): 17–32.

Munsil, Len. 2012. "Justice and Compassion: Applying Biblical Truth to the Problem of Illegal Immigration." *Regent Journal of International Law* 9: 11–18.

Murphie, Jeffrie G. 2017. "Christian Love and Criminal Punishment." *Agape, Justice, and Law: How Might Christian Love Shape Law?*, ed. Robert F. Cochran Jr. and Zachary R. Calo. New York: Cambridge University Press, pp. 151–65.

Murphy, John Patrick Michael. 1997. "National Bible Week (1997)." The Secular Web. https://infidels.org/library/modern/john_murphy/bibleweek.html. Accessed April 15, 2019.

Murphy-Gill, Meghan. 2017. "The Faith of Donald Trump." U.S. Catholic. January 19. https://www.uscatholic.org/articles/201701/faith-donald-trump-30910. Accessed April 16, 2019.

"Museum of the Bible Installs First Exhibit Item: An Exact Replica of the Liberty Bell." Press Release. https://www.charismanews.com/us/59303-museum-of-the-bible-installs-first-exhibit.

National Constitution Center Staff. 2017. "How Presidents Use Bibles at Inaugurations." Constitution Daily. January 20. https://constitutioncenter.org/blog/how-presidents-use-bibles-at-inaugurations/.

National Council of Churches. 1908. "The Social Creed of the Churches." December 4. https://nationalcouncilofchurches.us/common-witness/1908/social-creed.php.

Newcombe, Jerry. 2017. "A List of All the Presidents Who Mentioned God in an Inaugural Address." *Christian Post*. January 20. https://www.christianpost.com/news/a-list-of-all-the-presidents-who-mentioned-god-in-an-inaugural-address.html.

Newman, Judith H. 2016. "Tracing the Use of the Bible in Colonial Land Claims in North America." *The Bible in Political Debate: What Does It Really Say?*, ed. Frances Flannery and Rodney A. Werline. New York: Bloomsbury T&T Clark, pp. 127–40.

Newman, Roger. 2017. "When It Was Done Right: Justice Hugo Black, Religion and Alabama." *New American Journal*. December 5. https://www.newamericanjournal.net/tag/roger-newman/. Accessed April 22, 2019.

Newsome, Michael Dehaven. 2002. "Common School Religion: Judicial Narratives in a Protestant Empire." *Southern California Interdisciplinary Law Journal* 11: 219–37.

Newton, Richard. 2017. "The African American Bible: Bound in a Christian Nation." *Journal of Biblical Literature* 136 (Winter): 221–28.

Noll, Mark A. 2011. "William Jennings Bryan, Theodore Roosevelt, Woodrow Wilson and the King James Version of the Bible." *Theology* 114 (4): 251–59.

Noll, Mark A. 2012. "'Wee Shall Be as a Citty Upon a Hill': John Winthrop's Non-American Exceptionalism." *Review of Faith & International Affairs* 10 (May 24): 5–11.

Nutt, Rick. 2017. "United States Diplomatic Representation at the Vatican: The Presbyterian Reaction." *Journal of Presbyterian History* 95 (Fall/Winter): 62–73.

Obama, Barack. 2006. "'Call to Renewal' Keynote Address." June 28. http://obamaspeeches.com/081-Call-to-Renewal-Keynote-Address-Obama-Speech.htm.

Obama, Barack. 2015. "Remarks by the President in Eulogy for the Honorable Reverend Clementa Pinckney." June 26. https://obamawhitehouse.archives.gov/the-press-office/2015/06/26/remarks-president-eulogy-honorable-reverend-clementa-pinckney.

Obeidallah, Dean. 2019. "The Star of the Annual Muslim Convention Was a Jewish Man from Brooklyn." CNN. September 2. https://www.cnn.com/2019/09/01/opinions/bernie-sanders-muslim-american-support-obeidallah/index.html.

Ofulue, Nneka Ifeoma. 2002. "President Clinton and the White House Prayer Breakfast." *Journal of Communication and Religion* 25(1): 49–63.

Oliver, Kendrick. 2013. "The Apollo 8 Genesis Reading and Religion in the Space Age." *Astropolitics: The International Journal of Space Politics & Policy* 11(1–2): 116–21.

O'Neil, Tyler. 2017. "Trump Adds to Scripture in Inaugural Speech." PJ Media. January 20. https://pjmedia.com/faith/2017/01/20/trump-adds-to-scripture-in-inaugural-speech/.

Orr, Gabby. 2019. "'Render to God and Trump': Ralph Reed Calls for 2020 Obedience to Trump." *Politico*. October 9. https://www.politico.com/news/2019/10/09/ralph-reed-trump-book-040920.

Osler, Mark. 2007. "'Aseret Had'Varim in Tension: The Ten Commandments and the Bill of Rights." *Journal of Church and State* 49 (Autumn): 683–96.

Osler, Mark. 2013. "A Biblical Value in the Constitution: Mercy, Clemency, Faith and History." *University of St. Thomas Law Journal* 9: 769–82.

Ottoson, Robin Deich. 2010. "The Battle over the Flag: Protest, Community Opposition, and Silence in the Mennonite Colleges in Kansas during the Vietnam War." *Journal of Church and State* 52 (Autumn): 686–711.

Pahl, Jon. 2013. "America's King of Kings: The King James Bible and American Civil Religion." *The King James Version at 400*, ed. David G. Burke, John F. Kutsko, and Philip H. Towner. Atlanta, GA: Society of Biblical Literature, pp. 413–44.

Parke Caleb. 2019. "Pete Buttigieg Uses Bible Verse to Slam 'So-Called Conservative Christian' Republicans during Debate." Fox News. July 29. https://www.foxnews.com/politics/pete-buttigieg-democratic-debate-2020-bible-republicans-christian.

Pearl, Valerie, and Morris Pearl. 1990. "Governor John Winthrop on the Birth of the Antinomians' 'Monster': The Earliest Reports to Reach England and the Making of a Myth." *Proceedings of the Massachusetts Historical Society*, 3rd Series 102: 21–37.

Pears, Thomas C., Jr. 1939. "The Story of the Aitken Bible." *Journal of the Department of History (The Presbyterian Historical Society) of the Presbyterian Church in the U.S.A.* 18 (June): 225–41.

Pelikan, Jaroslav. 1989. "Jefferson and His Contemporaries." In Thomas Jefferson. *The Jefferson Bible: The Life and Morals of Jesus of Nazareth*. Boston: Beacon Press, pp. 149–67.

Pendergrass, Drew. 2017. "The Televangelist-in-Chief: Trump and the Prosperity Gospel." *Harvard Political Review*. November 12. www.https://harvardpolitics.com/culture/tevangelistinchief/.

Penn, William. 1682. "Charter of the Liberties and Frame of Government of Pennsylvania." Online Library of Liberty. https://oll.libertyfund.org/pages/1682-charter-of-the-liberties-and-frame-of-government-of-pennsylvania.

Perko, F. Michael. 2003. "Contemporary American Christian Attitudes to Israel Based on the Scriptures." *Israel Studies* 8 (Summer): 1–17.

Perl-Rosenthal, Nathan R. 2009. "The 'Divine Right of Republics': Hebraic Republicanism and the Debate over Kingless Government in Revolutionary America." *William and Mary Quarterly*, 3rd Series 66 (July): 535–64.

Perry, William Stevens, and Lawrence L. Brown. 1976. "The Alleged 'Toryism' of the Clergy of the United States at the Breaking Out of the War of the Revolution: An Historical Examination." *Historical Magazine of the Protestant Episcopal Church* 45 (June): 133–44.

Pestana, Carla Gardina. 1983. "The City upon a Hill under Siege: The Puritan Perception of the Quaker Threat to Massachusetts Bay, 1656–1661." *New England Quarterly* 56 (September): 323–53.

Peters, Jeremy W. 2019. "Pete Buttigieg, Gay and Christian, Challenges Religious Right on Their Own Turf." *New York Times*. April 10. https://www.nytimes.com/2019/04/10/us/politics/pete-buttigieg-sexuality-religion.html.

Peters, Jeremy W., and Maggie Haberman. 2019. "Paula White, Trump's Personal Pastor, Joins the White House." *New York Times*. October 31.

Petersen, Jonathan. 2016. "Bible Honored in US House of Representatives." BibleGateway. November 16. https://www.biblegateway.com/blog/2016/11/bible-honored-in-us-house-of-representatives/.

Peterson, Jonathan. R. 2017. "The Religious Content of the Presidents' Remarks at the National Prayer Breakfast, 1953–2016." *Congress & the Presidency* 44(2): 212–34.

Peterson, Mark A. 2002. "The Selling of Joseph: Bostonians, Antislavery, and the Protestant International, 1689–1733." *Massachusetts Historical Review* 4 (Race and Slavery): 1–22.

Peterson, Osler L. 1948. "Henry Wallace: A Divided Mind." *The Atlantic*. August. https://www.theatlantic.com/magazine/archive/1948/08/henry-wallace-a-divided-mind/306029/. Accessed May 8, 2019.

Phillips, William D., Jr. 1992. "Africa and the Atlantic Islands Meet the Garden of Eden: Christopher Columbus's View of America." *Journal of World History* 3 (Fall): 149–64.

Piar, Carlos R. 1996. "Cesar Chavez and La Causa: Toward a Hispanic Christian Social Ethic." *Annual of the Society of Christian Ethics* 16: 103–29.

Piatt, Christian. 2012. "Billy Graham: Punish America or Apologize to Sodom & Gomorrah." *Sojourners*. June 30. https://sojo.net/articles/billy-graham-punish-america-or-apologize-sodom-gomorrah.

Pierard, Richard V. 1980. "Billy Graham and the U.S. Presidency." *Journal of Church and State* 22 (Winter): 107–27.

Pieterse, Jan Nederveen. 1991. "A History of a Metaphor: Christian Zionism and the Politics of Apocalypse." *Archives de Sciences Sociales des Religions* 36 (June–September): 75–103.

Pilgrim, David. 2002 [edited in 2012]. "The Jezebel Stereotype." Ferris State University Jim Crow Museum of Racist Memorabilia. https://www.ferris.edu/HTMLS/news/jimcrow/jezebel/index.htm.

Pilkington, Ed. 2008. "Obama Angers Midwest Voters with Guns and Religion Remark." *Guardian*. April 14. https://www.theguardian.com/world/2008/apr/14/barackobama.uselections2008. Accessed March 30, 2019.

Plank, Geoffrey. 2017. "Quakers as Political Players in Early America." *William and Mary Quarterly* 74 (January): 35–42.

Plumstead, A. W. 1968. "An Introductory Essay." *The Wall and the Garden: Selected Massachusetts Election Sermons 1670–1775*, ed. A. W. Plumstead. Minneapolis: University of Minnesota Press, pp. 3–37.

PoliticalCartoons.com. https://politicalcartoons.com/?s=bible. Accessed May 24, 2019.

Posner, Sarah. 2008. "John Hagee's Controversial Gospel." The American Prospect. March 12. https://prospect.org/article/john-hagees-controversial-gospel.

Posner, Sarah. 2017. "Amazing Disgrace." The New Republic. March 10. https://newrepublic.com/article/140961/amazing/disgrace-donald-trump-hijacked-religious-right.

Posner, Sarah, and Julie Ingersoll. 2010. "Gun Ownership: 'An Obligation to God.'" *At the Tea Party: The Wing Nuts, Whack Jobs, and White-Whiteness of the New Republican Right . . . and Why We Should Take It Seriously*, ed. Laura Flanders. New York: OR Books, pp. 117–24.

Powell, Michael. 2008. "Following Months of Criticism, Obama Quits His Church." *New York Times*. June 1. https://www.nytimes.com/2008/06/01/us/politics/01obama.html. Accessed March 30, 2019.

Powers, Kirsten. 2019. "Mayor Pete Buttigieg's Countercultural Approach to Christianity Is What America Needs Now." *USA Today*. April 4. https://www.usatoday.com/story/opinion/2019/04/03/mayor-pete-buttigieg-christian-right-2020-democratic-primary-trump-column/3342767002/. Accessed April 23, 2019.

Pratt, John W. 1961. "Governor Seward and the New York City School Controversy, 1840–1842: A Milestone in the Advance of Nonsectarian Public Education." *New York History* 42 (October): 351–64.

Preble, Peter-Michael. 2016. "The Faith of John Kasich." HuffPost. March 10. https://www.huffpost.com/entry/the-faith-of-john-kasich_b_9413406.

Pruitt, Sarah. 2019. "Why the King James Bible of 1611 Remains the Most Popular Translation in History." History. March 22 [updated April 16, 2019]. https://www.history.com/news/king-james-bible-most-popular.

Przbyszewski, Linda. 2000. "The Religion of a Jurist: Justice David J. Brewer and the Christian Nation." *Journal of Supreme Court History* 25 (November): 228–42.

"Public Law 97–280 OCT. 4, 1982." National Liberty Alliance. https://www.nationallibertyalliance.org/sites/default/files/public_law_97-280_oct._4_1982_0.pdf.

Pyszczynski, Tom, Carl Henthron, Matt Motyl, and Kristel Gerow. 2010. "Is Obama the Anti-Christ? Racial Priming, Extreme Criticisms of Barack Obama, and Attitudes toward the 2008 US Presidential Candidates." *Journal of Experimental Social Psychology* 46: 863–66.

Rand, Lizabeth A. 2014. "A Rhetoric of Opposition: The Seventh-Day Adventist Church and the Sabbath Tradition." *Renovating Rhetoric in Christian Tradition*, ed. Elizabeth Vander Lei, Thomas Amorose, Beth Daniell, and Anne Ruggless Gere. Pittsburgh: University of Pittsburgh Press, pp. 17–27.

Rau, Andy. 2011. "What Does the Bible Say about Capital Punishment?" BibleGateway. September 27. https://www.biblegateway.com/blog/2011/09/what-does-the-bible-say-about-capital-punishment/.

Raymond, Matt. 2009. "The Lincoln Inaugural Bible, Chapter and Verse." Library of Congress Blog. January 14. https://blogs.loc.gov/loc/2009/01/the-lincoln-inaugural-bible-chapter-and-verse/.

Reagan, Ronald. 1986. "President Reagan's Remarks Following the Loss of the Space Shuttle Challenger and Her Crew." NASA. January 28. https://www.nasa.gov/audience/formedia/speeches/reagan_challenger.html.

Reavis, Jonathan. 2011. "To See the Negro Saved: The Religious Pragmatism of Booker T. Washington." *Lucerna* 10: 49–62. Accessed at https://mospace.umsystem.edu/xmlui/bitstream/handle/10355/48993/Lucerna%202016%20Volume%2010%20-%208-Reavis.pdf?sequence=1&isAllowed=y.

Reeves, Jay. 2019. "Buttigieg, Husband Attend Jimmy Carter's Sunday School Class." ABC News. May 5. https://abcnews.go.com/Politics/wireStory/buttigieg-husband-attend-jimmy-carters-sunday-school-class-62836105.

Reiff, Joseph T. 2013. "'Born of Conviction': White Mississippians Argue Civil Rights in 1963." *The Civil Rights Movement in Mississippi*, ed. Ted Ownby. Jackson: University Press of Mississippi, pp. 157–79.

Reimer, Neal. 1980. "Covenant and the Federal Constitution." *Publius* 10 (Fall): 135–48.

"Religion and the Founding of the American Republic. Religion and the Congress of the Confederation." Library of Congress Exhibitions. https://www.loc.gov/exhibits/religion/rel04.html.

Rentein, Alison Dundes. 2010. "Corporal Punishment and the Cultural Defense." *Law and Contemporary Problems* 73 (Spring): 253–79.

Richards, Peter Judson 2001. "'A Clear and Steady Channel': Isaac Backus and the Limits of Liberty." *Journal of Church and State* 43 (Summer): 447–82.

Rightmyer, Thomas Nelson. 1961. "The Holy Orders of Peter Muhlenberg." *Historical Magazine of the Protestant Episcopal Church* 30 (September): 183–97.

Ringenberg, William C. 1986. "Benjamin Harrison: The Religious Thought and Practice of a Presbyterian President." *American Presbyterians* 64 (Fall): 175–89.

Roach, David. 2019. "Trump's Bible Signing Called Southern Tradition." Baptist Press. March 11. www.bpnews.net/52551/trumps-bible-signing-called-souther-tradition.

Roberts, Kristofer. 2016. "Scripture in the Public Forum: The Fuller-Wayland Letters and the Debate Over Domestic Slavery." *Journal of Scriptural Reasoning*. March 9. http://jsr.shanti.virginia.edu/page/2/?s=Isaiah.

Robertson, David Brian. 2005. "Madison's Opponents and Constitutional Design." *American Political Science Review* 99 (May): 225–33.

Robertson, James I., Jr. "'Stonewall Jackson: Christian Soldier." Essential Civil War Curriculum. https://www.essentialcivilwarcurriculum.com/stonewall-jackson-christian-soldier.html. Accessed May 24, 2019.

Robertson, Pat. 2014. "Is Physical Punishment of Children Allowed in the Bible?" CBN. https://www1.cbn.com/questions/physical-punishment-allowed-bible.

Robles, Frances, and Jim Rutenberg. 2019. "The Evangelical, the 'Pool Boy,' the Comedian and Michael Cohen." *New York Times*. June 18.

Rocha, Veronica. 2019. "Pete Buttigieg: 'God Doesn't Have a Political Party.'" CNN. April 23. https://www.cnn.com/2019/04/23/politics/buttigieg-god-political-party/index.html.

Rodda, Chris. 2007. "PBS Show Gets It Right with the Story of Peter Muhlenberg's Robe." Talk to Action. August 4. www.talk2action.org/story/2007/8/4/201559/9741.

Roelofs, H. Mark. 1988. "Hebraic-Biblical Political Thinking." *Polity* 20 (Summer): 572–97.

Roelofs, H. Mark. 1991. "Teaching the Political Ideals of the Bible." *PS: Political Science and Politics* 24 (December): 712–15.

Rohrer, James R. 1987. "Sunday Mails and the Church-State Theme in Jacksonian America." *Journal of the Early Republic* 7 (Spring): 53–74.

Rolater, Fred S. 1977. "Charles Thomson, 'Prime Minister' of the United States." *Pennsylvania Magazine of History and Biography* 101 (July): 322–48.

Romero, Robert Chao. 2017. "The Spiritual Praxis of Cesar Chavez." *Perspectivas* 14 (Spring): 24–39.
Romero, Victor C. 2010. "Christian Realism and Immigration Reform." *University of St. Thomas Law Review* 7: 310–39.
Romney, Mitt. 2007. "Transcript: Mitt Romney's Faith Speech." NPR. December 6. https://www.npr.org/templates/story/story.php?storyID=16969460.
Roosevelt, Franklin D. 1933. "First Inaugural Address of Franklin D. Roosevelt." March 4. http://avalon.law.yale.edu/20th_century/froos1.asp.
Roosevelt, Franklin D. 1936. "Acceptance Speech at the Democratic National Convention (1936)." Teaching American History. July 27. https://teachingamericanhistory.org/library/document/acceptance-speech-at-the-democratic-national-convention-1936/.
Rosati, Kelly. 2019. "Today's Abortion Conversation: Where Do We Go from Here?" *Evanglicals* 5 (Fall): 14–17.
Rosen, Jeffrey. 2004. "John Ashcroft's Permanent Campaign." *The Atlantic*. April. https://www.theatlantic.com/magazine/archive/2004/04/john-ashcroft-s-permanent-campaign/302926/.
Rosenberg, Yair. 2013. "New Jersey Senate Candidate Cory Booker Knows His Torah, So What?" The Tablet. https://www.tabletmag.com/jewish-news-and-politics/140767/cory-bookers-jewish-story.
Rossinow, Doug. 2005. "The Radicalization of the Social Gospel: Harry F. Ward and the Search for a New Social Order, 1898–1936." *Religion and American Culture: A Journal of Interpretation* 15 (Winter): 63–106.
Rothman, Rozann. 1980. "The Impact of Covenant and Contract Theories on Conceptions of the U.S. Constitution." *Publius* 10 (Fall): 149–64.
Ruotsila, Markku. 2012. "Carl McIntire and the Fundamentalist Origins of the Christian Right." *Church History* 81 (June): 378–407.
Ruotsila, Markku. 2014. "Transnational Fundamentalist Anti-Communism: The International Council of Christian Churches." *Transnational Anti-Communism and the Cold War: Agents, Activities, and Networks*, ed. Luc van Dongen, Stephanie Roulin, and Giles Scott-Smith. New York: Palgrave Macmillan, pp. 235–50.
Ryan, William C. 1987. "The Historical Case for the Right of Sanctuary." *Journal of Church and State* 29 (Spring): 209–32.
Salon Staff. 2007. "The Hospital Room Showdown." Salon. May 15. https://www.salon.com/2007/05/15/comey_testimony/.
Sandeen, Ernest R. 1967. "Toward a Historical Interpretation of the Origins of Fundamentalism." *Church History* 36 (March): 66–83.
Sanders, Bernie. 2015. "Remarks at the Liberty University Convocation." October 3. https://medium.com/@BernieSanders/remarks-at-the-liberty-university-convocation-4b61c51a4b99. Accessed April 4, 2019. [Note: The transcript is not identical to the recorded speech.]
Sanders, Mary. 2016. "A Mighty Fortress Is Our Battle Hymn of the Republic: Episcopal Liturgy and American Civil Religion in the National Prayer Service on 14 September 2001." *Anglican and Episcopal History* 85 (March): 63–86.
Santoro, Anthony. 2008. "The Prophet in His Own Words: Nat Turner's Biblical Construction." *Virginia Magazine of History and Biography* 116(2): 114–49.
Sarna, Jonathan D. 1994. "'The Greatest Jew in the World since Jesus Christ': The Jewish Legacy of Louis D. Brandeis." *American Jewish History* 81 (Spring/Summer): 346–64.
Sarna, Jonathan D. 2017. "The Bible and Judaism in America." *The Oxford Handbook of the Bible in America*, ed. Paul C. Gutjahr. New York: Oxford University Press, pp. 505–16.

Sasse, Ben. 2018. "One of the Best Speeches You Will Ever Hear from the Senate Floor." Justin Taylor, The Gospel Coalition. October 4. https://www.thegospelcoalition.org/blogs/justin-taylor/one-best-speeches-will-ever-hear-senate-floor/.

Sawyer, Jeffrey K. 1990. "'Benefit of Clergy' in Maryland and Virginia." *American Journal of Legal History* 34 (January): 49–68.

Schaar, John H. 1991. "Liberty/Authority/Community in the Political Thought of John Winthrop." *Political Theory* 19 (November): 493–518.

Sewall, Samuel. "The Selling of Joseph: A Memorial (1700)." University of Nebraska-Lincoln. https://digitalcommons.unl.edu/cgi/viewcontent.cgi?article=1026&context=etas.

Schager, Nick. 2019. "A More Righteous Path: The Pro-Immigrant Bible-Belt Preachers Standing Up to Trump's Xenophobia." Daily Beast. July 13. https://www.thedailybeast.com/american-heretics-the-pro-immigrant-bible-belt-preachers-standing-up-to-trumps-xenophobia?ref=scroll.

Schallhorn, Kaitlyn. 2019. "New Lawmakers Used Historical Texts, Family Heirlooms during Swearing-In Ceremonies." Fox News. January 4. https://www.foxnews.com/politics/new-lawmakers-used-historical-texts-family-heirlooms-during-swearing-in-ceremonies.

Schapsmeier, Edward L., and Frederick H. Schapsmeier. 1970. "Henry A. Wallace: New Deal Philosopher." *The Historian* 32 (February): 177–90.

Schapsmeier, Edward L., and Frederick H. Schapsmeier. 1979. "Religion and Reform: A Case Study of Henry A. Wallace and Ezra Taft Benson." *Journal of Church and State* 21 (Autumn): 525–35.

Scheil, Andrew. 2016. *Babylon under Western Eyes: A Study of Allusion and Myth*. Toronto: University of Toronto Press.

Schiff, Stacy. 2015. "The Witches of Salem: Diabolical Doings in a Puritan village." *New Yorker*. August 31. https://www.newyorker.com/magazine/2015/09\07/the-witches-of-salem.

Schipper, Jeremy. 2019. "'Misconstruction of the Sacred Page': On Denmark Vesey's Biblical Interpretations." *Journal of Biblical Literature* 128(1): 23–38.

Schlereth, Eric R. 2007. "Fits of Political Religion: Stalking Infidelity and the Politics of Moral Reform in Antebellum America." *Early American Studies* 5 (Fall): 288–323.

Schlesinger, Arthur, Jr. 2005. "Forgetting Reinhold Niebuhr." *New York Times*. September 18. https://www.nytimes.com/2005/09/18/books/review/forgetting-reinhold-niebuhr.html.

Schor, Joel. 1979. "The Rivalry between Frederick Douglass and Henry Highland Garnet." *Journal of Negro History* 64 (Winter): 30–38.

Schur, Morris J. 1964. "The Theology of the Jehovah's Witnesses and Its Conflict with Earthly Governments." *Western Political Quarterly* 17 (September): 101–3.

Schweer, Howar. 1999. "The 'Science' of Legal Science: The Model of the Natural Sciences in Nineteenth-Century American Legal Education." *Law and History Review* 17 (Autumn): 421–66.

Schweitzer, Ivy. 2005. "John Winthrop's 'Model' of American Affiliation." *Early American Literature* 40(3): 441–69.

Scott, Eugenie C. 2016. "Creationism and Intelligent Design." *How Evolution Shapes Our Lives: Essays on Biology and Society*, ed. Jonathan B. Losos and Richard Lenski. Princeton, NJ: Princeton University Press, pp. 284–99.

Scott, William. 2004. "The Ethiopian Ethos in African American Thought." *International Journal of Ethiopian Studies* 1 (Winter/Spring): 40–57.

Seidel, Andrew L. 2018. "The White House Bible Study Group That Influenced Trump's Family Separation Policy." ThinkProgress. June 19. https://thinkprogress.org/white-house-bible-study-group-trump-child-separation-policy-24de236c4824/.

Seiglie, Mario. 2010. "Is Thanksgiving Rooted in a Biblical Festival?" Beyond Today. November 12. https://www.ucg.org/the-good-news/is-thanksgiving-rooted-in-a-biblical-festival.

Seitz-Wald, Alex. 2014. "Bernie Sanders Speaks at Liberty University." MSNBC. September 14 [updated September 14, 2015]. www.msnbc.com/msnbc/bernie-sanders-speaks-liberty-university.

Seller, Maxine S. 1968. "Isaac Leeser: A Jewish-Christian Dialogue in Antebellum Philadelphia." *Pennsylvania History: A Journal of Mid-Atlantic Studies* 35 (July): 231–42.

Seller, Maxine S. 1968. "Isaac Leeser's Views on the Restoration of a Jewish Palestine." *American Jewish Historical Quarterly* 58 (September): 118–35.

Senior, Donald. 2017. "The Bible and Catholicism." *The Oxford Handbook of the Bible in America*, ed. Paul C. Gutjahr. New York: Oxford University Press, pp. 517–30.

Sessions, Jeff. 2018. "Attorney General Sessions Addresses Recent Criticisms of Zero Tolerance by Church Leaders." U.S. Department of Justice. June 14. https://www.justice.gov/opa/speech/attorney-general-sessions-addresses-recent-criticisms-zero-tolerance-church-leaders.

Shalev, Eran. 2009. "'A Perfect Republic': The Mosaic Constitution in Revolutionary New England, 1775–1788." *New England Quarterly* (June): 235–63.

Shalev, Eran. 2010. "'Written in the Style of Antiquity': Pseudo-Biblicism and the Early American Republic, 1770–1830. *Church History* 79 (December): 800–26.

Shalev, Eran. 2013. "Evil Counselors, Corrupt Traitors, and Bad Kings: The Hebrew Bible and Political Critique." *Resistance to Tyrants, Obedience to God: Reason, Religion and Republicanism at the American Founding*, ed. Dustin Gish and Daniel Klinghard. Lanham, MD: Lexington Books, pp. 105–24.

Shalev, Eran. 2017. "The Bible and the Creation of the Nation." *The Oxford Handbook of The Bible in America*, ed. Paul C. Gutjahr. New York: Oxford University Press, pp. 347–57.

Shanahan, Ed. 2019. "$27 Million for Reparations over Slave Ties Pledged by Seminary." *New York Times*. October 21.

Shapiro, Aharon H. 1988. "Moses. Henry George's Inspiration." *American Journal of Economics and Sociology* 47 (October): 493–501.

Sheridan, Michael. 2012. "Florida Pastor Terry Jones Burns Copies of Koran outside Church." *New York Daily News*. April 29. https://www.nydailynews.com/news/national/florida-pastor-terry-jones-burns-copies-koran-church-article-1.1069458.

Sherkat, Darren E., and Christopher G. Ellison. 1997. "The Cognitive Structure of a Moral Crusade: Conservative Protestantism and Opposition to Pornography." *Social Forces* 75 (March): 957–80.

Sherwood, Yvonne. 2006. "Bush's Bible as a Liberal Bible (Strange Though That May Seem)." *Postscripts: The Journal of Sacred Texts and Contemporary Worlds* 2(1): 47–58.

Sherwood, Yvonne. 2008. "The God of Abraham and Exceptional States, or the Early Modern Rise of the Whig/Liberal Bible." *Journal of the American Academy of Religion* 76 (June): 312–43.

Shilliam, Robbie. 2012. "A Global Story of Psalms 68:31." November 7. https://robbieshilliam.wordpress.com/2012/11/07/a-global-story-of-psalms-6831/.

Shimron, Yonat. 2018. "Employees Quit American Bible Society over Sex and Marriage Rules." Religion News Service. May 29. https://religionnews.com/2018/05/29/american-bible-society-to-require-regular-church-attendance-strict-sexuality-codes/.

Shreve, Grant. 2017. "The Long, Winding History of the 'Battle Hymn of the Republic.'" JSTOR Daily Newsletter. October 20. https://daily.jstor.org/the-long-winding-history-of-the-battle-hymn-of-the-republic/.

Siker, Jeffrey S. n.d. "President Bush, Biblical Faith, and the Politics of Religion." SBL Forum. http://sbl-site.org/Article.aspx?ArticleID=151.
Siker, Jeffrey. 2012. "President Obama, the Bible, and Political Rhetoric." *Political Theology*. 12(5): 586–609.
Silk, Mark. 1984. "Notes on the Judeo-Christian Tradition in America." *American Quarterly* 36 (Spring): 65–85.
Simon, Ed. 2016. "The Remembrance of Amalek." *The Revealer: A Review of Religion & Media*. March 22. https://therevealer.org/the-remembrance-of-amalek/.
Sklar, Kathryn Kish. 2007. " 'The Throne of My Heart': Religion, Oratory, and Transatlantic Community in Angelina Grimke's Launching of Women's Rights, 1828–1838." *Women's Rights and Transatlantic Antislavery in the Era of Emancipation*, ed. Kathryn Kish Sklar and James Brewer Stewart. New Haven, CT: Yale University Press, pp. 211–41.
Slick, Matt. n.d. "John Hagee Denies Jesus Claimed to Be the Messiah." Christian Apologetics & Research Ministry. https://carm.org/john-hagee-denies-jesus-claimed-to-be-the-messiah.
Smith, Gary Scott. 1992. "Conservative Presbyterians: The Gospel, Social Reform, and the Church in the Progressive Ear." *American Presbyterians* 70 (Summer): 93–110.
Smith, Joseph. 1844. "Of the Powers and Policy of the Government of the United States." Nauvoo, IL: John Taylor. https://www.josephsmithpapers.org/transcript/general-smiths-views-of-the-power-and-policy-of-the-government-of-the-unite-states-7-february-1844. Accessed May 14, 2019.
Smith, Peter. 2013. "President Lincoln's Gettysburg Address Had Biblical Cadence." *Pittsburgh Post-Gazette*. November 18. https://www.post-gazette.com/Gettysburg-Stories/2013/11/19/Address-had-biblical-cadence/stories/201311190063. Accessed March 29, 2019.
Smith, Rogers M. 2008. "Religious Rhetoric and the Ethics of Public Discourse: The Case of George W. Bush." *Political Theory* 36 (April): 272–300.
Smith, Whitney. 2009. " 'One Nation under God': The Crusade to Capture the American Flag." *Proceedings: The XIX International Congress of Vexillology, York 23–37 July 2001*: 67–74. U.K. Flag Institute.
Smith, Willard H. "William Jennings Bryan and the Social Gospel." *Journal of American History* 53 (June): 41–60.
Smylie, James H. 1981. "The Bible, Race and the Changing South." *Journal of Southern Presbyterian History* 49 (Summer): 197–218.
Smylie, James H. 1995. "Madison and Witherspoon: Theological Roots of American Political Thought." *American Presbyterians* 73 (Fall): 155–64.
Smylie, James H. 1995. "'Uncle Tom's Cabin' Revisited: The Bible, the Romantic Imagination, and the Sympathies of Christ." *American Presbyterians* 73 (Fall): 165–76.
Smylie, James H. 1997. "America's Political Covenants, the Bible, and Calvinists." *Journal of Presbyterian History* 75 (Fall): 153–64.
Snyder, Edward D. 1951. "The Biblical Background of the 'Battle Hymn of the Republic.' " *New England Quarterly* 24 (June): 231–38.
Soloveichik, Meir Y. 2018. "Jimmy Carter: The Sunday-School Years." *Commentary Magazine*. October 28. https://www.jewishpress.com/indepth/opinion/jimmy-carter-the-sunday-school-years/2018/10/28/. Accessed May 6, 2019.
Spawn, Willman, and Carol Spawn. 1963. "The Aitken Shop: Identification of an Eighteenth-Century Bindery and Its Tools." *Papers of the Bibliographical Society of America* 57 (Fourth Quarter): 422–37.
Spencer, Aída Besançon. 1998. "Being a Stranger in a Time of Xenophobia." *Theology Today* 54 (January): 464–69.
Sporn, Jeremy B. 2009. "Legal Injection? The Constitutionality of the Bible in Capital Sentencing Deliberations." *Tulane Law Review* 83: 813–51.

Sprinkle, Preston M. 2014. "Romans 1 and Homosexuality: A Critical Review of James Brownson's 'Bible, Gender, Sexuality.'" *Bulletin for Biblical Research* 24: 515–28.

Stackhouse, John G., Jr. 2017. "The Bible and Evangelicalism." *The Oxford Handbook of the Bible in America*, ed. Paul C. Gutjahr. New York: Oxford University Press, pp. 558–74.

Staloff, Darren. 2014. "Deism and the Founders." *Faith and the Founders of the American Republic*. New York: Oxford University Press, pp. 13–33.

Starnes, Todd. 2012. "The Day the U.S. Military Burned the Bible in Afghanistan." Fox News. March 2 [updated May 7, 2015]. https://www.foxnews.com/opinion/the-day-the-us-military-burned-the-bible-in-afghanistan. Accessed March 31, 2019.

Stassen, Glen H. 2003. "It Is Time to Take Jesus Back: In Celebration of the Fiftieth Anniversary of H. Richard Niebuhr's 'Christ and Culture.'" *Journal of the Society of Christian Ethics* 23 (Spring/Summer): 133–43.

Stauffer, John. 2015. "'The Battle Hymn of the Republic': Origins, Influence, Legacies." *Exploring Lincoln: Great Historians Reappraise Our Greatest President*, ed. Harold Holzer, Craig L. Symonds, and Frank J. Williams. New York: Fordham University Press, pp. 123–45.

Steel, David A., Jr., and William J. Stuntz. 2006. "Christianity and the (Modest) Rule of Law." *University of Pennsylvania Journal of Constitutional Law* 8: 809–39.

Stein, Stephen J. 1975. "An Apocalyptic Rationale for the American Revolution." *Early American Literature* 9 (Winter): 211–25.

Steiner, Prudence L. June. "Benjamin Franklin's Biblical Hoaxes." *Proceedings of the American Philosophical Society* 131 (June): 183–96.

Stephens, Alexander H. 1861. "Cornerstone Speech." American Rhetoric Online Speech Bank. March 21. https://americanrhetoric.com/speeches/alexanderstephenscornerstone.htm.

Stern, Madeleine B. 1977. "The First Feminist Bible: The 'Alderney' Edition, 1876." *Quarterly Journal of the Library of Congress* 34 (January): 23–31.

Stevens, Paul. 1993. "'Leviticus Thinking' and the Rhetoric of Early Modern Colonialism." *Criticism* 35 (Summer): 441–61.

Stewart, Katherine. 2018. "Why Trump Reigns as King Cyrus." *New York Times*. December 31. https://www.nytimes.com/2018/12/31/opinion/trump-evangelicals-cyrus-king.html.

Stillwell, Ted W. 2018. "Truman's White House Bibles." *The Examiner* (Jackson County, Missouri). January 30. https://www.examiner.net/news/20180130/trumans-white-house-bibles.

Stoll, Ira. 2018. "The Revolutionary Gospel according to Samuel Adams." Historynet. May 3. https://www.historynet.com/revolutionary-gospel-according-samuel-adams.htm.

Stonestreet, John, and David Carlson. 2019. "The Manhattan Declaration 10 Years On." *Christian Post*. May 10. https://www.christianpost.com/voice/the-manhattan-declaration-10-years-on.html.

Stout, Harry S. "Religion in the Civil War: The Southern Perspective." TeacherServe. https://nationalhumanitiescenter.org/tserve/nineteen/nkeyinfo/cwsouth.htm.

Stowe, David W. 2014. "History, Memory, and Forgetting in Psalm 137." *The Bible in the Public Square: Its Enduring Influence in American Life*, ed. Mark Chancey, Carol Meyers, and Eric M. Meyers. Atlanta, GA: Society of Biblical Literature, pp. 137–57.

Sugg, John. 2005. "A Nation under God." Mother Jones. December. https://www.motherjones.com/politics/2005/12/nation-under-god/.

Sussman, Lance J. 1985. "Another Look at Isaac Leeser and the First Jewish Translation of the Bible in the United States." *Modern Judaism* 5 (May): 159–90.

Sutter, Richard L. 1976. "The Divine Dimension: John Adams and Religion in America." *Humboldt Journal of Social Relations* 4 (Fall/Winter): 42–46.
Sutton, Matthew Avery. 2019. "The Day Christian Fundamentalism Was Born." *New York Times*. May 25.
Swartz, David. 2019. "The National Prayer Breakfast and Evangelical Prophetic Witness." Patheos. January 30. https://www.patheos.com/blogs/anxiousbench/2019/01/the-national-prayer-breakfast-and-evangelical-prophetic-witness/.
Sweet, William W. 1935. "The English Bible in the Making of America." *Christian Education* 19 (October): 9–13.
Szasz, Ferenc M. 1971. "The Scopes Trial in Perspective." *Tennessee Historical Quarterly* 30 (Fall): 288–98.
Tanner, John S. "The King James Bible in America: Pilgrim, Prophet, President, Preacher." *Brigham Young University Studies* 50(3): 4–24.
Tarter, Brent. n.d. "Laws Divine, Morall and Martiall." Encyclopedia Virginia. https://www.encyclopediavirginia.org/Lawes_Divine_Morall_and_Martiall.
Taylor, Justin. 2013. "C. Everett Koop, Forceful U.S. Surgeon General, Dies at 96." *New York Times*. February 25.
Taylor, Justin. 2016. "An Interview with John Fea on His New History of the American Bible Society." The Gospel Coalition. March 23. https://www.thegospelcoalition.org/blogs/justin-taylor/an-interview-with-john-fea-on-his-new-history-of-the-american-bible-society/.
Taylor, Justin. 2017. "Christian History: How David Barton Is Doing It Wrong." The Gospel Coalition. May 12. https://www.thegospelcoalition.org/blogs/evangelical-history/christian-history-why-david-barton-is-doing-it-wrong/.
"Thanksgiving Day Proclamations 1789-Present." What So Proudly We Hail. https://www.whatsoproudlywehail.org/curriculum/the-american-calendar/thanksgiving-day-proclamations-1789-present.
Thebault, Reis. 2019. "GOP Legislator Prays for Forgiveness before Pennsylvania's First Muslim Woman Swears In." *Governing*. March 27. https://www.governing.com/topics/politics/GOP-Legislator-Prays-for-Forgiveness-Before-Pennsylvanias-First-Muslim-Woman-Swears-In.html.
Thompson, Dennis L. 1975. "The Basic Doctrines and Concepts of Reinhold Niebuhr's Political Thought." *Journal of Church and State* 17 (Spring): 275–99.
Thompson, Henry O. 1971. "Interracial Marriage and the Bible." *Negro History Bulletin* 34 (May): 103–6.
Thompson, Kenneth W. 1988. "The Religious Transformation of Politics and the Political Transformation of Religion." *Review of Politics* 50 (Autumn): 545–60.
Throckmorton, Warren. 2011. "The Cincinnati Bible Wars: When the KJV Was Removed from Public Schools." *Christian Post*. May 4. https://www.christianpost.com/news/the-cincinnati-bible-wars-when-the-kjv-was-removed-from-public-schools.html.
Tiro, Karim M. 1996. "Denominated 'SAVAGE': Methodism, Writing, and Identify in the Works of William Apess, a Pequoit." *American Quarterly* 48 (December): 653–79.
Titus, Herbert W. 2008. "The Bible and American Law." *Liberty University Law Review* 2: 305–27.
Tolbert, Mary Ann. 2006. "Marriage and Friendship in the Christian New Testament: Ancient Resources for Contemporary Same-Sex Unions." *Authorizing Marriage? Canon, Tradition, and Critique in the Blessing of Same-Sex Unions*, ed. Mark D. Jordan, Megan T. Sweeney, and David M. Mellott. Princeton, NJ: Princeton University Press, pp. 41–51.
Toulouse, Mark G. 1985. "The Development of a Cold Warrior: John Foster Dulles and the Soviet Union, 1945–1952." *American Presbyterians* 63 (Fall): 309–22.

Toulouse, Mark G. 1989. "Pat Robertson: Apocalyptic Theology and American Foreign Policy." *Journal of Church and State* 31 (Winter): 73–99.
Towner, Lawrence W. 1964. "The Sewall-Saffin Dialogue on Slavery." *William and Mary Quarterly* 21 (January): 40–52.
"Transcript of the Trial of Anne Hutchinson." 1637. http://bcs.bedfordstmartins.com/WebPub/history/mckayunderstanding1e/0312668872/Primary_Documents/US_History/Transcript%20of%20the%20Trial%20of%20Anne%20Hutchinson.pdf.
Truman, Harry S. 1934. "Longhand Note of Judge Harry S. Truman, May 14, 1934. President's Secretary's Files-Longhand Notes." Truman Library & Museum. May 14. https://www.trumanlibrary.org/whistlestop/study_collections/trumanpapers/psf/longhand/index.php?documentid=hst-psf_naid735402-01.
Turner, Laura. 2016. "How Kasich's Religion Is Hurting Him with Conservatives." *Politico*. March 15. https://www.politico.com/magazine/story/2016/03/john-kasich-2016-religion-213735.
"US Attorney General Quotes Bible to Defend Separating Families." 2018. BBC. June 15. https://www.bbc.com/news/world-us-canada-44499048.
Valeri, Mark. 1989. "The New Divinity and the American Revolution." *William and Mary Quarterly* 46 (October): 741–69.
Van Deburg, William L. 1975. "William Lloyd Garrison and the 'Pro-Slavery Priesthood': The Changing Beliefs of an Evangelical Reformer, 1830–1840." *Journal of the Academy of Religion* 43 (June): 224–37.
Van Engen, Abram C. 2013. "Origins and Last Farewells: Bible Wars, Textual Form, and the Making of American History." *New England Quarterly* 86 (December): 543–92.
Van Engen, Abram. 2017. "Review: A Medieval Puritan Welcomes the Early American Enlightenment: What Bible Commentaries Can Offer Postsecular and Literacy Studies." *Early American Literature* 52(2): 423–42.
Van Ness, Dan. "A Biblical Perspective on the Death Penalty." Prison Fellowship. https://www.prisonfellowship.org/resources/advocacy/sentencing/the-death-penalty/.
"Vice President Pence: The Verse above His Mantle." Museum of the Bible. https://www.museumofthebible.org/book/minutes/345.
Vile, John R. [1998]. "David and Ahab, Clinton and Nixon: Contemporary Lessons from Two Biblical Stories." www.leaderu.com/socialsciences/david-ahab.html.
Vile, John R. 2007. "Samuel Sewall: Defender of the Rule of Law?" *Noble Purposes: Nine Champions of the Rule of Law*, ed. Norman Gross. Athens: Ohio University Press, pp. 3–16.
Vile, John R., and Andrew Foshee. 1988. "Domestic Politics in the Book of Judges: The Story of Gibeah." *Journal of Political Science* 16 (Spring): 33–42.
Viney, Donald Wayne. 2010. "American Deism, Christianity, and the Age of Reason." *American Journal of Theology and Philosophy* 31 (May): 83–107.
Waggoner, Edward. 2017. "The Bible and the Military." *The Oxford Handbook of the Bible in America*, ed. Paul C. Gutjahr. New York: Oxford University Press, pp. 333–45.
Waligore, Joseph. 2016. "The Christian Deist Writings of Benjamin Franklin." *Pennsylvania Magazine of History and Biography* 140 (January): 7–29.
Walker, Albert B. Cleage, Jr. 2008. "Princes Shall Come Out of Egypt: A Theological Comparison of Marcus Garvey and Reverend Albert B. Cleague Jr." *Journal of Black Studies* 39 (November): 194–251.
Walker, Andrew T. 2015. "In Welcoming Sanders, Liberty University Shows the Left How to Handle Dissent." *National Review*. September 15. https://www.nationalreview.com/2015/09/bernie-sanders-liberty-university-greeted-warmly/.
"Washington Bible." http://www.masonicinfo.com/washington_bible.htm.

Washington, Booker T. 1900. "An Account of a Speech in Columbus, Ohio." *The Booker T. Washington Papers Collection*, 14 vols., ed. Louis R. Harlan and Raymond W. Smock. Champagne: University of Illinois Press, V: *1899–1900*, pp. 541–44.

Washington, George. "From George Washington to the Savannah, Ga., Hebrew Congregation 14 June 1790." Founders Online. https://founders.archives.gov/documents/Washington/05-05-02-0279.

Waskow, Arthur O. n.d. "Civil Disobedience in the Bible." https://www.myjewishlearning.com/article/civil-disobedience-in-the-bible/.

Wedgeworth, Steven. 2011–2012. "'The Two Sons of Oil' and the Limits of American Religious Dissent." *Journal of Law and Religion* 27(1): 141–61.

Wehner, Peter. 2019. "The Deepening Crisis in Evangelical Christianity." *The Atlantic*. July 5. https://www.theatlantic.com/ideas/archive/2019/07/evangelical-christians-face-deepening-crisisi/593353/.

Wehner, Peter. 2019. "Pete Buttigieg's Very Public Faith Is Challenging Assumptions." *The Atlantic*. April 10. https://www.theatlantic.com/ideas/archive/2019/04/buttigieg-wrong-about-christianity-and-progressivism/586810/.

Weiner, Rachel. 2012. "Conservative Bible Project Cuts Out Liberal Passages." HuffPost. January 4. https://www.huffpost.com/entry/conservative-bible-projec_n_310037.

Wetzel, Benjamin J. 2012. "Onward Christian Soldiers: Lyman Abbott's Justification of the Spanish-American War." *Journal of Church and State* 54 (Summer): 406–25.

Whittaker, David J. 1984. "Early Mormon Polygamy Defenses." *Journal of Mormon History* 11: 43–63.

Wicker, Christine. 2017. "FDR: When an Appeal to Scripture United a Divided Nation." Baptist News Global. January 31. https://baptistnews.com/article/fdr-when-an-appeal-to-scripture-united-a-divided-nation/#.XJjy8SJKiUk.

Wiegel, David. 2011. "And God Will Send Rick Perry." *Slate*. August 6. https://slate.com/news-and-politics/2011/08/rick-perry-leads-prayers-for-jobs-becomes-the-great-republican-hope.html.

Wiener, Jon. 2002. "Denmark Vesey: A New Verdict." The Nation. February 21. https://www.thenation.com/article/denmark-vesey-new-verdict/.

Wilcox, Clyde. 1987. "Popular Backing for the Old Christian Right: Explaining Support for the Christian Anti-Communist Crusade." *Journal of Social History* 21 (Autumn): 117–32.

Wilcox, Clyde. 2003. "Laying Up Treasures in Washington and in Heaven: The Christian Right and Evangelical Politics in the Twentieth Century and Beyond." *OAH Magazine of History* 17 (January) 23–29.

Wilder, Forrest. 2011. "Rick Perry's Army of God." *Texas Observer*. August 3. https://www.texasobserver.org/rick-perrys-army-of-god/.

Wilkerson, David. 1991. "Proclamations of Days of Thanksgiving, Fasting, and Prayer." World Challenge. February 1. https://worldchallenge.org/newsletter/1991/proclamations-for-days-of-thanksgiving-fasting-and-prayer.

Wilkins, Steven, and Diana L. Severance.; 2003. "A Man of Prayer: Stonewall Jackson." *Faith in God and Generals: An Anthology of Faith, Hope, and Love in the American Civil War*. Compiled by Ted Baehr and Susan Wales. Nashville, TN: Broadman & Holman, pp. 72–75.

Williams, George Huntston. 1959. "The Wilderness and Paradise in the History of the Church." *Church History* 28 (March): 3–24.

Williams, Michael J. n.d. "What Is Divine Providence? Is It Biblical?" https://www.whatchristianswanttoknow.com/what-is-divine-providence-is-it-biblical/.

Williams, Rhys H. 1999. "Visions of the Good Society and the Religious Roots of American Political Culture." *Sociology of Religion* 60 (Spring): 1–34.

Willsky, Lydia. 2014. "The (Un)Plain Bible: New Religious Movements and Alternative Scriptures in Nineteenth-century America." *Nova Religio: The Journal of Alternative and Emergent Religions* 17 (May): 13–36.
Wilson, Charles Reagan. 1984. "American Heavens: Apollo and the Civil Religion." *Journal of Church and State* 26 (Spring): 209–26.
Wilson, James. 1790. "Lectures on Law." *Collected Works of James Wilson*, Vol. I, ed. Mark David Hall and Kermit L. Hall. Indianapolis, IN: Liberty Fund, 2007, Chapter II: "Natural Law, Natural Rights, and American Constitutionalism." http://www.nlnrac.org/node/241.
Wilson, Woodrow. 1911. "The Bible and Progress, Address of Hon. Woodrow Wilson Governor of New Jersey in the Auditorium, Denver, Colo. on the Occasion of the Tercentenary Celebration of the Translation of the Bible into the English Language." May 7. http://frontiers.loc.gov/service/gdc/scd0001/2012/20120129002bi/20120129002bi.pdf.
Winship, Michael P. 2006. "Godly Republicanism and the Origins of the Massachusetts Polity." *William and Mary Quarterly*, 3rd Series 63 (July): 427–62.
Winston, Diane. 2017. "The History of the National Prayer Breakfast." *Smithsonian*. February 2. https://www.smithsonianmag.com/history/national-prayer-breakfast-what-does-its-history-reveal-180962017/.
Winthrop, John. 1630. "A Modell of Christian Charity." Collections of the Massachusetts Historical Society (Boston, 1838), 3rd Series 7: 31–48. Hanover Historical Texts Collection. https://history.hanover.edu/texts/winthmod.html.
Witherspoon, John. 1990. "The Dominion of Providence Over the Passions of Men." *The Selected Writings of John Witherspoon*, ed. Thomas Miller. Carbondale: Southern Illinois University Press, pp. 126–47.
Withington, Ann Fairfax, and Jack Schwartz. 1978. "The Political Trial of Anne Hutchinson." *New England Quarterly* 51 (June): 226–40.
Witte, John. 2010. "Puritan Sources of Enlightenment Liberty." *Religion, the Enlightenment, and the New Global Order*, ed. John M. Owen and J. Judd Owen. New York: Columbia University Press, pp. 140–73.
Wojdacz, Mariah. n.d. "Should Bibles Be Present in a Jury Deliberation Room?" LegalZoom. https://www.legalzoom.com/articles/should-bibles-be-present-in-a-jury-deliberation-room.
Wong, Edward. 2019. "The Rapture and the Real World: Mike Pompeo Blends Beliefs and Policy." *New York Times*. March 30.
Wood, Jerome H., Jr. 1977. "For Truth and Reputation: The New England Friends' Dispute with Isaac Backus." *New England Quarterly* 50 (September): 458–83.
Wood, Timothy L. 1998. "The Prophet and the Presidency: Mormonism and Politics in Joseph Smith's 1844 Presidential Campaign." *Journal of the Illinois State Historical Society* 93 (Summer): 167–93.
Woods, John A. 1967. "The Correspondence of Benjamin Rush and Granville Sharp 1773–1809." *Journal of American Studies* 2 (April): 1–38.
Worthen, Molly. 2008. "The Chalcedon Problem: Rousas John Rushdonny and the Origins of Christian Reconstructionism." *Church History* 77 (June): 399–437.
Worthen, Molly. 2015. "The Theological Origins of the Christian Right." *Faithful Republic: Religion and Politics in Modern America*, ed. Andrew Preston, Bruce J. Schulman, and Julian E. Zelizer. Philadelphia: University of Pennsylvania Press, pp. 101–16.
Wright, Jeremiah. 2003. "God Damn America." April 13. http://forums.sluggy.com/viewtopic.php?p=315691&sid=4b3e97ace4ee8cee02bd6850e52f50b7.
Wright, Jeremiah. 2008. "The Full Wright Transcript." *The Atlantic*. April 28. https://www.theatlantic.com/politics/archive/2008/04/the-full-wright-transcript/52865/.

Wright, Robin. 2019. "Pompeo and His Bible Define U.S. Policy in the Middle East." *New Yorker*. January 10. https://www.newyorker.com/news/our-columnists/pompeo-and-his-bible-define-us-policy-in-the-middle-east.
Wulf, Karin. 2012. "Bible, King, and Common Law: Genealogical Literacies and Family History Practices in British America." *Early American Studies* 10 (Fall): 467–502.
Yacovazzi, Cassandra L. 2013. "'Are You Allowed to Read the Bible in a Convent?': Protestant Perspectives on the Catholic Approach to Scripture in Convent Narratives, 1830–1860." *U.S. Catholic Historian* 31 (Summer): 23–46.
"Year of the Bible." https://www.allabouthistory.org/year-of-the-bible.htm.
Zastoupil, Lynn. 2009. "'Notorious and Convicted Mutilators': Rammohun Roy, Thomas Jefferson, and the Bible." *Journal of World History* 20 (September): 399–434.
Zavis, Alexandra. 2008. "U.S. Sniper Pulled from Iraq for Using Quran as a Target." *Baltimore Sun*. May 16. https://www.baltimoresun.com/news/bs-xpm-2008-05-19-0805190113-story.html. Accessed March 31, 2019.
Zeitz, Lisa Margaret. 1981. "Biblical Allusion and Imagery in Frederick Douglass' 'Narrative.'" *CLA Journal* 25 (September): 56–64.
Zgonganin, Sanja. 2005. "Quoting the Bible: The Use of Religious References in Judicial Decision-Making." *City of University of New York Law Review* 9 (Winter): 31–91.
Zlotowitz, Bernard M. 1988. "The Biblical and Rabbinic Underpinnings of the Constitution." *Judaism* 37 (Summer): 328–34.

Books, Theses, and Dissertations

Adams, John Quincy. 1848. *Letters of John Quincy Adams, to His Son, on the Bible and Its Teachings*. Auburn, NY: Derby, Miller. PDF accessed through Google.
Aikman, David. 2004. *A Man of Faith: The Spiritual Journey of George W. Bush*. Nashville, TN: W Publishing Group.
Allen, Ethan [and Thomas Young]. 1784. *Reason: The Only Oracle of Man: A Compendious System of Natural Religion*. Boston: J.P. Mendum, Cornhill, 1854. Accessed at libertyonline.hypermall.com/allen-reason.html.
Alter, Robert. *The Hebrew Bible: A Translation with Commentary*, 3 vols. New York: W. W. Norton.
Alumkal, Anthony. 2017. *Paranoid Science: The Christian Right's War on Reality*. New York: New York University Press.
Andrew, John A. 1992. *From Revivals to Removal: Jeremiah Evarts, the Cherokee Nation, and the Search for the Soul of America*. Athens: University of Georgia Press.
Areshidze, Giorgi. 2016. *Democratic Religion from Locke to Obama: Faith and the Civil Life of Democracy*. Lawrence: University Press of Kansas.
Ashcroft, John, with Gary Thomas. 1998. *Lessons from a Father to His Son*. Nashville, TN: Thomas Nelson.
Baker, Kelly J. 2011. *Gospel according to the Klan: The KKK's Appeal to Protestant America, 1915–1930*. Lawrence: University Press of Kansas.
Baldwiin, Alice M. 2014. *The New England Pulpit and the American Revolution*, ed. Joel McDurmon. Previously titled *The New England Clergy and the American Revolution*. Powder Springs, GA: American Vision Press.
Balkin, Jack, ed. 2007. *What Roe v. Wade Should Have Said: The Nation's Top Legal Experts Rewrite America's Most Controversial Decision*, 3rd ed. New York: NYU Press.
Balmer, Randall. 2008. *God in the White House: A History, How Faith Shaped the Presidency from John F. Kennedy to George W. Bush*. New York: HarperOne.
Barnhart, Joe Edward. 1986. *The Southern Baptist Holy War*. Austin: TexasMonthlyPress.
Barrett-Fox, Rebecca. 2016. *God Hates: Westboro Baptist Church, American Nationalism, and the Religious Right*. Lawrence: University Press of Kansas.

Bassard, Katherine Clay. 2010. *Transforming Scriptures: African American Women Writers and the Bible*. Athens: University of Georgia Press.
Beecher, Catharine E. 1837. *An Essay on Slavery and Abolitionism with Reference to the Duty of American Females*, 2nd ed. Philadelphia: Henry Perkins; Boston: Perkins & Marvin.
Beecher, Henry Ward. 1863. *Freedom and War. Discourses on Topics Suggested by the Times*. Boston: Ticknor and Fields.
Bercot, David. n.d. *In God We Don't Trust: A Look at the Founding of America in the Light of Jesus' Teachings*. Amberson, PA: Scroll.
Berens, John F. 1978. *Providence & Patriotism in Early America, 1640–1815*. Charlottesville: University Press of Virginia.
Berg, Herbert. 2009. *Elijah Muhammad and Islam*. New York: NYU Press.
Berk, Stephen E. 1974. *Calvinism versus Democracy: Timothy Dwight and the Origins of American Evangelical Orthodoxy*. Hamden, CT: Archon Books.
Berlinerblau, Jacques. 2008. *Thumpin' It: The Use and Abuse of the Bible in Today's Presidential Politics*. Louisville, KY: Westminster John Knox Press.
Beveridge, Albert J. 1907. *The Bible as Good Reading*. Philadelphia: Henry Altemus.
The Bible in the Public Schools. 1870. Cincinnati, OH: Robert Clarke. Reprinted by New York: Da Capo Press, 1967. Introduction by Robert G. McCloskey.
Black, C. Clifton. 2014. *Reading Scripture with the Saints*. Cambridge: Lutterworth Press.
Black, Hugo LaFayette. 1968. *A Constitutional Faith*. New York: Alfred A. Knopf.
Blanchard, J., and N. Rice. 1846. *A Debate on Slavery Held on the First, Second, Third and Sixth Days of October, 1845, in the City of Cincinnati, between Rev. J. Blanchard, and N.L. Rice*. Cincinnati: Wm. H. Moore; New York: Mark H. Newman.
Blum, Edward J., and Paul Harvey. 2014. *The Color of Christ: The Son of God and the Saga of Race in America*. Chapel Hill: University of North Carolina Press.
Boise, David, and Theodore B. Olson. 2014. *Redeeming the Dream: The Case for Marriage Equality*. New York: Viking.
Boritt, Gabor. 2006. *The Gettysburg Gospel: The Lincoln Speech That Nobody Knows*. New York: Simon & Schuster.
Boucher, Jonathan. 1793. *A View of the Causes and Consequences of the American Revolution; in Thirteen Discourses, Preached in North America between the Years 1763 and 1775: With an Historical Preface*. London: G.G. and J. Robinson. [Note: Readers may find an excerpted copy of Boucher's sermon on Civil Liberty, Passive Obedience, and Nonresistance on the Constitution Society website at https:///www.constitution.org/bcp/nonresis.htm.]
Boudinot, Elias. 1801. *The Age of Revelation: Or, The Age of Reason Shewn to Be an Age of Infidelity*. Philadelphia: Asbury Dickins. Reprinted by Power Springs, GA: American Vision Press.
Bowler, Kate. 2013. *Blessed: A History of the American Prosperity Gospel*. New York: Oxford University Press.
Bowman, Frank O., III. 2019. *High Crimes and Misdemeanors: A History of Impeachment for the Age of Trump*. New York: Cambridge University Press.
Brewer, David J. 1905. *The United States: A Christian Nation*. Philadelphia: John C. Winston.
Bright, Bill. 2008. *Your 5 Duties as a Christian Citizen*. Peachtree City, GA: New Life Resources.
Bruckberger, R. L. 1949. *Image of America*. New York: Viking Press.
Budziszewski, J. 1997. *Written on the Heart: The Case for Natural Law*. Downers Grove, IL: InterVarsity Press.

Byrd, James P. 2013. *Sacred Scripture, Sacred War: The Bible and the American Revolution*. New York: Oxford University Press.
Byrnes, Mark E. 1994. *Politics and Space: Image Making by NASA*. Westport, CT: Praeger.
Cahn, Jonathan. 2017. *The Paradigm*. Lake Mary, FL: FrontLine.
Callahan, Allen Dwight. 2006. *The Talking Book: African Americans and the Bible*. New Haven, CT: Yale University Press.
Calvert, Jane E. 2009. *Quaker Constitutionalism and the Political Thought of John Dickinson*. New York: Cambridge University Press.
Campbell, Gordon. 2010. *Bible: The Story of the King James Version 1611–2011*. New York: Oxford University Press.
Canipe, Lee. 2011. *A Baptist Democracy: Separating God and Caesar in the Land of the Free*. Macon, GA: Mercer University Press.
Canizares-Esguerra, Jorge. 2009. *Soundings in Atlantic History*. Cambridge, MA: Harvard University Press.
Carroll, M. Daniel. 2013. *Christians at the Border: Immigration, the Church, and the Bible*. Grand Rapids, MI: Brazos Press.
Carson, Ben, with Candy Carson. 2014. *One Nation: What We Can All Do to Save America's Future*. New York: Sentinel.
Carter, Jimmy. 1996. *Living Faith*. New York: Random House.
Carwardine, Richard J. 1997. *Evangelicals and Politics in Antebellum America*. Knoxville: University of Tennessee Press.
Case, Robert. 2018. *Esther & Trump*. Tacoma, WA: Saluda Press.
Charles, Mark, and Soong-Chan Rah. 2019. *Unsettling Truths: The Ongoing, Dehumanizing Legacy of the Doctrine of Discovery*. Downers Grove, IL: InterVarsity Press.
Clark, Victoria. 2007. *Allies for Armageddon*. New Haven, CT: Yale University Press.
Claxton, Nicholas James. March 2019. "The Niagara Creed: Its History, Theology, and Relevance." Submitted for PhD at Bob Jones University.
Closson, David. 2019. *Biblical Principles for Political Engagement: Worldview, Issues, and Voting*. Washington, DC: Family Research Council.
Cochran, Robert F., Jr., and David VanDrunen, eds. 2013. *Law and the Bible: Justice, Mercy and Legal Institutions*. Downers Grove, IL: InterVarsity Press.
Cohen Jared. 2019. *Accidental Presidents: Eight Men Who Changed America*. New York: Simon & Schuster.
Collins, Ace. 2003. *Songs Sung Red, White, and Blue: The Stories behind America's Best-Loved Patriotic Songs*. New York: HarperCollins.
Collins, John J. 2004. *Does the Bible Justify Violence?* Minneapolis, MN: Fortress Press.
Colson, Charles W. 1976. *Born Again*. Old Tappan, NJ. Chosen Books (Distributed by Fleming H. Revell).
Colson, Charles, and Nancy Pearcey. 1999. *How Now Shall We Live?* Wheaton, IL: Tyndale House.
Colson Charles, with Ellen Santilli Vaughn. 1992. *The Body*. Dallas, TX: Word Publishing.
Compolo, Tony. 2008. *Red Letter Christians: A Citizen's Guide to Faith and Politics*. Ventura, CA: Regal.
Compton, John W. 2014. *The Evangelical Origins of the Living Constitution*. Cambridge, MA: Harvard University Press.
Cone, James H. 2013. *The Cross and the Lynching Tree*. Maryknoll, NY: Orbis Books.
Constitution of the American Bible Society, formed by a Convention of Delegates, Held in the City of New York, May, 1816, Together with Their Address to the People of the United States; A Notice of Their Proceedings, and a List of Their Officers. 1816. New York: G. F. Hopkins.

Coogan, Michael. 2014. *The Ten Commandments: A Short History of an Ancient Text*. New Haven, CT: Yale University Press.
Cook, Jane Hampton. 2013. *American Phoenix: John Quincy and Louisa Adams, the War of 1812, and the Exile That Saved American Independence*. Nashville, TN: Thomas Nelson.
Cooper, Valerie C. 2011. *Word, Like Fire: Maria Stewart, the Bible, and the Rights of African Americans*. Charlottesville: University of Virginia Press.
Corrigan, John, and Lynn S. Neal. 2010. *Religious Intolerance in America: A Documentary History*. Chapel Hill: University of North Carolina Press.
Corwin, Edward S. 1965. *The "Higher Law" Background of American Constitutional Law*. Ithaca, NY: Cornell University Press.
Cousins, Norman, ed. 1958. *'In God We Trust": The Religious Beliefs and Ideas of the American Founding Fathers*. New York: Harper & Brothers.
Covington, Dennis. 1994. *Salvation on Sand Mountain: Snake Handling and Redemption in Southern Appalachia*. Reading, MA: Addison-Wesley.
Crocker, H. Mather. 1818. *Observations on the Real Rights of Women, with Their Appropriate Duties, Agreeable to Scripture, Reason, and Common Sense*. Boston: Printed for the author. From *Observations on the Real Rights of Women and Other Writings*. 2011. Constance J. Post, ed. Lincoln: University of Nebraska Press, pp. 71–144.
Curtis, Heather. D. 2019. *Holy Humanitarians: American Evangelicals and Global Aid*. Cambridge, MA: Harvard University Press.
Daly, John Patrick. 2002. *When Slavery Was Called Freedom: Evangelicalism, Proslavery, and the Causes of the Civil War*. Lexington: University Press of Kentucky.
Danforth, John. 2006. *Faith and Politics: How the "Moral Values" Debate Divides America and How to Move Forward Together*. New York: Viking.
Danforth, John. 2015. *The Relevance of Religion: How Faithful People Can Change Politics*. New York: Random House.
Danforth, Samuel. 1670. *A Brief Recognition of New England's Errand into the Wilderness*. Cambridge, MA: S.G. and M.F. From Danforth, Samuel, and Paul Royster (transcriber & editor). "A Brief Recognition of New-Englands Errand into the Wilderness: An Online Electronic Text Edition (1670)." Faculty Publications, UNL Libraries, 35. https://digitalcommons.unl.edu/libraryscience/35.
Daniell, David. 2003. *The Bible in English: Its History and Influence*. New Haven, CT: Yale University Press.
Davis, Deric H. 2000. *Religion and the Continental Congress, 1774–1789: Contributions to Original Intent*. New York: Oxford University Press.
Davis, Nancy J., and Robert V. Robinson. 2012. *Claiming Society for God: Religious Movements and Social Welfare*. Bloomington: Indiana University Press.
DeCaro, Louis A., Jr. 2002. *"Fire from the Midst of You": A Religious Life of John Brown*. New York: New York University Press.
Delgado, Sharon. 2017. *Love in a Time of Climate Change*. Minneapolis, MN: Augsburg Fortress.
Den Hartog, Jonathan J. 2015. *Patriotism & Piety: Federalist Politics and Religious Struggle in the New American Nation*. Charlottesville: University of Virginia Press.
Dershowitz, Alan M. 2000. *The Genesis of Justice: Ten Stories of Biblical Injustice That Led to the Ten Commandments and Modern Law*. New York: Time Warner.
Domnarski, William. 2006. *The Great Justices, 1941–54: Black, Douglas, Frankfurter, and Jackson in Chambers*. Ann Arbor: University of Michigan Press.
Dougherty, Keith I. 2001. *Collective Action under the Articles of Confederation*. Cambridge: Cambridge University Press.

Dreher, Rod. 2017. *The Benedict Option: A Strategy for Christians in a Post-Christian Nation*. New York: Sintenel.

D'Sousa, Dinesh. 2002. *What's So Great about America?* Washington, DC: Regnery.

Dunn, Charles W., ed. 1984. *American Political Theology: Historical Perspective and Theoretical Analysis*. New York: Praeger.

Duval, Patrick. 2011. *A Reason to Believe: Lessons from an Improbable Life*. New York: Broadway.

Dwight, Timothy. 1798. "The Duty of Americans, at the Present Crisis." July 4. https://www.consource.org/document/the-duty-of-americans-at-the-present-crisis-by-timothy-dwight-1798-7-4/.

Edwards, Jonathan. [1742]. *Some Thoughts Concerning the Present Revival of Religion in New England and the Way in Which It Ought to Be Acknowledged and Promoted, Humbly Offered to the Public in a Treatise on That Subject*. http://www.revival-library.org/index.php/catalogues-menu/1725/some-thoughts-concerning-the-present-revival-of-religion-in-new-england.

Eells, Robert, and Bartell Nyberg. 1979. *Lonely Walk: The Life of Senator Mark Hatfield*. Chappaqua, NY: Christian Herald Books.

Eels, Robert J. 1987. *Forgotten Saint: The Life of Theodore Frelinghuysen, A Case Study in Christian Leadership*. Lanham, MD: University Press of America.

Elazar, Daniel. 1995–1998. *The Covenant Tradition in Politics*, 3 vols. New Brunswick, NJ: Transaction.

Elmore, A. E. *Lincoln's Gettysburg Address: Echoes of the Bible and the Book of Common Prayer*. Carbondale: Southern Illinois University Press.

Ely, Ezra Stiles. 1828. *The Duty of Christian Freemen to Elect Christian Rules: A Discourse Delivered on the Fourth of July, 1827*. Philadelphia: William F. Geddes.

Esbeck, Carl H., and Jonathan J. Den Hartog, eds. 2019. *Disestablishment and Religious Dissent: Church-State Relations in the New American States, 1776–1833*. Columbia: University of Missouri Press.

Evangelical Immigration Table. 2019. *Thinking Biblically about Immigrants and Immigration Reform*. E-book.

[Evarts, Jeremiah]. 1829. *Essays on the Present Crisis in the Condition of the American Indians First Published in the National Intelligencer, under the Signature of William Penn*. Boston: Perkins & Marvin.

Farrand, Max, ed. 1966. *The Records of the Federal Convention of 1787*, 4 vols. New Haven, CT: Yale University Press.

Fea, John. 2016. *The Bible Cause: A History of the American Bible Society*. New York: Oxford University Press.

Fea, John. 2016. *Was America Founded as a Christian Nation?: A Historical Introduction*, rev. ed. Louisville, KY: Westminster John Knox Press.

Federer, William J. 2003. *The Ten Commandments and Their Influence on American Law*. St. Louis, MO: Amerisearch.

Feiler, Burce. 2009. *America's Prophet: Moses and the American Story*. New York: William Morrow.

Fellman, Michael. 2010. *In The Name of God and Country: Reconsidering Terrorism in American History*. New Haven, CT: Yale University Press.

Ferrell, Lori Anne. 2008. *The Bible and the People*. New Haven, CT: Yale University Press.

Fessenden, Tracy. 2007. *Culture and Redemption: Religion, the Secular and American Literature*. Princeton, NJ: Princeton University Press.

Findley, William. 2007. *Observations on "The Two Sons of Oil" Containing a Vindication of the American Constitutions, and Defending the Blessings of Religious Liberty and Toleration, against the Illiberal Strictures of the Rev. Samuel B. Wylie*, ed. with an introduction by John Caldwell. Indianapolis: Liberty Fund.

Finnis John. 2011. *Natural Law and Natural Rights*, 2nd ed. New York: Oxford University Press.

Finstuen, Andrew S. 2009. *Original Sin and Everyday Protestants: The Theology of Reinhold Niebuhr, Billy Graham, and Paul Tillich in an Age of Anxiety*. Chapel Hill: University of North Carolina Press.

Fischer, David Hackett. 2005. *Liberty and Freedom*. New York: Oxford University Press.

Fitzgerald, Frances. 2017. *The Evangelicals: The Struggle to Shape America*. New York: Simon & Schuster.

Flippin, J. Brooks. 2011. *Jimmy Carter, the Politics of Family, and the Rise of the Religious Right*. Athens: University of Georgia Press.

Fogleson, Robmer M., and Richard E. Rubenstein. 1969. *Mass Violence in America: Invasion at Harper's Ferry*. New York: Arno Press.

The Founders' Bible: The Origin of the Dream of Freedom. 2012. Signature Historian David Barton. Newbury Park, CA: Shiloh Road.

Franklin, Brian Russell. 2012. "America's Missions: The Home Missions Movement and the Story of the Early Republic." Submitted for PhD in history, Office of Graduate Studies at Texas A&M University.

Frazer, Gregg L. 2012. *The Religious Beliefs of America's Founders: Reason, Revelation, and Revolution*. Lawrence: University Press of Kansas.

Frazer, Gregg L. 2018. *God against the Revolution: The Loyalist Clergy's Case against the American Revolution*. Lawrence: University Press of Kansas.

Frelinghuysen, Theodore, and Henry Whiting Warner. 1838. *An Inquiry into the Moral and Religious Character of the American Government*. New York: Wiley and Putnam.

Frykholm, Amy. 2016. *Christian Understandings of the Future: The Historical Trajectory*. Minneapolis, MN: Augsburg Fortress.

Fuller, Richard, and Francis Wayland. 1860. *Domestic Slavery Considered as a Scriptural Institution: In a Correspondence between the Rev. Richard Fuller of Beauford, S.C., and the Rev. Francis Wayland, of Providence, R.I.*, rev. and corrected by the authors. New York: Sheldon.

Gamble, Richard M. 2003. *The War for Righteousness: Progressive Christianity, the Great War, and the Rise of the Messianic Nation*. Wilmington, DE: ISI Books.

Garnet, Henry Highland. 1865. *A Memorial Discourse; by Rev. Henry Highland Garnet, Delivered in the Hall of the House of Representatives, Washington City, D.C. on Sabbath, February 12, 1865, with an Introduction by James McCune Smith, M.D.* Philadelphia: Joseph M. Wilson.

Garrison, William Lloyd. [1852] 1968. *Selections from the Writings and Speeches of William Lloyd Garrison*. New York: Negro Universities Press. Reprint of R.F. Wallcut, 1852.

Garrow, David. 2004. *Bearing the Cross: Martin Luther King, Jr., and the Southern Christian Leadership Conference*. New York: William Morrow Paperbacks.

George, Robert P. 2001. *The Clash of Orthodoxies: Law, Religion, and Morality in Crisis*. Wilmington, DE: ISI Books.

Georgini, Sara. 2019. *Household Gods: The Religious Lives of the Adams Family*. New York: Oxford University Press.

Gibbs, Nancy, and Michael Duffy. 2008. *The Preacher and the Presidents: Billy Graham in the White House*. New York: Center Street.

Gilbert, Dan. 1936. *The Biblical Basis of the Constitution*. San Diego, CA: Danielle.

Goldstein, Warren. 2004. *William Sloane Coffin Jr: A Holy Impatience*. New Haven, CT: Yale University Press.

Gordon, Sarah Barringer. 2002. *The Mormon Question: Polygamy and Constitutional Conflict in Nineteenth-Century America*. Chapel Hill: University of North Carolina Press.

Gorman, Michael J. 1982. *Abortion and the Early Church: Christina, Jewish and Pagan Attitudes in the Greco-Roman World*. Downers Grove, IL: InterVarsity Press.

Gragg, Rod. 2010. *Forged in Faith: How Faith Shaped the Birth of the Nation, 1607–1776*. New York: Howard Books.

Gray, Thomas R. 1831. *The Confessions of Nat Turner, The Leader of the Late Insurrection in Southampton, VA*. Baltimore: Thomas R. Gray. Found at University of Nebraska DigitalCommons at https://digitalcommons.unl.edu/etas/15.

The Green Bible (NRSV). 2008. New York: HarperOne.

Greenleaf, Simon. [1846] n.d. *The Testimony of the Evangelists Examined by the Rules of Evidence Administered in Courts of Justice*. Holmen, WI: Suzeteo Enterprises. [Note: This version is a significantly shortened version of the original.]

Griffith, Elizabeth. 1984. *In Her Own Right: The Life of Elizabeth Cady Stanton*. New York: Oxford University Press.

Griffith, Sidney H. 2013. *The Bible in Arabic: The Scriptures of the "People of the Book" in the Language of Islam*. Princeton, NJ: Princeton University Press.

Grimke, Angelina Emily. 1836. *Appeal to Christian Women of the South*. New York: American Anti-Slavery Society. Website of National Women's History Museum.

Gruden, Wayne. 2010. *Politics according to the Bible: A Comprehensive Resource for Understanding Modern Political Issues in Light of Scripture*. Grand Rapids, MI: Zondervon.

Gunner, Goran, and Smith, Robert O., eds. *Comprehending Christian Zionism: Perspectives in Comparison*. Minneapolis, MN: Augsburg Fortress.

Gushee, David P. 2008. *The Future of Faith in American Politics: The Public Witness of the Evangelical Center*. Waco, TX: Baylor University Press.

Guthrie, D., and J. A. Motyer, eds. 1970. *The New Bible Commentary*, 3rd ed. Grand Rapids, MI: William B. Eerdmans.

Gutjahr, Paul C. 2012. *The "Book of Mormon": A Biography*. Princeton, NJ: Princeton University Press.

Gutterman, David S. 2005. *Prophetic Politics: Christian Social Movements and American Democracy*. Ithaca, NY: Cornell University Press.

Guyatt, Nicholas. 2007. *Providence and the Invention of the United States, 1607–1876*. New York: Cambridge University Press.

Hall, David W., ed. 1996. *Election Day Sermons*. Oak Ridge, TN: Kuyper Institute.

Hall, David W. 2003. *The Genevan Reformation and the American Founding*. Lanham, MD: Lexington Books.

Hall, Mark David. 2013. *Roger Sherman and the Creation of the American Republic*. New York: Oxford University Press.

Hall, Mark David. 2019. *Did America Have a Christian Founding?: Separating Modern Myth from Historical Truth*. Nashville, TN: Nelson Books.

Hallihan, C. P. 2010. *The Authorized Version: A Wonderful and Unfinished History*. London: Trinitarian Bible Society.

Hamilton, Alexander, James Madison, and John Jay. [1788] 1961. *The Federalist Papers*. New York: New American Library.

Hanson, Paul D. 2010. *Political Engagement as Biblical Mandate*. Cambridge: James Clarke.

Harder, Joseph D. 2014. " 'Heal Their Land': Evangelical Political Theology from the Great Awakening to the Moral Majority." PhD diss. in history, University of Nebraska.

Harmer, John L. 2016. *Jezebel, Willie, and the Voice*. Rochester, NY: Legends Library.
Hartnell, Anna. *Rewriting Exodus: American Futures from Du Bois to Obama*. Minneapolis, MN: Pluto Press.
Harvey, Paul. 2018. *Moses, Jesus, and the Trickster in the Evangelical South*. Athens: University of Georgia Press.
Hatch, Nathan O. 1989. *The Democratization of American Christianity*. New Haven, CT: Yale University Press.
Hatch, Nathan O., and Mark A. Noll, eds. 1982. *The Bible in America: Essays in Cultural History*. New York: Oxford University Press.
Hazony, Yoram. 2007. *The Dawn: Political Teachings of the Book of Esther*, 3rd printing. Jerusalem: Shalem Press.
Heclo, Hugh. 2007. *Christianity and Democracy in America*. Cambridge, MA: Harvard University Press.
Held, Shai. 2013. *Abraham Joshua Heschel: The Call of Transcendence*. Indianapolis: Indiana University Press.
Heltzel, Peter Goodwin. 2009. *Jesus and Justice: Evangelicals, Race, and American Politics*. New Haven, CT: Yale University Press.
Hempton, David. 2008. *Evangelical Disenchantment: Nine Portraits of Faith and Doubt*. New Haven, CT: Yale University Press.
Henderson, M. A. 1995. *Sowers of the Word: A 95-Year History of the Gideons International 1899–1994*. Nashville, TN: Gideons International.
Hendricks, J. Edwin. 1979. *Charles Thomson and the Making of a New Nation, 1729–1824*. Cranbury, NJ: Associated University Presses.
Heschel, Abraham Joshua. 1955. *God in Search of Man*. New York: Harper Torchbooks.
Hill, Christopher. 1993. *The English Bible and the Seventeenth-Century Revolution*. New York: Penguin Books.
Hill, Jim, and Rand Cheadle. 1996. *The Bible Tells Me So: Uses and Abuses of Holy Scripture*. New York: Anchor Books/Doubleday.
Hoffer, Peter Charles. 2011. *When Benjamin Franklin Met the Reverend Whitefield*. Baltimore, MD: Johns Hopkins University Press.
Holland, Matthew S. 2007. *Bonds of Affection: Civic Charity and the Making of America—Winthrop, Jefferson, and Lincoln*. Washington, DC: Georgetown University Press.
Holmes, David L. 2012. *The Faiths of the Postwar Presidents*. Athens: University of Georgia Press.
Hopkins, John H. [1863]. *Bible View of Slavery*. Philadelphia: Publisher unknown. https://ia902308.us.archive.org/33/items/bibleviewofslave00hopk/bibleviewofslave00hopk.pdf.
Howard-Pitney, David. 2005. *The African American Jeremiad: Appeals for Justice in America*, rev. ed. Philadelphia, PA: Temple University Press.
Howe, Ben. 2019. *The Immoral Majority: Why Evangelicals Chose Political Power over Christian Values*. New York: Broadside Books.
Hudnut-Beumler, James. 2018. *Strangers and Friends at the Welcome Table: Contemporary Christianities in the American South*. Chapel Hill: University of North Carolina Press.
Hughes, Richard T. 2009. *Christian America and the Kingdom of God*. Champaign: University of Illinois Press.
Hunter, James Davison *To Change the World: The Irony, Tragedy, and Possibility of Christianity in the Late Modern World*. New York: Oxford University Press.
Hutchinson, Robert J. 2007. *The Politically Incorrect Guide to the Bible*. Washington, DC: Regnery.
Hutson, James H., ed. 1987. *Supplement to Max Farrand's The Records of the Federal Convention of 1787*. New Haven, CT: Yale University Press.

Hutson, James. H. 1998. *Religion and the Founding of the American Republic*. Washington: Library of Congress.
Hyde, Carrie. 2018. *Civic Longing: The Speculative Origins of U.S. Citizenship*. Cambridge, MA: Harvard University Press.
Ilany, Ofri. 2018. *In Search of the Hebrew People: Bible and Nation in the German Enlightenment*. Indianapolis: Indiana University Press.
Jacoby, Stewart O. 1984. "The Religious Amendment Movement: God, People and Nation in the Gilded Age," 2 vols. PhD diss., University of Michigan.
Jay, John. [1788]. *An Address to the People of the State of New-York On the Subject of the Constitution, Agreed upon at Philadelphia, The 17th of September 1987*. New York: Samuel Loudon. Online Library of Liberty. https://oll.libertyfund.org/pages/1787-jay-address-to-the-people-of-n-y-pamphlet.
Jefferson, Thomas. [ca. 1820] 1989. *The Jefferson Bible: The Life and Morals of Jesus of Nazareth*. Boston: Beacon Press.
Jendrysik, Mark Stephen. 2008. *Modern Jeremiahs: Contemporary Visions of American Decline*. Lanham, MD: Lexington Books.
Jensen, Merrill. 1966. *The Articles of Confederation*. Madison: University of Wisconsin Press.
John Paul II. 1995. *The Gospel of Life (Evangelium Vitae)*. New York: Random House.
Johnson, James Turner, ed. 1985. *The Bible in American Law, Politics, and Political Rhetoric*. Philadelphia, PA: Fortress Press.
Jordan, Richard Lawrence. 2013. *The Second Coming of Paisley: Militant Fundamentalism and Ulster Politics*. New York: Syracuse University Press.
Joselit, Jenna Weissman. 2017. *Set in Stone: America's Embrace of the Ten Commandments*. New York: Oxford University Press.
Juster, Susan. 2016. *Sacred Violence in Early America*. Philadelphia: University of Pennsylvania Press.
Kabala, James S. 2013. *Church-State Relations in the Early American Republic, 1787–1846*. Brookfield, VT: Pickering and Chatto.
Kamrath, Angela E. 2014. *The Miracle of America: The Influence of the Bible on the Founding History and Principles of the United States of America for a People of Every Belief*. N.p.: Xulon Press.
Kasich, John. 2010. *Every Other Monday: Twenty Years of Life, Lunch, Faith, and Friendship*. New York: Atria.
Kazin, Michael. 2006. *A Godly Hero: The Life of William Jennings Bryan*. New York: Alfred A. Knopf.
Keane, John. 1995. *Tom Paine: A Political Life*. Boston, MA: Little, Brown.
Keillor, Steven J. 1996. *This Rebellious House: American History & the Truth of Christianity*. Downers Grove, IL: InterVarsity Press.
Kendall, Joshua. 2010. *The Forgotten Founding Father: Noah Webster's Obsession and the Creation of an American Culture*. New York: Berkeley Books.
Kendall, Willmoore, and George W. Carey. 1970. *The Basic Symbols of the American Political Tradition*. Baton Rouge: Louisiana State University Press.
Kennedy, Rick. 2015. *The First American Evangelical: A Short Life of Cotton Mather*. Grand Rapids, MI: Williama B. Eerdmans.
Kidd, Thomas S. 2019. *Who Is an Evangelical? The History of a Movement in Crisis*. New Haven, CT: Yale University Press.
Kilgore, John Mac. 2016. *Mania for Freedom: American Literatures of Enthusiasm from the Revolution to the Civil War*. Chapel Hill: University of North Carolina Press.
Koester, Nancy. 2015. *Introduction to the History of Christianity in the United States*, rev. and expanded. Minneapolis, MN: Augusburg Fortress.

Konvitz, Milton R. 1998. *Torah and Constitution: Essays in American Jewish Thought*. Syracuse, NY: Syracuse University Press.

Kramer, Justin. 1975. *Cast in America*. Los Angeles, CA: Justin Kramer.

Kramnick, Isaac, and R. Laurence Moore. 1996. *The Godless Constitution: The Case against Religious Correctness*. New York: W. W. Norton.

La Barre, Weston. 1969. *They Shall Take Up Serpents: Psychology of the Southern Snake-Handling Cult*. New York: Schocken Books.

Lambert, Frank. 2003. *The Founding Fathers and the Place of Religion in America*. Princeton, NJ: Princeton University Press.

Larson, Edward J. 1997. *Summer for the Gods: The Scopes Trial and America's Continuing Debate over Science and Religion*. Cambridge, MA: Harvard University Press.

Larson, Edward J. 2004. *Evolution: The Remarkable History of a Scientific Theory*. New York: Modern Library.

Leband, David, and Deborah Hendry Heinbuch. 1987. *Blue Laws: The History, Politics and Economics of Sunday Closing Laws*. Lanham, MD: Lexington Books.

Lee, Richard G., ed. 2009. *The American Patriot's Bible: The Word of God and the Shaping of America*. Nashville: Thomas Nelson.

Leiter, Yechiel J. M. 2018. *John Locke's Political Philosophy and the Hebrew Bible*. Cambridge: Cambridge University Press.

Leonard, Bill J. 2005. *Baptists in America*. New York: Columbia University Press.

Lieberman, Joe. 2011. *The Gift of Rest: Rediscovering the Beauty of the Sabbath*. New York: Howard Books.

Lieberman, Joe, with Ari D. Kahn. 2018. *With Liberty and Justice: The Fifty-Day Journey from Egypt to Sinai*. New Milford, CT: Maggid Books and OU Press.

Linder Robert D., and Richard V. Pierard. 1978. *Twilight of the Saints: Biblical Christianity & Civil Religion in America*. Downers Grove, IL: InterVarsity Press.

Lum, Kathryn Gin. 2014. *Damned Nation: Hell in American from Revolution to Reconstruction*. New York: Oxford University Press.

Mailer, Gideon. 2017. *John Witherspoon's American Revolution: Enlightenment and Religion from the Creation of Britain to the Founding of the United States*. Chapel Hill: University of North Carolina Press. Omohundro Institute of Early American History and Culture.

Mansfield, Stephen. 2008. *The Faith of Barack Obama*. Nashville, TN: Thomas Nelson.

Mansfield, Stephen. 2012. *Lincoln's Battle with God: A President's Struggle with Faith and What It Meant for America*. Nashville, TN: Thomas Nelson.

Marbury, Herbert Robinson. 2015. *Pillars of Cloud and Fire: The Politics of Exodus in African-American Biblical Interpretation*. New York: New York University Press.

Marsden, George M. 2003. *Jonathan Edwards: A Life*. New Haven, CT: Yale University Press.

Marshall, Peter, and David Manuel. 1977. *The Light and the Glory*. Old Tappan, NJ: Fleming H. Revell.

Marshall, Peter, and David Manuel. 1986. *From Sea to Shining Sea*. Old Tappan, NJ: Fleming H. Revell.

Martin, William. 2018. *A Prophet with Honor*, updated ed. Grand Rapids, MI: Zondervan.

Mason, Alpheus Thomas, and Gordon E. Baker. 1985. *Free Government in the Making: Readings in American Political Thought*, 4th ed. New York: Oxford University Press.

Mather, Increase [Boston Synod]. 1679. "The Necessity of Reformation." September 10. Boston: John Foster. Evans Early American Imprint Collection. https://quod.lib.umich.edu/cgi/t/text/text-idx?c=evans;cc=evans;view=toc;idno=N00203.0001.001.

Mathewes, Charles, and Christopher McKnight Nichols, eds. 2008. *Prophesies of Godlessness: Predictions of America's Imminent Secularization from the Puritans to the Present Day.* New York: Oxford University Press.
Matthews, Arthur H. 1992. *Standing Up, Standing Together: The Emergence of the National Association of Evangelicals.* Carol Stream, IL: National Association of Evangelicals.
Mayhew, Jonathan. 1750. *A Discourse Concerning Unlimited Submission and Non-Resistance to the Higher Powers: With Some Reflections on the Resistance Made to King Charles I. And on the Anniversary of His Death: In Which the Mysterious Doctrine of That Prince's Saintship and Martyrdom Is Unriddled.* University of Nebraska-Lincoln. Digital Commons. Accessed at https://digitalcommons.unl.edu/etas/44.
McConnell, Michael W., John H. Garvey, and Thomas C. Berg. 2002. *Religion and the Constitution.* New York: Aspen Law & Business.
McDougall, Walter A. 2019. *The Tragedy of U.S. Foreign Policy: How America's Civil Religion Betrayed the National Interest.* New Haven, CT: Yale University Press.
McGarvie, Mark Douglas. 2016. *Law and Religion in American History: Public Values and Private Conscience.* New York: Cambridge University Press.
McKenna, George. 2007. *The Puritan Narrative.* New Haven, CT: Yale University Press.
McLoughlin, William G. 1967. *Isaac Backus and the American Pietistic Tradition.* Boston: Little, Brown.
McLoughlin, William G. 1991. *Soul Liberty: The Baptists' Struggle in New England, 1630–1833.* Hanover, NH: Brown University Press.
McQueen, Alison. 2018. *Political Realism in Apocalyptic Times.* New York: Cambridge University Press.
Medved, Michael. 2019. *God's Hand on America: Divine Providence in the Modern Era.* New York: Crown Forum.
Metzger, Burce M. 2001. *The Bible in Translation: Ancient and English Versions.* Grand Rapids, MI: Baker Academic.
Meyers, Marvin, ed. 1973. *The Mind of the Founder: Sources of the Political Thought of James Madison.* Indianapolis, IN: Bobbs-Merrill.
Miller, Perry. *The New England Mind: The Seventeenth Century.* Cambridge, MA: Belknap Press.
Miller, Steven R. 2009. *Billy Graham and the Rise of the Republican South.* Philadelphia: University of Pennsylvania Press.
Montgomery, Leslie. 2019. *The Faith of Mike Pence.* New Kensington, PA: Whitaker House.
Montgomery, Scott L., and Daniel Chirot. 2015. *The Shape of the New: Four Big Ideas and How They Made the Modern World.* Princeton, NJ: Princeton University Press.
Moore, James P., Jr. 2005. *One Nation under God: The History of Prayer in America.* New York: Doubleday.
Moots, Glenn A. 2010. *Politics Reformed: The Anglo-American Legacy of Covenant Theology.* Columbia: University of Missouri Press.
Morgan, Edmund S. 1958. *The Puritan Dilemma: The Story of John Winthrop.* Boston: Little, Brown.
Morgan, Robert. 2020. *100 Bible Verses That Made America: Defining Moments That Shaped Our Enduring Foundation of Faith.* Nashville: Thomas Nelson.
Morris, Benjamin F. [1864] 2007. *The Christian Life and Character of the Civil Institutions of the United States.* Powder Springs, GA: American Vision.
Morton, Brian. 2008. *Woodrow Wilson: USA.* London: Haus.
Mosley, Carys. 2013. *Nationhood, Providence and Witness: Israel in Modern Theology and Social Theory.* Eugene, OR: Cascade Books.

Moss, Candida R., and Joel S. Baden. 2017. *Bible Nation: The United States of Holly Lobby*. Princeton, NJ: Princeton University Press.
Muhammad, Elijah. 1973. *Message to the Blackman in America*. Phoenix, AZ: Secretarius Memps.
Nation, Carry A. 1908. *The Use and Need of the Life of Carry A. Nation*. Topeka, KS: F. M. Steves & Sons, 1909.
National Association of Evangelicals. 2018. *For the Health of the Nation: An Evangelical Call to Civic Responsibility*. https://www.nae.net/for-the-health-of-the-nation/.
Nelson, Eric. 2010. *The Hebrew Republic: Jewish Sources and the Transformation of European Political Thought*. Cambridge, MA: Harvard University Press.
Neuhaus, Richard John. 1988. *The Naked Public Square: Religion and Democracy in America*. Grand Rapids, MI: William B. Eerdmans.
Newton, Merlin Owen. 1995. *Armed with the Constitution: Jehovah's Witnesses in Alabama and the U.S. Supreme Court, 1939–1946*. Tuscaloosa: University of Alabama Press.
Nichols-Belt, Tracy, with Gordon T. Belt. 2011. *Onward Christian Soldiers: Religion and the Army of Tennessee in the Civil War*. Charleston, SC: History Press.
Niebuhr, H. Richard. 1951. *Christ and Culture*. New York: Harper & Row.
Noll, Mark A. 1989. *Princeton and the Republic, 1768–1822: The Search for a Christian Enlightenment in the Era of Samuel Stanhope Smith*. Princeton, NJ: Princeton University Press.
Noll, Mark A. 2006. *The Civil War as a Theological Crisis*. Chapel Hill: University of North Carolina Press.
Noll, Mark A. 2008. *God and Race in American Politics*. Princeton, NJ: Princeton University Press.
Noll, Mark A. 2016. *In the Beginning Was the Word: The Bible in American Public Life, 1492–1783*. New York: Oxford University Press.
Offutt, William M., Jr. 1995. *Of "Good Laws" & "Good Men": Law and Society in the Delaware Valley, 1680–1710*. Urbana: University of Illinois Press.
Osler, Mark. 2009. *Jesus on Death Row: The Trial of Jesus and American Capital Punishment*. Nashville, TN: Abington Press.
Paige, John C. 1988. *The Liberty Bell of Independence National Historical Park: A Special History Study*, ed. David C. Kimball. Denver, CO: Denver Service Center, National Park Service, Department of the Interior.
Paine, Thomas. [1776] 1953. *Common Sense and Other Writings*, ed. Nelson F. Adkins. New York: Liberal Arts Press.
Pearsall, Sarah M. S. 2019. *Polygamy: An Early American History*. New Haven, CT: Yale University Press.
Peck, Garrett. 2009. *The Prohibition Hangover: Alcohol in America from Demon Rum to Cult Cabernet*. New Brunswick, NJ: Rutgers University Press.
Pelletier, Kevin. *Apocalyptic Sentimentalism: Love and Fear in U.S. Antebellum Literature*. Athens: University of Georgia Press.
Perry, Lewis. 2013. *Civil Disobedience: An American Tradition*. New Haven, CT: Yale University Press.
Peters, Shawn Francis. 2000. *Judging Jehovah's Witnesses: Religious Persecution and the Dawn of the Rights Revolution*. Lawrence: University Press of Kansas.
Peterson, Paul E. 2010. *Saving Schools: From Horace Mann to Virtual Learning*. Cambridge, MA: Harvard University Press.
Pillsbury, Parker. 1883. *Acts of the Anti-Slavery Apostles*. Concord, NH: Clague, Wegman, Schlicht.

Poole, W. Scott. 2009. *Satan in America: The Devil We Know*. Lanham, MD: Rowman & Littlefield.

Posner, Sarah. 2008. *God's Profits: Faith, Fraud, and the Republican Crusade for Values Voters*. Sausalito, CA: PoliPointPress.

Pottenger, John R. 2007. *Reaping the Whirlwind: Liberal Democracy and the Religious Axis*. Washington, DC: Georgetown University Press.

The Poverty and Justice Bible. 2008. Swindon: Bible Society.

Powell, Adam Clayton. 1967. *Keep the Faith Baby!* New York: Trident Press.

Powery, Emerson B., and Rodney S. Sadler Jr. 2016. *The Genesis of Liberation: Biblical Interpretation in the Antebellum Narratives of the Enslaved*. Louisville, KY: Westminster John Knox Press.

Presidential Inaugural Bibles: Catalogue of an Exhibition, November 17, 1968 through February 23, 1969. 1969. Washington, DC: Washington Cathedral.

Price, Robert M. 2013. *Politically Correct Bible*. eBookIt.com.

Prothero, Stephen. 2003. *American Jesus: How the Son of God Became a National Icon*. New York: Farrar, Straus and Giroux.

Rable, George C. 2010. *God's Almost Chosen Peoples: A Religious History of the American Civil War*. Chapel Hill: University of North Carolina Press.

Rauschenbusch, Walter. 1907. *Christianity and the Social Crisis*. New York: Hodder & Stoughton.

Reich, Michael. August 2014. "God's Involvement in American Politics (A Brief History and Present." Thesis for MA in English, Stony Brook University.

Reider, Jonathan. 2013. *Gospel of Freedom: Martin Luther King, Jr.'s Letter from Birmingham Jail and the Struggle That Changed a Nation*. New York: Bloomsbury Press.

Richard, Carl J. 2016. *The Founders and the Bible*. Lanham, MD: Rowman & Littlefield.

Robertson, David. 1999. *Denmark Vesey: The Buried Story of America's Largest Slave Rebellion and the Man Who Led It*. New York: Alfred A. Knopf.

Rodgers, Daniel T. 2018. *As a City on a Hill: The Story of America's Most Famous Lay Sermon*. Princeton, NJ: Princeton University Press.

Rosen, Leo, ed. 1975. *Religions of America*. New York: Simon & Schuster.

Rumberg, H. Rondel. 1993. *Stonewall Jackson's Verse*. Spout Spring, VA: Society for Biblical and Southern Studies.

Ruotsila, Markku. 2016. *Fighting Fundamentalist: Carl McIntire and the Politicization of American Fundamentalism*. New York: Oxford University Press.

Rush, Benjamin. 1947. *The Selected Writings of Benjamin Rush*, ed. Dagobert D. Runes. New York: Philosophical Library.

Rush, Benjamin. 1951. *Letters of Benjamin Rush*, 2 vols., ed. L. H. Butterfield. Princeton, NJ: Princeton University Press.

Rushdy, Ashraf H. A. 2012. *American Lynching*. New Haven, CT: Yale University Press.

Rushford, Jerry Bryant. August 1977. "Political Disciple: The Relationship Between James A. Garfield and the Disciples of Christ." PhD diss., University of California, Santa Barbara. Accessed through Pepperdine University Digital Commons.

Russell, C. Allyn. 1976. *Voices of American Fundamentalism: Seven Biographical Studies*. Philadelphia: Westminster Press.

Sandoff, Michelle. 2017. *Service in a Time of Suspicion: Experiences of Muslims Serving in the U.S. Military Post-9/11*. Iowa City: University of Iowa Press.

Sandoz, Ellis, ed. 1991. *Political Sermons of the American Founding Era, 1730–1805*. Indianapolis, IN: Liberty Fund.

Sasse, Ben. 2017. *The Vanishing American Adult: Our Coming-of-Age Crisis—and How to Rebuild a Culture of Self-Reliance*. New York: St. Martin's Press.

Sasse, Ben. 2018. *Them: Why We Hate Each Other—and How to Heal*. New York: St. Martin's Press.
Scalia, Antonin. 2019. *On Faith: Lessons From an American Believer*, ed. Christopher J. Scalia and Edward Whelan. New York: Crown Forum.
Schaeffer, Francis A. 1970. *Pollution and the Death of Man: The Christian View of Ecology*. Carol Stream, IL: Tyndale House.
Schaeffer, Francis A., and C. Everett Koop. 1979. *Whatever Happened to the Human Race?* Tappan: Fleming H. Revell.
Schlenther, Boyd Stanley. 1990. *Charles Thomson: A Patriot's Pursuit*. Newark: University of Delaware Press.
Schlereth, Eric R. 2013. *An Age of Infidels: The Politics of Religious Controversy in the Early United States*. Philadelphia: University of Pennsylvania Press.
Scholz, Susanne, and Pablo R. Andinach, eds. 2016. *La Violencia and the Hebrew Bible: The Politics and Histories of Biblical Hermeneutics on the American Continent*. Atlanta, GA: Society of Biblical Literature.
Seldes, Gilbert. [1927] 2012. *The Stammering Century*. New York: New York Review Books.
Sha'ban, Fuad. 2005. *For Zion's Sake: The Judeo-Christian Tradition in American Culture*. London: Pluto Press.
Shalev, Eran. 2013. *American Zion: The Old Testament as a Political Text from the Revolution to the Civil War*. New Haven, CT: Yale University Press.
Sherwood, Samuel. 1776. *The Church's Flight into the Wilderness: An Address on the Times. Containing Some Very Interesting and Important Observations on Scripture Prophesies: Shewing That Sundry of Them Plainly Related to Great-Britain and the American Colonies; and Are Fulfilling in the Present Day*. New York: S. Loudon. Found in Ellis Sandoz, ed. 1991. *Political Sermons of the Founding Era, 1730–1804*. Indianapolis, IN: Liberty Fund, pp. 495–527.
Shulman, George. 2008. *American Prophecy: Race and Redemption in American Political Culture*. Minneapolis: University of Minnesota Press.
Sider, Ronald J. 2008. *The Scandal of Evangelical Politics: Why Are Christians Missing the Chance to Really Change the World?* Grand Rapids, MI: Baker Books.
Skousen, Lesley. 2008. "Redefining Benefit of Clergy during the English Reformation: Royal Prerogative, Mercy, and the State." Thesis for MA in history, University of Wisconsin.
Smith, Erin A. 2015. *What Would Jesus Read? Popular Religious Books and Everyday Life in Twentieth-Century America*. Chapel Hill: North Carolina Press.
Smith, Frank J., ed. 2016. *Religion and Politics in America: An Encyclopedia of Church and State in American Life*, 2 vols. Santa Barbara: ABC-CLIO.
Smith, Gail K. 2018. *Above the American Renaissance: David S. Reynolds and the Spiritual Imagination in American Literary Studies*. Amherst; University of Massachusetts Press.
Smith, Gary Scott. 2006. *Faith and the Presidency: From George Washington to George W. Bush*. New York: Oxford University Press.
Smith, Gary Scott. 2015. *Religion in the Oval Office: The Religious Lives of American Presidents*. New York: Oxford University Press.
Smith, Steven B. 2012. *Political Philosophy*. New Haven, CT: Yale University Press.
Solberg, Winton U., ed. 1958. *The Federal Convention and the Formation of the Union of the American States*. Indianapolis, IN: Bobbs-Merrill.
Stahr, Walter. 2005. *John Jay: Founding Father*. New York: Hambleton and London.
Stanton, Elizabeth Cady. [1895]. *The Woman's Bible*. Lexington, KY: n.p.
Stauffer, John, and Benjamin Soskis. 2013. *The Battle Hymn of the Republic: A Biography of the Song That Marches On*. New York: Oxford University Press.

Stephens, Randall J., and Karl W. Giberson. 2011. *The Anointed: Evangelical Truth in a Secular Age*. Cambridge, MA: Harvard University Press.

Stewart, Maria W. 1987. *Maria W. Stewart, America's First Black Woman Political Writer: Essays and Speeches*, ed. and introduced by Marilyn Richardson. Bloomington: Indiana University Press.

Stewart, Matthew. 2014. *Nature's God: The Heretical Origins of the American Republic*. New York: W. W. Norton.

Stiles, Ezra. 1783. *The United States Elevated to Glory and Honor*, ed. Reiner Smolinski. DigitalCommons@University of Nebraska-Lincoln. http://digitalcommons.unl.edu/etas/41.

Stringfellow, Thornton. 1841. *A Brief Examination of Scripture Testimony on the Institution of Slavery*. Locust Grove, VA: Library of Congress. https://cdn.loc.gov/service/rbc/rbaapc/28100/28100.pdf.

Strub, Whitney. 2010. *Perversion for Profit: The Politics of Pornography and the Rise of the New Right*. New York: Columbia University Press.

Sullivan, Winnifred Fallers. 2009. *Prison Religion: Faith-Based Reform and the Constitution*. Princeton, NJ: Princeton University Press.

Sunday, Billy. 1970. *Billy Sunday Speaks*, ed. David Gullen. New York: Chelsea House.

Sutton, Matthew Avery. 2014. *American Apocalypse: A History of Modern Evangelicalism*. Cambridge, MA: Harvard University Press.

Swartley, Willard M. 1983. *Slavery Sabbath War and Women: Case Studies in Biblical Interpretation*. Scottdale, PA: Herald Press.

Talbot, Christine. 2013. *A Foreign Kingdom: Mormons and Polygamy in American Political Culture, 1852–1890*. Champaign: University of Illinois Press.

Taves, Ann. 2016. *Revelatory Events: Three Case Studies of the Emergency of New Spiritual Paths*. Princeton, NJ: Princeton University Press.

Tribe, Laurence H. 1990. *Abortion: The Clash of Absolutes*. New York: W. W. Norton.

Trueblood, Elton. 1973. *Abraham Lincoln: Theologian of American Anguish*. New York: HarperOne.

Truman, Harry, and Pope Pius XII. 1953. *Correspondence between President Truman and Pope Pius XII*, introduced by Myron C. Taylor. N.p.: Myron C. Taylor.

Turner, John G. 2012. *Brigham Young: Pioneer Prophet*. Cambridge, MA: Harvard University Press.

Tuveson, Ernest Lee. 1968. *Redeemer Nation: The Idea of America's Millennial Role*. Chicago: University of Chicago Press.

Unger, Harlow Giles. 1998. *The Life and Times of an American Patriot*. New York: John Wiley & Sons.

Unger, Walter. 1981. " 'Earnestly Contending for the Faith': The Role of the Niagara Bible Conference in the Emergence of American Fundamentalism, 1875–1900." PhD thesis, Simon Fraser University.

Viefhues-Bailey, Ludger H. 2010. *Between a Man and a Woman? Why Conservatives Oppose Same-Sex Marriage*. New York: Columbia University Press.

Vile, John R. 2014. *Re-Framers: 170 Eccentric, Visionary, and Patriotic Proposals to Rewrite the U.S. Constitution*. Santa Barbara, CA: ABC-CLIO.

Vile, John R. 2015. *Encyclopedia of Constitutional Amendments, Proposed Amendments, and Amending Issues, 1789–2015*, 2 vols., 4th ed. Santa Barbara, CA: ABC-CLIO.

Vile, John R., ed. 2015. *Founding Documents of America: Documents Decoded*. Santa Barbara, CA: ABC-CLIO.

Vile, John R., ed. 2016. *American Immigration and Citizenship: A Documentary History*. Lanham, MD: Rowman & Littlefield.

Vile, John R. 2016. *The Constitutional Convention of 1787: A Comprehensive Encyclopedia of America's Founding*, 2 vols., rev. 2nd ed. Clark, NJ: Talbot.

Vile, John R., ed. 2017. *The Jacksonian and Antebellum Eras: Documents Decoded*. Santa Barbara, CA: ABC-CLIO.

Vile, John R. ed. 2018. *The Civil War and Reconstruction Eras; Documents Decoded*. Santa Barbara, CA: ABC-CLIO.

Vile, John R. 2018. *Essential Supreme Court Decisions: Summaries of Leading Cases in U.S. Constitutional Law*, 17th ed. Lanham, MD: Rowman & Littlefield.

Vile, John R., ed. 2018. *Governmental Responses to Natural Disasters in the U.S.* Clark, NJ: Talbot.

Vile, John R. 2019. *A Constellation of Great Men: Exploring the Character Sketches of Dr. Benjamin Rush of Pennsylvania of the Signers of the Declaration of Independence*. Clark, NJ: Talbot.

Vile, John R. 2019. *The Declaration of Independence: America's First Founding Document in U.S. History and Culture*. Santa Barbara, CA: ABC-CLIO.

Vile, John R. 2019. *The Liberty Bell and Its Legacy: An Encyclopedia of an American Icon in U.S. History and Culture*. Santa Barbara, CA: ABC-CLIO.

Vile, John R. 2020. *America's National Anthem: The Star-Spangled Banner in U.S. History, Culture, and Law*. Santa Barbara, CA: ABC-CLIO.

Volk, Kyle G. 2014. *Moral Minorities and the Making of American Democracy*. New York: Oxford University Press.

Waldman, Steven. 2008. *Founding Faith: Providence, Politics, and the Birth of Religious Freedom in America*. New York: Random House.

Waldman, Steven. 2019. *Sacred Liberty: America's Long, Bloody, and Ongoing Struggle for Religious Freedom*. New York: HarperOne.

Walker, Clarence E., and Gregory D. Smithers. 2009. *The Preacher and the Politician: Jeremiah Wright, Barack Obama, and Race in America*. Charlottesville: University of Virginia Press.

Walker, David. 1830. *Walker's Appeal in Four Articles: Together with a Preamble, to the Coloured Citizens of the World, but in Particular, and Very Expressly, to Those of the United States of America*, 3rd ed. Boston: David Walker. Accessed at https://docsouth.unc.edu/nc/walker/walker.html.

Wallace, Henry A. 1934. *Statesmanship and Religion*. New York: Round Table Press.

Walters, Kerry S. 1992. *The American Deists: Voices of Reason and Dissent in the Early Republic*. Lawrence: University Press of Kansas.

Walzer, Michael. 1985. *Exodus and Revolution*. New York: Basic Books.

Walzer, Michael. 2012. *In God's Shadow: Politics in the Hebrew Bible*. New Haven, CT: Yale University Press.

[Ward, Nathaniel] de la Guard, Theodore. 1647. *The Simple Cobler of Aggawam in America*, 4th ed. London: Printed by J. D. & R. I. for Stephen Eawred, at the signe of the Bible in Popes Head-Alley.

Washington, Margaret. 2009. *Sojourner Truth's America*. Urbana: University of Illinois Press.

Watson, Henry C. 1852. *The Old Bell of Independence; or, Philadelphia in 1776*. Philadelphia: Linsay and Blakiston.

Webb, W. L. 1912. *Champ Clark*. New York: Neale.

Webster, Noah. 1834. *Value of the Bible and Excellence of the Christian Religion: For the Use of Families and Schools*. New Haven, CT: Durrie & Peck.

Wehner, Peter. 2019. *The Death of Politics: How to Heal Our Frayed Republic After Trump*. New York: HarperOne.

Weir, David A. 2005. *Early New England: A Covenanted Society*. Grand Rapids, MI: William B. Eerdmans.

Weld, Theodore Dwight. 1838. *The Bible against Slavery: An Inquiry into the Patriarchal and Mosaic Systems on the Subject of Human Rights*, 3rd ed. New York: American Anti-Slavery Society.
West, John G., Jr. 1996. *The Politics of Revelation and Reason: Religion and Civic Life in the New Nation*. Lawrence: University Press of Kansas.
Weyler, Karen A. 2013. *Empowering Words: Outsiders and Authorship in Early America*. Athens: University of Georgia Press.
Whitman, James Q. 2008. *The Origins of Reasonable Doubt: Theological Roots of the Criminal Trial*. New Haven, CT: Yale University Press.
Wildavsky, Aaron. 1984. *The Nursing Father: Moses as a Political Leader*. Tuscaloosa: University of Alabama Press.
Wiley, Tatha. 2009. *Creationism and the Conflict over Evolution*. Cambridge: James Clarke.
Williams, Elisha. [1742] 1967. *The Essential Rights and Liberties of Protestants. As Found in the Great Awakening: Documents Illustrating the Crisis and Its Consequence*, ed. Alan Heimert and Perry Miller. Indianapolis: Bobbs-Merrill.
Wills, Garry. 1984. *Cincinnatus: George Washington and the Enlightenment*. New York: Doubleday.
Wills, Garry. 2006. *Lincoln at Gettysburg: The Words That Remade America*. New York: Simon & Schuster.
Winder, Mike. 2019. *Favorite Scriptures of 100 American Leaders*. Springville, UT: Plain Sight.
Winters, Michael Sean. 2012. *God's Right Hand: How Jerry Falwell Made God a Republican and Baptized the American Right*. New York: HarperCollins.
Wolf, William J. 1959. *The Almost Chosen People: A Study of the Religion of Abraham Lincoln*. Garden City, NY: Doubleday.
Woolverton, John F., and James D. Bratt. 2019. *A Christian and a Democrat: A Religious Biography of Franklin D. Roosevelt*. Grand Rapids, MI: Eerdmans.
Yoder, John Howard. 1994. *The Politics of Jesus*. Grand Rapids, MI: Wm. B. Eerdmans.

Court Decisions

Abington School District v. Schempp, 374 U.S. 202 (1963).
Board of Education of Cincinnati v. Minor, 23 Ohio St. 211 (1872).
Bowers v. Hardwick, 478 U.S. 186 (1986).
Brown v. Board of Education, 347 U.S. 483 (1954).
Burstyn v. Wilson, 343 U.S. 495 (1952).
Cantwell v. Connecticut, 310 U.S. 296 (1940).
Chaplinsky v. New Hampshire, 315 U.S. 568 (1942).
Charles River Bridge v. Warren Bridge 11 Pet. (36 U.S.) 420 (1837).
Church of the Holy Trinity v. United States, 143 U.S. 457 (1892).
Commonwealth v. Cooke, 7 Am. L. Reg. 417 (Police Court of Boston, MA, 1859).
Commonwealth v. Kneeland, 37 Mass. 206 (1838).
Dickerson v. United States, 346 U.S. 389 (1953).
Edwards v. Aguillard, 482 U.S. 478 (1987).
Engel v. Vitale, 370 U.S. 421 (1962).
Epperson v. Arkansas, 393 U.S. 97 (1968).
Furman v. Georgia, 408 U.S. 238 (1972).
Gerke v. Purcell, 25 Ohio St. 229 (1874).
Gregg v. Georgia, 428 U.S. 153 (1976).
Griswold v. Connecticut, 381 U.S. 479 (1965).
Jerome B. Grubert, Inc. v. Great Lakes Dredge & Dock Co. 513 U.S. 427 (1995).
Johnson v. McIntosh 21 U.S. (Wheat) 543 (1823).

Lawrence v. Texas, 539 U.S. 558 (2003).
Lemon v. Kurtzman, 403 U.S. 602 (1971).
Lovell v. City of Griffin, 328 U.S. 303 (1938).
Loving v. Virginia, 388 U.S. 1 (1967).
McCollum v. Board of Education, 333 U.S. 203 (1948).
McCreary County v. American Civil Liberties Union, 545 U.S. 844 (2005).
McGowan v. Maryland, 366 U.S. 420 (1961).
Meyer v. Nebraska, 262 U.S. 390 (1923).
Miller v. California, 413 U.S. 15 (1973).
Minersville School District v. Gobitis, 310 U.S. 586 (1940).
New York v. Ferber, 458 U.S. 747 (1982).
Obergefell v. Hodges, 576 U.S. 644 (2015).
People v. Harlan, 209 P.3d616 (205).
People v. Ruggles, 8 Johns. 290 (NY 1811).
Planned Parenthood v. Casey, 505 U.S. 833 (1992).
Plessy v. Ferguson, 163 U.S. 537 (1896).
Powell v. McCormack, 395 U.S. 486 (1969).
Reynolds v. United States, 98 U.S. 145 (1879).
Roe v. Wade, 410 U.S. 113 (1973).
Snyder v. Phelps, 562 U.S. 433 (2011).
Stone v. Graham, 449 U.S. 39 (1980).
United States v. Lee, 455 U.S. 252 (1982).
United States v. Windsor, 570 U.S. 744 (2013)
Updegraph v. Commonwealth, 11 Serg. & Rawle 394 (PA 1824).
Van Orden v. Perry, 545 U.S. 677 (2005).
Vidal v. Girard's Executors, 43 U.S. 127 (1844).
West Virginia State Board of Education v. Barnette, 319 U.S. 624 (1943).
Wisconsin v. Yoder, 406 U.S. 205 (1972).
Youngstown Sheet & Tube Co. v. Sawyer, 343 U.S. 579 (1952).
Zorach v. Clauson, 343 U.S. 306 (1952).

Index to Biblical Citations

Books of the Old Testament

Apocrypha

Books of the New Testament

Note: The few books to which I have found no citations are relatively short, and some of the books (Genesis, Exodus, Psalms and Isaiah) to which there are quite a few citations are long. Similarly, although there are more references to the Old Testament than to the New, the former is considerably longer than the latter. Of the gospels, Matthew was quoted the most frequently, with a fair number of citations centering on the Sermon on the Mount in chapters 5–7. Note that some citations may be from the same individual, cited at different places in the book. Verses that stand out as being cited numerous times include Leviticus 25:10 (inscribed on the Liberty Bell); II Chronicles 7:14; Micah 6:8; and Galatians 5:1.

Index to Bible Names and Places

General Index

About the Author

John R. Vile, PhD, is professor of political science and dean of the University Honors College at Middle Tennessee State University. He has written and edited a variety of books on legal issues, the U.S. Constitution, and the American founding period. He has been selected by the Honor Society of Phi Kappa Phi, the nation's oldest and most selective all-discipline collegiate honor society, as the 2020–2022 Phi Kappa Phi Scholar. His books includes the following: *America's National Anthem: The Star-Spangled Banner in U.S. History, Culture and Law* (2020); *The Liberty Bell and Its Legacy: An Encyclopedia of an American Icon in U.S. History and Culture* (2020); *More than a Plea for a Declaration of Rights: The Constitutional and Political Thought of George Mason of Virginia* (2019); *A Constellation of Great Men: Restoring the Character Sketches of Dr. Benjamin Rush of Pennsylvania of the Signers of the Declaration of Independence* (2019); *The Declaration of Independence: America's First Founding Document in U.S. History and Culture* (2019); *The American Flag: An Encyclopedia of the Stars and Stripes in U.S. History, Culture, and Law* (2018); *Essential Supreme Court Decisions*, 17th ed. (2018); *Governmental Responses to Natural Disaster in the U.S.: A Documentary History* (2018); *The Civil War and Reconstruction Eras* (2018); *Encyclopedia of the First Amendment*, rev. online ed. (2017); *The Jacksonian and Antebellum Eras* (2017); *Constitutional Law in Contemporary America*, 2 vols. (2017); *The Constitutional Convention of 1787: A Comprehensive Encyclopedia of America's Founding*, 2 vols., 2nd ed. (2016); *Conventional Wisdom: The Alternative Article V Mechanism for Proposing Amendments to the U.S. Constitution* (2016); *The Early Republic* (2016); *American Immigration and Citizenship* (2016); *Encyclopedia of Constitutional Amendments, Proposed Amendments, and Amending Issues, 1789–2015*, 4th ed. (2015); *The United States Constitution: One Document, Many Choices* (2015); *Founding Documents of America: Documents Decoded* (2015); *A Companion to the United States Constitution and Its Amendments*, 6th ed. (2015); *The Wisest Council in the World: Restoring the Character Sketches by William Pierce of Georgia of the Delegates to the Constitutional Convention of 1787* (2015); *Re-Framers: 170 Eccentric, Visionary, and Patriotic Proposals to Rewrite the U.S. Constitution* (2014); *The Men Who Made the Constitution: Lives of the Delegates to the Constitutional Convention of 1787* (2013); *Encyclopedia of the Fourth Amendment* (2013); *The Writing and Ratification of the U.S. Constitution: Practical Virtue in Action* (2012); *Pleasing the Court: A Mock Trial Handbook*, 5th ed. (2012); *James Madison: Philosopher, Founder and Statesman* (2008); *The Encyclopedia of Civil Liberties in America* (2005); *Great American Judges: An Encyclopedia* (2003); *Great American Lawyers: An Encyclopedia* (2002); *Presidential Winners and Losers: Words of Victory and Concession* (2002); *History of the American Legal System:*

Interactive Encyclopedia (CD-ROM, 2000); *Tennessee Government and Politics* (1998); *Constitutional Change in the United States* (1994); *The Theory and Practice of Constitutional Change in America* (1993); *Contemporary Questions Surrounding the Constitutional Amending Process* (1993); *The Constitutional Amending Process in American Political Thought* (1992); and *Rewriting the United States Constitution* (1991).

www.ingramcontent.com/pod-product-compliance
Ingram Content Group UK Ltd.
Pitfield, Milton Keynes, MK11 3LW, UK
UKHW051029041026
15470UKWH00015B/1739

9 781538 141663